Merriam-Webster's
Pocket

Spanish-English
Dictionary

Merriam-Webster, Incorporated
Springfield, Massachusetts, U.S.A.

A GENUINE MERRIAM-WEBSTER

The name *Webster* alone is no guarantee of excellence. It is used by a number of publishers and may serve mainly to mislead an unwary buyer.

Merriam-Webster™ is the name you should look for when you consider the purchase of dictionaries or other fine reference books. It carries the reputation of a company that has been publishing since 1831 and is your assurance of quality and authority.

Printed in Canada
25th Printing   Webcom Inc. Toronto, ON   6/2019

Contents

Preface

MERRIAM-WEBSTER'S POCKET SPANISH-ENGLISH DICTIONARY is a concise reference to the core vocabulary of Spanish and English. Its 40,000 entries and over 50,000 translations provide up-to-date coverage of the basic vocabulary and idioms in both languages. In addition, the book includes many specifically Latin-American words and phrases.

IPA (International Phonetic Alphabet) pronunciations are given for all English words. Included as well are tables of irregular verbs in both languages and the most common Spanish and English abbreviations.

This book shares many details of presentation with our larger *Merriam-Webster's Spanish-English Dictionary,* but for reasons of conciseness it also has a number of features uniquely its own. Users need to be familiar with the following major features of this dictionary.

Main entries follow one another in strict alphabetical order, without regard to intervening spaces or hyphens. The Spanish letter combinations *ch* and *ll* are alphabetized within the letters *C* and *L;* however, the Spanish letter *ñ* is alphabetized separately between *N* and *O.*

Homographs (words spelled the same but having different meanings or parts of speech) are run on at a single main entry if they are closely related. Run-on homograph entries are replaced in the text by a boldfaced swung dash (as **haber** ... *v aux* ... — ∼ *nm* ...). Homographs of distinctly different origin (as **date¹** and **date²**) are given separate entries.

Run-on entries for related words that are not homographs may also follow the main entry. Thus we have the main entry **calcular** *vt* followed by run-on entries for — **calculador, -dora** *adj* ... — **calculadora** *nf* ... and — **cálculo** *nm.* However, if a related word falls later in the alphabet than a following unrelated main entry, it will be entered at its own place; **ear** and its run-on — **eardrum** precede the main entry **earl** which is followed by the main entry **earlobe.**

Variant spellings appear at the main entry separated by *or* (as **judgment** *or* **judgement, paralyze** *or Brit* **paralyse,** or **cacahuate** *or* **cacahuete**).

Inflected forms of English verbs, adjectives, adverbs, and nouns are shown when they are irregular (as **wage** ... **waged,**

waging; ride ... rode, ridden; good ... better, best; or **fly ...** *n,
pl* **flies**) or when there might be doubt about their spelling (as **ego
...** *n, pl* **egos**). Inflected forms of Spanish irregular verbs are
shown in the section Conjugation of Spanish Verbs on page 6a; numerical references to this table are included at the main entry (as
poseer {20} *vt*). Irregular plurals of Spanish nouns or adjectives
are shown at the main entry (as **ladrón, -drona** *n, mpl* **-drones**).

   Cross-references are provided to lead the user to the appropriate main entry (as **mice → mouse** or **sobrestimar → sobreestimar**).

   Pronunciation information is either given explicitly or implied
for all English words. Pronunciation of Spanish words is assumed
to be regular and is generally omitted; it is included, however, for
certain foreign borrowings (as **pizza** ['pitsa, 'pisa]). A full list of
the pronunciation symbols used appears on page 24a.

   The grammatical function of entry words is indicated by an italic **functional label** (as *vt, adj,* or *nm*). Italic **usage labels** may be
added at the entry or sense as well (as **timbre** *nm* ... **4** *Lat*
: postage stamp, **center** or *Brit* **centre** ... *n* ..., or **garra** *nf* ... **2**
fam : hand, paw). These labels are also included in the translations
(**bag** *n* ... **2** HANDBAG : bolso *m*, cartera *f Lat*).

   Usage notes are occasionally placed before a translation to clarify meaning or use (as **que** *conj* ... **2** (*in comparisons*) : than).

   Synonyms may appear before the translation word(s) in order to
provide context for the meaning of an entry word or sense (as **sitio**
nm ... **2** ESPACIO : room, space; or **meet** ... *vt* ... **2** SATISFY : satisfacer).

   Bold notes are sometimes used before a translation to introduce
a plural sense or a common phrase using the main entry word (as
mueble *nm* ... **2** **~s** *nmpl* : furniture, furnishings, or **call** ...
vt ... **2** **~ off** : cancelar). Note that when an entry word is repeated in a bold note, it is replaced by a swung dash.

Conjugation of Spanish Verbs

Simple Tenses

Tense	Regular Verbs Ending in -AR hablar	
PRESENT INDICATIVE	hablo	hablamos
	hablas	habláis
	habla	hablan
PRESENT SUBJUNCTIVE	hable	hablemos
	hables	habléis
	hable	hablen
PRETERIT INDICATIVE	hablé	hablamos
	hablaste	hablasteis
	habló	hablaron
IMPERFECT INDICATIVE	hablaba	hablábamos
	hablabas	hablabais
	hablaba	hablaban
IMPERFECT SUBJUNCTIVE	hablara	habláramos
	hablaras	hablarais
	hablara	hablaran
	or	
	hablase	hablásemos
	hablases	hablaseis
	hablase	hablasen
FUTURE INDICATIVE	hablaré	hablaremos
	hablarás	hablaréis
	hablará	hablarán
FUTURE SUBJUNCTIVE	hablare	habláremos
	hablares	hablareis
	hablare	hablaren
CONDITIONAL	hablaría	hablaríamos
	hablarías	hablaríais
	hablaría	hablarían
IMPERATIVE		hablemos
	habla	hablad
	hable	hablen
PRESENT PARTICIPLE (GERUND)	hablando	
PAST PARTICIPLE	hablado	

Regular Verbs Ending in -ER		Regular Verbs Ending in -IR	
comer		vivir	
como	comemos	vivo	vivimos
comes	coméis	vives	vivís
come	comen	vive	viven
coma	comamos	viva	vivamos
comas	comáis	vivas	viváis
coma	coman	viva	vivan
comí	comimos	viví	vivimos
comiste	comisteis	viviste	vivisteis
comió	comieron	vivió	vivieron
comía	comíamos	vivía	vivíamos
comías	comíais	vivías	vivíais
comía	comían	vivía	vivían
comiera	comiéramos	viviera	viviéramos
comieras	comierais	vivieras	vivierais
comiera	comieran	viviera	vivieran
or		*or*	
comiese	comiésemos	viviese	viviésemos
comieses	comieseis	vivieses	vivieseis
comiese	comiesen	viviese	viviesen
comeré	comeremos	viviré	viviremos
comerás	comeréis	vivirás	viviréis
comerá	comerán	vivirá	vivirán
comiere	comiéremos	viviere	viviéremos
comieres	comiereis	vivieres	viviereis
comiere	comieren	viviere	vivieren
comería	comeríamos	viviría	viviríamos
comerías	comeríais	vivirías	viviríais
comería	comerían	viviría	vivirían
	comamos		vivamos
come	comed	vive	vivid
coma	coman	viva	vivan
comiendo		viviendo	
comido		vivido	

Compound Tenses

1. Perfect Tenses

The perfect tenses are formed with *haber* and the past participle:

PRESENT PERFECT
> he hablado, etc. (*indicative*);
> haya hablado, etc. (*subjunctive*)

PAST PERFECT
> había hablado, etc. (*indicative*);
> hubiera hablado, etc. (*subjunctive*)
> *or*
> hubiese hablado, etc. (*subjunctive*)

PRETERIT PERFECT
> hube hablado, etc. (*indicative*)

FUTURE PERFECT
> habré hablado, etc. (*indicative*)

CONDITIONAL PERFECT
> habría hablado, etc. (*indicative*)

2. Progressive Tenses

The progressive tenses are formed with *estar* and the present participle:

PRESENT PROGRESSIVE
> estoy llamando, etc. (*indicative*);
> esté llamando, etc. (*subjunctive*)

IMPERFECT PROGRESSIVE
> estaba llamando, etc. (*indicative*);
> estuviera llamando, etc. (*subjunctive*)
> *or*
> estuviese llamando, etc. (*subjunctive*)

PRETERIT PROGRESSIVE
> estuve llamando, etc. (*indicative*)

FUTURE PROGRESSIVE
> estaré llamando, etc. (*indicative*)

CONDITIONAL PROGRESSIVE
    estaría llamando, etc. (*indicative*)

PRESENT PERFECT PROGRESSIVE
    he estado llamando, etc. (*indicative*);
    haya estado llamando, etc. (*subjunctive*)

PAST PERFECT PROGRESSIVE
    había estado llamando, etc. (*indicative*);
    hubiera estado llamando, etc. (*subjunctive*)
    or
    hubiese estado llamando, etc. (*subjunctive*)

Irregular Verbs

The *imperfect subjunctive*, the *future subjunctive*, the *conditional*, and most forms of the *imperative* are not included in the model conjugations, but can be derived as follows:

The *imperfect subjunctive* and the *future subjunctive* are formed from the third person plural form of the preterit tense by removing the last syllable (*-ron*) and adding the appropriate suffix:

PRETERIT INDICATIVE, THIRD PERSON PLURAL (querer)	quisieron
IMPERFECT SUBJUNCTIVE (querer)	quisiera, quisieras, etc. *or* quisiese, quisieses, etc.
FUTURE SUBJUNCTIVE (querer)	quisiere, quisieres, etc.

The conditional uses the same stem as the future indicative:

FUTURE INDICATIVE (poner)	pondré, pondrás, etc.
CONDITIONAL (poner)	pondría, pondrías, etc.

The third person singular, first person plural, and third person plural forms of the *imperative* are the same as the corresponding forms of the present subjunctive.

The second person singular form of the *imperative* is generally the same as the third person singular of the present indicative. Exceptions are noted in the model conjugations list.

The second person plural (*vosotros*) form of the *imperative* is formed by removing the final -r of the infinitive form and adding a -d (ex.: *oír → oíd*).

Model Conjugations of Irregular Verbs

The model conjugations below include the following simple tenses: the *present indicative* (*IND*), the *present subjunctive* (*SUBJ*), the *preterit indicative* (*PRET*), the *imperfect indicative* (*IMPF*), the *future indicative* (*FUT*), the second person singular form of the *imperative* (*IMPER*) when it differs from the third person singular of the present indicative, the *gerund* or *present participle* (*PRP*), and the *past participle* (*PP*). Each set of conjugations is preceded by the corresponding infinitive form of the verb, shown in bold type. Only tenses containing irregularities are listed, and the irregular verb forms within each tense are displayed in bold type.

Each irregular verb entry in the Spanish-English section of this dictionary is cross-referenced by number to one of the following model conjugations. These cross-reference numbers are shown in curly braces { } immediately following the entry's functional label.

1 **abolir** *(defective verb)* : *IND* abolimos, abolís *(other forms not used)*; *SUBJ* (not used); *IMPER* (only second person plural is used)

2 **abrir** : *PP* abierto

3 **actuar** : *IND* **actúo, actúas, actúa**, actuamos, actuáis, **actúan**; *SUBJ* **actúe, actúes, actúe**, actuemos, actuéis, **actúen**; *IMPER* **actúa**

4 **adquirir** : *IND* **adquiero, adquieres, adquiere**, adquirimos, adquirís, **adquieren**; *SUBJ* **adquiera, adquieras, adquiera**, adquiramos, adquiráis, **adquieran**; *IMPER* **adquiere**

5 **airar** : *IND* **aíro, aíras, aíra**, airamos, airáis, **aíran**; *SUBJ* **aíre, aíres, aíre**, airemos, airéis, **aíren**; *IMPER* **aíra**

6 **andar** : *PRET* **anduve, anduviste, anduvo, anduvimos, anduvisteis, anduvieron**

7 **asir** : *IND* **asgo**, ases, ase, asimos, asís, asen; *SUBJ* **asga, asgas, asga, asgamos, asgáis, asgan**

8 **aunar** : *IND* **aúno, aúnas, aúna**, aunamos, aunáis, **aúnan**; *SUBJ* **aúne, aúnes, aúne**, aunemos, aunéis, **aúnen**; *IMPER* **aúna**

9 **avergonzar** : *IND* **avergüenzo, avergüenzas, avergüenza**, avergonzamos, avergonzáis, **avergüenzan**; *SUBJ* **avergüence, avergüences, avergüence, avergoncemos, avergoncéis, avergüencen**; *PRET* **avergoncé**; *IMPER* **avergüenza**

10 **averiguar** : *SUBJ* **averigüe, averigües, averigüe, averigüe-mos, averigüéis, averigüen;** *PRET* **averigüé,** averiguaste, averiguó, averiguamos, averiguasteis, averiguaron

11 **bendecir** : *IND* **bendigo, bendices, bendice,** bendecimos, ben-decís, **bendicen;** *SUBJ* **bendiga, bendigas, bendiga, bendig-amos, bendigáis, bendigan;** *PRET* **bendije, bendijiste, bendi-jo, bendijimos, bendijisteis, bendijeron;** *IMPER* **bendice**

12 **caber** : *IND* **quepo,** cabes, cabe, cabemos, cabéis, caben; *SUBJ* **quepa, quepas, quepa, quepamos, quepáis, quepan;** *PRET* **cupe, cupiste, cupo, cupimos, cupisteis, cupieron;** *FUT* **cabré, cabrás, cabrá, cabremos, cabréis, cabrán**

13 **caer** : *IND* **caigo,** caes, cae, caemos, caéis, caen; *SUBJ* **caiga, caigas, caiga, caigamos, caigáis, caigan;** *PRET* **caí, caíste, cayó, caímos, caísteis, cayeron;** *PRP* **cayendo;** *PP* **caído**

14 **cocer** : *IND* **cuezo, cueces, cuece,** cocemos, cocéis, **cuecen;** *SUBJ* **cueza, cuezas, cueza, cozamos, cozáis, cuezan;** *IMPER* **cuece**

15 **coger** : *IND* **cojo,** coges, coge, cogemos, cogéis, cogen; *SUBJ* **coja, cojas, coja, cojamos, cojáis, cojan**

16 **colgar** : *IND* **cuelgo, cuelgas, cuelga,** colgamos, colgáis, **cuel-gan;** *SUBJ* **cuelgue, cuelgues, cuelgue, colguemos, colguéis, cuelguen;** *PRET* **colgué,** colgaste, colgó, colgamos, colgasteis, colgaron; *IMPER* **cuelga**

17 **concernir** *(defective verb; used only in the third person singu-lar and plural of the present indicative, present subjunctive, and imperfect subjunctive) see* 25 **discernir**

18 **conocer** : *IND* **conozco,** conoces, conoce, conocemos, conocéis, conocen; *SUBJ* **conozca, conozcas, conozca, conoz-camos, conozcáis, conozcan**

19 **contar** : *IND* **cuento, cuentas, cuenta,** contamos, contáis, **cuentan;** *SUBJ* **cuente, cuentes, cuente,** contemos, contéis, **cuenten;** *IMPER* **cuenta**

20 **creer** : *PRET* **creí, creíste, creyó, creímos, creísteis, creyeron;** *PRP* **creyendo;** *PP* **creído**

21 **cruzar** : *SUBJ* **cruce, cruces, cruce, crucemos, crucéis, cru-cen;** *PRET* **crucé,** cruzaste, cruzó, cruzamos, cruzasteis, cruzaron

22 **dar** : *IND* **doy,** das, da, damos, **dais,** dan; *SUBJ* **dé,** des, **dé,** demos, **deis,** den; *PRET* **di,** diste, dio, dimos, disteis, dieron

23 **decir** : *IND* **digo, dices, dice,** decimos, decís, **dicen;** *SUBJ* **diga, digas, diga, digamos, digáis, digan;** *PRET* **dije, dijiste, dijo,** dijimos, dijisteis, dijeron; *FUT* **diré, dirás, dirá, diremos, diréis, dirán;** *IMPER* **di;** *PRP* **diciendo;** *PP* **dicho**

24 **delinquir** : *IND* **delinco,** delinques, delinque, delinquimos, delinquís, delinquen; *SUBJ* **delinca, delincas, delinca, delincamos, delincáis, delincan**

25 **discernir** : *IND* **discierno, disciernes, discierne,** discernimos, discernís, **disciernen;** *SUBJ* **discierna, disciernas, discierna,** discernamos, discernáis, **disciernan;** *IMPER* **discierne**

26 **distinguir** : *IND* **distingo,** distingues, distingue, distinguimos, distinguís, distinguen; *SUBJ* **distinga, distingas, distinga, distingamos, distingáis, distingan**

27 **dormir** : *IND* **duermo, duermes, duerme,** dormimos, dormís, **duermen;** *SUBJ* **duerma, duermas, duerma, durmamos, durmáis, duerman;** *PRET* dormí, dormiste, **durmió,** dormimos, dormisteis, **durmieron;** *IMPER* **duerme;** *PRP* **durmiendo**

28 **elegir** : *IND* **elijo, eliges, elige,** elegimos, elegís, **eligen;** *SUBJ* **elija, elijas, elija, elijamos, elijáis, elijan;** *PRET* elegí, elegiste, **eligió,** elegimos, elegisteis, **eligieron;** *IMPER* **elige;** *PRP* **eligiendo**

29 **empezar** : *IND* **empiezo, empiezas, empieza,** empezamos, empezáis, **empiezan;** *SUBJ* **empiece, empieces, empiece, empecemos, empecéis, empiecen;** *PRET* **empecé,** empezaste, empezó, empezamos, empezasteis, empezaron; *IMPER* **empieza**

30 **enraizar** : *IND* **enraízo, enraízas, enraíza,** enraizamos, enraizáis, **enraízan;** *SUBJ* **enraíce, enraíces, enraíce, enraicemos, enraicéis, enraícen;** *PRET* **enraicé,** enraizaste, enraizó, enraizamos, enraizasteis, enraizaron; *IMPER* **enraíza**

31 **erguir** : *IND* **irgo** or **yergo, irgues** or **yergues, irgue** or **yergue,** erguimos, erguís, **irguen** or **yerguen;** *SUBJ* **irga** or **yerga, irgas** or **yergas, irga** or **yerga, irgamos, irgáis, irgan** or **yergan;** *PRET* erguí, erguiste, **irguió,** erguimos, erguisteis, **irguieron;** *IMPER* **irgue** or **yergue;** *PRP* **irguiendo**

32 **errar** : *IND* **yerro, yerras, yerra,** erramos, erráis, **yerran;** *SUBJ* **yerre, yerres, yerre,** erremos, erréis, **yerren;** *IMPER* **yerra**

33 **escribir** : *PP* **escrito**

34 estar : *IND* **estoy, estás, está,** estamos, estáis, **están;** *SUBJ* **esté, estés, esté,** estemos, estéis, **estén;** *PRET* **estuve, estuviste, estuvo, estuvimos, estuvisteis, estuvieron;** *IMPER* **está**

35 exigir : *IND* **exijo,** exiges, exige, exigimos, exigís, exigen; *SUBJ* **exija, exijas, exija, exijamos, exijáis, exijan**

36 forzar : *IND* **fuerzo, fuerzas, fuerza,** forzamos, forzáis, **fuerzan;** *SUBJ* **fuerce, fuerces, fuerce, forcemos, forcéis, fuercen;** *PRET* **forcé,** forzaste, forzó, forzamos, forzasteis, forzaron; *IMPER* **fuerza**

37 freír : *IND* **frío, fríes, fríe, freímos,** freís, **fríen;** *SUBJ* **fría, frías, fría, friamos, friáis, frían;** *PRET* freí, **freíste, frió, freímos, freísteis, frieron;** *IMPER* **fríe;** *PRP* **friendo;** *PP* **frito**

38 gruñir : *PRET* gruñí, gruñiste, **gruñó,** gruñimos, gruñisteis, **gruñeron;** *PRP* **gruñendo**

39 haber : *IND* **he, has, ha, hemos,** habéis, **han;** *SUBJ* **haya, hayas, haya, hayamos, hayáis, hayan;** *PRET* **hube, hubiste, hubo, hubimos, hubisteis, hubieron;** *FUT* **habré, habrás, habrá, habremos, habréis, habrán;** *IMPER* **he**

40 hacer : *IND* **hago,** haces, hace, hacemos, hacéis, hacen; *SUBJ* **haga, hagas, haga, hagamos, hagáis, hagan;** *PRET* **hice, hiciste, hizo, hicimos, hicisteis, hicieron;** *FUT* **haré, harás, hará, haremos, haréis, harán;** *IMPER* **haz;** *PP* **hecho**

41 huir : *IND* **huyo, huyes, huye,** huimos, huís, **huyen;** *SUBJ* **huya, huyas, huya, huyamos, huyáis, huyan;** *PRET* huí, huiste, **huyó,** huimos, huisteis, **huyeron;** *IMPER* **huye;** *PRP* **huyendo**

42 imprimir : *PP* **impreso**

43 ir : *IND* **voy, vas, va, vamos, vais, van;** *SUBJ* **vaya, vayas, vaya, vayamos, vayáis, vayan;** *PRET* **fui, fuiste, fue, fuimos, fuisteis, fueron;** *IMPF* **iba, ibas, iba, íbamos, ibais, iban;** *IMPER* **ve;** *PRP* **yendo;** *PP* **ido**

44 jugar : *IND* **juego, juegas, juega,** jugamos, jugáis, **juegan;** *SUBJ* **juegue, juegues, juegue, juguemos, juguéis, jueguen;** *PRET* **jugué,** jugaste, jugó, jugamos, jugasteis, jugaron; *IMPER* **juega**

45 lucir : *IND* **luzco,** luces, luce, lucimos, lucís, lucen; *SUBJ* **luzca, luzcas, luzca, luzcamos, luzcáis, luzcan**

46 morir : *IND* **muero, mueres, muere,** morimos, morís,

mueren; *SUBJ* **muera, mueras, muera, muramos, muráis, mueran;** *PRET* morí, moriste, **murió,** morimos, moristeis, murieron; *IMPER* **muere;** *PRP* **muriendo;** *PP* **muerto**

47 **mover :** *IND* **muevo, mueves, mueve,** movemos, movéis, **mueven;** *SUBJ* **mueva, muevas, mueva,** movamos, mováis, **muevan;** *IMPER* **mueve**

48 **nacer :** *IND* **nazco,** naces, nace, nacemos, nacéis, nacen; *SUBJ* **nazca, nazcas, nazca, nazcamos, nazcáis, nazcan**

49 **negar :** *IND* **niego, niegas, niega,** negamos, negáis, **niegan;** *SUBJ* **niegue, niegues, niegue, neguemos, neguéis, nieguen;** *PRET* **negué,** negaste, negó, negamos, negasteis, negaron; *IMPER* **niega**

50 **oír :** *IND* **oigo, oyes, oye,** oímos, oís, **oyen;** *SUBJ* **oiga, oigas, oiga, oigamos, oigáis, oigan;** *PRET* oí, **oíste, oyó,** oímos, oísteis, **oyeron;** *IMPER* **oye;** *PRP* **oyendo;** *PP* **oído**

51 **oler :** *IND* **huelo, hueles, huele,** olemos, oléis, **huelen;** *SUBJ* **huela, huelas, huela,** olamos, oláis, **huelan;** *IMPER* **huele**

52 **pagar :** *SUBJ* **pague, pagues, pague, paguemos, paguéis, paguen;** *PRET* **pagué,** pagaste, pagó, pagamos, pagasteis, pagaron

53 **parecer :** *IND* **parezco,** pareces, parece, parecemos, parecéis, parecen; *SUBJ* **parezca, parezcas, parezca, parezcamos, parezcáis, parezcan**

54 **pedir :** *IND* **pido, pides, pide,** pedimos, pedís, **piden;** *SUBJ* **pida, pidas, pida, pidamos, pidáis, pidan;** *PRET* pedí, pediste, **pidió,** pedimos, pedisteis, **pidieron;** *IMPER* **pide;** *PRP* **pidiendo**

55 **pensar :** *IND* **pienso, piensas, piensa,** pensamos, pensáis, **piensan;** *SUBJ* **piense, pienses, piense,** pensemos, penséis, **piensen;** *IMPER* **piensa**

56 **perder :** *IND* **pierdo, pierdes, pierde,** perdemos, perdéis, **pierden;** *SUBJ* **pierda, pierdas, pierda,** perdamos, perdáis, **pierdan;** *IMPER* **pierde**

57 **placer :** *IND* **plazco,** places, place, placemos, placéis, placen; *SUBJ* **plazca, plazcas, plazca, plazcamos, plazcáis, plazcan;** *PRET* plací, placiste, plació *or* **plugo,** placimos, placisteis, placieron *or* **pluguieron**

58 **poder :** *IND* **puedo, puedes, puede,** podemos, podéis, **pueden;** *SUBJ* **pueda, puedas, pueda,** podamos, podáis, **puedan;** *PRET*

pude, pudiste, pudo, pudimos, pudisteis, pudieron; *FUT* **podré, podrás, podrá, podremos, podréis, podrán;** *IMPER* **puede;** *PRP* **pudiendo**

59 **podrir** *or* **pudrir** : *PP* **podrido** *(all other forms based on pudrir)*

60 **poner** : *IND* **pongo,** pones, pone, ponemos, ponéis, ponen; *SUBJ* **ponga, pongas, ponga, pongamos, pongáis, pongan;** *PRET* **puse, pusiste, puso, pusimos, pusisteis, pusieron;** *FUT* **pondré, pondrás, pondrá, pondremos, pondréis, pondrán;** *IMPER* **pon;** *PP* **puesto**

61 **producir** : *IND* **produzco,** produces, produce, producimos, producís, producen; *SUBJ* **produzca, produzcas, produzca, produzcamos, produzcáis, produzcan;** *PRET* **produje, produjiste, produjo, produjimos, produjisteis, produjeron**

62 **prohibir** : *IND* **prohíbo, prohíbes, prohíbe,** prohibimos, prohibís, **prohíben;** *SUBJ* **prohíba, prohíbas, prohíba,** prohibamos, prohibáis, **prohíban;** *IMPER* **prohíbe**

63 **proveer** : *PRET* proveí, **proveíste, proveyó,** proveímos, proveísteis, **proveyeron;** *PRP* **proveyendo;** *PP* **provisto**

64 **querer** : *IND* **quiero, quieres, quiere,** queremos, queréis, **quieren;** *SUBJ* **quiera, quieras, quiera,** queramos, queráis, **quieran;** *PRET* **quise, quisiste, quiso, quisimos, quisisteis, quisieron;** *FUT* **querré, querrás, querrá, querremos, querréis, querrán;** *IMPER* **quiere**

65 **raer** : *IND* rao *or* **raigo** *or* **rayo,** raes, rae, raemos, raéis, raen; *SUBJ* **raiga** *or* **raya, raigas** *or* **rayas, raiga** *or* **raya, raigamos** *or* **rayamos, raigáis** *or* **rayáis, raigan** *or* **rayan;** *PRET* **raí, raíste, rayó, raímos, raísteis, rayeron;** *PRP* **rayendo;** *PP* **raído**

66 **reír** : *IND* **río, ríes, ríe, reímos,** reís, **ríen;** *SUBJ* **ría, rías, ría, riamos, riáis, rían;** *PRET* reí, **reíste, rió, reímos, reísteis, rieron;** *IMPER* **ríe;** *PRP* **riendo;** *PP* **reído**

67 **reñir** : *IND* **riño, riñes, riñe,** reñimos, reñís, **riñen;** *SUBJ* **riña, riñas, riña, riñamos, riñáis, riñan;** *PRET* reñí, reñiste, **riñó,** reñimos, reñisteis, **riñeron;** *PRP* **riñendo**

68 **reunir** : *IND* **reúno, reúnes, reúne,** reunimos, reunís, **reúnen;** *SUBJ* **reúna, reúnas, reúna,** reunamos, reunáis, **reúnan;** *IMPER* **reúne**

69 **roer** : *IND* roo *or* **roigo** *or* **royo,** roes, roe, roemos, roéis, roen;

SUBJ roa *or* roiga *or* roya, roas *or* roigas *or* royas, roa *or* roiga *or* roya, roamos *or* roigamos *or* royamos, roáis *or* roigáis *or* royáis, roan *or* roigan *or* royan; *PRET* roí, roíste, royó, roímos, roísteis, royeron; *PRP* royendo; *PP* roído

70 **romper** : *PP* **roto**

71 **saber** : *IND* **sé**, sabes, sabe, sabemos, sabéis, saben; *SUBJ* **sepa, sepas, sepa, sepamos, sepáis, sepan**; *PRET* **supe, supiste, supo, supimos, supisteis, supieron**; *FUT* **sabré, sabrás, sabrá, sabremos, sabréis, sabrán**

72 **sacar** : *SUBJ* **saque, saques, saque, saquemos, saquéis, saquen**; *PRET* **saqué**, sacaste, sacó, sacamos, sacasteis, sacaron

73 **salir** : *IND* **salgo**, sales, sale, salimos, salís, salen; *SUBJ* **salga, salgas, salga, salgamos, salgáis, salgan**; *FUT* **saldré, saldrás, saldrá, saldremos, saldréis, saldrán**; *IMPER* **sal**

74 **satisfacer** : *IND* **satisfago**, satisfaces, satisface, satisfacemos, satisfacéis, satisfacen; *SUBJ* **satisfaga, satisfagas, satisfaga, satisfagamos, satisfagáis, satisfagan**; *PRET* **satisfice, satisficiste, satisfizo, satisficimos**, satificisteis, **satisficieron**; *FUT* **satisfaré, satisfarás, satisfará, satisfaremos, satisfaréis, satisfarán**; *IMPER* **satisfaz** *or* **satisface**; *PP* **satisfecho**

75 **seguir** : *IND* **sigo, sigues, sigue**, seguimos, seguís, **siguen**; *SUBJ* **siga, sigas, siga, sigamos, sigáis, sigan**; *PRET* seguí, seguiste, **siguió**, seguimos, seguisteis, **siguieron**; *IMPER* **sigue**; *PRP* **siguiendo**

76 **sentir** : *IND* **siento, sientes, siente**, sentimos, sentís, **sienten**; *SUBJ* **sienta, sientas, sienta**, sintamos, sintáis, **sientan**; *PRET* sentí, sentiste, **sintió**, sentimos, sentisteis, **sintieron**; *IMPER* **siente**; *PRP* **sintiendo**

77 **ser** : *IND* **soy, eres, es, somos, sois, son**; *SUBJ* **sea, seas, sea, seamos, seáis, sean**; *PRET* **fui, fuiste, fue, fuimos, fuisteis, fueron**; *IMPF* **era, eras, era, éramos, erais, eran**; *IMPER* **sé**; *PRP* **siendo**; *PP* **sido**

78 **soler** (*defective verb; used only in the present, preterit, and imperfect indicative, and the present and imperfect subjunctive*) *see* 47 **mover**

79 **tañer** : *PRET* tañí, tañiste, **tañó**, tañimos, tañisteis, **tañeron**; *PRP* **tañendo**

80 **tener** : *IND* **tengo, tienes, tiene**, tenemos, tenéis, **tienen**; *SUBJ* **tenga, tengas, tenga, tengamos, tengáis, tengan**; *PRET* **tuve,**

tuviste, tuvo, tuvimos, tuvisteis, tuvieron; *FUT* **tendré, tendrás, tendrá, tendremos, tendréis, tendrán;** *IMPER* **ten**

81 **traer** : *IND* **traigo,** traes, trae, traemos, traéis, traen; *SUBJ* **traiga, traigas, traiga, traigamos, traigáis, traigan;** *PRET* **traje, trajiste, trajo, trajimos, trajisteis, trajeron;** *PRP* **trayendo;** *PP* **traído**

82 **trocar** : *IND* **trueco, truecas, trueca,** trocamos, trocáis, **truecan;** *SUBJ* **trueque, trueques, trueque,** troquemos, troquéis, **truequen;** *PRET* **troqué,** trocaste, trocó, trocamos, trocasteis, trocaron; *IMPER* **trueca**

83 **uncir** : *IND* **unzo,** unces, unce, uncimos, uncís, uncen; *SUBJ* **unza, unzas, unza, unzamos, unzáis, unzan**

84 **valer** : *IND* **valgo,** vales, vale, valemos, valéis, valen; *SUBJ* **valga, valgas, valga, valgamos, valgáis, valgan;** *FUT* **valdré, valdrás, valdrá, valdremos, valdréis, valdrán**

85 **variar** : *IND* **varío, varías, varía,** variamos, variáis, **varían;** *SUBJ* **varíe, varíes, varíe,** variemos, variéis, **varíen;** *IMPER* **varía**

86 **vencer** : *IND* **venzo,** vences, vence, vencemos, vencéis, vencen; *SUBJ* **venza, venzas, venza, venzamos, venzáis, venzan**

87 **venir** : *IND* **vengo, vienes, viene,** venimos, venís, **vienen;** *SUBJ* **venga, vengas, venga, vengamos, vengáis, vengan;** *PRET* **vine, viniste, vino, vinimos, vinisteis, vinieron;** *FUT* **vendré, vendrás, vendrá, vendremos, vendréis, vendrán;** *IMPER* **ven;** *PRP* **viniendo**

88 **ver** : *IND* **veo, ves, ve,** vemos, veis, ven; *PRET* **vi,** viste, vio, vimos, visteis, vieron; *IMPER* **ve;** *PRP* **viendo;** *PP* **visto**

89 **volver** : *IND* **vuelvo, vuelves, vuelve,** volvemos, volvéis, **vuelven;** *SUBJ* **vuelva, vuelvas, vuelva,** volvamos, volváis, **vuelvan;** *IMPER* **vuelve;** *PP* **vuelto**

90 **yacer** : *IND* **yazco** or **yazgo** or **yago,** yaces, yace, yacemos, yacéis, yacen; *SUBJ* **yazca** or **yazga** or **yaga, yazcas** or **yazgas** or **yagas, yazca** or **yazga** or **yaga, yazcamos** or **yazgamos** or **yagamos, yazcáis** or **yazgáis** or **yagáis, yazcan** or **yazgan** or **yagan;** *IMPER* **yace** or **yaz**

Irregular English Verbs

INFINITIVE	PAST	PAST PARTICIPLE
arise	arose	arisen
awake	awoke	awoken *or* awaked
be	was, were	been
bear	bore	borne
beat	beat	beaten *or* beat
become	became	become
befall	befell	befallen
begin	began	begun
behold	beheld	beheld
bend	bent	bent
beseech	beseeched *or* besought	beseeched *or* besought
beset	beset	beset
bet	bet	bet
bid	bade *or* bid	bidden *or* bid
bind	bound	bound
bite	bit	bitten
bleed	bled	bled
blow	blew	blown
break	broke	broken
breed	bred	bred
bring	brought	brought
build	built	built
burn	burned *or* burnt	burned *or* burnt
burst	burst	burst
buy	bought	bought
can	could	—
cast	cast	cast
catch	caught	caught
choose	chose	chosen
cling	clung	clung
come	came	come
cost	cost	cost
creep	crept	crept
cut	cut	cut
deal	dealt	dealt
dig	dug	dug
do	did	done
draw	drew	drawn

INFINITIVE	PAST	PAST PARTICIPLE
dream	dreamed *or* dreamt	dreamed *or* dreamt
drink	drank	drunk *or* drank
drive	drove	driven
dwell	dwelled *or* dwelt	dwelled *or* dwelt
eat	ate	eaten
fall	fell	fallen
feed	fed	fed
feel	felt	felt
fight	fought	fought
find	found	found
flee	fled	fled
fling	flung	flung
fly	flew	flown
forbid	forbade	forbidden
forecast	forecast	forecast
forego	forewent	foregone
foresee	foresaw	foreseen
foretell	foretold	foretold
forget	forgot	forgotten *or* forgot
forgive	forgave	forgiven
forsake	forsook	forsaken
freeze	froze	frozen
get	got	got *or* gotten
give	gave	given
go	went	gone
grind	ground	ground
grow	grew	grown
hang	hung	hung
have	had	had
hear	heard	heard
hide	hid	hidden *or* hid
hit	hit	hit
hold	held	held
hurt	hurt	hurt
keep	kept	kept
kneel	knelt *or* kneeled	knelt *or* kneeled
know	knew	known
lay	laid	laid
lead	led	led
lean	leaned	leaned
leap	leaped *or* leapt	leaped *or* leapt
learn	learned	learned

INFINITIVE	PAST	PAST PARTICIPLE
leave	left	left
lend	lent	lent
let	let	let
lie	lay	lain
light	lit *or* lighted	lit *or* lighted
lose	lost	lost
make	made	made
may	might	—
mean	meant	meant
meet	met	met
mow	mowed	mowed *or* mown
pay	paid	paid
put	put	put
quit	quit	quit
read	read	read
rend	rent	rent
rid	rid	rid
ride	rode	ridden
ring	rang	rung
rise	rose	risen
run	ran	run
saw	sawed	sawed *or* sawn
say	said	said
see	saw	seen
seek	sought	sought
sell	sold	sold
send	sent	sent
set	set	set
shake	shook	shaken
shall	should	—
shear	sheared	sheared *or* shorn
shed	shed	shed
shine	shone *or* shined	shone *or* shined
shoot	shot	shot
show	showed	shown *or* showed
shrink	shrank *or* shrunk	shrunk *or* shrunken
shut	shut	shut
sing	sang *or* sung	sung
sink	sank *or* sunk	sunk
sit	sat	sat
slay	slew	slain
sleep	slept	slept

INFINITIVE	PAST	PAST PARTICIPLE
slide	slid	slid
sling	slung	slung
smell	smelled *or* smelt	smelled *or* smelt
sow	sowed	sown *or* sowed
speak	spoke	spoken
speed	sped *or* speeded	sped *or* speeded
spell	spelled	spelled
spend	spent	spent
spill	spilled	spilled
spin	spun	spun
spit	spit *or* spat	spit *or* spat
split	split	split
spoil	spoiled	spoiled
spread	spread	spread
spring	sprang *or* sprung	sprung
stand	stood	stood
steal	stole	stolen
stick	stuck	stuck
sting	stung	stung
stink	stank *or* stunk	stunk
stride	strode	stridden
strike	struck	struck
swear	swore	sworn
sweep	swept	swept
swell	swelled	swelled *or* swollen
swim	swam	swum
swing	swung	swung
take	took	taken
teach	taught	taught
tear	tore	torn
tell	told	told
think	thought	thought
throw	threw	thrown
thrust	thrust	thrust
tread	trod	trodden *or* trod
wake	woke	woken *or* waked
waylay	waylaid	waylaid
wear	wore	worn
weave	wove *or* weaved	woven *or* weaved
wed	wedded	wedded
weep	wept	wept
will	would	—

INFINITIVE	PAST	PAST PARTICIPLE
win	won	won
wind	wound	wound
withdraw	withdrew	withdrawn
withhold	withheld	withheld
withstand	withstood	withstood
wring	wrung	wrung
write	wrote	written

Abbreviations in this Work

adj	adjective	*nmf*	masculine or feminine noun
adv	adverb		
adv phr	adverbial phrase	*nmfpl*	plural noun invariable for gender
algn	alguien (someone)		
art	article	*nmfs & pl*	noun invariable for both gender and number
Brit	Great Britain		
conj	conjunction	*nmpl*	masculine plural noun
conj phr	conjunctive phrase	*nms & pl*	invariable singular or plural masculine noun
esp	especially		
etc	et cetera	*npl*	plural noun
f	feminine	*ns & pl*	noun invariable for plural
fam	familiar or colloquial	*pl*	plural
fpl	feminine plural	*pp*	past participle
interj	interjection	*prep*	preposition
Lat	Latin America	*prep phr*	prepositional phrase
m	masculine	*pron*	pronoun
mf	masculine or feminine	*s.o.*	someone
mpl	masculine plural	*sth*	something
n	noun	*usu*	usually
nf	feminine noun	*v*	verb
nfpl	feminine plural noun	*v aux*	auxiliary verb
nfs & pl	invariable singular or plural feminine noun	*vi*	intransitive verb
		v impers	impersonal verb
nm	masculine noun	*vr*	reflexive verb
		vt	transitive verb

Pronunciation Symbols

VOWELS

æ	ask, bat, glad
ɑ	cot, bomb
a	*New England* **au**nt, *British* **a**sk, gl**a**ss, *Spanish* c**a**sa
ɛ	egg, bet, fed
ə	about, javelin, Alabama
ə	when italicized as in əl, əm, ən, indicates a syllabic pronunciation of the consonant as in bottle, prism, button
i	very, any, thirty, *Spanish* piña
iː	eat, bead, bee
ɪ	id, bid, pit
o	Ohio, yellower, potato, *Spanish* óvalo
oː	oats, own, zone, blow
ɔ	awl, maul, caught, paw
ʊ	sure, should, could
uː	boot, few, coo
ʌ	under, putt, bud
eɪ	eight, wade, bay
aɪ	ice, bite, tie
aʊ	out, gown, plow
ɔɪ	oyster, coil, boy
ː	indicates that the preceding vowel is long. Long vowels are almost always diphthongs in English, but not in Spanish.

STRESS MARKS

ˈ	high stress	**pen**manship
ˌ	low stress	penman**ship**

CONSONANTS

b	baby, labor, cab
d	day, ready, kid
dʒ	just, badger, fudge
ð	then, either, bathe
f	foe, tough, buff
g	go, bigger, bag
h	hot, aha
j	yes, vineyard
k	cat, keep, lacquer, flock
l	law, hollow, boil
m	mat, hemp, hammer, rim
n	new, tent, tenor, run
ŋ	rung, hang, swinger
p	pay, lapse, top
r	rope, burn, tar
s	sad, mist, kiss
ʃ	shoe, mission, slush
t	toe, button, mat
t̩	indicates that some speakers of English pronounce this sound as a voiced alveolar flap [ɾ], as in later, catty, battle
tʃ	choose, batch
θ	thin, ether, bath
v	vat, never, cave
w	wet, software
z	zoo, easy, buzz
ʒ	azure, beige
h, k, p, t	when italicized indicate sounds which are present in the pronunciation of some speakers of English but absent in the pronunciation of others, so that *whence* [ˈhwɛnts] can be pronounced as [ˈhwɛns], [ˈhwɛnts], or [ˈwɛns]

Spanish-English
Dictionary

A

a¹ *nf* : a, first letter of the Spanish alphabet

a² *prep* **1** : to **2 ~ las dos** : at two o'clock **3 al día siguiente** : (on) the following day **4 ~ pie** : on foot **5 de lunes ~ viernes** : from Monday until Friday **6 tres veces ~ la semana** : three times per week **7 ~ la** : in the manner of, like

abadía *nf* : abbey

abajo *adv* **1** : down, below, downstairs **2 ~ de** *Lat* : under, beneath **3 de ~** : (at the) bottom **4 hacia ~** : downwards

abalanzarse {21} *vr* : hurl oneself, rush

abandonar *vt* **1** : abandon, leave **2** RENUNCIAR A : give up — **abandonarse** *vr* **1** : neglect oneself **2 ~ a** : give oneself over to — **abandonado, -da** *adj* **1** : abandoned, deserted **2** DESCUIDADO : slovenly — **abandono** *nm* **1** : abandonment, neglect **2 por ~** : by default

abanico *nm* : fan — **abanicar** {72} *vt* : fan

abaratar *vt* : lower the price of — **abaratarse** *vr* : become cheaper

abarcar {72} *vt* **1** : cover, embrace **2** *Lat* : monopolize

abarrotar *vt* : pack, cram — **abarrotes** *nmpl Lat* **1** : groceries **2 tienda de ~** : grocery store

abastecer {53} *vt* : supply, stock — **abastecimiento** *nm* : supply, provisions — **abasto** *nm* **1** : supply **2 no dar ~** : be unable to cope with

abatir *vt* **1** : knock down, shoot down **2** DEPRIMIR : depress — **abatirse** *vr* **1** : get depressed **2 ~ sobre** : swoop down on — **abatido, -da** *adj* : dejected, depressed — **abatimiento** *nm* : depression, dejection

abdicar {72} *v* : abdicate — **abdicación** *nf, pl* **-ciones** : abdication

abdomen *nm, pl* **-dómenes** : abdomen — **abdominal** *adj* : abdominal

abecé *nm* : ABC — **abecedario** *nm* : alphabet

abedul *nm* : birch

abeja *nf* : bee — **abejorro** *nm* : bumblebee

aberración *nf, pl* **-ciones** : aberration

abertura *nf* : opening

abeto *nm* : fir (tree)

abierto, -ta *adj* : open

abigarrado, -da *adj* : multicolored

abismo *nm* : abyss, chasm — **abismal** *adj* : vast, enormous

abjurar *vi* **~ de** : abjure

ablandar *vt* : soften (up) — **ablandarse** *vr* : soften

abnegarse {49} *vr* : deny oneself — **abnegado, -da** *adj* : self-sacrificing — **abnegación** *nf, pl* **-ciones** : self-denial

abochornar *vt* : embarrass — **abochornarse** *vr* : get embarrassed

abofetear *vt* : slap

abogado, -da *n* : lawyer — **abogacía** *nf* : legal profession — **abogar** {52} *vi* **~ por** : plead for, defend

abolengo *nm* : lineage

abolir {1} *vt* : abolish — **abolición** *nf, pl* **-ciones** : abolition

abollar *vt* : dent — **abolladura** *nf* : dent

abominar *vt* : abominate — **abominable** *adj* : abominable — **abominación** *nf, pl* **-ciones** : abomination

abonar *vt* **1** : pay (a bill, etc.) **2** : fertilize (the soil) — **abonarse** *vr* : subscribe — **abonado, -da** *n* : subscriber — **abono** *nm* **1** : payment, installment **2** FERTILIZANTE : fertilizer **3** : season ticket (to the theater, etc.)

abordar *vt* **1** : tackle (a problem) **2** : accost, approach (a person) **3** *Lat* : board — **abordaje** *nm* : boarding

aborigen *nmf, pl* **-rígenes** : aborigine — **~** *adj* : aboriginal, native

aborrecer {53} *vt* : abhor, detest — **aborrecible** *adj* : hateful — **aborrecimiento** *nm* : loathing

abortar *vi* : have a miscarriage — *vt* : abort — **aborto** *nm* : abortion, miscarriage

abotonar *vt* : button — **abotonarse** *vr* : button up

abovedado, -da *adj* : vaulted

abrasar *vt* : burn, scorch — **abrasarse** *vr* : burn up — **abrasador, -dora** *adj* : burning

abrasivo, -va *adj* : abrasive — **abrasivo** *nm* : abrasive

abrazar {21} *vt* : hug, embrace — **abrazarse** *vr* : embrace — **abraza-**

dera *nf* : clamp — **abrazo** *nm* : hug, embrace

abrebotellas *nms & pl* : bottle opener — **abrelatas** *nms & pl* : can opener

abrevadero *nm* : watering trough

abreviar *vt* 1 : shorten, abridge 2 : abbreviate (a word) — **abreviación** *nf*, *pl* -ciones : shortening — **abreviatura** *nf* : abbreviation

abridor *nm* : bottle opener, can opener

abrigar {52} *vt* 1 : wrap up (in clothing) 2 ALBERGAR : cherish, harbor — **abrigarse** *vr* : dress warmly — **abrigado, -da** *adj* 1 : sheltered 2 : warm, wrapped up (of persons) — **abrigo** *nm* 1 : coat, overcoat 2 REFUGIO : shelter, refuge

abril *nm* : April

abrillantar *vt* : polish, shine

abrir {2} *vt* 1 : open 2 : unlock, undo — *vi* : open up — **abrirse** *vr* 1 : open up 2 : clear up (of weather)

abrochar *vt* : button, fasten — **abrocharse** *vr* : fasten, do up

abrogar {52} *vt* : annul, repeal

abrumar *vt* : overwhelm — **abrumador, -dora** *adj* : overwhelming, oppressive

abrupto, -ta *adj* 1 ESCARPADO : steep 2 ÁSPERO : rugged, harsh 3 REPENTINO : abrupt

absceso *nm* : abscess

absolución *nf*, *pl* -ciones 1 : absolution 2 : acquittal (in law)

absoluto, -ta *adj* 1 : absolute, unconditional 2 **en absoluto** : not at all — **absolutamente** *adv* : absolutely

absolver {89} *vt* 1 : absolve 2 : acquit (in law)

absorber *vt* 1 : absorb 2 : take up (time, energy, etc.) — **absorbente** *adj* 1 : absorbent 2 INTERESANTE : absorbing — **absorción** *nf*, *pl* -ciones : absorption — **absorto, -ta** *adj* : absorbed, engrossed

abstemio, -mia *adj* : abstemious — ～ *n* : teetotaler

abstenerse {80} *vr* : abstain, refrain — **abstención** *nf*, *pl* -ciones : abstention — **abstinencia** *nf* : abstinence

abstracción *nf*, *pl* -ciones : abstraction — **abstracto, -ta** *adj* : abstract — **abstraer** {81} *vt* : abstract — **abstraerse** *vr* : lose oneself in thought — **abstraído, -da** *adj* : preoccupied

absurdo, -da *adj* : absurd, ridiculous — **absurdo** *nm* : absurdity

abuchear *vt* : boo, jeer — **abucheo** *nm* : booing

abuelo, -la *n* 1 : grandfather, grand-

mother 2 **abuelos** *nmpl* : grandparents

abulia *nf* : apathy, lethargy

abultar *vi* : bulge, be bulky — *vt* : enlarge, expand — **abultado, -da** *adj* : bulky

abundar *vi* : abound, be plentiful — **abundancia** *nf* : abundance — **abundante** *adj* : abundant

aburrir *vt* : bore — **aburrirse** *vr* : get bored — **aburrido, -da** *adj* 1 : bored 2 TEDIOSO : boring — **aburrimiento** *nm* : boredom

abusar *vi* 1 : go too far 2 ～ **de** : abuse — **abusivo, -va** *adj* : outrageous, excessive — **abuso** *nm* : abuse

abyecto, -ta *adj* : abject, wretched

acá *adv* : here, over here

acabar *vi* 1 : finish, end 2 ～ **de** : have just (done something) 3 ～ **con** : put an end to 4 ～ **por** : end up (doing sth) — *vt* : finish — **acabarse** *vr* : come to an end — **acabado, -da** *adj* 1 : finished, perfect 2 AGOTADO : old, worn-out — **acabado** *nm* : finish

academia *nf* : academy — **académico, -ca** *adj* : academic

acaecer {53} *vi* : happen, occur

acallar *vt* : quiet, silence

acalorar *vt* : stir up, excite — **acalorarse** *vr* : get worked up — **acalorado, -da** *adj* : emotional, heated

acampar *vi* : camp — **acampada** *nf* **ir de** ～ : go camping

acanalado, -da *adj* 1 : grooved 2 : corrugated (of iron, etc.)

acantilado *nm* : cliff

acaparar *vt* 1 : hoard 2 MONOPOLIZAR : monopolize

acápite *nm* *Lat* : paragraph

acariciar *vt* 1 : caress 2 : cherish (hopes, ideas, etc.)

ácaro *nm* : mite

acarrear *vt* 1 : haul, carry 2 OCASIONAR : give rise to — **acarreo** *nm* : transport

acaso *adv* 1 : perhaps, maybe 2 **por si** ～ : just in case

acatar *vt* : comply with, respect — **acatamiento** *nm* : compliance, respect

acatarrarse *vr* : catch a cold

acaudalado, -da *adj* : wealthy, rich

acaudillar *vt* : lead

acceder *vi* 1 : agree 2 ～ **a** : gain access to, enter

acceso *nm* 1 : access 2 ENTRADA : entrance 3 : attack, bout (of an illness) — **accesible** *adj* : accessible

accesorio *nm* : accessory — **accesorio, -ria** *adj* : incidental

accidentado, -da *adj* 1 : eventful, turbulent 2 : rough, uneven (of land, etc.) 3 HERIDO : injured — ~ *n* : accident victim

accidental *adj* : accidental — **accidentarse** *vr* : have an accident — **accidente** *nm* 1 : accident 2 : unevenness (of land)

acción *nf*, *pl* **-ciones** 1 : action ACTO : act, deed 3 : share, stock (in finance) — **accionar** *vt* : activate — *vi* : gesticulate — **accionista** *nmf* : stockholder

acebo *nm* : holly

acechar *vt* : watch, stalk — **acecho** *nm* **estar al ~ por** : be on the lookout for

aceite *nm* 1 : oil — **aceitar** *vt* : oil — **aceitera** *nf* 1 : oilcan 2 : cruet (in cookery) 3 *Lat* : oil refinery — **aceitoso, -sa** *adj* : oily

aceituna *nf* : olive

acelerar *v* : accelerate — **acelerarse** *vr* : hurry up — **aceleración** *nf*, *pl* **-ciones** : acceleration — **acelerador** *nm* : accelerator

acelga *nf* : (Swiss) chard

acentuar {3} *vt* 1 : accent 2 ENFATIZAR : emphasize, stress — **acentuarse** *vr* : stand out — **acento** *nm* 1 : accent 2 ÉNFASIS : stress, emphasis

acepción *nf*, *pl* **-ciones** : sense, meaning

aceptar *vt* : accept — **aceptable** *adj* : acceptable — **aceptación** *nf*, *pl* **-ciones** 1 : acceptance 2 ÉXITO : success

acequia *nf* : irrigation ditch

acera *nf* : sidewalk

acerbo, -ba *adj* : harsh, caustic

acerca *prep* **~ de** : about, concerning

acercar {72} *vt* : bring near or closer — **acercarse** *vr* : approach, draw near

acero *nm* 1 : steel 2 **~ inoxidable** : stainless steel

acérrimo, -ma *adj* 1 : staunch, steadfast 2 : bitter (of an enemy)

acertar {55} *vt* : guess correctly — *vi* 1 ATINAR : be accurate 2 **~ a** : manage to — **acertado, -da** *adj* : correct, accurate

acertijo *nm* : riddle

acervo *nm* : heritage

acetona *nf* : acetone, nail-polish remover

achacar {72} *vt* : attribute, impute

achacoso, -sa *adj* : sickly

achaparrado, -da *adj* : squat, stocky

achaque *nm* : aches and pains

achatar *vt* : flatten

achicar {72} *vt* 1 : make smaller 2 ACOBARDAR : intimidate 3 : bail out

(water) — **achicarse** *vr* : become intimidated

achicharrar *vt* : scorch, burn to a crisp

achicoria *nf* : chicory

aciago, -ga *adj* : fateful, unlucky

acicalar *vt* : dress up, adorn — **acicalarse** *vr* : get dressed up

acicate *nm* 1 : spur 2 INCENTIVO : incentive

ácido, -da *adj* : acid, sour — **acidez** *nf*, *pl* **-deces** : acidity — **ácido** *nm* : acid

acierto *nm* 1 : correct answer 2 HABILIDAD : skill, sound judgment

aclamar *vt* : acclaim — **aclamación** *nf*, *pl* **-ciones** : acclaim, applause

aclarar *vt* 1 CLARIFICAR : clarify, explain 2 : rinse (clothing) 3 **~ la voz** : clear one's throat — *vi* : clear up — **aclararse** *vr* : become clear — **aclaración** *nf*, *pl* **-ciones** : explanation — **aclaratorio, -ria** *adj* : explanatory

aclimatar *vt* : acclimatize — **aclimatarse** *vr* **~ a** : get used to — **aclimatación** *nf*, *pl* **-ciones** : acclimatization

acné *nm* : acne

acobardar *vt* : intimidate — **acobardarse** *vr* : become frightened

acodarse *vr* **~ en** : lean (one's elbows) on

acoger {15} *vt* 1 REFUGIAR : shelter 2 RECIBIR : receive, welcome — **acogerse** *vr* 1 : take refuge 2 **~ a** : resort to — **acogedor, -dora** *adj* : cozy, welcoming — **acogida** *nf* 1 : welcome 2 REFUGIO : refuge

acolchar *vt* : pad

acólito *nm* MONAGUILLO : altar boy

acometer *vt* 1 : attack 2 EMPRENDER : undertake — *vi* **~ contra** : rush against — **acometida** *nf* : attack, assault

acomodar *vt* 1 ADAPTAR : adjust 2 COLOCAR : put, make a place for — **acomodarse** *vr* 1 : settle in 2 **~ a** : adapt to — **acomodado, -da** *adj* : well-to-do — **acomodaticio, -cia** *adj* : accommodating, obliging — **acomodo** *nm* : job, position

acompañar *vt* 1 : accompany 2 ADJUNTAR : enclose — **acompañamiento** *nm* : accompaniment — **acompañante** *nmf* 1 COMPAÑERO : companion 2 : accompanist (in music)

acompasado, -da *adj* : rhythmic, measured

acondicionar *vt* : fit out, equip — **acondicionado, -da** *adj* : equipped

acongojar *vt* : distress, upset — **acongojarse** *vr* : get upset

aconsejar *vt* : advise — **aconsejable** *adj* : advisable

acontecer {53} *vi* : occur, happen — **acontecimiento** *nm* : event

acopiar *vt* : gather, collect — **acopio** *nm* : collection, stock

acoplar *vt* : couple, connect — **acoplarse** *vr* : fit together — **acoplamiento** *nm* : connection, coupling

acorazado, -da *adj* : armored — **acorazado** *nm* : battleship

acordar {19} *vt* **1** : agree (on) **2** *Lat* : award — **acordarse** *vr* : remember

acorde *adj* **1** : in agreement **2** ~ **con** : in keeping with — ~ *nm* : chord (in music)

acordeón *nm, pl* **-deones** : accordion

acordonar *vt* **1** : cordon off **2** : lace up (shoes)

acorralar *vt* : corner, corral

acortar *vt* : shorten, cut short — **acortarse** *vr* : get shorter

acosar *vt* : hound, harass — **acoso** *nm* : harassment

acostar {19} *vt* : put to bed — **acostarse** *vr* **1** : go to bed **2** TUMBARSE : lie down

acostumbrar *vt* : accustom — *vi* ~ **a** : be in the habit of — **acostumbrarse** *vr* ~ **a** : get used to — **acostumbrado, -da** *adj* **1** HABITUADO : accustomed **2** HABITUAL : usual

acotar *vt* **1** ANOTAR : annotate **2** DELIMITAR : mark off (land) — **acotación** *nf, pl* **-ciones** : marginal note — **acotado, -da** *adj* : enclosed

acre *adj* **1** : pungent **2** MORDAZ : harsh, biting

acrecentar {55} *vt* : increase — **acrecentamiento** *nm* : growth, increase

acreditar *vt* **1** : accredit, authorize **2** PROBAR : prove — **acreditarse** *vr* : prove oneself — **acreditado, -da** *adj* **1** : reputable **2** : accredited (in politics, etc.)

acreedor, -dora *adj* : worthy — ~ *n* : creditor

acribillar *vt* **1** : riddle, pepper **2** ~ **a** : harass with

acrílico *nm* : acrylic

acrimonia *nf or* **acritud** *nf* **1** : pungency **2** RESENTIMIENTO : bitterness, acrimony

acrobacia *nf* : acrobatics — **acróbata** *nmf* : acrobat — **acrobático, -ca** *adj* : acrobatic

acta *nf* **1** : certificate **2** : minutes *pl* (of a meeting)

actitud *nf* **1** : attitude **2** POSTURA : posture, position

activar *vt* **1** : activate **2** ESTIMULAR : stimulate, speed up — **actividad** *nf* : activity — **activo, -va** *adj* : active — **activo** *nm* : assets *pl*

acto *nm* **1** ACCIÓN : act, deed **2** : act (in theater) **3 en el** ~ : right away

actor *nm* : actor — **actriz** *nf, pl* **-trices** : actress

actual *adj* : present, current — **actualidad** *nf* **1** : present time **2** ~ **es** *nfpl* : current affairs — **actualizar** {21} *vt* : modernize — **actualización** *nf, pl* **-ciones** : modernization — **actualmente** *adv* : at present, nowadays

actuar {3} *vi* **1** : act, perform **2** ~ **de** : act as

acuarela *nf* : watercolor

acuario *nm* : aquarium

acuartelar *vt* : quarter (troops)

acuático, -ca *adj* : aquatic, water

acuchillar *vt* : knife, stab

acudir *vi* **1** : go, come **2** ~ **a** : be present at, attend **3** ~ **a** : turn to

acueducto *nm* : aqueduct

acuerdo *nm* **1** : agreement **2 de** ~ : OK, all right **3 de** ~ **con** : in accordance with **4 estar de** ~ : agree

acumular *vt* : accumulate — **acumularse** *vr* : pile up — **acumulación** *nf, pl* **-ciones** : accumulation — **acumulador** *nm* : storage battery — **acumulativo, -va** *adj* : cumulative

acunar *vt* : rock

acuñar *vt* **1** : mint (money) **2** : coin (a word)

acuoso, -sa *adj* : watery

acupuntura *nf* : acupuncture

acurrucarse {72} *vr* : curl up, nestle

acusar *vt* **1** : accuse **2** MOSTRAR : reveal, show — **acusación** *nf, pl* **-ciones** : accusation, charge — **acusado, -da** *adj* : prominent, marked — ~ *n* : defendant

acuse *nm* ~ **de recibo** : acknowledgment of receipt

acústica *nf* : acoustics — **acústico, -ca** *adj* : acoustic

adagio *nm* **1** REFRÁN : adage, proverb **2** : adagio (in music)

adaptar *vt* **1** : adapt **2** AJUSTAR : adjust, fit — **adaptarse** *vr* ~ **a** : adapt to — **adaptable** *adj* : adaptable — **adaptación** *nf, pl* **-ciones** : adaptation — **adaptador** *nm* : adapter (in electricity)

adecuar {8} *vt* : adapt, make suitable — **adecuarse** *vr* ~ **a** : be appropriate for — **adecuado, -da** *adj* : suitable, appropriate

adelantar *vt* 1 : advance, move forward 2 PASAR : overtake 3 : pay in advance — **adelantarse** *vr* 1 : move forward, get ahead 2 : be fast (of a clock) — **adelantado, -da** *adj* 1 : advanced, ahead 2 : fast (of a clock) 3 **por** ~ : in advance — **adelante** *adv* 1 : ahead, forward 2 ¡~! : come in! 3 **más** ~ : later on, further on — **adelanto** *nm* 1 : advance 2 *or* ~ **de dinero** : advance payment

adelgazar {21} *vt* : make thin — *vi* : lose weight

ademán *nm, pl* -**manes** 1 GESTO : gesture 2 ~**es** *nmpl* : manners 3 **en** ~ **de** : as if to

además *adv* 1 : besides, furthermore 2 ~ **de** : in addition to, as well as

adentro *adv* : inside, within — **adentrarse** *vr* ~ **en** : go into, get inside of

adepto, -ta *n* : follower, supporter

aderezar {21} *vt* : season, dress — **aderezo** *nm* : dressing, seasoning

adeudar *vt* 1 : debit 2 DEBER : owe — **adeudo** *nm* 1 DÉBITO : debit 2 *Lat* : debt

adherirse {76} *vr* 1 : adhere, stick — **adherencia** *nf* : adherence — **adhesión** *nf, pl* -**siones** 1 : adhesion 2 APOYO : support — **adhesivo, -va** *adj* : adhesive — **adhesivo** *nm* : adhesive

adición *nf, pl* -**ciones** : addition — **adicional** *adj* : additional

adicto, -ta *adj* : addicted — ~ *n* : addict

adiestrar *vt* : train

adinerado, -da *adj* : wealthy

adiós *nm, pl* **adioses** 1 : farewell 2 ¡~! : good-bye!

aditamento *nm* : attachment, accessory

aditivo *nm* : additive

adivinar *vt* 1 : guess 2 PREDECIR : foretell — **adivinación** *nf, pl* -**ciones** : guessing, prediction — **adivinanza** *nf* : riddle — **adivino, -na** *n* : fortune-teller

adjetivo *nm* : adjective

adjudicar {72} *vt* : award — **adjudicarse** *vr* : appropriate — **adjudicación** *nf, pl* -**ciones** : awarding

adjuntar *vt* : enclose (with a letter, etc.) — **adjunto, -ta** *adj* : enclosed, attached — ~ *n* : assistant

administración *nf, pl* -**ciones** 1 : administration 2 : administering (of a drug, etc.) 3 DIRECCIÓN : management — **administrador, -dora** *n* : administrator, manager — **administrar** *vt* 1 : manage, run 2 : administer (a drug, etc.) — **administrativo, -va** *adj* : administrative

admirar *vt* : admire — **admirarse** *vr* : be amazed — **admirable** *adj* : admirable — **admiración** *nf, pl* -**ciones** 1 : admiration 2 ASOMBRO : amazement — **admirador, -dora** *n* : admirer

admitir *vt* 1 : admit 2 ACEPTAR : accept — **admisible** *adj* : admissible, acceptable — **admisión** *nf, pl* -**siones** 1 : admission 2 ACEPTACIÓN : acceptance

ADN *nm* : DNA

adobe *nm* : adobe

adobo *nm* : marinade

adoctrinar *vt* : indoctrinate — **adoctrinamiento** *nm* : indoctrination

adolecer {53} *vi* ~ **de** : suffer from

adolescente *adj & nmf* : adolescent — **adolescencia** *nf* : adolescence

adonde *conj* : where

adónde *adv* : where

adoptar *vt* : adopt (a child), take (a decision) — **adopción** *nf, pl* -**ciones** : adoption — **adoptivo, -va** *adj* : adopted, adoptive

adoquín *nm, pl* -**quines** : cobblestone

adorar *vt* : adore, worship — **adorable** *adj* : adorable — **adoración** *nf, pl* -**ciones** : adoration, worship

adormecer {53} *vt* 1 : make sleepy 2 ENTUMECER : numb — **adormecerse** *vr* : doze off — **adormecimiento** *nm* : drowsiness — **adormilarse** *vr* : doze

adornar *vt* : decorate, adorn — **adorno** *nm* : ornament, decoration

adquirir {4} *vt* 1 : acquire 2 COMPRAR : purchase — **adquisición** *nf, pl* -**ciones** 1 : acquisition 2 COMPRA : purchase

adrede *adv* : intentionally, on purpose

adscribir {33} *vt* : assign, appoint

aduana *nf* : customs (office) — **aduanero, -ra** *adj* : customs — ~ *n* : customs officer

aducir {61} *vt* : cite, put forward

adueñarse *vr* ~ **de** : take possession of

adular *vt* : flatter — **adulación** *nf, pl* -**ciones** : adulation, flattery — **adulador, -dora** *adj* : flattering — ~ *n* : flatterer

adulterar *vt* : adulterate

adulterio *nm* : adultery — **adúltero, -ra** *n* : adulterer

adulto, -ta *adj & n* : adult

adusto, -ta *adj* : stern, severe

advenedizo, -za *n* : upstart

advenimiento *nm* : advent, arrival

adverbio *nm* : adverb — **adverbial** *adj* : adverbial

adversario, -ria *n* : adversary, opponent — **adverso, -sa** *adj* : adverse — **adversidad** *nf* : adversity

advertir {76} *vt* **1** AVISAR : warn **2** NOTAR : notice — **advertencia** *nf* : warning

adviento *nm* : Advent

adyacente *adj* : adjacent

aéreo, -rea *adj* : aerial, air

aerobic *nm* : aerobics *pl*

aerodinámico, -ca *adj* : aerodynamic

aeródromo *nm* : airfield

aerolínea *nf* : airline

aeromozo, -za *n* : flight attendant, steward *m*, stewardess *f*

aeronave *nf* : aircraft

aeropuerto *nm* : airport

aerosol *nm* : aerosol, spray

afable *adj* : affable — **afabilidad** *nf* : affability

afán *nm, pl* **afanes 1** ANHELO : eagerness **2** EMPEÑO : effort, hard work — **afanarse** *vr* : toil — **afanosamente** *adv* : industriously, busily — **afanoso, -sa** *adj* **1** : eager **2** TRABAJOSO : arduous

afear *vt* : make ugly, disfigure

afección *nf, pl* **-ciones** : ailment, complaint

afectar *vt* : affect — **afectación** *nf, pl* **-ciones** : affectation — **afectado, -da** *adj* : affected

afectivo, -va *adj* : emotional

afecto *nm* : affection — **afecto, -ta** *adj* ~ **a** : fond of — **afectuoso, -sa** *adj* : affectionate, caring

afeitar *vt* : shave — **afeitarse** *vr* : shave — **afeitada** *nf* : shave

afeminado, -da *adj* : effeminate

aferrarse {55} *vr* : cling, hold on

afianzar {21} *vt* : secure, strengthen — **afianzarse** *vr* : become established

afiche *nm Lat* : poster

afición *nf, pl* **-ciones 1** : penchant, fondness PASATIEMPO : hobby — **aficionado, -da** *n* **1** ENTUSIASTA : enthusiast, fan **2** AMATEUR : amateur — **aficionarse** *vr* ~ **a** : become interested in

afilar *vt* : sharpen — **afilado, -da** *adj* : sharp — **afilador** *nm* : sharpener

afiliarse *vr* ~ **a** : join, become a member of — **afiliación** *nf, pl* **-ciones** : affiliation — **afiliado, -da** *adj* : affiliated

afín *adj, pl* **afines** : related, similar — **afinidad** *nf* : affinity, similarity

afinar *vt* **1** : tune **2** PULIR : perfect, refine

afirmar *vt* **1** : state, affirm **2** REFORZAR : strengthen — **afirmación** *nf, pl* **-ciones** : statement, affirmation — **afirmativo, -va** *adj* : affirmative

afligir {35} *vt* **1** : afflict **2** APENAR : distress — **afligirse** *vr* : grieve — **aflic-** **ción** *nf, pl* **-ciones** : grief, sorrow — **afligido -da** *adj* : sorrowful, distressed

aflojar *vt* : loosen, slacken — *vi* : ease up — **aflojarse** *vr* : become loose, slacken

aflorar *vi* : come to the surface, emerge — **afloramiento** *nm* : outcrop

afluencia *nf* : influx — **afluente** *nm* : tributary

afortunado, -da *adj* : fortunate, lucky — **afortunadamente** *adv* : fortunately

afrentar *vt* : insult — **afrenta** *nf* : affront, insult

africano, -na *adj* : African

afrontar *vt* : confront, face

afuera *adv* **1** : out **2** : outside, outdoors — **afueras** *nfpl* : outskirts

agachar *vt* : lower — **agacharse** *vr* : crouch, stoop

agalla *nf* **1** BRANQUIA : gill **2 tener ~s** *fam* : have guts

agarrar *vt* **1** ASIR : grasp **2** *Lat* : catch — **agarrarse** *vr* : hold on, cling — **agarradera** *nf Lat* : handle — **agarrado, -da** *adj fam* : stingy — **agarre** *nm* : grip, grasp — **agarrón** *nm, pl* **-rones** : tug, pull

agasajar *vt* : fête, wine and dine — **agasajo** *nm* : lavish attention

ágave *nm* : agave

agazaparse *vr* : crouch down

agencia *nf* : agency, office — **agente** *nmf* : agent, officer

agenda *nf* **1** : agenda **2** LIBRETA : notebook

ágil *adj* : agile — **agilidad** *nf* : agility

agitar *vt* **1** : agitate, shake **2** : wave, flap (wings, etc.) **3** PERTURBAR : stir up — **agitarse** *vr* **1** : toss about **2** INQUIETARSE : get upset — **agitación** *nf, pl* **-ciones** : agitation, shaking **2** INTRANQUILIDAD : restlessness — **agitado, -da** *adj* **1** : agitated, excited **2** : choppy, rough (of the sea)

aglomerar *vt* : amass — **aglomerarse** *vr* : crowd together

agnóstico, -ca *adj & n* : agnostic

agobiar *vt* **1** : oppress **2** ABRUMAR : overwhelm — **agobiado, -da** *adj* : weary, weighed down — **agobiante** *adj* : oppressing, oppressive

agonizar {21} *vi* : be dying — **agonía** *nf* **1** : death throes **2** PENA : agony — **agonizante** *adj* : dying

agorero, -ra *adj* : ominous

agostar *vt* : wither

agosto *nm* : August

agotar *vt* **1** : deplete, use up **2** CANSAR : exhaust, weary — **agotarse** *vr* **1**

: run out, give out **2** CANSARSE : get tired — **agotado, -da** *adj* **1** CANSADO : exhausted **2** : sold out — **agotador, -dora** *adj* : exhausting — **agotamiento** *nm* : exhaustion

agraciado, -da *adj* **1** : attractive **2** AFORTUNADO : fortunate

agradar *vi* : be pleasing — **agradable** *adj* : pleasant, agreeable — **agrado** *nm* **1** : taste, liking **2** con ~ : with pleasure

agradecer {53} *vt* : be grateful for, thank — **agradecido, -da** *adj* : grateful — **agradecimiento** *nm* : gratitude

agrandar *vt* : enlarge — **agrandarse** *vr* : grow larger

agrario, -ria *adj* : agrarian, agricultural

agravar *vt* **1** : make heavier **2** EMPEORAR : aggravate, worsen — **agravarse** *vr* : get worse

agraviar *vt* : insult — **agravio** *nm* : insult

agredir {1} *vt* : attack

agregar {52} *vt* : add, attach — **agregado, -da** *n* : attaché — **agregado** *nm* : aggregate

agresión *nf, pl* **-siones** : aggression, attack — **agresividad** *nf* : aggressiveness — **agresivo, -va** *adj* : aggressive — **agresor, -sora** *n* : aggressor, attacker

agreste *adj* : rugged, wild

agriar *vt* : sour — **agriarse** *vr* **1** : turn sour (of milk, etc.) **2** : become embittered

agrícola *adj* : agricultural — **agricultura** *nf* : agriculture, farming — **agricultor, -tora** *n* : farmer

agridulce *adj* **1** : bittersweet **2** : sweet-and-sour (in cooking)

agrietar *vt* : crack — **agrietarse** *vr* **1** : crack **2** : chap

agrimensor, -sora *n* : surveyor

agrio, agria *adj* : sour

agrupar *vt* : group together — **agruparse** *vr* : form a group — **agrupación** *nf, pl* **-ciones** : group, association — **agrupamiento** *nm* : grouping

agua *nf* **1** : water **2** ~ **oxigenada** : hydrogen peroxide **3** ~**s negras** *or* ~**s residuales** : sewage

aguacate *nm* : avocado

aguacero *nm* : downpour

aguado, -da *adj* **1** : watery **2** *Lat fam* : soft, flabby — **aguar** {10} *vt* **1** : water down, dilute **2** ~ **la fiesta** *fam* : spoil the party

aguafuerte *nm* : etching

aguanieve *nf* : sleet

aguantar *vt* **1** SOPORTAR : bear, withstand **2** SOSTENER : hold — *vi* : hold out, last — **aguantarse** *vr* **1** : resign oneself **2** CONTENERSE : restrain oneself — **aguante** *nm* **1** : patience **2** RESISTENCIA : endurance

aguardar *vt* : await

aguardiente *nm* : clear brandy

aguarrás *nm* : turpentine

agudo, -da *adj* **1** : acute, sharp **2** : shrill, high-pitched (in music) — **agudeza** *nf* **1** : sharpness **2** : witticism

agüero *nm* : augury, omen

aguijón *nm, pl* **-jones** **1** : stinger (of an insect) **2** ESTÍMULO : goad, stimulus — **aguijonear** *vt* : goad

águila *nf* : eagle

aguja *nf* **1** : needle **2** : hand (of a clock) **3** : spire (of a church)

agujero *nm* : hole

agujeta *nf* **1** *Lat* : shoelace **2** ~**s** *nfpl* : (muscular) stiffness

aguzar {21} *vt* **1** : sharpen **2** ~ **el oído** : prick up one's ears

ahí *adv* **1** : there **2** por ~ : somewhere, thereabouts

ahijado, -da *n* : godchild, godson *m*, goddaughter *f*

ahínco *nm* : eagerness, zeal

ahogar {52} *vt* **1** : drown **2** ASFIXIAR : smother — **ahogarse** *vr* **1** : drown — **ahogo** *nm* : breathlessness

ahondar *vt* : deepen — *vi* : elaborate, go into detail

ahora *adv* **1** : now **2** ~ **mismo** : right now

ahorcar {72} *vt* : hang, kill by hanging — **ahorcarse** *vr* : hang oneself

ahorita *adv* *Lat fam* : right now

ahorrar *vt* : save, spare — *vi* : save up — **ahorrarse** *vr* : spare oneself — **ahorro** *nm* : saving

ahuecar {72} *vt* **1** : hollow out **2** : cup (one's hands)

ahumar {8} *vt* **1** : smoke, cure — **ahumado, -da** *adj* : smoked

ahuyentar *vt* : scare away, chase away

airado, -da *adj* : irate, angry

aire *nm* **1** : air **2** ~ **acondicionado** : air-conditioning **3 al** ~ **libre** : in the open air, outdoors — **airear** *vt* : air, air out

aislar {5} *vt* **1** : isolate **2** : insulate (in electricity) — **aislamiento** *nm* **1** : isolation **2** : (electrical) insulation

ajar *vt* **1** : crumple, wrinkle **2** ESTROPEAR : spoil

ajedrez *nm* : chess

ajeno, -na *adj* **1** : someone else's **2** EXTRAÑO : alien **3** ~ **a** : foreign to

ajetreado, -da *adj* : hectic, busy —

ajetrearse *vr* : bustle about — **ajetreo** *nm* : hustle and bustle

ají *nm*, *pl* **ajíes** *Lat* : chili pepper

ajo *nm* : garlic

ajustar *vt* 1 : adjust, adapt 2 ACORDAR : agree on 3 SALDAR : settle — **ajustarse** *vr* : fit, conform — **ajustable** *adj* : adjustable — **ajustado, -da** *adj* 1 : close, tight 2 CEÑIDO : tight-fitting — **ajuste** *nm* : adjustment

ajusticiar *vt* : execute, put to death

al (*contraction of* **a** *and* **el**) → **a**²

ala *nf* 1 : wing 2 : brim (of a hat)

alabanza *nf* : praise — **alabar** *vt* : praise

alacena *nf* : cupboard, larder

alacrán *nm*, *pl* **-cranes** : scorpion

alado, -da *adj* : winged

alambre *nm* : wire

alameda *nf* 1 : poplar grove 2 : tree-lined avenue — **álamo** *nm* : poplar

alarde *nm* : show, display — **alardear** *vi* : boast

alargar {52} *vt* 1 : extend, lengthen 2 PROLONGAR : prolong — **alargarse** *vr* : become longer — **alargador** *nm* : extension cord

alarido *nm* : howl, shriek

alarmar *vt* : alarm — **alarma** *nf* : alarm — **alarmante** *adj* : alarming

alba *nf* : dawn

albahaca *nf* : basil

albañil *nm* : bricklayer, mason

albaricoque *nm* : apricot

albedrío *nm* **libre ~** : free will

alberca *nf* 1 : reservoir, tank 2 *Lat* : swimming pool

albergar {52} *vt* : house, lodge — **albergue** *nm* 1 : lodging 2 REFUGIO : shelter 3 **~ juvenil** : youth hostel

albóndiga *nf* : meatball

alborear *v impers* : dawn — **albor** *nm* : dawning — **alborada** *nf* : dawn

alborotar *vt* : excite, stir up — *vi* : make a racket — **alborotarse** *vr* : get excited — **alborotado, -da** *adj* : excited, agitated — **alborotador, -dora** *n* : agitator, rioter — **alboroto** *nm* : ruckus

alborozar {21} *vt* : gladden — **alborozo** *nm* : joy

álbum *nm* : album

alcachofa *nf* : artichoke

alcalde, -desa *n* : mayor

alcance *nm* 1 : reach 2 ÁMBITO : range, scope

alcancía *nf* : money box

alcantarilla *nf* : sewer, drain

alcanzar {21} *vt* 1 : reach 2 LLEGAR A : catch up with 3 LOGRAR : achieve, at-

tain — *vi* 1 : suffice, be enough 2 **~ a** : manage to

alcaparra *nf* : caper

alcázar *nm* : fortress, castle

alce *nm* : moose, European elk

alcoba *nf* : bedroom

alcohol *nm* : alcohol — **alcohólico, -ca** *adj* & *n* : alcoholic — **alcoholismo** *nm* : alcoholism

aldaba *nf* : door knocker

aldea *nf* : village — **aldeano, -na** *n* : villager

aleación *nf*, *pl* **-ciones** : alloy

aleatorio, -ria *adj* : random

aleccionar *vt* : instruct, teach

aledaño, -ña *adj* : bordering — **aledaños** *nmpl* : outskirts

alegar {52} *vt* : assert, allege — *vi Lat* : argue — **alegato** *nm* 1 : allegation (in law) 2 *Lat* : argument

alegoría *nf* : allegory — **alegórico, -ca** *adj* : allegorical

alegrar *vt* : make happy, cheer up — **alegrarse** *vr* : be glad — **alegre** *adj* 1 CONTENTO : glad, happy 2 : colorful, bright — **alegremente** *adv* : happily — **alegría** *nf* : joy, cheer

alejar *vt* 1 : remove, move away 2 ENAJENAR : estrange — **alejarse** *vr* : move away, drift apart — **alejado, -da** *adj* : remote — **alejamiento** *nm* 1 : removal 2 : estrangement (of persons)

alemán, -mana *adj*, *mpl* **-manes** : German — **alemán** *nm* : German (language)

alentar {55} *vt* : encourage — **alentador, -dora** *adj* : encouraging

alergia *nf* : allergy — **alérgico, -ca** *adj* : allergic

alero *nm* : eaves *pl*

alertar *vt* : alert — **alerta** *adv* : on the alert — **alerta** *adj* & *nf* : alert

aleta *nf* 1 : fin, flipper 2 : small wing

alevosía *nf* : treachery — **alevoso, -sa** *adj* : treacherous

alfabeto *nm* : alphabet — **alfabético, -ca** *adj* : alphabetical — **alfabetismo** *nm* : literacy — **alfabetizar** {21} *vt* 1 : teach literacy 2 : alphabetize

alfalfa *nf* : alfalfa

alfarería *nf* : pottery

alféizar *nm* : sill, windowsill

alfil *nm* : bishop (in chess)

alfiler *nm* 1 : pin 2 BROCHE : brooch — **alfiletero** *nm* : pincushion

alfombra *nf* : carpet, rug — **alfombrilla** *nf* : small rug, mat

alga *nf* : seaweed

álgebra *nf* : algebra

algo *pron* **1** : something **2** ~ **de** : some, a little — ~ *adv* : somewhat, rather
algodón *nm, pl* **-dones** : cotton
alguacil *nm* : constable, bailiff
alguien *pron* : somebody, someone
alguno, -na *adj* (**algún** *before masculine singular nouns*) **1** : some, any **2** (*in negative constructions*) : not any, not at all **3 algunas veces** : sometimes — ~ *pron* **1** : one, someone, somebody **2 algunos, -nas** *pron pl* : some, a few
alhaja *nf* : jewel
alharaca *nf* : fuss
aliado, -da *n* : ally — ~ *adj* : allied — **alianza** *nf* : alliance — **aliarse** {85} *vr* : form an alliance
alias *adv & nm* : alias
alicaído, -da *adj* : depressed
alicates *nmpl* : pliers
aliciente *nm* **1** : incentive **2** : attraction (to a place)
alienar *vt* : alienate — **alienación** *nf, pl* **-ciones** : alienation
aliento *nm* **1** : breath **2** ÁNIMO : encouragement, strength
aligerar *vt* **1** : lighten **2** APRESURAR : hasten, quicken
alimaña *nf* : pest, vermin
alimentar *vt* : feed, nourish — **alimentarse** *vr* ~ **con** : live on — **alimentación** *nf, pl* **-ciones** **1** : feeding **2** NUTRICIÓN : nourishment — **alimenticio, -cia** *adj* : nourishing — **alimento** *nm* : food, nourishment
alinear *vt* : align, line up — **alinearse** *vr* ~ **con** : align oneself with — **alineación** *nf, pl* **-ciones** **1** : alignment **2** : lineup (in sports)
aliño *nm* : dressing, seasoning — **aliñar** *vt* : season, dress
alisar *vt* : smooth
alistarse *vr* : join up, enlist — **alistamiento** *nm* : enlistment
aliviar *vt* : relieve, soothe — **aliviarse** *vr* : recover, get better — **alivio** *nm* : relief
aljibe *nm* : cistern, tank
allá *adv* **1** : there, over there **2 más** ~ : farther away **3 más** ~ **de** : beyond
allanar *vt* **1** : smooth, level out **2** *Spain* : break into (a house) **3** *Lat* : raid — **allanamiento** *nm* **1** *Spain* : breaking and entering **2** *Lat* : raid
allegado, -da *n* : close friend, relation
allí *adv* : there, over there
alma *nf* : soul
almacén *nm, pl* **-cenes** **1** : warehouse **2** *Lat* : shop, store **3 grandes almacenes** : department store — **alma-**
cenamiento *or* **almacenaje** *nm* : storage — **almacenar** *vt* : store
almádena *nf* : sledgehammer
almanaque *nm* : almanac
almeja *nf* : clam
almendra *nf* **1** : almond **2** : kernel (of nuts, fruit, etc.)
almiar *nm* : haystack
almíbar *nm* : syrup
almidón *nm, pl* **-dones** : starch — **almidonar** *vt* : starch
almirante *nm* : admiral
almohada *nf* : pillow — **almohadilla** *nf* : small pillow, pad — **almohadón** *nm, pl* **-dones** : bolster, large cushion
almorranas *nfpl* : hemorrhoids, piles
almorzar {36} *vi* : have lunch — *vt* : have for lunch — **almuerzo** *nm* : lunch
alocado, -da *adj* : crazy, wild
áloe *or* **aloe** *nm* : aloe
alojar *vt* : house, lodge — **alojarse** *vr* : lodge, room — **alojamiento** *nm* : lodging, accommodations *pl*
alondra *nf* : lark
alpaca *nf* : alpaca
alpinismo *nm* : mountain climbing — **alpinista** *nmf* : mountain climber
alpiste *nm* : birdseed
alquilar *vt* : rent, lease — **alquilarse** *vr* : be for rent — **alquiler** *nm* : rent, rental
alquitrán *nm, pl* **-tranes** : tar
alrededor *adv* **1** : around, about **2** ~ **de** : approximately — **alrededor de** *prep phr* : around — **alrededores** *nmpl* : outskirts
alta *nf* : discharge (of a patient)
altanería *nf* : haughtiness — **altanero, -ra** *adj* : haughty
altar *nm* : altar
altavoz *nm, pl* **-voces** : loudspeaker
alterar *vt* **1** : alter, modify **2** PERTURBAR : disturb — **alterarse** *vr* : get upset — **alteración** *nf, pl* **-ciones** **1** : alteration **2** ALBOROTO : disturbance — **alterado, -da** *adj* : upset
altercado *nm* : altercation, argument
alternar *vi* **1** : alternate **2** ~ **con** : socialize with — *vt* : alternate — **alternarse** *vr* : take turns — **alternativa** *nf* : alternative — **alternativo, -va** *adj* : alternating, alternative — **alterno, -na** *adj* : alternate
Alteza *nf* : Highness
altiplano *nm* : high plateau
altitud *nf* : altitude
altivez *nf, pl* **-veces** : haughtiness — **altivo, -va** *adj* : haughty
alto, -ta *adj* **1** : tall, high **2** RUIDOSO

: loud — **alto** *adv* 1 ARRIBA : high 2
: loud, loudly — **~** *nm* 1 ALTURA
: height, elevation 2 : stop, halt —
interj : halt!, stop! — **altoparlante** *nm*
Lat : loudspeaker

altruista *adj* : altruistic — **altruismo**
nm : altruism

altura *nf* 1 : height 2 ALTITUD : altitude
3 **a la ~ de** : near, up by

alubia *nf* : kidney bean

alucinar *vi* : hallucinate — **alucinación**
nf, pl **-ciones** : hallucination

alud *nm* : avalanche

aludir *vi* : allude, refer — **aludido, -da**
adj **darse por ~** : take it personally

alumbrar *vt* 1 : light, illuminate 2 PARIR
: give birth to — **alumbrado** 1
: (electric) lighting — **alumbramiento** *nm* : childbirth

aluminio *nm* : aluminum

alumno, -na *n* : pupil, student

alusión *nf, pl* **-siones** : allusion

aluvión *nm, pl* **-viones** : flood, barrage

alzar {21} *vt* : lift, raise — **alzarse** *vr*
: rise (up) — **alza** *nf* : rise — **alza-
miento** *nm* : uprising

ama → amo

amabilidad *nf* : kindness — **amable**
adj : kind, nice

amaestrar *vt* : train

amagar {52} *vt* 1 : show signs of 2
AMENAZAR : threaten — *vi* : be immi-
nent — **amago** *nm* 1 INDICIO : sign 2
AMENAZA : threat

amainar *vi* : abate

amamantar *v* : breast-feed, nurse

amanecer {53} *v impers* : dawn — *vi*
: wake up — **~** *nm* 1 : dawn, daybreak

amanerado *adj* : affected, mannered

amansar *vt* 1 : tame 2 APACIGUAR
: soothe — **amansarse** *vr* : calm down

amante *adj* **~ de** : fond of — **~** *nmf*
: lover

amañar *vt* : rig, tamper with

amapola *nf* : poppy

amar *vt* : love

amargar {52} *vt* : make bitter — **amar-
gado, -da** *adj* : embittered — **amargo, -ga** *adj* : bitter — **amargo** *nm*
: bitterness — **amargura** *nf* : bitterness, grief

amarillo, -lla *adj* : yellow — **amarillo**
nm : yellow

amarrar *vt* 1 : moor 2 ATAR : tie up

amasar *vt* 1 : knead 2 : amass (a fortune, etc.)

amateur *adj & nmf* : amateur

amatista *nf* : amethyst

ambages *nmpl* **sin ~** : without hesitation, straight to the point

ámbar *nm* : amber

ambición *nf, pl* **-ciones** : ambition —
ambicionar *vt* : aspire to — **ambicioso, -sa** *adj* : ambitious

ambiente *nm* 1 AIRE : atmosphere 2
MEDIO : environment, surroundings *pl*
— **ambiental** *adj* : environmental

ambigüedad *nf* : ambiguity — **ambiguo, -gua** *adj* : ambiguous

ámbito *nm* : domain, sphere

ambos, -bas *adj & pron* : both

ambulancia *nf* : ambulance

ambulante *adj* : traveling, itinerant

ameba *nf* : amoeba

amedrentar *vt* : intimidate

amén *nm* 1 : amen 2 **~ de** : in addition
to

amenazar {21} *vt* : threaten — **amenaza** *nf* : threat, menace

amenizar {21} *vt* : make pleasant, enliven — **ameno, -na** *adj* : pleasant

americano, -na *adj* : American

ameritar *vt Lat* : deserve

ametralladora *nf* : machine gun

amianto *nm* : asbestos

amiba → ameba

amígdala *nf* : tonsil — **amigdalitis** *nf*
: tonsilitis

amigo, -ga *adj* : friendly, close — **~** *n*
: friend — **amigable** *adj* : friendly

amilanar *vt* : daunt — **amilanarse** *vr*
: lose heart

aminorar *vt* : diminish

amistad *nf* : friendship — **amistoso,
-sa** *adj* : friendly

amnesia *nf* : amnesia

amnistía *nf* : amnesty

amo, ama *n* 1 : master *m*, mistress *f* 2
ama de casa : homemaker, housewife 3 **ama de llaves** : housekeeper

amodorrado, -da *adj* : drowsy

amolar {19} *vt* 1 : grind, sharpen 2 MO-
LESTAR : annoy

amoldar *vt* : adapt, adjust —
amoldarse *vr* **~ a** : adapt to

amonestar *vt* : admonish, warn —
amonestación *nf, pl* **-ciones** : admo-
nition, warning

amoníaco *or* **amoniaco** *nm* : ammonia

amontonar *vt* : pile up — **amontonarse** *vr* : pile up (of things), form a
crowd (of persons)

amor *nm* : love

amordazar {21} *vt* : gag

amorío *nm* : love affair — **amoroso,
-sa** *adj* 1 : loving 2 *Lat* : sweet, lovable

amortado, -da *adj* : black-and-blue

amortiguar {10} *vt* : muffle, soften,
tone down — **amortiguador** *nm*
: shock absorber

amortizar {21} vt : pay off — **amortización** nf : repayment

amotinar vt : incite (to riot) — **amotinarse** vr : riot, rebel

amparar vt : shelter, protect — **ampararse** vr 1 ~ **de** : take shelter from 2 ~ **en** : have recourse to — **amparo** nm : refuge, protection

ampliar {85} vt 1 : expand 2 : enlarge (a photograph) — **ampliación** nf, pl **-ciones** 1 : expansion, enlargement 2 : extension (of a building)

amplificar {72} vt : amplify — **amplificador** nm : amplifier

amplio, -plia adj : broad, wide, ample — **amplitud** nf 1 : breadth, extent 2 ESPACIOSIDAD : spaciousness

ampolla nf 1 : blister 2 : vial, ampoule — **ampollarse** vr : blister

ampuloso, -sa adj : pompous

amputar vt : amputate — **amputación** nf, pl **-ciones** : amputation

amueblar vt : furnish (a house, etc.)

amurallar vt : wall in

anacardo nm : cashew nut

anaconda nf : anaconda

anacrónico, -ca adj : anachronistic — **anacronismo** nm : anachronism

ánade nmf : duck

anagrama nm : anagram

anales nmpl : annals

analfabeto, -ta adj & n : illiterate — **analfabetismo** nm : illiteracy

analgésico nm : painkiller, analgesic

analizar {21} vt : analyze — **análisis** nm : analysis — **analítico, -ca** adj : analytical, analytic

analogía nf : analogy — **análogo, -ga** adj : analogous

ananá or ananás nm, pl **-nás** : pineapple

anaquel nm : shelf

anaranjado, -da adj : orange-colored

anarquía nf : anarchy — **anarquista** adj & nmf : anarchist

anatomía nf : anatomy — **anatómico, -ca** adj : anatomic, anatomical

anca nf 1 : haunch 2 ~**s de rana** : frogs' legs

ancestral adj : ancestral

ancho, -cha adj : wide, broad, ample — **ancho** nm : width

anchoa nf : anchovy

anchura nf : width, breadth

anciano, -na adj : aged, elderly — ~ n : elderly person

ancla nf : anchor — **anclar** v : anchor

andadas nfpl 1 : tracks 2 **volver a las** ~ : go back to one's old ways

andadura nf : walking, journey

andaluz, -luza adj & n, mpl **-luces** : Andalusian

andamio nm : scaffold

andanada nf 1 : volley 2 **soltar una** ~ : reprimand

andanzas nfpl : adventures

andar {6} vi 1 CAMINAR : walk 2 IR : go, travel 3 FUNCIONAR : run, work 4 ~ **en** : rummage around in 5 ~ **por** : be approximately — vt : cover, travel — ~ nm : gait, walk

andén nm, pl **-denes** 1 : (train) platform 2 Lat : sidewalk

andino, -na adj : Andean

andorrano, -na adj : Andorran

andrajos nmpl : tatters — **andrajoso, -sa** adj : ragged

anécdota nf : anecdote

anegar {52} vt : flood — **anegarse** vr 1 : be flooded 2 AHOGARSE : drown

anemia nf : anemia — **anémico, -ca** adj : anemic

anestesia nf : anesthesia — **anestésico, -ca** adj : anesthetic — **anestésico** nm : anesthetic

anexar vt : annex, attach — **anexo, -xa** adj : attached — **anexo** nm : annex

anfibio, -bia adj : amphibious — **anfibio** nm : amphibian

anfiteatro nm : amphitheater

anfitrión, -triona n, mpl **-triones** : host, hostess f

ángel nm : angel — **angelical** adj : angelic, angelical

angloparlante adj : English-speaking

anglosajón, -jona adj, mpl **-jones** : Anglo-Saxon

angosto, -ta adj : narrow

anguila nf : eel

ángulo nm 1 : angle 2 ESQUINA : corner — **angular** adj : angular — **anguloso, -sa** adj : angular

angustiar vt 1 : anguish, distress 2 INQUIETAR : worry — **angustiarse** vr : get upset — **angustia** nf 1 : anguish 2 INQUIETUD : worry — **angustioso, -sa** adj 1 : anguished 2 INQUIETANTE : distressing

anhelar vt : yearn for, crave — **anhelante** adj : yearning, longing — **anhelo** nm : longing

anidar vi : nest

anillo nm : ring

ánima n : soul

animación nf, pl **-ciones** 1 VIVEZA : liveliness 2 BULLICIO : hustle and bustle — **animado, -da** adj : cheerful, animated — **animador, -dora** n 1 : (television) host 2 : cheerleader

animadversión *nf*, *pl* **-siones** : animosity

animal *nm* : animal — ~ *nmf* : brute, beast — ~ *adj* : brutish

animar *vt* 1 ALENTAR : encourage 2 ALEGAR : cheer up — **animarse** *vr* 1 : liven up 2 ~ **a** : get up the nerve to

ánimo *nm* 1 : spirit, soul 2 HUMOR : mood, spirits *pl* 3 ALIENTO : encouragement

animosidad *nf* : animosity, ill will

animoso, -sa *adj* : spirited, brave

aniquilar *vt* : annihilate — **aniquilación** *n*, *pl* **-ciones** : annihilation

anís *nm* : anise

aniversario *nm* : anniversary

ano *nm* : anus

anoche *adv* : last night

anochecer {53} *vi* : get dark — ~ *nm* : dusk, nightfall

anodino, -na *adj* : insipid, dull

anomalía *nf* : anomaly

anonadado, -da *adj* : dumbfounded

anónimo, -ma *adj* : anonymous — **anonimato** *nm* : anonymity

anorexia *nf* : anorexia

anormal *adj* : abnormal — **anormalidad** *nf* : abnormality

anotar *vt* 1 : annotate 2 APUNTAR : jot down — **anotación** *nf*, *pl* **-ciones** : annotation, note

anquilosarse *vr* 1 : become paralyzed 2 ESTANCARSE : stagnate — **anquilosamiento** *nm* 1 : paralysis 2 ESTANCAMIENTO : stagnation

ansiar {85} *vt* : long for — **ansia** *nf* 1 INQUIETUD : uneasiness 2 ANGUSTIA : anguish 3 ANHELO : longing — **ansiedad** *nf* : anxiety — **ansioso, -sa** *adj* 1 : anxious 2 DESEOSO : eager

antagónico, -ca *adj* : antagonistic — **antagonismo** *nm* : antagonism — **antagonista** *nmf* : antagonist

antaño *adv* : yesteryear, long ago

antártico, -ca *adj* : antarctic

ante¹ *nm* 1 : elk, moose 2 GAMUZA : suede

ante² *prep* 1 : before, in front of 2 : in view of 3 ~ **todo** : above all

anteanoche *adv* : the night before last

anteayer *adv* : the day before yesterday

antebrazo *nm* : forearm

anteceder *vt* : precede — **antecedente** *adj* : previous, prior — ~ *nm* : precedent — **antecesor, -sora** *n* 1 : ancestor 2 PREDECESOR : predecessor

antedicho, -cha *adj* : aforesaid

antelación *nf*, *pl* **-ciones** 1 : advance notice 2 **con** ~ : in advance

antemano *adv* **de** ~ : beforehand

antena *nf* : antenna

antenoche → **anteanoche**

anteojos *nmpl* 1 : glasses, eyeglasses 2 ~ **bifocales** : bifocals

antepasado, -da *n* : ancestor

antepecho *nm* : ledge

antepenúltimo, -ma *adj* : third from last

anteponer {60} *vt* 1 : place before 2 PREFERIR : prefer

anterior *adj* 1 : previous, earlier 2 DELANTERO : front — **anterioridad** *nf* **con** ~ : beforehand, in advance — **anteriormente** *adv* : previously

antes *adv* 1 : before, earlier 2 ANTERIORMENTE : previously 3 PRIMERO : first 4 MEJOR : rather 5 ~ **de** : before, previous to 6 ~ **que** : before

antesala *nf* : waiting room

antiaéreo, -rea *adj* : antiaircraft

antibiótico *nm* : antibiotic

anticipar *vt* 1 : move up (a date, etc.) 2 : pay in advance — **anticiparse** *vr* 1 : be early 2 ADELANTARSE : get ahead — **anticipación** *nf*, *pl* **-ciones** 1 : anticipation 2 **con** ~ : in advance — **anticipado, -da** *adj* 1 : advance, early 2 **por** ~ : in advance — **anticipo** *nm* 1 : advance (payment) 2 : foretaste

anticoncepción *nf*, *pl* **-ciones** : contraception — **anticonceptivo, -va** *adj* : contraceptive — **anticonceptivo** *nm* : contraceptive

anticongelante *nm* : antifreeze

anticuado, -da *adj* : antiquated, outdated

anticuario, -ria *n* : antique dealer — **anticuario** *nm* : antique shop

anticuerpo *nm* : antibody

antídoto *nm* : antidote

antier → **anteayer**

antiestético, -ca *adj* : unsightly

antifaz *nm*, *pl* **-faces** : mask

antífona *nf* : anthem

antigualla *nf* : relic, old thing

antiguo, -gua *adj* 1 : ancient, old 2 ANTERIOR : former 3 ANTICUADO : old-fashioned 4 **muebles antiguos** : antique furniture — **antiguamente** *adv* 1 : long ago 2 ANTES : formerly — **antigüedad** *nf* 1 : antiquity 2 : seniority (in the workplace) 3 ~**es** *nfpl* : antiques

antihigiénico, -ca *adj* : unsanitary

antihistamínico *nm* : antihistamine

antiinflamatorio, -ria *adj* : anti-inflammatory

antílope *nm* : antelope

antinatural *adj* : unnatural

antipatía *nf* : aversion, dislike — **antipático, -ca** *adj* : unpleasant

antirreglamentario, -ria *adj* : unlawful

antirrobo, -ba *adj* : antitheft

antisemita *adj* : anti-Semitic — **antisemitismo** *nm* : anti-Semitism

antiséptico, -ca *adj* : antiseptic — **antiséptico** *nm* : antiseptic

antisocial *adj* : antisocial

antítesis *nf* : antithesis

antojarse *vr* 1 APETECER : crave 2 PARECER : seem, appear — **antojadizo, -za** *adj* : capricious — **antojo** *nm* : whim, craving

antología *nf* : anthology

antorcha *nf* : torch

antro *nm* : dive, den

antropófago, -ga *nmf* : cannibal

antropología *nf* : anthropology

anual *adj* : annual, yearly — **anualidad** *nf* : annuity — **anuario** *nm* : yearbook, annual

anudar *vt* : knot — **anudarse** *vr* : tie, knot

anular *vt* : annul, cancel — **anulación** *nf, pl* -**ciones** : annulment, cancellation

anunciar *vt* 1 : announce 2 : advertise (products) — **anunciante** *nmf* : advertiser — **anuncio** *nm* 1 : announcement 2 *or* ~ **publicitario** : advertisement

anzuelo *nm* 1 : fishhook 2 **morder el** ~ : take the bait

añadir *vt* : add — **añadidura** *nf* 1 : additive, addition 2 **por** ~ : in addition, furthermore

añejo, -ja *adj* : aged, vintage

añicos *nmpl* **hacer(se)** ~ : smash to pieces

añil *adj & nm* : indigo (color)

año *nm* 1 : year 2 **Año Nuevo** : New Year

añorar *vt* : long for, miss — **añoranza** *nf* : nostalgia

añoso, -sa *adj* : aged, old

aorta *nf* : aorta

apabullar *vt* : overwhelm

apacentar {55} *vt* : pasture, graze

apachurrar *vt Lat* : crush

apacible *adj* : gentle, mild

apaciguar {10} *vt* : appease, pacify — **apaciguarse** *vr* : calm down

apadrinar *vt* 1 : be a godparent to 2 : sponsor (an artist, etc.)

apagar {52} *vt* 1 : turn or switch off 2 EXTINGUIR : extinguish, put out — **apagarse** *vr* 1 EXTINGUIRSE : go out 2 : die down — **apagado, -da** *adj* 1 : off, out 2 : dull, subdued (of colors, sounds, etc.) — **apagador** *nm Lat*

: (light) switch — **apagón** *nm, pl* -**gones** : blackout

apalancar {72} *vt* 1 LEVANTAR : jack up 2 ABRIR : pry open — **apalancamiento** *nm* : leverage

apalear *vt* : beat up, thrash

aparador *nm* 1 : sideboard 2 *Lat* : shop window

aparato *nm* 1 : machine, appliance, apparatus 2 : system (in anatomy) 3 OSTENTACIÓN : ostentation — **aparatoso, -sa** *adj* 1 : ostentatious 2 ESPECTACULAR : spectacular

aparcar {72} *v Spain* : park — **aparcamiento** *nm Spain* 1 : parking 2 : parking lot

aparcero, -ra *n* : sharecropper

aparear *vt* : mate, pair up — **aparearse** *vr* : mate

aparecer {53} *vi* 1 : appear 2 PRESENTARSE : show up — **aparecerse** *vr* : appear

aparejar *vt* 1 : rig (a ship) 2 : harness (an animal) — **aparejado, -da** *adj* **llevar** ~ : entail — **aparejo** *nm* 1 : equipment, gear 2 : harness (for an animal) 3 : rigging (for a ship)

aparentar *vt* 1 : seem 2 FINGIR : feign — **aparente** *adj* : apparent, seeming

aparición *nf, pl* -**ciones** 1 : appearance 2 FANTASMA : apparition — **apariencia** *nf* 1 : appearance, look 2 **en** ~ : apparently

apartado *nm* 1 : section, paragraph 2 ~ **postal** : post office box

apartamento *nm* : apartment

apartar *vt* 1 ALEJAR : move away 2 SEPARAR : set aside, separate — **apartarse** *vr* 1 : move away 2 DESVIARSE : stray — **aparte** *adv* 1 : apart, separately 2 ADEMÁS : besides

apasionar *vt* : excite, fascinate — **apasionarse** *vr* : get excited — **apasionado, -da** *adj* : passionate, excited — **apasionante** *adj* : exciting

apatía *nf* : apathy — **apático, -ca** *adj* : apathetic

apearse *vr* 1 : dismount 2 : get out of or off (a vehicle)

apedrear *vt* : stone

apegarse {52} *vr* ~ **a** : become attached to, grow fond of — **apegado, -da** *adj* : devoted — **apego** *nm* : fondness

apelar *vi* 1 : appeal 2 ~ **a** : resort to — **apelación** *nf, pl* -**ciones** : appeal

apellido *nm* : last name, surname — **apellidarse** *vr* : have for a last name

apenar *vt* : sadden — **apenarse** *vr* 1 : grieve 2 *Lat* : become embarrassed

apenas *adv* : hardly, scarcely — **∼** *conj* : as soon as

apéndice *nm* : appendix — **apendicitis** *nf* : appendicitis

apercibir *vt* 1 : warn 2 *Lat* : notice — **apercibirse** *vr* **∼ de** : notice — **apercibimiento** *nm* : warning

aperitivo *nm* 1 : appetizer 2 : aperitif

apero *nm* : tool, implement

apertura *nf* : opening

apesadumbrar *vt* : sadden — **apesadumbrarse** *vr* : be weighed down

apestar *vi* : stink — **apestoso, -sa** *adj* : stinking, foul

apetecer {53} *vt* : crave, long for — **apetecible** *adj* : appealing

apetito *nm* : appetite — **apetitoso, -sa** *adj* : appetizing

ápice *nm* 1 : apex, summit 2 PIZCA : bit, smidgen

apilar *vt* : pile up — **apilarse** *vr* : pile up

apiñar *vt* : pack, cram — **apiñarse** *vr* : crowd together

apio *nm* : celery

apisonadora *nf* : steamroller

aplacar {72} *vt* : appease, placate — **aplacarse** *vr* : calm down

aplanar *vt* : flatten, level

aplastar *vt* : crush — **aplastante** *adj* : overwhelming

aplaudir *v* : applaud — **aplauso** *nm* 1 : applause 2 : acclaim

aplazar {21} *vt* : postpone, defer — **aplazamiento** *nm* : postponement

aplicar {72} *vt* : apply — **aplicarse** *vr* : apply oneself — **aplicable** *adj* : applicable — **aplicación** *nf, pl* **-ciones** : application — **aplicado, -da** *adj* : diligent

aplomo *nm* : aplomb

apocarse {72} *vr* : belittle oneself — **apocado, -da** *adj* : timid — **apocamiento** *nm* : timidity

apodar *vt* : nickname

apoderar *vt* : empower — **apoderarse** *vr* **∼ de** : seize — **apoderado, -da** *n* : agent, proxy

apodo *nm* : nickname

apogeo *nm* : peak, height

apología *nf* : defense, apology

apoplegía *nf* : stroke, apoplexy

aporrear *vt* : bang on, beat

aportar *vt* : contribute — **aportación** *nf, pl* **-ciones** : contribution

apostar¹ {19} *v* : bet, wager

apostar² *vt* : station, post

apostillar *vt* : annotate — **apostilla** *nf* : note

apóstol *nm* : apostle

apóstrofo *nm* : apostrophe

apostura *nf* : elegance, grace

apoyar *vt* 1 : support 2 INCLINAR : lean, rest — **apoyarse** *vr* **∼ en** : lean on, rest on — **apoyo** *nm* : support

apreciar *vt* 1 ESTIMAR : appreciate 2 EVALUAR : appraise — **apreciable** *adj* : considerable — **apreciación** *nf, pl* **-ciones** 1 : appreciation 2 VALORACIÓN : appraisal — **aprecio** *nm* 1 : appraisal 2 ESTIMA : esteem

aprehender *vt* : apprehend — **aprehensión** *nf, pl* **-siones** : apprehension, capture

apremiar *vt* — urge — *vi* : be urgent — **apremiante** *adj* : pressing, urgent — **apremio** *nm* : urgency

aprender *v* : learn — **aprenderse** *vr* : memorize

aprendiz, -diza *n, mpl* **-dices** : apprentice, trainee — **aprendizaje** *nm* : apprenticeship

aprensión *nf, pl* **-siones** : apprehension, dread — **aprensivo, -va** *adj* : apprehensive

apresar *vt* : capture, seize — **apresamiento** *nm* : seizure, capture

aprestar *vt* : make ready — **aprestarse** *vr* : get ready

apresurar *vt* : speed up — **apresurarse** *vr* : hurry — **apresuradamente** *adv* : hurriedly, hastily — **apresurado, -da** *adj* : in a rush

apretar {55} *vt* 1 : press, push (a button) 2 : tighten (a knot, etc.) 3 ESTRECHAR : squeeze — *vi* 1 : press (down) 2 : fit too tightly — **apretón** *nm, pl* **-tones** 1 : squeeze 2 **∼ de manos** : handshake — **apretado, -da** *adj* 1 : tight 2 *fam* : tightfisted

aprieto *nm* : predicament, jam

aprisa *adv* : quickly

aprisionar *vt* : imprison

aprobar {19} *vt* 1 : approve of 2 : pass (an exam, etc.) — *vi* : pass — **aprobación** *nf, pl* **-ciones** : approval

apropiarse *vr* **∼ de** : take possession of, appropriate — **apropiación** *nf, pl* **-ciones** : appropriation — **apropiado, -da** *adj* : appropriate

aprovechar *vt* : take advantage of, make good use of — *vi* : be of use — **aprovecharse** *vr* **∼ de** : take advantage of — **aprovechado, -da** *adj* 1 : diligent 2 OPORTUNISTA : opportunistic

aproximar *vt* : bring closer — **aproximarse** *vr* : approach — **aproximación** *nf, pl* **-ciones** : approximation — **aproximadamente** *adv*

: approximately — **aproximado, -da** *adj* : approximate

apto, -ta *adj* **1** : suitable **2** CAPAZ : capable — **aptitud** *nf* : aptitude, capability

apuesta *nf* : bet, wager

apuesto, -ta *adj* : elegant, good-looking

apuntalar *vt* : prop up, shore up

apuntar *vt* **1** : aim, point **2** ANOTAR : jot down **3** SEÑALAR : point at **4** : prompt (in theater) — **apuntarse** *vr* **1** : sign up **2** : score, chalk up (a victory, etc.) — **apunte** *nm* : note

apuñalar *vt* : stab

apurar *vt* **1** : hurry, rush **2** AGOTAR : use up **3** PREOCUPAR : trouble — **apurarse** *vr* **1** : worry **2** *Lat* : hurry up — **apuradamente** *adv* : with difficulty — **apurado, -da** *adj* **1** : needy **2** DIFÍCIL : difficult **3** *Lat* : rushed — **apuro** *nm* **1** : predicament, jam **2** *Lat* : hurry

aquejar *vt* : afflict

aquel, aquella *adj, mpl* **aquellos** : that, those

aquél, aquélla *pron, mpl* **aquéllos 1** : that (one), those (ones) **2** : the former

aquello *pron* : that, that matter

aquí *adv* **1** : here **2** AHORA : now **3** por ~ : hereabouts

aquietar *vt* : calm — **aquietarse** *vr* : calm down

ara *nf* **1** : altar **2 en ~s de** : for the sake of

árabe *adj* **1** : Arab, Arabic — ~ *nm* : Arabic (language)

arado *nm* : plow

arancel *nm* : tariff

arándano *nm* : blueberry

araña *nf* **1** : spider **2** LÁMPARA : chandelier

arañar *v* : scratch, claw — **arañazo** *nm* : scratch

arar *v* : plow

arbitrar *v* **1** : arbitrate **2** : referee, umpire (in sports) — **arbitraje** *nm* : arbitration — **arbitrario, -ria** *adj* : arbitrary — **arbitrio** *nm* **1** : (free) will **2** JUICIO : judgment — **árbitro, -tra** *n* **1** : arbitrator **2** : referee, umpire (in sports)

árbol *nm* **1** : tree — **arboleda** *nf* : grove

arbusto *nm* : shrub, bush

arca *nf* **1** : ark **2** COFRE : chest

arcada *nf* **1** : arcade **2 ~s** *nfpl* : retching

arcaico, -ca *adj* : archaic

arcano, -na *adj* : arcane, secret

arce *nm* : maple tree

archipiélago *nm* : archipelago

archivar *vt* : file — **archivador** *nm* : filing cabinet — **archivo** *nm* **1** : file **2** : archives *pl*

arcilla *nf* : clay

arco *nm* **1** : arch **2** : bow (in sports, music, etc.) **3** : arc (in geometry) **4 ~ iris** : rainbow

arder *vi* : burn

ardid *nm* : scheme, ruse

ardiente *adj* **1** : burning **2** FOGOSO : ardent

ardilla *nf* **1** : squirrel **2 ~ listada** : chipmunk

ardor *nm* **1** : burning **2** ENTUSIASMO : passion, ardor

arduo, -dua *adj* : arduous

área *nf* : area

arena *nf* **1** : sand **2** PALESTRA : arena — **arenoso, -sa** *adj* : sandy, gritty

arenque *nm* : herring

arete *nm* *Lat* : earring

argamasa *nf* : mortar

argentino, -na *adj* : Argentinian, Argentine

argolla *nf* : hoop, ring

argot *nm* : slang

argüir {41} *vt* **1** : argue **2** DEMOSTRAR : prove, show — *vi* : argue

argumentar *vt* : argue, contend — **argumentación** *nf, pl* **-ciones** : (line of) argument — **argumento** *nm* **1** : argument, reasoning **2** TRAMA : plot, story line

árido, -da *adj* : dry, arid — **aridez** *nf, pl* **-deces** : aridity

arisco, -ca *adj* : surly

aristocracia *nf* : aristocracy — **aristócrata** *nmf* : aristocrat — **aristocrático, -ca** *adj* : aristocratic

aritmética *nf* : arithmetic — **aritmético, -ca** *adj* : arithmetic, arithmetical

armar *vt* **1** : arm **2** MONTAR : assemble — **arma** *nf* **1** : arm, weapon **2 ~ de fuego** : firearm — **armada** *nf* : navy — **armado, -da** *adj* : armed — **armadura** *nf* **1** : armor **2** ARMAZÓN : framework — **armamento** *nm* : armament, arms *pl*

armario *nm* **1** : (clothes) closet **2** : cupboard, cabinet

armazón *nmf, pl* **-zones** : frame, framework

armisticio *nm* : armistice

armonizar {21} *vt* **1** : harmonize **2** : reconcile (differences, etc.) — *vi* : harmonize, go together — **armonía** *nf* : harmony — **armónica** *nf* : harmonica — **armónico, -ca** *adj* : harmonic — **armonioso, -sa** *adj* : harmonious

arnés *nm, pl* **-neses** : harness

aro nm **1** : hoop, ring **2** *Lat* : earring

aroma nm : aroma, scent — **aromático, -ca** adj : aromatic

arpa nf : harp

arpón nm, pl **-pones** : harpoon

arquear vt : arch, bend — **arquearse** vr : bend, bow

arqueología nf : archaeology — **arqueológico, -ca** adj : archaeological — **arqueólogo, -ga** n : archaeologist

arquero, -ra n **1** : archer **2** PORTERO : goalkeeper, goalie

arquetipo nm : archetype

arquitectura nf : architecture — **arquitecto, -ta** n : architect — **arquitectónico, -ca** adj : architectural

arrabal nm **1** : slum **2** ~**es** nmpl : outskirts

arracimarse vr : cluster together

arraigar {52} vi : take root, become established — **arraigarse** vr : settle down — **arraigado, -da** adj : deeply rooted, well established — **arraigo** nm : roots pl

arrancar {72} vt **1** : pull out, tear off **2** : start (an engine), boot (a computer) — vi **1** : start an engine **2** : get going — **arranque** nm **1** : starter (of a car) **2** ARREBATO : outburst **3** punto de ~ : starting point

arrasar vt **1** : destroy, devastate **2** LLENAR : fill to the brim

arrastrar vt **1** : drag **2** ATRAER : draw, attract — vi : hang down, trail — **arrastrarse** vr **1** : crawl, creep **2** HUMILLARSE : grovel — **arrastre** nm **1** : dragging **2** : trawling (for fish)

arrear vt : urge on

arrebatar vt **1** : snatch, seize **2** CAUTIVAR : captivate — **arrebatarse** vr : get carried away — **arrebatado, -da** adj : hotheaded, rash — **arrebato** nm : outburst

arreciar vi : intensify, worsen

arrecife nm : reef

arreglar vt **1** COMPONER : fix **2** ORDENAR : tidy up **3** SOLUCIONAR : solve, work out — **arreglarse** vr **1** : get dressed (up) **2** arreglárselas fam : get by, manage — **arreglado, -da** adj **1** : fixed, repaired **2** ORDENADO : tidy **3** SOLUCIONADO : settled, sorted out **4** ATAVIADO : smart, dressed-up — **arreglo** nm **1** : arrangement **2** REPARACIÓN : repair **3** ACUERDO : agreement

arremangarse {52} vr : roll up one's sleeves

arremeter vi : attack, charge — **arremetida** nf : attack, onslaught

arremolinarse vr **1** : crowd around, mill about **2** : swirl (about)

arrendar {55} vt : rent, lease — **arrendador, -dora** n : landlord, landlady f — **arrendamiento** nm : rent, rental — **arrendatario, -ria** n : tenant, renter

arrepentirse {76} vr **1** : regret, be sorry **2** : repent (for one's sins) — **arrepentido, -da** adj : repentant — **arrepentimiento** nm : regret, repentance

arrestar vt : arrest, detain — **arresto** nm : arrest

arriar vt : lower

arriba adv **1** (indicating position) : above, overhead **2** (indicating direction) : up, upwards **3** : upstairs (of a house) **4** ~ de : more than **5** de ~ abajo : from top to bottom

arribar vi **1** : arrive **2** : dock, put into port — **arribista** nmf : parvenu, upstart — **arribo** nm : arrival

arriendo → **arrendamiento**

arriesgar {52} vt : risk, venture — **arriesgarse** vr : take a chance — **arriesgado, -da** adj : risky

arrimar vt : bring closer, draw near — **arrimarse** vr : approach

arrinconar vt **1** : corner, box in **2** ABANDONAR : push aside

arrobar vt : entrance — **arrobarse** vr : be enraptured — **arrobamiento** nm : rapture, ecstasy

arrodillarse vr : kneel (down)

arrogancia nf : arrogance — **arrogante** adj : arrogant

arrojar vt **1** : hurl, cast **2** EMITIR : give off, spew out **3** PRODUCIR : yield — **arrojarse** vr : throw oneself — **arrojado, -da** adj : daring — **arrojo** nm : boldness, courage

arrollar vt **1** : sweep away **2** DERROTAR : crush, overwhelm **3** : run over (with a vehicle) — **arrollador, -dora** adj : overwhelming

arropar vt : clothe, cover (up) — **arroparse** vr : wrap oneself up

arroyo nm **1** RIACHUELO : stream **2** : gutter (in a street)

arroz nm, pl **arroces** : rice

arrugar {52} vt : wrinkle, crease — **arrugarse** vr : get wrinkled — **arruga** nf : wrinkle, crease

arruinar vt : ruin, wreck — **arruinarse** vr **1** : be ruined **2** EMPOBRECERSE : go bankrupt

arrullar vt : lull to sleep — vi : coo — **arrullo** nm **1** : lullaby **2** : cooing (of doves)

arrumbar vt : lay aside

arsenal nm : arsenal

arsénico nm : arsenic

arte nmf (usually m in singular, f in plural) **1** : art **2** HABILIDAD : skill **3** ASTUCIA : cunning, cleverness **4** → **bello**

artefacto nm : artifact, device

arteria nf : artery

artesanía nf **1** : craftsmanship **2** : handicrafts pl — **artesanal** adj : handmade — **artesano, -na** n : artisan, craftsman

ártico, -ca adj : arctic

articular vt : articulate — **articulación** nf, pl -**ciones** : articulation, pronunciation **2** COYUNTURA : joint

artículo nm **1** : article **2** ~s de primera necesidad : essentials **3** ~s de tocador : toiletries

artífice nmf : artisan, craftsman

artificial adj : artificial

artificio nm **1** HABILIDAD : skill **2** APARATO : device **3** ARDID : artifice, ruse — **artificioso, -sa** adj : cunning, deceptive

artillería nf : artillery

artilugio nm : gadget

artimaña nf : ruse, trick

artista nmf **1** : artist **2** ACTOR : actor, actress f — **artístico, -ca** adj : artistic

artritis nms & pl : arthritis — **artrítico, -ca** adj : arthritic

arveja nf Lat : pea

arzobispo nm : archbishop

as nm : ace

asa nf : handle

asado, -da adj : roasted, grilled — **asado** nm : roast — **asador** nm : spit — **asaduras** nfpl : offal, entrails

asalariado, -da n : wage earner — ~ adj : salaried

asaltar vt **1** : assault **2** ROBAR : mug, rob — **asaltante** nmf **1** : assailant **2** ATRACADOR : mugger, robber — **asalto** nm **1** : assault **2** ROBO : mugging, robbery

asamblea nf : assembly, meeting

asar vt : roast, grill — **asarse** vr fam : roast, feel the heat

asbesto nm : asbestos

ascender {56} vi **1** : ascend, rise up **2** : be promoted (in a job) **3** ~ a : amount to — vt : promote — **ascendencia** nf : ancestry, descent — **ascendiente** nmf : ancestor — ~ nm : influence — **ascensión** nf, pl -**siones** : ascent — **ascenso** nm **1** : ascent, rise **2** : promotion (in a job) — **ascensor** nm : elevator

asco nm **1** : disgust **2** hacer ~s de : turn up one's nose at **3** me da ~ : it makes me sick

ascua nf **1** : ember **2** estar en ~s fam : be on edge

asear vt **1** : clean, tidy up — **asearse** vr : get cleaned up — **aseado, -da** adj : clean, tidy

asediar vt **1** : besiege **2** ACOSAR : harass — **asedio** nm **1** : siege **2** ACOSO : harassment

asegurar vt **1** : assure **2** FIJAR : secure **3** : insure (a car, house, etc.) — **asegurarse** vr : make sure

asemejarse vr **1** : be similar **2** ~ a : look like, resemble

asentar {55} vt **1** : set down **2** INSTALAR : set up, establish **3** Lat : state — **asentarse** vr **1** : settle **2** ESTABLECERSE : settle down — **asentado, -da** adj : settled, established

asentir {76} vi : assent, agree — **asentimiento** nm : assent

aseo nm : cleanliness

asequible adj : accessible, attainable

aserrar {55} vt : saw — **aserradero** nm : sawmill — **aserrín** nm, pl -**rrines** : sawdust

asesinar vt **1** : murder **2** : assassinate — **asesinato** nm **1** : murder **2** : assassination — **asesino, -na** n **1** : murderer, killer **2** : assassin

asesorar vt : advise, counsel — **asesorarse** vr ~ de : consult — **asesor, -sora** n : advisor, consultant — **asesoramiento** nm : advice, counsel

asestar {55} vt **1** : aim (a weapon) **2** : deal (a blow)

aseverar vt : assert — **aseveración** nf, pl -**ciones** : assertion

asfalto nm : asphalt

asfixiar vt **1** : asphyxiate, suffocate — **asfixiarse** vr : suffocate — **asfixia** nf : asphyxiation, suffocation

así adv **1** : like this, like that, thus **2** ~ de : so, that (much) **3** ~ que : so, therefore **4** ~ que : as soon as **5** ~ como : as well as — ~ adj : such, like that — ~ conj AUNQUE : even though

asiático, -ca adj : Asian, Asiatic

asidero nm : handle

asiduo, -dua adj : frequent, regular

asiento nm : seat

asignar vt **1** : assign, allocate **2** DESTINAR : appoint — **asignación** nf, pl -**ciones** **1** : assignment **2** SUELDO : salary, pay — **asignatura** nf : subject, course

asilo nm **1** : asylum, home **2** REFUGIO : refuge, shelter — **asilado, -da** n : inmate

asimilar vt : assimilate — **asimilarse** vr ~ a : resemble

asimismo *adv* 1 : similarly, likewise 2 TAMBIÉN : as well, also

asir {7} *vt* : seize, grasp — **asirse** *vr* ~ a : cling to

asistir *vi* ~ a : attend, be present at — *vt* : assist — **asistencia** *nf* 1 : attendance 2 AYUDA : assistance — **asistente** *nmf* 1 : assistant 2 los ~s : those present

asma *nf* : asthma — **asmático, -ca** *adj* : asthmatic

asno *nm* : ass, donkey

asociar *vt* : associate — **asociarse** *vr* 1 : form a partnership 2 ~ a : join, become a member of — **asociación** *nf, pl* **-ciones** : association — **asociado, -da** *adj* : associate, associated — ~ *n* : associate, partner

asolar {19} *vt* : devastate

asomar *vt* : show, stick out — *vi* : appear, show — **asomarse** *vr* 1 : appear 2 : stick one's head out (of a window)

asombrar *vt* : amaze, astonish — **asombrarse** *vr* : be amazed — **asombro** *nm* : amazement, astonishment — **asombroso, -sa** *adj* : amazing, astonishing

asomo *nm* 1 : hint, trace 2 ni por ~ : by no means

aspaviento *nm* : exaggerated gestures, fuss

aspecto *nm* 1 : aspect 2 APARIENCIA : appearance, look

áspero, -ra *adj* : rough, harsh — **aspereza** *nf* : roughness, harshness

aspersión *nf, pl* **-siones** : sprinkling — **aspersor** *nm* : sprinkler

aspiración *nf, pl* **-ciones** 1 : breathing in 2 ANHELO : aspiration

aspiradora *nf* : vacuum cleaner

aspirar *vi* ~ a : aspire to — *vt* : inhale, breathe in — **aspirante** *nmf* : applicant, candidate

aspirina *nf* : aspirin

asquear *vt* : sicken, disgust

asquerosidad *nf* : filth, foulness — **asqueroso, -sa** *adj* : disgusting, sickening

asta *nf* 1 : flagpole 2 CUERNO : antler, horn 3 : shaft (of a spear) — **astado, -da** *adj* : horned

asterisco *nm* : asterisk

asteroide *nm* : asteroid

astigmatismo *nm* : astigmatism

astillar *vt* : splinter — **astilla** *nf* : splinter, chip

astillero *nm* : shipyard

astral *adj* : astral

astringente *adj & nm* : astringent

astro *nm* 1 : heavenly body 2 : star (of movies, etc.)

astrología *nf* : astrology

astronauta *nmf* : astronaut — **astronáutica** *nf* : astronautics

astronave *nf* : spaceship

astronomía *nf* : astronomy — **astronómico, -ca** *adj* : astronomical — **astrónomo, -ma** *n* : astronomer

astucia *nf* 1 : astuteness 2 ARDID : cunning, guile — **astuto, -ta** *adj* 1 : astute 2 TAIMADO : crafty

asueto *nm* : time off, break

asumir *vt* : assume — **asunción** *nf, pl* **-ciones** : assumption

asunto *nm* 1 : matter, affair 2 NEGOCIO : business

asustar *vt* : scare, frighten — **asustarse** *vr* ~ de : be frightened of — **asustadizo, -za** *adj* : jumpy, skittish — **asustado, -da** *adj* : frightened, afraid

atacar {72} *v* : attack — **atacante** *nmf* : attacker

atado *nm* : bundle

atadura *nf* : tie, bond

atajar *vt* : block, cut off — *vi* ~ por : take a shortcut through — **atajo** *nm* : shortcut

atañer {79} *vi* ~ a : concern, have to do with

ataque *nm* 1 : attack, assault 2 ACCESO : fit 3 ~ de nervios : nervous breakdown

atar *vt* : tie up, tie down — **atarse** *vr* : tie (up)

atardecer {53} *v impers* : get dark — ~ *nm* : late afternoon, dusk

atareado, -da *adj* : busy

atascar {72} *vt* 1 : block, clog 2 ESTORBAR : hinder — **atascarse** *vr* 1 OBSTRUIRSE : become obstructed 2 : get bogged down — **atasco** *nm* 1 : blockage 2 EMBOTELLAMIENTO : traffic jam

ataúd *nm* : coffin

ataviar {85} *vt* : dress (up) — **ataviarse** *vr* : dress up — **atavío** *nm* : attire

atemorizar {21} *vt* : frighten — **atemorizarse** *vr* : get scared

atención *nf, pl* **-ciones** 1 : attention 2 prestar ~ : pay attention 3 llamar la ~ : attract attention — *interj* : attention!, watch out!

atender {56} *vt* 1 : attend to 2 CUIDAR : look after 3 : heed (advice, etc.) — *vi* : pay attention

atenerse {80} *vr* ~ a : abide by

atentamente *adv* 1 : attentively 2 le saluda ~ : sincerely yours

atentar {55} *vi* ~ **contra** : make an attempt on — **atentado** *nm* : attack

atento, -ta *adj* 1 : attentive, mindful 2 CORTÉS : courteous

atenuar {3} *vt* 1 : dim (lights), tone down (colors, etc.) 2 DISMINUIR : lessen — **atenuante** *nmf* : extenuating circumstances

ateo, atea *adj* : atheistic — ~ *n* : atheist

aterciopelado, -da *adj* : velvety, downy

aterido, -da *adj* : frozen stiff

aterrar {55} *vt* : terrify — **aterrador, -dora** *adj* : terrifying

aterrizar {21} *vi* : land — **aterrizaje** *nm* : landing

aterrorizar {21} *vt* : terrify

atesorar *vt* : hoard, amass

atestar {55} *vt* 1 : crowd, pack 2 : testify to (in law) — **atestado, -da** *adj* : stuffed, packed

atestiguar {10} *vt* : testify to

atiborrar *vt* : stuff, cram — **atiborrarse** *vr* : stuff oneself

ático *nm* 1 : penthouse 2 DESVÁN : attic

atildado, -da *adj* : smart, neat

atinar *vi* : be on target

atípico, -ca *adj* : atypical

atirantar *vt* : tighten

atisbar *vt* 1 : spy on 2 VISLUMBRAR : catch a glimpse of — **atisbo** *nm* : sign, hint

atizar {57} *vt* 1 : poke (a fire) 2 : rouse, stir up (passions, etc.) — **atizador** *nm* : poker

atlántico, -ca *adj* : Atlantic

atlas *nm* : atlas

atleta *nmf* : athlete — **atlético, -ca** *adj* : athletic — **atletismo** *nm* : athletics

atmósfera *nf* : atmosphere — **atmosférico, -ca** *adj* : atmospheric

atolondrado, -da *adj* 1 : scatterbrained 2 ATURDIDO : bewildered, dazed

átomo *nm* : atom — **atómico, -ca** *adj* : atomic — **atomizador** *nm* : atomizer

atónito, -ta *adj* : astonished, amazed

atontar *vt* : stun, daze

atorar *vt* : block — **atorarse** *vr* : get stuck

atormentar *vt* : torment, torture — **atormentarse** *vr* : torment oneself, agonize — **atormentador, -dora** *n* : tormenter

atornillar *vt* : screw

atorrante *nmf* *Lat* : bum, loafer

atosigar {52} *vt* : harass, annoy

atracar {72} *vi* : dock, land — *vt* : hold up, mug — **atracarse** *vr fam* ~ **de** : gorge oneself with — **atracadero**

nm : dock, pier — **atracador, -dora** *n* : robber, mugger

atracción *nf, pl* **-ciones** : attraction

atraco *nm* : holdup, robbery

atractivo, -va *adj* : attractive — **atractivo** *nm* : attraction, appeal

atraer {81} *vt* : attract

atragantarse *vr* : choke

atrancar {72} *vt* : block, bar — **atrancarse** *vr* : get blocked, get stuck

atrapar *vt* : trap, capture

atrás *adv* 1 DETRÁS : back, behind 2 ANTES : before, earlier 3 **para** ~ *or* **hacia** ~ : backwards

atrasar *vt* 1 : put back (a clock) 2 DEMORAR : delay — *vi* : lose time — **atrasarse** *vr* : fall behind — **atrasado, -da** *adj* 1 : late, overdue 2 : backward (of countries, etc.) 3 : slow (of a clock) — **atraso** *nm* 1 RETRASO : delay 2 : backwardness 3 ~s *nmpl* : arrears

atravesar {55} *vt* 1 CRUZAR : cross 2 TRASPASAR : pierce 3 : lay across (a road, etc.) 4 : go through (a situation) — **atravesarse** *vr* : be in the way

atrayente *adj* : attractive

atreverse *vr* : dare — **atrevido, -da** *adj* 1 : bold 2 INSOLENTE : insolent — **atrevimiento** *nm* 1 : boldness 2 DESCARO : insolence

atribuir {41} *vt* 1 : attribute 2 : confer (powers, etc.) — **atribuirse** *vr* : take credit for

atribular *vt* : afflict, trouble

atributo *nm* : attribute

atrincherar *vt* : entrench — **atrincherarse** *vr* : dig oneself in

atrocidad *nf* : atrocity

atronador, -dora *adj* : thunderous

atropellar *vt* 1 : run over 2 : violate, abuse (a person) — **atropellarse** *vr* : rush — **atropellado, -da** *adj* : hasty — **atropello** *nm* : abuse, outrage

atroz *adj, pl* **atroces** : atrocious

atuendo *nm* : attire

atufar *vt* : vex — **atufarse** *vr* : get angry

atún *nm, pl* **atunes** : tuna

aturdir *vt* 1 : stun, shock 2 CONFUNDIR : bewilder — **aturdido, -da** *adj* : dazed, bewildered

audaz *adj, pl* **-daces** : bold, daring — **audacia** *nf* : boldness, audacity

audible *adj* : audible

audición *nf, pl* **-ciones** 1 : hearing 2 : audition (in theater, etc.)

audiencia *nf* : audience

audífono *nm* 1 : hearing aid 2 ~s *nmpl* *Lat* : headphones, earphones

audiovisual *adj* : audiovisual

auditar vt : audit — **auditor, -tora** n : auditor
auditorio nm **1** : auditorium **2** PÚBLICO : audience
auge nm **1** : peak **2** : (economic) boom
augurar vt : predict, foretell — **augurio** nm : omen
augusto, -ta adj : august
aula nf : classroom
aullar {8} vi : howl — **aullido** nm : howl
aumentar vt : increase, raise — vi : increase, grow — **aumento** nm : increase, rise
aun adv **1** : even **2** ~ **así** : even so
aún adv **1** : still, yet **2 más** ~ : furthermore
aunar {8} vt : join, combine — **aunarse** vr : unite
aunque conj **1** : though, although, even if **2** ~ **sea** : at least
aureola nf **1** : halo **2** FAMA : aura
auricular nm **1** : telephone receiver **2** ~**es** nmpl : headphones
aurora nf : dawn
ausentarse vr : leave, go away — **ausencia** nf : absence — **ausente** adj : absent — ~ nmf **1** : absentee **2** : missing person (in law)
auspicios nmpl : sponsorship, auspices
austero, -ra adj : austere — **austeridad** nf : austerity
austral adj : southern
australiano, -na adj : Australian
austriaco or **austríaco, -ca** adj : Austrian
auténtico, -ca adj : authentic, genuine — **autenticidad** nf : authenticity
auto nm : auto, car
autoayuda nf : self-help
autobiografía nf : autobiography — **autobiográfico, -ca** adj : autobiographical
autobús nm, pl **-buses** : bus
autocompasión nf : self-pity
autocontrol nm : self-control
autocracia nf : autocracy
autóctono, -na adj : indigenous, native
autodefensa nf : self-defense
autodidacta adj : self-taught
autodisciplina nf : self-discipline
autoestop → **autostop**
autografiar vt : autograph — **autógrafo** nm : autograph
autómata nm : automaton
automático, -ca adj : automatic — **tomatización** nf, pl **-ciones** : automation — **automatizar** {21} vt : automate
automotor, -triz adj, fpl **-trices** : self-propelled

automóvil nm : automobile — **automovilista** nmf : motorist — **automovilístico, -ca** adj : automobile, car
autonomía nf : autonomy — **autónomo, -ma** adj : autonomous
autopista nf : expressway, highway
autopropulsado, -da adj : self-propelled
autopsia nf : autopsy
autor, -tora n **1** : author **2** : perpetrator (of a crime)
autoridad nf : authority — **autoritario, -ria** adj : authoritarian
autorizar {21} vt : authorize, approve — **autorización** nf, pl **-ciones** : authorization — **autorizado, -da** adj **1** PERMITIDO : authorized **2** : authoritative
autorretrato nm : self-portrait
autoservicio nm **1** : self-service restaurant **2** SUPERMERCADO : supermarket
autostop nm **1** : hitchhiking **2 hacer** ~ : hitchhike — **autostopista** nmf : hitchhiker
autosuficiente adj : self-sufficient
auxiliar vt : aid, assist — ~ adj : auxiliary — ~ nmf **1** : assistant, helper **2** ~ **de vuelo** : flight attendant — **auxilio** nm **1** : aid, assistance **2 primeros** ~**s** : first aid
avalancha nf : avalanche
avalar vt : guarantee, endorse — **aval** nm : guarantee, endorsement
avanzar {21} v : advance, move forward — **avance** nm : advance — **avanzado, -da** adj : advanced
avaricia nf : greed, avarice — **avaricioso, -sa** adj : avaricious, greedy — **avaro, -ra** adj : miserly — ~ n : miser
avasallar vt : overpower, subjugate — **avasallador, -dora** adj : overwhelming
ave nf : bird
avecinarse vr : approach
avecindarse vr : settle, take up residence
avellana nf : hazelnut
avena nf **1** : oats pl **2** or **harina de** ~ : oatmeal
avenida nf : avenue
avenir {87} vt : reconcile, harmonize — **avenirse** vr : agree, come to terms
aventajar vt : be ahead of, surpass
aventar {55} vt **1** : fan **2** : winnow (grain) **3** Lat : throw, toss
aventurar vt : venture, risk — **aventurarse** vr : take a risk — **aventura** nf **1** : adventure **2** RIESGO : risk **3** AMORÍO : love affair — **aventurado, -da** adj

: risky — **aventurero, -ra** *adj* : adventurous — **~** *n* : adventurer

avergonzar {9} *vt* : shame, embarrass — **avergonzarse** *vr* : be ashamed, be embarrassed

averiar {85} *vt* : damage — **averiarse** *vr* : break down — **avería** *nf* 1 : damage 2 : breakdown (of an automobile) — **averiado, -da** *adj* 1 : damaged, faulty 2 : broken down (of an automobile)

averiguar {10} *vt* 1 : find out 2 INVESTIGAR : investigate — **averiguación** *nf, pl* **-ciones** : investigation, inquiry

aversión *nf, pl* **-siones** : aversion, dislike

avestruz *nm, pl* **-truces** : ostrich

aviación *nf, pl* **-ciones** : aviation — **aviador, -dora** *n* : aviator

aviar {85} *vt* : prepare, make ready

ávido, -da *adj* : eager, avid — **avidez** *nf, pl* **-deces** : eagerness

avío *nm* 1 : preparation, provision 2 **~s** *nmpl* : gear, equipment

avión *nm, pl* **aviones** : airplane — **avioneta** *nf* : light airplane

avisar *vt* 1 : notify 2 ADVERTIR : warn — **aviso** *nm* 1 : notice 2 ADVERTENCIA : warning 3 *Lat* : advertisement, ad 4 **estar sobre ~** : be on the alert

avispa *nf* : wasp — **avispón** *nm, pl* **-pones** : hornet

avispado, -da *adj fam* : clever, sharp

avistar *vt* : catch sight of

avivar *vt* 1 : enliven, brighten 2 : arouse (desire, etc.) 3 : intensify (pain)

axila *nf* : underarm, armpit

axioma *nm* : axiom

ay *interj* 1 : oh! 2 : ouch!, ow!

ayer *adv* : yesterday — **~** *nm* : yesteryear, days gone by

ayote *nm Lat* : pumpkin

ayudar *vt* : help, assist — **ayudarse** *vr* **~ de** : make use of — **ayuda** *nf* : help, assistance — **ayudante** *nmf* : helper, assistant

ayunar *vi* : fast — **ayunas** *nfpl* **en ~** : fasting — **ayuno** *nm* : fast

ayuntamiento *nm* 1 : town hall, city hall (building) 2 : town or city council

azabache *nm* : jet

azada *nf* : hoe — **azadonar** *vt* : hoe

azafata *nf* : stewardess *f*

azafrán *nm, pl* **-franes** : saffron

azalea *nf* : azalea

azar *nm* 1 : chance 2 **al ~** : at random — **azaroso, -sa** *adj* : hazardous (of a journey, etc.), eventful (of a life)

azorar *vt* 1 : alarm 2 DESCONCERTAR : embarrass — **azorarse** *vr* : get embarrassed

azotar *vt* : beat, whip — **azote** *nm* 1 LÁTIGO : whip, lash 2 CALAMIDAD : scourge

azotea *nf* : flat or terraced roof

azteca *adj* : Aztec

azúcar *nmf* : sugar — **azucarado, -da** *adj* : sugary — **azucarera** *nf* : sugar bowl — **azucarero, -ra** *adj* : sugar

azufre *nm* : sulphur

azul *adj & nm* : blue — **azulado, -da** *adj* : bluish

azulejo *nm* 1 : ceramic tile 2 *Lat* : bluebird

azur *n* : azure, sky blue

azuzar {21} *vt* : incite, urge on

B

b *nf* : b, second letter of the Spanish alphabet

babear *vi* : drool, slobber — **baba** *nf* : saliva, drool

babel *nmf* : bedlam

babero *nm* : bib

babor *nm* : port (side)

babosa *nf* : slug — **baboso, -sa** *adj* 1 : slimy 2 *Lat fam* : silly

babucha *nf* : slipper

babuino *nm* : baboon

bacalao *nm* : cod

bache *nm* 1 : pothole, rut 2 DIFICULTADES : bad time

bachiller *nmf* : high school graduate — **bachillerato** *nm* : high school diploma

bacon *nm Spain* : bacon

bacteria *nf* : bacterium

bagaje *nm* : baggage, luggage

bagatela *nf* : trinket

bagre *nm* : catfish

bahía *nf* : bay

bailar *v* : dance — **bailarín, -rina** *n, mpl* **-rines** : dancer — **baile** *nm* 1 : dance 2 FIESTA : dance party, ball

bajar *vt* 1 : bring down, lower 2 DESCENDER : go down, come down — *vi* : descend, drop — **bajarse** *vr* **~ de** : get out of, get off — **baja** *nf* 1 : fall, drop 2 CESE : dismissal 3 PERMISO : sick leave 4 : (military) casualty — **bajada** *nf* 1 : descent, drop 2 PENDIENTE : slope

bajeza *nf* : lowness, meanness
bajío *nm* : sandbank, shoal
bajo, -ja *adj* **1** : low, lower **2** : short (in stature) **3** : soft, faint (of sounds) **4** VIL : base, vile — **bajo** *adv* **1** : low **2** **habla más ~** : speak more softly — **~** *nm* **1** : ground floor **2** DOBLADILLO : hem **3** : bass (in music) — **~** *prep* : under, below — **bajón** *nm*, *pl* **-jones** : sharp drop, slump
bala *nf* **1** : bullet **2** : bale (of cotton, etc.)
balada *nf* : ballad
balancear *vt* **1** : balance **2** : swing (one's arms, etc.), rock (a boat) — **balancearse** *vr* : swing, sway — **balance** *nm* **1** : balance **2** : balance sheet — **balanceo** *nm* : swaying, rocking
balancín *nm*, *pl* **-cines** **1** : seesaw **2** MECEDORA : rocking chair
balanza *nf* : scales *pl*, balance
balar *vi* : bleat
balaustrada *nf* : balustrade, banister
balazo *nm* **1** DISPARO : shot **2** : bullet wound
balbucear *vi* **1** : stammer, stutter **2** : babble (of a baby) — **balbuceo** *nm* : stammering, muttering, babbling
balcón *nm*, *pl* **-cones** : balcony
balde *nm* **1** : bucket, pail **2 en ~** : in vain
baldío, -día *adj* **1** : uncultivated **2** INÚTIL : useless — **baldío** *nm* : wasteland
baldosa *nf* : floor tile
balear *vt* *Lat* : shoot (at) — **baleo** *nm* *Lat* : shot, shooting
balido *nm* : bleat
balín *nm*, *pl* **-lines** : pellet
balística *nf* : ballistics — **balístico, -ca** *adj* : ballistic
baliza *nf* **1** : buoy **2** : beacon (for aircraft)
ballena *nf* : whale
ballesta *nf* **1** : crossbow **2** : spring (of an automobile)
ballet *nm* : ballet
balneario *nm* : spa
balompié *nm* : soccer
balón *nm*, *pl* **-lones** : ball — **baloncesto** *nm* : basketball — **balonvolea** *nm* : volleyball
balsa *nf* **1** : raft **2** ESTANQUE : pond, pool
bálsamo *nm* : balsam, balm — **balsámico, -ca** *adj* : soothing
baluarte *nm* : bulwark, bastion
bambolear *vi* : sway, swing — **bambolearse** *vr* : sway, rock
bambú *nm*, *pl* **-búes** *or* **-bús** : bamboo
banal *adj* : banal
banana *nf* *Lat* : banana — **banano** *nm* *Lat* : banana
banca *nf* **1** : banking **2** BANCO : bench — **bancario, -ria** *adj* : bank, banking

— **bancarrota** *nf* : bankruptcy —
banco *nm* **1** : bank **2** BANCA : stool, bench, pew **3** : school (of fish)
banda *nf* **1** : band, strip **2** : band (in music) **3** PANDILLA : gang **4** : flock (of birds) **5 ~ sonora** : sound track — **bandada** *nf* : flock (of birds), school (of fish)
bandazo *nm* : lurch
bandeja *nf* : tray, platter
bandera *nf* : flag, banner
banderilla *nf* : banderilla
banderín *nm*, *pl* **-rines** : pennant, small flag
bandido, -da *n* : bandit
bando *nm* **1** : proclamation, edict **2** PARTIDO : faction, side
bandolero, -ra *n* : bandit
banjo *nm* : banjo
banquero, -ra *n* : banker
banqueta *nf* **1** : stool, footstool **2** *Lat* : sidewalk
banquete *nm* : banquet
bañar *vt* **1** : bathe, wash **2** SUMERGIR : immerse **3** CUBRIR : coat, cover — **bañarse** *vr* **1** : take a bath **2** : go swimming — **bañera** *nf* : bathtub — **bañista** *nmf* : bather — **baño** *nm* **1** : bath, swim **2** BAÑERA : bathtub **3** **¿donde está el ~?** : where is the bathroom? **4 ~ María** : double boiler
baqueta *nf* **1** : ramrod **2 ~s** *nfpl* : drumsticks
bar *nm* : bar, tavern
barajar *vt* **1** : shuffle (cards) **2** CONSIDERAR : consider — **baraja** *nf* : deck of cards
baranda *nf* : rail, railing — **barandal** *nm* : handrail, banister
barato, -ta *adj* : cheap — **barato** *adv* : cheap, cheaply — **barata** *nf* *Lat* : sale, bargain — **baratija** *nf* : trinket — **baratillo** *nm* : secondhand store, flea market
barba *nf* **1** : beard, stubble **2** BARBILLA : chin
barbacoa *nf* : barbecue
barbaridad *nf* **1** : barbarity, cruelty **2** **¡qué ~!** : that's outrageous! — **barbarie** *nf* : barbarism, savagery — **bárbaro, -ra** *adj* : barbaric
barbecho *nm* : fallow land
barbero, -ra *n* : barber — **barbería** *nf* : barbershop
barbilla *nf* : chin
barbudo, -da *adj* : bearded
barca *nf* **1** : boat **2 ~ de pasaje** : ferryboat — **barcaza** *nf* : barge — **barco** *nm* : boat, ship
barítono *nm* : baritone

barman *nm* : bartender
barnizar {21} *vt* **1** : varnish **2** : glaze (ceramics) — **barniz** *nm, pl* **-nices 1** : varnish **2** : glaze (on ceramics)
barómetro *nm* : barometer
barón *nm, pl* **-rones** : baron — **baronesa** *nf* : baroness
barquero *nm* : boatman
barquillo *nm* : wafer, cone
barra *nf* **1** : bar, rod, stick **2** : counter (of a bar, etc.)
barraca *nf* **1** : hut, cabin **2** CASETA : booth, stall
barranco *nm or* **barranca** *nf* : ravine, gorge, gully
barredera *nf* : street-sweeping machine
barrenar *vt* : drill — **barrena** *nf* : drill, auger
barrer *v* : sweep
barrera *nf* : barrier
barreta *nf* : crowbar
barriada *nf* : district, quarter
barrica *nf* : cask, keg
barricada *nf* : barricade
barrido *nm* : sweep, sweeping
barriga *nf* : belly
barril *nm* **1** : barrel, keg **2 de ~** : draft
barrio *nm* **1** : neighborhood **2 ~ bajo** : slums *pl*
barro *nm* **1** : mud **2** ARCILLA : clay **3** GRANO : pimple, blackhead — **barroso, -sa** *adj* : muddy
barrote *nm* : bar (on a window)
barrunto *nm* **1** : suspicion **2** INDICIO : sign, indication
bártulos *nmpl* : things, belongings
barullo *nm* : racket, ruckus
basa *nf* : base, pedestal — **basar** *vt* : base — **basarse** *vr* **~ en** : be based on
báscula *nf* : scales *pl*
base *nf* **1** : base **2** FUNDAMENTO : basis, foundation **3 ~ de datos** : database — **básico, -ca** *adj* : basic
basquetbol *or* **básquetbol** *nm Lat* : basketball
bastar *vi* : be enough, suffice — **bastante** *adv* **1** : fairly, rather **2** SUFICIENTE : enough — **~** *adj* : enough, sufficient — **~** *pron* : enough
bastardo, -da *adj & n* : bastard
bastidor *nm* **1** : frame **2** : wing (in theater) **3 entre ~es** : behind the scenes, backstage
bastilla *nf* : hem
bastión *nf, pl* **-tiones** : bastion, stronghold
basto, -ta *adj* : coarse, rough
bastón *nm, pl* **-tones 1** : cane, walking stick **2** : baton (in parades)

basura *nf* : garbage, rubbish — **basurero, -ra** *n* : garbage collector
bata *nf* **1** : bathrobe, housecoat **2** : smock (of a doctor, laboratory worker, etc.)
batalla *nf* : battle, fight — **batalla** *nf* **1** : battle, fight, struggle **2 de ~** : ordinary, everyday — **batallón** *nm, pl* **-llones** : battalion
batata *nf* : yam, sweet potato
batear *v* : bat, hit — **bate** *nm* : baseball bat — **bateador, -dora** *n* : batter, hitter
batería *nf* **1** : battery **2** : drums *pl* **3 ~ de cocina** : kitchen utensils *pl*
batir *vt* **1** : beat, whip **2** DERRIBAR : knock down — **batirse** *vr* : fight — **batido** *nm* : milk shake — **batidor** *nm* : eggbeater, whisk — **batidora** *nf* : electric mixer
batuta *nf* : baton
baúl *nm* : trunk, chest
bautismo *nm* : baptism — **bautismal** *adj* : baptismal — **bautizar** {21} *vt* : baptize — **bautizo** *nm* : baptism, christening
baya *nf* : berry
bayeta *nf* : cleaning cloth
bayoneta *nf* : bayonet
bazar *nm* : bazaar
bazo *nm* : spleen
bazofia *nf fam* : rubbish, hogwash
beato, -ta *adj* : blessed
bebé *nm* : baby
beber *v* : drink — **bebedero** *nm* : watering trough — **bebedor, -dora** *n* : (heavy) drinker — **bebida** *nf* : drink, beverage — **bebido, -da** *adj* : drunk
beca *nf* : grant, scholarship
becerro, -rra *n* : calf
befa *nf* : jeer, taunt
beige *adj & nm* : beige
beisbol *or* **béisbol** *nm* : baseball — **beisbolista** *nmf* : baseball player
beldad *nf* : beauty
belga *adj* : Belgian
belén *nf, pl* **-lenes** : Nativity scene
beliceño, -ña *adj* : Belizean
bélico, -ca *adj* : military, war — **belicoso, -sa** *adj* : warlike
beligerancia *nf* : belligerence — **beligerante** *adj & nmf* : belligerent
belleza *nf* : beauty — **bello, -lla** *adj* **1** : beautiful **2 bellas artes** : fine arts
bellota *nf* : acorn
bemol *adj & nm* : flat (in music)
bendecir {11} *vt* **1** : bless **2 ~ la mesa** : say grace — **bendición** *nf, pl* **-ciones** : benediction, blessing — **bendito, -ta** *adj* : blessed, holy **2** DI-

CHOSO : fortunate **3 ¡bendito sea Dios!** : thank goodness!

benefactor, -tora n : benefactor

beneficiar vt : benefit, assist — **beneficiarse** vr : benefit, profit — **beneficiario, -ria** n : beneficiary — **beneficio** nm **1** : gain, profit **2** BIEN : benefit — **beneficioso, -sa** adj : beneficial — **benéfico, -ca** adj : charitable

benemérito, -ta adj : worthy

beneplácito nm : approval, consent

benévolo, -la adj : benevolent, kind — **benevolencia** nf : benevolence, kindness

bengala nf or **luz de ∼** : flare

benigno, -na adj **1** : mild **2** : benign (in medicine) — **benignidad** nf : mildness, kindness

benjamín, -mina n, mpl **-mines** : youngest child

beodo, -da adj & n : drunk

berenjena nf : eggplant

berrear vi **1** : bellow, low **2** : bawl, howl (of a person) — **berrido** nm **1** : bellowing **2** : howl, scream (of a person)

berro nm : watercress

berza nf : cabbage

besar vt : kiss — **besarse** vr : kiss (each other) — **beso** nm : kiss

bestia nf : beast, animal — **bestial** adj : bestial, brutal — **bestialidad** nf : brutality

betabel nm Lat : beet

betún nm, pl **-tunes** : shoe polish

bianual adj : biannual

biberón nm, pl **-rones** : baby's bottle

Biblia nf : Bible — **bíblico, -ca** adj : biblical

bibliografía nf : bibliography — **bibliográfico, -ca** adj : bibliographic, bibliographical

biblioteca nf : library — **bibliotecario, -ria** n : librarian

bicarbonato nm **∼ de soda** : baking soda

bicentenario nm : bicentennial

bíceps nms & pl : biceps

bicho nm : small animal, bug

bicicleta nf : bicycle — **bici** nf fam : bike

bicolor adj : two-tone

bidón nm, pl **-dones** : large can, drum

bien adv **1** : well, good **2** CORRECTAMENTE : correctly, right **3** MUY : very, quite **4** DE BUENA GANA : willingly **5 ∼ que** : although **6 más ∼** : rather — **bien** adj **1** : all right, well **2** AGRADABLE : pleasant, nice **3** SATISFACTORIO : satisfactory **4** CORRECTO : correct, right — **bien** nm **1** : good **2 ∼es** nmpl : property, goods

bienal adj & nf : biennial

bienaventurado, -da adj : blessed, fortunate

bienestar nm : welfare, well-being

bienhechor, -chora n : benefactor

bienintencionado, -da adj : well-meaning

bienvenido, -da adj : welcome — **bienvenida** nf **1** : welcome **2 dar la ∼ a** : welcome (s.o.)

bife nm Lat : steak

bifocales nmpl : bifocals

bifurcarse {72} vr : fork — **bifurcación** nf, pl **-ciones** : fork, branch

bigamia nf : bigamy

bigote nm **1** : mustache **2 ∼s** nmpl : whiskers (of an animal)

bikini nm : bikini

bilingüe adj : bilingual

bilis nf : bile

billar nm : pool, billiards

billete nm **1** : bill, banknote **2** BOLETO : ticket — **billetera** nf : billfold, wallet

billón nm, pl **-llones** : trillion

bimensual, -suale adj : twice a month — **bimestral** adj : bimonthly

binario, -ria adj : binary

bingo nm : bingo

binoculares nmpl : binoculars

biodegradable adj : biodegradable

biofísica nf : biophysics

biografía nf : biography — **biográfico, -ca** adj : biographical — **biógrafo, -fa** n : biographer

biología nf : biology — **biológico, -ca** adj : biological, biologic — **biólogo, -ga** n : biologist

biombo nm : folding screen

biomecánica nf : biomechanics

biopsia nf : biopsy

bioquímica nf : biochemistry — **bioquímico, -ca** adj : biochemical

biotecnología nf : biotechnology

bipartidista adj : bipartisan

bípedo nm : biped

biquini → bikini

birlar vt fam : swipe, pinch

bis adv **1** : twice (in music) **2** : A (in an address) — **∼** nm : encore

bisabuelo, -la n : great-grandfather m, great-grandmother f

bisagra nf : hinge

bisecar {72} vt : bisect

biselar vt : bevel

bisexual adj : bisexual

bisiesto adj **año ∼** : leap year

bisnieto, -ta n : great-grandson m, great-granddaughter f

bisonte nm : bison, buffalo

bisoño, -ña n : novice

bistec *nm* : steak
bisturí *nm* : scalpel
bisutería *nf* : costume jewelry
bit *nm* : bit (unit of information)
bizco, -ca *adj* : cross-eyed
bizcocho *nm* : sponge cake
bizquear *vi* : squint — **bizquera** *nf* : squint
blanco, -ca *adj* : white — **blanco, -ca** *n* : white person — **blanco** *nm* **1** : white **2** DIANA : target, bull's-eye **3** : blank (space) — **blancura** *nf* : whiteness
blandir {1} *vt* : wave, brandish
blando, -da *adj* **1** : soft, tender **2** DÉBIL : weak-willed **3** INDULGENTE : lenient — **blandura** *nf* **1** : softness, tenderness **2** DEBILIDAD : weakness **3** INDULGENCIA : leniency
blanquear *vt* **1** : whiten, bleach **2** : launder (money) — *vi* : turn white — **blanqueador** *nm Lat* : bleach
blasfemar *vi* : blaspheme — **blasfemia** *nf* : blasphemy — **blasfemo, -ma** *adj* : blasphemous
bledo *nm* **no me importa un ∼** *fam* : I couldn't care less
blindaje *nm* : armor, armor plating — **blindado, -da** *adj* : armored
bloc *nm, pl* **blocs** : (writing) pad
bloquear *vt* **1** OBSTRUIR : block, obstruct **2** : blockade — **bloque** *nm* **1** : block **2** : bloc (in politics) — **bloqueo** *nm* **1** OBSTRUCCIÓN : blockage **2** : blockade
blusa *nf* : blouse — **blusón** *nm, pl* **-sones** : smock
boato *nm* : showiness
bobina *nf* : bobbin, reel
bobo, -ba *adj* : silly, stupid — **∼** *n* : fool, simpleton
boca *nf* **1** : mouth **2** ENTRADA : entrance **3 ∼ arriba** : faceup **4 ∼ abajo** : facedown, prone **5 ∼ de riego** : hydrant
bocacalle *nf* : entrance (to a street)
bocado *nm* **1** : bite, mouthful **2** : bit (of a bridle) — **bocadillo** *nm Spain* : sandwich
bocajarro *nm* **a ∼** : point-blank
bocallave *nf* : keyhole
bocanada *nf* **1** : swallow, swig **2** : puff, gust (of smoke, wind, etc.)
boceto *nm* : sketch, outline
bochorno *nm* **1** VERGÜENZA : embarrassment **2** : muggy weather — **bochornoso, -sa** *adj* **1** VERGONZOSO : embarrassing **2** : muggy, sultry
bocina *nf* **1** : horn **2** : mouthpiece (of a telephone) — **bocinazo** *nm* : honk, toot
boda *nf* : wedding
bodega *nf* **1** : wine cellar **2** : warehouse

3 : hold (of a ship or airplane) **4** *Lat* : grocery store
bofetear *vt* : slap — **bofetada** *nf or* **bofetón** *nm* : slap (in the face)
boga *nf* : fashion, vogue
bohemio, -mia *adj & n* : bohemian
boicotear *vt* : boycott — **boicot** *nm, pl* **-cots** : boycott
boina *nf* : beret
bola *nf* **1** : ball **2** *fam* : fib
bolera *nf* : bowling alley
boleta *nf Lat* : ticket — **boletería** *nf Lat* : ticket office
boletín *nm, pl* **-tines 1** : bulletin **2 ∼ de noticias** : news release
boleto *nm* : ticket
boliche *nm* **1** : bowling **2** BOLERA : bowling alley
bolígrafo *nm* : ballpoint pen
bolillo *nm* : bobbin
boliviano, -na *adj* : Bolivian
bollo *nm* : bun, sweet roll
bolo *nm* **1** : bowling pin **2 ∼s** *nmpl* : bowling
bolsa *nf* **1** : bag **2** *Lat* : pocketbook, purse **3 la Bolsa** : the stock market — **bolsillo** *nm* : pocket — **bolso** *nm Spain* : pocketbook, handbag
bomba *nf* **1** : bomb **2 ∼ de gasolina** : gas pump
bombachos *nmpl* : baggy trousers
bombardear *vt* : bomb, bombard — **bombardeo** *nm* : bombing, bombardment — **bombardero** *nm* : bomber (airplane)
bombear *vt* : pump — **bombero, -ra** *n* : firefighter
bombilla *nf* : lightbulb — **bombillo** *nm Lat* : lightbulb
bombo *nm* **1** : bass drum **2 a ∼s y platillos** : with a great fanfare
bombón *nm, pl* **-bones** : candy, chocolate
bonachón, -chona *adj, mpl* **-chones** *fam* : good-natured
bonanza *nf* **1** : fair weather (at sea) **2** PROSPERIDAD : prosperity
bondad *nf* : goodness, kindness — **bondadoso, -sa** *adj* : kind, good
boniato *nm* : sweet potato
bonificación *nf, pl* **-ciones 1** : bonus, extra **2** DESCUENTO : discount
bonito, -ta *adj* : pretty, lovely
bono *nm* **1** : bond **2** VALE : voucher
boquear *vi* : gasp — **boqueada** *nf* : gasp
boquerón *nm, pl* **-rones** : anchovy
boquete *nm* : gap, opening
boquiabierto, -ta *adj* : open-mouthed, speechless

boquilla *nf* : mouthpiece (of a musical instrument)

borbollar *vi* : bubble

borbotar *or* **borbotear** *vi* : boil, bubble, gurgle — **borbotón** *nm, pl* **-tones 1** : spurt **2 salir a borbotones** : gush out

bordar *v* : embroider — **bordado** *nm* : embroidery, needlework

borde *nm* **1** : border, edge **2 al ~ de** : on the verge of — **bordear** *vt* : border — **bordillo** *nm* : curb

bordo *nm* **a ~** : aboard, on board

borla *nf* **1** : pom-pom, tassel **2** : powder puff

borracho, -cha *adj & n* : drunk — **borrachera** *nf* : drunkenness

borrar *vt* : erase, blot out — **borrador** *nm* **1** : rough draft **2** : eraser (for a blackboard)

borrascoso, -sa *adj* : stormy

borrego, -ga *n* : lamb, sheep — **borrego** *nm Lat* : false rumor, hoax

borrón *nm, pl* **-rrones 1** : smudge, blot **2 ~ y cuenta nueva** : let's forget about it — **borroso, -sa** *adj* **1** : blurry, smudgy **2** INDISTINTO : vague, hazy

bosque *nm* : woods, forest — **boscoso, -sa** *adj* : wooded

bosquejar *vt* : sketch (out) — **bosquejo** *nm* : outline, sketch

bostezar {21} *vi* : yawn — **bostezo** *nm* : yawn

bota *nf* : boot

botánica *nf* : botany — **botánico, -ca** *adj* : botanical

botar *vt* **1** : throw, hurl **2** *Lat* : throw away **3** : launch (a ship) — *vi* : bounce

bote *nm* **1** : small boat **2** *Spain* : can **3** TARRO : jar **4** SALTO : bounce, jump

botella *nf* : bottle

botín *nm, pl* **-tines 1** : ankle boot **2** DESPOJOS : booty, plunder

botiquín *nm, pl* **-quines 1** : medicine cabinet **2** : first-aid kit

botón *nm, pl* **-tones 1** : button **2** YEMA : bud — **botones** *nmfs & pl* : bellhop

botulismo *nm* : botulism

boutique *nf* : boutique

bóveda *nf* : vault

boxear *vi* : box — **boxeador, -dora** *n* : boxer — **boxeo** *nm* : boxing

boya *nf* : buoy — **boyante** *adj* **1** : buoyant **2** PRÓSPERO : prosperous, thriving

bozal *nm* **1** : muzzle **2** : halter (for a horse)

bracear *vi* **1** : wave one's arms **2** NADAR : swim, crawl

bracero, -ra *n* : day laborer

bragas *nfpl Spain* : panties

braguета *nf* : fly, pants zipper

braille *adj & nm* : braille

bramante *nm* : twine, string

bramar *vi* **1** : bellow, roar **2** : howl (of the wind) — **bramido** *nm* : bellow, roar

brandy *nm* : brandy

branquia *nf* : gill

brasa *nf* : ember

brasier *nm Lat* : brassiere

brasileño, -ña *adj* : Brazilian

bravata *nf* **1** : boast, bravado **2** AMENAZA : threat

bravo, -va *adj* **1** : fierce, savage **2** : rough (of the sea) **3** *Lat* : angry — *interj* : bravo!, well done! — **bravura** *nf* **1** FEROCIDAD : fierceness **2** VALENTÍA : bravery

braza *nf* **1** : breaststroke **2** : fathom (measurement) — **brazada** *nf* : stroke (in swimming)

brazalete *nm* **1** : bracelet **2** : (cloth) armband

brazo *nm* **1** : arm **2** : branch (of a river, etc.) **3 ~ derecho** : right-hand man **4 ~s** *nmpl* : hands, laborers

brea *nf* : tar

brebaje *nm* : concoction

brecha *nf* : breach, gap

brécol *nm* : broccoli

bregar {52} *vi* **1** LUCHAR : struggle **2** TRABAJAR : work hard — **brega** *nf* **andar a la ~** : struggle

breña *nf* *or* **breñal** *nm* : scrubland, brush

breve *adj* **1** : brief, short **2 en ~** : shortly, in short — **brevedad** *nf* : brevity, shortness — **brevemente** *adv* : briefly

brezal *nm* : moor, heath — **brezo** *nm* : heather

bricolaje *or* **bricolage** *nm* : do-it-yourself

brida *nf* : bridle

brigada *nf* **1** : brigade **2** EQUIPO : gang, team, squad

brillar *vi* : shine, sparkle — **brillante** *adj* : brilliant, shiny — *~ nm* : diamond — **brillantez** *nf* : brilliance — **brillo** *nm* **1** : luster, shine **2** ESPLENDOR : splendor — **brilloso, -sa** *adj* : shiny

brincar {72} *vi* : jump about, frolic — **brinco** *nm* : jump, skip

brindar *vi* : drink a toast — *vt* : offer, provide — **brindarse** *vr* : offer one's assistance — **brindis** *nm* : drink, toast

brío *nm* **1** : force, determination **2** ÁNIMO : spirit, verve — **brioso, -sa** *adj* : spirited, lively

brisa *nf* : breeze

británico, -ca *adj* : British

brizna *nf* **1** : strand, thread **2** : blade (of grass)

brocado *nm* : brocade

brocha *nf* : paintbrush

broche *nm* **1** : fastener, clasp **2** ALFILER : brooch

brocheta *nf* : skewer

brócoli *nm* : broccoli

bromear *vi* : joke, fool around — **broma** *nf* : joke, prank — **bromista** *adj* : fun-loving, joking — ∼ *nmf* : joker, prankster

bronca *nf fam* : fight, row

bronce *nm* : bronze — **bronceado, -da** *adj* : suntanned — **bronceado** *nm* : tan — **broncearse** *vr* : get a suntan

bronco, -ca *adj* **1** : harsh, rough **2** : untamed, wild (of a horse)

bronquitis *nf* : bronchitis

broqueta *nf* : skewer

brotar *vi* **1** : bud, sprout **2** : stream, gush (of a river, tears, etc.) **3** : arise (of feelings, etc.) **4** : break out (in medicine) — **brote** *nm* **1** : outbreak **2** : sprout, bud, shoot (of plants)

brujería *nf* : witchcraft — **bruja** *nf* **1** : witch **2** *fam* : old hag — **brujo** *nm* : warlock, sorcerer — **brujo, -ja** *adj* : bewitching

brújula *nf* : compass

bruma *nf* : haze, mist — **brumoso, -sa** *adj* : hazy, misty

bruñir {38} *vt* : burnish, polish

brusco, -ca *adj* **1** SÚBITO : sudden, abrupt **2** TOSCO : brusque, rough — **brusquedad** *nf* : abruptness, brusqueness

brutal *adj* : brutal — **brutalidad** *nf* : brutality

bruto, -ta *adj* **1** : brutish, stupid **2** : crude (of petroleum, etc.), uncut (of diamonds) **3** *peso* ∼ : gross weight — ∼ *n* : brute

bucal *adj* : oral

bucear *vi* **1** : dive, swim underwater **2** ∼ **en** : delve into — **buceo** *nm* : (underwater) diving

bucle *nm* : curl

budín *nm, pl* **-dines** : pudding

budismo *nm* : Buddhism — **budista** *adj & nmf* : Buddhist

buenamente *adv* **1** : easily **2** VOLUNTARIAMENTE : willingly

buenaventura *nf* : good luck **2 decir la** ∼ **a uno** : tell s.o.'s fortune

bueno, -na *adj* (**buen** *before masculine singular nouns*) **1** : good **2** AMABLE : kind **3** APROPIADO : appropriate **4** SALUDABLE : well, healthy **5** : nice, fine (of weather) **6 buenos días** : hello, good day **7 buenas noches** : good night **8 buenas tardes** : good afternoon, good evening — **bueno** *interj* : OK!, all right!

buey *nm* : ox, steer

búfalo *nm* : buffalo

bufanda *nf* : scarf

bufar *vi* : snort — **bufido** *nm* : snort

bufet *or* **bufé** *nm* : buffet-style meal

bufete *nm* **1** : law practice **2** MESA : writing desk

bufo, -fa *adj* : comic — **bufón, -fona** *n, mpl* **-fones** : buffoon, jester — **bufonada** *nf* : wisecrack

buhardilla *nf* : attic, garret

búho *nm* : owl

buitre *nm* : vulture

bujía *nf* : spark plug

bulbo *nm* : bulb (of a plant)

bulevar *nm* : boulevard

búlgaro, -ra *adj* : Bulgarian

bulla *nf* : uproar, racket

bulldozer *nm* : bulldozer

bullicio *nm* **1** : uproar **2** AJETREO : hustle and bustle — **bullicioso, -sa** *adj* : noisy, boisterous

bullir {38} *vi* **1** : boil **2** AJETREARSE : bustle, stir

bulto *nm* **1** : package, bundle **2** VOLUMEN : bulk, size **3** FORMA : form, shape **4** PROTUBERANCIA : lump, swelling

bumerán *nm, pl* **-ranes** : boomerang

buñuelo *nm* : fried pastry

buque *nm* : ship

burbujear *vi* : bubble — **burbuja** *nf* : bubble

burdel *nm* : brothel

burdo, -da *adj* : coarse, rough

burgués, -guesa *adj & n, mpl* **-gueses** : bourgeois — **burguesía** *nf* : bourgeoisie

burlar *vt* : trick, deceive — **burlarse** *vr* ∼ **de** : make fun of — **burla** *nf* **1** MOFA : mockery, ridicule **2** BROMA : joke, trick

burlesco, -ca *adj* : comic, funny

burlón, -lona *adj, mpl* **-lones** : mocking

burocracia *nf* : bureaucracy — **burócrata** *nmf* : bureaucrat — **burocrático, -ca** *adj* : bureaucratic

burro, -rra *n* **1** : donkey **2** *fam* : dunce — ∼ *adj* : stupid — **burro** *nm* **1** : sawhorse **2** *Lat* : stepladder

bus *nm* : bus

buscar {72} *vt* **1** : look for, seek **2 ir a** ∼ **a uno** : fetch s.o. — *vi* : search — **busca** *nf* : search — **búsqueda** *nf* : search

busto *nm* : bust (in sculpture)
butaca *nf* **1** : armchair **2** : (theater) seat
butano *nm* : butane

buzo *nm* : diver
buzón *nm, pl* **-zones** : mailbox
byte ['bait] *nm* : byte

C

c *nf* : c, third letter of the Spanish alphabet
cabal *adj* **1** : exact **2** COMPLETO : complete — **cabales** *nmpl* **no estar en sus** ~ : not be in one's right mind
cabalgar {52} *vi* : ride — **cabalgata** *nf* : cavalcade
cabalia *nf* : mackerel
caballería *nf* **1** : cavalry **2** CABALLO : horse, mount — **caballeriza** *nf* : stable
caballero *nm* **1** : gentleman **2** : knight (rank) — **caballerosidad** *nf* : chivalry — **caballeroso, -sa** *adj* : chivalrous
caballete *nm* **1** : ridge (of a roof) **2** : easel (for a canvas) **3** : bridge (of the nose)
caballito *nm* **1** : rocking horse **2** ~s *nmpl* : merry-go-round
caballo *nm* **1** : horse **2** : knight (in chess) **3** ~ **de fuerza** : horsepower
cabaña *nf* : cabin, hut
cabaret *nm, pl* **-rets** : nightclub, cabaret
cabecear *vi* **1** : shake one's head, nod **2** : pitch, lurch (of a boat)
cabecera *nf* **1** : head (of a bed, etc.) **2** : heading (in a text) **3 médico de** ~ : family doctor
cabecilla *nmf* : ringleader
cabello *nm* : hair — **cabelludo, -da** *adj* : hairy
caber {12} *vi* **1** : fit, go (into) **2 no cabe duda** : there's no doubt
cabestro *nm* : halter
cabeza *nf* **1** : head **2 de** ~ : head first — **cabezada** *nf* **1** : butt (of the head) **2 dar** ~**s** : nod off
cabezal *nm* : bolster, headrest
cabida *nf* **1** : room, capacity **2 dar** ~ **a** : accomodate, find room for
cabina *nf* **1** : booth **2** : cab (of a truck, etc.) **3** : cabin, cockpit (of an airplane)
cabizbajo, -ja *adj* : downcast
cable *nm* : cable
cabo *nm* **1** : end, stub **2** TROZO : bit **3** : corporal (in the military) **4** : cape (in geography) **5 al fin y al** ~ : after all **6 llevar a** ~ : carry out, do
cabra *nf* : goat

cabriola *nf* **1** : leap, skip **2 hacer** ~**s** : prance around
cabrito *nm* : kid (goat)
cacahuate *or* **cacahuete** *nm* : peanut
cacao *nm* **1** : cacao (tree) **2** : cocoa (drink)
cacarear *vi* : crow, cackle — *vt fam* : boast about
cacería *nf* : hunt
cacerola *nf* : pan, saucepan
cacharro *nm* **1** *fam* : thing, piece of junk **2** *fam* : jalopy **3** ~**s** *nmpl* : pots and pans
cachear *vt* : search, frisk
cachemir *nm or* **cachemira** *nf* : cashmere
cachete *nm Lat* : cheek — **cachetada** *nf Lat* : slap
cacho *nm* **1** *fam* : piece, bit **2** *Lat* : horn
cachorro, -rra *n* **1** : cub **2** PERRITO : puppy
cactus *or* **cacto** *nm* : cactus
cada *adj* : each, every
cadalso *nm* : scaffold
cadáver *nm* : corpse
cadena *nf* **1** : chain **2** : (television) channel **3** ~ **de montaje** : assembly line
cadencia *nf* : cadence
cadera *nf* : hip
cadete *nmf* : cadet
caducar {72} *vi* : expire — **caducidad** *nf* : expiration
caer {13} *vi* **1** : fall, drop **2** ~ **bien a uno** : be to one's liking **3 dejar** ~ : drop **4 me cae bien** : I like her, I like him — **caerse** *vr* : drop, fall (down)
café *nm* **1** : coffee **2** : café — *adj Lat* : brown — **cafetera** *nf* : coffeepot — **cafetería** *nf* : coffee shop, cafeteria — **cafeína** *nf* : caffeine
caída *nf* **1** : fall, drop **2** PENDIENTE : slope
caimán *nm, pl* **-manes** : alligator
caja *nf* **1** : box, case **2** : checkout counter, cashier's desk (in a store) **3** ~ **fuerte** : safe **4** ~ **registradora** : cash register — **cajero, -ra** *n* **1** : cashier **2** : (bank) teller — **cajetilla** *nf* : pack (of cigarettes) — **cajón** *nm, pl* **-jones 1**

: drawer (in furniture) **2** : large box, crate

cajuela *nf Lat* : trunk (of a car)

cal *nf* : lime

cala *nf* : cove

calabaza *nf* **1** : pumpkin, squash, gourd **2 dar ~s a** *fam* : give the brush-off to — **calabacín** *nm, pl* **-cines** *or* **calabacita** *nf Lat* : zucchini

calabozo *nm* **1** : prison **2** CELDA : cell

calamar *nm* : squid

calambre *nm* **1** ESPASMO : cramp **2** : (electric) shock

calamidad *nf* : calamity

calar *vt* **1** : soak (through) **2** PERFORAR : pierce — **calarse** *vr* : get drenched

calavera *nf* : skull

calcar {72} *vt* **1** : trace **2** IMITAR : copy, imitate

calcetín *nm, pl* **-tines** : sock

calcinar *vt* : char

calcio *nm* : calcium

calcomanía *nf* : decal

calcular *vt* : calculate, estimate — **calculador, -dora** *adj* : calculating — **calculadora** *nf* : calculator — **cálculo** *nm* **1** : calculation **2** : calculus (in mathematics and medicine) **3 ~ biliar** : gallstone

caldera *nf* **1** : cauldron **2** : boiler (for heating, etc.) — **caldo** *nm* : broth, stock

calefacción *nf, pl* **-ciones** : heating, heat

calendario *nm* : calendar

calentar {55} *vt* : heat (up), warm (up) — **calentarse** *vr* : get warm, heat up — **calentador** *nm* : heater — **calentura** *nf* : temperature, fever

calibre *nm* **1** : caliber **2** DIÁMETRO : bore, diameter — **calibrar** *vt* : calibrate

calidad *nf* **1** : quality **2 en ~ de** : as, in the capacity of

cálido, -da *adj* : hot, warm

calidoscopio *nm* : kaleidoscope

caliente *adj* **1** : hot **2** ACALORADO : heated, fiery

calificar {72} *vt* **1** : qualify **2** EVALUAR : rate **3** : grade (an exam, etc.) — **calificación** *nf, pl* **-ciones** **1** : qualification **2** EVALUACIÓN : rating **3** NOTA : grade — **calificativo, -va** *adj* : qualifying — **calificativo** *nm* : qualifier, epithet

caligrafía *nf* : penmanship

calistenia *nf* : calisthenics

cáliz *nm, pl* **-lices** : chalice

caliza *nf* : limestone

callar *vi* : keep quiet, be silent — *vt* **1** : silence, hush **2** OCULTAR : keep secret — **callarse** *vr* : remain silent — **callado, -da** *adj* : quiet, silent

calle *nf* : street, road — **callejear** *vi* : wander about the streets — **callejero, -ra** *adj* **1** : street **2 perro callejero** : stray dog — **callejón** *nm, pl* **-jones 1** : alley **2 ~ sin salida** : dead-end street

callo *nm* : callus, corn

calma *nf* : calm, quiet — **calmante** *adj* : soothing — **~** *nm* : tranquilizer — **calmar** *vt* : calm, soothe — **calmarse** *vr* : calm down — **calmo, -ma** *adj Lat* : calm — **calmoso, -sa** *adj* **1** : calm **2** LENTO : slow

calor *nm* **1** : heat, warmth **2 tener ~** : be hot — **caloría** *nf* : calorie

calumnia *nf* : slander, libel — **calumniar** *vt* : slander, libel

caluroso, -sa *adj* **1** : hot **2** : warm, enthusiastic (of applause, etc.)

calvo, -va *adj* : bald — **calvicie** *nf* : baldness

calza *nf* : wedge

calzada *nf* : roadway

calzado *nm* : footwear — **calzar** {21} *vt* **1** : wear (shoes) **2** : put shoes on (s.o.)

calzones *nmpl Lat* : panties — **calzoncillos** *nmpl* : underpants, briefs

cama *nf* : bed

camada *nf* : litter, brood

camafeo *nm* : cameo

cámara *nf* **1** : chamber **2** *or* **~ fotográfica** : camera **3** : house (in government)

camarada *nmf* : comrade — **camaradería** *nf* : camaraderie

camarero, -ra *n* **1** : waiter, waitress *f* **2** : steward *m*, stewardess *f* (on a ship, etc.) — **camarera** *nf* : chambermaid *f*

camarón *nm, pl* **-rones** : shrimp

camarote *nm* : cabin, stateroom

cambiar *vt* **1** : change **2** CANJEAR : exchange — *vi* **1** : change **2** : shift gears (of an automobile) — **cambiarse** *vr* **1** : change (clothing) **2** : move (to a new address) — **cambiable** *adj* : changeable — **cambio** *nm* **1** : change **2** CANJE : exchange **3 en ~** : on the other hand

camello *nm* : camel

camilla *nf* : stretcher — **camillero** *nm* : orderly (in a hospital)

caminar *vi* : walk — *vt* : cover (a distance) — **caminata** *nf* : hike

camino *nm* **1** : road, path **2** RUTA : way **3 a medio ~** : halfway (there) **4 ponerse en ~** : set out

camión *nm, pl* **-miones 1** : truck **2** *Lat*

: bus — **camionero, -ra** *n* 1 : truck driver 2 *Lat* : bus driver — **camioneta** *nm* : light truck, van

camisa *nf* 1 : shirt 2 ~ **de fuerza** : straitjacket — **camiseta** *nf* : T-shirt, undershirt — **camisón** *nm*, *pl* **-sones** : nightshirt, nightgown

camorra *nf fam* : fight, trouble

camote *nm Lat* : sweet potato

campamento *nm* : camp

campana *nf* : bell — **campanada** *nf* : stroke (of a bell), peal — **campanario** *nm* : bell tower — **campanilla** *nf* : (small) bell

campaña *nf* 1 : countryside 2 : (military or political) campaign

campeón, -peona *n*, *mpl* **-peones** : champion — **campeonato** *nm* : championship

campesino, -na *n* : peasant, farm laborer — **campestre** *adj* : rural, rustic

camping *nm* 1 : campsite 2 **hacer ~** : go camping

campiña *nf* : countryside

campo *nm* 1 : field 2 CAMPIÑA : countryside, country 3 CAMPAMENTO : camp

camuflaje *nm* : camouflage — **camuflar** *vt* : camouflage

cana *nf* : gray hair

canadiense *adj* : Canadian

canal *nm* 1 : canal MEDIO : channel 3 : (radio or television) channel — **canalizar** {21} *vt* : channel

canalete *nm* : paddle (of a canoe)

canalla *nf* : rabble — ~ *nmf fam* : swine, bastard

canapé *nm* 1 : canapé 2 SOFÁ : sofa, couch

canario *nm* : canary

canasta *nf* : basket — **canasto** *nm* : large basket

cancelar *vt* 1 : cancel 2 : pay off, settle (a debt) — **cancelación** *nf*, *pl* **-ciones** 1 : cancellation 2 : payment in full (of a debt)

cáncer *nm* : cancer — **canceroso, -sa** *adj* : cancerous

cancha *nf* : court, field (for sports)

canciller *nm* : chancellor

canción *nf*, *pl* **-ciones** 1 : song 2 ~ **de cuna** : lullaby — **cancionero** *nm* : songbook

candado *nm* : padlock

candela *nf* : candle — **candelabro** *nm* : candelabra — **candelero** *nm* 1 : candlestick 2 **estar en el ~** : be in the limelight

candente *adj* : red-hot

candidato, -ta *n* : candidate — **candidatura** *nf* : candidacy

cándido, -da *adj* : naïve — **candidez** *nf* 1 : simplicity 2 INGENUIDAD : naïveté

candil *nm* 1 : oil lamp — **candilejas** *nfpl* : footlights

candor *nm* : naïveté, innocence

canela *nf* : cinnamon

cangrejo *nm* : crab

canguro *nm* : kangaroo

caníbal *nmf* : cannibal — **canibalismo** *nm* : cannibalism

canicas *nfpl* : (game of) marbles

canino, -na *adj* : canine — **canino** *nm* : canine (tooth)

canjear *vt* : exchange — **canje** *nm* : exchange, trade

cano, -na *adj* : gray, gray-haired

canoa *nf* : canoe

canon *nm*, *pl* **cánones** : canon

canonizar {21} *vt* : canonize

canoso, -sa *adj* : gray, gray-haired

cansar *vt* : tire (out) — *vi* : be tiring — **cansarse** *vr* : get tired — **cansado, -da** *adj* 1 : tired 2 PESADO : tiresome — **cansancio** *nm* : fatigue, weariness

cantalupo *nm* : cantaloupe

cantar *v* : sing — ~ *nm* : song — **cantante** *nmf* : singer

cántaro *nm* 1 : pitcher, jug 2 **llover a ~s** *fam* : rain cats and dogs

cantera *nf* : quarry (excavation)

cantidad *nf* 1 : quantity, amount 2 **una ~ de** : lots of

cantimplora *nf* : canteen, water bottle

cantina *nf* 1 : canteen, cafeteria 2 *Lat* : tavern, bar

canto *nm* 1 : singing, song 2 BORDE, LADO : edge 3 **de ~** : on end, sideways 4 ~ **rodado** : boulder — **cantor, -tora** *adj* 1 : singing 2 **pájaro ~** : songbird — ~ *n* : singer

caña *nf* 1 : cane, reed 2 ~ **de pescar** : fishing pole

cáñamo *nm* : hemp

cañería *nf* : pipes, piping — **caño** *nm* 1 : pipe 2 : spout (of a fountain) — **cañón** *nm*, *pl* **-ñones** 1 : cannon 2 : barrel (of a gun) 3 : canyon (in geography)

caoba *nf* : mahogany

caos *nm* : chaos — **caótico, -ca** *adj* : chaotic

capa *nf* 1 : cape, cloak 2 : coat (of paint, etc.), coating (in cooking) 3 ESTRATO : layer, stratum 4 : (social) class

capacidad *nf* 1 : capacity 2 APTITUD : ability

capacitar *vt* : train, qualify — **capacitación** *nf*, *pl* **-ciones** : training

caparazón nm, pl **-zones** : shell
capataz nmf, pl **-taces** : foreman
capaz adj, pl **-paces** 1 : capable, able 2 ESPACIOSO : spacious
capellán nm, pl **-llanes** : chaplain
capilla nf : chapel
capital adj 1 : capital 2 PRINCIPAL : chief, principal — ~ nm : capital (assets) — ~ nf : capital (city) — **capitalismo** nm : capitalism — **capitalista** adj & nmf : capitalist, capitalistic — **capitalizar** {21} vt : capitalize
capitán, -tana n, mpl **-tanes** : captain
capitolio nm : capitol
capitular vi : capitulate, surrender — **capitulación** nf, pl **-ciones** : surrender
capítulo nm : chapter
capó nm : hood (of a car)
capote nm : cloak, cape
capricho nm : whim, caprice — **caprichoso, -sa** adj : whimsical, capricious
cápsula nf : capsule
captar vt 1 : grasp 2 ATRAER : gain, attract (interest, etc.) 3 : harness (waters)
capturar vt : capture, seize — **captura** nf : capture, seizure
capucha nf : hood (of clothing)
capullo nm 1 : cocoon 2 : (flower) bud
caqui adj & nm : khaki
cara nf 1 : face 2 ASPECTO : appearance 3 fam : nerve, gall 4 ~ a or de ~ a : facing
carabina nf : carbine
caracol nm 1 : snail 2 Lat : conch 3 RIZO : curl
carácter nm, pl **-racteres** 1 : character 2 ÍNDOLE : nature — **característica** nf : characteristic — **característico, -ca** adj : characteristic — **caracterizar** {21} vt : characterize
caramba interj : oh my!, good grief!
carámbano nm : icicle
caramelo nm 1 : caramel 2 DULCE : candy
carátula nf 1 CARETA : mask 2 : jacket (of a record, etc.) 3 Lat : face (of a watch)
caravana nf 1 : caravan 2 REMOLQUE : trailer
caray → caramba
carbohidrato nm : carbohydrate
carbón nm, pl **-bones** 1 : coal 2 : charcoal (for drawing) — **carboncillo** nm : charcoal — **carbonero, -ra** adj : coal — **carbonizar** {21} vt : char — **carbono** nm : carbon — **carburador** nm : carburetor — **carburante** nm : fuel
carcajada nf : loud laugh, guffaw

cárcel nf : jail, prison — **carcelero, -ra** n : jailer
carcinógeno nm : carcinogen
carcomer vt : eat away at — **carcomido, -da** adj : worm-eaten
cardenal nm 1 : cardinal 2 CONTUSIÓN : bruise
cardíaco or **cardiaco, -ca** adj : cardiac, heart
cárdigan nm, pl **-gans** : cardigan
cardinal adj : cardinal
cardiólogo, -ga n : cardiologist
cardo nm : thistle
carear vt : bring face-to-face
carecer {53} vi ~ **de** : lack — **carencia** nf : lack, want — **carente** adj ~ **de** : lacking (in)
carestía nf 1 : high cost 2 ESCASEZ : dearth, scarcity
careta nf : mask
cargar {52} vt 1 : load 2 : charge (a battery, a purchase, etc.) 3 LLEVAR : carry 4 ~ **de** : burden with — vi 1 : load 2 ~ **con** : pick up, carry away — **carga** nf 1 : load 2 CARGAMENTO : freight, cargo 3 RESPONSABILIDAD : burden 4 : charge (in electricity, etc.) — **cargado, -da** adj 1 : loaded, burdened 2 PESADO : heavy, stuffy 3 : charged (of a battery) 4 FUERTE : strong, concentrated — **cargamento** nm : cargo, load — **cargo** nm 1 : charge 2 PUESTO : position, office
cariarse vr : decay (of teeth)
caribe adj : Caribbean
caricatura nf 1 : caricature 2 : (political) cartoon — **caricaturizar** vt : caricature
caricia nf : caress
caridad nf 1 : charity 2 LIMOSNA : alms pl
caries nfs & pl : cavity (in a tooth)
cariño nm 1 : affection, love — **cariñoso, -sa** adj : affectionate, loving
carisma nf : charisma — **carismático, -ca** adj : charismatic
caritativo, -va adj : charitable
cariz nm, pl **-rices** : appearance, aspect
carmesí adj & nm : crimson
carmín nm, pl **-mines** or ~ **de labios** : lipstick
carnada nf : bait
carnal adj 1 : carnal 2 primo ~ : first cousin
carnaval nm : carnival
carne nf 1 : meat 2 : flesh (of persons or fruits) 3 ~ **de cerdo** : pork 4 ~ **de gallina** : goose bumps 5 ~ **de ternera** : veal
carné nm → carnet

carnero *nm* **1** : ram, sheep **2** : mutton (in cooking)

carnet *nm* **1** ~ **de conducir** : driver's license **2** ~ **de identidad** : identification card, ID

carnicería *nf* **1** : butcher shop **2** MATANZA : slaughter — **carnicero, -ra** *n* : butcher

carnívoro, -ra *adj* : carnivorous — **carnívoro** *nm* : carnivore

carnoso, -sa *adj* : fleshy

caro, -ra *adj* : expensive QUERIDO : dear — **caro** *adv* : dearly

carpa *nf* **1** : carp TIENDA : tent

carpeta *nf* : folder

carpintería *nf* : carpentry — **carpintero, -ra** *n* : carpenter

carraspear *vi* : clear one's throat — **carraspera** *nf* **1** : hoarseness **2 tener** ~ : have a frog in one's throat

carrera *nf* **1** : running, run **2** COMPETICIÓN : race **3** : course (of studies) **4** PROFESIÓN : career, profession

carreta *nf* : cart, wagon

carrete *nm* : reel, spool

carretera *nf* : highway, road

carretilla *nf* : wheelbarrow

carril *nm* **1** : lane (of a road) **2** : rail (for a railroad)

carrillo *nm* : cheek

carrito *nm* : cart, trolley

carrizo *nm* : reed

carro *nm* **1** : wagon, cart **2** *Lat* : automobile, car — **carrocería** *nf* : body (of an automobile)

carroña *nf* : carrion

carroza *nf* **1** : carriage **2** : float (in a parade)

carruaje *nm* : carriage

carrusel *nm* : merry-go-round, carousel

carta *nf* **1** : letter **2** NAIPE : playing card **3** : charter (of an organization, etc.) **4** MENÚ : menu **5** MAPA : map, chart

cartel *nm* : poster, bill — **cartelera** *nf* : billboard

cartera *nf* **1** : briefcase **2** BILLETERA : wallet **3** *Lat* : pocketbook, handbag — **carterista** *nmf* : pickpocket

cartero, -ra *nm* : mail carrier, mailman *m*

cartílago *nm* : cartilage

cartilla *nf* **1** : primer, reader **2** : booklet, record (of a savings account, etc.)

cartón *nm*, *pl* **-tones 1** : cardboard **2** : carton (of cigarettes, etc.)

cartucho *nm* : cartridge

casa *nf* **1** : house **2** HOGAR : home **3** EMPRESA : company, firm **4** ~ **flotante** : houseboat

casar *vt* : marry — *vi* : go together,

match up — **casarse** *vr* **1** : get married **2** ~ **con** : marry — **casado, -da** *adj* : married — **casamiento** *nm* **1** : marriage **2** BODA : wedding

cascabel *nm* : small bell

cascada *nf* : waterfall

cascanueces *nms* & *pl* : nutcracker

cascar {72} *vt* : crack (a shell, etc.) — **cascarse** *vr* : crack, chip — **cáscara** *nf* : skin, peel, shell — **cascarón** *nm*, *pl* **-rones** : eggshell

casco *nm* **1** : helmet **2** : hull (of a boat) **3** : hoof (of a horse) **4** : fragment (of ceramics, etc.) **5** : center (of a town) **6** ENVASE : empty bottle

caserío *nm* **1** *Spain* : country house **2** POBLADO : hamlet

casero, -ra *adj* **1** : homemade **2** DOMÉSTICO : domestic, household — ~ *n* : landlord, landlady *f*

caseta *nf* : booth, stall

casete → **cassette**

casi *adv* **1** : almost, nearly **2** (*in negative phrases*) : hardly

casilla *nf* **1** : compartment, pigeonhole **2** CASETA : booth **3** : box (on a form)

casino *nm* **1** : casino **2** : (social) club

caso *nm* **1** : case **2 en** ~ **de** : in the event of **3 hacer** ~ : pay attention **4 no venir al** ~ : be beside the point

caspa *nf* : dandruff

cassette *nmf* : cassette

casta *nf* **1** : lineage, descent **2** : breed (of animals) **3** : caste (in India)

castaña *nf* : chestnut

castañetear *vi* : chatter (of teeth)

castaño, -ña *adj* : chestnut (color)

castañuela *nf* : castanet

castellano *nm* : Spanish, Castilian (language)

castidad *nf* : chastity

castigar {52} *vt* **1** : punish **2** : penalize (in sports) — **castigo** *nm* **1** : punishment **2** : penalty (in sports)

castillo *nm* : castle

casto, -ta *adj* : chaste, pure — **castizo, -za** *adj* : pure, traditional (in style)

castor *nm* : beaver

castrar *vt* : castrate

castrense *adj* : military

casual *adj* : chance, accidental — **casualidad** *nf* **1** : coincidence **2 por** ~ *or* **de** ~ : by chance — **casualmente** *adv* : by chance

cataclismo *nm* : cataclysm

catalán, -lana *adj*, *mpl* **-lanes** : Catalan — **catalán** *nm* : Catalan (language)

catalizador *nm* : catalyst

catalogar {52} *vt* : catalog, classify — **catálogo** *nm* : catalog

catapulta *nf* : catapult

catar *vt* : taste, sample

catarata *nf* **1** : waterfall **2** : cataract (in medicine)

catarro *nm* RESFRIADO : cold

catástrofe *nf* : catastrophe, disaster — **catastrófico, -ca** *adj* : catastrophic, disastrous

catecismo *nm* : catechism

cátedra *nf* : chair (at a university)

catedral *nf* : cathedral

catedrático, -ca *n* : professor

categoría *nf* **1** : category **2** RANGO : rank **3** de ~ : first-rate — **categórico, -ca** *adj* : categorical

católico, -ca *adj & n* : Catholic — **catolicismo** *nm* : Catholicism

catorce *adj & nm* : fourteen — **catorceavo** *nm* : fourteenth

catre *nm* : cot

cauce *nm* **1** : riverbed **2** VÍA : channel, means *pl*

caucho *nm* : rubber

caución *nf, pl* **-ciones** : security, guarantee

caudal *nm* **1** : volume of water, flow **2** RIQUEZA : wealth

caudillo *nm* : leader, commander

causar *vt* : cause, provoke — **causa** *nf* **1** : cause **2** RAZÓN : reason **3** : case (in law) **4** a ~ de : because of

cáustico, -ca *adj* : caustic

cautela *nf* : caution — **cauteloso, -sa** *adj* : cautious — **cautelosamente** *adv* : cautiously, warily

cautivar *vt* **1** : capture **2** ENCANTAR : captivate — **cautiverio** *nm* : captivity — **cautivo, -va** *adj & n* : captive

cauto, -ta *adj* : cautious

cavar *v* : dig

caverna *nf* : cavern, cave

cavidad *nf* : cavity

cavilar *vi* : ponder

cayado *nm* : crook, staff

cazar {21} *vt* **1** : hunt **2** ATRAPAR : catch, bag — *vi* : go hunting — **caza** *nf* **1** : hunt, hunting **2** : game (animals) — **cazador, -dora** *n* : hunter

cazo *nm* **1** : saucepan **2** CUCHARÓN : ladle — **cazuela** *nf* : casserole

CD *nm* : CD, compact disc

cebada *nf* : barley

cebar *vt* **1** : bait **2** : feed, fatten (animals) **3** : prime (a firearm, etc.) — **cebo** *nm* **1** CARNADA : bait **2** : charge (of a firearm)

cebolla *nf* : onion — **cebolleta** *nf* : scallion, green onion — **cebollino** *nm* : chive

cebra *nf* : zebra

cecear *vi* : lisp — **ceceo** *nm* : lisp

cedazo *nm* : sieve

ceder *vi* **1** : yield, give way **2** DISMINUIR : diminish, abate — *vt* : cede, hand over

cedro *nm* : cedar

cédula *nf* : document, certificate

cegar {49} *vt* **1** : blind **2** TAPAR : block, stop up — *vi* : be blinded, go blind — **ceguera** *nf* : blindness

ceja *nf* : eyebrow

cejar *vi* : give in, back down

celada *nf* : trap, ambush

celador, -dora *n* : guard, warden

celda *nf* : cell (of a jail)

celebrar *vt* **1** : celebrate **2** : hold (a meeting), say (Mass) **3** ALEGRARSE DE : be happy about — **celebrarse** *vr* : take place — **celebración** *nf, pl* **-ciones** : celebration — **célebre** *adj* : famous, celebrated — **celebridad** *nf* : celebrity

celeridad *nf* : swiftness, speed

celeste *adj* **1** : celestial, heavenly **2** *or* **azul** ~ : sky blue — **celestial** *adj* : celestial, heavenly

celibato *nm* : celibacy — **célibe** *adj* : celibate

celo *nm* **1** : zeal **2** en ~ : in heat **3** ~s *nmpl* : jealousy **4** tener ~s : be jealous

celofán *nm, pl* **-fanes** : cellophane

celoso, -sa *adj* **1** : jealous **2** DILIGENTE : zealous

célula *nf* : cell — **celular** *adj* : cellular

celulosa *nf* : cellulose

cementerio *nm* : cemetery

cemento *nm* **1** : cement **2** ~ **armado** : reinforced concrete

cena *nf* : supper, dinner

cenagal *nm* : bog, quagmire — **cenagoso** *adj* : swampy

cenar *vi* : have dinner, have supper — *vt* : have for dinner or supper

cenicero *nm* : ashtray

cenit *nm* : zenith

ceniza *nf* : ash

censo *nm* : census

censurar *vt* **1** : censor **2** REPROBAR : censure, criticize — **censura** *nf* **1** : censorship **2** REPROBACIÓN : censure, criticism

centavo *nm* **1** : cent **2** : centavo (unit of currency)

centellear *vi* : sparkle, twinkle — **centella** *nf* **1** : flash **2** CHISPA : spark — **centelleo** *nm* : twinkling, sparkle

centenar *nm* : hundred — **centenario** *nm* : centennial

centeno *nm* : rye

centésimo, -ma *adj* : hundredth

centígrado *adj* : centigrade, Celsius

centigramo *nm* : centigram

centímetro *nm* : centimeter

centinela *nmf* : sentinel, sentry

central *adj* : central — ~ *nf* : main office, headquarters — **centralita** *nf* : switchboard — **centralizar** {21} *vt* : centralize

centrar *vt* : center — **centrarse** *vr* ~ **en** : focus on — **céntrico, -ca** *adj* : central — **centro** *nm* **1** : center **2** : downtown (of a city) **3** ~ **de mesa** : centerpiece

centroamericano, -na *adj* : Central American

ceñir {67} *vt* **1** : encircle **2** : fit (s.o.) tightly — **ceñirse** *vr* ~ **a** : limit oneself to — **ceñido, -da** *adj* : tight

ceño *nm* **1** : frown **2 fruncir el** ~ : knit one's brow, frown

cepillo *nm* **1** : brush **2** : (carpenter's) plane **3** ~ **de dientes** : toothbrush — **cepillar** *vt* **1** : brush **2** : plane (wood)

cera *nf* **1** : wax, beeswax **2** : floor wax, furniture wax

cerámica *nf* **1** : ceramics *pl* **2** : (piece of) pottery

cerca¹ *nf* : fence — **cercado** *nm* : enclosure

cerca² *adv* **1** : close, near **2** ~ **de** : near, close to **3** ~ **de** : nearly, almost — **cercano, -na** *adj* : near, close — **cercanía** *nf* : proximity **2** ~**s** *nfpl* : outskirts

cercar {72} *vt* **1** : fence in **2 RODEAR** : surround

cerciorarse *vr* ~ **de** : make sure of

cerco *nm* **1** : circle, ring **2 ASEDIO** : siege **3** *Lat* : fence

cerda *nf* : bristle

cerdo *nm* **1** : pig, hog **2** ~ **macho** : boar

cereal *adj & nm* : cereal

cerebro *nm* : brain — **cerebral** *adj* : cerebral

ceremonia *nf* : ceremony — **ceremonial** *adj* : ceremonial — **ceremonioso, -sa** *adj* : ceremonious

cereza *nf* : cherry

cerilla *nf* : match — **cerillo** *nm Lat* : match

cerner {56} *or* **cernir** *vt* : sift — **cernerse** *vr* **1** : hover **2** ~ **sobre** : loom over — **cernidor** *nm* : sieve

cero *nm* : zero

cerrar {55} *vt* **1** : close, shut **2** : turn off (a faucet, etc.) **3** : bring to an end — *vi* **1** : close up, lock up **2** : close down (a business, etc.) — **cerrarse** *vr* **1**

: close, shut **2 TERMINAR** : come to a close, end — **cerrado, -da** *adj* **1** : closed, shut, locked **2** : overcast (of weather) **3** : sharp (of a curve) **4** : thick, broad (of an accent) — **cerradura** *nf* : lock — **cerrajero, -ra** *n* : locksmith

cerro *nm* : hill

cerrojo *nm* : bolt, latch

certamen *nm, pl* **-támenes** : competition, contest

certero, -ra *adj* : accurate, precise

certeza *nf* : certainty — **certidumbre** *nf* : certainty

certificar {72} *vt* **1** : certify **2** : register (mail) — **certificado, -da** *adj* : certified, registered — **certificado** *nm* : certificate

cervato *nm* : fawn

cerveza *nf* **1** : beer **2** ~ **de barril** : draft beer — **cervecería** *nf* **1** : brewery **2 BAR** : beer hall, bar

cesar *vi* : cease, stop — *vt* : dismiss, lay off — **cesación** *nf, pl* **-ciones** : cessation, suspension — **cesante** *adj* **1** : laid off **2** *Lat* : unemployed — **cesantía** *nf Lat* : unemployment

cesárea *nf* : cesarean (section)

cese *nm* **1** : cessation, stop **2 DESTITUCIÓN** : dismissal

césped *nm* : lawn, grass

cesta *nf* : basket — **cesto** *nm* **1** : (large) basket **2** ~ **de basura** : wastebasket

cetro *nm* : scepter

chabacano *nm Lat* : apricot

chabola *nf Spain* : shack, shanty

chacal *nm* : jackal

cháchara *nf fam* : gabbing, chatter

chacra *nf Lat* : (small) farm

chafar *vt fam* : flatten, crush

chal *nm* : shawl

chaleco *nm* : vest

chalet *nm Spain* : house

chalupa *nf* **1** : small boat **2** *Lat* : small stuffed tortilla

chamarra *nf* : jacket

chamba *nf Lat fam* : job

champaña *or* **champán** *nm* : champagne

champiñón *nm, pl* **-ñones** : mushroom

champú *nm, pl* **-pús** *or* **-púes** : shampoo

chamuscar {72} *vt* : scorch

chance *nm Lat* : chance, opportunity

chancho *nm Lat* : pig

chanclos *nmpl* : galoshes

chantaje *nm* : blackmail — **chantajear** *vt* : blackmail

chanza *nf* : joke, jest

chapa *nf* **1** : sheet, plate **2 INSIGNIA** : badge — **chapado, -da** *adj* **1** : plated

2 chapado a la antigua : old-fashioned

chaparrón nm, pl **-rrones** : downpour

chapotear vi : splash

chapucero, -ra adj : shoddy, sloppy — **chapuza** nf : botched job

chapuzón nm, pl **-zones** : dip, short swim

chaqueta nf : jacket

charca nf : pond — **charco** nm : puddle

charlar vi : chat — **charla** nf : chat, talk — **charlatán, -tana** adj, mpl **-tanes** : talkative — ~ n 1 : chatterbox 2 FARSANTE : charlatan

charol nm 1 : patent leather 2 BARNIZ : varnish

chasco nm 1 : trick, joke 2 DECEPCIÓN : disappointment

chasis nms & pl : chassis

chasquear vt 1 : click (the tongue), snap (one's fingers) 2 : crack (a whip) — **chasquido** nm 1 : click, snap 2 : crack (of a whip)

chatarra nf : scrap (metal)

chato, -ta adj 1 : pug-nosed 2 APLANADO : flat

chauvinismo nm : chauvinism — **chauvinista** adj : chauvinist, chauvinistic

chaval, -vala n : kid, boy m, girl f

checo, -ca adj : Czech — **checo** nm : Czech (language)

chef nm : chef

cheque nm : check — **chequera** nf : checkbook

chequear vt Lat 1 : check, inspect, verify 2 : check in (baggage) — **chequeo** nm 1 : (medical) checkup 2 Lat : check, inspection

chica → **chico**

chicano, -na adj : Chicano, Mexican-American

chícharo nm Lat : pea

chicharrón nm, pl **-rrones** : pork rind

chichón nm, pl **-chones** : bump

chicle nm : chewing gum

chico, -ca adj : little, small — ~ n : child, boy m, girl f

chiflar vt : whistle at, boo — vi Lat : whistle — **chiflado, -da** adj fam : crazy, nuts — **chiflido** nm : whistling

chile nm : chili pepper

chileno, -na adj : Chilean

chillar vi 1 : shriek, scream 2 CHIRRIAR : screech, squeal — **chillido** nm 1 : scream 2 CHIRRIDO : screech, squeal — **chillón, -llona** adj, mpl **-llones** : shrill, loud

chimenea nf 1 : chimney 2 HOGAR : fireplace

chimpancé nm : chimpanzee

chinche nf : bedbug

chino, -na adj : Chinese — **chino** nm : Chinese (language)

chiquillo, -lla n : kid, child

chiquito, -ta adj : tiny — ~ n : little child, tot

chiribita nf : spark

chiripa nf 1 : fluke 2 **de** ~ : by sheer luck

chirivía nf : parsnip

chirriar {85} vi 1 : squeak, creak 2 : screech (of brakes, etc.) — **chirrido** nm 1 : squeak, creak 2 : screech (of brakes)

chisme nm : (piece of) gossip — **chismear** vi : gossip — **chismoso, -sa** adj : gossipy — ~ n : gossip

chispear vi 1 : spark — **chispa** nf : spark

chisporrotear vi : crackle, sizzle — **chisporroteo** nm : crackle

chiste nm : joke, funny story — **chistoso, -sa** adj : funny, witty

chivo, -va n : kid, young goat

chocar {72} vi 1 : crash, collide 2 ENFRENTARSE : clash — **chocante** adj 1 : striking, shocking 2 Lat : unpleasant, rude

choclo nm Lat : ear of corn, corncob

chocolate nm : chocolate

chofer or **chófer** nm 1 : chauffeur 2 CONDUCTOR : driver

choque nm 1 : shock 2 : crash, collision (of vehicles) 3 CONFLICTO : clash

chorizo nm : chorizo, sausage

chorrear vi 1 : drip 2 BROTAR : pour out, gush — **chorro** nm 1 : stream, jet 2 HILO : trickle

chovinismo → **chauvinismo**

choza nf : hut, shack

chubasco nm : downpour, squall

chuchería nf 1 : knickknack, trinket 2 DULCE : sweet

chueco, -ca adj Lat : crooked

chuleta nf : cutlet, chop

chulo, -la adj fam : cute, pretty

chupar vt : suck 2 ABSORBER : absorb 3 fam : guzzle — vi : suckle — **chupada** nf : suck, sucking — **chupete** nm 1 : pacifier 2 Lat : lollipop

churro nm 1 : fried dough 2 fam : botch, mess

chusco, -ca adj : funny

chusma nf : riffraff, rabble

chutar vi : shoot (in soccer)

cianuro nm : cyanide

cicatriz nf, pl **-trices** : scar — **cicatrizar** {21} vi : form a scar, heal

cíclico, -ca adj : cyclical

ciclismo nm : cycling — **ciclista** nmf : cyclist

ciclo *nm* : cycle

ciclón *nm, pl* **-clones** : cyclone

ciego, -ga *adj* : blind — **ciegamente** *adv* : blindly

cielo *nm* 1 : sky 2 : heaven (in religion)

ciempiés *nms & pl* : centipede

cien *adj* : a hundred, hundred — ~ *nm* : one hundred

ciénaga *nf* : swamp, bog

ciencia *nf* 1 : science 2 a ~ **cierta** : for a fact

cieno *nm* : mire, mud, silt

científico, -ca *adj* : scientific — ~ *n* : scientist

ciento *adj* (*used in compound numbers*) : one hundred — ~ *nm* 1 : hundred, group of a hundred 2 **por** ~ : percent

cierre *nm* 1 : closing, closure 2 BROCHE : fastener, clasp

cierto, -ta *adj* 1 : true SEGURO : certain 3 **por** ~ : as a matter of fact

ciervo, -va *n* : deer, stag *m*, hind *f*

cifra *nf* 1 : number, figure 2 : sum (of money, etc.) 3 CLAVE : code, cipher — **cifrar** *vt* 1 : write in code 2 ~ **la esperanza en** : pin all one's hopes on

cigarrillo *nm* : cigarrette — **cigarro** *nm* 1 : cigarette 2 PURO : cigar

cigüeña *nf* : stork

cilantro *nm* : cilantro, coriander

cilindro *nm* : cylinder — **cilíndrico, -ca** *adj* : cylindrical

cima *nf* : peak, summit

címbalo *nm* : cymbal

cimbrar *or* **cimbrear** *vt* : shake, rock — **cimbrarse** *or* **cimbrearse** *vr* : sway

cimentar {55} *vt* 1 : lay the foundation of 2 : cement, strengthen (relations, etc.) — **cimientos** *nmpl* : base, foundation(s)

cinc *nm* : zinc

cincel *nm* : chisel — **cincelar** *vt* : chisel

cinco *adj & nm* : five

cincuenta *adj & nm* : fifty — **cincuentavo, -va** *adj* : fiftieth — **cincuentavo** *nm* : fiftieth

cine *nm* : cinema, movies *pl* — **cinematográfico, -ca** *adj* : movie, film

cínico, -ca *adj* : cynical — ~ *n* : cynic — **cinismo** *nm* : cynicism

cinta *nf* 1 : ribbon, band 2 ~ **adhesiva** : adhesive tape 3 ~ **métrica** : tape measure 4 ~ **magnetofónica** : magnetic tape

cinto *nm* : belt, girdle — **cintura** *nf* : waist — **cinturón** *nm, pl* **-rones** 1 : belt 2 ~ **de seguridad** : seat belt

ciprés *nm, pl* **-preses** : cypress

circo *nm* : circus

circuito *nm* : circuit

circulación *nf, pl* **-ciones** 1 : circulation 2 TRÁFICO : traffic — **circular** *vi* 1 : circulate 2 : drive (a vehicle) — ~ *adj* : circular

círculo *nm* : circle

circuncidar *vt* : circumcise — **circuncisión** *nf, pl* **-siones** : circumcision

circundar *vt* : surround

circunferencia *nf* : circumference

circunscribir {33} *vt* : confine, limit — **circunscribirse** *vr* ~ **a** : limit oneself to — **circunscripción** *nf, pl* **-ciones** : district, constituency

circunspecto, -ta *adj* : circumspect, cautious

circunstancia *nf* : circumstance — **circunstancial** *adj* : chance — **circunstante** *nmf* 1 : bystander 2 **los** ~**s** : those present

circunvalación *nf, pl* **-ciones** 1 : encircling 2 **carretera de** ~ : bypass

cirio *nm* : candle

ciruela *nf* : plum 2 ~ **pasa** : prune

cirugía *nf* : surgery — **cirujano, -na** *n* : surgeon

cisma *nf* : schism

cisne *nm* : swan

cisterna *nf* : cistern

cita *nf* 1 : appointment, date 2 REFERENCIA : quote, quotation — **citación** *nf, pl* **-ciones** : summons — **citar** *vt* 1 : quote, cite 2 CONVOCAR : make an appointment with 3 : summon (in law) — **citarse** *vr* ~ **con** : arrange to meet

cítrico *nm* : citrus (fruit)

ciudad *nf* : city, town — **ciudadano, -na** *n* 1 : citizen 2 HABITANTE : resident — **ciudadanía** *nf* : citizenship

cívico, -ca *adj* : civic

civil *adj* : civil — ~ *nmf* : civilian — **civilidad** *nf* : civility — **civilización** *nf, pl* **-ciones** : civilization — **civilizar** {21} *vt* : civilize

cizaña *nf* : discord, rift

clamar *vi* : clamor, cry out — **clamor** *nm* : clamor, outcry — **clamoroso, -sa** *adj* : clamorous, loud

clan *nm* : clan

clandestino, -na *adj* : clandestine, secret

clara *nf* : egg white

claraboya *nf* : skylight

claramente *adv* : clearly

clarear *v impers* 1 : dawn 2 ACLARAR : clear up — *vi* : be transparent

claridad *nf* 1 : clarity, clearness 2 LUZ : light

clarificar {72} *vt* : clarify — **clarificación** *nf, pl* **-ciones** : clarification

clarín *nm, pl* **-rines** : bugle

clarinete *nm* : clarinet
clarividente *adj* 1 : clairvoyant 2 PERSPICAZ : perspicacious — **clarividencia** *nf* 1 : clairvoyance 2 PERSPICACIA : farsightedness
claro *adv* 1 : clearly 2 POR SUPUESTO : of course, surely — ~ *nm* 1 : clearing, glade 2 ~ **de luna** : moonlight — **claro, -ra** *adj* 1 : clear, bright 2 : light (of colors) 3 EVIDENTE : clear, evident
clase *nf* 1 : class 2 TIPO : sort, kind
clásico, -ca *adj* : classic, classical — **clásico** *nm* : classic
clasificar {72} *vt* 1 : classify, sort out 2 : rate, rank (a hotel, a team, etc.) — **clasificarse** *vr* : qualify (in competitions) — **clasificación** *nf, pl* **-ciones** 1 : classification 2 : league (in sports)
claudicar {72} *vi* : back down
claustro *nm* : cloister
claustrofobia *nf* : claustrophobia — **claustrofóbico, -ca** *adj* : claustrophobic
cláusula *nf* : clause
clausurar *vt* : close (down) — **clausura** *nf* : closure, closing
clavado *nm Lat* : dive
clavar *vt* 1 : nail, hammer 2 HINCAR : drive in, plunge
clave *nf* 1 CIFRA : code 2 SOLUCIÓN : key 3 : clef (in music) — ~ *adj* : key
clavel *nm* : carnation
clavicémbalo *nm* : harpsichord
clavícula *nf* : collarbone
clavija *nf* 1 : peg, pin 2 : (electric) plug
clavo *nm* 1 : nail 2 : clove (spice)
claxon *nm, pl* **cláxones** : horn (of an automobile)
clemencia *nf* : clemency, mercy — **clemente** *adj* : merciful
clerical *adj* : clerical — **clérigo, -ga** *n* : clergyman, cleric — **clero** *nm* : clergy
cliché *nm* 1 : cliché 2 : negative (of a photograph)
cliente, -ta *n* : customer, client — **clientela** *nf* : clientele, customers *pl*
clima *nm* 1 : climate 2 AMBIENTE : atmosphere — **climático, -ca** *adj* : climatic
climatizar {21} *vt* : air-condition — **climatizado, -da** *adj* : air-conditioned
clímax *nm* : climax
clínica *nf* : clinic — **clínico, -ca** *adj* : clinical
clip *nm, pl* **clips** : (paper) clip
cloaca *nf* : sewer
cloquear *vi* : cluck — **cloqueo** *nm* : cluck, clucking
cloro *nm* : chlorine

clóset *nm Lat, pl* **clósets** : (built-in) closet, cupboard
club *nm* : club
coacción *nf, pl* **-ciones** : coercion — **coaccionar** *vt* : coerce
coagular *v* : clot, coagulate — **coagularse** *vr* : coagulate — **coágulo** *nm* : clot
coalición *nf, pl* **-ciones** : coalition
coartada *nf* : alibi
coartar *vt* : restrict, limit
cobarde *nmf* : coward — ~ *adj* : cowardly — **cobardía** *nf* : cowardice
cobaya *nf* : guinea pig
cobertizo *nm* : shelter, shed
cobertor *nm* : bedspread
cobertura *nf* 1 : cover 2 : coverage (of news, etc.)
cobijar *vt* : shelter — **cobijarse** *vr* : take shelter — **cobija** *nf Lat* : blanket — **cobijo** *nm* : shelter
cobra *nf* : cobra
cobrar *vt* 1 : charge, collect 2 : earn (a salary, etc.) 3 ADQUIRIR : acquire, gain 4 : cash (a check) — *vi* : be paid — **cobrador, -dora** *n* 1 : collector 2 : conductor (of a bus, etc.)
cobre *nm* : copper
cobro *nm* : collection (of money), cashing (of a check)
cocaína *nf* : cocaine
cocción *nf, pl* **-ciones** : cooking
cocear *vi* : kick
cocer {14} *vt* 1 : cook 2 HERVIR : boil
coche *nm* 1 : car, automobile 2 : coach (of a train) 3 ~ **de caballos** : carriage 4 ~ **fúnebre** : hearse — **cochecito** *nm* : baby carriage, stroller — **cochera** *nf* : garage, carport
cochino, -na *n* : pig, hog — ~ *adj fam* : dirty, filthy — **cochinada** *nf fam* : dirty thing — **cochinillo** *nm* : piglet
cocido, -da *adj* 1 : boiled, cooked 2 **bien ~** : well-done — **cocido** *nm* : stew
cociente *nm* : quotient
cocina *nf* 1 : kitchen 2 : (kitchen) stove 3 : (art of) cooking, cuisine — **cocinar** *v* : cook — **cocinero, -ra** *n* : cook, chef
coco *nm* : coconut
cocodrilo *nm* : crocodile
coctel *or* **cóctel** *nm* 1 : cocktail 2 FIESTA : cocktail party
codazo *nm* 1 : nudge 2 **dar un ~ a** : elbow, nudge
codicia *nf* : greed — **codiciar** *vt* : covet — **codicioso, -sa** *adj* : covetous, greedy

código *nm* 1 : code 2 ~ **postal** : zip code 3 ~ **morse** : Morse code

codo *nm* : elbow

codorniz *nf, pl* -**nices** : quail

coexistir *vi* : coexist

cofre *nm* : chest, coffer

coger {15} *vt* 1 : take (hold of) 2 ATRAPAR : catch 3 : pick up (from the ground) 4 : pick (fruit, etc.) — **cogerse** *vr* : hold on

cohechar *vt* : bribe — **cohecho** *nm* : bribe, bribery

coherencia *nf* : coherence — **coherente** *adj* : coherent — **cohesión** *nf*, -**siones** : cohesion

cohete *nm* : rocket

cohibir {62} *vt* 1 : restrict 2 : inhibit (a person) — **cohibirse** *vr* : feel inhibited — **cohibido, -da** *adj* : inhibited, shy

coincidir *vi* 1 : coincide 2 ~ **con** : agree with — **coincidencia** *nf* : coincidence

cojear *vi* 1 : limp 2 : wobble (of furniture, etc.) — **cojera** *nf* : limp

cojín *nm, pl* -**jines** : cushion — **cojinete** *nm* 1 : pad, cushion 2 : bearing (of a machine)

cojo, -ja *adj* 1 : lame 2 : wobbly (of furniture) — ~ *n* : lame person

col *nf* 1 : cabbage 2 ~ **de Bruselas** : Brussels sprout

cola *nf* 1 : tail 2 FILA : line (of people) 3 : end (of a line) 4 PEGAMENTO : glue 5 ~ **de caballo** : ponytail

colaborar *vi* : collaborate — **colaboración** *nf, pl* -**ciones** : collaboration — **colaborador, -dora** *n* 1 : collaborator 2 : contributor (to a periodical)

colada *nf Spain* 1 : laundry 2 **hacer la** ~ : do the washing

colador *nm* : colander, strainer

colapso *nm* : collapse

colar {19} *vt* : strain, filter — **colarse** *vr* : sneak in, gate-crash

colcha *nf* : bedspread, quilt — **colchón** *nm, pl* -**chones** : mattress — **colchoneta** *nf* : mat

colear *vi* : wag its tail

colección *nf, pl* -**ciones** : collection — **coleccionar** *vt* : collect — **coleccionista** *nmf* : collector — **colecta** *nf* : collection (of donations)

colectividad *nf* : community — **colectivo, -va** *adj* : collective — **colectivo** *nm* 1 : collective 2 *Lat* : city bus

colector *nm* : sewer

colega *nmf* : colleague

colegio *nm* 1 : school 2 : (professional) college — **colegial, -giala** *n* : schoolboy *m*, schoolgirl *f*

colegir {28} *vt* : gather

cólera *nm* : cholera — ~ *nf* : anger, rage — **colérico, -ca** *adj* 1 : bad-tempered 2 FURIOSO : angry

colesterol *nm* : cholesterol

coleta *nf* : pigtail

colgar {16} *vt* 1 : hang 2 ~ : hang up (a telephone) 3 : hang out (laundry) — *vi* : hang up — **colgante** *adj* : hanging — ~ *nm* : pendant

colibrí *nm* : hummingbird

cólico *nm* : colic

coliflor *nf* : cauliflower

colilla *nf* : (cigarette) butt

colina *nf* : hill

colindar *vi* ~ **con** : be adjacent to — **colindante** *adj* : adjacent

coliseo *nm* : coliseum

colisión *nf, pl* -**siones** : collision — **colisionar** *vi* ~ **contra** : collide with

collar *nm* 1 : necklace 2 : collar (for pets)

colmar *vt* 1 : fill to the brim 2 : fulfill (a wish, etc.) 3 ~ **de** : shower with — **colmado, -da** *adj* : heaping

colmena *nf* : beehive

colmillo *nm* 1 : canine (tooth) 2 : fang (of a dog, etc.), tusk (of an elephant)

colmo *nm* 1 : height, limit 2 **¡eso es el** ~ **!** : that's the last straw!

colocar {72} *vt* 1 PONER : place, put 2 : find a job for — **colocarse** *vr* 1 SITUARSE : position oneself 2 : get a job — **colocación** *nf, pl* -**ciones** 1 : placement, placing 2 EMPLEO : position, job

colombiano, -na *adj* : Colombian

colon *nm* : (intestinal) colon

colonia *nf* 1 : colony 2 PERFUME : cologne 3 *Lat* : residential area — **colonial** *adj* : colonial — **colonizar** {21} *vt* : colonize — **colonización** *nf, pl* -**ciones** : colonization — **colono, -na** *n* : settler, colonist

coloquial *adj* : colloquial — **coloquio** *nm* 1 : talk, discussion 2 CONGRESO : conference

color *nm* : color — **colorado, -da** *adj* : red — **colorear** *vt* : color — **colorete** *nm* : rouge — **colorido** *nm* : colors *pl*, coloring

colosal *adj* : colossal

columna *nf* 1 : column 2 ~ **vertebral** : spine, backbone — **columnista** *nmf* : columnist

columpiar *vt* : push (on a swing) — **columpiarse** *vr* : swing — **columpio** *nm* : swing

coma[1] *nm* : coma

coma[2] *nf* : comma

comadre *nf* 1 : godmother of one's child, mother of one's godchild 2 *fam*

: (female) friend — **comadrear** *vi fam*
: gossip
comadreja *nf* : weasel
comadrona *nf* : midwife
comandancia *nf* : command headquarters, command — **comandante** *nmf* 1
: commander 2 : major (in the military) — **comando** *nm* 1 : commando
2 *Lat* : command
comarca *nf* : region, area
combar *vt* : bend, curve
combatir *vt* : combat, fight against — *vi*
: fight — **combate** *nm* 1 : combat 2
: fight (in boxing) — **combatiente**
nmf : combatant, fighter
combinar *vt* 1 : combine 2 : put together, match (colors, etc.) — **combinarse** *vr* : get together — **combinación**
nf, pl **-ciones** 1 : combination 2 : connection (in travel)
combustible *nm* : fuel — *adj* : combustible — **combustión** *nf, pl* **-tiones**
: combustion
comedia *nf* : comedy
comedido, -da *adj* : moderate
comedor *nm* : dining room
comensal *nmf* : diner, dinner guest
comentar *vt* : comment on, discuss 2
MENCIONAR : mention — **comentario**
nm 1 : comment, remark 2 ANÁLISIS
: commentary — **comentarista** *nmf*
: commentator
comenzar {29} *v* : begin, start
comer *vt* 1 : eat 2 *fam* : eat up, eat into
— *vi* 1 : eat 2 CENAR : have a meal 3
dar de ~ : feed — **comerse** *vr* : eat
up
comercio *nm* 1 : commerce, trade 2 NEGOCIO : business — **comercial** *adj*
: commercial — **comercializar** {21}
vt : market — **comerciante** *nmf* : merchant, dealer — **comerciar** *vi* : do
business, trade
comestible *adj* : edible — **comestibles** *nmpl* : groceries, food
cometa *nm* : comet — ~ *nf* : kite
cometer *vt* 1 : commit 2 ~ **un error**
: make a mistake — **cometido** *nm*
: assignment, task
comezón *nf, pl* **-zones** : itchiness, itching
comicios *nmpl* : elections
cómico, -ca *adj* : comic, comical — ~
n : comic, comedian
comida *nf* 1 ALIMENTO : food 2 *Spain*
: lunch 3 *Lat* : dinner 4 **tres** ~**s al día**
: three meals a day
comienzo *nm* : beginning
comillas *nfpl* : quotation marks
comino *nm* : cumin

comisario, -ria *n* : commissioner —
comisaría *nf* : police station
comisión *nf, pl* **-siones** 1 : commission
2 COMITÉ : committee
comité *nm* : committee
como *conj* 1 : as, since 2 **sí** : if — ~
prep 1 : like, as 2 **así** ~ : as well as —
~ *adv* 1 : as 2 APROXIMADAMENTE
: around, about
cómo *adv* 1 : how 2 ~ **no** : by all
means 3 **¿**~ **te llamas?** : what's your
name?
cómoda *nf* : chest of drawers
comodidad *nf* : comfort, convenience
comodín *nm, pl* **-dines** : joker (in playing cards)
cómodo, -da *adj* 1 : comfortable 2 ÚTIL
: handy, convenient
comoquiera *adv* 1 : in any way 2 ~
que : however
compacto, -ta *adj* : compact
compadecer {53} *vt* : feel sorry for —
compadecerse *vr* ~ **de** : take pity on
compadre *nm* 1 : godfather of one's
child, father of one's godchild 2 *fam*
: buddy
compañero, -ra *n* : companion, partner
— **compañerismo** *nm* : companionship
compañía *nf* : company
comparar *vt* : compare — **comparable**
adj : comparable — **comparación** *nf,
pl* **-ciones** : comparison — **comparativo, -va** *adj* : comparative
comparecer *vi* : appear (before a court,
etc.)
compartimiento *or* **compartimento**
nm : compartment
compartir *vt* : share
compás *nm, pl* **-pases** 1 : compass 2
: rhythm, time (in music)
compasión *nf, pl* **-siones** : compassion, pity — **compasivo, -va** *adj*
: compassionate
compatible *adj* : compatible — **compatibilidad** *nf* : compatibility
compatriota *nmf* : compatriot, fellow
countryman
compeler *vt* : compel
compendiar *vt* : summarize — **compendio** *nm* : summary
compensar *vt* : compensate for —
compensación *nf, pl* **-ciones** : compensation
competir {54} *vi* : compete — **competencia** *nf* 1 : competition, rivalry 2 CAPACIDAD : competence — **competente**
adj : competent — **competición** *nf, pl*
-ciones : competition — **competidor,
-dora** *n* : competitor

compilar *vt* : compile

compinche *nmf fam* : friend, chum

complacer {57} *vt* : please — **complacerse** *vr* ~ **en** : take pleasure in — **complaciente** *adj* : obliging, helpful

complejidad *nf* : complexity — **complejo, -ja** *adj* : complex — **complejo** *nm* : complex

complementar *vt* : complement — **complementario, -ria** *adj* : complementary — **complemento** *nm* 1 : complement 2 : object (in grammar)

completar *vt* : complete — **completo, -ta** *adj* 1 : complete 2 PERFECTO : perfect 3 LLENO : full — **completamente** *adv* : completely

complexión *nf, pl* **-xiones** : constitution, build

complicar {72} *vt* 1 : complicate 2 IMPLICAR : involve — **complicación** *nf, pl* **-ciones** : complication — **complicado, -da** *adj* : complicated, complex

cómplice *nmf* : accomplice — ~ *adj* : conspiratorial, knowing

complot *nm, pl* **-plots** : conspiracy, plot

componer {60} *vt* 1 : make up, compose 2 : compose, write (a song) 3 ARREGLAR : fix, repair — **componerse** *vr* ~ **de** : consist of — **componente** *adj & nm* : component, constituent

comportarse *vr* : behave — **comportamiento** *nm* : behavior

composición *nf, pl* **-ciones** : composition — **compositor, -tora** *n* : composer, songwriter

compostura *nf* 1 : composure 2 REPARACIÓN : repair

comprar *vt* : buy, purchase — **compra** *nf* 1 : purchase 2 **ir de** ~**s** : go shopping — **comprador, -dora** *n* : buyer, shopper

comprender *vt* 1 : comprehend, understand 2 ABARCAR : cover, include — **comprensible** *adj* : understandable — **comprensión** *nf, pl* **-siones** : understanding — **comprensivo, -va** *adj* : understanding

compresa *nf* 1 : compress 2 *or* ~ **higiénica** : sanitary napkin

compresión *nf, pl* **-siones** : compression — **comprimido** *nm* : pill, tablet — **comprimir** *vt* : compress

comprobar {19} *vt* 1 VERIFICAR : check 2 DEMOSTRAR : prove — **comprobación** *nf, pl* **-ciones** : verification, check — **comprobante** *nm* 1 : proof 2 RECIBO : receipt, voucher

comprometer *vt* 1 : compromise 2 ARRIESGAR : jeopardize 3 OBLIGAR : commit, put under obligation — **comprometerse** *vr* 1 : commit oneself 2 ~ **con** : get engaged to — **comprometedor, -dora** *adj* : compromising — **comprometido, -da** *adj* 1 : compromising, awkward 2 : engaged (to be married) — **compromiso** *nm* 1 : obligation, commitment 2 : (marriage) engagement 3 ACUERDO : agreement 4 APURO : awkward situation

compuesto, -ta *adj* 1 : compound 2 ~ **de** : made up of, consisting of — **compuesto** *nm* : compound

compulsivo, -va *adj* : compelling, urgent

computar *vt* : compute, calculate — **computadora** *nf or* **computador** *nm* 1 : computer 2 ~ **portátil** : laptop computer — **cómputo** *nm* : calculation

comulgar {52} *vi* : receive Communion

común *adj, pl* **-munes** 1 : common 2 ~ **y corriente** : ordinary 3 **por lo** ~ : generally

comuna *nf* : commune — **comunal** *adj* : communal

comunicar {72} *vt* : communicate — **comunicarse** *vr* 1 : communicate 2 ~ **con** : get in touch with — **comunicación** *nf, pl* **-ciones** : communication — **comunicado** *nm* : communiqué — **comunicativo, -va** *adj* : communicative

comunidad *nf* : community

comunión *nf, pl* **-niones** : communion, Communion

comunismo *nm* : Communism — **comunista** *adj & nmf* : Communist

con *prep* 1 : with 2 A PESAR DE : in spite of 3 *(before an infinitive)* : by 4 ~ **(tal) que** : so long as

cóncavo, -va *adj* : concave

concebir {54} *v* : conceive — **concebible** *adj* : conceivable

conceder *vt* 1 : grant, bestow 2 ADMITIR : concede

concejal, -jala *n* : councilman, alderman

concentrar *vt* : concentrate — **concentrarse** *vr* : concentrate — **concentración** *nf, pl* **-ciones** : concentration

concepción *nf, pl* **-ciones** : conception — **concepto** *nm* 1 : concept 2 OPINIÓN : opinion

concernir {17} *vi* ~ **a** : concern — **concerniente** *adj* ~ **a** : concerning

concertar {55} *vt* 1 : arrange, coordinate 2 *(used before an infinitive)* : agree 3 : harmonize (in music) — *vi* : be in harmony

concesión *nf, pl* **-siones 1** : concession **2** : awarding (of prizes, etc.)

concha *nf* : shell

conciencia *nf* **1** : conscience **2** CONOCIMIENTO : consciousness, awareness — **concientizar** {21} *vt Lat* : make aware — **concientizarse** *vr Lat* ~ **de** : realize

concienzudo, -da *adj* : conscientious

concierto *nm* **1** : concert **2** : concerto (musical composition)

conciliar *vt* : reconcile — **conciliación** *nf, pl* **-ciones** : reconciliation

concilio *nm* : council

conciso, -sa *adj* : concise

conciudadano, -na *n* : fellow citizen

concluir {41} *vt* : conclude — *vi* : come to an end — **conclusión** *nf, pl* **-siones** : conclusion — **concluyente** *adj* : conclusive

concordar {19} *vi* : agree — *vt* : reconcile — **concordancia** *f* : agreement — **concordia** *nf* : harmony, concord

concretar *vt* : make concrete, specify — **concretarse** *vr* : become definite, take shape — **concreto, -ta** *adj* **1** : concrete **2** DETERMINADO : specific **3 en** ~ : specifically — **concreto** *nm Lat* : concrete

concurrir *vi* **1** : come together, meet **2** ~ **a** : take part in — **concurrencia** *nf* : audience, turnout — **concurrido, -da** *adj* : busy, crowded

concursar *vi* : compete, participate — **concursante** *nmf* : competitor — **concurso** *nm* **1** : competition **2** CONCURRENCIA : gathering **3** AYUDA : help, cooperation

condado *nm* : county

conde, -desa *n* : count *m*, countess *f*

condenar *vt* **1** : condemn, damn **2** : sentence (a criminal) — **condena** *nf* **1** : condemnation **2** SENTENCIA : sentence — **condenación** *nf, pl* **-ciones** : condemnation, damnation

condensar *vt* : condense — **condensación** *nf, pl* **-ciones** : condensation

condesa *nf* → **conde**

condescender {56} *vi* **1** : acquiesce, agree **2** ~ **a** : condescend to — **condescendiente** *adj* : condescending

condición *nf, pl* **-ciones 1** : condition, state **2** CALIDAD : capacity, position — **condicional** *adj* : conditional

condimento *nm* : condiment, seasoning

condolerse {47} *vr* : sympathize — **condolencia** *nf* : condolence

condominio *nm* **1** : joint ownership **2** *Lat* : condominium

condón *nm, pl* **-dones** : condom

conducir {61} *vt* **1** DIRIGIR : direct, lead **2** MANEJAR : drive — *vi* **1** : drive **2** ~ **a** : lead to — **conducirse** *vr* : behave

conducta *nf* : behavior, conduct

conducto *nm* : conduit, duct

conductor, -tora *n* : driver

conectar *vt* **1** : connect **2** ENCHUFAR : plug in — *vi* : connect

conejo, -ja *n* : rabbit — **conejera** *nf* : (rabbit) hutch

conexión *nf, pl* **-xiones** : connection — **conexo, -xa** *adj* : connected

confabularse *vr* : conspire, plot

confeccionar *vt* : make (up), prepare — **confección** *nf, pl* **-ciones 1** : making, preparation **2** : tailoring, dressmaking

confederación *nf, pl* **-ciones** : confederation

conferencia *nf* **1** : lecture **2** REUNIÓN : conference

conferir {76} *vt* : confer, bestow

confesar {55} *v* : confess — **confesarse** *vr* : go to confession — **confesión** *nf, pl* **-siones 1** : confession **2** CREDO : religion, creed

confeti *nm* : confetti

confiar {85} *vi* : trust — *vt* : entrust — **confiable** *adj* : trustworthy, reliable — **confiado, -da** *adj* **1** : confident **2** CRÉDULO : trusting — **confianza** *nf* **1** : trust **2** : confidence (in oneself)

confidencia *nf* : confidence, secret — **confidencial** *adj* : confidential — **confidencialidad** *nf* : confidentiality — **confidente** *nmf* **1** : confidant, confidante *f* **2** : (police) informer

configuración *nf, pl* **-ciones** : configuration, shape

confín *nm, pl* **-fines** : boundary, limit — **confinar** *vt* **1** : confine **2** DESTERRAR : exile

confirmar *vt* : confirm — **confirmación** *nf, pl* **-ciones** : confirmation

confiscar {72} *vt* : confiscate

confitería *nm* : candy store

confitura *nf* : jam

conflagración *nf, pl* **-ciones 1** : war, conflict **2** INCENDIO : fire

conflicto *nm* : conflict

confluencia *nf* : junction, confluence

conformar *vt* : shape, make up — **conformarse** *vr* **1** RESIGNARSE : resign oneself **2** ~ **con** : content oneself with — **conforme** *adj* **1** : content, satisfied **2** ~ **a** : in accordance with — ~ *conj* : as — **conformidad** *nf* **1** : agreement **2** RESIGNACIÓN : resignation

confortar *vt* : comfort — **confortable** *adj* : comfortable

confrontar *vt* **1** : confront **2** COMPARAR : compare — *vi* : border — **confrontarse** *vr* ~ **con** : face up to — **confrontación** *nf*, *pl* **-ciones** : confrontation

confundir *vt* : confuse, mix up — **confundirse** *vr* : make a mistake, be confused — **confusión** *nf*, *pl* **-siones** : confusion — **confuso, -sa** *adj* **1** : confused **2** INDISTINTO : hazy, indistinct — **congelar** *vt* : freeze — **congelarse** *vr* : freeze — **congelación** *nf*, *pl* **-ciones** : freezing — **congelado, -da** *adj* : frozen — **congelador** *nm* : freezer

congeniar *vi* : get along

congestión *nf*, *pl* **-tiones** : congestion — **congestionado, -da** *adj* : congested

congoja *nf* : anguish, grief

congraciarse *vr* : ingratiate oneself

congratular *vt* : congratulate

congregar {52} *vt* : bring together — **congregarse** *vr* : congregate — **congregación** *nf*, *pl* **-ciones** : congregation, gathering

congreso *nm* : congress — **congresista** *nmf* : member of congress

conjeturar *vt* : guess, conjecture — **conjetura** *nf* : guess, conjecture

conjugar {52} *vt* : conjugate — **conjugación** *nf*, *pl* **-ciones** : conjugation

conjunción *nf*, *pl* **-ciones** : conjunction

conjunto, -ta *adj* : joint — **conjunto** *nm* **1** : collection **2** : outfit (of clothing) **3** GRUPO : band **4 en ~** : as a whole

conjurar *vt* : ward off — *vi* : conspire, plot

conllevar *vt* : entail

conmemorar *vt* : commemorate — **conmemoración** *nf*, *pl* **-ciones** : commemoration — **conmemorativo, -va** *adj* : commemorative

conmigo *pron* : with me

conminar *vt* : threaten

conmiseración *nf*, *pl* **-ciones** : pity, commiseration

conmocionar *vt* : shock — **conmoción** *nf*, *pl* **-ciones** : shock, upheaval **2 or ~ cerebral** : concussion

conmover {47} *vt* **1** : move, touch **2** SACUDIR : shake (up) — **conmoverse** *vr* : be moved — **conmovedor, -dora** *adj* : moving, touching

conmutador *nm* **1** : (electric) switch **2** *Lat* : switchboard

cono *nm* : cone

conocer {18} *vt* **1** : know **2** : meet (a person), get to know (a city, etc.) **3** RECONOCER : recognize — **conocerse** *vr* **1** : meet, get to know each other **2** : know oneself — **conocedor, -dora** *adj* & *n* : expert — **conocido, -da** *adj* : well-known — ~ *n* : acquaintance — **conocimiento** *nm* **1** : knowledge **2** SENTIDO : consciousness

conque *conj* : so

conquistar *vt* : conquer — **conquista** *nf* : conquest — **conquistador, -dora** *adj* : conquering — **conquistador** *nm* : conqueror

consabido, -da *adj* **1** : well-known **2** HABITUAL : usual

consagrar *vt* **1** : consecrate **2** DEDICAR : devote — **consagración** *nf*, *pl* **-ciones** : consecration

consciencia *nf* → **conciencia** — **consciente** *adj* : conscious, aware

consecución *nf*, *pl* **-ciones** : attainment

consecuencia *nf* **1** : consequence **2 en ~** : accordingly — **consecuente** *adj* : consistent

consecutivo, -va *adj* : consecutive

conseguir {75} *vt* **1** : get, obtain **2 ~ hacer algo** : manage to do sth

consejo *nm* **1** : advice, counsel **2** : council (assembly) — **consejero, -ra** *n* : adviser, counselor

consenso *nm* : consensus

consentir {76} *vt* **1** : allow, permit **2** MIMAR : pamper, spoil — *vi* : consent — **consentimiento** *nm* : consent, permission

conserje *nmf* : caretaker, janitor

conservar *vt* **1** : preserve **2** GUARDAR : keep, conserve — **conservarse** *vr* : keep — **conserva** *nf* **1** : preserve(s) **2 ~s** *nfpl* : canned goods — **conservación** *nf*, *pl* **-ciones** : conservation, preservation — **conservador, -dora** *adj* & *n* : conservative — **conservatorio** *nm* : conservatory

considerar *vt* **1** : consider **2** RESPETAR : respect — **considerable** *adj* : considerable — **consideración** *nf*, *pl* **-ciones** **1** : consideration **2** RESPETO : respect — **considerado, -da** *adj* **1** : considerate **2** RESPETADO : respected

consigna *nf* **1** ESLOGAN : slogan **2** ORDEN : orders **3** : checkroom (for baggage)

consigo *pron* : with her, with him, with you, with oneself

consiguiente *adj* **1** : consequent **2 por ~** : consequently

consistir *vi* ~ **en 1** : consist of **2** : lie in, consist in — **consistencia** *nf* : consistency — **consistente** *adj* **1** : firm, solid **2** ~ **en** : consisting of

consolar {19} *vt* : console, comfort — **consolarse** *vr* : console oneself — **consolación** *nf, pl* **-ciones** : consolation

consolidar *vt* : consolidate — **consolidación** *nf, pl* **-ciones** : consolidation

consomé *nm* : consommé

consonante *adj* : consonant, harmonious — ~ *nf* : consonant

consorcio *nm* : consortium

conspirar *vi* : conspire, plot — **conspiración** *nf, pl* **-ciones** : conspiracy — **conspirador, -dora** *n* : conspirator

constancia *nf* **1** : record, evidence **2** PERSEVERANCIA : perseverance — **constante** *adj* : constant — **constantemente** *adv* : constantly, continually

constar *vi* **1** : be evident, be clear **2** ~ **de** : consist of

constatar *vt* **1** : verify **2** AFIRMAR : state, affirm

constelación *nf, pl* **-ciones** : constellation

consternación *nf, pl* **-ciones** : consternation

constipado, -da *adj estar* ~ : have a cold — **constipado** *nm* : cold — **constiparse** *vr* : catch a cold

constituir {41} *vt* **1** FORMAR : constitute, form **2** FUNDAR : establish, set up — **constituirse** *vr* ~ **en** : set oneself up as — **constitución** *nf, pl* **-ciones** : constitution — **constitucional** *adj* : constitutional — **constitutivo, -va** *adj* : constituent — **constituyente** *adj & nm* : constituent

constreñir {67} *vt* **1** : force, compel **2** RESTRINGIR : restrict, limit

construir {41} *vt* : build, construct — **construcción** *nf, pl* **-ciones** : construction, building — **constructivo, -va** *adj* : constructive — **constructor, -tora** *n* : builder

consuelo *nm* : consolation, comfort

consuetudinario, -ria *adj* : customary

cónsul *nmf* : consul — **consulado** *nm* : consulate

consultar *vt* : consult — **consulta** *nf* : consultation — **consultor, -tora** *n* : consultant — **consultorio** *nm* : office (of a doctor or dentist)

consumar *vt* **1** : consummate, complete **2** : commit (a crime)

consumir *vt* : consume — **consumirse** *vr* : waste away — **consumición** *nf, pl* **-ciones** : consumption **2** : drink (in a restaurant) — **consumido, -da** *adj* : thin, emaciated — **consumidor, -dora** *n* : consumer — **consumo** *nm* : consumption

contabilidad *nf* **1** : accounting, bookkeeping **2** : accountancy (profession) — **contable** *nmf Spain* : accountant, bookkeeper

contactar *vi* ~ **con** : get in touch with, contact — **contacto** *nm* : contact

contado, -da *adj* : numbered, few — **contado** *nm* **al** ~ : (in) cash

contador, -dora *n Lat* : accountant — **contador** *nm* : meter

contagiar *vt* **1** : infect **2** : transmit (a disease) — **contagiarse** *vr* **1** : be contagious **2** : become infected (with a disease) — **contagio** *nm* : contagion, infection — **contagioso, -sa** *adj* : contagious, infectious

contaminar *vt* : contaminate, pollute — **contaminación** *nf, pl* **-ciones** : contamination, pollution

contar {19} *vt* **1** : count **2** NARRAR : tell — *vi* **1** : count **2** ~ **con** : rely on, count on

contemplar *vt* **1** MIRAR : look at, behold **2** CONSIDERAR : contemplate — **contemplación** *nf, pl* **-ciones** : contemplation

contemporáneo, -nea *adj & n* : contemporary

contender {56} *vi* : contend, compete — **contendiente** *nmf* : competitor

contener {80} *vt* **1** : contain **2** RESTRINGIR : restrain, hold back — **contenerse** *vr* : restrain oneself — **contenedor** *nm* : container — **contenido, -da** *adj* : restrained — **contenido** *nm* : contents *pl*

contentar *vt* : please, make happy — **contentarse** *vr* ~ **con** : be satisfied with — **contento, -ta** *adj* : glad, happy, contented

contestar *vt* : answer — *vi* : reply, answer back — **contestación** *nf, pl* **-ciones** : answer, reply

contexto *nm* : context

contienda *nf* **1** COMBATE : dispute, fight **2** COMPETICIÓN : contest

contigo *pron* : with you

contiguo, -gua *adj* : adjacent

continente *nm* : continent — **continental** *adj* : continental

contingencia *nf* : contingency — **contingente** *adj & nm* : contingent

continuar {3} *v* : continue — **continuación** *nf, pl* **-ciones 1** : continuation **2 a** ~ : next, then — **continuidad** *nf* : continuity — **continuo, -nua** *adj* **1**

: continuous, steady **2** FRECUENTE : continual

contorno *nm* **1** : outline **2** ~**s** *nmpl* : surrounding area

contorsión *nf, pl* -**siones** : contortion

contra *prep* **1** : against **2 en** ~ : against — ~ **nm los pros y los** ~**s** : the pros and cons

contraatacar {72} *v* : counterattack — **contraataque** *nm* : counterattack

contrabajo *nm* : double bass

contrabalancear *vt* : counterbalance

contrabandista *nmf* : smuggler — **contrabando** *nm* **1** : smuggling **2** : contraband (goods)

contracción *nf, pl* -**ciones** : contraction

contrachapado *nm* : plywood

contradecir {11} *vt* : contradict — **contradicción** *nf, pl* -**ciones** : contradiction — **contradictorio, -ria** *adj* : contradictory

contraer {81} *vt* **1** : contract **2** ~ **matrimonio** : get married — **contraerse** *vr* : contract, tighten up

contrafuerte *nm* : buttress

contragolpe *nm* : backlash

contralto *nmf* : contralto

contrapartida *nf* : compensation

contrapelo : a ~ *adv phr* : the wrong way

contrapeso *nm* : counterbalance

contraponer {60} *vt* **1** : counter, oppose **2** COMPARAR : compare

contraproducente *adj* : counterproductive

contrariar {85} *vt* **1** : oppose **2** MOLESTAR : vex, annoy — **contrariedad** *nf* **1** : obstacle **2** DISGUSTO : annoyance — **contrario, -ria** *adj* **1** OPUESTO : opposite **2 al contrario** : on the contrary **3 ser** ~ **a** : be opposed to

contrarrestar *vt* : counteract

contrasentido *nm* : contradiction (in terms)

contraseña *nf* : password

contrastar *vt* **1** : check, verify **2** RESISTIR : resist — *vi* : contrast — **contraste** *nm* : contrast

contratar *vt* **1** : contract for **2** : hire, engage (workers)

contratiempo *nm* **1** : mishap **2** DIFICULTAD : setback

contrato *nm* : contract — **contratista** *nmf* : contractor

contraventana *nf* : shutter

contribuir {41} *vi* **1** : contribute **2** : pay taxes — **contribución** *nf, pl* -**ciones** **1** : contribution **2** IMPUESTO : tax — **contribuyente** *nmf* **1** : contributor **2** : taxpayer

contrincante *nmf* : opponent

contrito, -ta *adj* : contrite

controlar *vt* **1** : control **2** COMPROBAR : monitor, check — **control** *nm* **1** : control **2** VERIFICACIÓN : inspection, check — **controlador, -dora** *n* : controller

controversia *nf* : controversy

contundente *adj* **1** : blunt **2** : forceful, convincing (of arguments, etc.)

contusión *nf, pl* -**siones** : bruise

convalecencia *nf* : convalescence — **convaleciente** *adj & nmf* : convalescent

convencer {86} *vt* **1** : convince, persuade — **convencerse** *vr* : be convinced — **convencimiento** *nm* : conviction, belief

convención *nf, pl* -**ciones** : convention — **convencional** *adj* : conventional

convenir {87} *vi* **1** : be suitable, be advisable **2 en** ~ : agree on — **conveniencia** *nf* **1** : convenience **2** : suitability (of an action, etc.) — **conveniente** *adj* **1** : convenient **2** ACONSEJABLE : suitable, advisable **3** PROVECHOSO : useful — **convenio** *nm* : agreement, pact

convento *nm* : convent, monastery

converger {15} *or* **convergir** *vi* : converge

conversar *vi* : converse, talk — **conversación** *nf, pl* -**ciones** : conversation

conversión *nf, pl* -**siones** : conversion — **converso, -sa** *n* : convert

convertir {76} *vt* : convert — **convertirse** *vr* ~ **en** : turn into — **convertible** *adj & nm* : convertible

convexo, -xa *adj* : convex

convicción *nf, pl* -**ciones** : conviction — **convicto, -ta** *adj* : convicted

convidar *vt* : invite — **convidado, -da** *n* : guest

convincente *adj* : convincing

convite *nm* **1** : invitation **2** : banquet

convivir *vi* : live together — **convivencia** *nf* : coexistence, living together

convocar {72} *vt* : convoke, call together

convulsión *nf, pl* -**siones** **1** : convulsion **2** TRASTORNO : upheaval — **convulsivo, -va** *adj* : convulsive

conyugal *adj* : conjugal — **cónyuge** *nmf* : spouse, partner

coñac *nm* : cognac, brandy

cooperar *vi* : cooperate — **cooperación** *nf* : cooperation — **cooperativa** *nf* : cooperative, co-op — **cooperativo, -va** *adj* : cooperative

coordenada *nf* : coordinate
coordinar *vt* : coordinate — **coordinación** *nf, pl* **-ciones** : coordination — **coordinador, -dora** *n* : coordinator
copa *nf* 1 : glass, goblet 2 : cup (in sports) 3 **tomar una ~** : have a drink
copia *nf* : copy — **copiar** *vt* : copy
copioso, -sa *adj* : copious, abundant
copla *nf* 1 : (popular) song 2 ESTROFA : verse, stanza
copo *nm* 1 : flake 2 *or* **~ de nieve** : snowflake
coquetear *vi* : flirt — **coqueteo** *nm* : flirting, flirtation — **coqueto, -ta** *adj* : flirtatious — **~** *n* : flirt
coraje *nm* 1 : valor, courage 2 IRA : anger
coral¹ *nm* : coral
coral² *adj* : choral — **~** *nf* : choir, chorale
Corán *nm* **el ~** : the Koran
coraza *nf* 1 : armor plating 2 : shell
corazón *nm, pl* **-zones** 1 : heart 2 : core (of fruit) 3 **mi ~** : my darling — **corazonada** *nf* 1 : hunch 2 IMPULSO : impulse
corbata *nf* : tie, necktie
corchete *nm* 1 : hook and eye, clasp 2 : square bracket (punctuation mark)
corcho *nm* : cork
cordel *nm* : cord, string
cordero *nm* : lamb
cordial *adj* : cordial — **cordialidad** *nf* : cordiality
cordillera *nf* : mountain range
córdoba *nf* : córdoba (Nicaraguan unit of currency)
cordón *nm, pl* **-dones** 1 : cord 2 **~ policial** : (police) cordon 3 **cordones** *nmpl* : shoelaces
cordura *nf* : sanity
corear *vt* : chant
coreografía *nf* : choreography
cornamenta *nf* : antlers *pl*
corneta *nf* : bugle
coro *nm* 1 : chorus 2 : (church) choir
corona *nf* 1 : crown 2 : wreath, garland (of flowers) — **coronación** *nf, pl* **-ciones** : coronation — **coronar** *vt* : crown
coronel *nm* : colonel
coronilla *nf* 1 : crown (of the head) 2 **estar hasta la ~** : be fed up
corporación *nf, pl* **-ciones** : corporation
corporal *adj* : corporal, bodily
corporativo, -va *adj* : corporate
corpulento, -ta *adj* : stout
corral *nm* 1 : farmyard 2 : pen, corral (for animals) 3 *or* **corralito** : playpen

correa *nf* 1 : strap, belt 2 : leash (for a dog, etc.)
corrección *nf, pl* **-ciones** 1 : correction 2 : correctness, propriety (of manners) — **correccional** *nm* : reformatory — **correctivo, -va** *adj* : corrective — **correcto, -ta** *adj* 1 : correct, right 2 CORTÉS : polite
corredizo, -za *adj* : sliding
corredor, -dora *n* 1 : runner, racer 2 AGENTE : agent, broker — **corredor** *nm* : corridor, hallway
corregir {28} *vt* : correct — **corregirse** *vr* : mend one's ways
correlación *nf, pl* **-ciones** : correlation
correo *nm* 1 : mail 2 **~ aéreo** : airmail
correr *vi* 1 : run, race 2 : flow (of a river, etc.) 3 : pass (of time) — *vt* 1 : run 2 RECORRER : travel over, cover 3 : draw (curtains) — **correrse** *vr* 1 : move along 2 : run (of colors)
corresponder *vi* 1 : correspond 2 PERTENECER : belong 3 ENCAJAR : fit 4 **~ a** : reciprocate, repay — **corresponderse** *vr* : write to each other — **correspondencia** *nf* 1 : correspondence 2 : connection (of a train, etc.) — **correspondiente** *adj* : corresponding, respective — **corresponsal** *nmf* : correspondent
corretear *vi* : run about, scamper
corrida *nf* 1 : run 2 *or* **~ de toros** : bullfight — **corrido, -da** *adj* 1 : straight, continuous 2 *fam* : worldly
corriente *adj* 1 : current 2 NORMAL : common, ordinary 3 : running (of water, etc.) — **~** *nf* 1 : current (of water, electricity, etc.), draft (of air) 2 TENDENCIA : tendency, trend — **~** *nm* **al ~** 1 : up-to-date 2 ENTERADO : aware, informed
corrillo *nm* : clique, circle — **corro** *nm* : ring, circle (of people)
corroborar *vt* : corroborate
corroer {69} *vt* 1 : corrode (of metals) 2 : erode, wear away — **corroerse** *vr* : corrode
corromper *vt* 1 : corrupt 2 PUDRIR : rot — **corrompido, -da** *adj* : corrupt
corrosión *nf, pl* **-siones** : corrosion — **corrosivo, -va** *adj* : corrosive
corrupción *nf, pl* **-ciones** : corruption 2 DESCOMPOSICIÓN : decay, rot — **corrupto, -ta** *adj* : corrupt
corsé *nm* : corset
cortar *vt* 1 : cut 2 RECORTAR : cut out 3 QUITAR : cut off — *vi* : cut — **cortarse** *vr* 1 : cut oneself 2 : be cut off (on the telephone) 3 : curdle (of milk) 4 **~ el pelo** : have one's hair cut — **cortada**

nf Lat : cut — **cortante** *adj* : cutting, sharp

cortauñas *nms & pl* : nail clippers

corte[1] *nm* **1** : cutting **2** ESTILO : cut, style **3 ~ de pelo** : haircut

corte[2] *nf* **1** : court **2 hacer la ~ a** : court, woo — **cortejar** *vt* : court, woo

cortejo *nm* **1** : entourage **2** NOVIAZGO : courtship **3 ~ fúnebre** : funeral procession

cortés *adj* : courteous, polite — **cortesía** *nf* : courtesy, politeness

corteza *nf* **1** : bark **2** : crust (of bread) **3** : rind, peel (of fruit)

cortina *nm* : curtain

corto, -ta *adj* **1** : short **2** ESCASO : scarce **3** *fam* : timid, shy **4 ~ de vista** : near-sighted — **cortocircuito** *nm* : short circuit

corvo, -va *adj* : curved, bent

cosa *nf* **1** : thing **2** ASUNTO : matter, affair **3 ~ de** : about **4 poca ~** : nothing much

cosechar *v* : harvest, reap — **cosecha** *nf* **1** : harvest, crop **2** : vintage (of wine)

coser *v* : sew

cosmético, -ca *adj* : cosmetic — **cosmético** *nm* : cosmetic

cósmico, -ca *adj* : cosmic

cosmopolita *adj* : cosmopolitan

cosmos *nm* : cosmos

cosquillas *nfpl* **1** : tickling **2 hacer ~** : tickle — **cosquilleo** *nm* : tickling sensation, tingle

costa *nf* **1** : coast, shore **2 a toda ~** : at any cost

costado *nm* **1** : side **2 al ~** : alongside

costar {19} *v* : cost

costarricense *or* **costarriqueño, -ña** *adj* : Costa Rican

coste *nm* → **costo** — **costear** *vt* : pay for

costero, -ra *adj* : coastal

costilla *nf* **1** : rib **2** CHULETA : chop, cutlet

costo *nm* : cost, price — **costoso, -sa** *adj* : costly

costra *nf* : scab

costumbre *nf* **1** : custom, habit **2 de ~** : usual

costura *nf* **1** : sewing, dressmaking **2** PUNTADAS : seam — **costurera** *nf* : dressmaker

cotejar *vt* : compare

cotidiano, -na *adj* : daily

cotizar {21} *vt* : quote, set a price on — **cotización** *nf, pl* **-ciones** : quotation, price — **cotizado, -da** *adj* : in demand

coto *nm* : enclosure, reserve

cotorra *nf* **1** : small parrot **2** *fam* : chatterbox — **cotorrear** *vi fam* : chatter, gab

coyote *nm* : coyote

coyuntura *nf* **1** : joint **2** SITUACIÓN : situation, moment

coz *nm, pl* **coces** : kick (of an animal)

cráneo *nm* : cranium, skull

cráter *nm* : crater

crear *vt* : create — **creación** *nf, pl* **-ciones** : creation — **creativo, -va** *adj* : creative — **creador, -dora** *n* : creator

crecer {53} *vi* **1** : grow **2** AUMENTAR : increase — **crecido, -da** *adj* **1** : full-grown **2** : large (of numbers) — **creciente** *adj* **1** : growing, increasing **2** : crescent (of the moon) — **crecimiento** *nm* **1** : growth **2** AUMENTO : increase

credenciales *nfpl* : credentials

credibilidad *nf* : credibility

crédito *nm* : credit

credo *nm* : creed

crédulo, -la *adj* : credulous, gullible

creer {20} *v* **1** : believe **2** SUPONER : suppose, think — **creerse** *vr* : regard oneself as — **creencia** *nf* : belief — **creíble** *adj* : believable, credible — **creído, -da** *adj fam* : conceited

crema *nf* : cream

cremación *nf, pl* **-ciones** : cremation

cremallera *nf* : zipper

cremoso, -sa *adj* : creamy

crepe *nf* : crepe, pancake

crepitar *vi* : crackle

crepúsculo *nm* : twilight, dusk

crespo, -pa *adj* : curly, frizzy

crespón *nm, pl* **-pones** : crepe (fabric)

cresta *nf* **1** : crest **2** : comb (of a rooster)

cretino, -na *n* : cretin

creyente *nmf* : believer

criar {85} *vt* **1** : nurse (a baby) **2** EDUCAR : bring up, rear **3** : raise, breed (animals) — **cría** *nf* **1** : breeding, rearing **2** : young animal — **criadero** *nm* : farm, hatchery — **criado, -da** *n* : servant, maid *f* — **criador, -dora** *n* : breeder — **crianza** *nf* : upbringing, rearing

criatura *nf* **1** : creature **2** NIÑO : baby, child

crimen *nm, pl* **crímenes** : crime — **criminal** *adj & nmf* : criminal

críquet *nm* : cricket (game)

crin *nf* : mane

criollo, -lla *adj & n* : Creole

cripta *nf* : crypt

crisantemo *nm* : chrysanthemum

crisis *nf* 1 : crisis 2 ~ **nerviosa** : nervous breakdown

crispar *vt* 1 : tense (muscles), clench (one's fist) 2 IRRITAR : irritate, set on edge — **crisparse** *vr* : tense up

cristal *nm* 1 : crystal 2 VIDRIO : glass, piece of glass — **cristalería** *nf* : glassware — **cristalino, -na** *adj* : crystalline — **cristalino** *nm* : lens (of the eye) — **cristalizar** {21} *vi* : crystallize

cristiano, -na *adj* & *n* : Christian — **cristianismo** *nm* : Christianity — **Cristo** *nm* : Christ

criterio *nm* 1 : criterion 2 JUICIO : judgment, opinion

criticar {72} *vt* : criticize — **crítica** *nf* 1 : criticism 2 RESEÑA : review, critique — **crítico, -ca** *adj* : critical — ~ *n* : critic, reviewer

croar *vi* : croak

cromo *nm* : chromium, chrome

cromosoma *nm* : chromosome

crónica *nf* 1 : chronicle 2 : (news) report

crónico, -ca *adj* : chronic

cronista *nmf* : reporter, newscaster

cronología *nf* : chronology — **cronológico, -ca** *adj* : chronological

cronometrar *vt* : time, clock — **cronómetro** *nm* : chronometer, stopwatch

croqueta *nf* : croquette

croquis *nms & pl* : (rough) sketch

cruce *nm* 1 : crossing 2 : crossroads, intersection 3 ~ **peatonal** : crosswalk

crucero *nm* 1 : cruise 2 : cruiser (ship)

crucial *adj* : crucial

crucificar {72} *vt* : crucify — **crucifijo** *nm* : crucifix — **crucifixión** *nf, pl* -**fixiones** : crucifixion

crucigrama *nm* : crossword puzzle

crudo, -da *adj* 1 : harsh, crude 2 : raw (of food) — **crudo** *nm* : crude oil

cruel *adj* : cruel — **crueldad** *nf* : cruelty

crujir *vi* : rustle, creak, crackle, crunch — **crujido** *nm* : rustle, creak, crackle, crunch — **crujiente** *adj* : crunchy, crisp

cruzar {21} *vt* 1 : cross 2 : exchange (words) — **cruzarse** *vr* 1 : intersect 2 : pass each other — **cruz** *nf, pl* **cruces** : cross — **cruzada** *nf* : crusade — **cruzado, -da** *adj* : crossed — **cruzado** *nm* : crusader

cuaderno *nm* : notebook

cuadra *nf* 1 : stable 2 *Lat* : (city) block

cuadrado, -da *adj* : square — **cuadrado** *nm* : square

cuadragésimo, -ma *adj* : fortieth, forty- — ~ *n* : fortieth, forty- (in a series)

cuadrar *vi* 1 : conform, agree 2 : add up, tally (numbers) — *vt* : square — **cuadrarse** *vr* : stand at attention

cuadrilátero *nm* 1 : quadrilateral 2 : ring (in sports)

cuadrilla *nf* : gang, group

cuadro *nm* 1 : square 2 PINTURA : painting 3 DESCRIPCIÓN : picture, description 4 : staff, management (of an organization) 5 CUADRADO : check, square 6 : (baseball) diamond

cuadrúpedo *nm* : quadruped

cuádruple *adj* : quadruple — **cuadruplicar** {72} *vt* : quadruple

cuajar *vi* 1 : curdle 2 COAGULAR : clot, coagulate 3 : set (of pudding, etc.) 4 AFIANZARSE : catch on — *vt* 1 : curdle 2 ~ **de** : fill with

cual *pron* 1 **el** ~, **la** ~, **los** ~**es**, **las** ~**es** : who, whom, which 2 **lo** ~ : which 3 **cada** ~ : everyone, everybody — ~ *prep* : like, as

cuál *pron* : which (one), what (one) — ~ *adj* : which, what

cualidad *nf* : quality, trait

cualquiera (**cualquier** *before nouns*) *adj, pl* **cualesquiera** : any, whatever — ~ *pron, pl* **cualesquiera** : anyone, whatever

cuán *adv* : how

cuando *conj* 1 : when 2 SI : since, if 3 ~ **más** : at the most 4 **de vez en** ~ : from time to time — ~ *prep* : during, at the time of

cuándo *adv* 1 : when 2 **¿desde** ~? : since when?

cuantía *nf* 1 : quantity, extent 2 IMPORTANCIA : importance — **cuantioso, -sa** *adj* : abundant, considerable

cuanto *adv* 1 : as much as 2 ~ **antes** : as soon as possible 3 **en** ~ : as soon as 4 **en** ~ **a** : as for, as regards — **cuanto, -ta** *adj* : as many, whatever — ~ *pron* 1 : as much as, all that, everything 2 **unos cuantos, unas cuantas** : a few

cuánto *adv* : how much, how many — **cuánto, -ta** *adj* : how much, how many — ~ *pron* : how much, how many

cuarenta *adj & nm* : forty — **cuarentavo, -va** *adj* : fortieth — **cuarentavo** *nm* : fortieth

cuarentena *nf* : quarantine

Cuaresma *nf* : Lent

cuartear *vt* : quarter, divide up — **cuartearse** *vr* : crack, split

cuartel *nm* 1 : barracks *pl* 2 ~ **general** : headquarters 3 **no dar** ~ : show no mercy

cuarteto *nm* : quartet
cuarto, -ta *adj* : fourth — ~ *n* : fourth (in a series) — **cuarto** *nm* 1 : quarter, fourth 3 HABITACIÓN : room
cuarzo *nm* : quartz
cuatro *adj & nm* : four — **cuatrocientos, -tas** *adj* : four hundred — **cuatrocientos** *nms & pl* : four hundred
cuba *nf* : cask, barrel
cubano, -na *adj* : Cuban
cubeta *nf* 1 : keg, cask 2 *Lat* : pail, bucket
cúbico, -ca *adj* : cubic, cubed — **cubículo** *nm* : cubicle
cubierta *nf* 1 : cover, covering 2 : (automobile) tire 3 : deck (of a ship) — **cubierto** *nm* 1 : cutlery, place setting 2 a ~ : under cover
cubo *nm* 1 : cube 2 *Spain* : pail, bucket 3 : hub (of a wheel)
cubrecama *nm* : bedspread
cubrir {2} *vt* : cover — **cubrirse** *vr* 1 : cover oneself 2 : cloud over
cucaracha *nf* : cockroach
cuchara *nf* : spoon — **cucharada** *nf* : spoonful — **cucharilla** *or* **cucharita** *nf* : teaspoon — **cucharón** *nm, pl* **-rones** : ladle
cuchichear *vi* : whisper — **cuchicheo** *nm* : whisper
cuchilla *nf* 1 : (kitchen) knife 2 ~ **de afeitar** : razor blade — **cuchillada** *nf* : stab, knife wound — **cuchillo** *nm* : knife
cuclillas *nfpl* **en** ~ : squatting, crouching
cuco *nm* : cuckoo — **cuco, -ca** *adj fam* : pretty, cute
cucurucho *nm* : ice-cream cone
cuello *nm* 1 : neck 2 : collar (of clothing)
cuenca *nf* 1 : river basin 2 : (eye) socket — **cuenco** *nm* 1 : bowl 2 CONCAVIDAD : hollow
cuenta *nf* 1 : calculation, count 2 : (bank) account 3 FACTURA : check, bill 4 : bead (for a necklace, etc.) 5 **darse** ~ : realize 6 **tener en** ~ : bear in mind
cuento *nm* 1 : story, tale 2 ~ **de hadas** : fairy tale
cuerda *nf* 1 : cord, rope, string 2 ~**s vocales** : vocal cords 3 **dar** ~ **a** : wind up
cuerdo, -da *adj* : sane, sensible
cuerno *nm* 1 : horn 2 : antlers *pl* (of a deer)
cuero *nm* 1 : leather, hide 2 ~ **cabelludo** : scalp
cuerpo *nm* 1 : body 2 : corps (in the military, etc.)

cuervo *nm* : crow
cuesta *nf* 1 : slope 2 **a** ~**s** : on one's back 3 ~ **abajo** : downhill 4 ~ **arriba** : uphill
cuestión *nf, pl* **-tiones** : matter, affair — **cuestionar** *vt* : question — **cuestionario** *nm* 1 : questionnaire 2 : quiz (in school)
cueva *nf* : cave
cuidar *vt* 1 : take care of, look after 2 : pay attention to (details, etc.) — *vi* 1 ~ **de** : look after 2 ~ **de que** : make sure that — **cuidarse** *vr* : take care of oneself — **cuidado** *nm* 1 : care 2 PREOCUPACIÓN : worry, concern 3 **tener** ~ : be careful 4 ¡**cuidado**! : watch out!, careful! — **cuidadoso, -sa** *adj* : careful — **cuidadosamente** *adv* : carefully
culata *nf* : butt (of a gun) — **culatazo** *nm* : kick, recoil
culebra *nf* : snake
culinario, -ria *adj* : culinary
culminar *vi* : culminate — **culminación** *nf, pl* **-ciones** : culmination
culo *nm fam* : backside, bottom
culpa *nf* 1 : fault, blame 2 PECADO : sin 3 **echar la** ~ **a** : blame 4 **tener la** ~ : be at fault — **culpabilidad** *nf* : guilt — **culpable** *adj* : guilty — *nmf* : culprit, guilty party — **culpar** *vt* : blame
cultivar *vt* : cultivate — **cultivo** *nm* 1 : farming, cultivation 2 ~**s** : crops
culto, -ta *adj* : cultured, educated — **culto** *nm* 1 : worship 2 : (religious) cult — **cultura** *nf* : culture — **cultural** *adj* : cultural
cumbre *nf* : summit, top
cumpleaños *nms & pl* : birthday
cumplido, -da *adj* 1 : complete, full 2 CORTÉS : courteous — **cumplido** *nm* : compliment, courtesy
cumplimentar *vt* 1 : congratulate 2 CUMPLIR : carry out — **cumplimiento** *nm* : carrying out, performance
cumplir *vt* 1 : accomplish, carry out 2 : keep (a promise), observe (a law, etc.) 3 : reach (a given age) — *vi* 1 : expire, fall due 2 ~ **con el deber** : do one's duty — **cumplirse** *vr* 1 : expire REALIZARSE : come true
cúmulo *nm* 1 : heap, pile 2 : cumulus (cloud)
cuna *nf* 1 : cradle 2 ORIGEN : birthplace
cundir *vi* 1 PROPAGARSE : spread, propagate 2 : go a long way
cuneta *nf* : ditch (in a road), gutter (in a street)
cuña *nf* : wedge

cuñado, -da *n* : brother-in-law *m*, sister-in-law *f*

cuota *nf* 1 : fee, dues 2 CUPO : quota 3 *Lat* : installment, payment

cupo *nm* 1 : quota, share 2 *Lat* : capacity, room

cupón *nm*, *pl* -pones : coupon

cúpula *nf* : dome, cupola

cura *nf* 1 : cure, treatment — ~ *nm* : priest — curación *nf*, *pl* -ciones : healing — curar *vt* 1 : cure 2 : dress (a wound) 3 CURTIR : tan (hides) — curarse *vr* : get well

curiosear *vi* 1 : snoop, pry 2 : browse (in a store) — *vt* : look over — curiosidad *nf* : curiosity — curioso, -sa *adj* 1 : curious, inquisitive 2 RARO : unusual, strange

currículum *nm*, *pl* -lums *or* currículo *nm* : résumé, curriculum vitae

cursar *vt* 1 : take (a course), study 2 ENVIAR : send, pass on

cursi *adj fam* : affected, pretentious

cursiva *nf* : italics *pl*

curso *nm* 1 : course 2 : (school) year 3 en ~ : under way 4 en ~ : current

curtir *vt* 1 : tan 2 : harden (skin, features, etc.) — curtiduría *nf* : tannery

curva *nf* 1 : curve, bend 2 ~ de nivel : contour — curvo, -va *adj* : curved, bent

cúspide *nf* : apex, peak

custodia *nf* 1 : custody — custodiar *vt* : guard, look after — custodio, -dia *n* : guardian

cutáneo, -nea *adj* : skin

cutícula *nf* : cuticle

cutis *nm & pl* : skin, complexion

cuyo, -ya *adj* 1 : whose, of whom, of which 2 en cuyo caso : in which case

D

d *nf* : d, fourth letter of the Spanish alphabet

dádiva *nf* : gift, handout — dadivoso, -sa *adj* : generous

dado, -da *adj* 1 : given 2 dado que : provided that, since — dados *nmpl* : dice

daga *nf* : dagger

daltónico, -ca *adj* : color-blind

dama *nf* 1 : lady 2 ~s *nfpl* : checkers

damnificar {72} *vt* : damage, injure

danés, -nesa *adj* : Danish — danés *nm* : Danish (language)

danzar {21} *v* : dance — danza *nf* : dance, dancing

dañar *vt* : damage, harm — dañarse *vr* 1 : be damaged 2 : hurt oneself — dañino, -na *adj* : harmful — daño *nm* 1 : damage, harm 2 ~s y perjuicios : damages

dar {22} *vt* 1 : give 2 PRODUCIR : yield, produce 3 : strike (the hour) 4 MOSTRAR : show — *vi* 1 ~ como : consider, regard as 2 ~ con : run into, meet 3 ~ contra : knock against 4 ~ para : be enough for — darse *vr* 1 : happen 2 ~ contra : bump into 3 ~ por : consider oneself 4 dárselas de : pose as

dardo *nm* : dart

dársena *nf* : dock

datar *vt* : date — *vi* ~ de : date from

dátil *nm* : date (fruit)

dato *nm* 1 : fact 2 ~s *nmpl* : data

de *prep* 1 : of 2 ~ Managua : from Managua 3 ~ niño : as a child 4 ~ noche : at night 5 las tres ~ la mañana : three o'clock in the morning 6 más ~ 10 : more than 10

deambular *vi* : wander about, stroll

debajo *adv* 1 : underneath 2 ~ de : under, underneath 3 por ~ : below, beneath

debatir *vt* : debate — debatirse *vr* : struggle — debate *nm* : debate

deber *vt* : owe — *v aux* 1 : have to, should 2 (*expressing probability*) : must — deberse *vr* ~ a : be due to — ~ *nm* 1 : duty 2 ~es *nmpl* : homework — debido, -da *adj* ~ a : due to, owing to

débil *adj* : weak, feeble — debilidad *nf* : weakness — debilitar *vt* : weaken — debilitarse *vr* : get weak — débilmente *adv* : weakly, faintly

débito *nm* 1 : debit 2 DEUDA : debt

debutar *vi* : debut — debut *nm*, *pl* ~s : debut — debutante *nf* : debutante *f*

década *nf* : decade

decadencia *nf* : decadence — decadente *adj* : decadent

decaer {13} *vi* : decline, weaken

decano, -na *n* : dean

decapitar *vt* : behead

decena *nf* : ten, about ten

decencia *nf* : decency

decenio *nm* : decade

decente *adj* : decent

decepcionar *vt* : disappoint — **decepción** *nf, pl* -**ciones** : disappointment
decibelio *or* **decibel** *nm* : decibel
decidir *vt* : decide, determine — *vi* : decide — **decidirse** *vr* : make up one's mind — **decididamente** *adv* : definitely, decidedly — **decidido, -da** *adj* : determined, resolute
decimal *adj* : decimal
décimo, -ma *adj & n* : tenth
decimoctavo, -va *adj* : eighteenth — ∼ *n* : eighteenth (in a series)
decimocuarto, -ta *adj* : fourteenth — ∼ *n* : fourteenth (in a series)
decimonoveno, -na *or* **decimonono, -na** *adj* : nineteenth — ∼ *n* : nineteenth (in a series)
decimoquinto, -ta *adj* : fifteenth — ∼ *n* : fifteenth (in a series)
decimoséptimo, -ma *adj* : seventeenth — ∼ *n* : seventeenth (in a series)
decimosexto, -ta *adj* : sixteenth — ∼ *n* : sixteenth (in a series)
decimotercero, -ra *adj* : thirteenth — ∼ *n* : thirteenth (in a series)
decir {23} *vt* **1** : say **2** CONTAR : tell **3 es** ∼ : that is to say **4 querer** ∼ : mean — **decirse** *vr* **1** : tell oneself **2 ¿cómo se dice...?** : how do you say...? — ∼ *nm* : saying, expression
decisión *nf, pl* -**siones** : decision — **decisivo, -va** *adj* : decisive
declarar *vt* : declare — *vi* : testify — **declararse** *vr* **1** : declare oneself **2** : break out (of a fire, an epidemic, etc.) — **declaración** *nf, pl* -**ciones** : statement
declinar *v* : decline
declive *nm* **1** : decline **2** PENDIENTE : slope
decolorar *vt* : bleach — **decolorarse** *vr* : fade
decoración *nf, pl* -**ciones** : decoration — **decorado** *nm* : stage set — **decorar** *vt* : decorate — **decorativo, -va** *adj* : decorative
decoro *nm* : decency, decorum — **decoroso, -sa** *adj* : decent, proper
decrecer {53} *vi* : decrease
decrépito, -ta *adj* : decrepit
decretar *vt* : decree — **decreto** *nm* : decree
dedal *nm* : thimble
dedicar {72} *vt* : dedicate — **dedicarse** *vr* ∼ **a** : devote oneself to — **dedicación** *nf, pl* -**ciones** : dedication — **dedicatoria** *nf* : dedication, inscription
dedo *nm* **1** : finger **2** ∼ **del pie** : toe
deducir {61} *vt* **1** INFERIR : deduce **2**

DESCONTAR : deduct — **deducción** *nf, pl* -**ciones** : deduction
defecar {72} *vi* : defecate
defecto *nm* : defect — **defectuoso, -sa** *adj* : defective, faulty
defender {56} *vt* : defend — **defenderse** *vr* : defend oneself — **defensa** *nf* : defense — **defensiva** *nf* : defensive — **defensivo, -va** *adj* : defensive — **defensor, -sora** *n* **1** : defender **2** *or* **abogado defensor** : defense counsel
deferencia *nf* : deference — **deferente** *adj* : deferential
deficiencia *nf* : deficiency — **deficiente** *adj* : deficient
déficit *nm, pl* -**cits** : deficit
definir *vt* : define — **definición** *nf, pl* -**ciones** : definition — **definitivo, -va** *adj* **1** : definitive **2 en definitiva** : in short
deformar *vt* **1** : deform **2** : distort (the truth, etc.) — **deformación** *nf, pl* -**ciones** : distortion — **deforme** *adj* : deformed — **deformidad** *nf* : deformity
defraudar *vt* **1** : defraud **2** DECEPCIONAR : disappoint
degenerar *vi* : degenerate — **degenerado, -da** *adj* : degenerate
degradar *vt* **1** : degrade **2** : demote (in the military)
degustar *vt* : taste
dehesa *nf* : pasture
deidad *nf* : deity
dejar *vt* **1** : leave **2** ABANDONAR : abandon **3** PERMITIR : allow — *vi* ∼ **de** : quit — **dejado, -da** *adj* : slovenly, careless
dejo *nm* **1** : aftertaste **2** : (regional) accent
del (*contraction of* **de** *and* **el**) → **de**
delantal *nm* : apron
delante *adv* **1** : ahead **2** ∼ **de** : in front of
delantera *nf* **1** : front **2 tomar la** ∼ : take the lead — **delantero, -ra** *adj* : front, forward — ∼ *n* : forward (in sports)
delatar *vt* : denounce, inform against
delegar {52} *vt* : delegate — **delegación** *nf, pl* -**ciones** : delegation — **delegado, -da** *n* : delegate, representative
deleitar *vt* : delight, please — **deleite** *nm* : delight
deletrear *vt* : spell (out)
delfín *nm, pl* -**fines** : dolphin
delgado, -da *adj* : thin
deliberar *vi* : deliberate — **deliberación** *nf, pl* -**ciones** : deliberation

— **deliberado, -da** *adj* : deliberate, intentional

delicadeza *nf* **1** : delicacy, daintiness **2** SUAVIDAD : gentleness **3** TACTO : tact — **delicado, -da** *adj* **1** : delicate **2** SENSIBLE : sensible **3** DISCRETO : tactful

delicia *nf* : delight — **delicioso, -sa** *adj* **1** : delightful **2** RICO : delicious

delictivo, -va *adj* : criminal

delimitar *vt* : define, set the boundaries of

delincuencia *nf* : delinquency, crime — **delincuente** *adj & nmf* : delinquent, criminal — **delinquir** {24} *vi* : break the law

delirante *adj* : delirious — **delirar** *vi* **1** : be delirious **2** ~ **por** *fam* : rave about — **delirio** *nm* **1** : delirium **2** ~ **de grandeza** : delusions of grandeur

delito *nm* : crime

delta *nm* : delta

demacrado, -da *adj* : emaciated

demandar *vt* **1** : sue **2** PEDIR : demand **3** *Lat* : require — **demanda** *nf* **1** : lawsuit **2** PETICIÓN : request **3** **la oferta y la** ~ : supply and demand — **demandante** *nmf* : plaintiff

demás *adj* : rest of the other — ~ *pron* **1 lo (la, los, las)** ~ : the rest, others **2 por** ~ : extremely **3 por lo** ~ : otherwise **4 y** ~ : and so on

demasiado *adv* **1** : too **2** : too much — ~ *adj* : too much, too many

demencia *nf* : madness — **demente** *adj* : insane, mad

democracia *nf* : democracy — **demócrata** *nmf* : democrat — **democrático, -ca** *adj* : democratic

demoler {47} *vt* : demolish — **demolición** *nf, pl* **-ciones** : demolition

demonio *nm* : devil, demon

demorar *v* : delay — **demorarse** *vr* : take a long time — **demora** *nf* : delay

demostrar {19} *vt* **1** : demonstrate **2** MOSTRAR : show — **demostración** *nf, pl* **-ciones** : demonstration

demudar *vt* : change, alter

denegar {49} *vt* : deny, refuse — **denegación** *nf, pl* **-ciones** : denial, refusal

denigrar *vt* **1** : denigrate **2** INJURIAR : insult

denominador *nm* : denominator

denotar *vt* : denote, show

densidad *nf* : density — **denso, -sa** *adj* : dense

dental *adj* : dental — **dentado, -da** *adj* : toothed, notched — **dentadura** *nf* ~ **postiza** : dentures *pl* — **dentífrico** *nm* : toothpaste — **dentista** *nmf* : dentist

dentro *adv* **1** : in, inside **2** ~ **de poco** : soon, shortly **3 por** ~ : inside

denuedo *nm* : courage

denunciar *vt* **1** : denounce **2** : report (a crime) — **denuncia** *nf* **1** : accusation **2** : (police) report

departamento *nm* **1** : department **2** *Lat* : apartment

depender *vi* **1** : depend **2** ~ **de** : depend on — **dependencia** *nf* **1** : dependence, dependency **2** SUCURSAL : branch office — **dependiente** *adj* : dependent — **dependiente, -ta** *n* : clerk, salesperson

deplorar *vt* : deplore, regret

deponer {60} *vt* : remove from office, depose

deportar *vt* : deport — **deportación** *nf, pl* **-ciones** : deportation

deporte *nm* : sport, sports *pl* — **deportista** *nmf* : sportsman *m*, sportswoman *f* — **deportivo, -va** *adj* **1** : sporty **2 artículos deportivos** : sporting goods

depositar *vt* **1** : put, place **2** : deposit (in a bank, etc.) — **depósito** *nm* **1** : deposit **2** ALMACÉN : warehouse

depravado, -da *adj* : depraved

depreciarse *vr* : depreciate — **depreciación** *nf* : depreciation

depredador *nm* : predator

deprimir *vt* : depress — **deprimirse** *vr* : get depressed — **depresión** *nf, pl* **-siones** : depression

derecha *nf* **1** : right side **2** : right wing (in politics) — **derechista** *adj* : rightwing — **derecho** *nm* **1** : right **2** LEY : law — ~ *adv* : straight — **derecho, -cha** *adj* **1** : right, right-hand **2** VERTICAL : upright **3** RECTO : straight

deriva *nf* **1** : drift **2 a la** ~ : adrift — **derivación** *nf, pl* **-ciones** : derivation — **derivar** *vi* **1** : drift **2** ~ **de** : derive from

derramamiento *nm* ~ **de sangre** : bloodshed

derramar *vt* **1** : spill **2** : shed (tears, blood) — **derramarse** *vr* : overflow — **derrame** *nm* **1** : spilling **2** : discharge, hemorrhage

derrapar *vi* : skid — **derrape** : skid

derretir {54} *vt* : melt, thaw — **derretirse** *vr* **1** : melt, thaw **2** ~ **por** *fam* : be crazy about

derribar *vt* **1** : demolish **2** : bring down (a plane, a tree, etc.) **3** : overthrow (a government, etc.)

derrocar {72} *vt* : overthrow

derrochar *vt* : waste, squander — **der-**

rochador, -dora n : spendthrift — **derroche** nm : extravagance, waste

derrotar vt : defeat — **derrota** nf : defeat

derruir {41} vt : demolish, tear down

derrumbar vt : demolish, knock down — **derrumbarse** vr : collapse, break down — **derrumbamiento** nm : collapse — **derrumbe** nm : collapse

desabotonar vt : unbutton, undo

desabrido, -da adj : bland

desabrochar vt : unbutton, undo — **desabrocharse** vr : come undone

desacato nm 1 : disrespect 2 : contempt (of court) — **desacatar** vt : defy, disobey

desacertado, -da adj : mistaken, wrong — **desacertar** {55} vi : be mistaken — **desacierto** nm : mistake, error

desaconsejar vt : advise against — **desaconsejable** adj : inadvisable

desacreditar vt : discredit

desactivar vt : deactivate

desacuerdo nm : disagreement

desafiar {85} vt : defy, challenge — **desafiante** adj : defiant

desafilado, -da adj : blunt

desafinado, -da adj : out-of-tune, off-key

desafío nm : challenge, defiance

desafortunado, -da adj : unfortunate — **desafortunadamente** adv : unfortunately

desagradar vt : displease — **desagradable** adj : disagreeable, unpleasant

desagradecido, -da adj : ungrateful

desagrado nm 1 : displeasure 2 con ~ : reluctantly

desagravio nm : amends, reparation

desagregarse {52} vr : disintegrate

desaguar {10} vi : drain, empty — **desagüe** nm 1 : drainage 2 : drain (of a sink, etc.)

desahogar {52} vt 1 : relieve 2 : give vent to (anger, etc.) — **desahogarse** vr : let off steam, unburden oneself — **desahogado, -da** adj 1 : roomy 2 ADINERADO : comfortable, well-off — **desahogo** nm 1 : relief 2 con ~ : comfortably

desahuciar vt 1 : deprive of hope 2 DESALOJAR : evict — **desahucio** nm : eviction

desaire nm : snub, rebuff — **desairar** vt : snub, slight

desalentar {55} vt : discourage — **desaliento** nm : discouragement

desaliñado, -da adj : slovenly

desalmado, -da adj : heartless, cruel

desalojar vt 1 : evacuate 2 DESAHUCIAR : evict

desamparar vt : abandon — **desamparo** nm : abandonment, desertion

desamueblado, -da adj : unfurnished

desangrarse vr : lose blood, bleed to death

desanimar vt : discourage — **desanimarse** vr : get discouraged — **desanimado, -da** adj : downhearted, despondent — **desánimo** nm : discouragement

desanudar vr : untie

desaparecer {53} vi : disappear — **desaparecido, -da** n : missing person — **desaparición** nf, pl -**ciones** : disappearance

desapasionado, -da adj : dispassionate

desapego nm : indifference

desapercibido, -da adj : unnoticed

desaprobar {19} vt : disapprove of — **desaprobación** nf, pl -**ciones** : disapproval

desaprovechar vt : waste

desarmar vt 1 : disarm 2 DESMONTAR : dismantle, take apart — **desarme** nm : disarmament

desarraigar {52} vt : uproot, root out

desarreglar vt 1 : mess up 2 : disrupt (plans, etc.) — **desarreglado, -da** adj : disorganized — **desarreglo** nm : untidiness, disorder

desarrollar vt : develop — **desarrollarse** vr : take place — **desarrollo** nm : development

desarticular vt 1 : break up, dismantle 2 : dislocate (a bone)

desaseado, -da adj 1 : dirty 2 DESORDENADO : messy

desastre nm : disaster — **desastroso, -sa** adj : disastrous

desatar vt 1 : undo, untie 2 : unleash (passions) — **desatarse** vr 1 : come undone 2 DESENCADENARSE : break out, erupt

desatascar {72} vt : unclog

desatender {56} vt 1 : disregard 2 : neglect (an obligation, etc.) — **desatento, -ta** adj : inattentive

desatinado, -da adj : foolish, silly

desautorizado, -da adj : unauthorized

desavenencia nf : disagreement

desayunar vi : have breakfast — vt : have for breakfast — **desayuno** nm : breakfast

desbancar {72} vt : oust

desbarajuste nm : disorder, confusion

desbaratar vt : ruin, destroy — **desbaratarse** vr : fall apart

desbocarse {72} *vr* : run away, bolt

desbordar *vt* **1** : overflow **2** : exceed (limits) — **desbordarse** *vr* : overflow — **desbordamiento** *nm* : overflow

descabellado, -da *adj* : crazy

descafeinado, -da *adj* : decaffeinated

descalabrar *vt* : hit on the head — **descalabro** *nm* : misfortune, setback

descalificar {72} *vt* : disqualify — **descalificación** *nf, pl* **-ciones** : disqualification

descalzarse {21} *vr* : take off one's shoes — **descalzo, -za** *adj* : barefoot

descaminar *vt* : mislead, lead astray

descansar *v* : rest — **descanso** *nm* **1** : rest **2** : landing (of a staircase) **3** : intermission (in theater), halftime (in sports)

descapotable *adj & nm* : convertible

descarado, -da *adj* : insolent, shameless

descargar {52} *vt* **1** : unload **2** : discharge (a firearm, etc.) — **descarga** *nf* **1** : unloading **2** : discharge (of a firearm, of electricity, etc.) — **descargo** *nm* **1** : unloading **2** : discharge (of a duty, etc.) **3** : defense (in law)

descarnado, -da *adj* : scrawny, gaunt

descaro *nm* : insolence, nerve

descarrilar *vi* : derail — **descarrilarse** *vr* : be derailed

descartar *vt* : reject — **descartarse** *vr* : discard

descascarar *vt* : peel, shell, husk

descender {56} *vt* **1** : go down **2** BAJAR : lower — *vi* **1** : descend **2 ~ de** : be descended from — **descendencia** *nf* **1** : descendants *pl* **2** LINAJE : lineage, descent — **descendiente** *nmf* : descendant — **descenso** *nm* **1** : descent **2** : drop, fall (in level, in temperature, etc.)

descifrar *vt* : decipher, decode

descolgar {16} *vt* **1** : take down **2** : pick up, answer (the telephone)

descolorarse *vr* : fade — **descolorido, -da** *adj* : faded, discolored

descomponer {60} *vt* : break down — **descomponerse** *vr* **1** : rot, decompose **2** *Lat* : break down — **descompuesto, -ta** *adj Lat* : out of order

descomunal *adj* : enormous

desconcertar {55} *vt* : disconcert, confuse — **desconcertante** *adj* : confusing — **desconcierto** *nm* : confusion, bewilderment

desconectar *vt* : disconnect

desconfiar {85} *vi ~ de* : distrust — **desconfiado, -da** *adj* : distrustful — **desconfianza** *nf* : distrust

descongelar *vt* **1** : thaw, defrost **2** : unfreeze (assets)

descongestionante *nm* : decongestant

desconocer {18} *vt* : not know, fail to recognize — **desconocido, -da** *adj* : unknown — **~** *n* : stranger

desconsiderado, -da *adj* : inconsiderate

desconsolar *vt* : distress — **desconsolado, -da** *adj* : heartbroken — **desconsuelo** *nm* : grief, sorrow

descontar {19} *vt* : discount

descontento, -ta *adj* : dissatisfied — **descontento** *nm* : discontent

descontinuar *vt* : discontinue

descorazonado, -da *adj* : discouraged

descorrer *vt* : draw back

descortés *adj, pl* **-teses** : rude — **descortesía** *nf* : discourtesy, rudeness

descoyuntar *vt* : dislocate

descrédito *nm* : discredit

descremado, -da *adj* : nonfat, skim

describir {33} *vt* : describe — **descripción** *nf, pl* **-ciones** : description — **descriptivo, -va** *adj* : descriptive

descubierto, -ta *adj* **1** : exposed, uncovered **2 al descubierto** : in the open — **descubierto** *nm* **1** : deficit, overdraft

descubrir {2} *vt* **1** : discover **2** REVELAR : reveal — **descubrimiento** *nm* : discovery

descuento *nm* : discount

descuidar *vt* : neglect — **descuidarse** *vr* **1** : be careless **2** ABANDONARSE : let oneself go — **descuidado, -da** *adj* **1** : careless, sloppy **2** DESATENDIDO : neglected — **descuido** *nm* : neglect, carelessness

desde *prep* **1** : from (a place), since (a time) **2 ~ luego** : of course

desdén *nm* : scorn, disdain — **desdeñar** *vt* : scorn — **desdeñoso, -sa** *adj* : disdainful

desdicha *nf* **1** : misery **2** DESGRACIA : misfortune — **desdichado, -da** *adj* : unfortunate, unhappy

desear *vt* : wish, want — **deseable** *adj* : desirable

desecar *vt* : dry up

desechar *vt* **1** : throw away **2** RECHAZAR : reject — **desechable** *adj* : disposable — **desechos** *nmpl* : rubbish

desembarazarse {21} *vr ~ de* : get rid of

desembarcar {72} *vi* : disembark — *vt* : unload — **desembarcadero** *nm* : jetty, landing pier — **desembarco** *nm* : landing

desembocar {72} *vi ~ en* **1** : flow

into 2 : lead to (a result) — **desembocadura** *nf* 1 : mouth (of a river) 2 : opening, end (of a street)

desembolsar *vt* : pay out — **desembolso** *nm* : payment, outlay

desembragar *vi* : disengage the clutch

desempacar {72} *v Lat* : unpack

desempañe *vt* 1 : play (a role) 2 : redeem (from a pawnshop) — **desempeñarse** *vr* : get out of debt

desempleo *nm* : unemployment — **desempleado, -da** *adj* : unemployed

desempolvar *vt* : dust

desencadenar *vt* 1 : unchain 2 : trigger, unleash (protests, crises, etc.) — **desencadenarse** *vr* : break loose

desencajar *vt* : dislocate 2 DESCONECTAR : disconnect

desencanto *nm* : disillusionment

desenchufar *vt* : disconnect, unplug

desenfadado, -da *adj* : carefree, confident — **desenfado** *nm* : confidence, ease

desenfrenado, -da *adj* : unrestrained — **desenfreno** *nm* : abandon, lack of restraint

desenganchar *vt* : unhook

desengañar *vt* : disillusion — **desengaño** *nm* : disappointment

desenlace *nm* : ending, outcome

desenmarañar *vt* : disentangle

desenmascarar *vt* : unmask

desenredar *vt* : untangle — **desenredarse** *vr* ∼ **de** : extricate oneself from

desenrollar *vt* : unroll, unwind

desentenderse {56} *vr* ∼ **de** : want nothing to do with

desenterrar {55} *vt* : dig up, disinter

desentonar *vi* 1 : be out of tune 2 : clash (of colors, etc.)

desenvoltura *nf* : confidence, ease

desenvolver {89} *vt* : unfold, unwrap — **desenvolverse** *vr* : unfold, develop

desenvuelto, -ta *adj* : confident, self-assured

deseo *nm* : desire — **deseoso, -sa** *adj* : eager, anxious

desequilibrar *vt* : throw off balance — **desequilibrado, -da** *adj* : unbalanced — **desequilibrio** *nm* : imbalance

desertar *vt* : desert — **deserción** *nf, pl* **-ciones** : desertion — **desertor, -tora** *n* : deserter

desesperar *vt* : exasperate — *vi* : despair — **desesperarse** *vr* : become exasperated — **desesperación** *nf, pl* **-ciones** : desperation, despair — de-

sesperado, -da *adj* : desperate, hopeless

desestimar *vt* : reject

desfalcar {72} *vt* : embezzle — **desfalco** *nm* : embezzlement

desfallecer {53} *vi* 1 : weaken 2 DESMAYARSE : faint

desfavorable *adj* : unfavorable

desfigurar *vt* 1 : disfigure, mar 2 : distort (the truth)

desfiladero *nm* : mountain pass, gorge

desfilar *vi* : march, parade — **desfile** *nm* : parade, procession

desfogar {52} *vt* : vent — **desfogarse** *vr* : let off steam

desgajar *vt* : tear off, break apart — **desgajarse** *vr* : come off

desgana *nf* 1 : lack of appetite 2 : lack of enthusiasm, reluctance

desgarbado, -da *adj* : gawky, ungainly

desgarrar *vt* : tear, rip — **desgarrador, -dora** *adj* : heartbreaking — **desgarro** *nm* : tear

desgastar *vt* : wear away, wear down — **desgaste** *nm* : deterioration, wear and tear

desgracia *nf* 1 : misfortune 2 caer en ∼ : fall into disgrace 3 por ∼ : unfortunately — **desgraciadamente** *adv* : unfortunately — **desgraciado, -da** *adj* : unfortunate

deshabitado, -da *adj* : uninhabited

deshacer {40} *vt* 1 : undo 2 DESTRUIR : destroy, ruin 3 DISOLVER : dissolve 4 : break (an agreement), cancel (plans, etc.) — **deshacerse** *vr* 1 : come undone 2 ∼ **de** : get rid of 3 ∼ **en** : lavish, heap (praise, etc.) — **deshecho, -cha** *adj* 1 : undone 2 DESTROZADO : destroyed, ruined

desheredar *vt* : disinherit

deshidratar *vt* : dehydrate

deshielo *nm* : thaw

deshilachar *vt* : unravel — **deshilacharse** *vr* : fray

deshonesto, -ta *adj* : dishonest

deshonrar *vt* : dishonor, disgrace — **deshonra** *nf* : dishonor — **deshonroso, -sa** *adj* : dishonorable

deshuesar *vt* 1 : pit (a fruit) 2 : bone, debone (meat)

desidia *nf* 1 : indolence 2 DESASEO : sloppiness

desierto, -ta *adj* : deserted, uninhabited — **desierto** *nm* : desert

designar *vt* : designate — **designación** *nf, pl* **-ciones** : appointment (to an office, etc.)

designio *nm* : plan

desigual *adj* 1 : unequal 2 DISPAREJO

: uneven — **desigualdad** nf : inequality

desilusionar vt : disappoint, disillusion — **desilusión** nf, pl **-siones** : disappointment, disillusionment

desinfectar vt : disinfect — **desinfectante** adj & nm : disinfectant

desinflar vt : deflate — **desinflarse** vr : deflate, go flat

desinhibido, -da adj : uninhibited

desintegrar vt : disintegrate — **desintegrarse** vr : disintegrate — **desintegración** nf, pl **-ciones** : disintegration

desinteresado, -da adj : unselfish, generous — **desinterés** nm : unselfishness

desistir vi — **de** : give up

desleal adj : disloyal — **deslealtad** nf : disloyalty

desleír {66} vt : dilute, dissolve

desligar {52} vt 1 : untie 2 SEPARAR : separate — **desligarse** vr : extricate oneself

desliz nm, pl **-lices** : slip, mistake — **deslizar** {21} vt : slide, slip — **deslizarse** vr : slide, glide

deslucido, -da adj : dingy, tarnished

deslumbrar vt : dazzle — **deslumbrante** adj : dazzling, blinding

deslustrar vt : tarnish, dull

desmán nm, pl **-manes** : outrage, excess

desmandarse vr : get out of hand

desmantelar vt : dismantle

desmañado, -da adj : clumsy

desmayar vi : lose heart — **desmayarse** vr : faint — **desmayo** nm : faint

desmedido, -da adj : excessive

desmejorar vt : impair — vi : deteriorate

desmemoriado, -da adj : forgetful

desmentir {76} vt : deny — **desmentido** nm : denial

desmenuzar {21} vt 1 : crumble 2 EXAMINAR : scrutinize — **desmenuzarse** vr : crumble

desmerecer {53} vt : be unworthy of — vi : decline in value

desmesurado, -da adj : excessive

desmigajar vt : crumble

desmontar vt 1 : dismantle, take apart 2 ALLANAR : level — vi : dismount

desmoralizar {21} vt : demoralize

desmoronarse vr : crumble

desnivel nm : unevenness

desnudar vt : undress, strip — **desnudarse** vr : get undressed — **desnudez** nf, pl **-deces** : nudity, nakedness — **desnudo, -da** adj : nude, naked — **desnudo** nm : nude

desnutrición nf, pl **-ciones** : malnutrition

desobedecer {53} v : disobey — **desobediencia** nf : disobedience — **desobediente** adj : disobedient

desocupar vt : empty, vacate — **desocupado, -da** adj 1 : vacant 2 DESEMPLEADO : unemployed

desodorante adj & nm : deodorant

desolado, -da adj 1 : desolate 2 DESCONSOLADO : devastated, distressed — **desolación** nf, pl **-ciones** : desolation

desorden nm, pl **desórdenes** : disorder, mess — **desordenado, -da** adj : untidy — **desordenadamente** adv : in a disorderly way

desorganizar {21} vt : disorganize — **desorganización** nf, pl **-ciones** : disorganization

desorientar vt : disorient, confuse — **desorientarse** vr : lose one's way

desovar vi : spawn

despachar vt 1 : deal with (a task, etc.) 2 ENVIAR : dispatch, send 3 : wait on, serve (customers) — **despacho** nm 1 : dispatch, shipment 2 OFICINA : office

despacio adv : slowly

desparramar vt : spill, scatter, spread

despavorido, -da adj : terrified

despecho nm 1 : spite 2 a — **de** : despite, in spite of

despectivo, -va adj 1 : pejorative 2 DESPRECIATIVO : contemptuous

despedazar {21} vt : tear apart

despedir {54} vt 1 : see off 2 DESTITUIR : dismiss, fire 3 DESPRENDER : emit — **despedirse** vr : say good-bye — **despedida** nf : farewell, good-bye

despegar {52} vt : detach, unstick — vi : take off — **despegado, -da** adj : cold, distant — **despegue** nm : takeoff

despeinar vt : ruffle (hair) — **despeinado, -da** adj : disheveled, unkempt

despejar vt : clear, free — vi : clear up — **despejado, -da** adj 1 : clear, fair 2 LÚCIDO : clear-headed

despellejar vt : skin (an animal)

despensa nf : pantry, larder

despeñadero nm : precipice

desperdiciar vt : waste — **desperdicio** nm 1 : waste 2 —s nmpl : scraps

desperfecto nm : flaw, defect

despertar {55} vi : awaken, wake up — vt : wake, rouse — **despertador** nm : alarm clock

despiadado, -da adj : pitiless, merciless

despido *nm* : dismissal, layoff

despierto, -ta *adj* : awake

despilfarrar *vt* : squander — **despilfarrador, -dora** *n* : spendthrift — **despilfarro** *nm* : extravagance, wastefulness

despistar *vt* : throw off the track, confuse — **despistarse** *vr* : lose one's way — **despistado, -da** *adj* **1** : absentminded **2** DESORIENTADO : confused — **despiste** *nm* **1** : absentmindedness **2** ERROR : mistake

desplazar {21} *vt* : displace — **desplazarse** *vr* : travel

desplegar {49} *vt* : unfold, spread out — **despliegue** *nm* : display

desplomarse *vr* : collapse

desplumar *vt* **1** : pluck **2** *fam* : fleece

despoblado, -da *adj* : uninhabited, deserted — **despoblado** *nm* : deserted area

despojar *vt* : strip, deprive — **despojos** *nmpl* **1** : plunder **2** RESTOS : remains, scraps

desportillar *vt* : chip — **desportillarse** *vr* : chip — **desportilladura** *nf* : chip, nick

déspota *nmf* : despot

despotricar *vi* : rant (and rave)

despreciar *vt* : despise, scorn — **despreciable** *adj* **1** : despicable **2 una cantidad ~** : a negligible amount — **desprecio** *nm* : disdain, scorn

desprender *vt* **1** : detach, remove **2** EMITIR : give off — **desprenderse** *vr* **1** : come off **2** DEDUCIRSE : be inferred, follow — **desprendimiento** *nm* **~ de tierras** : landslide

despreocupado, -da *adj* : carefree, unconcerned

desprestigiar *vt* : discredit — **desprestigiarse** *vr* : lose face

desprevenido, -da *adj* : unprepared

desproporcionado, -da : out of proportion

despropósito *nm* : (piece of) nonsense, absurdity

desprovisto, -ta *adj* **~ de** : lacking in

después *adv* **1** : afterward **2** ENTONCES : then, next **3 ~ de** : after **4 después (de) que** : after **5 ~ de todo** : after all

despuntado, -da *adj* : blunt, dull

desquiciar *vt* : drive crazy

desquitarse *vr* **1** : retaliate **2 ~ con** : take it out on, get back at — **desquite** *nm* : revenge

destacar {72} *vt* : emphasize — *vi* : stand out — **destacado, -da** *adj* : outstanding

destapar *vt* : open, uncover — **destapador** *nm Lat* : bottle opener

destartalado, -da *adj* : dilapidated

destellar *vi* : flash, sparkle — **destello** *nm* : sparkle, twinkle, flash

destemplado, -da *adj* **1** : out of tune **2** MAL : out of sorts **3** : unpleasant (of weather)

desteñir {67} *vt* : fade, bleach — *vi* : run, fade — **desteñirse** *vr* : fade

desterrar {55} *vt* : banish, exile — **desterrado, -da** *n* : exile

destetar *vt* : wean

destiempo *adv* **a ~** : at the wrong time

destierro *nm* : exile

destilar *vt* : distill — **destilería** *nf* : distillery

destinar *vt* **1** : assign, allocate **2** NOMBRAR : appoint — **destinado, -da** *adj* : destined — **destinatario, -ria** *n* : addressee — **destino** *nm* **1** : destiny **2** RUMBO : destination

destituir {41} *vt* : dismiss — **destitución** *nf, pl* **-ciones** : dismissal

destornillar *vt* : unscrew — **destornillador** *nm* : screwdriver

destreza *nf* : skill, dexterity

destrozar {21} *vt* : destroy, wreck — **destrozos** *nmpl* : damage, destruction

destrucción *nf, pl* **-ciones** : destruction — **destructivo, -va** *adj* : destructive — **destruir** {41} *vt* : destroy

desunir *vt* : split, divide

desusado, -da *adj* **1** : obsolete **2** INSÓLITO : unusual — **desuso** *nm* **caer en ~** : fall into disuse

desvaído, -da *adj* **1** : pale, washed-out **2** BORROSO : vague, blurred

desvalido, -da *adj* : destitute, needy

desvalijar *vt* : rob

desván *nm, pl* **-vanes** : attic

desvanecer {53} *vt* : make disappear — **desvanecerse** *vr* **1** : vanish **2** DESMAYARSE : faint

desvariar {85} *vi* : be delirious — **desvarío** *nm* : delirium

desvelar *vt* : keep awake — **desvelarse** *vr* : stay awake — **desvelo** *nm* **1** : sleeplessness **2 ~s** *nmpl* : efforts

desvencijado, -da *adj* : dilapidated, rickety

desventaja *nf* : disadvantage

desventura *nf* : misfortune

desvergonzado, -da *adj* : shameless — **desvergüenza** *nf* : shamelessness

desvestir {54} *vt* : undress — **desvestirse** *vr* : get undressed

desviación *nf, pl* **-ciones 1** : deviation **2** : detour (in a road) — **desviar** {85} *vt* : divert, deflect — **desviarse** *vr* **1** : branch off **2** APARTARSE : stray — **desvío** *nm* : diversion, detour

detallar vt : detail — **detallado, -da** adj : detailed, thorough — **detalle** nm **1** : detail **2 al — :** retail — **~** nmf : retailer

detectar vt : detect — **detective** nmf : detective

detener {80} vt **1** : arrest, detain **2** PARAR : stop **3** RETRASAR : delay — **detenerse** vr **1** : stop **2** DEMORARSE : linger — **detención** nf, pl **-ciones** : arrest, detention

detergente nm : detergent

deteriorar vt : damage — **deteriorarse** vr : wear out, deteriorate — **deteriorado, -da** adj : damaged, worn — **deterioro** nm : deterioration, damage

determinar vt **1** : determine **2** MOTIVAR : bring about **3** DECIDIR : decide — **determinarse** vr : decide — **determinación** nf, pl **-ciones** : determination **2 tomar una — :** make a decision — **determinado, -da** adj **1** : determined **2** ESPECÍFICO : specific

detestar vt : detest

detonar vi : explode, detonate — **detonación** nf, pl **-ciones** : detonation

detrás adv **1** : behind **2 — de :** in back of **3 por — :** from behind

detrimento nm **en — de :** to the detriment of

deuda nf : debt — **deudor, -dora** n : debtor

devaluar {3} vt : devalue — **devaluarse** vr : depreciate

devastar vt : devastate — **devastador, -dora** adj : devastating

devenir {87} vi **1** : come about **2 — en** : become, turn into

devoción nf, pl **-ciones** : devotion

devolución nf, pl **-ciones** : return

devolver {89} vt **1** RESTITUIR : give back **2** : refund, pay back — vi : vomit — **devolverse** vr Lat : return, come back

devorar vt : devour

devoto, -ta adj : devout — **~** n : devotee

día nm **1** : day **2** : daytime **3 al — :** up-to-date **4 en pleno — :** in broad daylight

diabetes nf : diabetes — **diabético, -ca** adj & n : diabetic

diablo nm : devil — **diablillo** nm : imp, rascal — **diablura** nf : prank — **diabólico, -ca** adj : diabolic, diabolical

diafragma nm : diaphragm

diagnosticar {72} vt : diagnose — **diagnóstica, -ca** adj : diagnostic — **diagnóstico** nm : diagnosis

diagonal adj & nf : diagonal

diagrama nm : diagram

dial nm : dial (of a radio, etc.)

dialecto nm : dialect

dialogar {52} vi : have a talk — **diálogo** nm : dialogue

diamante nm : diamond

diámetro nm : diameter

diana nf **1** : reveille **2** BLANCO : target, bull's-eye

diario, -ria adj : daily — **diario** nm **1** : diary **2** PERIÓDICO : newspaper — **diariamente** adv : daily

diarrea nf : diarrhea

dibujar vt **1** : draw **2** DESCRIBIR : portray — **dibujante** nmf : draftsman m, draftswoman f — **dibujo** nm **1** : drawing **2 ~s animados :** (animated) cartoons

diccionario nm : dictionary

dicha nf **1** ALEGRÍA : happiness **2** SUERTE : good luck — **dicho** nm : saying, proverb — **dichoso, -sa** adj **1** : happy **2** AFORTUNADO : lucky

diciembre nm : December

dictar vt **1** : dictate **2** : pronounce (a sentence), deliver (a speech) — **dictado** nm : dictation — **dictador, -dora** n : dictator — **dictadura** nf : dictatorship

diecinueve adj & nm : nineteen — **diecinueveavo, -va** adj : nineteenth

dieciocho adj & nm : eighteen — **dieciochoavo, -va** or **dieciochavo, -va** adj : eighteenth

dieciséis adj & nm : sixteen — **dieciseisavo, -va** adj : sixteenth

diecisiete adj & nm : seventeen — **diecisieteavo, -va** adj : seventeenth

diente nm **1** : tooth **2** : prong, tine (of a fork, etc.) **3 ~ de ajo :** clove of garlic **4 ~ de león :** dandelion

diesel ['disel] adj & nm : diesel

diestra nf : right hand — **diestro, -tra** adj **1** : right **2** HÁBIL : skillful

dieta nf : diet — **dietético, -ca** adj : dietetic, dietary

diez adj & nm, pl **dieces** : ten

difamar vt : slander, libel — **difamación** nf, pl **-ciones** : slander, libel

diferencia nf : difference — **diferenciar** vt : distinguish between — **diferenciarse** vr : differ — **diferente** adj : different

diferir {76} vt : postpone — vi : differ

difícil adj : difficult — **dificultad** nf : difficulty — **dificultar** vt : hinder, obstruct

difteria nf : diphtheria

difundir vt **1** : spread (out) **2** : broadcast (television, etc.)

difunto, -ta *adj & n* : deceased

difusión *nf, pl* **-siones** : spreading

digerir {76} *vt* : digest — **digerible** *adj* : digestible — **digestión** *nf, pl* **-tiones** : digestion — **digestivo, -va** *adj* : digestive

dígito *nm* : digit — **digital** *adj* : digital

dignarse *vr* ~ **a** : deign to

dignatario, -ria *n* : dignitary — **dignidad** *nf* : dignity — **digno, -na** *adj* : worthy

digresión *nf*, *pl* **-siones** : digression

dilapidar *vt* : waste, squander

dilatar *vt* **1** : expand, dilate **2** PROLONGAR : prolong **3** POSPONER : postpone

dilema *nm* : dilemma

diligencia *nf* **1** : diligence **2** TRÁMITE : procedure, task — **diligente** *adj* : diligent

diluir {41} *vt* : dilute

diluvio *nm* **1** : flood **2** LLUVIA : downpour

dimensión *nf, pl* **-siones** : dimension

diminuto, -ta *adj* : minute, tiny

dimitir *vi* : resign — **dimisión** *nf, pl* **-siones** : resignation

dinámico, -ca *adj* : dynamic

dinamita *nf* : dynamite

dínamo *or* **dinamo** *nmf* : dynamo

dinastía *nf* : dynasty

dineral *nm* : large sum, fortune

dinero *nm* : money

dinosaurio *nm* : dinosaur

diócesis *nfs & pl* : diocese

dios, diosa *n* : god, goddess *f* — **Dios** *nm* : God

diploma *nm* : diploma — **diplomado, -da** *adj* : qualified, trained

diplomacia *nf* : diplomacy — **diplomático, -ca** *adj* : diplomatic — ~ *n* : diplomat

diputación *nf, pl* **-ciones** : delegation — **diputado, -da** *n* : delegate

dique *nm* : dike

dirección *nf, pl* **-ciones 1** : address **2** SENTIDO : direction **3** GESTIÓN : management **4** : steering (of an automobile) — **direccional** *nf Lat* : turn signal, blinker — **directa** *nf* : high gear — **directiva** *nf* : board of directors — **directivo, -va** *adj* : managerial — ~ *n* : manager, director — **directo, -ta** *adj* **1** : direct **2** DERECHO : straight — **director, -tora** *n* **1** : director, manager **2** : conductor (of an orchestra) — **directorio** *nm* : directory — **directriz** *nf, pl* **-trices** : guideline

dirigencia *nf* : leaders, leadership — **dirigente** *nmf* : director, leader

dirigible *nm* : dirigible, blimp

dirigir {35} *vt* **1** : direct, lead **2** : address (a letter, etc.) **3** ENCAMINAR : aim **4** : conduct (music) — **dirigirse** *vr* ~ **a** : go towards **2** ~ **a algn** : speak to s.o., write to s.o.

discernir {25} *vt* : discern, distinguish — **discernimiento** *nm* : discernment

disciplinar *vt* : discipline — **disciplina** *nf* : discipline

discípulo, -la *n* : disciple, follower

disco *nm* **1** : disc, disk **2** : discus (in sports) **3** ~ **compacto** : compact disc

discordante *adj* : discordant — **discordia** *nf* : discord

discoteca *nf* : disco, discotheque

discreción *nf, pl* **-ciones** : discretion

discrepancia *nf* **1** : discrepancy **2** DESACUERDO : disagreement — **discrepar** *vi* : differ, disagree

discreto, -ta *adj* : discreet

discriminar *vt* **1** : discriminate against **2** DISTINGUIR : distinguish — **discriminación** *nf, pl* **-ciones** : discrimination

disculpar *vt* : excuse, pardon — **disculparse** *vr* : apologize — **disculpa** *nf* **1** : apology **2** EXCUSA : excuse

discurrir *vi* **1** : pass, go by **2** REFLEXIONAR : ponder, reflect

discurso *nm* : speech, discourse

discutir *vt* **1** : discuss **2** CUESTIONAR : dispute — *vi* : argue — **discusión** *nf, pl* **-siones 1** : discussion **2** DISPUTA : argument — **discutible** *adj* : debatable

disecar {72} *vt* : dissect — **disección** *nf, pl* **-ciones** : dissection

diseminar *vt* : disseminate, spread

disentería *nf* : dysentery

disentir {76} *vi* ~ **de** : disagree with — **disentimiento** *nm* : disagreement, dissent

diseñar *vt* : design — **diseñador, -dora** *n* : designer — **diseño** *nm* : design

disertación *nf, pl* **-ciones 1** : lecture **2** : (written) dissertation

disfrazar {21} *vt* : disguise — **disfrazarse** *vr* ~ **de** : disguise oneself as — **disfraz** *nm, pl* **-fraces 1** : disguise **2** : costume (for a party, etc.)

disfrutar *vt* : enjoy — *vi* : enjoy oneself

disgustar *vt* : upset, annoy — **disgustarse** *vr* **1** : get annoyed **2** ENEMISTARSE : fall out (with s.o.) — **disgusto** *nm* **1** : annoyance, displeasure **2** RIÑA : quarrel

disidente *adj & nmf* : dissident

disimular *vt* : conceal, hide — *vi* : pretend — **disimulo** *nm* : pretense

disipar *vt* **1** : dispel **2** DERROCHAR : squander

diskette [dĭ'sket] *nm* : floppy disk, diskette

dislexia *nf* : dyslexia — **disléxico, -ca** *adj* : dyslexic

dislocar {72} *vt* : dislocate — **dislocarse** *vr* : become dislocated

disminuir {41} *vt* : reduce — *vi* : decrease, drop — **disminución** *nf, pl* **-ciones** : decrease

disociar *vt* : dissociate

disolver {89} *vt* : dissolve — **disolverse** *vr* : dissolve

disparar *vi* : shoot, fire — *vt* : shoot — **dispararse** *vr* : shoot up, skyrocket

disparatado, -da *adj* : absurd — **disparate** *nm* : nonsense, silly thing

disparejo, -ja *adj* : uneven — **disparidad** *nf* : difference, disparity

disparo *nm* : shot

dispensar *vt* **1** : dispense, distribute **2** DISCULPAR : excuse

dispersar *vt* : disperse, scatter — **dispersarse** *vr* : disperse — **dispersión** *nf, pl* **-siones** : scattering

disponer {60} *vt* **1** : arrange, lay out **2** ORDENAR : decide, stipulate — *vi* ~ **de** : have at one's disposal — **disponerse** *vr* ~ **a** : be ready to — **disponibilidad** *nf* : availability — **disponible** *adj* : available

disposición *nf, pl* **-ciones 1** : arrangement **2** APTITUD : aptitude **3** : order, provision (in law) **4 a** ~ **de** : at the disposal of

dispositivo *nm* : device, mechanism

dispuesto, -ta *adj* : prepared, ready

disputar *vi* **1** : argue COMPETIR : compete — *vt* : dispute — **disputa** *nf* : dispute, argument

disquete → diskette

distanciar *vt* : space out — **distanciarse** *vr* : grow apart — **distancia** *nf* : distance — **distante** *adj* : distant

distinguir {26} *vt* : distinguish — **distinguirse** *vr* : distinguish oneself, stand out — **distinción** *nf, pl* **-ciones** : distinction — **distintivo, -va** *adj* : distinctive — **distinto, -ta** *adj* **1** : different **2** CLARO : distinct, clear

distorsión *nf, pl* **-siones** : distortion

distraer {81} *vt* **1** : distract **2** DIVERTIR : entertain — **distraerse** *vr* **1** : get distracted **2** ENTRETENERSE : amuse oneself — **distracción** *nf, pl* **-ciones 1** : amusement **2** DESPISTE : absentmindedness — **distraído, -da** *adj* : distracted, absentminded

distribuir {41} *vt* : distribute — **distribución** *nf, pl* **-ciones** : distribution — **distribuidor, -dora** *n* : distributor

distrito *nm* : district

disturbio *nm* : disturbance

disuadir *vt* : dissuade, discourage — **disuasivo, -va** *adj* : deterrent

diurno, -na *adj* : day, daytime

divagar {52} *vi* : digress

diván *nm, pl* **-vanes** : divan, couch

divergir {35} *vi* **1** : diverge **2** ~ **en** : differ on

diversidad *nf* : diversity

diversificar {72} *vt* : diversify

diversión *nf, pl* **-siones** : fun, entertainment

diverso, -sa *adj* : diverse

divertir {76} *vt* : entertain — **divertirse** *vr* : enjoy oneself, have fun — **divertido, -da** *adj* : entertaining

dividendo *nm* : dividend

dividir *vt* **1** : divide **2** REPARTIR : distribute

divinidad *nf* : divinity — **divino, -na** *adj* : divine

divisa *nf* **1** : currency **2** EMBLEMA : emblem

divisar *vt* : discern, make out

división *nf, pl* **-siones** : division — **divisor** *nm* : denominator

divorciar *vt* : divorce — **divorciarse** *vr* : get a divorce — **divorciado, -da** *n* : divorcé *m*, divorcée *f* — **divorcio** *nm* : divorce

divulgar {52} *vt* **1** : divulge, reveal **2** PROPAGAR : spread, circulate

dizque *adv Lat* : supposedly, apparently

doblar {64} *vt* **1** : double **2** PLEGAR : fold **3** : turn (a corner) **4** : dub (a film) — *vi* : turn — **doblarse** *vr* **1** : double over **2** ~ **a** : give in to — **dobladillo** *nm* : hem — **doble** *adj* & *nm* : double — ~ *nmf* : stand-in, double — **doblemente** *adv* : doubly — **doblegar** {52} *vt* : force to yield — **doblegarse** *vr* : give in — **doblez** *nm, pl* **-bleces** : fold, crease

doce *adj* & *nm* : twelve — **doceavo, -va** *adj* : twelfth — **docena** *nf* : dozen

docente *adj* : teaching

dócil *adj* : docile

doctor, -tora *n* : doctor — **doctorado** *nm* : doctorate

doctrina *nf* : doctrine

documentar *vt* : document — **documentación** *nf, pl* **-ciones** : documentation — **documental** *adj* & *nm* : documentary — **documento** *nm* : document

dogma *nm* : dogma — **dogmático, -ca** *adj* : dogmatic

dólar *nm* : dollar

doler {47} vi 1 : hurt 2 me duelen los pies : my feet hurt — **dolerse** vr ~ de : complain about — **dolor** nm 1 : pain 2 PENA : grief 3 ~ de cabeza : headache 4 ~ de estómago : stomachache — **dolorido, -da** 1 : sore 2 AFLIGIDO : hurt — **doloroso, -sa** adj : painful

domar vt : tame, break in

domesticar {72} vt : domesticate, tame — **doméstico, -ca** adj : domestic

domicilio nm : home, residence

dominar vt 1 : dominate, control 2 : master (a subject, a language, etc.) — **dominarse** vr : control oneself — **dominación** nf, pl **-ciones** : domination — **dominante** adj : dominant

domingo nm 1 : Sunday — **dominical** adj periódico ~ : Sunday newspaper

dominio nm 1 : authority 2 : mastery (of a subject) 3 TERRITORIO : domain

dominó nm, pl **-nós** : dominoes pl (game)

don¹ nm : courtesy title preceding a man's first name

don² nm 1 : gift 2 TALENTO : talent — **donación** nf, pl **-ciones** : donation — **donador, -dora** n : donor

donaire nm : grace, charm

donar vt : donate — **donante** nmf : donor — **donativo** nm : donation

donde conj : where — ~ prep Lat : over by

dónde adv 1 : where 2 ¿de ~ eres? : where are you from? 3 ¿por ~? : whereabouts?

dondequiera adv 1 : anywhere 2 ~ que : wherever, everywhere

doña nf : courtesy title preceding a woman's first name

doquier adv por ~ : everywhere

dorar vt 1 : gild 2 : brown (food) — **dorado, -da** adj : gold, golden

dormir {27} vt : put to sleep — vi : sleep — **dormirse** vr : fall asleep — **dormido, -da** adj 1 : asleep 2 ENTUMECIDO : numb — **dormilón, -lona** n : sleepyhead, late riser — **dormitar** vi : doze — **dormitorio** nm 1 : bedroom 2 : dormitory (in a college)

dorso nm : back

dos adj & nm : two — **doscientos, -tas** adj : two hundred — **doscientos** nms & pl : two hundred

dosel nm : canopy

dosis nfs & pl : dose, dosage

dotar vt : provide, equip 2 ~ de : endow with — **dotación** nf, pl **-ciones** 1 : endowment, funding 2 PERSONAL : personnel — **dote** nf 1 : dowry 2 ~s nfpl : gift, talent

dragar {52} vt : dredge — **draga** nf : dredge

dragón nm, pl **-gones** : dragon

drama nm : drama — **dramático, -ca** adj : dramatic — **dramatizar** {21} vt : dramatize — **dramaturgo, -ga** n : dramatist, playwright

drástico, -ca adj : drastic

drenar vt : drain — **drenaje** nm : drainage

droga nf : drug — **drogadicto, -ta** n : drug addict — **drogar** {52} vt : drug — **drogarse** vr : take drugs — **droguería** nf : drugstore

dromedario nm : dromedary

dual adj : dual

ducha nf : shower — **ducharse** vr : take a shower

ducho, -cha adj : experienced, skilled

duda nf : doubt — **dudar** vt : doubt — vi ~ en : hesitate to — **dudoso, -sa** adj 1 : doubtful 2 SOSPECHOSO : questionable

duelo nm 1 : duel 2 LUTO : mourning

duende nm : elf, imp

dueño, -na n 1 : owner 2 : landlord, landlady f

dulce adj 1 : sweet 2 : fresh (of water) 3 SUAVE : mild, gentle — ~ nm : candy, sweet — **dulzura** nf : sweetness

duna nf : dune

dúo nm : duo, duet

duodécimo, -ma adj : twelfth — ~ n : twelfth (in a series)

dúplex nms & pl : duplex (apartment)

duplicar {72} vt 1 : double 2 : duplicate, copy (a document, etc.) — **duplicado, -da** adj : duplicate — **duplicado** nm : copy

duque nm : duke — **duquesa** nf : duchess

durabilidad nf : durability

duración nf, pl **-ciones** : duration, length

duradero, -ra adj : durable, lasting

durante prep 1 : during 2 ~ una hora : for an hour

durar vi : endure, last

durazno nm Lat : peach

duro, -ra adj : hard 2 SEVERO : harsh — **dureza** nf 1 : hardness 2 SEVERIDAD : harshness

E

e¹ *nf* : e, fifth letter of the Spanish alphabet

e² *conj* (*used instead of* **y** *before words beginning with* **i** *or* **hi**) : and

ebanista *nmf* : cabinetmaker

ébano *nm* : ebony

ebrio, -bria *adj* : drunk

ebullición *nf, pl* **-ciones** : boiling

echar *vt* **1** : throw, cast **2** EXPULSAR : expel, dismiss **3** : give off, emit (smoke, sparks, etc.) **4** BROTAR : sprout **5** PONER : put (on) **6** ~ **a perder** : spoil, ruin **7** ~ **de menos** : miss — **echarse** *vr* **1** : throw oneself **2** ACOSTARSE : lie down **3** ~ **a** : start (to)

eclesiástico, -ca *adj* : ecclesiastic — ~ *nm* : clergyman

eclipse *nm* : eclipse — **eclipsar** *vt* : eclipse

eco *nm* : echo

ecología *nf* **1** : ecology — **ecológico, -ca** *adj* : ecological — **ecologista** *nmf* : ecologist

economía *nf* **1** : economy **2** : economics (science) — **económico, -ca** *adj* **1** : economic, economical **2** BARATO : inexpensive — **economista** *nmf* : economist — **economizar** {21} *v* : save

ecosistema *nm* : ecosystem

ecuación *nf, pl* **-ciones** : equation

ecuador *nm* : equator

ecuánime *adj* **1** : even-tempered **2** : impartial (in law)

ecuatoriano, -na *adj* : Ecuadorian, Ecuadorean, Ecuadoran

ecuestre *adj* : equestrian

edad *nf* **1** : age **2 Edad Media** : Middle Ages *pl* **3** **¿qué ~ tienes?** : how old are you?

edición *nf, pl* **-ciones** **1** : publishing, publication **2** : edition (of a book, etc.)

edicto *nm* : edict

edificar {72} *vt* : build — **edificio** *nm* : building

editar *vt* **1** : publish **2** : edit (a film, a text, etc.) — **editor, -tora** *n* **1** : publisher **2** : editor — **editorial** *adj* : publishing — ~ *nm* : editorial — ~ *nf* : publishing house

edredón *nm, pl* **-dones** : (down) comforter, duvet

educar {72} *vt* **1** : educate **2** CRIAR : bring up, raise **3** : train (the body, the voice, etc.) — **educación** *nf, pl* **-ciones** **1** : education **2** MODALES : (good) manners *pl* — **educado, -da** *adj* : polite — **educador, -dora** *n* : educator — **educativo, -va** *adj* : educational

efectivo, -va *adj* **1** : effective **2** REAL : real — **efectivo** *nm* : cash — **efectivamente** *adv* **1** : really **2** POR SUPUESTO : yes, indeed — **efecto** *nm* **1** : effect **2 en ~** : in fact **3** ~**s** *nmpl* : goods, property — **efectuar** {3} *vt* : bring about, carry out

efervescente *adj* : effervescent — **efervescencia** *nf* : effervescence

eficaz *adj, pl* **-caces** **1** : effective **2** EFICIENTE : efficient — **eficacia** *nf* **1** : effectiveness **2** EFICIENCIA : efficiency — **eficiente** *adj* : efficient — **eficiencia** *nf* : efficiency

efímero, -ra *adj* : ephemeral

efusivo, -va *adj* : effusive

egipcio, -cia *adj* : Egyptian

ego *nm* : ego — **egocéntrico, -ca** *adj* : egocentric — **egoísmo** *nm* : egoism — **egoísta** *adj* : egoistic — ~ *nmf* : egoist

egresar *vi* : graduate — **egresado, -da** *n* : graduate — **egreso** *nm* : graduation, commencement

eje *nm* **1** : axis **2** : axle (of a wheel, etc.)

ejecutar *vt* **1** : execute, put to death **2** REALIZAR : carry out — **ejecución** *nf, pl* **-ciones** : execution — **ejecutivo, -va** *adj & n* : executive

ejemplar *adj* : exemplary — ~ *nm* **1** : copy, issue **2** EJEMPLO : example — **ejemplificar** {72} *vt* : exemplify — **ejemplo** *nm* **1** : example **2 por ~** : for example

ejercer {86} *vt* **1** : practice (a profession) **2** : exercise (a right, etc.) — *vi* ~ **de** : practice as, work as — **ejercicio** *nm* **1** : exercise **2** : practice (of a profession, etc.)

ejército *nm* : army

el, la *art, pl* **los, las** : the — **el** *pron* (*referring to masculine nouns*) **1** : the one **2** ~ **que** : he who, whoever, the one that

él *pron* : he, him

elaborar *vt* **1** : manufacture, produce **2** : draw up (a plan, etc.)

elástico, -ca *adj* : elastic — **elástico** *nm* : elastic — **elasticidad** *nf* : elasticity

elección *nf, pl* **-ciones 1** : election **2** SELECCIÓN : choice — **elector, -tora** *n* : voter — **electorado** *nm* : electorate — **electoral** *adj* : electoral

electricidad *nf* : electricity — **eléctrico, -ca** *adj* : electric, electrical — **electricista** *nmf* : electrician — **electrificar** {72} *vt* : electrify — **electrizar** {21} *vt* : electrify, thrill — **electrocutar** *vt* : electrocute

electrodo *nm* : electrode

electrodoméstico *nm* : electric appliance

electromagnético, -ca *adj* : electromagnetic

electrón *nm, pl* **-trones** : electron — **electrónico, -ca** *adj* : electronic — **electrónica** *nf* : electronics

elefante, -ta *n* : elephant

elegante *adj* : elegant — **elegancia** *nf* : elegance

elegía *nf* : elegy

elegir {28} *vt* **1** : elect **2** ESCOGER : choose, select — **elegible** *adj* : eligible

elemento *nm* : element — **elemental** *adj* **1** : elementary, basic **2** ESENCIAL : fundamental

elenco *nm* : cast (of actors)

elevar *vt* **1** : raise, lift **2** ASCENDER : elevate (in a hierarchy), promote — **elevarse** *vr* : rise — **elevación** *nf, pl* **-ciones** : elevation — **elevador** *nm* **1** : hoist **2** *Lat* : elevator

eliminar *vt* : eliminate — **eliminación** *nf, pl* **-ciones** : elimination

elipse *nf* : ellipse — **elíptico, -ca** *adj* : elliptical, elliptic

elite *or* **élite** *nf* : elite

elixir *or* **elíxir** *nm* : elixir

ella *pron* : she, her — **ello** *pron* : it — **ellos, ellas** *pron pl* **1** : they, them **2** de ellos, de ellas : theirs

elocuente *adj* : eloquent — **elocuencia** *nf* : eloquence

elogiar *vt* : praise — **elogio** *nm* : praise

eludir *vt* : avoid, elude

emanar *vi* ~ **de** : emanate from

emancipar *vt* : emancipate — **emanciparse** *vr* : free oneself — **emancipación** *nf, pl* **-ciones** : emancipation

embadurnar *vt* : smear, daub

embajada *nf* : embassy — **embajador, -dora** *n* : ambassador

embalar *vt* : wrap up, pack — **embalaje** *nm* : packing

embaldosar *vt* : pave with tiles

embalsamar *vt* : embalm

embalse *nm* : dam, reservoir

embarazar {21} *vt* **1** : make pregnant **2** IMPEDIR : restrict, hamper — **embarazada** *adj* : pregnant — **embarazo** *nm* **1** : pregnancy **2** IMPEDIMENTO : hindrance, obstacle — **embarazoso, -sa** *adj* : embarrassing

embarcar {72} *vt* : load — **embarcarse** *vr* : embark, board — **embarcación** *nf, pl* **-ciones** : boat, craft — **embarcadero** *nm* : pier, jetty — **embarco** *nm* : embarkation

embargar {52} *vt* **1** : seize, impound **2** : overwhelm (with emotion, etc.) — **embargo** *nm* **1** : embargo **2** : seizure (in law) **3** sin ~ : nevertheless

embarque *nm* : loading (of goods), boarding (of passengers)

embarrancar {72} *vi* : run aground

embarullarse *vr fam* : get mixed up

embaucar {72} *vt* : trick, swindle — **embaucador, -dora** *n* : swindler

embeber *vt* : absorb — *vi* : shrink — **embeberse** *vr* : become absorbed

embelesar *vt* : enchant, delight — **embelesado, -da** *adj* : spellbound

embellecer {53} *vt* : embellish, beautify

embestir {54} *vt* : attack, charge at — *vi* : charge, attack — **embestida** *nf* **1** : attack **2** : charge (of a bull)

emblema *nm* : emblem

embobar *vt* : amaze, fascinate

embocadura *nf* **1** : mouth (of a river, etc.) **2** : mouthpiece (of an instrument)

émbolo *nm* : piston

embolsarse *vr* : put in one's pocket

emborracharse *vr* : get drunk

emborronar *vt* **1** : smudge, blot **2** GARABATEAR : scribble

emboscar {72} *vt* : ambush — **emboscada** *nf* : ambush

embotar *vt* : dull, blunt

embotellar *vt* : bottle (up) — **embotellamiento** *nm* : traffic jam

embrague *nm* : clutch — **embragar** {52} *vi* : engage the clutch

embriagarse {52} *vr* : get drunk — **embriagado, -da** *adj* : intoxicated, drunk — **embriagador, -dora** *adj* : intoxicating — **embriaguez** *nf* : drunkenness

embrión *nm, pl* **-briones** : embryo

embrollo *nm* : tangle, confusion

embrujar *vt* : bewitch — **embrujo** *nm* : spell, curse

embrutecer {53} *vt* : brutalize

embudo *nm* : funnel

embuste *nm* : lie — **embustero, -ra** *adj* : lying — **~** *n* : liar, cheat

embutir *vt* : stuff — **embutido** *nm* : sausage, cold meat

emergencia *nf* : emergency

emerger {15} *vi* : emerge, appear

emigrar *vi* 1 : emigrate 2 : migrate (of animals) — **emigración** *nf, pl* **-ciones** 1 : emigration 2 : migration (of animals) — **emigrante** *adj & nmf* : emigrant

eminente *adj* : eminent — **eminencia** *nf* : eminence

emitir *vt* 1 : emit 2 EXPRESAR : express (an opinion, etc.) 3 : broadcast (on radio or television) 4 : issue (money, stamps, etc.) — **emisión** *nf, pl* **-siones** 1 : emission 2 : broadcast (on radio or television) 3 : issue (of money, etc.) — **emisora** *nf* : radio station

emoción *nf, pl* **-ciones** : emotion — **emocional** *adj* : emotional — **emocionante** *adj* 1 : moving, touching 2 APASIONANTE : exciting, thrilling — **emocionar** *vt* 1 : move, touch 2 APASIONAR : excite, thrill — **emocionarse** *vr* 1 : be moved 2 APASIONARSE : get excited — **emotivo, -va** *adj* 1 : emotional 2 CONMOVEDOR : moving

empacar {72} *vt Lat* : pack

empachar *vt* : give indigestion to — **empacharse** *vr* : get indigestion — **empacho** *nm* : indigestion

empadronarse *vr* : register to vote

empalagoso, -sa *adj* : excessively sweet, cloying

empalizada *nf* : palisade (fence)

empalmar *vt* : connect, link — *vi* : meet, converge — **empalme** *nm* 1 : connection, link 2 : junction (of a railroad, etc.)

empanada *nf* : pie, turnover — **empanadilla** *nf* : meat or seafood pie

empanar *vt* : bread (in cooking)

empantanar *vt* : flood — **empantanarse** *vr* 1 : become flooded 2 : get bogged down

empañar *vt* 1 : steam (up) 2 : tarnish (one's reputation, etc.) — **empañarse** *vr* : fog up

empapar *vt* : soak — **empaparse** *vr* : get soaking wet

empapelar *vt* : wallpaper

empaquetar *vt* : pack, package

emparedado, -da *adj* : walled in, confined — **emparedado** *nm* : sandwich

emparejar *vt* : match up, pair — **emparejarse** *vr* : pair off

emparentado, -da *adj* : related, kindred

empastar *vt* : fill (a tooth) — **empaste** *nm* : filling

empatar *vi* : result in a draw, be tied — **empate** *nm* : draw, tie

empedernido, -da *adj* : inveterate, hardened

empedrar {55} *vt* : pave (with stones) — **empedrado** *nm* : paving, pavement

empeine *nm* : instep

empeñar *vt* : pawn — **empeñarse** *vr* 1 : insist, persist 2 ENDEUDARSE : go into debt 3 ~ **en** : make an effort to — **empeñado, -da** *adj* 1 : determined, committed 2 ENDEUDADO : in debt — **empeño** *nm* 1 : determination, effort 2 **casa de ~s** : pawnshop

empeorar *vi* : get worse — *vt* : make worse

empequeñecer {53} *vt* : diminish, make smaller

emperador *nm* : emperor — **emperatriz** *nf, pl* **-trices** : empress

empezar {29} *v* : start, begin

empinar *vt* : raise — **empinarse** *vr* : stand on tiptoe — **empinado, -da** *adj* : steep

empírico, -ca *adj* : empirical

emplasto *nm* : poultice

emplazar {21} *vt* 1 : summon, subpoena 2 SITUAR : place, locate — **emplazamiento** *nm* 1 : location, site 2 CITACIÓN : summons, subpoena

emplear *vt* 1 : employ 2 USAR : use — **emplearse** *vr* 1 : get a job 2 USARSE : be used — **empleado, -da** *n* : employee — **empleador, -dora** *n* : employer — **empleo** *nm* 1 : occupation, job 2 USO : use

empobrecer {53} *vt* : impoverish — **empobrecerse** *vr* : become poor

empollar *v* : brood (eggs) — *vt* : incubate

empolvarse *vr* : powder one's face

empotrar *vt* : fit, build into — **empotrado, -da** *adj* : built-in

emprender *vt* : undertake, begin — **emprendedor, -dora** *adj* : enterprising

empresa *nf* 1 COMPAÑÍA : company, firm 2 TAREA : undertaking — **empresarial** *adj* : business, managerial — **empresario, -ria** *n* 1 : businessman *m*, businesswoman *f* 2 : impresario (in theater), promoter (in sports)

empujar *v* : push — **empuje** *nm* : impetus, drive — **empujón** *nm, pl* **-jones** : push, shove

empuñar *vt* : grasp, take hold of

emular *vt* : emulate

en *prep* 1 : in 2 DENTRO DE : into, inside

(of) **3** SOBRE : on **4** ~ **avión** : by plane **5** ~ **casa** : at home

enajenar vt : alienate — **enajenación** nf, pl **-ciones** : alienation

enagua nf : slip, petticoat

enaltecer {53} vt : praise, extol

enamorar vt : win the love of — **enamorarse** vr : fall in love — **enamorado, -da** adj : in love — ~ n : lover, sweetheart

enano, -na adj & n : dwarf

enarbolar vt : hoist, raise **2** : brandish (arms, etc.)

enardecer {53} vt : stir up, excite

encabezar {21} vt **1** : head, lead **2** : put a heading on (an article, a list, etc.) — **encabezamiento** nm **1** : heading **2** : headline (in a newspaper)

encabritarse vr : rear up

encadenar vt **1** : chain, tie (up) **2** ENLAZAR : connect, link

encajar vt : fit (together) — vi **1** : fit **2** CUADRAR : conform, tally — **encaje** nm : lace

encalar vt : whitewash

encallar vi : run aground

encaminar vt : direct, aim — **encaminarse** vr ~ **a** : head for — **encaminado, -da** adj ~ **a** : aimed at, designed to

encandilar vt : dazzle

encanecer {53} vi : turn gray

encantar vt : enchant, bewitch — vi me encanta esta canción : I love this song — **encantado, -da** adj **1** : delighted **2** HECHIZADO : bewitched — **encantador, -dora** adj : charming, delightful — **encantamiento** nm : enchantment, spell — **encanto** nm **1** : charm, fascination **2** HECHIZO : spell

encapotarse vr : cloud over — **encapotado, -da** adj : overcast

encapricharse vr ~ **con** : be infatuated with

encapuchado, -da adj : hooded

encaramar vt : lift up — **encaramarse** vr ~ **a** : climb up on

encarar vt : face, confront

encarcelar vt : imprison — **encarcelamiento** nm : imprisonment

encarecer {53} vt : increase, raise (price, value, etc.) — **encarecerse** vr : become more expensive

encargar {52} vt **1** : put in charge of **2** PEDIR : order — **encargarse** vr ~ **de** : take charge of — **encargado, -da** adj : in charge — ~ n : manager, person in charge — **encargo** nm **1** : errand **2** TAREA : assignment, task **3** PEDIDO : order

encariñarse vr ~ **con** : become fond of

encarnar vt : embody — **encarnación** nf, pl **-ciones** : embodiment — **encarnado, -da** adj **1** : incarnate **2** ROJO : red

encarnizarse {21} vr ~ **con** : attack viciously — **encarnizado, -da** adj : bitter, bloody

encarrilar vt : put on the right track

encasillar vt : pigeonhole

encauzar {21} vt : channel

encender {56} vt **1** : light, set fire to **2** PRENDER : switch on, start **3** AVIVAR : arouse (passions, etc.) — **encenderse** vr **1** : get excited **2** RUBORIZARSE : blush — **encendedor** nm : lighter — **encendido, -da** adj : lit, on — **encendido** nm : ignition (switch)

encerar vt : wax, polish — **encerado, -da** adj : waxed — **encerado** nm : blackboard

encerrar {55} vt **1** : lock up, shut away **2** CONTENER : contain

encestar vt : score (in basketball)

enchilada nf : enchilada

enchufar vt : plug in, connect — **enchufe** nm : plug, socket

encía nf : gum (tissue)

encíclica nf : encyclical

enciclopedia nf : encyclopedia — **enciclopédico, -ca** adj : encyclopedic

encierro nm **1** : confinement **2** : sit-in (at a university, etc.)

encima adv **1** : on top **2** ADEMÁS : as well, besides **3** ~ **de** : on, over, on top of **4** por ~ **de** : above, beyond

encinta adj : pregnant

enclenque adj : weak, sickly

encoger {15} v : shrink — **encogerse** vr **1** : shrink **2** : cower, cringe **3** ~ **de hombros** : shrug (one's shoulders) — **encogido, -da** adj **1** : shrunken **2** TÍMIDO : shy

encolar vt : glue, stick

encolerizar {21} vt : enrage, infuriate — **encolerizarse** vr : get angry

encomendar {55} vt : entrust

encomienda nf **1** : charge, mission **2** Lat : parcel

encono nm : rancor, animosity

encontrar {19} vt **1** : find **2** : meet, encounter (difficulties, etc.) — **encontrarse** vr **1** : meet **2** HALLARSE : find oneself, be — **encontrado, -da** adj : contrary, opposing

encorvar vt : bend, curve — **encorvarse** vr : bend over, stoop

encrespar vt **1** : curl **2** IRRITAR : irritate — **encresparse** vr **1** : curl one's hair

2 IRRITARSE : get annoyed **3** : become choppy (of the sea)

encrucijada *nf* : crossroads

encuadernar *vt* : bind (a book) — **encuadernación** *nf*, *pl* **-ciones** : bookbinding

encuadrar *vt* **1** : frame **2** ENCAJAR : fit **3** COMPRENDER : contain, include

encubrir {2} *vt* : conceal, cover (up) — **encubierto, -ta** *adj* : covert — **encubrimiento** *nm* : cover-up

encuentro *nm* : meeting, encounter

encuestar *vt* : poll, take a survey of — **encuesta** *nf* **1** : investigation, inquiry **2** SONDEO : survey — **encuestador, -dora** *n* : pollster

encumbrado, -da *adj* : eminent, distinguished

encurtir *vt* : pickle

endeble *adj* : weak, feeble — **endeblez** *nf* : weakness, frailty

endemoniado, -da *adj* : wicked

enderezar {21} *vt* **1** : straighten (out) **2** : put upright, stand on end

endeudarse *vr* : go into debt — **endeudado, -da** *adj* : indebted, in debt — **endeudamiento** *nm* : debt

endiablado, -da *adj* **1** : wicked, diabolical **2** : complicated, difficult

endibia *or* **endivia** *nf* : endive

endosar *vt* : endorse — **endoso** *nm* : endorsement

endulzar {21} *vt* **1** : sweeten **2** : soften, mellow (a tone, a response, etc.) — **endulzante** *nm* : sweetener

endurecer {53} *vt* : harden — **endurecerse** *vr* : become hardened

enema *nm* : enema

enemigo, -ga *adj* : hostile — **~** *n* : enemy — **enemistad** *nf* : enmity — **enemistar** *vt* : make enemies of — **enemistarse** *vr* ~ **con** : fall out with

energía *nf* : energy — **enérgico, -ca** *adj* : energetic, vigorous, forceful

enero *nm* : January

enervar *vt* **1** : enervate, weaken **2** *fam* : get on one's nerves

enésimo, -ma *adj* **por enésima vez** : for the umpteenth time

enfadar *vt* : annoy, make angry — **enfadarse** *vr* : get annoyed — **enfado** *nm* : anger, annoyance — **enfadoso, -sa** *adj* : annoying

enfatizar {21} *vt* : emphasize — **énfasis** *nms & pl* : emphasis — **enfático, -ca** *adj* : emphatic

enfermar *vi* : make sick — *vi* : get sick — **enfermedad** *nf* : sickness, disease — **enfermería** *nf* : infirmary — **enfermero, -ra** *n* : nurse — **enfermizo, -za**

adj : sickly — **enfermo, -ma** *adj* : sick — **~** *n* : sick person, patient

enflaquecer {53} *vi* : lose weight

enfocar {72} *vt* **1** : focus (on) **2** : consider (a problem, etc.) — **enfoque** *nm* : focus

enfrascarse {72} *vr* ~ **en** : immerse oneself in, get caught up in

enfrentar *vt* **1** : confront, face **2** : bring face to face — **enfrentarse** *vr* ~ **con** : confront, clash with — **enfrente** *adv* **1** : opposite **2** ~ **de** : in front of

enfriar {85} *vt* : chill, cool — **enfriarse** *vr* **1** : get cold **2** RESFRIARSE : catch a cold — **enfriamiento** *nm* **1** : cooling off **2** CATARRO : cold

enfurecer {53} *vt* : infuriate — **enfurecerse** *vr* : fly into a rage

enfurruñarse *vr fam* : sulk

engalanar *vt* : decorate — **engalanarse** *vr* : dress up

enganchar *vt* : hook, snag, catch — **engancharse** *vr* **1** : get caught **2** ALISTARSE : enlist

engañar *vt* **1** EMBAUCAR : trick, deceive **2** : cheat on, be unfaithful to — **engañarse** *vr* **1** : deceive oneself **2** EQUIVOCARSE : be mistaken — **engaño** *nm* : deception, deceit — **engañoso, -sa** *adj* : deceptive, deceitful

engatusar *vt* : coax, cajole

engendrar *vt* **1** : beget **2** : engender, give rise to (suspicions, etc.)

englobar *vt* : include, embrace

engomar *vt* : glue

engordar *vt* : fatten — *vi* : gain weight

engorroso, -sa *adj* : bothersome

engranar *v* : mesh, engage — **engranaje** *nm* : gears *pl*

engrandecer {53} *vt* **1** : enlarge **2** ENALTECER : exalt

engrapar *vt Lat* : staple — **engrapadora** *nf Lat* : stapler

engrasar *vt* : lubricate, grease — **engrase** *nm* : lubrication

engreído, -da *adj* : conceited

engrosar {19} *vt* : swell — *vi* : gain weight

engrudo *nm* : paste

engullir {38} *vt* : gulp down, gobble up

enhebrar *vt* : thread

enhorabuena *nf* : congratulations *pl*

enigma *nm* : enigma — **enigmático, -ca** *adj* : enigmatic

enjabonar *vt* : soap (up), lather

enjaezar {21} *vt* : harness

enjalbegar {52} *vt* : whitewash

enjambrar *vi* : swarm — **enjambre** *nm* : swarm

enjaular *vt* **1** : cage **2** *fam* : jail

enjuagar {52} *vt* : rinse — **enjuague** *nm* 1 : rinse 2 ~ **bucal** : mouthwash

enjugar {52} *vt* 1 : wipe away (tears) 2 : wipe out (debt)

enjuiciar *vt* 1 : prosecute 2 JUZGAR : try

enjuto, -ta *adj* : gaunt, lean

enlace *nm* 1 : bond, link 2 : junction (of a highway, etc.)

enlatar *vt* : can

enlazar {21} *vt* : join, link — *vi* ~ **con** : link up with

enlistarse *vr Lat* : enlist

enlodar *vt* : cover with mud

enloquecer {53} *vt* : drive crazy — **enloquecerse** *vr* : go crazy

enlosar *vt* : pave, tile

enlutarse *vr* : go into mourning

enmarañar *vt* 1 : tangle 2 COMPLICAR : complicate 3 CONFUNDIR : confuse — **enmarañarse** *vr* 1 : get tangled up 2 CONFUNDIRSE : become confused

enmarcar {72} *vt* : frame

enmascarar *vt* : mask

enmendar {55} *vt* 1 : amend 2 CORREGIR : emend, correct — **enmendarse** *vr* : mend one's ways — **enmienda** *nf* 1 : amendment 2 CORRECCIÓN : correction

enmohecerse {53} *vr* 1 : become moldy 2 OXIDARSE : rust

enmudecer {53} *vt* : silence — *vi* : fall silent

ennegrecer {53} *vt* : blacken

ennoblecer {53} *vt* : ennoble, dignify

enojar *vt* 1 : anger 2 MOLESTAR : annoy — **enojarse** *vr* ~ **con** : get upset with — **enojo** *nm* 1 : anger 2 MOLESTIA : annoyance — **enojoso, -sa** *adj* : annoying

enorgullecer {53} *vt* : make proud — **enorgullecerse** *vr* ~ **de** : pride oneself on

enorme *adj* : enormous — **enormemente** *adv* : enormously, extremely — **enormidad** *nf* : enormity

enraizar {30} *vi* : take root

enredadera *nf* : climbing plant, vine

enredar *vt* 1 : tangle up, entangle 2 CONFUNDIR : confuse 3 IMPLICAR : involve — **enredarse** *vr* 1 : become entangled 2 ~ **en** : get mixed up in — **enredo** *nm* 1 : tangle 2 EMBROLLO : confusion, mess — **enredoso, -sa** *adj* : tangled up, complicated

enrejado *nm* 1 : railing 2 REJILLA : grating, grille 3 : trellis (for plants)

enrevesado, -da *adj* : complicated

enriquecer {53} *vt* : enrich — **enriquecerse** *vr* : get rich

enrojecer {53} *vt* : redden — **enrojecerse** *vr* : blush

enrolar *vt* : enlist — **enrolarse** *vr* ~ **en** : enlist in

enrollar *vt* : roll up, coil

enroscar {72} *vt* 1 : roll up 2 ATORNILLAR : screw in

ensalada *nf* : salad

ensalzar {21} *vt* : praise

ensamblar *vt* : assemble, fit together

ensanchar *vt* 1 : widen 2 AMPLIAR : expand — **ensanche** *nm* 1 : widening 2 : (urban) expansion, development

ensangrentado, -da *adj* : bloody, bloodstained

ensañarse *vr* : act cruelly

ensartar *vt* : string, thread

ensayar *vi* : rehearse — *vt* : try out, test — **ensayo** *nm* 1 : essay 2 PRUEBA : trial, test 3 : rehearsal (in theater, etc.)

enseguida *adv* : right away, immediately

ensenada *nf* : inlet, cove

enseñar *vt* 1 : teach 2 MOSTRAR : show — **enseñanza** *nf* 1 EDUCACIÓN : education 2 INSTRUCCIÓN : teaching

enseres *nmpl* 1 : equipment 2 ~ **domésticos** : household goods

ensillar *vt* : saddle (up)

ensimismarse *vr* : lose oneself in thought

ensombrecer {53} *vt* : cast a shadow over, darken

ensoñación *nf, pl* **-ciones** : fantasy, daydream

ensordecer {53} *vt* : deafen — *vi* : go deaf — **ensordecedor, -dora** *adj* : deafening

ensortijar *vt* : curl

ensuciar *vt* : soil — **ensuciarse** *vr* : get dirty

ensueño *nm* : daydream, fantasy

entablar *vt* : initiate, start

entallar *vt* : tailor, fit (clothing) — *vi* : fit

entarimado *nm* : floorboards, flooring

ente *nm* 1 : being 2 ORGANISMO : body, organization

entender {56} *vt* 1 : understand 2 OPINAR : think, believe — *vi* 1 : understand 2 ~ **de** : know about, be good at — **entenderse** *vr* 1 : understand each other 2 LLEVARSE BIEN : get along well — ~ *nm* **a mí** ~ : in my opinion — **entendido, -da** *adj* 1 : understood 2 **eso se da por** ~ : that goes without saying 3 **tener** ~ : be under the impression — **entendimiento** *nm* 1 : understanding 2 INTELIGENCIA : intellect

enterar vt : inform — **enterarse** vr
: find out, learn — **enterado, -da** adj
: well-informed

entereza nf 1 HONRADEZ : integrity 2
FORTALEZA : fortitude 3 FIRMEZA : resolve

enternecer {53} vt : move, touch

entero, -ra adj 1 : whole 2 TOTAL : absolute, total 3 INTACTO : intact — **entero** nm : integer, whole number

enterrar {55} vt : bury

entibiar vt : cool (down) — **entibiarse**
vr : become lukewarm

entidad nf 1 : entity 2 ORGANIZACIÓN
: body, organization

entierro nm 1 : burial 2 : funeral (ceremony)

entomología nf : entomology — **ento-
mólogo, -ga** n : entomologist

entonar vt : sing, intone — vi : be in
tune

entonces adv 1 : then 2 **desde ~**
: since then

entornado, -da adj : half-closed, ajar

entorno nm : surroundings pl, environment

entorpecer {53} vt 1 : hinder, obstruct
2 : numb, dull (wits, reactions, etc.)

entrada nf 1 : entrance, entry 2 BILLETE
: ticket 3 COMIENZO : beginning 4 : inning (in baseball) 5 **~s** nfpl : income
6 **tener ~s** : have a receding hairline

entraña nf 1 : core, heart 2 **~s** nfpl
VÍSCERAS : entrails, innards — **en-
trañable** adj : close, intimate — **en-
trañar** vt : involve

entrar vi 1 : enter 2 EMPEZAR : begin —
vt : introduce, bring in

entre prep 1 : between 2 : among

entreabrir {2} vt : leave ajar — **entreabierto, -ta** adj : half-open, ajar

entreacto nm : intermission

entrecejo nm **fruncir el ~** : knit one's
brows, frown

entrecortado, -da adj : faltering (of the
voice), labored (of breathing)

entrecruzar {21} vi : intertwine

entredicho nm : doubt, question

entregar {52} vt : deliver, hand over —
entregarse vr : surrender — **entrega**
nf 1 : delivery 2 DEDICACIÓN : dedication, devotion 3 **~ inicial** : down payment

entrelazar {21} vt : intertwine — **entrelazarse** vr : become intertwined

entremés nm, pl **-meses** 1 : hors
d'oeuvre 2 : short play (in theater)

entremeterse → entrometerse

entremezclar vt : mix (up)

entrenar vt : train, drill — **entrenarse**

vr : train — **entrenador, -dora** n
: trainer, coach — **entrenamiento** nm
: training

entrepierna nf : crotch

entresacar {72} vt : pick out, select

entresuelo nm : mezzanine

entretanto adv : meanwhile — **~ nm**
en el ~ : in the meantime

entretener {80} vt 1 : entertain 2 DE-
SPISTAR : distract 3 RETRASAR : delay,
hold up — **entretenerse** vr 1 : amuse
oneself 2 DEMORARSE : dawdle — **en-
tretenido, -da** adj : entertaining —
entretenimiento nm 1 : entertainment, amusement 2 PASATIEMPO : pastime

entrever {88} vt : catch a glimpse of,
make out

entrevistar vt : interview — **entrevista**
nf : interview — **entrevistador, -dora**
n : interviewer

entristecer {53} vt : sadden

entrometerse vr : interfere — **entrometido, -da** adj : meddling, nosy
— n : meddler

entroncar {72} vi : be related, be connected

entumecer {53} vt : make numb — **entumecerse** vr : go numb — **entumecido, -da** adj 1 : numb 2 : stiff (of
muscles, etc.)

enturbiar vt : cloud — **enturbiarse** vr
: become cloudy

entusiasmar vt : fill with enthusiasm
— **entusiasmarse** vr : get excited —
entusiasmo nm : enthusiasm — **entusiasta** adj : enthusiastic — **~ nmf**
: enthusiast

enumerar vt : enumerate, list — **enumeración** nf, pl **-ciones** : enumera-
tion, count

enunciar vt : enunciate — **enun-
ciación** nf, pl **-ciones** : enunciation

envalentonar vt : make bold, encourage — **envalentonarse** vr : be brave

envanecerse {53} vr : become vain

envasar vt : package 2 : bottle, can —
envase nm 1 : packaging 2 RECIPIENTE
: container 3 : jar, bottle, can

envejecer {53} v : age — **envejecido,
-da** adj : aged, old — **envejecimiento**
nm : aging

envenenar vt : poison — **envene-
namiento** nm : poisoning

envergadura nf 1 ALCANCE : scope 2
: span (of wings, etc.)

envés nm, pl **-veses** : reverse side

enviar {85} vt : send — **enviado, -da** n
: envoy, correspondent

envidiar vt : envy — **envidia** nf : envy,

jealousy — **envidioso, -sa** *adj* : jealous, envious

envilecer {53} *vt* : degrade, debase — **envilecimiento** *nm* : degradation

envío *nm* **1** : sending, shipment **2** : remittance (of funds)

enviudar *vi* : be widowed

envolver {89} *vt* **1** : wrap **2** RODEAR : surround **3** IMPLICAR : involve — **envoltorio** *nm* or **envoltura** *nf* : wrapping, wrapper

enyesar *vt* **1** : plaster **2** ESCAYOLAR : put in a plaster cast

enzima *nf* : enzyme

épico, -ca *adj* : epic — **épica** *nf* : epic

epidemia *nf* : epidemic — **epidémico, -ca** *adj* : epidemic

epilepsia *nf* : epilepsy — **epiléptico, -ca** *adj* & *n* : epileptic

epílogo *nm* : epilogue

episodio *nm* : episode

epitafio *nm* : epitaph

epíteto *nm* : epithet

época *nf* **1** : epoch, period **2** ESTACIÓN : season

epopeya *nf* : epic poem

equidad *nf* : equity, justice

equilátero, -ra *adj* : equilateral

equilibrar *vt* : balance — **equilibrado, -da** *adj* : well-balanced — **equilibrio** *nm* **1** : balance, equilibrium **2** JUICIO : good sense

equinoccio *nm* : equinox

equipaje *nm* : baggage, luggage

equipar *vt* : equip

equiparar *vt* **1** IGUALAR : make equal **2** COMPARAR : compare — **equiparable** *adj* : comparable

equipo *nm* **1** : equipment **2** : team, crew (in sports, etc.)

equitación *nf, pl* **-ciones** : horseback riding

equitativo, -va *adj* : equitable, fair, just

equivaler {84} *vi* : be equivalent — **equivalencia** *nf* : equivalence — **equivalente** *adj* & *nm* : equivalent

equivocar {72} *vt* : mistake, confuse — **equivocarse** *vr* : make a mistake — **equivocación** *nf, pl* **-ciones** : error, mistake — **equivocado, -da** *adj* : mistaken, wrong

equívoco, -ca *adj* : ambiguous — **equívoco** *nm* : misunderstanding

era *nf* : era

erario *nm* : public treasury, funds *pl*

erección *nf, pl* **-ciones** : erection

erguir {31} *vt* : raise, lift — **erguirse** *vr* : rise (up) — **erguido, -da** *adj* : erect, upright

erigir {35} *vt* : build, erect — **erigirse** *vr* ~ **en** : set oneself up as

erizarse {21} *vr* : bristle, stand on end — **erizado, -da** *adj* : bristly

erizo *nm* **1** : hedgehog **2** ~ **de mar** : sea urchin

ermitaño, -ña *n* : hermit

erosionar *vt* : erode — **erosión** *nf, pl* **-siones** : erosion

erótico, -ca *adj* : erotic

erradicar {72} *vt* : eradicate

errar {32} *vt* : miss — *vi* **1** : be wrong, be mistaken **2** VAGAR : wander — **errado, -da** *adj Lat* : wrong, mistaken

errata *nf* : misprint

errático, -ca *adj* : erratic

error *nm* : error — **erróneo, -nea** *adj* : erroneous, mistaken

eructar *vi* : belch, burp — **eructo** *nm* : belch, burp

erudito, -ta *adj* : erudite, learned

erupción *nf, pl* **-ciones** : eruption **2** SARPULLIDO : rash

esa, ésa → **ese, ése**

esbelto, -ta *adj* : slender, slim

esbozar {21} *vt* : sketch, outline — **esbozo** *nm* : sketch, outline

escabechar *vt* : pickle — **escabeche** *nm* : brine (for pickling)

escabel *nm* : footstool

escabroso, -sa *adj* **1** : rugged, rough **2** ESPINOSO : thorny, difficult **3** ATREVIDO : shocking, risqué

escabullirse {38} *vr* : slip away, escape

escalar *vt* : climb, scale — *vi* : escalate — **escala** *nf* **1** : scale **2** ESCALERA : ladder **3** : stopover (of an airplane, etc.) — **escalada** *nf* : ascent, climb — **escalador, -dora** *n* ALPINISTA : mountain climber

escaldar *vt* : scald

escalera *nf* **1** : stairs *pl*, staircase **2** ESCALA : ladder **3** ~ **mecánica** : escalator

escalfar *vt* : poach

escalinata *nf* : flight of stairs

escalofrío *nm* : shiver, chill — **escalofriante** *adj* : chilling, horrifying

escalonar *vt* **1** : stagger, spread out **2** : terrace (land) — **escalón** *nm, pl* **-lones** : step, rung

escama *nf* **1** : scale (of fish or reptiles) **2** : flake (of skin) — **escamoso, -sa** *adj* : scaly

escamotear *vt* **1** : conceal **2** ~ **algo a algn** : rob s.o. of sth

escandalizar {21} *vt* : scandalize — **escandalizarse** *vr* : be shocked — **escándalo** *nm* **1** : scandal **2** ALBOROTO : scene, commotion — **escandaloso,**

-sa *adj* **1** : shocking, scandalous **2** RUI-DOSO : noisy

escandinavo, -va *adj* : Scandinavian

escáner *nm* : scanner

escaño *nm* **1** : seat (in a legislative body) **2** BANCO : bench

escapar *vi* : escape, run away — **escaparse** *vr* **1** : escape **2** : leak out (of gas, water, etc.) — **escapada** *nf* : escape

escaparate *nm* : store window

escapatoria *nf* : loophole, way out

escape *nm* **1** : leak (of gas, water, etc.) **2** : exhaust (from a vehicle)

escarabajo *nm* : beetle

escarbar *vt* **1** : dig, scratch, poke **2 ~ en** : pry into

escarcha *nf* : frost (on a surface)

escarlata *adj & nf* : scarlet — **escarlatina** *nf* : scarlet fever

escarmentar {55} *vi* : learn one's lesson — **escarmiento** *nm* : lesson, punishment

escarnecer {53} *vt* : ridicule, mock — **escarnio** *nm* : ridicule, mockery

escarola *nf* : escarole, endive

escarpa *nf* : steep slope — **escarpado, -da** *adj* : steep

escasear *vi* : be scarce — **escasez** *nf, pl* **-seces** : shortage, scarcity — **escaso, -sa** *adj* **1** : scarce **2 ~ de** : short of

escatimar *vt* : be sparing with, skimp on

escayolar *vt* : put in a plaster cast — **escayola** *nf* **1** : plaster (for casts) **2** : plaster cast

escena *nf* **1** : scene **2** ESCENARIO : stage — **escenario** *nm* **1** : setting, scene **2** ESCENA : stage — **escénico, -ca** *adj* : scenic

escepticismo *nm* : skepticism — **escéptico, -ca** *adj* : skeptical — **~** *n* : skeptic

esclarecer {53} *vt* : shed light on, clarify

esclavo, -va *n* : slave — **esclavitud** *nf* : slavery — **esclavizar** {21} *vt* : enslave

esclerosis *nf* **~ múltiple** : multiple sclerosis

esclusa *nf* : floodgate, lock (of a canal)

escoba *nf* : broom

escocer {14} *vi* : sting

escocés, -cesa *adj, mpl* **-ceses 1** : Scottish **2** : tartan, plaid — **escocés** *nm, pl* **-ceses** : Scotch (whiskey)

escoger {15} *vt* : choose — **escogido, -da** *adj* : choice, select

escolar *adj* : school — **~** *nmf* : student, pupil

escolta *nmf* : escort — **escoltar** *vt* : escort, accompany

escombros *nmpl* : ruins, rubble

esconder *vt* : hide, conceal — **esconderse** *vr* : hide — **escondidas** *nfpl* **1** *Lat* : hide-and-seek **2 a ~** : secretly, in secret — **escondite** *nm* **1** : hiding place **2** : hide-and-seek (game) — **escondrijo** *nm* : hiding place

escopeta *nf* : shotgun

escoplo *nm* : chisel

escoria *nf* **1** : slag **2** : dregs *pl* (of society, etc.)

escorpión *nm, pl* **-piones** : scorpion

escote *nm* **1** : (low) neckline **2 pagar a ~** : go Dutch

escotilla *nf* : hatchway

escribir {33} *v* : write — **escribirse** *vr* **1** : write to one another, correspond **2** : be spelled — **escribiente** *nmf* : clerk — **escrito, -ta** *adj* : written — **escritos** *nmpl* : writings — **escritor, -tora** *n* : writer — **escritorio** *nm* : desk — **escritura** *nf* **1** : handwriting **2** : deed (in law)

escroto *nm* : scrotum

escrúpulo *nm* : scruple — **escrupuloso, -sa** *adj* : scrupulous

escrutar *vt* **1** : scrutinize **2** : count (votes) — **escrutinio** *nm* **1** : scrutiny **2** : count (of votes)

escuadra *nf* **1** : square (instrument) **2** : fleet (of ships), squad (in the military) — **escuadrón** *nm, pl* **-drones** : squadron

escuálido, -da *adj* **1** : skinny **2** SUCIO : squalid

escuchar *vt* **1** : listen to **2** *Lat* : hear — *vi* : listen

escudo *nm* **1** : shield **2 or ~ de armas** : coat of arms

escudriñar *vt* : scrutinize, examine

escuela *nf* : school

escueto, -ta *adj* : plain, simple

esculpir *v* : sculpt — **escultor, -tora** *n* : sculptor — **escultura** *nf* : sculpture

escupir *v* : spit

escurrir *vt* **1** : drain **2** : wring out (clothes) — *vi* **1** : drain **2** : drip-dry (of clothes) — **escurrirse** *vr* **1** : drain **2** *fam* : slip away — **escurridizo, -da** *adj* : slippery, evasive — **escurridor** *nm* **1** : dish drainer **2** COLADOR : colander

ese, esa *adj, mpl* **esos** : that, those

ése, esa *pron, mpl* **ésos** : that one, those ones *pl*

esencia *nf* : essence — **esencial** *adj* : essential

esfera *nf* **1** : sphere **2** : dial (of a watch) — **esférico, -ca** *adj* : spherical

esfinge *nf* : sphinx

esforzar {36} *vt* : strain — **esforzarse** *vr* : make an effort — **esfuerzo** *nm* : effort

esfumarse *vr* : fade away, vanish

esgrimir *vt* **1** : brandish, wield **2** : make use of (an argument, etc.) — **esgrima** *nf* **1** : fencing **2 hacer ~** : fence

esguince *nm* : sprain, strain

eslabonar *vt* : link, connect — **eslabón** *nm*, *pl* **-bones** : link

eslavo, -va *adj* : Slavic

eslogan *nm*, *pl* **-lóganes** : slogan

esmaltar *vt* : enamel — **esmalte** *nm* **1** : enamel **2 ~ de uñas** : nail polish

esmerado, -da *adj* : careful

esmeralda *nf* : emerald

esmerarse *vr* : take great care

esmeril *nm* : emery

esmoquin *nm*, *pl* **-móquines** : tuxedo

esnob *nmf*, *pl* **esnobs** : snob — **~** *adj* : snobbish

eso *pron* (*neuter*) **1** : that **2 ¡~ es!** : that's it!, that's right! **3 en ~** : at that point, then

esófago *nm* : esophagus

esos, ésos → ese, ése

espabilarse *vr* **1** : wake up **2 DARSE PRISA** : get moving — **espabilado, -da** *adj* **1** : awake **2 LISTO** : bright, clever

espaciar *vt* : space out, spread out — **espacial** *adj* : space — **espacio** *nm* **1** : space **2 ~ exterior** : outer space — **espacioso, -sa** *adj* : spacious

espada *nf* **1** : sword **2 ~s** *nfpl* : spades (in playing cards)

espagueti *nm or* **espaguetis** *nmpl* : spaghetti

espalda *nf* **1** : back **2 ~s** *nfpl* : shoulders, back

espantar *vt* : scare, frighten — **espantarse** *vr* : become frightened — **espantajo** *nm or* **espantapájaros** *nms & pl* : scarecrow — **espanto** *nm* **1** : fright, fear — **espantoso, -sa** *adj* **1** : frightening, horrific **2 TERRIBLE** : awful, terrible

español, -ñola *adj* : Spanish — **español** *nm* : Spanish (language)

esparadrapo *nm* : adhesive bandage

esparcir {83} *vt* : scatter, spread — **esparcirse** *vr* **1** : be scattered, spread out **2 DIVERTIRSE** : enjoy oneself

espárrago *nm* : asparagus

espasmo *nm* : spasm — **espasmódico, -ca** *adj* : spasmodic

espátula *nf* : spatula

especia *nf* : spice

especial *adj & nm* : special — **especialidad** *nf* : specialty — **especialista** *nmf* : specialist — **especializarse** {21} *vr* **~ en** : specialize in — **especialmente** *adv* : especially

especie *nf* **1** : species **2 CLASE** : type, kind

especificar {72} *vt* : specify — **especificación** *nf*, *pl* **-ciones** : specification — **específico, -ca** *adj* : specific

espécimen *nm*, *pl* **especímenes** : specimen

espectáculo *nm* **1** : show, performance **2 VISIÓN** : spectacle, view — **espectacular** *adj* : spectacular — **espectador, -dora** *nmf* : spectator

espectro *nm* **1** : spectrum **2 FANTASMA** : ghost

especulación *nf*, *pl* **-ciones** : speculation

espejo *nm* : mirror — **espejismo** *nm* **1** : mirage **2 ILUSIÓN** : illusion

espeluznante *adj* : terrifying, hair-raising

esperar *vt* **1** : wait for **2 CONTAR CON** : expect **3 ~ que** : hope (that) — *vi* : wait — **espera** *nf* : wait — **esperanza** *nf* : hope, expectation — **esperanzado, -da** *adj* : hopeful — **esperanzar** {21} *vt* : give hope to

esperma *nmf* **1** : sperm **2 ~ de ballena** : blubber

esperpento *nm* : (grotesque) sight, fright

espesar *vt* : thicken — **espesarse** *vr* : thicken — **espeso, -sa** *adj* : thick, heavy — **espesor** *nm* : thickness, density — **espesura** *nf* **1 ESPESOR** : thickness **2** : thicket

espetar *vt* : blurt (out)

espiar {85} *vt* : spy on — *vi* : spy — **espía** *nmf* : spy

espiga *nf* : ear (of wheat, etc.)

espina *nf* **1** : thorn **2** : (fish) bone **3 ~ dorsal** : spine, backbone

espinaca *nf* **1** : spinach (plant) **2 ~s** *nfpl* : spinach (food)

espinazo *nm* : spine, backbone

espinilla *nf* **1** : shin **2 GRANO** : blackhead, pimple

espinoso, -sa *adj* **1** : prickly **2** : bony (of fish) **3** : difficult, thorny (of problems, etc.)

espionaje *nm* : espionage

espiral *adj & nf* : spiral

espirar *v* : breathe out, exhale

espíritu *nm* **1** : spirit **2 Espíritu Santo** : Holy Spirit — **espiritual** *adj* : spiritual — **espiritualidad** *nf* : spirituality

espita *nf* : spigot, faucet

espléndido, -da *adj* **1** : splendid **2 GE-**

NEROSO : lavish — **esplendor** *nm* : splendor

espliego *nm* : lavender

espolear *vt* : spur on

espoleta *nf* : fuse

espolvorear *vt* : sprinkle, dust

esponja *nf* **1** : sponge **2 tirar la ~** : throw in the towel — **esponjoso, -sa** *adj* : spongy

espontaneidad *nf* : spontaneity — **espontáneo, -nea** *adj* : spontaneous

espora *nf* : spore

esporádico, -ca *adj* : sporadic

esposo, -sa *n* : spouse, wife *f*, husband *m* — **esposar** *vt* : handcuff — **esposas** *nfpl* : handcuffs

esprintar *vi* : sprint (in sports) — **esprint** *nm* : sprint

espuela *nf* : spur

espumar *vt* : skim — **espuma** *nf* **1** : foam, froth **2** : (soap) lather **3** : head (on beer) — **espumoso, -sa** *adj* **1** : foamy, frothy **2** : sparkling (of wine)

esqueleto *nm* : skeleton

esquema *nm* : outline, sketch

esquí *nm* **1** : ski **2** : skiing (sport) **3 ~ acuático** : waterskiing — **esquiador, -dora** *n* : skier — **esquiar** {85} *vi* : ski

esquilar *vt* : shear

esquimal *adj* : Eskimo

esquina *nf* : corner

esquirol *nm* : strikebreaker, scab

esquivar *vt* **1** : evade, dodge (a blow) **2** EVITAR : avoid — **esquivo, -va** *adj* : shy, elusive

esquizofrenia *nf* : schizophrenia — **esquizofrénico, -ca** *adj* & *n* : schizophrenic

esta, ésta → **este¹, éste**

estable *adj* : stable — **estabilidad** *nf* : stability — **estabilizar** {21} *vt* : stabilize

establecer {53} *vt* : establish — **establecerse** *vr* : establish oneself, settle — **establecimiento** *nm* : establishment

establo *nm* : stable

estaca *nf* : stake — **estacada** *nf* **1** : (picket) fence **2 dejar en la ~** : leave in a lurch

estación *nf*, *pl* **-ciones 1** : season **2 ~ de servicio** : gas station — **estacionar** *v* : park — **estacionamiento** *nm* : parking — **estacionario, -ria** *adj* : stationary

estadía *nf* *Lat* : stay

estadio *nm* **1** : stadium **2** FASE : phase, stage

estadista *nmf* : statesman

estadística *nf* : statistics — **estadístico, -ca** *adj* : statistical

estado *nm* **1** : state **2 ~ civil** : marital status

estadounidense *adj* & *nmf* : American (from the United States)

estafar *vt* : swindle, defraud — **estafa** *nf* : swindle, fraud — **estafador, -dora** *n* : cheat, swindler

estallar *vi* **1** : explode **2** : break out (of war, an epidemic, etc.) **3 ~ en llamas** : burst into flames — **estallido** *nm* **1** : explosion **2** : report (of a gun) **3** : outbreak (of war, etc.)

estampar *vt* : stamp, print — **estampa** *nf* **1** : print, illustration **2** ASPECTO : appearance — **estampado, -da** *adj* : printed

estampida *nf* : stampede

estampilla *nf* : stamp

estancarse {72} *vr* **1** : stagnate **2** : come to a halt — **estancado, -da** *adj* : stagnant

estancia *nf* **1** : stay **2** HABITACIÓN : (large) room **3** *Lat* : (cattle) ranch

estanco, -ca *adj* : watertight

estándar *adj* & *nm* : standard — **estandarizar** {21} *vt* : standardize

estandarte *nm* : standard, banner

estanque *nm* **1** : pool, pond **2** : reservoir (for irrigation)

estante *nm* : shelf — **estantería** *nf* : shelves *pl*, bookcase

estaño *nm* : tin

estar {34} *v aux* : be — *vi* **1** : be **2** : be at home **3** QUEDARSE : stay, remain **4 ¿cómo estás?** : how are you? **5 ~ a** : cost **6 ~ bien (mal)** : be well (sick) **7 ~ para** : be in the mood for **8 ~ por** : be in favor of **9 ~ por** : be about to — **estarse** *vr* : stay, remain

estarcir {83} *vt* : stencil

estárter *nm* : choke (of an automobile)

estatal *adj* : state, national

estático, -ca *adj* **1** : static **2** INMÓVIL : unmoving, still — **estática** *nf* : static

estatua *nf* : statue

estatura *nf* : height

estatus *nm* : status, prestige

estatuto *nm* : statute — **estatutario, -ria** *adj* : statutory

este¹, esta *adj*, *mpl* **estos** : this, these

este² *adj* : eastern, east — **este** *nm* **1** : east **2** : east wind **3 el Este** : the Orient

éste, ésta *pron*, *mpl* **éstos 1** : this one, these ones *pl* **2** : the latter

estela *nf* **1** : wake (of a ship) **2** : trail (of smoke, etc.)

estera *nf* : mat

estéreo *adj* & *nm* : stereo — **estereofónico, -ca** *adj* : stereophonic

estereotipo *nm* : stereotype

estéril *adj* **1** : sterile **2** : infertile — **esterilidad** *nf* **1** : sterility **2** : infertility — **esterilizar** {21} *vt* : sterilize

estética *nf* : aesthetics — **estético, -ca** *adj* : aesthetic

estiércol *nm* : dung, manure

estigma *nm* : stigma — **estigmatizar** {21} *vt* : stigmatize

estilarse {21} *vr* : be in fashion

estilo *nm* **1** MANERA : fashion, manner — **estilista** *nmf* : stylist

estima *nf* : esteem, regard — **estimación** *nf, pl* **-ciones 1** : esteem **2** VALORACIÓN : estimate — **estimado, -da** *adj* **Estimado señor** : Dear Sir — **estimar** *vt* **1** : esteem, respect **2** VALORAR : value, estimate **3** CONSIDERAR : consider

estimular *vt* **1** : stimulate **2** ALENTAR : encourage — **estimulante** *adj* : stimulating — ~ *nm* : stimulant — **estímulo** *nm* : stimulus

estío *nm* : summertime

estipular *vt* : stipulate

estirar *vt* : stretch (out), extend — **estirado, -da** *adj* **1** : stretched, extended **2** ALTANERO : stuck-up, haughty — **estiramiento** *nm* ~ **facial** : face-lift — **estirón** *nm, pl* **-rones** : pull, tug

estirpe *nf* : lineage, stock

estival *adj* : summer

esto *pron* (*neuter*) **1** : this **2 en ~** : at this point **3 por ~** : for this reason

estofa *nf* **1** : class, quality **2 de baja ~** : low-class

estofar *vt* : stew — **estofado** *nm* : stew

estoicismo *nm* : stoicism — **estoico, -ca** *adj* : stoic, stoical — ~ *n* : stoic

estómago *nm* : stomach — **estomacal** *adj* : stomach

estorbar *vt* : obstruct — *vi* : get in the way — **estorbo** *nm* **1** : obstacle **2** MOLESTIA : nuisance

estornino *nm* : starling

estornudar *vi* : sneeze — **estornudo** *nm* : sneeze

estos, éstos → **este, éste**

estrabismo *nm* : squint

estrado *nm* : platform, stage

estrafalario, -ria *adj* : eccentric, bizarre

estragar {52} *vt* : devastate — **estragos** *nmpl* : ravages **2 hacer ~ en** *or* **causar ~ entre** : wreak havoc with

estragón *nm* : tarragon

estrangular *vt* : strangle — **estrangulación** *nf* : strangulation

estratagema *nf* : stratagem

estrategia *nf* : strategy — **estratégico, -ca** *adj* : strategic

estrato *nm* : stratum

estratosfera *nf* : stratosphere

estrechar *vt* **1** : narrow **2** : strengthen (a bond) **3** ABRAZAR : embrace **4 ~ la mano a uno** : shake s.o.'s hand — **estrecharse** *vr* : narrow — **estrechez** *nf, pl* **-checes 1** : narrowness **2 estrecheces** *nfpl* : financial problems — **estrecho, -cha** *adj* **1** : tight, narrow **2** ÍNTIMO : close — **estrecho** *nm* : strait

estrella *nf* **1** : star **2** DESTINO : destiny **3 ~ de mar** : starfish — **estrellado, -da** *adj* **1** : starry **2** : star-shaped

estrellar *v* : crash — **estrellarse** *vr* ~ **contre** : smash into

estremecer {53} *vt* : cause to shudder — *vi* : tremble, shake — **estremecerse** *vr* : shudder, shiver (with emotion) — **estremecimiento** *nm* : shaking, shivering

estrenar *vt* **1** : use for the first time **2** : premiere, open (a film, etc.) — **estrenarse** *vr* : make one's debut — **estreno** *nm* : debut, premiere

estreñirse {67} *vr* : be constipated — **estreñimiento** *nm* : constipation

estrépito *nm* : clamor, din — **estrepitoso, -sa** *adj* : noisy, clamorous

estrés *nm, pl* **estreses** : stress — **estresante** *adj* : stressful — **estresar** *vt* : stress (out)

estría *nf* : groove

estribaciones *nfpl* : foothills

estribar *vi* ~ **en** : stem from, lie in

estribillo *nm* : refrain, chorus

estribo *nm* **1** : stirrup **2** : running board (of a vehicle) **3** CONTRAFUERTE : buttress **4 perder los ~s** : lose one's temper

estribor *nm* : starboard

estricto, -ta *adj* : strict

estridente *adj* : strident, shrill

estrofa *nf* : stanza, verse

estropajo *nm* : scouring pad

estropear *vt* **1** : ruin, spoil **2** DAÑAR : damage — **estropearse** *vr* **1** : go bad **2** AVERIARSE : break down — **estropicio** *nm* : damage, havoc

estructura *nf* : structure — **estructural** *adj* : structural

estruendo *nm* : din, roar — **estruendoso, -sa** *adj* : thunderous

estrujar *vt* : squeeze

estuario *nm* : estuary

estuche *nm* : kit, case

estuco *nm* : stucco

estudiar *v* : study — **estudiante** *nmf* : student — **estudiantil** *adj* : student — **estudio** *nm* **1** : study **2** OFICINA

: studio, office **3** ~**s** *nmpl* : studies, education — **estudioso, -sa** *adj* : studious

estufa *nf* : stove, heater

estupefaciente *adj & nm* : narcotic — **estupefacto, -ta** *adj* : astonished

estupendo, -da *adj* : stupendous, marvelous

estúpido, -da *adj* : stupid — **estupidez** *nf, pl* **-deces** : stupidity

estupor *nm* **1** : stupor **2** ASOMBRO : amazement

etapa *nf* : stage, phase

etcétera : et cetera, and so on

éter *nm* : ether

etéreo, -rea *adj* : ethereal

eterno, -na *adj* : eternal — **eternidad** *nf* : eternity — **eternizarse** {21} *vr* : take forever

ética *nf* : ethics — **ético, -ca** *adj* : ethical

etimología *nf* : etymology

etíope *adj* : Ethiopian

etiqueta *nf* **1** : tag, label **2** PROTOCOLO : etiquette **3 de** ~ : formal, dressy — **etiquetar** *vt* : label

étnico, -ca *adj* : ethnic

eucalipto *nm* : eucalyptus

Eucaristía *nf* : Eucharist, communion

eufemismo *nm* : euphemism — **eufemístico, -ca** *adj* : euphemistic

euforia *nf* : euphoria — **eufórico, -ca** ' *adj* : euphoric

europeo, -pea *adj* : European

eutanasia *nf* : euthanasia

evacuar *vt* : evacuate, vacate — *vi* : have a bowel movement — **evacuación** *nf, pl* **-ciones** : evacuation

evadir *vt* : evade, avoid — **evadirse** *vr* : escape

evaluar {3} *vt* : evaluate — **evaluación** *nf, pl* **-ciones** : evaluation

evangelio *nm* : gospel — **evangélico, -ca** *adj* : evangelical — **evangelismo** *nm* : evangelism

evaporar *vt* : evaporate — **evaporarse** *vr* : evaporate, disappear — **evaporación** *nf, pl* **-ciones** : evaporation

evasión *nf, pl* **-siones** **1** : evasion **2** FUGA : escape — **evasiva** *nf* : excuse, pretext — **evasivo, -va** *adj* : evasive

evento *nm* : event

eventual *adj* **1** : temporary **2** POSIBLE : possible — **eventualidad** *nf* : possibility, eventuality

evidencia *nf* **1** : evidence, proof **2 poner en** ~ : demonstrate — **evidenciar** *vt* : demonstrate, show — **evidente** *adj* : evident — **evidentemente** *adv* : evidently, apparently

evitar *vt* **1** : avoid **2** IMPEDIR : prevent — **evitable** *adj* : avoidable

evocar {72} *vt* : evoke

evolución *nf, pl* **-ciones** : evolution — **evolucionar** *vi* : evolve

exacerbar *vt* **1** : exacerbate **2** IRRITAR : irritate

exacto, -ta *adj* : precise, exact — **exactamente** *adv* : exactly — **exactitud** *nf* : precision, accuracy

exagerar *v* : exaggerate — **exageración** *nf, pl* **-ciones** : exaggeration — **exagerado, -da** *adj* : exaggerated

exaltar *vt* **1** : exalt, extol **2** EXCITAR : excite, arouse — **exaltarse** *vr* : get worked-up — **exaltado, -da** *adj* : worked up, hotheaded

examen *nm, pl* **exámenes** **1** : examination, test **2** ANÁLISIS : investigation — **examinar** *vt* **1** : examine **2** ESTUDIAR : study, inspect — **examinarse** *vr* : take an exam

exánime *adj* : lifeless

exasperar *vt* : exasperate, irritate — **exasperación** *nf, pl* **-ciones** : exasperation

excavar *v* : excavate — **excavación** *nf, pl* **-ciones** : excavation

exceder *vt* : exceed, surpass — **excederse** *vr* : go too far — **excedente** *adj & nm* : surplus, excess

excelente *adj* : excellent — **excelencia** *nf* **1** : excellence **2 Su Excelencia** : His/Her Excellency

excéntrico, -ca *adj & n* : eccentric — **excentricidad** *nf* : eccentricity

excepción *nf, pl* **-ciones** : exception — **excepcional** *adj* : exceptional

excepto *prep* : except (for) — **exceptuar** {3} *vt* : exclude, except

exceso *nm* **1** : excess **2** ~ **de velocidad** : speeding — **excesivo, -va** *adj* : excessive

excitar *vt* : excite, arouse — **excitarse** *vr* : get excited — **excitable** *adj* : excitable — **excitación** *nf, pl* **-ciones** : excitement, agitation, arousal — **excitante** *adj* : exciting

exclamar *v* : exclaim — **exclamación** *nf, pl* **-ciones** : exclamation

excluir {41} *vt* : exclude — **exclusión** *nf, pl* **-siones** : exclusion — **exclusivo, -va** *adj* : exclusive

excomulgar {52} *vt* : excommunicate — **excomunión** *nf, pl* **-niones** : excommunication

excremento *nm* : excrement

exculpar *vt* : exonerate

excursión *nf, pl* **-siones** : excursion —

excursionista *nmf* **1** : tourist, sightseer **2** : hiker

excusar *vt* **1** : excuse **2** EXIMIR : exempt — **excusarse** *vr* : apologize — **excusa** *nf* **1** : excuse **2** DISCULPA : apology

exento, -ta *adj* : exempt

exequias *nfpl* : funeral rites

exhalar *vt* **1** : exhale **2** : give off (an odor, etc.)

exhaustivo, -va *adj* : exhaustive — **exhausto, -ta** *adj* : exhausted, worn-out

exhibir *vt* : exhibit, show — **exhibición** *nf, pl* **-ciones** : exhibition

exhortar *vt* : exhort, admonish

exigir {35} *vt* : demand, require — **exigencia** *nf* : demand, requirement — **exigente** *adj* : demanding

exiguo, -gua *adj* : meager

exiliar *vt* : exile — **exiliarse** *vr* : go into exile — **exiliado, -da** *adj* : exiled, in exile — **~** *n* : exile — **exilio** *nm* : exile

eximir *vt* : exempt

existir *vi* : exist — **existencia** *nf* **1** : existence **2** **~s** *nfpl* MERCANCÍA : goods, stock — **existente** *adj* : existing

éxito *nm* **1** : success, hit **2** **tener ~** : be successful — **exitoso, -sa** *adj Lat* : successful

éxodo *nm* : exodus

exorbitante *adj* : exorbitant

exorcizar {21} *vt* : exorcize — **exorcismo** *nm* : exorcism

exótico, -ca *adj* : exotic

expandir *vt* : expand — **expandirse** *vr* : spread — **expansión** *nf, pl* **-siones** : expansion — **expansivo, -va** *adj* : expansive

expatriarse {85} *vr* **1** : emigrate **2** EXILIARSE : go into exile — **expatriado, -da** *adj & n* : expatriate

expectativa *nf* **1** : expectation, hope **2** **~s** *nfpl* : prospects

expedición *nf, pl* **-ciones** : expedition

expediente *nm* **1** : expedient **2** DOCUMENTOS : file, record INVESTIGACIÓN : inquiry, proceedings

expedir {54} *vt* **1** : issue **2** ENVIAR : dispatch — **expedito, -ta** *adj* : free, clear

expeler *vt* : expel, eject

expendedor, -dora *n* : dealer, seller

expensas *nfpl* **1** : expenses **2 a ~ de** : at the expense of

experiencia *nf* : experience

experimentar *vi* : experiment — *vt* **1** : experiment with, test out **2** SENTIR : experience, feel — **experimentado, -da** *adj* : experienced — **experimental** *adj* : experimental — **experimento** *nm* : experiment

experto, -ta *adj & n* : expert

expiar {85} *vt* : atone for

expirar *vi* **1** : expire **2** MORIR : die

explayar *vt* : extend — **explayarse** *vr* **1** : spread out **2** HABLAR : speak at length

explicar {72} *vt* : explain — **explicarse** *vr* : understand — **explicación** *nf, pl* **-ciones** : explanation — **explicativo, -va** *adj* : explanatory

explícito, -ta *adj* : explicit

explorar *vt* : explore — **exploración** *nf, pl* **-ciones** : exploration — **explorador, -dora** *n* : explorer, scout — **exploratorio, -ria** *adj* : exploratory

explosión *nf, pl* **-siones 1** : explosion **2** : outburst (of anger, laughter, etc.) — **explosivo, -va** *adj* : explosive — **explosivo** *nm* : explosive

explotar *vt* **1** : exploit **2** : operate, run (a factory, etc.), work (a mine) — *vi* : explode — **explotación** *nf, pl* **-ciones 1** : exploitation **2** : running (of a business), working (of a mine)

exponer {60} *vt* **1** : expose **2** : explain, set out (ideas, theories, etc.) **3** EXHIBIR : exhibit, display — *vi* : exhibit — **exponerse** *vr* **~ a** : expose oneself to

exportar *vt* : export — **exportaciones** *nfpl* : exports — **exportador, -dora** *n* : exporter

exposición *nf, pl* **-ciones 1** : exposure **2** : exhibition (of objects, art, etc.) **3** : exposition, setting out (of ideas, etc.) — **expositor, -tora** *n* **1** : exhibitor **2** : exponent (of a theory, etc.)

exprés *nms & pl* **1** : express (train) **2 or café ~** : espresso

expresamente *adv* : expressly, on purpose

expresar *vt* : express — **expresarse** *vr* : express oneself — **expresión** *nf, pl* **-siones** : expression — **expresivo, -va** *adj* **1** : expressive **2** CARIÑOSO : affectionate

expreso, -sa *adj* : express — **expreso** *nm* : express train, express

exprimir *vt* **1** : squeeze **2** EXPLOTAR : exploit — **exprimidor** *nm* : squeezer, juicer

expuesto, -ta *adj* **1** : exposed **2** PELIGROSO : risky, dangerous

expulsar *vt* : expel, eject — **expulsión** *nf, pl* **-siones** : expulsion

exquisito, -ta *adj* **1** : exquisite **2** RICO : delicious — **exquisitez** *nf* **1** : exquisiteness **2** : delicacy, special dish

éxtasis *nms & pl* : ecstasy — **extático, -ta** *adj* : ecstatic

extender {56} *vt* **1** : spread out **2** : draw up (a document), write out (a check)

— **extenderse** vr **1** : extend, spread **2**
DURAR : last — **extendido, -da** adj **1**
: widespread **2** : outstretched (of arms,
wings, etc.)
extensamente adv : extensively
extensión nf, pl **-siones 1** : extension **2**
AMPLITUD : expanse **3** ALCANCE : range,
extent — **extenso, -sa** adj : extensive
extenuar {3} vt : exhaust, tire out
exterior adj **1** : exterior, external **2**
EXTRANJERO : foreign — ~ nm **1** : outside **2 en el ~** : abroad — **exteri-
orizar** {21} vr : show, reveal — **exteriormente** adv : outwardly, externally
exterminar vt : exterminate — **exterminación** nf, pl **-ciones** : extermination
— **exterminio** nm : extermination
externo, -na adj : external
extinguir {26} vt **1** : extinguish (a fire)
2 : put an end to, wipe out — **extinguirse** vr **1** : go out (of fire, light, etc.)
2 : become extinct — **extinción** nf, pl
-ciones : extinction — **extinguidor**
nm Lat : fire extinguisher — **extinto,
-ta** adj : extinct — **extintor** nm : fire
extinguisher
extirpar vt : remove, eradicate
extorsión nf, pl **-siones 1** : extortion **2**
MOLESTIA : trouble
extra adv : extra — ~ adj **1** ADICIONAL
: additional **2** : top-quality — ~ nmf
: extra (in movies) — ~ nm : extra
(expense)
extraditar vt : extradite
extraer {81} vt : extract — **extracción**
nf, pl **-ciones** : extraction — **extracto**
nm **1** : extract **2** RESUMEN : abstract,
summary

extranjero, -ra adj : foreign — ~ n
: foreigner — **extranjero** nm : foreign
countries pl
extrañar vt : miss (someone) — **ex-
trañarse** vr : be surprised — **ex-
trañeza** nf : surprise — **extraño, -ña**
adj **1** : foreign **2** RARO : strange, odd
— ~ n : stranger
extraoficial adj : unofficial
extraordinario, -ria adj : extraordinary
extrasensorial adj : extrasensory
extraterrestre adj & nmf : extraterrestrial
extravagante adj : extravagant, outrageous — **extravagancia** nf : extravagance, outlandishness
extraviar {85} vt : lose, misplace — **extraviarse** vr : get lost — **extravío** nm
: loss
extremar vt : carry to extremes — **ex-
tremarse** vr : do one's utmost — **extremadamente** adv : extremely — **ex-
tremado, -da** adj : extreme —
extremidad nf **1** : tip, end **2** ~**es** nfpl
: extremities — **extremista** adj & nmf
: extremist — **extremo, -ma** adj **1**
: extreme **2 en caso** ~ : as a last resort — **extremo** nm **1** : end **2 en** ~
: in the extreme, extremely **3 en ulti-
mo** ~ : as a last resort
extrovertido -da adj : extroverted —
~ n : extrovert
exuberante adj : exuberant — **exuberancia** nf : exuberance
exudar vi : exude
eyacular vi : ejaculate — **eyaculación**
nf, pl **-ciones** : ejaculation

F

f nf : f, sixth letter of the Spanish alphabet
fabricar {72} vt **1** : manufacture **2** CON-
STRUIR : build, construct **3** INVENTAR
: fabricate — **fábrica** nf : factory —
fabricación nf, pl **-ciones** : manufacture — **fabricante** nmf : manufacturer
fábula nf **1** : fable **2** MENTIRA : story, lie
fabuloso, -sa adj : fabulous
facción nf, pl **-ciones 1** : faction **2**
~**es** nfpl RASGOS : features
faceta nf : facet
facha nf : appearance, look
fachada nf : façade
facial adj : facial
fácil adj **1** : easy **2** PROBABLE : likely —
facilemente adv : easily, readily —

facilidad nf **1** : facility, ease **2** ~**es**
nfpl : facilities, services — **facilitar** vt
1 : facilitate **2** PROPORCIONAR : provide, supply
facsímil or **facsímile** nm **1** COPIA : facsimile, copy **2** : fax
factible adj : feasible
factor nm : factor
factoría nf : factory
factura nf **1** : bill, invoice **2** HECHURA
: making, manufacture — **facturar** vt
1 : bill for **2** : check in (baggage, etc.)
facultad nf **1** : faculty, ability **2** AUTORI-
DAD : authority **3** : school (of a university) — **facultativo, -va** adj : optional
faena nf **1** : task, job **2** ~**s domésticas**
: housework

fagot nm : bassoon

faisán nm, pl **-sanes** : pheasant

faja nf **1** : sash **2** : girdle, corset **3** : strip (of land)

fajo nm : bundle, sheaf

falda nf **1** : skirt **2** : side, slope (of a mountain)

falible adj : fallible

fálico, -ca adj : phallic

fallar vi : fail, go wrong — vt **1** : pronounce judgment on **2** ERRAR : miss —

falla nf **1** : flaw, defect **2** : (geological) fault

fallecer {53} vi : pass away, die — **fallecimiento** nm : demise, death

fallido, -da adj : failed, unsuccessful

fallo nm **1** : error **2** SENTENCIA : sentence, verdict

falo nm : phallus, penis

falsear vt : falsify, distort — **falsedad** nf **1** : falseness **2** MENTIRA : falsehood, lie — **falsificación** nf, pl **-ciones** : forgery, fake — **falsificador, -dora** n : forger — **falsificar** {72} vt **1** : counterfeit, forge **2** ALTERAR : falsify — **falso, -sa** adj **1** : false, untrue **2** FALSIFICADO : counterfeit, forged

falta nf **1** CARENCIA : lack **2** DEFECTO : defect, fault, error **3** AUSENCIA : absence **4** : offense, misdemeanor (in law) **5** : foul (in sports) **6** hacer ~ : be lacking, be needed **7** sin ~ : without fail — **faltar** vi **1** : be lacking, be needed **2** : be missing **3** QUEDAR : remain, be left **4** ¡no faltaba más! : don't mention it! — **falto, -ta** adj ~ **de** : lacking (in)

fama nf **1** : fame **2** REPUTACIÓN : reputation

famélico, -ca adj : starving

familia nf : family — **familiar** adj **1** : familial, family **2** CONOCIDO : familiar **3** : informal (of language, etc.) — ~ nmf : relation, relative — **familiaridad** nf : familiarity — **familiarizarse** {21} vr ~ **con** : familiarize oneself with

famoso, -sa adj : famous

fanático, -ca adj : fanatic, fanatical — ~ n : fanatic — **fanatismo** nm : fanaticism

fanfarria nf : fanfare

fanfarrón, -rrona adj, mpl **-rrones** fam : boastful — ~ n fam : braggart — **fanfarronear** vi : boast, brag

fango nm : mud, mire — **fangoso, -sa** adj : muddy

fantasear vi : fantasize, daydream — **fantasía** nf **1** : fantasy **2** IMAGINACIÓN : imagination

fantasma nm : ghost, phantom — **fantasmal** adj : ghostly

fantástico, -ca adj : fantastic

fardo nm : bundle

farfullar v : jabber, gabble

farmacéutico, -ca adj : pharmaceutical — ~ n : pharmacist — **farmacia** nf : drugstore, pharmacy

faro nm **1** : lighthouse **2** : headlight (of an automobile) — **farol** nm **1** LINTERNA : lantern **2** FAROLA : streetlight — **farola** nf **1** : lamppost **2** FAROL : streetlight

farsa nf : farce — **farsante** nmf : charlatan, fraud

fascículo nm : installment, part (of a publication)

fascinar vt : fascinate — **fascinación** nf, pl **-ciones** : fascination — **fascinante** adj : fascinating

fascismo nm : fascism — **fascista** adj & nmf : fascist

fase nf : phase

fastidiar vt : annoy, bother — vi : be annoying or bothersome — **fastidio** nm : annoyance — **fastidioso, -sa** adj : annoying, bothersome

fatal adj **1** : fateful **2** MORTAL : fatal **3** fam : awful, terrible — **fatalidad** nf **1** : fate, destiny **2** DESGRACIA : misfortune

fatídico, -ca adj : fateful, momentous

fatiga nf : fatigue — **fatigado, -da** adj : weary, tired — **fatigar** {52} vt : tire — **fatigarse** vr : get tired — **fatigoso, -sa** adj : fatiguing, tiring

fatuo, -tua adj **1** : fatuous **2** PRESUMIDO : conceited

fauna nf : fauna

favor nm **1** : favor **2 a ~ de** : in favor of **3 por ~** : please — **favorable** adj **1** : favorable **2 ser ~ a** : be in favor of — **favorecedor, -dora** adj : flattering — **favorecer** {53} vt **1** AYUDAR : favor **2** : look well on, suit — **favoritismo** nm : favoritism — **favorito, -ta** adj & n : favorite

fax nm : fax — **faxear** vt : fax

faz nf, pl **faces** : face, countenance

fe nf **1** : faith **2 dar ~ de** : bear witness to **3 de buena ~** : in good faith

fealdad nf : ugliness

febrero nm : February

febril adj : feverish

fecha nf **1** : date **2 ~ de caducidad** or **~ de vencimiento** : expiration date **3 ~ límite** : deadline — **fechar** vt : date, put a date on

fechoría nf : misdeed

fécula nf : starch (in food)

fecundar vt **1** : fertilize (an egg) **2** : make fertile — **fecundo, -da** adj : fertile

federación *nf, pl* **-ciones** : federation — **federal** *adj* : federal

felicidad *nf* **1** : happiness **2** ¡**~es!** : best wishes!, congratulations!, happy birthday! — **felicitación** *nf, pl* **-ciones** : congratulation — **felicitar** *vt* : congratulate — **felicitarse** *vr* **~ de** : be glad about

feligrés, -gresa *n, mpl* **-greses** : parishioner

felino, -na *adj & n* : feline

feliz *adj, pl* **-lices** **1** : happy **2** AFORTUNADO : fortunate **3 Feliz Navidad** : Merry Christmas

felpa *nf* **1** : plush **2** : terry cloth (for towels, etc.)

felpudo *nm* : doormat

femenino, -na *adj* **1** : feminine **2** : female (in biology) — **femenino** *nm* : feminine (in grammar) — **feminidad** *nf* : femininity — **feminismo** *nm* : feminism — **feminista** *adj & nmf* : feminist

fenómeno *nm* : phenomenon — **fenomenal** *adj* **1** : phenomenal **2** *fam* : fantastic, terrific

feo, fea *adj* **1** : ugly **2** DESAGRADABLE : unpleasant, nasty

féretro *nm* : coffin

feria *nf* **1** : fair, market **2** FIESTA : festival, holiday **3** *Lat fam* : small change — **feriado, -da** *adj* **día feriado** : public holiday

fermentar *v* : ferment — **fermentación** *nf, pl* **-ciones** : fermentation — **fermento** *nm* : ferment

feroz *adj, pl* **-roces** : ferocious, fierce — **ferocidad** *nf* : ferocity, fierceness

férreo, -rrea *adj* **1** : iron **2 vía férrea** : railroad track

ferretería *nf* : hardware store

ferrocarril *nm* : railroad, railway — **ferroviario, -ria** *adj* : rail, railroad

ferry *nm, pl* **ferrys** : ferry

fértil *adj* : fertile, fruitful — **fertilidad** *nf* : fertility — **fertilizante** *nm* : fertilizer — **fertilizar** *vt* : fertilize

fervor *nm* : fervor, zeal — **ferviente** *adj* : fervent

festejar *vt* **1** : celebrate **2** AGASAJAR : entertain, wine and dine — **festejo** *nm* : celebration, festivity

festín *nm, pl* **-tines** : banquet, feast

festival *nm* : festival — **festividad** *nf* : festivity — **festivo, -va** *adj* **1** : festive **2 día festivo** : holiday

fetiche *nm* : fetish

fétido, -da *adj* : foul-smelling, fetid

feto *nm* : fetus — **fetal** *adj* : fetal

feudal *adj* : feudal

fiable *adj* : reliable — **fiabilidad** *nf* : reliability

fiado, -da *adj* : on credit — **fiador, -dora** *n* : bondsman, guarantor

fiambres *nfpl* : cold cuts

fianza *nf* **1** : bail, bond **2 dar ~** : pay a deposit

fiar {85} *vt* **1** : guarantee **2** : sell on credit — *vi* **ser de ~** : be trustworthy — **fiarse** *vr* **~ de** : place trust in

fiasco *nm* : fiasco

fibra *nf* **1** : fiber **2 ~ de vidrio** : fiberglass

ficción *nf, pl* **-ciones** : fiction

ficha *nf* **1** : token **2** TARJETA : index card **3** : counter, chip (in games) — **fichar** *vt* : file, index — **fichero** *nm* **1** : card file **2** : filing cabinet

ficticio, -cia *adj* : fictitious

fidedigno, -na *adj* : reliable, trustworthy

fidelidad *nf* : fidelity, faithfulness

fideo *nm* : noodle

fiebre *nf* **1** : fever **2 ~ del heno** : hay fever **3 ~ palúdica** : malaria

fiel *adj* **1** : faithful, loyal **2** PRECISO : accurate, reliable — **~** *nm* **1** : pointer (of a scale) **2 los ~es** : the faithful — **fielmente** *adv* : faithfully

fieltro *nm* : felt

fiero, -ra *adj* **1** : fierce, ferocious — **fiera** *nf* : wild animal, beast

fierro *nm* *Lat* : iron (bar)

fiesta *nf* **1** : party **2** DIA FESTIVO : holiday, feast day

figura *nf* **1** : figure **2** FORMA : shape, form — **figurar** *vi* **1** : figure (in), be included (among) **2** DESTACAR : stand out — *vt* : represent — **figurarse** *vr* : imagine

fijar *vt* **1** : fasten, affix **2** CONCRETAR : set, fix — **fijarse** *vr* **1** : settle **2 ~ en** : notice, pay attention to — **fijo, -ja** *adj* **1** : fixed, firm **2** PERMANENTE : permanent

fila *nf* **1** : line, file, row **2 ponerse en ~** : line up

filantropía *nf* : philanthropy — **filantrópico, -ca** *adj* : philanthropic — **filántropo, -pa** *n* : philanthropist

filatelia *nf* : philately, stamp collecting

filete *nm* : fillet

filial *adj* : filial — **~** *nf* : affiliate, subsidiary

filigrana *nf* **1** : filigree **2** : watermark (on paper)

filipino, -na *adj* : Filipino

filmar *vt* : film, shoot — **filme** *or* **film** *nm* : film, movie

filo *nm* **1** : edge **2 dar ~ a** : sharpen

filón *nm, pl* **-lones** **1** : vein (of minerals) **2** *fam* : gold mine

filoso, -sa *adj* *Lat* : sharp

filosofía *nf* : philosophy — **filosófico, -ca** *adj* : philosophical — **filósofo, -fa** *n* : philosopher

filtrar *v* : filter — **filtrarse** *vr* : leak out, seep through — **filtro** *nm* : filter

fin *nm* **1** : end **2** OBJETIVO : purpose, aim **3** en ~ : well, in short **4** ~ de semana : weekend **5** por ~ : finally, at last

final *adj* : final — ~ *nm* : end, conclusion — ~ *nf* : final (in sports) — **finalidad** *nf* : purpose, aim — **finalista** *nmf* : finalist — **finalizar** {21} *v* : finish, end — **finalmente** *adv* : finally

financiar *vt* : finance, fund — **financiero, -ra** *adj* : financial — ~ *n* : financier — **finanzas** *nfpl* : finance

finca *nf* **1** : farm, ranch **2** *Lat* : country house

fingir {35} *v* : feign, pretend — **fingido, -da** *adj* : false, feigned

finito, -ta *adj* : finite

finlandés, -desa *adj* : Finnish

fino, -na *adj* **1** : fine **2** DELGADO : slender **3** REFINADO : refined **4** AGUDO : sharp, keen — **finura** *nf* **1** : fineness **2** REFINAMIENTO : refinement

firma *nf* **1** : signature **2** : (act of) signing **3** EMPRESA : firm, company

firmamento *nm* : firmament, sky

firmar *v* : sign

firme *adj* **1** : firm, resolute **2** ESTABLE : steady, stable — **firmeza** *nf* **1** : strength, resolve **2** ESTABILIDAD : firmness, stability

fiscal *adj* : fiscal — ~ *nmf* : district attorney — **fisco** *nm* : (national) treasury

fisgar {52} *vt* : pry into — *vi* : pry — **fisgón, -gona** *n*, *mpl* **-gones** : snoop, busybody

física *nf* : physics — **físico, -ca** *adj* : physical — ~ *n* : physicist — **físico** *nm* : physique

fisiología *nf* : physiology — **fisiológico, -ca** *adj* : physiological — **fisiólogo, -ga** *n* : physiologist

fisioterapia *nf* : physical therapy — **fisioterapeuta** *nmf* : physical therapist

fisonomía *nf* : features *pl*, appearance

fisura *nf* : fissure

fláccido, -da *or* **flácido, -da** *adj* : flaccid, flabby

flaco, -ca *adj* **1** : thin, skinny **2** DÉBIL : weak

flagrante *adj* : flagrant

flamante *adj* **1** : bright, brilliant **2** NUEVO : brand-new

flamenco, -ca *adj* **1** : flamenco (of music or dance) **2** : Flemish — **fla-**

menco *nm* **1** : flamingo **2** : flamenco (music or dance)

flaquear *vi* : weaken, flag — **flaqueza** *nf* **1** : thinness **2** DEBILIDAD : weakness

flash *nm* : flash

flatulencia *nf* : flatulence

flauta *nf* **1** : flute **2** ~ **dulce** : recorder — **flautín** *nm*, *pl* **-tines** : piccolo — **flautista** *nmf* : flutist

flecha *nf* : arrow

fleco *nm* **1** : fringe **2** *Lat* : bangs *pl*

flema *nf* : phlegm — **flemático, -ca** *adj* : phlegmatic

flequillo *nm* : bangs *pl*

fletar *vt* **1** : charter, rent **2** *Lat* : transport — **flete** *nm* **1** : charter **2** : shipping (charges) **3** *Lat* : transport, freight

flexible *adj* : flexible — **flexibilidad** *nf* : flexibility

flirtear *vi* : flirt

flojo, -ja *adj* **1** SUELTO : loose, slack **2** DÉBIL : weak **3** PEREZOSO : lazy — **flojera** *nf fam* : lethargy

flor *nf* : flower — **flora** *nf* : flora — **floral** *adj* : floral — **floreado, -da** *adj* : flowered — **florear** *vi Lat* : flower, bloom — **florecer** {53} *vi* **1** : bloom, blossom **2** PROSPERAR : flourish — **floreciente** *adj* : flourishing — **florero** *nm* : vase — **florido, -da** *adj* : flowery — **florista** *nmf* : florist — **floritura** *nf* : frill, flourish

flota *nf* : fleet

flotar *vi* : float — **flotador** *nm* **1** : float **2** : life preserver (for a swimmer) — **flotante** *adj* : floating, buoyant — **flote: a** ~ *adv phr* : afloat

flotilla *nf* : flotilla, fleet

fluctuar {3} *vi* : fluctuate — **fluctuación** *nf*, *pl* **-ciones** : fluctuation

fluir {41} *vi* : flow — **fluidez** *nf* **1** : fluidity **2** : fluency (of language, etc.) — **fluido, -da** *adj* **1** : fluid **2** : fluent (of language) — **fluido** *nm* : fluid — **flujo** *nm* : flow

fluorescente *adj* : fluorescent

fluoruro *nm* : fluoride

fluvial *adj* : river

fobia *nf* : phobia

foca *nf* : seal (animal)

foco *nm* **1** : focus **2** : spotlight, floodlight (in theater, etc.) **3** *Lat* : lightbulb

fofo, -fa *adj* : flabby

fogata *nf* : bonfire

fogón *nm*, *pl* **-gones** : burner

fogoso, -sa *adj* : ardent

folklore *nm* : folklore — **folklórico, -ca** *adj* : folk, traditional

follaje *nm* : foliage

folleto *nm* : pamphlet, leaflet

fomentar *vt* : promote, encourage — **fomento** *nm* : promotion, encouragement

fonda *nf* : boarding house

fondear *vt* : sound out, examine — *vi* : anchor

fondillos *nmpl* : seat (of pants, etc.)

fondo *nm* **1** : bottom **2** : rear, back, end **3** PROFUNDIDAD : depth **4** : background (of a painting, etc.) **5** *Lat* : slip, petticoat **6** ∼**s** *nmpl* : funds, resources **7 a** ∼ : thoroughly, in depth **8 en el** ∼ : deep down

fonético, -ca *adj* : phonetic — **fonética** *nf* : phonetics

fontanería *nf Spain* : plumbing — **fontanero, -ra** *n Spain* : plumber

footing ['futɪŋ] *nm* **1** : jogging **2 hacer** ∼ : jog

forajido, -da *n* : bandit, outlaw

foráneo, -nea *adj* : foreign, strange

forastero, -ra *n* : stranger, outsider

forcejear *vi* : struggle — **forcejeo** *nm* : struggle

forense *adj* : forensic

forja *nf* : forge — **forjar** *vt* **1** : forge **2** CREAR, FORMAR : build up, create

forma *nf* **1** : form, shape **2** MANERA : manner, way **3 en** ∼ : fit, healthy **4** ∼**s** *nfpl* : appearances, conventions — **formación** *nf, pl* **-ciones 1** : formation **2** EDUCACIÓN : training

formal *adj* **1** : formal **2** SERIO : serious **3** FIABLE : dependable, reliable — **formalidad** *nf* **1** : formality **2** SERIEDAD : seriousness **3** FIABILIDAD : reliability

formar *vt* **1** : form, shape **2** CONSTITUIR : constitute **3** EDUCAR : train, educate — **formarse** *vr* **1** DESARROLLARSE : develop, take shape **2** EDUCARSE : be educated

formato *nm* : format

formidable *adj* **1** : tremendous **2** *fam* : fantastic, terrific

fórmula *nf* : formula

formular *vt* **1** : formulate, draw up **2** : make, lodge (a complaint, etc.)

formulario *nm* : form

fornido, -da *adj* : well-built, burly

foro *nm* : forum

forraje *nm* : forage, fodder — **forrajear** *vi* : forage

forrar *vt* **1** : line (a garment) **2** : cover (a book) — **forro** *nm* **1** : lining CUBIERTA : book cover

fortalecer {53} *vt* : strengthen — **fortaleza** *nf* **1** : fortress **2** FUERZA : strength **3** : (moral) fortitude

fortificar {72} *vt* : fortify — **fortificación** *nf, pl* **-ciones** : fortification

fortuito, -ta *adj* : fortuitous, chance

fortuna *nf* **1** SUERTE : fortune, luck **2** RIQUEZA : wealth, fortune **3 por** ∼ : fortunately

forzar {36} *vt* **1** : force **2** : strain (one's eyes) — **forzosamente** *adv* : necessarily — **forzoso, -sa** *adj* : necessary, inevitable

fosa *nf* **1** : pit, ditch **2** TUMBA : grave **3** ∼**s nasales** : nostrils

fósforo *nm* **1** : phosphorus **2** CERILLA : match — **fosforescente** *adj* : phosphorescent

fósil *nm* : fossil

foso *nm* **1** : ditch **2** : pit (of a theater) **3** : moat (of a castle)

foto *nf* : photo

fotocopia *nf* : photocopy — **fotocopiadora** *nf* : photocopier — **fotocopiar** *vt* : photocopy

fotogénico, -ca *adj* : photogenic

fotografía *nf* **1** : photography **2** : photograph, picture — **fotografiar** {85} *vt* : photograph — **fotográfico, -ca** *adj* : photographic — **fotógrafo, -fa** *n* : photographer

fotosíntesis *nf* : photosynthesis

fracasar *vi* : fail — **fracaso** *nm* : failure

fracción *nf, pl* **-ciones 1** : fraction **2** : faction (in politics) — **fraccionamiento** *nm Lat* : housing development

fractura *nf* : fracture — **fracturarse** *vr* : fracture, break (a bone)

fragancia *nf* : fragrance, scent — **fragante** *adj* : fragrant

fragata *nf* : frigate

frágil *adj* **1** : fragile **2** DÉBIL : frail, delicate — **fragilidad** *nf* **1** : fragility **2** DEBILIDAD : frailty

fragmento *nm* : fragment

fragor *nm* : clamor, din

fragoso, -sa *adj* : rough, rugged

fragua *nf* : forge — **fraguar** {10} *vt* **1** : forge **2** IDEAR : concoct — *vi* : harden, solidify

fraile *nm* : friar, monk

frambuesa *nf* : raspberry

francés, -cesa *adj, mpl* **-ceses** : French — **francés** *nm* : French (language)

franco, -ca *adj* **1** : frank, candid **2** : free (in commerce) — **franco** *nm* : franc

francotirador, -dora *n* : sniper

franela *nf* : flannel

franja *nf* **1** : stripe, band **2** FLECO : fringe

franquear *vt* **1** : clear (a path, etc.) **2** : cross over (a doorstep, etc.) **3** : pay postage on (mail) — **franqueo** *nm* : postage

franqueza *nf* : frankness

frasco *nm* : small bottle, vial, flask

frase *nf* 1 : phrase 2 ORACIÓN : sentence

fraternal *adj* : brotherly, fraternal — **fraternidad** *nf* : brotherhood, fraternity — **fraternizar** {21} *vi* : fraternize — **fraterno, -na** *adj* : brotherly, fraternal

fraude *nm* : fraud — **fraudulento, -ta** *adj* : fraudulent

fray *nm* (*used in titles*) : brother, friar

frazada *nf Lat* : blanket

frecuencia *nf* 1 : frequency 2 **con ~** : often, frequently — **frecuentar** *vt* : frequent, haunt — **frecuente** *adj* : frequent

fregadero *nm* : kitchen sink

fregar {49} *vt* 1 : scrub, wash 2 *Lat fam* : annoy — *vi Lat fam* : be a pest

freír {37} *vt* : fry

fregona *nf Spain* : mop

frenar *vt* 1 : brake 2 RESTRINGIR : curb, check

frenesí *nm* : frenzy — **frenético, -ca** *adj* : frantic, frenzied

freno *nm* 1 : brake 2 : bit (of a bridle) 3 CONTROL : check, restraint

frente *nm* 1 : front 2 : facade (of a building) 3 **al ~ de** : at the head of 4 **~ a** : opposite 5 **de ~** : (facing) forward 6 **hacer ~ a** : face up to, brave — **~** *nf* : forehead

fresa *nf* : strawberry

fresco, -ca *adj* 1 : fresh 2 FRÍO : cool 3 *fam* : insolent, nervy — **fresco** *nm* 1 : fresh air 2 FRESCOR : coolness 3 : fresco (art or painting) — **frescor** *nm* : coolness, cool air — **frescura** *nf* 1 : freshness 2 FRÍO : coolness 3 *fam* : nerve, insolence

fresno *nm* : ash (tree)

frialdad *nf* 1 : coldness 2 INDIFERENCIA : indifference

fricción *nf, pl* **-ciones** 1 : friction 2 MASAJE : rubbing, massage — **friccionar** *vt* : rub

frigidez *nf* : frigidity

frigorífico *nm Spain* : refrigerator

frijol *nm Lat* : bean

frío, fría *adj* 1 : cold 2 INDIFERENTE : cool, indifferent — **frío** *nm* 1 : cold 2 INDIFERENCIA : coldness, indifference 3 **hacer ~** : be cold (outside) 4 **tener ~** : be cold, feel cold

frito, -ta *adj* 1 : fried 2 *fam* : fed up

frívolo, -la *adj* : frivolous — **frivolidad** *nf* : frivolity

fronda *nf* 1 : frond 2 *or* **~s** *nfpl* : foliage — **frondoso, -sa** *adj* : leafy

frontera *nf* : border, frontier — **fronterizo, -za** *adj* : border, on the border — **frontero, -ra** *adj* : facing, opposite

frotar *vt* : rub — **frotarse** *vr* **~ las manos** : rub one's hands

fructífero, -ra *adj* : fruitful

frugal *adj* : frugal, thrifty — **frugalidad** *adj* : frugality

fruncir {83} *vt* 1 : gather (in pleats) 2 **~ el ceño** : frown 3 **~ la boca** : purse one's lips

frustrar *vt* : frustrate — **frustrarse** *vr* : fail — **frustración** *nf, pl* **-ciones** : frustration — **frustrado, -da** *adj* 1 : frustrated 2 FRACASADO : failed, unsuccessful — **frustrante** *adj* : frustrating

fruta *nf* : fruit — **frutilla** *nf Lat* : strawberry — **fruto** *nm* 1 : fruit 2 RESULTADO : result, consequence

fucsia *adj & nm* : fuchsia

fuego *nm* 1 : fire 2 : flame, burner (on a stove) 3 **~s artificiales** *nmpl* : fireworks 4 **¿tienes fuego?** : have you got a light?

fuelle *nm* : bellows

fuente *nf* 1 : fountain 2 MANANTIAL : spring 3 ORIGEN : source 4 PLATO : platter, serving dish

fuera *adv* 1 : outside, out 2 : abroad, away 3 **~ de** : outside of, beyond 4 **~ de** : aside from, in addition to

fuerte *adj* 1 : strong 2 : bright (of colors), loud (of sounds) 3 EXTREMO : intense 4 DURO : hard — **~** *adv* 1 : strongly, hard 2 : loudly MUCHO : abundantly, a lot — **~** *nm* 1 : fort 2 ESPECIALIDAD : strong point

fuerza *nf* 1 : strength 2 VIOLENCIA : force 3 PODER : power, might 4 **~s armadas** *nfpl* : armed forces 5 **a ~ de** : by dint of 6 **a la ~** : necessarily

fuga *nf* 1 : flight, escape 2 : fugue (in music) 3 ESCAPE : leak — **fugarse** {52} *vr* : flee, run away — **fugaz** *adj, pl* **-gaces** : fleeting — **fugitivo, -va** *adj & n* : fugitive

fulano, -na *n* : so-and-so, what's-his-name, what's-her-name

fulgor *nm* : brilliance, splendor

fulminar *vt* 1 : strike with lightning 2 : strike down (with an illness, etc.) — **fulminante** *adj* : devastating

fumar *v* : smoke — **fumarse** *vr* 1 : smoke 2 *fam* : squander — **fumador, -dora** *n* : smoker

funámbulo, -la *n* : tightrope walker

función *nf, pl* **-ciones** 1 : function 2 TRABAJOS : duties *pl* 3 : performance, show (in theater) — **funcional** *adj* : functional — **funcionamiento** *nm* 1

: functioning **2 en ~** : in operation — **funcionar** *vi* **1** : function, run, work **2 no funciona** : out of order — **funcionario, -ria** *n* : civil servant, official

funda *nf* **1** : cover, sheath **2** *or* **~ de almohada** : pillowcase

fundar *vt* **1** ESTABLECER : found, establish **2** BASAR : base — **fundarse** *vr* **en** : be based on — **fundación** *nf, pl* **-ciones** : foundation — **fundador, -dora** *n* : founder — **fundamental** *adj* : fundamental, basic — **fundamentalmente** *adv* : basically — **fundamentar** *vt* **1** : lay the foundations for **2** BASAR : base — **fundamento** *nm* **1** : foundation **2 ~s** *nmpl* : fundamentals

fundir *vt* **1** : melt down, smelt **2** FUSIONAR : fuse, merge — **fundirse** *vr* **1** : blend, merge **2** DERRETIRSE : melt **3** : burn out (of a lightbulb) — **fundición** *nf, pl* **-ciones** **1** : smelting **2** : foundry

fúnebre *adj* **1** : funeral **2** LÚGUBRE : gloomy

funeral *adj* : funeral, funerary — **~** *nm* **1** : funeral **2 ~es** *nmpl* EXEQUIAS : funeral (rites) — **funeraria** *nf* : funeral home

funesto, ta *adj* : terrible, disastrous

fungir {35} *vi Lat* : act, function

furgón *nm, pl* **-gones 1** : van, truck **2** : freight car (of a train) **3 ~ de cola** : caboose — **furgoneta** *nf* : van

furia *nf* **1** CÓLERA : fury, rage **2** VIOLENCIA : violence — **furibundo, -da** *adj* : furious — **furioso, -sa** *adj* **1** : furious, irate **2** INTENSO : intense, violent — **furor** *nm* : fury

furtivo, -va *adj* : furtive

furúnculo *nm* : boil

fuselaje *nm* : fuselage

fusible *nm* : fuse

fusil *nm* : rifle — **fusilar** *vt* : shoot (by firing squad)

fusión *nf, pl* **-siones 1** : fusion **2** UNIÓN : union, merger — **fusionar** *vt* **1** : fuse **2** UNIR : merge — **fusionarse** *vr* : merge — **fusionarse** *vr* : merge

futbol *or* **fútbol** *nm* **1** : soccer **2 ~ americano** : football — **futbolista** *nmf* : soccer player, football player

fútil *adj* : trifling, trivial

futuro, -ra *adj* : future — **futuro** *nm* : future

G

g *nf* : g, seventh letter of the Spanish alphabet

gabán *nm, pl* **-banes** : topcoat, overcoat

gabardina *nf* **1** : trench coat, raincoat **2** : gabardine (fabric)

gabinete *nm* **1** : cabinet (in government) **2** : (professional) office

gacela *nf* : gazelle

gaceta *nf* : gazette

gachas *nfpl* : porridge

gacho, -cha *adj* : drooping

gaélico, -ca *adj* : Gaelic

gafas *nfpl* **1** : eyeglasses **2 ~ de sol** : sunglasses

gaita *nf* : bagpipes *pl*

gajo *nm* : segment (of fruit)

gala *nf* **1** : gala **2 de ~** : formal **3 hacer ~ de** : display, show off **4 ~s** *nfpl* : finery

galáctico, -ca *adj* : galactic

galán *nm, pl* **-lanes 1** : leading man (in theater) **2** *fam* : boyfriend

galante *adj* : gallant — **galantear** *vt* : court, woo — **galantería** *nf* **1** : gallantry **2** CUMPLIDO : compliment

galápago *nm* : (aquatic) turtle

galardón *nm, pl* **-dones** : reward

galaxia *nf* : galaxy

galera *nf* : galley

galería *nf* **1** : corridor **2** : gallery, balcony (in a theater)

galés, -lesa *adj, mpl* **-leses** : Welsh

galgo *nm* : greyhound

galimatías *nms & pl* : gibberish

gallardía *nf* **1** : bravery **2** ELEGANCIA : elegance — **gallardo, -da** *adj* **1** : brave **2** APUESTO : elegant, good-looking

gallego, -ga *adj* : Galician

galleta *nf* **1** : (sweet) cookie **2** : (salted) cracker

gallina *nf* **1** : hen **2 ~ de Guinea** : guinea fowl — **gallinero** *nm* : henhouse, (chicken) coop — **gallo** *nm* : rooster, cock

galón *nm, pl* **-lones 1** : gallon **2** : stripe (military insignia)

galopar *vi* : gallop — **galope** *nm* : gallop

galvanizar {21} *vt* : galvanize

gama *nf* **1** : range, spectrum **2** : scale (in music)

gamba *nf* : large shrimp, prawn

gamuza *nf* **1** : chamois (animal) **2** : chamois (leather), suede

gana *nf* **1** : desire, wish 2 APETITO : appetite **3 de buena ~** : willingly, heartily **4 de mala ~** : unwillingly **5 no me da la ~** : I don't feel like it **6 tener ~s de** : feel like, be in the mood for

ganado *nm* **1** : cattle *pl*, livestock **2 ~ ovino** : sheep *pl* **3 ~ porcino** : swine *pl* **— ganadería** *nf* **1** : cattle raising **2** GANADO : livestock

ganador, -dora *adj* : winning **— ~** *n* : winner

ganancia *nf* : profit

ganar *vt* **1** : earn **2** : win (in games, etc.) **3** CONSEGUIR : gain **4** ADQUERIR : get, obtain **5 ~ a algn** : win over s.o., beat s.o. **— vi** : win **— ganarse** *vr* **1** : win, gain **2 ~ la vida** : make a living

gancho *nm* **1** : hook **2** HORQUILLA : hairpin **3** *Lat* : (clothes) hanger

gandul, -dula *adj & n fam* : good-for-nothing **— gandul** *nm Lat* : pigeon pea

ganga *nf* : bargain

gangrena *nf* : gangrene

gángster *nmf* : gangster

ganso, -sa *n* : goose, gander *m* **— gansada** *nf* : silly thing, nonsense

gañir {38} *vi* : yelp **— gañido** *nm* : yelp

garabatear *v* : scribble **— garabato** *nm* : scribble

garaje *nm* : garage

garantizar {21} *vt* : guarantee **— garante** *nmf* : guarantor **— garantía** *nf* **1** : guarantee, warranty **2** FIANZA : surety

garapiñar *vt* : candy (fruits, etc.)

garbanzo *nm* : chickpea, garbanzo

garbo *nm* : grace, elegance **— garboso, -sa** *adj* : graceful, elegant

gardenia *nf* : gardenia

garfio *nm* : hook, gaff

garganta *nf* **1** : throat **2** CUELLO : neck **3** DESFILADERO : ravine, gorge **— gargantilla** *nf* : necklace

gárgara *nf* **1** : gargling, gargle **2 hacer ~s** : gargle

gárgola *nf* : gargoyle

garita *nf* **1** : sentry box **2** CABAÑA : cabin, hut

garito *nm* : gambling den

garra *nf* **1** : claw, talon **2** *fam* : hand, paw

garrafa *nf* : decanter, carafe **— garrafón** *nm, pl* **-fones** : large decanter or bottle

garrapata *nf* : tick

garrocha *nf* **1** : lance, pike **2** *Lat* : pole (in sports)

garrote *nm* : club, cudgel

garúa *nf Lat* : drizzle

gas *nm* **1** : gas **2 ~ lacrimógeno** : tear gas

gasa *nf* : gauze

gaseosa *nf* : soda, soft drink

gasolina *nf* : gasoline, gas **— gasoil** *or* **gasóleo** *nm* : diesel fuel **— gasolinera** *nf* : gas station, service station

gastar *vt* **1** : spend **2** CONSUMIR : consume, use up **3** DESPERDICIAR : squander, waste **— gastarse** *vr* **1** : spend **2** DETERIORARSE : wear out **— gastado, -da** *adj* **1** : spent **2** : worn-out (of clothing, etc.) **— gastador, -dora** *n* : spendthrift **— gasto** *nm* **1** : expense, expenditure **2 ~s generales** : overhead

gástrico, -ca *adj* : gastric

gastronomía *nf* : gastronomy **— gastrónomo, -ma** *n* : gourmet

gatas: a ~ *adv phr* : on all fours

gatear *vi* : crawl, creep

gatillo *nm* : trigger **— gatillero** *nm Mex* : gunman

gato, -ta *n* : cat **— gatito, -ta** *n* : kitten **— gato** *nm* : jack (for an automobile)

gaucho *nm* : gaucho

gaveta *nf* : drawer

gavilla *nf* **1** : sheaf **2** PANDILLA : gang

gaviota *nf* : gull, seagull

gay ['ge, 'gai] *adj* : gay (homosexual)

gaza *nf* : loop

gazpacho *nm* : gazpacho

géiser *nm* : geyser

gelatina *nf* : gelatin

gema *nf* : gem

gemelo, -la *adj & n* : twin **— gemelo** *nm* **1** : cuff link **2 ~s** *nmpl* : binoculars

gemir {54} *vi* : moan, groan, whine **— gemido** *nm* : moan, groan, whine

gen *or* **gene** *nm* : gene

genealogía *nf* : genealogy **— genealógico, -ca** *adj* : genealogical

generación *nf, pl* **-ciones** : generation

generador *nm* : generator

general *adj* **1** : general **2 en ~** *or* **por lo ~** : in general, generally **— ~** *nmf* : general **— generalidad** *nf* **1** : generalization **2** MAYORÍA : majority **— generalizar** {21} *vi* : generalize **— vt** : spread (out) **— generalizarse** *vr* : become widespread **— generalmente** *adv* : usually, generally

generar *vt* : generate

género *nm* **1** : kind, sort **2** : gender (in

grammar) **3 ~ humano** : human race — **genérico, -ca** adj : generic

generoso, -sa adj **1** : generous, unselfish **2** : ample (in quantity) — **generosidad** nf : generosity

génesis nfs & pl : genesis

genética nf : genetics — **genético, -ca** adj : genetic

genial adj **1** : brilliant **2** ESTUPENDO : great, terrific

genio nm **1** : genius **2** CARÁCTER : temper, disposition **3** : genie (in mythology)

genital adj : genital — **genitales** nmpl : genitals

genocidio nm : genocide

gente nf **1** : people **2** fam : relatives pl, folks pl **3 ser buena ~** : be nice, be kind

gentil adj **1** AMABLE : kind **2** : gentile (in religion) — **gentileza** nf : kindness, courtesy

gentío nm : crowd, mob

gentuza nf : riffraff, rabble

genuflexión nf, pl **-xiones** : genuflection

genuino, -na adj : genuine

geografía nf : geography — **geográfico, -ca** adj : geographic, geographical

geología nf : geology — **geológico, -ca** adj : geologic, geological

geometría nf : geometry — **geométrico, -ca** adj : geometric, geometrical

geranio nm : geranium

gerencia nf : management — **gerente** nmf : manager

geriatría nf : geriatrics — **geriátrico, -ca** adj : geriatric

germen nm, pl **gérmenes** : germ

germinar vi : germinate, sprout

gestación nf, pl **-ciones** : gestation

gesticular vi : gesticulate, gesture — **gesticulación** nf, pl **-ciones** : gesticulation

gestión nf, pl **-tiones 1** : procedure, step **2** ADMINISTRACIÓN : management — **gestionar** vt **1** : negotiate, work towards **2** ADMINISTRAR : manage, handle

gesto nm **1** : gesture **2 ~** : (facial) expression **3** MUECA : grimace

gigante adj & nm : giant — **gigantesco, -ca** adj : gigantic

gimnasia nf : gymnastics — **gimnasio** nm : gymnasium, gym — **gimnasta** nmf : gymnast

gimotear vi : whine, whimper

ginebra nf : gin

ginecología nf : gynecology — **ginecólogo, -ga** n : gynecologist

gira nf : tour

girar vi : turn (around), revolve — vt **1** : turn, twist, rotate **2** : draft (checks) **3** : transfer (funds)

girasol nm : sunflower

giratorio, -ria adj : revolving

giro nm **1** : turn, rotation **2** LOCUCIÓN : expression **3 ~ bancario** : bank draft **4 ~ postal** : money order

giroscopio nm : gyroscope

gis nm Lat : chalk

gitano, -na adj & n : Gypsy

glaciar nm : glacier — **glacial** adj : glacial, icy

gladiador nm : gladiator

glándula nf : gland

glasear vt : glaze, ice (cake, etc.) — **glaseado** nm : icing

glicerina nf : glycerin

globo nm **1** : globe **2** : balloon **3 ~ ocular** : eyeball — **global** adj **1** : global **2** TOTAL : total, overall

glóbulo nm : blood cell, corpuscle

gloria nf : glory

glorieta nf **1** : bower, arbor **2** Spain : rotary, traffic circle

glorificar {72} vt : glorify

glorioso, -sa adj : glorious

glosario nm : glossary

glotón, -tona adj, mpl **-tones** : gluttonous — ~ n : glutton — **glotonería** nf : gluttony

glucosa nf : glucose

gnomo ['nomo] nm : gnome

gobernar {55} v **1** : govern, rule **2** DIRIGIR : direct, manage **3** : steer (a boat, etc.) — **gobernación** nf, pl **-ciones** : governing, government — **gobernador, -dora** n : governor — **gobernante** adj : ruling, governing — ~ n : ruler, leader — **gobierno** nm : government

goce nm : enjoyment

gol nm : goal (in sports)

golf nm : golf — **golfista** nmf : golfer

golfo nm : gulf

golondrina nf **1** : swallow **2 ~ de mar** : tern

golosina nf : sweet, candy — **goloso, -sa** adj : fond of sweets

golpe nm **1** : blow **2** PUÑETAZO : punch **3** : knock (on a door, etc.) **4 de ~** : suddenly **5 de un ~** : all at once **6 ~ de estado** : coup d'etat — **golpear** vt **1** : hit, punch **2** : slam, bang (a door, etc.) — vi : knock (at a door)

goma nf **1** CAUCHO : rubber **2** PEGAMENTO : glue **3 or ~ elástica** : rubber band **4 ~ de mascar** : chewing gum **5 ~ de borrar** : eraser

gong nm : gong

gordo, -da *adj* **1** : fat, plump **2** GRUESO : thick **3** : fatty (of meat) **4** *fam* : big, serious — ~ *n* : fat person — **gorda** *nf Lat* : thick corn tortilla — **gordo** *nm* **1** GRASA : fat **2** : jackpot (in a lottery) — **gordura** *nf* : fatness, flab

gorgotear *vi* : gurgle, bubble

gorila *nm* : gorilla

gorjear *vi* **1** : chirp, tweet **2** : gurgle (of a baby) — **gorjeo** *nm* : chirping

gorra *nf* **1** : cap, bonnet **2 de** ~ *fam* : for free

gorrear *vt fam* : bum, scrounge

gorrión *nm, pl* **-rriones** : sparrow

gorro *nm* **1** : cap, bonnet **2 de** ~ *fam* : for free

gota *nf* **1** : drop **2** : gout (in medicine) — **gotear** *vi* : drip, leak — **goteo** *nm* : drip, dripping — **gotera** *nf* : leak

gótico, -ca *adj* : Gothic

gozar {21} *vi* **1** : enjoy oneself **2** ~ **de algo** : enjoy sth

gozne *nm* : hinge

gozo *nm* **1** : joy **2** PLACER : enjoyment, pleasure — **gozoso, -sa** *adj* : joyful, glad

grabar *vt* **1** : engrave **2** : record, tape — **grabación** *nf, pl* **-ciones** : recording — **grabado** *nm* : engraving — **grabadora** *nf* : tape recorder

gracia *nf* **1** : grace **2** FAVOR : favor, kindness **3** HUMOR : humor, wit **4** ~**s** *nfpl* : thanks **5 ¡(muchas)** ~**s!** : thank you (very much)! — **gracioso, -sa** *adj* **1** : funny, amusing

grada *nf* **1** : step, stair **2** : row (in a theater, etc.) **3** ~**s** *nfpl* : bleachers, grandstand — **gradación** *nf, pl* **-ciones** : gradation, scale — **gradería** *nf* : rows *pl*, stands *pl* — **grado** *nm* **1** : degree **2** : grade (in school) **3 de buen** ~ : willingly

graduar {3} *vt* **1** : regulate, adjust **2** MARCAR : calibrate **3** : confer a degree on (in education) — **graduarse** *vr* : graduate (from a school) — **graduación** *nf, pl* **-ciones 1** : graduation **2** : alcohol content, proof — **graduado, -da** *n* : graduate — **gradual** *adj* : gradual — **gradualmente** *adv* : little by little, gradually

gráfico, -ca *adj* : graphic — **gráfica** *nf* : graph — **gráfico** *nm* **1** : graph **2** : graphic (in computers)

gragea *nf* : pill, tablet

grajo *nm* : rook (bird)

gramática *nf* : grammar — **gramatical** *adj* : grammatical

gramo *nm* : gram

gran → **grande**

grana *nf* : scarlet

granada *nf* **1** : pomegranate **2** : grenade (in the military)

granate *nm* : garnet

grande *adj* (**gran** *before singular nouns*) **1** : large, big **2** ALTO : tall **3** : great (in quality, intensity, etc.) **4** *Lat* : grown-up — **grandeza** *nf* **1** : greatness **2** NOBLEZA : nobility — **grandiosidad** *nf* : grandeur — **grandioso, -sa** *adj* : grand, magnificent

granel : a ~ *adv phr* **1** : in bulk **2** : in abundance

granero *nm* : barn, granary

granito *nm* : granite

granizar {21} *v impers* : hail — **granizada** *nf* : hailstorm — **granizado** *nm* : iced drink — **granizo** *nm* : hail

granja *nf* : farm — **granjero, -ra** *n* : farmer

grano *nm* **1** : grain **2** SEMILLA : seed **3** : (coffee) bean **4** BARRO : pimple

granuja *nmf* : rascal

grapa *nf* : staple — **grapadora** *nf* : stapler — **grapar** *vt* : staple

grasa *nf* **1** : grease **2** : fat (in cooking, etc.) — **grasiento, -ta** *adj* : greasy, oily — **graso, -sa** *adj* : fatty, greasy, oily — **grasoso, -sa** *adj Lat* : greasy, oily

gratificar {72} *vt* **1** : give a tip or bonus to **2** SATISFACER : gratify, satisfy — **gratificación** *nf, pl* **-ciones 1** : bonus, tip, reward **2** SATISFACCIÓN : gratification

gratis *adv & adj* : free

gratitud *nf* : gratitude

grato, -ta *adj* : pleasant, agreeable

gratuito, -ta *adj* **1** : gratuitous, unwarranted **2** GRATIS : free

grava *nf* : gravel

gravar *vt* **1** : tax **2** CARGAR : burden — **gravamen** *nm, pl* **-vámenes 1** : burden, obligation **2** IMPUESTO : tax

grave *adj* **1** : grave, serious **2** : deep, low (of a voice, etc.) — **gravedad** *nf* : gravity

gravilla *nf* : gravel

gravitar *vi* **1** : gravitate **2** ~ **sobre** : weigh on — **gravitación** *nf, pl* **-ciones** : gravitation

gravoso, -sa *adj* : costly, burdensome

graznar *vi* : caw, squawk, honk — **graznido** *nm* : caw, quack, honk

gregario, -ria *adj* : gregarious

gremio *nm* : guild, (trade) union

greñas *nfpl* : shaggy hair, mop

griego, -ga *adj* : Greek — **griego** *nm* : Greek (language)

grieta *nf* : crack, crevice

grifo *nm Spain* : faucet, tap

grillete *nm* : shackle

grillo *nm* **1** : cricket **2 ~s** *nmpl* : fetters, shackles

grima *nf* **dar ~** : annoy, irritate

gringo, -ga *adj & n Lat fam* : Yankee, gringo

gripe *nf or* **gripa** *nf Lat* : flu, influenza

gris *adj & nm* : gray

gritar *v* : shout, scream, cry — **grito** *nm* **1** : shout, scream, cry **2 dar ~s** : shout

grosella *nf* : currant

grosería *nf* **1** : vulgar remark **2** DESCORTESÍA : rudeness — **grosero, -ra** *adj* **1** : coarse, vulgar **2** DESCORTÉS : rude

grosor *nm* : thickness

grotesco, -ca *adj* : grotesque, hideous

grúa *nf* : crane, derrick

grueso, -sa *adj* **1** : thick **2** CORPULENTO : stout, heavy — **gruesa** *nf* : gross — **grueso** *nm* **1** GROSOR : thickness **2** : main body, mass **3 en ~** : wholesale

grulla *nf* : crane (bird)

grumo *nm* : lump, clot — **grumoso, -sa** *adj* : lumpy

gruñir {38} *vi* **1** : growl, grunt **2** *fam* : grumble — **gruñido** *nm* **1** : growl, grunt **2** *fam* : grumble — **gruñón, -ñona** *adj, mpl* **-ñones** *fam* : grumpy, grouchy — **~ n** *fam* : grouch

grupa *nf* : rump, hindquarters *pl*

grupo *nm* : group

gruta *nf* : grotto

guacamayo *nm or* **guacamaya** *nf Lat* : macaw

guacamole *nm* : guacamole

guadaña *nf* : scythe

guagua *nf Lat* **1** : baby **2** AUTOBÚS : bus

guajolote, -ta *o* **guajolote, -ta** *n Lat* : turkey

guante *nm* : glove

guapo, -pa *adj* : handsome, good-looking

guaraní *nm* : Guarani (language of Paraguay)

guarda *nmf* **1** : keeper, custodian **2** GUARDIÁN : security guard — **guardabarros** *nms & pl* : fender — **guardabosque** *nmf* : forest ranger — **guardacostas** *nmfs & pl* : coast guard vessel — **guardaespaldas** *nmfs & pl* : bodyguard — **guardameta** *nmf* : goalkeeper — **guardapolvo** *nm* : overalls *pl* — **guardar** *vt* **1** : keep **2** PROTEGER : guard, protect **3** RESERVAR : save — **guardarse** *vr* **~ de 1** : refrain from **2** : guard against — **guardarropa** *nm* **1**

: cloakroom, checkroom **2** ARMARIO : wardrobe

guardería *nf* : nursery, day-care center

guardia *nf* **1** : guard, vigilence **2** TURNO : duty, watch — **~** *nmf* **1** : guard **2** *or* **~ municipal** : police officer — **guardián, -diana** *n, mpl* **-dianes 1** : guardian, keeper **2** GUARDA : security guard

guarecer {53} *vt* : shelter, protect — **guarecerse** *vr* : take shelter

guarida *nf* **1** : den, lair (of animals) **2** : hideout (of persons)

guarnecer {53} *vt* **1** : adorn, garnish **2** : garrison (an area) — **guarnición** *nf, pl* **-ciones 1** : garnish, trimming **2** : (military) garrison

guasa *nf fam* **1** : joke **2 de ~** : in jest — **guasón, -sona** *adj, mpl* **-sones** *fam* : joking, witty — **~ n** *fam* : joker

guatemalteco, -ca *adj* : Guatemalan

guayaba *nf* : guava

gubernamental *or* **gubernativo, -va** *adj* : governmental

guepardo *nm* : cheetah

güero, -ra *adj Lat* : blond, fair

guerra *nf* **1** : war, warfare **2** LUCHA : conflict, struggle — **guerrear** *vi* : wage war — **guerrero, -ra** *adj* **1** : war, fighting **2** BELICOSO : warlike — **~ n** : warrior — **guerrilla** *nf* : guerrilla warfare — **guerrillero, -ra** *adj & n* : guerrilla

gueto *nm* : ghetto

guiar {85} *vt* **1** : guide, lead **2** ACONSEJAR : advise — **guiarse** *vr* : be guided by, go by — **guía** *nf* **1** : guidebook **2** ORIENTACIÓN : guidance — **~** *nmf* : guide, leader

guijarro *nm* : pebble

guillotina *nf* : guillotine

guinda *nf* : morello (cherry)

guiñar *vi* : wink — **guiño** *nm* : wink

guión *nm, pl* **guiones 1** : script, screenplay **2** : hyphen, dash (in punctuation) — **guionista** *nmf* : scriptwriter, screenwriter

guirnalda *nf* : garland

guisa *nf* **1** : manner, fashion **2 a ~ de** : by way of **3 de tal ~** : in such a way

guisado *nm* : stew

guisante *nm* : pea

guisar *vt* : cook — **guiso** *nm* : stew, casserole

guitarra *nf* : guitar — **guitarrista** *nmf* : guitarist

gula *nf* : gluttony

gusano *nm* **1** : worm **2** : maggot (larva)

gustar *vt* **1** : taste **2** *Lat* : like — *vi* **1** : be pleasing **2 como guste** : as you like **3**

me gustan los dulces : I like sweets — **gusto** *nm* **1** : taste **2** PLACER : pleasure, liking **3 a** ~ : comfortable, at ease **4 al** ~ : to taste **5 mucho** ~ : pleased to meet you — **gustoso, -sa** *adj* **1** : tasty **2** AGRADABLE : pleasant **3 hacer algo** ~ : do sth willingly

gutural *adj* : guttural

H

h *nf* : h; eighth letter of the Spanish alphabet

haba *nf* : broad bean

habanero, -ra *adj* : Havanan — **habano** *nm* : Havana cigar

haber {39} *v aux* **1** : have, has **2** ~ **de** : must — *v impers* **1 hay** : there is, there are **2 hay que** : it is necessary (to) **3 ¿qué hay?** *or* **¿qué hubo?** : how's it going? — ~ *nm* **1** : assets *pl* **2** : credit side (in accounting) **3** ~**es** *nmpl* : income, earnings

habichuela *nf* **1** : bean **2** ~ **verde** : string bean

hábil *adj* **1** : able, skillful **2** LISTO : clever **3 horas** ~**es** : business hours — **habilidad** *nf* : ability, skill

habilitar *vt* **1** : equip, furnish **2** AUTORIZAR : authorize

habitar *vt* **1** : inhabit — *vi* : reside, dwell — **habitable** *adj* : habitable, inhabitable — **habitación** *nf, pl* **-ciones 1** : room, bedroom **2** MORADA : dwelling, abode **3** : habitat (in biology) — **habitante** *nmf* : inhabitant, resident — **hábitat** *nm* : habitat

hábito *nm* : habit — **habitual** *adj* : habitual, usual — **habituar** {3} *vt* : accustom, habituate — **habituarse** *vr* ~ **a** : get used to

hablar *vi* **1** : speak, talk **2** ~ **de** : mention, talk about **3** ~ **con** : talk to, speak with — *vt* **1** : speak (a language) **2** DISCUTIR : discuss — **hablarse** *vr* **1** : speak to each other **2 se habla inglés** : English spoken — **habla** *nf* **1** : speech **2** IDIOMA : language, dialect **3 de** ~ **inglesa** : English-speaking — **hablador, -dora** *adj* : talkative — ~ *n* : chatterbox — **habladuría** *nf* **1** : rumor **2** ~**s** *nfpl* : gossip — **hablante** *nmf* : speaker

hacedor, -dora *nm* : creator, maker

hacendado, -da *n* : landowner, rancher

hacer {40} *vt* **1** : do, perform **2** CONSTRUIR, CREAR : make **3** OBLIGAR : force, oblige — *vi* : act — *v impers* **1** ~ **calor/viento** : be hot/be windy **2** ~ **falta** : be necessary **hace mucho tiempo** : a long time ago **4 no lo hace** : it doesn't matter — **hacerse** *vr* **1** : VOLVERSE : become **2** : pretend (to be) **3** ~ **a** : get used to **4 se hace tarde** : it's getting late

hacha *nf* **1** : hatchet, ax **2** ANTORCHA : torch

hachís *nm* : hashish

hacia *prep* **1** : toward, towards **2** CERCA DE : near, around, about **3** ~ **abajo** : downward **4** ~ **adelante** : forward

hacienda *nf* **1** : estate, ranch **2** BIENES : property **3** *Lat* : livestock **4 Hacienda** : department of revenue

hacinar *vt* : stack

hada *nf* : fairy

hado *nm* : fate

halagar {52} *vt* : flatter — **halagador, -dora** *adj* : flattering — **halago** *nm* : flattery — **halagüeño, -ña** *adj* **1** : flattering **2** PROMETEDOR : promising

halcón *nm, pl* **-cones** : hawk, falcon

halibut *nm, pl* **-buts** : halibut

hálito *nm* : breath

hallar *vt* **1** : find **2** DESCUBRIR : discover, find out — **hallarse** *vr* : be, find oneself — **hallazgo** *nm* : discovery, find

halo *nm* : halo

hamaca *nf* : hammock

hambre *nf* **1** : hunger **2** INANICIÓN : starvation, famine **3 tener** ~ : be hungry — **hambriento, -ta** *adj* : hungry, starving — **hambruna** *nf* : famine

hamburguesa *nf* : hamburger

hampa *nf* : underworld — **hampón, -pona** *n, mpl* **-pones** : criminal, thug

hámster *nm* : hamster

hándicap *nm* : handicap (in sports)

hangar *nm* : hangar

haragán, -gana *adj, mpl* **-ganes** : lazy, idle — ~ *n* : slacker, idler — **haraganear** : be lazy, loaf

harapiento, -ta *adj* : ragged, in rags — **harapos** *nmpl* : rags, tatters

harina *nf* : flour

hartar *vt* **1** : glut, satiate **2** FASTIDIAR : annoy — **hartarse** *vr* **1** : gorge oneself **2** CANSARSE : get fed up — **harto, -ta** *adj* **1** : full, satiated **2** CANSADO : tired, fed up — **harto** *adv* : extremely, very — **hartura** *nf* **1** : surfeit **2** ABUNDANCIA : abundance, plenty

hasta *prep* **1** : until, up until (in time) **2**

: as far as, up to (in space) 3 ¡~
luego! : see you later! 4 ~ que : until
— ~ adv : even

hastiar {85} vt 1 : make weary, bore 2
ASQUEAR : sicken — hastiarse vr ~
de : get tired of — hastío nm 1 : weariness, tedium 2 REPUGNANCIA : disgust

hato nm 1 : flock, herd 2 : bundle (of
possessions)

haya nf : beech

haz nm, pl haces 1 : bundle, sheaf 2
: beam (of light)

hazaña nf : feat, exploit

hazmerreír nm fam : laughingstock

he {39} v impers ~ aquí : here is, here
are, behold

hebilla nf : buckle

hebra nf : strand, thread

hebreo, -brea adj : Hebrew — hebreo
nm : Hebrew (language)

hecatombe nm : disaster

hechizo nm 1 : spell 2 ENCANTO : charm,
fascination — hechicería nf : sorcery,
witchcraft — hechicero, -ra n : sorcerer, sorceress f — hechizar {21} vt 1
: bewitch 2 CAUTIVAR : charm

hecho, -cha adj 1 : made, done 2
: ready-to-wear (of clothing) 3 ~ y
derecho : full-fledged, mature —
hecho nm 1 : fact 2 SUCESO : event 3
ACTO : act, deed 4 de ~ : in fact —
hechura nf 1 : making, creation 2
FORMA : shape, form 3 : build (of the
body) 4 ARTESANÍA : workmanship

heder {56} vi : stink, reek — hedion-
dez nf, pl -deces : stench — hedion-
do, -da adj : stinking — hedor nm
: stench

helar {55} v : freeze — helarse vr
: freeze up, freeze over — helado, -da
adj 1 : freezing cold 2 CONGELADO
: frozen — helada nf : frost —
heladería nf : ice-cream parlor —
helado nm : ice cream — heladora nf
: freezer

helecho nm : fern

hélice nf 1 : propeller 2 ESPIRAL : spiral,
helix

helicóptero nm : helicopter

helio nm : helium

hembra nf : female 2 MUJER : woman

hemisferio nm : hemisphere

hemorragia nf 1 : hemorrhage 2 ~
nasal : nosebleed

hemorroides nfpl : hemorrhoids, piles

henchir {54} vt : stuff, fill

hender {56} vt : cleave, split — hendidura nf : crevice, fissure

henequén nm, pl -quenes : sisal

heno nm : hay

hepatitis nf : hepatitis

heraldo nm : herald

herbolario, -ria n : herbalist

heredar vt : inherit — heredad nm
: rural property, estate — heredero,
-ra n : heir, heiress f — hereditario,
-ria adj : hereditary

hereje nmf : heretic — herejía nf
: heresy

herencia nf 1 : inheritance 2 : heredity
(in biology)

herir {76} vt 1 : injure, wound 2 : hurt
(feelings, pride, etc.) — herida nf : injury, wound — herido, -da adj 1 : injured, wounded 2 : hurt (of feelings,
pride, etc.) — ~ n : injured person,
casualty

hermano, -na n : brother m, sister f —
hermanastro, -tra n : half brother m,
half sister f — hermandad f : brotherhood

hermético, -ca adj : hermetic, water-
tight

hermoso, -sa adj : beautiful, lovely —
hermosura nf : beauty

hernia nf : hernia

héroe nm : hero — heroico, -ca adj
: heroic — heroína nf 1 : heroine 2
: heroin (narcotic) — heroísmo nm
: heroism

herradura nf : horseshoe

herramienta nf : tool

herrero, -ra n : blacksmith

herrumbre nf : rust

hervir {76} v : boil — hervidero nm 1
: mass, swarm 2 : hotbed (of intrigue,
etc.) — hervidor nm : kettle — hervor
nm 1 : boiling 2 ENTUSIASMO : fervor,
ardor

heterogéneo, -nea adj : heterogeneous

heterosexual adj & nmf : heterosexual

hexágono nm : hexagon — hexagonal
adj : hexagonal

hez nf, pl heces : dregs pl, scum

hiato nm : hiatus

hibernar vi : hibernate — hibernación
nf, pl -ciones : hibernation

híbrido, -da adj : hybrid — híbrido nm
: hybrid

hidalgo, -ga n : nobleman m, noble-
woman f

hidratante adj : moisturizing

hidrato nm ~ de carbono : carbohydrate

hidráulico, -ca adj : hydraulic

hidroavión nm, pl -aviones : seaplane

hidroeléctrico, -ca adj : hydroelectric

hidrofobia nf : rabies

hidrógeno nm : hydrogen

hidroplano nm : hydroplane

hiedra *nf* **1** : ivy **2** ~ **venenosa** : poison ivy

hiel *nf* **1** : bile **2** AMARGURA : bitterness

hielo *nm* **1** : ice **2** FRIALDAD : coldness **3 romper el** ~ : break the ice

hiena *nf* : hyena

hierba *nf* **1** : herb **2** CÉSPED : grass **3 mala** ~ : weed — **hierbabuena** *nf* : mint

hierro *nm* **1** : iron **2** ~ **fundido** : cast iron

hígado *nm* : liver

higiene *nf* : hygiene — **higiénico, -ca** *adj* : hygienic

higo *nm* : fig

hijo, -ja *n* **1** : son *m*, daughter *f* **2 hijos** *nmpl* : children, offspring — **hijastro, -tra** *n* : stepson *m*, stepdaughter *f*

hilar *v* **1** : spin **2** ~ **delgado** : split hairs — **hilado** *nm* : yarn, thread

hilaridad *nf* : hilarity

hilera *nf* : file, row

hilo *nm* **1** : thread **2** LINO : linen **3** ALAMBRE : wire **4** : trickle (of water, etc.) **5** ~ **dental** : dental floss

hilvanar *vt* **1** : baste, tack **2** : put together (ideas, etc.)

himno *nm* **1** : hymn **2** ~ **nacional** : national anthem

hincapié *nm* **hacer** ~ **en** : emphasize, stress

hincar {72} *vt* : drive in, plunge — **hincarse** *vr* ~ **de rodillas** : kneel (down)

hinchar *vt Spain* : inflate, blow up — **hincharse** *vr* **1** : swell (up) **2** *Spain fam* : stuff oneself — **hinchado, -da** *adj* **1** : swollen **2** POMPOSO : pompous — **hinchazón** *nf, pl* -**zones** : swelling

hindú *adj & nmf, pl* -**dúes** : Hindu — **hinduismo** *nm* : Hinduism

hinojo *nm* : fennel

hiperactivo, -va *adj* : hyperactive

hipersensible *adj* : oversensitive

hipertensión *nf, pl* -**siones** : hypertension, high blood pressure

hípico, -ca *adj* : equestrian, horse

hipil → **huipil**

hipnosis *nfs & pl* : hypnosis — **hipnótico, -ca** *adj* : hypnotic — **hipnotismo** *nm* : hypnotism — **hipnotizador, -dora** *n* : hypnotist — **hipnotizar** {21} *vt* : hypnotize

hipo *nm* **1** : hiccup, hiccups *pl* **2 tener** ~ : have hiccups

hipocondríaco, -ca *adj* : hypochondriacal — ~ *n* : hypochondriac

hipocresía *nf* : hypocrisy — **hipócrita** *adj* : hypocritical — ~ *nmf* : hypocrite

hipodérmico, -ca *adj* : hypodermic

hipódromo *nm* : racetrack

hipopótamo *nm* : hippopotamus

hipoteca *nf* : mortgage — **hipotecar** {72} *vt* : mortgage

hipótesis *nfs & pl* : hypothesis — **hipotético, -ca** *adj* : hypothetical

hiriente *adj* : hurtful, offensive

hirsuto, -ta *adj* **1** : hairy **2** : bristly, wiry (of hair)

hirviente *adj* : boiling

hispano, -na *or* **hispánico, -ca** *adj & n* : Hispanic — **hispanoamericano, -na** *adj* : Latin-American — ~ *n* : Latin American — **hispanohablante** *or* **hispanoparlante** *adj* : Spanish-speaking

histeria *nf* : hysteria — **histérico, -ca** *adj* : hysterical — **histerismo** *nm* : hysteria

historia *nf* **1** : history **2** CUENTO : story — **historiador, -dora** *n* : historian — **historial** *nm* : record, background — **histórico, -ca** *adj* **1** : historical **2** IMPORTANTE : historic, important — **historieta** *nf* : comic strip

hito *nm* : milestone, landmark

hocico *nm* : snout, muzzle

hockey ['hɔke, -ki] *nm* : hockey

hogar *nm* **1** : home **2** CHIMENEA : hearth, fireplace — **hogareño, -ña** *adj* **1** : home-loving **2** DOMÉSTICO : home, domestic

hoguera *nf* : bonfire

hoja *nf* **1** : leaf **2** : sheet (of paper) **3** ~ **de afeitar** : razor blade — **hojalata** *nf* : tinplate — **hojaldre** *nm* : puff pastry — **hojear** *vt* : leaf through — **hojuela** *nf Lat* : flake

hola *interj* : hello!, hi!

holandés, -desa *adj, mpl* -**deses** : Dutch

holgado, -da *adj* **1** : loose, baggy **2** : comfortable (of an economic situation, a victory, etc.) — **holgazán, -zana** *adj, mpl* -**zanes** : lazy — ~ *n* : slacker, idler — **holgazanear** *vi* : laze about, loaf — **holgura** *nf* **1** : looseness **2** BIENESTAR : comfort, ease

hollín *nm, pl* -**llines** : soot

holocausto *nm* : holocaust

hombre *nm* **1** : man **2 el** ~ : mankind **3** ~ **de estado** : statesman **4** ~ **de negocios** : businessman

hombrera *nf* **1** : shoulder pad **2** : epaulet (of a uniform)

hombría *nf* : manliness

hombro *nm* : shoulder

hombruno, -na *adj* : mannish

homenaje *nm* **1** : homage **2 rendir ~ a** : pay tribute to

homeopatía *nf* : homeopathy

homicidio *nm* : homicide, murder — **homicida** *adj* : homicidal, murderous — ~ *nmf* : murderer

homogéneo, -nea *adj* : homogeneous

homólogo, -ga *adj* : equivalent — ~ *n* : counterpart

homosexual *adj & nmf* : homosexual — **homosexualidad** *nf* : homosexuality

hondo, -da *adj* : deep — **hondo** *adv* : deeply — **hondonada** *nf* : hollow — **hondura** *nf* : depth

hondureño, -ña *adj* : Honduran

honesto, -ta *adj* : decent, honorable — **honestidad** *nf* : honesty, integrity

hongo *nm* **1** : mushroom **2** : fungus (in botany and medicine)

honor *nm* : honor — **honorable** *adj* : honorable — **honorario, -ria** *adj* : honorary — **honorarios** *nmpl* : payment, fee — **honra** *nf* : honor — **honradez** *nf, pl* **-deces** : honesty, integrity — **honrado, -da** *adj* : honest, upright — **honrar** *vt* : honor — **honrarse** *vr* : be honored — **honroso, -sa** *adj* : honorable

hora *nf* **1** : hour **2** : (specific) time **3** CITA : appointment **4 a la última ~** : at the last minute **5 ~ punta** : rush hour **6 media ~** : half an hour **7 ¿qué ~ es?** : what time is it? **8 ~s de oficina** : office hours **9 ~s extraordinarias** : overtime

horario *nm* : schedule, timetable

horca *nf* **1** : gallows *pl* **2** : pitchfork (in agriculture)

horcajadas : a ~ *adv phr* : astride

horda *nf* : horde

horizonte *nm* : horizon — **horizontal** *adj* : horizontal

horma *nf* **1** : form, mold, last **2** : shoe tree

hormiga *nf* : ant

hormigón *nm, pl* **-gones** : concrete

hormigueo *nm* : tingling, pins and needles

hormiguero *nm* **1** : anthill **2** : swarm (of people)

hormona *nf* : hormone

horno *nm* **1** : oven (for cooking) **2** : small furnace, kiln — **hornada** *nf* : batch — **hornear** *vt* : bake — **hornillo** *nf* : portable stove

horóscopo *nm* : horoscope

horquilla *nf* **1** : hairpin, bobby pin **2** HORCA : pitchfork

horrendo, -da *adj* : horrendous, awful

horrible *adj* : horrible — **horripilante** *adj* : horrifying — **horror** *nm* **1** : horror, dread **2** ATROCIDAD : atrocity — **horrorizar** {21} *vt* : horrify, terrify — **horrorizarse** *vr* : be horrified — **horroroso, -sa** *adj* : horrifying, dreadful

hortaliza *nf* : (garden) vegetable — **hortelano, -na** *n* : truck farmer — **horticultura** *nf* : horticulture

hosco, -ca *adj* : sullen, gloomy

hospedar *vt* : put up, lodge — **hospedarse** *vr* : stay, lodge — **hospedaje** *nm* : lodging

hospital *nm* : hospital — **hospitalario, -ria** *adj* : hospitable — **hospitalidad** *nf* : hospitality — **hospitalizar** {21} *vt* : hospitalize

hostería *nf* : small hotel, inn

hostia *nf* : host (in religion)

hostigar {52} *vt* **1** : whip **2** ACOSAR : harass, pester

hostil *adj* : hostile — **hostilidad** *nf* : hostility

hotel *nm* : hotel — **hotelero, -ra** *adj* : hotel — ~ *n* : hotel manager, hotelier

hoy *adv* **1** : today **2 de ~ en adelante** : from now on **3 ~ (en) día** : nowadays **4 ~ mismo** : this very day

hoyo *nm* : hole — **hoyuelo** *nm* : dimple

hoz *nf, pl* **hoces** : sickle

huarache *nm* : huarache (sandal)

hueco, -ca *adj* **1** : hollow, empty **2** ESPONJOSO : soft, spongy **3** RESONANTE : resonant — **hueco** *nm* **1** : hollow, cavity **2** : recess (in a wall, etc.) **3 ~ de escalera** : stairwell

huelga *nf* **1** : strike **2 declararse en ~** : go on strike — **huelguista** *nmf* : striker

huella *nf* **1** : footprint **2** VESTIGIO : track, mark **3 ~ digital** *or* **~ dactilar** : fingerprint

huérfano, -na *n* : orphan — ~ *adj* : orphaned

huerta *nf* : truck farm — **huerto** *nm* **1** : vegetable garden **2** : (fruit) orchard

hueso *nm* **1** : bone **2** : pit, stone (of a fruit)

huésped, -peda *n* : guest — **huésped** *nm* : host (organism)

huesudo, -da *adj* : bony

huevo *nm* **1** : egg **2 ~s estrellados** : fried eggs **3 ~s revueltos** : scrambled eggs — **hueva** *nf* : roe

huida *nf* : flight, escape — **huidizo, -za** *adj* **1** : shy **2** FUGAZ : fleeting

huipil *nm Lat* : traditional embroidered blouse or dress

huir {41} *vi* **1** : escape, flee **2 ~ de** : shun, avoid

hule *nm* **1** : oilcloth **2** *Lat* : rubber

humano, -na *adj* **1** : human **2** COMPASIVO : humane — **humano** *nm* : human (being) — **humanidad** *nf* **1** : humanity, mankind **2** BENEVOLENCIA : humaneness **3 ~es** *nfpl* : humanities

humanismo *nm* **1** : humanism — **humanista** *nmf* : humanist — **humanitario, -ria** *adj & n* : humanitarian

humear *vi* : smoke, steam — **humareda** *nf* : cloud of smoke

humedad *nf* **1** : dampness **2** : humidity (in meteorology) — **humedecer** {53} *vt* : moisten, dampen — **humedecerse** *vr* : become moist — **húmedo, -da** *adj* **1** : moist, damp **2** : humid (in meteorology)

humildad *nf* : humility — **humilde** *adj* : humble — **humillación** *nf, pl* **-ciones** : humiliation — **humillante** *adj* : humiliating — **humillar** *vt* : humiliate — **humillarse** *vr* : humble oneself

humo *nm* **1** : smoke, steam, fumes **2 ~s** *nmpl* : airs, conceit

humor *nm* **1** : mood, temper **2** GRACIA : humor **3 de buen ~** : in a good mood — **humorismo** *nm* : humor, wit — **humorista** *nmf* : humorist, comedian — **humorístico, -ca** *adj* : humorous

hundir *vt* **1** : sink **2** : destroy, ruin (a building, plans, etc.) — **hundirse** *vr* **1** : sink **2** DERRUMBARSE : collapse — **hundido, -da** *adj* : sunken — **hundimiento** *nm* **1** : sinking **2** DERRUMBE : collapse

húngaro, -ra *adj* : Hungarian

huracán *nm, pl* **-canes** : hurricane

huraño, -ña *adj* : unsociable

hurgar {52} *vi* **~ en** : rummage around in

hurón *nm, pl* **-rones** : ferret

hurra *interj* : hurrah!, hooray!

hurtadillas: a ~ *adv phr* : stealthily, on the sly

hurtar *vt* : steal — **hurto** *nm* **1** ROBO : theft **2** : stolen property

husmear *vt* : sniff out, pry into — *vi* : nose around

huy *interj* : ow!, ouch!

I

i *nf* : i, ninth letter of the Spanish alphabet

ibérico, -ca *adj* : Iberian — **ibero, -ra** *or* **íbero, -ra** *adj* : Iberian

iceberg *nm, pl* **-bergs** : iceberg

icono *nm* : icon

ictericia *nf* : jaundice

ida *nf* **1** : outward journey **2 ~ y vuelta** : round-trip **3 ~s y venidas** : comings and goings

idea *nf* **1** : idea **2** OPINIÓN : opinion

ideal *adj & nm* : ideal — **idealismo** *nm* : idealism — **idealista** *adj* : idealistic — **~ nmf** : idealist — **idealizar** {21} *vt* : idealize

idear *vt* : devise, think up

ídem *nm* : the same, ditto

identidad *nf* : identity — **idéntico, -ca** *adj* : identical — **identificar** {72} *vt* : identify — **identificarse** *vr* **1** : identify oneself **2 ~ con** : identify with — **identificación** *nf, pl* **-ciones** : identification

ideología *nf* : ideology — **ideológico, -ca** *adj* : ideological

idílico, -ca *adj* : idyllic

idioma *nm* : language — **idiomático, -ca** *adj* : idiomatic

idiosincrasia *nf* : idiosyncrasy — **idiosincrásico, -ca** *adj* : idiosyncratic

idiota *adj* : idiotic — **~ nmf** : idiot — **idiotez** *nf* : idiocy

ídolo *nm* : idol — **idolatrar** *vt* : idolize — **idolatría** *nf* : idolatry

idóneo, -nea *adj* : suitable, fitting — **idoneidad** *nf* : fitness, suitability

iglesia *nf* : church

iglú *nm* : igloo

ignición *nf, pl* **-ciones** : ignition

ignífugo, -ga *adj* : fire-resistant, fireproof

ignorar *vt* **1** : ignore **2** DESCONOCER : be unaware of — **ignorancia** *nf* : ignorance — **ignorante** *adj* : ignorant — **~ nmf** : ignorant person

igual *adv* **1** : in the same way **2 por ~** : equally — **~ adj 1** IDÉNTICO : the same **3** LISO : smooth, even **4** SEMEJANTE : similar — **~ nmf** : equal, peer — **igualar** *vt* **1** : make equal **2** : be equal to **3** NIVELAR : level (off) — **igualdad** *nf* **1** : equality **2** UNIFORMI-

DAD : uniformity — **igualmente** *adv* : likewise

iguana *nf* : iguana

ijada *nf* : flank

ilegal *adj* : illegal

ilegible *adj* : illegible

ilegítimo, -ma *adj* : illegitimate — **ile-gitimidad** *nf* : illegitimacy

ileso, -sa *adj* : unharmed

ilícito, -ta *adj* : illicit

ilimitado, -da *adj* : unlimited

ilógico, -ca *adj* : illogical

iluminar *vt* : illuminate — **iluminarse** *vr* : light up — **iluminación** *nf, pl* **-ciones 1** : illumination **2** ALUMBRADO : lighting

ilusionar *vt* : excite — **ilusionarse** *vr* : get one's hopes up — **ilusión** *nf, pl* **-siones 1** : illusion **2** ESPERANZA : hope — **ilusionado, -da** *adj* : excited

iluso -sa *adj* : naïve, gullible — ～ *n* : dreamer, visionary — **ilusorio, -ria** *adj* : illusory

ilustrar *vt* **1** : illustrate **2** ACLARAR : explain — **ilustración** *nf, pl* **-ciones 1** : illustration **2** SABER : learning **3 la Ilustración** : the Enlightenment — **ilustrado, -da** *adj* **1** : illustrated **2** ERUDITO : learned — **ilustrador, -dora** *n* : illustrator

ilustre *adj* : illustrious

imagen *nf, pl* **imágenes** : image, picture

imaginar *vt* : imagine — **imaginarse** *vr* : imagine — **imaginación** *nf, pl* **-ciones** : imagination — **imaginario, -ria** *adj* : imaginary — **imaginativo, -va** *adj* : imaginative

imán *nm, pl* **imanes** : magnet — **imantar** *vt* : magnetize

imbécil *adj* : stupid, idiotic — ～ *nmf* : idiot

imborrable *adj* : indelible

imbuir {41} *vt* ～ **de** : imbue with

imitar *vt* **1** COPIAR : imitate, copy **2** : impersonate — **imitación** *nf, pl* **-ciones 1** COPIA : imitation, copy **2** : impersonation — **imitador, -dora** *n* : impersonator

impaciencia *nf* : impatience — **impacientar** *v* : make impatient, exasperate —**impacientarse** *vr* : grow impatient — **impaciente** *adj* : impatient

impacto *nm* : impact

impar *adj* : odd — ～ *nm* : odd number

imparcial *adj* : impartial — **imparcialidad** *nf* : impartiality

impartir *vt* : impart, give

impasible *adj* : impassive

impasse *nm* : impasse

impávido, -da *adj* : fearless

impecable *adj* : impeccable, spotless

impedir {54} *vt* **1** : prevent **2** DIFICULTAR : impede, hinder — **impedido, -da** *adj* : disabled — **impedimento** *nm* : obstacle, impediment

impeler *vt* : drive, propel

impenetrable *adj* : impenetrable

impenitente *adj* : unrepentant

impensable *adj* : unthinkable — **impensado, -da** *adj* : unexpected

imperar *vi* **1** : reign, rule **2** PREDOMINAR : prevail — **imperante** *adj* : prevailing

imperativo, -va *adj* : imperative — **imperativo** *nm* : imperative

imperceptible *adj* : imperceptible

imperdible *nm* : safety pin

imperdonable *adj* : unforgivable

imperfección *nf, pl* **-ciones** : imperfection — **imperfecto, -ta** *adj* : imperfect — **imperfecto** *nm* : imperfect (tense)

imperial *adj* : imperial — **imperialismo** *nm* : imperialism — **imperialista** *adj & nmf* : imperialist

impericia *nf* : lack of skill

imperio *nm* **1** : empire **2** DOMINIO : rule — **imperioso, -sa** *adj* **1** : imperious **2** URGENTE : pressing, urgent

impermeable *adj* **1** : waterproof **2** ～ **a** : impervious to — ～ *nm* : raincoat

impersonal *adj* : impersonal

impertinente *adj* : impertinent — **impertinencia** *nf* : impertinence

ímpetu *nm* **1** : impetus **2** ENERGÍA : energy, vigor **3** VIOLENCIA : force — **impetuoso, -sa** *adj* : impetuous — **impetuosidad** *nf* : impetuosity

impío, -pía *adj* : impious, ungodly

implacable *adj* : implacable

implantar *vt* **1** : implant **2** ESTABLECER : establish, introduce

implemento *nm* *Lat* : implement, tool

implicar {72} *vt* **1** : involve, implicate **2** SIGNIFICAR : imply — **implicación** *nf, pl* **-ciones** : implication

implícito, -ta *adj* : implicit

implorar *vt* : implore

imponer {60} *vt* **1** : impose **2** : command (respect, etc.) — *vi* : be imposing — **imponerse** *vr* **1** : assert oneself, command respect **2** PREVALECER : prevail — **imponente** *adj* : imposing, impressive — **imponible** *adj* : taxable

impopular *adj* : unpopular — **impopularidad** *nf* : unpopularity

importación *nf, pl* **-ciones 1** : importation **2 importaciones** *nfpl* : imports — **importado, -da** *adj* : imported — **importador, -dora** *adj* : importing — ～ *n* : importer

importancia *nf* : importance — **importante** *adj* : important — **importar** *vi* **1** : matter, be important **2** no me importa : I don't care — *vt* **1** : import ASCENDER A : amount to, cost

importe *nm* **1** : price **2** CANTIDAD : sum, amount

importunar *vt* : bother — **importuno, -na** *adj* **1** : inopportune **2** MOLESTO : bothersome

imposible *adj* : impossible — **imposibilidad** *nf* : impossibility

imposición *nf, pl* **-ciones** **1** : imposition **2** IMPUESTO : tax

impostor, -tora *n* : impostor

impotente *adj* : powerless, impotent — **impotencia** *nf* : impotence

impracticable *adj* **1** : impracticable **2** INTRANSITABLE : impassable

impreciso, -sa *adj* : vague, imprecise — **imprecisión** *nf, pl* **-siones** **1** : vagueness **2** ERROR : inaccuracy

impredecible *adj* : unpredictable

impregnar *vt* : impregnate

imprenta *nf* **1** : printing **2** : printing shop, press

imprescindible *adj* : essential, indispensable

impresión *nf, pl* **-siones** **1** : impression **2** IMPRENTA : printing — **impresionable** *adj* : impressionable — **impresionante** *adj* : impressive — **impresionar** *vt* **1** : impress **2** CONMOVER : affect, move — *vi* : make an impression — **impresionarse** *vr* **1** : be impressed **2** CONMOVERSE : be affected

impreso, -sa *adj* : printed — **impreso** *nm* **1** FORMULARIO : form **2** ~s *nmpl* : printed matter — **impresor, -sora** *n* : printer — **impresora** *nf* : (computer) printer

imprevisible *adj* : unforeseeable — **imprevisto, -ta** *adj* : unexpected, unforeseen

imprimir {42} *vt* **1** : print **2** DAR : impart, give

improbable *adj* : improbable — **improbabilidad** *nf* : improbability

improcedente *adj* : inappropriate

improductivo, -va *adj* : unproductive

improperio *nm* : insult

impropio, -pia *adj* **1** : inappropriate **2** INCORRECTO : incorrect

improvisar *v* : improvise — **improvisado, -da** *adj* : improvised, impromptu — **improvisación** *nf, pl* **-ciones** : improvisation — **improviso: de ~** *adv phr* : suddenly

imprudente *adj* : imprudent, rash —

imprudencia *nf* : imprudence, carelessness

impúdico, -ca *adj* : shameless, indecent

impuesto *nm* **1** : tax **2** ~ **sobre la renta** : income tax

impugnar *vt* : challenge, contest

impulsar *vt* : propel, drive — **impulsividad** *nf* : impulsiveness — **impulsivo, -va** *adj* : impulsive — **impulso** *nm* **1** : drive, thrust **2** MOTIVACIÓN : impulse

impune *adj* : unpunished — **impunidad** *nf* : impunity

impuro, -ra *adj* : impure — **impureza** *nf* : impurity

imputar *vt* : impute, attribute

inacabable *adj* : interminable, endless

inaccesible *adj* : inaccessible

inaceptable *adj* : unacceptable

inactivo, -va *adj* : inactive — **inactividad** *nf* : inactivity

inadaptado, -da *adj* : maladjusted — **~** *n* : misfit

inadecuado, -da *adj* **1** : inadequate **2** INAPROPIADO : inappropriate

inadmisible *adj* : inadmissible

inadvertido, -da *adj* **1** : unnoticed **2** DISTRAÍDO : distracted — **inadvertencia** *nf* : oversight

inagotable *adj* : inexhaustible

inaguantable *adj* : unbearable

inalámbrico, -ca *adj* : wireless, cordless

inalcanzable *adj* : unreachable, unattainable

inalterable *adj* **1** : unchangeable **2** : impassive (of character) **3** : fast (of colors)

inanición *nf, pl* **-ciones** : starvation, famine

inanimado, -da *adj* : inanimate

inaplicable *adj* : inapplicable

inapreciable *adj* : imperceptible

inapropiado, -da *adj* : inappropriate

inarticulado, -da *adj* : inarticulate

inasequible *adj* : unattainable

inaudito, -ta *adj* : unheard-of, unprecedented

inaugurar *vt* : inaugurate — **inauguración** *nf, pl* **-ciones** : inauguration — **inaugural** *adj* : inaugural

inca *adj* : Inca, Incan

incalculable *adj* : incalculable

incandescencia *nf* : incandescence — **incandescente** *adj* : incandescent

incansable *adj* : tireless

incapacitar *vt* : incapacitate, disable — **incapacidad** *nf* : incapacity, inability — **incapaz** *adj, pl* **-paces** : incapable

incautar *vt* : confiscate, seize

incendiar vt : set fire to, burn (down) — **incendiarse** vr : catch fire — **incendiario, -ria** adj : incendiary — ~ n : arsonist — **incendio** nm 1 : fire 2 ~ **premeditado** : arson

incentivo nm : incentive

incertidumbre nf : uncertainty

incesante adj : incessant

incesto nm : incest — **incestuoso, -sa** adj : incestuous

incidencia nf 1 : impact 2 SUCESO : incident — **incidental** adj : incidental — **incidente** nm : incident

incidir vi ~ **en** 1 : fall into (a habit, mistake, etc.) 2 INFLUIR EN : affect, influence

incienso nm : incense

incierto, -ta adj : uncertain

incinerar vt 1 : incinerate 2 : cremate (a corpse) — **incineración** nf, pl **-ciones** 1 : incineration 2 : cremation (of a corpse) — **incinerador** nm : incinerator

incipiente adj : incipient

incisión nf, pl **-siones** : incision

incisivo, -va adj : incisive — **incisivo** nm : incisor

incitar vt : incite, rouse

incivilizado, -da adj : uncivilized

inclinar vt : tilt, lean — **inclinarse** vr 1 : lean (over) 2 ~ **a** : be inclined to — **inclinación** nf, pl **-ciones** 1 : inclination 2 LADERA : incline, tilt

incluir {41} vt 1 : include 2 ADJUNTAR : enclose — **inclusión** nf, pl **-siones** : inclusion — **inclusive** adv : up to and including — **inclusivo, -va** adj : inclusive — **incluso** adv : even, in fact — **incluso, -sa** adj : enclosed

incógnito, -ta adj 1 : unknown 2 **de** ~ : incognito

incoherente adj : incoherent — **incoherencia** nf : incoherence

incoloro, -ra adj : colorless

incombustible adj : fireproof

incomible adj : inedible

incomodar vt 1 : inconvenience 2 ENFADAR : bother, annoy — **incomodarse** vr 1 : take the trouble 2 ENFADARSE : get annoyed — **incomodidad** nf : discomfort — **incómodo, -da** adj 1 : uncomfortable 2 INCONVENIENTE : inconvenient, awkward

incomparable adj : incomparable

incompatible adj : incompatible — **incompatibilidad** nf : incompatibility

incompetente adj : incompetent — **incompetencia** nf : incompetence

incompleto, -ta adj : incomplete

incomprendido, -da adj : misunderstood — **incomprensible** adj : incomprehensible — **incomprensión** nf, pl **-siones** : lack of understanding

incomunicado, -da adj 1 : isolated 2 : in solitary confinement

inconcebible adj : inconceivable

inconcluso, -sa adj : unfinished

incondicional adj : unconditional

inconformista adj & nmf : nonconformist

inconfundible adj : unmistakable

incongruente adj : incongruous

inconmensurable adj : vast, immeasurable

inconsciente adj 1 : unconscious, unaware 2 IRREFLEXIVO : reckless — ~ nm **el** ~ : the unconscious — **inconsciencia** nf 1 : unconsciousness 2 INSENSATEZ : thoughtlessness

inconsecuente adj : inconsistent — **inconsecuencia** nf : inconsistency

inconsiderado, -da adj : inconsiderate

inconsistente adj 1 : flimsy 2 : watery (of a sauce, etc.) 3 : inconsistent (of an argument) — **inconsistencia** nf : inconsistency

inconsolable adj : inconsolable

inconstante adj : changeable, unreliable — **inconstancia** nf : inconstancy

inconstitucional adj : unconstitutional

incontable adj : countless

incontenible adj : irrepressible

incontestable adj : indisputable

incontinente adj : incontinent — **incontinencia** nf : incontinence

inconveniente adj 1 : inconvenient 2 INAPROPIADO : inappropriate — ~ nm : obstacle, problem — **inconveniencia** nf 1 : inconvenience 2 : tactless remark

incorporar vt AGREGAR : incorporate, add 2 : mix (in cooking) — **incorporarse** vr 1 : sit up 2 ~ **a** : join — **incorporación** nf, pl **-ciones** : incorporation

incorrecto, -ta adj 1 : incorrect 2 DESCORTÉS : impolite

incorregible adj : incorrigible

incrédulo, -la adj : incredulous — **incredulidad** nf : incredulity, disbelief

increíble adj : incredible, unbelievable

incrementar vt : increase — **incremento** nm : increase

incriminar vt 1 : incriminate 2 ACUSAR : accuse

incrustar vt : set, inlay — **incrustarse** vr : become embedded

incubar vt : incubate — **incubadora** nf : incubator

incuestionable *adj* : unquestionable

inculcar {72} *vt* : instill

inculpar *vt* : accuse, charge

inculto, -ta *adj* 1 : uneducated 2 : uncultivated (of land)

incumplimiento *nm* 1 : noncompliance 2 ∼ **de contrato** : breach of contract

incurable *adj* : incurable

incurrir *vi* ∼ **en** 1 : incur (expenses, etc.) 2 : fall into, commit (crimes)

incursión *nf, pl* **-siones** : raid

indagar {52} *vt* : investigate — **indagación** *nf, pl* **-ciones** : investigation

indebido, -da *adj* : undue

indecente *adj* : indecent, obscene — **indecencia** *nf* : indecency, obscenity

indecible *adj* : inexpressible

indecisión *nf, pl* **-siones** : indecision — **indeciso, -sa** *adj* 1 : undecided 2 IRRESOLUTO : indecisive

indefenso, -sa *adj* : defenseless, helpless

indefinido, -da *adj* : indefinite — **indefinidamente** *adv* : indefinitely

indeleble *adj* : indelible

indemnizar {21} *vt* : indemnify, compensate — **indemnización** *nf, pl* **-ciones** : compensation

independiente *adj* : independent — **independencia** *nf* : independence — **independizarse** {21} *vr* : become independent

indescifrable *adj* : indecipherable

indescriptible *adj* : indescribable

indeseable *adj* : undesirable

indestructible *adj* : indestructible

indeterminado, -da *adj* : indeterminate

indicar {72} *vt* 1 : indicate 2 MOSTRAR : show — **indicación** *nf, pl* **-ciones** 1 : sign, indication 2 **indicaciones** *nfpl* : directions — **indicador** *nm* 1 : sign, signal 2 : gauge, dial, meter — **indicativo, -va** *adj* : indicative — **indicativo** *nm* : indicative (mood)

índice *nm* 1 : indication 2 : index (of a book, etc.) 3 : index finger 4 ∼ **de natalidad** : birth rate

indicio *nm* : indication, sign

indiferente *adj* 1 : indifferent 2 **me es** ∼ : it doesn't matter to me — **indiferencia** *nf* : indifference

indígena *adj* : indigenous, native — ∼ *nmf* : native

indigente *adj & nmf* : indigent — **indigencia** *nf* : poverty

indigestión *nf, pl* **-tiones** : indigestion — **indigesto, -ta** *adj* : indigestible

indignar *vt* : outrage, infuriate — **indignarse** *vr* : become indignant — **indignación** *nf, pl* **-ciones** : indignation

— **indignado, -da** *adj* : indignant — **indignidad** *nf* : indignity — **indigno, -na** *adj* : unworthy

indio, -dia *adj* 1 : American Indian 2 : Indian (from India)

indirecta *nf* 1 : hint 2 **lanzar una** ∼ : drop a hint — **indirecto, -ta** *adj* : indirect

indisciplina *nf* : lack of discipline — **indisciplinado, -da** *adj* : undisciplined

indiscreto, -ta *adj* : indiscreet — **indiscreción** *nf, pl* **-ciones** 1 : indiscretion 2 : tactless remark

indiscriminado, -da *adj* : indiscriminate

indiscutible *adj* : indisputable

indispensable *adj* : indispensable

indisponer {60} *vt* 1 : upset, make ill 2 ENEMISTAR : set against, set at odds — **indisponerse** *vr* 1 : become ill 2 ∼ **con** : fall out with — **indisposición** *nf, pl* **-ciones** : indisposition, illness — **indispuesto, -ta** *adj* : unwell, indisposed

indistinto, -ta *adj* : indistinct

individual *adj* : individual — **individualidad** *nf* : individuality — **individualizar** {21} *vt* : individualize — **individuo** *nm* : individual

indivisible *adj* : indivisible

índole *nf* 1 : nature, character 2 TIPO : type, kind

indolente *adj* : indolent, lazy — **indolencia** *nf* : indolence, laziness

indoloro, -ra *adj* : painless

indómito, -ta *adj* : indomitable

indonesio, -sia *adj* : Indonesian

inducir {61} *vt* 1 : induce 2 DEDUCIR : infer

indudable *adj* : beyond doubt — **indudablemente** *adv* : undoubtedly

indulgente *adj* : indulgent — **indulgencia** *nf* : indulgence

indultar *vt* : pardon, reprieve — **indulto** *nm* : pardon, reprieve

industria *nf* : industry — **industrial** *adj* : industrial — ∼ *nmf* : industrialist, manufacturer — **industrialización** *nf, pl* **-ciones** : industrialization — **industrializar** {21} *vt* : industrialize — **industrioso, -sa** *adj* : industrious

inédito, -ta *adj* : unpublished

inefable *adj* : inexpressible

ineficaz *adj, pl* **-caces** 1 : ineffective 2 INEFICIENTE : inefficient

ineficiente *adj* : inefficient — **ineficiencia** *nf* : inefficiency

inelegible *adj* : ineligible

ineludible *adj* : unavoidable, inescapable

inepto, -ta *adj* : inept — **ineptitud** *nf* : ineptitude

inequívoco, -ca *adj* : unequivocal

inercia *nf* : inertia

inerme *adj* : unarmed, defenseless

inerte *adj* : inert

inesperado, -da *adj* : unexpected

inestable *adj* : unstable — **inestabilidad** *nf* : instability

inevitable *adj* : inevitable

inexacto, -ta *adj* 1 : inexact 2 INCORRECTO : incorrect, wrong

inexistente *adj* : nonexistent

inexorable *adj* : inexorable

inexperiencia *nf* : inexperience — **inexperto, -ta** *adj* : inexperienced, unskilled

inexplicable *adj* : inexplicable

infalible *adj* : infallible

infame *adj* 1 : infamous, vile 2 *fam* : horrible — **infamia** *nf* : infamy, disgrace

infancia *nf* : infancy — **infanta** *nf* : infanta, princess — **infante** *nm* 1 : infante, prince 2 : infantryman (in the military) — **infantería** *nf* : infantry — **infantil** *adj* 1 : child's, children's 2 INMADURO : childish

infarto *nm* : heart attack

infatigable *adj* : tireless

infectar *vt* : infect — **infectarse** *vr* : become infected — **infección** *nf, pl* **-ciones** : infection — **infeccioso, -sa** *adj* : infectious — **infecto, -ta** *adj* 1 : infected 2 : foul, sickening

infecundo, -da *adj* : infertile

infeliz *adj, pl* **-lices** : unhappy — **infelicidad** *nf* : unhappiness

inferior *adj & nmf* : inferior — **inferioridad** *nf* : inferiority

inferir {76} *vt* 1 DEDUCIR : infer 2 : cause (harm or injury)

infernal *adj* : infernal, hellish

infestar *vt* : infest

infiel *adj* : unfaithful — **infidelidad** *nf* : infidelity

infierno *nm* 1 : hell 2 **el quinto ∼** *fam* : the middle of nowhere

infiltrar *vt* : infiltrate — **infiltrarse** *vr* : infiltrate

infinidad *nf* 1 : infinity 2 **una ∼ de** : countless — **infinitivo** *nm* : infinitive — **infinito, -ta** *adj* : infinite — **infinito** *nm* : infinity

inflación *nf, pl* **-ciones** : inflation — **inflacionario, -ria** *or* **inflacionista** *adj* : inflationary

inflamar *vt* : inflame — **inflamable** *adj* : flammable, inflammable — **inflamación** *nf, pl* **-ciones** : inflammation — **inflamatorio, -ria** *adj* : inflammatory

inflar *vt* 1 : inflate 2 EXAGERAR : exaggerate — **inflarse** *vr* **∼ de** : swell (up) with

inflexible *adj* : inflexible — **inflexión** *nf, pl* **-xiones** : inflection

infligir {35} *vt* : inflict

influencia *nf* : influence — **influenciar → influir**

influenza *nf* : influenza

influir {41} *vt* : influence — *vi* **∼ en** *or* **∼ sobre** : have an influence on — **influjo** *nm* : influence — **influyente** *adj* : influential

información *nf, pl* **-ciones** 1 : information 2 NOTICIAS : news 3 : directory assistance (on the telephone)

informal *adj* 1 : informal 2 IRRESPONSABLE : unreliable

informar *v* : inform — **informarse** *vr* : get information, find out — **informante** *nmf* : informant — **informática** *nf* : information technology — **informativo, -va** *adj* : informative — **informatizar** {21} *vt* : computerize

informe *adj* : shapeless — **∼** *nm* 1 : report 2 **∼s** *nmpl* : information, data 3 **∼s** *nmpl* : references (for employment)

infortunado, -da *adj* : unfortunate — **infortunio** *nm* : misfortune

infracción *nf, pl* **-ciones** : violation, infraction

infraestructura *nf* : infrastructure

infrahumano, -na *adj* : subhuman

infranqueable *adj* 1 : impassable 2 INSUPERABLE : insurmountable

infrarrojo, -ja *adj* : infrared

infrecuente *adj* : infrequent

infringir {35} *vt* : infringe

infructuoso, -sa *adj* : fruitless

infundado, -da *adj* : unfounded, baseless

infundir *vt* : instill, infuse — **infusión** *nf, pl* **-siones** : infusion

ingeniar *vt* : invent, think up

ingeniería *nf* : engineering — **ingeniero, -ra** *n* : engineer

ingenio *nm* 1 : ingenuity 2 AGUDEZA : wit 3 MÁQUINA : device, apparatus 4 **∼ azucarero** *Lat* : sugar refinery — **ingenioso, -sa** *adj* 1 : ingenious 2 AGUDO : clever, witty — **ingeniosamente** *adv* : cleverly

ingenuidad *nf* : naïveté, ingenuousness — **ingenuo, -nua** *adj* : naive

ingerir {76} *vt* : ingest, consume

ingle *nf* : groin

inglés, -glesa *adj, mpl* **-gleses** : English — **inglés** *nm* : English (language)

ingrato, -ta *adj* **1** : ungrateful **2 un trabajo ingrato** : a thankless task — **ingratitud** *nf* : ingratitude

ingrediente *nm* : ingredient

ingresar *vt* : deposit — *vi* ~ **en** : enter, be admitted into, join — **ingreso** *nm* **1** : entrance, entry **2** : admission (into a hospital, etc.) **3** ~**s** *nmpl* : income, earnings

inhábil *adj* **1** : unskillful, clumsy **2** ~ **para** : unsuited for — **inhabilidad** *nf* : unskillfulness

inhabitable *adj* : uninhabitable — **inhabitado, -da** *adj* : uninhabited

inhalar *vt* : inhale — **inhalación** *nf* : inhalation

inherente *adj* : inherent

inhibir *vt* : inhibit — **inhibición** *nf, pl* **-ciones** : inhibition

inhóspito, -ta *adj* : inhospitable

inhumano, -na *adj* : inhuman, inhumane — **inhumanidad** *nf* : inhumanity

iniciar *vt* : initiate, begin — **iniciación** *nf, pl* **-ciones** **1** : initiation **2** COMIENZO : beginning — **inicial** *adj & nf* : initial — **iniciativa** *nf* : initiative — **inicio** *nm* : start, beginning

inigualado, -da *adj* : unequaled

ininterrumpido, -da *adj* : uninterrupted

injerirse {76} *vr* : interfere — **injerencia** *nf* : interference

injertar *vt* : graft — **injerto** *nm* : graft

injuriar *vt* : insult — **injuria** *nf* : insult — **injurioso, -sa** *adj* : insulting, abusive

injusticia *nf* : injustice, unfairness — **injusto, -ta** *adj* : unfair, unjust

inmaculado, -da *adj* : immaculate

inmaduro, -ra *adj* **1** : immature **2** : unripe (of fruit) — **inmadurez** *nf* : immaturity

inmediaciones *nfpl* : surrounding area

inmediato, -ta *adj* **1** : immediate **2** CONTIGUO : adjoining **3 de** ~ : immediately, right away **4** ~ **a** : next to, close to — **inmediatamente** *adv* : immediately

inmejorable *adj* : excellent

inmenso, -sa *adj* : immense, vast — **inmensidad** *nf* : immensity

inmerecido, -da *adj* : undeserved

inmersión *nf, pl* **-siones** : immersion

inmigrar *vi* : immigrate — **inmigración** *nf, pl* **-ciones** : immigration — **inmigrante** *adj & nmf* : immigrant

inminente *adj* : imminent, impending — **inminencia** *nf* : imminence

inmiscuirse {41} *vr* : interfere

inmobiliario, -ria *adj* : real estate, property

inmodesto, -ta *adj* : immodest

inmoral *adj* : immoral — **inmoralidad** *nf* : immorality

inmortal *adj & nmf* : immortal — **inmortalidad** *nf* : immortality

inmóvil *adj* : motionless, still — **inmovilizar** {21} *vt* : immobilize

inmueble *nm* : building, property

inmundicia *nf* : filth, trash — **inmundo, -da** *adj* : dirty, filthy

inmunizar {21} *vt* : immunize — **inmune** *adj* : immune — **inmunidad** *nf* : immunity — **inmunización** *nf, pl* **-ciones** : immunization

inmutable *adj* : unchangeable

innato, -ta *adj* : innate

innecesario, -ria *adj* : unnecessary, needless

innegable *adj* : undeniable

innoble *adj* : ignoble

innovar *vt* : introduce — *vi* : innovate — **innovación** *nf, pl* **-ciones** : innovation — **innovador, -dora** *adj* : innovative — ~ *n* : innovator

innumerable *adj* : innumerable

inocencia *nf* : innocence — **inocente** *adj & nmf* : innocent — **inocentón, -tona** *adj, mpl* **-tones** : naive — ~ *n* : simpleton, dupe

inocular *vt* : inoculate — **inoculación** *nf, pl* **-ciones** : inoculation

inocuo, -cua *adj* : innocuous

inodoro, -ra *adj* : odorless — **inodoro** *nm* : toilet

inofensivo, -va *adj* : inoffensive, harmless

inolvidable *adj* : unforgettable

inoperable *adj* : inoperable

inoperante *adj* : ineffective

inopinado, -da *adj* : unexpected

inoportuno, -na *adj* : untimely, inopportune

inorgánico, -ca *adj* : inorganic

inoxidable *adj* **1** : rustproof **2 acero** ~ : stainless steel

inquebrantable *adj* : unwavering

inquietar *vt* : disturb, worry — **inquietarse** *vr* : worry — **inquietante** *adj* : disturbing, worrisome — **inquieto, -ta** *adj* : anxious, worried — **inquietud** *nf* : anxiety, worry

inquilino, -na *n* : tenant

inquirir {4} *vi* : make inquiries — *vt* : investigate

insaciable *adj* : insatiable

insalubre *adj* : unhealthy

insatisfecho, -cha *adj* 1 : unsatisfied 2 DESCONTENTO : dissatisfied

inscribir {33} *vt* 1 : enroll, register 2 GRABAR : inscribe, engrave — inscribirse *vr* : register — inscripción *nf, pl* -ciones 1 : inscription 2 REGISTRO : registration

insecto *nm* : insect — insecticida *nm* : insecticide

inseguro, -ra *adj* 1 : insecure 2 PELIGROSO : unsafe 3 DUDOSO : uncertain — inseguridad *nf* 1 : insecurity 2 PELIGRO : lack of safety 3 DUDA : uncertainty

inseminar *vt* : inseminate — inseminación *nf, pl* -ciones : insemination

insensato, -ta *adj* : senseless, foolish — insensatez *nf* : foolishness, thoughtlessness

insensible *adj* 1 : insensitive, unfeeling 2 : numb (in medicine) 3 IMPERCEPTIBLE : imperceptible — insensibilidad *nf* : insensitivity

inseparable *adj* : inseparable

insertar *vt* : insert

insidia *nf* : snare, trap — insidioso, -sa *adj* : insidious

insigne *adj* : noted, famous

insignia *nf* 1 : insignia, badge 2 BANDERA : flag

insignificante *adj* : insignificant, negligible

insincero, -ra *adj* : insincere

insinuar {3} *vt* : insinuate — insinuarse *vr* ~ en : worm one's way into — insinuación *nf, pl* -ciones : insinuation — insinuante *adj* : insinuating, suggestive

insípido, -da *adj* : insipid

insistir *v* : insist — insistencia *nf* : insistence — insistente *adj* : insistent

insociable *adj* : unsociable

insolación *nf, pl* -ciones : sunstroke

insolencia *nf* : insolence — insolente *adj* : insolent

insólito, -ta *adj* : rare, unusual

insoluble *adj* : insoluble

insolvencia *nf* : insolvency, bankruptcy — insolvente *adj* : insolvent, bankrupt

insomnio *nm* : insomnia — insomne *nmf* : insomniac

insondable *adj* : unfathomable

insonorizado, -da *adj* : soundproof

insoportable *adj* : unbearable

insospechado, -da *adj* : unexpected

insostenible *adj* : untenable

inspeccionar *vt* : inspect — inspección *nf, pl* -ciones : inspection — inspector, -tora *n* : inspector

inspirar *vt* : inspire — *vi* : inhale — inspirarse *vr* : be inspired — inspiración *nf, pl* -ciones 1 : inspiration 2 RESPIRACIÓN : inhalation — inspirador, -dora *adj* : inspirational

instalar *vt* : install — instalarse *vr* : settle — instalación *nf, pl* -ciones : installation

instancia *nf* : request 2 en última ~ : ultimately, as a last resort

instantáneo, -nea *adj* : instantaneous, instant — instantánea *nf* : snapshot — instante *nm* 1 : instant 2 a cada ~ : frequently, all the time 3 al ~ : immediately

instar *vt* : urge, press

instaurar *vt* : establish — instauración *nf, pl* -ciones : establishment

instigar {52} *vt* : incite, instigate — instigador, -dora *n* : instigator

instinto *nm* : instinct — instintivo, -va *adj* : instinctive

institución *nf, pl* -ciones : institution — institucional *adj* : institutional — institucionalizar {21} *vt* : institutionalize — instituir {41} *vt* : institute, establish — instituto *nm* : institute — institutriz *nf, pl* -trices : governess

instruir {41} *vt* : instruct — instrucción *nf, pl* -ciones 1 : instruction 2 instrucciones *nfpl* : instructions, directions — instructivo, -va *adj* : instructive — instructor, -tora *n* : instructor

instrumento *nm* : instrument — instrumental *adj* : instrumental

insubordinarse *vr* : rebel — insubordinado, -da *adj* : insubordinate — insubordinación *nf, pl* -ciones : insubordination

insuficiente *adj* : insufficient, inadequate — insuficiencia *nf* 1 : insufficiency, inadequacy 2 ~ cardíaca : heart failure

insufrible *adj* : insufferable

insular *adj* : insular, island

insulina *nf* : insulin

insulso, -sa *adj* 1 : insipid, bland 2 SOSO : dull

insultar *vt* : insult — insultante *adj* : insulting — insulto *nm* : insult

insuperable *adj* : insurmountable

insurgente *adj & nmf* : insurgent

insurrección *nf, pl* -ciones : insurrection, uprising

intachable *adj* : irreproachable

intacto, -ta *adj* : intact

intangible *adj* : intangible

integrar *vt* : integrate — integrarse *vr* : become integrated — integración

nf, pl **-ciones** : integration — **integral**
adj **1** : integral **2** pan ~ : whole grain
bread — **íntegro, -gra** *adj* **1** : honest,
upright **2** ENTERO : whole, complete —
integridad *nf* **1** RECTITUD : integrity **2**
TOTALIDAD : wholeness

intelecto *nm* : intellect — **intelectual**
adj & nmf : intellectual

inteligencia *nf* : intelligence — **inteligente** *adj* : intelligent — **inteligible** *adj* : intelligible

intemperie *nf* a la ~ : in the open air,
outside

intempestivo, -va *adj* : untimely, inopportune

intención *nf, pl* **-ciones** : intention, intent — **intencionado, -da** *adj* **1** : intended **2 bien** ~ : well-meaning **3
mal** ~ : malicious — **intencional** *adj*
: intentional

intensidad *nf* : intensity — **intensificar**
{72} *vt* : intensify — **intensificarse** *vr*
: intensify — **intensivo, -va** *adj* : intensive — **intenso, -sa** *adj* : intense

intentar *vt* : attempt, try — **intento** *nm*
1 : intention **2** TENTATIVA : attempt

interactuar {3} *vi* : interact — **interacción** *nf, pl* **-ciones** : interaction — **interactivo, -va** *adj* : interactive

intercalar *vt* : insert, intersperse

intercambio *nm* : exchange — **intercambiable** *adj* : interchangeable —
intercambiar *vt* : exchange, trade

interceder *vi* : intercede

interceptar *vt* : intercept — **intercep-
ción** *nf, pl* **-ciones** : interception

intercesión *nf, pl* **-siones** : interces-
sion

interés *nm, pl* **-reses** : interest — **interesado, -da** *adj* **1** : interested **2** EGO-
ISTA : selfish — **interesante** *adj* : interesting — **interesar** *vt* : interest —
vi : be of interest — **interesarse** *vr*
: take an interest

interfaz *nf, pl* **-faces** : interface

interferir {76} *vi* : interfere — *vt* : interfere with — **interferencia** *nf* : interference

interino, -na *adj* : temporary, interim —
interiormente *adv* : inwardly

interior *adj* : interior, inner — ~ *nm*
: interior, inside — **interiormente** *adv*
: inwardly

interjección *nf, pl* **-ciones** : interjection

interlocutor, -tora *n* : speaker

intermediario, -ria *adj & n* : intermediary

intermedio, -dia *adj* : intermediate —
intermedio *nm* : intermission

interminable *adj* : interminable, endless

intermisión *nf, pl* **-siones** : intermission, pause

intermitente *adj* : intermittent — ~
nm : blinker, turn signal

internacional *adj* : international

internar *vt* : commit, confine — **in-
ternarse** *vr* : penetrate — **internado**
nm : boarding school — **interno, -na**
adj : internal — ~ *n* **1** : boarder **2** : inmate (in a jail, etc.)

interponer {60} *vt* : interpose — **inter-
ponerse** *vr* : intervene

interpretar *vt* **1** : interpret **2** : play, perform (in theater, etc.) — **inter-
pretación** *nf, pl* **-ciones** : interpretation — **intérprete** *nmf* TRADUCTOR
: interpreter **2** : performer (of music)

interrogar {52} *vt* : interrogate, question — **interrogación** *nf, pl* **-ciones 1**
: interrogation **2 signo de** ~ : question mark — **interrogativo, -va** *adj*
: interrogative — **interrogatorio** *nm*
: interrogation, questioning

interrumpir *v* : interrupt — **interrupción** *nf, pl* **-ciones** : interruption —
interruptor *nm* : (electrical) switch

intersección *nf, pl* **-ciones** : intersection

intervalo *nm* : interval

intervenir {87} *vi* **1** : take part **2** MEDI-
AR : intervene — *vt* **1** : tap (a telephone) **2** INSPECCIONAR : audit **3** OPER-
AR : operate on — **intervención** *nf, pl*
-ciones 1 : intervention **2** : audit (in
business) **3** *o* **~ quirúrgica** : operation — **interventor, -tora** *n* : inspector, auditor

intestino *nm* : intestine — **intestinal**
adj : intestinal

intimar *vi* **~ con** : become friendly
with — **intimidad** *nf* **1** : private life **2**
AMISTAD : intimacy

intimidar *vt* : intimidate

íntimo, -ma *adj* **1** : intimate, close **2** PRI-
VADO : private

intolerable *adj* : intolerable — **intolerancia** *nf* : intolerance — **intolerante**
adj : intolerant

intoxicar {72} *vt* : poison — **intoxi-
cación** *nf, pl* **-ciones** : poisoning

intranquilizar {21} *vt* : make uneasy —
intranquilizarse *vr* : be anxious — **intranquilidad** *nf* : uneasiness, anxiety
— **intranquilo, -la** *adj* : uneasy, worried

intransigente *adj* : unyielding, intran-
sigent

intransitable *adj* : impassable

intransitivo, -va *adj* : intransitive
intrascendente *adj* : unimportant, insignificant
intravenoso, -sa *adj* : intravenous
intrépido, -da *adj* : intrepid, fearless
intrigar {52} *v* : intrigue — **intriga** *nf* : intrigue — **intrigante** *adj* : intriguing
intrincado, -da *adj* : intricate, involved
intrínseco, -ca *adj* : intrinsic — **intrínsecamente** *adv* : intrinsically, inherently
introducción *nf, pl* **-ciones** : introduction — **introducir** {61} *vt* 1 : introduce 2 METER : insert — **introducirse** *vr* ~ **en** : penetrate, get into — **introductorio, -ria** *adj* : introductory
intromisión *nf, pl* **-siones** : interference
introvertido, -da *adj* : introverted — ~ *n* : introvert
intrusión *nf, pl* **-siones** : intrusion — **intruso, -sa** *adj* : intrusive — ~ *n* : intruder
intuir {41} *vt* : sense — **intuición** *nf, pl* **-ciones** : intuition — **intuitivo, -va** *adj* : intuitive
inundar *vt* : flood — **inundarse** *vr* ~ **de** : be inundated with — **inundación** *nf, pl* **-ciones** : flood
inusitado, -da *adj* : unusual, uncommon
inútil *adj* 1 : useless 2 INVÁLIDO : disabled — **inutilidad** *nf* : uselessness — **inutilizar** {21} *vt* 1 : make useless 2 INCAPACITAR : disable
invadir *vt* : invade
invalidez *nf, pl* **-deces** 1 : invalidity 2 : disability (in medicine) — **inválido, -da** *adj & n* : invalid
invalorable *adj Lat* : invaluable
invariable *adj* : invariable
invasión *nf, pl* **-siones** : invasion — **invasor, -sora** *adj* : invading — ~ *n* : invader
invencible *adj* : invincible
inventar *vt* 1 : invent 2 : fabricate, make up (a word, an excuse, etc.) — **invención** *nf, pl* **-ciones** 1 : invention 2 MENTIRA : lie, fabrication
inventario *nm* : inventory
inventiva *nf* : inventiveness — **inventivo, -va** *adj* : inventive — **inventor, -tora** *n* : inventor
invernadero *nm* : greenhouse
invernal *adj* : winter
inverosímil *adj* : unlikely
inversión *nf, pl* **-siones** 1 : inversion, reversal 2 : investment (of money, time, etc.)

inverso, -sa *adj* 1 : inverse 2 CONTRARIO : opposite 3 **a la inversa** : the other way around, inversely
inversor, -sora *n* : investor
invertebrado, -da *adj* : invertebrate — **invertebrado** *nm* : invertebrate
invertir {76} *vt* 1 : invert, reverse 2 : invest (money, time, etc.) — *vi* : make an investment
investidura *nf* : investiture
investigar {52} *vt* 1 : investigate 2 ESTUDIAR : research — *vi* ~ **sobre** : do research into — **investigación** *nf, pl* **-ciones** 1 : investigation 2 ESTUDIO : research — **investigador, -dora** *n* : investigator, researcher
investir {54} *vt* : invest
inveterado, -da *adj* : deep-seated, inveterate
invicto, -ta *adj* : undefeated
invierno *nm* : winter
invisible *adj* : invisible — **invisibilidad** *nf* : invisibility
invitar *vt* : invite — **invitación** *nf, pl* **-ciones** : invitation — **invitado, -da** *n* : guest
invocar {72} *vt* : invoke — **invocación** *nf, pl* **-ciones** : invocation
involuntario, -ria *adj* : involuntary
invulnerable *adj* : invulnerable
inyectar *vt* : inject — **inyección** *nf, pl* **-ciones** : injection, shot — **inyectado, -da** *adj* **ojos inyectados** : bloodshot eyes
ion *nm* : ion — **ionizar** {21} *vt* : ionize
ir {43} *vi* 1 : go 2 FUNCIONAR : work, function 3 CONVENIR : suit 4 **¿cómo te va?** : how are you? 5 ~ **con prisa** : be in a hurry 6 ~ **por** : follow, go along 7 **vamos** : let's go — *v aux* 1 ~ **a** : be going to, be about to 2 ~ **caminando** : take a walk 3 **vamos a ver** : we shall see — **irse** *vr* : go away, be gone
ira *nf* : rage, anger — **iracundo, -da** *adj* : irate, angry
iraní *adj* : Iranian
iraquí *adj* : Iraqi
iris *nms & pl* 1 : iris (of the eye) 2 **arco** ~ : rainbow
irlandés, -desa *adj, mpl* **-deses** : Irish
ironía *nf* : irony — **irónico, -ca** *adj* : ironic, ironical
irracional *adj* : irrational
irradiar *vt* : radiate, irradiate
irrazonable *adj* : unreasonable
irreal *adj* : unreal
irreconciliable *adj* : irreconcilable
irreconocible *adj* : unrecognizable
irrecuperable *adj* : irretrievable

irreductible *adj* : unyielding
irreemplazable *adj* : irreplaceable
irreflexivo, -va *adj* : rash, unthinking
irrefutable *adj* : irrefutable
irregular *adj* : irregular — **irregularidad** *nf* : irregularity
irrelevante *adj* : irrelevant
irreparable *adj* : irreparable
irreprimible *adj* : irrepressible
irreprochable *adj* : irreproachable
irresistible *adj* : irresistible
irresoluto, -ta *adj* : indecisive, irresolute
irrespetuoso, -sa *adj* : disrespectful
irresponsable *adj* : irresponsible — **irresponsabilidad** *nf* : irresponsibility
irreverente *adj* : irreverent
irreversible *adj* : irreversible
irrevocable *adj* : irrevocable
irrigar {52} *vt* : irrigate — **irrigación** *nf, pl* **-ciones** : irrigation

irrisorio, -ria *adj* : laughable, ridiculous
irritar *vt* : irritate — **irritarse** *vr* : get annoyed — **irritable** *adj* : irritable — **irritación** *nf, pl* **-ciones** : irritation — **irritante** *adj* : irritating
irrompible *adj* : unbreakable
irrumpir *vi* **~ en** : burst into
isla *nf* : island
islámico, -ca *adj* : Islamic, Muslim
islandés, -desa *adj, mpl* **-deses** : Icelandic
isleño, -ña *n* : islander
israelí *adj* : Israeli
istmo *nm* : isthmus
italiano, -na *adj* : Italian — **italiano** *nm* : Italian (language)
itinerario *nm* : itinerary
izar {21} *vt* : hoist, raise
izquierda *nf* : left — **izquierdista** *adj & nmf* : leftist — **izquierdo, -da** *adj* : left

J

j *nf* : j, tenth letter of the Spanish alphabet
jabalí *nm, pl* **-líes** : wild boar
jabalina *nf* : javelin
jabón *nm, pl* **-bones** : soap — **jabonar** *vt* : soap (up) — **jabonera** *nf* : soap dish — **jabonoso, -sa** *adj* : soapy
jaca *nf* : pony
jacinto *nm* : hyacinth
jactarse *vr* : boast, brag — **jactancia** *nf* : boastfulness, bragging — **jactancioso, -sa** *adj* : boastful
jadear *vi* : pant, gasp — **jadeante** *adj* : panting, breathless — **jadeo** *nm* : gasp, panting
jaez *nm, pl* **jaeces 1** : harness **2 jaeces** *nmpl* : trappings
jaguar *nm* : jaguar
jaiba *nf* *Lat* : crab
jalapeño *nm* *Lat* : jalapeño pepper
jalar *v* *Lat* : pull, tug
jalea *nf* : jelly
jaleo *nm fam* **1** : uproar, racket **2 armar un ~** : raise a ruckus
jalón *nm, pl* **-lones** *Lat* : pull, tug
jamaicano, -na *or* **jamaiquino, -na** *adj* : Jamaican
jamás *adv* **1** : never **2 para siempre ~** : for ever and ever
jamelgo *nm* : nag (horse)
jamón *nm, pl* **-mones 1** : ham **2 ~ serrano** : cured ham
Januká *nmf* : Hanukkah

japonés, -nesa *adj, mpl* **-neses** : Japanese — **japonés** *nm* : Japanese (language)
jaque *nm* **1** : check (in chess) **2 ~ mate** : checkmate
jaqueca *nf* : headache, migraine
jarabe *nm* : syrup
jardín *nm, pl* **-dines 1** : garden **2 ~ infantil** *or* **~ de niños** *Lat* : kindergarten — **jardinería** *nf* : gardening — **jardinero, -ra** *n* : gardener
jarra *nf* : pitcher, jug — **jarro** *nm* : pitcher — **jarrón** *nm, pl* **-rrones** : vase
jaula *nf* : cage
jauría *nf* : pack of hounds
jazmín *nm, pl* **-mines** : jasmine
jazz ['jas, 'dʒas] *nm* : jazz
jeans ['jins, 'dʒins] *nmpl* : jeans
jefe, -fa *n* **1** : chief, leader **2** PATRÓN : boss **3 ~ de cocina** : chef — **jefatura** *nf* **1** : leadership **2** SEDE : headquarters
jengibre *nm* : ginger
jeque *nm* : sheikh, sheik
jerarquía *nf* **1** : hierarchy **2** RANGO : rank — **jerárquico, -ca** *adj* : hierarchical
jerez *nm, pl* **-reces** : sherry
jerga *nf* **1** : coarse cloth **2** ARGOT : jargon, slang
jerigonza *nf* **1** : jargon **2** GALIMATÍAS : gibberish

jeringa or **jeringuilla** nf : syringe — **jeringar** {52} vt fam : annoy, pester
jeroglífico nm : hieroglyphic
jersey nm, pl **-seys** : jersey
jesuita adj & nm : Jesuit
Jesús nm : Jesus
jilguero nm : goldfinch
jinete nmf : horseman, horsewoman f, rider
jirafa nf : giraffe
jirón nm, pl **-rones** : shred, tatter
jitomate nm Lat : tomato
jockey ['ʝoki, 'dʒo-] nmf, pl **-keys** [-kis] : jockey
jocoso, -sa adj : humorous, jocular
jofaina nf : washbowl
jolgorio nm : merrymaking
jornada nf 1 : day's journey 2 : working day — **jornal** nm : day's pay — **jornalero, -ra** n : day laborer
joroba nf : hump — **jorobado, -da** adj : hunchbacked, humpbacked — ~ n : hunchback — **jorobar** vt fam : annoy
jota nf 1 : iota, jot 2 **no veo ni ~** : I can't see a thing
joven adj, pl **jóvenes** : young — ~ nmf : young man m, young woman f, youth
jovial adj : jovial, cheerful
joya nf : jewel — **joyería** nf : jewelry store — **joyero, -ra** n : jeweler — **joyero** nm : jewelry box
juanete nm : bunion
jubilación nf, pl **-ciones** : retirement — **jubilado, -da** adj : retired — ~ nmf : retiree — **jubilar** vt : retire, pension off — **jubilarse** vr : retire — **jubileo** nm : jubilee
júbilo nm : joy, jubilation — **jubiloso, -sa** adj : joyous, jubilant
judaísmo nm : Judaism
judía nf 1 : bean 2 or **~ verde** : green bean, string bean
judicial adj : judicial
judío, -día adj : Jewish — ~ n : Jew
judo ['ʝuðo, 'dʒu-] nm : judo
juego nm 1 : game 2 : playing (of children, etc.) 3 or **~s de azar** : gambling 4 CONJUNTO : set 5 **estar en ~** : be at stake 6 **fuera de ~** : offside (in sports) 7 **hacer ~** : go together, match 8 **~ de manos** : conjuring trick 9 **poner en ~** : bring into play
juerga nf fam : spree, binge
jueves nms & pl : Thursday
juez nmf, pl **jueces** 1 : judge 2 ÁRBITRO : umpire, referee

jugar {44} vi 1 : play 2 : gamble (in a casino, etc.) 3 APOSTAR : bet 4 **~ (al)** tenis : play tennis — vt : play — **jugarse** vr : risk, gamble (away) — **jugada** nf 1 : play, move 2 TRETA : (dirty) trick — **jugador, -dora** n 1 : player 2 : gambler
juglar nm : minstrel
jugo nm 1 : juice 2 SUSTANCIA : substance, essence — **jugoso, -sa** adj 1 : juicy 2 SUSTANCIAL : substantial, important
juguete nm : toy — **juguetear** vi : play — **juguetería** nf : toy store — **juguetón, -tona** adj, mpl **-tones** : playful
juicio nm 1 : judgment 2 RAZÓN : reason, sense 3 **a mi ~** : in my opinion — **juicioso, -sa** adj : wise, sensible
julio nm : July
junco nm : reed, rush
jungla nf : jungle
junio nm : June
juntar vt UNIR : join, unite 2 REUNIR : collect — **juntarse** vr 1 : join (together) 2 REUNIRSE : meet, get together — **junta** nf 1 : board, committee 2 REUNIÓN : meeting 3 : (political) junta 4 : joint, gasket — **junto, -ta** adj 1 : joined PRÓXIMO : close, adjacent 3 (used adverbially) : together 4 **~ a** : next to 5 **~ con** : together with — **juntura** nf : joint
Júpiter nm : Jupiter
jurar vt 1 : swear 2 **~ en falso** : commit perjury — **jurado** nm 1 : jury 2 : juror, member of a jury — **juramento** nm : oath
jurídico, -ca adj : legal
jurisdicción nf, pl **-ciones** : jurisdiction
jurisprudencia nf : jurisprudence
justamente adv 1 : fairly, justly 2 PRECISAMENTE : precisely, exactly
justicia nf : justice, fairness
justificar {72} vt 1 : justify 2 DISCULPAR : excuse, vindicate — **justificación** nf, pl **-ciones** : justification
justo, -ta adj 1 : just, fair 2 EXACTO : exact 3 APRETADO : tight — **justo** adv 1 : just, exactly 2 **~ a tiempo** : just in time
juvenil adj : youthful — **juventud** nf 1 : youth 2 JÓVENES : young people
juzgar {52} vt 1 : try (a case in court) 2 ESTIMAR : judge, consider 3 **a ~ por** : judging by — **juzgado** nm : court, tribunal

K

k *nf* : k, eleventh letter of the Spanish alphabet
kaki → **caqui**
karate *or* **kárate** *nm* : karate
kilo *nm* : kilo — **kilogramo** *nm* : kilogram

kilómetro *nm* : kilometer — **kilometraje** *nm* : distance in kilometers, mileage — **kilométrico, -ca** *adj fam* : endless
kilovatio *nm* : kilowatt
kiosco *nm* → **quiosco**

L

l *nf* : l, twelfth letter of the Spanish alphabet
la *pron vt* 1 : her, it 2 (*formal*) : you 3 ~ **que** : the one who —— *art* → **el**
laberinto *nm* : labyrinth, maze
labia *nf fam* : gift of gab
labio *nm* : lip
labor *nf* 1 : work, labor 2 TAREA : task 3 ~**es domésticas** : housework — **laborable** *adj* **día** ~ : business day — **laborar** *vi* : work — **laboratorio** *nm* : laboratory, lab — **laborioso, -sa** *adj* : laborious
labrar *vt* 1 : cultivate, till 2 : work (metals), carve (stone, wood) 3 CAUSAR : cause, bring about — **labrado, -da** *adj* 1 : cultivated, tilled 2 : carved, wrought — **labrador, -dora** *n* : farmer — **labranza** *nf* : farming
laca *nf* 1 : lacquer 2 : hair spray
lacayo *nm* : lackey
lacerar *vt* : lacerate
lacio, -cia *adj* 1 : limp 2 : straight (of hair)
lacónico, -ca *adj* : laconic
lacra *nf* : scar
lacrar *vt* : seal — **lacre** *nm* : sealing wax
lacrimógeno, -na *adj* **gas lacrimógeno** : tear gas — **lacrimoso, -sa** *adj* : tearful
lácteo, -tea *adj* 1 : dairy 2 **Vía Láctea** : Milky Way
ladear *vt* : tilt — **ladearse** *vr* : lean
ladera *nf* : slope, hillside
ladino, -na *adj* : crafty
lado *nm* 1 : side 2 **al** ~ : next door, nearby 3 **al** ~ **de** : beside, next to 4 **de** ~ : sideways 5 **por otro** ~ : on the other hand 6 **por todos** ~**s** : everywhere, all around
ladrar *vi* : bark — **ladrido** *nm* : bark
ladrillo *nm* : brick

ladrón, -drona *n, mpl* **-drones** : thief
lagarto *nm* : lizard — **lagartija** *nf* : (small) lizard
lago *nm* : lake
lágrima *nf* : tear
laguna *nf* 1 : lagoon 2 VACÍO : gap
laico, -ca *adj* : lay, secular — ~ *n* : layman *m*, layperson
lamentar *vt* 1 : regret, be sorry about 2 **lo lamento** : I'm sorry — **lamentarse** *vr* : lament — **lamentable** *adj* 1 : deplorable 2 TRISTE : sad, pitiful — **lamento** *nm* : lament, moan
lamer *vt* 1 : lick 2 ~ : lap (against) — **lamida** *nf* : lick
lámina *nf* 1 PLANCHA : sheet 2 DIBUJO : plate, illustration — **laminar** *vt* : laminate
lámpara *nf* : lamp
lampiño, -ña *adj* : beardless, hairless
lana *nf* 1 : wool 2 **de** ~ : woolen
lance *nm* 1 : event, incident 2 : throw (of dice, etc.) 3 RIÑA : quarrel
lanceta *nf* : lancet
lancha *nf* : boat, launch 2 ~ **motora** : motorboat
langosta *nf* 1 : lobster 2 : locust (insect) — **langostino** *nm* : prawn, crayfish
languidecer [53] *vi* : languish — **languidez** *nf, pl* **-deces** : languor — **lánguido, -da** *adj* : languid, listless
lanilla *nf* : nap (of fabric)
lanudo, -da *adj* : woolly
lanza *nf* : spear, lance
lanzar [21] *vt* 1 : throw 2 : shoot (a glance), give (a sigh, etc.) 3 : launch (a missile, a project) — **lanzarse** *vr* : throw oneself — **lanzamiento** *nm* : throwing, launching
lapicero *nm* : (mechanical) pencil
lápida *nf* : tombstone

lapidar *vt* : stone
lápiz *nm, pl* **-pices 1** : pencil **2** ~ **de labios** : lipstick
lapso *nm* : lapse (of time) — **lapsus** *nms & pl* : lapse, slip (of the tongue)
largar {52} *vt* **1** AFLOJAR : loosen, slacken **2** *fam* : give — **largarse** *vr fam* : go away, beat it — **largo, -ga** *adj* **1** : long **2 a la larga** : in the long run **3 a lo largo** : lengthwise **4 a lo largo de** : along — **a lo largo de** *nm* : length — **largometraje** *nm* : feature film — **largueza** *nf* : generosity
laringe *nf* : larynx — **laringitis** *nfs & pl* : laryngitis
larva *nf* : larva
las → **el**
lascivo, -va *adj* : lascivious, lewd
láser *nm* : laser
lastimar *vt* : hurt — **lastimarse** *vr* : hurt oneself — **lástima** *nf* **1** : pity **2 dar** ~ : be pitiful **3 me dan** ~ : I feel sorry for them **4 ¡qué** ~! : what a shame! — **lastimero, -ra** *adj* : pitiful, wretched — **lastimoso, -sa** *adj* : pitiful, terrible
lastre *nm* : ballast
lata *nf* **1** : tinplate **2** : (tin) can **3** *fam* : nuisance, bore **4 dar (la) lata** *a fam* : bother, annoy
latente *adj* : latent
lateral *adj* : side, lateral
latido *nm* **1** : beat, throb **2** ~ **del corazón** : heartbeat
latifundio *nm* : large estate
látigo *nm* : whip — **latigazo** *nm* : lash
latín *nm* : Latin (language)
latino, -na *adj* **1** : Latin **2** : Latin-American — ~ *n* : Latin American — **latinoamericano, -na** *adj* : Latin-American — ~ *n* : Latin American
latir *vi* : beat, throb
latitud *nf* : latitude
latón *nm, pl* **-tones** : brass
latoso, -sa *adj fam* : annoying
laúd *nm* : lute
laudable *adj* : laudable
laureado, -da *adj* : prize-winning
laurel *nm* **1** : laurel **2** : bay leaf (in cooking)
lava *nf* : lava
lavar *vt* : wash — **lavarse** *vr* **1** : wash oneself **2** ~ **las manos** : wash one's hands — **lavable** *adj* : washable — **lavabo** *nm* **1** : sink **2** RETRETE : lavatory, toilet — **lavadero** *nm* : laundry room — **lavado** *nm* : wash, washing — **lavadora** *nf* : washing machine — **lavamanos** *nms & pl* : washbowl — **lavandería** *nf* : laundry (service) — **lavaplatos** *nms & pl* : dishwasher **2**

Lat : kitchen sink — **lavativa** *nf* : enema — **lavatorio** *nm* : lavatory, washroom — **lavavajillas** *nms & pl* : dishwasher
laxante *adj & nm* : laxative — **laxo, -xa** *adj* : loose
lazo *nm* **1** VÍNCULO : link, bond **2** LAZADA : bow **3** : lasso, lariat — **lazada** *nf* : bow, loop
le *pron* **1** : (to) her, (to) him, (to) it **2** (*formal*) : (to) you **3** (*as direct object*) : him, you
leal *adj* : loyal, faithful — **lealtad** *nf* : loyalty, allegiance
lebrel *nm* : hound
lección *nf, pl* **-ciones 1** : lesson **2** : lecture (in a classroom)
leche *nf* **1** : milk **2** ~ **descremada** *or* ~ **desnatada** : skim milk **3** ~ **en polvo** : powdered milk — **lechera** *nf* : milk jug — **lechería** *nf* : dairy store — **lechero, -ra** *adj* : dairy — ~ *n* : milkman *m*, milk dealer
lecho *nm* : bed
lechón, -chona *n, mpl* **-chones** : suckling pig
lechoso, -sa *adj* : milky
lechuga *nf* : lettuce
lechuza *nf* : owl
lector, -tora *n* : reader — **lectura** *nf* **1** : reading **2** ESCRITOS : reading matter
leer {20} *v* : read
legación *nf, pl* **-ciones** : legation
legado *nm* **1** : legacy **2** ENVIADO : legate, emissary
legajo *nm* : dossier, file
legal *adj* : legal — **legalidad** *nf* : legality — **legalizar** {21} *vt* : legalize — **legalización** *nf, pl* **-ciones** : legalization
legar {52} *vt* : bequeath
legendario, -ria *adj* : legendary
legible *adj* : legible
legión *nf, pl* **-giones** : legion — **legionario, -ria** *n* : legionnaire
legislar *vi* : legislate — **legislación** *nf, pl* **-ciones** : legislation — **legislador, -dora** *n* : legislator — **legislatura** *nf* : legislature
legítimo, -ma *adj* **1** : legitimate **2** GENUINO : authentic — **legitimidad** *nf* : legitimacy
lego, -ga *adj* **1** : secular, lay **2** IGNORANTE : ignorant — ~ *n* : layman *m*, layperson
legua *nf* : league
legumbre *nf* : vegetable
leído, -da *adj* : well-read
lejano, -na *adj* : distant, far away — **lejanía** *nf* : distance
lejía *nf* : bleach

lejos *adv* **1** : far (away) **2 a lo ~** : in the distance **3 de ~** or **desde ~** : from afar **4 ~ de** : far from

lelo, -la *adj* : silly, stupid

lema *nm* : motto

lencería *nf* **1** : linen **2** : (women's) lingerie

lengua *nf* **1** : tongue **2** IDIOMA : language **3 morderse la ~** : hold one's tongue

lenguado *nm* : sole, flounder

lenguaje *nm* : language

lengüeta *nf* **1** : tongue (of a shoe) **2** : reed (of a musical instrument)

lengüetada *nf* **beber a ~s** : lap (up)

lente *nmf* **1** : lens **2 ~s** *nmpl* : eyeglasses **3 ~s de contacto** : contact lenses

lenteja *nf* : lentil — **lentejuela** *nf* : sequin

lento, -ta *adj* : slow — **lento** *adv* : slowly — **lentitud** *nf* : slowness

leña *nf* : firewood — **leñador, -dora** *n* : lumberjack, woodcutter — **leño** *nm* : log

león, -ona *n, mpl* **leones** : lion, lioness *f*

leopardo *nm* : leopard

leotardo *nm* : leotard, tights *pl*

lepra *nf* : leprosy — **leproso, -sa** *n* : leper

lerdo, -da *adj* **1** TORPE : clumsy **2** TONTO : slow-witted

les *pron* **1** : (to) them, (to) you **2** (*as direct object*) : them, you

lesbiano, -na *adj* : lesbian — **lesbiana** *nf* : lesbian — **lesbianismo** *nm* : lesbianism

lesión *nf, pl* **-siones** : lesion, wound — **lesionado, -da** *adj* : injured, wounded — **lesionar** *vt* **1** : injure, wound **2** DAÑAR : damage

letal *adj* : lethal

letanía *nf* : litany

letárgico, -ca *adj* : lethargic — **letargo** *nm* : lethargy

letra *nf* **1** : letter **2** ESCRITURA : handwriting **3** : lyrics *pl* (of a song) **4 ~ de cambio** : bill of exchange **5 ~s** *nfpl* : arts — **letrado, -da** *adj* : learned — **letrero** *nm* : sign, notice

letrina *nf* : latrine

leucemia *nf* : leukemia

levadizo, -za *adj* **puente levadizo** : drawbridge

levadura *nf* **1** : yeast **2 ~ en polvo** : baking powder

levantar *vt* **1** : lift, raise **2** RECOGER : pick up **3** CONSTRUIR : erect, put up **4** ENCENDER : rouse, stir up **5 ~ la mesa** *Lat* : clear the table — **levan-**

tarse *vr* **1** : rise, stand up **2** : get out of bed **3** SUBLEVARSE : rise up — **levantamiento** *nm* **1** : raising, lifting **2** SUBLEVACIÓN : uprising

levante *nm* **1** : east **2** : east wind

levar *vt* **~ anclas** : weigh anchor

leve *adj* **1** : light, slight **2** : minor, trivial (of wounds, sins, etc.) — **levedad** *nf* : lightness — **levemente** *adv* : lightly, slightly

léxico *nm* : vocabulary, lexicon

ley *nf* **1** : law **2 de (buena) ~** : genuine, pure (of metals)

leyenda *nf* **1** : legend **2** : caption (of an illustration, etc.)

liar {85} *vt* **1** : bind, tie (up) **2** : roll (a cigarette) **3** CONFUNDIR : confuse, muddle — **liarse** *vr* : get mixed up

libanés, -nesa *adj, mpl* **-neses** : Lebanese

libelo *nm* **1** : libel **2** : petition (in court)

libélula *nf* : dragonfly

liberación *nf, pl* **-ciones** : liberation, deliverance

liberal *adj & nmf* : liberal — **liberalidad** *nf* : generosity, liberality

liberar *vt* : liberate, free — **libertad** *nf* **1** : freedom, liberty **2 ~ bajo fianza** : bail **3 ~ condicional** : parole **4 en ~** : free — **libertar** *vt* : set free

libertinaje *nm* : licentiousness — **libertino, -na** *n* : libertine

libido *nf* : libido

libio, -bia *adj* : Libyan

libra *nf* **1** : pound **2 ~ esterlina** : pound sterling

librar *vt* **1** : free, save **2** : wage, fight (a battle) **3** : draw, issue (a check, etc.) — **librarse** *vr* **~ de** : free oneself from, get rid of

libre *adj* **1** : free **2** : unoccupied (of space), spare (of time) **3 al aire ~** : in the open air **4 ~ de impuestos** : tax-free

librea *nf* : livery

libro *nm* **1** : book **2 ~ de bolsillo** : paperback — **librería** *nf* : bookstore — **librero, -ra** *n* : bookseller — **librero** *nm Lat* : bookcase — **libreta** *nf* : notebook

licencia *nf* **1** : license, permit **2** PERMISO : permission **3** : (military) leave — **licenciado, -da** *n* **1** : graduate **2** *Lat* : lawyer — **licenciar** *vt* : dismiss, discharge — **licenciarse** *vr* : graduate — **licenciatura** *nf* : degree

licencioso, -sa *adj* : licentious

liceo *nm* : high school

licitar *vt* : bid for

lícito, -ta *adj* **1** : lawful, legal **2** JUSTO : just, fair

licor *nm* **1** : liquor **2** : liqueur — **licorera** *nf* : decanter

licuadora *nf* : blender — **licuado** *nm* : milk shake — **licuar** {3} *vt* : liquefy

lid *nf* **1** : fight **2 en buena ~** : fair and square

líder *nmf* : leading — *nmf* : leader — **liderato** *or* **liderazgo** *nm* : leadership

lidia *nf* : bullfight — **lidiar** *v* : fight

liebre *nf* : hare

lienzo *nm* **1** : cotton or linen cloth **2** : canvas (for a painting) **3** PARED : wall

liga *nf* **1** : league **2** *Lat* : rubber band **3** : garter (for stockings) — **ligadura** *nf* **1** ATADURA : tie, bond **2** : ligature (in medicine or music) — **ligamento** *nm* : ligament — **ligar** {52} *vt* : bind, tie (up)

ligero, -ra *adj* **1** : light, lightweight **2** LEVE : slight **3** ÁGIL : agile **4** FRÍVOLO : lighthearted, superficial — **ligeramente** *adv* : lightly, slightly — **ligereza** *nf* **1** : lightness **2** : flippancy (of character), thoughtlessness (of actions) **3** AGILIDAD : agility

lija *nf* : sandpaper — **lijar** *vt* : sand

lila *nf* : lilac

lima *nf* **1** : file **2** : lime (fruit) **3 ~ para uñas** : nail file — **limar** *vt* : file

limbo *nm* : limbo

limitar *vt* : limit — *vi* **~ con** : border on — **limitación** *nf, pl* **-ciones** : limitation, limit — **límite** *nm* **1** : limit **2** CONFÍN : boundary, border **3 ~ de velocidad** : speed limit **4 fecha ~** : deadline — **limítrofe** *adj* : bordering

limo *nm* : slime, mud

limón *nm, pl* **-mones 1** : lemon **2 ~ verde** *Lat* : lime — **limonada** *nf* : lemonade

limosna *nf* **1** : alms **2 pedir ~** : beg — **limosnero, -ra** *n* : beggar

limpiabotas *nmfs & pl* : bootblack

limpiaparabrisas *nms & pl* : windshield wiper

limpiar *vt* **1** : clean, wipe (away) **2 ~ en seco** : dry-clean — **limpieza** *nf* **1** : cleanliness **2** : (act of) cleaning — **limpio** *adv* : cleanly, fairly — **limpio, -pia** *adj* **1** : clean, neat **2** HONRADO : honest **3** NETO : net, clear

limusina *nf* : limousine

linaje *nm* : lineage, ancestry

linaza *nf* : linseed

lince *nm* : lynx

linchar *vt* : lynch

lindar *vi* **~ con** : border on — **lindante**

adj : bordering — **linde** *nmf or* **lindero** *nm* : boundary

lindo, -da *adj* **1** : pretty, lovely **2 de lo lindo** *fam* : a lot

línea *nf* **1** : line **2 ~ de conducta** : course of action **3 en ~** : on-line **4 guardar la ~** : watch one's figure — **lineal** *adj* : linear

lingote *nm* : ingot

lingüista *nmf* : linguist — **lingüística** *nf* : linguistics — **lingüístico, -ca** *adj* : linguistic

linimento *nm* : liniment

lino *nm* **1** : flax (plant) **2** : linen (fabric)

linóleo *nm* : linoleum

linterna *nf* **1** FAROL : lantern **2** : flashlight

lío *nm* **1** : bundle **2** *fam* : mess, trouble **3** *fam* : (love) affair

liofilizar {21} *vt* : freeze-dry

liquen *nm* : lichen

liquidar *vt* **1** : liquefy **2** : liquidate (merchandise, etc.) **3** : settle, pay off (a debt, etc.) — **liquidación** *nf, pl* **-ciones 1** : liquidation **2** REBAJA : clearance sale — **líquido, -da** *adj* **1** : liquid **2** NETO : net — **líquido** *nm* : liquid

lira *nf* : lyre

lírico, -ca *adj* : lyric, lyrical — **lírica** *nf* : lyric poetry

lirio *nm* : iris

lisiado, -da *adj* : disabled — **~** *n* : disabled person — **lisiar** *vt* : disable, cripple

liso, -sa *adj* **1** : smooth **2** PLANO : flat **3** SENCILLO : plain **4 pelo ~** : straight hair

lisonjear *vt* : flatter — **lisonja** *nf* : flattery

lista *nf* **1** : stripe **2** ENUMERACIÓN : list **3** : menu (in a restaurant) — **listado, -da** *adj* : striped

listo, -ta *adj* **1** : clever, smart **2** PREPARADO : ready

listón *nm, pl* **-tones 1** : ribbon **2** : strip (of wood)

lisura *nf* : smoothness

litera *nf* : bunk bed, berth

literal *adj* : literal

literatura *nf* : literature — **literario, -ria** *adj* : literary

litigar {52} *vi* : litigate — **litigio** *nm* **1** : litigation **2 en ~** : in dispute

litografía *nf* **1** : lithography **2** : lithograph (picture)

litoral *adj* : coastal — **~** *nm* : shore, seaboard

litro *nm* : liter

liturgia nf : liturgy — **litúrgico, -ca** adj : liturgical

liviano, -na adj 1 LIGERO : light 2 IN-CONSTANTE : fickle

lívido, -da adj : livid

llaga nf : sore, wound

llama nf 1 : flame 2 : llama (animal)

llamar vt 1 : call 2 : call up (on the telephone) — vi 1 : phone, call 2 : knock, ring (at the door) — **llamarse** vr 1 : be called 2 ¿cómo te llamas? : what's your name? — **llamada** nf : call — **llamado, -da** adj : named, called — **llamamiento** nm : call, appeal

llamarada nf 1 : blaze 2 : flushing (of the face)

llamativo, -va adj : flashy, showy

llamear vi : flame, blaze

llano, -na adj 1 : flat 2 : straightforward (of a person, a message, etc.) 3 SEN-CILLO : plain, simple — **llano** nm : plain — **llaneza** nf : simplicity

llanta nf 1 : rim (of a wheel) 2 Lat : tire

llanto nm : crying, weeping

llanura nf : plain

llave nf 1 : key 2 Lat : faucet 3 INTER-RUPTOR : switch 4 cerrar con ~ : lock 5 ~ inglesa : monkey wrench — **llavero** nm : key chain

llegar {52} vi 1 : arrive, come 2 ALCAN-ZAR : reach 3 BASTAR : be enough 4 ~ a : manage to 5 ~ a ser : become — **llegada** nf : arrival

llenar vt : fill (up), fill in — **lleno, -na** adj 1 : full 2 de lleno : completely — **lleno** nm : full house

llevar vt 1 : take, carry 2 CONDUCIR : lead 3 : wear (clothing, etc.) 4 TENER : have 5 **llevo una hora aquí** : I've been here for an hour — **llevarse** vr 1 : take (away) 2 ~ bien : get along well — **llevadero, -ra** adj : bearable

llorar vi : cry, weep — **lloriquear** vi : whimper, whine — **lloro** nm 1 : crying — **llorón, -rona** n, mpl -rones : crybaby, whiner — **lloroso, -sa** adj : tearful

llover {47} v impers : rain — **llovizna** nf : drizzle — **lloviznar** v impers : drizzle

lluvia nf : rain — **lluvioso, -sa** adj : rainy

lo pron 1 : him, it 2 (formal, masculine) : you 3 ~ que : what, that which — ~ art 1 : the best — ~ mejor : the best (part) 3 **sé ~ bueno que eres** : I know how good you are

loa nf : praise — **loable** adj : praiseworthy — **loar** vt : praise

lobo, -ba n : wolf

lóbrego, -ga adj : gloomy

lóbulo nm : lobe

local adj : local — ~ nm : premises pl — **localidad** nf : town, locality — **localizar** {21} vt 1 : localize 2 ENCON-TRAR : locate — **localizarse** vr : be located

loción nf, pl -ciones : lotion

loco, -ca adj 1 : crazy, insane 2 a lo loco : wildly, recklessly 3 **volverse ~** : go mad — ~ n 1 : crazy person, lunatic 2 **hacerse el loco** : act the fool

locomoción nf, pl -ciones : locomotion — **locomotora** nf : engine, locomotive

locuaz adj, pl -cuaces : talkative, loquacious

locución nf, pl -ciones : expression, phrase

locura nf 1 : insanity, madness 2 INSEN-SATEZ : crazy act, folly

locutor, -tora n : announcer

locutorio nm : phone booth

lodo nm : mud — **lodazal** nm : quagmire

logaritmo nm : logarithm

lógica nf : logic — **lógico, -ca** adj : logical — **logística** nf : logistics pl

logotipo nm : logo

lograr vt 1 : achieve, attain 2 CONSEGUIR : get, obtain 3 ~ hacer : manage to do — **logro** nm : achievement, success

loma nf : hill, hillock

lombriz nf, pl -brices : worm

lomo nm 1 : back (of an animal) 2 : spine (of a book) 3 ~ de cerdo : pork loin

lona nf : canvas

loncha nf : slice of bacon, etc.)

lonche nm Lat : lunch — **lonchería** nf Lat : luncheonette

longaniza nf : sausage

longevidad nf : longevity — **longevo, -va** adj : long-lived

longitud nf 1 : longitude 2 LARGO : length

lonja ~ loncha

loro nm : parrot

los, las pron 1 : them 2 : you 3 **los que, las que** : those who, the ones who — **los** art → el

losa nf 1 : flagstone 2 or ~ sepulcral : tombstone

lote nm 1 : batch, lot 2 Lat : plot of land

lotería nf : lottery

loto nm : lotus

loza nf : crockery, earthenware

lozano, -na adj 1 : healthy-looking, vigorous 2 : luxuriant (of plants) — **lozanía** nf 1 : (youthful) vigor 2 : luxuriance (of plants)

lubricar {72} vt : lubricate — **lubri-**

cante *adj* : lubricating — ~ *nm* : lubricant

lucero *nm* : bright star

luchar *vi* 1 : fight, struggle 2 : wrestle (in sports) — **lucha** *nf* 1 : struggle, fight 2 : wrestling (sport) — **luchador, -dora** *n* : fighter, wrestler

lucidez *nf, pl* **-deces** : lucidity — **lúcido, -da** *adj* : lucid

lucido, -da *adj* : magnificent, splendid

luciérnaga *nf* : firefly, glowworm

lucir {45} *vi* 1 : shine 2 *Lat* : appear, seem — *vt* 1 : wear, sport 2 OSTENTAR : show off — **lucirse** *vr* 1 : shine, excel 2 PRESUMIR : show off — **lucimiento** *nm* 1 : brilliance 2 ÉXITO : brilliant performance, success

lucrativo, -va *adj* : lucrative — **lucro** *nm* : profit

luego *adv* 1 : then 2 : later (on) 3 desde ~ : of course 4 ¡hasta ~! : see you later! 5 ~ que : as soon as — ~ *conj* : therefore

lugar *nm* 1 : place 2 ESPACIO : space, room 3 dar ~ a : give rise to 4 en ~ de : instead of 5 tener ~ : take place

lugarteniente *nmf* : deputy

lúgubre *adj* : gloomy

lujo *nm* 1 : luxury 2 de ~ : deluxe — **lujoso, -sa** *adj* : luxurious

lujuria *nf* : lust

lumbre *nf* 1 : fire 2 poner en la ~ : put on the stove

luminoso, -sa *adj* : shining, luminous

luna *nf* 1 : moon 2 : (window) glass 3 ESPEJO : mirror 4 ~ de miel : honeymoon — **lunar** *adj* : lunar — ~ *nm* : mole, beauty spot

lunes *nms & pl* : Monday

lupa *nf* : magnifying glass

lúpulo *nm* : hops

lustrar *vt* : shine, polish — **lustre** *nm* 1 BRILLO : luster, shine 2 ESPLENDOR : glory — **lustroso, -sa** *adj* : lustrous, shiny

luto *nm* 1 : mourning 2 estar de ~ : be in mourning

luxación *nf, pl* **-ciones** : dislocation

luz *nf, pl* **luces** 1 : light 2 : lighting (in a room, etc.) 3 *fam* : electricity 4 a la ~ de : in light of 5 dar a ~ : give birth 6 sacar a la ~ : bring to light

M

m *nf* : m, 13th letter of the Spanish alphabet

macabro, -bra *adj* : macabre

macarrón *nm, pl* **-rrones** 1 : macaroon 2 macarrones *nmpl* : macaroni

maceta *nf* : flowerpot

machacar {72} *vt* : crush, grind — *vi* ~ **sobre** : go on about — **machacón, -cona** *adj, mpl* **-cones** : tiresome, boring

machete *nm* : machete — **machetear** *vt* : hack with a machete

macho *adj* 1 : male 2 *fam* : macho — ~ *nm* 1 : male 2 *fam* : he-man — **machista** *nm* : male chauvinist

machucar {72} *vt* 1 : beat, crush 2 : bruise (fruit)

macizo, -za *adj* : solid — **macizo** *nm* ~ de flores : flower bed

mácula *nf* : stain

madeja *nf* : skein, hank

madera *nf* 1 : wood 2 : lumber (for construction) 3 ~ dura : hardwood — **madero** *nm* : piece of lumber, plank

madre *nf* 1 : mother 2 ~ política : mother-in-law — **madrastra** *nf* : stepmother

madreselva *nf* : honeysuckle

madriguera *nf* : burrow, den

madrileño, -ña *adj* : of or from Madrid

madrina *nf* 1 : godmother 2 : bridesmaid (at a wedding)

madrugada *nf* : dawn, daybreak — **madrugador, -dora** *n* : early riser

madurar *v* 1 : mature 2 : ripen (of fruit) — **madurez** *nf, pl* **-reces** 1 : maturity 2 : ripeness (of fruit) — **maduro, -ra** *adj* 1 : mature 2 : ripe (of fruit)

maestría *nf* : mastery, skill — **maestro, -tra** *adj* : masterly, skilled — ~ *n* 1 : teacher (in grammar school) 2 EXPERTO : expert, master

Mafia *nf* : Mafia

magia *nf* : magic — **mágico, -ca** *adj* : magic, magical

magisterio *nm* : teachers *pl*, teaching profession

magistrado, -da *n* : magistrate, judge

magistral *adj* 1 : masterful 2 : magisterial (of an attitude, etc.)

magnánimo, -ma *adj* : magnanimous — **magnanimidad** *nf* : magnanimity

magnate *nmf* : magnate, tycoon

magnesia *nf* : magnesia — **magnesio** *nm* : magnesium

magnético, -ca *adj* : magnetic — **mag-**

netismo nm : magnetism — **magnetizar** {21} vt : magnetize

magnetófono nm : tape recorder

magnificencia nf : magnificence — **magnífico, -ca** adj : magnificent

magnitud nf : magnitude

magnolia nf : magnolia

mago, -ga n 1 : magician 2 **los Reyes Magos** : the Magi

magro, -gra adj 1 : lean MEZQUINO : poor, meager

magullar vt : bruise — **magulladura** nf : bruise

mahometano, -na adj : Islamic, Muslim — ~ n : Muslim

maicena nf : cornstarch

maíz nm : corn

maja nf : pestle

majadero, -ra adj : foolish, silly — ~ n : fool

majar vt : crush

majestad nf 1 : majesty 2 **Su Majestad** : His/Her Majesty — **majestuoso, -sa** adj : majestic

majo, -ja adj 1 : nice 2 GUAPO : good-looking

mal adv 1 : badly, poorly 2 INCORRECTAMENTE : incorrectly 3 DIFÍCILMENTE : with difficulty, hardly 4 **de ~ en peor** : from bad to worse 5 **menos ~** : it's just as well — ~ nm 1 : evil 2 DAÑO : harm, damage 3 ENFERMEDAD : illness — ~ adj → **malo**

malabarismo nm : juggling — **malabarista** nmf : juggler

malacostumbrar vt : spoil, pamper — **malacostumbrado, -da** adj : spoiled

malaria nf : malaria

malasio, -sia adj : Malaysian

malaventura nf : misfortune — **malaventurado, -da** adj : unfortunate

malayo, -ya adj : Malay, Malayan

malcriado, -da adj : bad-mannered, spoiled

maldad nf 1 : evil 2 : evil deed

maldecir {11} vt : curse, damn — vi 1 : curse, swear 2 ~ **de** : speak ill of — **maldición** nf, pl **-ciones** : curse — **maldito, -ta** adj fam : damned

maleable adj : malleable

maleante nmf : crook

malecón nm, pl **-cones** : jetty

maleducado, -da adj : rude

maleficio nm : curse — **maléfico, -ca** adj : evil, harmful

malentendido nm : misunderstanding

malestar nm 1 : discomfort 2 INQUIETUD : uneasiness

maleta nf 1 : suitcase 2 **hacer la ~** : pack one's bags — **maletero, -ra** n

: porter — **maletero** nm : trunk (of an automobile) — **maletín** nm, pl **-tines** 1 PORTAFOLIO : briefcase 2 : overnight bag

malévolo, -la adj : malevolent — **malevolencia** nf : malevolence

maleza nf 1 : underbrush 2 MALAS HIERBAS : weeds pl

malgastar vt : waste, squander

malhablado, -da adj : foul-mouthed

malhechor, -chora n : criminal, delinquent

malhumorado, -da adj : bad-tempered, cross

malicia nf : malice — **malicioso, -sa** adj : malicious

maligno, -na adj 1 : malignant 2 PERNICIOSO : harmful, evil

malla nf 1 : mesh 2 ~ **s** nfpl : tights

malo, -la adj (**mal** before masculine singular nouns) 1 : bad 2 : poor (in quality) 3 ENFERMO : unwell 4 **estar de malas** : be in a bad mood — ~ n : villain, bad guy (in movies, etc.)

malograr vt : waste — **malograrse** vr 1 FRACASAR : fail 2 : die young — **malogro** nm : failure

maloliente adj : smelly

malpensado, -da adj : malicious, nasty

malsano, -na adj : unhealthy

malsonante adj : rude

malta nf : malt

maltratar vt : mistreat

maltrecho, -cha adj : battered

malvado, -da adj : evil, wicked

malvavisco nm : marshmallow

malversar vt : embezzle — **malversación** nf, pl **-ciones** : embezzlement

mama nf : teat (of an animal), breast (of a woman)

mamá nf fam : mom, mama

mamar vi 1 : suckle 2 **dar de ~ a** : breast-feed — vt 1 : suckle, nurse 2 : learn from childhood, grow up with — **mamario, -ria** adj : mammary

mamarracho nm fam : mess, sight

mambo nm : mambo

mamífero, -ra adj : mammalian — **mamífero** nm : mammal

mamografía nf : mammogram

mampara nf : screen, room divider

mampostería nf : masonry

manada nf : flock, herd, pack 2 **en ~** : in droves

manantial nm 1 : spring 2 ORIGEN : source

manar vi 1 : flow 2 ~ **en** : be rich in —

manchar vt 1 : stain, spot, mark 2 : tarnish (a reputation, etc.) — **mancharse** vr : get dirty — **mancha** nf : stain

mancillar *vt* : sully, stain

manco, -ca *adj* : one-armed, one-handed

mancomunar *vt* : combine, join — **mancomunarse** *vr* : unite — **mancomunidad** *nf* : union

mandar *vt* 1 : command, order 2 ENVIAR : send 3 *Lat* : hurl, throw — *vi* 1 : be in charge 2 ¿mande? *Lat* : yes?, pardon? — **mandadero, -ra** *nm* : messenger — **mandado** *nm* : errand — **mandamiento** *nm* 1 : order, warrant 2 : commandment (in religion)

mandarina *nf* : mandarin orange, tangerine

mandato *nm* 1 : term of office 2 ORDEN : mandate — **mandatorio, -ria** *n* 1 : leader (in politics) 2 : agent (in law)

mandíbula *nf* : jaw, jawbone

mandil *nm* : apron

mando *nm* 1 : command, leadership 2 al ~ de : in charge of 3 ~ a distancia : remote control

mandolina *nf* : mandolin

mandón, -dona *adj*, *mpl* **-dones** : bossy

manecilla *nf* : hand (of a clock), pointer

manejar *vt* 1 : handle, operate 2 : manage (a business, etc.) 3 : manipulate (a person) 4 *Lat* : drive (a car) — **manejarse** *vr* 1 : manage, get by 2 *Lat* : behave — **manejo** *nm* 1 : handling, use 2 : management (of a business, etc.)

manera *nf* 1 : way, manner 2 de ~ que : so that 3 de ninguna ~ : by no means 4 de todas ~s : anyway

manga *nf* 1 : sleeve 2 MANGUERA : hose

mango *nm* 1 : hilt, handle 2 : mango (fruit)

mangonear *vt fam* : boss around — *vi* 1 : be bossy 2 HOLGAZANEAR : loaf, fool around

manguera *nf* : hose

maní *nm*, *pl* **-níes** *Lat* : peanut

manía *nf* 1 : mania, obsession 2 MODA PASAJERA : craze, fad 3 ANTIPATÍA : dislike — **maníaco, -ca** *adj* : maniacal — ~ *n* : maniac

maniatar *vt* : tie the hands of

maniático, -ca *adj* : obsessive, fussy — ~ *n* : fussy person, fanatic

manicomio *nm* : insane asylum

manicura *nf* : manicure — **manicuro, -ra** *n* : manicurist

manido, -da *adj* : stale, hackneyed

manifestar {55} *vt* 1 : demonstrate, show 2 DECLARAR : express, declare — **manifestarse** *vr* 1 : become evident 2 : demonstrate (in politics) — **mani-**

festación *nf*, *pl* **-ciones** 1 : manifestation, sign 2 : demonstration (in politics) — **manifestante** *nmf* : protester, demonstrator — **manifiesto, -ta** *adj* : manifest, evident — **manifiesto** *nm* : manifesto

manija *nf* : handle

manillar *nm* : handlebars *pl*

maniobra *nf* : maneuver — **maniobrar** *v* : maneuver

manipular *vt* 1 : manipulate 2 MANEJAR : handle — **manipulación** *nf*, *pl* **-ciones** : manipulation

maniquí *nmf*, *pl* **-quíes** : mannequin, model — ~ *nm* : mannequin, dummy

manirroto, -ta *adj* : extravagant — ~ *n* : spendthrift

manivela *nf* : crank

manjar *nm* : delicacy, special dish

mano *nf* 1 : hand 2 : coat (of paint, etc.) 3 a ~ *or* a la ~ : at hand, nearby 4 dar la ~ : shake hands 5 de segunda ~ : secondhand 6 ~ de obra : labor, manpower

manojo *nm* : bunch

manopla *nf* : mitten

manosear *vt* 1 : handle excessively 2 : fondle (a person)

manotazo *nm* : slap

mansalva: a ~ *adv phr* : at close range, without risk

mansarda *nf* : attic

mansedumbre *nf* 1 : gentleness 2 : tameness (of an animal)

mansión *nf*, *pl* **-siones** : mansion

manso, -sa *adj* 1 : gentle 2 : tame (of an animal)

manta *nf* 1 : blanket 2 *Lat* : poncho

manteca *nf* : lard, fat — **mantecoso, -sa** *adj* : greasy

mantel *nm* : tablecloth — **mantelería** *nf* : table linen

mantener {80} *vt* 1 : support 2 CONSERVAR : preserve 3 : keep up, maintain (relations, correspondence, etc.) 4 AFIRMAR : affirm — **mantenerse** *vr* 1 : support oneself 2 ~ firme : hold one's ground — **mantenimiento** *nm* 1 : maintenance 2 SUSTENTO : sustenance

mantequilla *nf* : butter — **mantequera** *nf* : churn — **mantequería** *nf* : dairy

mantilla *nf* : mantilla

manto *nm* : cloak

mantón *nm*, *pl* **-tones** : shawl

manual *adj* : manual — ~ *nm* : manual, handbook

manubrio *nm* 1 : handle, crank 2 *Lat* : handlebars *pl*

manufactura *nf* 1 : manufacture 2
  FÁBRICA : factory
manuscrito *nm* : manuscript — **manu-**
  scrito, -ta *adj* : handwritten
manutención *nf, pl* -**ciones** : maintenance
manzana *nf* 1 : apple 2 : (city) block —
  manzanar *nm* : apple orchard —
  manzano *nm* : apple tree
maña *nf* 1 : skill 2 ASTUCIA : cunning,
  guile
mañana *adv* : tomorrow — ~ *nm* el ~
  : the future — ~ *nf* : morning
mañoso, -sa *adj* 1 : skillful 2 *Lat*
  : finicky
mapa *nm* : map — **mapamundi** *nm*
  : map of the world
mapache *nm* : raccoon
maqueta *nf* : model, mock-up
maquillaje *nm* : makeup — **maquil-**
  larse *vr* : put on makeup
máquina *nf* 1 : machine 2 LOCOMOTORA
  : locomotive 3 a toda ~ : at full
  speed 4 ~ de escribir : typewriter —
  maquinación *nf, pl* -**ciones** : machi-
  nation — **maquinal** *adj* : mechanical
  — **maquinaria** *nf* 1 : machinery 2
  : mechanism, works *pl* (of a watch,
  etc.) — **maquinilla** *nf* : small machine
  — **maquinista** *nmf* 1 : machinist 2
  : (railroad) engineer
mar *nmf* 1 : sea 2 alta ~ : high seas *pl*
maraca *nf* : maraca
maraña *nf* 1 : thicket 2 ENREDO : tangle,
  mess
maratón *nm, pl* -**tones** : marathon
maravilla *nf* 1 : wonder, marvel 2
  : marigold (flower) — **maravillar** *vt*
  : astonish — **maravillarse** *vr* : be
  amazed — **maravilloso, -sa** *adj* : marvelous
marca *nf* 1 : mark 2 : brand (on livestock) 3 or ~ de fábrica : trademark
  4 : record (in sports) — **marcado, -da**
  adj : marked — **marcador** *nm* 1
  : scoreboard 2 *Lat* : marker, felt-
  tipped pen
marcapasos *nms & pl* : pacemaker
marcar {72} *vt* 1 : mark 2 : brand (livestock) 3 INDICAR : indicate, show 4
  : dial (a telephone, etc.) 5 : score (in
  sports) — *vi* 1 : score 2 : dial (on the
  telephone, etc.)
marchar *vi* 1 : go 2 CAMINAR : walk 3
  FUNCIONAR : work, run — **marcharse**
  vr : leave, go — **marcha** *nf* 1 : march 2
  PASO : pace, speed 3 : gear (of an automobile) 4 poner en ~ : put in motion
marchitarse *vr* : wither, wilt — **mar-**
  chito, -ta *adj* : withered

marcial *adj* : martial, military
marco *nm* 1 : frame 2 : goalposts *pl* (in
  sports) 3 ENTORNO : setting, framework
marea *nf* : tide — **marear** *vt* 1 : make
  nauseous or dizzy 2 CONFUNDIR : confuse — **marearse** *vr* 1 : become nau-
  seated or dizzy 2 CONFUNDIRSE : get
  confused — **mareado, -da** *adj* 1 : sick,
  nauseous 2 ATURDIDO : dazed, dizzy
maremoto *nm* : tidal wave
mareo *nm* 1 : nausea, seasickness 2
  VÉRTIGO : dizziness
marfil *nm* : ivory
margarina *nf* : margarine
margarita *nf* : daisy
margen *nm, pl* **márgenes** 1 : edge,
  border 2 : margin (of a page, etc.) —
  marginado, -da *adj* 1 : alienated 2
  clases marginadas : underclass —
  ~ *n* : outcast — **marginal** *adj* : marginal — **marginar** *vt* : ostracize, exclude
mariachi *nm* : mariachi musician or
  band
maridaje *nm* : marriage, union — **mari-**
  do *nm* : husband
marihuana or mariguana or marijuana *nf* : marijuana
marimba *nf* : marimba
marina *nf* 1 : coast 2 or ~ de guerra
  : navy, fleet
marinada *nf* : marinade — **marinar** *vt*
  : marinate
marinero, -ra *adj* 1 : sea, marine 2
  : seaworthy (of a ship) — **marinero**
  nm : sailor — **marino, -na** *adj* : marine — **marino** *nm* : seaman, sailor
marioneta *nf* : puppet, marionette
mariposa *nf* 1 : butterfly 2 ~ noctur-
  na : moth
mariquita *nf* : ladybug
marisco *nm* 1 : shellfish 2 ~s *nmpl*
  : seafood
marisma *nf* : salt marsh
marítimo, -ma *adj* : maritime, shipping
mármol *nm* : marble
marmota *nf* ~ de América : groundhog
marquesina *nf* : marquee, (glass)
  canopy
marrano, -na *n* 1 : pig, hog 2 *fam* : slob
marrar *vt* : miss (a target) — *vi* : fail
marrón *adj & nm, pl* -**rrones** : brown
marroquí *adj* : Moroccan
marsopa *nf* : porpoise
marsupial *nm* : marsupial
Marte *nm* : Mars
martes *nms & pl* : Tuesday
martillo *nm* 1 : hammer 2 ~ neumáti-

co : jackhammer — **martillar** or **mar-tillear** v : hammer

mártir nmf : martyr — **martirio** nm : martyrdom — **martirizar** {21} vt : martyr 2 ATORMENTAR : torment

marxismo nm : Marxism — **marxista** adj & nmf : Marxist

marzo nm : March

mas conj : but

más adv 1 : more 2 **el/la/lo ~** : (the) most 3 (in negative constructions) : (any) longer 4 **¡qué día ~ bonito!** : what a beautiful day! — ~ adj 1 : more 2 : most 3 **¿quién ~?** : who else? — ~ prep : plus — ~ pron 1 **a lo ~** : at most 2 **de ~** : extra, spare 3 **~ o menos** : more or less 4 **¿tienes ~?** : do you have more?

masa nf 1 : mass, volume 2 : dough (in cooking) 3 **~s** nfpl : people, masses

masacre nf : massacre

masaje nm : massage — **masajear** vt : massage

mascar {72} v : chew

máscara nf : mask — **mascarada** nf : masquerade — **mascarilla** nf : mask (in medecine, etc.)

mascota nf : mascot

masculino, -na adj 1 : masculine, male 2 VARONIL : manly 3 : masculine (in grammar) — **masculinidad** nf : masculinity

mascullar v : mumble

masilla nf : putty

masivo, -va adj : mass, large-scale

masón nm, pl **-sones** : Mason, Freemason — **masónico, -ca** adj : Masonic

masoquismo nm : masochism — **masoquista** adj : masochistic — ~ nmf : masochist

masticar {72} v : chew

mástil nm 1 : mast 2 ASTA : flagpole 3 : neck (of a stringed instrument)

mastín nm, pl **-tines** : mastiff

masturbarse vr : masturbate — **masturbación** nf, pl **-ciones** : masturbation

mata nf : bush, shrub

matadero nm : slaughterhouse

matador nm : matador, bullfighter

matamoscas nms & pl : flyswatter

matar vt 1 : kill 2 : slaughter (animals) — **matarse** vr 1 : be killed 2 SUICIDARSE : commit suicide — **matanza** nf : slaughter, killing

matasanos nms & pl fam : quack

matasellos nms & pl : postmark

mate adj : matte, dull — ~ nm 1 : maté 2 **jaque ~** : checkmate

matemáticas nfpl : mathematics — **matemático, -ca** adj : mathematical — ~ n : mathematician

materia nf 1 ASUNTO : matter 2 MATERIAL : material — **material** adj 1 : material 2 **daños ~es** : property damage — ~ nm 1 : material 2 EQUIPO : equipment, gear — **materialismo** nm : materialism — **materialista** adj : materialistic — **materializar** {21} vt : bring to fruition — **materializarse** vr : materialize — **materialmente** adv : absolutely

maternal adj : maternal — **maternidad** nf 1 : motherhood 2 : maternity hospital — **materno, -na** adj 1 : maternal 2 **lengua materna** : mother tongue

matinal adj : morning

matinée or **matiné** nf : matinee

matiz nm, pl **-tices** 1 : nuance 2 : hue, shade (of colors) — **matizar** {21} vt 1 : blend (colors) 2 : qualify (a statement, etc.) 3 **~ de** : tinge with

matón nm, pl **-tones** 1 : bully 2 CRIMINAL : gangster, hoodlum

matorral nm : thicket

matraca nf 1 : rattle, noisemaker 2 **dar la ~ a** : pester

matriarcado nm : matriarchy

matrícula nf 1 : list, roll, register 2 INSCRIPCIÓN : registration 3 : license plate (of an automobile) — **matricular** vt : register — **matricularse** vr : register, matriculate

matrimonio nm 1 : marriage 2 PAREJA : (married) couple — **matrimonial** adj : marital

matriz nf, pl **-trices** 1 : matrix 2 : uterus, womb (in anatomy)

matrona nf : matron

matutino, -na adj : morning

maullar {8} vi : meow — **maullido** nm : meow

maxilar nm : jaw, jawbone

máxima nf : maxim

máxime adv : especially

máximo, -ma adj : maximum, highest — **máximo** nm 1 : maximum 2 **al ~** : to the full

maya adj : Mayan

mayo nm : May

mayonesa nf : mayonnaise

mayor adj 1 (comparative of **grande**) : bigger, larger, greater, older 2 (superlative of **grande**) : biggest, largest, greatest, oldest 3 **al por ~** : wholesale 4 **~ de edad** : of (legal) age — ~ nmf 1 : major (in the military) 2 ADULTO : adult 3 **~es** nmfpl : grownups — **mayoral** nm : foreman

mayordomo *nm* : butler

mayoreo *nm Lat* : wholesale

mayoría *nf* : majority

mayorista *adj* : wholesale — ~ *nmf* : wholesaler

mayormente *adv* : primarily

mayúscula *nf* : capital letter — **mayúsculo, -la** *adj* 1 : capital, uppercase 2 **un fallo mayúsculo** : a terrible mistake

maza *nf* : mace (weapon)

mazapán *nm, pl* -**panes** : marzipan

mazmorra *nf* : dungeon

mazo *nm* 1 : mallet 2 MAJA : pestle

mazorca *nf* ~ **de maíz** : corncob

me *pron* 1 (*direct object*) : me 2 (*indirect object*) : to me, for me, from me 3 (*reflexive*) : myself, to myself, for myself, from myself

mecánica *nf* : mechanics — **mecánico, -ca** *adj* : mechanical — ~ *n* : mechanic

mecanismo *nm* : mechanism — **mecanización** *nf, pl* -**ciones** : mechanization — **mecanizar** {21} *vt* : mechanize

mecanografiar {85} *vt* : type — **mecanografía** *nf* : typing — **mecanógrafo, -fa** *n* : typist

mecate *nm Lat* : rope

mecedora *nf* : rocking chair

mecenas *nmfs & pl* : patron, sponsor — **mecenazgo** *nm* : patronage, sponsorship

mecer {86} *vt* 1 : rock 2 : push (on a swing) — **mecerse** *vr* : rock, swing

mecha *nf* 1 : fuse (of a bomb, etc.) 2 : wick (of a candle)

mechero *nm* 1 : burner 2 *Spain* : cigarette lighter

mechón *nm, pl* -**chones** : lock (of hair)

medalla *nf* : medal — **medallón** *nm, pl* -**llones** : medallion 2 : locket (jewelry)

media *nf* 1 : average 2 ~**s** *nfpl* : stockings 3 **a** ~**s** : by halves, halfway

mediación *nf, pl* -**ciones** : mediation

mediado, -da *adj* 1 : half full, half empty, half over 2 : halfway through — **mediados** *nmpl* **a** ~ **de** : halfway through, in the middle of

mediador, -dora *n* : mediator

medialuna *nf* 1 : crescent 2 : croissant (pastry)

medianamente *adv* : fairly

medianero, -ra *adj* **pared medianera** : dividing wall

mediano, -na *adj* 1 : medium, average 2 MEDIOCRE : mediocre

medianoche *nf* : midnight

mediante *prep* : through, by means of

mediar *vi* 1 : be in the middle 2 INTERVENIR : mediate 3 ~ **entre** : be between

medicación *nf, pl* -**ciones** : medication — **medicamento** *nm* : medicine — **medicar** {72} *vt* : medicate — **medicarse** *vr* : take medicine — **medicina** *nf* : medicine — **medicinal** *adj* : medicinal

medición *nf, pl* -**ciones** : measurement

médico, -ca *adj* : medical — ~ *n* : doctor, physician

medida *nf* 1 : measurement, measure 2 MODERACIÓN : moderation 3 GRADO : extent, degree 4 **tomar** ~**s** : take steps — **medidor** *nm Lat* : meter, gauge

medieval *adj* : medieval

medio, -dia *adj* 1 : half 2 MEDIANO : average 3 **una media hora** : half an hour 4 **la clase media** : the middle class — **medio** *adv* : half — ~ *nm* 1 : half 2 MANERA : means *pl*, way 3 **en** ~ **de** : in the middle of 4 ~ **ambiente** : environment 5 ~**s** *nmpl* : means, resources

mediocre *adj* : mediocre, average — **mediocridad** *nf* : mediocrity

mediodía *nm* : noon, midday

medioevo *nm* : Middle Ages

medir {54} *vt* 1 : measure 2 CONSIDERAR : weigh, consider — **medirse** *vr* : be moderate

meditar *vi* : meditate, contemplate — *vt* 1 : think over, consider 2 PLANEAR : plan, work out — **meditación** *nf, pl* -**ciones** : meditation

mediterráneo, -nea *adj* : Mediterranean

medrar *vt* : flourish, thrive

medroso, -sa *adj* : fearful

médula *nf* 1 : marrow 2 ~ **espinal** : spinal cord

medusa *nf* : jellyfish

megabyte *nm* : megabyte

megáfono *nm* : megaphone

mejicano → mexicano

mejilla *nf* : cheek

mejillón *nm, pl* -**llones** : mussel

mejor *adv* 1 (*comparative*) : better 2 (*superlative*) : best 3 **a lo** ~ : maybe, perhaps — ~ *adj* 1 (*comparative of* **bueno** *or* **bien**) : better 2 (*superlative of* **bueno** *or* **bien**) : best 3 **lo** ~ : the best thing 4 **tanto** ~ : so much the better — **mejora** *nf* : improvement

mejorana *nf* : marjoram

mejorar *vt* : improve — *vi* : improve, get better

mejunje *nm* : concoction, brew

melancolía *nf* : melancholy — **melancólico, -ca** *adj* : melancholic, melancholy

melaza *nf* : molasses

melena *nf* **1** : long hair **2** : mane (of a lion)

melindroso, -sa *adj* **1** : affected **2** *Lat* : finicky

mella *nf* : chip, nick — **mellado, -da** *adj* : chipped, jagged

mellizo, -za *adj & n* : twin

melocotón *nm, pl* **-tones** : peach

melodía *nf* : melody — **melódico, -ca** *adj* : melodic

melodrama *nm* : melodrama — **melodramático, -ca** *adj* : melodramatic

melón *nm, pl* **-lones** : melon

meloso, -sa *adj* **1** : sweet, honeyed **2** EMPALAGOSO : cloying

membrana *nf* : membrane

membrete *nm* : letterhead, heading

membrillo *nm* : quince

membrudo, -da *adj* : muscular, burly

memorable *adj* : memorable

memorándum *or* **memorando** *nm, pl* **-dums** *or* **-dos 1** : memorandum **2** AGENDA : notebook

memoria *nf* **1** : memory **2** RECUERDO : remembrance **3** INFORME : report **de ∼** : by heart **5 ∼s** *nfpl* : memoirs — **memorizar** {21} *vt* : memorize

mena *nf* : ore

menaje *nm* : household goods *pl*, furnishings *pl*

mencionar *vt* : mention, refer to — **mención** *nf, pl* **-ciones** : mention

mendaz *adj, pl* **-daces** : lying

mendigar {52} *vi* : beg — *vt* : beg for — **mendicidad** *nf* : begging — **mendigo, -ga** *n* : beggar

mendrugo *nm* : crust (of bread)

menear *vt* **1** : move, shake **2** : sway (one's hips) **3** : wag (a tail) — **menearse** *vr* **1** : sway, shake, move **2** *fam* : hurry up

menester *nm* **ser ∼** : be necessary — **menesteroso, -sa** *adj* : needy

menguar *vi* **1** : diminish, lessen — *vi* **1** : decline, decrease **2** : wane (of the moon) — **mengua** *nf* : decrease, decline

menopausia *nf* : menopause

menor *adj* **1** (*comparative of* **pequeño**) : smaller, lesser, younger **2** (*superlative of* **pequeño**) : smallest, least, youngest **3** : minor (in music) **4 al por ∼** : retail — *nm, nf* : minor, juvenile

menos *adv* **1** (*comparative*) : less **2** (*superlative*) : least **3 ∼ de** : fewer than — **∼** *adj* **1** (*comparative*) : less, fewer **2** (*superlative*) : least, fewest — **∼** *prep* **1** : minus **2** EXCEPTO : except — **∼** *pron* **1** : less, fewer **2 al ∼** *or* **por lo ∼** : at least **3 a ∼ que** : unless —

menoscabar *vt* **1** : lessen **2** ESTROPEAR : harm, damage — **menospreciar** *vt* **1** DESPRECIAR : scorn **2** SUBESTIMAR : undervalue — **menosprecio** *nm* : contempt

mensaje *nm* : message — **mensajero, -ra** *n* : messenger

menso, -sa *adj Lat fam* : foolish, stupid

menstruar {3} *vi* : menstruate — **menstruación** *nf* : menstruation

mensual *adj* : monthly — **mensualidad** *nf* **1** : monthly payment **2** : monthly salary

mensurable *adj* : measurable

menta *nf* **1** : mint, peppermint **2 ∼ verde** : spearmint

mental *adj* : mental — **mentalidad** *nf* : mentality

mentar {55} *vt* : mention, name

mente *nf* : mind

mentir {76} *vi* : lie — **mentira** *nf* : lie — **mentirilla** *nf* : fib — **mentiroso, -sa** *adj* : lying — **∼** *n* : liar

mentís *nms & pl* : denial

mentol *nm* : menthol

mentón *nm, pl* **-tones** : chin

menú *nm, pl* **-nús** : menu

menudear *vi* : occur frequently — **menudeo** *nm Lat* : retail, retailing

menudillos *nmpl* : giblets

menudo, -da *adj* **1** : small, insignificant **2 a ∼** : often

meñique *nm or* **dedo ∼** : little finger, pinkie

meollo *nm* **1** : marrow **2** ESENCIA : essence, core

mercado *nm* **1** : market **2 ∼ de valores** : stock market — **mercadería** *nf* : merchandise, goods *pl*

mercancía *nf* : merchandise, goods *pl* — **mercante** *nmf* : merchant, dealer — **mercantil** *adj* : commercial

mercenario, -ria *adj & n* : mercenary

mercería *nf* : notions store

mercurio *nm* : mercury

Mercurio *nm* : Mercury (planet)

merecer {53} *vt* : deserve — *vi* : be worthy — **merecedor, -dora** *adj* : deserving, worthy — **merecido** *nm* **recibir su ∼** : get one's just deserts

merendar {55} *vi* : have an afternoon snack — *vt* : have as an afternoon snack — **merendero** *nm* **1** : snack bar **2** : picnic area

merengue *nm* **1** : meringue **2** : merengue (dance)

meridiano, -na *adj* 1 : midday 2 CLARO : crystal-clear — **meridiano** *nm* : meridian — **meridional** *adj* : southern

merienda *nf* : afternoon snack, tea

mérito *nm* : merit, worth — **meritorio, -ria** *adj* : deserving — ~ *n* : intern, trainee

mermar *vi* : decrease — *vt* : reduce, cut down — **merma** *nf* : decrease

mermelada *nf* : marmalade, jam

mero, -ra *adj* 1 : mere, simple 2 *Lat fam* (*used as an intensifier*) : very, real — **mero** *adv Lat fam* 1 : nearly, almost 2 **aquí** ~ : right here

merodear *vi* 1 : maraud 2 — **por** : prowl about (a place)

mes *nm* : month

mesa *nf* 1 : table 2 COMITÉ : committee, board

mesarse *vr* ~ **los cabellos** : tear one's hair

meseta *nf* : plateau

Mesías *nm* : Messiah

mesilla *nf* : small table

mesón *nm, pl* **-sones** : inn — **mesonero, -ra** *n* : innkeeper

mestizo, -za *adj* 1 : of mixed ancestry 2 HÍBRIDO : hybrid — ~ *n* : person of mixed ancestry

mesura *nf* : moderation — **mesurado, -da** *adj* : moderate, restrained

meta *nf* : goal, objective

metabolismo *nm* : metabolism

metafísica *nf* : metaphysics — **metafísico, -ca** *adj* : metaphysical

metáfora *nf* : metaphor — **metafórico, -ca** *adj* : metaphoric, metaphorical

metal *nm* 1 : metal 2 : brass section (in an orchestra) — **metálico, -ca** *adj* : metallic, metal — **metalurgia** *nf* : metallurgy

metamorfosis *nfs & pl* : metamorphosis

metano *nm* : methane

meteúra *vr* ~ **de pata** *fam* : blunder

meteoro *nm* : meteor — **meteórico, -ca** *adj* : meteoric — **meteorito** *nm* : meteorite — **meteorología** *nf* : meteorology — **meteorólogo, -ga** *adj* : meteorological, meteorologic — ~ *n* : meteorologist

meter *vt* 1 : put (in) 2 : place (in a job, etc.) 3 ENREDAR : involve 4 CAUSAR : make, cause 5 : spread (a rumor) 6 *Lat* : strike (a blow) — **meterse** *vr* 1 : get in, enter 2 ~ **en** : get involved in, meddle in 3 ~ **con** *fam* : pick a fight with

meticuloso, -sa *adj* : meticulous

método *nm* : method — **metódico, -ca**

adj : methodical — **metodología** *nf* : methodology

metomentodo *nmf fam* : busybody

metralla *nf* : shrapnel — **metralleta** *nf* : submachine gun

métrico, -ca *adj* : metric, metrical

metro *nm* 1 : meter 2 : subway (train)

metrópoli *nf or* **metrópolis** *nfs & pl* : metropolis — **metropolitano, -na** *adj* : metropolitan

mexicano, -na *adj* : Mexican — **mexicoamericano, -na** *adj* : Mexican-American

mezcla *nf* 1 : mixture 2 ARGAMASA : mortar — **mezclar** *vt* 1 : mix, blend 2 CONFUNDIR : mix up, muddle 3 INVOLUCRAR : involve — **mezclarse** *vr* 1 : get mixed up 2 : mingle (socially) — **mezcolanza** *nf* : mixture

mezclilla *nf Lat* : denim

mezquino, -na *adj* 1 : mean, petty 2 ESCASO : meager — **mezquindad** *nf* : meanness, stinginess

mezquita *nf* : mosque

mezquite *nm* : mesquite

mi *adj* : my

mí *pron* 1 : me 2 *or* ~ **mismo**, ~ **misma** : myself 3 **a** ~ **no me importa** : it doesn't matter to me

miajas → **migajas**

miau *nm* : meow

mica *nf* : mica

mico *nm* : (long-tailed) monkey

microbio *nm* : microbe, germ — **microbiología** *nf* : microbiology

microbús *nm, pl* **-buses** : minibus

microcosmos *nms & pl* : microcosm

microfilm *nm, pl* **-films** : microfilm

micrófono *nm* : microphone

microondas *nms & pl* : microwave (oven)

microorganismo *nm* : microorganism

microscopio *nm* : microscope — **microscópico, -ca** *adj* : microscopic

miedo *nm* 1 : fear 2 **dar** ~ : be frightening — **miedoso, -sa** *adj* : fearful

miel *nf* : honey

miembro *nm* 1 : member 2 EXTREMIDAD : limb, extremity

mientras *adv or* ~ **tanto** : meanwhile, in the meantime — ~ *conj* 1 : while, as 2 ~ **que** : while, whereas 3 ~ **viva** : as long as I live

miércoles *nms & pl* : Wednesday

mies *nf* : (ripe) corn, grain

miga *nf* 1 : crumb — **migajas** *nfpl* 1 : breadcrumbs 2 SOBRAS : leftovers

migración *nf, pl* **-ciones** : migration

migraña *nf* : migraine

migrar *vi* : migrate

mijo *nm* : millet

mil *adj & nm* : thousand

milagro *nm* : miracle — **milagroso, -sa** *adj* : miraculous

milenio *nm* : millennium

milésimo, -ma *adj* : thousandth

milicia *nf* **1** : militia **2** : military (service)

miligramo *nm* : milligram

mililitro *nm* : milliliter

milímetro *nm* : millimeter

militante *adj & nmf* : militant

militar *adj* : military — *nmf* : soldier — **militarizar** {21} *vt* : militarize

milla *nf* : mile

millar *nm* : thousand

millón *nm, pl* **-llones 1** : million **2 mil millones** : billion — **millonario, -ria** *n* : millionaire — **millonésimo, -ma** *adj* : millionth

mimar *vt* : pamper, spoil

mimbre *nm* : wicker

mímica *nf* **1** : mime, sign language **2** IMITACIÓN : mimicry

mimo *nm* : pampering — *~ nmf* : mime

mina *nf* **1** : mine **2** : lead (for pencils) — **minar** *vt* **1** : mine **2** DEBILITAR : undermine

mineral *adj* : mineral — *~ nm* **1** : mineral **2** : ore (of a metal)

minería *nf* : mining — **minero, -ra** *adj* : mining — *~ nm* : miner

miniatura *nf* : miniature

minifalda *nf* : miniskirt

minifundio *nm* : small farm

minimizar {21} *vt* : minimize

mínimo, -ma *adj* **1** : minimum **2** MINÚSCULO : minute **3 en lo más** *~* : in the slightest — **mínimo** *nm* : minimum

minino, -na *n fam* : pussycat

ministerio *nm* : ministry — **ministro, -tra** *n* **1** : minister, secretary **2 primer ministro** : prime minister

minoría *nf* : minority

minorista *adj* : retail — *~ nmf* : retailer

minoritario, -ria *adj* : minority

minucia *nf* : trifle, small detail — **minucioso, -sa** *adj* **1** : detailed **2** METICULOSO : thorough

minué *nm* : minuet

minúsculo, -la *adj* : minuscule, tiny

minusvalía *nf* : handicap, disability — **minusválido, -da** *adj* : disabled

minuta *nf* **1** : bill, fee **2** BORRADOR : rough draft

minuto *nm* : minute — **minutero** *nm* : minute hand

mío, mía *adj* **1** : mine **2 una amiga mía** : a friend of mine — *~ pron* **el mío, la mía** : mine, my own

miope *adj* : nearsighted

mirar *vt* **1** : look at **2** OBSERVAR : watch **3** CONSIDERAR : consider — *vi* **1** : look **2 ~ a** : face, overlook **3 ~ por** : look after — **mirarse** *vr* **1** : look at oneself **2** : look at each other — **mira** *nf* **1** : sight (of a firearm or instrument) **2** INTENCIÓN : aim, objective — **mirada** *nf* : look — **mirado, -da** *adj* **1** : careful **2** CONSIDERADO : considerate **3 bien** *~* : well thought of — **mirador** *nm* **1** BALCÓN : balcony **2** : lookout, vantage point — **miramiento** *nm* : consideration

mirlo *nm* : blackbird

misa *nf* : Mass

miscelánea *nf* : miscellany

miserable *adj* **1** : poor **2** LASTIMOSO : miserable, wretched — **miseria** *nf* **1** : poverty **2** DESGRACIA : misfortune, misery

misericordia *nf* : mercy — **misericordioso, -sa** *adj* : merciful

mísero, -ra *adj* : wretched, miserable

misil *nm* : missile

misión *nf, pl* **-siones** : mission — **misionero, -ra** *adj & n* : missionary

mismo, -ma *adv* (*used for emphasis*) : right, exactly — **mismo, -ma** *adj* **1** : same **2** (*used for emphasis*) : very **3** : -self **4 por lo** *~* : for that reason

misoginia *nf* : misogyny — **misógino** *nm* : misogynist

misterio *nm* : mystery — **misterioso, -sa** *adj* : mysterious

mística *nf* : mysticism — **místico, -ca** *adj* : mystic, mystical — *~ n* : mystic

mitad *nf* **1** : half **2** MEDIO : middle

mítico, -ca *adj* : mythical, mythic

mitigar {52} *vt* : mitigate

mitin *nm, pl* **mítines** : (political) meeting

mito *nm* : myth — **mitología** *nm* : mythology — **mitológico, -ca** *adj* : mythological

mixto, -ta *adj* **1** : mixed, joint **2** : coeducational (of a school)

mnemónico, -ca *adj* : mnemonic

mobiliario *nm* : furniture

mocasín *nm, pl* **-sines** : moccasin

mochila *nf* : backpack, knapsack

moción *nf, pl* **-ciones** : motion

moco *nm* **1** : mucus **2 limpiarse los** *~***s** : wipe one's nose — **mocoso, -sa** *n fam* : kid, brat

moda *nf* **1** : fashion, style **2 a la** *~ or* **de** *~* : in style, fashionable **3 ~ pasajera** : fad — **modal** *adj* : modal — **modales** *nmpl* : manners — **modalidad** *nf* : type, kind

modelar *vt* : model, mold — **modelo** *adj* : model — ~ *nm* : model, pattern — ~ *nmf* : model, mannequin

módem *or* **modem** ['mo̬ðem] *nm* : modem

moderar *vt* **1** : moderate **2** : reduce (speed, etc.) **3** PRESIDIR : chair (a meeting) — **moderarse** *vr* : restrain oneself — **moderación** *nf, pl* -**ciones** : moderation — **moderado, -da** *adj* & *n* : moderate — **moderador, -dora** *n* : moderator, chairperson

moderno, -na *adj* : modern — **modernismo** *nm* : modernism — **modernizar** {21} *vt* : modernize

modesto, -ta *adj* : modest — **modestia** *nf* : modesty

modificar {72} *vt* : modify, alter — **modificación** *nf, pl* -**ciones** : alteration

modismo *nm* : idiom

modista *nmf* **1** : dressmaker **2** : (fashion) designer

modo *nm* **1** : way, manner **2** : mood (in grammar) **3** : mode (in music) **4 a ~ de** : by way of **5 de ~ que** : so (that) **6 de todos ~s** : in any case, anyway

modorra *nf* : drowsiness

modular *vt* : modulate — **modulación** *nf, pl* -**ciones** : modulation

módulo *nm* : module, unit

mofa *nf* : ridicule, mockery — **mofarse** *vr* ~ **de** : make fun of

mofeta *nf* : skunk

moflete *nm fam* : fat cheek — **mofletudo, -da** *adj fam* : fat-cheeked, chubby

mohín *nm, pl* -**hines** : grimace — **mohino, -na** *adj* : sulky

moho *nm* **1** : mold, mildew **2** ÓXIDO : rust — **mohoso, -sa** *adj* **1** : moldy **2** OXIDADO : rusty

moisés *nm, pl* -**seses** : bassinet, cradle

mojar *vt* **1** : wet, moisten **2** : dunk (food) — **mojarse** *vr* : get wet — **mojado, -da** *adj* : wet, damp

mojigato, -ta *adj* : prudish — ~ *n* : prude

mojón *nm, pl* -**jones** : boundary stone, marker

molar *nm* : molar

moldear *vt* : mold, shape — **molde** *nm* : mold, form — **moldura** *nf* : molding

mole[1] *nf* : mass, bulk

mole[2] *nm* **1** : Mexican chili sauce **2** : meat served with mole

molécula *nf* : molecule — **molecular** *adj* : molecular

moler {47} *vt* : grind, crush

molestar *vt* **1** : annoy, bother **2 no ~** : do not disturb — *vi* : be a nuisance — **molestarse** *vr* **1** : bother **2** OFENDERSE

: take offense — **molestia** *nf* **1** : annoyance, nuisance **2** MALESTAR : discomfort — **molesto, -ta** *adj* **1** : annoyed **2** FASTIDIOSO : annoying **3** INCÓMODO : in discomfort — **molestoso, -sa** *adj* : bothersome, annoying

molido, -da *adj* **1** : ground (of meat, etc.) **2** *fam* : worn out, exhausted

molino *nm* **1** : mill **2 ~ de viento** : windmill — **molinero, -ra** *n* : miller — **molinillo** *nm* : grinder, mill

mollera *nf* **1** : crown (of the head) **2** *fam* : brains *pl*

molusco *nm* : mollusk

momento *nm* **1** : moment, instant **2** : (period of) time **3** : momentum (in physics) **4 de ~** : for the moment **5 de un ~ a otro** : any time now — **momentáneamente** *adv* : momentarily — **momentáneo, -nea** *adj* **1** : momentary **2** PASAJERO : temporary

momia *nf* : mummy

monaguillo *nm* : altar boy

monarca *nmf* : monarch — **monarquía** *nf* : monarchy

monasterio *nm* : monastery — **monástico, -ca** *adj* : monastic

mondadientes *nms & pl* : toothpick

mondar *vt* : peel

mondongo *nm* : innards *pl*, guts *pl*

moneda *nf* **1** : coin **2** : currency (of a country) — **monedero** *nm* : change purse

monetario, -ria *adj* : monetary

monitor *nm* : monitor

monja *nf* : nun — **monje** *nm* : monk

mono, -na *n* **1** : monkey — ~ *adj fam* : lovely, cute

monogamia *nf* : monogamy — **monógamo -ma** *adj* : monogamous

monografía *nf* : monograph

monograma *nm* : monogram

monolingüe *adj* : monolingual

monólogo *nm* : monologue

monopatín *nm, pl* -**tines** : scooter, skateboard

monopolio *nm* : monopoly — **monopolizar** {21} *vt* : monopolize

monosílabo *nm* : monosyllable — **monosilábico, -ca** *adj* : monosyllabic

monoteísmo *nm* : monotheism — **monoteísta** *adj* : monotheistic

monotonía *nf* : monotony — **monótono, -na** *adj* : monotonous

monóxido *nm* ~ **de carbono** : carbon monoxide

monstruo *nm* : monster — **monstruosidad** *nf* : monstrosity — **monstruoso, -sa** *adj* : monstrous

monta *nf* : importance, value

montaje *nm* **1** : assembly **2** : staging (in theater), editing (of films)

montaña *nf* **1** : mountain **2** ~ **rusa** : roller coaster — **montañero, -ra** *n* : mountain climber — **montañoso, -sa** *adj* : mountainous

montar *vt* **1** : mount **2** ESTABLECER : establish **3** ENSAMBLAR : assemble, put together **4** : stage (a performance) **5** : cock (a gun) — *vi* **1** ~ **a caballo** : ride horseback **2** ~ **en bicicleta** : get on a bicycle

monte *nm* **1** : mountain **2** BOSQUE : woodland **3** *or* ~ **bajo** : scrubland **4** ~ **de piedad** : pawnshop

montés *adj, pl* **-teses** : wild (of animals or plants)

montículo *nm* : mound, hillock

montón *nm, pl* **-tones 1** : heap, pile **2** **un** ~ **de** *fam* : lots of

montura *nf* **1** : mount (horse) **2** SILLA : saddle **3** : frame (of glasses)

monumento *nm* : monument — **monumental** *adj* : monumental, huge

monzón *nm, pl* **-zones** : monsoon

moño *nm* **1** : bun (of hair) **2** *Lat* : bow (knot)

mora *nf* **1** : mulberry **2** ZARZAMORA : blackberry

morada *nf* : residence, dwelling

morado, -da *adj* : purple — **morado** *nm* : purple

moral *adj* : moral — ~ *nf* **1** : ethics, morals *pl* **2** ÁNIMO : morale — **moraleja** *nf* : moral (of a story) — **moralidad** *nf* : morality — **moralista** *adj* : moralistic — ~ *nmf* : moralist

morar *vi* : live, reside

morboso, -sa *adj* : morbid

mordaz *adj* : caustic, scathing — **mordacidad** *nf* : bite, sharpness

mordaza *nf* : gag

morder {47} *v* : bite — **mordedura** *nf* : bite (of an animal)

mordisquear *vt* : nibble (on) — **mordisco** *nm* : nibble, bite

moreno, -na *adj* **1** : dark-haired, brunette **2** : dark-skinned — ~ *n* **1** : brunette **2** : dark-skinned person

moretón *nm, pl* **-tones** : bruise

morfina *nf* : morphine

morir {46} *vi* **1** : die **2** APAGARSE : die out, go out — **morirse** *vr* **1** ~ **de** : die of **2** ~ **por** : be dying for — **moribundo, -da** *adj* : dying

moro, -ra *adj* : Moorish — ~ *n* : Moor

moroso, -sa *adj* : delinquent, in arrears — **morosidad** *nf* : delinquency (in payment)

morral *nm* : backpack

morriña *nf* : homesickness

morro *nm* : snout

morsa *nf* : walrus

morse *nm* : Morse code

mortaja *nf* : shroud

mortal *adj* **1** : mortal **2** : deadly (of a wound, an enemy, etc.) — ~ *nmf* : mortal — **mortalidad** *nf* : mortality — **mortandad** *nf* : death toll

mortero *nm* : mortar

mortífero, -ra *adj* : deadly, lethal

mortificar {72} *vt* **1** : mortify **2** ATORMENTAR : torment — **mortificarse** *vr* : be distressed

mosaico *nm* : mosaic

mosca *nf* : fly

moscada *adj* → **nuez**

mosquearse *vr fam* **1** : become suspicious **2** ENFADARSE : get annoyed

mosquito *nm* : mosquito — **mosquitero** *nm* **1** : (window) screen **2** : mosquito net

mostacho *nm, pl* **-chones** : macaroon

mostaza *nf* : mustard

mostrador *nm* : counter (in a store)

mostrar {19} *vt* : show — **mostrarse** *vr* : show oneself, appear

mota *nf* : spot, speck — **moteado, -da** *adj* : speckled, spotted

mote *nm* : nickname

motel *nm* : motel

motín *nm, pl* **-tines 1** : riot, uprising **2** : mutiny (of troops)

motivo *nm* **1** : motive, cause **2** : motif (in art, music, etc.) — **motivación** *nf, pl* **-ciones** : motivation — **motivar** *vt* **1** : cause **2** IMPULSAR : motivate

moto *nf* : motorcycle, motorbike — **motocicleta** *nf* : motorcycle — **motociclista** *nmf* : motorcyclist

motor, -triz *or* **-tora** *adj* : motor — **motor** *nm* : motor, engine — **motorista** *nmf* **1** : motorcyclist **2** *Lat* : motorist

mover {47} *vt* **1** : move, shift **2** : shake (the head) **3** PROVOCAR : provoke — **moverse** *vr* **1** : move (over) **2** APRESURARSE : get a move on — **movedizo, -za** *adj* : movable, shifting — **movible** *adj* : movable

móvil *adj* : mobile — ~ *nm* **1** MOTIVO : motive **2** : mobile — **movilidad** *nf* : mobility — **movilizar** {21} *vt* : mobilize

movimiento *nm* **1** : movement, motion **2** ~ **sindicalista** : labor movement

mozo, -za *adj* : young — ~ *n* **1** : young man *m*, young woman *f* **2** *Lat* : waiter *m*, waitress *f*

muchacho, -cha *n* : kid, boy *m*, girl *f*

muchedumbre *nf* : crowd

mucho *adv* 1 : very much, a lot 2 : long, a long time — mucho, -cha *adj* 1 : a lot of, many, much 2 muchas veces : often — ~ *pron* : a lot, many, much

mucosidad *nf* : mucus

muda *nf* 1 : molting (of animals) 2 : change (of clothing) — mudanza *nf* 1 : change 2 TRASLADO : move, change of residence — mudar *v* 1 : molt, shed 2 CAMBIAR : change — mudarse *vr* 1 : change (one's clothes) 2 TRASLADARSE : move (one's residence)

mudo, -da *adj* 1 : mute 2 SILENCIOSO : silent

mueble *nm* 1 : piece of furniture 2 ~s *nmpl* : furniture, furnishings

mueca *nf* 1 : grimace, face 2 hacer ~s : makes faces

muela *nf* 1 : tooth, molar 2 ~ de juicio : wisdom tooth

muelle *adj* : soft — ~ *nm* 1 : wharf, jetty 2 RESORTE : spring

muérdago *nm* : mistletoe

muerte *nf* : death — muerto, -ta *adj* 1 : dead 2 : dull (of colors, etc.) — ~ *nm* : dead person, deceased

muesca *nf* : nick, notch

muestra *nf* 1 : sample 2 SEÑAL : sign, show

mugir {35} *vi* : moo, bellow — mugido *nm* : mooing, bellowing

mugre *nf* : grime, filth — mugriento, -ta *adj* : filthy, grimy

muguete *nm* : lily of the valley

mujer *nf* 1 : woman 2 ESPOSA : wife 3 ~ de negocios : businesswoman

mulato, -ta *adj & n* : mulatto

muleta *nf* 1 : crutch 2 APOYO : prop, support

mullido, -da *adj* : soft, spongy

mulo, -la *n* : mule

multa *nf* : fine — multar *vt* : fine

multicolor *adj* : multicolored

multicultural *adj* : multicultural

multimedia *adj* : multimedia

multinacional *adj* : multinational

multiplicar {72} *v* : multiply — multiplicarse *vr* : multiply, reproduce — múltiple *adj* : multiple — multipli-

cación *nf, pl* -ciones : multiplication — múltiplo *nm* : multiple

multitud *nf* : crowd, multitude

mundo *nm* 1 : world 2 todo el ~ : everyone, everybody — mundanal *adj* : worldly — mundano, -na *adj* 1 : worldly, earthly 2 la vida mundana : high society — mundial *adj* : world, worldwide

municiones *nfpl* : ammunition

municipal *adj* : municipal — municipio *nm* 1 : municipality 2 AYUNTAMIENTO : town council

muñeca *nf* 1 : doll 2 : wrist (in anatomy) — muñeco *nm* 1 : boy doll 2 MANIQUÍ : dummy, puppet

muñon *nm, pl* -ñones : stump (of an arm or leg)

mural *adj & nm* : mural — muralla *nf* : wall, rampart

murciélago *nm* : bat (animal)

murmullo *nm* 1 : murmur, murmuring 2 : rustling (of leaves, etc.)

murmurar *vi* 1 : murmur, whisper 2 CRITICAR : gossip

muro *nm* : wall

musa *nf* : muse

musaraña *nf* : shrew

músculo *nm* : muscle — muscular *adj* : muscular — musculatura *nf* : muscles *pl* — musculoso, -sa *adj* : muscular

muselina *nf* : muslin

museo *nm* : museum

musgo *nm* : moss — musgoso, -sa *adj* : mossy

música *nf* : music — musical *adj* : musical — músico, -ca *adj* : musical — ~ *n* : musician

musitar *vt* : mumble

muslo *nm* : thigh

musulmán, -mana *adj & n, mpl* -manes : Muslim

mutar *v* : mutate — mutación *nf, pl* -ciones : mutation — mutante *adj & nmf* : mutant

mutilar *vt* : mutilate — mutilación *nf, pl* -ciones : mutilation

mutuo, -tua *adj* : mutual

muy *adv* 1 : very, quite 2 DEMASIADO : too

N

n *nf* : n, 14th letter of the Spanish alphabet
nabo *nm* : turnip
nácar *nm* : mother-of-pearl
nacer {48} *vi* **1** : be born **2** : hatch (of an egg), sprout (of a plant) **3** SURGIR : arise, spring up — **nacido, -da** *adj & n* **recién** ~ : newborn — **naciente** *adj* **1** : new, growing **2** : rising (of the sun) — **nacimiento** *nm* **1** : birth **2** : source (of a river) **3** ORIGEN : beginning **4** BELÉN : Nativity scene
nación *nf, pl* **-ciones** : nation, country — **nacional** *adj* : national — ~ *nmf* : national, citizen — **nacionalidad** *nf* : nationality — **nacionalismo** *nm* : nationalism — **nacionalista** *adj & nmf* : nationalist — **nacionalizar** {21} *vt* **1** : nationalize **2** : naturalize (as a citizen) — **nacionalizarse** *vr* : become naturalized
nada *pron* **1** : nothing **2 de** ~ : you're welcome **3** ~ **más** : nothing else, nothing more — ~ *adv* : not at all — ~ **nf la** ~ : nothingness
nadar *v* : swim — **nadador, -dora** *n* : swimmer
nadería *nf* : small thing, trifle
nadie *pron* : nobody, no one
nado: a ~ *adv phr* : swimming
nafta *nf Lat* : gasoline
naipe *nm* : playing card
nalgas *nfpl* : buttocks, bottom
nana *nf* : lullaby
naranja *adj & nm* : orange (color) — ~ *nf* : orange (fruit) — **naranjal** *nm* : orange grove — **naranjo** *nm* : orange tree
narciso *nm* : narcissus, daffodil
narcótico, -ca *adj* : narcotic — **narcótico** *nm* : narcotic — **narcotizar** {21} *vt* : drug — **narcotraficante** *nmf* : drug trafficker — **narcotráfico** *nm* : drug trafficking
nariz *nf, pl* **-rices 1** : nose **2** OLFATO : sense of smell **3 narices** *nfpl* : nostrils
narrar *vt* : narrate, tell — **narración** *nf, pl* **-ciones** : narration — **narrador, -dora** *n* : narrator — **narrativa** *nf* : narrative, storytelling
nasal *adj* : nasal
nata *nf Spain* : cream

natación *nf, pl* **-ciones** : swimming
natal *adj* : native, birth — **natalicio** *nm* : birthday — **natalidad** *nf* : birthrate
natillas *nfpl* : custard
natividad *nf* : birth, nativity
nativo, -va *adj & n* : native
natural *adj* **1** : natural **2** NORMAL : normal **3** ~ **de** : native of, from — ~ *nm* **1** : temperament **2** NATIVO : native — **naturaleza** *nf* : nature — **naturalidad** *nf* : naturalness — **naturalista** *adj* : naturalistic — **naturalización** *nf, pl* **-ciones** : naturalization — **naturalizar** {21} *vt* : naturalize — **naturalizarse** *vr* : become naturalized — **naturalmente** *adv* **1** : naturally **2** POR SUPUESTO : of course
naufragar {52} *vi* **1** : be shipwrecked **2** FRACASAR : fail — **naufragio** *nm* : shipwreck — **náufrago, -ga** *adj* : shipwrecked — ~ *n* : castaway
náusea *nf* **1** : nausea **2 dar** ~**s** : nauseate **3** ~**s matutinas** : morning sickness — **nauseabundo, -da** *adj* : nauseating
náutico, -ca *adj* : nautical
navaja *nf* : pocketknife, penknife
naval *adj* : naval
nave *nf* **1** : ship **2** : nave (of a church) **3** ~ **espacial** : spaceship
navegar {52} *v* : navigate, sail — **navegable** *adj* : navigable — **navegación** *nf, pl* **-ciones** : navigation — **navegante** *adj* : sailing, seafaring — ~ *nmf* : navigator
Navidad *nf* **1** : Christmas **2 feliz** ~ : Merry Christmas — **navideño, -ña** *adj* : Christmas
naviero, -ra *adj* : shipping
nazi *adj & nmf* : Nazi — **nazismo** *nm* : Nazism
neblina *nf* : mist
nebuloso, -sa *adj* **1** : hazy, misty, foggy **2** VAGO : vague, nebulous
necedad *nf* **1** : stupidity **2 decir** ~**es** : talk nonsense
necesario, -ria *adj* : necessary — **necesariamente** *adv* : necessarily — **necesidad** *nf* **1** : need, necessity **2** POBREZA : poverty **3** ~**es** *nfpl* : hardships — **necesitado, -da** *adj* : needy — **necesitar** *vt* : need — *vi* ~ **de** : have need of

necio, -cia *adj* : silly, dumb
necrología *nf* : obituary
néctar *nm* : nectar
nectarina *nf* : nectarine
neerlandés, -desa *adj, mpl* **-deses** : Dutch — **neerlandés** *nm* : Dutch (language)
nefasto, -ta *adj* **1** : ill-fated **2** *fam* : terrible, awful
negar {49} *vt* **1** : deny **2** REHUSAR : refuse **3** : disown (a person) — **negarse** *vr* : refuse — **negación** *nf, pl* **-ciones 1** : denial **2** : negation (in grammar) — **negativa** *nf* **1** : denial RECHAZO : refusal — **negativo, -va** *adj* : negative — **negativo** *nm* : negative (of a photograph)
negligente *adj* : negligent — **negligencia** *nf* : negligence
negociar *vt* : negotiate — *vi* : deal, do business — **negociable** *adj* : negotiable — **negociación** *nf, pl* **-ciones** : negotiation — **negociante** *nmf* : businessman *m*, businesswoman *f* — **negocio** *nm* **1** : business **2** TRANSACCIÓN : deal **3 ~s** : business, commerce
negro, -gra *adj* : black, dark — **~** *n* : dark-skinned person — **negro** *nm* : black (color) — **negrura** *nf* : blackness — **negruzco, -ca** *adj* : blackish
nene, -na *n fam* : baby, small child
nenúfar *nm* : water lily
neón *nm* : neon
neoyorquino, -na *adj* : of or from New York
nepotismo *nm* : nepotism
Neptuno *nm* : Neptune
nervio *nm* **1** : nerve **2** : sinew (in meat) **3** VIGOR : vigor, energy **4 tener ~s** : be nervous — **nerviosismo** *nm* : nervousness — **nervioso, -sa** *adj* **1** : nervous, anxious **2 sistema nervioso** : nervous system
nervudo, -da *adj* : sinewy
neto, -ta *adj* **1** : clear, distinct **2** : net (of weight, salaries, etc.)
neumático *nm* : tire
neumonía *nf* : pneumonia
neurología *nf* : neurology — **neurológico, -ca** *adj* : neurological, neurologic — **neurólogo, -ga** *n* : neurologist
neurosis *nfs & pl* : neurosis — **neurótico, -ca** *adj & n* : neurotic
neutral *adj* : neutral — **neutralidad** *nf* : neutrality — **neutralizar** {21} *vt* : neutralize — **neutro, -tra** *adj* **1** : neutral **2** : neuter (in biology and grammar)
neutrón *nm, pl* **-trones** : neutron
nevar {55} *v impers* : snow — **nevada**

nf : snowfall — **nevado, -da** *adj* **1** : snow-covered, snowy **2** : snow-white — **nevasca** *nf* : snowstorm
nevera *nf* : refrigerator
nevisca *nf* : light snowfall, flurry
nexo *nm* : link, connection
ni *conj* **1** : neither, nor **2 ~ que** : as if **3 ~ siquiera** : not even
nicaragüense *adj* : Nicaraguan
nicho *nm* : niche
nicotina *nf* : nicotine
nidada *nf* : brood (of chicks, etc.)
nido *nm* **1** : nest GUARIDA : hiding place, den
niebla *nf* : fog, mist
nieto, -ta *n* **1** : grandson *m*, granddaughter *f* **2 nietos** *nmpl* : grandchildren
nieve *nf* : snow
nigeriano, -na *adj* : Nigerian
nilón *or* **nilon** *nm, pl* **-lones** : nylon
nimio, -mia *adj* : insignificant, trivial — **nimiedad** *nf* **1** : trifle **2** INSIGNIFICANCIA : triviality
ninfa *nf* : nymph
ninguno, -na (**ningún** *before masculine singular nouns*) *adj* : no, not any — **~** *pron* **1** : neither, none **2** : no one, nobody
niña *nf* **1** : pupil (of the eye) **2 la ~ de los ojos** : the apple of one's eye
niño, -ña *n* : child, boy *m*, girl *f* — **~** *adj* **1** : young **2** INFANTIL : immature, childish — **niñero, -ra** *n* : baby-sitter, nanny — **niñez** *nf, pl* **-ñeces** : childhood
nipón, -pona *adj* : Japanese
níquel *nm* : nickel
nítido, -da *adj* : clear, sharp — **nitidez** *nf, pl* **-deces** : clarity, sharpness
nitrato *nm* : nitrate
nitrógeno *nm* : nitrogen
nivel *nm* **1** : level, height **2 ~ de vida** : standard of living — **nivelar** *vt* : level (out)
no *adv* **1** : not **2** (*in answer to a question*) : no **3 ¡como ~!** : of course! **4 ~ bien** : as soon as **5 ~ fumador** : non-smoker — **~** *nm* : no
noble *adj & nmf* : noble — **nobleza** *nf* : nobility
noche *nf* **1** : night, evening **2 buenas ~s** : good evening, good night **3 de ~** *or* **por la ~** : at night **4 hacerse de ~** : get dark — **Nochebuena** *nf* : Christmas Eve — **nochecita** *nf* : dusk — **Nochevieja** *nf* : New Year's Eve
noción *nf, pl* **-ciones 1** : notion, concept **2 nociones** *nfpl* : rudiments
nocivo, -va *adj* : harmful, noxious

nocturno, -na *adj* **1** : night **2** : nocturnal (of animals, etc.) — **nocturno** *nm* : nocturne

nogal *nm* **1** : walnut tree **2** ~ **americano** : hickory

nómada *nmf* : nomad — ~ *adj* : nomadic

nomás *adv Lat* : only, just

nombrar *vt* **1** : appoint **2** CITAR : mention — **nombrado, -da** *adj* : famous, well-known — **nombramiento** *nm* : appointment, nomination — **nombre** *nm* **1** : name **2** SUSTANTIVO : noun **3** FAMA : fame, renown **4** ~ **de pila** : first name

nómina *nf* : payroll

nominal *adj* : nominal

nominar *vt* : nominate — **nominación** *nf, pl* -**ciones** : nomination

nomo *nm* : gnome

non *adj* : odd, not even — ~ *nm* : odd number

nonagésimo, -ma *adj & n* : ninetieth

nopal *nm* : nopal, prickly pear

nordeste *or* **noreste** *adj* **1** : northeastern **2** : northeasterly (of wind, etc.) — ~ *nm* : northeast

nórdico, -ca *adj* : Scandinavian

noreste → nordeste

noria *nf* **1** : waterwheel **2** : Ferris wheel (at a fair, etc.)

norma *nf* : rule, norm, standard — **normal** *adj* **1** : normal **2 escuela** ~ : teacher-training college — **normalidad** *nf* : normality — **normalizar** {21} *vt* **1** : normalize **2** ESTANDARIZAR : standardize — **normalizarse** *vr* : return to normal — **normalmente** *adv* : ordinarily, generally

noroeste *adj* **1** : northwestern **2** : northwesterly (of wind, etc.) — ~ *nm* : northwest

norte *adj* : north, northern — ~ *nm* **1** : north **2** : north wind

norteamericano, -na *adj* : North American

norteño, -ña *adj* : northern

noruego, -ga *adj* : Norwegian — **noruego** *nm* : Norwegian (language)

nos *pron* **1** (*direct object*) : us **2** (*indirect object*) : to us, for us, from us **3** (*reflexive*) : ourselves **4** : each other, one another

nosotros, -tras *pron* **1** (*subject*) : we **2** (*object*) : us **3** *or* ~ **mismos** : ourselves

nostalgia *nf* **1** : nostalgia **2 sentir** ~ **por** : be homesick for — **nostálgico, -ca** *adj* : nostalgic

nota *nf* **1** : note **2** : grade, mark (in school) **3** CUENTA : bill, check — **notable** *adj* : noteworthy, notable — **notar** *vt* : notice — **notarse** *vr* : be evident, seem

notario, -ria *n* : notary (public)

noticia *nf* **1** : news item, piece of news **2** ~**s** *nfpl* : news — **noticiario** *nm* : newscast — **noticiero** *nm Lat* : newscast

notificar {72} *vt* : notify — **notificación** *nf, pl* -**ciones** : notification

notorio, -ria *adj* **1** : obvious **2** CONOCIDO : well-known — **notoriedad** *nf* : fame, notoriety

novato, -ta *adj* : inexperienced — ~ *n* : beginner, novice

novecientos, -tas *adj* : nine hundred — **novecientos** *nms & pl* : nine hundred

novedad *nf* **1** : newness, innovation **2** NOTICIAS : news **3** ~**s** : novelties, latest news — **novedoso, -sa** *adj* : original, novel

novela *nf* **1** : novel **2** : soap opera (on television) — **novelesco, -ca** *adj* **1** : fictional **2** FANTÁSTICO : fabulous — **novelista** *nmf* : novelist

noveno, -na *adj* : ninth — **noveno** *nm* : ninth

noventa *adj & nm* : ninety — **noventavo, -va** *adj* : ninetieth — **noventavo** *nm* : ninetieth

novia → novio

noviazgo *nm* : engagement

novicio, -cia *n* : novice

noviembre *nm* : November

novillo, -lla *n* : young bull *m*, heifer *f*

novio, -via *n* **1** : boyfriend *m*, girlfriend *f* **2** PROMETIDO : fiancé *m*, fiancée *f* **3** : bridegroom *m*, bride *f* (at a wedding)

novocaína *nf* : novocaine

nube *nf* **1** : cloud — **nubarrón** *nm, pl* -**rrones** : storm cloud — **nublado, -da** *adj* **1** : cloudy **2** ENTURBIADO : clouded, dim — **nublado** *nm* : storm cloud — **nublar** *vt* **1** : cloud **2** OSCURECER : obscure — **nublarse** *vr* : get cloudy — **nuboso, -sa** *adj* : cloudy

nuca *nf* : nape, back of the neck

núcleo *nm* **1** : nucleus **2** CENTRO : center, core — **nuclear** *adj* : nuclear

nudillo *nm* : knuckle

nudismo *nm* : nudism — **nudista** *adj & nmf* : nudist

nudo *nm* **1** : knot **2** : crux, heart (of a problem, etc.) — **nudoso, -sa** *adj* : knotty, gnarled

nuera *nf* : daughter-in-law

nuestro, -tra *adj* : our — ~ *pron* (*with definite article*) : ours, our own

nuevamente *adv* : again, anew

nueve *adj & nm* : nine
nuevo, -va *adj* **1** : new **2 de nuevo** : again, once more
nuez *nf, pl* **nueces 1** : nut **2** *or* ~ **de nogal** : walnut **3** ~ **de Adán** : Adam's apple **4** ~ **moscada** : nutmeg
nulo, -la *adj* **1** *or* ~ **y sin efecto** : null and void **2** INCAPAZ : useless, inept — **nulidad** *nf* **1** : nullity **2 es una** ~ *fam* : he's a total loss
numerar *vt* — **numeración** *nf, pl* **-ciones 1** : numbering **2** NÚMEROS : numbers *pl*, numerals *pl* — **numeral** *adj* : numeral — **número** *nm* **1** : number, numeral **2** : issue (of a

publication) **3 sin** ~ : countless —
numérico, -ca *adj* : numerical — **numeroso, -sa** *adj* : numerous
nunca *adv* **1** : never, ever **2** ~ **más** : never again **3** ~ **jamás** : never ever
nupcial *adj* : nuptial, wedding — **nupcias** *nfpl* : nuptials, wedding
nutria *nf* : otter
nutrir *vt* **1** ALIMENTAR : feed, nourish **2** FOMENTAR : fuel, foster — **nutrición** *nf, pl* **-ciones** : nutrition — **nutrido, -da** *adj* **1** : nourished **2** ABUNDANTE : considerable, abundant — **nutriente** *nm* : nutrient — **nutritivo, -va** *adj* : nourishing, nutritious

O

o¹ *nf* : o, 16th letter of the Spanish alphabet
o² *conj* (**u** *before words beginning with o- or ho-*) **1** : or, either **2** ~ **sea** : in other words
oasis *nms & pl* : oasis
obcecar {72} *vt* : blind (by emotions) — **obcecarse** *vr* : become stubborn
obedecer {53} *vt* : obey — *vi* **1** : obey **2** ~ **a** : respond to **3** ~ **a** : be due to — **obediencia** *nf* : obedience — **obediente** *adj* : obedient
obertura *nf* : overture
obeso, -sa *adj* : obese — **obesidad** *nf* : obesity
obispo *nm* : bishop
objetar *v* : object — **objeción** *nf, pl* **-ciones** : objection
objeto *nm* : object — **objetivo, -va** *adj* : objective — **objetivo** *nm* **1** : objective, goal **2** : lens (in photography, etc.)
objetor, -tora *n* ~ **de conciencia** : conscientious objector
oblicuo, -cua *adj* : oblique
obligar {52} *vt* : require, oblige — **obligarse** *vr* : commit oneself (to do something) — **obligación** *nf, pl* **-ciones** : obligation — **obligado, -da** *adj* **1** : obliged **2** FORZOSO : obligatory — **obligatorio, -ria** *adj* : mandatory
oblongo, -ga *adj* : oblong
oboe *nm* : oboe — *nmf* : oboist
obra *nf* **1** : work, deed **2** : work (of art, literature, etc.) **3** CONSTRUCCIÓN : construction work **4** ~ **maestra** : masterpiece **5** ~**s públicas** : public works — **obrar** *vt* : work, produce — *vi* : act, behave — **obrero, -ra** *adj* **la clase obrera** : the working class — ~ *n* : worker, laborer

obsceno, -na *adj* : obscene — **obscenidad** *nf* : obscenity
obsequiar *vt* : give, present — **obsequio** *nm* : gift, present
observar *vt* **1** : observe, watch **2** ADVERTIR : notice **3** ACATAR : observe, obey **4** COMENTAR : remark — **observación** *nf, pl* **-ciones** : observation — **observador, -dora** *adj* : observant — ~ *n* : observer — **observancia** *nf* : observance — **observatorio** *nm* : observatory
obsesionar *vt* : obsess — **obsesionarse** *vr* : be obsessed — **obsesión** *nf, pl* **-siones** : obsession — **obsesivo, -va** *adj* : obsessive — **obseso, -sa** *adj* : obsessed
obsoleto, -ta *adj* : obsolete
obstaculizar {21} *vt* : hinder — **obstáculo** *nm* : obstacle
obstante: no ~ *conj phr* : nevertheless, however — ~ *prep phr* : in spite of, despite
obstar {21} *vi* ~ **a** *or* ~ **para** : stop, prevent
obstetricia *nf* : obstetrics — **obstetra** *nmf* : obstetrician
obstinarse *vr* : be stubborn — **obstinado, -da** *adj* **1** : obstinate, stubborn **2** TENAZ : persistent
obstruir {41} *vt* : obstruct — **obstrucción** *nf, pl* **-ciones** : obstruction
obtener {80} *vt* : obtain, get
obtuso, -sa *adj* : obtuse
obviar *vt* : get around, avoid
obvio, -via *adj* : obvious — **obviamente** *adv* : obviously, clearly
oca *nf* : goose
ocasión *nf, pl* **-siones 1** : occasion **2** OPORTUNIDAD : opportunity **3** GANGA

: bargain — **ocasional** *adj* **1** : occasional **2** ACCIDENTAL : accidental, chance — **ocasionar** *vt* : cause

ocaso *nm* **1** : sunset **2** DECADENCIA : decline

occidente *nm* **1** : west **2 el Occidente** : the West — **occidental** *adj* : western, Western

océano *nm* : ocean — **oceanografía** *nf* : oceanography

ochenta *adj & nm* : eighty

ocho *adj & nm* : eight — **ochocientos, -tas** *adj* : eight hundred — **ochocientos** *nms & pl* : eight hundred

ocio *nm* **1** : free time, leisure **2** INACTIVIDAD : idleness — **ociosidad** *nf* : idleness, inactivity — **ocioso, -sa** *adj* **1** : idle, inactive **2** INÚTIL : useless

ocre *adj & nm* : ocher

octágono *nm* : octagon — **octagonal** *adj* : octagonal

octava *nf* : octave

octavo, -va *adj & n* : eighth

octeto *nm* : byte

octogésimo, -ma *adj & n* : eightieth

octubre *nm* : October

ocular *adj* : ocular, eye — **oculista** *nmf* : ophthalmologist

ocultar *vt* : conceal, hide — **ocultarse** *vr* : hide — **oculto, -ta** *adj* : hidden, occult

ocupar *vt* **1** : occupy **2** : hold (a position, etc.) **3** : provide work for — **ocuparse** *vr* **1 ~ de** : concern oneself with **2 ~ de** : take care of (children, etc.) — **ocupación** *nf, pl* **-ciones 1** : occupation **2** EMPLEO : job — **ocupado, -da** *adj* **1** : busy **2** : occupied (of a place) **3 señal de ocupado** : busy signal — **ocupante** *nmf* : occupant

ocurrir *vi* : occur, happen — **ocurrirse** *vr* **~ a** : occur to — **ocurrencia** *nf* **1** : occurrence, event **2** SALIDA : witty remark, quip

oda *nf* : ode

odiar *vt* : hate — **odio** *nm* : hatred — **odioso, -sa** *adj* : hateful

odisea *nf* : odyssey

odontología *nf* : dentistry, dental surgery — **odontólogo, -ga** *n* : dentist, dental surgeon

oeste *adj* : west, western — *~ nm* **1** : west **2 el Oeste** : the West

ofender *v* : offend — **ofenderse** *vr* : take offense — **ofensa** *nf* : offense, insult — **ofensiva** *nf* : offensive — **ofensivo, -va** *adj* : offensive

oferta *nf* **1** : offer **2 de ~** : on sale **3 ~ y demanda** : supply and demand

oficial *adj* : official — *~ nmf* **1** : skilled worker **2** : officer (in the military)

oficina *nf* : office — **oficinista** *nmf* : office worker

oficio *nm* : trade, profession — **oficioso, -sa** *adj* : unofficial

ofrecer {53} *vt* **1** : offer **2** : provide, present (an opportunity, etc.) — **ofrecerse** *vr* : volunteer — **ofrecimiento** *nm* : offer

ofrenda *nf* : offering

oftalmología *nf* : ophthalmology — **oftalmólogo, -ga** *n* : ophthalmologist

ofuscar {72} *vt* **1** : blind, dazzle **2** CONFUNDIR : confuse — **ofuscarse** *vr* **~ con** : be blinded by — **ofuscación** *nf, pl* **-ciones 1** : blindness **2** CONFUSIÓN : confusion

ogro *nm* : ogre

oír {50} *vi* : hear — *vt* **1** : hear **2** ESCUCHAR : listen to **3 ¡oiga!** *or* **¡oye!** : excuse me!, listen! — **oídas: de ~** *adv phr* : by hearsay — **oído** *nm* **1** : ear **2** : (sense of) hearing **3 duro de ~** : hard of hearing

ojal *nm* : buttonhole

ojalá *interj* : I hope so!, if only!

ojear *vt* : eye, look at — **ojeada** *nf* : glimpse, glance

ojeriza *nf* **1** : ill will **2 tener ~ a** : have a grudge against

ojo *nm* **1** : eye **2** PERSPICACIA : shrewdness **3** : span (of a bridge) **4 ¡~!** : look out!, pay attention!

ola *nf* : wave — **oleada** *nf* : wave, surge — **oleaje** *nm* : swell (of the sea)

olé *interj* : bravo!

oleada *nf* : wave, swell — **oleaje** *nm* : waves *pl*, surf

óleo *nm* **1** : oil **2** CUADRO : oil painting — **oleoducto** *nm* : oil pipeline

oler {51} *vt* : smell — *vi* **1** : smell **2 ~ a** : smell of — **olerse** *vr fam* : have a hunch about

olfatear *vt* : sniff **2** OLER : sense, sniff out — **olfato** *nm* **1** : sense of smell **2** PERSPICACIA : nose, instinct

Olimpíada *or* **Olimpiada** *nf* : Olympics *pl*, Olympic Games *pl* — **olímpico, -ca** *adj* : Olympic

oliva *nf* : olive — **olivo** *nm* : olive tree

olla *nf* **1** : pot **2 ~ podrida** : (Spanish) stew

olmo *nm* : elm

olor *nm* : smell — **oloroso, -sa** *adj* : fragrant

olvidar *vt* **1** : forget **2** DEJAR : leave (behind) — **olvidarse** *vr* : forget — **olvidadizo, -za** *adj* : forgetful — **olvido** *nm* **1** : forgetfulness **2** DESCUIDO : oversight

ombligo *nm* : navel

omelette *nmf Lat* : omelet

ominoso, -sa *adj* : ominous

omitir *vt* : omit — **omisión** *nf, pl* **-siones** : omission

ómnibus *nm, pl* **-bus** *or* **-buses** : bus

omnipotente *adj* : omnipotent

omóplato *or* **omoplato** *nm* : shoulder blade

once *adj & nm* : eleven — **onceavo, -va** *adj & n* : eleventh

onda *nf* : wave — **ondear** *vi* : ripple — **ondulación** *nf, pl* **-ciones** : undulation — **ondulado, -da** *adj* : wavy — **ondular** *vt* : wave (hair) — *vi* : undulate, ripple

ónice *nmf or* **ónix** *nm* : onyx

onza *nf* : ounce

opaco, -ca *adj* **1** : opaque **2** DESLUSTRA-DO : dull

ópalo *nm* : opal

opción *nf, pl* **-ciones** : option — **opcional** *adj* : optional

ópera *nf* : opera

operar *vt* **1** : operate on **2** *Lat* : operate, run (a machine) — *vi* **1** : operate **2** NE-GOCIAR : deal, do business — **operarse** *vr* **1** : have an operation **2** OCUR-RIR : take place — **operación** *nf, pl* **-ciones 1** TRANSACCIÓN : transaction, deal — **operacional** *adj* : operational — **operador, -dora** *n* **1** : operator **2** : cameraman (for television, etc.)

opereta *nf* : operetta

opinar *vt* : think — *vi* : express an opinion — **opinión** *nf, pl* **-niones** : opinion

opio *nm* : opium

oponer {60} *vt* **1** : raise, put forward (arguments, etc.) **2** ~ **resistencia** : put up a fight — **oponerse** *vr* ~ **a** : oppose, be against — **oponente** *nmf* : opponent

oporto *nm* : port (wine)

oportunidad *nf* : opportunity — **oportunista** *nmf* : opportunist — **oportuno, -na** *adj* **1** : opportune, timely **2** APROPIADO : suitable

opositor, -tora *n* **1** : opponent **2** : candidate (for a position) — **oposición** *nf, pl* **-ciones** : opposition

oprimir *vt* **1** : press, squeeze **2** TIRANIZAR : oppress — **opresión** *nf, pl* **-siones 1** : oppression **2** ~ **de pecho** : tightness in the chest — **opresivo, -va** *adj* : oppressive — **opresor, -sora** *n* : oppressor

optar *vi* **1** ~ **a** : apply for **2** ~ **por** : choose, opt for

óptica *nf* **1** : optics **2** : optician's (shop) — **óptico, -ca** *adj* : optical — ~ *n* : optician

optimismo *nm* : optimism — **optimista** *adj* : optimistic — ~ *nmf* : optimist

optometría *nf* : optometry — **optometrista** *nmf* : optometrist

opuesto *adj* **1** : opposite CONTRADIC-TORIO : opposed, conflicting

opulencia *nf* : opulence — **opulento, -ta** *adj* : opulent

oración *nf, pl* **-ciones 1** : prayer **2** FRASE : sentence, clause

oráculo *nm* : oracle

orador, -dora *n* : speaker

oral *adj* : oral

orar *vi* : pray

órbita *nf* **1** : orbit (in astronomy) **2** : eye socket — **orbitar** *vi* : orbit

orden *nm, pl* **órdenes 1** : order **2** ~ **del día** : agenda (at a meeting) **3** ~ **público** : law and order — ~ *nf, pl* **órdenes 1** : order (of food) **2** ~ **religiosa** : religious order **3** ~ **de compra** : purchase order

ordenador *nm Spain* : computer

ordenar *vt* **1** : order, command **2** AR-REGLAR : put in order **3** : ordain (a priest) — **ordenanza** *nm* : orderly (in the armed forces) — ~ *nf* : ordinance, regulation

ordeñar *vt* : milk

ordinal *adj & nm* : ordinal

ordinario, -ria *adj* **1** : ordinary **2** GROSERO : common, vulgar

orear *vt* : air

orégano *nm* : oregano

oreja *nf* : ear

orfanato *or* **orfelinato** *nm* : orphanage

orfebre *nmf* : goldsmith, silversmith

orgánico, -ca *adj* : organic

organigrama *nm* : flowchart

organismo *nm* **1** : organism **2** ORGANI-ZACIÓN : agency, organization

organista *nmf* : organist

organizar {21} *vt* : organize — **organizarse** *vr* : get organized — **organización** *nf, pl* **-ciones** : organization — **organizador, -dora** *n* : organizer

órgano *nm* : organ

orgasmo *nm* : orgasm

orgía *nf* : orgy

orgullo *nm* : pride — **orgulloso, -sa** *adj* : proud

orientación *nf, pl* **-ciones 1** : orientation **2** DIRECCIÓN : direction **3** CONSEJO : guidance

oriental *adj* **1** : eastern **2** : oriental — ~ *nmf* : Oriental

orientar *vt* **1** : orient, position **2** GUIAR : guide, direct — **orientarse** *vr* **1** : orient oneself **2** ~ **hacia** : turn towards

oriente *nm* **1** : east, East **2 el Oriente** : the Orient

orificio *nm* : orifice, opening

origen *nm, pl* **orígenes** : origin — **original** *adj & nm* : original — **originalidad** *nf* : originality — **originar** *vt* : give rise to — **originarse** *vr* : originate, arise — **originario, -ria** *adj* ~ **de** : native of

orilla *nf* **1** : border, edge **2** : bank (of a river), shore (of the sea)

orinar *vi* : urinate — **orina** *nf* : urine

oriol *nm* : oriole

oriundo, -da *adj* ~ **de** : native of

orla *nf* : border

ornamental *adj* : ornamental — **ornamento** *nm* : ornament

ornar *vt* : adorn

ornitología *nf* : ornithology

oro *nm* : gold

orquesta *nf* : orchestra — **orquestar** *vt* : orchestrate

orquídea *nf* : orchid

ortiga *nf* : nettle

ortodoxia *nf* : orthodoxy — **ortodoxo, -xa** *adj* : orthodox

ortografía *nf* : spelling

ortopedia *nf* : orthopedics — **ortopédico, -ca** *adj* : orthopedic

oruga *nf* : caterpillar

orzuelo *nm* : sty (in the eye)

os *pron pl Spain* **1** (*direct or indirect object*) : you, to you **2** (*reflexive*) : yourselves, to yourselves **3** : each other, to each other

osado, -da *adj* : bold, daring — **osadía** *nf* **1** : boldness, daring **2** DESCARO : audacity, nerve

osamenta *nf* : skeleton

osar *vi* : dare

oscilar *vi* **1** : swing, sway **2** FLUCTUAR : fluctuate — **oscilación** *nf, pl* **-ciones 1** : swinging **2** FLUCTUACIÓN : fluctuation

oscuro, -ra *adj* **1** : dark **2** : obscure (of ideas, persons, etc.) **3 a oscuras** : in the dark — **oscurecer** {53} *vt* **1** : darken **2** : confuse, cloud (the mind)

3 al ~ : at nightfall — *v impers* : get dark — **oscurecerse** *vr* : grow dark — **oscuridad** *nf* **1** : darkness **2** : obscurity (of ideas, persons, etc.)

óseo, ósea *adj* : skeletal, bony

oso, osa *n* **1** : bear **2** ~ **de peluche** *or* ~ **de felpa** : teddy bear

ostensible *adj* : evident, obvious

ostentar *vt* **1** : flaunt, display **2** POSEER : have, hold — **ostentación** *nf, pl* **-ciones** : ostentation — **ostentoso, -sa** *adj* : ostentatious, showy

osteopatía *nf* : osteopathy — **osteópata** *nmf* : osteopath

osteoporosis *nf* : osteoporosis

ostra *nf* : oyster

ostracismo *nm* : ostracism

otear *vt* : scan, survey

otoño *nm* : autumn, fall — **otoñal** *adj* : autumn, fall

otorgar {52} *vt* **1** : grant, award **2** : draw up (a legal document)

otro, otra *adj* **1** : another, other **2 otra vez** : again — *pron* **1** : another (one), other (one) **2 los otros, las otras** : the others, the rest

ovación *nf, pl* **-ciones** : ovation

óvalo *nm* : oval — **oval** *or* **ovalado, -da** *adj* : oval

ovario *nm* : ovary

oveja *nf* **1** : sheep, ewe **2** ~ **negra** : black sheep

overol *nm Lat* : overalls *pl*

ovillo *nm* **1** : ball (of yarn) **2 hacerse un** ~ : curl up (into a ball)

ovni *or* **OVNI** *nm* (*objeto volador no identificado*) : UFO

ovular *vi* : ovulate — **ovulación** *nf, pl* **-ciones** : ovulation

oxidar *vi* : rust — **oxidarse** *vr* : get rusty — **oxidación** *nf, pl* **-ciones** : rusting — **oxidado, -da** *adj* : rusty — **óxido** *nm* : rust

oxígeno *nm* : oxygen

oye → **oír**

oyente *nmf* **1** : listener **2** : auditor (student)

ozono *nm* : ozone

P

p *nf* : p, 17th letter of the Spanish alphabet

pabellón *nm, pl* **-llones 1** : pavilion **2** : block, building (in a hospital complex, etc.) **3** : summerhouse (in a garden, etc.) **4** BANDERA : flag

pabilo *nm* : wick

pacer {48} *v* : graze

paces → **paz**

paciencia *nf* : patience — **paciente** *adj & nmf* : patient

pacificar {72} *vt* : pacify, calm — **paci-**

ficarse *vr* : calm down — **pacífico, -ca** *adj* : peaceful, pacific — **pacifismo** *nm* : pacifism — **pacifista** *adj & nmf* : pacifist

pacotilla *nf* **de ~** : second-rate, trashy

pacto *nm* : pact, agreement — **pactar** *vt* : agree on — *vi* : come to an agreement

padecer {53} *vt* : suffer, endure — *vi* **~ de** : suffer from — **padecimiento** *nm* : suffering

padre *nm* **1** : father **2 ~s** *nmpl* : parents — **~** *adj Lat fam* : great, fantastic — **padrastro** *nm* : stepfather — **padrino** *nm* **1** : godfather **2** : best man (at a wedding)

padrón *nm, pl* **-drones** : register, roll

paella *nf* : paella

paga *nf* : pay, wages *pl* — **pagadero, -ra** *adj* : payable

pagano, -na *adj & n* : pagan, heathen

pagar {52} *vt* : pay, pay for — *vi* : pay — **pagaré** *nm* : IOU

página *nf* : page

pago *nm* : payment

país *nm* **1** : country, nation **2** REGIÓN : region, land — **paisaje** *nm* : scenery, landscape — **paisano, -na** *n* : compatriot

paja *nf* **1** : straw **2** *fam* : nonsense

pájaro *nm* **1** : bird **2 ~ carpintero** : woodpecker — **pajarera** *nf* : aviary

pajita *nf* : (drinking) straw

pala *nf* **1** : shovel, spade **2** : blade (of an oar or a rotor) **3** : paddle, racket (in sports)

palabra *nf* **1** : word **2** HABLA : speech **3 tener la ~** : have the floor — **palabrota** *nf* : swearword

palacio *nm* **1** : palace, mansion **2 ~ de justicia** : courthouse

paladar *nm* : palate — **paladear** *vt* : savor

palanca *nf* **1** : lever, crowbar **2** *fam* : leverage, influence **3 ~ de cambio** *or* **~ de velocidades** : gearshift

palangana *nf* : washbowl

palco *nm* : box (in a theater)

palestino, -na *adj* : Palestinian

paleta *nf* **1** : small shovel, trowel **2** : palette (in art) **3** : paddle (in sports, etc.)

paletilla *nf* : shoulder blade

paliar *vt* : alleviate, ease — **paliativo, -va** *adj* : palliative

pálido, -da *adj* : pale — **palidecer** {53} *vi* : turn pale — **palidez** *nf, pl* **-deces** : paleness, pallor

palillo *nm* **1** : small stick **2** *or* **~ de dientes** : toothpick

paliza *nf* : beating

palma *nf* **1** : palm (of the hand) **2** : palm (tree or leaf) **3 batir ~s** : clap, applaud — **palmada** *nf* **1** : pat, slap **2 ~s** *nfpl* : clapping

palmera *nf* : palm tree

palmo *nm* **1** : span, small amount **2 ~ a ~** : bit by bit

palmotear *vi* : applaud — **palmoteo** *nm* : clapping, applause

palo *nm* **1** : stick **2** MANGO : shaft, handle **3** MÁSTIL : mast **4** POSTE : pole **5** GOLPE : blow **6** : suit (of cards)

paloma *nf* : pigeon, dove — **palomilla** *nf* : moth — **palomitas** *nfpl* : popcorn

palpar *vt* : feel, touch — **palpable** *adj* : palpable

palpitar *vi* : palpitate, throb — **palpitación** *nf, pl* **-ciones** : palpitation

palta *nf Lat* : avocado

paludismo *nm* : malaria

pampa *nf* : pampa

pan *nm* **1** : bread **2** : loaf (of bread, etc.) **3 ~ tostado** : toast

pana *nf* : corduroy

panacea *nf* : panacea

panadería *nf* : bakery, bread shop — **panadero, -ra** *n* : baker

panal *nm* : honeycomb

panameño, -ña *adj* : Panamanian

pancarta *nf* : placard, banner

pancito *nm Lat* : (bread) roll

páncreas *nms & pl* : pancreas

panda *nmf* : panda

pandemonio *nm* : pandemonium

pandero *nm* : tambourine — **pandereta** *nf* : (small) tambourine

pandilla *nf* : gang

panecillo *nm Spain* : (bread) roll

panel *nm* : panel

panfleto *nm* : pamphlet

pánico *nm* : panic

panorama *nm* : panorama — **panorámico, -ca** *adj* : panoramic

panqueque *nm Lat* : pancake

pantaletas *nfpl Lat* : panties

pantalla *nf* **1** : screen **2** : lampshade

pantalón *nm, pl* **-lones 1** *or* **pantalones** *nmpl* : pants *pl*, trousers *pl* **2 pantalones vaqueros** : jeans

pantano *nm* **1** : swamp, marsh **2** EMBALSE : reservoir — **pantanoso, -sa** *adj* : marshy, swampy

pantera *nf* : panther

pantimedias *nfpl Lat* : panty hose

pantomima *nf* : pantomime

pantorrilla *nf* : calf (of the leg)

pantufla *nf* : slipper

panza *nf* : belly, paunch — **panzón, -zona** *adj, mpl* **-zones** : potbellied

pañal *nm* : diaper
paño *nm* **1** : cloth **2** TRAPO : rag, dust cloth **3** ~ **de cocina** : dishcloth **4** ~ **higiénico** : sanitary napkin **5** ~ **s menores** : underwear
pañuelo *nm* **1** : handkerchief **2** : scarf, kerchief
papa[1] *nm* : pope
papa[2] *nf Lat* **1** : potato **2** ~ **s fritas** : potato chips, french fries
papá *nm fam* **1** : dad, pop **2** ~ **s** *nmpl* : parents, folks
papada *nf* : double chin
papagayo *nm* : parrot
papal *adj* : papal
papalote *nm Lat* : kite
papanatas *nmfs & pl fam* : simpleton
papaya *nf* : papaya
papel *nm* **1** : paper, sheet of paper **2** : role, part (in theater, etc.) **3** ~ **de aluminio** : aluminum foil **4** ~ **higiénico** *or* ~ **de baño** : toilet paper **5** ~ **de lija** : sandpaper **6** ~ **pintado** : wallpaper — **papeleo** *nm* : paperwork, red tape — **papelera** *nf* : wastebasket — **papelería** *nf* : stationery store — **papeleta** *nf* : ticket, slip **2** : ballot paper (paper)
paperas *nfpl* : mumps
papilla *nf* **1** : baby food, pap **2 hacer** ~ : smash to bits
paquete *nm* **1** : package, parcel **2** : pack (of cigarettes, etc.)
paquistaní : Pakistani
par *nm* **1** : pair, couple **2** : par (in golf) **3** NOBLE : peer **4 abierto de** ~ **en** ~ : wide open **5 sin** ~ : without equal — ~ *adj* : even (in number) — ~ *nf* **1** : par **2 a la** ~ **que** : at the same time as
para *prep* **1** : for **2** HACIA : towards **3** : (in order) to **4** : around, by (a time) **5** ~ **adelante** : forwards **6** ~ **atrás** : backwards **7** ~ **que** : so (that), in order that
parabienes *nmpl* : congratulations
parábola *nf* : parable
parabrisas *nms & pl* : windshield
paracaídas *nms & pl* : parachute — **paracaidista** *nmf* **1** : parachutist **2** : paratrooper (in the military)
parachoques *nms & pl* : bumper
parada *nf* **1** : stop **2** : (act of) stopping **3** DESFILE : parade — **paradero** *nm* **1** : whereabouts **2** *Lat* : bus stop — **parado, -da** *adj* **1** : idle, stopped **2** *Lat* : standing (up) **3 bien (mal) parado** : in good (bad) shape
paradoja *nf* : paradox
parafernalia *nf* : paraphernalia

parafina *nf* : paraffin
parafrasear *vt* : paraphrase — **paráfrasis** *nfs & pl* : paraphrase
paraguas *nms & pl* : umbrella
paraguayo, -ya *adj* : Paraguayan
paraíso *nm* : paradise
paralelo, -la *adj* : parallel — **paralelo** *nm* : parallel — **paralelismo** *nm* : similarity
parálisis *nfs & pl* : paralysis — **paralítico, -ca** *adj* : paralytic — **paralizar** {21} *vt* : paralyze
parámetro *nm* : parameter
páramo *nm* : barren plateau
parangón *nm, pl* **-gones 1** : comparison **2 sin** ~ : matchless
paraninfo *nm* : auditorium, hall
paranoia *nf* : paranoia — **paranoico, -ca** *adj & n* : paranoid
parapeto *nm* : parapet, rampart
parapléjico, -ca *adj & n* : paraplegic
parar *vt* **1** : stop **2** *Lat* : stand, prop — *vi* **1** : stop **2 ir a** ~ : end up, wind up — **pararse** *vr* **1** : stop **2** *Lat* : stand up
pararrayos *nms & pl* : lightning rod
parásito, -ta *adj* : parasitic — **parásito** *nm* : parasite
parasol *nm* : parasol
parcela *nf* : parcel, tract (of land) — **parcelar** *vt* : parcel (up)
parche *nm* : patch
parcial *adj* **1** : partial **2 a tiempo** ~ : part-time — **parcialidad** *nf* : partiality, bias
parco, -ca *adj* : sparing, frugal
pardo, -da *adj* : brownish grey
parear *vt* : pair (up)
parecer {53} *vi* **1** : seem, look **2** ASEMEJARSE a : look like, seem like **3 me parece que** : I think that, in my opinion **4 ¿qué te parece?** : what do you think? **5 según parece** : apparently — **parecerse** *vr* ~ a : resemble — ~ *nm* **1** : opinion **2** ASPECTO : appearance **3 al** ~ : apparently — **parecido, -da** *adj* **1** : similar **2 bien parecido** : good-looking — **parecido** *nm* : resemblance, similarity
pared *nf* : wall
parejo, -ja *adj* **1** : even, smooth **2** SEMEJANTE : similar — **pareja** *nf* **1** : couple, pair **2** : partner (person)
parentela *nf* : relatives *pl*, kin — **parentesco** *nm* : relationship, kinship
paréntesis *nms & pl* **1** : parenthesis **2** DIGRESIÓN : digression **3 entre** ~ : by the way
paria *nmf* : outcast
paridad *nf* : equality
pariente *nmf* : relative, relation

parir *vi* : give birth, have a baby — *vt* : give birth to

parking *nm* : parking lot

parlamentar *vi* : discuss — **parlamentario, -ria** *adj* : parliamentary — **~** *n* : member of parliament — **parlamento** *nm* : parliament

parlanchín, -china *adj, mpl* **-chines** : talkative, chatty — **~** *n* : chatterbox

parlotear *vi fam* : chatter — **parloteo** *nm fam* : chatter

paro *nm* **1** : stoppage, shutdown **2** DESEMPLEO : unemployment **3** *Lat* : strike **4 ~ cardíaco** : cardiac arrest

parodia *nf* : parody — **parodiar** *vt* : parody

párpado *nm* : eyelid — **parpadear** *vi* **1** : blink **2** : flicker (of light), twinkle (of stars) — **parpadeo** *nm* **1** : blink **2** : flicker (of light), twinkling (of stars)

parque *nm* **1** : park **2 ~ de atracciones** : amusement park

parqué *nm* : parquet

parquear *vt Lat* : park

parquedad *nf* : frugality, moderation

parquímetro *nm* : parking meter

parra *nf* : grapevine

párrafo *nm* : paragraph

parranda *nf fam* : party, spree

parrilla *nf* **1** : broiler, grill **2** : grate (of a chimney, etc.) — **parrillada** *nf* : barbecue

párroco *nm* : parish priest — **parroquia** *nf* **1** : parish **2** : parish church — **parroquial** *adj* : parochial — **parroquiano, -na** *nm* **1** : parishioner **2** CLIENTE : customer

parsimonia *nf* **1** : calm **2** FRUGALIDAD : thrift — **parsimonioso, -sa** *adj* **1** : calm, unhurried **2** FRUGAL : thrifty

parte *nf* **1** : part **2** PORCIÓN : share **3** LADO : side **4** : party (in negotiations, etc.) **5 de ~** : on behalf of **6 ¿de ~ de quién?** : who is speaking? **7 en alguna ~** : somewhere **8 en todas ~s** : everywhere **9 tomar ~** : take part — **~** *nm* **1** : report **2 ~ meteorológico** : weather forecast

partero, -ra *n* : midwife

partición *nf, pl* **-ciones** : division, sharing

participar *vi* **1** : participate, take part **2 ~ en** : have a share in — *vt* : notify — **participación** *nf, pl* **-ciones** : participation **2** : share, interest (in a fund, etc.) **3** NOTICIA : notice — **participante** *adj* : participating — **~** *nmf* : participant — **partícipe** *nmf* : participant

participio *nm* : participle

partícula *nf* : particle

particular *adj* **1** : particular **2** PRIVADO : private — **~** *nm* **1** : matter **2** PERSONA : individual — **particularidad** *nf* : peculiarity — **particularizar** {21} *vt* : distinguish, characterize — *vi* : go into details

partir *vt* **1** : split, divide **2** ROMPER : break, crack **3** REPARTIR : share (out) — *vi* **1** : depart **2 ~ de** : start from **3 a ~ de** : as of, from — **partirse** *vr* **1** : split (open) **2** RAJARSE : crack — **partida** *nf* **1** : departure **2** : entry, item (in a register, etc.) **3** JUEGO : game **4** : group (of persons) **5 mala ~** : dirty trick **6 ~ de nacimiento** : birth certificate — **partidario, -ria** *n* : follower, supporter — **partido** *nm* **1** : (political) party **2** : game, match (in sports) **3** PARTIDARIOS : following **4 sacar ~ de** : make the most of

partitura *nf* : (musical) score

parto *nm* **1** : childbirth **2 estar de ~** : be in labor

parvulario *nm* : nursery school

pasa *nf* **1** : raisin **2 ~ de Corinto** : currant

pasable *adj* : passable

pasada *nf* **1** : pass, wipe, coat (of paint, etc.) **2 de ~** : in passing **3 mala ~** : dirty trick — **pasadizo** *nm* : corridor — **pasado, -da** *adj* **1** : past **2** PODRIDO : bad, spoiled **3** ANTICUADO : out-of-date **4 el año pasado** : last year — **pasado** *nm* : past

pasador *nm* **1** CERROJO : bolt **2** : barrette (for the hair)

pasaje *nm* **1** : passage **2** BILLETE : ticket, fare **3** PASILLO : passageway **4** PASAJEROS : passengers *pl* — **pasajero, -ra** *adj* : passing — **~** *n* : passenger

pasamanos *nms & pl* : handrail, banister

pasaporte *nm* : passport

pasar *vi* **1** : pass, go (by) **2** ENTRAR : come in **3** SUCEDER : happen **4** TERMINARSE : be over, end **5 ~ de** : exceed **6 ¿qué pasa?** : what's the matter? — *vt* **1** : pass **2** : spend (time) **3** CRUZAR : cross **4** TOLERAR : tolerate **5** SUFRIR : go through, suffer **6** : show (a movie, etc.) **7 pasarlo bien** : have a good time **8 ~ por alto** : overlook, omit — **pasarse** *vr* **1** : pass, go away **2** ESTROPEARSE : spoil, go bad **3** OLVIDARSE : slip one's mind **4** EXCEDERSE : go too far

pasarela *nf* **1** : footbridge **2** : gangway (on a ship)

pasatiempo *nm* : pastime, hobby
Pascua *nf* 1 : Easter (Christian feast) 2 : Passover (Jewish feast) 3 NAVIDAD : Christmas
pase *nm* : pass
pasear *vi* : take a walk, go for a ride — *vt* 1 : take for a walk 2 EXHIBIR : parade, show off — **pasearse** *vr* : go for a walk, go for a ride — **paseo** *nm* 1 : walk, ride 2 *Lat* : outing
pasillo *nm* : passage, corridor
pasión *nf*, *pl* **-siones** : passion
pasivo, -va *adj* : passive — **pasivo** *nm* : liabilities *pl*
pasmar *vt* : astonish, amaze — **pasmarse** *vr* : be astonished — **pasmado, -da** *adj* : stunned, flabbergasted — **pasmo** *nm* : astonishment — **pasmoso, -sa** *adj* : astonishing
paso¹, -sa *adj* : dried (of fruit)
paso² *nm* 1 : step 2 HUELLA : footprint 3 RITMO : pace 4 CRUCE : crossing 5 PASAJE : passage, way through 6 : (mountain) pass 7 **de** ~ : in passing
pasta *nf* 1 : paste 2 MASA : dough 3 *or* ~ **s** : pasta 4 ~ **de dientes** *or* ~ **dentífrica** : toothpaste
pastar *v* : graze
pastel *nm* 1 : cake 2 EMPANADA : pie 3 : pastel (crayon) — **pastelería** *nf* : pastry shop
pasteurizar {21} *vt* : pasteurize
pastilla *nf* 1 : pill, tablet 2 : bar (of chocolate, soap, etc.) 3 ~ **para la tos** : lozenge, cough drop
pasto *nm* 1 : pasture 2 *Lat* : grass, lawn — **pastor, -tora** *n* 1 : shepherd 2 : pastor (in religion) — **pastoral** *adj* : pastoral
pata *nf* 1 : paw, leg (of an animal) 2 : foot, leg (of furniture) 3 **meter la** ~ *fam* : put one's foot in it — **patada** *nf* 1 : kick 2 : stamp (of the foot) — **patalear** *vi* 1 : kick 2 : stamp (one's feet)
patata *nf Spain* : potato
patear *vt* : kick — *vi* 1 : kick 2 : stamp (one's feet)
patentar *vt* : patent — **patente** *adj* : obvious, patent — ~ *nf* : patent
paternal *adj* : fatherly, paternal — **paternidad** *nf* 1 : fatherhood 2 : paternity (in law) — **paterno, -na** *adj* : paternal
patético, -ca *adj* : pathetic, moving
patillas *nfpl* : sideburns
patinar *vi* 1 : skate 2 RESBALAR : slip, slide — **patín** *nm*, *pl* **-tines** : skate — **patinador, -dora** *n* : skater — **patinaje** *nm* : skating — **patinazo** *nm* 1 : skid 2 *fam* : blunder — **patinete** *nm* : scooter

patio *nm* 1 : courtyard, patio 2 *or* ~ **de recreo** : playground
pato, -ta *n* 1 : duck 2 **pagar el pato** *fam* : take the blame — **patito, -ta** *n* : duckling
patología *nf* : pathology — **patológico, -ca** *adj* : pathological
patraña *nf* : hoax
patria *nf* : native land
patriarca *nm* : patriarch
patrimonio *nm* 1 : inheritance 2 : (historical or cultural) heritage
patriota *adj* : patriotic — ~ *nmf* : patriot — **patriótico, -ca** *adj* : patriotic — **patriotismo** *nm* : patriotism
patrocinador, -dora *n* : sponsor — **patrocinar** *vt* : sponsor — **patrocinio** *nm* : sponsorship
patrón, -trona *n*, *mpl* **-trones** 1 : patron 2 JEFE : boss 3 : landlord, landlady *f* (of a boarding house, etc.) — **patrón** *nm*, *pl* **-trones** : pattern (in sewing) — **patronato** *nm* 1 : patronage 2 FUNDACIÓN : foundation, trust
patrulla *nf* 1 : patrol 2 : (police) cruiser — **patrullar** *v* : patrol
paulatino, -na *adj* : gradual
pausa *nf* : pause, break — **pausado, -da** *adj* : slow, deliberate
pauta *nf* : guideline
pavimento *nm* : pavement — **pavimentar** *vt* : pave
pavo, -va *n* 1 : turkey 2 **pavo real** : peacock
pavonearse *vr* : strut, swagger
pavor *nm* : dread, terror — **pavoroso, -sa** *adj* : terrifying
payaso, -sa *n* : clown — **payasada** *nf* : antic, buffoonery — **payasear** *vi Lat fam* : clown (around)
paz *nf*, *pl* **paces** 1 : peace 2 **dejar en** ~ : leave alone 3 **hacer las paces** : make up, reconcile
peaje *nm* : toll
peatón *nm*, *pl* **-tones** : pedestrian
peca *nf* : freckle
pecado *nm* : sin — **pecador, -dora** *n* : sinner — **pecaminoso, -sa** *adj* : sinful — **pecar** {72} *vi* : sin
pecera *nf* : fishbowl, fish tank
pecho *nm* 1 : chest 2 MAMA : breast 3 CORAZÓN : heart, courage 4 **dar el** ~ : breast-feed 5 **tomar a** ~ : take to heart — **pechuga** *nf* : breast (of fowl)
pecoso, -sa *adj* : freckled
pectoral *adj* : pectoral
peculiar *adj* 1 : particular 2 RARO : peculiar, odd — **peculiaridad** *nf* : peculiarity

pedagogía *nf* : education, pedagogy — **pedagogo, -ga** *n* : educator, teacher
pedal *nm* : pedal — **pedalear** *vi* : pedal
pedante *adj* : pedantic, pompous
pedazo *nm* 1 : piece, bit 2 hacerse ~s : fall to pieces
pedernal *nm* : flint
pedestal *nm* : pedestal
pediatra *nmf* : pediatrician
pedigrí *nm* : pedigree
pedir {54} *vt* 1 : ask for, request 2 : order (food, merchandise, etc.) — *vi* 1 : ask 2 ~ prestado : borrow — **pedido** *nm* 1 : order 2 hacer un ~ : place an order
pedregoso, -sa *adj* : rocky, stony
pedrería *nf* : precious stones *pl*
pegar {52} *vt* 1 : stick, glue, paste 2 : sew on (a button, etc.) 3 JUNTAR : bring together 4 GOLPEAR : hit, strike 5 PROPINAR : deal (a blow, etc.) 6 : transmit (an illness) 7 ~ un grito : let out a scream — *vi* 1 : adhere, stick 2 GOLPEAR : hit — **pegarse** *vr* 1 : hit oneself, hit each other 2 ADHERIRSE : stick, adhere 3 CONTAGIARSE : be transmitted — **pegadizo, -za** *adj* 1 : catchy 2 CONTAGIOSO : contagious — **pegajoso, -sa** *adj* 1 : sticky 2 *Lat* : catchy — **pegamento** *nm* : glue
peinar *vt* : comb — **peinarse** *vr* : comb one's hair — **peinado** *nm* : hairstyle, hairdo — **peine** *nm* : comb — **peineta** *nf* : ornamental comb
pelado, -da *adj* 1 : shorn, hairless 2 : peeled (of fruit, etc.) 3 *fam* : bare 4 *fam* : broke, penniless
pelaje *nm* : coat (of an animal), fur
pelar *vt* 1 : cut the hair of (a person) 2 MONDAR : peel (fruit) 3 : pluck (a chicken, etc.), skin (an animal) — **pelarse** *vr* 1 : peel 2 *fam* : get a haircut
peldaño *nm* 1 : step (of stairs) 2 : rung (of a ladder)
pelear *vi* 1 : fight 2 DISCUTIR : quarrel — **pelearse** *vr* : have a fight — **pelea** *nf* 1 : fight 2 DISCUSIÓN : quarrel
peletería *nf* : fur shop
peliagudo, -da *adj* : tricky, difficult
pelícano *nm* : pelican
película *nf* : movie, film
peligro *nm* 1 : danger 2 RIESGO : risk — **peligroso, -sa** *adj* : dangerous
pelirrojo, -ja *adj* : red-haired — ~ *n* : redhead
pellejo *nm* : skin, hide
pellizcar {72} *vt* : pinch — **pellizco** *nm* : pinch
pelo *nm* 1 : hair 2 : coat, fur (of an animal) 3 : pile, nap (of fabric) 4 con ~s

y señales : in great detail 5 no tener ~ en la lengua *fam* : not to mince words 6 tomar el ~ a algn *fam* : pull someone's leg — **pelón, -lona** *adj fam, mpl* -lones : bald
pelota *nf* : ball
pelotón *nm, pl* -tones : squad, detachment
peltre *nm* : pewter
peluca *nf* : wig
peluche *nm* 1 : plush 2 oso de ~ : teddy bear
peludo, -da *adj* : hairy, furry
peluquería *nf* : hairdresser's, barber shop — **peluquero, -ra** *n* : barber, hairdresser
pelusa *nf* : fuzz, lint
pelvis *nfs & pl* : pelvis
pena *nf* 1 : penalty 2 TRISTEZA : sorrow 3 DOLOR : suffering, pain 4 *Lat* : embarrassment 5 a duras ~s : with great difficulty 6 ¡qué ~! : what a shame! 7 valer la ~ : be worthwhile
penacho *nm* 1 : crest, tuft 2 : plume (ornament)
penal *adj* : penal — ~ *nm* : prison, penitentiary — **penalidad** *nf* 1 : hardship 2 : penalty (in law) — **penalizar** {21} *vt* : penalize
penalty *nm* : penalty (in sports)
penar *vt* : punish — *vi* : suffer
pendenciero, -ra *adj* : quarrelsome
pender *vi* : hang — **pendiente** *adj* 1 : pending 2 estar ~ de : be watching out for — ~ *nf* : slope — ~ *nm Spain* : earring
pendón *nm, pl* -dones : banner
péndulo *nm* : pendulum
pene *nm* : penis
penetrar *vi* 1 : penetrate 2 ~ en : go into — *vt* 1 : penetrate 2 : pierce (one's heart, etc.) 3 ENTENDER : fathom, grasp — **penetración** *nf, pl* -ciones 1 : penetration 2 PERSPICACIA : insight — **penetrante** *adj* 1 : penetrating 2 : sharp (of odors, etc.), piercing (of sounds) 3 : deep (of a wound, etc.)
penicilina *nf* : penicillin
península *nf* : peninsula — **peninsular** *adj* : peninsular
penitencia *nf* 1 : penitence 2 CASTIGO : penance — **penitenciaría** *nf* : penitentiary — **penitente** *adj & nmf* : penitent
penoso, -sa *adj* 1 : painful, distressing 2 TRABAJOSO : difficult 3 *Lat* : shy
pensar {55} *vi* 1 : think 2 ~ en : think about — *vt* 1 : think 2 CONSIDERAR : think about 3 ~ hacer algo : intend to do sth — **pensador, -dora** *n*

: thinker — **pensamiento** *nm* 1
: thought 2 : pansy (flower) — **pen-sativo, -va** *adj* : pensive, thoughtful
pensión *nf, pl* **-siones** 1 : boarding
house 2 : (retirement) pension 3 ~ **alimenticia** : alimony — **pensionista**
nmf 1 : lodger 2 JUBILADO : retiree
pentágono *nm* : pentagon
pentagrama *nm* : staff (in music)
penúltimo, -ma *adj* : next to last, penultimate
penumbra *nf* : half-light
penuria *nf* : dearth, shortage
peña *nf* : rock, crag — **peñasco** *nm*
: crag, large rock — **peñón** *nm, pl*
-ñones : craggy rock
peón *nm, pl* **peones** 1 : laborer, peon 2
: pawn (in chess)
peonía *nf* : peony
peor *adv* 1 (*comparative of* **mal**)
: worse 2 (*superlative of* **mal**) : worst
— ~ *adj* 1 (*comparative of* **malo**)
: worse 2 (*superlative of* **malo**) : worst
pepino *nm* : cucumber — **pepinillo** *nm*
: pickle, gherkin
pepita *nf* 1 : seed, pip 2 : nugget (of
gold, etc.)
pequeño, -ña *adj* : small, little — **pequeñez** *nf, pl* **-ñeces** 1 : smallness 2
NIMIEDAD : trifle
pera *nf* : pear — **peral** *nm* : pear tree
percance *nm* : mishap, setback
percatarse *vr* ~ **de** : notice
percepción *nf, pl* **-ciones** : perception
— **perceptible** *adj* : perceptible
percha *nf* 1 : perch (for birds) 2 : (coat)
hanger 3 ~ : coatrack (on a wall)
percibir *vt* 1 : perceive 2 : receive (a
salary, etc.)
percusión *nf, pl* **-siones** : percussion
perder {56} *vt* 1 : lose 2 : miss (an opportunity, etc.) 3 DESPERDICIAR : waste
(time) — *vi* : lose — **perderse** *vr* 1
: get lost 2 DESAPARECER : disappear 3
DESPERDICIARSE : be wasted — **perdedor, -dora** *n* : loser — **pérdida** *nf* 1
: loss 2 ESCAPE : leak 3 ~ **de tiempo**
: waste of time — **perdido, -da** *adj* 1
: lost 2 **un caso perdido** *fam* : a hopeless case
perdigón *nm, pl* **-gones** : shot, pellet
perdiz *nf, pl* **-dices** : partridge
perdón *nm, pl* **-dones** : forgiveness,
pardon — **perdón** *interj* : sorry! —
perdonar *vt* 1 DISCULPAR : forgive 2
: pardon (in law)
perdurar *vi* : last, endure — **perdurable** *adj* : lasting
perecer {53} *vi* : perish, die — **perecedero, -ra** *adj* : perishable

peregrinación *nf, pl* **-ciones** *or* **peregrinaje** *nm* : pilgrimage — **peregrino, -na** *adj* 1 : migratory 2 RARO : unusual, odd — ~ *n* : pilgrim
perejil *nm* : parsley
perenne *adj & nm* : perennial
pereza *nf* : laziness — **perezoso, -sa**
adj : lazy
perfección *nf, pl* **-ciones** : perfection
— **perfeccionar** *vt* 1 : perfect 2 MEJORAR : improve — **perfeccionista** *nmf*
: perfectionist — **perfecto, -ta** *adj*
: perfect
perfidia *nf* : treachery — **pérfido, -da**
adj : treacherous
perfil *nm* 1 : profile 2 CONTORNO : outline 3 ~ **es** *nmpl* RASGOS : features —
perfilar *vt* : outline — **perfilarse** *vr* 1
: be outlined 2 CONCRETARSE : take
shape
perforar *vt* 1 : perforate 2 : drill, bore (a
hole) — **perforación** *nf, pl* **-ciones**
: perforation — **perforadora** *nf*
: (paper) punch
perfume *nm* : perfume, scent — **perfumar** *vt* : perfume — **perfumarse** *vr*
: put perfume on
pergamino *nm* : parchment
pericia *nf* : skill
periferia *nf* : periphery, outskirts (of a
city, etc.) — **periférico, -ca** *adj* : peripheral
perilla *nf* 1 : goatee 2 *Lat* : knob 3 **venir
de** ~ **s** *fam* : come in handy
perímetro *nm* : perimeter
periódico, -ca *adj* : periodic — **periódico** *nm* : newspaper — **periodismo** *nm* : journalism — **periodista** *nmf*
: journalist
período *or* **periodo** *nm* : period
periquito *nm* : parakeet
periscopio *nm* : periscope
perito, -ta *adj & n* : expert
perjudicar {72} *vt* : harm, damage —
perjudicial *adj* : harmful — **perjuicio**
nm 1 : harm, damage 2 **en** ~ **de** : to
the detriment of
perjurar *vi* : perjure oneself — **perjurio**
nm : perjury
perla *nf* 1 : pearl 2 **de** ~ **s** *fam* : great,
just fine
permanecer {53} *vi* : remain — **permanencia** *nf* 1 : permanence 2 : stay,
staying (in a place) — **permanente**
adj : permanent — ~ *nf* : permanent
(wave)
permeable *adj* : permeable
permitir *vt* 1 : permit, allow 2 **¿me permite?** : may I? — **permitirse** *vr*
: allow oneself — **permisible** *adj*

: permissible, allowable — **permisivo, -va** *adj* : permissive — **permiso** *nm* **1** : permission **2** : permit, license (document) **3** : leave (in the military) **4 con ~** : excuse me
permuta *nf* : exchange
pernicioso, -sa *adj* : pernicious, destructive
pero *conj* : but — **~** *nm* **1** : fault **2** REPARO : objection
perorar *vi* : make a speech — **perorata** *nf* : (long-winded) speech
perpendicular *adj & nf* : perpendicular
perpetrar *vt* : perpetrate
perpetuar {3} *vt* : perpetuate — **perpetuo, -tua** *adj* : perpetual
perplejo, -ja *adj* : perplexed — **perplejidad** *nf* : perplexity
perro, -rra *n* **1** : dog, bitch *f* **2 perro caliente** : hot dog — **perrera** *nf* : kennel
perseguir {75} *vt* **1** : pursue, chase **2** ACOSAR : persecute — **persecución** *nf, pl* **-ciones 1** : pursuit, chase **2** ACOSO : persecution
perseverar *vi* : persevere — **perseverancia** *nf* : perseverance
persiana *nf* : (venetian) blind
persistir *vi* : persist — **persistencia** *nf* : persistence — **persistente** *adj* : persistent
persona *nf* : person — **personaje** *nm* **1** : character (in literature, etc.) **2** : important person, celebrity — **personal** *adj* : personal — **~** *nm* : personnel, staff — **personalidad** *nf* : personality — **personificar** {72} *vi* : personify
perspectiva *nf* **1** : perspective **2** VISTA : view **3** POSIBILIDAD : prospect, outlook
perspicacia *nf* : shrewdness, insight — **perspicaz** *adj, pl* **-caces** : shrewd, discerning
persuadir *vt* : persuade — **persuadirse** *vr* : become convinced — **persuasión** *nf, pl* **-siones** : persuasion — **persuasivo, -va** *adj* : persuasive
pertenecer {53} *vi* **~ a** : belong to — **perteneciente** *adj* **~ a** : belonging to — **pertenencia** *nf* **1** : ownership **2 ~s** *nfpl* : belongings
pertinaz *adj, pl* **-naces 1** OBSTINADO : obstinate **2** PERSISTENTE : persistent
pertinente *adj* : pertinent, relevant — **pertinencia** *nf* : relevance
perturbar *vt* : disturb — **perturbación** *nf, pl* **-ciones** : disturbance
peruano, -na *adj* : Peruvian
pervertir {76} *vt* : pervert — **perversión** *nf, pl* **-siones** : perversion —

perverso, -sa *adj* : perverse — **pervertido, -da** *adj* : perverted, depraved — **~** *n* : pervert
pesa *nf* **1** : weight **2 ~s** : weights (in sports) — **pesadez** *nf, pl* **-deces 1** : heaviness **2** *fam* : tediousness, drag
pesadilla *nf* : nightmare
pesado, -da *adj* **1** : heavy **2** LENTO : sluggish **3** MOLESTO : annoying **4** ABURRIDO : tedious **5** DURO : tough, difficult — **~** *n fam* : bore, pest — **pesadumbre** *nf* : grief, sorrow
pésame *nm* : condolences *pl*
pesar *vt* : weigh — *vi* **1** : weigh, be heavy **2** INFLUIR : carry weight **3 pese a** : despite — **~** *nm* **1** : sorrow, grief **2** REMORDIMIENTO : remorse **3 a ~ de** : in spite of
pescado *nm* : fish — **pesca** *nf* **1** : fishing **2** PECES : fish *pl*, catch **3 ir de ~** : go fishing — **pescadería** *nf* : fish market — **pescador, -dora** *n, mpl* **-dores** : fisherman — **pescar** {72} *vt* **1** : fish for **2** *fam* : catch (a cold, etc.) **3** *fam* : catch hold of, nab — *vi* : fish
pescuezo *nm* : neck (of an animal)
pese a → *pesar*
pesebre *nm* : manger
pesero *nm Lat* : minibus
peseta *nf* : peseta
pesimismo *nm* : pessimism — **pesimista** *adj* : pessimistic — **~** *nmf* : pessimist
pésimo, -ma *adj* : awful
peso *nm* **1** : weight **2** CARGA : burden **3** : peso (currency) **4 ~ pesado** : heavyweight
pesquero, -ra *adj* : fishing
pesquisa *nf* : inquiry
pestaña *nf* : eyelash — **pestañear** *vi* : blink — **pestañeo** *nm* : blink
peste *nf* **1** : plague **2** *fam* : stench, stink **3** *Lat fam* : cold, bug — **pesticida** *nm* : pesticide — **pestilencia** *nf* **1** : stench **2** PLAGA : pestilence
pestillo *nm* : bolt, latch
petaca *nf Lat* : suitcase
pétalo *nm* : petal
petardo *nm* : firecracker
petición *nf, pl* **-ciones** : petition, request
petirrojo *nm* : robin
petrificar {72} *vt* : petrify
petróleo *nm* : oil, petroleum — **petrolero, -ra** *adj* : oil — **petrolero** *nm* : oil tanker
petulante *adj* : insolent, arrogant
peyorativo, -va *adj* : pejorative
pez *nm, pl* **peces 1** : fish **2 ~ de col-**

ores : goldfish 3 ~ **espada** : swordfish 4 ~ **gordo** *fam* : big shot

pezón *nm, pl* **-zones** : nipple

pezuña *nf* : hoof

piadoso, -sa *adj* 1 : compassionate 2 DEVOTO : pious, devout

piano *nm* : piano — **pianista** *nmf* : pianist, piano player

piar {85} *vi* : chirp, tweet

pibe, -ba *n Lat fam* : kid, child

pica *nf* 1 : pike, lance 2 : spade (in playing cards)

picado, -da *adj* 1 : perforated 2 : minced, chopped (of meat, etc.) 3 : decayed (of teeth) 4 : choppy (of the sea) 5 *fam* : annoyed — **picada** *nf* 1 : bite, sting 2 *Lat* : sharp descent — **picadillo** *nm* : minced meat — **picadura** *nf* 1 : sting, bite 2 : (moth) hole

picante *adj* : hot, spicy

picaporte *nm* 1 : door handle 2 ALDABA : door knocker 3 PESTILLO : latch

picar {72} *vt* 1 : sting, bite 2 : peck at, nibble on (food) 3 PERFORAR : prick, puncture 4 TRITURAR : chop, mince — *vi* 1 : bite, take the bait 2 ESCOCER : sting, itch 3 COMER : nibble 4 : be spicy (of food) — **picarse** *vr* 1 : get a cavity 2 ENFADARSE : take offense

picardía *nf* 1 : craftiness 2 TRAVESURA : prank — **picaresco, -ca** *adj* 1 : picaresque 2 TRAVIESO : roguish — **pícaro, -ra** *adj* 1 : mischievous 2 MALICIOSO : villainous — ~ *n* : rascal, scoundrel

picazón *nf, pl* **-zones** : itch

pichón, -chona *n, mpl* **-chones** : (young) pigeon

picnic *nm, pl* **-nics** : picnic

pico *nm* 1 : beak 2 CIMA : peak 3 PUNTA : (sharp) point 4 : pick, pickax (tool) 5 **las siete y** ~ : a little after seven — **picotazo** *nm* : peck — **picotear** *vt* : peck — *vi fam* : nibble, pick — **picudo, -da** *adj* : pointy

pie *nm* 1 : foot (in anatomy) 2 : base, bottom, stem 3 **al** ~ **de la letra** : word for word 4 **dar** ~ **a** : give rise to 5 **de** ~ : standing (up) 6 **de** ~**s a cabeza** : from top to bottom

piedad *nf* 1 : pity, mercy 2 DEVOCIÓN : piety

piedra *nf* 1 : stone 2 : flint (of a lighter) 3 GRANIZO : hailstone 4 ~ **angular** : cornerstone 5 → **pómez**

piel *nf* 1 : skin 2 CUERO : leather 3 PELO : fur, pelt

pienso *nm* : feed, fodder

pierna *nf* : leg

pieza *nf* 1 : piece, part 2 *or* ~ **de teatro** : play 3 HABITACIÓN : room

pigmento *nm* : pigment — **pigmentación** *nf, pl* **-ciones** : pigmentation

pigmeo, -mea *adj* : pygmy

pijama *nm* : pajamas *pl*

pila *nf* 1 : battery 2 MONTÓN : pile 3 FREGADERO : sink 4 : basin (of a fountain, etc.)

pilar *nm* : pillar

píldora *nf* : pill

pillar *vt* 1 : catch 2 : get (a joke, etc.) — **pillaje** *nm* : pillage — **pillo, -lla** *adj* : crafty — ~ *n* : rascal, scoundrel

piloto *nmf* : pilot — **pilotar** *vt* : pilot

pimienta *nf* : pepper (condiment) — **pimiento** *nm* : pepper (fruit) — **pimentero** *nm* : pepper shaker — **pimentón** *nm, pl* **-tones** 1 : paprika 2 : cayenne pepper

pináculo *nm* : pinnacle

pincel *nm* : paintbrush

pinchar *v* 1 : pierce, prick 2 : puncture (a tire, etc.) 3 INCITAR : goad — **pinchazo** *nm* 1 : prick 2 : puncture (of a tire, etc.)

pingüino *nm* : penguin

pino *nm* : pine (tree)

pintar *v* : paint — **pintarse** *vr* : put on makeup — **pinta** *nf* 1 : spot 2 : pint (measure) 3 *fam* : appearance — **pintada** *nf* : graffiti — **pinto, -ta** *adj* : speckled, spotted — **pintor, -tora** *n, mpl* **-tores** : painter — **pintoresco, -ca** *adj* : picturesque, quaint — **pintura** *nf* 1 : paint 2 CUADRO : painting

pinza *nf* 1 : clothespin 2 : claw, pincer (of a crab, etc.) 3 ~**s** *nfpl* : tweezers

pinzón *nm, pl* **-zones** : finch

piña *nf* 1 : pine cone 2 ANANÁS : pineapple

piñata *nf* : piñata

piñón *nm, pl* **-ñones** : pine nut

pío¹, pía *adj* 1 : pious 2 : piebald (of a horse)

pío² *nm* : peep, chirp

piojo *nm* : louse

pionero, -ra *n* : pioneer

pipa *nf* 1 : pipe (for smoking) 2 *Spain* : seed, pip

pique *nm* 1 : grudge 2 RIVALIDAD : rivalry 3 **irse a** ~ : sink, founder

piqueta *nf* : pickax

piquete *nm* : picket (line) — **piquetear** *v* : picket

piragua *nf* : canoe

pirámide *nf* : pyramid

piraña *nf* : piranha

pirata *adj* 1 : bootleg, pirated — ~ *nmf* : pirate — **piratear** *vt* 1 : bootleg, pirate 2 : hack into (a computer)

piropo *nm* : (flirtatious) compliment

pirueta *nf* : pirouette

pirulí *nm* : (cone-shaped) lollipop

pisada *nf* **1** : footstep **2** HUELLA : footprint

pisapapeles *nms & pl* : paperweight

pisar *vt* **1** : step on **2** HUMILLAR : walk all over, abuse — *vi* : step, tread

piscina *nf* **1** : swimming pool **2** : (fish) pond

piso *nm* **1** : floor, story **2** *Lat* : floor (of a room) **3** *Spain* : apartment

pisotear *vt* : trample (on)

pista *nf* **1** : trail, track **2** INDICIO : clue **3** ~ **de aterrizaje** : runway, airstrip **4** ~ **de baile** : dance floor **5** ~ **de hielo** : ice-skating rink

pistacho *nm* : pistachio

pistola *nf* **1** : pistol, gun **2** PULVERIZADOR : spray gun — **pistolera** *nf* : holster — **pistolero** *nm* : gunman

pistón *nm, pl* **-tones** : piston

pito *nm* **1** SILBATO : whistle **2** CLAXON : horn — **pitar** *vi* **1** : blow a whistle **2** : beep, honk (of a horn) — *vi* : whistle at — **pitido** *nm* **1** : whistle, whistling **2** : beep (of a horn) — **pitillo** *nm fam* : cigarette

pitón *nm, pl* **-tones** : python

pitorro *nm* : spout

pivote *nm* : pivot

piyama *nmf Lat* : pajamas *pl*

pizarra *nf* **1** : slate **2** ENCERADO : blackboard — **pizarrón** *nm, pl* **-rrones** *Lat* : blackboard

pizca *nf* **1** : pinch (of salt) **2** ÁPICE : speck, tiny bit **3** *Lat* : harvest

pizza ['pitsa, 'pisa] *nf* : pizza — **pizzería** *nf* : pizzeria

placa *nf* **1** : sheet, plate **2** INSCRIPCIÓN : plaque **3** : (police) badge

placenta *nf* : placenta

placer {57} *vt* : please — ~ *nm* : pleasure — **placentero, -ra** *adj* : pleasant, agreeable

plácido, -da *adj* : placid, calm

plaga *nf* **1** : plague **2** CALAMIDAD : disaster — **plagar** {52} *vt* : plague, infest

plagiar *vt* : plagiarize — **plagio** *nm* : plagiarism

plan *nm* **1** : plan **2 en** ~ **de** : as **3 no te pongas en ese** ~ *fam* : don't be that way

plana *nf* **1** : page **2 en primera** ~ : on the front page

plancha *nf* **1** : iron (for ironing) **2** : grill (for cooking) **3** LÁMINA : sheet, plate — **planchar** *v* : iron — **planchado** *nm* : ironing

planear *vt* : plan — *vi* : glide — **planeador** *nm* : glider

planeta *nm* : planet

planicie *nf* : plain

planificar {72} *vt* : plan — **planificación** *nf, pl* **-ciones** : planning

planilla *nf Lat* : list, roster

plano, -na *adj* : flat — **plano** *nm* **1** : map, plan **2** : plane (surface) **3** NIVEL : level **4 de** ~ : flatly, outright **5** **primer** ~ : foreground, close-up (in photography)

planta *nf* **1** : plant **2** PISO : floor, story **3** : sole (of the foot) — **plantación** *nf, pl* **-ciones 1** : plantation **2** : (action of) planting — **plantar** *vt* **1** : plant **2** PONER : deal, land — **plantarse** *vr* : stand firm

plantear *vt* **1** : expound, set forth **2** : raise (a question) **3** CAUSAR : create, pose (a problem) — **plantearse** *vr* : think about, consider

plantel *nm* **1** : staff, team **2** *Lat* : educational institution

plantilla *nf* **1** : insole **2** PATRÓN : pattern, template **3** : staff (of a business, etc.)

plasma *nf* : plasma

plástico, -ca *adj* : plastic — **plástico** *nm* : plastic

plata *nf* **1** : silver **2** *Lat fam* : money **3** ~ **de ley** : sterling silver

plataforma *nf* **1** : platform **2** ~ **petrolífera** : oil rig **3** ~ **de lanzamiento** : launching pad

plátano *nm* **1** : banana **2** : plantain

platea *nf* : orchestra, pit (in a theater)

plateado, -da *adj* **1** : silver, silvery (color) **2** : silver-plated

platicar {72} *vi* : talk, chat — **plática** *nf* : chat, conversation

platija *nf* : flatfish, flounder

platillo *nm* **1** : saucer **2** CÍMBALO : cymbal **3** *Lat* : dish, course

platino *nm* : platinum

plato *nm* **1** : plate, dish **2** : course (of a meal) **3** ~ **principal** : entrée

platónico, -ca *adj* : platonic

playa *nf* **1** : beach, seashore **2** ~ **de estacionamiento** *Lat* : parking lot

plaza *nf* **1** : square, plaza **2** : seat (in transportation) **3** PUESTO : post, position **4** MERCADO : market, marketplace **5** ~ **de toros** : bullring

plazo *nm* **1** : period, term **2** PAGO : installment **3 a largo** ~ : long-term

plazoleta *or* **plazuela** *nf* : small square

pleamar *nf* : high tide

plebe *nf* : common people — **plebeyo, -ya** *adj & nm* : plebeian

plegar {49} *vt* : fold, bend — **plegarse** *vr* **1** : give in, yield **2** : jackknife (of a

truck) — **plegable** or **plegadizo, -za**
adj : folding, collapsible

plegaria nf : prayer

pleito nm 1 : lawsuit 2 Lat : dispute, fight

plenilunio nm : full moon

pleno, -na adj 1 : full, complete 2 **en plena forma** : in top form 3 **en pleno día** : in broad daylight — **plenitud** nf : fullness, abundance

pleuresía nf : pleurisy

pliego nm : sheet (of paper) — **pliegue** nm 1 : crease, fold 2 : pleat (in fabric)

plisar vt : pleat

plomería nf Lat : plumbing — **plomero, -ra** n Lat : plumber

plomo nm 1 : lead 2 FUSIBLE : fuse

pluma nf 1 : feather 2 : (fountain) pen — **plumaje** nm : plumage — **plumero** nm : feather duster — **plumilla** nf : nib — **plumón** nm 1, pl **-mones** : down

plural adj & nm : plural — **pluralidad** nf : plurality

pluriempleo nm **hacer ~** : have more than one job

plus nm : bonus

plusvalía nf : appreciation, capital gain

plutocracia nf : plutocracy

Plutón nm : Pluto

plutonio nm : plutonium

pluvial adj : rain

poblar {19} vt 1 : settle, colonize 2 HABITAR : inhabit — **poblarse** vr : become crowded — **población** nf, pl **-ciones** 1 : city, town, village 2 HABITANTES : population — **poblado, -da** adj 1 : populated 2 : thick, bushy (of a beard, eyebrows, etc.) — **poblado** nm : village

pobre adj 1 : poor 2 **¡~ de mí!** : poor me! — **~** nmf 1 : poor person 2 **los ~s** : the poor 3 **¡pobre!** : poor thing! — **pobreza** nf : poverty

pocilga nf : pigsty

poción nf, pl **-ciones** or **pócima** nf : potion

poco, -ca adj 1 : little, not much, (a) few 2 **pocas veces** : rarely — **~** pron 1 : little, few 2 **hace poco** : not long ago 3 **poco a poco** : bit by bit, gradually 4 **por poco** : nearly, just about 5 **un poco** : a little, a bit — **poco** adv : little, not much

podar vt : prune

poder {58} v aux 1 : be able to, can 2 (expressing possibility) : might, may 3 (expressing permission) : can, may 4 **¿cómo puede ser?** : how can it be? 5 **¿puedo pasar?** : may I come in? — vi 1 : be possible 2 **~ con** : cope with, manage 3 **no puedo más** : I've

had enough — **~** nm : power 2 POSESIÓN : possession — **poderío** nm : power — **poderoso, -sa** adj : powerful

podólogo, -ga n : chiropodist

podrido, -da adj : rotten

poema nm : poem — **poesía** nf : poetry POEMA : poem — **poeta** nmf : poet — **poético, -ca** adj : poetic

póker nm → **póquer**

polaco, -ca adj : Polish

polar adj : polar — **polarizar** {21} vt : polarize

polea nf : pulley

polémica nf : controversy — **polémico, -ca** adj : controversial — **polemizar** vt : argue

polen nm, pl **pólenes** : pollen

policía nf : police — **~** nmf : police officer, policeman m, policewoman f — **policíaco, -ca** adj 1 : police 2 **novela policíaca** : detective story

poliéster nm : polyester

poligamia nf : polygamy — **polígamo, -ma** n : polygamist

polígono nm : polygon

polilla nf : moth

polio or **poliomielitis** nf : polio, poliomyelitis

politécnico, -ca adj : polytechnic

política nf 1 : politics 2 POSTURA : policy — **político, -ca** adj 1 : political 2 **hermano político** : brother-in-law — **~** n : politician

póliza nf or **~ de seguros** : insurance policy

polizón nm, pl **-zones** : stowaway

pollo, -lla n 1 : chicken, chick 2 : chicken (for cooking) — **pollera** nf Lat : skirt — **pollería** nf : poultry shop — **pollito, -ta** n : chick

polo nm 1 : pole 2 : polo (sport) 3 **~ norte** : North Pole

poltrona nf : easy chair

polución nf, pl **-ciones** : pollution

polvo nm 1 : powder 2 SUCIEDAD : dust 3 **~s** nmpl : face powder 4 **hacer ~** fam : crush, shatter — **polvareda** nf : cloud of dust — **polvera** nf : compact (for powder) — **pólvora** nf : gunpowder — **polvoriento, -ta** adj : dusty

pomada nf : ointment

pomelo nm : grapefruit

pómez nm or **piedra ~** nf : pumice

pomo nm : knob, doorknob

pompa nf 1 : (soap) bubble 2 ESPLENDOR : pomp 3 **~s fúnebres** : funeral — **pomposo, -sa** adj 1 : pompous 2 ESPLÉNDIDO : splendid

pómulo nm : cheekbone

ponchar *vt Lat* : puncture — **ponchadura** *nf Lat* : puncture
ponche *nm* : punch (drink)
poncho *nm* : poncho
ponderar *vt* **1** : consider **2** ALABAR : speak highly of
poner {60} *vt* **1** : put **2** AGREGAR : add **3** CONTRIBUIR : contribute **4** SUPONER : suppose **5** DISPONER : arrange, set out **6** : give (a name), call **7** ENCENDER : turn on **8** ESTABLECER : set up, establish **9** : lay (eggs) — *vi* : lay eggs — **ponerse** *vr* **1** : move (into a position) **2** : put on (clothing, etc.) **3** : set (of the sun) **4 ~ furioso** : become angry
poniente *nm* **1** OCCIDENTE : west **2** : west wind
pontífice *nm* : pontiff
pontón *nm*, *pl* **-tones** : pontoon
ponzoña *nf* : poison, venom
popa *nf* **1** : stern **2 a ~** : astern
popelín *nm*, *pl* **-lines** : poplin
popote *nm Lat* : (drinking) straw
populacho *nm* : rabble, masses *pl*
popular *adj* **1** : popular **2** : colloquial (of language) — **popularidad** *nf* : popularity — **popularizar** {21} *vt* : popularize — **populoso, -sa** *adj* : populous
póquer *nm* : poker (card game)
por *prep* **1** : for **2** (*indicating an approximate time*) : around, during **3** (*indicating an approximate place*) : around, about **4** A TRAVÉS DE : through, along **5** A CAUSA DE : because of **6** (*indicating rate or ratio*) : per **7** *or* **~ medio de** : by means of **8** : times (in mathematics) **9** SEGÚN : as for, according to **10 estar ~** : be about to **11 ~ ciento** : percent **12 ~ favor** : please **13 ~ lo tanto** : therefore **14 ¿por qué?** : why?
porcelana *nf* : porcelain, china
porcentaje *nm* : percentage
porción *nf*, *pl* **-ciones** : portion, piece
pordiosero, -ra *n* : beggar
porfiar {85} *vi* : insist — **porfiado, -da** *adj* : obstinate, persistent
pormenor *nm* : detail
pornografía *nf* : pornography — **pornográfico, -ca** *adj* : pornographic
poro *nm* : pore — **poroso, -sa** *adj* : porous
poroto *nm Lat* : bean
porque *conj* **1** : because **2** *or* **por que** : in order that — **porqué** *nm* : reason
porquería *nf* **1** SUCIEDAD : filth **2** : shoddy thing, junk
porra *nf* : nightstick, club — **porrazo** *nm* : blow, whack

portaaviones *nms & pl* : aircraft carrier
portada *nf* **1** : facade **2** : title page (of a book), cover (of a magazine)
portador, -dora *n* : bearer
portaequipajes *nms & pl* : luggage rack
portafolio *or* **portafolios** *nm*, *pl* **-lios 1** : portfolio **2** MALETÍN : briefcase
portal *nm* **1** : doorway **2** VESTÍBULO : hall, vestibule
portamonedas *nms & pl* : purse
portar *vt* : carry, bear — **portarse** *vr* : behave
portátil *adj* : portable
portaviones *nm* → **portaaviones**
portavoz *nmf*, *pl* **-voces** : spokesperson, spokesman *m*, spokeswoman *f*
portazo *nm* **dar un ~** : slam the door
porte *nm* **1** : transport, freight **2** ASPECTO : bearing, appearance **3 ~ pagado** : postage paid
portento *nm* : marvel, wonder — **portentoso, -sa** *adj* : marvelous
porteño, -ña *adj* : of or from Buenos Aires
portería *nf* **1** : superintendent's office **2** : goal, goalposts *pl* (in sports) — **portero, -ra** *n* **1** : goalkeeper, goalie **2** CONSERJE : janitor, superintendent
portezuela *nf* : door (of an automobile)
pórtico *nm* : portico
portilla *nf* : porthole
portugués, -guesa *adj*, *mpl* **-gueses** : Portuguese — **portugués** *nm* : Portuguese (language)
porvenir *nm* : future
pos: en ~ de *adv phr* : in pursuit of
posada *nf* : inn
posaderas *nfpl fam* : backside, bottom
posar *vi* : pose — *vt* : place, lay — **posarse** *vr* : settle, rest
posavasos *nms & pl* : coaster
posdata *nf* : postscript
pose *nf* : pose
poseer {20} *vt* : possess, own — **poseedor, -dora** *n* : possessor, owner — **poseído, -da** *adj* : possessed — **posesión** *nf*, *pl* **-siones** : possession — **posesionarse** *vr* **~ de** : take possession of, take over — **posesivo, -va** *adj* : possessive
posguerra *nf* : postwar period
posibilidad *nf* : possibility — **posibilitar** *vt* : make possible — **posible** *adj* **1** : possible **2 de ser ~** : if possible
posición *nf*, *pl* **-ciones** : position — **posicionar** *vt* : position — **posicionarse** *vr* : take a stand
positivo, -va *adj* : positive
poso *nm* : sediment, (coffee) grounds

posponer {60} *vt* **1** : postpone **2** RELEGAR : put behind, subordinate

postal *adj* : postal — ~ *nf* : postcard

postdata → **posdata**

poste *nm* : post, pole

póster *nm, pl* **-ters** : poster

postergar {52} *vt* **1** : pass over **2** APLAZAR : postpone

posteridad *nf* : posterity — **posterior** *adj* **1** : later, subsequent **2** TRASERO : back, rear — **posteriormente** *adv* : subsequently, later

postigo *nm* **1** : small door **2** CONTRAVENTANA : shutter

postizo, -za *adj* : artificial, false

postrarse *vr* : prostrate oneself — **postrado, -da** *adj* : prostrate

postre *nm* : dessert

postular *vt* **1** : advance, propose **2** *Lat* : nominate — **postulado** *nm* : postulate

póstumo, -ma *adj* : posthumous

postura *nf* : position, stance

potable *adj* : drinkable, potable

potaje *nm* : thick vegetable soup

potasio *nm* : potassium

pote *nm* : jar

potencia *nf* : power — **potencial** *adj* & *nm* : potential — **potente** *adj* : powerful

potro, -tra *n* : colt *m*, filly *f* — **potro** *nm* : horse (in gymnastics)

pozo *nm* **1** : well **2** : shaft (in a mine)

práctica *nf* **1** : practice **2 en la ~** : in practice — **practicable** *adj* : practicable, feasible — **practicante** *adj* : practicing — ~ *nmf* : practitioner — **practicar** {72} *vt* **1** : practice **2** REALIZAR : perform, carry out — *vi* : practice — **práctico, -ca** *adj* : practical

pradera *nf* : grassland, prairie — **prado** *nm* : meadow

pragmático, -ca *adj* : pragmatic

preámbulo *nm* : preamble

precario, -ria *adj* : precarious

precaución *nf, pl* **-ciones 1** : precaution **2** PRUDENCIA : caution, care **3 con ~** : cautiously

precaver *vt* : guard against — **precavido, -da** *adj* : prudent, cautious

preceder *v* : precede — **precedencia** *nf* : precedence, priority — **precedente** *adj* : preceding, previous — ~ *nm* : precedent

precepto *nm* : precept

preciado, -da *adj* : prized, valuable — **preciarse** *vr* ~ **de** : pride oneself on, boast about

precinto *nm* : seal

precio *nm* : price, cost — **preciosidad** *nf* **1** VALOR : value **2** : beautiful thing — **precioso, -sa** *adj* **1** HERMOSO : beautiful **2** VALIOSO : precious

precipicio *nm* : precipice

precipitar *vt* **1** : hasten, speed up **2** ARROJAR : hurl — **precipitarse** *vr* **1** APRESURARSE : rush **2** : act rashly **3** ARROJARSE : throw oneself — **precipitación** *nf, pl* **-ciones 1** : precipitation **2** PRISA : haste — **precipitadamente** *adv* : in a rush, hastily — **precipitado, -da** *adj* : hasty

preciso, -sa *adj* **1** : precise **2** NECESARIO : necessary — **precisamente** *adv* : precisely, exactly — **precisar** *vt* **1** : specify, determine **2** NECESITAR : require — **precisión** *nf, pl* **-siones 1** : precision **2** NECESIDAD : necessity

preconcebido, -da *adj* : preconceived

precoz *adj, pl* **-coces 1** : early **2** : precocious (of children)

precursor, -sora *n* : forerunner

predecesor, -sora *n* : predecessor

predecir {11} *vt* : foretell, predict

predestinado, -da *adj* : predestined

predeterminar *vt* : predetermine

prédica *nf* : sermon

predicado *nm* : predicate

predicar {72} *v* : preach — **predicador, -dora** *n* : preacher

predicción *nf, pl* **-ciones 1** : prediction **2** PRONÓSTICO : forecast

predilección *nf, pl* **-ciones** : preference — **predilecto, -ta** *adj* : favorite

predisponer {60} *vt* : predispose — **predisposición** *nf, pl* **-ciones** : predisposition

predominar *vi* : predominate — **predominante** *adj* : predominant, prevailing — **predominio** *nm* : predominance

preeminente *adj* : preeminent

prefabricado, -da *adj* : prefabricated

prefacio *nm* : preface

preferir {76} *vt* : prefer — **preferencia** *nf* **1** : preference **2 de ~** : preferably — **preferente** *adj* : preferential — **preferible** *adj* : preferable — **preferido, -da** *adj* : favorite

prefijo *nm* **1** : prefix **2** *Spain* : area code

pregonar *vt* : proclaim, announce

pregunta *nf* **1** : question **2 hacer ~s** : ask questions — **preguntar** *v* : ask — **preguntarse** *vr* : wonder

prehistórico, -ca *adj* : prehistoric

prejuicio *nm* : prejudice

preliminar *adj* & *nm* : preliminary

preludio *nm* : prelude

prematrimonial *adj* : premarital

prematuro, -ra *adj* : premature
premeditar *vt* : premeditate — **premeditación** *nf, pl* **-ciones** : premeditation
premenstrual *adj* : premenstrual
premio *nm* **1** : prize RECOMPENSA : reward **3** ~ **gordo** : jackpot — **premiado, -da** *adj* : prizewinning — **premiar** *vt* **1** : award a prize to **2** RECOMPENSAR : reward
premisa *nf* : premise
premonición *nf, pl* **-ciones** : premonition
premura *nf* : haste, urgency
prenatal *adj* : prenatal
prenda *nf* **1** : piece of clothing **2** GARANTÍA : pledge **3** : forfeit (in a game) — **prendar** *vt* : captivate — **prendarse** *vr* ~ **de** : fall in love with
prender *vt* **1** SUJETAR : pin, fasten **2** APRESAR : capture **3** : light (a match, etc.) **4** *Lat* : turn on (a light, etc.) — *vi* **1** : take root **2** ARDER : catch, burn (of fire) — **prenderse** *vr* : catch fire — **prendedor** *nm Lat* : brooch, pin
prensa *nf* : press — **prensar** *vt* : press
preñado, -da *adj* **1** : pregnant **2** ~ **de** : filled with
preocupar *vt* : worry — **preocuparse** *vr* **1** : worry **2** ~ **de** : take care of — **preocupación** *nf, pl* **-ciones** : worry
preparar *vt* : prepare — **prepararse** *vr* : get ready — **preparación** *nf, pl* **-ciones** : preparation — **preparado, -da** *adj* : prepared, ready — **preparado** *nm* : preparation — **preparativo, -va** *adj* : preparatory, preliminary — **preparativos** *nmpl* : preparations — **preparatorio, -ria** *adj* : preparatory
preposición *nf, pl* **-ciones** : preposition
prepotente *adj* : arrogant, domineering
prerrogativa *nf* : prerogative
presa *nf* **1** : catch, prey **2** DIQUE : dam **3** hacer ~ **en** : seize
presagiar *vt* : presage, forebode — **presagio** *nm* **1** : omen **2** PREMONICIÓN : premonition
presbítero *nm* : presbyter, priest
prescribir {33} *vt* : prescribe — **prescripción** *nf, pl* **-ciones** : prescription
presencia *nf* **1** : presence **2** ASPECTO : appearance — **presenciar** *vt* : be present at, witness
presentar *vt* **1** OFRECER : offer, give **3** MOSTRAR : show **4** : introduce (persons) — **presentarse** *vr* **1** : show up **2** : arise, come up (of a

problem, etc.) **3** : introduce oneself — **presentación** *nf, pl* **-ciones 1** : presentation **2** : introduction (of persons) **3** ASPECTO : appearance — **presentador, -dora** *n* : presenter, host (of a television program, etc.)
presente *adj* **1** : present **2** tener ~ : keep in mind — ~ *nm* **1** : present **2** entre los ~**s** : among those present
presentir {76} *vt* : have a presentiment of — **presentimiento** *nm* : premonition
preservar *vt* : preserve, protect — **preservación** *nf, pl* **-ciones** : preservation — **preservativo** *nm* : condom
presidente, -ta *n* **1** : president **2** : chair, chairperson (of a meeting) — **presidencia** *nf* **1** : presidency **2** : chairmanship (of a meeting) — **presidencial** *adj* : presidential
presidio *nm* : prison — **presidiario, -ria** *n* : convict
presidir *vt* **1** : preside over, chair **2** PREDOMINAR : dominate
presión *nf, pl* **-siones 1** : pressure **2** ~ **arterial** : blood pressure **3** hacer ~ : press — **presionar** *vt* **1** : press **2** COACCIONAR : put pressure on
preso, -sa *adj* : imprisoned — ~ *n* : prisoner
prestar *vt* **1** : lend, loan **2** : give (aid) **3** ~ **atención** : pay attention — **prestado, -da** *adj* **1** : borrowed, on loan **2** pedir ~ : borrow — **prestamista** *nmf* : moneylender — **préstamo** *nm* : loan
prestidigitación *nf, pl* **-ciones** : sleight of hand — **prestidigitador, -dora** *n* : magician
prestigio *nm* : prestige — **prestigioso, -sa** *adj* : prestigious
presto, -ta *adj* : prompt, ready — **presto** *adv* : promptly, right away
presumir *vi* : presume — *vi* : boast, show off — **presumido, -da** *adj* : conceited, vain — **presunción** *nf, pl* **-ciones 1** : presumption **2** VANIDAD : vanity — **presunto, -ta** *adj* : presumed, alleged — **presuntuoso, -sa** *adj* : conceited
presuponer {60} *vt* : presuppose — **presupuesto** *nm* **1** : budget, estimate **2** SUPUESTO : assumption
presuroso, -sa *adj* : hasty, quick
pretender *vt* **1** : try to **2** AFIRMAR : claim **3** CORTEJAR : court, woo **4** ~ que : expect — **pretencioso, -sa** *adj* : pretentious — **pretendido** *adj* : supposed — **pretendiente** *nmf* **1** : candidate **2** : pretender (to a throne) — ~

nm : suitor — **pretensión** *nf, pl* **-siones 1** INTENCIÓN : intention, aspiration **2** : claim (to a throne, etc.) **3 pretensiones** *nfpl* : pretensions

pretérito *nm* : past (in grammar)

pretexto *nm* : pretext, excuse

prevalecer {53} *vi* : prevail — **prevaleciente** *adj* : prevailing, prevalent

prevenir {87} *vt* **1** : prevent **2** AVISAR : warn — **prevenirse** {87} *vr* ~ **contra** *or* ~ **de** : take precautions against — **prevención** *nf, pl* **-ciones 1** : prevention **2** PRECAUCIÓN : precaution **3** PREJUICIO : prejudice — **prevenido, -da** *adj* **1** : prepared, ready **2** PRECAVIDO : cautious — **preventivo, -va** *adj* : preventive

prever {88} *vt* **1** : foresee **2** PLANEAR : plan

previo, -via *adj* : previous, prior

previsible *adj* : foreseeable — **previsión** *nf, pl* **-siones 1** : foresight **2** PREDICCIÓN : prediction, forecast — **previsor, -sora** *adj* : farsighted, prudent

prieto, -ta *adj* **1** CEÑIDO : tight **2** *Lat fam* : dark-skinned

prima *nf* **1** : bonus **2** : (insurance) premium **3** → **primo**

primario, -ria *adj* **1** : primary **2 escuela primaria** : elementary school

primate *nm* : primate

primavera *nf* **1** : spring (season) **2** : primrose (flower) — **primaveral** *adj* : spring

primero, -ra *adj* (**primer** *before masculine singular nouns*) **1** : first **2** MEJOR : top, leading **3** PRINCIPAL : main, basic **4 de primera** : first-rate — ~ *n* **1** : first (person or thing) — **primero** *adv* **1** : first **2** MÁS BIEN : rather, sooner

primitivo, -va *adj* : primitive

primo, -ma *n* : cousin

primogénito, -ta *adj* & *n* : firstborn

primor *nm* : beautiful thing

primordial *adj* : basic, fundamental

primoroso, -sa *adj* **1** : exquisite, fine **2** HÁBIL : skillful

princesa *nf* : princess

principado *nm* : principality

principal *adj* : main, principal

príncipe *nm* : prince

principio *nm* **1** : principle **2** COMIENZO : beginning, start **3** ORIGEN : origin **4 al** ~ : at first **5 a** ~**s de** : at the beginning of — **principiante** *nmf* : beginner

pringar {52} *vt* : spatter (with grease) — **pringoso, -sa** *adj* : greasy

prioridad *nf* : priority

prisa *nf* **1** : hurry, rush **2 a** ~ *or* **de** ~

: quickly **3 a toda** ~ : as fast as possible **4 darse** ~ : hurry **5 tener** ~ : be in a hurry

prisión *nf, pl* **-siones 1** : prison **2** ENCARCELAMIENTO : imprisonment — **prisionero, -ra** *n* : prisoner

prisma *nm* : prism — **prismáticos** *nmpl* : binoculars

privar *vt* **1** : deprive **2** PROHIBIR : forbid **3** *Lat* : knock out — **privarse** *vr* : deprive oneself — **privación** *nf, pl* **-ciones** : deprivation — **privado, -da** *adj* : private — **privativo, -va** *adj* : exclusive

privilegio *nm* : privilege — **privilegiado, -da** *adj* : privileged

pro *prep* : for, in favor of — ~ *nm* **1** : pro, advantage **2 en** ~ **de** : for, in support of **3 los pros y los contras** : the pros and cons

proa *nf* : bow, prow

probabilidad *nf* : probability — **probable** *adj* : probable, likely — **probablemente** *adv* : probably

probar {19} *vt* **1** : try, test **2** : try on (clothing) **3** DEMOSTRAR : prove **4** DEGUSTAR : taste — *vi* : try — **probarse** *vr* : try on (clothing) — **probeta** *nf* : test tube

problema *nm* : problem — **problemático, -ca** *adj* : problematic

proceder *vi* **1** : proceed, act **2** : be appropriate **3** ~ **de** : come from — **procedencia** *nf* : origin — **procedente** *adj* ~ **de** : coming from, originating in — **procedimiento** *nm* **1** : procedure, method **2** : proceedings *pl* (in law)

procesar *vt* **1** : prosecute **2** : process (data) — **procesador** *nm* ~ **de textos** : word processor — **procesamiento** *nm* : processing — **procesión** *nf, pl* **-siones** : procession — **proceso** *nm* **1** : process **2** : trial, proceedings *pl* (in law)

proclamar *vt* : proclaim — **proclama** *nf* : proclamation — **proclamación** *nf, pl* **-ciones** : proclamation

procrear *vt* : procreate — **procreación** *nf, pl* **-ciones** : procreation

procurar *vt* **1** : try, endeavor **2** CONSEGUIR : obtain, procure — **procurador, -dora** *n* : attorney

prodigar {52} *vt* : lavish — **prodigio** *nm* : wonder, prodigy — **prodigioso, -sa** *adj* : prodigious

pródigo, -ga *adj* : extravagant, prodigal

producir {61} *vt* **1** : produce **2** CAUSAR : cause **3** : yield, bear (interest, fruit, etc.) — **producirse** *vr* : take place —

producción *nf, pl* **-ciones** : production — **productividad** *nf* : productivity — **productivo, -va** *adj* : productive — **producto** *nm* : product — **productor, -tora** *n* : producer

proeza *nf* : exploit

profanar *vt* : profane, desecrate — **profanación** *nf, pl* **-ciones** : desecration — **profano, -na** *adj* : profane

profecía *nf* : prophecy

proferir {76} *vt* **1** : utter **2** : hurl (insults)

profesar *vt* **1** : profess **2** : practice (a profession, etc.) — **profesión** *nf, pl* **-siones** : profession — **profesional** *adj & nmf* : professional — **profesor, -sora** *n* **1** : teacher **2** : professor (at a university, etc.) — **profesorado** *nm* **1** : teaching profession **2** PROFESORES : faculty

profeta *nm* : prophet — **profético, -ca** *adj* : prophetic — **profetisa** *nf* **1** : (female) prophet — **profetizar** {21} *vt* : prophesy

prófugo, -ga *adj & n* : fugitive

profundo, -da *adj* **1** HONDO : deep **2** : profound (of thoughts, etc.) — **profundamente** *adv* : deeply, profoundly — **profundidad** *nf* : depth — **profundizar** {21} *vt* : study in depth

profuso, -sa *adj* : profuse — **profusión** *nf, pl* **-siones** : profusion

progenie *nf* : progeny, offspring

programa *nm* **1** : program **2** : curriculum (in education) — **programación** *nf, pl* **-ciones** : programming — **programador, -dora** *n* : programmer — **programar** *vt* **1** : schedule **2** : program (a computer, etc.)

progreso *nm* : progress — **progresar** *vi* : (make) progress — **progresión** *nf, pl* **-ciones** : progression — **progresista** *adj & nmf* : progressive — **progresivo, -va** *adj* : progressive, gradual

prohibir {62} *vt* : prohibit, forbid — **prohibición** *nf, pl* **-ciones** : ban, prohibition — **prohibido, -da** *adj* : forbidden — **prohibitivo, -va** *adj* : prohibitive

prójimo *nm* : neighbor, fellow man

prole *nf* : offspring

proletariado *nm* : proletariat — **proletario, -ria** *adj & n* : proletarian

proliferar *vi* : proliferate — **proliferación** *nf, pl* **-ciones** : proliferation — **prolífico, -ca** *adj* : prolific

prolijo, -ja *adj* : wordy, long-winded

prólogo *nm* : prologue, foreword

prolongar {52} *vt* **1** : prolong **2** ALARGAR : lengthen — **prolongarse** *vr* : last, continue — **prolongación** *nf, pl* **-ciones** : extension

promedio *nm* : average

promesa *nf* : promise — **prometedor, -dora** *adj* : promising, hopeful — **prometer** *vt* : promise — *vi* : show promise — **prometerse** *vr* : get engaged — **prometido, -da** *adj* : engaged — ~ *n* : fiancé *m*, fiancée *f*

prominente *adj* : prominent — **prominencia** *nf* : prominence

promiscuo, -cua *adj* : promiscuous — **promiscuidad** *nf* : promiscuity

promocionar *vt* : promote — **promoción** *nf, pl* **-ciones** : promotion

promontorio *nm* : promontory

promover {47} *vt* **1** : promote **2** CAUSAR : cause — **promotor, -tora** *n* : promoter

promulgar {52} *vt* **1** : proclaim **2** : enact (a law)

pronombre *nm* : pronoun

pronosticar {72} *vt* : predict, forecast — **pronóstico** *nm* **1** : prediction, forecast **2** : (medical) prognosis

pronto, -ta *adj* **1** : quick, prompt **2** PREPARADO : ready — **pronto** *adv* **1** : soon **2** RAPIDAMENTE : quickly, promptly **3** de ~ : suddenly **4** por lo ~ : for the time being **5** tan ~ como : as soon as

pronunciar *vt* **1** : pronounce **2** : give, deliver (a speech) — **pronunciarse** *vr* **1** : declare oneself **2** SUBLEVARSE : revolt — **pronunciación** *nf, pl* **-ciones** : pronunciation

propagación *nf, pl* **-ciones** : propagation

propaganda *nf* **1** : propaganda **2** PUBLICIDAD : advertising

propagar {52} *vt* : propagate, spread — **propagarse** *vr* : propagate

propano *nm* : propane

proparse *vr* : go too far

propensión *nf, pl* **-siones** : inclination, propensity — **propenso, -sa** *adj* : prone, inclined

propiamente *adv* : exactly

propicio, -cia *adj* : favorable, propitious

propiedad *nf* **1** : property **2** PERTINENCIA : ownership, possession — **propietario, -ria** *n* : owner, proprietor

propina *nf* : tip

propinar *vt* : give, deal (a blow, etc.)

propio, -pia *adj* **1** : own **2** APROPIADO : proper, appropriate **3** CARACTERÍSTICO : characteristic, typical **4** MISMO : himself, herself, oneself

proponer {60} *vt* **1** : propose **2** : nominate (a person) — **proponerse** *vr* : propose, intend

proporción *nf, pl* **-ciones** : proportion — **proporcionado, -da** *adj* : proportionate — **proporcional** *adj* : proportional — **proporcionar** *vt* 1 : provide 2 AJUSTAR : adapt, proportion

proposición *nf, pl* **-ciones** : proposal, proposition

propósito *nm* 1 : purpose, intention 2 a ~ : incidentally, by the way 3 a ~ : on purpose, intentionally

propuesta *nf* 1 : proposal 2 : offer (of employment, etc.)

propulsar *vt* 1 : propel, drive 2 PROMOVER : promote — **propulsión** *nf, pl* **-siones** : propulsion

prorrogar {52} *vt* 1 : extend APLAZAR : postpone — **prórroga** *nf* 1 : extension, deferment 2 : extension (in sports)

prorrumpir *vi* : burst forth, break out

prosa *nf* : prose

proscribir {33} *vt* 1 : prohibit, ban 2 DESTERRAR : exile — **proscripción** *nf, pl* **-ciones** 1 : ban 2 DESTIERRO : banishment — **proscrito, -ta** *adj* : banned — ~ *n* : exile, outlaw

proseguir {75} *v* : continue — **prosecución** *nf, pl* **-ciones** : continuation

prospección *nf, pl* **-ciones** : prospecting, exploration

prospecto *nm* : prospectus

prosperar *vi* : prosper, thrive — **prosperidad** *nf* : prosperity — **próspero, -ra** *adj* : prosperous, flourishing

prostituir {41} *vt* : prostitute — **prostitución** *nf, pl* **-ciones** : prostitution — **prostituta** *nf* : prostitute

protagonista *nmf* : protagonist — **protagonizar** *vt* : star in

proteger {15} *vt* : protect — **protegerse** *vr* : protect oneself — **protección** *nf, pl* **-ciones** : protection — **protector, -tora** *adj* : protective — ~ *n* : protector — **protegido, -da** *n* : protégé

proteína *nf* : protein

protesta *v* : protest — **protesta** *nf* : protest — **protestante** *adj & nmf* : Protestant

protocolo *nm* : protocol

prototipo *nm* : prototype

protuberancia *nf* : protuberance — **protuberante** *adj* : protuberant

provecho *nm* 1 : benefit, advantage 2 ¡buen ~! : enjoy your meal! — **provechoso, -sa** *adj* : profitable, beneficial

proveer {63} *vt* : provide, supply — **proveedor, -dora** *n* : supplier

provenir {87} *vi* ~ **de** : come from

proverbio *nm* : proverb — **proverbial** *adj* : proverbial

providencia *nf* 1 : providence 2 PRECAUCIÓN : precaution — **providencial** *adj* : providential

provincia *nf* : province — **provincial** *adj* : provincial — **provinciano, -na** *adj* : provincial, parochial

provisión *nf, pl* **-siones** : provision — **provisional** *adj* : provisional

provocar {72} *vt* 1 : provoke, cause 2 IRRITAR : irritate — **provocación** *nf, pl* **-ciones** : provocation — **provocativo, -va** *adj* : provocative

próximo, -ma *adj* 1 CERCANO : near 2 SIGUIENTE : next — **próximamente** *adv* : shortly, soon — **proximidad** *nf* 1 : proximity 2 ~es *nfpl* : vicinity

proyectar *vt* 1 : plan 2 LANZAR : throw, hurl 3 : cast (light) 4 : show (a film) — **proyección** *nf, pl* **-ciones** : projection — **proyectil** *nm* : missile — **proyecto** *nm* : plan, project — **proyector** *nm* : projector

prudencia *nf* : prudence, care — **prudente** *adj* : prudent, sensible

prueba *nf* 1 : proof, evidence 2 : test (in education, medicine, etc.) 3 : event (in sports) 4 a ~ **de agua** : waterproof

psicoanálisis *nm* : psychoanalysis — **psicoanalista** *nmf* : psychoanalyst — **psicoanalizar** {21} *vt* : psychoanalyze

psicología *nf* : psychology — **psicológico, -ca** *adj* : psychological — **psicólogo, -ga** *n* : psychologist

psicópata *nmf* : psychopath

psicosis *nfs & pl* : psychosis

psicoterapia *nf* : psychotherapy — **psicoterapeuta** *nmf* : psychotherapist

psicótico, -ca *adj & n* : psychotic

psiquiatría *nf* : psychiatry — **psiquiatra** *nmf* : psychiatrist — **psiquiátrico, -ca** *adj* : psychiatric

psíquico, -ca *adj* : psychic

púa *nf* 1 : sharp point 2 : tooth (of a comb) 3 : thorn (of a plant), quill (of a porcupine, etc.) 4 : (guitar) pick

pubertad *nf* : puberty

publicar {72} *vt* 1 : publish 2 DIVULGAR : divulge, disclose — **publicación** *nf, pl* **-ciones** : publication

publicidad *nf* 1 : publicity 2 : advertising (in marketing) — **publicista** *nmf* : publicist — **publicitar** *vt* 1 : publicize 2 : advertise (a product, etc.) — **publicitario, -ria** *adj* : advertising

público, -ca *adj* : public — **público** *nm* 1 : public 2 : audience (of theater, etc.), spectators *pl* (of sports)

puchero *nm* 1 : (cooking) pot 2 GUISADO : stew 3 **hacer ~s** : pout

púdico, -ca *adj* : modest

pudiente *adj* : wealthy

pudín *nm, pl* **-dines** : pudding

pudor *nm* : modesty — **pudoroso, -sa** *adj* : modest

pudrir {59} *vt* **1** : rot **2** *fam* : annoy — **pudrirse** *vr* : rot

pueblo *nm* **1** : town, village **2** NACIÓN : people, nation

puente *nm* **1** : bridge **2 hacer ～** : have a long weekend **3 ～ levadizo** : drawbridge

puerco, -ca *n* **1** : pig **2 puerco espín** : porcupine — **～** *adj* : dirty, filthy

pueril *adj* : childish

puerro *nm* : leek

puerta *nf* **1** : door, gate **2 a ～ cerrada** : behind closed doors

puerto *nm* **1** : port **2** : (mountain) pass **3** REFUGIO : haven

puertorriqueño, -ña *adj* : Puerto Rican

pues *conj* **1** : since, because **2** POR LO TANTO : so, therefore **3** (*used interjectionally*) : well, then

puesta *nf* **1 ～ a punto** : tune-up **2 ～ de sol** : sunset **3 ～ en marcha** : starting up — **puesto, -ta** *adj* **1** : put, set **2** VESTIDO : dressed — **puesto** *nm* **1** : place **2** EMPLEO : position, job **3** : stand, stall (in a market) **4 ～ avanzado** : outpost — **～ que** *conj* : since, given that

púgil *nm* : boxer

pugnar *vi* : fight — **pugna** *nf* : fight, battle

pulcro, -cra *adj* : tidy, neat

pulga *nf* **1** : flea **2 tener malas ～s** : have a bad temper

pulgada *nf* : inch — **pulgar** *nm* **1** : thumb **2** : big toe

pulir *vt* **1** : polish **2** REFINAR : touch up, perfect

pulla *nf* : cutting remark, gibe

pulmón *nm, pl* **-mones** : lung — **pulmonar** *adj* : pulmonary — **pulmonía** *nf* : pneumonia

pulpa *nf* : pulp

pulpería *nf Lat* : grocery store

púlpito *nm* : pulpit

pulpo *nm* : octopus

pulsar *vt* **1** : press (a button), strike (a key) **2** : play (music) — **pulsación** *nf, pl* **-ciones 1** : beat, throb **2** : keystroke (on a typewriter, etc.)

pulsera *nf* : bracelet

pulso *nm* **1** : pulse **2** : steadiness (of hand)

pulular *vi* : swarm

pulverizar {21} *vt* **1** : pulverize, crush **2** : spray (a liquid) — **pulverizador** *nm* : atomizer, spray

puma *nf* : puma

punitivo, -va *adj* : punitive

punta *nf* **1** : tip, end **2** : point (of a needle, etc.) **3 ～ del dedo** : fingertip **4 sacar ～ a** : sharpen

puntada *nf* **1** : stitch **2 ～s** *nfpl* : seam

puntal *nm* : prop, support

puntapié *nm* : kick

puntear *vt* : pluck (a guitar)

puntería *nf* : aim, marksmanship

puntiagudo, -da *adj* : sharp, pointed

puntilla *nf* **1** : lace edging **2 de ～s** : on tiptoe

punto *nm* **1** : dot, point **2** : period (in punctuation) **3** ASUNTO : item, question **4** LUGAR : spot, place **5** MOMENTO : moment **6** : point (in a score) **7** PUNTADA : stitch **8 a las dos en ～** : at two o'clock sharp **9 dos ～s** : colon **10 hasta cierto ～** : up to a point **11 ～ de partida** : starting point **12 ～ muerto** : deadlock **13 ～ y coma** : semicolon

puntuación *nf, pl* **-ciones 1** : punctuation **2** : scoring, score (in sports)

puntual *adj* **1** : prompt, punctual **2** EXACTO : accurate, exact — **puntualidad** *nf* **1** : punctuality **2** EXACTITUD : accuracy

puntuar {3} *vt* : punctuate — *vi* : score (in sports)

punzar {21} *vt* : prick, puncture — **punzada** *nf* **1** PINCHAZO : prick **2** : sharp pain — **punzante** *adj* **1** : sharp **2** MORDAZ : biting, caustic

puñado *nm* **1** : handful **2 a ～** : by the handful

puñal *nm* : dagger — **puñalada** *nf* : stab

puño *nm* **1** : fist **2** : cuff (of a shirt) **3** : handle, hilt (of a sword, etc.) — **puñetazo** *nm* : punch (with the fist)

pupila *nf* : pupil (of the eye)

pupitre *nm* : desk

puré *nm* **1** : purée **2 ～ de papas** *or* **～ de patatas** *Spain* : mashed potatoes

pureza *nf* : purity

purga *nf* : purge — **purgar** {52} *vt* : purge — **purgatorio** *nm* : purgatory

purificar {72} *vt* : purify — **purificación** *nf, pl* **-ciones** : purification

puritano, -na *adj* : puritanical — **～** *n* : puritan

puro, -ra *adj* **1** : pure **2** SIMPLE : plain, simple **3** *Lat fam* : only, just — **puro** *nm* : cigar

púrpura *nf* : purple — **purpúreo, -rea** *adj* : purple

pus *nm* : pus

pusilánime *adj* : cowardly

puta *nf* : whore

putrefacción *nf, pl* **-ciones** : putrefaction, rot — **pútrido, -da** *adj* : putrid, rotten

Q

q *nf* : q, 18th letter of the Spanish alphabet

que *conj* **1** : that **2** (*in comparisons*) : than **3** (*introducing a reason or cause*) : so that, or else **4 es ~** : the thing is that **5 yo ~ tú** : if I were you — *pron* **1** (*referring to persons*) : who, whom **2** (*referring to things*) : that, which **3 el (la, lo, las, los) ~** : he (she, it, they) who, whoever, the one(s) that

qué *adv* **1** : how, what **2 ¡~ lindo!** : how lovely! — *adj* : what, which — *pron* **1** : what **2 ¿~ crees?** : what do you think?

quebrar {55} *vt* : break — *vi* : go bankrupt — **quebrarse** *vr* : break — **quebrada** *nf* : ravine, gorge — **quebradizo, -za** *adj* : breakable, fragile — **quebrado, -da** *adj* **1** : bankrupt **2** : rough, uneven (of land, etc.) **3** ROTO : broken — **quebrado** *nm* : fraction — **quebradura** *nf* : crack, fissure — **quebrantar** *vt* **1** : break **2** DEBILITAR : weaken — **quebranto** *nm* **1** : harm, damage **2** AFLICCIÓN : grief, pain

queda *nf* → **toque**

quedar *vi* PERMANECER : remain, stay **2** ESTAR : be **3** FALTAR : be left **4** : fit, look (of clothing, etc.) **5 no queda lejos** : it's not far **6 ~ en** : agree to, agree on — **quedarse** *vr* **1** : stay **2 ~ con** : keep

quedo, -da *adj* : quiet, still — **quedo** *adv* : softly, quietly

quehacer *nm* **1** : task **2 ~es** *nmpl* : chores

queja *nf* : complaint — **quejarse** *vr* **1** : complain **2** GEMIR : moan, groan — **quejido** *nm* : moan, whimper — **quejoso, -sa** *adj* : complaining, whining

quemar *vt* **1** : burn **2** MALGASTAR : squander — *vi* : burn — **quemarse** *vr* **1** : burn oneself **2** : burn (up) **3** : get sunburned — **quemado, -da** *adj* **1** : burned **2** AGOTADO : burned-out **3 estar ~** : be fed up — **quemador** *nm* : burner — **quemadura** *nf* : burn — **quemarropa: a ~** *adj & adv phr* : point-blank

querella *nf* **1** : dispute, quarrel **2** : charge (in law)

querer {64} *vt* **1** : want **2** AMAR : love **3**

~ decir : mean **4 ¿quieres pasarme la leche?** : please pass the milk **5 sin ~** : unintentionally — **~** *nm* : love — **querido, -da** *adj* : dear, beloved — *n* **1** : darling **2** AMANTE : lover

queroseno *nm* : kerosene

querubín *nm, pl* **-bines** : cherub

queso *nm* : cheese — **quesadilla** *nf Lat* : quesadilla

quicio *nm* **1 estar fuera de ~** : be beside oneself **2 sacar de ~** : drive crazy

quiebra *nf* **1** : break **2** BANCARROTA : bankruptcy

quien *pron, pl* **quienes 1** (*subject*) : who **2** (*object*) : whom **3** (*indefinite*) : whoever, anyone, some people

quién *pron, pl* **quiénes 1** (*subject*) : who **2** (*object*) : whom **3 ¿de ~ es este lápiz?** : whose pencil is this?

quienquiera *pron, pl* **quienesquiera** : whoever, whomever

quieto, -ta *adj* **1** : calm, quiet **2** INMÓVIL : still — **quietud** *nf* : stillness

quijada *nf* : jaw, jawbone (of an animal)

quilate *nm* : carat, karat

quilla *nf* : keel

quimera *nf* : illusion — **quimérico, -ca** *adj* : fanciful

química *nf* : chemistry — **químico, -ca** *adj* : chemical — *n* : chemist

quince *adj & nm* : fifteen — **quinceañero, -ra** *n* : fifteen-year-old, teenager — **quincena** *nf* : two-week period, fortnight — **quincenal** *adj* : semimonthly, twice a month

quincuagésimo, -ma *adj & n* : fiftieth

quinientos, -tas *adj* : five hundred — **quinientos** *nms & pl* : five hundred

quinina *nf* : quinine

quinqué *nm* : oil lamp

quinta *nf* : country house, villa

quintaesencia *nf* : quintessence

quinteto *nm* : quintet

quinto, -ta *adj & n* : fifth — **quinto** *nm* : fifth

quiosco *nm* : kiosk, newsstand

quiropráctico, -ca *n* : chiropractor

quirúrgico, -ca *adj* : surgical

quisquilloso, -sa *adj* : fastidious, fussy

quiste *nm* : cyst

quitar *vt* **1** : remove, take away **2** : take off (clothes) **3** : get rid of, relieve (pain, etc.) — **quitarse** *vr* **1** : withdraw, leave **2** : take off (one's clothes) **3** ~ **de** : give up (a habit) **4** ~ **de encima** : get rid of — **quitaesmalte** *nm* : nail-polish remover — **quita-**

manchas *nms & pl* : stain remover — **quitanieves** *nm* : snowplow — **quitasol** *nm* : parasol
quizá *or* **quizás** *adv* : maybe, perhaps

R

r *nf* : r, 19th letter of the Spanish alphabet
rábano *nm* **1** : radish **2** ~ **picante** : horseradish
rabí *nmf, pl* **-bíes** : rabbi
rabia *nf* **1** : rage, anger **2** : rabies (disease) — **rabiar** *vi* **1** : be furious **2** : be in great pain **3** ~ **por** : be dying for — **rabioso, -sa** *adj* **1** : enraged, furious **2** : rabid, having rabies
rabino, -na *n* : rabbi
rabo *nm* **1** : tail **2 el ~ del ojo** : the corner of one's eye
racha *nf* **1** : gust of wind **2** SERIE : series, string — **racheado, -da** *adj* : gusty
racial *adj* : racial
racimo *nm* : bunch, cluster
raciocinio *nm* : reason, reasoning
ración *nf, pl* **-ciones 1** : share, ration **2** : helping (of food)
racional *adj* : rational — **racionalizar** {21} *vt* : rationalize
racionar *vt* : ration — **racionamiento** *nm* : rationing
racismo *nm* : racism — **racista** *adj & nmf* : racist
radar *nm* : radar
radiación *nf, pl* **-ciones** : radiation
radiactivo, -va *adj* : radioactive — **radiactividad** *nf* : radioactivity
radiador *nm* : radiator
radiante *adj* : radiant
radical *adj & nmf* : radical
radicar {72} *vi* ~ **en** : lie in, be rooted in
radio *nm* **1** : radius **2** : spoke (of a wheel) **3** : radium (element) — ~ *nmf* : radio
radioactivo, -va *adj* : radioactive — **radioactividad** *nf* : radioactivity
radiodifusión *nf, pl* **-siones** : broadcasting — **radioemisora** *nf* : radio station — **radioescucha** *nmf* : listener — **radiofónico, -ca** *adj* : radio
radiografía *nf* : X ray — **radiografiar** {85} *vt* : x-ray
radiología *nf* : radiology — **radiólogo, -ga** *n* : radiologist
raer {65} *vt* : scrape off
ráfaga *nf* **1** : gust (of wind) **2** : flash (of light)

raído, -da *adj* : worn, shabby
raíz *nf, pl* **raíces 1** : root **2** ORIGEN : origin, source **3 echar raíces** : take root
raja *nf* **1** : crack, slit **2** RODAJA : slice — **rajar** *vt* : crack, split — **rajarse** *vr* **1** : crack, split open **2** *fam* : back out
rajatabla: a ~ *adv phr* : strictly, to the letter
ralea *nf* : sort, kind
ralentí *nm* : neutral (gear)
rallar *vt* : grate — **rallador** *nm* : grater
rama *nf* : branch — **ramaje** *nm* : branches *pl* — **ramal** *nm* **1** : branch (of a railroad, etc.) — **ramificarse** {72} *vr* : branch (off) — **ramillete** *nm* **1** : bouquet **2** GRUPO : cluster, bunch — **ramo** *nm* **1** : branch **2** RAMILLETE : bouquet
rampa *nf* : ramp, incline
rana *nf* **1** : frog **2** ~ **toro** : bullfrog
rancho *nm* : ranch, farm — **ranchero, -ra** *n* : rancher, farmer
rancio, -cia *adj* **1** : rancid **2** : aged (of wine)
rango *nm* **1** : rank **2** : (social) standing
ranúnculo *nm* : buttercup
ranura *nf* : groove, slot
rapar *vt* **1** : shave **2** : crop (hair)
rapaz *adj, pl* **-paces** : rapacious, predatory
rápido, -da *adj* : rapid, quick — **rápidamente** *adv* : rapidly, fast — **rapidez** *nf* : speed — **rápido** *adv* : quickly, fast — ~ *nm* **1** : express train **2** ~**s** *nmpl* : rapids
rapiña *nf* **1** : plunder **2 ave de** ~ : bird of prey
rapsodia *nf* : rhapsody
raptar *vt* : kidnap — **rapto** *nm* : kidnapping — **raptor, -tora** *n* : kidnapper
raqueta *nf* : racket (in sports)
raro, -ra *adj* **1** : rare **2** EXTRAÑO : odd, strange — **raramente** *adv* : rarely, infrequently — **rareza** *nf* : rarity
ras *nm* **a** ~ **de** : level with
rascacielos *nms & pl* : skyscraper
rascar {72} *vt* **1** : scratch **2** RASPAR : scrape — **rascarse** *vr* : scratch oneself
rasgar {52} *vt* : rip, tear — **rasgarse** *vr* : rip

rasgo *nm* **1** : stroke (of a pen) **2** CARAC-
TERÍSTICA : trait, characteristic **3** ~**s**
nmpl FACCIONES : features

rasguear *vt* : strum

rasguñar *vt* : scratch — **rasguño** *nm*
: scratch

raso, -sa *adj* **1** : level, flat **2** : low (of a
flight) **3 soldado raso** : private (in the
army) — **raso** *nm* : satin

raspar *vt* **1** : scrape **2** LIMAR : file down,
smooth — *vi* : be rough — **raspadura**
nf **1** : scratch **2** ~**s** *nfpl* : scrapings

rastra *nf* **1** : rake **2 a** ~**s** : unwillingly
— **rastrear** *vt* : track, trace — **ras-
trero, -ra** *adj* **1** : creeping **2** DESPRE-
CIABLE : despicable — **rastrillar** *vt*
: rake — **rastrillo** *nm* : rake — **rastro**
nm **1** : trail, track **2** SEÑAL : sign

rasurar *vt* *Lat* : shave — **rasurarse** *vr*
Lat : shave

rata *nf* : rat

ratear *vt* : steal — **ratero, -ra** *n* : thief

ratificar {72} *vt* : ratify — **ratificación**
nf, pl **-ciones** : ratification

rato *nm* **1** : while **2 al poco** ~ : shortly after **3 pasar el** ~ : pass the time

ratón *nm, pl* **-tones** : mouse — **ratonera** *nf* : mousetrap

raudal *nm* **1** : torrent **2 a** ~**es** : in
abundance — **raudo, -da** *adj* : swift

raya *nf* **1** : line **2** LISTA : stripe **3** : part
(in the hair) — **rayar** *vt* : scratch — *vi*
1 al ~ **el día** : at daybreak **2** ~ **en**
: border on — **rayarse** *vr* : get
scratched

rayo *nm* **1** : ray, beam **2** : bolt of lightning **3** ~**s X** : X rays

rayón *nm* : rayon

raza *nf* **1** : (human) race **2** : breed (of
animals) **3 de** ~ : thoroughbred,
pedigreed

razón *nf, pl* **-zones 1** : reason **2 dar** ~
: inform **3 en** ~ **de** : because of **4
tener** ~ : be right — **razonable** *adj*
: reasonable — **razonamiento** *nm*
: reasoning — **razonar** *v* : reason,
think

reacción *nf, pl* **-ciones** : reaction —
reaccionar *vi* : react — **reaccionario,
-ria** *adj & n* : reactionary

reacio, -cia *adj* : resistant, stubborn

reactivar *vt* : reactivate, revive

reactor *nm* **1** : jet (airplane) **2** ~ **nuclear** : nuclear reactor

reajustar *vt* : readjust — **reajuste** *nm*
: readjustment

real *adj* **1** : royal **2** VERDADERO : real,
true

realce *nm* **1** : relief **2 dar** ~ : highlight

realeza *nf* : royalty

realidad *nf* **1** : reality **2 en** ~ : actually, in fact

realismo *nm* : realism — **realista** *adj*
: realistic — ~ *nmf* : realist

realizar {21} *vt* **1** : carry out **2** : achieve
(a goal) **3** : produce (a film or play) **4**
: realize (a profit) — **realizarse** *vr* **1**
: fulfill oneself **2** : come true (of a
dream, etc.) — **realización** *nf, pl*
-ciones : execution, realization

realmente *adv* : really, actually

realzar {21} *vt* : highlight, enhance

reanimar *vt* : revive

reanudar *vt* : resume, renew — **reanudarse** *vr* : resume

reaparecer {53} *vi* : reappear — **rea-
parición** *nf, pl* **-ciones** : reappearance

reavivar *vt* : revive

rebajar *vt* **1** : lower, reduce **2** HUMILLAR
: humiliate — **rebajarse** *vr* **1** : humble
oneself **2** ~ **a** : stoop to — **rebaja** *nf*
1 : reduction **2** DESCUENTO : discount **3**
~**s** *nfpl* : sales

rebanada *nf* : slice

rebanar *vt* : slice

rebaño *nm* **1** : herd **2** : flock (of sheep)

rebasar *vt* : surpass, exceed

rebatir *vt* : refute

rebelarse *vr* : rebel — **rebelde** *adj* : rebellious — ~ *nmf* : rebel — **rebeldía**
nf : rebelliousness — **rebelión** *nf, pl*
-liones : rebellion

reblandecer *vt* : soften

rebobinar *vt* : rewind

rebosar *vt* **1** : overflow **2** ~ **de** : be
bursting with — *vi* : overflow with

rebotar *vi* : bounce, rebound — **rebote**
nm **1** : bounce **2 de** ~ : on the rebound

rebozar {21} *vt* : coat in batter

rebuscado, -da *adj* : pretentious

rebuznar *vi* : bray

recabar *vt* **1** : obtain, collect **2** ~ **fondos** : raise money

recado *nm* **1** MENSAJE : message **2**
Spain : errand

recaer {13} *vi* **1** : relapse **2** ~ **sobre**
: fall on — **recaída** *nf* : relapse

recalcar {72} *vt* : emphasize, stress

recalcitrante *adj* : recalcitrant

recalentar {55} *vt* **1** : overheat **2** : re-
heat, warm up (food) — **recalentarse**
vr : overheat

recámara *nf* **1** : chamber (of a firearm)
2 *Lat* : bedroom

recambio *nm* **1** : spare part **2** : refill (for
a pen, etc.)

recapitular *vt* : recapitulate, sum up —
recapitulación *nf, pl* **-ciones** : reca-
pitulation

recargar {52} *vt* **1** : overload **2**

: recharge (a battery), reload (a firearm, etc.) — **recargado, -da** *adj* : overly elaborate — **recargo** *nm* : surcharge

recato *nm* : modesty — **recatado, -da** *adj* : modest, demure

recaudar *vt* : collect — **recaudación** *nf, pl* **-ciones** : collection — **recaudador, -dora** *n* ~ **de impuestos** : tax collector

recelar *vt* : distrust, fear — **recelo** *nm* : distrust, suspicion — **receloso, -sa** *adj* : distrustful, suspicious

recepción *nf, pl* **-ciones** : reception — **recepcionista** *nmf* : receptionist

receptáculo *nm* : receptacle

receptivo, -va *adj* : receptive — **receptor, -tora** *n* : recipient — **receptor** *nm* : receiver (of a radio, etc.)

recesión *nf, pl* **-siones** : recession

receso *nm* Lat : recess, adjournment

receta *nf* 1 : recipe 2 : prescription (in medicine)

rechazar {21} *vt* 1 : reject, refuse 2 REPELER : repel 3 : reflect (light) — **rechazo** *nm* 1 : rejection

rechinar *vi* 1 : squeak, creak 2 : grind, gnash (one's teeth)

rechoncho, -cha *adj fam* : chubby

recibir *vt* 1 : receive 2 ACOGER : welcome — *vi* : receive visitors — **recibidor** *nm* : vestibule, entrance hall — **recibimiento** *nm* : reception, welcome — **recibo** *nm* : receipt

reciclar *vt* 1 : recycle 2 : retrain (workers) — **reciclaje** *nm* : recycling

recién *adv* 1 : newly, recently 2 ~ **casados** : newlyweds — **reciente** *adj* : recent — **recientemente** *adv* : recently

recinto *nm* 1 : enclosure 2 ÁREA : area, site

recio, -cia *adj* : tough, strong

recipiente *nm* : container, receptacle — ~ *nmf* : recipient

recíproco, -ca *adj* : reciprocal, mutual

recitar *vt* : recite — **recital** *nm* : recital

reclamar *vt* : demand, ask for — *vi* : complain — **reclamación** *nf, pl* **-ciones** 1 : claim, demand 2 QUEJA : complaint — **reclamo** *nm* 1 : lure (in hunting) 2 Lat : inducement, attraction

reclinar *vt* : rest, lean — **reclinarse** *vr* : recline, lean back

recluir {41} *vt* : confine, lock up — **recluirse** *vr* : shut oneself away — **reclusión** *nf, pl* **-siones** : imprisonment — **recluso, -sa** *n* : prisoner

recluta *nmf* : recruit — **reclutamiento** *nm* : recruitment — **reclutar** *vt* : recruit, enlist

recobrar *vt* : recover, regain — **recobrarse** *vr* ~ **de** : recover from

recodo *nm* : bend

recoger {15} *vt* 1 : collect, gather 2 COGER : pick up 3 LIMPIAR, ORDENAR : clean up, tidy (up) — **recogerse** *vr* : retire, withdraw — **recogedor** *nm* : dustpan — **recogido, -da** *adj* : quiet, secluded

recolección *nf, pl* **-ciones** 1 : collection 2 COSECHA : harvest

recomendar {55} *vt* : recommend — **recomendación** *nf, pl* **-ciones** : recommendation

recompensar *vt* : reward — **recompensa** *nf* : reward

reconciliar *vt* : reconcile — **reconciliarse** *vr* : be reconciled — **reconciliación** *nf, pl* **-ciones** : reconciliation

recóndito, -ta *adj* : hidden

reconfortar *vt* : comfort

reconocer {18} *vt* 1 : recognize 2 ADMITIR : admit 3 EXAMINAR : examine — **reconocible** *adj* : recognizable — **reconocido, -da** *adj* 1 : recognized, accepted 2 AGRADECIDO : grateful — **reconocimiento** *nm* 1 : recognition 2 AGRADECIMIENTO : gratitude 3 : (medical) examination

reconsiderar *vt* : reconsider

reconstruir {41} *vt* : reconstruct — **reconstrucción** *nf, pl* **-ciones** : reconstruction

recopilar *vt* RECOGER : collect, gather 2 : compile — **recopilación** *nf, pl* **-ciones** : collection, compilation

récord *nm, pl* **-cords** : record

recordar {19} *vt* 1 ACORDARSE DE : remember 2 : remind — *vi* : remember — **recordatorio** *nm* : reminder

recorrer *vt* 1 : travel through 2 : cover (a distance) — **recorrido** *nm* 1 : journey, trip 2 TRAYECTO : route, course

recortar *vt* 1 : reduce 2 CORTAR : cut (out) 3 : trim (hair) — **recortarse** *vr* : stand out — **recorte** *nm* 1 : cut, cutting 2 ~**s de periódicos** : newspaper clippings

recostar {19} *vt* : lean, rest — **recostarse** *vr* : lie down

recoveco *nm* 1 : bend 2 RINCÓN : nook, corner

recrear *vt* 1 : recreate 2 ENTRETENER : entertain — **recrearse** *vr* : to enjoy oneself — **recreativo, -va** *adj* : recreational — **recreo** *nm* 1 : recreation, amusement 2 : recess, break (at school)

recriminar *vt* : reproach
recrudecer {53} *vi* : worsen — **recrudecerse** *vr* : intensify, get worse
rectángulo *nm* : rectangle — **rectangular** *adj* : rectangular
rectificar {72} *vt* **1** : rectify, correct **2** AJUSTAR : straighten (out) — **rectitud** *nf* **1** : straightness **2** : (moral) rectitude — **recto, -ta** *adj* **1** : straight **2** INTEGRO : upright, honorable — **recto** *nm* : rectum
rector, -tora *adj* : governing, managing — **~** *n* : rector — **rectoría** *nf* : rectory
recubrir {2} *vt* : cover, coat
recuento *nm* : count, recount
recuerdo *nm* **1** : memory **2** : souvenir, remembrance (of a journey, etc.) **3** **~s** *nmpl* SALUDOS : regards
recuperar *vt* **1** : recover, retrieve **2** **el tiempo perdido** : make up for lost time — **recuperarse** *vr* **de** : recover from — **recuperación** *nf, pl* **-ciones 1** : recovery **2** **~ de datos** : data retrieval
recurrir *vi* **a** : turn to (a person), resort to (force, etc.) — **recurso** *nm* **1** : recourse, resort **2** : appeal (in law) **3** **~s** *nmpl* : resources
red *nf* **1** : net **2** SISTEMA : network, system **3 la Red** : the Internet
redactar *vt* : write (up), draft — **redacción** *nf, pl* **-ciones 1** : writing, drafting **2** : editing (of a newspaper, etc.) — **redactor, -tora** *n* : editor
redada *nf* **1** : (police) raid **2** : catch (in fishing)
redescubrir {2} *vt* : rediscover
redención *nf, pl* **-ciones** : redemption — **redentor, -tora** *adj* : redeeming
redil *nm* : fold, pen
rédito *nm* : interest, yield
redoblar *vt* : redouble
redomado, -da *adj* : out-and-out
redondear *vt* **1** : make round **2** : round off (a number, etc.) — **redonda** *nf* **1** : whole note (in music) **2 a la ~** : in the surrounding area — **redondel** *nm* **1** : ring, circle **2** : bullring — **redondo, -da** *adj* **1** : round **2** PERFECTO : excellent
reducir {61} *vt* : reduce — **reducirse** *vr* **a** : come down to, amount to — **reducción** *nf, pl* **-ciones** : reduction — **reducido, -da** *adj* **1** : reduced, limited **2** PEQUEÑO : small
redundante *adj* : redundant — **redundancia** *nf* : redundancy
reedición *nf, pl* **-ciones** : reprint
reembolsar *vt* : refund, reimburse,

repay — **reembolso** *nm* : refund, reimbursement
reemplazar {21} *vt* : replace — **reemplazo** *nm* : replacement
reencarnación *nf, pl* **-ciones** : reincarnation
reencuentro *nm* : reunion
reestructurar *vt* : restructure
refaccionar *vt Lat* : repair, renovate — **refacciones** *nfpl Lat* : repairs, renovations
referir {76} *vt* **1** : tell **2** REMITIR : refer — **referirse** *vr* **a** : refer to — **referencia** *nf* **1** : reference **2 hacer ~ a** : refer to — **referéndum** *nm, pl* **-dums** : referendum — **referente** *adj* **~ a** : concerning
refinar *vt* : refine — **refinado, -da** *adj* : refined — **refinamiento** *nm* : refinement — **refinería** *nf* : refinery
reflector *nm* **1** : reflector **2** : spotlight, searchlight, floodlight
reflejar *vt* : reflect — **reflejarse** *vr* : be reflected — **reflejo** *nm* **1** : reflection **2** : (physical) reflex **3 ~s** *nmpl* : highlights (in hair)
reflexionar *vi* : reflect, think — **reflexión** *nf, pl* **-xiones** : reflection, thought — **reflexivo, -va** *adj* **1** : reflective, thoughtful **2** : reflexive (in grammar)
reflujo *nm* : ebb (tide)
reforma *nf* **1** : reform **2 ~s** *nfpl* : renovations — **reformador, -dora** *n* : reformer — **reformar** *vt* **1** : reform **2** : renovate, repair (a house, etc.) — **reformarse** *vr* : mend one's ways — **reformatorio** *nm* : reformatory
reforzar {36} *vt* : reinforce
refrán *nm, pl* **-franes** : proverb, saying
refregar {49} *vt* : scrub
refrenar *vt* **1** : rein in (a horse) **2** CONTENER : restrain — **refrenarse** *vr* : restrain oneself
refrendar *vt* : approve, endorse
refrescar {72} *vt* **1** : refresh, cool **2** : brush up on (knowledge) — *vi* : turn cooler — **refrescante** *adj* : refreshing — **refresco** *nm* : soft drink
refriega *nf* : scuffle, skirmish
refrigerar *vt* **1** : refrigerate **2** CLIMATIZAR : air-condition — **refrigeración** *nf, pl* **-ciones** : refrigeration **2** AIRE ACONDICIONADO : air-conditioning — **refrigerador** *nmf Lat* : refrigerator — **refrigerio** *nm* : refreshments *pl*
refrito, -ta *adj* : refried — **refrito** *nm* : rehash
refuerzo *nm* : reinforcement
refugiar *vt* : shelter — **refugiarse** *vr* : take refuge — **refugiado, -da** *n*

: refugee — **refugio** nm : refuge, shelter

refulgir {35} vi : shine brightly

refunfuñar vi : grumble, groan

refutar vt : refute

regadera nf 1 : watering can 2 Lat : shower head, shower

regalar vt : give (as a gift) — **regalarse** vr ~ **con** : treat oneself to

regaliz nm, pl **-lices** : licorice

regalo nm 1 : gift, present 2 PLACER : pleasure, delight

regañadientes : a ~ adv phr : reluctantly, unwillingly

regañar vt : scold — vi 1 QUEJARSE : grumble 2 Spain : quarrel — **regañón, -ñona** adj, mpl **-ñones** fam : grumpy, irritable

regar {49} vt 1 : irrigate, water 2 ESPARCIR : scatter

regatear vt 1 : haggle over 2 ESCATIMAR : skimp on — vi : bargain, haggle

regazo nm : lap (of a person)

regenerar vt : regenerate

regentar vt : run, manage

régimen nm, pl **regímenes** 1 : regime 2 DIETA : diet 3 ~ **de vida** : lifestyle

regimiento nm : regiment

regio, -gia adj : royal, regal

región nf, pl **-giones** : region, area — **regional** adj : regional

regir {28} vt 1 : rule 2 ADMINISTRAR : manage, run 3 DETERMINAR : govern, determine — vi : apply, be in force — **regirse** vr ~ **por** : be guided by

registrar vt 1 : register 2 GRABAR : record, tape 3 : search (a house, etc.), frisk (a person) — **registrarse** vr 1 : register 2 : be recorded (of temperatures, etc.) — **registrador, -dora** adj **caja registradora** : cash register — ~ n : registrar — **registro** nm 1 : registration 2 : register (book) 3 : registry (office) 4 : range (of a voice, etc.) 5 INSPECCIÓN : search

regla nf 1 : rule, regulation 2 : ruler (for measuring) 3 MENSTRUACIÓN : period — **reglamentación** nf, pl **-ciones** 1 : regulation 2 REGLAS : rules pl — **reglamentar** vt : regulate — **reglamentario, -ria** adj : regulation, official — **reglamento** nm : regulations pl, rules pl

regocijar vt : gladden, delight — **regocijarse** vr : rejoice — **regocijo** nm : delight, rejoicing

regodearse vr : be delighted — **regodeo** nm : delight

regordete adj fam : chubby

regresar vi : return, come back, go back — vt Lat : give back — **regresión** nf, pl **-siones** : regression — **regresivo, -va** adj : regressive — **regreso** nm 1 : return 2 **estar de ~** : be back, be home again

reguero nm 1 : irrigation ditch 2 SEÑAL : trail, trace 3 **correr como un ~ de pólvora** : spread like wildfire

regular adj 1 : regular 2 MEDIANO : medium, average 3 **por lo ~** : in general — ~ vt : regulate, control — **regulación** nf, pl **-ciones** : regulation, control — **regularidad** nf : regularity — **regularizar** {21} vt : normalize, make regular

rehabilitar vt 1 : rehabilitate 2 : reinstate (s.o. in a position) 3 : renovate (a building, etc.) — **rehabilitación** nf 1 : rehabilitation 2 : reinstatement (in a position) 3 : renovation (of a building, etc.)

rehacer {40} vt 1 : redo 2 REPARAR : repair — **rehacerse** vr 1 : recover 2 ~ **de** : get over

rehén nm, pl **-henes** : hostage

rehuir {41} vt : avoid, shun

rehusar {8} v : refuse

reimprimir vt : reprint — **reimpresión** nf, pl **-siones** : reprinting, reprint

reina nf : queen — **reinado** nm : reign — **reinante** adj : reigning — **reinar** vi 1 : reign 2 PREVALECER : prevail

reincidir vi : backslide, relapse

reino nm : kingdom, realm

reintegrar vt 1 : reinstate 2 : refund (money), reimburse (expenses, etc.) — **reintegrarse** vr ~ **a** : return to — **reintegro** nm : reimbursement

reír {66} vi : laugh — vt : laugh at — **reírse** vr : laugh

reiterar vt : repeat, reiterate

reivindicar {72} vt 1 : claim 2 RESTAURAR : restore

reja nf : grille, grating — **rejilla** nf : grille, grate, screen

rejuvenecer {53} vt : rejuvenate — **rejuvenecerse** vr : be rejuvenated

relación nf, pl **-ciones** 1 : relation, connection 2 COMUNICACIÓN : relationship, relations pl 3 RELATO : account 4 LISTA : list 5 **con ~ a** or **en ~ a** : in relation to — **relacionar** vt : relate, connect — **relacionarse** vr ~ **con** : be connected to, interact with

relajar vt : relax — **relajarse** vr : relax — **relajación** nf, pl **-ciones** : relaxation — **relajado, -da** adj 1 : relaxed 2 : dissolute, lax (in behavior)

relamerse vr : smack one's lips, lick its chops

relámpago *nm* : flash of lightning — **relampaguear** *vi* : flash

relatar *vt* : relate, tell

relativo, -va *adj* **1** : relative **2 en lo relativo a** : with regard to — **relatividad** *nf* : relativity

relato *nm* **1** : account, report **2** CUENTO : story, tale

releer {20} *vt* : reread

relegar {52} *vt* : relegate

relevante *adj* : outstanding, important

relevar *vt* **1** : relieve, take over from **2** ~ **de** : exempt from — **relevo** *nm* **1** : relief, replacement **2 carrera de** ~**s** : relay race

relieve *nm* **1** : relief (in art, etc.) **2** IMPORTANCIA : prominence, importance **3 poner en** ~ : emphasize

religión *nf, pl* **-giones** : religion — **religioso, -sa** *adj* : religious — ~ *n* : monk *m*, nun *f*

relinchar *vi* : neigh, whinny — **relincho** *nm* : neigh, whinny

reliquia *nf* **1** : relic **2** ~ **de familia** : family heirloom

rellenar *vt* **1** : refill **2** : stuff, fill (in cooking) — **relleno, -na** *adj* : stuffed, filled — **relleno** *nm* : stuffing, filling

reloj *nm* **1** : clock **2** *or* ~ **de pulsera** : wristwatch **3** ~ **de arena** : hourglass **4 como un** ~ : like clockwork

relucir {45} *vi* **1** : glitter, shine **2 sacar a** ~ : bring up, mention — **reluciente** *adj* : brilliant, shining

relumbrar *vi* : shine brightly

remachar *vt* **1** : rivet **2** RECALCAR : stress, drive home — **remache** *nm* : rivet

remanente *nm* : remainder, surplus

remanso *nm* : pool

remar *vi* : row

rematar *vt* **1** : conclude, finish up **2** MATAR : finish off **3** LIQUIDAR : sell off cheaply **4** *Lat* : auction — *vi* **1** : shoot (in sports) **2** TERMINAR : end — **rematado, -da** *adj* : utter, complete — **remate** *nm* **1** : shot (in sports) **2** FIN : end

remedar *vt* : imitate, mimic

remediar *vt* **1** : remedy, repair **2** : solve (a problem) **3** EVITAR : avoid — **remedio** *nm* **1** : remedy, cure **2** SOLUCIÓN : solution **3 sin** ~ : hopeless

rememorar *vi* : recall

remendar {55} *vt* : mend

remesa *nf* **1** : remittance **2** : shipment (of merchandise)

remezón *nm, pl* **-zones** *Lat* : mild earthquake, tremor

remiendo *nm* : mend, patch

remilgado, -da *adj* **1** : prudish **2** AFEC-

TADO : affected — **remilgo** *nm* : primness, affectation

reminiscencia *nf* : reminiscence

remisión *nf, pl* **-siones** : remission

remiso, -sa *adj* **1** : reluctant **2** NEGLIGENTE : remiss

remitir *vt* **1** : send, remit **2** ~ **a** : refer to, direct to — *vi* **1** : subside, let up — **remite** *nm* : return address — **remitente** *nmf* : sender (of a letter, etc.)

remo *nm* : paddle, oar

remodelar *vt* **1** : remodel **2** : restructure (an organization)

remojar *vt* : soak, steep — **remojo** *nm* : **poner en** ~ : soak

remolacha *nf* : beet

remolcar {72} *vt* : tow, tug — **remolcador** *nm* : tugboat

remolino *nm* **1** : whirlwind, whirlpool **2** : crowd (of people) **3** : cowlick (of hair)

remolque *nm* **1** : towing, tow **2** : trailer (vehicle)

remontar *vt* **1** : overcome **2** SUBIR : go up — **remontarse** *vr* **1** : soar **2** ~ **a** : date from, go back to

rémora *nf* : hindrance

remorder {47} *vt* : trouble, worry — **remordimiento** *nm* : remorse

remoto, -ta *adj* : remote — **remotamente** *adv* : remotely, slightly

remover {47} *vt* **1** : stir **2** : move around, turn over (earth, embers, etc.) **3** REAVIVIR : bring up again **4** DESPEDIR : fire, dismiss

remunerar *vt* : remunerate

renacer {48} *vi* : be reborn, revive — **renacimiento** *nm* **1** : rebirth, revival **2 el Renacimiento** : the Renaissance

renacuajo *nm* : tadpole, pollywog

rencilla *nf* : quarrel

renco, -ca *adj* *Lat* : lame

rencor *nm* **1** : rancor, hostility **2 guardar** ~ : hold a grudge — **rencoroso, -sa** *adj* : resentful

rendición *nf, pl* **-ciones** : surrender — **rendido, -da** *adj* **1** : submissive **2** AGOTADO : exhausted

rendija *nf* : crack, split

rendir {54} *vt* **1** : render, give **2** PRODUCIR : yield, produce **3** CANSAR : exhaust — *vi* : make progress, go a long way — **rendirse** *vr* : surrender, give up — **rendimiento** *nm* **1** : performance **2** : yield, return (in finance, etc.)

renegar {49} *vt* : deny — *vi* **1** QUEJARSE : grumble **2** ~ **de** ABJURAR : renounce, disown — **renegado, -da** *n* : renegade

renglón *nm, pl* **-glones 1** : line (of writing) **2** *Lat* : line (of products)
reno *nm* : reindeer
renombre *nm* : renown — **renombrado, -da** *adj* : famous, renowned
renovar {19} *vt* **1** : renew, restore **2** : renovate (a building, etc.) — **renovación** *nf, pl* **-ciones 1** : renewal **2** : renovation (of a building, etc.)
renquear *vi* : limp, hobble
rentar *vt* **1** : produce, yield **2** *Lat* : rent — **renta** *nf* **1** : income **2** ALQUILER : rent **3 impuesto sobre la ~** : income tax — **rentable** *adj* : profitable
renunciar *vi* **1** : resign **2 ~ a** : renounce, relinquish — **renuncia** *nf* **1** : renunciation **2** DIMISIÓN : resignation
reñir {67} *vi* **1 ~ con** : argue with, fall out with — *vt* **1** : scold **2** DISPUTAR : fight — **reñido, -da** *adj* **1** : hard-fought **2 ~ con** : on bad terms with
reo, rea *n* **1** : accused, defendant **2** CULPABLE : culprit
reojo *nm* **de ~** : out of the corner of one's eye
reorganizar {21} *vt* : reorganize
repantigarse {52} *vr* : sprawl out
reparar *vt* **1** : repair, fix **2** : make amends for (an offense, etc.) — *vi* **1 ~ en** ADVERTIR : take notice of **2 ~ en** CONSIDERAR : consider — **reparación** *nf, pl* **-ciones 1** : reparation, amends **2** ARREGLO : repair — **reparo** *nm* **1** : reservation, objection **2 poner ~s a** : object to
repartir *vt* **1** : allocate **2** DISTRIBUIR : distribute **3** ESPARCIR : spread — **repartición** *nf, pl* **-ciones** : distribution — **repartidor, -dora** *n* : delivery person, distributor — **reparto** *nm* **1** : allocation **2** DISTRIBUCIÓN : delivery **3** : cast (of characters)
repasar *vt* **1** : review, go over **2** ZURCIR : mend — **repaso** *nm* **1** : review **2** : mending (of clothes)
repeler *vt* **1** : repel **2** REPUGNAR : disgust — **repelente** *adj* : repellent, repulsive
repente *nm* **1** : fit, outburst **2 de ~** : suddenly — **repentino, -na** *adj* : sudden
repercutir *vi* **1** : reverberate **2 ~ en** : have repercussions on — **repercusión** *nf, pl* **-siones** : repercussion
repertorio *nm* : repertoire
repetir {54} *vt* **1** : repeat **2** : have a second helping of (food) — **repetirse** *vr* **1** : repeat oneself **2** : recur (of an event, etc.) — **repetición** *nf, pl* **-ciones** : repetition **2** : rerun, repeat (of a program, etc.) — **repetido, -da**

adj **1** : repeated **2 repetidas veces** : repeatedly, time and again — **repetitivo, -va** *adj* : repetitive, repetitious
repicar {72} *vt* : ring — *vi* : ring out, peal — **repique** *nm* : ringing, pealing
repisa *nf* **1** : shelf, ledge **2 ~ de ventana** : windowsill
replegar {49} *vt* **1** : fold — **replegarse** *vr* : retreat, withdraw
repleto, -ta *adj* **1** : replete, full **2 ~ de** : packed with
replicar {72} *vt* : reply, retort — *vi* : answer back — **réplica** *nf* **1** RESPUESTA : reply **2** COPIA : replica, reproduction
repliegue *nm* **1** : fold **2** : (military) withdrawal
repollo *nm* : cabbage
reponer {60} *vt* **1** : replace **2** REPLICAR : reply — **reponerse** *vr* : recover
reportar *vt* **1** : yield, bring **2** *Lat* : report — **reportaje** *nm* : article, (news) report — **reporte** *nm* *Lat* : report — **reportero, -ra** *n* : reporter
reposar *vi* **1** DESCANSAR : rest **2** : stand, settle (of liquids, dough, etc.) — **reposado, -da** *adj* : calm, relaxed — **reposición** *nf, pl* **-ciones** : replacement **2** : rerun, repeat (of a program, etc.) — **reposo** *nm* : rest
repostar *vt* **1** : stock up on **2** : refuel (an airplane, etc.) — *vi* : fill up, refuel
reprender *vt* : reprimand, scold — **reprensible** *adj* : reprehensible
represalia *nf* : reprisal **2 tomar ~s** : retaliate
represar *vt* : dam
representar *vt* **1** : represent **2** : perform (a play, etc.) **3** APARENTAR : look, appear as — **representación** *nf, pl* **-ciones** : representation **2** : performance (of a play, etc.) **3 en ~ de** : on behalf of — **representante** *nmf* **1** : representative **2** ACTOR : performer — **representativo, -va** *adj* : representative
represión *nf, pl* **-siones** : repression
reprimenda *nf* : reprimand
reprimir *vt* **1** : repress **2** : suppress (a rebellion, etc.)
reprobar {19} *vt* **1** : reprove, condemn **2** *Lat* : fail (an exam, etc.)
reprochar *vt* : reproach — **reprocharse** *vr* : reproach oneself — **reproche** *nm* : reproach
reproducir {61} *vt* : reproduce — **reproducirse** *vr* **1** : breed, reproduce **2** : recur (of an event, etc.) — **reproducción** *nf, pl* **-ciones** : reproduction — **reproductor, -tora** *adj* : reproductive
reptil *nm* : reptile

república *nf* : republic — **republicano, -na** *adj & n* : republican

repudiar *vt* : repudiate

repuesto *nm* : spare (auto) part

repugnar *vt* : disgust — **repugnancia** *nf* : disgust — **repugnante** *adj* : disgusting

repujar *vt* : emboss

repulsivo, -va *adj* : repulsive

reputar *vt* : consider, deem — **reputación** *nf, pl* -ciones : reputation

requerir {76} *vt* 1 : require 2 : summon, send for (a person)

requesón *nm, pl* -sones : cottage cheese

réquiem *nm* : requiem

requisito *nm* 1 : requirement 2 ~ previo : prerequisite

res *nf* 1 : beast, animal 2 *Lat or* carne de ~ : beef

resabio *nm* 1 VICIO : bad habit, vice 2 DEJO : aftertaste

resaca *nf* 1 : undertow 2 tener ~ : have a hangover

resaltar *vi* 1 : stand out 2 hacer ~ : bring out, highlight — *vt* : emphasize

resarcir {83} *vt* : compensate, repay — **resarcirse** *vr* ~ de : make up for

resbalar *vi* 1 : slip, slide 2 : skid (of an automobile) — **resbalarse** *vr* : slip, skid — **resbaladizo, -za** *adj* : slippery — **resbalón** *nm, pl* -lones : slip — **resbaloso, -sa** *adj Lat* : slippery

rescatar *vt* 1 : rescue, ransom 2 RECUPERAR : recover, get back — **rescate** *nm* 1 : rescue 2 : ransom (money) 3 RECUPERACIÓN : recovery

rescindir *vt* : cancel — **rescisión** *nf, pl* -siones : cancellation

rescoldo *nm* : embers *pl*

resecar {72} *vt* : dry (out) — **resecarse** *vr* : dry up — **reseco, -ca** *adj* : dry, dried-up

resentirse {76} *vr* 1 : suffer, be weakened 2 OFENDERSE : be offended 3 ~ de : feel the effects of — **resentido, -da** *adj* : resentful — **resentimiento** *nm* : resentment

reseñar *vt* 1 : review 2 DESCRIBIR : describe — **reseña** *nf* 1 : review, report 2 DESCRIPCIÓN : description

reservar *vt* 1 : reserve 2 GUARDAR : keep, save — **reservarse** *vr* 1 : save oneself 2 : keep for oneself — **reserva** *nf* 1 : reservation 2 PROVISIÓN : reserve 3 de ~ : spare, in reserve — **reservación** *nf, pl* -ciones : reservation — **reservado, -da** *adj* 1 : reserved 2 : confidential (of a document, etc.)

resfriar {85} *vt* : cool — **resfriarse** *vr* 1 : cool off 2 CONSTIPARSE : catch a cold — **resfriado** *nm* CATARRO : cold — **resfrío** *nm Lat* : cold

resguardar *vt* : protect — **resguardarse** *vr* : protect oneself — **resguardo** *nm* 1 : protection 2 RECIBO : receipt

residir *vi* 1 : reside, live 2 ~ en : lie in — **residencia** *nf* 1 : residence 2 or ~ universitaria : dormitory — **residencial** *adj* : residential — **residente** *adj & nmf* : resident

residuo *nm* 1 : residue 2 ~s *nmpl* : waste — **residual** *adj* : residual

resignar *vt* : resign — **resignarse** *vr* ~ a : resign oneself to — **resignación** *nf, pl* -ciones : resignation

resina *nf* 1 : resin 2 : epoxídica : epoxy

resistir *vt* 1 AGUANTAR : stand, bear 2 : withstand (temptation, etc.) — *vi* : resist — **resistirse** *vr* ~ a : be resistant to — **resistencia** *nf* 1 : resistance 2 AGUANTE : endurance, stamina — **resistente** *adj* : resistant, strong, tough

resma *nf* : ream

resollar {19} *vi* : breathe heavily, pant

resolver {89} *vt* 1 : resolve 2 DECIDIR : decide — **resolverse** *vr* : make up one's mind — **resolución** *nf, pl* -ciones : resolution 2 DECISIÓN : decision 3 FIRMEZA : determination, resolve

resonar {19} *vi* : resound — **resonancia** *nf* 1 : resonance 2 CONSECUENCIAS : impact, repercussions *pl* — **resonante** *adj* : resonant, resounding

resoplar *vi* 1 : puff, pant 2 : snort (with annoyance)

resorte *nm* 1 MUELLE : spring 2 tocar ~s : pull strings

respaldar *vt* : back, endorse — **respaldarse** *vr* : lean back — **respaldo** *nm* 1 : back (of a chair, etc.) 2 APOYO : support, backing

respectar *vt* : concern, relate to — **respectivo, -va** *adj* : respective — **respecto** *nm* 1 al ~ : in this respect 2 ~ a : in regard to, concerning

respetar *vt* : respect — **respetable** *adj* : respectable — **respeto** *nm* 1 : respect 2 presentar sus ~s : pay one's respects — **respetuoso, -sa** *adj* : respectful

respingo *nm* : start, jump

respirar *v* : breathe — **respiración** *nf, pl* -ciones : respiration, breathing — **respiratorio, -ria** *adj* : respiratory — **respiro** *nm* 1 : breath 2 DESCANSO : respite, break

resplandecer {53} *vi* : shine — **resplandeciente** *adj* : shining, gleaming — **resplandor** *nm* 1 : brilliance, gleam 2 : flash (of lightning, etc.)

responder *vt* : answer, reply — *vi* 1 : answer 2 REPLICAR : answer back 3 ~ a : respond to 4 ~ de : answer for (something)

responsable *adj* : responsible — **responsabilidad** *nf* : responsibility

respuesta *nf* 1 : answer, reply 2 REACCIÓN : response

resquebrajar *vt* : split, crack — **resquebrajarse** *vr* : crack

resquicio *nm* 1 : crack, crevice 2 VESTIGIO : trace, glimmer

resta *nf* : subtraction

restablecer {53} *vt* : reestablish, restore — **restablecerse** *vr* : recover — **restablecimiento** *nm* : restoration, recovery

restallar *vi* : crack, crackle

restar *vt* 1 : deduct, subtract 2 DISMINUIR : minimize — *vi* : be left — **restante** *adj* 1 : remaining 2 **lo** ~ : the rest

restauración *nf*, *pl* -**ciones** : restoration

restaurante *nm* : restaurant

restaurar *vt* : restore

restituir {41} *vt* : return, restore — **restitución** *nf*, *pl* -**ciones** : restitution

resto *nm* 1 : rest, remainder 2 ~**s** *nmpl* : leftovers 3 or ~**s mortales** : mortal remains

restregar {49} *vt* : rub, scrub — **restregarse** *vr* : rub

restringir {35} *vt* : restrict, limit — **restricción** *nf*, *pl* -**ciones** : restriction, limitation — **restrictivo**, -**va** *adj* : restrictive

resucitar *vt* : resuscitate, revive — *vi* : come back to life

resuelto, -**ta** *adj* : determined, resolved

resuello *nm* : heavy breathing, panting

resultar *vi* 1 : succeed, work out 2 SALIR : turn out (to be) 3 ~ **de** : be the result of 4 ~ **en** : result in — **resultado** *nm* : result, outcome

resumir *v* : summarize, sum up — **resumen** *nm*, *pl* -**súmenes** 1 : summary 2 **en** ~ : in short

resurgir {35} *vi* : reappear, revive — **resurgimiento** *nm* : resurgence — **resurrección** *nf*, *pl* -**ciones** : resurrection

retahíla *nf* : string, series

retal *nm* : remnant

retardar *vt* 1 RETRASAR : delay 2 POSPONER : postpone

retazo *nm* 1 : remnant, scrap 2 : fragment (of a text, etc.)

retener {80} *vt* 1 : retain, keep 2 : withhold (funds, etc.) 3 DETENER : detain — **retención** *nf*, *pl* -**ciones** 1 : retention 2 : deduction, withholding (of funds)

reticente *adj* : reluctant — **reticencia** *nf* : reluctance

retina *nf* : retina

retintín *nm*, *pl* -**tines** 1 : tinkling, jingle 2 **con** ~ : sarcastically

retirar *vt* 1 : remove, take away 2 : withdraw (funds, statements, etc.) — **retirarse** *vr* 1 : retreat, withdraw 2 JUBILARSE : retire — **retirada** *nf* 1 : withdrawal 2 **batirse en** ~ : beat a retreat — **retirado**, -**da** *adj* 1 : remote, secluded 2 JUBILADO : retired — **retiro** *nm* 1 : retreat 2 JUBILACIÓN : retirement 3 *Lat* : withdrawal

reto *nm* : challenge, dare

retocar {72} *vt* : touch up

retoño *nm* : sprout, shoot

retoque *nm* 1 : retouching 2 **el último** ~ : the finishing touch

retorcer {14} *vt* 1 : twist, contort 2 : wring out (clothes, etc.) — **retorcerse** *vr* 1 : get twisted up 2 : squirm, writhe (in pain) — **retorcijón** *nm*, *pl* -**jones** : cramp, spasm — **retorcimiento** *nm* : twisting, wringing out

retórica *nf* : rhetoric — **retórico**, -**ca** *adj* : rhetorical

retornar *v* : return — **retorno** *nm* : return

retozar {21} *vi* : frolic, romp — **retozón**, -**zona** *adj* : playful, frisky

retractarse *vr* 1 : withdraw, back down 2 ~ **de** : take back, retract

retraer {81} *vt* : retract — **retraerse** *vr* : withdraw — **retraído**, -**da** *adj* : withdrawn, shy

retrasar *vt* 1 : delay, hold up 2 APLAZAR : postpone 3 : set back (a clock) — **retrasarse** *vr* 1 : be late 2 : fall behind (in work, etc.) — **retrasado**, -**da** *adj* 1 : retarded 2 : in arrears (of payments) 3 : backward (of a country) 4 : slow (of a clock) — **retraso** *nm* 1 : delay 2 SUBDESARROLLO : backwardness 3 ~ **mental** : mental retardation

retratar *vt* 1 : portray 2 FOTOGRAFIAR : photograph 3 DIBUJAR : paint a portrait of — **retrato** *nm* 1 : portrayal 2 DIBUJO : portrait 3 FOTOGRAFÍA : photograph

retrete *nm* : restroom, toilet

retribuir {41} *vt* 1 : pay 2 RECOMPENSAR : reward — **retribución** *nf*, *pl*

-ciones 1 : payment **2** RECOMPENSA : reward

retroactivo, -va *adj* : retroactive

retroceder *vi* **1** : go back, turn back **2** CEDER : back down — **retroceso** *nm* **1** : backward movement **2** : backing down

retrógrado, -da *adj & nmf* : reactionary

retrospectiva *nf* : hindsight — **retrospectivo, -va** *adj* : retrospective

retrovisor *nm* : rearview mirror

retumbar *vi* : resound, reverberate, rumble

reumatismo *nm* : rheumatism

reunir {68} *vt* **1** : unite, join **2** TENER : have, possess **3** RECOGER : gather, collect — **reunirse** *vr* : meet, gather — **reunión** *nf, pl* **-niones 1** : meeting **2** : (social) gathering, reunion

revalidar *vt* : confirm, ratify

revancha *nf* **1** : revenge **2** : rematch (in sports)

revelar *vt* **1** : reveal, disclose **2** : develop (film) — **revelación** *nf, pl* **-ciones** : revelation — **revelado** *nm* : developing (of film) — **revelador, -dora** *adj* : revealing

reventar {55} *v* **1** : burst, blow up — **reventarse** *vr* : burst — **reventón** *nm, pl* **-tones** : blowout, flat tire

reverberar *vi* : reverberate — **reverberación** *nf, pl* **-ciones** : reverberation

reverenciar *vt* : revere — **reverencia** *nf* **1** : bow, curtsy **2** VENERACIÓN : reverence — **reverendo, -da** *adj & nmf* : reverend — **reverente** *adj* : reverent

reversa *nf Lat* : reverse (gear)

reverso *nm* **1** : back, reverse **2 el ~ de la medalla** : the complete opposite — **reversible** *adj* : reversible

revertir {76} *vi* **1** : revert **2 ~ en** : result in

revés *nm, pl* **-veses 1** : back, wrong side **2** CONTRATIEMPO : setback **3** BOFETADA : slap **4** : backhand (in sports) **5 al ~** : the other way around, upside down, inside out

revestir {54} *vt* **1** : coat, cover **2** ASUMIR : take on, assume — **revestimiento** *nm* : covering, coating

revisar *vt* **1** : examine, inspect **2** : check over, overhaul (machinery, etc.) **3** MODIFICAR : revise — **revisión** *nf, pl* **-siones 1** : revision **2** INSPECCIÓN : inspection, check — **revisor, -sora** *n* : inspector

revistar *vt* : review, inspect (troops, etc.) — **revista** *nf* **1** : magazine, jour-

nal **2** : revue (in theater) **3 pasar ~** : review, inspect

revivir *vi* : revive, come alive again — *vt* : relive

revocar {72} *vt* : revoke

revolcar {82} *vt* : knock over, knock down — **revolcarse** *vr* : roll around

revolotear *vi* : flutter, flit — **revoloteo** *nm* : fluttering, flitting

revoltijo *nm* : mess, jumble

revoltoso, -sa *adj* : rebellious

revolución *nf, pl* **-ciones** : revolution — **revolucionar** *vt* : revolutionize — **revolucionario, -ria** *adj & n* : revolutionary

revolver {89} *vt* **1** : mix, stir **2** : upset (one's stomach) **3** DESORGANIZAR : mess up — **revolverse** *vr* **1** : toss and turn **2** VOLVERSE : turn around

revólver *nm* : revolver

revuelo *nm* : commotion

revuelta *nf* : uprising, revolt — **revuelto, -ta** *adj* **1** : choppy, rough **2** DESORDENADO : messed up **3 huevos revueltos** : scrambled eggs

rey *nm* : king

reyerta *nf* : brawl, fight

rezagarse {52} *vr* : fall behind, lag

rezar {21} *vi* **1** : pray **2** DECIR : say — *vt* : say, recite — **rezo** *nm* : prayer

rezongar {52} *vi* : gripe, grumble

rezumar *v* : ooze

ría *nf* : estuary

riachuelo *nm* : brook, stream

riada *nf* : flood

ribera *nf* : bank, shore

ribete *nm* : border, trim — **ribete** *nm* **1** : border, trim **2** : embellishment

rico, -ca *adj* **1** : rich, wealthy **2** ABUNDANTE : abundant **3** SABROSO : rich, tasty — *n* : rich person

ridiculizar {21} *vt* : ridicule — **ridículo, -la** *adj* : ridiculous — **ridículo** *nm* **1 hacer el ~** : make a fool of oneself **2 poner en ~** : ridicule

riego *nm* : irrigation

riel *nm* : rail

rienda *nf* **1** : rein **2 dar ~ suelta a** : give free rein to

riesgo *nm* : risk

rifa *nf* : raffle — **rifar** *vt* : raffle (off) — **rifarse** *vr fam* : fight over

rifle *nm* : rifle

rígido, -da *adj* **1** : rigid, stiff **2** SEVERO : harsh, strict — **rigidez** *nf, pl* **-deces 1** : rigidity, stiffness **2** SEVERIDAD : harshness, strictness

rigor *nm* **1** : rigor, harshness **2** EXACTITUD : precision **3 de ~** : essential, obligatory — **riguroso, -sa** *adj* : rigorous

rima *nf* 1 : rhyme 2 ~**s** *nfpl* : verse, poetry — **rimar** *vi* : rhyme

rimbombante *adj* : showy, pompous

rímel *nm* : mascara

rincón *nm, pl* -**cones** : corner, nook

rinoceronte *nm* : rhinoceros

riña *nf* 1 : fight, brawl 2 DISPUTA : dispute, quarrel

riñón *nm, pl* -**ñones** : kidney

río *nm* 1 : river 2 TORRENTE : torrent, stream

riqueza *nf* 1 : wealth 2 ABUNDANCIA : richness 3 ~**s naturales** : natural resources

risa *nf* 1 : laughter, laugh 2 **dar** ~ **a algn** : make s.o. laugh 3 **morirse de la** ~ *fam* : die laughing

risco *nm* : crag, cliff

risible *adj* : laughable

ristra *nf* : string, series

risueño, -ña *adj* : cheerful, smiling

ritmo *nm* 1 : rhythm 2 VELOCIDAD : pace, speed — **rítmico, -ca** *adj* : rhythmical

rito *nm* : rite, ritual — **ritual** *adj & nm* : ritual

rival *adj & nmf* : rival — **rivalidad** *nf* : rivalry, competition — **rivalizar** {21} *vi* ~ **con** : rival, compete with

rizar {21} *vt* 1 : curl 2 : ripple (a surface) — **rizarse** *vr* : curl — **rizado, -da** *adj* 1 : curly 2 : choppy (of water) — **rizo** *nm* 1 : curl 2 : ripple (in water) 3 : loop (in aviation)

róbalo *nm* : bass (fish)

robar *vt* 1 : steal 2 : burglarize (a house, etc.) 3 SECUESTRAR : kidnap — **robo** *nm* : robbery, theft

roble *nm* : oak

robot *nm, pl* -**bots** : robot — **robótica** *nf* : robotics

robustecer {53} *vt* : make stronger, strengthen — **robusto, -ta** *adj* : robust, sturdy

roca *nf* : rock, boulder

roce *nm* 1 : rubbing, chafing 2 RASGUÑO : graze, scratch 3 **tener un** ~ **con** : have a brush with

rociar {85} *vt* : spray, sprinkle — **rocío** *nm* : dew

rocoso, -sa *adj* : rocky

rodaja *nf* : slice

rodar {19} *vi* 1 : roll, roll down, roll along 2 GIRAR : turn, go around 3 : travel (of a vehicle) 4 : film (of movies, etc.) — *vt* 1 : film, shoot 2 : break in (a vehicle) — **rodaje** *nm* 1 : filming, shooting 2 : breaking in (of a vehicle)

rodear *vt* 1 : surround, encircle 2 *Lat* : round up (cattle) — **rodearse** *vr* ~ **de** : surround oneself with — **rodeo** *nm* 1 : rodeo, roundup 2 DESVÍO : detour 3 **andar con** ~**s** : beat around the bush

rodilla *nf* : knee

rodillo *nm* 1 : roller 2 : rolling pin (for pastry)

roer {69} *vt* 1 : gnaw 2 ATORMENTAR : eat away at, torment — **roedor** *nm* : rodent

rogar {16} *vt* : beg, request — *vi* : pray

rojo, -ja *adj* 1 : red 2 **ponerse** ~ : blush — **rojo** *nm* : red — **rojez** *nf* : redness — **rojizo, -za** *adj* : reddish

rollizo, -za *adj* : plump, chubby

rollo *nm* 1 : roll, coil 2 *fam* : boring speech, lecture

romance *nm* 1 : romance 2 : Romance (language)

romano, -na *adj & n* : Roman

romántico, -ca *adj* : romantic — **romanticismo** *nm* : romanticism

romería *nf* : pilgrimage, procession

romero *nm* : rosemary

romo, -ma *adj* : blunt, dull

rompecabezas *nms & pl* : puzzle

romper {70} *vt* 1 : break 2 RASGAR : rip, tear 3 : break off (relations), break (a contract) — *vi* 1 : break (of the day, waves, etc.) 2 ~ **a** : begin to, burst out with 3 ~ **con** : break off with — **romperse** *vr* : break

ron *nm* : rum

roncar {72} *vi* : snore — **ronco, -ca** *adj* : hoarse

ronda *nf* 1 : rounds *pl*, patrol 2 : round (of drinks, etc.) — **rondar** *vt* 1 : patrol 2 : hang around (a place) 3 : be approximately (an age, a number, etc.) — *vi* 1 : be on patrol 2 MERODEAR : prowl about

ronquera *nf* : hoarseness

ronquido *nm* : snore

ronronear *vi* : purr — **ronroneo** *nm* : purr, purring

ronzar {21} *vt* : munch, crunch

roña *nf* 1 : mange 2 SUCIEDAD : dirt, filth — **roñoso, -sa** *adj* 1 : mangy 2 SUCIO : dirty 3 *fam* : stingy

ropa *nf* 1 : clothes *pl*, clothing 2 ~ **interior** : underwear — **ropaje** *nm* : robes *pl*, regalia — **ropero** *nm* : wardrobe, closet

rosa *nf* : rose (flower) — ~ *adj* : rose-colored — ~ *nm* : rose (color) — **rosado, -da** *adj* 1 : pink 2 **vino rosado** : rosé — **rosado** *nm* : pink (color) — **rosal** *nm* : rosebush

rosario *nm* : rosary
rosbif *nm* : roast beef
rosca *nf* **1** : thread (of a screw) **2** ESPIRAL : ring, coil
roseta *nf* : rosette
rosquilla *nf* : doughnut
rostro *nm* : face
rotación *nf*, *pl* **-ciones** : rotation — **rotativo, -va** *adj* : rotary, revolving
roto, -ta *adj* : broken, torn
rotonda *nf* : traffic circle, rotary
rótula *nf* : kneecap
rótulo *nm* **1** : heading, title **2** ETIQUETA : label, sign
rotundo, -da *adj* : categorical, absolute
rotura *nf* : break, tear, fracture
rozar {21} *vt* **1** : graze, touch lightly **2** APROXIMARSE DE : touch on, border on — *vi* : scrape, rub — **rozarse** *vr* **1** : rub, chafe **2 ~ con** *fam* : rub elbows with — **rozadura** *nf* : scratch
rubí *nm*, *pl* **rubíes** : ruby
rubicundo, -da *adj* : ruddy
rubio, -bia *adj* & *n* : blond
rubor *nm* : flush, blush — **ruborizarse** {21} *vr* : blush
rúbrica *nf* **1** : flourish (in writing) **2** TÍTULO : title, heading
rudeza *nf* : roughness, coarseness
rudimentos *nmpl* : rudiments, basics — **rudimentario, -ria** *adj* : rudimentary
rudo, -da *adj* **1** : rough, harsh **2** GROSERO : coarse, unpolished
rueda *nf* **1** CORRO : circle, ring **3** RODAJA : (round) slice **4** **ir sobre ~s** : go smoothly — **ruedo** *nm* : bullring

ruego *nm* : request
rugir {35} *vi* : roar — **rugido** *nm* : roar
rugoso, -sa *adj* **1** : rough **2** ARRUGADO : wrinkled
ruibarbo *nm* : rhubarb
ruido *nm* : noise — **ruidoso, -sa** *adj* : loud, noisy
ruina *nf* **1** : ruin, destruction **2** COLAPSO : collapse **3 ~s** *nfpl* : ruins, remains — **ruinoso, -sa** *adj* : run-down, dilapidated
ruiseñor *nm* : nightingale
ruleta *nf* : roulette
rulo *nm* : curler, roller
rumano, -na *adj* : Romanian, Rumanian
rumba *nf* : rumba
rumbo *nm* **1** : direction, course **2** ESPLENDIDEZ : lavishness **3** **con ~ a** : bound for, heading for **4** **perder el ~** : go off course
rumiar *vt* : mull over — *vi* : chew the cud — **rumiante** *adj* & *nm* : ruminant
rumor *nm* **1** : rumor **2** MURMULLO : murmur — **rumorearse** *or* **rumorarse** *vr* : be rumored — **rumoroso, -sa** *adj* : murmuring, babbling
ruptura *nf* **1** : break, rupture **2** : breach (of a contract) **3** : breaking off (of relations)
rural *adj* : rural
ruso, -sa *adj* : Russian — **ruso** *nm* : Russian (language)
rústico, -ca *adj* **1** : rural, rustic **2** **en rústica** : in paperback
ruta *nf* : route
rutina *nf* : routine — **rutinario, -ria** *adj* : routine

S

s *nf* : s, 20th letter of the Spanish alphabet
sábado *nm* : Saturday
sábana *nf* : sheet
sabandija *nf* : bug
saber {71} *vt* **1** : know **2** SER CAPAZ DE : know how to, be able to **3** ENTERARSE : learn, find out **4 a ~** : namely — *vi* **1** : taste **2 ~ de** : know about — **~** *nm* : knowledge — **sabelotodo** *nmf fam* : know-it-all — **sabido, -da** *adj* : well-known — **sabiduría** *nf* **1** : wisdom **2** CONOCIMIENTO : learning, knowledge — **sabiendas : a ~** *adv phr* : knowingly — **sabio, -bia** *adj* **1** : learned **2** PRUDENTE : wise, sensible

sabor *nm* : flavor, taste — **saborear** *vt* : savor
sabotaje *nm* : sabotage — **saboteador, -dora** *n* : saboteur — **sabotear** *vt* : sabotage
sabroso, -sa *adj* : delicious, tasty
sabueso *nm* **1** : bloodhound **2** *fam* : sleuth
sacacorchos *nms* & *pl* : corkscrew
sacapuntas *nms* & *pl* : pencil sharpener
sacar {72} *vt* **1** : take out **2** OBTENER : get, obtain **3** EXTRAER : extract, withdraw **4** : bring out (a book, a product, etc.) **5** : take (photos), make (copies) **6** QUITAR : remove **7 ~ adelante** : bring up (children), carry out (a project,

etc.) **8 ~ la lengua** : stick out one's tongue — *vi* : serve (in sports)
sacarina *nf* : saccharin
sacerdote, -tisa *n* : priest *m*, priestess *f* — **sacerdocio** *nm* : priesthood — **sacerdotal** *adj* : priestly
saciar *vt* : satisfy
saco *nm* **1** : bag, sack **2** : sac (in anatomy) **3** *Lat* : jacket
sacramento *nm* : sacrament — **sacramental** *adj* : sacramental
sacrificar {72} *vt* : sacrifice — **sacrificarse** *vr* : sacrifice oneself — **sacrificio** *nm* : sacrifice
sacrilegio *nm* : sacrilege — **sacrílego, -ga** *adj* : sacrilegious
sacro, -cra *adj* : sacred — **sacrosanto, -ta** *adj* : sacrosanct
sacudir *vt* **1** : shake **2** GOLPEAR : beat **3** CONMOVER : shake up, shock — **sacudirse** *vr* : shake off — **sacudida** *nf* **1** : shaking **2** : jolt (of a train, etc.), tremor (of an earthquake) **3** : (emotional) shock
sádico, -ca *adj* : sadistic — **~** *n* : sadist — **sadismo** *nm* : sadism
saeta *nf* : arrow
safari *nm* : safari
sagaz *adj, pl* **-gaces** : shrewd, sagacious — **sagacidad** *nf* : shrewdness
sagrado, -da *adj* : sacred, holy
sal *nf* : salt
sala *nf* **1** : room, hall **2** : living room (of a house) **3 ~ de espera** : waiting room
salar *vt* : salt — **salado, -da** *adj* **1** : salty **2** GRACIOSO : witty **3 agua salada** : salt water
salario *nm* : salary, wage
salchicha *nf* : sausage — **salchichón** *nf, pl* **-chones** : salami-like cold cut
saldar *vt* **1** : settle, pay off **2** VENDER : sell off — **saldo** *nm* **1** : balance (of an account) **2 ~s** *nmpl* : remainders, sale items
salero *nm* : saltshaker
salir {73} *vi* **1** : go out, come out **2** PARTIR : leave **3** APARECER : appear **4** RESULTAR : turn out **5** : rise (of the sun) **6 ~ adelante** : get by **7 ~ con** : go out with, date **8 ~ de** : come from — **salirse** *vr* **1** : leave **2** ESCAPARSE : leak out, escape **3** SOLTARSE : come off **4 ~ con la suya** : get one's own way — **salida** *nf* **1** : exit **2** : (action of) leaving, departure **3** SOLUCIÓN : way out **4** : leak (of gas, liquid, etc.) **5** OCURRENCIA : witty remark **6 ~ de emergencia** : emergency exit **7 ~ del sol** : sunrise — **saliente** *adj* **1** : departing, outgoing **2** DESTACADO : outstanding

saliva *nf* : saliva
salmo *nm* : psalm
salmón *nm, pl* **-mones** : salmon
salmuera *nf* : brine
salón *nm, pl* **-lones** **1** : lounge, sitting room **2 ~ de belleza** : beauty salon **3 ~ de clase** : classroom
salpicar {72} *vt* **1** : splash, spatter **2 ~ de** : pepper with — **salpicadera** *nf* *Lat* : fender — **salpicadura** *nf* : splash
salsa *nf* **1** : sauce **2** : (meat) gravy **3** : salsa (music)
saltamontes *nms & pl* : grasshopper
saltar *vi* **1** : jump, leap **2** REBOTAR : bounce **3** : come off (of a button, etc.) **4** ROMPERSE : shatter **5** ESTALLAR : explode, blow up — **~** *vt* **1** : jump (over) **2** OMITIR : skip, miss — **saltarse** *vr* **1** : come off **2** OMITIR : skip, miss
saltear *vt* : sauté
saltimbanqui *nmf* : acrobat
salto *nm* **1** : jump, leap **2** : dive (into water) **3 ~ de agua** : waterfall — **saltón, -tona** *adj, mpl* **-tones** : bulging, protruding
salud *nf* **1** : health **2 ¡salud!** : here's to your health! **3 ¡salud!** *Lat* : bless you! (when someone sneezes) — **saludable** *adj* : healthy
saludar *vt* **1** : greet, say hello to **2** : salute (in the military) — **saludo** *nm* **1** : greeting **2** : (military) salute **3 ~s** : best wishes, regards
salva *nf* **~ de aplausos** : round of applause
salvación *nf, pl* **-ciones** : salvation
salvado *nm* : bran
salvador, -dora *n* : savior, rescuer
salvadoreño, -ña *adj* : (El) Salvadoran
salvaguardar *vt* : safeguard
salvaje *adj* **1** : wild **2** PRIMITIVO : savage, primitive — **~** *nmf* : savage
salvar *vt* **1** : save, rescue **2** RECORRER : cover, travel **3** SUPERAR : overcome — **salvarse** *vr* : save oneself — **salvavidas** *nms & pl* **1** : life preserver **2 ~ bote ~** : lifeboat
salvia *nf* : sage (plant)
salvo, -va *adj* : safe — **salvo** *prep* **1** : except (for), save **2 ~ que** : unless
samba *nf* : samba
San → santo
sanar *vt* : heal, cure — *vi* : recover — **sanatorio** *nm* **1** : sanatorium **2** HOSPITAL : clinic, hospital
sanción *nf, pl* **-ciones** : sanction — **sancionar** *vt* : sanction
sandalia *nf* : sandal
sándalo *nm* : sandalwood
sandía *nf* : watermelon

sandwich ['sandwitʃ, 'saŋgwitʃ] *nm, pl* **-wiches** [-dwitʃes, -gwi-] : sandwich

saneamiento *nm* : sanitation

sangrar *vt* 1 : bleed 2 : indent (a paragraph) — *vi* : bleed — **sangrante** *adj* : bleeding — **sangre** *nf* 1 : blood 2 **a fría** : in cold blood — **sangriento, -ta** *adj* : bloody

sanguijuela *nf* : leech

sanguinario, -ria *adj* : bloodthirsty — **sanguíneo, -nea** *adj* : blood

sano, -na *adj* 1 : healthy 2 : (morally) wholesome 3 ENTERO : intact 4 **sano y salvo** : safe and sound — **sanidad** *nf* 1 : health 2 : public health, sanitation — **sanitario, -ria** *adj* : sanitary, health — **sanitario** *nm Lat* : toilet

santiamén **en un** ~ : in no time at all

santo, -ta *adj* 1 : holy 2 **Santo, Santa (San** *before masculine names except those beginning with D or T*) : Saint — ~ *n* : saint — **santo** *nm* 1 : saint's day 2 *Lat* : birthday — **santidad** *nf* : holiness, sanctity — **santiguarse** {10} *vr* : cross oneself — **santuario** *nm* : sanctuary

saña *nf* 1 : fury 2 BRUTALIDAD : viciousness

sapo *nm* : toad

saque *nm* : serve (in tennis, etc.), throw-in (in soccer)

saquear *vt* : sack, loot — **saqueador, -dora** *n* : looter — **saqueo** *nm* : sacking, looting

sarampión *nm* : measles *pl*

sarape *nm Lat* : serape

sarcasmo *nm* : sarcasm — **sarcástico, -ca** *adj* : sarcastic

sardina *nf* : sardine

sardónico, -ca *adj* : sardonic

sargento *nmf* : sergeant

sarpullido *nm* : rash

sartén *nmf, pl* **-tenes** : frying pan

sastre, -tra *n* : tailor — **sastrería** *nf* 1 : tailoring 2 : tailor's shop

Satanás *nm* : Satan — **satánico, -ca** *adj* : satanic

satélite *nm* : satellite

sátira *nf* : satire — **satírico, -ca** *adj* : satirical

satisfacer {74} *vt* 1 : satisfy 2 CUMPLIR : fulfill, meet 3 PAGAR : pay — **satisfacerse** *vr* 1 : be satisfied 2 VENGARSE : take revenge — **satisfacción** *nf, pl* **-ciones** : satisfaction — **satisfactorio, -ria** *adj* : satisfactory — **satisfecho, -cha** *adj* : satisfied

saturar *vt* : saturate — **saturación** *nf, pl* **-ciones** : saturation

Saturno *nm* : Saturn

sauce *nm* : willow

sauna *nf* : sauna

savia *nf* : sap

saxofón *nm, pl* **-fones** : saxophone

sazón *nf, pl* **-zones** 1 : seasoning 2 MADUREZ : ripeness 3 **a la** ~ : at that time, then 4 **en** ~ : ripe, in season — **sazonar** *vt* : season

se *pron* 1 (*reflexive*) : himself, herself, itself, oneself, yourself, yourselves, themselves 2 (*indirect object*) : (to) him, (to) her, (to) you, (to) them 3 : each other, one another 4 ~ **dice que** : it is said that 5 ~ **habla inglés** : English spoken

sebo *nm* 1 : fat 2 : tallow (for candles, etc.) 3 : suet (for cooking)

secar {72} *v* : dry — **secarse** *vr* : dry (up) — **secador** *nm* : hair dryer — **secadora** *nf* : (clothes) dryer

sección *nf, pl* **-ciones** : section

seco, -ca *adj* 1 : dry 2 : dried (of fruits, etc.) 3 TAJANTE : sharp, brusque 4 : thin, skinny 5 **a secas** : simply, just 6 **en seco** : suddenly

secretar *vt* : secrete — **secreción** *nf, pl* **-ciones** : secretion

secretario, -ria *n* : secretary — **secretaría** *nf* : secretariat

secreto, -ta *adj* : secret — **secreto** *nm* 1 : secret 2 **en** ~ : in confidence

secta *nf* : sect

sector *nm* : sector

secuaz *nmf, pl* **-cuaces** : follower, henchman

secuela *nf* : consequence

secuencia *nf* : sequence

secuestrar *vt* 1 : kidnap 2 : hijack (an airplane, etc.) 3 EMBARGAR : confiscate, seize — **secuestrador, -dora** *n* 1 : kidnapper 2 : hijacker (of an airplane, etc.) — **secuestro** *nm* 1 : kidnapping 2 : hijacking (of an airplane, etc.) 3 : seizure (of goods)

secular *adj* : secular

secundar *vt* : support, second — **secundario, -ria** *adj* : secondary

sed *nf* 1 : thirst 2 **tener** ~ : be thirsty

seda *nf* : silk

sedal *nm* : fishing line

sedar *vt* : sedate — **sedante** *adj & nm* : sedative

sede *nf* 1 : seat, headquarters 2 **Santa Sede** : Holy See

sedentario, -ria *adj* : sedentary

sedición *nf, pl* **-ciones** : sedition — **sedicioso, -sa** *adj* : seditious

sediento, -ta *adj* : thirsty

sedimento *nm* : sediment

sedoso, -sa *adj* : silky, silken

seducir {61} *vt* **1** : seduce **2** ATRAER : captivate, charm — **seducción** *nf, pl* **-ciones** : seduction — **seductor, -tora** *adj* **1** : seductive **2** ENCANTADOR : charming — **~** *n* : seducer

segar {49} *vt* : reap — **segador, -dora** *n* : reaper, harvester

seglar *adj* : lay, secular — **~** *nm* : layperson, layman *m*, laywoman *f*

segmento *nm* : segment

segregar {52} *vt* : segregate — **segregación** *nf, pl* **-ciones** : segregation

seguir {75} *vt* : follow — *vi* **1** : go on, continue — **seguida: en ~** *adv phr* : right away — **seguido** *adv* **1** : straight (ahead) **2** *Lat* : often — **seguido, -da** *adj* **1** : continuous **2** CONSECUTIVO : consecutive — **seguidor, -dora** *n* : follower

según *prep* : according to — **~** *adv* : it depends — **~** *conj* : as, just as

segundo, -da *adj* : second — **~** *n* : second (one) — **segundo** *nm* : second (unit of time)

seguro, -ra *adj* **1** : safe **2** FIRME : secure **3** CIERTO : sure, certain **4** FIABLE : reliable — **seguramente** *adv* : for sure, surely — **seguridad** *nf* **1** : safety **2** GARANTÍA : security **3** CERTEZA : certainty **4** CONFIANZA : confidence — **seguro** *adv* : certainly — **~** *nm* **1** : insurance **2** : safety (device)

seis *adj & nm* : six — **seiscientos, -tas** *adj* : six hundred — **seiscientos** *nms & pl* : six hundred

seísmo *nm* : earthquake

selección *nf, pl* **-ciones** : selection — **seleccionar** *vt* : select, choose — **selectivo, -va** *adj* : selective — **selecto, -ta** *adj* : choice, select

sellar *vt* **1** : seal **2** TIMBRAR : stamp — **sello** *nm* **1** : seal **2** TIMBRE : stamp **3** *or* **~ distintivo** : hallmark

selva *nf* **1** : jungle **2** BOSQUE : forest

semáforo *nm* : traffic light

semana *nf* **1** : week — **semanal** *adj* : weekly — **semanario** *nf* : weekly

semántica *nf* : semantics — **semántico, -ca** *adj* : semantic

semblante *nm* **1** : countenance, face **2** APARIENCIA : look

sembrar {55} *vt* **1** : sow **2 ~ de** : strew with

semejar *vi* : resemble — **semejarse** *vr* : look alike — **semejante** *adj* **1** : similar **2** TAL : such — **~** *nm* : fellowman — **semejanza** *nf* : similarity

semen *nm* : semen — **semental** *nm* **1** : stud **2 caballo ~** : stallion

semestre *nm* : semester

semiconductor *nm* : semiconductor

semifinal *nf* : semifinal

semilla *nf* : seed — **semillero** *nm* **1** : nursery (for plants) **2** HERVIDERO : hotbed, breeding ground

seminario *nm* **1** : seminary **2** CURSO : seminar, course

sémola *nf* : semolina

senado *nm* : senate — **senador, -dora** *n* : senator

sencillo, -lla *adj* **1** : simple **2** ÚNICO : single — **sencillez** *nf* : simplicity

senda *nf* *or* **sendero** *nm* : path, way

sendos, -das *adj pl* : each, both

senil *adj* : senile

seno *nm* **1** : breast, bosom **2** : sinus (in anatomy) **3 ~ materno** : womb

sensación *nf, pl* **-ciones** : feeling, sensation — **sensacional** *adj* : sensational — **sensacionalista** *adj* : sensationalistic, lurid

sensato, -ta *adj* : sensible — **sensatez** *nf* : good sense

sensible *adj* **1** : sensitive **2** APRECIABLE : considerable, significant — **sensibilidad** *nf* : sensitivity — **sensitivo, -va** *or* **sensorial** *adj* : sense, sensory

sensual *adj* : sensual, sensuous — **sensualidad** *nf* : sensuality

sentar {55} *vt* **1** : seat, sit **2** ESTABLECER : establish, set — *vi* **1** : suit **2 ~ bien a** : agree with (of food or drink) — **sentarse** *vr* : sit (down) — **sentado, -da** *adj* **1** : sitting, seated **2 dar por sentado** : take for granted

sentencia *nf* **1** FALLO : sentence, judgment **2** MÁXIMA : saying — **sentenciar** *vt* : sentence

sentido, -da *adj* **1** : heartfelt, sincere **2** SENSIBLE : touchy, sensitive — **sentido** *nm* **1** : sense **2** CONOCIMIENTO : consciousness **3** DIRECCIÓN : direction **4 doble ~** : double entendre **5 ~ común** : common sense **6 ~ del humor** : sense of humor **7 ~ único** : one-way

sentimiento *nm* **1** : feeling, emotion **2** PESAR : regret — **sentimental** *adj* : sentimental — **sentimentalismo** *nm* : sentimentality

sentir {76} *vt* **1** : feel **2** OÍR : hear **3** LAMENTAR : be sorry for **4 lo siento** : I'm sorry — *vi* : feel — **sentirse** *vr* : feel

seña *nf* **1** : signal **2 ~s** *nfpl* DIRECCIÓN : address **3 ~s particulares** : distinguishing marks

señal *nf* **1** : signal **2** AVISO, INDICIO : sign **3** DEPÓSITO : deposit **4 dar ~es**

de : show signs of **5 en ~ de** : as a token of — **señalado, -da** *adj* : notable — **señalar** *vt* **1** INDICAR : indicate, point out **2** MARCAR : mark **3** FIJAR : fix, set — **señalarse** *vr* : distinguish oneself

señor, -ñora *n* **1** : gentleman *m*, man *m*, lady *f*, woman *f* **2** : Sir *m*, Madam *f* **3** : Mr. *m*, Mrs. *f* **4 señora** : wife *f* **5 el Señor** : the Lord — **señorial** *adj* : stately — **señorita** *nf* **1** : young lady, young woman **2** : Miss

señuelo *nm* **1** : decoy **2** TRAMPA : bait, lure

separar *vt* **1** : separate **2** QUITAR : detach, remove **3** APARTAR : move away **4** DESTITUIR : dismiss — **separarse** *vr* **1** APARTARSE : separate **2** : part company — **separación** *nf, pl* **-ciones** : separation — **separado, -da** *adj* **1** : separate **2** : separated (of persons) **3 por separado** : separately

septentrional *adj* : northern

séptico, -ca *adj* : septic

septiembre *nm* : September

séptimo, -ma *adj* : seventh — **~** *n* : seventh

sepulcro *nm* : tomb, sepulchre — **sepultar** *vt* : bury — **sepultura** *nf* **1** : burial **2** TUMBA : grave

sequedad *nf* : dryness — **sequía** *nf* : drought

séquito *nm* : retinue, entourage

ser {77} *vi* **1** : be **2 a no ~ que** : unless **3 ¿cuánto es?** : how much is it? **4 es más** : what's more **5 ~ de** : belong to **6 ~ de** : come from **7 son las diez** : it's ten o'clock — **~** *nm* **1** ENTE : being **2 ~ humano** : human being

serbio, -bia *adj* : Serb, Serbian

serenar *vt* : calm — **serenarse** *vr* : calm down — **serenata** *nf* : serenade — **serenidad** *nf* : serenity — **sereno, -na** *adj* **1** : serene, calm **2** : fair, clear (of weather) — **sereno** *nm* : night watchman

serie *nf* **1** : series **2 fabricación en ~** : mass production **3 fuera de ~** : extraordinary — **serial** *nm* : serial

serio, -ria *adj* **1** : serious **2** RESPONSABLE : reliable **3 en serio** : seriously — **seriedad** *nf* : seriousness

sermón *nm, pl* **-mones** : sermon — **sermonear** *vt* : lecture, reprimand

serpentear *vi* : twist, wind — **serpiente** *nf* **1** : serpent, snake **2 ~ de cascabel** : rattlesnake

serrado, -da *adj* : serrated

serrano, -na *adj* **1** : mountain **2 jamón serrano** : cured ham

serrar {55} *vt* : saw — **serrín** *nm, pl* **-rrines** : sawdust — **serrucho** *nm* : saw, handsaw

servicio *nm* **1** : service **2 ~s** *nmpl* : restroom — **servicial** *adj* : obliging, helpful — **servidor, -dora** *n* **1** : servant **2 su seguro servidor** : yours truly — **servidumbre** *nf* **1** : servitude **2** CRIADOS : help, servants *pl* — **servil** *adj* : servile

servilleta *nf* : napkin

servir {54} *vt* : serve — *vi* **1** : work, function **2** VALER : be of use — **servirse** *vr* **1** : help oneself **2 sírvase sentarse** : please have a seat

sesenta *adj* & *nm* : sixty

sesgo *nm* : bias, slant

sesión *nf, pl* **-siones 1** : session **2** : showing (of a film), performance (of a play)

seso : brain — **sesudo, -da** *adj* **1** : sensible **2** *fam* : brainy

seta *nf* : mushroom

setecientos, -tas *adj* : seven hundred — **setecientos** *nms & pl* : seven hundred

setenta *adj* & *nm* : seventy

setiembre *nm* → **septiembre**

seto *nm* **1** : fence **2 ~ vivo** : hedge

seudónimo *nm* : pseudonym

severo, -ra *adj* **1** : harsh, severe **2** : strict (of a teacher, etc.) — **severidad** *nf* : severity

sexagésimo, -ma *adj* & *n* : sixtieth

sexo *nm* : sex — **sexismo** *nm* : sexism — **sexista** *adj* & *nmf* : sexist

sexteto *nm* : sextet

sexto, -ta *adj* & *n* : sixth

sexual *adj* : sexual — **sexualidad** *nf* : sexuality

sexy *adj, pl* **sexy** *or* **sexys** : sexy

si *conj* **1** : if **2** (*in indirect questions*) : whether **3 ~ bien** : although **4 ~ no** : otherwise, or else

sí¹ *adv* **1** : yes **2 creo que ~** : I think so **3 porque ~** *fam* : (just) because — **~** *nm* : consent

sí² *pron* **1 de por ~** *or* **en ~** : by itself, in itself, per se **2 fuera de ~** : beside oneself **3 para ~ (mismo)** : to himself, to herself, for himself, for herself **4 entre ~** : among themselves

sico- → **psico-**

SIDA *or* **sida** *nm* : AIDS

siderurgia *nf* : iron and steel industry

sidra *nf* : (hard) cider

siega *nf* **1** : harvesting **2** : harvest (time)

siembra *nf* **1** : sowing **2** : sowing season

siempre *adv* **1** : always **2** *Lat* : still **3 para ~** : forever, for good **4 ~ que** : whenever, every time **5 ~ que** *or* **~ y cuando** : provided that

sien *nf* : temple

sierra *nf* **1** : saw **2** CORDILLERA : mountain range **3 la ~** : the mountains *pl*

siervo, -va *n* : slave

siesta *nf* : nap, siesta

siete *adj & nm* : seven

sífilis *nf* : syphilis

sifón *nm, pl* **-fones** : siphon

sigilo *nm* : secrecy

sigla *nf* : acronym, abbreviation

siglo *nm* **1** : century **2 hace ~s** : for ages

significar {72} *vt* **1** : mean, signify **2** EXPRESAR : express — **significación** *nf, pl* **-ciones 1** : significance, importance **2** : meaning (of a word, etc.) — **significado, -da** *adj* : well-known — **significado** *nm* : meaning — **significativo, -va** *adj* : significant

signo *nm* **1** : sign **2 ~ de admiración** : exclamation point **3 ~ de interrogación** : question mark

siguiente *adj* : next, following

sílaba *nf* : syllable

silbar *v* **1** : whistle **2** ABUCHEAR : hiss, boo — **silbato** *nm* : whistle — **silbido** *nm* **1** : whistle, whistling **2** ABUCHEO : hiss, booing

silenciar *vt* : silence — **silenciador** *nm* : muffler — **silencio** *nm* : silence — **silencioso, -sa** *adj* : silent, quiet

silicio *nm* : silicon

silla *nf* **1** : chair **2 ~ de montar** : saddle **3 ~ de ruedas** : wheelchair — **sillón** *nm, pl* **-llones** : armchair, easy chair

silo *nm* : silo

silueta *nf* **1** : silhouette **2** CONTORNO : outline, shape

silvestre *adj* : wild

silvicultura *nf* : forestry

símbolo *nm* : symbol — **simbólico, -ca** *adj* : symbolic — **simbolismo** *nm* : symbolism — **simbolizar** {21} *vt* : symbolize

simetría *nf* : symmetry — **simétrico, -ca** *adj* : symmetrical, symmetric

simiente *nf* : seed

símil *nm* **1** : simile **2** COMPARACIÓN : comparison — **similar** *adj* : similar, alike

simio *nm* : ape

simpatía *nf* **1** : liking, affection **2** AMABILIDAD : friendliness — **simpático, -ca** *adj* **1** : nice, likeable **2** AMABLE : pleasant, kind — **simpatizante** *nmf*

: sympathizer — **simpatizar** {21} *vi* **1** : get along, hit it off **2 ~ con** : sympathize with

simple *adj* **1** SENCILLO : simple **2** MERO : pure, sheer **3** TONTO : simpleminded — ~ *n* : fool, simpleton — **simpleza** *nf* **1** : simpleness **2** TONTERÍA : silly thing — **simplicidad** *nf* : simplicity — **simplificar** {72} *vt* : simplify

simposio *or* **simposium** *nm* : symposium

simular *vt* **1** : simulate **2** FINGIR : feign — **simulacro** *nm* : simulation, drill

simultáneo, -nea *adj* : simultaneous

sin *prep* **1** : without **2 ~ que** : without

sinagoga *nf* : synagogue

sincero, -ra *adj* : sincere — **sinceramente** *adv* : sincerely — **sinceridad** *nf* : sincerity

síncopa *nf* : syncopation

sincronizar {21} *vt* : synchronize

sindicato *nm* : (labor) union — **sindical** *adj* : union, labor

síndrome *nm* : syndrome

sinfín *nm* **1** : endless number **2 un ~ de** : no end of

sinfonía *nf* : symphony — **sinfónico, -ca** *adj* : symphonic

singular *adj* **1** : exceptional, outstanding **2** PECULIAR : peculiar **3** : singular (in grammar) — ~ *nm* : singular — **singularizar** {21} *vt* : single out — **singularizarse** *vr* : stand out

siniestro, -tra *adj* **1** : sinister **2** IZQUIERDO : left — **siniestro** *nm* : disaster

sinnúmero *nm* → **sinfín**

sino *conj* **1** : but, rather **2** EXCEPTO : except, save

sinónimo, -ma *adj* : synonymous — **sinónimo** *nm* : synonym

sinopsis *nfs & pl* : synopsis

sinrazón *nf, pl* **-zones** : wrong

sintaxis *nfs & pl* : syntax

síntesis *nfs & pl* : synthesis — **sintético, -ca** *adj* : synthetic — **sintetizar** {21} *vt* **1** : synthesize **2** RESUMIR : summarize

síntoma *nm* : symptom — **sintomático, -ca** *adj* : symptomatic

sintonía *nf* **1** : tuning in (of a radio) **2 en ~ con** : in tune with — **sintonizar** {21} *vt* : tune (in) to

sinuoso, -sa *adj* : winding

sinvergüenza *nmf* : scoundrel

sionismo *nm* : Zionism

siquiera *adv* **1** : at least **2 ni ~** : not even — ~ *conj* : even if

sirena *nf* **1** : mermaid **2** : siren (of an ambulance, etc.)

sirio, -ria *adj* : Syrian

sirviente, -ta *n* : servant, maid *f*

sisear *vi* : hiss — **siseo** *nm* : hiss

sismo *nm* : earthquake — **sísmico, -ca** *adj* : seismic

sistema *nm* **1** : system **2 por ~** : systematically — **sistemático, -ca** *adj* : systematic

sitiar *vt* : besiege

sitio *nm* **1** : place, site **2** ESPACIO : room, space **3** CERCO : siege **4 en cualquier ~** : anywhere

situar {3} *vt* : situate, place — **situarse** *vr* **1** : be located **2** ESTABLECERSE : get oneself established — **situación** *nf, pl* **-ciones** : situation, position — **situado, -da** *adj* : situated, placed

slip *nm* : briefs *pl*, underpants *pl*

smoking *nm* : tuxedo

so *prep* : under

sobaco *nm* : armpit

sobar *vt* **1** : finger, handle **2** : knead (dough) — **sobado, -da** *adj* : worn, shabby

soberanía *nf* : sovereignty — **soberano, -na** *adj & n* : sovereign

soberbia *nf* : pride, arrogance — **soberbio, -bia** *adj* : proud, arrogant

sobornar *vt* : bribe — **soborno** *nm* **1** : bribe **2** : (action of) bribery

sobrar *vi* **1** : be more than enough **2** RESTAR : be left over — **sobra** *nf* **1** : surplus **2 de ~** : to spare **3 ~s** *nfpl* : leftovers — **sobrado, -da** *adj* : more than enough — **sobrante** *adj* : remaining

sobre[1] *nm* : envelope

sobre[2] *prep* **1** : on, on top of **2** POR ENCIMA DE : over, above **3** ACERCA DE : about **4 ~ todo** : especially, above all

sobrecama *nmf Lat* : bedspread

sobrecargar {52} *vt* : overload, overburden

sobrecoger {15} *vt* : startle — **sobrecogerse** *vr* : be startled

sobrecubierta *nf* : dust jacket

sobredosis *nfs & pl* : overdose

sobreentender {56} *vt* : infer, understand — **sobreentenderse** *vr* : be understood

sobreestimar *vt* : overestimate

sobregiro *nm* : overdraft

sobrellevar *vt* : endure, bear

sobremesa *nf* **de ~** : after-dinner

sobrenatural *adj* : supernatural

sobrenombre *nm* : nickname

sobrentender → **sobreentender**

sobrepasar *vt* : exceed

sobreponer {60} *vt* **1** : superimpose **2** ANTEPONER : put before — **sobreponerse** *vr* **~ a** : overcome

sobresalir {73} *vi* **1** : protrude **2** DESTACARSE : stand out — **sobresaliente** *adj* : outstanding

sobresaltar *vt* : startle — **sobresaltarse** *vr* : start, jump up — **sobresalto** *nm* : fright

sobrestimar → **sobreestimar**

sobretodo *nm* : overcoat

sobrevenir {87} *vi* : happen, ensue

sobrevivencia *nf* → **supervivencia**

sobreviviente *adj & nmf* → **superviviente**

sobrevivir *vi* : survive — *vt* : outlive

sobrevolar {19} *vt* : fly over

sobriedad *nf* **1** : sobriety **2** MODERACIÓN : restraint

sobrino, -na *n* : nephew *m*, niece *f*

sobrio, -bria *adj* : sober

socarrón, -rrona *adj, mpl* **-rrones** : sarcastic

socavar *vt* : undermine

sociable *adj* : sociable — **social** *adj* : social — **socialismo** *nm* : socialism — **socialista** *adj & nmf* : socialist — **sociedad** *nf* **1** : society **2** EMPRESA : company **3 ~ anónima** : incorporated company — **socio, -cia** *n* **1** : partner **2** MIEMBRO : member — **sociología** *nf* : sociology — **sociólogo, -ga** *n* : sociologist

socorrer *vt* : help — **socorrista** *nmf* : lifeguard — **socorro** *nm* : help

soda *nf* : soda (water)

sodio *nf* : sodium

sofá *nm* : couch, sofa

sofisticación *nf, pl* **-ciones** : sophistication — **sofisticado, -da** *adj* : sophisticated

sofocar {72} *vt* **1** : suffocate, smother **2** : put out (a fire), stifle (a rebellion, etc.) — **sofocarse** *vr* **1** : suffocate **2** *fam* : get upset — **sofocante** *adj* : suffocating, stifling

sofreír {66} *vt* : sauté

soga *nf* : rope

soja *nf* → **soya**

sojuzgar *vt* : subdue, subjugate

sol *nm* **1** : sun **2 hacer ~** : be sunny

solamente *adv* : only, just

solapa *nf* **1** : lapel (of a jacket) **2** : flap (of an envelope) — **solapado, -da** *adj* : secret, underhanded

solar[1] *adj* : solar, sun

solar[2] *nm* : lot, site

solariego, -ga *adj* : ancestral

solaz *nm, pl* **-laces 1** : solace **2** DESCANSO : relaxation — **solazarse** {21} *vr* : relax

soldado *nm* **1** : soldier **2 ~ raso** : private

soldar {19} *vt* : weld, solder — **solda-**

dor *nm* : soldering iron — **soldador, -dora** *n* : welder

soleado, -da *adj* : sunny

soledad *nf* : loneliness, solitude

solemne *adj* : solemn — **solemnidad** *nf* : solemnity

soler {78} *vi* **1** : be in the habit of **2 suele llegar tarde** : he usually arrives late

solicitar *vt* **1** : request, solicit **2** : apply for (a job, etc.) — **solicitante** *nmf* : applicant — **solícito, -ta** *adj* : solicitous, obliging — **solicitud** *nf* **1** : concern **2** PETICIÓN : request **3** : application (for a job, etc.)

solidaridad *nf* : solidarity

sólido, -da *adj* **1** : solid **2** : sound (of an argument, etc.) — **sólido** *nm* : solid — **solidez** *nf* : solidity — **solidificar** {72} *vt* : solidify — **solidificarse** *vr* : solidify, harden

soliloquio *nm* : soliloquy

solista *nmf* : soloist

solitario, -ria *adj* **1** : solitary **2** AISLADO : lonely, deserted — ~ *n* : recluse — **solitaria** *nf* : tapeworm — **solitario** *nm* : solitaire

sollozar {21} *vi* : sob — **sollozo** *nm* : sob

solo, -la *adj* **1** : alone **2** AISLADO : lonely **3 a solas** : alone, by oneself — **solo** *nm* : solo

sólo *adv* : just, only

solomillo *nm* : sirloin

solsticio *nm* : solstice

soltar {19} *vt* **1** : release **2** DEJAR CAER : let go of, drop **3** DESATAR : unfasten, undo — **soltarse** *vr* **1** : break free **2** DESATARSE : come undone

soltero, -ra *adj* : single, unmarried — ~ *n* **1** : bachelor *m*, single woman *f* **2 apellido de soltera** : maiden name

soltura *nf* **1** : looseness **2** : fluency (in language) **3** AGILIDAD : agility, ease

soluble *adj* : soluble

solución *nf*, *pl* **-ciones** : solution — **solucionar** *vt* : solve, resolve

solventar *vt* **1** : settle, pay **2** RESOLVER : resolve — **solvente** *adj & nm* : solvent

sombra *nf* **1** : shadow **2** : shade (of a tree, etc.) **3** ~s *nfpl* : darkness, shadows — **sombreado, -da** *adj* : shady

sombrero *nm* : hat

sombrilla *nf* : parasol, umbrella

sombrío, -bría *adj* : dark, somber, gloomy

somero, -ra *adj* : superficial

someter *vt* **1** : subjugate **2** SUBORDINAR : subordinate **3** : subject (to treatment, etc.) **4** PRESENTAR : submit, present — **someterse** *vr* **1** : submit, yield **2** ~ **a** : undergo

somnífero, -ra *adj* : soporific — **somnífero** *nm* : sleeping pill — **somnoliento, -ta** *adj* : drowsy, sleepy

somos → **ser**

son[1] → **ser**

son[2] *nm* **1** : sound **2 en** ~ **de** : as, in the manner of

sonajero *nm* : (baby's) rattle

sonámbulo, -la *n* : sleepwalker

sonar {19} *vi* **1** : sound **2** : ring (as a bell) **3** : look or sound familiar **4** ~ **a** : sound like — **sonarse** *vr* or ~ **las narices** : blow one's nose

sonata *nf* : sonata

sondear *vt* **1** : sound, probe **2** : survey, sound out (opinions, etc.) — **sondeo** *nm* **1** : sounding, probing **2** ENCUESTA : survey, poll

soneto *nm* : sonnet

sónico, -ca *adj* : sonic

sonido *nm* : sound

sonoro, -ra *adj* **1** : resonant, sonorous **2** RUIDOSO : loud

sonreír {66} *vi* : smile — **sonreírse** *vr* : smile — **sonriente** *adj* : smiling — **sonrisa** *nf* : smile

sonrojar *vt* : cause to blush — **sonrojarse** *vr* : blush — **sonrojo** *nm* : blush

sonrosado, -da *adj* : rosy, pink

sonsacar {72} *vt* : wheedle (out)

soñar {19} *v* **1** : dream **2** ~ **con** : dream about **3** ~ **despierto** : daydream — **soñador, -dora** *adj* : dreamy — ~ *n* : dreamer — **soñoliento, -ta** *adj* : sleepy, drowsy

sopa *nf* : soup

sopesar *vt* : weigh, consider

soplar *vi* : blow — *vt* : blow out, blow off, blow up — **soplete** *nm* : blowtorch — **soplo** *nm* : puff, gust

soplón, -plona *n*, *pl* **-plones** *fam* : sneak

sopor *nm* : drowsiness — **soporífero, -ra** *adj* : soporific

soportar *vt* **1** SOSTENER : support **2** AGUANTAR : bear — **soporte** *nm* : support

soprano *nmf* : soprano

sor *nf* : Sister (in religion)

sorber *vt* **1** : sip **2** ABSORBER : absorb **3** CHUPAR : suck up — **sorbete** *nm* : sherbet — **sorbo** *nm* : sip, swallow **2 beber a** ~**s** : sip

sordera *nf* : deafness

sórdido, -da *adj* : sordid, squalid

sordo, -da *adj* **1** : deaf **2** : muted (of a

sound) — **sordomudo, -da** n : deaf-mute

sorna nf : sarcasm

sorprender vt : surprise — **sorprenderse** vr : be surprised — **sorprendente** adj : surprising — **sorpresa** nf : surprise

sortear vt 1 : raffle off, draw lots for 2 ESQUIVAR : dodge — **sorteo** nm : drawing, raffle

sortija nf 1 : ring 2 : ringlet (of hair)

sortilegio nm 1 HECHIZO : spell 2 HECHICERÍA : sorcery

sosegar {49} vt 1 : calm, pacify — **sosegarse** vr : calm down — **sosegado, -da** adj : calm, tranquil — **sosiego** nm : calm

soslayo: de ~ adv phr : obliquely, sideways

soso, -sa adj 1 : insipid, tasteless 2 ABURRIDO : dull

sospechar vt : suspect — **sospecha** nf : suspicion — **sospechoso, -sa** adj : suspicious — ~ n : suspect

sostener {80} vt 1 : support 2 SUJETAR : hold 3 MANTENER : sustain, maintain — **sostenerse** vr 1 : stand (up) 2 CONTINUAR : remain 3 SUSTENTARSE : support oneself — **sostén** nm, pl **-tenes** 1 APOYO : support 2 SUSTENTO : sustenance 3 : brassiere, bra — **sostenido, -da** adj 1 : sustained 2 : sharp (in music) — **sostenido** nm : sharp

sótano nm : basement

soterrar {55} vt 1 : bury 2 ESCONDER : hide

soto nm : grove

soviético, -ca adj : Soviet

soy → ser

soya nf : soy

Sr. nm : Mr. — **Sra.** nf : Mrs., Ms. — **Srta.** or **Srita.** nf : Miss, Ms.

su adj 1 : his, her, its, their, one's 2 (formal) : your

suave adj 1 : soft 2 LISO : smooth 3 APACIBLE : gentle, mild — **suavidad** nf 1 : softness, smoothness 2 APACIBILIDAD : mildness, gentleness — **suavizar** {21} vt : soften, smooth

subalimentado, -da adj : undernourished, underfed

subalterno, -na adj 1 SUBORDINADO : subordinate 2 SECUNDARIO : secondary — ~ n : subordinate

subarrendar {55} vt : sublet

subasta nf : auction — **subastar** vt : auction (off)

subcampeón, -peona n, mpl **-peones** : runner-up

subcomité nm : subcommittee

subconsciente adj & nm : subconscious

subdesarrollado, -da adj : underdeveloped

subdirector, -tora n : assistant manager

súbdito, -ta n : subject

subdividir vt : subdivide — **subdivisión** nf, pl **-siones** : subdivision

subestimar vt : underestimate

subir vt 1 : climb, go up 2 LLEVAR : bring up, take up 3 AUMENTAR : raise — vi 1 : go up, come up 2 ~ a : get in (a car), get on (a bus, etc.) — **subirse** vr 1 : climb (up) 2 ~ a : get in (a car), get on (a bus, etc.) 3 ~ a la cabeza : go to one's head — **subida** nf 1 : ascent, climb 2 AUMENTO : rise 3 PENDIENTE : slope — **subido, -da** adj 1 : bright, strong 2 ~ de tono : risqué

súbito, -ta adj 1 : sudden 2 de súbito : all of a sudden, suddenly

subjetivo, -va adj : subjective

subjuntivo, -va adj : subjunctive — **subjuntivo** nm : subjunctive (case)

sublevar vt : stir up, incite to rebellion — **sublevarse** vr : rebel — **sublevación** nf, pl **-ciones** : uprising, rebellion

sublime adj : sublime

submarino, -na adj : underwater — **submarino** nm : submarine — **submarinismo** nm : scuba diving

subordinar vt : subordinate — **subordinado, -da** adj & n : subordinate

subproducto nm : by-product

subrayar vt 1 : underline 2 ENFATIZAR : emphasize, stress

subrepticio, -cia adj : surreptitious

subsanar vt 1 : rectify, correct 2 : make up for (a deficiency), overcome (an obstacle)

subscribir → suscribir

subsidio nm : subsidy, benefit

subsiguiente adj : subsequent

subsistir vi 1 : live, subsist 2 SOBREVIVIR : survive — **subsistencia** nf : subsistence

substancia nf → sustancia

subterfugio nm : subterfuge

subterráneo, -nea adj : underground, subterranean — **subterráneo** nm : underground passage

subtítulo nm : subtitle

suburbio nm 1 : suburb 2 : slum (outside a city) — **suburbano, -na** adj : suburban

subvencionar vt : subsidize — **sub-**

vención *nf, pl* **-ciones** : subsidy, grant

subvertir {76} *vt* : subvert — **subversión** *nf, pl* **-siones** : subversion — **subversivo, -va** *adj & n* : subversive

subyacente *adj* : underlying

subyugar {52} *vt* : subjugate, subdue

succión *nf, pl* **-ciones** : suction — **succionar** *vt* : suck up, draw in

sucedáneo *nm* : substitute

suceder *vi* 1 : happen, occur 2 ~ **a** : follow 3 **suceda lo que suceda** : come what may — **sucesión** *nf, pl* **-siones** : succession — **sucesivo, -va** *adj* : successive — **suceso** *nm* 1 : event 2 INCIDENTE : incident — **sucesor, -sora** *n* : successor

suciedad *nf* 1 : dirtiness 2 MUGRE : dirt, filth

sucinto, -ta *adj* : succinct, concise

sucio, -cia *adj* : dirty, filthy

suculento, -ta *adj* : succulent

sucumbir *vi* : succumb

sucursal *nf* : branch (of a business)

sudadera *nf* : sweatshirt — **sudado, -da** *adj* : sweaty

sudafricano, -na *adj* : South African

sudamericano, -na *adj* : South American

sudar *vi* : sweat

sudeste → **sureste**

sudoeste → **suroeste**

sudor *nm* : sweat — **sudoroso, -sa** *adj* : sweaty

sueco, -ca *adj* : Swedish — **sueco** *nm* : Swedish (language)

suegro, -gra *n* 1 : father-in-law *m*, mother-in-law *f* 2 **suegros** *nmpl* : in-laws

suela *nf* : sole (of a shoe)

sueldo *nm* : salary, wage

suelo *nm* 1 : ground 2 : floor (in a house) 3 TIERRA : soil, land

suelto, -ta *adj* : loose, free — **suelto** *nm* : loose change

sueño *nm* 1 : dream 2 **coger el** ~ : get to sleep 3 **tener** ~ : be sleepy

suero *nm* 1 : whey 2 : serum (in medicine)

suerte *nf* 1 : luck, fortune 2 AZAR : chance 3 DESTINO : fate 4 CLASE : sort, kind 5 **por** ~ : luckily 6 **tener** ~ : be lucky

suéter *nm* : sweater

suficiencia *nf* 1 CAPACIDAD : competence, proficiency 2 PRESUNCIÓN : smugness — **suficiente** *adj* 1 : enough, sufficient 2 PRESUNTUOSO : smug — **suficientemente** *adv* : enough

sufijo *nm* : suffix

sufragio *nm* : suffrage, vote

sufrir *vt* 1 : suffer 2 SOPORTAR : bear, stand — *vi* : suffer — **sufrido, -da** *adj* 1 : long-suffering 2 : sturdy, serviceable (of clothing) — **sufrimiento** *nm* : suffering

sugerir {76} *vt* : suggest — **sugerencia** *nf* : suggestion — **sugestión** *nf, pl* **-tiones** : suggestion — **sugestionable** *adj* : impressionable — **sugestionar** *vt* : influence — **sugestivo, -va** *adj* 1 : suggestive 2 ESTIMULANTE : interesting, stimulating

suicidio *nm* : suicide — **suicida** *adj* : suicidal — ~ *nmf* : suicide (victim) — **suicidarse** *vr* : commit suicide

suite *nf* : suite

suizo, -za *adj* : Swiss

sujetar *vt* 1 : hold (on to) 2 FIJAR : fasten 3 DOMINAR : subdue — **sujetarse** *vr* 1 ~ **a** : hold on to, cling to 2 ~ **a** : abide by — **sujeción** *nf, pl* **-ciones** 1 : fastening 2 DOMINACIÓN : subjection — **sujetador** *nm* *Spain* : brassiere, bra — **sujetapapeles** *nms & pl* : paper clip — **sujeto, -ta** *adj* 1 : fastened 2 ~ **a** : subject to — **sujeto** *nm* 1 : individual 2 : subject (in grammar)

sulfuro *nm* : sulfur — **sulfúrico, -ca** *adj* : sulfuric

sultán *nm, pl* **-tanes** : sultan

suma *nf* 1 : sum, total 2 : addition (in mathematics) 3 **en** ~ : in short — **sumamente** *adv* : extremely — **sumar** *vt* 1 : add (up) 2 TOTALIZAR : add up to, total — *vi* : add up — **sumarse** *vr* ~ **a** : join

sumario, -ria *adj* : concise — **sumario** *nm* 1 : summary 2 : indictment (in law)

sumergir {35} *vt* : submerge, plunge — **sumergirse** *vr* : be submerged — **sumergible** *adj* : waterproof (of a watch, etc.)

sumidero *nm* : drain

suministrar *vt* : supply, provide — **suministro** *nm* : supply, provision

sumir *vt* : plunge, immerse — **sumirse** *vr* ~ **en** : sink into

sumisión *nf, pl* **-siones** : submission — **sumiso, -sa** *adj* : submissive

sumo, -ma *adj* 1 : highest, supreme 2 **de suma importancia** : of great importance

suntuoso, -sa *adj* : sumptuous, lavish

super *or* **súper** *nm fam* : supermarket

superabundancia *nf* : overabundance

superar *vt* 1 : surpass, outdo 2 VENCER : overcome — **superarse** *vr* : improve oneself

superávit *nm* : surplus
superestructura *nf* : superstructure
superficie *nf* **1** : surface **2** ÁREA : area
— **superficial** *adj* : superficial
superfluo, -flua *adj* : superfluous
superintendente *nmf* : supervisor, superintendent
superior *adj* **1** : superior **2** : upper (of a floor, etc.) **3** ~ **a** : above, higher than — ~ *nm* : superior — **superioridad** *nf* : superiority
superlativo, -va *adj* : superlative — **superlativo** *nm* : superlative
supermercado *nm* : supermarket
superpoblado, -da *adj* : overpopulated
supersónico, -ca *adj* : supersonic
superstición *nf*, *pl* **-ciones** : superstition — **supersticioso, -sa** *adj* : superstitious
supervisar *vt* : supervise, oversee — **supervisión** *nf*, *pl* **-siones** : supervision — **supervisor, -sora** *n* : supervisor
supervivencia *nf* : survival — **superviviente** *adj* : surviving — ~ *nmf* : survivor
suplantar *vt* : supplant, replace
suplemento *nm* : supplement — **suplementario, -ria** *adj* : supplementary
suplente *adj & nmf* : substitute
suplicar {72} *vt* : beg, entreat — **súplica** *nf* : plea, entreaty
suplicio *nm* : ordeal, torture
suplir *vt* **1** : make up for **2** REEMPLAZAR : replace
supo, etc. → **saber**
suponer {60} *vt* **1** : suppose, assume **2** SIGNIFICAR : mean **3** IMPLICAR : involve, entail — **suposición** *nf*, *pl* **-ciones** : supposition
supositorio *nm* : suppository
supremo, -ma *adj* : supreme — **supremacía** *nf* : supremacy
suprimir *vt* **1** : suppress, eliminate **2** : delete (text) — **supresión** *nf*, *pl* **-siones** **1** : suppression, elimination **2** : deletion (of text)
supuesto, -ta *adj* **1** : supposed, alleged **2 por supuesto** : of course — ~ *nm* : assumption — **supuestamente** *adv* : allegedly
sur *nm* **1** : south, South **2** : south wind **3 del** ~ : south, southerly
surafricano, -na → **sudafricano**
suramericano, -na → **sudamericano**
surcar {72} *vt* **1** : plow (earth) **2** : cut through (air, water, etc.) — **surco** *nm* : groove, furrow, rut
sureño, -ña *adj* : southern, Southern — ~ *n* : Southerner

sureste *adj* **1** : southeast, southeastern **2** : southeasterly (of wind, etc.) — ~ *nm* : southeast, Southeast
surf *or* **surfing** *nm* : surfing
surgir {35} *vi* **1** : arise **2** APARECER : appear — **surgimiento** *nm* : rise, emergence
suroeste *adj* **1** : southwest, southwestern **2** : southwesterly (of wind, etc.) — ~ *nm* : southwest, Southwest
surtir *vt* **1** : supply, provide **2** ~ **efecto** : have an effect — **surtirse** *vr* ~ **de** : stock up on — **surtido, -da** *adj* **1** : assorted, varied **2** : stocked (with merchandise) — **surtido** *nm* : assortment, selection — **surtidor** *nm* : gas pump
susceptible *adj* **1** : susceptible, sensitive **2** ~ **de** : capable of — **susceptibilidad** *nf* : sensitivity
suscitar *vt* : provoke, arouse
suscribir {33} *vt* **1** : sign (a formal document) **2** RATIFICAR : endorse — **suscribirse** *vr* ~ **a** : subscribe to — **suscripción** *nf*, *pl* **-ciones** : subscription — **suscriptor, -tora** *n* : subscriber
susodicho, -cha *adj* : aforementioned
suspender *vt* **1** : suspend **2** COLGAR : hang **3** *Spain* : fail (an exam, etc.) — **suspensión** *nf*, *pl* **-siones** : suspension — **suspenso** *nm* **1** *Spain* : failure (in an exam, etc.) **2** *Lat* : suspense
suspicaz *adj*, *pl* **-caces** : suspicious
suspirar *vi* : sigh — **suspiro** *nm* : sigh
sustancia *nf* **1** : substance **2 sin** ~ : shallow, lacking substance — **sustancial** *adj* : substantial, significant — **sustancioso, -sa** *adj* : substantial, solid
sustantivo *nm* : noun
sustentar *vt* **1** : support **2** ALIMENTAR : sustain, nourish **3** MANTENER : maintain — **sustentarse** *vr* : support oneself — **sustentación** *nf*, *pl* **-ciones** : support — **sustento** *nm* **1** : means of support, livelihood **2** ALIMENTO : sustenance
sustituir {41} *vt* : replace, substitute — **sustitución** *nf*, *pl* **-ciones** : replacement, substitution — **sustituto, -ta** *n* : substitute
susto *nm* : fright, scare
sustraer {81} *vt* **1** : remove, take away **2** : subtract (in mathematics) — **sustraerse** *vr* ~ **a** : avoid, evade — **sustracción** *nf*, *pl* **-ciones** : subtraction
susurrar *vi* **1** : whisper **2** : murmur (of water) **3** : rustle (of leaves, etc.) — *vt* : whisper — **susurro** *nm* **1** : whisper **2**

: murmur (of water) **3** : rustle, rustling (of leaves, etc.)

sutil *adj* **1** : delicate, fine **2** : subtle (of fragrances, differences, etc.) — **sutileza** *nf* : subtlety

sutura *nf* : suture

suyo, -ya *adj* **1** : his, her, its, one's, theirs **2** (*formal*) : yours **3 un primo suyo** : a cousin of his/hers — **~** *pron* **1** : his, hers, its (own), one's own, theirs **2** (*formal*) : yours

switch *nm Lat* : switch

T

t *nf* : t, 21st letter of the Spanish alphabet

taba *nf* : anklebone

tabaco *nm* : tobacco — **tabacalero, -ra** *adj* : tobacco

tábano *nm* : horsefly

taberna *nf* : tavern

tabicar {72} *vt* : wall up — **tabique** *nm* : thin wall, partition

tabla *nf* **1** : board, plank **2** LISTA : table, list **3 ~ de planchar** : ironing board **4 ~s** *nfpl* : stage, boards *pl* — **tablado** *nm* **1** : flooring **2** PLATAFORMA : platform **3** : (theater) stage — **tablero** *nm* **1** : bulletin board **2** : board (in games) **3** PIZARRA : blackboard **4 ~ de instrumentos** : dashboard, instrument panel

tableta *nf* **1** : tablet, pill **2** : bar (of chocolate)

tablilla *nf* : slat — **tablón** *nm, pl* **-lones 1** : plank, beam **2 ~ de anuncios** : bulletin board

tabú *adj* : taboo — **tabú** *nm, pl* **-búes** or **-bús** : taboo

tabular *vt* : tabulate

taburete *nm* : stool

tacaño, -na *adj* : stingy, miserly

tacha *nf* **1** : flaw, defect **2 sin ~** : flawless

tachar *vt* **1** : cross out, delete **2 ~ de** : accuse of, label as

tachón *nm, pl* **-chones** : stud, hobnail — **tachuela** *nf* : tack, hobnail

tácito, -ta *adj* : tacit

taciturno, -na *adj* : taciturn

taco *nm* **1** : stopper, plug **2** *Lat* : heel (of a shoe) **3** : cue (in billiards) **4** : taco (in cooking)

tacón *nm, pl* **-cones** : heel (of a shoe) **2 de ~ alto** : high-heeled

táctica *nf* : tactic, tactics *pl* — **táctico, -ca** *adj* : tactical

tacto *nm* **1** : (sense of) touch, feel **2** DELICADEZA : tact

tafetán *nm, pl* **-tanes** : taffeta

tailandés, -desa *adj* : Thai

taimado, -da *adj* : crafty, sly

tajar *vt* : cut, slice — **tajada** *nf* **1** : slice **2 sacar ~** *fam* : get one's share — **tajante** *adj* : categorical — **tajo** *nm* **1** : cut, gash **2** ESCARPA : steep cliff

tal *adv* **1** : so, in such a way **2 con ~ que** : provided that, as long as **3 ¿qué ~?** : how are you?, how's it going? — **~** *adj* **1** : such, such a **2 ~ vez** : maybe, perhaps — **~** *pron* **1** : such a one, such a thing **2 ~ para cual** : two of a kind

taladrar *vt* : drill — **taladro** *nm* : drill

talante *nm* **1** HUMOR : mood **2** VOLUNTAD : willingness

talar *vt* : cut down, fell

talco *nm* : talcum powder

talego *nm* : sack

talento *nm* : talent — **talentoso, -sa** *adj* : talented

talismán *nm, pl* **-manes** : talisman, charm

talla *nf* **1** : sculpture, carving **2** ESTATURA : height **3** : size (in clothing) — **tallar** *vt* **1** : sculpt, carve **2** : measure (someone's height)

tallarín *nf, pl* **-rines** : noodle

talle *nm* **1** : waist, waistline **2** FIGURA : figure **3** : measurements *pl* (of clothing)

taller *nm* **1** : workshop **2** : studio (of an artist)

tallo *nm* : stalk, stem

talón *nm, pl* **-lones 1** : heel (of the foot) **2** : stub (of a check) — **talonario** *nm* : checkbook

taltuza *nf* : gopher

tamal *nm* : tamale

tamaño, -ña *adj* : such, such a big — **tamaño** *nm* **1** : size **2 de ~ natural** : life-size

tambalearse *vr* **1** : teeter, wobble **2** : stagger, totter (of persons)

también *adv* : too, as well, also

tambor *nm* : drum — **tamborilear** *vi* : drum

tamiz *nm* : sieve — **tamizar** {21} *vt* : sift

tampoco *adv* : neither, not either

tampón *nm, pl* **-pones 1** : tampon **2** : ink pad (for stamping)

tan *adv* **1** : so, so very **2 ~ pronto como** : as soon as **3 ~ sólo** : only, merely

tanda *nf* **1** TURNO : turn, shift **2** GRUPO : batch, lot, series

tangente *nf* : tangent

tangible *adj* : tangible

tango *nm* : tango

tanque *nm* : tank

tantear *vt* **1** : feel, grope **2** SOPESAR : size up, weigh — *vi* : feel one's way — **tanteador** *nm* : scoreboard — **tanteo** *nm* **1** : weighing, sizing up **2** PUNTUACIÓN : scoring (in sports)

tanto *adv* **1** : so much **2** (*in expressions of time*) : so long — ~ *nm* **1** : certain amount **2** : goal, point (in sports) **3** un ~ : somewhat, rather — **tanto, -ta** *adj* **1** : so much, so many **2** (*in comparisons*) : as much, as many **3** *fam* : however many — ~ *pron* **1** : so much, so many **2 entre** ~ : meanwhile **3 por lo** ~ : therefore

tañer {79} *vt* **1** : ring (a bell) **2** : play (a musical instrument)

tapa *nf* **1** : cover, top, lid **2** *Spain* : snack

tapacubos *nms & pl* : hubcap

tapar *vt* **1** : cover, put a lid on **2** OCULTAR : block out **3** ENCUBRIR : cover up — **tapadera** *nf* **1** : cover, lid **2** : front (to hide a deception)

tapete *nm* **1** : small rug, mat **2** : cover (for a table)

tapia *nf* : (adobe) wall, garden wall — **tapiar** *vt* **1** : wall in **2** : block off (a door, etc.)

tapicería *nf* **1** : upholstery **2** TAPIZ : tapestry — **tapicero, -ra** *n* : upholsterer

tapioca *nf* : tapioca

tapiz *nm, pl* **-pices** : tapestry — **tapizar** {21} *vt* : upholster

tapón *nm, pl* **-pones** **1** : cork **2** : cap (for a bottle, etc.) **3** : plug, stopper (for a sink)

tapujo *nm* **sin** ~**s** : openly, outright

taquigrafía *nf* : stenography, shorthand — **taquígrafo, -fa** *n* : stenographer

taquilla *nf* **1** : box office **2** RECAUDACIÓN : earnings *pl*, take — **taquillero, -ra** *adj* **un éxito taquillero** : a box-office hit

tarántula *nf* : tarantula

tararear *vt* : hum

tardar *vi* **1** : take a long time, be late **2 a más** ~ : at the latest — *vt* : take (time) — **tardanza** *nf* : lateness, delay — **tarde** *adv* **1** : late **2** ~ **o temprano** : sooner or later — ~ *nf* **1** : afternoon, evening **2 ¡buenas** ~**s!** : good afternoon!, good evening! **3 en la** ~ **o por la** ~ : in the afternoon, in the evening — **tardío, -día** *adj* : late, tardy — **tardo, -da** *adj* : slow

tarea *nf* **1** : task, job **2** : homework (in education)

tarifa *nf* **1** : fare, rate **2** LISTA : price list **3** ARANCEL : duty, tariff

tarima *nf* : platform, stage

tarjeta *nf* **1** : card **2** ~ **de crédito** : credit card **3** ~ **postal** : postcard

tarro *nm* : jar, pot

tarta *nf* **1** : cake **2** TORTA : tart

tartamudear *vi* : stammer, stutter — **tartamudeo** *nm* : stammer, stutter

tartán *nm, adj pl* **-tanes** : tartan, plaid

tártaro *nm* : tartar

tarugo *nm* **1** : block (of wood) **2** *fam* : blockhead, dunce

tasa *nf* **1** : rate **2** IMPUESTO : tax **3** VALORACIÓN : appraisal — **tasación** *nf, pl* **-ciones** : appraisal — **tasar** *vt* **1** : set the price of **2** VALORAR : appraise, value

tasca *nf* : cheap bar, dive

tatuar {3} *vt* : tattoo — **tatuaje** *nm* : tattoo, tattooing

taurino, -na *adj* : bull, bullfighting — **tauromaquia** *nf* : (art of) bullfighting

taxi *nm, pl* **taxis** : taxi, taxicab — **taxista** *nmf* : taxi driver

taza *nf* **1** : cup **2** : (toilet) bowl — **tazón** *nm, pl* **-zones** : bowl

te *pron* **1** (*direct object*) : you **2** (*indirect object*) : for you, to you, from you **3** (*reflexive*) : yourself, for yourself, to yourself, from yourself

té *nm* : tea

teatro *nm* : theater — **teatral** *adj* : theatrical

techo *nm* **1** : roof **2** : ceiling (of a room) **3** LÍMITE : upper limit, ceiling — **techumbre** *nf* : roofing

tecla *nf* : key (of a musical instrument or a machine) — **teclado** *nm* : keyboard — **teclear** *vt* : type in, enter

técnica *nf* **1** : technique, skill **2** TECNOLOGÍA : technology — **técnico, -ca** *adj* : technical — ~ *n* : technician

tecnología *nf* : technology — **tecnológico, -ca** *adj* : technological

tecolote *nm Lat* : owl

tedio *nm* : boredom — **tedioso, -sa** *adj* : tedious, boring

teja *nf* : tile — **tejado** *nm* : roof

tejer *v* **1** : knit, crochet **2** : weave (on a loom)

tejido *nm* **1** : fabric, cloth **2** : tissue (of the body)

tejón *nm, pl* **-jones** : badger

tela *nf* **1** : fabric, material **2** ~ **de araña** : spiderweb — **telar** *nm* : loom — **telaraña** *nf* : spiderweb, cobweb

tele *nf fam* : TV, television

telecomunicación *nf, pl* **-ciones** : telecommunication

teledifusión *nf, pl* **-siones** : television broadcasting

teledirigido, -da *adj* : remote-controlled

telefonear *v* : telephone, call — **telefónico, -ca** *adj* : telephone — **telefonista** *nmf* : telephone operator — **teléfono** *nm* **1** : telephone **2 llamar por ~** : make a phone call

telegrafiar {85} *v* : telegraph — **telegráfico, -ca** *adj* : telegraphic — **telégrafo** *nm* : telegaph

telegrama *nm* : telegram

telenovela *nf* : soap opera

telepatía *nf* : telepathy — **telepático, -ca** *adj* : telepathic

telescopio *nm* : telescope — **telescópico, -ca** *adj* : telescopic

telespectador, -dora *n* : (television) viewer

telesquí *nm, pl* **-squís** : ski lift

televidente *nmf* : (television) viewer

televisión *nf, pl* **-siones** : television, TV — **televisar** *vt* : televise — **televisor** *nm* : television set

telón *nm, pl* **-lones 1** : curtain (in theater) **2 ~ de fondo** : backdrop, background

tema *nm* : theme

temblar {55} *vi* **1** : tremble, shiver **2** : shake (of a building, the ground, etc.) — **temblor** *nm* **1** : shaking, trembling **2 or ~ de tierra** : tremor, earthquake — **tembloroso, -sa** *adj* : trembling, shaky

temer *vt* : fear, dread — *vi* : be afraid — **temerario, -ria** *adj* : reckless — **temeridad** *nf* **1** : recklessness **2** : rash act — **temeroso, -sa** *adj* : fearful — **temor** *nm* : fear, dread

temperamento *nm* : temperament — **temperamental** *adj* : temperamental

temperatura *nf* : temperature

tempestad *nf* : storm — **tempestuoso, -sa** *adj* : stormy

templar *vt* **1** : temper (steel) **2** : moderate (temperature) **3** : tune (a musical instrument) — **templarse** *vr* : warm up, cool down — **templado, -da** *adj* **1** : temperate, mild **2** TIBIO : lukewarm **3** VALIENTE : courageous — **templanza** *nf* **1** : moderation **2** : mildness (of weather)

templo *nm* : temple, synagogue

tempo *nm* : tempo

temporada *nf* **1** : season, time **2** PERÍODO : period, spell — **temporal** *adj* **1** : temporal **2** PROVISIONAL : temporary — *~ nm* : storm — **temporero, -ra** *n* : temporary or seasonal worker

temporizador *nm* : timer

temprano, -na *adj* : early — **temprano** *adv* : early

tenaz {61} *adj, pl* **-naces** : tenacious — **tenaza** *nf or* **tenazas** *nfpl* **1** : pliers **2** : tongs (for the fireplace, etc.) **3** : claw (of a crustacean)

tendedero *nm* : clothesline

tendencia *nf* : tendency, trend

tender {56} *vt* **1** : spread out, stretch out **2** : hang out (clothes) **3** : lay (cables, etc.) **4** : set (a trap) — *vi* **~ a** : have a tendency towards — **tenderse** *vr* : stretch out, lie down

tendero, -ra *n* : shopkeeper

tendido *nm* **1** : laying (of cables, etc.) **2** : seats *pl*, stand (at a bullfight)

tendón *nm, pl* **-dones** : tendon

tenebroso, -sa *adj* **1** : gloomy, dark **2** SINIESTRO : sinister

tenedor, -dora *n* **1** : holder **2 ~ de libros** : bookkeeper — **tenedor** *nm* : table fork — **teneduría** *nf* **~ de libros** : bookkeeping

tener {80} *vt* **1** : have, possess **2** SUJETAR : hold **3** TOMAR : take **4 ~ frío (hambre,** *etc.***)** : be cold (hungry, etc.) **5 ~ ... años** : be ... years old **6 ~ por** : think, consider — *v aux* **1 ~ que** : have to, ought to **2 tenía pensado escribirte** : I've been thinking of writing to you — **tenerse** *vr* **1** : stand up **2 ~ por** : consider oneself

tenería *nf* : tannery

tengo → tener

tenia *nf* : tapeworm

teniente *nmf* : lieutenant

tenis *nms & pl* **1** : tennis **2 ~** *nmpl* : sneakers — **tenista** *nmf* : tennis player

tenor *nm* **1** : tenor **2** : tone, sense (in style)

tensar *vt* **1** : tense, make taut **2** : draw (a bow) — **tensarse** *vr* : become tense — **tensión** *nf, pl* **-siones 1** : tension **2 ~ arterial** : blood pressure — **tenso, -sa** *adj* : tense

tentación *nf, pl* **-ciones** : temptation

tentáculo *nm* : tentacle

tentar {55} *vt* **1** : feel, touch **2** ATRAER : tempt — **tentador, -dora** *adj* : tempting

tentativa *nf* : attempt

tentempié *nm fam* : snack

tenue *adj* **1** : tenuous **2** : faint, weak (of sounds) **3** : light, fine (of thread, rain, etc.)

teñir {67} *vt* **1** : dye **2 ~ de** : tinge with

teología *nf* : theology — **teólogo, -ga** *n* : theologian

teorema nm : theorem

teoría nf : theory — **teórico, -ca** adj : theoretical

tequila nm : tequila

terapia nf 1 : therapy 2 ~ **ocupacional** : occupational therapy — **terapeuta** nmf : therapist — **terapéutico, -ca** adj : therapeutic

tercermundista adj : third-world

tercero, -ra adj (tercer before masculine singular nouns) 1 : third 2 **el Tercer Mundo** : the Third World — ~ n : third (in a series)

terciar vt : sling (sth over one's shoulders), tilt (a hat) — vi 1 : intervene 2 ~ **en** : take part in

tercio nm : third

terciopelo nm : velvet

terco, -ca adj : obstinate, stubborn

tergiversar vt : distort, twist

termal adj : thermal, hot — **termas** nfpl : hot springs

terminar vt : conclude, finish — vi 1 : finish 2 ACABARSE : come to an end — **terminarse** vr 1 : run out 2 ACABARSE : come to an end — **terminación** nf, pl **-ciones** : termination, conclusion — **terminal** adj : terminal, final — ~ nm (in some regions f) : (electric or electronic) terminal — ~ nf (in some regions m) : terminal, station — **término** nm 1 : end 2 PLAZO : period, term 3 ~ **medio** : happy medium 4 ~**s** nmpl : terms — **terminología** nf : terminology

termita nf : termite

termo nm : thermos

termómetro nm : thermometer

termóstato nm : thermostat

ternero, -ra n : calf — **ternera** nf : veal

ternura nf : tenderness

terquedad nf : obstinacy, stubbornness

terracota nf : terra-cotta

terraplén nm, pl **-plenes** : embankment

terráqueo, -quea adj : earth, terrestrial

terrateniente nmf : landowner

terraza nf 1 : terrace 2 BALCÓN : balcony

terremoto nm : earthquake

terreno nm 1 : terrain 2 SUELO : earth, ground 3 SOLAR : plot, tract of land — **terreno, -na** adj : earthly — **terrestre** adj : terrestrial

terrible adj : terrible

terrier nm : terrier

territorio nm : territory — **territorial** adj : territorial

terrón nm, pl **-rones** 1 : clod (of earth) 2 ~ **de azúcar** : lump of sugar

terror nm : terror — **terrorífico, -ca** adj

: terrifying — **terrorismo** nm : terrorism — **terrorista** adj & nmf : terrorist

terroso, -sa adj : earthy

terso, -sa adj 1 : smooth 2 : polished, flowing (of a style) — **tersura** nf : smoothness

tertulia nf : gathering, group

tesis nfs & pl : thesis

tesón nm : persistence, tenacity

tesoro nm 1 : treasure 2 : thesaurus (book) 3 **el Tesoro** : the Treasury — **tesorero, -ra** n : treasurer

testaferro nm : figurehead

testamento nm : testament, will — **testamentario, -ria** n : executor, executrix f — **testar** vi : draw up a will

testarudo, -da adj : stubborn

testículo nm : testicle

testificar {72} v : testify — **testigo** nmf 1 : witness 2 ~ **ocular** : eyewitness — **testimoniar** vi : testify — **testimonio** nm : testimony

tétano or **tétanos** nm : tetanus

tetera nf : teapot

tetilla nf 1 : teat, nipple (of a man) 2 : nipple (of a baby bottle) — **tetina** nf : nipple (of a baby bottle)

tétrico, -ca adj : somber, gloomy

textil adj & nm : textile

texto nm : text — **textual** adj 1 : textual 2 EXACTO : literal, exact

textura nf : texture

tez nf, pl **teces** : complexion

ti pron 1 : you 2 ~ **mismo, ~ misma** : yourself

tía → tío

tianguis nms & pl Lat : open-air market

tibio, -bia adj : lukewarm

tiburón nm, pl **-rones** : shark

tic nm : tic

tiempo nm 1 : time 2 ÉPOCA : age, period 3 : weather (in meteorology) 4 : halftime (in sports) 5 : tempo (in music) 6 : tense (in grammar)

tienda nf 1 : store, shop 2 or ~ **de campaña** : tent

tiene → tener

tienta nf **andar a** ~**s** : feel one's way, grope around

tierno, -na adj 1 : tender, fresh, young 2 CARIÑOSO : affectionate

tierra nf 1 : land 2 SUELO : ground, earth 3 or ~ **natal** : native land 4 **la Tierra** : the Earth 5 **por** ~ : overland 6 ~ **adentro** : inland

tieso, -sa adj 1 : stiff, rigid 2 ERGUIDO : erect 3 ENGREÍDO : haughty

tiesto nm : flowerpot

tifoideo, -dea adj **fiebre tifoidea** : typhoid fever

tifón nm, pl **-fones** : typhoon

tifus nm : typhus

tigre, -gresa n 1 : tiger, tigress f 2 Lat : jaguar

tijera nf or **tijeras** nfpl : scissors — **tijeretada** nf : cut, snip

tildar vt ~ **de** : brand as, call

tilde nf 1 : tilde 2 ACENTO : accent mark

tilo nm : linden (tree)

timar vt : swindle, cheat

timbre nm 1 : bell 2 : tone, timbre (of a voice, etc.) 3 SELLO : seal, stamp 4 Lat : postage stamp — **timbrar** vt : stamp

tímido, -da adj : timid, shy — **timidez** nf : timidity, shyness

timo nm fam : swindle, hoax

timón nm 1 : rudder 2 **coger el** ~ : take the helm, take charge

tímpano nm 1 : eardrum 2 ~s nmpl : timpani, kettledrums

tina nf 1 : vat 2 BAÑERA : bathtub

tinieblas nfpl 1 : darkness 2 **estar en** ~ **sobre** : be in the dark about

tino nm 1 : good judgment, sense 2 TACTO : tact

tinta nf 1 : ink 2 **saberlo de buena** ~ : have it on good authority — **tinte** nm 1 : dye, coloring 2 MATIZ : overtone — **tintero** nm : inkwell

tintinear vi : jingle, tinkle, clink — **tintineo** nm : jingle, tinkle, clink

tinto, -ta adj 1 : dyed, stained 2 : red (of wine)

tintorería nf : dry cleaner (service)

tintura nf 1 : dye, tint 2 ~ **de yodo** : tincture of iodine

tiña nf : ringworm

tío, tía n : uncle m, aunt f

tiovivo nm : merry-go-round

típico, -ca adj : typical

tiple nm : soprano

tipo nm 1 : type, kind 2 FIGURA : figure (of a woman), build (of a man) 3 : rate (of interest, etc.) 4 : (printing) type, typeface — **tipo, -pa** n fam : guy m, gal f

tipografía nf : typography, printing — **tipográfico, -ca** adj : typographical — **tipógrafo, -fa** n : printer

tique or **tíquet** nm : ticket — **tiquete** nm Lat : ticket

tira nf 1 : strip, strap 2 ~ **cómica** : comic strip

tirabuzón nf, pl **-zones** 1 : corkscrew 2 RIZO : curl, coil

tirada nf 1 : throw 2 DISTANCIA : distance 3 IMPRESIÓN : printing, issue — **tirador** nm : handle, knob — **tirador, -dora** n : marksman m, markswoman f

tiranía nf : tyranny — **tiránico, -ca** adj : tyrannical — **tiranizar** {21} vt : tyrannize — **tirano, -na** adj : tyrannical — ~ n : tyrant

tirante adj 1 : taut, tight 2 : tense (of a situation, etc.) — ~ nm 1 : (shoulder) strap 2 ~s nmpl : suspenders

tirar vt 1 : throw 2 DESECHAR : throw away 3 DERRIBAR : knock down 4 DISPARAR : shoot, fire 5 IMPRIMIR : print — vi 1 : pull 2 DISPARAR : shoot 3 ATRAER : attract 4 fam : get by, manage 5 ~ **a** : tend towards — **tirarse** vr 1 : throw oneself 2 fam : spend (time)

tiritar vi : shiver

tiro nm 1 : shot, gunshot 2 : shot, kick (in sports) 3 : team (of horses, etc.) 4 **a** ~ : within range

tiroides nmf : thyroid (gland)

tirón nm, pl **-rones** 1 : pull, yank 2 **de un** ~ : in one go

tirotear vt : shoot at — **tiroteo** nm : shooting

tisis nfs & pl : tuberculosis

títere nm : puppet

titilar vi : flicker

titiritero, -ra n 1 : puppeteer 2 ACRÓBATA : acrobat

titubear vi 1 : hesitate 2 BALBUCEAR : stutter, stammer — **titubeante** adj : hesitant, faltering — **titubeo** nm : hesitation

titular vt : title, call — **titularse** vr 1 : be called, be titled 2 LICENCIARSE : receive a degree — ~ adj : titular, official — ~ nm : headline — ~ nmf : holder, incumbent — **título** nm 1 : title 2 : degree, qualification (in education)

tiza nf : chalk

tiznar vt : blacken (with soot, etc.) — **tizne** nm : soot

toalla nf : towel — **toallero** nm : towel rack

tobillo nm : ankle

tobogán nm, pl **-ganes** 1 : toboggan, sled 2 : slide (in a playground, etc.)

tocadiscos nms & pl : record player

tocado, -da adj fam : touched, not all there — **tocado** nm : headgear, headdress

tocador nm : dressing table

tocar {72} vt 1 : touch, feel 2 MENCIONAR : touch on, refer to 3 : play (a musical instrument) — vi 1 : knock, ring 2 ~ **en** : touch on, border on

tocayo, -ya n : namesake

tocino nm 1 : bacon 2 : salt pork (for cooking) — **tocineta** nf Lat : bacon

tocólogo, -ga n : obstetrician

tocón nm, pl **-cones** : stump (of a tree)

todavía *adv* **1** AÚN : still **2** (*in comparisons*) : even **3** ~ **no** : not yet

todo, -da *adj* **1** : all CADA, CUALQUIER : every, each **3** **a toda velocidad** : at top speed **4** **todo el mundo** : everyone, everybody — ~ *pron* **1** : everything, all **2** **todos, -das** *pl* : everybody, everyone, all — **todo** *nm* : whole — **todopoderoso, -sa** *adj* : almighty, all-powerful

toga *nf* **1** : toga **2** : gown, robe (of a judge, etc.)

toldo *nm* : awning, canopy

tolerar *vt* : tolerate — **tolerancia** *nf* : tolerance — **tolerante** *adj* : tolerant

toma *nf* **1** : capture **2** DOSIS : dose **3** : take (in film) **4** ~ **de corriente** : wall socket, outlet **5** ~ **y daca** : give-and-take — **tomar** *vt* **1** : take **2** : have (food or drink) **3** CAPTURAR : capture, seize **4** ~ **el sol** : sunbathe **5** ~ **tierra** : land — *vi* : drink (alcohol) — **tomarse** *vr* **1** : take (time, etc.) **2** : drink, eat, have (food or drink)

tomate *nm* : tomato

tomillo *nm* : thyme

tomo *nm* : volume

ton *nm* **sin** ~ **ni son** : without rhyme or reason

tonada *nf* : tune

tonel *nm* : barrel, cask

tonelada *nf* : ton — **tonelaje** *nm* : tonnage

tónica *nf* **1** : tonic (water) **2** TENDENCIA : trend, tone — **tónico, -ca** *adj* : tonic — **tónico** *nm* : tonic (in medicine)

tono *nm* **1** : tone **2** : shade (of colors) **3** : key (in music)

tontería *nf* **1** : silly thing or remark **2** ESTUPIDEZ : foolishness **3** **decir** ~**s** : talk nonsense — **tonto, -ta** *adj* **1** : stupid, silly **2** **a tontas y a locas** : haphazardly — ~ *n* : fool, idiot

topacio *nm* : topaz

toparse *vr* ~ **con** : run into, come across

tope *nm* **1** : limit, end **2** *or* ~ **de puerta** : doorstop **3** *Lat* : bump — ~ *adj* : maximum

tópico, -ca *adj* **1** : topical, external **2** MANIDO : trite — **tópico** *nm* : cliché

topo *nm* : mole (animal)

toque *nm* **1** : (light) touch **2** : ringing, peal (of a bell) **3** ~ **de queda** : curfew **4** ~ **de diana** : reveille — **toquetear** *vt* : finger, handle

tórax *nms & pl* : thorax

torbellino *nm* : whirlwind

torcer {14} *vt* **1** : twist, bend **2** : wring (out) — *vi* : turn —

torcerse *vr* **1** : twist, sprain **2** FRUSTRARSE : go wrong **3** DESVIARSE : go astray — **torcedura** *nf* **1** : twisting **2** ESGUINCE : sprain — **torcido, -da** *adj* : twisted, crooked

tordo, -da *adj* : dappled — **tordo** *nm* : thrush (bird)

torear *vt* **1** : fight (bulls) **2** ELUDIR : dodge, sidestep — *vi* : fight bulls — **toreo** *nm* : bullfighting — **torero, -ra** *n* : bullfighter

tormenta *nf* **1** : storm — **tormento** *nm* **1** : torture **2** ANGUSTIA : torment, anguish — **tormentoso, -sa** *adj* : stormy

tornado *nm* : tornado

tornar *vt* CONVERTIR : render, turn — *vi* : go back, return — **tornarse** *vr* : become, turn into

torneo *nm* : tournament

tornillo *nm* : screw

torniquete *nm* **1** : turnstile **2** : tourniquet (in medicine)

torno *nm* **1** : winch **2** : (carpenter's) lathe **3** ~ **de alfarero** : (potter's) wheel **4** ~ **de banco** : vise **5** **en** ~ **a** : around, about

toro *nm* **1** : bull **2** ~**s** *nmpl* : bullfight

toronja *nf* : grapefruit

torpe *adj* **1** : clumsy, awkward **2** ESTÚPIDO : stupid, dull

torpedear *vt* : torpedo — **torpedo** *nm* : torpedo

torpeza *nf* **1** : clumsiness, awkwardness **2** ESTUPIDEZ : slowness, stupidity

torre *nf* **1** : tower **2** : turret (on a ship, etc.) **3** : rook, castle (in chess)

torrente *nm* **1** : torrent **2** ~ **sanguíneo** : bloodstream — **torrencial** *adj* : torrential

tórrido, -da *adj* : torrid

torsión *nf*, *pl* **-siones** : twisting

torta *nf* **1** : torte, cake **2** *Lat* : sandwich

tortazo *nm fam* : blow, wallop

tortícolis *nfs & pl* : stiff neck

tortilla *nf* **1** : tortilla **2** *or* ~ **de huevo** : omelet

tórtola *nf* : turtledove

tortuga *nf* **1** : turtle, tortoise **2** ~ **de agua dulce** : terrapin

tortuoso, -sa *adj* : tortuous, winding

tortura *nf* : torture — **torturar** *vt* : torture

tos *nf* **1** : cough **2** ~ **ferina** : whooping cough

tosco, -ca *adj* : rough, coarse

toser *vi* : cough

tosquedad *nf* : coarseness

tostar {19} *vt* **1** : toast **2** BRONCEAR : tan — **tostarse** *vr* : get a tan — **tostada**

nf **1** : piece of toast **2** *Lat* : tostada —
tostador *nm* : toaster
tostón *nm, pl* **-tones** *Lat* : fried plantain chip
total *adj & nm* : total — ~ *adv* : so,
after all — **totalidad** *nf* : whole — **totalitario, -ria** *adj & n* : totalitarian —
totalitarismo *nm* : totalitarianism —
totalizar {21} *vt* : total, add up to
tóxico, -ca *adj* : toxic, poisonous —
tóxico *nm* : poison — **toxicomanía** *nf*
: drug addiction — **toxicómano, -na** *n*
: drug addict — **toxina** *nf* : toxin
tozudo, -da *adj* : stubborn
traba *nf* : obstacle, hindrance
trabajar *vi* **1** : work **2** : act, perform (in
theater, etc.) — *vt* **1** : work (metal) **2**
: knead (dough) **3** MEJORAR : work on,
work at — **trabajador, -dora** *adj*
: hard-working — ~ *n* : worker —
trabajo *nm* **1** : work **2** EMPLEO : job **3**
TAREA : task **4** ESFUERZO : effort **5**
costar ~ : be difficult **6** ~ en
equipo : teamwork **7** ~s *nmpl*
: hardships, difficulties — **trabajoso,
-sa** *adj* : hard, laborious
trabalenguas *nms & pl* : tongue twister
trabar *vt* **1** : join, connect **2** OBSTACULIZAR : impede **3** : strike up (a conversation, etc.) **4** : thicken (sauces) —
trabarse *vr* **1** : jam **2** ENREDARSE : become entangled **3** se le traba la
lengua : he gets tongue-tied
trabucar {72} *vt* : mix up
tracción *nf* : traction
tractor *nm* : tractor
tradición *nf, pl* **-ciones** : tradition —
tradicional *adj* : traditional
traducir {61} *vt* : translate — **traducción** *nf, pl* **-ciones** : translation — **traductor, -tora** *n* : translator
traer {81} *vt* **1** : bring **2** CAUSAR : cause,
bring about **3** CONTENER : carry, have **4**
LLEVAR : wear — **traerse** *vr* **1** : bring
along **2** traérselas : be difficult
traficar {72} *vi* ~ en : traffic in —
traficante *nmf* : dealer, trafficker —
tráfico *nm* **1** : trade (of merchandise)
2 : traffic (of vehicles)
tragaluz *nf, pl* **-luces** : skylight
tragar {52} *vt* : swallow **2** *fam* : put up
with — *vi* : swallow — **tragarse** *vr* **1**
: swallow **2** ABSORBER : absorb, swallow up
tragedia *nf* : tragedy — **trágico, -ca** *adj*
: tragic
trago *nm* **1** : swallow, swig **2** *fam*
: drink, liquor — **tragón, -gona** *adj*
fam : greedy — ~ *nmf fam* : glutton
traicionar *vt* : betray — **traición** *nf, pl*

-**ciones 1** : betrayal **2** : treason (in
law) — **traidor, -dora** *adj* : traitorous,
treacherous — ~ *n* : traitor
trailer *nm* : trailer
traje *nm* **1** : dress, costume **2** : (man's)
suit **3** ~ de baño : bathing suit
trajinar *vi fam* : rush around — **trajín**
nm, pl **-jines** *fam* : hustle and bustle
trama *nf* **1** : plot **2** : weave, weft (of fabric) — **tramar** *vt* **1** : plot, plan **2**
: weave (fabric)
tramitar *vt* : negotiate — **trámite** *nm*
: procedure, step
tramo *nm* **1** : stretch, section **2** : flight
(of stairs)
trampa *nf* **1** : trap **2** hacer ~s : cheat
— **trampear** *vi* : cheat
trampilla *nf* : trapdoor
trampolín *nm, pl* **-lines 1** : diving board
2 : trampoline (in a gymnasium, etc.)
tramposo, -sa *adj* : crooked, cheating
— ~ *n* : cheat, swindler
tranca *nf* **1** : cudgel, club **2** : bar (for a
door or window)
trance *nm* **1** : critical juncture **2** : (hypnotic) trance **3** en ~ de : in the
process of
tranquilo, -la *adj* : calm, tranquil —
tranquilidad *nf* : tranquility, peace —
tranquilizante *nm* : tranquilizer —
tranquilizar {21} *vt* : calm, soothe —
tranquilizarse *vr* : calm down
trans- *see also* tras-
transacción *nf, pl* **-ciones** : transaction
transatlántico, -ca *adj* : transatlantic
— **transatlántico** *nm* : ocean liner
transbordador *nm* **1** : ferry **2** ~ espacial : space shuttle — **transbordar** *vt*
: transfer — *vi* : change (of trains, etc.)
— **transbordo** *nm* hacer ~ : change
(trains, etc.)
transcribir {33} *vt* : transcribe —
transcripción *nf, pl* **-ciones** : transcription
transcurrir *vi* : elapse, pass — **transcurso** *nm* : course, progression
transeúnte *nmf* : passerby
transferir {76} *vt* : transfer — **transferencia** *nf* : transfer, transference
transformar *vt* **1** : transform, change **2**
CONVERTIR : convert — **transformarse** *vr* : be transformed — **transformación** *nf, pl* **-ciones** : transformation — **transformador** *nm*
: transformer
transfusión *nf, pl* **-siones** : transfusion
transgredir {1} *vt* : transgress —
transgresión *nf* : transgression
transición *nf, pl* **-ciones** : transition
transido, -da *adj* : overcome, stricken

transigir {35} *vi* : give in, compromise
transistor *nm* : transistor
transitar *vi* : go, travel — **transitable** *adj* : passable
transitivo, -va *adj* : transitive
tránsito *nm* 1 : transit 2 TRÁFICO : traffic 3 **hora de máximo ~** : rush hour — **transitorio, -ria** *adj* : transitory
transmitir *vt* 1 : transmit 2 : broadcast (radio, TV, etc.) 3 CEDER : pass on — **transmisión** *nf, pl* **-siones** 1 : broadcast 2 TRANSFERENCIA : transfer 3 : transmission (of an automobile) — **transmisor** *nm* : transmitter
transparentarse *vr* : be transparent — **transparente** *adj* : transparent
transpirar *vi* : perspire, sweat — **transpiración** *nf, pl* **-ciones** : perspiration, sweat
transponer {60} *vt* : transpose, move — **transponerse** *vr* 1 : set (of the sun, etc.) 2 DORMITAR : doze off
transportar *vt* : transport, carry — **transportarse** *vr* : get carried away — **transporte** *nm* : transport, transportation
transversal *adj* **corte ~** : cross section
tranvía *nm* : streetcar, trolley
trapear *vt Lat* : mop
trapecio *nm* : trapeze
trapisonda *nf* : scheme, plot
trapo *nm* 1 : cloth, rag 2 **~s** *nmpl fam* : clothes
tráquea *nf* : trachea, windpipe
traquetear *vi* : rattle around, shake — **traqueteo** *nm* : rattling
tras *prep* 1 DESPUÉS DE : after 2 DETRÁS DE : behind
tras- *see also* **trans-**
trascender {56} *vi* 1 : leak out, become known 2 EXTENDERSE : spread 3 **~ de** : transcend — **trascendencia** *nf* : importance — **trascendental** *adj* 1 : transcendental 2 IMPORTANTE : important
trasegar *vt* : move around
trasero, -ra *adj* : rear, back — **trasero** *nm* : buttocks
trasfondo *nm* 1 : background 2 : undercurrent (of suspicion, etc.)
trasladar *vt* 1 : transfer, move 2 POSPONER : postpone — **trasladarse** *vr* : move, relocate — **traslado** *nm* 1 : transfer, move 2 COPIA : copy
traslapar *vt* : overlap — **traslaparse** *vr* : overlap
traslucirse {45} *vr* 1 : be translucent 2 REVELARSE : be revealed — **traslúcido, -da** *adj* : translucent

trasnochar *vi* : stay up all night
traspasar *vt* 1 : pierce, go through 2 EXCEDER : go beyond 3 ATRAVESAR : cross, go across 4 : transfer (a business, etc.) — **traspaso** *nm* : transfer, sale
traspié *nm* 1 : stumble, trip 2 ERROR : blunder
trasplantar *vt* : transplant — **trasplante** *nm* : transplant
trasquilar *vt* : shear
traste *nm* 1 : fret (on a guitar, etc.) 2 *Lat* : (kitchen) utensil 3 **dar al ~ con** : ruin 4 **irse al ~** : fall through
trastos *nmpl fam* : pieces of junk, stuff
trastornar *vt* 1 : disturb, disrupt 2 VOLVER LOCO : drive crazy — **trastornarse** *vr* : go crazy — **trastornado, -da** *adj* : disturbed, deranged — **trastorno** *nm* 1 : disturbance, disruption 2 : (medical or psychological) disorder
trastrocar *vt* : change, switch around
tratable *adj* : friendly, sociable
tratar *vi* 1 **~ con** : deal with 2 **~ de** : try to 3 **~ de** *or* **~ sobre** : be about, concern 4 **~ en** : deal in — *vt* 1 : treat 2 MANEJAR : deal with, handle — **tratarse** *vr* **~ de** : be about, concern — **tratado** *nm* 1 : treatise 2 CONVENIO : treaty — **tratamiento** *nm* : treatment — **trato** *nm* 1 : treatment 2 ACUERDO : deal, agreement 3 **~s** *nmpl* : dealings
trauma *nm* : trauma — **traumático, -ca** *adj* : traumatic
través *nm* 1 **a ~ de** : across, through 2 **de ~** : sideways
travesaño *nm* : crosspiece
travesía *nf* : voyage, crossing (of the sea)
travesura *nf* 1 : prank 2 **~s** *nfpl* : mischief — **travieso, -sa** *adj* : mischievous, naughty
trayecto *nm* 1 : trajectory, path 2 VIAJE : journey 3 RUTA : route — **trayectoria** *nf* : path, trajectory
traza *nf* 1 : design, plan 2 ASPECTO : appearance — **trazado** *nm* 1 : outline, sketch 2 DISEÑO : plan, layout — **trazar** {21} *vt* 1 : trace, outline 2 : draw up (a plan, etc.) — **trazo** *nm* : stroke, line
trébol *nm* 1 : clover, shamrock 2 **~es** *nmpl* : clubs (in playing cards)
trece *adj & nm* : thirteen — **treceavo, -va** *adj* : thirteenth — **treceavo** *nm* : thirteenth (fraction)
trecho *nm* 1 : stretch, period 2 DISTANCIA : distance 3 **de ~ a ~** : at intervals

tregua *nf* 1 : truce 2 **sin ~** : without respite

treinta *adj & nm* : thirty — **treintavo, -va** *adj* : thirtieth — **treintavo** *nm* : thirtieth (fraction)

tremendo, -da *adj* : tremendous, enormous

trementina *nf* : turpentine

trémulo, -la *adj* : trembling, flickering

tren *nm* 1 : train 2 **~ de aterrizaje** : landing gear

trenza *nf* 1 : braid, pigtail — **trenzar** {21} *vt* : braid — **trenzarse** *vr Lat* : get involved

trepar *vi* 1 : climb 2 : creep, spread (of a plant) — **treparse** *vr* : climb (up) — **trepador, -dora** *adj* : climbing — **trepadora** *nf* 1 : climbing plant 2 *fam* : social climber

trepidar *vi* : shake, vibrate

tres *adj & nm* : three — **trescientos, -tas** *adj* : three hundred — **trescientos** *nms & pl* : three hundred

treta *nf* : trick

triángulo *nm* : triangle — **triangular** *adj* : triangular

tribu *nf* : tribe — **tribal** *adj* : tribal

tribulación *nf, pl* **-ciones** : tribulation

tribuna *nf* 1 : dais, platform 2 : grandstand, bleachers *pl* (in a stadium)

tribunal *nm* : court, tribunal

tributar *vt* : pay, render — *vi* : pay taxes — **tributo** *nm* 1 : tribute 2 IMPUESTO : tax

triciclo *nm* : tricycle

tricolor *adj* : tricolored

tridimensional *adj* : three-dimensional

trigésimo, -ma *adj & n* : thirtieth

trigo *nm* : wheat

trigonometría *nf* : trigonometry

trillado, -da *adj* : trite

trillar *vt* : thresh — **trilladora** *nf* : threshing machine

trillizo, -za *n* : triplet

trilogía *nf* : trilogy

trimestral *adj* : quarterly

trinar *vi* : warble

trinchar *vt* : carve

trinchera *nf* 1 : trench, ditch 2 IMPERMEABLE : trench coat

trineo *nm* : sled, sleigh

trinidad *nf* : trinity

trino *nm* : trill, warble

trío *nm* : trio

tripa *nf* 1 : gut, intestine 2 **~s** *nfpl fam* : belly, tummy

triple *adj & nm* : triple — **triplicar** {72} *vt* : triple

trípode *nm* : tripod

tripular *vt* : man — **tripulación** *nf, pl* **-ciones** : crew — **tripulante** *nmf* : crew member

tris *nm* **estar en un ~ de** : be within an inch of

triste *adj* 1 : sad 2 SOMBRÍO : dismal, gloomy 3 MISERABLE : sorry, miserable — **tristeza** *nf* : sadness, grief

tritón *nm, pl* **-tones** : newt

triturar *vt* : crush, grind

triunfar *vi* : triumph, win — **triunfal** *adj* : triumphal — **triunfante** *adj* : triumphant — **triunfo** *nm* : triumph, victory

trivial *adj* : trivial

triza *nf* 1 : shred, bit 2 **hacer ~s** : smash to pieces

trocar {82} *vt* 1 CONVERTIR : change 2 INTERCAMBIAR : exchange

trocha *nf* : path, trail

trofeo *nm* : trophy

trombón *nm, pl* **-bones** 1 : trombone 2 : trombonist (musician)

trombosis *nf* : thrombosis

trompa *nf* 1 : trunk (of an elephant), snout 2 : horn (musical instrument) 3 : tube (in anatomy)

trompeta *nf* : trumpet — **trompetista** *nmf* : trumpet player

trompo *nm* : top (toy)

tronada *nf* : thunderstorm — **tronar** {19} *vi* : thunder, rage — *vt Lat fam* : shoot — *v impers* : thunder

tronchar *vt* 1 : snap 2 TRUNCAR : cut short

tronco *nm* 1 : trunk (of a tree) 2 : torso (of a person) 3 **dormir como un ~** : sleep like a log

trono *nm* : throne

tropa *nf* : troops *pl*, soldiers *pl*

tropel *nm* : mob

tropezar {29} *vi* 1 : trip, stumble 2 **~ con** : come up against, run into — **tropezón** *nm, pl* **-zones** 1 : stumble 2 EQUIVOCACIÓN : mistake, slip

trópico *nm* : tropic — **tropical** *adj* : tropical

tropiezo *nm* 1 CONTRATIEMPO : snag, setback 2 EQUIVOCACIÓN : mistake, slip

trotar *vi* 1 : trot 2 *fam* : rush about — **trote** *nm* 1 : trot 2 *fam* : rush, bustle 3 **al ~** : at a trot, quickly

trozo *nm* : piece, bit, chunk

trucha *nf* : trout

truco *nm* 1 : knack 2 ARDID : trick

trueno *nm* : thunder

trueque *nm* : barter, exchange

trufa *nf* : truffle

truncar {72} *vt* 1 : cut short 2 : thwart, spoil (plans, etc.)

tu *adj* : your
tú *pron* : you
tuba *nf* : tuba
tuberculosis *nf* : tuberculosis
tubo *nm* **1** : tube, pipe **2** ~ **de escape** : exhaust pipe (of a vehicle) **3** ~ **de desagüe** : drainpipe — **tubería** *nf* : pipes *pl*, tubing
tuerca *nf* : nut (for a screw)
tuerto, -ta *adj* : one-eyed, blind in one eye
tuétano *nm* : marrow
tufo *nm* **1** : vapor **2** *fam* : stench, stink
tugurio *nm* : hovel
tulipán *nm, pl* **-panes** : tulip
tullido, -da *adj* : crippled, paralyzed
tumba *nf* : tomb, grave
tumbar *vt* : knock down, knock over — **tumbarse** *vr* : lie down — **tumbo** *nm* **dar** ~**s** : jolt, bump around
tumor *nm* : tumor
tumulto *nm* **1** : commotion, tumult **2** MOTÍN : riot — **tumultuoso, -sa** *adj* : tumultuous
tuna *nf* : prickly pear
túnel *nm* : tunnel
túnica *nf* : tunic
tupé *nm* : toupee
tupido, -da *adj* : dense, thick
turba *nf* **1** : peat **2** MUCHEDUMBRE : mob, throng

turbación *nf, pl* **-ciones 1** : disturbance **2** CONFUSIÓN : confusion
turbante *nm* : turban
turbar *vt* **1** : disturb, upset **2** CONFUNDIR : confuse, bewilder
turbina *nf* : turbine
turbio, -bia *adj* **1** : cloudy, murky **2** : blurred (of vision, etc.) — **turbión** *nm, pl* **-biones** : squall
turbulencia *nf* : turbulence — **turbulento, -ta** *adj* : turbulent
turco, -ca *adj* : Turkish — **turco** *nm* : Turkish (language)
turista *nmf* : tourist — **turismo** *nm* : tourism, tourist industry — **turístico, -ca** *adj* : tourist, travel
turnarse *vr* : take turns, alternate — **turno** *nm* **1** : turn **2** ~ **de noche** : night shift
turquesa *nf* : turquoise
turrón *nm, pl* **-rrones** : nougat
tutear *vt* : address as *tú*
tutela *nf* **1** : guardianship (in law) **2** **bajo la** ~ **de** : under the protection of
tuteo *nm* : addressing as *tú*
tutor, -tora *n* **1** : guardian **2** : tutor (in education)
tuyo, -ya *adj* : yours, of yours — ~ *pron* **1** **el tuyo, la tuya, lo tuyo, los tuyos, las tuyas** : yours **2** **los tuyos** : your family, your friends

U

u¹ *nf* : u, 22d letter of the Spanish alphabet
u² *conj* (*used before words beginning with o- or ho-*) : or
uapití *nm* : American elk, wapiti
ubicar {72} *vt* *Lat* **1** COLOCAR : place, position **2** LOCALIZAR : find — **ubicarse** *vr* : be located
ubre *nf* : udder
Ud., Uds. → **usted**
ufanarse *vr* ~ **de** : boast about — **ufano, -na** *adj* **1** : proud **2** ENGREÍDO : self-satisfied
ujier *nm* : usher
úlcera *nf* : ulcer
ulterior *adj* : later, subsequent — **ulteriormente** *adv* : subsequently
últimamente *adv* : lately, recently
ultimar *vt* **1** : complete, finish **2** *Lat* : kill — **ultimátum** *nm, pl* **-tums** : ultimatum
último, -ma *adj* **1** : last **2** : latest, most

recent (in time) **3** : farthest (in space) **4** **por último** : finally
ultrajar *vt* : outrage, insult — **ultraje** *nm* : outrage, insult
ultramar *nm* **de** ~ **or en** ~ : overseas — **ultramarino, -na** *adj* : overseas — **ultramarinos** *nmpl* **tienda de** ~ : grocery store
ultranza: a ~ *adv phr* : to the extreme — **a** ~ *adj phr* : out-and-out, complete
ultrasonido *nm* : ultrasound
ultravioleta *adj* : ultraviolet
ulular *vi* **1** : hoot (of an owl) **2** : howl (of a wolf, the wind, etc.) — **ululato** *nm* : hoot (of an owl)
umbilical *adj* : umbilical
umbral *nm* : threshold
un, una *art, mpl* **unos 1** : a, an **2** **unos** *or* **unas** : some, a few **3** **unos** *or* **unas** *pl* : about, approximately — **un** *adj* → **uno**

unánime *adj* : unanimous — **unanimidad** *nf* : unanimity
uncir {83} *vt* : yoke
undécimo, -ma *adj & n* : eleventh
ungir {35} *vt* : anoint — **ungüento** *nm* : ointment
único, -ca *adj* **1** : only, sole **2** EXCEPCIONAL : unique — **~ n** : only one — **únicamente** *adv* : only
unicornio *nm* : unicorn
unidad *nf* **1** : unit ARMONÍA : unity — **unido, -da** *adj* **1** : united **2** : close (of friends, etc.)
unificar {72} *vt* : unify — **unificación** *nf, pl* **-ciones** : unification
uniformar *vt* **1** : standardize **2** : put into uniform — **uniformado, -da** *adj* : uniformed — **uniforme** *adj & nm* : uniform — **uniformidad** *nf* : uniformity
unilateral *adj* : unilateral
unir *vt* **1** : unite, join **2** COMBINAR : combine, mix together — **unirse** *vr* **1** : join together **2 ~ a** : join — **unión** *nf, pl* **uniones 1** : union **2** JUNTURA : joint, coupling
unísono *nm* **al ~** : in unison
unitario, -ria *adj* : unitary
universal *adj* : universal
universidad *nf* : university, college — **universitario, -ria** *adj* : university, college
universo *nm* : universe
uno, una (**un** *before masculine singular nouns*) *adj* : one — **~** *pron* **1** : one **2 unos, unas** *pl* : some **3 uno(s) a otro(s)** : one another, each other **4 uno y otro** : both — **uno** *nm* : one (number)
untar *vt* **1** : smear, grease **2** *fam* : bribe — **untuoso, -sa** *adj* : greasy, sticky
uña *nf* **1** : nail, fingernail **2** : claw (of a cat, etc.), hoof (of a horse, etc.)
uranio *nm* : uranium

Urano *nm* : Uranus
urbano, -na *adj* : urban, city — **urbanidad** *nf* : politeness, courtesy — **urbanización** *nf, pl* **-ciones** : housing development — **urbanizar** *vt* : develop, urbanize — **urbe** *nf* : large city
urdir *vt* **1** : warp **2** PLANEAR : plot — **urdimbre** *nf* : warp (of a fabric)
urgir {35} *v impers* : be urgent, be pressing — **urgencia** *nf* **1** : urgency **2** EMERGENCIA : emergency — **urgente** *adj* : urgent
urinario, -ria *adj* : urinary — **urinario** *nm* : urinal (place)
urna *nf* **1** : urn **2** : ballot box (for voting)
urraca *nf* : magpie
uruguayo, -ya *adj* : Uruguayan
usar *vt* **1** : use **2** LLEVAR : wear — **usarse** *vr* EMPLEARSE : be used **2** : be worn, be in fashion — **usado, -da** *adj* **1** : used **2** GASTADO : worn, worn-out — **usanza** *nf* : custom, usage — **uso** *nm* **1** : use **2** DESGASTE : wear and tear **3** USANZA : custom, usage
usted *pron* **1** (*used in formal address; often written as* **Ud.** *or* **Vd.**) : you **2 ~es** *pl* (*often written as* **Uds.** *or* **Vds.**) : you (all)
usual *adj* : usual
usuario, -ria *n* : user
usura *nf* : usury — **usurero, -ra** *n* : usurer
usurpar *vt* : usurp
utensilio *nm* : utensil, tool
útero *nm* : uterus, womb
utilizar {21} *vt* : use, utilize — **útil** *adj* : useful — **útiles** *nmpl* : implements, tools — **utilidad** *nf* : utility, usefulness — **utilitario, -ria** *adj* : utilitarian — **utilización** *nf, pl* **-ciones** : utilization, use
uva *nf* : grape

V

v *nf* : v, 23d letter of the Spanish alphabet
va → ir
vaca *nf* : cow
vacaciones *nfpl* **1** : vacation **2 estar de ~** : be on vacation **3 irse de ~** : go on vacation
vacante *adj* : vacant — **~** *nf* : vacancy
vaciar {85} *vt* **1** : empty (out) **2** AHUECAR : hollow out **3** : cast, mold (a statue, etc.)

vacilar *vi* **1** : hesitate, waver **2** : flicker (of light) **3** TAMBALEARSE : be unsteady, wobble **4** *fam* : joke, fool around — **vacilación** *nf, pl* **-ciones** : hesitation — **vacilante** *adj* **1** : hesitant **2** OSCILANTE : unsteady
vacío, -cía *adj* : empty — **vacío** *nm* **1** : void **2** : vacuum (in physics) **3** HUECO : space, gap
vacuna *nf* : vaccine — **vacunación** *nf,*

pl **-ciones** : vaccination — **vacunar** *vt* : vaccinate

vacuno, -na *adj* : bovine

vadear *vt* : ford — **vado** *nm* : ford

vagabundear *vi* : wander — **vagabundo, -da** *adj* **1** : vagrant **2** : stray (of a dog, etc.) — *n* : hobo, bum — **vagancia** *nf* **1** : vagrancy **2** PEREZA : laziness, idleness — **vagar** {52} *vi* : roam, wander

vagina *nf* : vagina

vago, -ga *adj* **1** : vague **2** PEREZOSO : lazy, idle — *n* : idler, loafer

vagón *nm*, *pl* **-gones** : car (of a train)

vahído *nm* : dizzy spell

vaho *nm* **1** : breath **2** VAPOR : vapor, steam

vaina *nf* **1** : sheath, scabbard **2** : pod (in botany) **3** *Lat fam* : bother, pain

vainilla *nf* : vanilla

vaivén *nm*, *pl* **-venes** **1** : swinging, swaying **2** : coming and going (of people, etc.) **3 vaivenes** *nmpl* : ups and downs

vajilla *nf* : dishes *pl*

vale *nm* **1** : voucher **2** PAGARÉ : IOU — **valedero, -ra** *adj* : valid

valentía *nf* : courage, bravery

valer {84} *vt* **1** : be worth **2** COSTAR : cost **3** GANAR : gain, earn **4** EQUIVALER A : be equal to — *vi* **1** : have value, cost **2** SER VÁLIDO : be valid, count **3** SERVIR : be of use **4 hacerse ~** : assert oneself **5 más vale** : it's better — **valerse** *vr* **1 ~ de** : take advantage of **2 ~ solo** *or* **~ por sí mismo** : look after oneself

valeroso, -sa *adj* : courageous

valga, etc. → **valer**

valía *nf* : worth

validar *vt* : validate — **validez** *nf* : validity — **válido, -da** *adj* : valid

valiente *adj* **1** : brave **2** (*used ironically*) : fine, great

valija *nf* : case, valise

valioso, -sa *adj* : valuable

valla *nf* **1** : fence **2** : hurdle (in sports) — **vallar** *vt* : put a fence around

valle *nm* : valley

valor *nm* **1** : value, worth **2** VALENTÍA : courage, valor **3 objetos de ~** : valuables **4 sin ~** : worthless **5 ~es** *nmpl* : values, principles **6 ~es** *nmpl* : securities, bonds — **valoración** *nf*, *pl* **-ciones** : valuation — **valorar** *vt* : evaluate, assess

vals *nm* : waltz

válvula *nf* : valve

vamos → **ir**

vampiro *nm* : vampire

van → **ir**

vanagloriarse *vr* : boast, brag

vándalo *nm* : vandal — **vandalismo** : vandalism

vanguardia *nf* **1** : vanguard **2** : avant-garde (in art, music, etc.) **3 a la ~** : at/in the forefront

vanidad *nf* : vanity — **vanidoso, -sa** *adj* : vain, conceited

vano, -na *adj* **1** INÚTIL : vain, useless **2** SUPERFICIAL : empty, hollow **3 en vano** : in vain

vapor *nm* **1** : steam, vapor **2 al ~** : steamed — **vaporizador** *nm* : vaporizer — **vaporizar** {21} *vt* : vaporize

vaquero, -ra *n* : cowboy *m*, cowgirl *f* — **vaqueros** *nmpl* : jeans

vara *nf* **1** : stick, rod **2** : staff (of office)

varado, -da *adj* : stranded

variar {85} *vt* **1** : vary **2** CAMBIAR : change, alter — *vi* : vary, change — **variable** *adj* & *nf* : variable — **variación** *nf*, *pl* **-ciones** : variation — **variado, -da** *adj* : varied — **variante** *nf* : variant

varicela *nf* : chicken pox

varicoso, -sa *adj* : varicose

variedad *nf* : variety

varilla *nf* : rod, stick

vario, -ria *adj* **1** : varied **2 ~s** *pl* : several

varita *nf* : wand

variz *nf*, *pl* **-rices** *or* **várices** : varicose vein

varón *nm*, *pl* **-rones** **1** : man, male **2** NIÑO : boy — **varonil** *adj* : manly

vas → **ir**

vasco, -ca *adj* : Basque — **vasco** *nm* : Basque (language)

vasija *nf* : container, vessel

vaso *nm* **1** : glass **2** : vessel (in anatomy)

vástago *nm* **1** : offspring, descendent **2** BROTE : shoot **3** VARILLA : rod

vasto, -ta *adj* : vast

vaticinar *vt* : prophesy, predict — **vaticinio** *nm* : prophecy

vatio *nm* : watt

vaya, etc. → **ir**

Vd., Vds. → **usted**

ve, etc. → **ir**, **ver**

vecinal *adj* : local

vecino, -na *n* **1** : neighbor **2** HABITANTE : resident, inhabitant — **~** *adj* : neighboring — **vecindad** *nf* : neighborhood, vicinity — **vecindario** *nm* **1** : neighborhood **2** VECINOS : community, residents *pl*

vedar *vt* : prohibit — **veda** *nf* **1** : prohibition, ban **2** : closed season (for hunting and fishing) — **vedado** *nm* : preserve (for game, etc.)

vega *vt* : fertile lowland

vegetal *nm* : vegetable, plant — ~ *adj* : vegetable — **vegetación** *nf, pl* **-ciones** : vegetation — **vegetar** *vi* : vegetate — **vegetariano, -na** *adj & n* : vegetarian

vehemente *adj* : vehement

vehículo *nm* : vehicle

veinte *adj & nm* : twenty — **veinteavo, -va** *adj* : twentieth — **veinteavo** *nm* : twentieth — **veintena** *nf* : group of twenty, score

vejar *vt* : mistreat, humiliate — **vejación** *nf, pl* **-ciones** : humiliation

vejez *nf* : old age

vejiga *nf* **1** : bladder **2** AMPOLLA : blister

vela *nf* **1** : candle **2** : sail (of a ship) **3** VIGILIA : vigil **4 pasar la noche en ~** : have a sleepless night

velada *nf* : evening (party)

velar *vt* **1** : hold a wake over **2** CUIDAR : watch over **3** : blur (a photograph) **4** OCULTAR : veil, mask — *vi* **1** : stay awake **2 ~ por** : watch over — **velado, -da** *adj* **1** : veiled, hidden **2** : blurred (of a photograph)

velero *nm* : sailing ship

veleta *nf* : weather vane

vello *nm* **1** : body hair **2** PELUSA : down, fuzz — **vellón** *nm, pl* **-llones** : fleece — **velloso, -sa** *adj* : downy, fluffy — **velludo, -da** *adj* : hairy

velo *nm* : veil

veloz *adj, pl* **-loces** : fast, quick — **velocidad** *nf* **1** : speed, velocity **2** MARCHA : gear (of an automobile) — **velocímetro** *nm* : speedometer

vena *nf* **1** : vein **2** : grain (of wood) **3** DISPOSICIÓN : mood **4 tener ~ de** : have a talent for

venado *nm* **1** : deer **2** : venison (in cooking)

vencer {86} *vt* **1** : beat, defeat **2** SUPERAR : overcome — *vi* **1** : win **2** CADUCAR : expire — **vencerse** *vr* **1** : collapse, give way — **vencedor, -dora** *adj* : winning — ~ *n* : winner — **vencido, -da** *adj* **1** : beaten, defeated **2** CADUCADO : expired **3** : due, payable (in finance) **4 darse por ~** : give up — **vencimiento** *nm* **1** : expiration **2** : maturity (of a loan)

venda *nf* **1** : bandage — **vendaje** *nm* : bandage, dressing — **vendar** *vt* **1** : bandage **2 ~ los ojos** : blindfold

vendaval *nm* : gale

vender *vt* : sell — **venderse** *vr* **1** : be sold **2 se vende** : for sale — **vende-**

dor, -dora *n* **1** : seller **2** : salesman *m*, saleswoman *f* (in a store)

vendimia *nf* : grape harvest

vendrá, etc. → **venir**

veneno *nm* **1** : poison **2** : venom (of a snake, etc.) — **venenoso, -sa** *adj* : poisonous

venerar *vt* : venerate, revere — **venerable** *adj* : venerable — **veneración** *nf, pl* **-ciones** : veneration, reverence

venéreo, -rea *adj* : venereal

venezolano, -na *adj* : Venezuelan

venga → **venir**

vengar {52} *vt* : avenge — **vengarse** *vr* : get even, take revenge — **venganza** *nf* : vengeance, revenge — **vengativo, -va** *adj* : vindictive, vengeful

venia *nf* **1** : permission **2** : pardon (in law)

venial *adj* : venial, petty

venir {87} *vi* **1** : come **2** LLEGAR : arrive **3** HALLARSE : be, appear **4** QUEDAR : fit **5 que viene** : coming, next **6 ~ a ser** : turn out to be **7 ~ bien** : be suitable — **venirse** *vr* **1** : come **2 ~ abajo** : fall apart, collapse — **venida** *nf* **1** : arrival, coming **2** REGRESO : return — **venidero, -ra** *adj* : coming

venta *nf* **1** : sale, selling **2 en ~** : for sale

ventaja *nf* : advantage — **ventajoso, -sa** *adj* : advantageous

ventana *nf* **1** : window **2 ~ de la nariz** : nostril — **ventanilla** *nf* **1** : window (of a vehicle or airplane) **2** : ticket window, box office (of a theater, etc.)

ventilar *vt* : ventilate, air (out) — **ventilación** *nf, pl* **-ciones** : ventilation — **ventilador** *nm* : fan, ventilator

ventisca *nf* : blizzard — **ventisquero** *nm* : snowdrift

ventoso, -sa *adj* : windy — **ventosidad** *nf* : wind, flatulence

ventrílocuo, -cua *n* : ventriloquist

ventura *nf* **1** : fortune, luck **2** SATISFACCIÓN : happiness **3 a la ~** : at random — **venturoso, -sa** *adj* : fortunate, happy

ver {88} *vt* **1** : see **2** : watch (television, etc.) — *vi* **1** : see **2 a ~** *or* **vamos a ~** : let's see **3 no tener nada que ~ con** : have nothing to do with **4 ya veremos** : we'll see — **verse** *vr* **1** : see oneself **2** HALLARSE : find oneself **3** ENCONTRARSE : see each other, meet

vera *nf* **1** : side, edge **2** : bank (of a river)

veracidad *nf* : truthfulness

verano *nm* : summer — **veraneante** *nmf* : summer vacationer — **veranear**

vi : spend the summer — **veraniego, -ga** *adj* : summer

veras *nfpl* **de ~** : really

veraz *adj, pl* **-races** : truthful

verbal *adj* : verbal

verbena *nf* : festival, fair

verbo *nm* : verb — **verboso, -sa** *adj* : verbose

verdad *nf* 1 : truth 2 **de ~** : really, truly 3 **¿verdad?** : right?, isn't that so? — **verdaderamente** *adv* : really, truly — **verdadero, -dera** *adj* : true, real

verde *adj* 1 : green 2 : dirty, risqué (of a joke, etc.) — **~** *nm* : green — **verdor** *nm* : greenness

verdugo *nm* 1 : executioner, hangman 2 : cruel person, tyrant

verdura *nf* : vegetable(s), green(s)

vereda *nf* 1 : path, trail 2 *Lat* : sidewalk

veredicto *nm* : verdict

vergüenza *nf* 1 : shame 2 TIMIDEZ : bashfulness, shyness — **vergonzoso, -sa** *adj* 1 : shameful 2 TÍMIDO : bashful, shy

verídico, -ca *adj* : true, truthful

verificar {72} *vt* 1 : verify, confirm 2 EXAMINAR : test, check out — **verificarse** *vr* 1 : take place 2 : come true (of a prophecy, etc.) — **verificación** *nf, pl* **-ciones** : verification

verja *nf* 1 : (iron) gate 2 : rails *pl* (of a fence) 3 ENREJADO : grating, grille

vermut *nm, pl* **-muts** : vermouth

vernáculo, -la *adj* : vernacular

verosímil *adj* 1 : probable, likely 2 CREÍBLE : credible

verraco *nm* : boar

verruga *nf* : wart

versar *vi* **~ sobre** : deal with, be about — **versado, -da** *adj* **~ en** : versed in

versátil *adj* 1 : versatile 2 VOLUBLE : fickle

versión *nf, pl* **-siones** 1 : version 2 TRADUCCIÓN : translation

verso *nm* 1 : poem, verse 2 : line (of poetry)

vértebra *nf* : vertebra

verter {56} *vt* 1 : pour (out) 2 DERRAMAR : spill 3 TIRAR : dump — *vi* : flow — **vertedero** *nm* 1 : dump, landfill 2 DESAGÜE : drain, outlet

vertical *adj & nf* : vertical

vértice *nm* : vertex, apex

vertiente *nf* : slope

vértigo *nm* : vertigo, dizziness — **vertiginoso, -sa** *adj* : dizzy

vesícula *nf* 1 : blister 2 **~ biliar** : gallbladder

vestíbulo *nm* : vestibule, hall, foyer

vestido *nm* 1 : dress 2 ROPA : clothing, clothes *pl*

vestigio *nm* : vestige, trace

vestir {54} *vt* 1 : dress, clothe 2 LLEVAR : wear — *vi* : dress — **vestirse** *vr* : get dressed — **vestimenta** *nf* : clothing — **vestuario** *nm* 1 : wardrobe, clothes *pl* 2 : dressing room (in a theater), locker room (in sports)

veta *nf* 1 : vein, seam 2 : grain (of wood)

vetar *vt* : veto

veteado, -da *adj* : streaked, veined

veterano, -na *adj & n* : veteran

veterinaria *nf* : veterinary medicine — **veterinario, -ria** *adj* : veterinary — **~** *n* : veterinarian

veto *nm* : veto

vetusto, -ta *adj* : ancient

vez *nf, pl* **veces** 1 : time 2 TURNO : turn 3 **a la ~** : at the same time 4 **a veces** : sometimes 5 **de una ~** : all at once 6 **de una ~ para siempre** : once and for all 7 **de ~ en cuando** : from time to time 8 **dos veces** : twice 9 **en ~ de** : instead of 10 **una ~** : once

vía *nf* 1 : way, road, route 2 MEDIO : means 3 : track, line (of a railroad) 4 : (anatomical) tract 5 **en ~ de** : in the process of — **~** *prep* : via

viable *adj* : viable, feasible — **viabilidad** *nf* : viability

viaducto *nm* : viaduct

viajar *vi* : travel — **viajante** *nmf* : traveling salesperson — **viaje** *nm* : trip, journey — **viajero, -ra** *adj* : traveling — **~** *n* 1 : traveler 2 PASAJERO : passenger

vial *adj* : road, traffic

víbora *nf* : viper

vibrar *vi* : vibrate — **vibración** *nf, pl* **-ciones** : vibration — **vibrante** *adj* : vibrant

vicario, -ria *n* : vicar

vicepresidente, -ta *n* : vice president

viceversa *adv* : vice versa

vicio *nm* 1 : vice 2 MALA COSTUMBRE : bad habit 3 DEFECTO : defect — **viciado, -da** *adj* 1 : corrupt 2 : stuffy, stale (of air, etc.) — **viciar** *vt* 1 : corrupt 2 ESTROPEAR : spoil, pollute — **vicioso, -sa** *adj* : depraved, corrupt

vicisitud *nf* : vicissitude

víctima *nf* : victim

victoria *nf* : victory — **victorioso, -sa** *adj* : victorious

vid *nf* : vine, grapevine

vida *nf* 1 : life 2 DURACIÓN : lifetime 3 **de por ~** : for life 4 **estar con ~** : be alive

video *or* **vídeo** *nm* **1** : video **2** : VCR, videocassette recorder

vidrio *nm* : glass — **vidriado** *nm* : glaze — **vidriar** *vt* : glaze — **vidriera** *nf* **1** : stained-glass window **2** : glass door **3** *Lat* : shopwindow — **vidrioso, -sa** *adj* **1** : delicate (of a subject, etc.) **2** **ojos vidriosos** : glassy eyes

vieira *nf* : scallop

viejo, -ja *adj* : old — ~ *n* **1** : old man *m*, old woman *f* **2 hacerse** ~ : get old

viene, etc. → **venir**

viento *nm* : wind

vientre *nm* **1** : abdomen, belly **2** MATRIZ : womb **3** INTESTINO : bowels *pl*

viernes *nms & pl* **1** : Friday **2 Viernes Santo** : Good Friday

viga *nf* : beam, girder

vigencia *nf* **1** : validity **2 entrar en** ~ : go into effect — **vigente** *adj* : valid, in force

vigésimo, -ma *adj & n* : twentieth

vigía *nmf* : lookout

vigilar *vt* : look after, watch over — ~ *vi* : keep watch — **vigilancia** *nf* **1** : vigilance **2 bajo** ~ : under surveillance — **vigilante** *adj* : vigilant — ~ *nmf* : watchman, guard — **vigilia** *nf* **1** : wakefulness **2** : vigil (in religion)

vigor *nm* **1** : vigor **2 entrar en** ~ : go into effect — **vigorizante** *adj* : invigorating — **vigoroso, -sa** *adj* : vigorous

VIH *nm* : HIV

vil *adj* : vile, despicable — **vileza** *nf* **1** : vileness **2** : despicable act — **vilipendiar** *vt* : revile

villa *nf* **1** : town, village **2** : villa (house)

villancico *nm* : (Christmas) carol

villano, -na *n* : villain

vilo en ~ : suspended, in the air

vinagre *nm* : vinegar — **vinagrera** *nf* : cruet — **vinagreta** *nf* : vinaigrette

vincular *vt* : tie, link — **vínculo** *nm* : link, bond

vindicar *vt* **1** : vindicate **2** VENGAR : avenge

vino¹, etc. → **venir**

vino² *nm* : wine

viña *nf or* **viñedo** *nm* : vineyard

vio, etc. → **ver**

viola *nf* : viola

violar *vt* **1** : violate (a law, etc.) **2** : rape (a person) — **violación** *nf, pl* **-ciones 1** : violation, offense **2** : rape (of a person)

violencia *nf* : violence, force — **violentar** *vt* **1** : force **2** : break into (a house, etc.) — **violentarse** *vr* **1** : force one-

self **2** AVERGONZARSE : be embarrassed — **violento, -ta** *adj* **1** : violent **2** INCÓMODO : awkward, embarrassing

violeta *adj & nm* : violet (color) — ~ *nf* : violet (flower)

violín *nm, pl* **-lines** : violin — **violinista** *nmf* : violinist — **violoncelista** *or* **violonchelista** *nmf* : cellist — **violoncelo** *or* **violonchelo** *nm* : cello, violoncello

virar *vi* : turn, change direction — **viraje** *nm* **1** : turn, swerve **2** CAMBIO : change

virgen *adj & nmf, pl* **vírgenes** : virgin — **virginal** *adj* : virginal — **virginidad** *nf* : virginity

viril *adj* : virile — **virilidad** *nf* : virility

virtual *adj* : virtual

virtud *nf* **1** : virtue **2 en** ~ **de** : by virtue of — **virtuoso, -sa** *adj* : virtuous — ~ *n* : virtuoso

viruela *nf* **1** : smallpox **2 picado de** ~**s** : pockmarked

virulento, -ta *adj* : virulent

virus *nms & pl* : virus

visa *nf Lat* : visa — **visado** *nm Spain* : visa

vísceras *nfpl* : entrails — **visceral** *adj* : visceral

viscoso, -sa *adj* : viscous — **viscosidad** *nf* : viscosity

visera *nf* : visor

visible *adj* : visible — **visibilidad** *nf* : visibility

visión *nf, pl* **-siones 1** : eyesight **2** APARICIÓN, ILUSIÓN : vision, illusion **3** PUNTO DE VISTA : view, perspective — **visionario, -ria** *adj & n* : visionary

visitar *vt* : visit — **visita** *nf* **1** : visit **2 tener** ~ : have company — **visitante** *adj* : visiting — ~ *nmf* : visitor

vislumbrar *vt* : make out, discern — **vislumbre** *nf* **1** : glimpse, sign **2** RESPLANDOR : glimmer, gleam

viso *nm* **1** : sheen **2 tener** ~**s de** : seem, show signs of

visón *nm, pl* **-sones** : mink

víspera *nf* : eve, day before

vista *nf* **1** : vision, eyesight **2** MIRADA : look, gaze **3** PANORAMA : view, vista **4** : hearing (in court) **5 a primera** ~ *or* **a simple** ~ : at first sight **6 hacer la** ~ **gorda** : turn a blind eye **7 perder de** ~ : lose sight of — **vistazo** *nm* **1** : glance **2 echar un** ~ : have a look

visto, -ta *adj* **1** : clear, obvious **2** COMÚN : commonly seen **3 estar bien** ~ : be approved of **4 estar mal** ~ : be frowned upon **5 nunca** ~ : unheard-of **6 por lo visto** : apparently **7 visto que** : since, given that — **visto** *nm* ~ **bueno** : approval — *pp* → **ver**

vistoso, -sa *adj* : colorful, bright

visual *adj* : visual — **visualizar** {21} *vt* : visualize

vital *adj* : vital — **vitalicio, -cia** *adj* : life, for life — **vitalidad** *nf* : vitality

vitamina *nf* : vitamin

viticultor, -tora *n* : winegrower — **viticultura** *nf* : wine growing

vitorear *vt* : cheer, acclaim

vítreo, -trea *adj* : glassy

vitrina *nf* **1** : showcase, display case **2** *Lat* : shopwindow

vituperar *vt* : censure — **vituperio** *nm* : censure

viudo, -da *n* : widower *m*, widow *f* — ~ *adj* : widowed — **viudez** *nf* : widowerhood, widowhood

viva *nm* **dar** ~**s** : cheer

vivacidad *nf* : vivacity, liveliness

vivamente *adv* **1** : vividly **2** PROFUNDAMENTE : deeply, acutely

vivaz *adj, pl* **-vaces 1** : lively, vivacious **2** AGUDO : vivid, sharp

víveres *nmpl* : provisions, supplies

vivero *nm* **1** : nursery (for plants) **2** : (fish) hatchery, (oyster) bed

viveza *nf* **1** : liveliness **2** : vividness (of colors, descriptions, etc.) **3** ASTUCIA : sharpness (of mind) — **vívido, -da** *adj* : vivid

vividor, -dora *n* : freeloader

vivienda *nf* **1** : housing **2** MORADA : dwelling

viviente *adj* : living

vivificar {72} *vt* : enliven

vivir *vi* **1** : live, be alive **2** ~ **de** : live on — *vt* : experience, live (through) — ~ *nm* **1** : life, lifestyle **2 de mal** ~ : disreputable — **vivo, -va** *adj* **1** : alive **2** INTENSO : intense, bright **3** ANIMADO : lively **4** ASTUTO : sharp, quick **5 en vivo** : live

vocablo *nm* : word — **vocabulario** *nm* : vocabulary

vocación *nf, pl* **-ciones** : vocation — **vocacional** *adj* : vocational

vocal *adj* : vocal — ~ *nmf* : member (of a committee, etc.) — ~ *nf* : vowel — **vocalista** *nmf* : singer, vocalist

vocear *v* : shout — **vocerío** *nm* : shouting

vociferar *vi* : shout

vodka *nmf* : vodka

volar {19} *vi* **1** : fly **2** : blow away (of papers, etc.) **3** *fam* : disappear **4 irse volando** : rush off — *vt* : blow up — **volador, -dora** *adj* : flying — **volan-**

das: en ~ *adv phr* : in the air —

volante *adj* : flying — ~ *nm* **1** : steering wheel **2** : shuttlecock (in badminton) **3** : flounce (of fabric) **4** *Lat* : flier, circular

volátil *adj* : volatile

volcán *nm, pl* **-canes** : volcano — **volcánico, -ca** *adj* : volcanic

volcar {82} *vt* **1** : upset, knock over **2** VACIAR : empty out — *vi* : overturn — **volcarse** *vr* **1** : overturn, tip over **2** ~ **en** : throw oneself into

voleibol *nm* : volleyball

voltaje *nm* : voltage

voltear *vt* : turn over, turn upside down — **voltearse** *vr* *Lat* : turn (around) — **voltereta** *nf* : somersault

voltio *nm* : volt

voluble *adj* : fickle

volumen *nm, pl* **-lúmenes** : volume — **voluminoso, -sa** *adj* : voluminous

voluntad *nf* **1** : will **2** DESEO : wish **3** INTENCIÓN : intention **4 a** ~ : at will **5 buena** ~ : goodwill **6 mala** ~ : ill will **7 fuerza de** ~ : willpower — **voluntario, -ria** *adj* : voluntary — ~ *n* : volunteer — **voluntarioso, -sa** *adj* **1** : willing **2** TERCO : stubborn, willful

voluptuoso, -sa *adj* : voluptuous

volver {89} *vi* **1** : return, come or go back **2** ~ **a** : return to, do again **3** ~ **en sí** : come to — *vt* **1** : turn, turn over, turn inside out **2** CONVERTIR EN : turn (into) **3** ~ **loco** : drive crazy — **volverse** *vr* **1** : turn (around) **2** HACERSE : become

vomitar *vi* : vomit — *vt* **1** : vomit **2** : spew (out) — **vómito** *nm* **1** : (action of) vomiting **2** : vomit

voraz *adj, pl* **-races** : voracious

vos *pron* *Lat* : you

vosotros, -tras *pron* *Spain* : you, yourselves

votar *vi* : vote — *vt* : vote for — **votación** *nf, pl* **-ciones** : vote, voting — **votante** *nmf* : voter — **voto** *nm* **1** : vote **2** : vow (in religion)

voy → **ir**

voz *nf, pl* **voces 1** : voice **2** GRITO : shout, yell **3** VOCABLO : word, term **4** RUMOR : rumor **5 dar voces** : shout **6 en** ~ **alta** : loudly **7 en** ~ **baja** : softly

vuelco *nm* : upset, overturning

vuelo *nm* **1** : flight **2** : (action of) flying **3** : flare (of clothing) **4 al** ~ : on the wing

vuelta *nf* **1** : turn **2** REVOLUCIÓN : circle, revolution **3** CURVA : bend, curve **4** REGRESO : return **5** : round, lap (in sports)

6 PASEO : walk, drive, ride **7** REVÉS : back, other side **8** *Spain* : change **9 dar — s** : spin **10 estar de —** : be back — **vuelto** *nm Lat* : change
vuestro, -tra *adj Spain* : your, of yours — **~** *pron Spain (with definite article)* : yours

vulgar *adj* **1** : vulgar **2** CORRIENTE : common — **vulgaridad** *nf* **1** : vulgarity **2** BANALIDAD : banality — **vulgo** *nm* **el —** : the masses, common people
vulnerable *adj* : vulnerable — **vulnerabilidad** *nf* : vulnerability

WXYZ

w *nf* : w, 24th letter of the Spanish alphabet
wáter *nm Spain* : toilet
whisky *nm, pl* **-skys** *or* **-skies** : whiskey

x *nf* : x, 25th letter of the Spanish alphabet
xenofobia *nf* : xenophobia
xilófono *nm* : xylophone

y¹ *nf* : y, 26th letter of the Spanish alphabet
y² *conj* : and
ya *adv* **1** : already **2** AHORA : (right) now **3** MÁS TARDE : later, soon **4 ~ no** : no longer **5 ~ que** : now that, since, inasmuch as
yacer {90} *vi* : lie (on or in the ground) — **yacimiento** *nm* : bed, deposit
yanqui *adj & nmf* : Yankee
yate *nm* : yacht
yegua *nf* : mare
yelmo *nm* : helmet
yema *nf* **1** : bud, shoot **2** : yolk (of an egg) **3** *or* **~ del dedo** : fingertip
yerba *nf* **1** *or* **~ mate** : maté **2** → **hierba**
yermo, -ma *adj* : barren, deserted → **yermo** *nm* : wasteland
yerno *nm* : son-in-law
yerro *nm* : blunder, mistake
yerto, -ta *adj* : stiff
yesca *nf* : tinder
yeso *nm* **1** : gypsum **2** : plaster (for art, construction)
yo *pron* **1** *(subject)* : I **2** *(object)* : me **3 soy ~** : it is I, it's me — **~** *nm* : ego, self
yodo *nm* : iodine
yoga *nm* : yoga
yogurt *or* **yogur** *nm* : yogurt
yuca *nf* : yucca
yugo *nm* : yoke (of oxen)
yugoslavo, -va *adj* : Yugoslavian
yugular *adj* : jugular
yunque *nm* : anvil
yunta *nf* : yoke

yuxtaponer {60} *vt* : juxtapose — **yuxtaposición** *nf, pl* **-ciones** : juxtaposition

z *nf* : z, 27th letter of the Spanish alphabet
zacate *nm Lat* : grass
zafar *vt Lat* : loosen, untie — **zafarse** *vr* **1** : come undone **2** : get free of (an obligation, etc.)
zafio, -fia *adj* : coarse
zafiro *nm* : sapphire
zaga *nf* **a la ~** *or* **en ~** : behind, in the rear
zaguán *nm, pl* **-guanes** : (entrance) hall
zaherir {76} *vt* : hurt (s.o.'s feelings)
zaino, -na *adj* : chestnut (color)
zalamería *nf* : flattery — **zalamero, -ra** *adj* : flattering — **~** *n* : flatterer
zambullirse {38} *vr* : dive, plunge — **zambullida** *nf* : dive, plunge
zanahoria *nf* : carrot
zancada *nf* : stride, step — **zancadilla** *nf* **1** : trip, stumble **2 hacer una ~ a algn** : trip s.o. up
zancos *nmpl* : stilts
zancudo *nm Lat* : mosquito
zángano, -na *n fam* : lazy person, slacker — **zángano** *nm* : drone (bee)
zanja *nf* : ditch, trench — **zanjar** *vt* : settle, resolve
zapallo *nm Lat* : pumpkin — **zapallito** *nm Lat* : zucchini
zapapico *nm* : pickax
zapato *nm* : shoe — **zapatería** *nf* : shoe store — **zapatero, -ra** *n* : shoemaker, cobbler — **zapatilla** *nf* **1** : slipper **2** : sneaker (for sports, etc.)
zar *nm* : czar
zarandear *vt* **1** : sift **2** SACUDIR : shake
zarcillo *nm* : earring
zarpa *nf* : paw
zarpar *vi* : set sail, raise anchor
zarza *nf* : bramble — **zarzamora** *nf* : blackberry
zigzag *nm, pl* **-zags** *or* **-zagues** : zigzag — **zigzaguear** *vi* : zigzag

zinc *nm* : zinc
zíper *nm Lat, pl* **-cones** : zipper
zircón *nm, pl* **-cones** : zircon
zócalo *nm* **1** : base (of a column, etc.) **2** : baseboard (of a wall) **3** *Lat* : main square, plaza
zodíaco *nm* : zodiac
zona *nf* : zone, area
zoo *nm* : zoo — **zoología** *nf* : zoology — **zoológico, -ca** *adj* : zoological — **zoológico** *nm* : zoo — **zoólogo, -ga** *n* : zoologist
zopilote *nm Lat* : buzzard
zoquete *nmf fam* : oaf, blockhead

zorrillo *nm Lat* : skunk
zorro, -rra *n* : fox, vixen *f* — ~ *adj* : foxy, sly
zozobra *nf* : anxiety, worry — **zozobrar** *vi* : capsize
zueco *nm* : clog (shoe)
zumbar *vi* : buzz — *vt fam* : hit, beat — **zumbido** *nm* : buzzing
zumo *nf* : juice
zurcir {83} *vt* : darn, mend
zurdo, -da *adj* : left-handed — ~ *n* : left-handed person — **zurda** *nf* : left hand
zutano, -na → fulano

English-Spanish
Dictionary

A

a¹ ['eɪ] *n, pl* **a's** *or* **as** ['eɪz] : a *f*, primera letra del alfabeto inglés

a² [ə, 'eɪ] *art* (**an** [ən, æn] *before vowel or silent h*) **1** : un *m*, una *f* **2** PER : por, a la, al

aback [ə'bæk] *adv* **be taken ~** : quedarse desconcertado

abacus ['æbəkəs] *n, pl* **abaci** [æbə,saɪ, -,kiː] *or* **abacuses** : ábaco *m*

abandon [ə'bændən] *vt* **1** DESERT : abandonar **2** GIVE UP : renunciar a — **~** *n* : desenfreno *m* — **abandonment** [ə'bændənmənt] *n* : abandono *m*

abashed [ə'bæʃt] *adj* : avergonzado

abate [ə'beɪt] *vi* **abated; abating** : amainar, disminuir

abattoir ['æbə,twɑr] *n* : matadero *m*

abbey ['æbi] *n, pl* **-beys** : abadía *f* — **abbot** ['æbət] *n* : abad *m*

abbreviate [ə'briːvi,eɪt] *vt* **-ated; -ating** : abreviar — **abbreviation** [ə,briːvi-'eɪʃən] *n* : abreviatura *f*, abreviación *f*

abdicate ['æbdɪ,keɪt] *v* **-cated; -cating** : abdicar — **abdication** [,æbdɪ'keɪ,ən] *n* : abdicación *f*

abdomen ['æbdəmən, æb'doːmən] *n* : abdomen *m*, vientre *m* — **abdominal** [æb'dɑmənəl] *adj* : abdominal

abduct [æb'dʌkt] *vt* : secuestrar — **abduction** [æb'dʌkʃən] *n* : secuestro *m*

aberration [,æbə'reɪʃən] *n* : aberración *f*

abet [ə'bɛt] *vt* **abetted; abetting** *or* **aid and ~** : ser cómplice de

abeyance [ə'beɪənts] *n* : desuso *m*

abhor [əb'hɔr, æb-] *vt* **-horred; -horring** : aborrecer

abide [ə'baɪd] *v* **abode** [ə'boːd] *or* **abided; abiding** *vt* : soportar, tolerar — *vi* **1** DWELL : morar **2 ~ by** : atenerse a

ability [ə'bɪləti] *n, pl* **-ties 1** CAPABILITY : aptitud *f*, capacidad *f* **2** SKILL : habilidad *f*

abject ['æb,dʒɛkt, æb'-] *adj* : miserable, desdichado

ablaze [ə'bleɪz] *adj* : en llamas

able ['eɪbəl] *adj* **abler; ablest 1** CAPABLE : capaz, hábil **2** COMPETENT : competente

abnormal [æb'nɔrməl] *adj* : anormal — **abnormality** [,æbnɔr'mæləti, -nɔr-] *n, pl* **-ties** : anormalidad *f*

aboard [ə'bord] *adv* : a bordo — **~** *prep* : a bordo de

abode *n* : morada *f*, domicilio *m*

abolish [ə'bɑlɪʃ] *vt* : abolir, suprimir — **abolition** [,æbə'lɪʃən] *n* : abolición *f*

abominable [ə'bɑmənəbəl] *adj* : abominable, aborrecible — **abomination** [ə,bɑmə'neɪʃən] *n* : abominación *f*

aborigine [,æbə'rɪdʒəni] *n* : aborigen *mf*

abort [ə'bɔrt] *vt* : abortar — **abortion** [ə'bɔrʃən] *n* : aborto *m* — **abortive** [ə'bɔrtɪv] *adj* UNSUCCESSFUL : malogrado

abound [ə'baʊnd] *vi* **~ in** : abundar en

about [ə'baʊt] *adv* **1** APPROXIMATELY : aproximadamente, más o menos **2** AROUND : alrededor **3 be ~ to** : estar a punto de **4 be up and ~** : estar levantado — **~** *prep* **1** AROUND : alrededor de **2** CONCERNING : acerca de, sobre

above [ə'bʌv] *adv* : arriba — **~** *prep* **1** : encima de **2 ~ all** : sobre todo — **aboveboard** *adj* : honrado

abrasive [ə'breɪsɪv] *adj* **1** : abrasivo **2** BRUSQUE : brusco, mordaz

abreast [ə'brɛst] *adv* **1** : al lado de **2 keep ~ of** : mantenerse al corriente de

abridge [ə'brɪdʒ] *vt* **abridged; abridging** : abreviar

abroad [ə'brɔd] *adv* **1** : en el extranjero **2** WIDELY : por todas partes **3 go ~** : ir al extranjero

abrupt [ə'brʌpt] *adj* **1** SUDDEN : repentino **2** BRUSQUE : brusco

abscess ['æb,sɛs] *n* : absceso *m*

absence ['æbsənts] *n* **1** : ausencia *f* **2** LACK : falta *f*, carencia *f* — **absent** ['æbsənt] *adj* : ausente — **absentee** [,æbsən'tiː] *n* : ausente *mf* — **absent-minded** [,æbsənt'maɪndəd] *adj* : distraído, despistado

absolute ['æbsə,luːt, ,æbsə'luːt] *adj* : absoluto — **absolutely** [,æbsə'luːtli] *adv* : absolutamente

absolve [əb'zɑlv, æb-, -'sɑlv] *vt* **-solved; -solving** : absolver

absorb [əb'zɔrb, æb-, -'sɔrb] *vt* : absorber — **absorbent** [əb'zɔrbənt, æb-, -'sɔr-] *adj* : absorbente — **absorption** [əb'zɔrpʃən, æb-, -'sɔrp-] *n* : absorción *f*

abstain [əb'steɪn, æb-] *vi* **~ from** : abstenerse de — **abstinence** ['æbstənənts] *n* : abstinencia *f*

abstract [æb'strækt, 'æb,-] *adj* : abstracto — ~ *vt* : extraer — ~ ['æb,strækt] *n* : resumen *m* — **abstraction** [æb'strækʃən] *n* : abstracción *f*

absurd [əb'sərd, -'zərd] *adj* : absurdo — **absurdity** [əb'sərdəti, -'zərdəti] *n, pl* **-ties** : absurdo *m*

abundant [ə'bʌndənt] *adj* : abundante — **abundance** [ə'bʌndəns] *n* : abundancia *f*

abuse [ə'bjuːz] *vt* **abused; abusing** 1 MISUSE : abusar de 2 MISTREAT : maltratar 3 REVILE : insultar — ~ [ə'bjuːs] *n* 1 : abuso *m* 2 INSULTS : insultos *mpl* — **abusive** [ə'bjuːsɪv] *adj* : injurioso

abut [ə'bʌt] *vi* **abutted; abutting** — ~ **on** : colindar con

abyss [ə'bɪs, 'æbɪs] *n* : abismo *m* — **abysmal** [ə'bɪzməl] *adj* : atroz, pésimo

academy [ə'kædəmi] *n, pl* **-mies** : academia *f* — **academic** [,ækə'dɛmɪk] *adj* 1 : académico 2 THEORETICAL : teórico

accelerate [ɪk'sɛləˌreɪt, æk-] *v* **-ated; -ating** : acelerar — **acceleration** [ɪk,sɛlə'reɪʃən, æk-] *n* : aceleración *f*

accent [æk,sɛnt, æk'sɛnt] *vt* : acentuar — ~ ['æk,sɛnt, ,sɛnt] *n* : acento *m* — **accentuate** [ɪk'sɛntʃəˌeɪt, æk-] *vt* **-ated; -ating** : acentuar, subrayar

acceptable [ɪk'sɛpt, æk-] *vt* : aceptar — **acceptable** [ɪk'sɛptəbəl, æk-] *adj* : aceptable — **acceptance** [ɪk'sɛptəns, æk-] *n* 1 : aceptación *f* 2 APPROVAL : aprobación *f*

access ['æk,sɛs] *n* : acceso *m* — **accessible** [ɪk'sɛsəbəl, æk-] *adj* : accesible, asequible

accessory *n, pl* **-ries** 1 : accesorio *m* 2 ACCOMPLICE : cómplice *mf*

accident ['æksədənt] *n* 1 MISHAP : accidente *m* 2 CHANCE : casualidad *f* — **accidental** [,æksə'dɛntəl] *adj* : accidental — **accidentally** [,æksə'dɛntəli, -'dɛntli] *adv* 1 BY CHANCE : por casualidad 2 UNINTENTIONALLY : sin querer

acclaim [ə'kleɪm] *vt* : aclamar — ~ *n* : aclamación *f*

acclimatize [ə'klaɪməˌtaɪz] *vt* **-tized; -tizing** : aclimatar

accommodate [ə'kɑmə,deɪt] *vt* **-dated; -dating** 1 ADAPT : acomodar, adaptar 2 SATISFY : complacer, satisfacer 3 HOLD : tener cabida para — **accommodation** [ə,kɑmə'deɪʃən] *n* 1 : adaptación *f* 2 ~s *npl* LODGING : alojamiento *m*

accompany [ə'kʌmpəni, -'kʌm-] *vt* **-nied; -nying** : acompañar

accomplice [ə'kɑmpləs, -'kʌm-] *n* : cómplice *mf*

accomplish [ə'kɑmplɪʃ, -'kʌm-] *vt* : re-alizar, llevar a cabo — **accomplishment** [ə'kɑmplɪʃmənt, -'kʌm-] *n* 1 COMPLETION : realización *f* 2 ACHIEVEMENT : logro *m*, éxito *m*

accord *n* 1 AGREEMENT : acuerdo *m* 2 of one's own ~ : voluntariamente — **accordance** [ə'kɔrdəns] *n* **in ~ with** : conforme a, de acuerdo con — **accordingly** [ə'kɔrdɪŋli] *adv* : en consecuencia — **according to** [ə'kɔrdɪŋ] *prep* : según

accordion [ə'kɔrdiən] *n* : acordeón *m*

accost [ə'kɔst] *vt* : abordar

account [ə'kaʊnt] *n* 1 : cuenta *f* 2 REPORT : relato *m*, informe *m* 3 WORTH : importancia *f* 4 on ~ of : a causa de, debido a 5 on no ~ : de ninguna manera — ~ *vi* **for** : dar cuenta de, explicar — **accountable** [ə'kaʊntəbəl] *adj* : responsable — **accountant** [ə'kaʊntənt] *n* : contador *m*, -dora *f Lat*; contable *mf Spain* — **accounting** [ə'kaʊntɪŋ] *n* : contabilidad *f*

accrue [ə'kruː] *vi* **-crued; -cruing** : acumularse

accumulate [ə'kjuːmjəˌleɪt] *v* **-lated; -lating** *vt* : acumular — *vi* : acumularse — **accumulation** [ə,kjuːmjə'leɪʃən] *n* : acumulación *f*

accurate ['ækjərət] *adj* : exacto, preciso — **accuracy** ['ækjərəsi] *n* : exactitud *f*, precisión *f*

accuse [ə'kjuːz] *vt* **-cused; -cusing** : acusar — **accusation** [,ækjə'zeɪʃən] *n* : acusación *f*

accustomed [ə'kʌstəmd] *adj* 1 : acostumbrado 2 **become ~ to** : acostumbrarse a

ace ['eɪs] *n* : as *m*

ache ['eɪk] *vi* **ached; aching** : doler — ~ *n* : dolor *m*

achieve [ə'tʃiːv] *vt* **achieved; achieving** : lograr, realizar — **achievement** [ə'tʃiːvmənt] *n* : logro *m*, éxito *m*

acid ['æsəd] *adj* : ácido — ~ *n* : ácido *m*

acknowledge [ɪk'nɑlɪdʒ, æk-] *vt* **-edged; -edging** 1 ADMIT : admitir 2 RECOGNIZE : reconocer 3 ~ **receipt of** : acusar recibo de — **acknowledgment** [ɪk'nɑlɪdʒmənt, æk-] *n* 1 : reconocimiento *m* 2 THANKS : agradecimiento *m* 3 ~ **of receipt** : acuse *m* de recibo

acne ['ækni] *n* : acné *m*

acorn ['eɪkɔrn, -kəm] *n* : bellota *f*

acoustic [ə'kuːstɪk] *or* **acoustical** [-stɪkəl] *adj* : acústico — **acoustics** [ə'kuːstɪks] *ns & pl* : acústica *f*

acquaint [ə'kweɪnt] *vt* ~ **s.o. with**

: poner a algn al corriente de **2 be ~ed with** : conocer a (una persona), saber (un hecho) — **acquaintance** [ə'kweintən*t*s] *n* **1** : conocimiento *m* **2** : conocido *m*, -da *f* (persona)

acquire [ə'kwair] *vt* **-quired; -quiring** : adquirir — **acquisition** [ækwə'zɪʃən] *n* : adquisición *f*

acquit [ə'kwɪt] *vt* **-quitted; -quitting** : absolver

acre ['eɪkər] *n* : acre *m* — **acreage** ['eɪkərɪdʒ] *n* : superficie *f* en acres

acrid ['ækrəd] *adj* : acre

acrobat ['ækrəˌbæt] *n* : acróbata *mf* — **acrobatic** [ˌækrə'bætɪk] *adj* : acrobático

acronym ['ækrəˌnɪm] *n* : siglas *fpl*

across [ə'krɔs] *adv* **1** : de un lado a otro **2** CROSSWISE : a través **3 go ~** : atravesar — **~** *prep* **1** : a través de **2 ~ the street** : al otro lado de la calle

acrylic [ə'krɪlɪk] *n* : acrílico *m*

act ['ækt] *vi* **1** : actuar **2** PRETEND : fingir **3** FUNCTION : funcionar **4 ~ as** : servir de — *vt* : interpretar (un papel) — **~** *n* **1** ACTION : acto *m*, acción *f* **2** DECREE : ley *f* **3** : acto *m* (en una obra de teatro), número *m* (en un espectáculo) — **acting** *adj* : interino

action ['ækʃən] *n* **1** : acción *f* **2** LAWSUIT : demanda *f* **3 take ~** : tomar medidas

activate ['æktəˌveɪt] *vt* **-vated; -vating** : activar

active ['æktɪv] *adj* **1** : activo **2** LIVELY : enérgico **3 ~ volcano** : volcán *m* en actividad — **activity** [æk'tɪvəti] *n, pl* **-ties** : actividad *f*

actor ['æktər] *n* : actor *m* — **actress** ['æktrəs] *n* : actriz *f*

actual ['æktʃuəl] *adj* : real, verdadero — **actually** ['æktʃuəli, -æli] *adv* : realmente, en realidad

acupuncture ['ækjuˌpʌŋktʃər] *n* : acupuntura *f*

acute [ə'kjut] *adj* **acuter; acutest 1** : agudo **2** PERCEPTIVE : perspicaz

ad ['æd] → **advertisement**

adamant ['ædəmənt, -ˌmænt] *adj* : inflexible

adapt [ə'dæpt] *vt* : adaptar — *vi* : adaptarse — **adaptable** [ə'dæptəbəl] *adj* : adaptable — **adaptation** [ˌædæp'teɪʃən, -dəp-] *n* : adaptación *f* — **adapter** [ə'dæptər] *n* : adaptador *m*

add ['æd] *vt* **1** : añadir **2 ~ up** : sumar — *vi* : sumar

addict ['ædɪkt] *n* **1** : adicto *m*, -ta *f* **2 or drug~** : drogadicto *m*, -ta *f*; toxicómano *m*, -na *f* — **addiction** [ə'dɪkʃən] *n* : dependencia *f*

addition [ə'dɪʃən] *n* **1** : suma *f* (en matemáticas) **2** ADDING : adición *f* **3 in ~** : además — **additional** [ə'dɪʃənəl] *adj* : adicional — **additive** ['ædəˌtɪv] *n* : aditivo *m*

address [ə'dres] *vt* **1** : dirigirse a (una persona) **2** : ponerle la dirección a (una carta) **3** : tratar (un asunto) — **~** ['dres, ə'dres] *n* **1** : dirección *f*, domicilio *m* **2** SPEECH : discurso *m*

adept [ə'dept] *adj* : experto, hábil

adequate ['ædɪkwət] *adj* : adecuado, suficiente

adhere [æd'hɪr, əd-] *vi* **-hered; -hering 1** STICK : adherirse **2 ~ to** : observar — **adherence** [æd'hɪrən*t*s, əd-] *n* **1** : adhesión *f* **2** : observancia *f* (de una ley, etc.) — **adhesive** [æd'hi:sɪv, əd-, -zɪv] *adj* : adhesivo — *n* : adhesivo *m*

adjacent [ə'dʒeɪsənt] *adj* : adyacente, contiguo

adjective ['ædʒɪktɪv] *n* : adjetivo *m*

adjoining [ə'dʒɔɪnɪŋ] *adj* : contiguo, vecino

adjourn [ə'dʒərn] *vt* : aplazar, suspender — *vi* : suspenderse

adjust [ə'dʒʌst] *vt* : ajustar, arreglar — *vi* : adaptarse — **adjustable** [ə'dʒʌstəbəl] *adj* : ajustable — **adjustment** [ə'dʒʌstmənt] *n* : ajuste *m* (a una máquina, etc.), adaptación *f* (de una persona)

ad–lib ['æd'lɪb] *v* **-libbed; -libbing** : improvisar

administer [æd'mɪnəstər, əd-] *vt* : administrar — **administration** [ædˌmɪnə'streɪʃən, əd-] *n* : administración *f* — **administrative** [æd'mɪnəˌstreɪtɪv, əd-] *adj* : administrativo — **administrator** [æd'mɪnəˌstreɪtər, əd-] *n* : administrador *m*, -dora *f*

admirable ['ædmərəbəl] *adj* : admirable

admiral ['ædmərəl] *n* : almirante *m*

admire [æd'maɪr] *vt* **-mired; -miring** : admirar — **admiration** [ˌædmə'reɪʃən] *n* : admiración *f* — **admirer** [æd'maɪrər] *n* : admirador *m*, -dora *f*

admit [æd'mɪt, əd-] *vt* **-mitted; -mitting 1** : admitir, dejar entrar **2** ACKNOWLEDGE : reconocer — **admission** [æd'mɪʃən] *n* **1** ADMITTANCE : entrada *f*, admisión *f* **2** ACKNOWLEDGMENT : reconocimiento *m* — **admittance** [æd'mɪtən*t*s, əd-] *n* : admisión *f*, entrada *f*

admonish [æd'mɒnɪʃ, əd-] *vt* : amonestar, reprender

ado [ə'du:] *n* **1** : alboroto *m*, bulla *f* **2 without further ~** : sin más (preámbulos)

adolescent [ˌædəlˈesənt] n : adolescente mf — **adolescence** [ˌædəlˈesənts] n : adolescencia f

adopt [əˈdɑpt] vt : adoptar — **adoption** [əˈdɑpʃən] n : adopción f

adore [əˈdor] vt **adored; adoring 1** : adorar **2** LIKE, LOVE : encantarle (algo a uno) — **adorable** [əˈdorəbəl] adj : adorable — **adoration** [ˌædəˈreɪʃən] n : adoración f

adorn [əˈdɔrn] vt : adornar — **adornment** [əˈdɔrnmənt] n : adorno m

adrift [əˈdrɪft] adj & adv : a la deriva

adroit [əˈdrɔɪt] adj : diestro, hábil

adult [əˈdʌlt, ˈæˌdʌlt] adj : adulto — ~ n : adulto m, -ta f

adultery [əˈdʌltəri] n, pl -teries : adulterio m

advance [ædˈvæns, əd-] v -**vanced; -vancing** vt : adelantar — vi : avanzar, adelantarse — ~ n **1** : avance m **2** PROGRESS : adelanto m **3 in ~** : por adelantado — **advancement** [ædˈvænsmənt, əd-] n : adelanto m, progreso m

advantage [ædˈvæntɪdʒ, æd-] n **1** : ventaja f **2 take ~ of** : aprovecharse de — **advantageous** [ˌædˌvænˈteɪdʒəs, -vən-] adj : ventajoso

advent [ˈædˌvent] n **1** ARRIVAL : llegada f **2 Advent** : Adviento m

adventure [ædˈventʃər, əd-] n : aventura f — **adventurous** [ædˈventʃərəs, əd-] adj **1** : intrépido **2** RISKY : arriesgado

adverb [ˈædˌvərb] n : adverbio m

adversary [ˈædvərˌseri] n, pl -**saries** : adversario m, -ria f

adverse [ædˈvərs, ˈæd-] adj : adverso, desfavorable — **adversity** [ædˈvərsəti, əd-] n, pl -**ties** : adversidad f

advertise [ˈædvərˌtaɪz] v -**tised; -tising** vt : anunciar — vi : hacer publicidad — **advertisement** [ˌædvərˈtaɪzmənt] n : anuncio m — **advertiser** [ˈædvərˌtaɪzər] n : anunciante mf — **advertising** [ˈædvərˌtaɪzɪŋ] n : publicidad f

advice [ædˈvaɪs] n : consejo m

advise [ædˈvaɪz, əd-] vt -**vised; -vising 1** COUNSEL : aconsejar, asesorar **2** RECOMMEND : recomendar **3** INFORM : informar — **advisable** [ædˈvaɪzəbəl, əd-] adj : aconsejable — **adviser** [ædˈvaɪzər, əd-] n : consejero m, -ra f; asesor m, -sora f — **advisory** [ædˈvaɪzəri, əd-] adj : consultivo

advocate [ˈædvəˌkeɪt] vt -**cated; -cating** : recomendar — ~ [ˈædvəkət] n : defensor m, -sora f

aerial [ˈæriəl] adj : aéreo — ~ n : antena f

aerobics [ˌærˈoːbɪks] ns & pl : aeróbic m

aerodynamic [ˌærˌoːdarˈnæmɪk] adj : aerodinámico

aerosol [ˈærəˌsɔl] n : aerosol m

aesthetic [esˈθetɪk] adj : estético

afar [əˈfɑr] adv : lejos

affable [ˈæfəbəl] adj : afable

affair [əˈfær] n **1** : asunto m, cuestión f **2** or **love ~** : amorío m, aventura f

affect [əˈfekt, æ-] vt **1** : afectar **2** FEIGN : fingir — **affection** [əˈfekʃən] n : afecto m, cariño m — **affectionate** [əˈfekʃənət] adj : afectuoso, cariñoso

affinity [əˈfɪnəti] n, pl -**ties** : afinidad f

affirm [əˈfərm] vt : afirmar — **affirmative** [əˈfɔrmətɪv] adj : afirmativo

affix [əˈfɪks] vt : fijar, pegar

afflict [əˈflɪkt] vt : afligir — **affliction** [əˈflɪkʃən] n : aflicción f

affluent [ˈæˌfluːənt; æˈfluː-, ə-] adj : próspero, adinerado

afford [əˈfɔrd] vt **1** : tener los recursos para, permitirse (el lujo de) **2** PROVIDE : brindar

affront [əˈfrʌnt] n : afrenta f

afloat [əˈfloːt] adv & adj : a flote

afoot [əˈfʊt] adj : en marcha

afraid [əˈfreɪd] adj **1 be ~** : tener miedo **2 I'm ~ not** : me temo que no

African [ˈæfrɪkən] adj : africano

after [ˈæftər] adv AFTERWARD : después **2** BEHIND : detrás, atrás — ~ conj : después de (que) — ~ prep **1** : después de **2 ~ all** : después de todo **3 it's ten ~ five** : son las cinco y diez

aftereffect [ˈæftərəˌfekt] n : efecto m secundario

aftermath [ˈæftərˌmæθ] n : consecuencias fpl

afternoon [ˌæftərˈnuːn] n : tarde f

afterward [ˈæftərwərd] or **afterwards** [-wərdz] adv : después, más tarde

again [əˈgen, -ˈgɪn] adv **1** : otra vez, de nuevo **2 ~ and ~** : una y otra vez **3 then ~** : por otra parte

against [əˈgenst, -ˈgɪnst] prep : contra, en contra de

age [ˈeɪdʒ] n **1** : edad f **2** ERA : era f, época f **3 be of ~** : ser mayor de edad **4 for ~s** : hace siglos **5 old ~** : vejez f — ~ vi **aged; aging** : envejecer — **aged** adj **1** [ˈeɪdʒəd, ˈeɪdʒd] OLD : anciano, viejo **2** [ˈeɪdʒd] **children ~ 10 to 17** : niños de 10 a 17 años

agency [ˈeɪdʒənti] n, pl -**cies** : agencia f

agenda [əˈdʒendə] n : orden m del día

agent [ˈeɪdʒənt] n : agente mf, representante mf

aggravate [ˈægrəˌveɪt] vt -**vated; -vating**

1 WORSEN : agravar, empeorar **2** AN-
NOY : irritar

aggregate ['ægrɪgət] *adj* : total, global
— ~ *n* : total *m*

aggression [ə'greʃən] *n* : agresión *f* —
aggressive [ə'gresɪv] *adj* : agresivo —
aggressor [ə'gresər] *n* : agresor *m*,
-sora *f*

aghast [ə'gæst] *adj* : horrorizado

agile ['ædʒəl] *adj* : ágil — **agility** [ə-
'dʒɪləṭi] *n, pl* -ties : agilidad *f*

agitate ['ædʒə,teɪt] *v* -tated; -tating *vt* **1**
SHAKE : agitar **2** TROUBLE : inquietar —
agitation [ædʒə'teɪʃən] *n* : agitación *f*,
inquietud *f*

agnostic [æg'nɑstɪk] *n* : agnóstico *m*,
-ca *f*

ago [ə'go:] *adv* **1** : hace **2** long ~ : hace
mucho tiempo

agony ['ægəni] *n, pl* -nies **1** PAIN : dolor
m **2** ANGUISH : angustia *f* — **agonize**
['ægə,naɪz] *vi* -nized; -nizing : atormentarse — **agonizing** ['ægə,naɪzɪŋ]
adj : angustioso

agree [ə'gri:] *v* agreed; agreeing *vt* **1**
: acordar **2** ~ that : estar de acuerdo
de que — *vi* **1** : estar de acuerdo **2**
CORRESPOND : concordar **3** ~ to : acceder a **4** this climate ~s with me
: este clima me sienta bien — **agreeable** [ə'gri:əbəl] *adj* **1** PLEASING
: agradable **2** WILLING : dispuesto —
agreement [ə'gri:mənt] *n* : acuerdo *m*

agriculture ['ægrɪ,kʌltʃər] *n* : agricultura
f — **agricultural** [ægrɪ'kʌltʃərəl] *adj*
: agrícola

aground [ə'graʊnd] *adv* run ~ : encallar

ahead [ə'hed] *adv* **1** IN FRONT : delante,
adelante **2** BEFOREHAND : por adelantado **3** LEADING : a la delantera **4** get ~
: adelantar — **ahead of** *prep* **1** : delante de, antes de **2** get ~ of : adelantarse a

aid [eɪd] *vt* : ayudar — ~ *n* : ayuda *f*,
asistencia *f*

AIDS [eɪdz] *n* : SIDA *m*, sida *m*

ail [eɪl] *vi* : estar enfermo — **ailment**
['eɪlmənt] *n* : enfermedad *f*

aim [eɪm] *vt* : apuntar (un arma), dirigir
(una observación) — *vi* **1** : apuntar **2**
ASPIRE : aspirar — ~ *n* **1** : puntería *f* **2**
GOAL : propósito *m*, objetivo *m* —
aimless ['eɪmləs] *adj* : sin objetivo

air ['ær] *vt or* ~ **out** : airear **2** EXPRESS
: expresar **3** BROADCAST : emitir — ~
n **1** : aire *m* **2 be on the** ~ : estar en
el aire — **air-conditioning** [ærkən-
'dɪʃənɪŋ] *n* : aire *m* acondicionado —
air conditioned ['ærkən,dɪʃənd] *n*

: climatizado — **aircraft** ['ær,kræft] *ns*
& *pl* **1** : avión *m*, aeronave *f* **2** ~ **carrier** : portaaviones *m* — **air force** *n*
: fuerza *f* aérea — **airline** ['ær,laɪn] *n*
: aerolínea *f*, línea *f* aérea — **airliner**
['ær,laɪnər] *n* : avión *m* de pasajeros —
airmail *n* : correo *m* aéreo — **airplane**
['ær,pleɪn] *n* : avión *m* — **airport** ['ær-
,port] *n* : aeropuerto *m* — **airstrip** ['ær-
,strɪp] *n* : pista *f* de aterrizaje — **air-
tight** ['ær'taɪt] *adj* : hermético — **airy**
['æri] *adj* **airier** [-iər]; **-est** : aireado,
bien ventilado

aisle ['aɪl] *n* **1** : pasillo *m* **2** : nave *f* lateral (de una iglesia)

ajar [ə'dʒɑr] *adj* : entreabierto

akin [ə'kɪn] *adj* ~ **to** : semejante a

alarm [ə'lɑrm] *n* **1** : alarma *f* **2** ANXIETY
: inquietud *f* — *vt* : alarmar, asustar —
alarm clock *n* : despertador *m*

alas [ə'læs] *interj* : ¡ay!

album ['ælbəm] *n* : álbum *m*

alcohol ['ælkə,hɔl] *n* : alcohol *m* — **alcoholic** [,ælkə'hɔlɪk] *adj* : alcohólico
— ~ *n* : alcohólico *m*, -ca *f* — **alcoholism** ['ælkəhɔ,lɪzəm] *n* : alcoholismo *m*

alcove ['æl,ko:v] *n* : nicho *m*, hueco *m*

ale ['eɪl] *n* : cerveza *f*

alert [ə'lərt] *adj* **1** WATCHFUL : alerta,
atento **2** LIVELY : vivo — ~ *n* : alerta *f*
— ~ *vt* : alertar, poner sobre aviso

alfalfa [æl'fælfə] *n* : alfalfa *f*

alga ['ælgə] *n, pl* -gae ['æl,dʒi:] : alga *f*

algebra ['ældʒəbrə] *n* : álgebra *f*

alias ['eɪliəs] *adv* : alias — ~ *n* : alias *m*

alibi ['ælə,baɪ] *n* : coartada *f*

alien ['eɪliən] *adj* : extranjero — ~ *n* **1**
FOREIGNER : extranjero *m*, -ra *f* **2** EX-
TRATERRESTRIAL : extraterrestre *mf*

alienate ['eɪliə,neɪt] *vt* -ated; -ating
: enajenar — **alienation** [,eɪliə'neɪæən]
n : enajenación *f*

alight [ə'laɪt] *vi* **1** LAND : posarse **2** ~
from : apearse de

align [ə'laɪn] *vt* : alinear — **alignment**
[ə'laɪnmənt] *n* : alineación *f*

alike [ə'laɪk] *adv* : igual, del mismo
modo — ~ *adj* : parecido

alimony ['ælə,mo:ni] *n, pl* -nies : pensión *f* alimenticia

alive [ə'laɪv] *adj* **1** LIVING : vivo,
viviente **2** LIVELY : animado, activo

all ['ɔl] *adv* **1** COMPLETELY : todo, completamente **2** ~ **the better** : tanto
mejor **3** ~ **the more** : aún más, todavía más — ~ *adj* : todo — ~ *pron*
1 : todo, -da **2** ~ **in** ~ : en general **3**
not at ~ : de ninguna manera —

all–around [ˌɔlə'raʊnd] *adj* VERSATILE : completo

allay [ə'leɪ] *vt* **1** ALLEVIATE : aliviar **2** CALM : aquietar

allege [ə'lɛdʒ] *vt* -leged; -leging : alegar — **allegation** [ˌælɪ'geɪʃən] *n* : alegato *m*, acusación *f* — **alleged** [ə'lɛdʒd, ə'lɛdʒəd] *adj* : presunto — **allegedly** [ə'lɛdʒədli] *adv* : supuestamente

allegiance [ə'liːdʒənts] *n* : lealtad *f*

allegory ['ælə,gori] *n*, *pl* **-ries** : alegoría *f* — **allegorical** [ˌælə'gorɪkəl] *adj* : alegórico

allergy ['ælərdʒi] *n*, *pl* **-gies** : alergia *f* — **allergic** [ə'lordʒɪk] *adj* : alérgico

alleviate [ə'liːviˌeɪt] *vt* -ated; -ating : aliviar

alley ['æli] *n*, *pl* **-leys** : callejón *m*

alliance [ə'laɪənts] *n* : alianza *f*

alligator ['ælə,geɪtər] *n* : caimán *m*

allocate ['ælə,keɪt] *vt* -cated; -cating : asignar — **allocation** [ˌælə'keɪʃən] *n* : asignación *f*, reparto *m*

allot [ə'lɑt] *vt* -lotted; -lotting : asignar — **allotment** [ə'lɑtmənt] *n* : reparto *m*, asignación *f*

allow [ə'laʊ] *vt* **1** PERMIT : permitir **2** GRANT : dar, conceder **3** ADMIT : admitir **4** CONCEDE : reconocer — *vi* ~ **for** : tener en cuenta — **allowance** [ə'laʊənts] *n* **1** : pensión *f*, subsidio *m* **2 make ~s for** : tener en cuenta, disculpar

alloy ['æˌlɔɪ, ə'lɔɪ] *n* : aleación *f*

all right *adv* **1** YES : sí, de acuerdo **2** WELL : bien **3** DEFINITELY : bien, sin duda — ~ *adj* : bien, bueno

allude [ə'luːd] *vi* -luded; -luding : aludir

allure [ə'lʊr] *vt* -lured; -luring : atraer — **alluring** [ə'lʊrɪŋ] *adj* : atrayente, seductor

allusion [ə'luːʒən] *n* : alusión *f*

ally [ə'laɪ, 'æˌlaɪ] *vt* -lied; -lying ~ **oneself with** : aliarse con — ~ ['æˌlaɪ, ə'laɪ] *n* : aliado *m*, -da *f*

almanac ['ɔlmə,næk, 'æl-] *n* : almanaque *m*

almighty [ɔl'maɪti] *adj* : omnipotente, todopoderoso

almond ['ɑmənd, 'ɑl-, 'æ-, 'æl-] *n* : almendra *f*

almost ['ɔl,moːst, ɔl'moːst] *adv* : casi

alms ['ɑmz, 'ɑlmz, 'ælmz] *ns & pl* : limosna *f*

alone [ə'loːn] *adv* : sólo, solamente, únicamente — ~ *adj* : solo

along [ə'lɔŋ] *adv* **1** FORWARD : adelante **2** ~ **with** : con, junto con **3 all** ~ : desde el principio — ~ *prep* : por, a lo largo de — **alongside** [ə'lɔŋ,saɪd]

adv : al costado — ~ *or* ~ **of** *prep* : al lado de

aloof [ə'luːf] *adj* : distante, reservado

aloud [ə'laʊd] *adv* : en voz alta

alphabet ['ælfə,bɛt] *n* : alfabeto *m* — **alphabetical** [ˌælfə'bɛtɪkəl] *or* **alphabetic** [-'bɛtɪk] *adj* : alfabético

already [ɔl'rɛdi] *adv* : ya

also ['ɔl,soː] *adv* : también, además

altar ['ɔltər] *n* : altar *m*

alter ['ɔltər] *vt* : alterar, modificar — **alteration** [ˌɔltə'reɪʃən] *n* : alteración *f*, modificación *f*

alternate ['ɔltərnət] *adj* : alterno — ~ ['ɔltər,neɪt] *vt* -nated; -nating : alternar — **alternating current** [-'kərənt] : corriente *f* alterna — **alternative** [ɔl'tərnətɪv] *adj* : alternativo — ~ *n* : alternativa *f*

although [ɔl'ðoː] *conj* : aunque

altitude ['æltə,tuːd, -,tjuːd] *n* : altitud *f*

altogether [ˌɔltə'gɛðər] *adv* **1** COMPLETELY : completamente, del todo **2** ON THE WHOLE : en suma, en general

aluminum [ə'luːmɪnəm] *n* : aluminio *m*

always ['ɔl,wiz, -,weɪz] *adv* **1** : siempre **2** FOREVER : para siempre

am → **be**

amass [ə'mæs] *vt* : amasar, acumular

amateur ['æmə,tʃər, -tər, -,tʊr, -,tjʊr] *adj* : amateur — ~ *n* : amateur *mf*; aficionado *m*, -da *f*

amaze [ə'meɪz] *vt* amazed; amazing : asombrar — **amazement** [ə'meɪzmənt] *n* : asombro *m* — **amazing** [ə'meɪzɪŋ] *adj* : asombroso

ambassador [æm'bæsədər] *n* : embajador *m*, -dora *f*

amber ['æmbər] *n* : ámbar *m*

ambiguous [æm'bɪgjuəs] *adj* : ambiguo — **ambiguity** [ˌæmbə'gjuːəti] *n*, *pl* **-ties** : ambigüedad *f*

ambition [æm'bɪʃən] *n* : ambición *f* — **ambitious** [æm'bɪʃəs] *adj* : ambicioso

ambivalence [æm'bɪvələnts] *n* : ambivalencia *f* — **ambivalent** [æm'bɪvələnt] *adj* : ambivalente

amble ['æmbəl] *vi* *or* ~ **along** : andar sin prisa

ambulance ['æmbjələnts] *n* : ambulancia *f*

ambush ['æm,bʊʃ] *vt* : emboscar — ~ *n* : emboscada *f*

amen ['eɪ'mɛn, 'ɑ-] *interj* : amén

amenable [ə'miːnəbəl, -'mɛ-] *adj* ~ **to** : receptivo a

amend [ə'mɛnd] *vt* : enmendar — **amendment** [ə'mɛndmənt] *n* : enmienda *f* — **amends** [ə'mɛndz] *ns & pl* **make ~ for** : reparar

amenities [ə'menəțiz, -mi:-] *npl* : servicios *mpl*, comodidades *fpl*
American [ə'merɪkən] *adj* : americano
amethyst ['æməθəst] *n* : amatista *f*
amiable ['eɪmiəbəl] *adj* : amable, agradable
amicable ['æmɪkəbəl] *adj* : amigable, amistoso
amid [ə'mɪd] *or* **amidst** [ə'mɪdst] *prep* : en medio de, entre
amiss [ə'mɪs] *adv* 1 : mal 2 **take sth** ~ : tomar algo a mal — ~ *adj* 1 **WRONG** : malo 2 **something is** ~ : algo anda mal
ammonia [ə'moːnjə] *n* : amoníaco *m*
ammunition [,æmjə'nɪʃən] *n* : municiones *fpl*
amnesia [æm'niːʒə] *n* : amnesia *f*
amnesty ['æmnəsti] *n, pl* **-ties** : amnistía *f*
among [ə'mʌŋ] *prep* : entre
amorous ['æmərəs] *adj* : amoroso
amount [ə'maʊnt] *vi* 1 ~ **to** : equivaler a 2 ~ **to** **TOTAL** : sumar, ascender a — ~ *n* : cantidad *f*
amphibian [æm'fɪbiən] *n* : anfibio *m* — **amphibious** [æm'fɪbiəs] *adj* : anfibio
amphitheater ['æmfə,θiːəțər] *n* : anfiteatro *m*
ample ['æmpəl] *adj* **-pler; -plest** 1 **SPACIOUS** : amplio, extenso 2 **ABUNDANT** : abundante
amplify ['æmplə,faɪ] *vt* **-fied; -fying** : amplificar — **amplifier** ['æmplə,faɪər] *n* : amplificador *m*
amputate ['æmpjə,teɪt] *vt* **-tated; -tating** : amputar — **amputation** [,æmpjə'teɪʃən] *n* : amputación *f*
amuse [ə'mjuːz] *vt* **amused; amusing** 1 : hacer reír, divertir 2 **ENTERTAIN** : entretener — **amusement** [ə'mjuːzmənt] *n* : diversión *f* — **amusing** *adj* : divertido
an → **a**[2]
analogy [ə'nælədʒi] *n, pl* **-gies** : analogía *f* — **analogous** [ə'næləgəs] *adj* : análogo
analysis [ə'næləsəs] *n, pl* **-yses** [-,siːz] : análisis *m* — **analytic** [,ænə'lɪțɪk] *or* **analytical** [-țɪkəl] *adj* : analítico — **analyze** ['ænə,laɪz] *vt* **-lyzed; -lyzing** : analizar
anarchy ['ænərki, -nɑr-] *n* : anarquía *f*
anatomy [ə'næțəmi] *n, pl* **-mies** : anatomía *f* — **anatomic** [,ænə'tɑmɪk] *or* **anatomical** [-mɪkəl] *adj* : anatómico
ancestor ['æn,sestər] *n* : antepasado *m*, -da *f* — **ancestral** [æn'sestrəl] *adj* : ancestral — **ancestry** ['æn,sestri] *n* 1 **DE-**

SCENT : linaje *m*, abolengo *m* 2 **ANCESTORS** : antepasados *mpl*, -das *fpl*
anchor ['æŋkər] *n* 1 : ancla *f* 2 : presentador *m*, -dora *f* (en televisión) — ~ *vt* 1 : anclar 2 **FASTEN** : sujetar — *vi* : anclar
anchovy ['æn,tʃoːvi, æn'tʃoː-] *n, pl* **-vies** *or* **-vy** : anchoa *f*
ancient ['eɪntʃənt] *adj* : antiguo, viejo
and ['ænd] *conj* 1 : y (e *before words beginning with i- or hi-*) 2 **come** ~ **see** : ven a ver 3 **more** ~ **more** : cada vez más 4 **try** ~ **finish it soon** : trata de terminarlo pronto
anecdote ['ænɪk,doːt] *n* : anécdota *f*
anemia [ə'niːmiə] *n* : anemia *f* — **anemic** [ə'niːmɪk] *adj* : anémico
anesthesia [,ænəs'θiːʒə] *n* : anestesia *f* — **anesthetic** [,ænəs'θeṭɪk] *adj* : anestésico — ~ *n* : anestésico *m*
anew [ə'nuː, -'njuː] *adv* : de nuevo, nuevamente
angel ['eɪndʒəl] *n* : ángel *m* — **angelic** [æn'dʒelɪk] *or* **angelical** [-lɪkəl] *adj* : angélico
anger ['æŋgər] *vt* : enojar, enfadar — ~ *n* : ira *f*, enojo *m*, enfado *m*
angle *n* 1 : ángulo *m* 2 **POINT OF VIEW** : perspectiva *f*, punto *m* de vista — **angler** ['æŋglər] *n* : pescador *m*, -dora *f*
Anglo-Saxon [,æŋgloː'sæksən] *adj* : anglosajón
angry ['æŋgri] *adj* **-grier; -est** : enojado, enfadado
anguish ['æŋgwɪʃ] *n* : angustia *f*
angular ['æŋgjələr] *adj* 1 : angular 2 ~ **features** : rasgos *mpl* angulosos
animal ['ænəməl] *n* : animal *m*
animate ['ænəmət] *adj* : animado — ~ ['ænə,meɪt] *vt* **-mated; -mating** : animar — **animated** *adj* 1 : animado 2 ~ **cartoon** : dibujos *mpl* animados — **animation** [,ænə'meɪʃən] *n* : animación *f*
animosity [,ænə'mɑsəți] *n, pl* **-ties** : animosidad *f*
anise ['ænəs] *n* : anís *m*
ankle ['æŋkəl] *n* : tobillo *m*
annals ['ænəlz] *npl* : anales *mpl*
annex [ə'neks, 'æ,neks] *vt* : anexar — ~ ['æ,neks, -nəks] *n* : anexo *m*
annihilate [ə'naɪə,leɪt] *vt* **-lated; -lating** : aniquilar — **annihilation** [ə,naɪə'leɪʃən] *n* : aniquilación *f*
anniversary [,ænə'vərsəri] *n, pl* **-ries** : aniversario *m*
annotate ['ænə,teɪt] *vt* **-tated; -tating** : anotar — **annotation** [,ænə'teɪʃən] *n* : anotación *f*
announce [ə'naʊns] *vt* **-nounced;**

-nouncing : anunciar — **announcement** [ə'naʊnsmənt] n : anuncio m —
announcer [ə'naʊnsər] n : locutor m, -tora f
annoy [ə'nɔɪ] vt : fastidiar, molestar — **annoyance** [ə'nɔɪəns] n : fastidio m, molestia f — **annoying** [ə'nɔɪɪŋ] adj : molesto, fastidioso
annual ['ænjʊəl] adj : anual — ~ n : anuario m
annuity [ə'nuːəti] n, pl -ties : anualidad f
annul [ə'nʌl] vt annulled; annulling : anular — **annulment** [ə'nʌlmənt] n : anulación f
anoint [ə'nɔɪnt] vt : ungir
anomaly [ə'nɑməli] n, pl -lies : anomalía f
anonymous [ə'nɑnəməs] adj : anónimo — **anonymity** [ænə'nɪməti] n : anonimato m
another [ə'nʌðər] adj 1 : otro 2 in a minute : en un minuto más — ~ pron : otro, otra
answer ['ænsər] n 1 REPLY : respuesta f, contestación f 2 SOLUTION : solución f — ~ vt 1 : contestar a, responder a 2 ~ the door : abrir la puerta — vi : contestar, responder
ant ['ænt] n : hormiga f
antagonize [æn'tægə,naɪz] vt -nized; -nizing : provocar la enemistad de — **antagonism** [æn'tægə,nɪzəm] n : antagonismo m
antarctic [ænt'ɑrktɪk, -'ɑrtɪk] adj : antártico
antelope ['æntəl,op] n, pl -lope or -lopes : antílope m
antenna [æn'tenə] n, pl -nae [-,niː, -,naɪ] or -nas : antena f
anthem ['ænθəm] n : himno m
anthology [æn'θɑlədʒi] n, pl -gies : antología f
anthropology [ænθrə'pɑlədʒi] n : antropología f
antibiotic [æntibai'ɑṭɪk, æntaɪ-, -bi-] adj : antibiótico — ~ n : antibiótico m
antibody ['ænti,bɑdi] n, pl -bodies : anticuerpo m
anticipate [æn'tɪsə,peɪt] vt -pated; -pating 1 FORESEE : anticipar, prever 2 EXPECT : esperar — **anticipation** [æn,tɪsə'peɪʃən] n : anticipación f, expectación f
antics ['æntɪks] npl : payasadas fpl
antidote ['ænti,dot] n : antídoto m
antifreeze ['ænti,friːz] n : anticongelante m
antipathy [æn'tɪpəθi] n, pl -thies : antipatía f

antiquated ['æntə,kweɪṭəd] adj : anticuado
antique [æn'tiːk] adj : antiguo — ~ n : antigüedad f — **antiquity** [æn'tɪkwəṭi] n, pl -ties : antigüedad f
anti–Semitic [,æntisə'mɪṭɪk, ,æntaɪ-] adj : antisemita
antiseptic [,æntə'septɪk] adj : antiséptico — ~ n : antiséptico m
antisocial [,ænti'soːʃəl, ,æntaɪ-] adj 1 : antisocial 2 UNSOCIABLE : poco sociable
antithesis [æn'tɪθəsɪs] n, pl -eses [-,siːz] : antítesis f
antlers ['æntlərz] npl : cornamenta f
antonym ['æntə,nɪm] n : antónimo m
anus ['eɪnəs] n : ano m
anvil ['ænvəl, -vɪl] n : yunque m
anxiety [æŋk'zaɪəṭi] n, pl -eties 1 APPREHENSION : inquietud f, ansiedad f 2 EAGERNESS : anhelo m — **anxious** ['æŋkʃəs] adj 1 WORRIED : inquieto, preocupado 2 EAGER : ansioso — **anxiously** ['æŋkʃəsli] adv : con ansiedad
any ['eni] adv 1 SOMEWHAT : algo, un poco 2 it's not ~ good : no sirve para nada 3 we can't wait ~ longer : no podemos esperar más — ~ adj 1 : alguno 2 (in negative constructions) : ningún 3 WHATEVER : cualquier 4 in ~ case : en todo caso — ~ pron 1 : alguno, -na 2 : ninguno, -na 3 do you want ~ more rice? : ¿quieres más arroz?
anybody ['eni,bʌdi, -,bɑ-] → anyone
anyhow ['eni,haʊ] adv 1 : de todas formas 2 HAPHAZARDLY : de cualquier modo
anymore [,eni'mor] adv not ~ : ya no
anyone ['eni,wan] pron 1 SOMEONE : alguien 2 WHOEVER : quienquiera 3 I don't see ~ : no veo a nadie
anyplace ['eni,pleɪs] → anywhere
anything ['eni,θɪŋ] pron 1 SOMETHING : algo, alguna cosa 2 (in negative constructions) : nada 3 WHATEVER : cualquier cosa, lo que sea
anytime ['eni,taɪm] adv : en cualquier momento
anyway ['eni,weɪ] → anyhow
anywhere ['eni,hwer] adv 1 : en cualquier parte, dondequiera 2 (used in questions) : en algún sitio 3 I can't find it ~ : no lo encuentro por ninguna parte
apart [ə'pɑrt] adv 1 : aparte 2 ~ from : excepto, aparte de 3 fall ~ : deshacerse, hacerse pedazos 4 live ~ : vivir separados 5 take ~ : desmontar, desmantelar

apartment [ə'pɑrtmənt] *n* : apartamento *m*

apathy ['æpəθi] *n* : apatía *f* — **apathetic** [ˌæpə'θεtɪk] *adj* : apático, indiferente

ape *n* : simio *m*

aperture ['æpərˌtʃər, -ˌtʃur] *n* : abertura *f*

apex ['eɪˌpεks] *n, pl* **apexes** *or* **apices** ['eɪpəˌsiːz, 'æ-] : ápice *m*, cumbre *f*

apiece [ə'piːs] *adv* : cada uno

aplomb [ə'plɑm, -'plʌm] *n* : aplomo *m*

apology [ə'pɑlədʒi] *n, pl* **-gies** : disculpa *f* — **apologetic** [əˌpɑlə'dʒεtɪk] *adj* : lleno de disculpas — **apologize** [ə'pɑləˌdʒaɪz] *vi* **-gized; -gizing** : disculparse, pedir perdón

apostle [ə'pɑsəl] *n* : apóstol *m*

apostrophe [ə'pɑstrəˌfiː] *n* : apóstrofo *m*

appall [ə'pɔl] *vt* : horrorizar — **appalling** [ə'pɔlɪŋ] *adj* : horroroso

apparatus [ˌæpə'ræt̬əs, -'reɪ-] *n, pl* **-tuses** *or* **-tus** : aparato *m*

apparel [ə'pærəl] *n* : ropa *f*

apparent [ə'pærənt] *adj* **1** OBVIOUS : claro, evidente **2** SEEMING : aparente — **apparently** [ə'pærəntli] *adv* : al parecer, por lo visto

apparition [ˌæpə'rɪʃən] *n* : aparición *f*

appeal [ə'piːl] *vi* **1** ~ **for** : solicitar **2** ~ **to** : apelar a (la bondad de algn, etc.) **3** ~ **to** ATTRACT : atraer a — ~ *n* **1** : apelación *f* (en derecho) **2** REQUEST : llamamiento *m* **3** ATTRACTION : atractivo *m* — **appealing** [ə'piːlɪŋ] *adj* : atractivo

appear [ə'pɪr] *vi* **1** : aparecer **2** : comparecer (ante un tribunal), actuar (en el teatro) **3** SEEM : parecer — **appearance** [ə'pɪrəns] *n* **1** : aparición *f* **2** LOOK : apariencia *f*, aspecto *m*

appease [ə'piːz] *vt* **-peased; -peasing** : apaciguar, aplacar

appendix [ə'pendɪks] *n, pl* **-dixes** *or* **-dices** [-də,siːz] : apéndice *m* — **appendicitis** [əˌpendə'saɪt̬əs] *n* : apendicitis *f*

appetite ['æpəˌtaɪt] *n* : apetito *m* — **appetizer** ['æpəˌtaɪzər] *n* : aperitivo *m* — **appetizing** ['æpəˌtaɪzɪŋ] *adj* : apetitoso

applaud [ə'plɔd] *v* : aplaudir — **applause** [ə'plɔz] *n* : aplauso *m*

apple ['æpəl] *n* : manzana *f*

appliance [ə'plaɪəns] *n* : aparato *m*

apply [ə'plaɪ] *v* **-plied; -plying** *vt* **1** : aplicar **2** ~ **oneself** : aplicarse — *vi* **1** : aplicarse **2** ~ **for** : solicitar, pedir — **applicable** ['æplɪkəbəl, ə'plɪkə-] *adj* : aplicable — **applicant** ['æplɪkənt] *n* : solicitante *mf*; candidato *m*, -ta *f* — **application** [ˌæplə'keɪʃən] *n* **1** : aplicación *f* **2** : solicitud *f* (para un empleo, etc.)

appoint [ə'pɔɪnt] *vt* **1** NAME : nombrar **2** FIX, SET : fijar, señalar — **appointment** [ə'pɔɪntmənt] *n* **1** APPOINTING : nombramiento *m* **2** ENGAGEMENT : cita *f*

apportion [ə'pɔrʃən] *vt* : distribuir, repartir

appraise [ə'preɪz] *vt* **-praised; -praising** : evaluar, valorar — **appraisal** [ə'preɪzəl] *n* : evaluación *f*

appreciate [ə'priːʃiˌeɪt, -'priː-] *v* **-ated; -ating** *vt* **1** VALUE : apreciar **2** UNDERSTAND : darse cuenta de **3 I** ~ **your help** : te agradezco tu ayuda — *vi* : aumentar en valor — **appreciation** [əˌpriːʃi'eɪʃən, -priː-] *n* **1** GRATITUDE : agradecimiento *m* **2** VALUING : apreciación *f*, valoración *f* — **appreciative** [ə'priːʃət̬ɪv, -priː-, ə'priːʃiˌeɪ-] *adj* **1** : apreciativo **2** GRATEFUL : agradecido

apprehend [ˌæprɪ'hεnd] *vt* **1** ARREST : aprehender, detener **2** DREAD : temer **3** COMPREHEND : comprender — **apprehension** [ˌæprɪ'hεnʃən] *n* **1** ARREST : detención *f*, aprehensión *f* **2** ANXIETY : aprensión *f*, temor *m* — **apprehensive** [ˌæprɪ'hεnsɪv] *adj* : aprensivo, inquieto

apprentice [ə'prentɪs] *n* : aprendiz *m*, -diza *f*

approach [ə'proʊtʃ] *vt* **1** NEAR : acercarse a **2** : dirigirse a (algn), abordar (un problema, etc.) — *vi* : acercarse — ~ *n* **1** NEARING : acercamiento *m* **2** POSITION : enfoque *m* **3** ACCESS : acceso *m* — **approachable** [ə'proʊtʃəbəl] *adj* : accesible, asequible

appropriate [ə'proʊpriˌeɪt] *vt* **-ated; -ating** : apropiarse de — ~ [ə'proʊpriːət] *adj* : apropiado

approve [ə'pruːv] *vt* **-proved; -proving** : aprobar — **approval** [ə'pruːvəl] *n* : aprobación *f*

approximate [ə'prɑksəmət] *adj* : aproximado — ~ [ə'prɑksəˌmeɪt] *vt* **-mated; -mating** : aproximarse a — **approximately** [ə'prɑksəmətli] *adv* : aproximadamente

apricot ['æprɪˌkɑt, 'eɪ-] *n* : albaricoque *m*, chabacano *m Lat*

April ['eɪprəl] *n* : abril *m*

apron ['eɪprən] *n* : delantal *m*

apropos [ˌæprə'poʊ, 'æprəˌpoʊ] *adv* : a propósito

apt ['æpt] *adj* **1** FITTING : apto, apropiado **2** LIABLE : propenso — **aptitude** ['æptəˌtuːd, -ˌtjuːd] *n* : aptitud *f*

aquarium [ə'kwæriəm] *n, pl* **-iums** *or* **-ia** [-iə] : acuario *m*

aquatic [ə'kwɑtɪk, -'kwæ-] *adj* : acuático

aqueduct ['ækwəˌdʌkt] *n* : acueducto *m*

Arab ['ærəb] *adj* : árabe — **Arabic** ['ærəbɪk] *adj* : árabe — *n* : árabe *m* (idioma)

arbitrary ['ɑrbəˌtreri] *adj* : arbitrario

arbitrate ['ɑrbəˌtreɪt] *v* **-trated; -trating** : arbitrar — **arbitration** [ˌɑrbə'treɪʃən] *n* : arbitraje *m*

arc ['ɑrk] *n* : arco *m*

arcade [ɑr'keɪd] *n* **1** : arcada *f* **2 shopping ~** : galería *f* comercial

arch ['ɑrtʃ] *n* : arco *m* — *vt* : arquear — *vi* : arquearse

archaeology *or* **archeology** [ˌɑrki-'ɑlədʒi] *n* : arqueología *f* — **archaeological** [ˌɑrkiə'lɑdʒɪkəl] *adj* : arqueológico — **archaeologist** [ˌɑrki'ɑlədʒɪst] *n* : arqueólogo *m*, -ga *f*

archaic [ɑr'keɪɪk] *adj* : arcaico

archbishop [ˌɑrtʃ'bɪʃəp] *n* : arzobispo *m*

archery ['ɑrtʃəri] *n* : tiro *m* al arco

archipelago [ˌɑrkə'peləˌgo, ˌɑrtʃə-] *n, pl* **-goes** *or* **-gos** [-goːz] : archipiélago *m*

architecture ['ɑrkəˌtektʃər] *n* : arquitectura *f* — **architect** ['ɑrkəˌtekt] *n* : arquitecto *m*, -ta *f* — **architectural** [ˌɑrkə'tektʃərəl] *adj* : arquitectónico

archives ['ɑrkaɪvz] *npl* : archivo *m*

archway ['ɑrtʃˌweɪ] *n* : arco *m* (de entrada)

arctic ['ɑrktɪk, 'ɑrt-] *adj* : ártico

ardent ['ɑrdənt] *adj* : ardiente, fervoroso — **ardor** ['ɑrdər] *n* : ardor *m*, fervor *m*

arduous ['ɑrdʒuəs] *adj* : arduo

are → be

area ['æriə] *n* **1** REGION : área *f*, zona *f* **2** FIELD : campo *m* **3 ~ code** : código *m* de la zona *Lat*, prefijo *m* *Spain*

arena [ə'riːnə] *n* : arena *f*, ruedo *m*

aren't ['ɑrnt, 'ɑrənt] (*contraction of* **are not**) → be

Argentine ['ɑrdʒənˌtaɪn, -ˌtiːn] *or* **Argentinean** *or* **Argentinian** [ˌɑrdʒən'tɪniən] *adj* : argentino

argue ['ɑrˌgjuː] *v* **-gued; -guing** *vi* **1** QUARREL : discutir **2 ~ against** : argumentar contra — *vt* : argumentar, sostener — **argument** ['ɑrgjəmənt] *n* **1** QUARREL : disputa *f*, discusión *f* **2** REASONING : argumentos *mpl*

arid ['ærəd] *adj* : árido — **aridity** [ə'rɪdəˌti, æ-] *n* : aridez *f*

arise [ə'raɪz] *vi* **arose** [ə'roːz]; **arisen** [ə'rɪzən]; **arising 1** : levantarse **2 ~ from** : surgir de

aristocracy [ˌærə'stɑkrəsi] *n, pl* **-cies** : aristocracia *f* — **aristocrat** [ə'rɪstə-

ˌkræt] *n* : aristócrata *mf* — **aristocratic** [əˌrɪstə'krætɪk] *adj* : aristocrático

arithmetic [ə'rɪθməˌtɪk] *n* : aritmética *f*

ark ['ɑrk] *n* : arca *f*

arm ['ɑrm] *n* **1** : brazo *m* **2** WEAPON : arma *f* — *vt* : armar — **armament** ['ɑrməmənt] *n* : armamento *m* — **armchair** ['ɑrmˌtʃer] *n* : sillón *m* — **armed** ['ɑrmd] *adj* **1 ~ forces** : fuerzas *fpl* armadas **2 ~ robbery** : robo *m* a mano armada

armistice ['ɑrməstɪs] *n* : armisticio *m*

armor *or Brit* **armour** ['ɑrmər] *n* : armadura *f* — **armored** *or Brit* **armoured** ['ɑrmərd] *adj* : blindado, acorazado — **armory** *or Brit* **armoury** ['ɑrmri, 'ɑrməri] : arsenal *m*

armpit ['ɑrmˌpɪt] *n* : axila *f*, sobaco *m*

army ['ɑrmi] *n, pl* **-mies** : ejército *m*

aroma [ə'roːmə] *n* : aroma *m* — **aromatic** [ˌærə'mætɪk] *adj* : aromático

around [ə'raʊnd] *adv* **1** : de circunferencia **2** NEARBY : por ahí **3** APPROXIMATELY : más o menos, aproximadamente **4 all ~** : por todos lados, todo alrededor **5 turn ~** : voltearse — *prep* **1** SURROUNDING : alrededor de **2** THROUGHOUT : por **3** NEAR : cerca de **4 ~ the corner** : a la vuelta de la esquina

arouse [ə'raʊz] *vt* **aroused; arousing 1** AWAKE : despertar **2** EXCITE : excitar

arrange [ə'reɪndʒ] *vt* **-ranged; -ranging 1** : arreglar, poner en orden — **arrangement** [ə'reɪndʒmənt] *n* **1** ORDER : arreglo *m* **2 ~s** *npl* : preparativos *mpl*

array [ə'reɪ] *n* : selección *f*, surtido *m*

arrears [ə'rɪrz] *npl* **1** : atrasos *mpl* **2 be in ~** : estar atrasado en pagos

arrest [ə'rest] *vt* : detener — *n* **1** : arresto *m*, detención *f* **2 under ~** : detenido

arrive [ə'raɪv] *vi* **-rived; -riving** : llegar — **arrival** [ə'raɪvəl] *n* : llegada *f*

arrogance ['ærəgəns] *n* : arrogancia *f* — **arrogant** ['ærəgənt] *adj* : arrogante

arrow ['æro] *n* : flecha *f*

arsenal ['ɑrsənəl] *n* : arsenal *m*

arsenic ['ɑrsənɪk] *n* : arsénico *m*

arson ['ɑrsən] *n* : incendio *m* premeditado

art ['ɑrt] *n* **1** : arte *m* **2 ~s** *npl* : letras *fpl* (en educación) **3 fine ~s** : bellas artes *fpl*

artefact *Brit* → **artifact**

artery ['ɑrtəri] *n, pl* **-teries** : arteria *f*

artful ['ɑrtfəl] *adj* : astuto, taimado

arthritis [ɑr'θraɪtəs] *n, pl* **-tides** [ɑr'θrɪtəˌdiz] : artritis *f* — **arthritic** [ɑr'θrɪtɪk] *adj* : artrítico

artichoke ['ɑrt̬ə,t̬ʃo:k] n : alcachofa f

article ['ɑrt̬ɪkəl] n : artículo m

articulate [ɑrˈtɪkjə,leɪt] vt -lated; -lating : articular — ~ [ɑrˈtɪkjələt] adj be ~ : expresarse bien

artifact or Brit **artefact** ['ɑrt̬ə,fækt] n : artefacto m

artificial [,ɑrt̬əˈfɪʃəl] adj : artificial

artillery [ɑrˈtɪləri] n, pl **-leries** : artillería f

artisan ['ɑrt̬əzən, -sən] n : artesano m, -na f

artist ['ɑrt̬ɪst] n : artista mf — **artistic** [ɑrˈtɪstɪk] adj : artístico

as [æz] adv 1 : tan, tanto 2 ~ **much** : tanto como 3 ~ **tall** : tan alto como 4 ~ **well** : también — ~ conj 1 WHILE : mientras 2 (referring to manner) : como 3 SINCE : ya que — ~ prep 1 : de LIKE : como — ~ pron : que

asbestos [æzˈbestəs, æs-] n : asbesto m, amianto m

ascend [əˈsend] vi : ascender, subir — ~ vt : subir (a) — **ascent** [əˈsent] n : ascensión f, subida f

ascertain [,æsərˈteɪn] vt : averiguar, determinar

ascribe [əˈskraɪb] vt -cribed; -cribing : atribuir

as for prep : en cuanto a

ash[1] ['æʃ] n : ceniza f

ash[2] n : fresno m (árbol)

ashamed [əˈʃeɪmd] adj : avergonzado, apenado Lat

ashore [əˈʃor] adv 1 : en tierra 2 **go** ~ : desembarcar

ashtray ['æʃ,treɪ] n : cenicero m

Asian ['eɪʒən, -ʃən] adj : asiático

aside [əˈsaɪd] adv 1 : a un lado 2 APART : aparte 3 **set** ~ : guardar — **aside from** prep 1 BESIDES : además de 2 EXCEPT : aparte de, menos

as if conj : como si

ask ['æsk] vt 1 : preguntar 2 REQUEST : pedir 3 INVITE : invitar — vi : preguntar

askance [əˈskænts] adv **look** ~ : mirar de soslayo

askew [əˈskju:] adj : torcido, ladeado

asleep [əˈsli:p] adj 1 : dormido 2 **fall** ~ : dormirse, quedarse dormido

as of prep : desde, a partir de

asparagus [əˈspærəgəs] n : espárrago m

aspect ['æˌspekt] n : aspecto m

asphalt ['æsˌfɑlt] n : asfalto m

asphyxiate [æsˈfɪksi,eɪt] v -ated; -ating vt : asfixiar — **asphyxiation** [æsˌfɪksi'eɪʃən] n : asfixia f

aspire [əˈspaɪr] vi -pired; -piring : aspirar — **aspiration** [,æspəˈreɪʃən] n : aspiración f

aspirin ['æsprən, 'æspə-] n, pl **aspirin** or **aspirins** : aspirina f

ass ['æs] n 1 : asno m 2 IDIOT : imbécil mf, idiota mf

assail [əˈseɪl] vt : atacar, asaltar — **assailant** [əˈseɪlənt] n : asaltante mf, atacante mf

assassin [əˈsæsən] n : asesino m, -na f — **assassinate** [əˈsæsən,eɪt] vt -nated; -nating : asesinar — **assassination** [ə,sæsən'eɪʃən] n : asesinato m

assault [əˈsɔlt] n 1 : ataque m, asalto m 2 : agresión f (contra algn) — ~ vt : atacar, asaltar

assemble [əˈsembəl] v -bled; -bling vt 1 GATHER : reunir, juntar 2 CONSTRUCT : montar — vi : reunirse — **assembly** [əˈsembli] n, pl **-blies** 1 MEETING : reunión f, asamblea f 2 CONSTRUCTING : montaje m

assent [əˈsent] vi : asentir, consentir — ~ n : asentimiento m

assert [əˈsərt] vt 1 : afirmar 2 ~ **oneself** : hacerse valer — **assertion** [əˈsərʃən] n : afirmación f — **assertive** [əˈsərt̬ɪv] adj : firme, enérgico

assess [əˈses] vt : evaluar, valorar — **assessment** [əˈsesmənt] n : evaluación f, valoración f

asset [əˈset] n 1 : ventaja f, recurso m 2 ~**s** npl : bienes mpl, activo m

assiduous [əˈsɪdʒuəs] adj : asiduo

assign [əˈsaɪn] vt 1 APPOINT : designar, nombrar 2 ALLOT : asignar — **assignment** [əˈsaɪnmənt] n 1 TASK : misión f 2 HOMEWORK : tarea f 3 ASSIGNING : asignación f

assimilate [əˈsɪmə,leɪt] vt -lated; -lating : asimilar

assist [əˈsɪst] vt : ayudar — **assistance** [əˈsɪstənts] n : ayuda f — **assistant** [əˈsɪstənt] n : ayudante mf

associate [əˈso:ʃi,eɪt, -si-] v -ated; -ating vt : asociar — vi : asociarse — ~ [əˈso:ʃiət, -siət] n : asociado m, -da f; socio m, -cia f — **association** [ə,so:ʃi'eɪʃən, -si-] n : asociación f

as soon as conj : tan pronto como

assorted [əˈsɔrt̬əd] adj : surtido — **assortment** [əˈsɔrtmənt] n : surtido m, variedad f

assume [əˈsu:m] vt -sumed; -suming 1 SUPPOSE : suponer 2 UNDERTAKE : asumir 3 TAKE ON : adquirir, tomar — **assumption** [əˈsʌmpʃən] n : suposición f

assure [əˈʃor] vt -sured; -suring : asegurar — **assurance** [əˈʃorənts] n 1

CERTAINTY : certeza *f*, garantía *f* **2** CONFIDENCE : confianza *f*, seguridad *f* (de sí mismo)

asterisk ['æstə,rɪsk] *n* : asterisco *m*

asthma ['æzmə] *n* : asma *m*

as though → **as if**

as to *prep* : sobre, acerca de

astonish [ə'stɑnɪʃ] *vt* : asombrar — **astonishing** [ə'stɑnɪʃɪŋ] *adj* : asombroso — **astonishment** [ə'stɑnɪʃmənt] *n* : asombro *m*

astound [ə'staʊnd] *vt* : asombrar, pasmar — **astounding** [ə'staʊndɪŋ] *adj* : asombroso, pasmoso

astray [ə'streɪ] *adv* **1 go ~** : extraviarse **2 lead ~** : llevar por mal camino

astrology [ə'strɑlədʒi] *n* : astrología *f*

astronaut ['æstrə,nɔt] *n* : astronauta *mf*

astronomy [ə'strɑnəmi] *n, pl* **-mies** : astronomía *f* — **astronomer** [ə-'strɑnəmər] *n* : astrónomo *m*, -ma *f* — **astronomical** [æstrə'nɑmɪkəl] *adj* : astronómico

astute [ə'stut, -'stjut] *adj* : astuto, sagaz — **astuteness** [ə'stutnəs, -'stjut-] *n* : astucia *f*

as well as *conj* : tanto como — **~** *prep* : además de, aparte de

asylum [ə'saɪləm] *n* **1** : asilo *m* **2** INSANE **~** : manicomio *m*

at ['æt] *prep* **1** : a **2 ~ home** : en casa **3 ~ night** : en la noche, por la noche **4 ~ two o'clock** : a las dos **5 be angry ~** : estar enojado con **6 laugh ~** : reírse de — **at all** *adv* **not ~** : en absoluto, nada

ate → **eat**

atheist ['eɪθiɪst] *n* : ateo *m*, atea *f* — **atheism** ['eɪθi,ɪzəm] *n* : ateísmo *m*

athlete ['æθ,lit] *n* : atleta *mf* — **athletic** [æθ'letɪk] *adj* : atlético — **athletics** [æθ'letɪks] *ns & pl* : atletismo *m*

atlas ['ætləs] *n* : atlas *m*

atmosphere ['ætmə,sfɪr] *n* **1** : atmósfera *f* **2** AMBIENCE : ambiente *m* — **atmospheric** [,ætməs'fɪrɪk, -'sfer-] *adj* : atmosférico

atom ['ætəm] *n* : átomo *m* — **atomic** [ə-'tɑmɪk] *adj* : atómico

atomizer ['ætə,maɪzər] *n* : atomizador *m*

atone [ə'toʊn] *vi* **atoned; atoning ~ for** : expiar

atrocity [ə'trɑsəti] *n, pl* **-ties** : atrocidad *f* — **atrocious** [ə'troʊʃəs] *adj* : atroz

atrophy ['ætrəfi] *vi* **-phied; -phying** : atrofiarse

attach [ə'tætʃ] *vt* **1** : sujetar, atar **2** : adjuntar (un documento, etc.) **3 ~ importance to** : atribuir importancia a **4 become ~ed to s.o.** : encariñarse

con algn — **attachment** [ə'tætʃmənt] *n* **1** ACCESSORY : accesorio *m* **2** FONDNESS : cariño *m*

attack [ə'tæk] *v* : atacar — **~** *n* : ataque *m* — **attacker** [ə'tækər] *n* : agresor *m*, -sora *f*

attain [ə'teɪn] *vt* : lograr, alcanzar — **attainment** [ə'teɪnmənt] *n* : logro *m*

attempt [ə'tempt] *vt* : intentar — **~** *n* : intento *m*

attend [ə'tend] *vt* : asistir a — *vi* **1** : asistir **2 ~ to** : ocuparse de — **attendance** [ə'tendənts] *n* **1** : asistencia *f* **2** TURNOUT : concurrencia *f* — **attendant** *n* : encargado *m*, -da *f*; asistente *mf*

attention [ə'tentʃən] *n* **1** : atención *f* **2 pay ~** : prestar atención, hacer caso — **attentive** [ə'tentɪv] *adj* : atento

attest [ə'test] *vt* : atestiguar

attic ['ætɪk] *n* : desván *m*

attire [ə'taɪr] *n* : atavío *m*

attitude ['ætə,tud, -,tjud] *n* **1** : actitud *f* **2** POSTURE : postura *f*

attorney [ə'tərni] *n, pl* **-neys** : abogado *m*, -da *f*

attract [ə'trækt] *vt* : atraer — **attraction** [ə'trækʃən] *n* **1** : atracción *f* **2** APPEAL : atractivo *m* — **attractive** [ə'træktɪv] *adj* : atractivo, atrayente

attribute [ə'trɪbjut] *n* : atributo *m* — **~** [ə'trɪbjut] *vt* **-tributed; -tributing** : atribuir, imputar

auburn [ɔbərn] *adj* : castaño rojizo

auction ['ɔkʃən] *n* : subasta *f* — **~** *vt* or **~ off** : subastar

audacious [ɔ'deɪʃəs] *adj* : audaz — **audacity** [ɔ'dæsəti] *n, pl* **-ties** : audacia *f*, atrevimiento *m*

audible ['ɔdəbəl] *adj* : audible

audience ['ɔdiənts] *n* **1** INTERVIEW : audiencia *f* **2** PUBLIC : público *m*

audiovisual [,ɔdioʊ'vɪʒəl] *adj* : audiovisual

audition [ɔ'dɪʃən] *n* : audición *f*

auditor ['ɔdətər] *n* **1** : auditor *m*, -tora *f* (de finanzas) **2** STUDENT : oyente *mf*

auditorium [,ɔdə'toriəm] *n, pl* **-riums** or **-ria** [-riə] : auditorio *m*

augment [ɔg'ment] *vt* : aumentar

augur ['ɔgər] *vi* **~ well** : ser de buen agüero

August ['ɔgəst] *n* : agosto *m*

aunt ['ænt, 'ɑnt] *n* : tía *f*

aura ['ɔrə] *n* : aura *f*

auspices ['ɔspəsəz, -,siz] *npl* : auspicios *mpl*

auspicious [ɔ'spɪʃəs] *adj* : propicio, prometedor

austere [ɔ'stɪr] adj : austero — **austerity** [ɔ'sterəti] n, pl -ties : austeridad f

Australian [ɔ'streɪljən] adj : australiano

authentic [ə'θentɪk, ɔ-] adj : auténtico

author ['ɔθər] n : autor m, -tora f

authority [ə'θɔrəti, ɔ-] n, pl -ties : autoridad f — **authoritarian** [ɔ,θɔrə'teriən, ɔ-] adj : autoritario — **authoritative** [ə'θɔrə,teɪtɪv, ɔ-] adj 1 RELIABLE : autorizado 2 DICTATORIAL : autoritario — **authorization** [,ɔθərə'zeɪʃən] n : autorización f — **authorize** ['ɔθə,raɪz] vt -rized; -rizing : autorizar

autobiography [,ɔṭəbaɪ'agrəfi] n, pl -phies : autobiografía f — **autobiographical** [,ɔṭə,baɪə'græfɪkəl] adj : autobiográfico

autograph ['ɔṭə,græf] n : autógrafo m — ~ vt : autografiar

automatic [,ɔṭə'mætɪk] adj : automático — **automate** ['ɔṭə,meɪt] vt -mated; -mating : automatizar — **automation** [,ɔṭə'meɪʃən] n : automatización f

automobile [,ɔṭəmo'bi:l, -'mo:bi:l] n : automóvil m

autonomy [ɔ'tanəmi] n, pl -mies : autonomía f — **autonomous** [ɔ'tanəməs] adj : autónomo

autopsy ['ɔ,tapsi, -təp-] n, pl -sies : autopsia f

autumn ['ɔṭəm] n : otoño m

auxiliary [ɔg'zɪljəri, -'zɪləri] adj : auxiliar — ~ n, pl -ries : auxiliar mf

avail [ə'veɪl] vt ~ **oneself of** : aprovecharse de — ~ n **to no** ~ : en vano — **available** [ə'veɪləbəl] adj : disponible — **availability** [ə,veɪlə'bɪləṭi] n, pl -ties : disponibilidad f

avalanche ['ævə,læntʃ] n : avalancha f

avarice ['ævərəs] n : avaricia f

avenge [ə'vendʒ] vt avenged; avenging : vengar

avenue ['ævə,nu:, -,nju:] n 1 : avenida f 2 MEANS : vía f

average ['ævrɪdʒ, 'ævə-] n : promedio m — ~ adj 1 MEAN : medio 2 ORDINARY : regular, ordinario — ~ vt -aged; -aging 1 : hacer un promedio de 2 or ~ **out** : calcular el promedio de

averse [ə'vərs] adj **be ~ to** : sentir aversión por — **aversion** [ə'vərʒən] n : aversión f

avert [ə'vərt] vt 1 AVOID : evitar, prevenir 2 ~ **one's eyes** : apartar los ojos

aviation [,eɪvi'eɪʃən] n : aviación f — **aviator** ['eɪvi,eɪṭər] n : aviador m, -dora f

avid ['ævɪd] adj : ávido — **avidly** adv : con avidez

avocado [,ævə'kado, ,avə-] n, pl -dos : aguacate m

avoid [ə'vɔɪd] vt : evitar — **avoidable** [ə'vɔɪdəbəl] adj : evitable

await [ə'weɪt] vt : esperar

awake [ə'weɪk] v **awoke** [ə'wo:k]; **awoken** [ə'wo:kən] or **awaked**; **awaking** : despertar — ~ adj : despierto — **awaken** [ə'weɪkən] v → **awake**

award [ə'wɔrd] vt 1 : otorgar, conceder (un premio, etc.) 2 : adjudicar (daños y perjuicios) — ~ n 1 PRIZE : premio m 2 : adjudicación f

aware [ə'wær] adj **be ~ of** : estar consciente de — **awareness** [ə'wærnəs] n : conciencia f

away [ə'weɪ] adv 1 (referring to distance) : de aquí, de distancia 2 **far** ~ : lejos 3 **give** ~ : regalar 4 **go** ~ : irse 5 **right** ~ : en seguida 6 **take** ~ : quitar — ~ adj 1 ABSENT : ausente 2 ~ **game** : partido m fuera de casa

awe [ɔ] n : temor m reverencial — **awesome** ['ɔsəm] adj : imponente, formidable

awful ['ɔfəl] adj 1 : terrible, espantoso 2 **an ~ lot** : muchísimo — **awfully** ['ɔfəli] adv : terriblemente

awhile [ə'hwaɪl] adv : un rato

awkward ['ɔkwərd] adj 1 CLUMSY : torpe 2 EMBARRASSING : embarazoso, delicado 3 DIFFICULT : difícil — **awkwardly** adv 1 : con dificultad 2 CLUMSILY : de manera torpe

awning ['ɔnɪŋ] n : toldo m

awry [ə'raɪ] adj 1 ASKEW : torcido 2 **go** ~ : salir mal

ax or **axe** ['æks] n : hacha f

axiom ['æksiəm] n : axioma m

axis ['æksɪs] n, pl **axes** [-,si:z] : eje m

axle ['æksəl] n : eje m

B

b ['bi:] *n*, *pl* **b's** *or* **bs** ['bi:z] : b, segunda letra del alfabeto inglés

babble ['bæbəl] *vi* **-bled; -bling 1** : balbucear 2 MURMUR : murmurar — ~ *n* : balbuceo *m* (de bebé), murmullo *m* (de voces, de un arroyo)

baboon [bæ'bu:n] *n* : babuino *m*

baby ['beɪbi] *n*, *pl* **-bies** : bebé *m*; niño *m*, -ña *f* — **baby** *vt* **-bied; -bying** : mimar, consentir — **babyish** ['beɪbiɪʃ] *adj* : infantil — **baby-sit** ['beɪbi̇ˌsɪt] *vi* **-sat** [-ˌsæt]; **-sitting** : cuidar a los niños

bachelor ['bætʃələr] *n* **1** : soltero *m* **2** GRADUATE : licenciado *m*, -da *f*

back ['bæk] *n* **1** : espalda *f* **2** REVERSE : reverso *m*, dorso *m*, revés *m* **3** REAR : fondo *m*, parte *f* trasera **4** : defensa *mf* (en deportes) — ~ *adv* **1** : atrás 2 be ~ : estar de vuelta **3** go ~ : volver **4** two years ~ : hace dos años — ~ *adj* **1** REAR : de atrás, trasero **2** OVERDUE : atrasado — ~ *vt* **1** SUPPORT : apoyar **2** *or* ~ **up** : darle marcha atrás a (un vehículo) — *vi* **1** ~ **down** : volverse atrás **2** ~ **up** : retroceder — **backache** ['bækˌeɪk] *n* : dolor *m* de espalda — **backbone** ['bækˌboːn] *n* : columna *f* vertebral — **backfire** ['bækˌfaɪr] *vi* **-fired; -firing** : petardear — **background** ['bækˌgraʊnd] *n* **1** : fondo *m* (de un cuadro, etc.), antecedentes *mpl* (de una situación) **2** EXPERIENCE : formación *f* — **backhand** ['bækˌhænd] *adv* : de revés, con el revés — **backhanded** ['bækˌhændəd] *adj* : indirecto — **backing** ['bækɪŋ] *n* : apoyo *m*, respaldo *m* — **backlash** ['bækˌlæʃ] *n* : reacción *f* violenta — **backlog** ['bækˌlɔg] *n* : atrasos *mpl* — **backpack** ['bækˌpæk] *n* : mochila *f* — **backstage** [bækˈsteɪdʒ, ˈbæk-] *adv* & *adj* : entre bastidores — **backtrack** ['bækˌtræk] *vi* : dar marcha atrás — **backup** ['bækˌʌp] *n* **1** SUPPORT : respaldo *m*, apoyo *m* **2** : copia *f* de seguridad (para computadoras) — **backward** ['bækwərd] *or* **backwards** [-wərdz] *adv* **1** : hacia atrás **2 do it** ~ : hacerlo al revés **3 fall** ~ : caer de espaldas **4 bend over** ~**s** : hacer todo lo posible — **backward** *adj* **1** : hacia atrás **2** RETARDED : retrasado

3 SHY : tímido **4** UNDERDEVELOPED : atrasado

bacon ['beɪkən] *n* : tocino *m*, tocineta *f* *Lat*, bacon *m* *Spain*

bacteria [bæk'tɪriːə] *n pl* : bacterias *fpl*

bad ['bæd] *adj* **worse** ['wərs]; **worst** ['wərst] **1** : malo **2** ROTTEN : podrido **3** SEVERE : grave **4 from** ~ **to worse** : de mal en peor **5 too** ~! : ¡qué lástima! — ~ *adv* → **badly**

badge ['bædʒ] *n* : insignia *f*, chapa *f*

badger ['bædʒər] *n* : tejón *m* — ~ *vt* : acosar

badly ['bædli] *adv* **1** : mal **2** SEVERELY : gravemente **3 want** ~ : desear mucho

baffle ['bæfəl] *vt* **-fled; -fling** : desconcertar

bag ['bæg] *n* **1** : bolsa *f*, saco *m* **2** HANDBAG : bolso *m*, cartera *f* *Lat* **3** SUITCASE : maleta *f* — ~ *vt* **bagged; bagging** : ensacar, poner en una bolsa

baggage ['bægɪdʒ] *n* : equipaje *m*

baggy ['bægi] *adj* **-gier; -est** : holgado

bail ['beɪl] *n* : fianza *f* — ~ *vt* **1** : achicar (agua de un bote) **2** ~ **out** RELEASE : poner en libertad bajo fianza **3** ~ **out** EXTRICATE : sacar de apuros

bailiff ['beɪləf] *n* : alguacil *mf*

bait ['beɪt] *vt* **1** : cebar **2** HARASS : acosar — ~ *n* : cebo *m*, carnada *f*

bake ['beɪk] *vt* **baked; baking** *vt* : cocer al horno — *vi* : cocerse (al horno) — **baker** ['beɪkər] *n* : panadero *m*, -ra *f* — **bakery** ['beɪkəri] *n*, *pl* **-ries** : panadería *f*

balance ['bæləns] *n* **1** SCALES : balanza *f* **2** COUNTERBALANCE : contrapeso *m* **3** EQUILIBRIUM : equilibrio *m* **4** REMAINDER : resto *m* **5** *or* **bank** ~ : saldo *m* — ~ *v* **-anced; -ancing** *vt* **1** : hacer el balance de (una cuenta) **2** EQUALIZE : equilibrar **3** WEIGH : sopesar — *vi* **1** : sostenerse en equilibrio **2** : cuadrar (dícese de una cuenta)

balcony ['bælkəni] *n*, *pl* **-nies** : balcón *m* **2** : galería *f* (de un teatro)

bald ['bɔld] *adj* **1** : calvo **2** WORN : pelado **3 the** ~ **truth** : la pura verdad

bale ['beɪl] *n* : bala *f*, fardo *m*

baleful ['beɪlfəl] *adj* : siniestro

balk ['bɔk] *vi* ~ **at** : resistirse a

ball ['bɔl] *n* 1 : pelota *f*, bola *f*, balón *m* 2 DANCE : baile *m* 3 ~ **of string** : ovillo *m* de cuerda

ballad ['bæləd] *n* : balada *f*

ballast *n* : lastre *m*

ball bearing *n* : cojinete *m* de bola

ballerina [,bælə'ri:nə] *n* : bailarina *f*

ballet [bæ'leɪ, 'bæ,leɪ] *n* : ballet *m*

ballistic [bə'lɪstɪk] *adj* : balístico

balloon [bə'lu:n] *n* : globo *m*

ballot ['bælət] *n* 1 : papeleta *f* (de voto) 2 VOTING : votación *f*

ballpoint pen ['bɔl,pɔɪnt] *n* : bolígrafo *m*

ballroom ['bɔl,ru:m, -,rʊm] *n* : sala *f* de baile

balm ['bɑm, 'bɔlm] *n* : bálsamo *m* — **balmy** ['bɑmi, 'bɔl-] *adj* **balmier; -est** : templado, agradable

baloney [bə'loʊni] *n* NONSENSE : tonterías *fpl*

bamboo [bæm'bu:] *n* : bambú *m*

bamboozle [bæm'bu:zəl] *vt* **-zled; -zling** : engañar, embaucar

ban ['bæn] *vt* **banned; banning** : prohibir — ~ *n* : prohibición *f*

banal [bə'nɔl, bə'næl, 'beɪnəl] *adj* : banal

banana [bə'nænə] *n* : plátano *m*, banana *f Lat*, banano *m Lat*

band ['bænd] *n* 1 STRIP : banda *f* 2 GROUP : banda *f*, grupo *m*, conjunto *m* — ~ *vi* ~ **together** : unirse, juntarse

bandage ['bændɪdʒ] *n* : vendaje *m*, venda *f* — ~ *vt* **-daged; -daging** : vendar

bandit ['bændət] *n* : bandido *m*, -da *f*

bandy ['bændi] *vt* **-died; -dying** ~ **about** : circular, repetir

bang ['bæŋ] *vt* 1 STRIKE : golpear 2 SLAM : cerrar de un golpe — *vi* 1 SLAM : cerrarse de un golpe 2 ~ **on** : golpear — ~ *n* 1 BLOW : golpe *m* 2 NOISE : estrépito *m* 3 SLAM : portazo *m*

bangle ['bæŋgəl] *n* : brazalete *m*, pulsera *f*

bangs ['bæŋz] *npl* : flequillo *m*

banish ['bænɪʃ] *vt* : desterrar

banister ['bænəstər] *n* : pasamanos *m*, barandal *m*

bank ['bæŋk] *n* 1 : banco *m* 2 : orilla *f*, ribera *f* (de un río) 3 EMBANKMENT : terraplén *m* — ~ *vt* : depositar — *vi* 1 : ladearse (dícese de un avión) 2 ~ **on** : contar con — **banker** ['bæŋkər] *n* : banquero *m*, -ra *f* — **banking** ['bæŋkɪŋ] *n* : banca *f*

bankrupt ['bæŋ,krʌpt] *adj* : en bancarrota, en quiebra — **bankruptcy** ['bæŋ,krʌptsi] *n, pl* **-cies** : quiebra *f*, bancarrota *f*

banner ['bænər] *n* : bandera *f*, pancarta *f*

banquet ['bæŋkwət] *n* : banquete *m*

banter ['bæntər] *n* : bromas *fpl* — *vi* : hacer bromas

baptize [bæp'taɪz, 'bæp,taɪz] *vt* **-tized; -tizing** : bautizar — **baptism** ['bæp,tɪzəm] *n* : bautismo *m*

bar ['bɑr] *n* 1 : barra *f* 2 BARRIER : barrera *f*, obstáculo *m* 3 COUNTER : mostrador *m*, barra *f* 4 TAVERN : bar *m* 5 **behind** ~**s** : entre rejas 6 ~ **of soap** : pastilla *f* de jabón — ~ *vt* **barred; barring** 1 OBSTRUCT : obstruir, bloquear 2 EXCLUDE : excluir 3 PROHIBIT : prohibir — ~ *prep* 1 : excepto 2 ~ **none** : sin excepción

barbarian [bɑr'bæriən] *n* : bárbaro *m*, -ra *f*

barbecue ['bɑrbɪ,kju:] *vt* **-cued; -cuing** : asar a la parrilla — ~ *n* : barbacoa *f*

barbed wire ['bɑrbd'waɪr] *n* : alambre *m* de púas

barber ['bɑrbər] *n* : barbero *m*, -ra *f*

bare ['bær] *adj* 1 : desnudo 2 EMPTY : vacío 3 MINIMUM : mero, esencial — **barefoot** ['bær,fʊt] *or* **barefooted** [-,fʊtəd] *adv & adj* : descalzo — **barely** ['bærli] *adv* : apenas, por poco

bargain ['bɑrgən] *n* 1 AGREEMENT : acuerdo *m* 2 BUY : ganga *f* — ~ *vi* 1 : regatear, negociar 2 ~ **for** : contar con

barge ['bɑrdʒ] *n* : barcaza *f* — ~ *vi* **barged; barging** ~ **in** : entrometerse, interrumpir

baritone ['bærə,toʊn] *n* : barítono *m*

bark[1] ['bɑrk] *vi* : ladrar — ~ *n* : ladrido *m* (de un perro)

bark[2] *n* : corteza *f* (de un árbol)

barley ['bɑrli] *n* : cebada *f*

barn ['bɑrn] *n* : granero *m* — **barnyard** ['bɑrn,jɑrd] *n* : corral *m*

barometer [bə'rɑmətər] *n* : barómetro *m*

baron ['bærən] *n* : barón *m* — **baroness** ['bærənɪs, -,nɛs, -,nɛs] *n* : baronesa *f*

barracks ['bærəks] *ns & pl* : cuartel *m*

barrage [bə'rɑʒ, -'rɑdʒ] *n* 1 : descarga *f* (de artillería) 2 : aluvión *m* (de preguntas, etc.)

barrel ['bærəl] *n* 1 : barril *m*, tonel *m* 2 : cañón *m* (de un arma de fuego)

barren ['bærən] *adj* : estéril

barricade ['bærə,keɪd, ,bærə'-] *vt* **-caded; -cading** : cerrar con barricadas — ~ *n* : barricada *f*

barrier ['bæriər] *n* : barrera *f*

barring ['bɑrɪŋ] *prep* : salvo

barrio ['bɑrio, 'bær-] *n* : barrio *m*

bartender ['bɑr,tɛndər] n : camarero m, -ra f

barter ['bɑrtər] vt : cambiar, trocar — ~ n : trueque m

base ['beɪs] n, pl **bases** : base f — ~ vt **based; basing** : basar, fundamentar — ~ adj **baser; basest** : vil

baseball ['beɪs,bɔl] n : beisbol m, béisbol m

basement ['beɪsmənt] n : sótano m

bash ['bæʃ] vt : golpear violentamente — ~ n **1** BLOW : golpe m **2** PARTY : fiesta f

bashful ['bæʃfəl] adj : tímido, vergonzoso

basic ['beɪsɪk] adj : básico, fundamental — **basically** ['beɪsɪkli] adv : fundamentalmente

basil ['beɪzəl, 'bæzəl] n : albahaca f

basin ['beɪsən] n **1** WASHBOWL : palangana f, lavabo m **2** : cuenca f (de un río)

basis ['beɪsəs] n, pl **bases** [-,siːz] : base f

bask ['bæsk] vi — **in the sun** : tostarse al sol

basket ['bæskət] n : cesta f, cesto m — **basketball** ['bæskət,bɔl] n : baloncesto m, basquetbol m Lat

bass¹ ['bæs] n, pl **bass** or **basses** : róbalo m (pesca)

bass² ['beɪs] n : bajo m (tono, voz, instrumento)

bassoon [bə'suːn, bæ-] n : fagot m

bastard ['bæstərd] n : bastardo m, -da f

baste ['beɪst] vt **basted; basting 1** STITCH : hilvanar **2** : bañar (carne)

bat¹ ['bæt] n : murciélago m (animal)

bat² n : bate m — ~ vt **batted; batting** : batear

batch ['bætʃ] n : cesta f, cesto m — **basketball** ['bæʃ] n : hornada f (de pasteles, etc.), lote m (de mercancías), montón m (de trabajo), grupo m (de personas)

bath ['bæθ, 'bɑθ] n, pl **baths** ['bæðz, 'bɑθs, 'bɑðz, 'bɑθs] **1** : baño m **2** BATHROOM : baño m, cuarto m de baño **3 take a ~** : bañarse — **bathe** ['beɪð] v **bathed; bathing** vt : bañar, lavar — vi : bañarse — **bathrobe** ['bæθ,roːb] n : bata f (de baño) — **bathroom** ['bæθ,ruːm, -,rʊm] n : baño m, cuarto m de baño — **bathtub** ['bæθ,tʌb] n : bañera f, tina f (de baño)

baton [bə'tɑn] n : batuta f

battalion [bə'tæljən] n : batallón m

batter ['bætər] vt **1** BEAT : golpear **2** MISTREAT : maltratar — ~ n **1** : masa f para rebozar **2** HITTER : bateador m, -dora f

battery ['bæʈəri] n, pl **-teries** : batería f, pila f (de electricidad)

battle ['bæʈəl] n **1** : batalla f **2** STRUGGLE : lucha f — ~ vi **-tled; -tling** : luchar — **battlefield** ['bæʈəl,fiːld] n : campo m de batalla — **battleship** ['bæʈəl,ʃɪp] n : acorazado m

bawl ['bɔl] vi : llorar a gritos

bay¹ ['beɪ] n INLET : bahía f

bay² n or ~ **leaf** : laurel m

bay³ vi : aullar — ~ n : aullido m

bayonet [,beɪə'nɛt, 'beɪə,nɛt] n : bayoneta f

bay window n : ventana f en saliente

bazaar [bə'zɑr] n **1** : bazar m **2** SALE : venta f benéfica

be ['biː] v **was** ['wʌz, 'wɑz], **were** ['wər]; **been** ['bɪn]; **being; am** ['æm], **is** ['ɪz], **are** ['ɑr] vi **1** : ser **2** (expressing location) : estar **3** (expressing existence) : ser, existir **4** (expressing a state of being) : estar, tener — v impers **1** (indicating time) : ser **2** (indicating a condition) : hacer, estar — v aux **1** (expressing occurrence) : ser **2** (expressing possibility) : poderse **3** (expressing obligation) : deber **4** (expressing progression) : estar

beach ['biːtʃ] n : playa f

beacon ['biːkən] n : faro m

bead ['biːd] n **1** : cuenta f **2** DROP : gota f **3** ~**s** NECKLACE : collar m

beak ['biːk] n : pico m

beam ['biːm] n **1** : viga f (de madera, etc.) **2** RAY : rayo m — ~ vi SHINE : brillar — vt BROADCAST : transmitir, emitir

bean ['biːn] n **1** : habichuela f, frijol m **2 coffee** ~ : grano m **3 string** ~ : judía f

bear¹ ['bær] n, pl **bears** or **bear** : oso m, osa f

bear² v **bore** ['bɔr]; **borne** ['bɔrn]; **bearing** vt **1** CARRY : portar **2** ENDURE : soportar — vi — **right/left** : doble a la derecha/a la izquierda — **bearable** ['bærəbəl] adj : soportable

beard ['bɪrd] n : barba f

bearer ['bærər] n : portador m, -dora f

bearing ['bærɪŋ] n **1** MANNER : comportamiento m **2** SIGNIFICANCE : relación f, importancia f **3 get one's** ~**s** : orientarse

beast ['biːst] n : bestia f

beat ['biːt] v **beat; beaten** ['biːtən] or **beat; beating** vt **1** HIT : golpear **2** : batir (huevos, etc.) **3** DEFEAT : derrotar — vi : latir (dícese del corazón) — ~ n **1** : golpe m **2** : latido m (del corazón) **3** RHYTHM : ritmo m, tiempo m — **beating** ['biːtɪŋ] n **1** : paliza f **2** DEFEAT : derrota f

beauty ['bjuːṭi] *n*, *pl* **-ties** : belleza *f* — **beautiful** ['bjuːṭɪfəl] *adj* : hermoso, lindo — **beautifully** ['bjuːṭɪfəli] *adv* WONDERFULLY : maravillosamente — **beautify** ['bjuːṭɪˌfaɪ] *vt* **-fied; -fying** : embellecer

beaver ['biːvər] *n* : castor *m*

because [brˈkʌz, -ˈkɔz] *conj* : porque — **because of** *prep* : por, a causa de, debido a

beckon ['bɛkən] *vt* : llamar, hacer señas a — *vi* : hacer una seña

become [brˈkʌm] *v* **-came** [-ˈkeɪm]; **-come; -coming** *vi* 1 : hacerse, ponerse — *vt* SUIT : favorecer — **becoming** [brˈkʌmɪŋ] *adj* 1 SUITABLE : apropiado 2 FLATTERING : favorecedor

bed ['bɛd] *n* 1 : cama *f* 2 : cauce *m* (de un río), fondo *m* (del mar) 3 : macizo *m* (de flores) 4 **go to ~** : irse a la cama — **bedclothes** ['bɛdˌkloːz, -ˌkloːðz] *npl* : ropa *f* de cama

bedlam ['bɛdləm] *n* : confusión *f*, caos *m*

bedraggled [brˈdrægəld] *adj* : desaliñado, sucio

bedridden ['bɛdˌrɪdən] *adj* : postrado en cama

bedroom ['bɛdˌruːm, -ˌrʊm] *n* : dormitorio *m*, recámara *f* *Lat*

bedspread ['bɛdˌsprɛd] *n* : colcha *f*

bedtime ['bɛdˌtaɪm] *n* : hora *f* de acostarse

bee ['biː] *n* : abeja *f*

beech ['biːtʃ] *n*, *pl* **beeches** *or* **beech** : haya *f*

beef ['biːf] *n* : carne *f* de vaca, carne *f* de res *Lat* — **beefsteak** ['biːfˌsteɪk] *n* : bistec *m*

beehive ['biːˌhaɪv] *n* : colmena *f*

beeline ['biːˌlaɪn] *n* **make a ~ for** : irse derecho a

beep ['biːp] *n* : pitido *m* — *vi* ~ : pitar

beer ['biːr] *n* : cerveza *f*

beet ['biːt] *n* : remolacha *f*

beetle ['biːtəl] *n* : escarabajo *m*

before [brˈfoːr] *adv* 1 : antes 2 **the month ~** : el mes anterior — *prep* 1 (*in space*) : delante de, ante 2 (*in time*) : antes de — *conj* : antes de que — **beforehand** [brˈfoːrˌhænd] *adv* : antes

befriend [brˈfrɛnd] *vt* : hacerse amigo de

beg ['bɛg] *v* **begged; begging** *vt* 1 : pedir, mendigar 2 ENTREAT : suplicar — *vi* : mendigar, pedir limosna — **beggar** ['bɛgər] *n* : mendigo *m*, -ga *f*

begin [brˈgɪn] *v* **-gan** [-ˈgæn]; **-gun** [-ˈgʌn]; **-ginning** : empezar, comenzar — **beginner** [brˈgɪnər] *n* : principiante

mf — **beginning** [brˈgɪnɪŋ] *n* : principio *m*, comienzo *m*

begrudge [brˈgrʌdʒ] *vt* **-grudged; -grudging** 1 : dar de mala gana 2 ENVY : envidiar

behalf [brˈhæf, -ˈhaf] *n* **on ~ of** : de parte de, en nombre de

behave [brˈheɪv] *vi* **-haved; -having** : comportarse, portarse — **behavior** [brˈheɪvjər] *n* : comportamiento *m*, conducta *f*

behind [brˈhaɪnd] *adv* 1 : detrás 2 **fall ~** : atrasarse — *prep* 1 : atrás de, detrás de 2 **be ~ schedule** : ir retrasado 3 **her friends are ~ her** : tiene el apoyo de sus amigos

behold [brˈhoːld] *vt* **-held; -holding** : contemplar

beige ['beɪʒ] *adj* & *nm* : beige

being ['biːɪŋ] *n* 1 : ser *m* 2 **come into ~** : nacer

belated [brˈleɪṭəd] *adj* : tardío

belch ['bɛltʃ] *vi* : eructar — *n* : eructo *m*

Belgian ['bɛldʒən] *adj* : belga

belie [brˈlaɪ] *vt* **-lied; -lying** : contradecir, desmentir

belief [bəˈliːf] *n* 1 TRUST : confianza *f* 2 CONVICTION : creencia *f*, convicción *f* 3 FAITH : fe *f* — **believable** [bəˈliːvəbəl] *adj* : creíble — **believe** [bəˈliːv] *v* **-lieved; -lieving** : creer — **believer** [bəˈliːvər] *n* : creyente *mf*

belittle [brˈlɪṭəl] *vt* **-littled; -littling** : menospreciar

Belizean [bəˈliːziən] *adj* : beliceño *m*, -ña *f*

bell ['bɛl] *n* 1 : campana *f* 2 : timbre *m* (de teléfono, de la puerta, etc.)

belligerent [bəˈlɪdʒərənt] *adj* : beligerante

bellow ['bɛˌloː] *vi* : bramar, mugir — *vt or* ~ **out** : gritar

bellows ['bɛˌloːz] *ns* & *pl* : fuelle *m*

belly ['bɛli] *n*, *pl* **-lies** : vientre *m*

belong [brˈlɔŋ] *vi* 1 ~ **to** : pertenecer a, ser propiedad de 2 ~ **to** : ser miembro de (un club, etc.) 3 **where does it ~** : ¿dónde va? — **belongings** [brˈlɔŋɪŋz] *npl* : pertenencias *fpl*, efectos *mpl* personales

beloved [brˈlʌvəd, -ˈlʌvd] *adj* : querido, amado — *n* : querido *m*, -da *f*

below [brˈloː] *adv* : abajo — *prep* 1 : abajo de, debajo de 2 ~ **average** : por debajo del promedio 3 ~ **zero** : bajo cero

belt ['bɛlt] *n* 1 : cinturón *m* 2 BAND, STRAP : cinta *f*, correa *f* 3 AREA : frente *m*, zona *f* — *vt* **1** : ceñir con un cinturón **2** THRASH : darle una paliza a

bench ['bentʃ] *n* **1** : banco *m* **2** WORKBENCH : mesa *f* de trabajo **3** COURT : tribunal *m*

bend ['bend] *v* **bent** ['bent]; **bending** *vt* : doblar, torcer — *vi* **1** : torcerse **2** ~ **over** : inclinarse — *n* : curva *f*, ángulo *m*

beneath [bɪ'niːθ] *adv* : abajo, debajo — ~ *prep* : bajo, debajo de

benediction [,benə'dɪkʃən] *n* : bendición *f*

benefactor ['benə,fæktər] *n* : benefactor *m*, -tora *f*

benefit ['benəfɪt] *n* **1** ADVANTAGE : ventaja *f*, provecho *m* **2** AID : asistencia *f*, beneficio *m* — ~ *vt* : beneficiar — *vi* beneficiarse — **beneficial** [,benə-'fɪʃəl] *adj* : beneficioso — **beneficiary** [,benə'fɪʃəri, -'fɪʃəri] *n*, *pl* **-ries** : beneficiario *m*, -ria *f*

benevolent [bə'nevələnt] *adj* : benévolo

benign [bɪ'naɪn] *adj* **1** KIND : benévolo, amable **2** : benigno (en medicina)

bent ['bent] *adj* **1** : encorvado **2 be ~ on** : estar empeñado en — ~ *n* : aptitud *f*, inclinación *f*

bequeath [bɪ'kwiːθ, -'kwiːð] *vt* : legar — **bequest** [bɪ'kwest] *n* : legado *m*

berate [bɪ'reɪt] *vt* **-rated; -rating** : reprender, regañar

bereaved [bɪ'riːvd] *adj* : desconsolado, a luto

beret [bə'reɪ] *n* : boina *f*

berry ['beri] *n*, *pl* **-ries** : baya *f*

berserk [bər'sərk, -'zərk] *adj* **1** : enloquecido **2 go ~** : volverse loco

berth ['bərθ] *n* **1** MOORING : atracadero *m* **2** BUNK : litera *f*

beseech [bɪ'siːtʃ] *vt* **-sought** [-'sɔt] *or* **-seeched; -seeching** : suplicar, implorar

beset [bɪ'set] *vt* **-set; -setting 1** HARASS : acosar **2** SURROUND : rodear

beside [bɪ'saɪd] *prep* **1** : al lado de, junto a **2 be ~ oneself** : estar fuera de sí — **besides** [bɪ'saɪdz] *adv* : además — ~ *prep* **1** : además de **2** EXCEPT : excepto

besiege [bɪ'siːdʒ] *vt* **-sieged; -sieging** : asediar

best ['best] *adj* (*superlative of* **good**) : mejor — ~ *adv* (*superlative of* **well**) : mejor — ~ *n* **1 at ~** : a lo más **2 do one's ~** : hacer todo lo posible **3 the ~** : lo mejor — **best man** *n* : padrino *m* (de boda)

bestow [bɪ'stoː] *vt* : otorgar, conceder

bet ['bet] *n* : apuesta *f* — *v* **bet; bet-**

ting *vt* : apostar — *vi* ~ **on sth** : apostarle a algo

betray [bɪ'treɪ] *vt* : traicionar — **betrayal** [bɪ'treɪəl] *n* : traición *f*

better ['betər] *adj* (*comparative of* **good**) **1** : mejor **2 get ~** : mejorar — ~ *adv* (*comparative of* **well**) **1** : mejor **2 all the ~** : tanto mejor — ~ *n* **1 the ~** : el mejor, la mejor **2 get the ~ of** : vencer a — ~ *vt* **1** IMPROVE : mejorar **2** SURPASS : superar

between [bɪ'twiːn] *prep* : entre — ~ *adv or* **in ~** : en medio

beverage ['bevrɪdʒ, 'bevə-] *n* : bebida *f*

beware [bɪ'wær] *vi* ~ **of** : tener cuidado con

bewilder [bɪ'wɪldər] *vt* : desconcertar — **bewilderment** [bɪ'wɪldərmənt] *n* : desconcierto *m*

bewitch [bɪ'wɪtʃ] *vt* : hechizar, encantar

beyond [bɪ'jɑnd] *adv* : más allá, más lejos (en el espacio), más adelante (en el tiempo) — ~ *prep* : más allá de

bias ['baɪəs] *n* **1** PREJUDICE : prejuicio *m* **2** TENDENCY : inclinación *f*, tendencia *f* — **biased** ['baɪəst] *adj* : parcial

bib ['bɪb] *n* : babero *m* (para niños)

Bible ['baɪbəl] *n* : Biblia *f* — **biblical** ['bɪblɪkəl] *adj* : bíblico

bibliography [,bɪbli'ɑgrəfi] *n*, *pl* **-phies** : bibliografía *f*

bicarbonate of soda [baɪˈkɑrbənət, ,neɪt] *n* : bicarbonato *m* de soda

biceps ['baɪ,seps] *ns & pl* : bíceps *m*

bicker ['bɪkər] *vi* : reñir

bicycle ['baɪsɪkəl, -sɪ-] *n* : bicicleta *f* — ~ *vi* **-cled; -cling** : ir en bicicleta

bid ['bɪd] *vt* **bade** ['bæd, 'beɪd] *or* **bid; bidden** ['bɪdən] *or* **bid; bidding 1** OFFER : ofrecer **2** ~ **farewell** : decir adiós — ~ *n* **1** OFFER : oferta *f* **2** ATTEMPT : intento *m*, tentativa *f*

bide ['baɪd] *vt* **bode** ['boːd] *or* **bided; bided; biding** ~ **one's time** : esperar el momento oportuno

bifocals ['baɪfoːkəlz] *npl* : anteojos *mpl* bifocales

big ['bɪg] *adj* **bigger; biggest** : grande

bigamy ['bɪgəmi] *n* : bigamia *f*

bigot ['bɪgət] *n* : intolerante *mf* — **bigotry** ['bɪgətri] *n*, *pl* **-tries** : intolerancia *f*, fanatismo *m*

bike ['baɪk] *n* **1** BICYCLE : bici *f fam* **2** MOTORCYCLE : moto *f*

bikini [bɪ'kiːni] *n* : bikini *m*

bile ['baɪl] *n* : bilis *f*

bilingual [baɪ'lɪŋgwəl] *adj* : bilingüe

bill ['bɪl] *n* **1** BEAK : pico *m* **2** INVOICE : cuenta *f*, factura *f* **3** BANKNOTE : billete *m* **4** LAW : proyecto *m* de ley, ley *f*

— ~ vt : pasarle la cuenta a — **billboard** ['bɪl,bɔrd] n : cartelera f — **billfold** ['bɪl,foʊld] n : billetera f, cartera f

billiards ['bɪljərdz] n : billar m

billion ['bɪljən] n, pl **billions** or **billion** : mil millones mpl

billow ['bɪlo] vi : ondular, hincharse

billy goat ['bɪlɪgoʊt] n : macho m cabrío

bin ['bɪn] n : cubo m, cajón m

binary ['baɪnəri, -neri] adj : binario m

bind ['baɪnd] vt **bound** ['baʊnd], **binding** 1 TIE : atar 2 OBLIGATE : obligar 3 UNITE : unir 4 BANDAGE : vendar 5 : encuadernar (un libro) — **binder** ['baɪndər] n FOLDER : carpeta f — **binding** ['baɪndɪŋ] n : encuadernación f (de libros)

binge ['bɪndʒ] n : juerga f fam

bingo ['bɪŋgo] n, pl **-gos** : bingo m

binoculars [bəˈnɑkjələrz, baɪ-] npl : binoculares mpl, gemelos mpl

biochemistry [,baɪoˈkemɪstri] n : bioquímica f

biography [baɪˈɑgrəfi, bi:-] n, pl **-phies** : biografía f — **biographer** [baɪˈɑgrəfər] n : biógrafo m, -fa f — **biographical** [,baɪəˈgræfɪkəl] adj : biográfico

biology [baɪˈɑlədʒi] n : biología f — **biological** [-dʒɪkəl] adj : biológico — **biologist** [baɪˈɑlədʒɪst] n : biólogo m, -ga f

birch ['bərtʃ] n : abedul m

bird ['bərd] n : pájaro m (pequeño), ave f (grande)

birth ['bərθ] n 1 : nacimiento m, parto m 2 give ~ to : dar a luz a — **birthday** ['bərθdeɪ] n : cumpleaños m — **birthmark** ['bərθmɑrk] n : mancha f de nacimiento — **birthplace** ['bərθpleɪs] n : lugar m de nacimiento — **birthrate** ['bərθreɪt] n : índice m de natalidad

biscuit ['bɪskət] n : bizcocho m

bisect ['baɪsɛkt, baɪ-] vt : bisecar

bisexual [,baɪˈsɛkʃəwəl, -ˈsɛkʃəl] adj : bisexual

bishop ['bɪʃəp] n : obispo m

bison ['baɪzən, -sən] ns & pl : bisonte m

bit¹ ['bɪt] n : bocado m (de una brida)

bit² ['bɪt] n 1 : trozo m, pedazo m 2 : bit m (de información) 3 **a** ~ : un poco

bitch ['bɪtʃ] n : perra f — ~ vi COMPLAIN : quejarse, reclamar

bite ['baɪt] v **bit** ['bɪt]; **bitten** ['bɪtən]; **biting** vt 1 : morder 2 STING : picar — vi : morder — n 1 : picadura f (de un insecto), mordedura f (de un animal) 2 SNACK : bocado m — **biting** adj 1 PENETRATING : cortante, penetrante 2 CAUSTIC : mordaz

bitter ['bɪtər] adj 1 : amargo 2 it's ~ cold : hace un frío glacial 3 to the ~ end : hasta el final — **bitterness** ['bɪtərnəs] n : amargura f

bizarre [bəˈzɑr] adj : extraño

black ['blæk] adj : negro — ~ n 1 : negro m (color) 2 : negro m, -gra f (persona) — **black-and-blue** [,blækənˈblu:] adj : amoratado — **blackberry** ['blækberi] n, pl **-ries** : mora f — **blackbird** ['blækbərd] n : mirlo m — **blackboard** ['blækbɔrd] n : pizarra f, pizarrón m Lat — **blacken** ['blækən] vt : ennegrecer — **blackmail** ['blækmeɪl] n : chantaje m — ~ vt : chantajear — **black market** n : mercado m negro — **blackout** ['blækaʊt] n 1 : apagón m (de poder eléctrico) 2 FAINT : desmayo m — **blacksmith** ['blæksmɪθ] n : herrero m — **blacktop** ['blæktɑp] n : asfalto m

bladder ['blædər] n : vejiga f

blade ['bleɪd] n 1 : hoja f (de un cuchillo), cuchilla f (de un patín) 2 : pala f (de un remo, una hélice, etc.) 3 ~ **of grass** : brizna f (de hierba)

blame ['bleɪm] vt **blamed; blaming** : culpar, echar la culpa a — ~ n : culpa f — **blameless** ['bleɪmləs] adj : inocente

bland ['blænd] adj : soso, insulso

blank ['blæŋk] adj 1 : en blanco (dícese de un papel), liso (dícese de una pared) 2 EMPTY : vacío — ~ n : espacio m en blanco

blanket ['blæŋkət] n 1 : manta f, cobija f Lat 2 ~ **of snow** : manto m de nieve — ~ vt : cubrir

blare ['blær] vi **blared; blaring** : resonar

blasphemy ['blæsfəmi] n, pl **-mies** : blasfemia f

blast ['blæst] n 1 GUST : ráfaga f 2 EXPLOSION : explosión f 3 : toque m (de trompeta, etc.) — ~ vt BLOW UP : volar — **blast-off** ['blæst,ɔf] n : despegue m

blatant ['bleɪtənt] adj : descarado

blaze ['bleɪz] n 1 FIRE : fuego m 2 BRIGHTNESS : resplandor m, brillantez f 3 ~ **of anger** : arranque m de cólera — ~ v **blazed; blazing** vi : arder, brillar — vt ~ **a trail** : abrir un camino

blazer ['bleɪzər] n : chaqueta f deportiva

bleach ['bli:tʃ] vt : blanquear, decolorar — ~ n : lejía f, blanqueador m Lat — **bleachers** ['bli:tʃərz] ns & pl : gradas fpl

bleak ['bli:k] adj 1 DESOLATE : desolado 2 GLOOMY : triste, sombrío

bleary-eyed ['blɪri,aɪd] adj : con los ojos nublados

bleat ['bli:t] vi : balar — ~ n : balido m

bleed ['bliːd] v **bled** ['bled]; **bleeding** : sangrar

blemish ['blemɪʃ] vt : manchar, marcar — ~ n : mancha f, marca f

blend ['blend] vt : mezclar, combinar — ~ n : mezcla f, combinación f — **blender** ['blendər] n : licuadora f

bless ['bles] vt **blessed** ['blest]; **blessing** : bendecir — **blessed** ['blesəd] or **blest** ['blest] adj : bendito — **blessing** ['blesɪŋ] n : bendición f

blew → **blow**

blind ['blaɪnd] adj : ciego — ~ vt 1 : cegar, dejar ciego 2 DAZZLE : deslumbrar — ~ n 1 : persiana f (para una ventana) 2 **the** ~ : los ciegos — **blindfold** ['blaɪnd,foːld] vt : vendar los ojos — ~ n : venda f (para los ojos) — **blindly** ['blaɪndli] adv : ciegamente — **blindness** ['blaɪndnəs] n : ceguera f

blink ['blɪŋk] vi 1 : parpadear 2 FLICKER : brillar intermitentemente — ~ n : parpadeo m — **blinker** ['blɪŋkər] n : intermitente m, direccional f Lat

bliss ['blɪs] n : dicha f, felicidad f (absoluta) — **blissful** ['blɪsfəl] adj : feliz

blister ['blɪstər] n : ampolla f — ~ vi : ampollarse

blitz ['blɪts] n : bombardeo m aéreo

blizzard ['blɪzərd] n : ventisca f (de nieve)

bloated ['bloːtəd] adj : hinchado

blob ['blɑb] n 1 DROP : gota f 2 SPOT : mancha f

block ['blɑk] n 1 : bloque m 2 OBSTRUCTION : obstrucción f 3 : manzana f, cuadra f Lat (de edificios) 4 or **building** ~ : cubo m de construcción — ~ vt : obstruir, bloquear — **blockade** [blɑ'keɪd] n : bloqueo m — **blockage** ['blɑkɪdʒ] n : obstrucción f

blond or **blonde** ['blɑnd] adj : rubio — ~ n : rubio m, -bia f

blood ['blʌd] n : sangre f — **bloodhound** ['blʌd,haʊnd] n : sabueso m — **blood pressure** n : tensión f (arterial) — **bloodshed** ['blʌd,ʃed] n : derramamiento m de sangre — **bloodshot** ['blʌd,ʃɑt] adj : inyectado de sangre — **bloodstained** ['blʌd,steɪnd] adj : manchado de sangre — **bloodstream** ['blʌd,striːm] n : sangre f, torrente m sanguíneo — **bloody** ['blʌdi] adj **bloodier; -est** : ensangrentado, sangriento

bloom ['bluːm] n 1 : flor f 2 **in full** ~ : en plena floración — ~ vi : florecer

blossom ['blɑsəm] n : flor f — ~ vi : florecer

blot ['blɑt] n 1 : borrón m (de tinta, etc.)

2 BLEMISH : mancha f — ~ vt **blotted; blotting** 1 : emborronar 2 DRY : secar

blotch ['blɑtʃ] n : mancha f, borrón m — **blotchy** ['blɑtʃi] adj **blotchier; -est** : lleno de manchas

blouse ['blaʊs, 'blaʊz] n : blusa f

blow ['bloː] v **blew** ['bluː]; **blown** ['bloːn]; **blowing** vi 1 : soplar 2 SOUND : sonar 3 or ~ **out** : fundirse (dícese de un fusible eléctrico), reventarse (dícese de una llanta) — vt 1 : soplar 2 SOUND : tocar, sonar 3 BUNGLE : echar a perder — ~ n : golpe m — **blowout** ['bloː,aʊt] n : reventón m — **blow up** vi 1 : estallar, hacer explosión — vt 1 EXPLODE : volar 2 INFLATE : inflar

blubber ['blʌbər] n : esperma f de ballena

bludgeon ['blʌdʒən] vt : aporrear

blue ['bluː] adj **bluer; bluest** 1 : azul 2 MELANCHOLY : triste — ~ n : azul m — **blueberry** ['bluː,beri] n, pl **-ries** : arándano m — **bluebird** ['bluː,bərd] n : azulejo m — **blue cheese** n : queso m azul — **blueprint** ['bluː,prɪnt] n PLAN : proyecto m — **blues** ['bluːz] npl 1 SADNESS : tristeza f 2 : blues m (en música)

bluff ['blʌf] vi : hacer un farol — ~ n : farol m

blunder ['blʌndər] vi : meter la pata fam — ~ n : metedura f de pata fam

blunt ['blʌnt] adj 1 DULL : desafilado 2 DIRECT : directo, franco

blur ['blər] n : imágen f borrosa — ~ vt **blurred; blurring** : hacer borroso

blurb ['blərb] n : nota f publicitaria

blurt ['blərt] vt or ~ **out** : espetar

blush ['blʌʃ] n : rubor m — ~ vi : ruborizarse

blustery ['blʌstəri] adj : borrascoso, tempestuoso

boar ['bor] n : cerdo m macho

board ['bord] n 1 PLANK : tabla f, tablón m 2 COMMITTEE : junta f, consejo m 3 : tablero m (de juegos) 4 **room and** ~ : comida y alojamiento — ~ vt 1 : subir a bordo de (una nave, un avión, etc.), subir a (un tren) 2 LODGE : hospedar 3 ~ **up** : cerrar con tablas — **boarder** ['bordər] n : huésped mf

boast ['boːst] n : jactancia f — ~ vi : alardear, jactarse — **boastful** ['boːstfəl] adj : jactancioso

boat ['boːt] n : barco m (grande), barca f (pequeña)

bob ['bɑb] vi **bobbed; bobbing** or ~ **up and down** : subir y bajar

bobbin ['bɑbən] n : bobina f, carrete m

bobby pin ['bɑbi,pɪn] n : horquilla f

body ['bɑdi] *n, pl* **bodies 1** : cuerpo *m* **2** CORPSE : cadáver *m* **3** : carrocería (de un automóvil, etc.) **4** COLLECTION : conjunto *m* **5 ~ of water** : masa *f* de agua — **bodily** *adj* : corporal — **bodyguard** ['bɑdiˌgɑrd] *n* : guardaespaldas *mf*

bog ['bɑg, 'bɔg] *n* : ciénaga *f* — **~** *vt* **bogged; bogging** *or* **~ down** : empantanarse

bogus ['boːgəs] *adj* : falso

boil ['bɔil] *v* : hervir — **boiler** ['bɔilər] *n* : caldera *f*

bold ['boːld] *adj* **1** DARING : audaz **2** IMPUDENT : descarado — **boldness** ['boːldnəs] *n* : audacia *f*

Bolivian [bə'liviən] *adj* : boliviano *m*, -na *f*

bologna [bə'loːni] *n* : salchicha *f* ahumada

bolster ['boːlstər] *vt* **-stered; -stering** *or* **~ up** : reforzar

bolt ['boːlt] *n* **1** LOCK : cerrojo *m* **2** SCREW : tornillo *m* **3 ~ of lightning** : relámpago *m*, rayo *m* — **~** *vt* **1** FASTEN : atornillar **2** LOCK : echar el cerrojo a — *vi* FLEE : salir corriendo

bomb ['bɑm] *n* : bomba *f* — **~** *vt* : bombardear — **bombard** [bɑm'bɑrd, bəm-] *vt* : bombardear — **bombardment** [bɑm'bɑrdmənt] *n* : bombardeo *m* — **bomber** ['bɑmər] *n* : bombardero *m*

bond ['bɑnd] *n* **1** TIE : vínculo *m*, lazo *m* **2** SURETY : fianza *f* **3** : bono *m* (en finanzas) — **~** *vi* : adherirse

bondage ['bɑndidʒ] *n* : esclavitud *f*

bone ['boːn] *n* : hueso *m* — **~** *vt* **boned; boning** : deshuesar

bonfire ['bɑnˌfair] *n* : hoguera *f*

bonus ['boːnəs] *n* **1** PAY : prima *f* **2** BENEFIT : beneficio *m* adicional

bony ['boːni] *adj* **bonier; -est 1** : huesudo **2** : lleno de espinas (dícese de pescados)

boo ['buː] *n, pl* **boos** : abucheo *m* — **~** *vt* : abuchear

book ['bʊk] *n* **1** : libro *m* **2** NOTEBOOK : libreta *f*, cuaderno *m* — **~** *vt* : reservar — **bookcase** ['bʊkˌkeis] *n* : estantería *f* — **bookkeeping** ['bʊkˌkiːpiŋ] *n* : teneduría *f* de libros, contabilidad *f* — **booklet** ['bʊklət] *n* : folleto *m* — **bookmark** ['bʊkˌmɑrk] *n* : marcador *m* de libros — **bookseller** ['bʊkˌselər] *n* : librero *m*, -ra *f* — **bookshelf** ['bʊkˌʃelf] *n, pl* **-shelves** : estante *m* — **bookstore** ['bʊkˌstor] *n* : librería *f*

boom ['buːm] *vi* **1** : tronar, resonar **2** PROSPER : estar en auge, prosperar —

~ *n* **1** : bramido *m*, estruendo *m* **2** : auge *m* (económico)

boon ['buːn] *n* : ayuda *f*, beneficio *m*

boost ['buːst] *vt* **1** LIFT : levantar **2** INCREASE : aumentar — **~** *n* **1** INCREASE : aumento *m* **2** ENCOURAGEMENT : estímulo *m*

boot ['buːt] *n* : bota *f*, botín *m* — **~** *vt* **1** : dar una patada a **2** *or* **~ up** : cargar (un ordenador)

booth ['buːθ] *n, pl* **booths** ['buːðz, 'buːθs] : cabina *f* (de teléfono, de votar), caseta *f* (de información)

booty ['buːti] *n, pl* **-ties** : botín *m*

booze ['buːz] *n* : trago *m*, bebida *f* (alcohólica)

border ['bɔrdər] *n* **1** EDGE : borde *m*, orilla *f* **2** TRIM : ribete *m* **3** FRONTIER : frontera *f*

bore¹ ['bor] *vt* **bored; boring** DRILL : taladrar

bore² *vt* TIRE : aburrir — **~** *n* : pesado *m*, -da *f am* (persona), lata *f am* (cosa, situación) — **boredom** ['bordəm] *n* : aburrimiento *m* — **boring** ['boriŋ] *adj* : aburrido, pesado

born ['bɔrn] *adj* **1** : nacido **2 be ~** : nacer

borough ['bərə] *n* : distrito *m* municipal

borrow ['bɑro] *vt* : pedir prestado, tomar prestado

Bosnian ['bɑzniən, 'bɔz-] *adj* : bosnio *m*, -nia *f*

bosom ['bʊzəm, 'buː-] *n* BREAST : pecho *m*, seno *m* — **~** *adj* **~ friend** : amigo *m* íntimo

boss ['bɔs] *n* : jefe *m*, -fa *f*; patrón *m*, -trona *f* — **~** *vt* SUPERVISE : dirigir — **bossy** ['bɔsi] *adj* **bossier; -est** : autoritario

botany ['bɑtəni] *n* : botánica *f* — **botanical** [bə'tænikəl] *adj* : botánico

botch ['bɑtʃ] *vt* : hacer una chapuza de, estropear

both ['boːθ] *adj* : ambos, los dos, las dos — **~** *pron* : ambos *m*, -bas *f*; los dos, las dos

bother ['bɑðər] *vt* **1** TROUBLE : preocupar **2** PESTER : molestar, fastidiar — *vi* **~ to** : molestarse en — **~** *n* : molestia *f*

bottle ['bɑtəl] *n* **1** : botella *f*, frasco *m* **2** *or* **baby ~** : biberón *m* — **~** *vt* **bottled; bottling** : embotellar — **bottleneck** ['bɑtəlˌnek] *n* : embotellamiento *m*

bottom ['bɑtəm] *n* **1** : fondo *m* (de una caja, del mar, etc.), pie *m* (de una escalera, una montaña, etc.), final *m* (de una lista) **2** BUTTOCKS : nalgas *fpl*, trasero *m* — **~** *adj* : más bajo, inferior, de abajo — **bottomless** ['bɑtəmləs] *adj* : sin fondo

bough ['bau] *n* : rama *f*

bought → **buy**

bouillon ['buːjɑn; 'buljɑn, -jɔn] *n* : caldo *m*

boulder ['boːldər] *n* : canto *m* rodado

boulevard ['buləvɑrd, 'buː-] *n* : bulevar *m*

bounce ['bauns] *v* **bounced; bouncing** *vt* : hacer rebotar — *vi* : rebotar — ~ *n* : rebote *m*

bound[1] ['baund] *adj* **be** ~ **for** : ir rumbo a

bound[2] *adj* **1** OBLIGED : obligado **2** DETERMINED : decidido **3 be** ~ **to** : tener que

bound[3] *n* **out of** ~**s** : (en) zona prohibida — **boundary** ['baundri, -dəri] *n*, *pl* **-aries** : límite *m* — **boundless** ['baundləs] *adj* : sin límites

bouquet ['boːkeɪ, buː-] *n* : ramo *m*

bourgeois ['burˌʒwɑ, burˌʒwɑ] *adj* : burgués

bout ['baut] *n* **1** : combate *m* (en deportes) **2** : ataque *m* (de una enfermedad) **3** : período *m* (de actividad)

bow[1] ['bau] *vi* : inclinarse — *vt* ~ **one's head** : inclinar la cabeza — ~ ['bau] *n* : reverencia *f*, inclinación *f*

bow[2] ['boː] *n* **1** : arco *m* **2 tie a** ~ : hacer un lazo

bow[3] ['bau] *n* : proa *f* (de un barco)

bowels ['bauəls] *npl* **1** : intestinos *mpl* **2** DEPTHS : entrañas *fpl*

bowl[1] ['boːl] *n* : tazón *m*, cuenco *m*

bowl[2] *vi* : jugar a los bolos — **bowling** ['boːlɪŋ] *n* : bolos *mpl*

box[1] ['bɑks] *vi* FIGHT : boxear — **boxer** ['bɑksər] *n* : boxeador *m*, -dora *f* — **boxing** ['bɑksɪŋ] *n* : boxeo *m*

box[2] *n* **1** : caja *f*, cajón *m* **2** : palco *m* (en el teatro) — ~ *vt* : empaquetar — **box office** *n* : taquilla *f*, boletería *f* *Lat*

boy ['boɪ] *n* : niño *m*, chico *m*

boycott ['boɪˌkɑt] *vt* : boicotear — ~ *n* : boicot *m*

boyfriend ['boɪˌfrɛnd] *n* : novio *m*

bra ['brɑ] → **brassiere**

brace ['breɪs] *n* **1** SUPPORT : abrazadera *f* **2** ~**s** *npl* : aparatos *mpl* (para dientes) — ~ *vi* : **oneself for** : prepararse para

bracelet ['breɪslət] *n* : brazalete *m*

bracket ['brækət] *n* **1** SUPPORT : soporte *m* **2** : corchete *m* (marca de puntuación) **3** CATEGORY : categoría *f* — ~ *vt* **1** : poner entre corchetes **2** CATEGORIZE : catalogar

brag ['bræg] *vi* **bragged; bragging** : jactarse

braid ['breɪd] *vt* : trenzar — ~ *n* : trenza *f*

braille ['breɪl] *n* : braille *m*

brain ['breɪn] *n* **1** : cerebro *m* **2** ~**s** *npl* : inteligencia *f* — **brainstorm** ['breɪnˌstɔrm] *n* : idea *f* genial — **brainwash** ['breɪnˌwɑʃ, -ˌwɔʃ] *vt* : lavar el cerebro — **brainy** ['breɪni] *adj* **brainier; -est** : inteligente, listo

brake ['breɪk] *n* : freno *m* — ~ *v* **braked; braking** : frenar

bramble ['bræmbəl] *n* : zarza *f*

bran ['bræn] *n* : salvado *m*

branch ['bræntʃ] *n* **1** : rama *f* (de una planta) **2** DIVISION : ramal *m* (de un camino, etc.), sucursal *f* (de una empresa), agencia *f* (del gobierno) — ~ *vi* **or** ~ **off** : ramificarse, bifurcarse

brand ['brænd] *n* **1** : marca *f* (de ganado) **2 or** ~ **name** : marca *f* de fábrica — ~ *vt* **1** : marcar (ganado) **2** LABEL : tachar, tildar

brandish ['brændɪʃ] *vt* : blandir

brand-new ['brændˈnuː, -ˈnjuː] *adj* : flamante

brandy ['brændi] *n*, *pl* **-dies** : brandy *m*, coñac *m*

brass ['bræs] *n* **1** : latón *m* **2** : metales *mpl* (de una orquesta)

brassiere [brəˈzɪr, brɑ-] *n* : sostén *m*, brasier *m* *Lat*

brat ['bræt] *n* : mocoso *m*, -sa *f* *fam*

bravado [brəˈvɑdo] *n*, *pl* **-does or -dos** : bravuconadas *fpl*

brave ['breɪv] *adj* **braver; bravest** : valiente, valeroso — ~ *vt* **braved; braving** : afrontar, hacer frente a — ~ *n* : guerrero *m* indio — **bravery** ['breɪvəri] *n* : valor *m*, valentía *f*

brawl ['brɔl] *n* : pelea *f*, reyerta *f*

brawn ['brɔn] *n* : músculos *mpl* — **brawny** ['brɔni] *adj* **brawnier; -est** : musculoso

bray ['breɪ] *vi* : rebuznar

brazen ['breɪzən] *adj* : descarado

Brazilian [brəˈzɪljən] *adj* : brasileño *m*, -ña *f*

breach ['briːtʃ] *n* **1** VIOLATION : infracción *f*, violación *f* **2** GAP : brecha *f*

bread ['brɛd] *n* **1** : pan *m* **2** ~ **crumbs** : migajas *fpl*

breadth ['brɛdθ] *n* : anchura *f*

break ['breɪk] *v* **broke** ['broːk]; **broken** ['broːkən]; **breaking** *vt* **1** : romper, quebrar **2** VIOLATE : infringir, violar **3** INTERRUPT : interrumpir **4** SURPASS : batir (un récord, etc.) **5** ~ **a habit** : quitarse una costumbre **6** ~ **the news** : dar la noticia — *vi* **1** : romperse, quebrarse **2** ~ **away** : escapar 3 **~ down** : estropearse (dícese de una máquina), fallar (dícese de un sistema, etc.) 4 **~ into** : entrar en 5 **~ off** : interrumpirse 6 **~ out of** : escaparse de 7 **~ up** SEPARATE : separarse — **~** n 1 : ruptura f, fractura f 2 GAP : interrupción f, claro m (entre las nubes) 3 **lucky ~** : golpe m de suerte 4 **take a ~** : tomar(se) un descanso — **breakable** ['breɪkəbəl] adj : quebradizo, frágil — **breakdown** ['breɪk-ˌdaʊn] n 1 : avería f (de máquinas), interrupción f (de comunicaciones), fracaso m (de negociaciones) 2 or **nervous ~** : crisis f nerviosa

breakfast ['brɛkfəst] n : desayuno m

breast ['brɛst] n 1 : seno m (de una mujer) 2 CHEST : pecho m — **breast–feed** ['brɛst,fiːd] vt **-fed** [-ˌfɛd]; **-feeding** : amamantar

breath ['brɛθ] n : aliento m, respiración f — **breathe** ['briːð] v **breathed**; **breathing** : respirar — **breathless** ['brɛθləs] adj : sin aliento, jadeante — **breathtaking** ['brɛθˌteɪkɪŋ] adj : impresionante

breed ['briːd] v **bred** ['brɛd]; **breeding** vt 1 : criar (animales) 2 ENGENDER : engendrar, producir — vi : reproducirse — **~** n 1 : raza f 2 CLASS : clase f, tipo m

breeze ['briːz] n : brisa f — **breezy** ['briːzi] adj **breezier; -est** 1 WINDY : ventoso 2 NONCHALANT : despreocupado

brevity ['brɛvəti] n, pl **-ties** : brevedad f

brew ['bruː] vt : hacer (cerveza, etc.), preparar (té) — vi 1 : fabricar cerveza 2 : amenazar (dícese de una tormenta) — **brewery** ['bruːəri, 'bruɾi] n, pl **-eries** : cervecería f

bribe ['braɪb] vt **bribed; bribing** : sobornar m — **~** n : soborno m — **bribery** ['braɪbəri] n, pl **-eries** : soborno m

brick ['brɪk] n : ladrillo m — **bricklayer** ['brɪkˌleɪər] n : albañil mf

bride ['braɪd] n : novia f — **bridal** ['braɪdəl] adj : nupcial, de novia — **bridegroom** ['braɪdˌgruːm] n : novio m — **bridesmaid** ['braɪdzˌmeɪd] n : dama f de honor

bridge ['brɪdʒ] n 1 : puente m 2 : caballete m (de la nariz) 3 : bridge m (juego de naipes) — **~** vt **bridged; bridging** 1 : tender un puente sobre 2 **~ the gap** : salvar las diferencias

bridle ['braɪdəl] n : brida f — **~** vt **-dled; -dling** : embridar

brief ['briːf] adj : breve — **~** n 1 : resumen m, sumario m 2 **~s** npl UN-

DERPANTS : calzoncillos mpl — **~** vt : dar órdenes a, instruir — **briefcase** ['briːfˌkeɪs] n : portafolio m, maletín m — **briefly** ['briːfli] adv : brevemente

bright ['braɪt] adj 1 : brillante, claro 2 CHEERFUL : alegre, animado 3 INTELLIGENT : listo, inteligente — **brighten** ['braɪtən] vi 1 : hacerse más brillante 2 or **~ up** : animarse, alegrarse — vt 1 ILLUMINATE : iluminar 2 ENLIVEN : alegrar, animar

brilliant ['brɪljənt] adj : brillante — **brilliance** ['brɪljənts] n 1 BRIGHTNESS : resplandor m, brillantez f 2 INTELLIGENCE : inteligencia f

brim ['brɪm] n 1 : borde m (de una taza, etc.) 2 : ala f (de un sombrero) — **~** vi **brimmed; brimming** or **~ over** : desbordarse, rebosar

brine ['braɪn] n : salmuera f

bring ['brɪŋ] vt **brought** ['brɔt]; **bringing** 1 : traer 2 **~ about** : ocasionar 3 **~ around** PERSUADE : convencer 4 **~ back** : devolver 5 **~ down** : derribar 6 **~ on** CAUSE : provocar 7 **~ out** : sacar 8 **~ to an end** : terminar (con) 9 **~ up** REAR : criar 10 **~ up** MENTION : sacar

brink ['brɪŋk] n : borde m

brisk ['brɪsk] adj 1 FAST : rápido 2 LIVELY : enérgico

bristle ['brɪsəl] n : cerda f (de un animal), pelo m (de una planta) — **~** vi **-tled; -tling** : erizarse

British ['brɪtɪʃ] adj : británico

brittle ['brɪtəl] adj **-tler; -tlest** : frágil, quebradizo

broach ['broːtʃ] vt : abordar

broad ['brɔd] adj 1 WIDE : ancho 2 GENERAL : general 3 **in ~ daylight** : en pleno día

broadcast ['brɔdˌkæst] vt **-cast; -casting** : emitir — **~** n : emisión f

broaden ['brɔdən] vt : ampliar, ensanchar — vi : ensancharse — **broadly** ['brɔdli] adv : en general — **broad-minded** ['brɔdˈmaɪndəd] adj : de miras amplias, tolerante

broccoli ['brɑkəli] n : brócoli m, brécol m

brochure ['broˈʃʊr] n : folleto m

broil ['brɔɪl] vt : asar a la parrilla

broke ['broːk] → **break** — **~** adj : pelado fam — **broken** ['broːkən] adj : roto, quebrado — **brokenhearted** [ˌbroːkənˈhɑrtəd] adj : desconsolado, con el corazón destrozado

broker ['broːkər] n : corredor m, -dora f

bronchitis [brɑnˈkaɪtəs, brɑŋ-] n : bronquitis f

bronze ['brɒnz] n : bronce m

brooch ['broʧ, 'bruːʧ] n : broche m

brood ['bruːd] n : nidada f (de pájaros), camada f (de mamíferos) — vi 1 INCUBATE : empollar 2 **~ about** : dar vueltas a, pensar demasiado en

brook ['brʊk] n : arroyo m

broom ['bruːm, 'brʊm] n : escoba f — **broomstick** ['bruːmˌstɪk, 'brʊm-] n : palo m de escoba

broth ['brɒθ] n, pl **broths** ['brɒθs, 'brɒðz] : caldo m

brothel ['brɒθəl, 'brɔ-] n : burdel m

brother ['brʌðər] n : hermano m — **brotherhood** ['brʌðərˌhʊd] n : fraternidad f — **brother-in-law** ['brʌðərɪnˌlɔ] n, pl **brothers-in-law** : cuñado m — **brotherly** ['brʌðərli] adj : fraternal

brought → **bring**

brow ['braʊ] n 1 EYEBROW : ceja f 2 FOREHEAD : frente f 3 : cima f (de una colina)

brown ['braʊn] adj : marrón, castaño (dícese del pelo), moreno (dícese de la piel) — ~ n : marrón m — ~ vt : dorar (en cocinar)

browse ['braʊz] vi **browsed; browsing** : mirar, echar un vistazo

bruise ['bruːz] vt **bruised; bruising** 1 : contusionar, magullar (a una persona) 2 : machucar (frutas) — ~ n : cardenal m, magulladura f

brunch ['brʌnʧ] n : brunch m

brunet or **brunette** [bruː'net] adj : moreno — ~ n : moreno m, -na f

brunt ['brʌnt] n **bear the ~ of** : aguantar el mayor impacto de

brush ['brʌʃ] n 1 : cepillo m, pincel m (de artista), brocha f (de pintor) 2 UNDERBRUSH : maleza f — ~ vt 1 : cepillar 2 GRAZE : rozar 3 **~ aside** : rechazar 4 **~ off** DISREGARD : hacer caso omiso de — vi **~ up on** : repasar — **brush-off** ['brʌʃˌɔf] n **give the ~ to** : dar calabazas a

brusque ['brʌsk] adj : brusco

brutal ['bruːtəl] adj : brutal — **brutality** [bruː'tæləti] n, pl **-ties** : brutalidad f

brute ['bruːt] adj : bruto — n : bestia f; bruto m, -ta f

bubble ['bʌbəl] n : burbuja f — ~ vi **-bled; -bling** : burbujear

buck ['bʌk] n, pl **buck** or **bucks** 1 : animal m macho, ciervo m (macho) 2 DOLLAR : dólar m — ~ vi 1 : corcovear (dícese de un caballo) 2 **~ up** : animarse, levantar el ánimo — vt OPPOSE : oponerse a, ir en contra de

bucket ['bʌkət] n : cubo m

buckle ['bʌkəl] n : hebilla f — ~ v **-led;**

-ling vt 1 FASTEN : abrochar 2 BEND : combar, torcer — vi 1 : combarse, torcerse 2 : doblarse (dícese de las rodillas)

bud ['bʌd] n 1 : brote m 2 or **flower ~** : capullo m — ~ vi **budded; budding** : brotar, hacer brotes

Buddhism ['buːˌdɪzəm, 'bʊ-] n : budismo m — **Buddhist** ['buːdɪst, 'bʊ-] adj : budista — ~ n : budista mf

buddy ['bʌdi] n, pl **-dies** : compañero m, -ra f

budge ['bʌdʒ] vi **budged; budging** : MOVE : moverse 2 YIELD : ceder

budget ['bʌdʒət] n : presupuesto m — ~ vi : presupuestar — **budgetary** ['bʌdʒəˌteri] adj : presupuestario

buff ['bʌf] n 1 : beige m, color m de ante 2 ENTHUSIAST : aficionado m, -da f — ~ adj : beige — ~ vt POLISH : pulir

buffalo ['bʌfəˌlo] n, pl **-lo** or **-loes** : búfalo m

buffet [bʌ'feɪ, ˌbuː-] n 1 : bufé m (comida) 2 SIDEBOARD : aparador m

bug ['bʌg] n 1 INSECT : bicho m, insecto m 2 FLAW : defecto m 3 GERM : microbio m 4 MICROPHONE : micrófono m (oculto) — ~ vt **bugged; bugging** 1 PESTER : fastidiar, molestar 2 : ocultar micrófonos en (una habitación, etc.)

buggy ['bʌgi] n, pl **-gies** 1 CARRIAGE : calesa f 2 or **baby ~** : cochecito m (para niños)

bugle ['bjuːgəl] n : clarín m, corneta f

build ['bɪld] v **built** ['bɪlt], **building** vt 1 : construir 2 DEVELOP : desarrollar — vi 1 or **~ up** INTENSIFY : aumentar, intensificar 2 or **~ up** ACCUMULATE : acumularse — n PHYSIQUE : físico m, complexión f — **builder** ['bɪldər] n : constructor m, -tora f — **building** ['bɪldɪŋ] n 1 STRUCTURE : edificio m 2 CONSTRUCTION : construcción f — **built-in** ['bɪlt'ɪn] adj : empotrado

bulb ['bʌlb] n 1 : bulbo m (de una planta) 2 LIGHTBULB : bombilla f

bulge ['bʌldʒ] vi **bulged; bulging** : sobresalir — ~ n : bulto m, protuberancia f

bulk ['bʌlk] n 1 VOLUME : volumen m, bulto m 2 **in ~** : en grandes cantidades — **bulky** ['bʌlki] adj **bulkier; -est** : voluminoso

bull ['bʊl] n 1 : toro m 2 MALE : macho m

bulldog ['bʊlˌdɔg] n : buldog m

bulldozer ['bʊlˌdoːzər] n : bulldozer m

bullet ['bʊlət] n : bala f

bulletin ['bʊlətən, -lətən] n : boletín m — **bulletin board** n : tablón m de anuncios

bulletproof ['bʊlətˌpruːf] *adj* : a prueba de balas

bullfight ['bʊlˌfaɪt] *n* : corrida *f* (de toros) — **bullfighter** ['bʊlˌfaɪtər] *n* : torero *m*, -ra *f*; matador *m*

bullion ['bʊljən] *n* : oro *m* en lingotes, plata *f* en lingotes

bull's-eye ['bʊlzˌaɪ] *n*, *pl* **bull's-eyes** : diana *f*

bully ['bʊli] *n*, *pl* **-lies** : matón *m* — ~ *vt* **-lied; -lying** : intimidar

bum ['bʌm] *n* : vagabundo *m*, -da *f*

bumblebee ['bʌmbəlˌbiː] *n* : abejorro *m*

bump ['bʌmp] *n* 1 BULGE : bulto *m*, protuberancia *f* 2 IMPACT : golpe *m* 3 JOLT : sacudida *f* — ~ *vt* : chocar contra — *vi* ~ **into** MEET : encontrarse con — **bumper** ['bʌmpər] *n* : parachoques *mpl* — ~ *adj* : extraordinario, récord — **bumpy** ['bʌmpi] *adj* **bumpier; -est** 1 : desigual, lleno de baches (dícese de un camino) 2 a ~ **flight** : un vuelo agitado

bun ['bʌn] *n* : bollo *m*

bunch ['bʌntʃ] *n* : grupo *m* (de personas), racimo *m* (de frutas, etc.), ramo *m* (de flores), manojo *m* (de llaves) — ~ *vi* or ~ **up** : amontonarse, agruparse

bundle ['bʌndəl] *n* 1 : lío *m*, bulto *m*, atado *m*, haz *m* (de palos) 2 PARCEL : paquete *m* 3 ~ **of nerves** : manojo *m* de nervios — ~ *vt* **-dled; -dling** or ~ **up** : liar, atar

bungalow ['bʌŋgəˌloː] *n* : casa *f* de un solo piso

bungle ['bʌŋgəl] *vt* **-gled; -gling** : echar a perder

bunion ['bʌnjən] *n* : juanete *m*

bunk ['bʌŋk] *n* or **bunk bed** : litera *f*

bunny ['bʌni] *n*, *pl* **-nies** : conejo *m*, -ja *f*

buoy ['buːi, 'bɔɪ] *n* : boya *f* — ~ *vt* or ~ **up** HEARTEN : animar, levantar el ánimo a — **buoyant** ['bɔɪənt, 'buːjənt] *adj* 1 : boyante, flotante 2 LIGHTHEARTED : alegre, optimista

burden ['bərdən] *n* : carga *f* — ~ *vt* ~ **s.o. with** : cargar a algn con — **burdensome** ['bərdənsəm] *adj* : oneroso

bureau ['bjʊro] *n* 1 : cómoda *f* (mueble) 2 : departamento *m* (del gobierno) 3 AGENCY : agencia *f* — **bureaucracy** [bjʊˈrɑkrəsi] *n*, *pl* **-cies** : burocracia *f* — **bureaucrat** ['bjʊrəˌkræt] *n* : burócrata *mf* — **bureaucratic** [bjʊrəˈkrætɪk] *adj* : burocrático

burglar ['bərglər] *n* : ladrón *m*, -drona *f* — **burglarize** ['bərgləˌraɪz] *vt* **-ized; -izing** : robar — **burglary** ['bərgləri] *n*, *pl* **-glaries** : robo *m*

burgundy ['bərgəndi] *n*, *pl* **-dies** : borgoña *m*, vino *m* de Borgoña

burial ['beriəl] *n* : entierro *m*

burly ['bərli] *adj* **-lier; -liest** : fornido

burn ['bərn] *v* **burned** ['bərnd, 'bərnt] or **burnt** ['bərnt]; **burning** *vt* 1 : quemar 2 or ~ **down** : incendiar 3 ~ **up** : consumir — *vi* 1 : arder (dícese de un fuego), quemarse (dícese de la comida, etc.) 2 : estar encendido (dícese de una luz) 3 ~ **out** : apagarse — ~ *n* : quemadura *f* — **burner** ['bərnər] *n* : quemador *m*

burnish ['bərnɪʃ] *vt* : pulir

burp ['bərp] *vi* : eructar — ~ *n* : eructo *m*

burro ['bəro, 'bʊr-] *n*, *pl* **-os** : burro *m*

burrow ['bəro] *n* : madriguera *f* — ~ *vi* 1 : cavar 2 ~ **into** : hurgar en

bursar ['bərsər] *n* : tesorero *m*, -ra *f*

burst ['bərst] *v* **burst** or **bursted; bursting** *vi* : reventarse — *vt* : reventar — ~ *n* 1 EXPLOSION : estallido *m*, explosión *f* 2 OUTBURST : arranque *m*, arrebato *m* 3 ~ **of laughter** : carcajada *f*

bury ['beri] *vt* **buried; burying** 1 INTER : enterrar 2 HIDE : esconder

bus ['bʌs] *n*, *pl* **buses** or **busses** : autobús *m*, bus *m* — ~ *v* **bused** or **bussed** ['bʌst]; **busing** or **bussing** ['bʌsɪŋ] *vt* : transportar en autobús — *vi* : viajar en autobús

bush ['bʊʃ] *n* SHRUB : arbusto *m*, mata *f*

bushel ['bʊʃəl] *n* : medida *f* de áridos igual a 35.24 litros

bushy ['bʊʃi] *adj* **bushier; -est** : poblado, espeso

busily ['bɪzəli] *adv* : afanosamente

business ['bɪznəs, -nəz] *n* 1 COMMERCE : negocios *mpl*, comercio *m* 2 COMPANY : empresa *f*, negocio *m* 3 **it's none of your** ~ : no es asunto tuyo — **businessman** ['bɪznəsˌmæn, -nəz-] *n*, *pl* **-men** [-mən, -ˌmen] : empresario *m*, hombre *m* de negocios — **businesswoman** ['bɪznəsˌwʊmən, -nəz-] *n*, *pl* **-women** [-ˌwɪmən] : empresaria *f*, mujer *f* de negocios

bust[1] ['bʌst] *vt* BREAK : romper

bust[2] *n* 1 : busto *m* (en la escultura) 2 BREASTS : pecho *m*, senos *mpl*

bustle ['bʌsəl] *vi* **-tled; -tling** or ~ **about** : ir y venir, ajetrearse — ~ *n* or **hustle and** ~ : bullicio *m*, ajetreo *m*

busy ['bɪzi] *adj* **busier; -est** 1 : ocupado 2 BUSTLING : concurrido

but ['bʌt] *conj* 1 : pero 2 **not one** ~ **two** : no uno sino dos — ~ *prep* : excepto, menos

butcher ['butʃər] n : carnicero m, -ra f — ~ vt 1 : matar 2 BOTCH : hacer una carnicería de

butler ['bʌtlər] n : mayordomo m

butt ['bʌt] vt : embestir (con los cuernos), darle un cabezazo a — vi ~ **in** : interrumpir — ~ n 1 BUTTING : embestida f (de cuernos) 2 TARGET : blanco m 3 : extremo m, culata f (de un rifle), colilla f (de un cigarrillo)

butter ['bʌtər] n : mantequilla f — ~ vt : untar con mantequilla

buttercup ['bʌtər,kʌp] n : ranúnculo m

butterfly ['bʌtər,flaɪ] n, pl **-flies** : mariposa f

buttocks ['bʌtəks, -təks] npl : nalgas fpl

button ['bʌtən] n : botón m — ~ vt : abotonar — vi or ~ **up** : abotonarse — **buttonhole** ['bʌtən,hoʊl] n : ojal m — ~ vt **-holed; -holing** : acorralar

buy ['baɪ] vt **bought** ['bɔt]; **buying** : comprar — ~ n : compra f — **buyer** ['baɪər] n : comprador m, -dora f

buzz ['bʌz] vi : zumbar — ~ n : zumbido m

buzzard ['bʌzərd] n : buitre m

buzzer ['bʌzər] n : timbre m

by ['baɪ] prep 1 NEAR : cerca de 2 VIA : por 3 PAST : por, por delante de 4 DURING : de, durante 5 (in expressions of time) : para 6 (indicating cause or agent) : por, de, a — ~ adv 1 ~ **and** ~ : poco después 2 ~ **and large** : en general 3 **go** ~ : pasar 4 **stop** ~ : pasar por casa

bygone ['baɪ,gɔn] adj : pasado — ~ n **let** ~ **s be** ~ **s** : lo pasado, pasado está

bypass ['baɪ,pæs] n : carretera f de circunvalación — ~ vt : evitar

by-product ['baɪ,prɑdəkt] n : subproducto m

bystander ['baɪ,stændər] n : espectador m, -dora f

byte ['baɪt] n : byte m, octeto m

byword ['baɪ,wərd] n **be a** ~ **for** : ser sinónimo de

C

c ['si:] n, pl **c's** or **cs** ['si:z] : c, tercera letra del alfabeto inglés

cab ['kæb] n 1 : taxi m 2 : cabina f (de un camión, etc.)

cabbage ['kæbɪdʒ] n : col f, repollo m

cabin ['kæbən] n 1 : cabaña f 2 : cabina f (de un avión, etc.), camarote m (de un barco)

cabinet ['kæbnət] n 1 CUPBOARD : armario m 2 : gabinete m (del gobierno) 3 or **medicine** ~ : botiquín m

cable ['keɪbəl] n : cable m — **cable television** n : televisión f por cable

cackle ['kækəl] vi **-led; -ling** 1 CLUCK : cacarear 2 LAUGH : reírse a carcajadas

cactus ['kæktəs] n, pl **cacti** [-taɪ] or **-tuses** : cactus m

cadence ['keɪdənts] n : cadencia f, ritmo m

cadet [kə'dɛt] n : cadete mf

café [kæˈfeɪ, kə-] n : café m, cafetería f — **cafeteria** [ˌkæfəˈtɪriə] n : restaurante m autoservicio, cantina f

caffeine ['kæ,fi:n] n : cafeína f

cage ['keɪdʒ] n : jaula f — ~ vt **caged; caging** : enjaular

cajole [kəˈdʒoʊl] vt **-joled; -joling** : engatusar

cake ['keɪk] n 1 : pastel m, torta f 2 : pastilla f (de jabón) 3 **take the** ~ : ser el colmo — **caked** ['keɪkt] adj ~ **with** : cubierto de

calamity [kəˈlæmət̬i] n, pl **-ties** : calamidad f

calcium ['kælsiəm] n : calcio m

calculate ['kælkjəˌleɪt] v **-lated; -lating** : calcular — **calculating** ['kælkjəˌleɪt̬ɪŋ] adj : calculador — **calculation** [ˌkælkjəˈleɪʃən] n : cálculo m — **calculator** ['kælkjəˌleɪt̬ər] n : calculadora f

calendar ['kæləndər] n : calendario m

calf¹ ['kæf, 'kaf] n, pl **calves** ['kævz, 'kavz] 1 : becerro m, -rra f; ternero m, -ra f (de vacunos) 2 : cría f (de otros mamíferos)

calf² n, pl **calves** : pantorrilla f (de la pierna)

caliber or **calibre** ['kæləbər] n : calibre m

call ['kɔl] vi 1 : llamar 2 VISIT : pasar, hacer (una) visita 3 ~ **for** : requerir — vt 1 : llamar 2 ~ **off** : cancelar — ~ n 1 : llamada f 2 SHOUT : grito m 3 VISIT : visita f 4 DEMAND : petición f — **calling** ['kɔlɪŋ] n : vocación f

callous ['kæləs] adj : insensible, cruel

calm ['kɑm, 'kɑlm] n : calma f, tranquilidad f — vi : calmar — vi or ~ **down** : calmarse — ~ adj : tranquilo, en calma — **calmly** ['kɑmli, 'kɑlm-] adv : con calma

calorie ['kæləri] *n* : caloría *f*

came → **come**

camel ['kæməl] *n* : camello *m*

camera ['kæmrə, 'kæmərə] *n* : cámara *f*

camouflage ['kæmə,flaʒ, -,flɑʒ] *n* : camuflaje *m* — ~ *vt* **-flaged; -flaging** : camuflar

camp ['kæmp] *n* **1** : campamento *m* **2** FACTION : bando *m* — ~ *vi* : acampar, ir de camping

campaign [kæm'peɪn] *n* : campaña *f* — ~ *vi* : hacer (una) campaña

camping ['kæmpɪŋ] *n* : camping *m*

campus ['kæmpəs] *n* : ciudad *f* universitaria

can¹ ['kæn] *v aux, past* **could** ['kʊd]; *present s & pl* **can 1** (*expressing possibility or permission*) : poder **2** (*expressing knowledge or ability*) : saber **3** *that cannot be!* : ¡no puede ser!

can² ['kæn] *n* : lata *f* — ~ *vt* **canned; canning** : enlatar

Canadian [kə'neɪdiən] *adj* : canadiense

canal [kə'næl] *n* : canal *m*

canary [kə'neri] *n, pl* **-naries** : canario *m*

cancel ['kæntsəl] *vt* **-celed** *or* **-celled; -celing** *or* **-celling** : cancelar — **cancellation** [,kæntsə'leɪʃən] *n* : cancelación *f*

cancer ['kæntsər] *n* : cáncer *m* — **cancerous** ['kæntsərəs] *adj* : canceroso

candelabra [,kændə'lɑbrə, -'læ-] *n, pl* **-bra** *or* **-bras** : candelabro *m*

candid ['kændɪd] *adj* : franco

candidate ['kændə,deɪt, -dət] *n* : candidato *m*, -ta *f* — **candidacy** ['kændədəsi] *n, pl* **-cies** : candidatura *f*

candle ['kændəl] *n* : vela *f* — **candlestick** ['kændəl,stɪk] *n* : candelero *m*

candor *or Brit* **candour** ['kændər] *n* : franqueza *f*

candy ['kændi] *n, pl* **-dies** : dulce *m*, caramelo *m*

cane ['keɪn] *n* **1** : bastón *m* (para andar), vara *f* (para castigar) **2** REED : caña *f*, mimbre *m* — ~ *vt* **caned; caning 1** : tapizar con mimbre **2** FLOG : azotar

canine ['keɪ,naɪn] *n or* ~ **tooth** : colmillo *m*, diente *m* canino — ~ *adj* : canino

canister ['kænəstər] *n* : lata *f*, bote *m* Spain

cannibal ['kænəbəl] *n* : caníbal *mf*

cannon ['kænən] *n, pl* **-nons** *or* **-non** : cañón *m*

cannot (can not) ['kæn,ɑt, kə'nɑt] → **can¹**

canny ['kæni] *adj* **cannier; -est** : astuto

canoe [kə'nu:] *n* : canoa *f*, piragua *f* — ~ *vi* **-noed; -noeing** : ir en canoa

canon ['kænən] *n* : canon *m* — **canonize** ['kænə,naɪz] *vt* **-ized; -izing** : canonizar

can opener *n* : abrelatas *m*

canopy ['kænəpi] *n, pl* **-pies** : dosel *m*

can't ['kænt, 'kɑnt] (*contraction of* **can not**) → **can¹**

cantaloupe ['kæntəl,o:p] *n* : melón *m*, cantalupo *m*

cantankerous [kæn'tæŋkərəs] *adj* : irritable, irascible

canteen [kæn'ti:n] *n* **1** FLASK : cantimplora *f* **2** CAFETERIA : cantina *f*

canter ['kæntər] *vi* : ir a medio galope — ~ *n* : medio galope *m*

canvas ['kænvəs] *n* **1** : lona *f* (tela) **2** : lienzo *m* (de pintar)

canvass ['kænvəs] *vt* **1** : solicitar votos de, hacer campaña entre **2** POLL : sondear — ~ *n* **1** : solicitación *f* (de votos) **2** POLL : sondeo *m*

canyon ['kænjən] *n* : cañón *m*

cap *n* **1** : gorra *f*, gorro *m* **2** TOP : tapa *f*, tapón *m* (de botellas) **3** LIMIT : tope *m* — ~ ['kæp] *vt* **capped; capping 1** COVER : tapar, cubrir **2** OUTDO : superar

capable ['keɪpəbəl] *adj* : capaz, competente — **capability** [,keɪpə'bɪləti] *n, pl* **-ties** : capacidad *f*

capacity [kə'pæsəti] *n, pl* **-ties 1** : capacidad *f* **2** ROLE : calidad *f*

cape¹ ['keɪp] *n* : cabo *m* (en geografía)

cape² *n* CLOAK : capa *f*

caper¹ ['keɪpər] *n* : alcaparra *f*

caper² *n* PRANK : broma *f*, travesura *f*

capital ['kæpətəl] *adj* **1** : capital **2** : mayúsculo (dícese de las letras) — ~ *n* **1** *or* ~ **city** : capital *f* **2** WEALTH : capital *m* **3** *or* ~ **letter** : mayúscula *f* — **capitalism** ['kæpətəl,ɪzəm] *n* : capitalismo *m* — **capitalist** ['kæpətəl,ɪst] *or* **capitalistic** [,kæpətəl'ɪstɪk] *adj* : capitalista — **capitalize** ['kæpətəl,aɪz] *vt* **-ized; -izing** FINANCE : capitalizar **2** : escribir con mayúscula — *vi* ~ **on** : sacar partido de

capitol ['kæpətəl] *n* : capitolio *m*

capitulate [kə'pɪtʃə,leɪt] *vi* **-lated; -lating** : capitular

capsize ['kæp,saɪz, kæp'saɪz] *v* **-sized; -sizing** *vt* : hacer volcar — *vi* : zozobrar, volcar(se)

capsule ['kæpsəl, -su:l] *n* : cápsula *f*

captain ['kæptən] *n* : capitán *m*, -tana *f*

caption ['kæpʃən] *n* **1** : leyenda *f* (al pie de una ilustración) **2** SUBTITLE : subtítulo *m*

captivate ['kæptə,veɪt] *vt* **-vated; -vating** : cautivar, encantar

captive ['kæptɪv] *adj* : cautivo — **~** *n* : cautivo *m*, -va *f* — **captivity** [kæp-'tɪvəṭi] *n* : cautiverio *m*

capture ['kæpʃər] *n* : captura *f*, apresamiento *m* — **~** *vt* **-tured; -turing 1** SEIZE : capturar, apresar **2 ~ one's interest** : captar el interés de uno

car ['kar] *n* **1** : automóvil *m*, coche *m*, carro *m* *Lat 2 or* **railroad** — : vagón *m*

carafe [kə'ræf, -'raf] *n* : garrafa *f*

caramel ['kɑrməl, 'kærəməl, -,mel] *n* : caramelo *m*, azúcar *f* quemada

carat ['kærət] *n* : quilate *m*

caravan ['kærə,væn] *n* : caravana *f*

carbohydrate [,kɑrbo'haɪ,dreɪt, -drət] *n* : carbohidrato *m*, hidrato *m* de carbono

carbon ['kɑrbən] *n* : carbono *m* — **carbon copy** *n* : copia *f*, duplicado *m*

carburetor ['kɑrbə,reɪṭər, -bjə-] *n* : carburador *m*

carcass ['kɑrkəs] *n* : cuerpo *m* (de un animal muerto)

card ['kɑrd] *n* **1** : tarjeta *f* **2** *or* **playing ~** : carta *f*, naipe *m* — **cardboard** ['kɑrd,bɔrd] *n* : cartón *m*

cardiac ['kɑrdi,æk] *adj* : cardíaco

cardigan ['kɑrdɪgən] *n* : cárdigan *m*

cardinal ['kɑrdənəl] *n* : cardenal *m* — **~** *adj* : cardinal, fundamental

care ['kær] *n* **1** : cuidado *m* **2** WORRY : preocupación **3 take ~ of** : cuidar (de) — **~** *vi* **cared; caring 1** : preocuparse, inquietarse **2 ~ for** TEND : cuidar (de), atender **3 ~ for** LIKE : querer **4 I don't ~** : no me importa

career [kə'rɪr] *n* : carrera *f* — **~** *vi* : ir a toda velocidad

carefree ['kær,fri:, ,kær-] *adj* : despreocupado

careful ['kærfəl] *adj* : cuidadoso — **carefully** ['kærfəli] *adv* : con cuidado, cuidadosamente — **careless** ['kærləs] *adj* : descuidado — **carelessness** ['kærləsnəs] *n* : descuido *m*

caress [kə'res] *n* : caricia *f* — **~** *vt* : acariciar

cargo ['kɑrgo:] *n*, *pl* **-goes** *or* **-gos** : cargamento *m*, carga *f*

caricature ['kærɪkə,tʃʊr] *n* : caricatura *f* — **~** *vt* **-tured; -turing** : caricaturizar

caring ['kærɪŋ] *adj* : solícito, afectuoso

carnage ['kɑrnɪdʒ] *n* : matanza *f*, carnicería *f*

carnal ['kɑrnəl] *adj* : carnal

carnation [kɑr'neɪʃən] *n* : clavel *m*

carnival ['kɑrnəvəl] *n* : carnaval *m*

carol ['kærəl] *n* : villancico *m*

carp ['kɑrp] *vi* **~ at** : quejarse de

carpenter ['kɑrpəntər] *n* : carpintero *m*,

-ra *f* — **carpentry** ['kɑrpəntri] *n* : carpintería *f*

carpet ['kɑrpət] *n* : alfombra *f*

carriage ['kærɪdʒ] *n* **1** : transporte *m* (de mercancías) **2** BEARING : porte *m* **3** *or* **baby ~** : cochecito *m* **4** *or* **horse-drawn ~** : carruaje *m*, coche *m*

carrier ['kæriər] *n* **1** : transportista *mf*, empresa *f* de transportes **2** : portador *m*, -dora *f* (de una enfermedad)

carrot ['kærət] *n* : zanahoria *f*

carry ['kæri] *v* **-ried; -rying** *vt* **1** : llevar **2** TRANSPORT : transportar **3** STOCK : vender **4** ENTAIL : acarrear, implicar **5 ~ oneself** : portarse — *vi* : oírse (dícese de sonidos) — **carry away** *vt* **get carried away** : exaltarse, entusiasmarse — **carry on** *vt* CONDUCT : realizar — *vi* **1** : portarse inapropiadamente **2** CONTINUE : seguir, continuar — **carry out** *vt* **1** PERFORM : llevar a cabo, realizar **2** FULFILL : cumplir

cart ['kɑrt] *n* : carreta *f*, carro *m* — **~** *vt* *or* **~ around** : acarrear

cartilage ['kɑrṭəlɪdʒ] *n* : cartílago *m*

carton ['kɑrtən] *n* : caja *f* (de cartón)

cartoon [kɑr'tu:n] *n* **1** : caricatura *f* **2** COMIC STRIP : historieta *f* **3** *or* **animated ~** : dibujos *mpl* animados

cartridge ['kɑrtrɪdʒ] *n* : cartucho *m*

carve ['kɑrv] *vt* **carved; carving 1** : tallar, esculpir **2** : trinchar (carne)

case ['keɪs] *n* **1** : caso *m* **2** BOX : caja *f* **3 in any ~** : en todo caso **4 in ~ of** : en caso de **5 just in ~** : por si acaso

cash ['kæʃ] *n* : efectivo *m*, dinero *m* en efectivo — **~** *vt* : convertir en efectivo, cobrar

cashew ['kæ,ʃu:, kə'ʃu:] *n* : anacardo *m*

cashier [kæ'ʃɪr] *n* : cajero *m*, -ra *f*

cashmere ['kæʒ,mɪr, 'kæʃ-] *n* : cachemira *f*

cash register *n* : caja *f* registradora

casino [kə'si:,no:] *n*, *pl* **-nos** : casino *m*

cask ['kæsk] *n* : barril *m*

casket ['kæskət] *n* : ataúd *m*

casserole ['kæsə,roːl] *n* **1** *or* **~ dish** : cazuela *f* **2** : guiso *m* (comida)

cassette [kə'set, kæ-] *n* : cassette *mf*

cast ['kæst] *vt* **cast; casting 1** THROW : arrojar, lanzar **2** : depositar (un voto) **3** : repartir (papeles dramáticos) **4** MOLD : fundir — **~** *n* **1** : elenco *m*, reparto *m* (de actores) **2** *or* **plaster ~** : molde *m* de yeso, escayola *f*

castanets [,kæstə'nets] *npl* : castañuelas *fpl*

castaway ['kæstə,weɪ] *n* : náufrago *m*, -ga *f*

cast iron *n* : hierro *m* fundido

castle ['kæsəl] n 1 : castillo m 2 : torre f (en ajedrez)

castrate ['kæs,treɪt] vt -trated; -trating : castrar

casual ['kæʒuəl] adj 1 CHANCE : casual, fortuito 2 INDIFFERENT : despreocupado 3 INFORMAL : informal — **casually** ['kæʒuəli, 'kæʒəli] adv 1 : de manera despreocupada 2 INFORMALLY : informalmente

casualty ['kæʒuəlti, 'kæʒəl-] n, pl -ties 1 : accidente m 2 VICTIM : víctima f; herido m, -da f 3 **casualties** npl : bajas fpl (militares)

cat ['kæt] n : gato m, -ta f

catalog or **catalogue** ['kæt̬əlɔg] n : catálogo m — ~ vt -loged or -logued; -loging or -loguing : catalogar

catapult ['kæt̬əpʌlt, -pʊlt] n : catapulta f

cataract ['kæt̬ərækt] n : catarata f

catastrophe [kə'tæstrəfi] n : catástrofe f — **catastrophic** [kæt̬ə'strɑfɪk] adj : catastrófico

catch ['kætʃ, 'kɛtʃ] v **caught** ['kɔt]; **catching** vt 1 CAPTURE, TRAP : capturar, atrapar 2 SURPRISE : sorprender 3 GRASP : agarrar, captar 4 SNAG : enganchar 5 : tomar (un tren, etc.) 6 **~ a cold** : resfriarse — vi 1 SNAG : engancharse 2 **~ fire** : prender fuego — **catching** ['kætʃɪŋ, 'kɛtʃ-] adj : contagioso — **catchy** ['kætʃi, 'kɛ-] adj **catchier; -est** : pegadizo, pegajoso Lat

category ['kæt̬əgori] n, pl -ries : categoría f — **categorical** [kæt̬ə'gorɪkəl] adj : categórico

cater ['keɪt̬ər] vi 1 : proveer comida 2 **~ to** : atender a — **caterer** ['keɪt̬ərər] n : proveedor m, -dora f de comida

caterpillar ['kæt̬ər,pɪlər] n : oruga f

catfish ['kæt,fɪʃ] n : bagre m

cathedral [kə'θi:drəl] n : catedral f

catholic ['kæθəlɪk] adj 1 : universal 2 **Catholic** : católico — **catholicism** [kə'θɑlə,sɪzəm] n : catolicismo m

cattle ['kæt̬əl] npl : ganado m (vacuno)

caught → **catch**

cauldron ['kɔldrən] n : caldera f

cauliflower ['kɑlɪ,flauər, 'kɔ-] n : coliflor f

cause ['kɔz] n 1 : causa f 2 REASON : motivo m — ~ vt **caused; causing** : causar

caustic ['kɔstɪk] adj : cáustico

caution ['kɔʃən] n 1 WARNING : advertencia f 2 CARE : precaución f, cautela f — ~ vt : advertir — **cautious** ['kɔʃəs] adj : cauteloso, precavido —

cautiously ['kɔʃəsli] adv : con precaución

cavalier [,kævə'lɪr] adj : arrogante, desdeñoso

cavalry ['kævəlri] n, pl -ries : caballería f

cave ['keɪv] n : cueva f — ~ vi **caved; caving** or **~ in** : hundirse

cavern ['kævərn] n : caverna f

cavity ['kævət̬i] n, pl -ties 1 : cavidad f 2 : caries f (dental)

cavort [kə'vort] vi : brincar

CD [,si:'di:] n : CD m, disco m compacto

cease ['si:s] v **ceased; ceasing** vt : dejar de — vi : cesar — **cease-fire** ['si:s'faɪr] n : alto m el fuego — **ceaseless** ['si:sləs] adj : incesante

cedar ['si:dər] n : cedro m

ceiling ['si:lɪŋ] n : techo m

celebrate ['sɛlə,breɪt] v -brated; -brating vt : celebrar — vi : divertirse — **celebrated** ['sɛlə,breɪt̬əd] adj : célebre — **celebration** [,sɛlə'breɪʃən] n 1 : celebración f 2 FESTIVITY : fiesta f — **celebrity** [sə'lɛbrət̬i] n, pl -ties : celebridad f

celery ['sɛləri] n, pl -eries : apio m

cell ['sɛl] n 1 : célula f 2 : celda f (en una cárcel, etc.)

cellar ['sɛlər] n 1 BASEMENT : sótano m 2 : bodega f (de vinos)

cello ['tʃɛ,lo:] n, pl -los : violoncelo m

cellular ['sɛljələr] adj : celular

cement [sɪ'mɛnt] n : cemento m — ~ vt : cementar

cemetery ['sɛmə,t̬ɛri] n, pl -teries : cementerio m

censor ['sɛnsər] vt : censurar — **censorship** ['sɛnsər,ʃɪp] n : censura f — **censure** ['sɛntʃər] n : censura f — ~ vt -sured; -suring : censurar, criticar

census ['sɛnsəs] n : censo m

cent ['sɛnt] n : centavo m

centennial [sɛn'tɛniəl] n : centenario m

center or Brit **centre** ['sɛntər] n : centro m — ~ v **centered** or Brit **centred**; **centering** or Brit **centring** vt : centrar — vi **~ on** : centrarse en

centigrade ['sɛntə,greɪd, 'sɑn-] adj : centígrado

centimeter ['sɛntə,mit̬ər, 'sɑn-] n : centímetro m

centipede ['sɛntə,pi:d] n : ciempiés m

central ['sɛntrəl] adj 1 : central 2 **a ~ location** : un lugar céntrico — **centralize** ['sɛntrə,laɪz] vt -ized; -izing : centralizar

centre ['sɛntər] → **center**

century ['sɛntʃəri] n, pl -ries : siglo m

ceramics [sə'ræmɪks] npl : cerámica f

cereal ['sɪriəl] *n* : cereal *m*

ceremony ['serə,moni] *n, pl* **-nies** : ceremonia *f* — **ceremonial** [,serə'moniəl] *adj* : ceremonial

certain ['sərtən] *adj* **1** : cierto **2 be ~ of** : estar seguro de **3 for ~** : seguro, con toda seguridad **4 make ~ of** : asegurarse de — **certainly** ['sərtənli] *adv* : desde luego, por supuesto — **certainty** ['sərtənti] *n, pl* **-ties** : certeza *f*, seguridad *f*

certify ['sərtə,faɪ] *vt* **-fied; -fying** : certificar — **certificate** [sər'tɪfɪkət] *n* : certificado *m*, partida *f*, acta *f*

chafe ['tʃeɪf] *v* **chafed; chafing** *vi* : rozarse — *vt* : rozar

chain ['tʃeɪn] *n* **1** : cadena *f* **2 ~ of events** : serie *f* de acontecimientos — *~ vt* : encadenar

chair ['tʃer] *n* **1** : silla *f* **2** : cátedra *f* (en una universidad) — *~ vt* : presidir — **chairman** ['tʃerman] *n, pl* **-men** [-mən, -mɛn] : presidente *m* — **chairperson** ['tʃer,pərsən] *n* : presidente *m*, -ta *f*

chalk ['tʃɔk] *n* : tiza *f*, gis *m* Lat

challenge ['tʃælɪndʒ] *vt* **-lenged; -lenging 1** DISPUTE : disputar, poner en duda **2** DARE : desafiar — *~ n* : reto *m*, desafío *m* — **challenging** ['tʃælɪndʒɪŋ] *adj* : estimulante

chamber ['tʃeɪmbər] *n* : cámara *f* — **chambermaid** ['tʃeɪmbər,meɪd] *n* : camarera *f*

champagne [ʃæm'peɪn] *n* : champaña *m*, champán *m*

champion ['tʃæmpiən] *n* : campeón *m*, -peona *f* — *~ vt* : defender — **championship** ['tʃæmpiən,ʃɪp] *n* : campeonato *m*

chance ['tʃæns] *n* **1** LUCK : azar *m*, suerte *f* **2** OPPORTUNITY : oportunidad *f* **3** LIKELIHOOD : probabilidad *f* **4 by ~** : por casualidad **5 take a ~** : arriesgarse — *~ vt* **chanced; chancing** RISK : arriesgar — *~ adj* : fortuito

chandelier [,ʃændə'lɪr] *n* : araña *f* (de luces)

change ['tʃeɪndʒ] *v* **changed; changing** *vt* **1** : cambiar **2** SWITCH : cambiar de — *vi* **1** : cambiar **2** *or* **~ clothes** : cambiarse (de ropa) — *~ n* : cambio *m* — **changeable** ['tʃeɪndʒəbəl] *adj* : cambiable

channel ['tʃænəl] *n* **1** : canal *m* **2** : cauce *m* (de un río) **3** MEANS : vía *f*, medio *m*

chant ['tʃænt] *v* : cantar — *~ n* : canto *m*

chaos ['keɪɑs] *n* : caos *m* — **chaotic** [keɪ'ɑtɪk] *adj* : caótico

chap[1] ['tʃæp] *vi* **chapped; chapping** : agrietarse

chap[2] *n* : tipo *m* *fam*

chapel ['tʃæpəl] *n* : capilla *f*

chaperon *or* **chaperone** ['ʃæpə,roːn] *n* : acompañante *mf*

chaplain ['tʃæplɪn] *n* : capellán *m*

chapter ['tʃæptər] *n* : capítulo *m*

char ['tʃɑr] *vt* **charred; charring** : carbonizar

character ['kærɪktər] *n* **1** : carácter *m* **2** : personaje *m* (en una novela, etc.) — **characteristic** [,kærɪktə'rɪstɪk] *adj* : característico — *~ n* : característica *f* — **characterize** ['kærɪktə,raɪz] *vt* **-ized; -izing** : caracterizar

charcoal ['tʃɑr,koːl] *n* : carbón *m*

charge ['tʃɑrdʒ] *n* **1** : carga *f* (eléctrica) **2** COST : precio *m* **3** BURDEN : carga *f*, peso *m* **4** ACCUSATION : cargo *m*, acusación *f* **5 in ~ of** : encargado de **6 take ~ of** : hacerse cargo de — *~ v* **charged; charging** *vt* **1** : cargar **2** ENTRUST : encargar **3** COMMAND : ordenar, mandar **4** ACCUSE : acusar — *vi* **1** : cargar **2 ~ too much** : cobrar demasiado

charisma [kə'rɪzmə] *n* : carisma *m* — **charismatic** [,kærəz'mætɪk] *adj* : carismático

charity ['tʃærəti] *n, pl* **-ties 1** : organización *f* benéfica **2** GOODWILL : caridad *f*

charlatan ['ʃɑrlətən] *n* : charlatán *m*, -tana *f*

charm ['tʃɑrm] *n* **1** : encanto *m* **2** SPELL : hechizo *m* — *~ vt* : encantar, cautivar — **charming** ['tʃɑrmɪŋ] *adj* : encantador

chart ['tʃɑrt] *n* **1** MAP : carta *f* **2** DIAGRAM : gráfico *m*, tabla *f* — *~ vt* : trazar un mapa de

charter ['tʃɑrtər] *n* : carta *f* — *~ vt* : alquilar, fletar

chase ['tʃeɪs] *n* : persecución *f* — *~ vt* **chased; chasing 1** PURSUE : perseguir **2** *or* **~ away** : ahuyentar

chasm ['kæzəm] *n* : abismo *m*

chaste ['tʃeɪst] *adj* **chaster; -est** : casto — **chastity** ['tʃæstəti] *n* : castidad *f*

chat ['tʃæt] *vi* **chatted; chatting** : charlar — *~ n* : charla *f* — **chatter** ['tʃæt̬ər] *vi* **1** : parlotear *fam* **2** : castañetear (dícese de los dientes) — *~ n* : parloteo *m*, cháchara *f* — **chatterbox** ['tʃæt̬ər,bɑks] *n* : parlanchín *m*, -china *f* — **chatty** ['tʃæti] *adj* **chattier; chattiest 1** : parlanchín **2** INFORMAL : familiar

chauffeur ['ʃoːfər, ʃoʊ'fər] *n* : chofer *mf*

chauvinist ['ʃoːvənɪst] *or* **chauvinistic**

[ʃoːvɪˈnɪstɪk] *adj* : chauvinista, patriotero

cheap [ˈtʃiːp] *adj* **1** INEXPENSIVE : barato **2** SHODDY : de mala calidad — ~ *adv* : barato — **cheapen** [ˈtʃiːpən] *vt* : rebajar — **cheaply** [ˈtʃiːpli] *adv* : barato, a precio bajo

cheat [ˈtʃiːt] *vt* : defraudar, estafar — *vi* **1** : hacer trampa(s) **2** ~ **on s.o.** : engañar a algn — ~ *or* **cheater** [ˈtʃiːtər] *n* : tramposo *m*, -sa *f*

check [ˈtʃɛk] *n* **1** RESTRAINT : freno *m* **2** INSPECTION : inspección *f*, comprobación *f* **3** DRAFT : cheque *m* **4** BILL : cuenta *f* **5** : jaque *m* (en ajedrez) **6** : tela a cuadros — ~ *vt* **1** RESTRAIN : frenar, contener **2** INSPECT : revisar **3** VERIFY : comprobar **4** : dar jaque (en ajedrez) **5** : enregistrarse (en un hotel) **6** ~ **out** : irse (de un hotel) **7** ~ **out** VERIFY : verificar, comprobar

checkers [ˈtʃɛkərz] *n* : damas *fpl*

checkmate [ˈtʃɛkˌmeɪt] *n* : jaque *m* mate

checkpoint [ˈtʃɛkˌpɔɪnt] *n* : puesto *m* de control

checkup [ˈtʃɛkˌʌp] *n* : chequeo *m*, examen *m* médico

cheek [ˈtʃiːk] *n* : mejilla *f*

cheer [ˈtʃɪr] *n* **1** CHEERFULNESS : alegría *f* **2** APPLAUSE : aclamación *f* **3** ~ **s!** : ¡salud! — ~ *vt* **1** GLADDEN : alegrar **2** APPLAUD, SHOUT : aclamar, aplaudir — **cheerful** [ˈtʃɪrfəl] *adj* : alegre

cheese [ˈtʃiːz] *n* : queso *m*

cheetah [ˈtʃiːtə] *n* : guepardo *m*

chef [ˈʃɛf] *n* : chef *m*

chemical [ˈkɛmɪkəl] *adj* : químico — ~ *n* : sustancia *f* química — **chemist** [ˈkɛmɪst] *n* : químico *m*, -ca *f* — **chemistry** [ˈkɛmɪstri] *n*, *pl* **-tries** : química *f*

cheque [ˈtʃɛk] *Brit* → **check**

cherish [ˈtʃɛrɪʃ] *vt* **1** : querer, apreciar **2** HARBOR : abrigar (un recuerdo, una esperanza, etc.)

cherry [ˈtʃɛri] *n*, *pl* **-ries** : cereza *f*

chess [ˈtʃɛs] *n* : ajedrez *m*

chest [ˈtʃɛst] *n* **1** BOX : cofre *m* **2** : pecho *m* (del cuerpo) **3** *or* ~ **of drawers** : cómoda *f*

chestnut [ˈtʃɛsnʌt] *n* : castaña *f*

chew [ˈtʃuː] *vt* : masticar, mascar — **chewing gum** *n* : chicle *m*

chic [ˈʃiːk] *adj* : elegante

chick [ˈtʃɪk] *n* : polluelo *m*, -la *f* — **chicken** [ˈtʃɪkən] *n* : pollo *m* — **chicken pox** *n* : varicela *f*

chicory [ˈtʃɪkəri] *n*, *pl* **-ries 1** : endivia *f* (para ensaladas) **2** : achicoria *f* (aditivo de café)

chief [ˈtʃiːf] *adj* : principal — ~ *n* : jefe

m, -fa *f* — **chiefly** [ˈtʃiːfli] *adv* : principalmente

child [ˈtʃaɪld] *n*, *pl* **children** [ˈtʃɪldrən] **1** : niño *m*, -ña *f* **2** OFFSPRING : hijo *m*, -ja *f* — **childbirth** [ˈtʃaɪldˌbərθ] *n* : parto *m* — **childhood** [ˈtʃaɪldˌhʊd] *n* : infancia *f*, niñez *f* — **childish** [ˈtʃaɪldɪʃ] *adj* : infantil — **childlike** [ˈtʃaɪldˌlaɪk] *adj* : infantil, inocente — **childproof** [ˈtʃaɪldˌpruːf] *adj* : a prueba de niños

Chilean [ˈtʃɪliən, tʃɪˈleɪən] *adj* : chileno

chili *or* **chile** *or* **chilli** [ˈtʃɪli] *n*, *pl* **chilies** *or* **chiles** *or* **chillies 1** *or* ~ **pepper** : chile *m* **2** : chile *m* con carne

chill [ˈtʃɪl] *n* **1** CHILLINESS : frío *m* **2 catch a** ~ : resfriarse **3 there's a** ~ **in the air** : hace fresco — ~ *adj* : frío — ~ *v* : enfriar — **chilly** [ˈtʃɪli] *adj* **chillier; -est** : fresco, frío

chime [ˈtʃaɪm] *vi* **chimed; chiming** : repicar, sonar — ~ *n* : carillón *m*

chimney [ˈtʃɪmni] *n*, *pl* **-neys** : chimenea *f*

chimpanzee [ˌtʃɪmpænˈziː, ˌtʃɪm-; tʃɪmˈpænzi, ˌtʃɪm-] *n* : chimpancé *m*

chin [ˈtʃɪn] *n* : barbilla *f*

china [ˈtʃaɪnə] *n* : porcelana *f*, loza *f* — **Chinese** [ˈtʃaɪˈniːz, -ˈniːs] *adj* : chino — ~ *n* : chino *m* (idioma)

chink [ˈtʃɪŋk] *n* : grieta *f*

chip [ˈtʃɪp] *n* **1** : astilla *f* (de madera o vidrio), lasca *f* (de piedra) **2** : ficha *f* (de póker, etc.) **3** NICK : desportilladura *f* **4** *or* **computer** ~ : chip *m* **5** *or* **potato chips** — ~ *v* **chipped; chipping** *vt* : desportillar — *vi* **1** : desportillarse **2** ~ **in** : contribuir

chipmunk [ˈtʃɪpˌmʌŋk] *n* : ardilla *f* listada

chiropodist [kəˈrɑpədɪst, ʃə-] *n* : podólogo *m*, -ga *f*

chiropractor [ˈkaɪrəˌpræktər] *n* : quiropráctico *m*, -ca *f*

chirp [ˈtʃərp] *vi* : piar, gorjear

chisel [ˈtʃɪzəl] *n* : cincel *m* (para piedras, etc.), formón *m*, escoplo *m* (para madera) — ~ *vt* **-eled** *or* **-elled; -eling** *or* **-elling** : cincelar, tallar

chit [ˈtʃɪt] *n* : nota *f*

chitchat [ˈtʃɪtˌtʃæt] *n* : cháchara *f fam*

chivalrous [ˈʃɪvəlrəs] *adj* : caballeroso — **chivalry** [ˈʃɪvəlri] *n*, *pl* **-ries** : caballerosidad *f*

chive [ˈtʃaɪv] *n* : cebollino *m*

chlorine [ˈklɔriːn] *n* : cloro *m*

chock-full [ˈtʃɑkˈfʊl, ˈtʃɑk-] *adj* : repleto, atestado

chocolate [ˈtʃɑkələt, ˈtʃɔk-] *n* : chocolate *m*

choice [ˈtʃɔɪs] *n* **1** : elección *f*, selección

f **2** PREFERENCE : preferencia *f* — ~ *adj* **choicer; -est** : selecto

choir ['kwaɪr] *n* : coro *m*

choke ['tʃoːk] *v* **choked; choking** *vt* **1** : asfixiar, estrangular **2** BLOCK : atascar — *vi* : asfixiarse, atragantarse (con comida) — ~ *n* : estárter *m* (de un motor)

choose ['tʃuːz] *v* **chose** ['tʃoːz]; **chosen** ['tʃoːzən]; **choosing** *vt* **1** SELECT : escoger, elegir **2** DECIDE : decidir — *vi* : escoger — **choosy** *or* **choosey** ['tʃuːzi] *adj* **choosier; -est** : exigente

chop ['tʃɑp] *vt* **chopped; chopping 1** : cortar, picar (carne, etc.) **2** ~ **down** : talar — ~ *n* : chuleta *f* (de cerdo, etc.) — **choppy** ['tʃɑpi] *adj* **-pier; -est** : picado, agitado

chopsticks ['tʃɑpˌstɪks] *npl* : palillos *mpl*

chord ['kɔrd] *n* : acorde *m* (en música)

chore ['tʃor] *n* **1** : tarea *f* **2 household** ~**s** : faenas *fpl* domésticas

choreography [ˌkori'ɑɡrəfi] *n, pl* **-phies** : coreografía *f*

chortle ['tʃɔrtəl] *vi* **-tled; -tling** : reírse (con satisfacción o júbilo)

chorus ['korəs] *n* **1** : coro *m* (grupo de personas) **2** REFRAIN : estribillo *m*

chose, chosen → **choose**

christen ['krɪsən] *vt* : bautizar — **christening** ['krɪsənɪŋ] *n* : bautizo *m*

Christian ['krɪstʃən] *n* : cristiano *m*, -na *f* — ~ *adj* : cristiano — **Christianity** [ˌkrɪstʃi'ænəti, ˌkrɪstʃæ-] *n* : cristianismo *m*

Christmas ['krɪsməs] *n* : Navidad *f*

chrome ['kroːm] *n* : cromo *m*

chronic ['krɑnɪk] *adj* : crónico

chronicle ['krɑnɪkəl] *n* : crónica *f*

chronology [krə'nɑlədʒi] *n, pl* **-gies** : cronología *f* — **chronological** [ˌkrɑnə'lɑdʒɪkəl] *adj* : cronológico

chrysanthemum [krɪ'sænθəməm] *n* : crisantemo *m*

chubby ['tʃʌbi] *adj* **-bier; -est** : regordete *fam*, rechoncho *fam*

chuck ['tʃʌk] *vt* : tirar, arrojar

chuckle ['tʃʌkəl] *vi* **-led; -ling** : reírse (entre dientes) — ~ *n* : risa *f* ahogada

chum ['tʃʌm] *n* : amigo *m*, -ga *f*, compinche *mf fam* — **chummy** ['tʃʌmi] *adj* **-mier; -est** : muy amigable

chunk ['tʃʌŋk] *n* : trozo *m*, pedazo *m*

church ['tʃərtʃ] *n* : iglesia *f*

churn ['tʃərn] *n* : mantequera *f* — ~ *vt* **1** : agitar **2** ~ **out** : producir en grandes cantidades

chute ['ʃuːt] *n* **1** : vertedor *m* **2** SLIDE : tobogán *m*

cider ['saɪdər] *n* : sidra *f*

cigar [sɪ'ɡɑr] *n* : puro *m* — **cigarette** [ˌsɪɡə'rɛt, 'sɪɡəˌrɛt] *n* : cigarrillo *m*, cigarro *m*

cinch ['sɪntʃ] *n* **it's a** ~ : es pan comido

cinema ['sɪnəmə] *n* : cine *m*

cinnamon ['sɪnəmən] *n* : canela *f*

cipher ['saɪfər] *n* **1** ZERO : cero *m* **2** CODE : cifra *f*

circa ['sərkə] *prep* : hacia

circle ['sərkəl] *n* : círculo *m* — ~ *v* **-cled; -cling** *vt* **1** : dar vueltas alrededor de **2** : trazar un círculo alrededor de (un número, etc.) — *vi* : dar vueltas

circuit ['sərkət] *n* : circuito *m* — **circuitous** [ˌsər'kjuːətəs] *adj* : tortuoso

circular ['sərkjələr] *adj* : circular — ~ *n* LEAFLET : circular *f*

circulate ['sərkjəˌleɪt] *v* **-lated; -lating** *vt* : hacer circular — *vi* : circular — **circulation** [ˌsərkjə'leɪʃən] *n* **1** : circulación *f* **2** : tirada *f* (de una publicación)

circumcise ['sərkəmˌsaɪz] *vt* **-cised; -cising** : circuncidar — **circumcision** [ˌsərkəm'sɪʒən, 'sərkəm-] *n* : circuncisión *f*

circumference [sər'kʌmfrənts] *n* : circunferencia *f*

circumspect ['sərkəmˌspɛkt] *adj* : circunspecto, prudente

circumstance ['sərkəmˌstænts] *n* **1** : circunstancia *f* **2 under no** ~**s** : bajo ningún concepto

circus ['sərkəs] *n* : circo *m*

cistern ['sɪstərn] *n* : cisterna *f*

cite ['saɪt] *vt* **cited; citing** : citar — **citation** [saɪ'teɪʃən] *n* : citación *f*

citizen ['sɪtəzən] *n* : ciudadano *m*, -na *f* — **citizenship** ['sɪtəzənˌʃɪp] *n* : ciudadanía *f*

citrus ['sɪtrəs] *n, pl* **-rus** *or* **-ruses** *or* ~ **fruit** : cítrico *m*

city ['sɪti] *n, pl* **cities** : ciudad *f*

civic ['sɪvɪk] *adj* : cívico — **civics** ['sɪvɪks] *ns & pl* : civismo *m*

civil ['sɪvəl] *adj* : civil — **civilian** [sə'vɪljən] *n* : civil *mf* — **civility** [sə'vɪləti] *n, pl* **-ties** : cortesía *f* — **civilization** [ˌsɪvələ'zeɪʃən] *n* : civilización *f* — **civilize** ['sɪvəˌlaɪz] *vt* **-lized; -lizing** : civilizar

clad ['klæd] *adj* ~ **in** : vestido de

claim ['kleɪm] *vt* **1** DEMAND : reclamar **2** MAINTAIN : afirmar, sostener **3** ~ **responsibility** : atribuirse la responsabilidad — ~ *n* **1** DEMAND : demanda *f*, reclamación *f* **2** ASSERTION : afirmación *f*

clam ['klæm] *n* : almeja *f*

clamber ['klæmbər] *vi* : trepar (con torpeza)

clammy ['klæmi] *adj* **-mier; -est** : húmedo y algo frío

clamor ['klæmər] *n* : clamor *m* — ~ *vi* : clamar

clamp ['klæmp] *n* : abrazadera *f* — ~ *vt* : sujetar con abrazaderas — ~ *vi* — **down on** : reprimir

clan ['klæn] *n* : clan *m*

clandestine [klæn'destɪn] *adj* : clandestino

clang ['klæŋ] *n* : ruido *m* metálico

clap ['klæp] *v* **clapped; clapping** *vt* 1 : aplaudir 2 **~ one's hands** : dar palmadas — *vi* : aplaudir — ~ *n* : palmada *f*

clarify ['klærə,faɪ] *vt* **-fied; -fying** : aclarar — **clarification** [,klærəfə'keɪʃən] *n* : clarificación *f*

clarinet [,klærə'nɛt] *n* : clarinete *m*

clarity ['klærəti] *n* : claridad *f*

clash ['klæʃ] *vi* 1 : chocar, enfrentarse 2 CONFLICT : estar en conflicto — ~ *n* 1 CRASH : choque *m* 2 CONFLICT : conflicto *m*

clasp ['klæsp] *n* : broche *m*, cierre *m* — ~ *vt* 1 : abrazar (a una persona), agarrar (una cosa) 2 FASTEN : abrochar

class ['klæs] *n* : clase *f*

classic ['klæsɪk] *or* **classical** ['klæsɪkəl] *adj* : clásico — ~ *n* : clásico *m*

classify ['klæsə,faɪ] *vt* **-fied; -fying** : clasificar — **classification** [,klæsəfə'keɪʃən] *n* : clasificación *f* — **classified** ['klæsə,faɪd] *adj* RESTRICTED : secreto

classmate ['klæs,meɪt] *n* : compañero *m*, -ra *f* de clase

classroom ['klæs,ru:m] *n* : aula *f*, salón *m* de clase

clatter ['klætər] *vi* : hacer ruido — ~ *n* : estrépito *m*

clause ['klɔz] *n* : cláusula *f*

claustrophobia [,klɔstrə'fobiə] *n* : claustrofobia *f*

claw ['klɔ] *n* : garra *f*, uña *f* (de un gato), pinza *f* (de un crustáceo) — ~ *vt* : arañar

clay ['kleɪ] *n* : arcilla *f*

clean ['kli:n] *adj* 1 : limpio 2 UNADULTERATED : puro 3 SPOTLESS : impecable — ~ *vt* : limpiar — ~ *adv* : limpio — **cleaner** ['kli:nər] *n* 1 : limpiador *m*, -dora *f* 2 DRY CLEANER : tintorería *f* — **cleanliness** ['klɛnlinəs] *n* : limpieza *f* — **cleanse** ['klɛnz] *vt* **cleansed; cleansing** : limpiar, purificar

clear ['klɪr] *adj* 1 : claro 2 TRANSPARENT : transparente 3 UNOBSTRUCTED : despejado, libre — ~ *vt* 1 : despejar (una superficie), desatascar (un tubo, etc.) 2 EXONERATE : absolver 3 : saltar por encima de (un obstáculo) 4 **~ the table** : levantar la mesa 5 **~ up** RESOLVE : aclarar, resolver — *vi* 1 **~ up** BRIGHTEN : despejarse (dícese del tiempo, etc.) 2 **~ up** VANISH : desaparecer (dícese de una infección, etc.) — ~ *adv* 1 **make oneself ~** : explicarse 2 **stand ~!** : ¡aléjate! — **clearance** ['klɪrəns] *n* 1 SPACE : espacio *m* (libre) 2 AUTHORIZATION : autorización *f* 3 **~ sale** : liquidación *f* — **clearing** ['klɪrɪŋ] *n* : claro *m* — **clearly** ['klɪrli] *adv* 1 DISTINCTLY : claramente 2 OBVIOUSLY : obviamente

cleaver ['kli:vər] *n* : cuchillo *m* de carnicero

clef ['klɛf] *n* : clave *f*

cleft ['klɛft] *n* : hendidura *f*, grieta *f*

clement ['klɛmənt] *adj* : clemente — **clemency** ['klɛmənsi] *n* : clemencia *f*

clench ['klɛntʃ] *vt* : apretar

clergy ['klərdʒi] *n*, *pl* **-gies** : clero *m* — **clergyman** ['klərdʒimən] *n*, *pl* **-men** [-mən, -,mɛn] : clérigo *m* — **clerical** ['klɛrɪkəl] *adj* 1 : clerical 2 **~ work** : trabajo *m* de oficina

clerk ['klərk, *Brit* 'klɑrk] *n* 1 : oficinista *mf*; empleado *m*, -da *f* de oficina 2 SALESPERSON : dependiente *m*, -ta *f*

clever ['klɛvər] *adj* 1 SKILLFUL : ingenioso, hábil 2 SMART : listo, inteligente — **cleverly** ['klɛvərli] *adv* : ingeniosamente — **cleverness** ['klɛvərnəs] *n* 1 SKILL : ingenio *m* 2 INTELLIGENCE : inteligencia *f*

cliché [kli'ʃeɪ] *n* : cliché *m*

click ['klɪk] *vt* : chasquear — *vi* 1 : chasquear 2 GET ALONG : llevarse bien — ~ *n* : chasquido *m*

client ['klaɪənt] *n* : cliente *m*, -ta *f* — **clientele** [,klaɪən'tɛl, ,kli:-] *n* : clientela *f*

cliff ['klɪf] *n* : acantilado *m*

climate ['klaɪmət] *n* : clima *m*

climax ['klaɪ,mæks] *n* : clímax *m*, punto *m* culminante

climb ['klaɪm] *vt* : escalar, subir a, trepar a — *vi* 1 RISE : subir 2 *or* **~ up** : subirse, treparse — ~ *n* : subida *f*

clinch ['klɪntʃ] *vt* : cerrar (un acuerdo, etc.)

cling ['klɪŋ] *vi* **clung** ['klʌŋ]; **clinging** : adherirse, pegarse

clinic ['klɪnɪk] *n* : clínica *f* — **clinical** ['klɪnɪkəl] *adj* : clínico

clink ['klɪŋk] *vi* : tintinear

clip ['klɪp] *vt* **clipped; clipping** 1 CUT

: cortar, recortar **2** FASTEN : sujetar (con un clip) — ~ n **1** FASTENER : clip m **2 at a good** ~ : a buen trote **3** ~ **paper clip** — **clippers** ['klɪpərz] npl **1** : maquinilla f para cortar el pelo **2 or nail** ~ : cortauñas m

cloak ['klok] n : capa f

clock ['klɑk] **1** : reloj m (de pared) **2 around the** ~ : las veinticuatro horas — **clockwise** ['klɑk,waɪz] adv & adj : en el sentido de las agujas del reloj — **clockwork** ['klɑk,wərk] n **1** : mecanismo m de relojería **2 like** ~ : con precisión

clog ['klɑg] n : zueco m — v **clogged; clogging** vt : atascar, obstruir — vi or ~ **up** : atascarse

cloister ['klɔɪstər] n : claustro m

close¹ ['kloːz] v **closed; closing** vt : cerrar — vi **1** : cerrarse **2** TERMINATE : terminar **3** ~ **in** : acercarse — ~ n : final m

close² ['kloːs] adj **closer; closest 1** NEAR : cercano, próximo **2** INTIMATE : íntimo **3** STRICT : estricto **4** STUFFY : sofocante **5 a** ~ **game** : un juego reñido — ~ adv : cerca, de cerca — **closely** ['kloːsli] adv : cerca, de cerca — **closeness** ['kloːsnəs] n **1** NEARNESS : cercanía f **2** INTIMACY : intimidad f

closet ['klɑzət] n : armario m, clóset m Lat

closure ['kloːʒər] n : cierre m

clot ['klɑt] n : coágulo m — v **clotted; clotting** vt : coagular, cuajar — vi : coagularse

cloth ['klɔθ] n, pl **cloths** ['klɔðz, 'klɔθs] **1** FABRIC : tela f **2** RAG : trapo m — **clothe** ['kloːð] vt **clothed** or **clad** ['klæd]; **clothing** : vestir — **clothes** ['kloz, 'kloːðz] npl **1** : ropa f **2 put on one's** ~ : vestirse — **clothespin** ['kloːz,pɪn] n : pinza f (para la ropa) — **clothing** ['kloːðɪŋ] n : ropa f

cloud ['klaʊd] n : nube f — ~ vt : nublar — vi or ~ **over** : nublarse — **cloudy** ['klaʊdi] adj **cloudier; -est** : nublado

clout ['klaʊt] n **1** BLOW : golpe m, tortazo m fam **2** INFLUENCE : influencia f

clove ['kloːv] n **1** : clavo m **2** : diente m (de ajo)

clover ['kloːvər] n : trébol m

clown ['klaʊn] n : payaso m, -sa f — or ~ **around** vi : payasear

cloying ['klɔɪŋ] adj : empalagoso

club ['klʌb] n **1** : garrote m, porra f **2** ASSOCIATION : club m **3** ~ **s** mpl : tréboles mpl (en los naipes) — ~ vt **clubbed; clubbing** : aporrear

cluck ['klʌk] vi : cloquear

clue ['kluː] n **1** : pista f, indicio m **2 I haven't got a** ~ : no tengo la menor idea

clump ['klʌmp] n : grupo m (de arbustos)

clumsy ['klʌmzi] adj **-sier; -est** : torpe — **clumsiness** ['klʌmzinəs] n : torpeza f

cluster ['klʌstər] n : grupo m, racimo m (de uvas, etc.) — ~ vi : agruparse

clutch ['klʌtʃ] vt : agarrar, asir — ~ **at** : tratar de agarrar — ~ n : embrague m, clutch m Lat (de un automóvil)

clutter ['klʌtər] vt : llenar desordenadamente — ~ n : desorden m, revoltijo m

coach ['koːtʃ] n **1** CARRIAGE : carruaje m, carroza f **2** : vagón m de pasajeros (de un tren) **3** BUS : autobús m **4** : pasaje m aéreo de segunda clase **5** TRAINER : entrenador m, -dora f — vt : entrenar (a un atleta), dar clases particulares a (un alumno)

coagulate [koˈægjəˌleɪt] v **-lated; -lating** vt : coagular — vi : coagularse

coal ['koːl] n : carbón m

coalition [ˌkoːəˈlɪʃən] n : coalición f

coarse ['kors] adj **coarser; -est 1** : tosco, basto **2** CRUDE, VULGAR : grosero, ordinario — **coarseness** ['korsnəs] n : aspereza f, tosquedad f

coast ['koːst] n : costa f — vi : ir en punto muerto (dícese de un automóvil), deslizarse (dícese de una bicicleta) — **coastal** ['koːstəl] adj : costero

coaster ['koːstər] n : posavasos m

coast guard n : guardacostas mpl

coastline ['koːstˌlaɪn] n : litoral m

coat ['koːt] n **1** : abrigo m **2** : pelaje m (de un animal) **3** : mano f (de pintura) — ~ vt : cubrir, revestir — **coating** ['koːtɪŋ] n : capa f — **coat of arms** : escudo m de armas

coax ['koːks] vt : engatusar

cob ['kɑb] → **corncob**

cobblestone ['kɑbəlˌstoːn] n : adoquín m

cobweb ['kɑbˌwɛb] n : telaraña f

cocaine [koˈkeɪn, 'koːˌkeɪn] n : cocaína f

cock ['kɑk] n **1** ROOSTER : gallo m **2** FAUCET : grifo m **3** : martillo m (de un arma de fuego) — ~ vt **1** : amartillar (un arma de fuego) **2** ~ **one's head** : ladear la cabeza — **cockeyed** ['kɑkˌaɪd] adj **1** ASKEW : ladeado **2** ABSURD : absurdo

cockpit ['kɑkˌpɪt] n : cabina f

cockroach ['kɑkˌroːtʃ] n : cucaracha f

cocktail ['kɑk,teɪl] *n* : coctel *m*, cóctel *m*

cocky ['kɑki] *adj* **cockier; -est** : engreído, arrogante

cocoa ['ko:ko:] *n* **1** : cacao *m* **2** : chocolate *m* (bebida)

coconut ['ko:kə,nʌt] *n* : coco *m*

cocoon [kə'ku:n] *n* : capullo *m*

cod ['kɑd] *ns & pl* : bacalao *m*

coddle ['kɑdəl] *vt* **-dled; -dling** : mimar

code ['ko:d] *n* : código *m*

coeducational [,ko:edʒə'keɪʃənəl] *adj* : mixto

coerce [ko'ərs] *vt* **-erced; -ercing** : coaccionar, forzar — **coercion** [ko'ərʒən, -ʃən] *n* : coacción *f*

coffee ['kɔfi] *n* : café *m* — **coffeepot** ['kɔfi,pɑt] *n* : cafetera *f*

coffer ['kɔfər] *n* : cofre *m*

coffin ['kɔfən] *n* : ataúd *m*, féretro *m*

cog ['kɑg] *n* : diente *m* (de una rueda)

cogent ['ko:dʒənt] *adj* : convincente, persuasivo

cognac ['ko:n,jæk] *n* : coñac *m*

cogwheel ['kɑg,hwi:l] *n* : rueda *f* dentada

coherent [ko'hɪrənt] *adj* : coherente

coil ['kɔɪl] *vt* : enrollar — *vi* : enrollarse — ～ *n* **1** ROLL : rollo *m* **2** : tirabuzón *m* (de pelo), espiral *f* (de humo)

coin ['kɔɪn] *n* : moneda *f* — ～ *vt* : acuñar

coincide [,ko:n'saɪd, 'ko:n,saɪd] *vi* **-cided; -ciding** : coincidir — **coincidence** [ko'ɪnsədəns] *n* : coincidencia *f*, casualidad *f* — **coincidental** [ko,ɪnsə'dentəl] *adj* : casual, fortuito

coke ['ko:k] *n* : coque *m* (combustible)

colander ['kɑləndər, 'kʌ-] *n* : colador *m*

cold ['ko:ld] *adj* **1** : frío **2 be** ～ : tener frío **3 it's** ～ **today** : hace frío hoy — ～ *n* **1** : frío *m* **2** : resfriado *m* (en medicina) **3 catch a** ～ : resfriarse

coleslaw ['ko:l,slɔ] *n* : ensalada *f* de col

colic ['kɑlɪk] *n* : cólico *m*

collaborate [kə'læbə,reɪt] *vi* **-rated; -rating** : colaborar — **collaboration** [kə,læbə'reɪʃən] *n* : colaboración *f* — **collaborator** [kə'læbə,reɪtər] *n* : colaborador *m*, -dora *f*

collapse [kə'læps] *vi* **-lapsed; -lapsing** **1** : derrumbarse, hundirse **2** : sufrir un colapso (físico o mental) — ～ *n* **1** FALL : derrumbamiento *m* **2** BREAKDOWN : colapso *m* — **collapsible** [kə'læpsəbəl] *adj* : plegable

collar ['kɑlər] *n* : cuello *m* (de camisa, etc.), collar *m* (para animales) — **collarbone** ['kɑlər,bo:n] *n* : clavícula *f*

colleague ['kɑli:g] *n* : colega *m f*

collect [kə'lekt] *vt* **1** GATHER : reunir **2** : coleccionar, juntar (timbres, etc.) **3**

: recaudar (fondos, etc.) — *vi* **1** ACCUMULATE : acumularse, juntarse **2** CONGREGATE : congregarse, reunirse — *adv* **call** ～ : llamar a cobro revertido, llamar por cobrar *Lat* — **collection** [kə'lekʃən] *n* **1** : colección *f* **2** : colecta *f* (de contribuciones) — **collective** [kə'lektɪv] *adj* : colectivo — **collector** [kə'lektər] *n* **1** : coleccionista *m f* **2** : cobrador *m*, -dora *f* (de deudas)

college ['kɑlɪdʒ] *n* **1** : instituto *m* (a nivel universitario) **2** : colegio *m* (electoral, etc.)

collide [kə'laɪd] *vi* **-lided; -liding** : chocar, colisionar — **collision** [kə'lɪʒən] *n* : choque *m*, colisión *f*

colloquial [kə'lo:kwiəl] *adj* : coloquial, familiar

cologne [kə'lo:n] *n* : colonia *f*

Colombian [kə'lʌmbiən] *adj* : colombiano

colon¹ ['ko:lən] *n*, *pl* **colons** *or* **cola** [-lə] : colon *m* (en anatomía)

colon² *n*, *pl* **colons** : dos puntos *mpl* (signo de puntuación)

colonel ['kərnəl] *n* : coronel *m*

colony ['kɑləni] *n*, *pl* **-nies** : colonia *f* — **colonial** [kə'lo:niəl] *adj* : colonial — **colonize** ['kɑlə,naɪz] *vt* **-nized; -nizing** : colonizar

color *or Brit* **colour** ['kʌlər] *n* : color *m* — ～ *vt* : colorear, pintar — *vi* **1** BLUSH : sonrojarse — **color-blind** *or Brit* **colour-blind** ['kʌlər,blaɪnd] *adj* : daltónico — **colored** *or Brit* **coloured** ['kʌlərd] *adj* : de color — **colorful** *or Brit* **colourful** ['kʌlərfəl] *adj* **1** : de vivos colores **2** PICTURESQUE : pintoresco — **colorless** *or Brit* **colourless** ['kʌlərləs] *adj* : incoloro

colossal [kə'lɑsəl] *adj* : colosal

colt ['ko:lt] *n* : potro *m*

column ['kɑləm] *n* : columna *f* — **columnist** ['kɑləmnɪst, -ləmɪst] *n* : columnista *f*

coma ['ko:mə] *n* : coma *m*

comb ['ko:m] *n* **1** : peine *m* **2** : cresta *f* (de un gallo) — ～ *vt* : peinar

combat ['kɑm,bæt] *n* : combate *m* — ～ [kəm'bæt, 'kɑm,bæt] *vt* **-bated** *or* **-batted; -bating** *or* **-batting** : combatir — **combatant** [kəm'bætənt] *n* : combatiente *m f*

combine [kəm'baɪn] *v* **-bined; -bining** — *vt* : combinar — *vi* : combinarse — ～ ['kɑm,baɪn] *n* HARVESTER : cosechadora *f* — **combination** [,kɑmbə'neɪʃən] *n* : combinación *f*

combustion [kəm'bʌstʃən] *n* : combustión *f*

come ['kʌm] *vi* **came** ['keɪm]; **come**; **coming 1** : venir **2** ARRIVE : llegar **3** ~ **about** : suceder **4** ~ **back** : regresar, volver **5** ~ **from** : venir de, provenir de **6** ~ **in** : entrar **7** ~ **out** : salir **8** ~ **to** REVIVE : volver en sí **9** ~ **on!** : ¡ándale! **10** ~ **up** OCCUR : surgir **11 how** ~? : ¿por qué? — **comeback** ['kʌm,bæk] *n* **1** RETURN : retorno *m* **2** RETORT : réplica *f*

comedy ['kɑmədi] *n, pl* **-dies** : comedia *f* — **comedian** [kə'miːdiən] *n* : cómico *m*, -ca *f*

comet ['kɑmət] *n* : cometa *m*

comfort ['kʌmpfərt] *vt* : consolar — ~ *n* **1** : comodidad *f* **2** SOLACE : consuelo *m* — **comfortable** ['kʌmpfərʈəbəl, 'kʌmpfʈə-] *adj* : cómodo

comic ['kɑmɪk] *or* **comical** [kɑmɪkəl] *adj* : cómico — ~ *n* **1** COMEDIAN : cómico *m*, -ca *f* **2** *or* ~ **book** : revista *f* de historietas, cómic *m* — **comic strip** *n* : tira *f* cómica, historieta *f*

coming ['kʌmɪŋ] *adj* : próximo, que viene

comma ['kɑmə] *n* : coma *f*

command [kə'mænd] *vt* **1** ORDER : ordenar, mandar **2** : estar al mando de (un barco, etc.) **3** ~ **respect** : inspirar (el) respeto — *vi* : dar órdenes — ~ *n* **1** ORDER : orden *f* **2** LEADERSHIP : mando *m* **3** MASTERY : maestría *f*, dominio *m* — **commander** [kə'mændər] *n* : comandante *mf* — **commandment** [kə'mændmənt] *n* : mandamiento *m*

commemorate [kə'memə,reɪt] *vt* **-rated; -rating** : conmemorar — **commemoration** [kə,memə'reɪʃən] *n* : conmemoración *f*

commence [kə'mɛnts] *v* **-menced; -mencing** : comenzar, empezar — **commencement** [kə'mɛntsmənt] *n* **1** BEGINNING : comienzo *m* **2** GRADUATION : ceremonia *f* de graduación

commend [kə'mɛnd] *vt* **1** ENTRUST : encomendar **2** PRAISE : alabar — **commendable** [kə'mɛndəbəl] *adj* : loable

comment ['kɑ,mɛnt] *n* : comentario *m*, observación *f* — *vi* : hacer comentarios — **commentary** ['kɑmən,tɛri] *n, pl* **-taries** : comentario *m* — **commentator** ['kɑmən,tɛɪtər] *n* : comentarista *mf*

commerce ['kɑmərs] *n* : comercio *m* — **commercial** [kə'mərʃəl] *adj* : comercial — ~ *n* : anuncio *m*, aviso *m Lat* — **commercialize** [kə'mərʃə,laɪz] *vt* **-ized; -izing** : comercializar

commiserate [kə'mɪzə,reɪt] *vi* **-ated; -ating** : compadecerse

commission [kə'mɪʃən] *n* : comisión *f* — ~ *vt* : encargar (una obra de arte) — **commissioner** [kə'mɪʃənər] *n* : comisario *m*, -ria *f*

commit [kə'mɪt] *vt* **-mitted; -mitting 1** ENTRUST : confiar **2** : cometer (un crimen) **3** : internar (a algn en un hospital) **4** ~ **oneself** : comprometerse **5** ~ **to memory** : aprender de memoria — **commitment** [kə'mɪtmənt] *n* : compromiso *m*

committee [kə'mɪti] *n* : comité *m*, comisión *f*

commodity [kə'mɑdəʈi] *n, pl* **-ties** : artículo *m* de comercio, producto *m*

common ['kɑmən] *adj* **1** : común **2** ORDINARY : ordinario, común y corriente — ~ **in** ~ : en común — **commonly** ['kɑmənli] *adv* : comúnmente — **commonplace** ['kɑmən,pleɪs] *adj* : común, banal — **common sense** *n* : sentido *m* común

commotion [kə'moːʃən] *n* : alboroto *m*, jaleo *m*

commune¹ ['kɑ,mjuːn, kə'mjuːn] *n* : comuna *f* — **communal** [kə'mjuːnəl] *adj* : comunal

commune² [kə'mjuːn] *vi* **-muned; -muning** ~ **with** : comunicarse con

communicate [kə'mjuːnə,keɪt] *v* **-cated; -cating** *vt* : comunicar — *vi* : comunicarse — **communicable** [kə'mjuːnɪkəbəl] *adj* : transmisible — **communication** [kə,mjuːnə'keɪʃən] *n* : comunicación *f* — **communicative** [kə'mjuːnɪ,keɪtɪv, -kəʈɪv] *adj* : comunicativo

communion [kə'mjuːnjən] *n* : comunión *f*

Communism ['kɑmjə,nɪzəm] *n* : comunismo *m* — **Communist** ['kɑmjə,nɪst] *adj* : comunista — ~ *n* : comunista *mf*

community [kə'mjuːnəʈi] *n, pl* **-ties** : comunidad *f*

commute [kə'mjuːt] *v* **-muted; -muting** *vt* : conmutar, reducir (una sentencia) — *vi* : viajar de la residencia al trabajo

compact [kəm'pækt, 'kɑm,pækt] *adj* : compacto — ~ ['kɑm,pækt] *n* **1** *or* ~ **car** : auto *m* compacto **2** *or* **powder** ~ : polvera *f* — **compact disc** ['kɑm,pækt'dɪsk] *n* : disco *m* compacto

companion [kəm'pænjən] *n* : compañero *m*, -ra *f* — **companionship** [kəm'pænjən,ʃɪp] *n* : compañerismo *m*

company ['kʌmpəni] *n, pl* **-nies** *f* **1** : compañía *f* **2** GUESTS : visita *f*

compare [kəm'pær] *v* **-pared; -paring**

vt : comparar — *vi* ~ **with** : poderse comparar con — **comparable** [ˈkɑmpərəbəl] *adj* : comparable — **comparative** [kəmˈpærətɪv] *adj* : comparativo, relativo — **comparison** [kəmˈpærəsən] *n* : comparación *f*

compartment [kəmˈpɑrtmənt] *n* : compartimiento *m*

compass [ˈkʌmpəs, ˈkɑm-] *n* 1 : compás *m* 2 **points of the** ~ : puntos *mpl* cardinales

compassion [kəmˈpæʃən] *n* : compasión *f* — **compassionate** [kəmˈpæʃənət] *adj* : compasivo

compatible [kəmˈpæţəbəl] *adj* : compatible, afín — **compatibility** [kəmˌpæţəˈbiləţi] *n* : compatibilidad *f*

compel [kəmˈpɛl] *vt* **-pelled; -pelling** : obligar — **compelling** [kəmˈpɛlɪŋ] *adj* : convincente

compensate [ˈkɑmpənˌseit] *v* **-sated; -sating** *vi* ~ **for** : compensar — *vt* : indemnizar, compensar — **compensation** [ˌkɑmpənˈseiʃən] *n* : compensación *f*, indemnización *f*

compete [kəmˈpiːt] *vi* **-peted; -peting** : competir — **competent** [ˈkɑmpəţənt] *adj* : competente — **competition** [ˌkɑmpəˈtiʃən] *n* 1 : competencia *f* 2 CONTEST : concurso *m* — **competitor** [kəmˈpɛţəţər] *n* : competidor *m*, -dora *f*

compile [kəmˈpaɪl] *vt* **-piled; -piling** : compilar, recopilar

complacency [kəmˈpleisənsi] *n* : satisfacción *f* consigo mismo — **complacent** [kəmˈpleisənt] *adj* : satisfecho de sí mismo

complain [kəmˈpleɪn] *vi* : quejarse — **complaint** [kəmˈpleɪnt] *n* 1 : queja *f* 2 AILMENT : enfermedad *f*

complement [ˈkɑmpləmənt] *n* : complemento *m* — ~ [ˈkɑmpləˌmɛnt] *vt* : complementar — **complementary** [ˌkɑmpləˈmɛntəri] *adj* : complementario

complete [kəmˈpliːt] *adj* **-pleter; -est** 1 WHOLE : completo, entero 2 FINISHED : terminado 3 TOTAL : total — ~ *vt* **-pleted; -pleting** : completar — **completion** [kəmˈpliːʃən] *n* : conclusión *f*

complex [kɑmˈplɛks, kəm-; ˈkɑmˌplɛks] *adj* : complejo — ~ [ˈkɑmˌplɛks] *n* : complejo *m*

complexion [kəmˈplɛkʃən] *n* : cutis *m*, tez *f*

complexity [kəmˈplɛksəţi, kɑm-] *n, pl* **-ties** : complejidad *f*

compliance [kəmˈplaɪənts] *n* 1 : acatamiento *m* 2 **in** ~ **with** : conforme a — **compliant** [kəmˈplaɪənt] *adj* : sumiso

complicate [ˈkɑmpləˌkeit] *vt* **-cated;**

-cating : complicar — **complicated** [ˈkɑmpləˌkeiţəd] *adj* : complicado — **complication** [ˌkɑmpləˈkeiʃən] *n* : complicación *f*

compliment [ˈkɑmpləmənt] *n* 1 : cumplido *m* 2 ~**s** *npl* : saludos *mpl* — ~ [ˈkɑmpləˌmɛnt] *vt* : felicitar — **complimentary** [ˌkɑmpləˈmɛntəri] *adj* 1 FLATTERING : halagador, halagüeño 2 FREE : de cortesía, gratis

comply [kəmˈplaɪ] *vi* **-plied; -plying** ~ **with** : cumplir, obedecer

component [kəmˈpoːnənt, ˈkɑmˌpoː-] *n* : componente *m*

compose [kəmˈpoːz] *vt* **-posed; -posing** 1 : componer 2 ~ **oneself** : serenarse — **composer** [kəmˈpoːzər] *n* : compositor *m*, -tora *f* — **composition** [ˌkɑmpəˈziʃən] *n* 1 : composición *f* 2 ESSAY : ensayo *m* — **composure** [kəmˈpoːʒər] *n* : calma *f*

compound[1] [kɑmˈpaʊnd, kəm-; ˈkɑmˌpaʊnd] *vt* 1 COMPOSE : componer 2 : agravar (un problema, etc.) — ~ [ˈkɑmˌpaʊnd; kɑmˈpaʊnd, kəm-] *adj* : compuesto — ~ [ˈkɑmˌpaʊnd] *n* : compuesto *m*

compound[2] [ˈkɑmˌpaʊnd] *n* ENCLOSURE : recinto *m*

comprehend [ˌkɑmprɪˈhɛnd] *vt* : comprender — **comprehension** [ˌkɑmprɪˈhɛntʃən] *n* : comprensión *f* — **comprehensive** [ˌkɑmprɪˈhɛntsɪv] *adj* 1 INCLUSIVE : incluso 2 BROAD : amplio

compress [kəmˈprɛs] *vt* : comprimir — **compression** [kəmˈprɛʃən] *n* : compresión *f*

comprise [kəmˈpraɪz] *vt* **-prised; -prising** : comprender

compromise [ˈkɑmprəˌmaɪz] *n* : acuerdo *m*, arreglo *m* — ~ *v* **-mised; -mising** *vi* : llegar a un acuerdo — *vt* : comprometer

compulsion [kəmˈpʌlʃən] *n* 1 COERCION : coacción *f* 2 URGE : impulso *m* — **compulsive** [kəmˈpʌlsɪv] *adj* : compulsivo — **compulsory** [kəmˈpʌlsəri] *adj* : obligatorio

compute [kəmˈpjuːt] *vt* **-puted; -puting** : computar — **computer** [kəmˈpjuːţər] *n* : computadora *f*, computador *m*, ordenador *m* Spain — **computerize** [kəmˈpjuːţəˌraɪz] *vt* **-ized; -izing** : informatizar

comrade [ˈkɑmˌræd] *n* : camarada *mf*

con [ˈkɑn] *vt* **conned; conning** : estafar — ~ *n* 1 SWINDLE : estafa *f* 2 **the pros and** ~**s** : los pros y los contras

concave [kɑnˈkeiv, ˈkɑnˌkeiv] *adj* : cóncavo

conceal [kən'si:l] vt : ocultar

concede [kən'si:d] vt -ceded; -ceding : conceder, admitir

conceit [kən'si:t] n : vanidad f — **conceited** [kən'si:t̬əd] adj : engreído

conceive [kən'si:v] v -ceived; -ceiving vt : concebir — vi ~ of : concebir — **conceivable** [kən'si:vəbəl] adj : concebible

concentrate ['kɑnsən‚treɪt] v -trated; -trating vt : concentrar — vi : concentrarse — **concentration** [‚kɑnsən-'treɪʃən] n : concentración f

concept ['kɑn‚sɛpt] n : concepto m — **conception** [kən'sɛpʃən] n : concepción f

concern [kən'sərn] vt 1 : concernir 2 ~ **oneself about** : preocuparse por — ~ n 1 AFFAIR : asunto m 2 WORRY : preocupación f 3 BUSINESS : negocio m — **concerned** [kən'sərnd] adj 1 ANXIOUS : ansioso 2 **as far as I'm** ~ : en cuanto a mí — **concerning** [kən'sərnɪŋ] prep : con respecto a

concert ['kɑn‚sərt] n : concierto m — **concerted** [kən'sərt̬əd] adj : concertado

concession [kən'sɛʃən] n : concesión f

concise [kən'saɪs] adj : conciso

conclude [kən'klu:d] v -cluded; -cluding : concluir — **conclusion** [kən'klu:ʒən] n : conclusión f — **conclusive** [kən'klu:sɪv] adj : concluyente

concoct [kən'kɑkt, kɑn-] vt 1 PREPARE : confeccionar 2 DEVISE : inventarse, tramar — **concoction** [kən'kɑkʃən] n : mezcla f, brebaje m

concourse [kɑn‚kors] n : vestíbulo m, salón m

concrete [kɑn'kri:t, 'kɑn‚kri:t] adj : concreto — ~ ['kɑn‚kri:t, kɑn'kri:t] n : hormigón m, concreto m Lat

concur [kən'kər] vi concurred; concurring AGREE : estar de acuerdo

concussion [kən'kʌʃən] n : conmoción f cerebral

condemn [kən'dɛm] vt : condenar — **condemnation** [‚kɑn‚dɛm'neɪʃən] n : condenación f

condense [kən'dɛns] v -densed; -densing vt : condensar — vi : condensarse — **condensation** [‚kɑnden-'seɪʃən, -dən-] n : condensación f

condescending [‚kɑndrɪ'sendɪŋ] adj : condescendiente

condiment ['kɑndəmənt] n : condimento m

condition [kən'dɪʃən] n 1 : condición f 2 **in good** ~ : en buen estado — **conditional** [kən'dɪʃənəl] adj : condicional

condolences [kən'do:lənt̬səz] npl : pésame m

condom ['kɑndəm] n : condón m

condominium [‚kɑndə'mɪniəm] n, pl -ums : condominio m Lat

condone [kən'do:n] vt -doned; -doning : aprobar

conducive [kən'du:sɪv, -'dju:-] adj : propicio, favorable

conduct ['kɑn‚dʌkt] n : conducta f — ~ [kən'dʌkt] vt 1 DIRECT, GUIDE : conducir, dirigir 2 CARRY OUT : llevar a cabo 3 ~ **oneself** : conducirse, comportarse — **conductor** [kən'dʌktər] n : revisor m, -sora f (en un tren); cobrador m, -dora f (en un autobús); director m, -tora f (de una orquesta)

cone ['ko:n] n 1 : cono m 2 or **ice-cream** ~ : cucurucho m, barquillo m Lat

confection [kən'fɛkʃən] n : dulce m

confederation [kən‚fedə'reɪʃən] n : confederación f

confer [kən'fər] v -ferred; -ferring vt : conferir, otorgar — vi ~ **with** : consultar — **conference** ['kɑnfrənts, -fərənts] n : conferencia f

confess [kən'fɛs] vt : confesar — vi 1 : confesarse 2 ~ **to** : confesar, admitir — **confession** [kən'fɛʃən] n : confesión f

confetti [kən'fet̬i] n : confeti m

confide [kən'faɪd] v -fided; -fiding : confiar — **confidence** ['kɑnfədənts] n 1 TRUST : confianza f 2 SELF-ASSURANCE : confianza f en sí mismo 3 SECRET : confidencia f — **confident** ['kɑnfədənt] adj 1 SURE : seguro 2 SELF-ASSURED : confiado, seguro de sí mismo — **confidential** [‚kɑnfə'dentʃəl] adj : confidencial

confine [kən'faɪn] vt -fined; -fining 1 LIMIT : confinar, limitar 2 IMPRISON : encerrar — **confines** ['kɑn‚faɪnz] npl : confines mpl

confirm [kən'fərm] vt : confirmar — **confirmation** [‚kɑnfər'meɪʃən] n : confirmación f — **confirmed** adj : inveterado

confiscate ['kɑnfə‚skeɪt] vt -cated; -cating : confiscar

conflict ['kɑn‚flɪkt] n : conflicto m — ~ [kən'flɪkt] vi : estar en conflicto, oponerse

conform [kən'fɔrm] vi 1 COMPLY : ajustarse 2 ~ **with** : corresponder a — **conformity** [kən'fɔrmət̬i] n, pl -ties : conformidad f

confound [kən'faʊnd, kɑn-] vt : confundir, desconcertar

confront [kən'frʌnt] vt : afrontar, encarar — **confrontation** [kanfrən'teɪʃən] n : confrontación f

confuse [kən'fjuːz] vt **-fused; -fusing** : confundir — **confusing** [kən'fjuːzɪŋ] adj : confuso, desconcertante — **confusion** [kən'fjuːʒən] n : confusión f, desconcierto m

congeal [kən'dʒiːl] vi : coagularse

congenial [kən'dʒiːniəl] adj : agradable

congested [kən'dʒɛstəd] adj : congestionado — **congestion** [kən'dʒɛstʃən] n : congestión f

congratulate [kən'grædʒəˌleɪt, -'grætʃə-] vt **-lated; -lating** : felicitar — **congratulations** [kənˌgrædʒə'leɪʃən, -grætʃə-] npl : felicitaciones fpl

congregate ['kaŋgrɪˌgeɪt] vi **-gated; -gating** : congregarse — **congregation** [kaŋgrɪ'geɪʃən] n : feligreses mpl (en religión)

congress ['kaŋgrəs] n : congreso m — **congressional** [kən'grɛʃənəl, kaŋ-] adj : del congreso — **congressman** ['kaŋgrəsmən] n, pl **-men** [-mən, -ˌmɛn] : congresista mf

conjecture [kən'dʒɛktʃər] n : conjetura f, presunción f — v **-tured; -turing** vt : conjeturar — vi : hacer conjeturas

conjugal ['kandʒɪgəl, kən'dʒuː-] adj : conyugal

conjugate ['kandʒəˌgeɪt] vt **-gated; -gating** : conjugar — **conjugation** [kandʒə'geɪʃən] n : conjugación f

conjunction [kən'dʒʌŋkʃən] n **1** : conjunción f **2 in ~ with** : en combinación con

conjure ['kandʒər, 'kʌn-] v **-jured; -juring** vi : hacer juegos de manos — vt or **~ up** : evocar

connect [kə'nɛkt] vi : conectarse — vt **1** JOIN : conectar, juntar **2** ASSOCIATE : asociar — **connection** [kə'nɛkʃən] n **1** : conexión f **2** : enlace m (con un tren, etc.) **3 ~s** npl : relaciones fpl (personas)

connoisseur [kanə'sər, -'sur] n : conocedor m, -dora f

connote [kə'noːt] vt **-noted; -noting** : connotar, implicar

conquer ['kaŋkər] vt : conquistar — **conqueror** ['kaŋkərər] n : conquistador m, -dora f — **conquest** ['kaŋˌkwɛst, 'kaŋ-] n : conquista f

conscience ['kantʃəns] n : conciencia f — **conscientious** [kantʃi'ɛntʃəs] adj : concienzudo

conscious ['kantʃəs] adj **1** AWARE : consciente **2** INTENTIONAL : intencional — **consciously** adv : deliberadamente

— **consciousness** ['kantʃəsnəs] n **1** AWARENESS : conciencia f **2 lose ~** : perder el conocimiento

consecrate ['kantsəˌkreɪt] vt **-crated; -crating** : consagrar — **consecration** [kantsə'kreɪʃən] n : consagración f

consecutive [kən'sɛkjətɪv] adj : consecutivo, sucesivo

consensus [kən'sɛntsəs] n : consenso m

consent [kən'sɛnt] vi : consentir — ~ n : consentimiento m

consequence ['kantsəˌkwɛnts, -kwənts] n **1** : consecuencia f **2 of no ~** : sin importancia — **consequent** ['kantsəkwənt, -ˌkwɛnt] adj : consiguiente — **consequently** ['kantsəkwəntli, -ˌkwɛnt-] adv : por consiguiente

conserve [kən'sərv] vt **-served; -serving** : conservar, preservar — **conservation** [kantsər'veɪʃən] n : conservación f — **conservative** [kən'sərvətɪv] adj **1** : conservador **2** CAUTIOUS : moderado, prudente — ~ n : conservador m, -dora f — **conservatory** [kən'sərvəˌtori] n, pl **-ries** : conservatorio m

consider [kən'sɪdər] vt **1** : considerar **2 all things considered** : teniéndolo todo en cuenta — **considerable** [kən'sɪdərəbəl] adj : considerable — **considerate** [kən'sɪdərət] adj : considerado — **consideration** [kənsɪdə'reɪʃən] n **1** : consideración f **2 take into ~** : tener en cuenta — **considering** [kən'sɪdərɪŋ] prep : teniendo en cuenta

consign [kən'saɪn] vt **1** : relegar **2** SEND : enviar — **consignment** [kən'saɪnmənt] n : envío m

consist [kən'sɪst] vi **1 ~ in** : consistir en **2 ~ of** : constar de, componerse de — **consistency** [kən'sɪstəntsi] n, pl **-cies** **1** TEXTURE : consistencia f **2** COHERENCE : coherencia f **3** UNIFORMITY : regularidad f — **consistent** [kən'sɪstənt] adj **1** UNCHANGING : constante, regular **2 ~ with** : consecuente con

console [kən'soːl] vt **-soled; -soling** : consolar — **consolation** [kantsə'leɪʃən] n : consuelo m **2 ~ prize** : premio m de consolación

consolidate [kən'saləˌdeɪt] vt **-dated; -dating** : consolidar — **consolidation** [kənˌsalə'deɪʃən] n : consolidación f

consonant ['kantsənənt] n : consonante f

conspicuous [kən'spɪkjuəs] adj **1** OBVIOUS : visible, evidente **2** STRIKING : llamativo — **conspicuously** [kən'spɪkjuəsli] adv : de manera llamativa

conspire [kən'spaɪr] *vi* **-spired; -spiring** : conspirar — **conspiracy** [kən'spɪrəsi] *n, pl* **-cies** : conspiración *f*

constant ['kɑnstənt] *adj* : constante — **constantly** ['kɑnstəntli] *adv* : constantemente

constellation [,kɑnstə'leɪʃən] *n* : constelación *f*

constipated ['kɑnstə,peɪtəd] *adj* : estreñido — **constipation** [,kɑnstə'peɪʃən] *n* : estreñimiento *m*

constituent [kən'stɪtʃuənt] *n* **1** COMPONENT : componente *m* **2** VOTER : elector *m*, -tora *f*; votante *mf*

constitute ['kɑnstə,tuːt, -,tjuːt] *vt* **-tuted; -tuting** : constituir — **constitution** [,kɑnstə'tuːʃən, -'tjuː-] *n* : constitución *f* — **constitutional** [,kɑnstə'tuːʃənəl, -'tjuː-] *adj* : constitucional

constrain [kən'streɪn] *vt* : restringir — **constraint** [kən'streɪnt] *n* : restricción *f*, limitación *f*

construct [kən'strʌkt] *vt* : construir — **construction** [kən'strʌkʃən] *n* : construcción *f* — **constructive** [kən'strʌktɪv] *adj* : constructivo

construe [kən'struː] *vt* **-strued; -struing** : interpretar

consul ['kɑnsəl] *n* : cónsul *mf* — **consulate** ['kɑnsələt] *n* : consulado *m*

consult [kən'sʌlt] *v* : consultar — **consultant** [kən'sʌltənt] *n* : asesor *m*, -sora *f*; consultor *m*, -tora *f* — **consultation** [,kɑnsəl'teɪʃən] *n* : consulta *f*

consume [kən'suːm] *vt* **-sumed; -suming** : consumir — **consumer** [kən'suːmər] *n* : consumidor *m*, -dora *f* — **consumption** [kən'sʌmpʃən] *n* : consumo *m*

contact ['kɑn,tækt] *n* : contacto *m* — ~ ['kɑn,tækt, kən'-] *vt* : ponerse en contacto con — **contact lens** ['kɑn,tækt'lenz] *n* : lente *mf* (de contacto)

contagious [kən'teɪdʒəs] *adj* : contagioso

contain [kən'teɪn] *vt* **1** : contener **2** ~ **oneself** : contenerse — **container** [kən'teɪnər] *n* : recipiente *m*, envase *m*

contaminate [kən'tæmə,neɪt] *vt* **-nated; -nating** : contaminar — **contamination** [kən,tæmə'neɪʃən] *n* : contaminación *f*

contemplate ['kɑntəm,pleɪt] *v* **-plated; -plating** *vt* **1** : contemplar **2** CONSIDER : considerar, pensar en — *vi* : reflexionar — **contemplation** [,kɑntəm'pleɪʃən] *n* : contemplación *f*

contemporary [kən'tempə,reri] *adj* : contemporáneo — ~ *n, pl* **-raries** : contemporáneo *m*, -nea *f*

contempt [kən'tempt] *n* : desprecio *m* —

contemptible [kən'temptəbəl] *adj* : despreciable — **contemptuous** [kən'temptʃuəs] *adj* : desdeñoso

contend [kən'tend] *vi* **1** COMPETE : contender, competir **2** ~ **with** : enfrentarse a — *vt* : sostener, afirmar — **contender** [kən'tendər] *n* : contendiente *mf*

content¹ ['kɑntent] *n* **1** : contenido *m* **2 table of** ~**s** : índice *m* de materias **content²** [kən'tent] *adj* : contento — ~ *vt* ~ **oneself with** : contentarse con — **contented** [kən'tentəd] *adj* : satisfecho, contento

contention [kən'tentʃən] *n* **1** DISPUTE : disputa *f* **2** OPINION : argumento *m*, opinión *f*

contentment [kən'tentmənt] *n* : satisfacción *f*

contest [kən'test] *vt* : disputar — ~ ['kɑn,test] *n* **1** STRUGGLE : contienda *f* **2** COMPETITION : concurso *m*, competencia *f* — **contestant** [kən'testənt] *n* : concursante *mf*, contendiente *mf*

context ['kɑn,tekst] *n* : contexto *m*

continent ['kɑntənənt] *n* : continente *m* — **continental** [,kɑntən'entəl] *adj* : continental

contingency [kən'tɪndʒənsi] *n, pl* **-cies** : contingencia *f*

continue [kən'tɪnjuː] *v* **-tinued; -tinuing** : continuar — **continual** [kən'tɪnjuəl] *adj* : continuo, constante — **continuation** [kən,tɪnjuˈeɪʃən] *n* : continuación *f* — **continuity** [,kɑntən'uːəti, -'juː-] *n, pl* **-ties** : continuidad *f* — **continuous** [kən'tɪnjuəs] *adj* : continuo

contort [kən'tɔrt] *vt* : retorcer — **contortion** [kən'tɔrʃən] *n* : contorsión *f*

contour ['kɑn,tʊr] *n* **1** : contorno *m* **2** ~ **line** : curva *f* de nivel

contraband ['kɑntrə,bænd] *n* : contrabando *m*

contraception [,kɑntrə'sepʃən] *n* : anticoncepción *f* — **contraceptive** [,kɑntrə'septɪv] *adj* : anticonceptivo — ~ *n* : anticonceptivo *m*

contract ['kɑn,trækt] *n* : contrato *m* — ~ [kən'trækt] *vi* : contraer — *vi* : contraerse — **contraction** [kən'trækʃən] *n* : contracción *f* — **contractor** [kən'træktər, kən'træk-] *n* : contratista *mf*

contradiction [,kɑntrə'dɪkʃən] *n* : contradicción *f* — **contradict** [,kɑntrə'dɪkt] *vt* : contradecir — **contradictory** [,kɑntrə'dɪktəri] *adj* : contradictorio

contraption [kən'træpʃən] *n* : artilugio *m*, artefacto *m*

contrary ['kɑn,treri] *n, pl* **-traries 1** : contrario *m* **2 on the** ~ : al contrario

— ~ ['kɑntri] adj 1 : contrario, opuesto 2 ~ to : en contra de
contrast [kən'træst] v : contrastar — ~ ['kɑn,træst] n : contraste m
contribute [kən'trɪbjət] v -uted; -uting : contribuir — contribution [,kɑntrə'bju:ʃən] n : contribución f — contributor [kən'trɪbjətər] n 1 : contribuyente mf 2 : colaborador m, -dora f (en periodismo)
contrite [kən'traɪt, 'kɑn,traɪt] adj : arrepentido
contrive [kən'traɪv] vt -trived; -triving 1 DEVISE : idear 2 ~ to do sth : lograr hacer algo
control [kən'tro:l] vt -trolled; -trolling : controlar — ~ n 1 : control m 2 ~s npl : mandos mpl
controversy ['kɑntrə,vərsi] n, pl -sies : controversia f — controversial [,kɑntrə'vərʃəl, -siəl] adj : polémico
convalescence [,kɑnvə'lesənts] n : convalecencia f — convalescent [,kɑnvə'lesənt] adj : convaleciente — ~ n : convaleciente mf
convene [kən'viːn] v -vened; -vening : convocar — vi : reunirse
convenience [kən'viːnjənts] n : conveniencia f, comodidad f — convenient [kən'viːnjənt] adj : conveniente
convent ['kɑnvənt, -,vent] n : convento m
convention [kən'ventʃən] n : convención f — conventional [kən'ventʃənəl] adj : convencional
converge [kən'vərdʒ] vi -verged; -verging : converger, convergir
converse¹ [kən'vərs] vi -versed; -versing : conversar — conversation [,kɑnvər'seɪʃən] n : conversación f — conversational [,kɑnvər'seɪʃənəl] adj : familiar
converse² [kən'vərs, 'kɑn,vərs] adj : contrario, opuesto — conversely [kən'vərsli, 'kɑn,vərs-] adv : a la inversa
conversion [kən'vərʒən] n : conversión f — convert [kən'vərt] vt : convertir — vi : convertirse — convertible [kən'vərtəbəl] adj : convertible — ~ n : descapotable m, convertible m Lat
convex [kɑn'veks, 'kɑn,-, kən'-] adj : convexo
convey [kən'veɪ] vt 1 TRANSPORT : llevar, transportar 2 TRANSMIT : comunicar
convict [kən'vɪkt] vt : declarar culpable a — ~ ['kɑn,vɪkt] n : presidiario m, -ria f — conviction [kən'vɪkʃən] n 1 : condena f (de un acusado) 2 BELIEF : convicción f

convince [kən'vɪnts] vt -vinced; -vincing : convencer — convincing [kən'vɪntsɪŋ] adj : convincente
convoke [kən'voːk] vt -voked; -voking : convocar
convoluted ['kɑnvə,luːtəd] adj : complicado
convulsion [kən'vʌlʃən] n : convulsión f — convulsive [kən'vʌlsɪv] adj : convulsivo
cook ['kʊk] n : cocinero m, -ra f — vi : cocinar, guisar — vt : preparar (comida) — cookbook ['kʊk,bʊk] n : libro m de cocina
cookie or cooky ['kʊki] n, pl -ies : galleta f (dulce)
cooking n : cocina f
cool ['kuːl] adj 1 : fresco 2 CALM : tranquilo 3 UNFRIENDLY : frío — ~ vt : enfriar — vi : enfriarse — ~ n 1 : fresco m 2 COMPOSURE : calma f — cooler ['kuːlər] n : nevera f portátil — coolness ['kuːlnəs] n : frescura f
coop ['kuːp, 'kʊp] n : gallinero m — ~ vt or ~ up : encerrar
cooperate [koʊ'ɑpə,reɪt] vi -ated; -ating : cooperar — cooperation [koʊ,ɑpə'reɪʃən] n : cooperación f — cooperative [koʊ'ɑpərəṭɪv, -,ɑpə,reɪṭɪv] adj : cooperativo
coordinate [koʊ'ɔrdən,eɪt] v -nated; -nating vt : coordinar — coordination [koʊ,ɔrdən'eɪʃən] n : coordinación f
cop ['kɑp] n 1 : poli mf fam 2 the ~s : la poli fam
cope ['koːp] vi coped; coping 1 : arreglárselas 2 ~ with : hacer frente a, poder con
copier ['kɑpiər] n : fotocopiadora f
copious ['koːpiəs] adj : copioso
copper ['kɑpər] n : cobre m
copy ['kɑpi] n, pl copies 1 : copia f 2 : ejemplar m (de un libro), número m (de una revista) — ~ vt copied; copying 1 DUPLICATE : hacer una copia de 2 IMITATE : copiar — copyright ['kɑpi,raɪt] n : derechos mpl de autor
coral ['kɔrəl] n : coral m
cord ['kɔrd] n 1 : cuerda f 2 or electric ~ : cable m (eléctrico)
cordial ['kɔrdʒəl] adj : cordial
corduroy ['kɔrdə,rɔɪ] n : pana f
core ['kɔr] n 1 : corazón m (de una fruta) 2 CENTER : núcleo m, centro m
cork ['kɔrk] n : corcho m — corkscrew ['kɔrk,skruː] n : sacacorchos m
corn ['kɔrn] n 1 : grano m 2 or Indian ~ : maíz m 3 : callo m (del pie) — corncob ['kɔrn,kɑb] n : mazorca f

corner ['kɔrnər] n : ángulo m, rincón m (en una habitación), esquina f (de una intersección) — vt **1** TRAP : acorralar **2** MONOPOLIZE : acaparar (un mercado) — **cornerstone** ['kɔrnər,ston] n : piedra f angular

cornmeal ['kɔrn,mil] n : harina f de maíz — **cornstarch** ['kɔrn,stɑrtʃ] n : maicena f

corny ['kɔrni] adj : cursi, sentimental

coronary ['kɔrə,neri] n, pl **-naries** : trombosis f coronaria

coronation [,kɔrə'neiʃən] n : coronación f

corporal ['kɔrpərəl] n : cabo m

corporation [,kɔrpə'reiʃən] n : sociedad f anónima, compañía f — **corporate** ['kɔrpərət] adj : corporativo

corps [kɔr] n, pl **corps** ['kɔrz] : cuerpo m

corpse ['kɔrps] n : cadáver m

corpulent ['kɔrpjələnt] adj : obeso, gordo

corpuscle ['kɔr,pʌsəl] n : glóbulo m

corral [kə'ræl] n : corral m — vt **-ralled; -ralling** : acorralar

correct [kə'rɛkt] vt : corregir — adj : correcto — **correction** [kə'rɛkʃən] n : corrección f

correlation [,kɔrə'leiʃən] n : correlación f

correspond [,kɔrə'spɑnd] vi **1** WRITE : corresponderse **2 — to** : corresponder a — **correspondence** [,kɔrə'spɑndəns] n : correspondencia f

corridor ['kɔrədər, -,dɔr] n : pasillo m

corroborate [kə'rɑbə,reit] vt **-rated; -rating** : corroborar

corrode [kə'roːd] v **-roded; -roding** vt : corroer — vi : corroerse — **corrosion** [kə'roːʒən] n : corrosión f — **corrosive** [kə'roːsiv] adj : corrosivo

corrugated ['kɔrə,geitəd] adj : ondulado

corrupt [kə'rʌpt] vt : corromper — adj : corrupto, corrompido — **corruption** [kə'rʌpʃən] n : corrupción f

corset ['kɔrsət] n : corsé m

cosmetic [kɑz'mɛtɪk] n : cosmético m — adj : cosmético

cosmic ['kɑzmɪk] adj : cósmico

cosmopolitan [,kɑzmə'pɑlətən] adj : cosmopolita

cosmos ['kɑzmɔs, -,moːs, -,mɑs] n : cosmos m

cost [kɔst] n : costo m, coste m — vi **cost; costing 1** : costar **2 how much does it ~?** : ¿cuánto cuesta?, ¿cuánto vale?

Costa Rican [,kɔstə'riːkən] adj : costarricense

costly ['kɔstli] adj : costoso

costume [kɑs,tuːm, -,tjuːm] n **1** OUTFIT : traje m **2** DISGUISE : disfraz m

cot ['kɑt] n : catre m

cottage ['kɑtɪdʒ] n : casita f (de campo) — **cottage cheese** n : requesón m

cotton ['kɑtən] n : algodón m

couch ['kautʃ] n : sofá m

cough ['kɔf] vi : toser — n : tos f

could ['kud] → **can¹**

council ['kaunsəl] n **1** : concejo m **2** or **city —** : ayuntamiento m — **councillor** or **councilor** ['kaunsələr] n : concejal m, -jala f

counsel n **1** ADVICE : consejo m **2** LAWYER : abogado m, -da f — v ['kaunsəl] vt **-seled** or **-selled; -seling** or **-selling** : aconsejar — **counselor** or **counsellor** ['kaunsələr] n : consejero m, -ra f

count¹ ['kaunt] vt : contar — vi **1** : contar **2 — on** : contar con **3 that doesn't ~** : eso no vale — n **1** : recuento m **2 keep ~ of** : llevar la cuenta de

count² n : conde m (noble)

counter¹ ['kauntər] n **1** : mostrador m (de un negocio) **2** TOKEN : ficha f (de un juego)

counter² ['kauntər] v — vi : oponerse a — vt : contraatacar — adv **— to** : contrario a — **counteract** [,kauntər'ækt] vt : contrarrestar — **counterattack** ['kauntərə,tæk] n : contraataque m — **counterbalance** ['kauntər,bæləns] n : contrapeso m — **counterclockwise** [,kauntər'klɑk,waiz] adv & adj : en sentido opuesto a las agujas del reloj — **counterfeit** ['kauntər,fit] vt : falsificar — adj : falsificado — n : falsificación f — **counterpart** ['kauntər,pɑrt] n : homólogo m (de una persona), equivalente m (de una cosa) — **counterproductive** [,kauntərprə'dʌktiv] adj : contraproducente

countess ['kauntɪs] n : condesa f

countless ['kauntləs] adj : incontable, innumerable

country ['kʌntri] n, pl **-tries 1** NATION : país m **2** COUNTRYSIDE : campo m — adj : campestre, rural — **countryman** ['kʌntrimən] n, pl **-men** [-mən, -,men] or **fellow —** : compatriota mf — **countryside** ['kʌntri,said] n : campo m, campiña f

county ['kaunti] n, pl **-ties** : condado m

coup ['kuː] n, pl **coups** ['kuːz] or **— d'etat** : golpe m (de estado)

couple ['kʌpəl] n **1** : pareja f (de per-

sonas) **2 a ~ of** : un par de — **~** vt
-pled; -pling : acoplar, unir

coupon ['ku:pɑn, 'kju:-] n : cupón m

courage ['kʌrɪdʒ] n : valor m — **courageous** [kəˈreɪdʒəs] adj : valiente

courier ['kuriər, 'kəriər] n : mensajero m,
-ra f

course ['kors] n **1** : curso m **2** : plato m
(de una cena) **3** or **golf ~** : campo m
de golf **4 in the ~ of** : en el transcurso de **5 of ~** : desde luego, por
supuesto

court ['kort] n **1** : corte f (de un rey, etc.)
2 : cancha f, pista f (en deportes) **3** TRI-
BUNAL : corte f, tribunal m — **~** vt
: cortejar

courteous ['kərtiəs] adj : cortés —
courtesy ['kərtəsi] n, pl **-sies** : cortesía f

courthouse ['korthaus] n : palacio m de
justicia, juzgado m — **courtroom**
['kort,ru:m] n : sala f (de un tribunal)

courtship ['kort,ʃɪp] n : cortejo m, noviazgo m

courtyard ['kort,jɑrd] n : patio m

cousin ['kʌzən] n : primo m, -ma f

cove ['ko:v] n : ensenada f, cala f

covenant ['kʌvənənt] n : pacto m, convenio m

cover ['kʌvər] vt **1** : cubrir **2** or **~ up**
: encubrir, ocultar **3** TREAT : tratar —
~ n **1** : cubierta f **2** SHELTER : abrigo
m, refugio m **3** LID : tapa f **4** : cubierta
f (de un libro), portada f (de una revista) **5 ~s** npl BEDCLOTHES : mantas
fpl, cobijas fpl Lat **6 take ~** : ponerse
a cubierto **7 under ~ of** : al amparo
de — **coverage** ['kʌvərɪdʒ] n : cobertura f — **covert** ['ko:vərt, 'kʌvərt] adj
: encubierto — **cover-up** ['kʌvər,ʌp] n
: encubrimiento f

covet ['kʌvət] vt : codiciar — **covetous**
['kʌvətəs] adj : codicioso

cow ['kau] n : vaca f — **~** vt : intimidar,
acobardar

coward ['kauərd] n : cobarde mf —
cowardice ['kauərdɪs] n : cobardía f —
cowardly ['kauərdli] adj : cobarde

cowboy ['kau,bɔɪ] n : vaquero m

cower ['kauər] vi : encogerse (de miedo)

coy ['kɔɪ] adj : tímido y coqueto

coyote [kaɪˈoːti, ˈkaɪˌoːt] n, pl **coyotes**
or **coyote** : coyote m

cozy ['koːzi] adj **-zier; -est** : acogedor

crab ['kræb] n : cangrejo m, jaiba f Lat

crack ['kræk] vt **1** SPLIT : rajar, partir
2 : cascar (nueces, huevos) **3** : chasquear (un látigo, etc.) **4** — **down on**
: tomar medidas enérgicas contra —
vi **1** SPLIT : rajarse, agrietarse **2**

: chasquear (dícese de un látigo) **3** —
up : sufrir una crisis nerviosa — **~** n
1 CRACKING : chasquido m, crujido m **2**
CREVICE : raja f, grieta f **3 have a ~ at**
: intentar

cracker ['krækər] n : galleta f (de soda,
etc.)

crackle ['krækəl] vi **-led; -ling** : crepitar,
chisporrotear — **~** n : crujido m,
chisporroteo m

cradle ['kreɪdəl] n : cuna f — **~** vt
-dled; -dling : acunar

craft ['kræft] n **1** TRADE : oficio m **2** CUN-
NING : astucia f **3** → **craftsmanship 4**
pl usually **craft** BOAT : embarcación f
— **craftsman** ['kræftsmən] n, pl **-men**
[-mən, -ˌmen] : artesano m, -na f —
craftsmanship ['kræftsmən,ʃɪp] n
: artesanía f, destreza f — **crafty**
['kræfti] adj **craftier; -est** : astuto,
taimado

crag ['kræg] n : peñasco m

cram ['kræm] v **crammed; cramming**
vt **1** STUFF : embutir **2 ~ with** : atiborrar de — vi : estudiar a última hora

cramp ['kræmp] n **1** : calambre m, espasmo m (de los músculos) **2 ~s** npl
: retorcijones mpl

cranberry ['kræn,beri] n, pl **-berries**
: arándano m (rojo y agrio)

crane ['kreɪn] n **1** : grulla f (ave) **2** : grúa
f (máquina) — **~** vt **craned; craning**
: estirar (el cuello)

crank ['kræŋk] n **1** : manivela f **2** ECCEN-
TRIC : excéntrico m, -ca f — **cranky**
['kræŋki] adj **crankier; -est** : malhumorado

crash ['kræʃ] vi **1** : caerse con estrépito
2 COLLIDE : estrellarse, chocar — vt
: estrellar — **~** n **1** DIN : estrépito m **2**
COLLISION : choque m

crass ['kræs] adj : burdo, grosero

crate ['kreɪt] n : cajón m (de madera)

crater ['kreɪtər] n : cráter m

crave ['kreɪv] vt **craved; craving** : ansiar — **craving** ['kreɪvɪŋ] n : ansia f

crawl ['krɔl] vi : arrastrarse, gatear
(dícese de un bebé) — **~** n : paso a
paso lento

crayon ['kreɪɑn, -ən] n : lápiz m de cera

craze ['kreɪz] n : moda f pasajera, manía
f

crazy ['kreɪzi] adj **-zier; -est 1** : loco **2
go ~** : volverse loco — **craziness**
['kreɪzinəs] n : locura f

creak ['kri:k] vi : chirriar, crujir — **~** n
: chirrido m, crujido m

cream ['kri:m] n : crema f, nata f Spain
— **cream cheese** : queso m crema

— **creamy** ['kri:mi] *adj* **creamier; -est** : cremoso

crease ['kri:s] *n* : pliegue *m*, raya *f* (del pantalón) — ~ *vt* **creased; creasing** : plegar, poner una raya en (el pantalón)

create [kri'eɪt] *vt* **-ated; -ating** : crear — **creation** [kri'eɪʃən] *n* : creación *f* — **creative** [kri'eɪtɪv] *adj* : creativo — **creator** [kri'eɪtər] *n* : creador *m*, -dora *f* — **creature** ['kri:tʃər] *n* : criatura *f*, animal *m*

credence ['kri:dənts] *n* **lend ~ to** : dar crédito a

credentials [kri'dentʃəlz] *npl* : credenciales *fpl*

credible ['krɛdəbəl] *adj* : creíble — **credibility** [ˌkrɛdə'bɪləti] *n* : credibilidad *f*

credit ['krɛdɪt] *n* **1** : crédito *m* **2** RECOGNITION : reconocimiento *m* **3 be a ~ to** : ser el orgullo de — ~ *vt* **1** BELIEVE : creer **2** : abonar (en una cuenta) **3 ~ s.o. with sth** : atribuir algo a algn — **credit card** *n* : tarjeta *f* de crédito

credulous ['krɛdʒələs] *adj* : crédulo

creed ['kri:d] *n* : credo *m*

creek ['kri:k, 'krɪk] *n* : arroyo *m*, riachuelo *m*

creep ['kri:p] *vi* **crept** ['krɛpt]; **creeping** **1** CRAWL : arrastrarse **2** SLINK : ir a hurtadillas — ~ *n* **1** CRAWL : paso *m* lento **2 the ~s** : escalofríos *mpl* — **creeping** *adj* ~ **plant** : planta *f* trepadora

cremate ['kri:meɪt] *vt* **-mated; -mating** : incinerar

crescent ['krɛsənt] *n* : media luna *f*

cress ['krɛs] *n* : berro *m*

crest ['krɛst] *n* : cresta *f* — **crestfallen** ['krɛstˌfɔlən] *adj* : alicaído

crevice ['krɛvɪs] *n* : grieta *f*

crew ['kru:] *n* **1** : tripulación *f* (de una nave) **2** TEAM : equipo *m*

crib ['krɪb] *n* : cuna *f* (de un bebé)

cricket ['krɪkət] *n* **1** : grillo *m* (insecto) **2** : críquet *m* (juego)

crime ['kraɪm] *n* : crimen *m* — **criminal** ['krɪmənəl] *adj* : criminal — ~ *n* : criminal *mf*

crimp ['krɪmp] *vt* : rizar

crimson ['krɪmzən] *n* : carmesí *m*

cringe ['krɪndʒ] *vi* **cringed; cringing** : encogerse

crinkle ['krɪŋkəl] *vt* **-kled; -kling** : arrugar

cripple ['krɪpəl] *vt* **-pled; -pling 1** DISABLE : lisiar, dejar inválido **2** INCAPACITATE : inutilizar, paralizar

crisis ['kraɪsɪs] *n, pl* **crises** [-ˌsi:z] : crisis *f*

crisp ['krɪsp] *adj* **1** CRUNCHY : crujiente **2** : frío y vigorizante (dícese del aire) — **crispy** ['krɪspi] *adj* **crispier; -est** : crujiente

crisscross ['krɪsˌkrɔs] *vt* : entrecruzar

criterion [kraɪ'tɪriən] *n, pl* **-ria** [-ə] : criterio *m*

critic ['krɪtɪk] *n* : crítico *m*, -ca *f* — **critical** ['krɪtɪkəl] *adj* : crítico — **criticism** ['krɪtəˌsɪzəm] *n* : crítica *f* — **criticize** ['krɪtəˌsaɪz] *vt* **-cized; -cizing** : criticar

croak ['kro:k] *vi* : croar

crock ['krɑk] *n* : vasija *f* de barro — **crockery** ['krɑkəri] *n* : vajilla *f*, loza *f*

crocodile ['krɑkəˌdaɪl] *n* : cocodrilo *m*

crony ['kro:ni] *n, pl* **-nies** : amigote *m* *fam*

crook ['kruk] *n* **1** STAFF : cayado *m* **2** THIEF : ratero *m*, -ra *f*; ladrón *m*, -drona *f* **3** BEND : pliegue *m* — **crooked** ['kru:kəd] *adj* **1** BENT : torcido, chueco *Lat* **2** DISHONEST : deshonesto

crop ['krɑp] *n* **1** WHIP : fusta *f* **2** HARVEST : cosecha *f* **3** : cultivo *m* (de maíz, tabaco, etc.) — ~ *v* **cropped; cropping** *vt* TRIM : recortar, cortar — *vi* ~ **up** : surgir

cross ['krɔs] *n* **1** : cruz *f* **2** HYBRID : cruce *m* — ~ *vt* **1** : cruzar, atravesar **2** CROSSBREED : cruzar **3** *or* ~ **out** : tachar — ~ *adj* **1** : que atraviesa **2** ANGRY : enojado — **crossbreed** ['krɔsˌbrɪd] *vt* **-bred** [-bred]; **-breeding** : cruzar — **cross-examine** *vt* : interrogar — **cross-eyed** ['krɔsˌaɪd] *adj* : bizco — **cross fire** *n* : fuego *m* cruzado — **crossing** ['krɔsɪŋ] *n* **1** INTERSECTION : cruce *m*, paso *m* **2** VOYAGE : travesía *f* (del mar) — **cross-reference** [ˌkrɔs'refrənts, -'refərənts] *n* : referencia *f* — **crossroads** ['krɔsˌro:dz] *n* : cruce *m* — **cross section** *n* **1** : corte *m* transversal **2** SAMPLE : muestra *f* representativa — **crosswalk** ['krɔsˌwɔk] *n* : cruce *m* peatonal, paso *m* de peatones — **crossword puzzle** ['krɔsˌwərd] *n* : crucigrama *m*

crotch ['krɑtʃ] *n* : entrepierna *f*

crouch ['kraʊtʃ] *vi* : agacharse

crouton ['kru:ˌtɑn] *n* : crutón *m*

crow ['kro:] *n* : cuervo *m* — ~ *vi* **crowed** *or Brit* **crew; crowing** : cacarear

crowbar ['kro:ˌbɑr] *n* : palanca *f*

crowd ['kraʊd] *vi* : amontonarse — *vt* : atestar, llenar — ~ *n* : multitud *f*, muchedumbre *f*

crown ['kraun] *n* **1** : corona *f* **2** : cima *f* (de una colina) — ~ *vt* : coronar

crucial ['kru:ʃəl] *adj* : crucial

crucify ['kru:səˌfaɪ] *vt* **-fied; -fying** : crucificar — **crucifix** ['kru:səˌfɪks] *n* : crucifijo *m* — **crucifixion** [ˌkru:sə'fɪkʃən] *n* : crucifixión *f*

crude ['kru:d] *adj* **cruder; -est 1** RAW : crudo **2** VULGAR : grosero **3** ROUGH : tosco, rudo

cruel ['kru:əl] *adj* **-eler** *or* **-eller; -elest** *or* **-ellest** : cruel — **cruelty** ['kru:əlti] *n, pl* **-ties** : crueldad *f*

cruet ['kru:ət] *n* : vinagrera *f*

cruise ['kru:z] *vi* **cruised; cruising 1** : hacer un crucero **2** : ir a velocidad de crucero — ~ *n* : crucero *m* — **cruiser** ['kru:zər] *n* **1** WARSHIP : crucero *m* **2** : patrulla *f* (de policía)

crumb ['krʌm] *n* : miga *f*, migaja *f*

crumble ['krʌmbəl] *v* **-bled; -bling** *vt* : desmenuzar — *vi* : desmenuzarse, desmoronarse

crumple ['krʌmpəl] *vt* **-pled; -pling** : arrugar

crunch ['krʌntʃ] *vt* : ronzar (con los dientes), hacer crujir (con los pies, etc.) — **crunchy** ['krʌntʃi] *adj* **crunchier; -est** : crujiente

crusade [kru:'seɪd] *n* : cruzada *f*

crush ['krʌʃ] *vt* : aplastar, apachurrar *Lat* — ~ *n* **have a** ~ **on** : estar chiflado por

crust ['krʌst] *n* : corteza *f*

crutch ['krʌtʃ] *n* : muleta *f*

crux ['krʌks, 'kruks] *n* : quid *m*

cry ['kraɪ] *vi* **cried; crying 1** SHOUT : gritar **2** WEEP : llorar — ~ *n, pl* **cries** : grito *m*

crypt ['krɪpt] *n* : cripta *f*

crystal ['krɪstəl] *n* : cristal *m*

cub ['kʌb] *n* : cachorro *m*, -rra *f*

Cuban ['kju:bən] *adj* : cubano

cube ['kju:b] *n* : cubo *m* — **cubic** ['kju:bɪk] *adj* : cúbico

cubicle ['kju:bɪkəl] *n* : cubículo *m*

cuckoo ['ku:ku:, 'ku-] *n* : cuco *m*, cuclillo *m*

cucumber ['kju:ˌkʌmbər] *n* : pepino *m*

cuddle ['kʌdəl] *v* **-dled; -dling** *vi* : acurrucarse, abrazarse — *vt* : abrazar

cudgel ['kʌdʒəl] *n* : porra *f* — ~ *vt* **-geled** *or* **-gelled; -geling** *or* **-gelling** : aporrear

cue¹ ['kju:] *n* SIGNAL : señal *f*

cue² *n* : taco *m* (de billar)

cuff¹ ['kʌf] *n* **1** : puño *m* (de una camisa) **2** ~**s** *npl* → **handcuffs**

cuff² *vt* : bofetear — ~ *n* SLAP : bofetada *f*

cuisine [kwɪ'zi:n] *n* : cocina *f*

culinary ['kʌləˌneri, 'kjulə-] *adj* : culinario

cull ['kʌl] *vt* : seleccionar, entresacar

culminate ['kʌlməˌneɪt] *vi* **-nated; -nating** : culminar — **culmination** [ˌkʌlmə'neɪʃən] *n* : culminación *f*

culprit ['kʌlprɪt] *n* : culpable *mf*

cult ['kʌlt] *n* : culto *m*

cultivate ['kʌltəˌveɪt] *vt* **-vated; -vating** : cultivar — **cultivation** [ˌkʌltə'veɪʃən] *n* : cultivo *m*

culture ['kʌltʃər] *n* **1** : cultura *f* **2** : cultivo *m* (en biología) — **cultural** ['kʌltʃərəl] *adj* : cultural — **cultured** ['kʌltʃərd] *adj* : culto

cumbersome ['kʌmbərsəm] *adj* : torpe (y pesado), difícil de manejar

cumulative ['kju:mjələtɪv, -ˌleɪtɪv] *adj* : acumulativo

cunning ['kʌnɪŋ] *adj* : astuto, taimado — ~ *n* : astucia *f*

cup ['kʌp] *n* **1** : taza *f* **2** TROPHY : copa *f*

cupboard ['kʌbərd] *n* : alacena *f*, armario *m*

curator ['kjurˌeɪtər, kju'reɪtər] *n* : conservador *m*, -dora *f*; director *m*, -tora *f*

curb ['kərb] *n* **1** RESTRAINT : freno *m* **2** : borde *m* de la acera — ~ *vt* : refrenar

curdle ['kərdəl] *v* **-dled; -dling** *vi* : cuajarse — *vt* : cuajar

cure ['kjur] *n* : cura *f*, remedio *m* — ~ *vt* **cured; curing** : curar

curfew ['kərˌfju:] *n* : toque *m* de queda

curious ['kjuriəs] *adj* : curioso — **curio** ['kjuri.o:] *n, pl* **-rios** : curiosidad *f* — **curiosity** [ˌkjuri'osəti] *n, pl* **-ties** : curiosidad *f*

curl ['kərl] *vt* **1** : rizar **2** COIL : enrollar, enroscar — *vi* **1** : rizarse **2** ~ **up** : acurrucarse — ~ *n* : rizo *m* — **curler** ['kərlər] *n* : rulo *m* — **curly** ['kərli] *adj* **curlier; -est** : rizado

currant ['kərənt] *n* **1** : grosella *f* (fruta) **2** RAISIN : pasa *f* de Corinto

currency ['kərənsi] *n, pl* **-cies 1** MONEY : moneda *f* **2 gain** ~ : ganar aceptación

current ['kərənt] *adj* **1** PRESENT : actual **2** PREVALENT : corriente — ~ *n* : corriente *f*

curriculum [kə'rɪkjələm] *n, pl* **-la** [-lə] : plan *m* de estudios

curry ['kəri] *n, pl* **-ries** : curry *m*

curse ['kərs] *n* : maldición *f* — ~ *v* **cursed; cursing** : maldecir

cursor ['kərsər] *n* : cursor *m*

cursory ['kərsəri] *adj* : superficial

curt ['kərt] *adj* : corto, seco

curtail [kər'teɪl] *vt* : acortar
curtain ['kərtən] *n* : cortina *f* (de una ventana), telón *m* (en un teatro) — **~** *n* : reverencia *f*
curtsy ['kərtsi] *vi* **-sied** *or* **-seyed;** **-sying** *or* **-seying** : hacer una reverencia — **~** *n* : reverencia *f*
curve ['kərv] *v* **curved; curving** *vi* : hacer una curva — *vt* : encorvar — **~** *n* : curva *f*
cushion ['kuʃən] *n* : cojín *m* — **~** *vt* : amortiguar
custard ['kʌstərd] *n* : natillas *fpl*
custody ['kʌstədi] *n, pl* **-dies** 1 : custodia *f* 2 **be in ~** : estar detenido — **custodian** [kʌ'stoːdiən] *n* : custodio *m*, -dia *f*; guardián, -diana *f*
custom ['kʌstəm] *n* : costumbre *f* — **customary** ['kʌstəˌmeri] *adj* : habitual, acostumbrado — **customer** ['kʌstəmər] *n* : cliente *m*, -ta *f* — **customs** ['kʌstəmz] *npl* : aduana *f*
cut ['kʌt] *v* **cut; cutting** *vt* 1 cortar 2 REDUCE : reducir, rebajar 3 **~ oneself** : cortarse 4 **~ up** : cortar en pedazos — *vi* 1 : cortar 2 **~ in** : interrumpir

~ *n* 1 : corte *m* 2 REDUCTION : rebaja *f*, reducción *f*
cute ['kjuːt] *adj* **cuter; -est** : mono *fam*, lindo
cutlery ['kʌtləri] *n* : cubiertos *mpl*
cutlet ['kʌtlət] *n* : chuleta *f*
cutting ['kʌtɪŋ] *adj* : cortante, mordaz
cyanide ['saɪəˌnaɪd, -nɪd] *n* : cianuro *m*
cycle ['saɪkəl] *n* 1 : ciclo *m* 2 BICYCLE : bicicleta *f* — **~** *vi* **-cled; -cling** : ir en bicicleta — **cyclic** ['saɪklɪk, 'sɪ-] *or* **cyclical** [-klɪkəl] *adj* : cíclico — **cyclist** ['saɪklɪst] *n* : ciclista *mf*
cyclone ['saɪˌkloːn] *n* : ciclón *m*
cylinder ['sɪləndər] *n* : cilindro *m* — **cylindrical** [sə'lɪndrɪkəl] *adj* : cilíndrico
cymbal ['sɪmbəl] *n* : platillo *m*, címbalo *m*
cynic ['sɪnɪk] *n* : cínico *m*, -ca *f* — **cynical** ['sɪnɪkəl] *adj* : cínico — **cynicism** ['sɪnəˌsɪzəm] *n* : cinismo *m*
cypress ['saɪprəs] *n* : ciprés *m*
cyst ['sɪst] *n* : quiste *m*
czar ['zɑr, 'sɑr] *n* : zar *m*
Czech ['tʃɛk] *adj* : checo — **~** *n* : checo *m* (idioma)

D

d ['diː] *n, pl* **d's** *or* **ds** ['diːz] : d *f*, cuarta letra del alfabeto inglés
dab ['dæb] *n* : toque *m* — **~** *vt* **dabbed; dabbing** : dar toques ligeros a, aplicar suavemente
dabble ['dæbəl] *vi* **-bled; -bling** **~ in** : interesarse superficialmente en — **dabbler** *n* : aficionado *m*, -da *f*
dad ['dæd] *n* : papá *m fam* — **daddy** ['dædi] *n, pl* **-dies** : papá *m fam*
daffodil ['dæfəˌdɪl] *n* : narciso *m*
dagger ['dægər] *n* : daga *f*, puñal *m*
daily ['deɪli] *adj* : diario — **~** *adv* : diariamente
dainty ['deɪnti] *adj* **-tier; -est** : delicado
dairy ['dæri] *n, pl* **-ies** 1 : lechería *f* (tienda) 2 *or* **~ farm** : granja *f* lechera
daisy ['deɪzi] *n, pl* **-sies** : margarita *f*
dam ['dæm] *n* : presa *f* — **~** *vt* **dammed; damming** : represar
damage ['dæmɪdʒ] *n* 1 : daño *m*, perjuicio *m* 2 **~s** *npl* : daños y perjuicios *mpl* — **~** *vt* **-aged; -aging** : dañar
damn ['dæm] *vt* 1 CONDEMN : condenar 2 CURSE : maldecir — **~** *n* **not give a ~** : no importarse un comino *fam* — *or* **damned** ['dæmd] *adj* : maldito *fam*
damp ['dæmp] *adj* : húmedo — **dampen** ['dæmpən] *vt* 1 MOISTEN : humede-

cer 2 DISCOURAGE : desalentar, desanimar — **dampness** ['dæmpnəs] *n* : humedad *f*
dance ['dæns] *v* **danced; dancing** : bailar — **~** *n* : baile *m* — **dancer** ['dænsər] *n* : bailarín *m*, -rina *f*
dandelion ['dændəˌlaɪən] *n* : diente *m* de león
dandruff ['dændrəf] *n* : caspa *f*
dandy ['dændi] *adj* **-dier; -est** : de primera, excelente
danger ['deɪndʒər] *n* : peligro *m* — **dangerous** ['deɪndʒərəs] *adj* : peligroso
dangle ['dæŋgəl] *v* **-gled; -gling** *vi* HANG : colgar, pender — *vt* : hacer oscilar
Danish ['deɪnɪʃ] *adj* : danés — **~** *n* : danés *m* (idioma)
dank ['dæŋk] *adj* : frío y húmedo
dare ['dær] *v* **dared; daring** *vt* : desafiar — *vi* : osar — **~** *n* : desafío *m* — **daredevil** ['dærˌdɛvəl] *n* : persona *f* temeraria — **daring** ['dærɪŋ] *adj* : atrevido, audaz — **~** *n* : audacia *f*
dark ['dɑrk] *adj* 1 : oscuro 2 : moreno (dícese del pelo o de la piel) 3 GLOOMY : sombrío 4 **get ~** : hacerse de noche — **darken** ['dɑrkən] *vt* : oscurecer — *vi* : oscurecerse — **darkness** ['dɑrknəs] *n* : oscuridad *f*

darling ['dɑrlɪŋ] *n* BELOVED : querido *m*, -da *f* — *adj* : querido

darn ['dɑrn] *vt* : zurcir — *adj* : maldito *fam*

dart ['dɑrt] *n* 1 : dardo *m* 2 **~s** *npl* : juego *m* de dardos — *~ vi* : precipitarse

dash ['dæʃ] *vt* 1 SMASH : romper 2 HURL : lanzar 3 **~ off** : hacer (algo) rápidamente — *vi* : lanzarse, irse corriendo — *~ n* 1 : guión *m* largo (signo de puntuación), pizca *f* 3 RACE : carrera *f* — **dashboard** ['dæʃ,bord] *n* : tablero *m* de instrumentos — **dashing** ['dæʃɪŋ] *adj* : gallardo, apuesto

data ['deɪt̬ə, 'dæ-, 'dɑ-] *ns & pl* : datos *mpl* — **database** ['deɪt̬ə,beɪs, 'dæ-, 'dɑ-] *n* : base *f* de datos

date¹ ['deɪt] *n* : dátil *m* (fruta)

date² *n* 1 : fecha *f* 2 APPOINTMENT : cita *f* — *v* **dated; dating** *vt* 1 : fechar (una carta, etc.) 2 : salir con (algn) — *vi* **~ from** : datar de — **dated** ['deɪt̬əd] *adj* : pasado de moda

daub ['dɔb] *vt* : embadurnar

daughter ['dɔt̬ər] *n* : hija *f* — **daughter-in-law** ['dɔt̬ərɪn,lɔ] *n*, *pl* **daughters-in-law** : nuera *f*

daunt ['dɔnt] *vt* : intimidar

dawdle ['dɔdəl] *vi* **-dled; -dling** : entretenerse, perder tiempo

dawn ['dɔn] *vi* 1 : amanecer 2 **it ~ed on him that** : cayó en la cuenta de que — *~ n* : amanecer *m*

day ['deɪ] *n* 1 : día *m* 2 *or* working **~** : jornada *f* 3 **the ~ before** : el día anterior 4 **the ~ before yesterday** : anteayer 5 **the ~ after** : el día siguiente 6 **the ~ after tomorrow** : pasada mañana — **daybreak** ['deɪ,breɪk] *n* : amanecer *m* — **daydream** ['deɪ,dri:m] *n* : ensueño *m* — *vi* : soñar despierto — **daylight** ['deɪ,laɪt] *n* : luz *f* del día — **daytime** ['deɪ,taɪm] *n* : día *m*

daze ['deɪz] *vt* **dazed; dazing** : aturdir — *~ n* **in a ~** : aturdido

dazzle ['dæzəl] *vt* **-zled; -zling** : deslumbrar

dead ['dɛd] *adj* 1 LIFELESS : muerto *m* 2 NUMB : entumecido — *~ n* 1 **in the ~ of night** : en plena noche 2 **the ~** : los muertos — *~ adv* ABSOLUTELY : absolutamente — **deaden** ['dɛdən] *vt* 1 : atenuar (dolores) 2 MUFFLE : amortiguar — **dead end** ['dɛd'ɛnd] *n* : callejón *m* sin salida — **deadline** ['dɛd,laɪn] *n* : fecha *f* límite — **deadlock** ['dɛd,lɑk] *n* : punto *m* muerto — **deadly**

['dɛdli] *adj* **-lier; -est** 1 : mortal, letal 2 ACCURATE : certero, preciso

deaf ['dɛf] *adj* : sordo — **deafen** ['dɛfən] *vt* : ensordecer — **deafness** ['dɛfnəs] *n* : sordera *f*

deal ['di:l] *n* 1 TRANSACTION : trato *m*, transacción *f* 2 : reparto *m* (de naipes) 3 **a good ~** : mucho — *~ v* **dealt; dealing** *vt* 1 : dar 2 : repartir, dar (naipes) 3 **~ a blow** : asestar un golpe — *vi* 1 : dar, repartir (en juegos de naipes) 2 **~ in** : comerciar en 3 **~ with** CONCERN : tratar de 4 **~ with s.o.** : tratar con algn — **dealer** ['di:lər] *n* : comerciante *mf* — **dealings** *npl* : trato *m*, relaciones *fpl*

dean ['di:n] *n* : decano *m*, -na *f*

dear ['dɪr] *adj* : querido — *~ n* : querido *m*, -da *f* — **dearly** ['dɪrli] *adv* 1 : mucho 2 **pay ~** : pagar caro

death ['dɛθ] *n* : muerte *f*

debar ['dɪ'bɑr] *vt* : excluir

debate [dɪ'beɪt] *n* : debate *m*, discusión *f* — *vt* **-bated; -bating** : debatir, discutir

debit ['dɛbɪt] *vt* : adeudar, cargar — *~ n* : débito *m*, debe *m*

debris [də'bri:, deɪ-; 'deɪbri:] *n*, *pl* **-bris** [-'bri:z, -,bri:z] : escombros *mpl*

debt ['dɛt] *n* : deuda *f* — **debtor** ['dɛt̬ər] *n* : deudor *m*, -dora *f*

debunk [dɪ'bʌŋk] *vt* : desmentir

debut [deɪ'bju:, 'deɪ,bju:] *n* : debut *m* — *vi* : debutar

decade ['dɛ,keɪd, dɛ'keɪd] *n* : década *f*

decadence ['dɛkədəns] *n* : decadencia *f* — **decadent** ['dɛkədənt] *adj* : decadente

decal ['di:,kæl, dɪ'kæl] *n* : calcomanía *f*

decanter [dɪ'kæntər] *n* : licorera *f*

decapitate [dɪ'kæpə,teɪt] *vt* **-tated; -tating** : decapitar

decay [dɪ'keɪ] *vi* 1 DECOMPOSE : descomponerse 2 DETERIORATE : deteriorarse 3 : cariarse (dícese de los dientes) — *~ n* 1 : descomposición *f* 2 : deterioro *m* (de un edificio, etc.) 3 : caries *f* (de los dientes)

deceased [dɪ'si:st] *adj* : difunto — *~ n* **the ~** : el difunto, la difunta

deceive [dɪ'si:v] *vt* **-ceived; -ceiving** : engañar — **deceit** [dɪ'si:t] *n* : engaño *m* — **deceitful** [dɪ'si:tfəl] *adj* : engañoso

December [dɪ'sɛmbər] *n* : diciembre *m*

decent ['di:sənt] *adj* 1 : decente 2 KIND : bueno, amable — **decency** ['di:səntsi] *n*, *pl* **-cies** : decencia *f*

deception [dɪ'sɛpʃən] *n* : engaño *m* — **deceptive** [dɪ'sɛptɪv] *adj* : engañoso

decide [dɪ'saɪd] v **-cided; -ciding** vt : decidir — vi : decidirse — **decided** [dɪ'saɪdəd] adj **1** UNQUESTIONABLE : indudable **2** RESOLUTE : decidido — **decidedly** [dɪ'saɪdədli] adv **1** DEFINITELY : decididamente **2** RESOLUTELY : con decisión

decimal ['dɛsəməl] adj : decimal — n : número m decimal — **decimal point** n : coma f decimal

decipher [dɪ'saɪfər] vt : descifrar

decision [dɪ'sɪʒən] n : decisión f — **decisive** [dɪ'saɪsɪv] adj **1** RESOLUTE : decidido **2** CONCLUSIVE : decisivo

deck ['dɛk] n **1** : cubierta f (de un barco) **2** or ~ **of cards** : baraja f (de naipes) **3** TERRACE : entarimado m

declare [dɪ'klær] vt **-clared; -claring** : declarar — **declaration** [ˌdɛkləˈreɪʃən] n : declaración f

decline [dɪ'klaɪn] v **-clined; -clining** REFUSE : declinar, rehusar — vi DECREASE : disminuir — ~ n **1** DETERIORATION : decadencia f, deterioro m **2** DECREASE : disminución f

decode [dɪ'koːd] vt **-coded; -coding** : descodificar

decompose [ˌdiːkəmˈpoːz] vt **-posed; -posing** : descomponer — vi : descomponerse

decongestant [ˌdiːkənˈdʒɛstənt] n : descongestionante m

decorate ['dɛkəˌreɪt] vt **-rated; -rating** : decorar — **decor** or **décor** [deɪˈkor, ˈdeɪˌkor] n : decoración f — **decoration** [ˌdɛkəˈreɪʃən] n : decoración f — **decorator** ['dɛkəˌreɪtər] n : decorador m, -dora f

decoy ['diːˌkɔɪ, dɪ'-] n : señuelo m

decrease [dɪ'kriːs] v **-creased; -creasing** : disminuir — ~ ['diːˌkriːs] n : disminución f

decree [dɪ'kriː] n : decreto m — ~ vt **-creed; -creeing** : decretar

decrepit [dɪ'krɛpɪt] adj **1** FEEBLE : decrépito **2** DILAPIDATED : ruinoso

dedicate ['dɛdɪˌkeɪt] vt **-cated; -cating** : dedicar **2** ~ **oneself to** : consagrarse a — **dedication** [ˌdɛdɪˈkeɪʃən] n **1** DEVOTION : dedicación f **2** INSCRIPTION : dedicatoria f

deduce [dɪ'duːs, -'djuːs] vt **-duced; -ducing** : deducir — **deduct** [dɪ'dʌkt] vt : deducir — **deduction** [dɪ'dʌkʃən] n : deducción f

deed ['diːd] n : acción f, hecho m

deem ['diːm] vt : considerar, juzgar

deep ['diːp] adj : hondo, profundo — ~ adv **1** DEEPLY : profundamente **2** ~ **down** : en el fondo **3 dig** ~ : cavar hondo — **deepen** ['diːpən] vt : ahondar — vi : hacerse más profundo — **deeply** ['diːpli] adv : hondo, profundamente

deer ['dɪr] ns & pl : ciervo m

deface [dɪ'feɪs] vt **-faced; -facing** : desfigurar

default [dɪ'fɔlt, 'diːˌfɔlt] n **by** ~ : en rebeldía — ~ vi **1** ~ **on** : no pagar (una deuda) **2** : no presentarse (en deportes)

defeat [dɪ'fiːt] vt **1** BEAT : vencer, derrotar **2** FRUSTRATE : frustrar — ~ n : derrota f

defect ['diːˌfɛkt, dɪ'fɛkt] n : defecto m — ~ [dɪ'fɛkt] vi : desertar — **defective** [dɪ'fɛktɪv] adj : defectuoso

defend [dɪ'fɛnd] vt : defender — **defendant** [dɪ'fɛndənt] n : acusado m, -da f — **defense** or Brit **defence** [dɪ'fɛns, 'diːˌfɛns] n : defensa f — **defenseless** or Brit **defenceless** adj : indefenso — **defensive** [dɪ'fɛnsɪv] adj : defensivo — ~ n **on the** ~ : a la defensiva

defer [dɪ'fər] v **-ferred; -ferring** vt : diferir, aplazar — vi ~ **to** : deferir a — **deference** ['dɛfərəns] n : deferencia f — **deferential** [ˌdɛfəˈrɛntʃəl] adj : deferente

defiance [dɪ'faɪəns] n **1** : desafío m **2 in** ~ **of** : a despecho de — **defiant** [dɪ'faɪənt] adj : desafiante

deficiency [dɪ'fɪʃənsi] n, pl **-cies** : deficiencia f — **deficient** [dɪ'fɪʃənt] adj : deficiente

deficit ['dɛfəsɪt] n : déficit m

defile [dɪ'faɪl] vt **-filed; -filing 1** DIRTY : ensuciar **2** DESECRATE : profanar

define [dɪ'faɪn] vt **-fined; -fining** : definir — **definite** ['dɛfənɪt] adj **1** : definido **2** CERTAIN : seguro, incuestionable — **definition** [ˌdɛfəˈnɪʃən] n : definición f — **definitive** [dɪ'fɪnətɪv] adj : definitivo

deflate [dɪ'fleɪt] v **-flated; -flating** vt : desinflar (una llanta, etc.) — vi : desinflarse

deflect [dɪ'flɛkt] vt : desviar — vi : desviarse

deform [dɪ'fɔrm] vt : deformar — **deformity** [dɪ'fɔrməti] n, pl **-ties** : deformidad f

defraud [dɪ'frɔd] vt : defraudar

defrost [dɪ'frɔst] vt : descongelar — vi : descongelarse

deft ['dɛft] adj : hábil, diestro

defy [dɪ'faɪ] vt **-fied; -fying 1** CHALLENGE : desafiar **2** RESIST : resistir

degenerate [dɪ'dʒɛnəˌreɪt] vi : degenerar — ~ [dɪ'dʒɛnərət] adj : degenerado

degrade 237 depend

degrade [dɪ'greɪd] *vt* -graded; -grading
: degradar — **degrading** *adj* : degradante

degree [dɪ'gri:] *n* 1 : grado *m* 2 *or* academic ~ : título *m*

dehydrate [di'haɪˌdreɪt] *vt* -drated; -drating : deshidratar

deign ['deɪn] *vi* ~ to : dignarse (a)

deity ['di:əti, 'deɪ-] *n, pl* -ties : deidad *f*

dejected [dɪ'dʒɛktəd] *adj* : abatido — **dejection** [dɪ'dʒɛkʃən] *n* : abatimiento *m*

delay [dɪ'leɪ] *n* : retraso *m* — ~ *vt* 1 POSTPONE : aplazar 2 HOLD UP : retrasar — *vi* : demorar

delectable [dɪ'lɛktəbəl] *adj* : delicioso

delegate [dɛləˌgeɪt, -gət] *n* : delegado *m*, -da *f* — ['dɛləˌgeɪt] *vt* -gated; -gating : delegar — **delegation** [dɛlɪ'geɪʃən] *n* : delegación *f*

delete [dɪ'li:t] *vt* -leted; -leting : borrar

deliberate [dɪ'lɪbəˌreɪt] *vt* -ated; -ating : deliberar sobre — *vi* : deliberar — [dɪ'lɪbərət] *adj* : deliberado — **deliberately** [dɪ'lɪbərətli] *adv* INTENTIONALLY : a propósito — **deliberation** [dɪˌlɪbə-'reɪʃən] *n* : deliberación *f*

delicacy ['dɛlɪkəsi] *n, pl* -cies 1 : delicadeza *f* 2 FOOD : manjar *m*, exquisitez *f* — **delicate** ['dɛlɪkət] *adj* : delicado

delicatessen [ˌdɛlɪkə'tɛsən] *n* : charcutería *f*

delicious [dɪ'lɪʃəs] *adj* : delicioso

delight [dɪ'laɪt] *n* : placer *m*, deleite *m* — ~ *vt* : deleitar, encantar — *vi* — in : deleitarse con — **delightful** [dɪ-'laɪtfəl] *adj* : delicioso, encantador

delinquent [dɪ'lɪŋkwənt] *adj* : delincuente — ~ *n* : delincuente *mf*

delirious [dɪ'lɪriəs] *adj* : delirante — **delirium** [dɪ'lɪriəm] *n* : delirio *m*

deliver [dɪ'lɪvər] *vt* 1 DISTRIBUTE : entregar, repartir 2 FREE : liberar 3 : asistir en el parto de (un niño) 4 : pronunciar (un discurso, etc.) 5 DEAL : asestar (un golpe, etc.) — **delivery** [dɪ'lɪvəri] *n, pl* -eries 1 DISTRIBUTION : entrega *f*, reparto *m* 2 LIBERATION : liberación *f* 3 CHILDBIRTH : parto *m*, alumbramiento *m*

delude [dɪ'lu:d] *vt* -luded; -luding 1 : engañar 2 ~ oneself : engañarse

deluge ['dɛljuːdʒ, -juːʒ] *n* 1 : diluvio *m*

delusion [dɪ'luːʒən] *n* : ilusión *f*

deluxe [dɪ'lʌks, -'lʊks] *adj* : de lujo

delve ['dɛlv] *vi* delved; delving 1 : escarbar 2 ~ into PROBE : investigar

demand [dɪ'mænd] *n* 1 REQUEST : petición *f* 2 CLAIM : reclamación *f*, exigen-

cia *f* 3 → supply — ~ *vt* : exigir — **demanding** *adj* : exigente

demean [dɪ'miːn] *vt* ~ oneself : rebajarse

demeanor [dɪ'miːnər] *n* : comportamiento *m*

demented [dɪ'mɛntəd] *adj* : demente, loco

demise [dɪ'maɪz] *n* : fallecimiento *m*

democracy [dɪ'mɑkrəsi] *n, pl* -cies : democracia *f* — **democrat** ['dɛmə-ˌkræt] *n* : demócrata *mf* — **democratic** [ˌdɛmə'krætɪk] *adj* : democrático

demolish [dɪ'mɑlɪʃ] *vt* : demoler — **demolition** [ˌdɛmə'lɪʃən, ˌdiː-] *n* : demolición *f*

demon ['diːmən] *n* : demonio *m*

demonstrate ['dɛmənˌstreɪt] *v* -strated; -strating *vt* : demostrar — *vi* RALLY : manifestarse — **demonstration** [ˌdɛmən'streɪʃən] *n* 1 : demostración *f* 2 RALLY : manifestación *f*

demoralize [dɪ'mɔrəˌlaɪz] *vt* -ized; -izing : desmoralizar

demote [dɪ'moʊt] *vt* -moted; -moting : bajar de categoría

demure [dɪ'mjʊr] *adj* : recatado

den ['dɛn] *n* LAIR : guarida *f*

denial [dɪ'naɪəl] *n* 1 : negación *f*, rechazo *m* 2 REFUSAL : denegación *f*

denim ['dɛnəm] *n* : tela *f* vaquera, mezclilla *f* Lat

denomination [dɪˌnɑmə'neɪʃən] *n* 1 : confesión *f* (religiosa) 2 : valor *m* (de una moneda)

denounce [dɪ'naʊnts] *vt* -nounced; -nouncing : denunciar

dense ['dɛnts] *adj* denser; -est 1 THICK : denso 2 STUPID : estúpido — **density** ['dɛntsəti] *n, pl* -ties : densidad *f*

dent ['dɛnt] *vt* : abollar — ~ *n* : abolladura *f*

dental ['dɛntəl] *adj* : dental — **dental floss** *n* : hilo *m* dental — **dentist** ['dɛntɪst] *n* : dentista *mf* — **dentures** ['dɛntʃərz] *npl* : dentadura *f* postiza

deny [dɪ'naɪ] *vt* -nied; -nying 1 : negar 2 REFUSE : denegar

deodorant [di'oːdərənt] *n* : desodorante *m*

depart [dɪ'pɑrt] *vi* 1 : salir 2 ~ from : apartarse de (la verdad, etc.)

department [dɪ'pɑrtmənt] *n* : sección *f* (de una tienda, etc.), departamento *m* (de una empresa, etc.), ministerio *m* (del gobierno) — **department store** *n* : grandes almacenes *mpl*

departure [dɪ'pɑrtʃər] *n* 1 : salida *f* 2 DEVIATION : desviación *f*

depend [dɪ'pɛnd] *vi* 1 ~ on : depender

de 2 — **on s.o.** : contar con algn 3
that ~**s** : eso depende — **dependable** [dɪ'pɛndəbəl] *adj* : digno de confianza — **dependence** [dɪ'pɛndənts] *n*
: dependencia *f* — **dependent** [dɪ'pɛndənt] *adj* : dependiente

depict [dɪ'pɪkt] *vt* **1** PORTRAY : representar **2** DESCRIBE : describir

deplete [dɪ'pliːt] *vt* **-pleted; -pleting**
: agotar, reducir

deplore [dɪ'plɔr] *vt* **-plored; -ploring**
: deplorar, lamentar — **deplorable**
[dɪ'plɔrəbəl] *adj* : lamentable

deploy [dɪ'plɔɪ] *vt* : desplegar

deport [dɪ'pɔrt] *vt* : deportar, expulsar
(de un país) — **deportation** [ˌdiˌpɔr-
'teɪʃən] *n* : deportación *f*

depose [dɪ'poːz] *vt* **-posed; -posing**
: deponer

deposit [dɪ'pɑzət] *vt* **-ited; -iting** : depositar — ~ *n* **1** : depósito *m* **2** DOWN
PAYMENT : entrega *f* inicial

depot [*in sense 1 usu* 'deˌpo, *2 usu* 'diː-]
n **1** WAREHOUSE : almacén *m*, depósito
m **2** STATION : terminal *mf*

depreciate [dɪ'priːʃieɪt] *vi* **-ated; -ating**
: depreciarse — **depreciation** [dɪ-
ˌpriːʃieɪʃən] *n* : depreciación *f*

depress [dɪ'prɛs] *vt* **1** : deprimir **2** PRESS
: apretar — **depressed** [dɪ'prɛst] *adj*
: abatido, deprimido — **depressing**
[dɪ'prɛsɪŋ] *adj* : deprimente — **depression** [dɪ'prɛʃən] *n* : depresión *f*

deprive [dɪ'praɪv] *vt* **-prived; -priving**
: privar

depth [dɛpθ] *n, pl* **depths** [dɛpθs,
'dɛps] **1** : profundidad *f* **2 in the ~s of
night** : en lo más profundo de la noche

deputy ['dɛpjuti] *n, pl* **-ties** : suplente
mf; sustituto *m*, -ta *f*

derail [dɪ'reɪl] *vt* : hacer descarrilar

deranged [dɪ'reɪndʒd] *adj* : trastornado

derelict ['dɛrəˌlɪkt] *adj* : abandonado

deride [dɪ'raɪd] *vt* **-rided; -riding** : burlarse de — **derision** [dɪ'rɪʒən] *n* : mofa
f

derive [dɪ'raɪv] *vi* **-rived; -riving** : derivar — **derivation** [ˌdɛrə'veɪʃən] *n* : derivación *f*

derogatory [dɪ'rɑgəˌtɔri] *adj* : despectivo

descend [dɪ'sɛnd] *v* : descender, bajar
— **descendant** [dɪ'sɛndənt] *n* : descendiente *mf* —**descent** [dɪ'sɛnt] *n* **1**
: descenso *m* **2** LINEAGE : descendencia *f*

describe [dɪ'skraɪb] *vt* **-scribed; -scribing** : describir — **description** [dɪ-
'skrɪpʃən] *n* : descripción *f* — **descriptive** [dɪ'skrɪptɪv] *adj* : descriptivo

desecrate ['dɛsɪˌkreɪt] *vt* **-crated;
-crating** : profanar

desert ['dɛzərt] *n* : desierto *m* — ~ *adj*
~ **island** : isla *f* desierta — ~ [dɪ-
'zərt] *vt* : abandonar — *vi* : desertar —
deserter [dɪ'zərtər] *n* : desertor *m*,
-tora *f*

deserve [dɪ'zərv] *vt* **-served; -serving**
: merecer

design [dɪ'zaɪn] *vt* **1** DEVISE : diseñar **2**
PLAN : proyectar — ~ *n* **1** : diseño *m*
2 PLAN : plan *m*, proyecto *m*

designate ['dɛzɪgˌneɪt] *vt* **-nated;
-nating** : nombrar, designar

designer [dɪ'zaɪnər] *n* : diseñador *m*,
-dora *f*

desire [dɪ'zaɪr] *vt* **-sired; -siring** : desear — ~ *n* : deseo *m* — **desirable** [dɪ-
'zaɪrəbəl] *adj* : deseable

desk [dɛsk] *n* : escritorio *m*, pupitre *m*
(en la escuela)

desolate ['dɛsələt, -zə-] *adj* : desolado

despair [dɪ'spær] *vi* : desesperar — ~ *n*
: desesperación *f*

desperate ['dɛspərət] *adj* : desesperado
— **desperation** [ˌdɛspə'reɪʃən] *n* : desesperación *f*

despise [dɪ'spaɪz] *vt* **-spised; -spising**
: despreciar — **despicable** [dɪ-
'spɪkəbəl, 'dɛspɪ-] *adj* : despreciable

despite [dɪ'spaɪt] *prep* : a pesar de

despondent [dɪ'spɑndənt] *adj* : desanimado

dessert [dɪ'zərt] *n* : postre *m*

destination [ˌdɛstə'neɪʃən] *n* : destino *m*
— **destined** [dɪ'stɛnd] *adj* **1** : destinado **2 — for** : con destino a — **destiny**
['dɛstəni] *n, pl* **-nies** : destino *m*

destitute ['dɛstəˌtuːt, -ˌtjuːt] *adj* : indigente

destroy [dɪ'strɔɪ] *vt* : destruir — **destruction** [dɪ'strʌkʃən] *n* : destrucción *f*
— **destructive** [dɪ'strʌktɪv] *adj* : destructivo

detach [dɪ'tætʃ] *vt* : separar — **detached** [dɪ'tætʃt] *adj* **1** : separado **2** IMPARTIAL : objetivo

detail [dɪ'teɪl, 'diːˌteɪl] *n* **1** : detalle *m* **2 go
into** ~ : entrar en detalles — ~ *vt*
: detallar — **detailed** *adj* : detallado

detain [dɪ'teɪn] *vt* **1** : detener (un prisionero) **2** DELAY : entretener

detect [dɪ'tɛkt] *vt* : detectar — **detection** [dɪ'tɛkʃən] *n* : detección *f*, descubrimiento *m* — **detective** [dɪ'tɛktɪv]
n : detective *mf*

detention [dɪ'tɛntʃən] *n* : detención *m*

deter [dɪ'tər] *vt* **-terred; -terring** : disuadir

detergent [dɪ'tərdʒənt] *n* : detergente *m*

deteriorate [dɪ'tɪriə,reɪt] vi **-rated;** **-rating** : deteriorarse — **deterioration** [dɪ,tɪriə'reɪʃən] n : deterioro m

determine [dɪ'tərmən] vt **-mined;** **-mining** : determinar — **determined** [dɪ'tərmənd] adj RESOLUTE : decidido — **determination** [dɪ,tərmə'neɪʃən] n : determinación f

deterrent [dɪ'tərənt] n : medida f disuasiva

detest [dɪ'tɛst] vt : detestar — **detestable** [dɪ'tɛstəbəl] adj : odioso

detonate [dɛtən,eɪt] v **-nated; -nating** vt : hacer detonar — vi EXPLODE : detonar, estallar — **detonation** [,dɛtə'neɪʃən, 'dɛtə,-] n : detonación f

detour ['di:,tʊr, dɪ'tʊr] n 1 : desviación f 2 **make a ~** : dar un rodeo — **~** vi : desviarse

detract [dɪ'trækt] vi **~ from** : aminorar, restar importancia a

detrimental [,dɛtrə'mɛntəl] adj : perjudicial

devalue [dɪ'væl,ju:] vt **-ued; -uing** : devaluar

devastate ['dɛvə,steɪt] vt **-tated; -tating** : devastar — **devastating** adj : devastador — **devastation** [,dɛvə'steɪʃən] n : devastación f

develop [dɪ'vɛləp] vt 1 : desarrollar 2 **~ an illness** : contraer una enfermedad — vi 1 GROW : desarrollarse 2 HAPPEN : aparecer — **development** [dɪ'vɛləpmənt] n : desarrollo m

deviate ['di:vi,eɪt] v **-ated; -ating** vi : desviarse — **deviation** [,di:vi'eɪʃən] n : desviación f

device [dɪ'vaɪs] n : dispositivo m, mecanismo m

devil ['dɛvəl] n : diablo m, demonio m — **devilish** ['dɛvəlɪʃ] adj : diabólico

devious ['di:viəs] adj 1 CRAFTY : taimado 2 WINDING : tortuoso

devise [dɪ'vaɪz] vt **-vised; -vising** : idear, concebir

devoid [dɪ'vɔɪd] adj **~ of** : desprovisto de

devote [dɪ'voːt] vt **-voted; -voting** : consagrar, dedicar — **devoted** [dɪ'voːtəd] adj : leal — **devotee** [,dɛvə'ti:, -'teɪ] n : devoto m, -ta f — **devotion** [dɪ'voːʃən] n 1 : devoción f, dedicación f 2 : oración f (en religión)

devour [dɪ'vaʊər] vt : devorar

devout [dɪ'vaʊt] adj : devoto

dew ['du:, 'dju:] n : rocío m

dexterity [dɛk'stɛrəti] n, pl **-ties** : destreza f

diabetes [,daɪə'bi:ti:z] n : diabetes f —

diabetic [,daɪə'bɛtɪk] adj : diabético — **~** n : diabético m, -ca f

diabolic [,daɪə'bɑlɪk] or **diabolical** [-lɪkəl] adj : diabólico

diagnosis [,daɪəg'noːsɪs] n, pl **-noses** [-'noː,siːz] : diagnóstico m — **diagnose** ['daɪəg,noːs, ,daɪəg'noːs] vt **-nosed; -nosing** : diagnosticar — **diagnostic** [,daɪəg'nɑstɪk] adj : diagnóstico

diagonal [daɪ'ægənəl] adj : diagonal, en diagonal — **~** n : diagonal f

diagram ['daɪə,græm] n : diagrama m

dial ['daɪəl] n 1 : esfera f (de un reloj), dial m (de un radio, etc.) — **~** v **dialed** or **dialled** : marcar

dialect ['daɪə,lɛkt] n : dialecto m

dialogue ['daɪə,lɔg] n : diálogo m

diameter [daɪ'æmətər] n : diámetro m

diamond ['daɪmənd, 'daɪə-] n 1 : diamante m 2 : rombo m (forma) 3 or **baseball ~** : cuadro m, diamante m

diaper ['daɪpər, 'daɪə-] n : pañal m

diaphragm ['daɪə,fræm] n : diafragma m

diarrhea [,daɪə'riːə] n : diarrea f

diary ['daɪəri] n, pl **-ries** : diario m

dice ['daɪs] ns & pl : dados mpl (juego)

dictate ['dɪk,teɪt, dɪk'teɪt] vt **-tated; -tating** : dictar — **dictation** [dɪk'teɪʃən] n : dictado m — **dictator** ['dɪk,teɪtər] n : dictador m, -dora f — **dictatorship** [dɪk'teɪtər,ʃɪp, 'dɪk,-] n : dictadura f

dictionary ['dɪkʃə,nɛri] n, pl **-naries** : diccionario m

did → **do**

die¹ ['daɪ] vi **died** ['daɪd]; **dying** ['daɪɪŋ] 1 : morir 2 **~ down** : amainar, disminuir 3 **~ out** : extinguirse 4 **be dying for** : morirse por

die² ['daɪ] n 1 pl **dice** ['daɪs] : dado m (para jugar) 2 pl **dies** ['daɪz] MOLD : molde m

diesel ['diːzəl, -səl] n : diesel m

diet ['daɪət] n 1 FOOD : alimentación f 2 **go on a ~** : ponerse a régimen — **~** vi : estar a régimen

differ ['dɪfər] vi **-ferred; -ferring** 1 : diferir, ser distinto 2 DISAGREE : no estar de acuerdo — **difference** ['dɪfrənts, 'dɪfərənts] n : diferencia f — **different** ['dɪfrənt, 'dɪfərənt] adj : distinto, diferente — **differentiate** [,dɪfə'rɛntʃi,eɪt] v **-ated; -ating** vt : diferenciar — vi : distinguir — **differently** ['dɪfrəntli, 'dɪfərənt-] adv : de otra manera

difficult ['dɪfɪ,kʌlt] adj : difícil — **difficulty** ['dɪfɪ,kʌlti] n, pl **-ties** : dificultad f

diffident ['dɪfədənt] adj : tímido, que falta confianza

dig ['dɪg] v **dug** ['dʌg]; **digging** vt **1** : cavar **2** — **up** : desenterrar — vi : cavar — **~** n **1** GIBE : pulla f **2** EXCAVATION : excavación f

digest ['daɪˌdʒɛst] n : resumen m — ['daɪˌdʒɛst] vt **1** : digerir **2** SUMMARIZE : resumir — **digestible** [daɪˈdʒɛstəbəl, dɪ-] adj : digerible — **digestion** [daɪˈdʒɛstʃən, dɪ-] n : digestión f — **digestive** [daɪˈdʒɛstɪv, dɪ-] adj : digestivo

digit ['dɪdʒət] n **1** NUMERAL : dígito m, número m **2** FINGER, TOE : dedo m — **digital** ['dɪdʒətəl] adj : digital

dignity ['dɪgnəti] n, pl **-ties** : dignidad f — **dignified** ['dɪgnəˌfaɪd] adj : digno, decoroso

digress [daɪˈgrɛs, də-] vi : desviarse del tema, divagar — **digression** [daɪˈgrɛʃən, də-] n : digresión f

dike ['daɪk] n : dique m

dilapidated [dəˈlæpəˌdeɪtəd] adj : ruinoso

dilate [daɪˈleɪt, 'daɪˌleɪt] v **-lated; -lating** vt : dilatar — vi : dilatarse

dilemma [dɪˈlɛmə] n : dilema m

diligence ['dɪlədʒəns] n : diligencia f — **diligent** ['dɪlədʒənt] adj : diligente

dilute [daɪˈluːt, də-] vt **-luted; -luting** : diluir

dim ['dɪm] v **dimmed; dimming** vt : atenuar — vi : irse atenuando — adj **dimmer; dimmest 1** DARK : oscuro **2** FAINT : débil, tenue

dime ['daɪm] n : moneda f de diez centavos

dimension [dəˈmɛntʃən, daɪ-] n : dimensión f

diminish [dəˈmɪnɪʃ] v : disminuir

diminutive [dəˈmɪnjʊˌtɪv] adj : diminuto

dimple ['dɪmpəl] n : hoyuelo m

din ['dɪn] n : estrépito m

dine ['daɪn] vi **dined; dining** : cenar — **diner** ['daɪnər] n **1** : comensal mf (persona) **2** : cafetería f (restaurante)

dingy ['dɪndʒi] adj **-gier; -est** : sucio, deslucido

dinner ['dɪnər] n : cena f, comida f

dinosaur ['daɪnəˌsɔr] n : dinosaurio m

dint ['dɪnt] n **by ~ of** : a fuerza de

dip ['dɪp] v **dipped; dipping 1** : mojar — vi : bajar, descender — **~** n **1** DROP : descenso m, caída f **2** SWIM : chapuzón m **3** SAUCE : salsa f

diploma [dəˈploːmə] n, pl **-mas** : diploma m

diplomacy [dəˈploːməsi] n : diplomacia f — **diplomat** ['dɪpləˌmæt] n : diplomático m, -ca f — **diplomatic** [ˌdɪpləˈmætɪk] adj : diplomático

dire ['daɪr] adj **direr; direst 1** : grave, terrible **2** EXTREME : extremo

direct [dəˈrɛkt, daɪ-] vt **1** : dirigir **2** ORDER : mandar — **~** adj **1** STRAIGHT : directo **2** FRANK : franco — **~** adv : directamente — **direct current** : corriente f continua — **direction** [dəˈrɛkʃən, daɪ-] n **1** : dirección f **2** ask **~s** : pedir indicaciones — **directly** [dəˈrɛktli, daɪ-] adv **1** STRAIGHT : directamente **2** IMMEDIATELY : en seguida — **director** [dəˈrɛktər, daɪ-] n : director m, -tora f **2 board of ~s** : directorio m — **directory** [dəˈrɛktəri, daɪ-] n, pl **-ries** : guía f (telefónica)

dirt ['dərt] n **1** : suciedad f **2** SOIL : tierra f — **dirty** ['dərti] adj **dirtier; -est 1** : sucio **2** INDECENT : obsceno, cochino fam

disability [ˌdɪsəˈbɪləti] n, pl **-ties** : minusvalía f, invalidez f — **disable** [dɪsˈeɪbəl] vt **-abled; -abling** : incapacitar — **disabled** [dɪsˈeɪbəld] adj : minusválido

disadvantage [ˌdɪsədˈvæntɪdʒ] n : desventaja f

disagree [ˌdɪsəˈgriː] vi **1** : no estar de acuerdo (con algn) **2** CONFLICT : no coincidir — **disagreeable** [ˌdɪsəˈgriːəbəl] adj : desagradable — **disagreement** [ˌdɪsəˈgriːmənt] n **1** : desacuerdo m **2** ARGUMENT : discusión f

disappear [ˌdɪsəˈpɪr] vi : desaparecer — **disappearance** [ˌdɪsəˈpɪrəns] n : desaparición f

disappoint [ˌdɪsəˈpɔɪnt] vt : decepcionar, desilusionar — **disappointment** [ˌdɪsəˈpɔɪntmənt] n : decepción f, desilusión f

disapprove [ˌdɪsəˈpruːv] vi **-proved; -proving — ~ of** : desaprobar — **disapproval** [ˌdɪsəˈpruːvəl] n : desaprobación f

disarm [dɪsˈɑrm] vt : desarmar — **disarmament** [dɪsˈɑrməmənt] n : desarme m

disarray [ˌdɪsəˈreɪ] n : desorden m

disaster [dɪˈzæstər] n : desastre m — **disastrous** [dɪˈzæstrəs] adj : desastroso

disbelief [ˌdɪsbɪˈliːf] n : incredulidad f

disc — disk

discard [dɪsˈkɑrd, ˈdɪsˌkɑrd] vt : desechar, deshacerse de

discern [dɪˈsərn, -ˈzərn] vt : percibir, discernir — **discernible** [dɪˈsərnəbəl, -ˈzər-] adj : perceptible

discharge [dɪsˈtʃɑrdʒ, ˈdɪs-] vt **-charged; -charging 1** UNLOAD : descargar **2** RELEASE : liberar, poner en libertad **3** DISMISS : despedir **4**

CARRY OUT : cumplir con (una obligación) — ~ ['dɪstʃərdʒ, dɪs-] n 1 : descarga f (de electricidad), emisión f (de humo, etc.) 2 DISMISSAL : despido m 3 RELEASE : alta f (de un paciente), puesta f en libertad (de un preso) 4 : supuración f (en medicina)

disciple [dɪ'saɪpəl] n : discípulo m, -la f

discipline ['dɪsəplən] n 1 : disciplina f 2 PUNISHMENT : castigo m — ~ vt -plined; -plining 1 CONTROL : disciplinar 2 PUNISH : castigar

disclaim [dɪs'kleɪm] vt : negar

disclose [dɪs'kloz] vt -closed; -closing : revelar — **disclosure** [dɪs'kloʒər] n : revelación f

discomfort [dɪs'kʌmfərt] n 1 : incomodidad f 2 PAIN : malestar m 3 UNEASINESS : inquietud f

disconcert [,dɪskən'sərt] vt : desconcertar

disconnect [,dɪskə'nɛkt] vt : desconectar

disconsolate [dɪs'kɑntsələt] adj : desconsolado

discontented [,dɪskən'tɛntəd] adj : descontento

discontinue [,dɪskən'tɪnju:] vt -ued; -uing : suspender, descontinuar

discount ['dɪs,kaʊnt, dɪs-] n : descuento m, rebaja f — ~ vt 1 : descontar (precios) 2 DISREGARD : descartar

discourage [dɪs'kərɪdʒ] vt -aged; -aging : desalentar, desanimar — **discouragement** [dɪs'kərɪdʒmənt] n : desánimo m, desaliento m

discover [dɪs'kʌvər] vt : descubrir — **discovery** [dɪs'kʌvəri] n, pl -ries : descubrimiento m

discredit [dɪs'krɛdət] vt : desacreditar — ~ n : descrédito m

discreet [dɪs'kri:t] adj : discreto

discrepancy [dɪs'krɛpəntsi] n, pl -cies : discrepancia f

discretion [dɪs'krɛʃən] n : discreción f

discriminate [dɪs'krɪmə,neɪt] vi -nated; -nating 1 ~ against : discriminar 2 ~ between : distinguir entre — **discrimination** [dɪs,krɪmə'neɪʃən] n 1 PREJUDICE : discriminación f 2 DISCERNMENT : discernimiento m

discuss [dɪs'kʌs] vt : hablar de, discutir — **discussion** [dɪs'kʌʃən] n : discusión f

disdain [dɪs'deɪn] n : desdén m — ~ vt : desdeñar

disease [dɪ'zi:z] n : enfermedad f — **diseased** [dɪ'zi:zd] adj : enfermo

disembark [,dɪsɪm'bɑrk] vi : desembarcar

disengage [,dɪsɪn'geɪdʒ] vt -gaged;

-gaging 1 RELEASE : soltar 2 ~ the clutch : desembragar

disentangle [,dɪsɪn'tæŋgəl] vt -gled; -gling : desenredar

disfavor [dɪs'feɪvər] n : desaprobación f

disfigure [dɪs'fɪgjər] vt -ured; -uring : desfigurar

disgrace [dɪs'kreɪs] vt -graced; -gracing : deshonrar — ~ n 1 DISHONOR : deshonra f 2 SHAME : vergüenza f — **disgraceful** [dɪs'kreɪsfəl] adj : vergonzoso, deshonroso

disgruntled [dɪs'grʌntəld] adj : descontento

disguise [dɪs'gaɪz] vt -guised; -guising : disfrazar — ~ n : disfraz m

disgust [dɪs'kʌst] n : asco m, repugnancia f — ~ vt : asquear — **disgusting** [dɪs'kʌstɪŋ] adj : asqueroso

dish ['dɪʃ] n 1 : plato m 2 or serving ~ : fuente f 3 wash the ~es : lavar los platos — ~ vt or ~ up : servir — **dishcloth** ['dɪʃ,klɔθ] n : paño m de cocina (para secar), trapo m de fregar (para lavar)

dishearten [dɪs'hɑrtən] vt : desanimar

disheveled or **dishevelled** [dɪ'ʃɛvəld] adj : desaliñado, despeinado (dícese del pelo)

dishonest [dɪs'ɑnəst] adj : deshonesto — **dishonesty** [dɪs'ɑnəsti] n, pl -ties : falta f de honradez

dishonor [dɪs'ɑnər] n : deshonra f — ~ vt : deshonrar — **dishonorable** [dɪs'ɑnərəbəl] adj : deshonroso

dishwasher ['dɪʃ,wɔʃər] n : lavaplatos m, lavavajillas m

disillusion [,dɪsə'lu:ʒən] vt : desilusionar — **disillusionment** [,dɪsə'lu:ʒənmənt] n : desilusión f

disinfect [,dɪsɪn'fɛkt] vt : desinfectar — **disinfectant** [,dɪsɪn'fɛktənt] n : desinfectante m

disintegrate [dɪs'ɪntə,greɪt] vi -grated; -grating : desintegrarse

disinterested [dɪs'ɪntərəstəd, -,rɛs-] adj : desinteresado

disk or **disc** ['dɪsk] n : disco m

dislike [dɪs'laɪk] n : aversión f, antipatía f — ~ vt -liked; -liking 1 : tener aversión a 2 I ~ dancing : no me gusta bailar

dislocate ['dɪslo,keɪt, dɪs'lo:-] vt -cated; -cating : dislocar

dislodge [dɪs'lɑdʒ] vt -lodged; -lodging : sacar, desalojar

disloyal [dɪs'lɔɪəl] adj : desleal — **disloyalty** [dɪs'lɔɪəlti] n, pl -ties : deslealtad f

dismal ['dɪzməl] adj : sombrío, deprimente

dismantle [dɪs'mæntəl] vt -tled; -tling : desmontar, desarmar

dismay [dɪs'meɪ] vt : consternar — ~ n : consternación f

dismiss [dɪs'mɪs] vt 1 DISCHARGE : despedir, destituir 2 REJECT : descartar, rechazar — **dismissal** [dɪs'mɪsəl] n 1 : despido m (de un empleado), destitución f (de un funcionario) 2 REJECTION : rechazo m

dismount [dɪs'maʊnt] vi : desmontar

disobey [ˌdɪsə'beɪ] v : desobedecer — **disobedience** [ˌdɪsə'biːdiəns] n : desobediencia f — **disobedient** [-ənt] adj : desobediente

disorder [dɪs'ɔrdər] n 1 : desorden m 2 AILMENT : afección f, problema m — **disorderly** [dɪs'ɔrdərli] adj : desordenado

disorganize [dɪs'ɔrgəˌnaɪz] vt -nized; -nizing : desorganizar

disown [dɪs'oʊn] vt : renegar de

dispassionate [dɪs'pæʃənət] adj : desapasionado

dispatch [dɪs'pætʃ] vt : despachar, enviar

dispel [dɪs'pɛl] vt -pelled; -pelling : disipar

dispensation [ˌdɪspen'seɪʃən] n EXEMPTION : exención m, dispensa f

dispense [dɪs'pens] v -pensed; -pensing vt : repartir, distribuir — vi ~ with : prescindir de

disperse [dɪs'pərs] v -persed; -persing vt : dispersar — vi : dispersarse

displace [dɪs'pleɪs] vt -placed; -placing 1 : desplazar 2 REPLACE : reemplazar

display [dɪs'pleɪ] vt 1 EXHIBIT : exponer, exhibir 2 ~ anger : manifestar la ira — ~ n : muestra f, exposición f

displease [dɪs'pliːz] vt -pleased; -pleasing : desagradar — **displeasure** [dɪs'plɛʒər] n : desagrado m

dispose [dɪs'poʊz] v -posed; -posing : disponer — vi ~ of : deshacerse de — **disposable** [dɪs'poʊzəbəl] adj : desechable — **disposal** [dɪs'poʊzəl] n 1 REMOVAL : eliminación f 2 have at one's ~ : tener a su disposición — **disposition** [ˌdɪspə'zɪʃən] n 1 ARRANGEMENT : disposición f 2 TEMPERAMENT : temperamento m, carácter m

disprove [dɪs'pruːv] vt -proved; -proving : refutar

dispute [dɪs'pjuːt] v -puted; -puting QUESTION : cuestionar — vi ARGUE : discutir — ~ n : disputa f, conflicto m

disqualification [dɪsˌkwɑləfə'keɪʃən] n : descalificación f — **disqualify** [dɪs'kwɑləˌfaɪ] vt -fied; -fying : descalificar

disregard [ˌdɪsrɪ'gɑrd] vt : ignorar, hacer caso omiso de — ~ n : indiferencia f

disrepair [ˌdɪsrɪ'pær] n : mal estado m

disreputable [dɪs'repjʊtəbəl] adj : de mala fama

disrespect [ˌdɪsrɪ'spekt] n : falta f de respeto — **disrespectful** [ˌdɪsrɪ'spektfəl] adj : irrespetuoso

disrupt [dɪs'rʌpt] vt : trastornar, perturbar — **disruption** [dɪs'rʌpʃən] n : trastorno m

dissatisfaction [ˌdɪsˌsætəs'fækʃən] n : descontento m — **dissatisfied** [dɪs'sætəsˌfaɪd] adj : descontento

dissect [daɪ'sekt] vt : disecar

disseminate [dɪ'semənˌeɪt] vt -nated; -nating : diseminar, difundir

dissent [dɪ'sent] vi : disentir — ~ n : disentimiento m

dissertation [ˌdɪsər'teɪʃən] THESIS : tesis f

disservice [dɪs'sərvɪs] n do a ~ to : no hacer justicia a

dissident [dɪs'ədənt] n : disidente mf

dissimilar [dɪ'sɪmələr] adj : distinto

dissipate [dɪs'əˌpeɪt] vt -pated; -pating 1 DISPEL : disipar 2 SQUANDER : desperdiciar

dissolve [dɪ'zɑlv] v -solved; -solving vt : disolver — vi : disolverse

dissuade [dɪ'sweɪd] vt -suaded; -suading : disuadir

distance [dɪs'təns] n 1 : distancia f 2 in the ~ : a lo lejos — **distant** [dɪs'tənt] adj : distante

distaste [dɪs'teɪst] n : desagrado m — **distasteful** [dɪs'teɪstfəl] adj : desagradable

distend [dɪs'tend] vt : dilatar — vi : dilatarse

distill [dɪs'tɪl] or Brit **distil** vt -tilled; -tilling : destilar

distinct [dɪs'tɪŋkt] adj 1 DIFFERENT : distinto 2 CLEAR : claro — **distinction** [dɪs'tɪŋkʃən] n : distinción f — **distinctive** [dɪs'tɪŋktɪv] adj : distintivo

distinguish [dɪs'tɪŋgwɪʃ] vt : distinguir — **distinguished** [dɪs'tɪŋgwɪʃt] adj : distinguido

distort [dɪs'tɔrt] vt : deformar, distorsionar — **distortion** [dɪs'tɔrʃən] n : deformación f

distract [dɪs'trækt] vt : distraer — **distraction** [dɪs'trækʃən] n : distracción f

distraught [dɪs'trɔt] adj : muy afligido

distress [dɪs'tres] n 1 : angustia f, aflicción f 2 in ~ : en peligro — ~ vt

: afligir — **distressing** [dɪ'strɛsɪŋ] *adj* : penoso

distribute [dɪ'strɪ,bjuːt, -bjut] *vt* -**uted**; -**uting** : distribuir, repartir — **distribution** [,dɪstrə'bjuːʃən] *n* : distribución *f*

distributor [dɪ'strɪbjuːt̬ər] *n* : distribuidor *m*, -dora *f*

district ['dɪstrɪkt] *n* **1** REGION : región *f*, zona *f*, barrio *m* (de una ciudad) **2** : distrito *m* (zona política)

distrust [dɪs'trʌst] *n* : desconfianza *f* — ~ *vt* : desconfiar de

disturb [dɪs'tərb] *vt* **1** BOTHER : molestar, perturbar **2** WORRY : inquietar — **disturbance** [dɪs'tərbəns] *n* **1** COMMOTION : alboroto *m*, disturbio *m* **2** INTERRUPTION : interrupción *f*

disuse [dɪs'juːs] *n* **fall into** ~ : caer en desuso

ditch ['dɪtʃ] *n* : zanja *f*, cuneta *f* — ~ *vt* DISCARD : deshacerse de, botar

ditto ['dɪt̬oː] *n, pl* -**tos 1** : ídem *m* **2** ~ **marks** : comillas *fpl*

dive ['daɪv] *vi* **dived** *or* **dove** ['doːv]; **dived**; **diving 1** : zambullirse, tirarse al agua **2** DESCEND : bajar en picada (dícese de un avión, etc.) — ~ *n* **1** : zambullida *f*, clavado *m* *Lat* **2** DESCENT : descenso *m* en picada — **diver** ['daɪvər] *n* : saltador *m*, -dora *f*

diverge [də'vərdʒ, daɪ-] *vi* -**verged**; -**verging** : divergir

diverse [daɪ'vərs, də-, 'daɪˌvərs] *adj* : diverso — **diversify** [daɪ'vərsəˌfaɪ, də-] *vt* -**fied**; -**fying** *vt* : diversificar — *vi* : diversificarse

diversion [daɪ'vərʒən, də-] *n* **1** : desviación *f* **2** AMUSEMENT : diversión *f*, distracción *f*

diversity [daɪ'vərsət̬i, də-] *n, pl* -**ties** : diversidad *f*

divert [də'vərt, daɪ-] *vt* **1** : desviar **2** DISTRACT : distraer **3** AMUSE : divertir

divide [də'vaɪd] *v* -**vided**; -**viding** *vt* : dividir — *vi* : dividirse

dividend ['dɪvəˌdɛnd, -dənd] *n* : dividendo *m*

divine [də'vaɪn] *adj* -**viner**; -**est** : divino — **divinity** [də'vɪnət̬i] *n, pl* -**ties** : divinidad *f*

division [də'vɪʒən] *n* : división *f*

divorce [də'vɔrs] *n* : divorcio *m* — ~ *v* -**vorced**; -**vorcing** *vt* : divorciar — *vi* : divorciarse — **divorcée** [dɪˌvɔr'seɪ, -siː; -'vɔr-] *n* : divorciada *f*

divulge [də'vʌldʒ, daɪ-] *vt* -**vulged**; -**vulging** : revelar, divulgar

dizzy ['dɪzi] *adj* **dizzier**; -**est 1** : mareado **2 a** ~ **speed** : una velocidad ver-

tiginosa — **dizziness** ['dɪzinəs] *n* : mareo *m*, vértigo *m*

DNA [ˌdiːˌɛn'eɪ] *n* : AND *m*

do ['duː] *v* **did** ['dɪd]; **done** ['dʌn]; **doing**; **does** ['dʌz] *vt* **1** : hacer PREPARE : preparar — *v* **1** BEHAVE : hacer **2** FARE : estar, ir, andar **3** SUFFICE : ser suficiente **4** ~ **away with** : abolir, eliminar **5 how are you doing?** : ¿cómo estás? — *v aux* **1** *(used in interrogative sentences)* **do you know her?** : ¿la conoces? **2** *(used in negative statements)* **I don't know** : yo no se **3** *(used as a substitute verb to avoid repetition)* **do you speak English? yes, I do** : ¿habla inglés? sí

dock ['dɑk] *n* : muelle *m* — *vt* : descontar dinero de (un sueldo) — ~ *n* ANCHOR : fondear, atracar

doctor ['dɑktər] *n* **1** : doctor *m*, -tora *f* (en derecho, etc.) **2** PHYSICIAN : médico *m*, -ca; doctor *m*, -tora *f* — ~ *vt* ALTER : alterar, falsificar

doctrine ['dɑktrɪn] *n* : doctrina *f*

document ['dɑkjumənt] *n* : documento *m* — ~ ['dɑkjuˌment] *vt* : documentar — **documentary** [ˌdɑkju'mentəri] *n, pl* -**ries** : documental *m*

dodge ['dɑdʒ] *n* : artimaña *f*, truco *m* — ~ *v* **dodged**; **dodging** *vt* : esquivar, eludir — *vi* : echarse a un lado

doe ['doː] *n, pl* **does** *or* **doe** : gama *f*, cierva *f*

does → **do**

dog ['dɔg, 'dɑg] *n* : perro *m*, -rra *f* — ~ *vt* **dogged**; **dogging** : perseguir — **dogged** ['dɔgəd] *adj* : tenaz

dogma ['dɔgmə] *n* : dogma *m* — **dogmatic** [dɔg'mæt̬ɪk] *adj* : dogmático

doily ['dɔɪli] *n, pl* -**lies** : tapete *m*

doings ['duːɪŋz] *npl* : actividades *fpl*

doldrums ['doːldrəmz, 'dɑl-] *npl* **be in the** ~ : estar abatido

dole ['doːl] *n* : subsidio *m* de desempleo — ~ *vt* **doled**; **doling** *or* ~ **out** : repartir

doleful ['doːlfəl] *adj* : triste, lúgubre

doll ['dɑl, 'dɔl] *n* : muñeco *m*, -ca *f*

dollar ['dɑlər] *n* : dólar *m*

dolphin ['dɑlfən, 'dɔl-] *n* : delfín *m*

domain [doː'meɪn, də-] *n* **1** TERRITORY : dominio *m* **2** FIELD : campo *m*, esfera *f*

dome ['doːm] *n* : cúpula *f*

domestic [də'mestɪk] *adj* **1** : doméstico **2** INTERNAL : nacional — ~ *n* SERVANT : empleado *m* doméstico, empleada *f* doméstica — **domesticate** [də'mestɪˌkeɪt] *vt* -**cated**; -**cating** : domesticar

domination [ˌdɑmə'neɪʃən] *n* : dominación *f* — **dominant** ['dɑmənənt] *adj* : dominante — **dominate** ['dɑmə,neɪt] *v* -**nated;** -**nating** : dominar — **domineer** [,dɑmə'nɪr] *vi* : dominar, tiranizar

dominos ['dɑmə,noːz] *n* : dominó *m* (juego)

donate ['doː,neɪt, doː'-] *vt* -**nated;** -**nating** : donar, hacer un donativo de — **donation** [doː'neɪʃən] *n* : donativo *m*

done ['dʌn] → **do** — ~ *adj* **1** FINISHED : terminado, hecho **2** COOKED : cocido

donkey ['dɑŋki, 'dʌŋ-] *n, pl* -**keys** : burro *m*

donor ['doːnər] *n* : donante *mf*

don't ['doːnt] (*contraction of* **do not**) → **do**

doodle ['duːdəl] *v* -**dled;** -**dling** : garabatear — ~ *n* : garabato *m*

doom ['duːm] *n* : perdición *f*, fatalidad *f* — ~ *vt* : condenar

door ['dor] *n* **1** : puerta *f* **2** ENTRANCE : entrada *f* — **doorbell** ['dor,bɛl] *n* : timbre *m* — **doorknob** ['dor,nɑb] *n* : pomo *m* — **doorman** ['dorman] *n, pl* -**men** [-mən, -,mɛn] : portero *m* — **doormat** ['dor,mæt] *n* : felpudo *m* — **doorstep** ['dor,stɛp] *n* : umbral *m* — **doorway** ['dor,weɪ] *n* : entrada *f*, portal *m*

dope ['doːp] *n* **1** DRUG : droga *f* **2** IDIOT : idiota *mf* — ~ *vt* **doped; doping** : drogar

dormant ['dormənt] *adj* : inactivo, latente

dormitory ['dormə,tori] *n, pl* -**ries** : dormitorio *m*

dose ['doːs] *n* : dosis *f* — **dosage** ['doːsɪdʒ] *n* : dosis *f*

dot ['dɑt] *n* **1** : punto *m* **2 on the ~** : en punto

dote ['doːt] *vi* **doted; doting ~ on** : adorar

double ['dʌbəl] *adj* : doble — ~ *v* -**bled;** -**bling** *vt* : doblar — *vi* : doblarse — ~ *adv* : (el) doble — ~ *n* : doble *m* — **double bass** *n* : contrabajo *m* — **double-cross** [,dʌbəl-'krɔs] *vt* : traicionar — **doubly** ['dʌbli] *adv* : doblemente

doubt ['daut] *vt* **1** : dudar **2** DISTRUST : desconfiar de, dudar de — ~ *n* : duda *f* — **doubtful** ['dautfəl] *adj* : dudoso — **doubtless** ['dautləs] *adv* : sin duda

dough ['doː] *n* : masa *f* — **doughnut** ['doː,nʌt] *n* : rosquilla *f*, dona *f Lat*

douse ['daus, 'dauz] *vt* **doused; dousing 1** DRENCH : empapar, mojar **2** EXTINGUISH : apagar

dove¹ ['dʌv] → **dive**

dove² ['dʌv] *n* : paloma *f*

dowdy ['daudi] *adj* **dowdier; -est** : poco elegante

down ['daun] *adv* **1** DOWNWARD : hacia abajo **2 come/go ~** : bajar **3 ~ here** : aquí abajo **4 fall ~** : caer **5 lie ~** : acostarse **6 sit ~** : sentarse — ~ *prep* **1** ALONG : a lo largo de **2** THROUGH : a través de **3 ~ the hill** : cuesta abajo — ~ *adj* **1** DESCENDING : de bajada **2** DOWNCAST : abatido — ~ *n* : plumón *m* — **downcast** ['daun,kæst] *adj* : triste, abatido — **downfall** ['daun,fɔl] *n* : ruina *f* — **downhearted** ['daun,hɑrtəd] *adj* : desanimado — **downhill** ['daun'hɪl] *adv & adj* : cuesta abajo — **down payment** *n* : entrega *f* inicial — **downpour** ['daun,por] *n* : chaparrón *m* — **downright** ['daun,raɪt] *adv* : absolutamente — ~ *adj* : absoluto, categórico — **downstairs** ['daun'stærz] *adv* : abajo — ~ ['daun,stærz] *adj* : de abajo — **downstream** ['daun'striːm] *adv* : río abajo — **down-to-earth** ['daun,tu'ərθ] *adj* : realista — **downtown** [,daun'taun, 'daun,taun] *n* : centro *m* (de la ciudad) — ['daun'taun] *adv* : al centro, en el centro — ~ *adj* : del centro — **downward** ['daunwərd] *or* **downwards** [-wərdz] *adv & adj* : hacia abajo

dowry ['dauri] *n, pl* -**ries** : dote *f*

doze ['doːz] *vi* **dozed; dozing** : dormitar

dozen ['dʌzən] *n, pl* **dozens** *or* **dozen** : docena *f*

drab ['dræb] *adj* **drabber; drabbest** : monótono, apagado

draft ['dræft, 'drɑft] *n* **1** : corriente *f* de aire **2** *or* **rough ~** : borrador *m* **3** : conscripción *f* (military) **4** *or* **~ beer** : cerveza *f* de barril — ~ *vt* **1** SKETCH : hacer el borrador de **2** CONSCRIPT : reclutar — **drafty** ['dræfti] *adj* **draftier; -est** : con corrientes de aire

drag ['dræg] *v* **dragged; dragging** *vt* **1** : arrastrar **2** DREDGE : dragar — *vi* : arrastrar(se) — ~ *n* **1** RESISTANCE : resistencia *f* (aerodinámica) **2** BORE : pesadez *f*, plomo *m fam*

dragon ['drægən] *n* : dragón *m* — **dragonfly** ['drægən,flaɪ] *n, pl* -**flies** : libélula *f*

drain ['dreɪn] *vt* **1** EMPTY : vaciar, drenar **2** EXHAUST : agotar — *vi* **1** : escurrir(se) (se dice de los platos) **2** *or* **~ away** : desaparecer poco a poco — ~ *n* **1** : desagüe *m* **2** SEWER : alcantarilla *f* **3** DEPLETION : agotamiento *m* — **drainage** ['dreɪnɪdʒ] *n* : drenaje *m* — **drainpipe** ['dreɪn,paɪp] *n* : tubo *m* de desagüe

drama ['drɑmə, 'dræ-] *n* : drama *m* —

dramatic [drəˈmætɪk] *adj* : dramático — **dramatist** [ˈdræmətɪst, ˈdrɑ-] *n* : dramaturgo *m*, -ga *f* — **dramatize** [ˈdræmətaɪz, ˈdrɑ-] *vt* -**tized**; -**tizing** : dramatizar

drank → **drink**

drape [ˈdreɪp] *vt* **draped**; **draping** 1 COVER : cubrir (con tela) 2 HANG : drapear —**drapes** *npl* CURTAINS : cortinas *fpl*

drastic [ˈdræstɪk] *adj* : drástico

draught [ˈdræft, ˈdraft] → **draft**

draw [ˈdrɔ] *v* **drew** [ˈdruː]; **drawn** [ˈdrɔn]; **drawing** *vt* 1 PULL : tirar de 2 ATTRACT : atraer 3 SKETCH : dibujar, trazar 4 : sacar (una espada, etc.) 5 ~ **a conclusion** : llegar a una conclusión 6 ~ **up** DRAFT : redactar — *vi* 1 SKETCH : dibujar 2 ~ **near** : acercarse — **drawing** *n* 1 DRAWING : sorteo *m* 2 TIE : empate *m* 3 ATTRACTION : atracción *f* — **drawback** [ˈdrɔˌbæk] *n* : desventaja *f* — **drawer** [ˈdrɔr, ˈdrɔər] *n* : gaveta *f*, cajón *m* (en un mueble) — **drawing** [ˈdrɔɪŋ] *n* 1 LOTTERY : sorteo *m* 2 SKETCH : dibujo *m*

drawl [ˈdrɔl] *n* : habla *f* lenta y con vocales prolongadas

dread [ˈdred] *vt* : temer — ~ *n* : pavor *m*, temor *m* — **dreadful** [ˈdredfəl] *adj* : espantoso, terrible

dream [ˈdriːm] *n* : sueño *m* — ~ *v* **dreamed** [ˈdrɛmpt, ˈdriːmd] *or* **dreamt** [ˈdrɛmpt]; **dreaming** *vi* : soñar — *vt* 1 : soñar 2 ~ **up** : idear — **dreamer** [ˈdriːmər] *n* : soñador *m*, -dora *f* — **dreamy** [ˈdriːmi] *adj* **dreamier**; -**est** : soñador

dreary [ˈdrɪri] *adj* -**rier**; -**est** : sombrío, deprimente

dredge [ˈdredʒ] *vt* **dredged**; **dredging** : dragar — ~ *n* : draga *f*

dregs [ˈdregz] *npl* : heces *fpl*

drench [ˈdrentʃ] *vt* : empapar

dress [ˈdres] *vt* 1 : vestir 2 : preparar (pollo o pescado), aliñar (ensalada) — *vi* 1 : vestirse 2 ~ **up** : ponerse elegante — ~ *n* 1 CLOTHING : ropa *f* 2 : vestido *m* (de mujer) — **dresser** [ˈdresər] *n* : cómoda *f* con espejo — **dressing** [ˈdresɪŋ] *n* 1 : aliño *m* (de ensalada), relleno *m* (de pollo) 2 BANDAGE : vendaje *m* — **dressmaker** [ˈdresˌmeɪkər] *n* : modista *mf* — **dressy** [ˈdresi] *adj* **dressier**; -**est** : elegante

drew → **draw**

dribble [ˈdrɪbəl] *vi* -**bled**; -**bling** 1 DRIP : gotear 2 DROOL : babear 3 : driblar (en basquetbol) — ~ *n* 1 TRICKLE : goteo *m*, hilo *m* 2 DROOL : baba *f*

drier, driest → **dry**

drift [ˈdrɪft] *n* 1 MOVEMENT : movimiento *m* 2 HEAP : montón *m* (de arena, etc.), ventisquero *m* (de nieve) 3 MEANING : sentido *m* — *vi* 1 : ir a la deriva 2 ACCUMULATE : amontonarse

drill [ˈdrɪl] *n* 1 : taladro *m* 2 : ejercicio *m* (en educación), simulacro *m* (de incendio, etc.) — ~ *vt* 1 : perforar, taladrar 2 TRAIN : instruir por repetición — *vi* ~ **for** : perforar en busca de

drink [ˈdrɪŋk] *v* **drank** [ˈdræŋk]; **drunk** [ˈdrəŋk] *or* **drank**; **drinking** : beber — ~ *n* : bebida *f*

drip [ˈdrɪp] *vi* **dripped**; **dripping** : gotear — ~ *n* 1 DROP : gota *f* 2 DRIPPING : goteo *m*

drive [ˈdraɪv] *v* **drove** [ˈdroːv]; **driven** [ˈdrɪvən]; **driving** *vt* 1 : manejar 2 IMPEL : impulsar 3 ~ **crazy** : volver loco 4 ~ **s.o. to (do sth)** : llevar a algn a (hacer algo) — *vi* : manejar, conducir — ~ *n* 1 : paseo *m* (en coche) 2 CAMPAIGN : campaña *f* 3 VIGOR : energía *f* 4 NEED : instinto *m*

drivel [ˈdrɪvəl] *n* : tonterías *fpl*

driver [ˈdraɪvər] *n* : conductor *m*, -tora *f*; chofer *m*

driveway [ˈdraɪvˌweɪ] *n* : camino *m* de entrada

drizzle [ˈdrɪzəl] *n* : llovizna *f* — ~ *vi* -**zled**; -**zling** : lloviznar

drone [ˈdroːn] *n* 1 BEE : zángano *m* 2 HUM : zumbido *m* — ~ *vi* **droned**; **droning** 1 BUZZ : zumbar 2 *or* ~ **on** : hablar con monotonía

drool [ˈdruːl] *vi* : babear — ~ *n* : baba *f*

droop [ˈdruːp] *vi* : inclinarse (dícese de la cabeza), encorvarse (dícese de los escombros), marchitarse (dícese de las flores)

drop [ˈdrɑp] *n* 1 : gota *f* (de líquido) 2 DECLINE, FALL : caída *f* — ~ *v* **dropped**; **dropping** *vt* 1 : dejar caer 2 LOWER : bajar 3 ABANDON : abandonar, dejar 4 ~ **off** LEAVE : dejar — *vi* 1 FALL : caer(se) 2 DECREASE : bajar, descender 3 ~ **by** *or* ~ **in** : pasar

drought [ˈdraʊt] *n* : sequía *f*

drove → **drive**

droves [ˈdroːvz] *n* **in** ~ : en manada

drown [ˈdraʊn] *vt* : ahogar — *vi* : ahogarse

drowsy [ˈdraʊzi] *adj* **drowsier**; -**est** : somnoliento

drudgery [ˈdrʌdʒəri] *n*, *pl* -**eries** : trabajo *m* pesado

drug [ˈdrʌg] *n* 1 MEDICATION : medicamento *m* 2 NARCOTIC : droga *f*, estupefaciente *m* — ~ *vt* **drugged**; **drugging** : drogar — **drugstore** [ˈdrʌgˌstɔr] *n* : farmacia *f*

drum ['drʌm] n 1 : tambor m 2 or oil ~ : bidón m (de petróleo) — ~ v **drummed; drumming** 1 : tocar el tambor — vt : tamborilear con (los dedos, etc.) — **drumstick** ['drʌmˌstɪk] n 1 : palillo m (de tambor) 2 : muslo m (de pollo)

drunk ['drʌŋk] → **drink** — ~ adj : borracho — or **drunkard** ['drʌŋkərd] n : borracho m, -cha f — **drunken** ['drʌŋkən] adj : borracho, ebrio

dry ['draɪ] adj **drier; driest** : seco — ~ v **dried; drying** vt : secar — vi : secarse — **dry-clean** ['draɪˌkliːn] vt : limpiar en seco — **dry cleaner** n : tintorería f (servicio) — **dry cleaning** n : limpieza f en seco — **dryer** ['draɪər] n : secadora f — **dryness** ['draɪnəs] n : sequedad f, aridez f

dual ['duːəl, 'djuː-] adj : doble

dub ['dʌb] vt **dubbed; dubbing** 1 CALL : apodar 2 : doblar (una película)

dubious ['duːbiəs, 'djuː-] adj 1 UNCERTAIN : dudoso 2 QUESTIONABLE : sospechoso

duchess ['dʌtʃəs] n : duquesa f

duck ['dʌk] n, pl **duck** or **ducks** : pato m, -ta f — ~ vt 1 LOWER : agachar, bajar 2 EVADE : eludir, esquivar — vi : agacharse — **duckling** ['dʌklɪŋ] n : patito m, -ta f

duct ['dʌkt] n : conducto m

due ['duː, 'djuː] adj 1 PAYABLE : pagadero 2 APPROPRIATE : debido, apropiado 3 EXPECTED : esperado 4 ~ **to** : debido a — ~ n 1 **give s.o. their** ~ : hacer justicia a algn 2 ~**s** npl : cuota f — ~ adv ~ **east** : justo al este

duel ['duːəl, 'djuː-] n : duelo m

duet ['duːet, djuː-] n : dúo m

dug → **dig**

duke ['duːk, 'djuːk] n : duque m

dull ['dʌl] adj 1 STUPID : torpe 2 BLUNT : desafilado 3 BORING : aburrido 4 LACKLUSTER : apagado — ~ vt : entorpecer (los sentidos), aliviar (el dolor)

dumb ['dʌm] adj 1 MUTE : mudo 2 STUPID : estúpido

dumbfound or **dumfound** ['dʌmˈfaʊnd] vt : dejar sin habla

dummy ['dʌmi] n, pl **-mies** 1 SHAM : imitación f 2 MANNEQUIN : maniquí m 3 IDIOT : tonto m, -ta f

dump ['dʌmp] vt : descargar, verter — ~ n 1 : vertedero m, tiradero m Lat 2 **down in the** ~**s** : triste, deprimido

dumpling ['dʌmplɪŋ] n : bola f de masa hervida

dumpy ['dʌmpi] adj **dumpier; -est** : regordete

dunce ['dʌns] n : burro m, -rra f fam

dune ['duːn, 'djuːn] n : duna f

dung ['dʌŋ] n 1 : excrementos mpl 2 MANURE : estiércol m

dungarees [ˌdʌŋgəˈriː] npl JEANS : vaqueros mpl, jeans mpl

dungeon ['dʌndʒən] n : calabozo m

dunk ['dʌŋk] vt : mojar

duo ['duːoː, 'djuː-] n, pl **duos** : dúo m

dupe ['duːp, 'djuː-] vt **duped; duping** : engañar — ~ n : inocentón m, -tona f

duplex ['duːpleks, 'djuː-] n : casa f de dos viviendas, dúplex m

duplicate ['duːplɪkət, 'djuː-] adj : duplicado — ~ ['duːplɪˌkeɪt, 'djuː-] vt **-cated; -cating** : duplicar, hacer copias de — ~ ['duːplɪkət, 'djuː-] n : duplicado m, copia f

durable ['dʊrəbəl, 'djʊr-] adj : duradero

duration [dʊˈreɪʃən, djʊ-] n : duración f

duress [dʊˈres, djʊ-] n : coacción f

during ['dʊrɪŋ, 'djʊr-] prep : durante

dusk ['dʌsk] n : anochecer m, crepúsculo m

dust ['dʌst] n : polvo m — ~ vt 1 : quitar el polvo a 2 SPRINKLE : espolvorear — **dustpan** ['dʌstˌpæn] n : recogedor m — **dusty** ['dʌsti] adj **dustier; -est** : polvoriento

Dutch ['dʌtʃ] adj : holandés — ~ n 1 : holandés m (idioma) 2 **the** ~ : los holandeses

duty ['duːti, 'djuː-] n, pl **-ties** 1 OBLIGATION : deber m 2 TAX : impuesto m 3 **on** ~ : de servicio — **dutiful** ['duːtɪfəl, 'djuː-] adj : obediente

dwarf ['dwɔrf] n, pl **dwarfs** ['dwɔrfs] or **dwarves** ['dwɔrvz] : enano m, -na f — ~ vt : hacer parecer pequeño

dwell ['dwel] vi **dwelled** or **dwelt** ['dwelt]; **dwelling** 1 RESIDE : morar, vivir 2 ~ **on** : pensar demasiado en — **dweller** ['dwelər] n : habitante mf — **dwelling** ['dwelɪŋ] n : morada f, vivienda f

dwindle ['dwɪndəl] vi **-dled; -dling** : disminuir

dye ['daɪ] n : tinte m — ~ vt **dyed; dyeing** : teñir

dying → **die¹**

dynamic [daɪˈnæmɪk] adj : dinámico

dynamite ['daɪnəˌmaɪt] n : dinamita f

dynamo ['daɪnəˌmoː] n, pl **-mos** : dínamo m

dynasty ['daɪnəsti, -ˌnæs-] n, pl **-ties** : dinastía f

dysentery ['dɪsənˌteri] n, pl **-teries** : disentería f

E

e ['iː] *n, pl* **e's** *or* **es** ['iːz] : e *f*, quinta letra del alfabeto inglés

each ['iːtʃ] *adj* : cada — ~ *pron* **1** : cada uno *m*, cada una *f* **2** ~ **other** : el uno al otro **3 they hate** ~ **other** : se odian — ~ *adv* : cada uno, por persona

eager ['iːgər] *adj* **1** ENTHUSIASTIC : entusiasta **2** IMPATIENT : impaciente — **eagerness** ['iːgərnəs] *n* : entusiasmo *m*, impaciencia *f*

eagle ['iːgəl] *n* : águila *f*

ear ['ɪr] *n* **1** : oreja *f* **2** ~ **of corn** : mazorca *f*, choclo *m Lat* — **eardrum** ['ɪr‚drʌm] *n* : tímpano *m*

earl ['ərl] *n* : conde *m*

earlobe ['ɪr‚loːb] *n* : lóbulo *m* de la oreja

early ['ərli] *adv* **earlier; -est 1** : temprano **2 as** ~ **as possible** : lo más pronto posible **3 ten minutes** ~ : diez minutos de adelanto — ~ *adj* **earlier; -est 1** FIRST : primero **2** ANCIENT : primitivo, antiguo **3 an** ~ **death** : una muerte prematura **4 be** ~ : llegar temprano **5 in the** ~ **spring** : a principios de la primavera

earmark ['ɪr‚mɑrk] *vt* : destinar

earn ['ərn] *vt* **1** : ganar **2** DESERVE : merecer

earnest ['ərnəst] *adj* : serio — ~ *n* **in** ~ : en serio

earnings ['ərnɪŋz] *npl* **1** WAGES : ingresos *mpl* **2** PROFITS : ganancias *fpl*

earphone ['ɪr‚foːn] *n* : audífono *m*

earring ['ɪr‚rɪŋ] *n* : pendiente *m*, arete *m Lat*

earshot ['ɪr‚ʃɑt] *n* **within** ~ : al alcance del oído

earth ['ərθ] *n* : tierra *f* — **earthenware** ['ərθən‚wer, -ðən-] *n* : loza *f* — **earthly** ['ərθli] *adj* : terrenal — **earthquake** ['ərθ‚kweɪk] *n* : terremoto *m* — **earthworm** ['ərθ‚wərm] *n* : lombriz *f* (de tierra) — **earthy** ['ərθi] *adj* **earthier; -est 1** : terroso **2** COARSE, CRUDE : grosero

ease ['iːz] *n* **1** FACILITY : facilidad *f* **2** COMFORT : comodidad *f* **3 feel at** ~ : sentir cómodo — ~ *v* **eased; easing** *vt* **1** ALLEVIATE : aliviar, calmar **2** FACILITATE : facilitar — *vi* **1** : calmarse **2** ~ **up** : disminuir

easel ['iːzəl] *n* : caballete *m*

easily ['iːzəli] *adv* **1** : fácilmente, con fa-

cilidad **2** UNQUESTIONABLY : con mucho, de lejos *Lat*

east ['iːst] *adv* : al este — ~ *adj* : este, del este — ~ *n* **1** : este *m* **2 the East** : el Oriente

Easter ['iːstər] *n* : Pascua *f*

easterly ['iːstərli] *adv & adj* : del este

eastern ['iːstərn] *adj* **1** : del este **2 Eastern** : oriental, del este

easy ['iːzi] *adj* **easier; -est 1** : fácil **2** RELAXED : relajado — **easygoing** [‚iːzi'goːɪŋ] *adj* : tolerante, relajado

eat ['iːt] *v* **ate** ['eɪt]; **eaten** ['iːtən]; **eating** *vt* : comer — *vi* **1** : comer **2** ~ **into** CORRODE : corroer **3** ~ **into** DEPLETE : comerse — **eatable** ['iːtəbəl] *adj* : comestible

eaves ['iːvz] *npl* : alero *m* — **eavesdrop** ['iːvz‚drɑp] *vi* **-dropped; -dropping** : escuchar a escondidas

ebb ['eb] *n* : reflujo *m* — ~ *vi* **1** : bajar (dícese de la marea) **2** DECLINE : decaer

ebony ['ebəni] *n, pl* **-nies** : ébano *m*

eccentric [ɪk'sentrɪk] *adj* : excéntrico — ~ *n* : excéntrico *m*, -ca *f* — **eccentricity** [‚ɪkˌsen'trɪsəti] *n, pl* **-ties** : excentricidad *f*

echo ['ekoː] *n, pl* **echoes** : eco *m* — ~ *v* **echoed; echoing** *vt* : repetir — *vi* : hacer eco, resonar

eclipse [ɪ'klɪps] *n* : eclipse *m* — ~ *vt* **eclipsed; eclipsing** : eclipsar

ecology [ɪ'kɑlədʒi, ɛ-] *n, pl* **-gies** : ecología *f* — **ecological** [‚iːkə'lɑdʒɪkəl, ‚ekə-] *adj* : ecológico

economy [ɪ'kɑnəmi] *n, pl* **-mies** : economía *f* — **economic** [‚iːkə'nɑmɪk, ‚ekə-] *or* **economical** [‚iːkə'nɑmɪkəl, ‚ekə-] *adj* : económico — **economics** [‚iːkə'nɑmɪks, ‚ekə-] *n* : economía *f* — **economist** [ɪ'kɑnəmɪst] *n* : economista *mf* — **economize** [ɪ'kɑnə‚maɪz] *v* **-mized; -mizing** : economizar

ecstasy ['ekstəsi] *n, pl* **-sies** : éxtasis *m* — **ecstatic** [ek'stætɪk, ɪk-] *adj* : extático

Ecuadoran [‚ekwə'dorən] *or* **Ecuadorean** *or* **Ecuadorian** [‚ekwə'doriən] *adj* : ecuatoriano

edge ['edʒ] *n* **1** BORDER : borde *m* **2** : filo *m* (de un cuchillo) **3** ADVANTAGE : ventaja *f* — ~ *v* **edged; edging** *vt* : bordear, ribetear — *vi* : avanzar poco a poco — **edgewise** ['ɛdʒ,waɪz] *adv* : de lado — **edgy** ['ɛdʒi] *adj* **edgier; -est** : nervioso

edible ['ɛdəbəl] *adj* : comestible

edit ['ɛdɪt] *vt* : editar, redactar, corregir **2 ~ out** : suprimir, cortar — **edition** ['dɪʃən] *n* : edición *f* — **editor** ['ɛdɪ̩ər] *n* : director *m*, -tora *f* (de un periódico); redactor *m*, -tora *f* (de un libro) — **editorial** [ˌɛdɪˈtoriəl] *n* : editorial *m*

educate ['ɛdʒə,keɪt] *vt* **-cated; -cating 1** TEACH : educar, instruir **2** INFORM : informar — **education** [ˌɛdʒəˈkeɪʃən] *n* : educación *f* — **educational** [ˌɛdʒəˈkeɪʃənəl] *adj* **1** : educativo, instructivo **2** TEACHING : docente — **educator** ['ɛdʒə,keɪtər] *n* : educador *m*, -dora *f*

eel ['iːl] *n* : anguila *f*

eerie ['ɪri] *adj* **-rier; -est** : extraño e inquietante, misterioso

effect [ɪˈfɛkt] *n* **1** : efecto *m* **2 go into ~** : entrar en vigor — *vt* : efectuar, llevar a cabo — **effective** [ɪˈfɛktɪv] *adj* **1** : eficaz **2** ACTUAL : vigente — **effectiveness** [ɪˈfɛktɪvnəs] *n* : eficacia *f*

effeminate [əˈfɛmənət] *adj* : afeminado

effervescent [ˌɛfərˈvɛsənt] *adj* : efervescente

efficient [ɪˈfɪʃənt] *adj* : eficiente — **efficiency** [ɪˈfɪʃənsi] *n, pl* **-cies** : eficiencia *f*

effort ['ɛfərt] *n* **1** : esfuerzo *m* **2 it's not worth the ~** : no vale la pena — **effortless** ['ɛfərtləs] *adj* : fácil, sin esfuerzo

egg ['ɛg] *n* : huevo *m* — ~ *vt* ~ **on** : incitar — **eggplant** ['ɛg,plænt] *n* : berenjena *f* — **eggshell** ['ɛg,ʃɛl] *n* : cascarón *m*

ego ['iː,goː] *n, pl* **egos 1** SELF : yo, el yo *m* **2** SELF-ESTEEM : amor *m* propio — **egotism** ['iːgəˌtɪzəm] *n* : egotismo *m* — **egotist** ['iːgətɪst] *n* : egotista *mf* — **egotistic** [ˌiːgəˈtɪstɪk] *or* **egotistical** [-ˈtɪstɪkəl] *adj* : egotista

eiderdown ['aɪdər,daʊn] *n* **1** DOWN : plumón *m* **2** COMFORTER : edredón *m*

eight ['eɪt] *n* : ocho *m* — ~ *adj* : ocho — **eight hundred** *n* : ochocientos *m*

eighteen [eɪt'tiːn] *n* : dieciocho *m* — ~ *adj* : dieciocho — **eighteenth** [eɪtˈtiːnθ] *adj* : decimoctavo — ~ *n* **1** : decimoctavo *m*, -va *f* (en una serie) **2** : dieciochoavo *m*, dieciochoava parte *f*

eighth ['eɪtθ] *n* **1** : octavo *m*, -va *f* (en una serie) **2** : octavo *m*, octava parte *f* — ~ *adj* : octavo

eighty ['eɪti] *n, pl* **eighties** : ochenta *m* — **eightieth** *adj* : ochenta

either ['iːðər, 'aɪ-] *adj* **1** : cualquiera (de los dos) **2** (*in negative constructions*) : ninguno (de los dos) **3** EACH : cada — ~ *pron* **1** : cualquiera *mf* (de los dos) **2** (*in negative constructions*) : ninguno *m*, -na *f* (de los dos) **3** *or* ~ **one** : algún *m*, alguna *f* — ~ *conj* **1** : o **2** (*in negative constructions*) : ni

eject [ɪˈdʒɛkt] *vt* : expulsar, expeler

eke ['iːk] *vt* **eked; eking** *or* ~ **out** : ganar a duras penas

elaborate [ɪˈlæbərət] *adj* **1** DETAILED : detallado **2** COMPLEX : complicado — ~ [ɪˈlæbəˌreɪt] *v* **-rated; -rating** *vt* : elaborar — *vi* : entrar en detalles

elapse [ɪˈlæps] *vi* **elapsed; elapsing** : transcurrir

elastic [ɪˈlæstɪk] *adj* : elástico — ~ *n* **1** : elástico *m* **2** RUBBER BAND : goma *f* (elástica) — **elasticity** [ɪ,læsˈtɪsəti, iˌlæs-] *n, pl* **-ties** : elasticidad *f*

elated [ɪˈleɪtəd] *adj* : regocijado

elbow ['ɛl,boː] *n* : codo *m*

elder ['ɛldər] *adj* : mayor — ~ *n* **1** : mayor *mf* **2** : anciano *m*, -na *f* (de un tribu, etc.) — **elderly** ['ɛldərli] *adj* : mayor, anciano

elect [ɪˈlɛkt] *vt* : elegir — ~ *adj* : electo — **election** [ɪˈlɛkʃən] *n* : elección *f* — **electoral** [ɪˈlɛktərəl] *adj* : electoral — **electorate** [ɪˈlɛktərət] *n* : electorado *m*

electricity [ɪˌlɛkˈtrɪsəti] *n, pl* **-ties** : electricidad *f* — **electric** [ɪˈlɛktrɪk] *or* **electrical** [-trɪkəl] *adj* : eléctrico — **electrician** [ɪˌlɛkˈtrɪʃən] *n* : electricista *mf* — **electrify** [ɪˈlɛktrəˌfaɪ] *vt* **-fied; -fying** : electrificar — **electrocute** [ɪˈlɛktrəˌkjuːt] *vt* **-cuted; -cuting** : electrocutar

electron [ɪˈlɛk,tran] *n* : electrón *m* — **electronic** [ɪˌlɛkˈtranɪk] *adj* : electrónico — **electronic mail** *n* : correo *m* electrónico — **electronics** [ɪˌlɛkˈtranɪks] *n* : electrónica *f*

elegant ['ɛlɪgənt] *adj* : elegante — **elegance** ['ɛlɪgəns] *n* : elegancia *f*

element ['ɛləmənt] *n* **1** : elemento *m* **2 ~s** *npl* BASICS : elementos *mpl*, rudimentos *mpl* — **elementary** [ˌɛləˈmɛntri] *adj* : elemental — **elementary school** *n* : escuela *f* primaria

elephant ['ɛləfənt] *n* : elefante *m*, -ta *f*

elevate ['ɛlə,veɪt] *vt* **-vated; -vating** : elevar — **elevator** ['ɛlə,veɪtər] *n* : ascensor *m*

eleven [ɪˈlɛvən] *n* : once *m* — ~ *adj* : once — **eleventh** [ɪˈlɛvənθ] *adj* : undécimo — ~ *n* **1** : undécimo *m*, -ma *f* (en una serie) **2** : onceavo *m*, onceava parte *f*

elf ['elf] *n*, *pl* **elves** ['elvz] : duende *m*

elicit [ɪ'lɪsət] *vt* : provocar

eligible ['ɛlədʒəbəl] *adj* : elegible

eliminate [ɪ'lɪmə,neɪt] *vt* **-nated; -nating** : eliminar — **elimination** [ɪ,lɪmə'neɪʃən] *n* : eliminación *f*

elite [eɪ'liːt, i-] *n* : elite *f*

elk ['elk] *n* : alce *m* (de Europa), uapití *m* (de América)

elliptical [ɪ'lɪptɪkəl, ɛ-] *or* **elliptic** [-tɪk] *adj* : elíptico

elm ['elm] *n* : olmo *m*

elongate [ɪ'lɔŋ] *vt* **-gated; -gating** : alargar

elope [ɪ'loːp] *vi* **eloped; eloping** : fugarse — **elopement** [ɪ'loːpmənt] *n* : fuga *f*

eloquence ['ɛləkwənts] *n* : elocuencia *f* — **eloquent** ['ɛləkwənt] *adj* : elocuente

else ['ɛls] *adv* **1 how** ~ ? : ¿de qué otro modo? **2 where** ~ ? : ¿en qué otro sitio? **3 or** ~ : si no, de lo contrario — ~ *adj* **1 everyone** ~ : todos los demás **2 nobody** ~ : ningún otro, nadie más **3 nothing** ~ : nada más **4 what** ~ ? : ¿qué más? — **elsewhere** ['ɛls,ʰwɛr] *adv* : en otra parte

elude [ɪ'luːd] *vt* **eluded; eluding** : eludir, esquivar — **elusive** [ɪ'luːsɪv] *adj* : esquivo

elves → **elf**

emaciated [ɪ'meɪʃi,eɪtəd] *adj* : escuálido, demacrado

E–mail ['iː,meɪl] → **electronic mail**

emanate ['ɛmə,neɪt] *vi* **-nated; -nating** : emanar

emancipate [ɪ'mæntsə,peɪt] *vt* **-pated; -pating** : emancipar — **emancipation** [ɪ,mæntsə'peɪʃən] *n* : emancipación *f*

embalm [ɪm'bam, ɛm-, -'balm] *vt* : embalsamar

embankment [ɪm'bæŋkmənt, ɛm-] *n* : terraplén *m*, dique *m* (de un río)

embargo [ɪm'bargo, ɛm-] *n*, *pl* **-goes** : embargo *m*

embark [ɪm'bark, ɛm-] *vt* : embarcar — *vi* **1** : embarcarse **2** ~ **upon** : emprender — **embarkation** [,ɛm,bar'keɪʃən] *n* : embarque *m*, embarco *m*

embarrass [ɪm'bærəs, ɛm-] *vt* : avergonzar — **embarrassing** [ɪm'bærəsɪŋ, ɛm-] *adj* : embarazoso — **embarrassment** [ɪm'bærəsmənt, ɛm-] *n* : vergüenza *f*

embassy ['ɛmbəsi] *n*, *pl* **-sies** : embajada *f*

embed [ɪm'bɛd, ɛm-] *vt* **-bedded; -bedding** : incrustar, enterrar

embellish [ɪm'bɛlɪʃ, ɛm-] *vt* : adornar, embellecer — **embellishment** [ɪm'bɛlɪʃmənt, ɛm-] *n* : adorno *m*

embers ['ɛmbəz] *npl* : ascuas *fpl*

embezzle [ɪm'bɛzəl, ɛm-] *vt* **-zled; -zling** : desfalcar, malversar — **embezzlement** [ɪm'bɛzəlmənt, ɛm-] *n* : desfalco *m*, malversación *f*

emblem ['ɛmbləm] *n* : emblema *m*

embody [ɪm'badi, ɛm-] *vt* **-bodied; -bodying** : encarnar, personificar

emboss [ɪm'bas, ɛm-, -'bɔs] *vt* : repujar, grabar en relieve

embrace [ɪm'breɪs, ɛm-] *v* **-braced; -bracing** *vt* : abrazar — *vi* : abrazarse — ~ *n* : abrazo *m*

embroider [ɪm'brɔɪdər, ɛm-] *vt* : bordar — **embroidery** [ɪm'brɔɪdəri, ɛm-] *n*, *pl* **-deries** : bordado *m*

embryo ['ɛmbri,oː] *n*, *pl* **embryos** : embrión *m*

emerald ['ɛmrəld, 'ɛmə-] *n* : esmeralda *f*

emerge [ɪ'mərdʒ] *vi* **emerged; emerging** : salir, aparecer — **emergence** [ɪ'mərdʒənts] *n* : aparición *f*

emergency [ɪ'mərdʒəntsi] *n*, *pl* **-cies 1** : emergencia *f* **2** ~ **exit** : salida *f* de emergencia **3** ~ **room** : sala *f* de urgencias, sala *f* de guardia

emery ['ɛməri] *n*, *pl* **-eries 1** : esmeril *m* **2** ~ **board** : lima *f* de uñas

emigrant ['ɛmɪgrənt] *n* : emigrante *mf* — **emigrate** ['ɛmə,greɪt] *vi* **-grated; -grating** : emigrar — **emigration** [,ɛmə'greɪʃən] *n* : emigración *f*

eminence ['ɛmənənts] *n* : eminencia *f* — **eminent** ['ɛmənənt] *adj* : eminente

emission [ɪ'mɪʃən] *n* : emisión *f* — **emit** [ɪ'mɪt] *vt* **emitted; emitting** : emitir

emotion [ɪ'moːʃən] *n* : emoción *f* — **emotional** [ɪ'moːʃənəl] *adj* **1** : emocional **2 MOVING** : emotivo

emperor ['ɛmpərər] *n* : emperador *m*

emphasis ['ɛmfəsɪs] *n*, *pl* **-phases** [-,siːz] : énfasis *m* — **emphasize** ['ɛmfə,saɪz] *vt* **-sized; -sizing** : subrayar, hacer hincapié en — **emphatic** [ɪm-'fætɪk, ɛm-] *adj* : enérgico, categórico

empire ['ɛm,paɪr] *n* : imperio *m*

employ [ɪm'plɔɪ, ɛm-] *vt* : emplear — **employee** [ɪm,plɔɪ'iː, ɛm-, -'plɔɪ,iː] *n* : empleado *m*, -da *f* — **employer** [ɪm'plɔɪər, ɛm-] *n* : patrón *m*, -trona *f*; empleador *m*, -dora *f* — **employment** [ɪm'plɔɪmənt, ɛm-] *n* : trabajo *m*, empleo *m*

empower [ɪm'pauər, ɛm-] *vt* : autorizar

empress ['ɛmprəs] *n* : emperatriz *f*

empty ['ɛmpti] *adj* **emptier; -est 1** : vacío **2 MEANINGLESS** : vano — ~ *v*

-tied; -tying *vt* : vaciar — *vi* : vaciarse
— **emptiness** ['emptinəs] *n* : vacío *m*

emulate ['emjə,leit] *vt* **-lated; -lating**
: emular

enable [ɪ'neibəl, ɛ-] *vt* **-abled; -abling**
: hacer posible, permitir

enact [ɪ'nækt, ɛ-] *vt* **1** : promulgar (un ley o un decreto) **2** PERFORM : representar

enamel [ɪ'næməl] *n* : esmalte *m*

encampment [ɪn'kæmpmənt, ɛn-] *n* : campamento *m*

encase [ɪn'keis, ɛn-] *vt* **-cased; -casing** : encerrar, revestir

enchant [ɪn'tʃænt, ɛn-] *vt* : encantar — **enchanting** [ɪn'tʃæntɪŋ, ɛn-] *adj* : encantador — **enchantment** [ɪn'tʃænt-mənt, ɛn-] *n* : encanto *m*

encircle [ɪn'sərkəl, ɛn-] *vt* **-cled; -cling** : rodear

enclose [ɪn'kloiz, ɛn-] *vt* **-closed; -closing 1** SURROUND : encerrar, cercar **2** INCLUDE : adjuntar (a una carta) — **enclosure** [ɪn'kloiʒər, ɛn-] *n* **1** AREA : recinto *m* **2** : anexo *m* (con una carta)

encompass [ɪn'kʌmpəs, ɛn-, -'kam-] *vt* **1** ENCIRCLE : cercar **2** INCLUDE : abarcar

encore ['an,kor] *n* : bis *m*

encounter [ɪn'kauntər, ɛn-] *vt* : encontrar — ~ *n* : encuentro *m*

encourage [ɪn'kərɪdʒ, ɛn-] *vt* **-aged; -aging 1** : animar, alentar **2** FOSTER : promover, fomentar — **encouragement** [ɪn'kərɪdʒmənt, ɛn-] *n* **1** : aliento *m* **2** PROMOTION : fomento *m*

encroach [ɪn'krotʃ, ɛn-] *vi* — **on** : invadir, usurpar, quitar (el tiempo)

encyclopedia [ɪn,saɪklə'pi:diə, ɛn-] *n* : enciclopedia *f*

end ['end] *n* **1** : fin **2** EXTREMITY : extremo *m*, punta *f* **3 come to an** — : llegar a su fin **4 in the** — : por fin — ~ *vt* : terminar, poner fin a — *vi* : terminar(se)

endanger [ɪn'deindʒər, ɛn-] *vt* : poner en peligro

endearing [ɪn'dɪrɪŋ, ɛn-] *adj* : simpático

endeavor *or Brit* **endeavour** [ɪn'devər, ɛn-] *vt* — **to** : esforzarse por — ~ *n* : esfuerzo *m*

ending ['endɪŋ] *n* : final *m*, desenlace *m*

endive ['ɛn,daɪv, 'an,di:v] *n* : endibia *f*, endivia *f*

endless ['endləs] *adj* **1** INTERMINABLE : interminable **2** INNUMERABLE : innumerable **3** — **possibilities** : posibilidades *fpl* infinitas

endorse [ɪn'dors, ɛn-] *vt* **-dorsed; -dorsing 1** SIGN : endosar **2** APPROVE

: aprobar — **endorsement** [ɪn'dorsmənt, ɛn-] *n* APPROVAL : aprobación *f*

endow [ɪn'dau, ɛn-] *vt* : dotar

endure [ɪn'dur, ɛn-, -'djur] *v* **-dured; -during** *vt* **1** : soportar, aguantar — *vi* LAST : durar — **endurance** [ɪn'durənts, ɛn-, -'djur-] *n* : resistencia *f*

enemy ['enəmi] *n*, *pl* **-mies** : enemigo *m*, -ga *f*

energy ['enərdʒi] *n*, *pl* **-gies** : energía *f* — **energetic** [,enər'dʒetɪk] *adj* : enérgico

enforce [ɪn'fors, ɛn-] *vt* **-forced; -forcing 1** : hacer cumplir (un ley, etc.) **2** IMPOSE : imponer — **enforced** *adj* : forzoso — **enforcement** [ɪn'forsmənt, ɛn-] *n* : imposición *f* del cumplimiento

engage [ɪn'geidʒ, ɛn-] *v* **-gaged; -gaging** *vt* **1** : captar, atraer (la atención, etc.) **2** — **the clutch** : embragar — *vi* — **in** : dedicarse a, entrar en — **engagement** [ɪn'geidʒmənt, ɛn-] *n* **1** APPOINTMENT : cita *f*, hora *f* **2** BETROTHAL : compromiso *m* — **engaging** [ɪn'geidʒɪŋ, ɛn-] *adj* : atractivo

engine ['endʒən] *n* **1** : motor *m* **2** LOCOMOTIVE : locomotora *f* — **engineer** [,endʒə'nɪr] *n* **1** : ingeniero *m*, -ra *f* **2** : maquinista *mf* (de locomotoras) — ~ *vt* **1** CONSTRUCT : construir **2** CONTRIVE : tramar — **engineering** [,endʒə'nɪrɪŋ] *n* : ingeniería *f*

English ['ɪŋglɪʃ, 'ɪŋlɪʃ] *adj* : inglés — ~ *n* : inglés *m* (idioma) — **Englishman** ['ɪŋglɪʃmən, 'ɪŋlɪʃ-] *n* : inglés *m* — **Englishwoman** ['ɪŋglɪʃ,wumən, 'ɪŋlɪʃ-] *n* : inglesa *f*

engrave [ɪn'greiv, ɛn-] *vt* **-graved; -graving** : grabar — **engraving** [ɪn'greivɪŋ, ɛn-] *n* : grabado *m*

engross [ɪn'gros, ɛn-] *vt* : absorber

engulf [ɪn'gʌlf, ɛn-] *vt* : envolver

enhance [ɪn'hænts, ɛn-] *vt* **-hanced; -hancing** : aumentar, mejorar

enjoy [ɪn'dʒoi, ɛn-] *vt* **1** : disfrutar, gozar de **2** — **oneself** : divertirse — **enjoyable** [ɪn'dʒoiəbəl, ɛn-] *adj* : agradable — **enjoyment** [ɪn'dʒoimənt, ɛn-] *n* : placer *m*

enlarge [ɪn'lardʒ, ɛn-] *v* **-larged; -larging** *vt* : agrandar, ampliar — *vi* **1** : agrandarse **2** — **upon** : extenderse sobre — **enlargement** [ɪn'lardʒmənt, ɛn-] *n* : ampliación *f*

enlighten [ɪn'laitən, ɛn-] *vt* : aclarar, iluminar

enlist [ɪn'lɪst, ɛn-] *vt* **1** ENROLL : alistar **2** OBTAIN : conseguir — *vi* : alistarse

enliven [ɪn'laivən, ɛn-] *vt* : animar

enmity ['enmət̬i] *n, pl* **-ties** : enemistad *f*

enormous [ɪ'nɔrməs] *adj* : enorme

enough [ɪ'nʌf] *adj* : bastante, suficiente — ~ *adv* : bastante — ~ *pron* **1** : (lo) suficiente, (lo) bastante **2 it's not** ~ : no basta **3 I've had** ~ ! : ¡estoy harto!

enquire [ɪn'kwaɪr, ɛn-], **enquiry** [ɪn'kwaɪri, 'ɪn-, -kwəri; ɪn'kwaɪri, 'ɛn-] → **inquire, inquiry**

enrage [ɪn'reɪdʒ, ɛn-] *vt* **-raged; -raging** : enfurecer

enrich [ɪn'rɪtʃ, ɛn-] *vt* : enriquecer

enroll *or* **enrol** [ɪn'roːl, ɛn-] *v* **-rolled; -rolling** *vt* : matricular, inscribir — *vi* : matricularse, inscribirse

ensemble [ɑn'sɑmbəl] *n* : conjunto *m*

ensign ['ensən, 'en,saɪn] *n* **1** FLAG : enseña *f* **2** : alférez *mf* (de fragata)

enslave [ɪn'sleɪv, ɛn-] *vt* **-slaved; -slaving** : esclavizar

ensue [ɪn'suː, ɛn-] *vi* **-sued; -suing** : seguir, resultar

ensure [ɪn'ʃur, ɛn-] *vt* **-sured; -suring** : asegurar

entail [ɪn'teɪl, ɛn-] *vt* : suponer, conllevar

entangle [ɪn'tæŋgəl, ɛn-] *vt* **-gled; -gling** : enredar — **entanglement** [ɪn'tæŋgəlmənt, ɛn-] *n* : enredo *m*

enter ['ɛnt̬ər] *vt* **1** : entrar en **2** RECORD : inscribir — *vi* **1** : entrar **2** ~ **into** : firmar (un acuerdo), entablar (negociaciones, etc.)

enterprise ['ɛnt̬ər,praɪz] *n* **1** : empresa *f* **2** INITIATIVE : iniciativa *f* — **enterprising** ['ɛnt̬ər,praɪzɪŋ] *adj* : emprendedor

entertain [,ɛnt̬ər'teɪn] *vt* **1** AMUSE : entretener, divertir **2** CONSIDER : considerar **3** ~ **guests** : recibir invitados — **entertainment** [,ɛnt̬ər'teɪnmənt] *n* : entretenimiento *m*, diversión *f*

enthrall *or* **enthral** [ɪn'θrɔl, ɛn-] *vt* **-thralled; -thralling** : cautivar, embelesar

enthusiasm [ɪn'θuːzi,æzəm, ɛn-, -'θjuː-] *n* : entusiasmo *m* — **enthusiast** [ɪn'θuːzi,æst, ɛn-, -'θjuː-, -əst] *n* : entusiasta *mf* — **enthusiastic** [ɪn,θuːzi'æstɪk, ɛn-, -,θjuː-] *adj* : entusiasta

entice [ɪn'taɪs, ɛn-] *vt* **-ticed; -ticing** : atraer, tentar

entire [ɪn'taɪr, ɛn-] *adj* : entero, completo — **entirely** [ɪn'taɪrli, ɛn-] *adv* : completamente — **entirety** [ɪn'taɪrt̬i, ɛn-, -'taɪrt̬i] *n, pl* **-ties** : totalidad *f*

entitle [ɪn'taɪt̬əl, ɛn-] *vt* **-tled; -tling 1** NAME : titular **2** AUTHORIZE : dar derecho a — **entitlement** [ɪn'taɪt̬əlmənt, ɛn-] *n* : derecho *m*

entity ['ɛnt̬ət̬i] *n, pl* **-ties** : entidad *f*

entrails ['ɛn,treɪlz, -trəlz] *npl* : entrañas *fpl*, vísceras *fpl*

entrance¹ [ɪn'træns, ɛn-] *vt* **-tranced; -trancing** : encantar, fascinar

entrance² ['ɛntrəns] *n* : entrada *f* — **entrant** ['ɛntrənt] *n* : participante *mf*

entreat [ɪn'triːt, ɛn-] *vt* : suplicar

entrée *or* **entree** ['ɑn,treɪ, ɑn'-] *n* : plato *m* principal

entrepreneur [,ɑntrəprə'nər, -'njur] *n* : empresario *m*, -ria *f*

entrust [ɪn'trʌst, ɛn-] *vt* : confiar

entry ['ɛntri] *n, pl* **-tries 1** ENTRANCE : entrada *f* **2** NOTATION : entrada *f*, anotación *f*

enumerate [ɪ'nuːmə,reɪt, ɛ-, -'njuː-] *vt* **-ated; -ating** : enumerar

enunciate [ɪ'nʌnsi,eɪt, ɛ-] *vt* **-ated; -ating 1** STATE : enunciar **2** PRONOUNCE : articular

envelop [ɪn'vɛləp, ɛn-] *vt* : envolver — **envelope** ['ɛnvə,loːp, 'ɑn-] *n* : sobre *m*

envious ['ɛnviəs] *adj* : envidioso — **enviously** *adv* : con envidia

environment [ɪn'vaɪrənmənt, ɛn-, -'vaɪrəm-] *n* : medio *m* ambiente — **environmental** [ɪn,vaɪrən'mɛnt̬əl, ɛn-, -,vaɪrəm-] *adj* : ambiental — **environmentalist** [ɪn,vaɪrən'mɛnt̬əlɪst, ɛn-, -,vaɪrəm-] *n* : ecologista *mf*

envision [ɪn'vɪʒən, ɛn-] *vt* : prever, imaginar

envoy ['ɛn,vɔɪ, 'ɑn-] *n* : enviado *m*, -da *f*

envy ['ɛnvi] *n, pl* **envies** : envidia *f* — ~ *vt* **-vied; -vying** : envidiar

enzyme ['ɛn,zaɪm] *n* : enzima *f*

epic ['ɛpɪk] *adj* : épico — ~ *n* : epopeya *f*

epidemic [,ɛpə'dɛmɪk] *n* : epidemia *f* — ~ *adj* : epidémico

epilepsy ['ɛpə,lɛpsi] *n, pl* **-sies** : epilepsia *f* — **epileptic** [,ɛpə'lɛptɪk] *adj* : epiléptico — ~ *n* : epiléptico *m*, -ca *f*

episode ['ɛpə,soːd] *n* : episodio *m*

epitaph ['ɛpə,tæf] *n* : epitafio *m*

epitome [ɪ'pɪt̬əmi] *n* : personificación *f* — **epitomize** [ɪ'pɪt̬ə,maɪz] *vt* **-mized; -mizing** : ser la personificación de, personificar

epoch ['ɛpək, 'ɛ,pɑk, 'iːpək] *n* : época *f*

equal ['iːkwəl] *adj* **1** SAME : igual **2 be** ~ **to** : estar a la altura de (una tarea, etc.) — ~ *n* : igual *mf* — ~ *vt* **-qualed** *or* **-qualled; -qualing** *or* **-qualling** : igualar **2** : ser igual a (en matemáticas) — **equality** [ɪ'kwɑlət̬i] *n, pl* **-ties** : igualdad *f* — **equalize** ['iːkwə,laɪz] *vt* **-ized; -izing** : igualar — **equally** ['iːkwəli] *adv* **1** : igualmente **2** ~ **important** : igual de importante

equate [ɪ'kweɪt] *vt* **equated; equating** ~ **with** : equiparar con — **equation** [ɪ'kweɪʒən] *n* : ecuación *f*

equator [ɪ'kweɪt̬ər] *n* : ecuador *m*

equilibrium [ˌiːkwə'lɪbriəm, ˌɛ-] *n, pl* **-riums** *or* **-ria** [-briə] : equilibrio *m*

equinox ['iːkwə,nɑks, 'ɛ-] *n* : equinoccio *m*

equip [ɪ'kwɪp] *vt* **equipped; equipping** : equipar — **equipment** [ɪ'kwɪpmənt] *n* : equipo *m*

equity ['ɛkwəti] *n, pl* **-ties 1** FAIRNESS : equidad *f* **2 equities** *npl* STOCKS : acciones *fpl* ordinarias

equivalent [ɪ'kwɪvələnt] *adj* : equivalente — ~ *n* : equivalente *m*

era ['ɪrə, 'ɛrə, 'iːrə] *n* : era *f*, época *f*

eradicate [ɪ'rædə,keɪt] *vt* **-cated; -cating** : erradicar

erase [ɪ'reɪs] *vt* **erased; erasing** : borrar — **eraser** [ɪ'reɪsər] *n* **1** : goma *f* de borrar, borrador *m*

erect [ɪ'rɛkt] *adj* : erguido — ~ *vt* : erigir, levantar — **erection** [ɪ'rɛkʃən] *n* **1** BUILDING : construcción *f* **2** : erección *f* (en fisiología)

erode [ɪ'roːd] *vt* **eroded; eroding** : erosionar (el suelo), corroer (metales) — **erosion** [ɪ'roːʒən] *n* : erosión *f*, corrosión *f*

erotic [ɪ'rɑt̬ɪk] *adj* : erótico

err ['ɛr, 'ər] *vi* : equivocarse, errar

errand ['ɛrənd] *n* : mandado *m*, recado *m* Spain

erratic [ɪ'ræt̬ɪk] *adj* : errático, irregular

error ['ɛrər] *n* : error *m* — **erroneous** [ɪ'roːniəs, ɛ-] *adj* : erróneo

erupt [ɪ'rʌpt] *vi* **1** : hacer erupción (dícese de un volcán) **2** : estallar (dícese de la cólera, la violencia, etc.) — **eruption** [ɪ'rʌpʃən] *n* : erupción *f*

escalate ['ɛskəˌleɪt] *vi* **-lated; -lating** : intensificarse

escalator ['ɛskə,leɪt̬ər] *n* : escalera *f* mecánica

escapade ['ɛskə,peɪd] *n* : aventura *f*

escape [ɪ'skeɪp, ɛ-] *v* **-caped; -caping** *vt* : escapar a, evitar — *vi* : escaparse, fugarse — ~ *n* **1** : fuga *f* **2** ~ **from reality** : evasión *f* de la realidad — **escapee** [ɪ,skeɪˈpiː, ˌɛ-] *n* : fugitivo *m*, -va *f*

escort ['ɛsˌkɔrt] *n* **1** GUARD : escolta *f* **2** COMPANION : acompañante *mf* — ~ [ɪˈskɔrt, ɛ-] *vt* **1** : escoltar **2** ACCOMPANY : acompañar

Eskimo ['ɛskəˌmoː] *adj* : esquimal

especially [ɪ'spɛʃəli] *adv* : especialmente

espionage ['ɛspiəˌnɑʒ, -ˌnɑdʒ] *n* : espionaje *m*

espresso [ɛˈspreˌsoː] *n, pl* **-sos** : café *m* exprés

essay ['ɛˌseɪ] *n* : ensayo *m* (literario), composición *f* (académica)

essence ['ɛsənts] *n* : esencia *f* — **essential** [ɪˈsɛntʃəl] *adj* : esencial — ~ *n* **1** : elemento *m* esencial **2 the** ~**s** : lo indispensable

establish [ɪ'stæblɪʃ, ɛ-] *vt* : establecer — **establishment** [ɪ'stæblɪʃmənt, ɛ-] *n* : establecimiento *m*

estate [ɪ'steɪt, ɛ-] *n* **1** POSSESSIONS : bienes *mpl* **2** LAND, PROPERTY : finca *f*

esteem [ɪ'stiːm, ɛ-] *n* : estima *f* — ~ *vt* : estimar

esthetic [ɛs'θɛt̬ɪk] → aesthetic

estimate ['ɛstəˌmeɪt] *vt* **-mated; -mating** : calcular, estimar — ~ ['ɛstəmət] *n* **1** : cálculo *m* (aproximado) **2** *or* ~ **of costs** : presupuesto *m* — **estimation** [ˌɛstəˈmeɪʃən] *n* **1** JUDGMENT : juicio *m* **2** ESTEEM : estima *f*

estuary ['ɛstʃuˌweri] *n, pl* **-aries** : estuario *m*, ría *f*

eternal [ɪ'tərnəl, iː-] *adj* : eterno — **eternity** [ɪ'tərnət̬i, iː-] *n, pl* **-ties** : eternidad *f*

ether ['iːθər] *n* : éter *m*

ethical ['ɛθɪkəl] *adj* : ético — **ethics** ['ɛθɪks] *ns & pl* : ética *f*, moralidad *f*

ethnic ['ɛθnɪk] *adj* : étnico

etiquette ['ɛt̬ɪkət, -ˌkɛt] *n* : etiqueta *f*

Eucharist ['juːkərɪst] *n* : Eucaristía *f*

eulogy ['juːlədʒi] *n, pl* **-gies** : elogio *m*, panegírico *m*

euphemism ['juːfəˌmɪzəm] *n* : eufemismo *m*

euphoria [juˈforiə] *n* : euforia *f*

European [ˌjʊrəˈpiːən, -piːn] *adj* : europeo

evacuate [ɪ'vækjuˌeɪt] *vt* **-ated; -ating** : evacuar — **evacuation** [ɪˌvækjuˈeɪʃən] *n* : evacuación *f*

evade [ɪ'veɪd] *vt* **evaded; evading** : evadir, eludir

evaluate [ɪ'væljuˌeɪt] *vt* **-ated; -ating** : evaluar

evaporate [ɪ'væpəˌreɪt] *vi* **-rated; -rating** : evaporarse

evasion [ɪ'veɪʒən] *n* : evasión *f* — **evasive** [ɪ'veɪsɪv] *adj* : evasivo

eve ['iːv] *n* : víspera *f*

even ['iːvən] *adj* **1** REGULAR, STEADY : regular, constante **2** LEVEL : plano, llano **3** SMOOTH : liso **4** EQUAL : igual **5** ~ **number** : número *m* par **6 get** ~ **with** : desquitarse con — ~ *adv* **1** : hasta, incluso **2** ~ **better** : aún mejor, todavía mejor **3 ~ if** : aunque **4 ~ so** : aun así — **~** *vt* : igualar — *vi or* **out** : nivelarse

evening ['iːvnɪŋ] *n* : tarde *f*, noche *f*

event ['vɛnt] *n* **1** : acontecimiento *m*, suceso *m* **2** : prueba *f* (en deportes) **3 in the ~ of** : en caso de — **eventful** ['vɛntfəl] *adj* : lleno de incidentes

eventual ['vɛntʃʊəl] *adj* : final — **eventuality** [ˌvɛntʃʊˈæləti] *n, pl* **-ties** : eventualidad *f* — **eventually** [ɪ-'vɛntʃʊəli] *adv* : al fin, finalmente

ever ['ɛvər] *adv* **1** ALWAYS : siempre **2 ~ since** : desde entonces **3 hardly ~** : casi nunca **4 have you ~ done it?** : ¿lo has hecho alguna vez?

evergreen ['ɛvərˌgriːn] *n* : planta *f* de hoja perenne

everlasting [ˌɛvərˈlæstɪŋ] *adj* : eterno

every ['ɛvri] *adj* **1** EACH : cada **2 ~ month** : todos los meses **3 ~ other day** : cada dos días — **everybody** ['ɛvriˌbʌdi, -bɑ-] *pron* : todos *mpl*, -das *fpl*; todo el mundo — **everyday** [ˌɛvri-'deɪ, 'ɛvri-] *adj* : cotidiano, de todos los días — **everyone** ['ɛvriˌwʌn] → **everybody** — **everything** ['ɛvri ˌθɪŋ] *pron* : todo — **everywhere** ['ɛvri ˌhwɛr] *adv* : en todas partes, por todas partes

evict ['vɪkt] *vt* : desahuciar, desalojar — **eviction** ['vɪkʃən] *n* : desahucio *m*

evidence ['ɛvədəns] *n* **1** PROOF : pruebas *fpl* **2** TESTIMONY : testimonio *m*, declaración *f* — **evident** ['ɛvɪdənt] *adj* : evidente — **evidently** ['ɛvɪdəntli, ˌɛvɪ-'dɛntli] *adv* **1** OBVIOUSLY : obviamente **2** APPARENTLY : evidentemente, al parecer

evil ['iːvəl, -vɪl] *adj* **eviler** *or* **eviller; evilest** *or* **evillest** : malvado, malo — **~** *n* : mal *m*, maldad *f*

evoke ['voːk] *vt* **evoked; evoking** : evocar

evolution [ˌɛvəˈluːʃən, ˌiː-] *n* : evolución *f*, desarrollo *m* — **evolve** ['vɑlv] *vi* **evolved; evolving** : evolucionar, desarrollarse

exact [ɪg'zækt, ɛg-] *adj* : exacto, preciso — **~** *vt* : exigir — **exacting** [ɪg-'zæktɪŋ, ɛg-] *adj* : exigente — **exactly** [ɪg'zæktli, ɛg-] *adv* : exactamente

exaggerate [ɪg'zædʒəˌreɪt, ɛg-] *v* **-ated; -ating** : exagerar — **exaggeration** [ɪgˌzædʒəˈreɪʃən, ɛg-] *n* : exageración *f*

examine [ɪg'zæmən, ɛg-] *vt* **-ined; -ining** **1** : examinar **2** INSPECT : revisar **3** QUESTION : interrogar — **exam** [ɪg-'zæm, ɛg-] *n* : examen *m* — **examination** [ɪgˌzæməˈneɪʃən, ɛg-] *n* : examen *m*

example [ɪg'zæmpəl, ɛg-] *n* : ejemplo *m*

exasperate [ɪg'zæspəˌreɪt, ɛg-] *vt* **-ated; -ating** : exasperar — **exasperation** [ɪgˌzæspəˈreɪʃən, ɛg-] *n* : exasperación *f*

excavate ['ɛkskəˌveɪt] *vt* **-vated; -vating** : excavar — **excavation** [ˌɛkskəˈveɪʃən] *n* : excavación *f*

exceed [ɪk'siːd, ɛk-] *vt* : exceder, sobrepasar — **exceedingly** [ɪk'siːdɪŋli, ɛk-] *adv* : extremadamente

excel [ɪk'sɛl, ɛk-] *v* **-celled; -celling** *vi* : sobresalir — *vt* SURPASS : superar — **excellence** ['ɛksələns] *n* : excelencia *f* — **excellent** ['ɛksələnt] *adj* : excelente

except [ɪk'sɛpt] *prep or* **~ for** : excepto, menos, salvo — **~** *vt* : exceptuar — **exception** [ɪk'sɛpʃən] *n* : excepción *f* — **exceptional** [ɪk'sɛpʃənəl] *adj* : excepcional

excerpt ['ɛkˌsərpt, 'ɛgˌzərpt] *n* : extracto *m*

excess [ɪk'sɛs, 'ɛkˌsɛs] *n* : exceso *m* — **~** ['ɛkˌsɛs, ɪk'sɛs] *adj* : excesivo, de sobra — **excessive** [ɪk'sɛsɪv, ɛk-] *adj* : excesivo

exchange [ɪks'tʃeɪndʒ, ɛks-; 'ɛksˌtʃeɪndʒ] *n* **1** : intercambio *m* **2** : cambio *m* (en finanzas) — *vt* **-changed; -changing** : cambiar, intercambiar

excise [ɪk'saɪz, ɛk-] *n* **~ tax** : impuesto *m* interno, impuesto *m* sobre el consumo

excite [ɪk'saɪt, ɛk-] *vt* **-cited; -citing** : excitar, emocionar — **excited** [ɪk-'saɪtəd, ɛk-] *adj* : excitado, entusiasmado — **excitement** [ɪk'saɪtmənt, ɛk-] *n* : entusiasmo *m*, emoción *f*

exclaim [ɪks'kleɪm, ɛks-] *v* : exclamar — **exclamation** [ˌɛkskləˈmeɪʃən] *n* : exclamación *f* — **exclamation point** *n* : signo *m* de admiración

exclude [ɪks'kluːd, ɛks-] *vt* **-cluded; -cluding** : excluir — **excluding** [ɪks-'kluːdɪŋ, ɛks-] *prep* : excepto, con excepción de — **exclusion** [ɪks'kluːʒən, ɛks-] *n* : exclusión *f* — **exclusive** [ɪks-'kluːsɪv, ɛks-] *adj* : exclusivo

excrement ['ɛkskrəmənt] *n* : excremento *m*

excruciating [ɪk'skruːʃiˌeɪtɪŋ, ɛk-] *adj* : insoportable, atroz

excursion [ɪk'skərʒən, ɛk-] *n* : excursión *f*

excuse [ɪk'skjuːz, ɛk-] *vt* **-cused; -cusing** **1** : perdonar **2 ~ me** : perdóne, perdón — **~** [ɪk'skjuːs, ɛk-] *n* : excusa *f*

execute ['ɛksɪˌkjuːt] *vt* **-cuted; -cuting** : ejecutar — **execution** [ˌɛksɪˈkjuːʃən] *n* : ejecución *f* — **executioner** [ˌɛksɪ-'kjuːʃənər] *n* : verdugo *m*

executive [ɪgˈzekjət̬ɪv, eg-] : ejecutivo — ~ *n* **1** MANAGER : ejecutivo *m*, -va *f* **2** *or* ~ **branch** : poder *m* ejecutivo

exemplify [ɪgˈzemplə̩faɪ, eg-] *vt* **-fied;** **-fying** : ejemplificar — **exemplary** [ɪgˈzempləri, eg-] *adj* : ejemplar

exempt [ɪgˈzempt, eg-] *adj* : exento — ~ *vt* : dispensar — **exemption** [ɪgˈzempʃən, eg-] *n* : exención *f*

exercise [ˈeksərˌsaɪz] *n* : ejercicio *m* — ~ *v* **-cised; -cising** *vt* USE : ejercer, hacer uso de — *vi* : hacer ejercicio

exert [ɪgˈzərt, eg-] *vt* **1** : ejercer **2** ~ **oneself** : esforzarse — **exertion** [ɪgˈzərʃən, eg-] *n* : esfuerzo *m*

exhale [eksˈheɪl] *v* **-haled; -haling** : exhalar

exhaust [ɪgˈzɔst, eg-] *vt* **1** : agotar — ~ *n* **1** *or* ~ **fumes** : gases *mpl* de escape **2** *or* ~ **pipe** : tubo *m* de escape — **exhaustion** [ɪgˈzɔstʃən, eg-] *n* : agotamiento *m* — **exhaustive** [ɪgˈzɔstɪv, eg-] *adj* : exhaustivo

exhibit [ɪgˈzɪbət, eg-] *vt* **1** DISPLAY : exponer **2** SHOW : mostrar — ~ *n* **1** : objeto *m* expuesto **2** EXHIBITION : exposición *f* — **exhibition** [ˌeksəˈbɪʃən] *n* : exposición *f*

exhilarate [ɪgˈzɪləˌreɪt, eg-] *vt* **-rated;** **-rating** : alegrar — **exhilaration** [ɪgˌzɪləˈreɪʃən, eg-] *n* : regocijo *m*

exile [ˈegˌzaɪl, ˈeksˌaɪl] *n* **1** : exilio *m* **2** OUTCAST : exiliado *m*, -da *f* — ~ *vt* : exiliar — **exiled; exiling** : exiliar

exist [ɪgˈzɪst, eg-] *vi* : existir — **existence** [ɪgˈzɪstəns, eg-] *n* : existencia *f* — **existing** *adj* : existente

exit [ˈegzət, ˈeksət] *n* : salida *f* — ~ *vi* : salir

exodus [ˈeksədəs] *n* : éxodo *m*

exonerate [ɪgˈzɑnəˌreɪt, eg-] *vt* **-ated;** **-ating** : exonerar, disculpar

exorbitant [ɪgˈzɔrbətənt, eg-] *adj* : exorbitante, excesivo

exotic [ɪgˈzɑtɪk, eg-] *adj* : exótico

expand [ɪkˈspænd, ek-] *vt* **1** : ampliar, extender **2** : dilatar (metales, etc.) — *vi* **1** : ampliarse, extenderse **2** : dilatarse (dícese de metales, etc.) — **expanse** [ɪkˈspæns, ek-] *n* : extensión *f* — **expansion** [ɪkˈspænʃən, ek-] *n* : expansión *f*

expatriate [eksˈpeɪtriət, -ˌeɪt] *n* : expatriado *m*, -da *f* — ~ *adj* : expatriado

expect [ɪkˈspekt, ek-] *vt* **1** : esperar **2** REQUIRE : contar con — *vi* **be expecting** : estar embarazada — **expectancy** [ɪkˈspektənsi, ek-] *n, pl* **-cies** : esperanza *f* — **expectant** [ɪkˈspektənt, ek-] *adj* **1**

: expectante **2** ~ **mother** : futura madre *f* — **expectation** [ˌekˌspekˈteɪʃən] *n* : esperanza *f*

expedient [ɪkˈspiːdiənt, ek-] *adj* : conveniente — ~ *n* : expediente *m*, recurso *m*

expedition [ˌekspəˈdɪʃən] *n* : expedición *f*

expel [ɪkˈspel, ek-] *vt* **-pelled; -pelling** : expulsar (a una persona), expeler (humo, etc.)

expend [ɪkˈspend, ek-] *vt* : gastar — **expendable** [ɪkˈspendəbəl, ek-] *adj* : prescindible — **expenditure** [ɪkˈspendɪtʃər, ek-, -ˌtʃʊr] *n* : gasto *m* — **expense** [ɪkˈspens, ek-] *n* **1** : gasto *m* **2** ~**s** *npl* : gastos *mpl*, expensas *fpl* **3 at the** ~ **of** : a expensas de — **expensive** [ɪkˈspensɪv, ek-] *adj* : caro

experience [ɪkˈspɪriəns, ek-] *n* : experiencia *f* — ~ *vt* **-enced; -encing** : experimentar — **experienced** [ɪkˈspɪriənst, ek-] *adj* : experimentado

experiment [ɪkˈsperəmənt, ek-, -ˈspɪr-] *n* : experimento *m* — ~ *vi* : experimentar — **experimental** [ɪkˌsperəˈmentəl, ek-, -ˌspɪr-] *adj* : experimental

expert [ˈekˌspərt] *adj* : experto — ~ *n* [ˈekˌspərt] : experto *m*, -ta *f* — **expertise** [ˌekspərˈtiːz] *n* : pericia *f*, competencia *f*

expire [ɪkˈspaɪr, ek-] *vi* **-pired; -piring 1** : caducar, vencer **2** DIE : expirar, morir — **expiration** [ˌekspəˈreɪʃən] *n* : vencimiento *m*, caducidad *f*

explain [ɪkˈspleɪn, ek-] *vt* : explicar — **explanation** [ˌekspləˈneɪʃən] *n* : explicación *f* — **explanatory** [ɪkˈsplænəˌtori, ek-] *adj* : explicativo

explicit [ɪkˈsplɪsət, ek-] *adj* : explícito

explode [ɪkˈsploːd, ek-] *v* **-ploded;** **-ploding** *vt* : hacer explotar — *vi* : explotar, estallar

exploit [ˈekˌsplɔɪt] *n* : hazaña *f*, proeza *f* — ~ [ɪkˈsplɔɪt, ek-] *vt* : explotar — **exploitation** [ˌeksplɔɪˈteɪʃən] *n* : explotación *f*

exploration [ˌekspləˈreɪʃən] *n* : exploración *f* — **explore** [ɪkˈsplor, ek-] *vt* **-plored; -ploring** : explorar — **explorer** [ɪkˈsplorər, ek-] *n* : explorador *m*, -dora *f*

explosion [ɪkˈsploːʒən, ek-] *n* : explosión *f* — **explosive** [ɪkˈsploːsɪv, ek-] *adj* : explosivo — ~ *n* : explosivo *m*

export [ˈekˌsport, ˈekˌsport] *vt* : exportar — ~ *n* : exportación *f*

expose [ɪkˈspoːz, ek-] *vt* **-posed; -posing 1** : exponer **2** REVEAL : descubrir, revelar — **exposed** [ɪkˈspoːzd, ek-] *adj*

: expuesto, al descubierto — **exposure** [ɪk'spoʒər, ɛk-] n : exposición f

express [ɪk'spres, ɛk-] adj 1 SPECIFIC : expreso, específico 2 FAST : expreso, rápido — ~ adv : por correo urgente — ~ n or ~ **train** : expreso m — ~ vt : expresar — **expression** [ɪk'spreʃən, ɛk-] n : expresión f — **expressive** [ɪk'spresɪv, ɛk-] adj : expresivo — **expressly** [ɪk'spresli, ɛk-] adv : expresamente — **expressway** [ɪk'spres,weɪ, ɛk-] n : autopista f

expulsion [ɪk'spʌlʃən, ɛk-] n : expulsión f

exquisite [ɪk'skwɪzət, 'ɛk,skwɪ-] adj : exquisito

extend [ɪk'stend, ɛk-] vt 1 STRETCH : extender 2 LENGTHEN : prolongar 3 ENLARGE : ampliar 4 ~ **one's hand** : tender la mano — vi : extenderse — **extension** [ɪk'stentʃən, ɛk-] n 1 : extensión f 2 LENGTHENING : prolongación f 3 ANNEX : ampliación f, anexo m 4 ~ **cord** : alargador m — **extensive** [ɪk'stensɪv, ɛk-] adj : extenso — **extent** [ɪk'stent, ɛk-] n 1 SIZE : extensión f 2 DEGREE : alcance m, grado m 3 **to a certain** ~ : hasta cierto punto

extenuating [ɪk'stenjə,weɪtɪŋ, ɛk-] adj ~ **circumstances** : circunstancias fpl atenuantes

exterior [ɛk'stɪriər] adj : exterior — ~ n : exterior m

exterminate [ɪk'stərmə,neɪt, ɛk-] vt -nated; -nating : exterminar — **extermination** [ɪk,stərmə'neɪʃən, ɛk-] n : exterminación f

external [ɪk'stərnəl, ɛk-] adj : externo — **externally** [ɪk'stərnəli, ɛk-] adv : exteriormente

extinct [ɪk'stɪŋkt, ɛk-] adj : extinto — **extinction** [ɪk'stɪŋkʃən, ɛk-] n : extinción f

extinguish [ɪk'stɪŋgwɪʃ, ɛk-] vt : extinguir, apagar — **extinguisher** [ɪk'stɪŋgwɪʃər, ɛk-] n : extintor m

extol [ɪk'stoːl, ɛk-] vt -tolled; -tolling : ensalzar, alabar

extort [ɪk'stort, ɛk-] vt : arrancar (algo a algn) por la fuerza — **extortion** [ɪk'storʃən, ɛk-] n : extorsión f

extra ['ɛkstrə] adj : suplementario, de

más — ~ n : extra m — ~ adv 1 : extra, más 2 ~ **special** : super especial

extract [ɪk'strækt, ɛk-] vt : extraer, sacar — ~ ['ɛk,strækt] n : extracto m — **extraction** [ɪk'strækʃən, ɛk-] n : extracción f

extracurricular [ˌɛkstrəkə'rɪkjələr] adj : extracurricular

extradite ['ɛkstrə,daɪt] vt -dited; -diting : extraditar

extraordinary [ɪk'strordən,eri, ˌɛkstrə-'ord-] adj : extraordinario

extraterrestrial [ˌɛkstrətə'restriəl] adj : extraterrestre — ~ n : extraterrestre mf

extravagant [ɪk'strævɪgənt, ɛk-] adj 1 WASTEFUL : despilfarrador, derrochador 2 EXAGGERATED : extravagante, exagerado — **extravagance** [ɪk'strævɪgəns, ɛk-] n 1 WASTEFULNESS : derroche m, despilfarro m 2 LUXURY : lujo m 3 EXAGGERATION : extravagancia f

extreme [ɪk'striːm, ɛk-] adj : extremo — ~ n : extremo m — **extremely** [ɪk'striːmli, ɛk-] adv : extremadamente — **extremity** [ɪk'streməti, ɛk-] n, pl -ties : extremidad f

extricate ['ɛkstrə,keɪt] vt -cated; -cating : librar, (lograr) sacar

extrovert ['ɛkstrə,vərt] n : extrovertido m, -da f — **extroverted** ['ɛkstrə,vərtəd] adj : extrovertido

exuberant [ɪg'zuːbərənt, ɛg-] adj 1 JOYOUS : eufórico 2 LUSH : exuberante — **exuberance** [ɪg'zuːbərəns, ɛg-] n 1 JOYOUSNESS : euforia f 2 VIGOR : exuberancia f

exult [ɪg'zʌlt, ɛg-] vi : exultar

eye ['aɪ] n 1 : ojo m 2 VISION : visión f, vista f 3 GLANCE : mirada f — ~ vt : mirar — **eyeball** ['aɪ,bol] n : globo m ocular — **eyebrow** ['aɪ,braʊ] n : ceja f — **eyeglasses** ['aɪˌglæsəz] npl : anteojos mpl, lentes mpl — **eyelash** ['aɪˌlæʃ] n : pestaña f — **eyelid** ['aɪˌlɪd] n : párpado m — **eyesight** ['aɪˌsaɪt] n : vista f, visión f — **eyesore** ['aɪˌsor] n : monstruosidad f — **eyewitness** ['aɪ'wɪtnəs] n : testigo mf ocular

F

f ['ɛf] *n*, *pl* **f's** *or* **fs** ['ɛfs] : f, sexta letra del alfabeto inglés

fable ['feɪbəl] *n* : fábula *f*

fabric ['fæbrɪk] *n* : tela *f*, tejido *m*

fabulous ['fæbjələs] *adj* : fabuloso

facade [fə'sɑd] *n* : fachada *f*

face ['feɪs] *n* **1** : cara *f*, rostro *m* (de una persona) **2** APPEARANCE : fisonomía *f*, aspecto *m* **3** : cara *f* (de una moneda), fachada *f* (de un edificio) **4** ~ **value** : valor *m* nominal **5 in the ~ of** : en medio de, ante **6 lose ~** : desprestigiarse **7 make ~s** : hacer muecas — ~ **faced; facing** *vt* **1** ~ **to the north** : mirar hacia el norte — **facedown** ['feɪs,daun] *adv* : boca abajo — **faceless** ['feɪsləs] *adj* : anónimo — **face-lift** ['feɪs,lɪft] *n* : estiramiento *m* facial

facet ['fæsət] *n* : faceta *f*

face-to-face *adv & adj* : cara a cara

facial ['feɪʃəl] *adj* : de la cara, facial — ~ *n* : limpieza *f* de cutis

facetious [fə'siːʃəs] *adj* : gracioso, burlón

facility [fə'sɪləti] *n*, *pl* **-ties 1** EASE : facilidad *f* **2** CENTER : centro *m* **3 facilities** *npl* : comodidades *fpl*, servicios *mpl*

facsimile [fæk'sɪməli] *n* : facsímile *m*, facsímil *m*

fact ['fækt] *n* **1** : hecho *m* **2 in ~** : en realidad, de hecho

faction ['fækʃən] *n* : facción *f*, bando *m*

factor ['fæktər] *n* : factor *m*

factory ['fæktəri] *n*, *pl* **-ries** : fábrica *f*

factual ['fæktʃuəl] *adj* : basado en hechos

faculty ['fækəlti] *n*, *pl* **-ties** : facultad *f*

fad ['fæd] *n* : moda *f* pasajera, manía *f*

fade ['feɪd] *v* **faded; fading** *vi* **1** WITHER : marchitarse **2** DISCOLOR : destenirse, decolorarse **3** DIM : apagarse **4** VANISH : desvanecerse — *vt* : destenir

fail ['feɪl] *vi* **1** : fracasar (dícese de una empresa, un matrimonio, etc.) **2** BREAK DOWN : fallar **3** ~ **in** : faltar a, no cumplir con **4** FLUNK : suspender *Spain*, ser reprobado *Lat* **5** ~ **to do sth** : no hacer algo — *vt* **1** DISAPPOINT : fallar **2** FLUNK : suspender *Spain*, reprobar *Lat* — ~ **without** ~ : sin falta — **failing** ['feɪlɪŋ] *n* : defecto *m* — **failure** ['feɪljər] *n* **1** : fracaso *m* **2** BREAKDOWN : falla *f*

faint ['feɪnt] *adj* **1** WEAK : débil **2** INDISTINCT : tenue, indistinto **3 feel ~** : estar mareado — ~ *vi* : desmayarse — ~ *n* : desmayo *m* — **fainthearted** ['feɪnt,hɑrtəd] *adj* : cobarde, pusilánime — **faintly** ['feɪntli] *adv* **1** WEAKLY : débilmente **2** SLIGHTLY : ligeramente, levemente

fair¹ ['fær] *n* **1** : feria *f*

fair² *adj* **1** BEAUTIFUL : bello, hermoso **2** : bueno (dícese del tiempo) **3** JUST : justo **4** : rubio (dícese del pelo), blanco (dícese de la tez) **5** ADEQUATE : adecuado — ~ *adv* **play** ~ : jugar limpio — **fairly** ['færli] *adv* **1** JUSTLY : justamente **2** QUITE : bastante — **fairness** ['færnəs] *n* : justicia *f*

fairy ['færi] *n*, *pl* **fairies 1** : hada *f* **2** ~ **tale** : cuento *m* de hadas

faith ['feɪθ] *n*, *pl* **faiths** ['feɪθs, 'feɪðz] : fe *f* — **faithful** ['feɪθfəl] *adj* : fiel — **faithfully** *adv* : fielmente — **faithfulness** ['feɪθfəlnəs] *n* : fidelidad *f*

fake ['feɪk] *v* **faked; faking** *vt* **1** FALSIFY : falsificar, falsear **2** FEIGN : fingir — *vi* PRETEND : fingir — ~ *adj* : falso — ~ *n* **1** IMITATION : falsificación *f* **2** IMPOSTOR : impostor *m*, -tora *f*

falcon ['fælkən, 'fɔl-] *n* : halcón *m*

fall ['fɔl] *vi* **fell** ['fɛl]; **fallen** ['fɔlən]; **falling 1** : caer, bajar (dícese de los precios), descender (dícese de la temperatura) **2** ~ **asleep** : dormirse **3** ~ **back** : retirarse **4** ~ **back on** : recurrir a **5** ~ **down** : caerse **6** ~ **in love** : enamorarse **7** ~ **out** QUARREL : pelearse **8** ~ **through** : fracasar — ~ *n* **1** : caída *f*, bajada *f* (de precios), descenso *m* (de temperatura) **2** AUTUMN : otoño *m* **3** ~ *npl* WATERFALL : cascada *f*, catarata *f*

fallacy ['fæləsi] *n*, *pl* **-cies** : concepto *m* erróneo

fallible ['fæləbəl] *adj* : falible

fallow ['fæloʊ] *adj* **lie** ~ : estar en barbecho

false ['fɔls] *adj* **falser; falsest 1** : falso **2** ~ **alarm** : falsa alarma *f* **3** ~ **teeth** : dentadura *f* postiza — **falsehood** ['fɔls,hʊd] *n* : mentira *f* — **falseness**

['fɔlsnəs] *n* : falsedad *f* — **falsify** ['fɔlsə,faɪ] *vt* **-fied; fying** : falsificar, falsear

falter ['fɔltər] *vi* **-tered; -tering** 1 STUMBLE : tambalearse 2 WAVER : vacilar

fame [feɪm] *n* : fama *f*

familiar [fə'mɪljər] *adj* 1 : familiar 2 **be ~ with** : estar familiarizado con — **familiarity** [fə,mɪli'ærəti, -mɪl'jær-] *n, pl* **-ties** : familiaridad *f* — **familiarize** [fə'mɪljə,raɪz] *vt* **-ized; -izing ~ oneself** : familiarizarse

family ['fæməli, 'fæm-] *n, pl* **-lies** : familia *f*

famine ['fæmən] *n* : hambre *f*, hambruna *f*

famished ['fæmɪʃt] *adj* : famélico

famous ['feɪməs] *adj* : famoso

fan [fæn] *n* 1 : ventilador *m*, abanico *m* 2 : aficionado *m*, -da *f* (a un pasatiempo); admirador *m*, -dora *f* (de una persona) — **~** *vt* **fanned; fanning** : abanicar (a una persona), avivar (un fuego)

fanatic [fə'næt̬ɪk] *or* **fanatical** [-t̬ɪkəl] *adj* : fanático — *n* : fanático *m*, -ca *f* — **fanaticism** [fə'næt̬ə,sɪzəm] *n* : fanatismo *m*

fancy ['fænsi] *vt* **-cied; -cying** 1 IMAGINE : imaginarse 2 DESIRE : apetecerle (algo a uno) — **~** *adj* **-cier; -est** 1 ELABORATE : elaborado 2 LUXURIOUS : lujoso, elegante — **~** *n, pl* **-cies** 1 WHIM : capricho *m* 2 IMAGINATION : imaginación *f* 3 **take a ~ to** : aficionarse a (una cosa), tomar cariño a (una persona) — **fanciful** ['fænsɪfəl] *adj* 1 CAPRICIOUS : caprichoso 2 IMAGINATIVE : imaginativo

fanfare ['fæn,fær] *n* : fanfarria *f*

fang [fæŋ] *n* : colmillo *m* (de un animal), diente *m* (de una serpiente)

fantasy ['fæntəsi] *n, pl* **-sies** : fantasía *f* — **fantasize** ['fæntə,saɪz] *vi* **-sized; -sizing** : fantasear — **fantastic** [fæn'tæstɪk] *adj* : fantástico

far [fɑr] *adv* **farther** ['fɑrðər] *or* **further** ['fər-]; **farthest** *or* **furthest** [-ðəst] 1 : lejos 2 MUCH : muy, mucho 3 **as ~ as** : hasta (un lugar), con respecto a (un tema) 4 **by ~** : con mucho 5 **~ and wide** : por todas partes 6 **~ away** : a lo lejos 7 **~ from it!** : ¡todo lo contrario! 8 **so ~** : hasta ahora, todavía — **~** *adj* **farther** *or* **further; farthest** *or* **furthest** 1 REMOTE : lejano 2 EXTREME : extremo — **faraway** ['fɑrə,weɪ] *adj* : remoto, lejano

farce ['fɑrs] *n* : farsa *f*

fare ['fær] *vi* **fared; faring** : irle a uno —

~ *n* 1 : precio *m* del pasaje 2 FOOD : comida *f*

farewell [fær'wɛl] *n* : despedida *f* — **~** *adj* : de despedida

far-fetched ['fɑr'fɛtʃt] *adj* : improbable, exagerado

farm ['fɑrm] *n* : granja *f*, hacienda *f* — **~** *vt* : cultivar (la tierra), criar (animales) — *vi* : ser agricultor — **farmer** ['fɑrmər] *n* : agricultor *m*, -tora *f*; granjero *m*, -jera *f* — **farmhand** ['fɑrm,hænd] *n* : peón *m* — **farmhouse** ['fɑrm,haʊs] *n* : granja *f*, casa *f* de hacienda — **farming** ['fɑrmɪŋ] *n* : agricultura *f*, cultivo *m* (de plantas), crianza *f* (de animales) — **farmyard** ['fɑrm,jɑrd] *n* : corral *m*

far-off ['fɑr,ɔf, -ˈɔf] *adj* : lejano

far-reaching ['fɑr'riːtʃɪŋ] *adj* : de gran alcance

farsighted ['fɑr,saɪt̬əd] *adj* 1 : hipermétrope 2 PRUDENT : previsor

farther ['fɑrðər] *adv* 1 : más lejos 2 MORE : más — *adj* : más lejano — **farthest** *adv* 1 : lo más lejos 2 MOST : más — *adj* : más lejano

fascinate ['fæsən,eɪt] *vt* **-nated; -nating** : fascinar — **fascination** [,fæsən'eɪʃən] *n* : fascinación *f*

fascism ['fæ,ʃɪzəm] *n* : fascismo *m* — **fascist** ['fæʃɪst] *adj* : fascista — **~** *n* : fascista *mf*

fashion ['fæʃən] *n* 1 MANNER : manera *f* 2 STYLE : moda *f* 3 **out of ~** : pasada de moda — **fashionable** ['fæʃənəbəl] *adj* : de moda

fast¹ ['fæst] *vi* : ayunar — **~** *n* : ayuno *m*

fast² *adj* 1 SWIFT : rápido 2 SECURE : firme, seguro 3 : adelantado (dícese de un reloj) 4 **~ friends** : amigos *mpl* leales — **~** *adv* 1 SECURELY : firmemente 2 SWIFTLY : rápidamente 3 **~ asleep** : profundamente dormido

fasten ['fæsən] *vt* : sujetar (papeles, etc.), abrochar (una blusa, etc.), cerrar (una maleta, etc.) — *vi* : abrocharse, cerrar — **fastener** ['fæsənər] *n* : cierre *m*

fat ['fæt] *adj* **fatter; fattest** 1 : gordo 2 THICK : grueso — **~** *n* : grasa *f*

fatal ['feɪt̬əl] *adj* 1 : mortal 2 FATEFUL : fatal, fatídico — **fatality** [feɪ'tæləti, fə-] *n, pl* **-ties** : víctima *f* mortal

fate ['feɪt] *n* 1 : destino *m* 2 LOT : suerte *f* — **fateful** ['feɪtfəl] *adj* : fatídico

father ['fɑðər] *n* : padre *m* — **~** *vt* : engendrar — **fatherhood** ['fɑðər,hʊd] *n* : paternidad *f* — **father-in-law** ['fɑðərɪn,lɔ] *n, pl* **fathers-in-law** : suegro m — **fatherly** ['foðərli] adj : paternal

fathom ['fæðəm] vt : comprender

fatigue [fə'ti:g] n : fatiga f — ~ vt -tigued; -tiguing : fatigar

fatten ['fætən] vt : engordar — **fattening** adj : que engorda

fatty ['fæṭi] adj **fattier; -est** : graso

faucet ['fɔsət] n : llave f Lat, grifo m Spain

fault ['fɔlt] n 1 FLAW : defecto m 2 RESPONSIBILITY : culpa f 3 : falla f (geológica) — vt : encontrar defectos a — **faultless** ['fɔltləs] adj : impecable — **faulty** ['fɔlti] adj **faultier; -est** : defectuoso

fauna ['fɔnə] n : fauna f

favor or Brit **favour** ['feɪvər] n 1 : favor m 2 in ~ of : a favor de — ~ vt 1 : favorecer 2 SUPPORT : estar a favor de 3 PREFER : preferir — **favorable** or Brit **favourable** ['feɪvərəbəl] adj : favorable — **favorite** or Brit **favourite** ['feɪvərət] n : favorito m, -ta f — ~ adj : favorito — **favoritism** or Brit **favouritism** ['feɪvərə,tɪzəm] n : favoritismo m

fawn[1] ['fɔn] vi ~ **over** : adular

fawn[2] n : cervato m

fax ['fæks] n : fax m — ~ vt : faxear, enviar por fax

fear ['fɪr] v : temer — ~ n 1 : miedo m, temor m 2 for ~ of : por temor a — **fearful** ['fɪrfəl] adj 1 FRIGHTENING : espantoso 2 AFRAID : temeroso

feasible ['fi:zəbəl] adj : viable, factible

feast ['fi:st] n 1 BANQUET : banquete m, festín m 2 FESTIVAL : fiesta f — ~ v 1 : banquetear 2 ~ **upon** : darse un festín de

feat ['fi:t] n : hazaña f

feather ['feðər] n : pluma f

feature ['fi:tʃər] n 1 : rasgo m (de la cara) 2 CHARACTERISTIC : característica f 3 : artículo m (en un periódico) 4 ~ **film** : largometraje m — v ~ted; -turing vt 1 PRESENT : presentar 2 EMPHASIZE : destacar — vi : figurar

February ['fɛbjʊˌɛri, 'fɛbʊ-, 'fɛbrʊ-] n : febrero m

feces ['fi:siːz] npl : excremento mpl

federal ['fɛdrəl, -dərəl] adj : federal — **federation** [ˌfɛdə'reɪʃən] n : federación f

fed up adj : harto

fee ['fi:] n 1 : honorarios mpl 2 entrance ~ : entrada f

feeble ['fi:bəl] adj **-bler; -blest** 1 : débil 2 a ~ **excuse** : una pobre excusa

feed ['fi:d] v **fed** ['fɛd]; **feeding** 1 : dar

de comer a, alimentar 2 SUPPLY : alimentar — vi : comer, alimentarse — ~ n : pienso m

feel ['fi:l] v **felt** ['fɛlt]; **feeling** vt 1 : sentir (una sensación, etc.) 2 TOUCH : tocar, palpar 3 BELIEVE : creer — vi 1 : sentirse (bien, cansado, etc.) 2 SEEM : parecer 3 ~ **hot/thirsty** : tener calor/sed 4 ~ **like doing** : tener ganas de hacer — ~ n : tacto m, sensación f — **feeling** ['fi:lɪŋ] n 1 SENSATION : sensación f 2 EMOTION : sentimiento m 3 OPINION : opinión f 4 **hurt s.o.'s** ~**s** : herir los sentimientos de algn

feet → **foot**

feign ['feɪn] vt : fingir

feline ['fi:laɪn] adj : felino — ~ n : felino m, -na f

fell[1] → **fall**

fell[2] ['fɛl] vt : talar (un árbol)

fellow ['fɛ,lo:] n 1 COMPANION : compañero m, -ra f 2 MEMBER : socio m, -cia f 3 MAN : tipo m — **fellowship** ['fɛlo,ʃɪp] n 1 : compañerismo m 2 ASSOCIATION : fraternidad f 3 GRANT : beca f

felon ['fɛlən] n : criminal mf — **felony** ['fɛləni] n, pl **-nies** : delito m grave

felt[1] → **feel**

felt[2] ['fɛlt] n : fieltro m

female ['fi:,meɪl] adj : femenino — ~ n 1 : hembra f (animal) 2 WOMAN : mujer f

feminine ['fɛmənən] adj : femenino — **femininity** [ˌfɛmə'nɪnəṭi] n : feminidad f — **feminism** ['fɛmə,nɪzəm] n : feminismo m — **feminist** ['fɛmənəst] adj : feminista — ~ n : feminista mf

fence ['fɛns] n : cerca f, valla f, cerco m Lat — ~ v **fenced; fencing** vt or ~ **in** : vallar, cercar — vi : hacer esgrima — **fencing** ['fɛnsɪŋ] n : esgrima m (deporte)

fend ['fɛnd] vt ~ **off** : rechazar (un enemigo), eludir (una pregunta) — vi ~ **for oneself** : valerse por sí mismo

fender ['fɛndər] n : guardabarros mpl

fennel ['fɛnəl] n : hinojo m

ferment ['fɜrˌmɛnt] v : fermentar — **fermentation** [ˌfɜrmənˈteɪʃən, -ˌmɛn-] n : fermentación f

fern ['fɜrn] n : helecho m

ferocious [fəˈroːʃəs] adj : feroz — **ferocity** [fəˈrɑsəṭi] n : ferocidad f

ferret ['fɛrət] n : hurón m — ~ vt ~ **out** : descubrir

Ferris wheel ['fɛrɪs] n : noria f

ferry ['fɛri] vt **-ried; -rying** : transportar — ~ n, pl **-ries** : ferry m

fertile ['fərt̞əl] *adj* : fértil — **fertility** [fər-'tɪlət̞i] *n* : fertilidad *f* — **fertilize** ['fərt̞əl,aɪz] *vt* **-ized; -izing** : fecundar (un huevo), abonar (el suelo) — **fertilizer** ['fərt̞əl,aɪzər] *n* : fertilizante *m*, abono *m*

fervent ['fərvənt] *adj* : ferviente — **fervor** *or Brit* **fervour** ['fərvər] *n* : fervor *m*

fester ['fɛstər] *vi* : enconarse

festival ['fɛstəvəl] *n* **1** : fiesta *f* **2 film** : festival *m* de cine — **festive** ['fɛstɪv] *adj* : festivo — **festivity** [fɛs'tɪvət̞i] *n*, *pl* **-ties** : festividad *f*

fetch ['fɛtʃ] *vt* **1** : ir a buscar **2** : venderse por (un precio)

fête ['feɪt, 'fɛt] *n* : fiesta *f*

fetid ['fɛt̞əd] *adj* : fétido

fetish ['fɛt̞ɪʃ] *n* : fetiche *m*

fetters ['fɛt̞ərz] *npl* : grillos *mpl* — **fetter** ['fɛt̞ər] *vt* : encadenar

fetus ['fit̞əs] *n* : feto *m*

feud ['fjuːd] *n* : enemistad *f* (entre familiares) — *vi* : pelear

feudal ['fjuːdəl] *adj* : feudal — **feudalism** ['fjuːdəl,ɪzəm] *n* : feudalismo *m*

fever ['fiːvər] *n* : fiebre *f* — **feverish** ['fiːvərɪʃ] *adj* : febril

few ['fjuː] *adj* **1** : pocos **2 a** ~ **times** : varias veces — *pron* **1** : pocos **2 a** ~ : algunos, unos cuantos **3 quite a** ~ : muchos — **fewer** ['fjuːər] *adj & pron* : menos

fiancé, fiancée [fiː,ɑnˈseɪ, fiːˈɑn,seɪ] *n* : prometido *m*, -da *f*; novio *m*, -via *f*

fiasco [fiˈæs,koː] *n*, *pl* **-coes** : fiasco *m*

fib ['fɪb] *n* : mentirilla *f* — *vi* **fibbed; fibbing** : decir mentirillas

fiber *or* **fibre** ['faɪbər] *n* : fibra *f* — **fiberglass** ['faɪbər,glæs] *n* : fibra *f* de vidrio — **fibrous** ['faɪbrəs] *adj* : fibroso

fickle ['fɪkəl] *adj* : inconstante

fiction ['fɪkʃən] *n* : ficción *f* — **fictional** ['fɪkʃənəl] *or* **fictitious** [fɪkˈtɪʃəs] *adj* : ficticio

fiddle ['fɪdəl] *n* : violín *m* — *vi* **-dled; -dling** **1** : tocar el violín **2** ~ **with** : juguetear con

fidelity [fəˈdɛlət̞i, faɪ-] *n*, *pl* **-ties** : fidelidad *f*

fidget ['fɪdʒət] *vi* **1** : estarse inquieto, moverse **2** ~ **with** : juguetear con — **fidgety** ['fɪdʒət̞i] *adj* : inquieto, nervioso

field ['fiːld] *n* : campo *m* — *vt* : interceptar (una pelota), sortear (una pregunta) — **field glasses** *npl* : binoculares *mpl*, gemelos *mpl* — **field trip** *n* : viaje *m* de estudio

fiend ['fiːnd] *n* **1** : demonio *m* **2 FANATIC** : fanático *m*, -ca *f* — **fiendish** ['fiːndɪʃ] *adj* : diabólico

fierce ['fɪrs] *adj* **fiercer; -est 1** : feroz **2 INTENSE** : fuerte (dícese del viento), acalorado (dícese de un debate) — **fierceness** ['fɪrsnəs] *n* : ferocidad *f*

fiery ['faɪəri] *adj* **fierier; -est** **1 BURNING** : llameante **2 SPIRITED** : ardiente, fogoso — **fieriness** ['faɪərinəs] *n* : pasión *f*, ardor *m*

fifteen ['fɪf'tiːn] *n* : quince *m* — ~ *adj* : quince — **fifteenth** [fɪf'tiːnθ] *adj* : decimoquinto — ~ *n* **1** : decimoquinto *m*, -ta *f* (en una serie) **2** : quinceavo *m* (en matemáticas)

fifth ['fɪfθ] *n* **1** : quinto *m*, -ta *f* (en una serie) **2** : quinto *m* (en matemáticas) — ~ *adj* : quinto

fiftieth ['fɪftiəθ] *adj* : quincuagésimo — ~ *n* **1** : quincuagésimo *m*, -ma *f* (en una serie) **2** : cincuentavo *m* (en matemáticas)

fifty ['fɪfti] *n*, *pl* **-ties** : cincuenta *m* — ~ *adj* : cincuenta — **fifty-fifty** [ˈfɪfti-ˈfɪfti] *adv* : a medias, mitad y mitad — ~ *adj* ~ **a chance** : un cincuenta por ciento de posibilidades

fig ['fɪg] *n* : higo *m*

fight ['faɪt] *v* **fought** ['fɔt], **fighting** *vi* **1 BATTLE** : luchar **2 QUARREL** : pelear **3** ~ **back** : defenderse — *vt* : luchar contra — ~ *n* **1 STRUGGLE** : lucha *f* **2 QUARREL** : pelea *f* — **fighter** ['faɪt̞ər] *n* **1** : luchador *m*, -dora *f* **2** ~ *or* ~ **plane** : avión *m* de caza

figment ['fɪgmənt] *n* ~ **of the imagination** : producto *m* de la imaginación

figurative ['fɪgjərət̞ɪv, -gə-] *adj* : figurado

figure ['fɪgjər, -gər] *n* **1 NUMBER** : número *m*, cifra *f* **2 PERSON, SHAPE** : figura *f* **3** ~ **of speech** : figura *f* retórica **4 watch one's** ~ : cuidar la línea — *v* **-ured; -uring** *vt* : calcular — *vi* **1** : figurar **2 that** ~ **s!** : ¡no me extraña! — **figurehead** ['fɪgjər,hɛd, -gər-] *n* : testaferro *m* — **figure out** *vt* **1 UNDERSTAND** : entender **2 RESOLVE** : resolver

file¹ ['faɪl] *n* : lima *f* (instrumento) — *vt* **filed; filing** : limar

file² *vt* **filed; filing 1** : archivar (documentos) **2** ~ **charges** : presentar cargos — ~ *n* : archivo *m*

file³ *n* **LINE** : fila *f* — *vi* ~ **in/out** : entrar/salir en fila

fill ['fɪl] *vt* **1** : llenar, rellenar **2** : cumplir con (un requisito) **3** : tapar (un agujero), empastar (un diente) — *vi* **1** ~ **in for** : reemplazar **2** *or* ~ **up**

: llenarse — ~ **1** eat one's ~ : comer lo suficiente **2** have one's ~ of : estar harto de

fillet ['fɪlət, frleɪ, 'fɪleɪ] *n* : filete *m*

filling ['fɪlɪŋ] *n* **1** : relleno *m* **2** : empaste *m* (de dientes) **3** — ~ **station** → **service station**

filly ['fɪli] *n, pl* **-lies** : potra *f*

film ['fɪlm] *n* : película *f* — ~ *vt* : filmar

filter ['fɪltər] *n* : filtro *m* — ~ *vt* : filtrar

filth ['fɪlθ] *n* : mugre *f* — **filthy** ['fɪlθi] *adj* **filthier**, **-est 1** : mugriento **2** OBSCENE : obsceno

fin ['fɪn] *n* : aleta *f*

final ['faɪnəl] *adj* **1** LAST : último **2** DEFINITIVE : definitivo **3** ULTIMATE : final — ~ *n* **1** : final *f* (en deportes) **2** ~ s *npl* : exámenes *mpl* finales — **finalist** ['faɪnəlɪst] *n* : finalista *mf* — **finalize** ['faɪnəˌlaɪz] *vt* **-ized; -izing** : finalizar — **finally** ['faɪnəli] *adv* : finalmente

finance [fəˈnæns, ˈfaɪˌnæns] *n* **1** : finanzas *fpl* **2** ~ s *npl* : recursos *mpl* financieros — ~ *vt* **-nanced; -nancing** : financiar — **financial** [fəˈnænʧəl, faɪ-] *adj* : financiero — **financially** [fəˈnænʧəli, faɪ-] *adv* : económicamente

find ['faɪnd] *vt* **found** ['faʊnd]; **finding 1** LOCATE : encontrar **2** REALIZE : darse cuenta de **3** ~ **guilty** : declarar culpable **4** *or* ~ **out** : descubrir — *vi* ~ **out** : enterarse — ~ *n* : hallazgo *m* — **finding** ['faɪndɪŋ] *n* **1** FIND : hallazgo *m* **2** ~ s *npl* : conclusiones *fpl*

fine¹ ['faɪn] *n* : multa *f* — ~ *vt* **fined; fining** : multar

fine² *adj* **finer; -est 1** DELICATE : fino **2** EXCELLENT : excelente **3** SUBTLE : sutil **4** : bueno (dícese del tiempo) **5** ~ **print** : letra *f* menuda **6** it's ~ **with me** : me parece bien — ~ *adv* OK : bien — **fine arts** *npl* : bellas artes *fpl* — **finely** ['faɪnli] *adv* **1** EXCELLENTLY : excelentemente **2** PRECISELY : con precisión **3** MINUTELY : fino, menudo

finger ['fɪŋɡər] *n* : dedo *m* — ~ *vt* : tocar, toquetear — **fingernail** ['fɪŋɡərˌneɪl] *n* : uña *f* — **fingerprint** ['fɪŋɡərˌprɪnt] *n* : huella *f* digital — **fingertip** ['fɪŋɡərˌtɪp] *n* : punta *f* del dedo

finicky ['fɪnɪki] *adj* : maniático, mañoso *Lat*

finish ['fɪnɪʃ] *v* : acabar, terminar — ~ *n* **1** END : fin *m*, final *m* **2** *or* ~ **line** : meta *f* **3** SURFACE : acabado *m*

finite ['faɪˌnaɪt] *adj* : finito

fir ['fər] *n* : abeto *m*

fire ['faɪr] *n* **1** : fuego *m* **2** CONFLAGRATION : incendio *m* **3** catch ~ : incendiarse (dícese de bosques, etc.), pren-

derse (dícese de fósforos, etc.) **4** on ~ : en llamas **5** open ~ on : abrir fuego sobre — ~ *vt* **fired; firing 1** DISMISS : despedir **2** SHOOT : disparar — *vi* : disparar — **fire alarm** *n* : alarma *f* contra incendios — **firearm** ['faɪrˌɑrm] *n* : arma *f* de fuego — **firecracker** ['faɪrˌkrækər] *n* : petardo *m* — **fire engine** *n* : carro *m* de bomberos *Lat*, coche *m* de bomberos *Spain* — **fire escape** *n* : escalera *f* de incendios — **fire extinguisher** *n* : extintor *m* (de incendios) — **firefighter** ['faɪrˌfaɪtər] *n* : bombero *m*, **-ra** *f* — **firefly** ['faɪrˌflaɪ] *n, pl* **-flies** : luciérnaga *f* — **firehouse** → **fire station** — **fireman** ['faɪrmən] *n, pl* **-men** [-mən, -ˌmen] → **firefighter** — **fireplace** ['faɪrˌpleɪs] *n* : hogar *m*, chimenea *f* — **fireproof** ['faɪrˌpruːf] *adj* : ignífugo — **fireside** ['faɪrˌsaɪd] *n* : hogar *m* — **fire station** *n* : estación *f* de bomberos *Lat*, parque *m* de bomberos *Spain* — **firewood** ['faɪrˌwʊd] *n* : leña *f* — **fireworks** ['faɪrˌwərk] *npl* : fuegos *mpl* artificiales

firm¹ ['fərm] *n* : empresa *f*

firm² *adj* : firme — **firmly** ['fərmli] *adv* : firmemente — **firmness** ['fərmnəs] *n* : firmeza *f*

first ['fərst] *adj* **1** : primero **2** at ~ **sight** : a primera vista **3** for the ~ **time** : por primera vez — ~ *adv* **1** : primero **2** ~ **and foremost** : ante todo **3** ~ **of all** : en primer lugar — ~ *n* **1** : primero *m*, **-ra** *f* **2** at ~ : al principio — **first aid** *n* : primeros auxilios *mpl* — **first-class** ['fərstˌklæs] *adv* : en primera — ~ *adj* : de primera *f* — **firsthand** ['fərstˌhænd] *adv* : directamente — ~ *adj* : de primera mano — **firstly** ['fərstli] *adv* : en primer lugar — **first name** *n* : nombre *m* de pila — **first-rate** ['fərstˌreɪt] *adj* → **first-class**

fiscal ['fɪskəl] *adj* : fiscal

fish ['fɪʃ] *n, pl* **fish** *or* **fishes** : pez *m* (vivo), pescado *m* (para comer) — *vi* **1** : pescar **2** ~ **for** SEEK : buscar **3** **go** ~ **ing** : ir de pesca — **fisherman** ['fɪʃərmən] *n, pl* **-men** [-mən, -ˌmen] : pescador *m*, **-dora** *f* — **fishhook** ['fɪʃˌhʊk] *n* : anzuelo *m* — **fishing** ['fɪʃɪŋ] *n* : pesca *f* — **fishing pole** *n* : caña *f* de pescar — **fish market** *n* : pescadería *f* — **fishy** ['fɪʃi] *adj* **fishier, -est 1** : a pescado (dícese de sabores, etc.) **2** SUSPICIOUS : sospechoso

fist ['fɪst] *n* : puño *m*

fit¹ ['fɪt] *n* **1** : ataque *m* **2** he had a ~ : le dio un ataque

fit² *adj* **fitter; fittest 1** SUITABLE : apropiado **2** HEALTHY : en forma **3 be ~ for** : ser apto para — *v* **fitted; fitting** *vt* **1** : encajar en (un hueco, etc.) **2** *(relating to clothing)* : quedar bien a **3** SUIT : ser apropiado para **4** MATCH : coincidir con **5** *or* ~ **out** : equipar — *vi* **1** : caber (en una caja, etc.), encajar (en un hueco, etc.) **2** *or* ~ **in** BELONG : encajar **3 this dress doesn't ~** : me está vestido no me queda bien — *n* **it's a good fit** : me queda bien — **fitful** ['fɪtfəl] *adj* : irregular — **fitness** ['fɪtnəs] *n* **1** HEALTH : salud *f* **2** SUITABILITY : idoneidad *f* — **fitting** ['fɪtɪŋ] *adj* : apropiado

five [faɪv] *n* : cinco *m* — ~ *adj* : cinco — **five hundred** *n* : quinientos *m* — ~ *adj* : quinientos

fix [fɪks] *vt* **1** ATTACH : fijar, sujetar **2** REPAIR : arreglar **3** PREPARE : preparar — ~ *n* PREDICAMENT : aprieto *m*, apuro *m* — **fixed** ['fɪkst] *adj* : fijo — **fixture** ['fɪkstʃər] *n* : instalación *f*

fizz ['fɪz] *vi* : burbujear — ~ *n* : efervescencia *f*

fizzle ['fɪzəl] *vi* **-zled; -zling** *or* ~ **out** : quedar en nada

flabbergasted ['flæbərˌgæstəd] *adj* : estupefacto, pasmado

flabby ['flæbi] *adj* **-bier; -est** : fofo

flaccid ['flæksəd, 'flæsəd] *adj* : fláccido

flag¹ ['flæg] *vi* WEAKEN : flaquear

flag² *n* : bandera *f* — ~ *vt* **flagged; flagging** *or* ~ **down** : hacer señales de parada — **flagpole** ['flæg,poːl] *n* : asta *f*

flagrant ['fleɪgrənt] *adj* : flagrante

flair ['flær] *n* : don *m*, facilidad *f*

flake ['fleɪk] *n* : copo *m* (de nieve), escama *f* (de pintura, de la piel) — ~ *vi* **flaked; flaking** : pelarse

flamboyant [flæm'bɔɪənt] *adj* : extravagante

flame ['fleɪm] *n* **1** : llama *f* **2 burst into ~s** : estallar en llamas **3 go up in ~s** : incendiarse

flamingo [flə'mɪŋgo] *n, pl* **-gos** : flamenco *m*

flammable ['flæməbəl] *adj* : inflamable

flank ['flæŋk] *n* : ijada *m* (de un animal), flanco *m* (militar) — ~ *vt* : flanquear

flannel ['flænəl] *n* : franela *f*

flap ['flæp] *n* : solapa *f* (de un sobre, un libro, etc.), tapa *f* (de un recipiente) — ~ *v* **flapped; flapping** *vi* : agitarse — *vt* : batir, agitar

flapjack ['flæp,dʒæk] → **pancake**

flare ['flær] *vi* **flared; flaring 1** ~ **up** BLAZE : llamear **2** ~ **up** EXPLODE,

ERUPT : estallar, explotar — ~ *n* **1** BLAZE : llamarada *f* **2** SIGNAL : (luz *f* de) bengala *f*

flash ['flæʃ] *vi* **1** : brillar, destellar **2** ~ **past** : pasar como un rayo — *vt* **1** : dirigir (una luz) **2** SHOW : mostrar **3** ~ **a smile** : sonreír — ~ *n* **1** : destello *m* **2** ~ **of lightning** : relámpago *m* **3 in a ~** : de repente — **flashlight** ['flæʃˌlaɪt] *n* : linterna *f* — **flashy** ['flæʃi] *adj* **flashier; -est** : ostentoso

flask ['flæsk] *n* : frasco *m*

flat ['flæt] *adj* **flatter; flattest 1** LEVEL : plano, llano **2** DOWNRIGHT : categórico **3** FIXED : fijo **4** MONOTONOUS : monótono **5** : bemol (en la música) **6** ~ **tire** : neumático *m* desinflado — ~ *n* **1** : bemol *m* (en la música) **2** *Brit* APARTMENT : apartamento *m*, departamento *m Lat* **3** PUNCTURE : pinchazo *m* — ~ *adv* **1** : pelado *f* **2 in one hour ~** : en una hora justa — **flatly** ['flætli] *adv* : categóricamente — **flat-out** ['flæt'aʊt] *adj* **1** : frenético **2** DOWNRIGHT : categórico — **flatten** ['flætən] *vt* **1** LEVEL : aplanar, allanar **2** KNOCK DOWN : arrasar

flatter ['flætər] *vt* **1** : halagar **2** BECOME : favorecer — **flatterer** ['flætərər] *n* : adulador *m*, -dora *f* — **flattering** ['flætərɪŋ] *adj* **1** : halagador **2** BECOMING : favorecedor — **flattery** ['flætəri] *n, pl* **-ries** : halagos *mpl*

flaunt ['flɔnt] *vt* : hacer alarde de

flavor *or Brit* **flavour** ['fleɪvər] *n* : gusto *m*, sabor *m* — ~ *vt* : sazonar — **flavorful** *or Brit* **flavourful** ['fleɪvərfəl] *adj* : sabroso — **flavoring** *or Brit* **flavouring** ['fleɪvərɪŋ] *n* : condimento *m*, sazón *f*

flaw ['flɔ] *n* : defecto *m* — **flawless** ['flɔləs] *adj* : perfecto

flax ['flæks] *n* : lino *m*

flea ['fliː] *n* : pulga *f*

fleck ['flɛk] *n* **1** PARTICLE : mota *f* **2** SPOT : pinta *f*

flee ['fliː] *v* **fled** ['flɛd] **; fleeing** *vi* : huir — *vt* : huir de

fleece ['fliːs] *n* : vellón *m* — ~ *vt* **fleeced; fleecing 1** SHEAR : esquilar **2** DEFRAUD : desplumar

fleet ['fliːt] *n* : flota *f*

fleeting ['fliːtɪŋ] *adj* : fugaz

Flemish ['flɛmɪʃ] *adj* : flamenco

flesh ['flɛʃ] *n* **1** : carne *f* **2** PULP : pulpa *f* **3 in the ~** : en persona — **fleshy** ['flɛʃi] *adj* **fleshier; -est 1** : gordo **2** PULPY : carnoso

flew → **fly**

flex ['flɛks] *vt* : flexionar — **flexibility**

[ˌfleksəˈbɪlət̬i] n, pl **-ties** : flexibilidad f — **flexible** [ˈfleksəbəl] adj : flexible

flick [ˈflɪk] n : golpecito m — ~ vt : dar un golpecito a — vi **through** : hojear

flicker [ˈflɪkər] vi : parpadear — ~ n 1 : parpadeo m 2 **a ~ of hope** : un rayo de esperanza

flier [ˈflaɪər] n 1 AVIATOR : aviador m, -dora f 2 or **flyer** LEAFLET : folleto m, volante m Lat

flight[1] [ˈflaɪt] n 1 : vuelo m 2 TRAJECTORY : trayectoria f 3 **~ of stairs** : tramo m

flight[2] n ESCAPE : huida f

flimsy [ˈflɪmzi] adj **flimsier; -est** 1 LIGHT : ligero 2 SHAKY : poco sólido 3 **a ~ excuse** : una excusa floja

flinch [ˈflɪntʃ] vi **~ from** : encogerse ante

fling [ˈflɪŋ] vt **flung** [ˈflʌŋ]; **flinging** 1 : arrojar 2 **~ open** : abrir de un golpe — ~ n 1 AFFAIR : aventura f 2 **have a ~ at** : intentar

flint [ˈflɪnt] n : pedernal m

flip [ˈflɪp] v **flipped; flipping** vt 1 or **~ over** : dar la vuelta a 2 **~ a coin** : echarlo a cara o cruz — vi 1 or **~ over** : volcarse 2 **~ through** : hojear — n SOMERSAULT : voltereta f

flippant [ˈflɪpənt] adj : ligero, frívolo

flipper [ˈflɪpər] n : aleta f

flirt [ˈflərt] vi : coquetear — ~ n : coqueto m, -ta f — **flirtatious** [flərˈteɪʃəs] adj : coqueto

flit [ˈflɪt] vi **flitted; flitting** : revolotear

float [ˈfloʊt] n 1 : flotador m 2 : carroza f (en un desfile) — ~ vi : flotar — vt : hacer flotar

flock [ˈflɑk] n : rebaño m (de ovejas), bandada f (de pájaros) — ~ vi : congregarse

flog [ˈflɑg] vt **flogged; flogging** : azotar

flood [ˈflʌd] n 1 : inundación f 2 : torrente m (de palabras, de lágrimas, etc.) — ~ vt : inundar — **floodlight** [ˈflʌdˌlaɪt] n : foco m

floor [ˈflor] n 1 : suelo m, piso m Lat 2 STORY : piso m 3 **dance ~** : pista f de baile 4 **ground ~** : planta f baja — ~ vt 1 KNOCK DOWN : derribar 2 NONPLUS : desconcertar — **floorboard** [ˈflorˌbord] n : tabla f del suelo

flop [ˈflɑp] vi **flopped; flopping** 1 FLAP : agitarse 2 COLLAPSE : dejarse caer 3 FAIL : fracasar — ~ n FAILURE : fracaso m — **floppy** [ˈflɑpi] adj **-pier; -est** : flojo, flexible — **floppy disk** n : diskette m, disquete m

flora [ˈflorə] n : flora f — **floral** [ˈflorəl]

adj : floral — **florid** [ˈflorɪd] adj 1 FLOWERY : florido 2 RUDDY : rojizo — **florist** [ˈflorɪst] n : florista mf

floss [ˈflɑs] n **→ dental floss**

flounder[1] [ˈflaʊndər] n, pl **flounder** or **flounders** : platija f

flounder[2] vi 1 or **~ about** : resbalarse, revolcarse 2 : titubear (en un discurso)

flour [ˈflaʊər] n : harina f

flourish [ˈflərɪʃ] vi : florecer — vt BRANDISH : blandir — ~ n : floritura f — **flourishing** [ˈflərɪʃɪŋ] adj : floreciente

flout [ˈflaʊt] vt : desacatar, burlarse de

flow [ˈfloʊ] vi : fluir, correr — ~ n : flujo m, circulación f 2 : corriente f (de información, etc.)

flower [ˈflaʊər] n : flor f — ~ vi : florecer — **flowered** [ˈflaʊərd] adj : floreado — **flowerpot** [ˈflaʊərˌpɑt] n : maceta f — **flowery** [ˈflaʊəri] adj : florido

flown → fly

flu [ˈflu] n : gripe f

fluctuate [ˈflʌktʃuˌeɪt] vi **-ated; -ating** : fluctuar — **fluctuation** [ˌflʌktʃuˈeɪʃən] n : fluctuación f

fluency [ˈfluənsi] n : fluidez f — **fluent** [ˈfluənt] adj 1 : fluido 2 **be ~ in** : hablar con fluidez — **fluently** [ˈfluəntli] adv : con fluidez

fluff [ˈflʌf] n : pelusa f — **fluffy** [ˈflʌfi] adj **fluffier; -est** : de pelusa, velloso

fluid [ˈfluːɪd] adj : fluido — ~ n : fluido m

flung → fling

flunk [ˈflʌŋk] vt : reprobar Lat, suspender Spain — vi : ser reprobado Lat, suspender Spain

fluorescence [ˌflorˈɛsənts, ˌflor-] n : fluorescencia f — **fluorescent** [ˌflorˈɛsənt, ˌflor-] adj : fluorescente

flurry [ˈfləri] n, pl **-ries** 1 GUST : ráfaga f 2 or **snow ~** : nevisca f 3 **~ of questions** : aluvión m de preguntas

flush [ˈflʌʃ] vi BLUSH : ruborizarse, sonrojarse — vt **~ the toilet** : tirar de la cadena, jalarle a la cadena Lat — ~ n BLUSH : rubor m, sonrojo m — ~ adj **~ with** : a nivel con, a ras de — ~ adv : al mismo nivel, a ras

fluster [ˈflʌstər] vt : poner nervioso

flute [ˈfluːt] n : flauta f

flutter [ˈflʌt̬ər] vi 1 FLIT : revolotear 2 WAVE : ondear 3 or **~ about** : ir y venir — ~ n 1 : revoloteo m (de alas) 2 STIR : revuelo m

flux [ˈflʌks] n **be in a state of ~** : cambiar continuamente

fly[1] [ˈflaɪ] v **flew** [ˈfluː]; **flown** [ˈfloːn]; **flying** vi 1 : volar 2 TRAVEL : ir en avión 3 WAVE : ondear 4 RUSH : correr 5 ~

by : pasar volando — vt 1 PILOT : pilotar 2 : hacer volar (una cometa), enarbolar (una bandera) — ~ n, pl flies : bragueta f (de un pantalón)

fly² n, pl flies : mosca f (insecto)

flyer → flier

flying saucer n : platillo m volador Lat, platillo m volante Spain

flyswatter ['flaɪˌswɑtər] n : matamoscas m

foal ['foːl] n : potro m, -tra f

foam ['foːm] n : espuma f — vi : hacer espuma — foamy ['foːmi] adj foamier, -est : espumoso

focus ['foːkəs] n, pl -ci ['foːˌsaɪ, -ˌkaɪ] 1 : foco m 2 be in ~ : estar enfocado 3 ~ of attention : centro m de atención — ~ v -cused or -cussed; -cusing or -cussing vt 1 : enfocar (la atención, etc.) — vi ~ on : enfocar (con los ojos), concentrarse en (con la mente)

fodder ['fɑdər] n : forraje m

foe ['foː] n : enemigo m, -ga f

fog ['fɑg, 'fɔg] n : niebla f — v fogged, fogging vt : empañar — vi or ~ up : empañarse — foggy ['fɑgi, 'fɔ-] adj foggier, -est : nebuloso — foghorn ['fɑgˌhɔrn, 'fɔg-] n : sirena f de niebla

foil¹ ['fɔɪl] vt : frustrar

foil² n or aluminum ~ : papel m de aluminio

fold¹ ['foːld] n : redil m (para ovejas) 2 return to the ~ : volver al redil

fold² ['foːld] vt 1 : doblar, plegar 2 ~ one's arms : cruzar los brazos — vi 1 or ~ up : doblarse, plegarse 2 FAIL : fracasar — ~ n : pliegue m — folder ['foːldər] n : carpeta f

foliage ['foːliɪdʒ, -lidʒ] n : follaje m

folk ['foːk] n, pl folk or folks 1 : gente f 2 ~s npl PARENTS : padres mpl — ~ adj 1 : popular 2 ~ dance : danza f folklórica — folklore ['foːkˌlɔr] n : folklore m

follow ['fɑlo] vt 1 : seguir 2 UNDERSTAND : entender 3 ~ up : seguir — vi 1 : seguir 2 UNDERSTAND : entender 3 ~ up on : seguir con — follower ['fɑloər] n : seguidor m, -dora f — following ['fɑloɪŋ] adj : siguiente — ~ n : seguidores mpl — ~ prep : después de

folly ['fɑli] n, pl -lies : locura f

fond ['fɑnd] adj 1 : cariñoso 2 be ~ of sth : ser aficionado a algo 3 be ~ of s.o. : tener cariño a algn

fondle ['fɑndəl] vt -dled; -dling : acariciar

fondness ['fɑndnəs] n 1 LOVE : cariño m 2 LIKING : afición f

food ['fuːd] n : comida f, alimento m — foodstuffs ['fuːdˌstʌfs] npl : comestibles mpl

fool ['fuːl] n 1 : idiota mf 2 JESTER : bufón m, -fona f — ~ vi 1 JOKE : bromear 2 ~ around : perder el tiempo — vt TRICK : engañar — foolhardy ['fuːlˌhɑrdi] adj : temerario — foolish ['fuːlɪʃ] adj : tonto — foolishness ['fuːlɪʃnəs] n : tontería f — foolproof ['fuːlˌpruːf] adj : infalible

foot ['fut] n, pl feet ['fiːt] : pie m — footage ['futɪdʒ] n : secuencias fpl (cinemáticas) — football ['futˌbɔl] n : fútbol m americano — footbridge ['futˌbrɪdʒ] n : pasarela f, puente m peatonal — foothills ['futˌhɪlz] npl : estribaciones fpl — foothold ['futˌhoːld] n : punto m de apoyo — footing ['futɪŋ] n 1 BALANCE : equilibrio m 2 on equal ~ : en igualdad — footlights ['futˌlaɪts] npl : candilejas fpl — footnote ['futˌnoːt] n : nota f al pie de la página — footpath ['futˌpæθ] n : sendero m — footprint ['futˌprɪnt] n : huella f — footstep ['futˌstɛp] n : paso m — footstool ['futˌstuːl] n : escabel m — footwear ['futˌwær] n : calzado m

for ['fɔr] prep 1 (indicating purpose, etc.) : para 2 (indicating motivation, etc.) : por 3 (indicating duration) : durante 4 we walked ~ 3 miles : andamos 3 millas 5 AS FOR : con respecto a — ~ conj : puesto que, porque

forage ['fɔrɪdʒ] n : forraje m — ~ v -aged; -aging 1 : forrajear 2 ~ for : buscar

foray ['fɔreɪ] n : incursión f

forbid [fərˈbɪd] vt -bade [-ˈbæd, -ˈbeɪd] or -bad [-ˈbæd]; -bidden [-ˈbɪdən]; -bidding : prohibir — forbidding [fərˈbɪdɪŋ] adj : intimidante, severo

force ['fɔrs] n 1 : fuerza f 2 by ~ : por la fuerza 3 in ~ : en vigor, en vigencia 4 armed ~s : fuerzas fpl armadas — ~ vt forced; forcing 1 : forzar 2 OBLIGATE : obligar — forced ['fɔrst] adj : forzado, forzoso — forceful ['fɔrsfəl] adj : fuerte, energético

forceps ['fɔrsəps, -ˌsɛps] ns & pl : fórceps m

forcibly [-bli] adv : por la fuerza

ford ['fɔrd] n : vado m — ~ vt : vadear

fore ['fɔr] n 1 come to the ~ : empezar a destacarse

forearm ['fɔrˌɑrm] n : antebrazo m

foreboding [fɔrˈboːdɪŋ] n : premonición f, presentimiento m

forecast ['fɔr.kæst] vt **-cast; -casting** : predecir, pronosticar — ~ n : predicción f, pronóstico m

forefathers ['fɔr.fɑðərz] n : antepasados mpl

forefinger ['fɔr.fɪŋgər] n : índice m, dedo m índice

forefront ['fɔr.frʌnt] n **at/in the** ~ : a la vanguardia

forego [fɔr'go:] → forgo

foregone [fɔr'gɔn] adj ~ **conclusion** : resultado m inevitable

foreground ['fɔr.graʊnd] n : primer plano m

forehead ['fɔrəd, 'fɔr.hɛd] n : frente f

foreign ['fɔrən] adj 1 : extranjero 2 ~ **trade** : comercio m exterior — **foreigner** ['fɔrənər] n : extranjero m, -ra f

foreman ['fɔrmən] n, pl **-men** [-mən, -mɛn] : capataz mf

foremost ['fɔr.mo:st] adj : principal — ~ adv **first and** ~ : ante todo

forensic [fə'rɛnsɪk] adj : forense

forerunner ['fɔr.rʌnər] n : precursor m, -sora f

foresee [fɔr'si:] vt **-saw; -seen; -seeing** : prever — **foreseeable** [fɔr'si:əbəl] adj : previsible

foreshadow [fɔr'ʃædo:] vt : presagiar

foresight ['fɔr.saɪt] n : previsión f

forest ['fɔrəst] n : bosque m — **forestry** ['fɔrəstri] n : silvicultura f

foretaste ['fɔr.teɪst] n : anticipo m

foretell [fɔr'tɛl] vt **-told; -telling** : predecir

forethought ['fɔr.θɔt] n : reflexión f previa

forever [fə'rɛvər] adv **1** ETERNALLY : para siempre **2** CONTINUALLY : siempre, constantemente

forewarn [fɔr'wɔrn] vt : advertir, prevenir

foreword ['fɔr.wərd] n : prólogo m

forfeit ['fɔr.fət] n **1** PENALTY : pena f **2** : prenda f (en un juego) — ~ vt : perder

forge [fɔrdʒ] n : forja f — ~ v **forged; forging** vt **1** : forjar (metal, etc.) **2** COUNTERFEIT : falsificar — vi ~ **ahead** : avanzar, seguir adelante — **forger** ['fɔrdʒər] n : falsificador m, -dora f — **forgery** ['fɔrdʒəri] n, pl **-eries** : falsificación f

forget [fər'gɛt] v **-got** [-'gɑt]; **-gotten** [-'gɑtən] or **-got; -getting** vt : olvidar, olvidarse de — vi **1** : olvidarse **2 I forgot** : se me olvidó — **forgetful** [fər'gɛtfəl] adj : olvidadizo

forgive [fər'gɪv] vt **-gave** [-'geɪv]; **-given** [-'gɪvən]; **-giving** : perdonar — **forgiveness** [fər'gɪvnəs] n : perdón m

forgo or **forego** [fɔr'go:] vt **-went; -gone; -going** : privarse de, renunciar a

fork ['fɔrk] n **1** : tenedor m **2** PITCHFORK : horca f **3** : bifurcación f (de un camino, etc.) — vi : ramificarse, bifurcarse — vt ~ **over** : desembolsar

forlorn [fɔr'lɔrn] adj : triste

form ['fɔrm] n **1** : forma f **2** DOCUMENT : formulario m **3** KIND : tipo m — ~ vt **1** : formar **2** ~ **a habit** : adquirir un hábito — vi : formarse

formal ['fɔrməl] adj : formal — ~ n **1** BALL : baile m (formal) **2** or ~ **dress** : traje m de etiqueta — **formality** [fɔr'mæləti] n, pl **-ties** : formalidad f

format ['fɔr.mæt] n : formato m — ~ vt **-matted; -matting** : formatear

formation [fɔr'meɪʃən] n **1** : formación f **2** SHAPE : forma f

former ['fɔrmər] adj **1** PREVIOUS : antiguo, anterior **2** : primero (de dos) — **formerly** ['fɔrmərli] adv : anteriormente, antes

formidable ['fɔrmədəbəl, fɔr'mɪdə-] adj : formidable

formula ['fɔrmjələ] n, pl **-las** or **-lae** [-.li:, -.laɪ] **1** : fórmula f **2** or **baby** ~ : preparado m para biberón

forsake [fɔr'seɪk] vt **-sook** [-'sʊk]; **-saken** [-'seɪkən]; **-saking** : abandonar

fort ['fɔrt] n : fuerte m

forth ['fɔrθ] adv **1 and so** ~ : etcétera **2 back and** ~ → **back 3 from this day** ~ : de hoy en adelante — **forthcoming** [fɔrθ'kʌmɪŋ, 'fɔrθ-] adj **1** COMING : próximo **2** OPEN : comunicativo — **forthright** ['fɔrθ.raɪt] adj : directo, franco

fortieth ['fɔrtiəθ] adj : cuadragésimo — ~ n **1** : cuadragésimo m, -ma f (en una serie) **2** : cuarentavo m, cuarentava parte f

fortify ['fɔrtə.faɪ] vt **-fied; -fying** : fortificar — **fortification** [fɔrtəfə'keɪʃən] n : fortificación f

fortitude ['fɔrtə.tu:d, -.tju:d] n : fortaleza f

fortnight ['fɔrt.naɪt] n : quince días mpl, quincena f

fortress ['fɔrtrəs] n : fortaleza f

fortunate ['fɔrtʃənət] adj : afortunado — **fortunately** ['fɔrtʃənətli] adv : afortunadamente — **fortune** ['fɔrtʃən] n : fortuna f — **fortune-teller** ['fɔrtʃən.tɛlər] n : adivino m, -na f

forty ['fɔrti] n, pl **forties** : cuarenta m — ~ adj : cuarenta

forum ['forəm] *n*, *pl* **-rums** : foro *m*
forward ['fɔrwərd] *adj* 1 : hacia adelante (en dirección), delantero (en posición) 2 BRASH : descarado — **~** *adv* 1 : (hacia) adelante 2 **from this day ~** : de aquí en adelante — **~** *vt* : remitir, enviar — **~** *n* : delantero *m*, -ra *f* (en deportes) — **forwards** ['fɔrwərdz] *adv* → **forward**
fossil ['fɑsəl] *n* : fósil *m*
foster ['fɑstər] *adj* : adoptivo — **~** *vt* : promover, fomentar
fought → **fight**
foul ['faul] *adj* 1 REPULSIVE : asqueroso 2 **~ language** : palabrotas *fpl* 3 **~ play** : actos *mpl* criminales 4 **~ weather** : mal tiempo *m* — **~** *n* : falta *f* (en deportes) — **~** *vi* : cometer faltas (en deportes) — **~** *vt* : ensuciar
found¹ ['faund] → **find**
found² *vt* : fundar, establecer — **foundation** [faun'deɪʃən] *n* 1 : fundación *f* 2 BASIS : fundamento *m* 3 : cimientos *mpl* (de un edificio)
founder¹ ['faundər] *n* : fundador *m*, -dora *f*
founder² *vi* SINK : hundirse
fountain ['fauntən] *n* : fuente *f*
four ['for] *n* : cuatro *m* — **~** *adj* : cuatro — **fourfold** ['for,fold, -'fold] *adj* : cuádruple — **four hundred** *adj* : cuatrocientos — **~** *n* : cuatrocientos *m*
fourteen [for'tin] *n* : catorce *m* — **~** *adj* : catorce — **fourteenth** [for'tinθ] *adj* : decimocuarto — **~** *n* : decimocuarto *m*, -ta *f* (en una serie) 2 : catorceavo *m*, catorceava parte *f*
fourth ['forθ] *n* 1 : cuarto *m*, -ta *f* (en una serie) 2 : cuarto *m*, cuarta parte *f* — **~** *adj* : cuarto
fowl ['faul] *n*, *pl* **fowl** or **fowls** : ave *f*
fox ['fɑks] *n*, *pl* **foxes** : zorro *m*, -rra *f* — **~** *vt* TRICK : engañar — **foxy** ['fɑksi] *adj* **foxier; -est** SHREWD : astuto
foyer ['fɔɪər, 'fɔɪjeɪ] *n* : vestíbulo *m*
fraction ['frækʃən] *n* : fracción *f*
fracture ['fræktʃər] *n* : fractura *f* — **~** *vt* **-tured; -turing** : fracturar
fragile ['frædʒəl, -,dʒaɪl] *adj* : frágil
fragment ['frægmənt] *n* : fragmento *m*
fragrant ['freɪgrənt] *adj* : fragante — **fragrance** ['freɪgrəns] *n* : fragancia *f*, aroma *m*
frail ['freɪl] *adj* : débil, delicado
frame ['freɪm] *n* **framed; framing** ENCLOSE : enmarcar 2 COMPOSE, DRAFT : formular 3 INCRIMINATE : incriminar — **~** *n* 1 : armazón *mf* (de un edificio, etc.) 2 : marco *m* (de un cuadro, una puerta, etc.) 3 or **~s** *npl* : montura *f*

(para anteojos) 4 **~ of mind** : estado *m* de ánimo — **framework** ['freɪm,wɜrk] *n* : armazón *f*
franc ['fræŋk] *n* : franco *m*
frank ['fræŋk] *adj* : franco — **frankly** *adv* : francamente — **frankness** ['fræŋknəs] *n* : franqueza *f*
frantic ['fræntɪk] *adj* : frenético
fraternal [frə'tərnəl] *adj* : fraterno, fraternal — **fraternity** [frə'tərnəti] *n*, *pl* **-ties** : fraternidad *f* — **fraternize** ['frætər,naɪz] *vi* **-nized; -nizing** : confraternizar
fraud ['frɔd] *n* 1 DECEIT : fraude *m* 2 IMPOSTOR : impostor *m*, -tora *f* — **fraudulent** ['frɔdʒələnt] *adj* : fraudulento
fraught ['frɔt] *adj* **~ with** : lleno de, cargado de
fray¹ ['freɪ] *n* 1 **join the ~** : salir a la palestra 2 **return to the ~** : volver a la carga
fray² *vt* : crispar (los nervios) — *vi* : deshilacharse
freak ['frik] *n* 1 ODDITY : fenómeno *m* 2 ENTHUSIAST : entusiasta *mf* — **freakish** ['frikɪʃ] *adj* : anormal
freckle ['frekəl] *n* : peca *f*
free ['fri] *adj* **freer; freest** 1 : libre 2 or **~ of charge** : gratuito, gratis 3 LOOSE : suelto — **~** *vt* **freed; freeing** 1 : liberar, poner en libertad 2 RELEASE, UNFASTEN : soltar, desatar — **~** *adv* or **for ~** : gratis — **freedom** ['fridəm] *n* : libertad *f* — **freelance** ['fri,læns] *adj* : por cuenta propia — **freely** ['frili] *adv* 1 : libremente 2 LAVISHLY : con generosidad — **freeway** ['fri,weɪ] *n* : autopista *f* — **free will** *n* 1 : libre albedrío *m* 2 **of one's own ~** : por su propia voluntad
freeze ['friz] *v* **froze** ['froz]; **frozen** ['frozən]; **freezing** *vi* 1 : congelarse, helarse 2 STOP : quedarse inmóvil — *vt* : helar (agua, etc.), congelar (alimentos, precios, etc.) — **freeze-dry** ['friz,draɪ] *vt* **-dried; -drying** : liofilizar — **freezer** ['frizər] *n* : congelador *m* — **freezing** ['frizɪŋ] *adj* 1 CHILLY : helado 2 **it's freezing!** : ¡hace un frío espantoso!
freight ['freɪt] *n* 1 SHIPPING : porte *m*, flete *m* Lat 2 CARGO : carga *f*
French ['frentʃ] *adj* : francés — **~** *n* 1 : francés *m* (idioma) 2 **the ~** *npl* : los franceses — **Frenchman** ['frentʃmən] *n* : francés *m* — **Frenchwoman** ['frentʃ,wumən] *n* : francesa *f* — **french fries** ['frentʃ,fraɪz] *npl* : papas *fpl* fritas
frenetic [frɪ'nɛtɪk] *adj* : frenético

frenzy ['frenzi] n, pl **-zies** : frenesí m — **frenzied** ['frenzid] adj : frenético

frequent [fri'kwɛnt, 'frikwənt] vt : frecuentar — — ['frikwənt] adj : frecuente — **frequency** ['frikwənsi] n, pl **-cies** : frecuencia f — **frequently** adv : a menudo, frecuentemente

fresco ['freskoː] n, pl **-coes** or **-cos** : fresco m

fresh ['freʃ] adj **1** : fresco **2** IMPUDENT : descarado **3** CLEAN : limpio **4** NEW : nuevo **5 ~ water** : agua m dulce — **freshen** ['freʃən] vt : refrescar — vi **~ up** : arreglarse — **freshly** ['freʃli] adv : recién — **freshman** ['freʃmən] n, pl **-men** [-mən, -mɛn] : estudiante mf de primer año — **freshness** ['freʃnəs] n : frescura f

fret ['frɛt] vi **fretted; fretting** : preocuparse — **fretful** ['frɛtfəl] adj : nervioso, irritable

friar ['fraɪər] n : fraile m

friction ['frɪkʃən] n : fricción f

Friday ['fraɪdeɪ, -di] n : viernes m

friend ['frɛnd] n : amigo m, -ga f — **friendliness** ['frɛndlinəs] n : simpatía f — **friendly** ['frɛndli] adj **-lier; -est** : simpático, amable — **friendship** ['frɛndʃɪp] n : amistad f

frigate ['frɪgət] n : fragata f

fright ['fraɪt] n : miedo m, susto m — **frighten** ['fraɪtən] vt : asustar, espantar — **frightened** ['fraɪtənd] adj **1** : asustado, temeroso **2 be ~ of** : tener miedo de — **frightening** ['fraɪtənɪŋ] adj : espantoso — **frightful** ['fraɪtfəl] adj : espantoso, terrible

frigid ['frɪdʒɪd] adj : frío, glacial

frill ['frɪl] n **1** RUFFLE : volante m **2** LUXURY : lujo m

fringe ['frɪndʒ] n **1** : fleco m **2** EDGE : periferia f, margen m **3 ~ benefits** : incentivos mpl, extras mpl

frisk ['frɪsk] vt SEARCH : cachear, registrar — **frisky** ['frɪski] adj **friskier; -est** : retozón, juguetón

fritter ['frɪtər] n : buñuelo m — vt or **~ away** : malgastar (dinero), desperdiciar (tiempo)

frivolous ['frɪvələs] adj : frívolo — **frivolity** [frɪ'vɑləti] n, pl **-ties** : frivolidad f

frizzy ['frɪzi] adj **frizzier; -est** : rizado, crespo

fro ['froː] adv **to and ~** : → **to**

frock ['frɑk] n : vestido m

frog ['frɔg, 'frɑg] n **1** : rana f **2 have a ~ in one's throat** : tener carraspera

frolic ['frɑlɪk] vi **-icked; -icking** : retozar

from ['frʌm, 'frɑm] prep **1** : de **2** (indicating a starting point) : desde **3** (indicating a cause) : de, por **4 ~ now on** : a partir de ahora

front ['frʌnt] n **1** : parte f delantera **2** : delantera f (de un vestido, etc.), fachada f (de un edificio), frente m (militar) **3 cold ~** : frente m frío **4 in ~ of** : delante de, adelante de Lat — **~** vi or **~ on** : dar a, estar orientado a — adj **1** : delantero, de adelante **2 the ~ row** : la primera fila

frontier [frʌn'tɪr] n : frontera f

frost ['frɔst] n **1** : helada f **2** : escarcha f (en una superficie) — vt ICE : bañar (pasteles) — **frostbite** ['frɔstbaɪt] n : congelación f — **frosting** ['frɔstɪŋ] n ICING : baño m — **frosty** ['frɔsti] adj **frostier; -est** : cubierto de escarcha **2** CHILLY : helado, frío

froth ['frɔθ] n, pl **froths** ['frɔðs, 'frɔθs] : espuma f — **frothy** ['frɔθi] adj **frothier; -est** : espumoso

frown ['fraʊn] vi **1** : fruncir el ceño, fruncir el entrecejo **2 ~ at** : mirar con ceño **3 ~ upon** : desaprobar — **~** n : ceño m (fruncido)

froze, frozen → **freeze**

frugal ['frugəl] adj : frugal

fruit ['frut] n **1** : fruta f **2** PRODUCT, RESULT : fruto m — **fruitcake** ['frut,keɪk] n : pastel m de frutas — **fruitful** ['frutfəl] adj : fructífero — **fruition** [fru'ɪʃən] n **come to ~** : realizarse — **fruitless** ['frutləs] adj : infructuoso — **fruity** ['fruti] adj **fruitier; -est** : (con sabor) a fruta

frustrate ['frʌs,treɪt] vt **-trated; -trating** : frustrar — **frustrating** ['frʌs,treɪtɪŋ] adj : frustrante — **frustration** [frʌs'treɪʃən] n : frustración f

fry ['fraɪ] vt **fried; frying** : freír — **~** n, pl **fries 1 small ~** : gente f de poca monta **2 fries** npl → **french fries** — **frying pan** n : sartén mf

fudge ['fʌdʒ] n : dulce m blando de chocolate y leche

fuel ['fjuːəl] n : combustible m — vt **-eled** or **-elled; -eling** or **-elling 1** : alimentar (un horno), abastecer de combustible (un avión) **2** STIMULATE : estimular

fugitive ['fjuːdʒətɪv] n : fugitivo m, -va f

fulfill or **fulfil** [fʊl'fɪl] vt **-filled; -filling 1** : cumplir con (una obligación), desarrollar (potencial) **2** FILL, MEET : cumplir — **fulfillment** [fʊl'fɪlmənt] n **1** ACCOMPLISHMENT : cumplimiento m **2** SATISFACTION : satisfacción f

full ['fʊl, 'fəl] adj **1** FILLED : lleno **2** COMPLETE : complete, detallado **3** : redondo (dícese de la cara), amplio (dícese de ropa) **4 at ~ speed** : a toda velocidad **5 in ~ bloom** : en plena flor — ~ *adv* **1** DIRECTLY : de lleno **2 know ~ well** : saber muy bien — ~ *n* **1 pay in ~** : pagar en su totalidad **2 to the ~** : al máximo — **full-fledged** [ˈfʊlˈfledʒd] *adj* : hecho y derecho — **fully** [ˈfʊli] *adv* **1** COMPLETELY : completamente **2** AT LEAST : al menos, por lo menos

fumble [ˈfʌmbəl] *vi* -bled; -bling **1** RUMMAGE : hurgar **2 ~ with** : manejar con torpeza

fume [ˈfjuːm] *vi* fumed; fuming **1** SMOKE : echar humo, humear **2** RAGE : estar furioso — **fumes** *npl* : gases *mpl*

fumigate [ˈfjuːməgeɪt] *vt* -gated; -gating : fumigar

fun [ˈfʌn] *n* **1** AMUSEMENT : diversión *f* **2 have ~** : divertirse **3 make ~ of** : reírse de, burlarse de — ~ *adj* : divertido

function [ˈfʌŋkʃən] *n* **1** : función *f* **2** GATHERING : recepción *f*, reunión *f* social — ~ *vi* : funcionar — **functional** [ˈfʌŋkʃənəl] *adj* : funcional

fund [ˈfʌnd] *n* **1** : fondo *m* **2 ~s** *npl* RESOURCES : fondos *mpl* — ~ *vt* : financiar

fundamental [ˌfʌndəˈmentəl] *adj* : fundamental — **fundamentals** *npl* : fundamentos *mpl*

funeral [ˈfjuːnərəl] *adj* : funeral, fúnebre — ~ *n* : funeral *m*, funerales *mpl* — **funeral home** *or* **funeral parlor** *n* : funeraria *f*

fungus [ˈfʌŋgəs] *n*, *pl* fungi [ˈfʌnˌdʒaɪ, ˈfʌnˌgaɪ] : hongo *m*

funnel [ˈfʌnəl] *n* **1** : embudo *m* **2** SMOKESTACK : chimenea *f*

funny [ˈfʌni] *adj* funnier; -est **1** : divertido, gracioso **2** STRANGE : extraño, raro — **funnies** [ˈfʌniz] *npl* : tiras *fpl* cómicas

fur [ˈfər] *n* **1** : pelaje *m*, pelo *m* (de un animal) **2 ~** *or* **~ coat** : (prenda *f* de) piel *f* — ~ *adj* : de piel

furious [ˈfjʊriəs] *adj* : furioso

furnace [ˈfərnəs] *n* : horno *m*

furnish [ˈfərnɪʃ] *vt* **1** SUPPLY : proveer **2** : amueblar (una casa, etc.) — **furnishings** [ˈfərnɪʃɪŋz] *npl* : muebles *mpl*, mobiliario *m* — **furniture** [ˈfərnɪtʃər] *n* : muebles *mpl*, mobiliario *m*

furrow [ˈfəro] *n* : surco *m*

furry [ˈfəri] *adj* furrier; -est : peludo (dícese de un animal), de peluche (dícese de un juguete, etc.)

further [ˈfərðər] *adv* **1** FARTHER : más lejos **2** MOREOVER : además **3** MORE : más — ~ *vt* : promover, fomentar — ~ *adj* **1** FARTHER : más lejano **2** ADDITIONAL : adicional, más **3** UNTIL ~ **notice** : hasta nuevo aviso — **furthermore** [ˈfərðərˌmor] *adv* : además — **furthest** [ˈfərðəst] → **farthest**

fury [ˈfjʊri] *n*, *pl* -ries : furia *f*

fuse[1] *or* **fuze** [ˈfjuːz] *n* : mecha *f* (de una bomba, etc.)

fuse[2] *v* fused; fusing *vt* **1** MELT : fundir **2** UNITE : fusionar — *vi* : fundirse, fusionarse — ~ *n* **1** : fusible *m* **2 blow a ~** : fundir un fusible — **fusion** [ˈfjuːʒən] *n* : fusión *f*

fuss [ˈfʌs] *n* **1** : jaleo *m*, alboroto *m* **2 make a ~** : armar un escándalo — *vi* **1** WORRY : preocuparse **2** COMPLAIN : quejarse — **fussy** [ˈfʌsi] *adj* fussier; -est **1** IRRITABLE : irritable **2** ELABORATE : recargado **3** FINICKY : quisquilloso

futile [ˈfjuːtəl, ˈfjuːˌtaɪl] *adj* : inútil, vano — **futility** [fjuˈtɪləti] *n*, *pl* -ties : inutilidad *f*

future [ˈfjuːtʃər] *adj* : futuro — ~ *n* : futuro *m*

fuze → **fuse**[1]

fuzz [ˈfʌz] *n* : pelusa *f* — **fuzzy** [ˈfʌzi] *adj* fuzzier; -est **1** FURRY : con pelusa, peludo **2** BLURRY : borroso **3** VAGUE : confuso

G

g [ˈdʒiː] *n*, *pl* **g's** *or* **gs** [ˈdʒiːz] : g *f*, séptima letra del alfabeto inglés

gab [ˈgæb] *vi* gabbed; gabbing : charlar, cotorrear *fam* — ~ *n* CHATTER : charla *f*

gable [ˈgeɪbəl] *n* : aguilón *m*

gadget [ˈgædʒət] *n* : artilugio *m*

gag [ˈgæg] *v* gagged; gagging *vt* : amordazar — *vi* CHOKE : atragantarse — ~ *n* **1** : mordaza *f* **2** JOKE : chiste *m*

gage → **gauge**

gaiety [ˈgeɪəti] *n*, *pl* -eties : alegría *f* — **gaily** [ˈgeɪli] *adv* : alegremente

gain [ˈgeɪn] *n* **1** PROFIT : ganancia *f* **2** INCREASE : aumento *m* — ~ *vt* **1** OBTAIN : ganar, adquirir **2 ~ weight** : aumen-

tar de peso — *vi* **1** PROFIT : beneficiarse **2** : adelantar(se) (dícese de un reloj) —
gainful ['geɪnfəl] *adj* : lucrativo
gait ['geɪt] *n* : modo *m* de andar
gala ['geɪlə, 'gæ-, 'gɑ-] *n* : fiesta *f*
galaxy ['gæləksi] *n*, *pl* **-axies** : galaxia *f*
gale ['geɪl] *n* **1** : vendaval *f* **2** **~s** of laughter : carcajadas *fpl*
gall ['gɔl] *n* **have the ~ to** : tener el descaro de
gallant ['gælənt] *adj* **1** BRAVE : valiente **2** CHIVALROUS : galante
gallbladder ['gɔl,blædər] *n* : vesícula *f* biliar
gallery ['gæləri] *n*, *pl* **-leries** : galería *f*
gallon ['gælən] *n* : galón *m*
gallop ['gæləp] *vi* : galopar — **~** *n* : galope *m*
gallows ['gæ,loːz] *n*, *pl* **-lows** or **-lowses** [-,loːzəz] : horca *f*
gallstone ['gɔl,stoːn] *n* : cálculo *m* biliar
galore [gə'lor] *adj* : en abundancia
galoshes [gə'lɑʃ] *n* : galochas *fpl*, chanclos *mpl*
galvanize ['gælvə,naɪz] *vt* **-nized; -nizing** : galvanizar
gamble ['gæmbəl] *v* **-bled; -bling** **1** : jugar — *vt* : jugarse — **~** *n* **1** BET : apuesta *f* **2** RISK : riesga *f* — **gambler** ['gæmbələr] *n* : jugador *m*, -dora *f*
game ['geɪm] *n* **1** : juego *m* **2** MATCH : partido *m* **3** or **~ animals** : caza *f* — **~** *adj* READY : listo, dispuesto
gamut ['gæmət] *n* : gama *f*
gang ['gæŋ] *n* : banda *f*, pandilla *f* — *vi* **~ up on** : unirse contra
gangplank ['gæŋ,plæŋk] *n* : pasarela *f*
gangrene ['gæŋ,grin, 'gæn-; 'gæŋ'-, gæn'-] *n* : gangrena *f*
gangster ['gæŋstər] *n* : gángster *mf*
gangway ['gæŋ,weɪ] *n* → **gangplank**
gap ['gæp] *n* **1** OPENING : espacio *m* **2** INTERVAL : intervalo *m* **3** DISPARITY : brecha *f*, distancia *f* **4** DEFICIENCY : laguna *f*
gape ['geɪp] *vi* **gaped; gaping** **1** OPEN : estar abierto **2** STARE : mirar boquiabierto
garage [gə'rɑʒ, -'rɑdʒ] *n* : garaje *m* — *vt* **-raged; -raging** : dejar en un garaje
garb ['gɑrb] *n* : vestido *m*
garbage ['gɑrbɪdʒ] *n* : basura *f* — **garbage can** *n* : cubo *m* de la basura
garble ['gɑrbəl] *vt* **-bled; -bling** : tergiversar — **garbled** ['gɑrbəld] *adj* : confuso, incomprensible
garden ['gɑrdən] *n* : jardín *m* — *vi* : trabajar en el jardín — **gardener** ['gɑrdənər] *n* : jardinero *m*, -ra *f* — **gardening** ['gɑrdənɪŋ] *n* : jardinería *f*

gargle ['gɑrgəl] *vi* **-gled; -gling** : hacer gárgaras
garish ['gærɪʃ] *adj* : chillón
garland ['gɑrlənd] *n* : guirnalda *f*
garlic ['gɑrlɪk] *n* : ajo *m*
garment ['gɑrmənt] *n* : prenda *f*
garnish ['gɑrnɪʃ] *vt* : guarnecer — **~** *n* : adorno *m*, guarnición *f*
garret ['gærət] *n* : buhardilla *f*
garrison ['gærəsən] *n* : guarnición *f*
garrulous ['gærələs] *adj* : charlatán, parlanchín
garter ['gɑrtər] *n* : liga *f*
gas ['gæs] *n*, *pl* **gases** ['gæsəz] **1** : gas *m* **2** GASOLINE : gasolina *f* — **~** *v* **gassed; gassing** *vt* : asfixiar con gas — *vi* **~ up** : llenar el tanque con gasolina
gash ['gæʃ] *n* : tajo *m* — **~** *vt* : hacer un tajo en, cortar
gasket ['gæskət] *n* : junta *f*
gasoline ['gæsə,lin, ,gæsə'-] *n* : gasolina *f*
gasp ['gæsp] *vi* **1** : dar un grito ahogado **2** PANT : jadear — **~** *n* : grito *m* ahogado
gas station *n* : gasolinera *f*
gastric ['gæstrɪk] *adj* : gástrico
gastronomy [gæs'trɑnəmi] *n* : gastronomía *f*
gate ['geɪt] *n* **1** DOOR : puerta *f* **2** BARRIER : barrera *f* — **gateway** ['geɪt,weɪ] *n* : puerta *f*
gather ['gæðər] *vt* **1** ASSEMBLE : reunir **2** COLLECT : recoger **3** CONCLUDE : deducir **4** : fruncir (una tela) **5** **~ speed** : acelerar — *vi* : reunirse (dícese de personas), acumularse (dícese de cosas) — **gathering** ['gæðərɪŋ] *n* : reunión *f*
gaudy ['gɔdi] *adj* **gaudier; -est** : chillón, llamativo
gauge ['geɪdʒ] *n* **1** INDICATOR : indicador *m* **2** CALIBER : calibre *m* — **~** *vt* **gauged; gauging 1** MEASURE : medir **2** ESTIMATE : calcular, evaluar
gaunt ['gɔnt] *adj* : demacrado, descarnado
gauze ['gɔz] *n* : gasa *f*
gave → **give**
gawky ['gɔki] *adj* **gawkier; -est** : desgarbado
gay ['geɪ] *adj* **1** : alegre **2** HOMOSEXUAL : gay, homosexual
gaze ['geɪz] *vi* **gazed; gazing** : mirar (fijamente) — **~** *n* : mirada *f*
gazelle [gə'zɛl] *n* : gacela *f*
gazette [gə'zɛt] *n* : gaceta *f*
gear ['gɪr] *n* **1** EQUIPMENT : equipo *m* **2** POSSESSIONS : efectos *mpl* personales

3 : marcha f (de un vehículo) 4 or ~ wheel : rueda f dentada — ~ vt : orientar, adaptar — vi ~ up : prepararse — gearshift ['gɪr,ʃɪft] n : palanca f de cambio, palanca f de velocidades Lat

geese → goose

gelatin ['dʒɛlətən] n : gelatina f

gem ['dʒɛm] n : gema f, piedra f preciosa — gemstone ['dʒɛm,stoʊn] n : piedra f preciosa

gender ['dʒɛndər] n 1 SEX : sexo m 2 : género m (en la gramática)

gene ['dʒiːn] n : gen m, gene m

genealogy [,dʒiːniˈɑlədʒi, ,dʒɛ-, -ˈæ-] n, pl -gies : genealogía f

general ['dʒɛnrəl, 'dʒɛnə-] adj : general — ~ n 1 : general mf (militar) 2 in ~ : en general, por lo general — generalize ['dʒɛnrəˌlaɪz, 'dʒɛnərə-] v -ized; -izing : generalizar — generally ['dʒɛnrəli, 'dʒɛnərə-] adv : generalmente, en general — general practitioner n : médico m, -ca f de cabecera

generate ['dʒɛnəˌreɪt] vt -ated; -ating : generar — generation [,dʒɛnəˈreɪʃən] n : generación f — generator ['dʒɛnəˌreɪtər] n : generador m

generous ['dʒɛnərəs] adj 1 : generoso 2 AMPLE : abundante — generosity [,dʒɛnəˈrɑsəti] n, pl -ties : generosidad f

genetic [dʒəˈnɛtɪk] adj : genético — genetics [dʒəˈnɛtɪks] n : genética f

genial ['dʒiːniəl] adj : afable, simpático

genital ['dʒɛnətəl] adj : genital — genitals ['dʒɛnətəlz] npl : genitales mpl

genius ['dʒiːnjəs] n : genio m

genocide ['dʒɛnəˌsaɪd] n : genocidio m

genteel [dʒɛnˈtiːl] adj : refinado

gentle ['dʒɛntəl] adj -tler; -tlest 1 MILD : suave, dulce 2 LIGHT : ligero 3 a ~ hint : una indirecta discreta — gentleman ['dʒɛntəlmən] n, pl -men [-mən, -mɛn] 1 MAN : caballero m, señor m 2 a perfect ~ : un perfecto caballero — gentleness ['dʒɛntəlnəs] n : delicadeza f, ternura f

genuine ['dʒɛnjuwən] adj 1 AUTHENTIC : verdadero, auténtico 2 SINCERE : sincero

geography [dʒiˈɑgrəfi] n, pl -phies : geografía f — geographic [,dʒiːəˈgræfɪk] or geographical [-fɪkəl] adj : geográfico

geology [dʒiˈɑlədʒi] n : geología f — geologic [,dʒiːəˈlɑdʒɪk] or geological [-dʒɪkəl] adj : geológico

geometry [dʒiˈɑmətri] n, pl -tries : geometría f — geometric [,dʒiːəˈmɛtrɪk] or geometrical [-trɪkəl] adj : geométrico

geranium [dʒəˈreɪniəm] n : geranio m

geriatric [,dʒɛriˈætrɪk] adj : geriátrico — geriatrics [,dʒɛriˈætrɪks] n : geriatría f

germ ['dʒərm] n 1 : germen m 2 MICROBE : microbio m

German ['dʒərmən] n : alemán m — ~ n : alemán m (idioma)

germinate ['dʒərməˌneɪt] v -nated; -nating vi : germinar — vt : hacer germinar

gestation [dʒɛˈsteɪʃən] n : gestación f

gesture ['dʒɛstʃər] n : gesto m — ~ vi -tured; -turing 1 : hacer gestos 2 ~ to : hacer señas a

get ['gɛt] v got ['gɑt]; got or gotten ['gɑtən]; getting vt 1 OBTAIN : conseguir, obtener 2 RECEIVE : recibir 3 EARN : ganar 4 FETCH : traer 5 CATCH : coger, agarrar Lat 6 UNDERSTAND : entender 7 PREPARE : preparar 8 ~ one's hair cut : cortarse el pelo 9 ~ s.o. to do sth : lograr que uno haga algo 10 have got : tener 11 have got to : tener que — vi 1 BECOME : ponerse, hacerse 2 GO, MOVE : ir 3 PROGRESS : avanzar 4 ~ ahead : progresar 5 ~ at MEAN : querer decir 6 ~ away : escaparse 7 ~ away with : salir impune de 8 ~ back at : desquitarse con 9 ~ by : arreglárselas 10 ~ home : llegar a casa 11 ~ out : salir 12 ~ over : reponerse de, consolarse de 13 ~ together : reunirse 14 ~ up : levantarse — getaway ['gɛtəˌweɪ] n : fuga f, huida f — get-together n : reunión f

geyser ['gaɪzər] n : géiser m

ghastly ['gæstli] adj -lier; -est : horrible, espantoso

ghetto ['gɛtoʊ] n, pl -tos or -toes : gueto m

ghost ['goʊst] n : fantasma m, espectro m — ghostly ['goʊstli] adv : fantasmal

giant ['dʒaɪənt] n : gigante m, -ta f — ~ adj : gigantesco

gibberish ['dʒɪbərɪʃ] n : galimatías m, jerigonza f

gibe ['dʒaɪb] vi gibed; gibing ~ at : mofarse de — ~ n : pulla f, mofa f

giblets ['dʒɪbləts] npl : menudillos mpl

giddy ['gɪdi] adj -dier; -est : mareado, vertiginoso — giddiness ['gɪdinəs] n : vértigo m

gift ['gɪft] n 1 PRESENT : regalo m 2 TALENT : don m — gifted ['gɪftəd] adj : talentoso, de talento

gigantic [dʒaɪˈgæntɪk] adj : gigantesco

giggle ['gɪgəl] vi -gled; -gling : reírse tontamente — ~ n : risa f tonta

gild ['gɪld] vt **gilded** ['gɪldəd] or **gilt** ['gɪlt]; **gilding** : dorar

gill ['gɪl] n : agalla f, branquia f

gilt ['gɪlt] adj : dorado

gimmick ['gɪmɪk] n : truco m, ardid m

gin ['dʒɪn] n : ginebra f

ginger ['dʒɪndʒər] n : jengibre m — **ginger ale** n : refresco m de jengibre — **gingerbread** ['dʒɪndʒər,brɛd] n : pan m de jengibre — **gingerly** ['dʒɪndʒərli] adv : con cuidado, cautelosamente

giraffe [dʒəˈræf] n : jirafa f

girder ['gərdər] n : viga f

girdle ['gərdəl] n CORSET : faja f

girl ['gərl] n 1 : niña f, muchacha f, chica f — **girlfriend** ['gərl,frɛnd] n : novia f, amiga f

girth ['gərθ] n : circunferencia f

gist ['dʒɪst] n **get the ~ of** : comprender lo esencial de

give ['gɪv] v **gave** ['geɪv]; **given** ['gɪvən]; **giving** vt 1 : dar 2 INDICATE : señalar 3 PRESENT : presentar 4 **~ away** : regalar 5 **~ back** : devolver 6 **~ out** : repartir 7 **~ up smoking** : dejar de fumar — vi 1 YIELD : ceder 2 COLLAPSE : romperse 3 **~ out** : agotarse 4 **~ up** : rendirse — **given** ['gɪvən] adj 1 SPECIFIED : determinado 2 INCLINED : dado, inclinado — **given name** : nombre m de pila

glacier ['gleɪʃər] n : glaciar m

glad ['glæd] adj **gladder; gladdest** 1 : alegre, contento 2 **be ~** : alegrarse 3 **~ to meet you!** : ¡mucho gusto! — **gladden** ['glædən] vt : alegrar — **gladly** ['glædli] adv : con mucho gusto — **gladness** ['glædnəs] n : alegría f, gozo m

glade ['gleɪd] n : claro m

glamor or **glamour** ['glæmər] n : atractivo m, encanto m — **glamorous** ['glæmərəs] adj : atractivo

glance ['glæns] vi **glanced; glancing** 1 **~ at** : mirar, dar un vistazo a 2 **~ off** : rebotar en — **~** n : mirada f, vistazo m

gland ['glænd] n : glándula f

glare ['glær] vi **glared; glaring** 1 : brillar, relumbrar 2 **~ at** : lanzar una mirada feroz a — **~** n 1 : luz f deslumbrante 2 STARE : mirada f feroz — **glaring** ['glærɪŋ] adj 1 BRIGHT : deslumbrante 2 FLAGRANT : flagrante

glass ['glæs] n 1 : vidrio m, cristal m 2 **~ of milk** : un vaso de leche 3 **~es** npl SPECTACLES : anteojos mpl, lentes fpl — **~** adj : de vidrio — **glassware** ['glæs,wær] n : cristalería f — **glassy** ['glæsi] adj **glassier; -est** 1 : vítreo 2 **~ eyes** : ojos mpl vidriosos

glaze ['gleɪz] vt **glazed; glazing** 1 : poner vidrios a (una ventana, etc.) 2 : vidriar (cerámica) 3 ICE : glasear — **~** n 1 : vidriado m, barniz m (de cerámica) 2 ICING : glaseado m

gleam ['glim] n 1 : destello m 2 a **~ of hope** : un rayo de esperanza — **~** vi : destellar, relucir

glee ['gli:] n : alegría f — **gleeful** ['gli:fəl] adj : lleno de alegría

glib ['glɪb] adj **glibber; glibbest** 1 : de mucha labia 2 a **~ reply** : una respuesta simplista — **glibly** ['glɪbli] adv : con mucha labia

glide ['glaɪd] vi **glided; gliding** 1 : deslizarse (en una superficie), planear (en el aire) — **glider** ['glaɪdər] n : planeador m

glimmer ['glɪmər] vi : brillar con luz trémula — **~** n 1 : luz f trémula, luz f tenue

glimpse ['glɪmps] vt **glimpsed; glimpsing** : vislumbrar — **~** n : vislumbre f

glint ['glɪnt] vi : destellar — **~** n : destello m

glisten ['glɪsən] vi : brillar

glitter ['glɪtər] vi : relucir, brillar

gloat ['gloːt] vi **~ over** : regodearse con

globe ['gloːb] n : globo m — **global** ['gloːbəl] adj : global, mundial

gloom ['glum] n 1 DARKNESS : oscuridad f 2 SADNESS : tristeza f — **gloomy** ['glumi] adj **gloomier; -est** 1 DARK : sombrío, tenebroso 2 DISMAL : deprimente, lúgubre 3 PESSIMISTIC : pesimista

glory ['glori] n, pl **-ries** : gloria f — **glorify** ['glorə,faɪ] vt **-fied; -fying** : glorificar — **glorious** ['gloriəs] adj : glorioso, esplendído

gloss ['glɒs, 'glɑs] n : lustre m, brillo m — **~** vt **~ over** : minimizar (la importancia de algo)

glossary ['glɒsəri, 'glɑ-] n, pl **-ries** : glosario m

glossy ['glɒsi, 'glɑ-] adj **glossier; -est** : lustroso, brillante

glove ['glʌv] n : guante m

glow ['gloː] vi 1 : brillar, resplandecer 2 **~ with health** : rebosar de salud — **~** n : resplandor m, brillo m

glue ['glu:] n : pegamento m, cola f — **~** vt **glued; gluing** or **glueing** : pegar

glum ['glʌm] adj **glummer; glummest** : sombrío, triste

glut ['glʌt] n : superabundancia f, exceso m

glutton ['glʌtən] n : glotón m, -tona f — **gluttonous** ['glʌtənəs] adj : glotón — **gluttony** ['glʌtəni] n, pl **-tonies** : glotonería f

gnarled ['nɑrld] adj : nudoso

gnash ['næʃ] vt ~ **one's teeth** : hacer rechinar los dientes

gnat ['næt] n : jején m

gnaw ['nɔ] vt : roer

go ['goː] v **went** ['wɛnt], **gone** ['gɔn, 'gɑn]; **going; goes** ['goːz] vi 1 : ir 2 LEAVE : irse, salir 3 EXTEND : ir, extenderse 4 SELL : venderse 5 FUNCTION : funcionar, marchar 6 DISAPPEAR : desaparecer 7 ~ **back on one's word** : faltar a su palabra 8 ~ **crazy** : volverse loco 9 ~ **for** LIKE : gustar 10 ~ **off** EXPLODE : estallar 11 ~ **with** MATCH : armonizar con 12 ~ **without** : pasar sin — v aux **be going to** : ir a — ~ n, pl **goes** 1 **be on the** ~ : no parar 2 **have a** ~ **at** : intentar

goad ['goːd] vt : aguijonear (un animal), incitar (a una persona)

goal ['goːl] n 1 AIM : meta m, objetivo m 2 : gol m (en deportes) — **goalkeeper** ['goːlˌkiːpər] or **goalie** ['goːli] n : portero m, -ra f; arquero m, -ra f

goat ['goːt] n : cabra f

goatee [goːˈtiː] n : barbita f de chivo

gobble ['gɑbəl] vt **-bled; -bling** or ~ **up** : engullir

goblet ['gɑblət] n : copa f

goblin ['gɑblən] n : duende m

god ['gɑd, 'gɔd] n 1 : dios m 2 **God** : Dios m — **goddess** ['gɑdəs, 'gɔ-] n : diosa f — **godchild** ['gɑdˌtʃaɪld, 'gɔd-] n, pl **-children** : ahijado m, -da f — **godfather** ['gɑdˌfɑðər, 'gɔd-] n : padrino m — **godmother** ['gɑdˌmʌðər, 'gɔd-] n : madrina f — **godparents** ['gɑdˌpærənt, 'gɔd-] npl : padrinos mpl — **godsend** ['gɑdˌsɛnd, 'gɔd-] n : bendición f (del cielo)

goes → **go**

goggles ['gɑgəlz] npl : gafas fpl (protectoras), anteojos mpl

goings-on [goːɪŋˈzɑn, -ˈɔn] npl : sucesos mpl

gold ['goːld] n : oro m — **golden** ['goːldən] adj 1 : (hecho) de oro 2 : dorado, de color oro — **goldfish** ['goːldˌfiʃ] n : pez m de colores — **goldsmith** ['goːldˌsmiθ] n : orfebre mf

golf ['gɑlf, 'gɔlf] n : golf m — ~ vi : jugar (al) golf — **golf ball** n : pelota f de golf — **golf course** n : campo m de golf — **golfer** ['gɑlfər, 'gɔl-] n : golfista mf

gone ['gɔn] adj 1 : ido, pasado 2 DEAD : muerto 3 LOST : desaparecido

good ['gʊd] adj **better** ['bɛʈər], **best** ['bɛst] 1 : bueno 2 KIND : amable 3 ~ **afternoon (evening)** : buenas tardes 4 **be** ~ **at** : tener facilidad para 5 **feel** ~ : sentirse bien 6 ~ **for a cold** : beneficioso para los resfriados 7 **have a** ~ **time** : divertirse 8 ~ **morning** : buenos días 9 ~ **night** : buenas noches — ~ n 1 : bien m 2 GOODNESS : bondad f 3 ~**s** npl PROPERTY : bienes mpl, mercancías fpl 4 ~**s** npl WARES : mercancías fpl, mercaderías fpl 5 **for** ~ : para siempre — adv : bien — **good-bye** or **good-by** [gʊdˈbaɪ] n : adiós m — **Good Friday** n : Viernes m Santo — **good-looking** ['gʊdˈlʊkɪŋ] adj : bello, guapo — **goodness** ['gʊdnəs] n 1 : bondad f 2 **thank** ~ ! : ¡gracias a Dios!, ¡menos mal! — **goodwill** [ˌgʊdˈwɪl] n : buena voluntad f — **goody** ['gʊdi] n, pl **goodies** : golosina f

gooey ['guːi] adj **gooier; gooiest** : pegajoso

goof ['guːf] n : pifia f fam — ~ vi 1 or ~ **up** : cometer un error 2 ~ **around** : hacer tonterías

goose ['guːs] n, pl **geese** ['giːs] : ganso m, -sa f; oca f — **goose bumps** or **goose pimples** npl : carne f de gallina

gopher ['goːfər] n : taltuza f

gore[1] ['gor] n BLOOD : sangre f

gore[2] vt **gored; goring** : cornear

gorge ['gɔrdʒ] n RAVINE : cañon m — ~ vt **gorged; gorging** ~ **oneself** : hartarse

gorgeous ['gɔrdʒəs] adj : magnífico, espléndido

gorilla [gəˈrɪlə] n : gorila m

gory ['gori] adj **gorier; -est** : sangriento

gospel ['gɑspəl] n 1 : evangelio m 2 **the Gospel** : el Evangelio

gossip ['gɑsɪp] n 1 : chismoso m, -sa f (persona) 2 RUMOR : chisme m — ~ vi : chismear, contar chismes — **gossipy** ['gɑsɪpi] adj : chismoso

got → **get**

Gothic ['gɑθɪk] adj : gótico

gotten → **get**

gourmet ['gʊrˌmeɪ, gʊrˈmeɪ] n : gastrónomo m, -ma f

gout ['gaʊt] n : gota f

govern ['gʌvərn] v : gobernar — **governess** ['gʌvərnəs] n : institutriz f — **government** ['gʌvərnmənt] n : gobierno m — **governor** ['gʌvənər, 'gʌvərnər] n : gobernador m, -dora f

gown ['gaʊn] *n* **1** : vestido *m* **2** : toga *f* (de magistrados, etc.)

grab ['græb] *v* **grabbed; grabbing** *vt* : agarrar, arrebatar

grace ['greɪs] *n* **1** : gracia *f* **2 say ~** : bendecir la mesa — **~** *vt* **graced; gracing** **1** HONOR : honrar **2** ADORN : adornar — **graceful** ['greɪsfəl] *adj* : lleno de gracia, grácil — **gracious** ['greɪʃəs] *adj* : cortés, gentil

grade ['greɪd] *n* **1** QUALITY : calidad *f* **2** RANK : grado *m*, rango *m* (militar) **3** YEAR : grado *m*, año *m* (a la escuela) **4** MARK : nota *f* **5** SLOPE : cuesta *f* — **~** *vt* **graded; grading** **1** CLASSIFY : clasificar **2** MARK : calificar (exámenes, etc.) — **grade school → elementary school**

gradual ['grædʒʊəl] *adj* : gradual — **gradually** ['grædʒʊəli, 'grædʒəli] *adv* : gradualmente, poco a poco

graduate ['grædʒʊət] *n* : licenciado *m*, -da *f* (de la universidad), bachiller *mf* (de la escuela secundaria) — **~** ['grædʒʊeɪt] *v* **-ated; -ating** *vi* : graduarse, licenciarse — *vt* CALIBRATE : graduar — **graduation** [ˌgrædʒʊ-'eɪʃən] *n* : graduación *f*

graffiti [grəˈfiːt̬i, græ-] *npl* : graffiti *mpl*

graft ['græft] *n* : injerto *m* — **~** *vt* : injertar

grain ['greɪn] *n* **1** : grano *m* **2** CEREALS : cereales *mpl* **3** : veta *f*, vena *f* (de madera)

gram ['græm] *n* : gramo *m*

grammar ['græmər] *n* : gramática *f* — **grammar school → elementary school**

granite ['grænət] *n* : granito *m*

grant ['grænt] *vt* **1** : conceder **2** ADMIT : reconocer, admitir **3 take for granted** : dar (algo) por sentado — **~** *n* **1** SUBSIDY : subvención *f* **2** SCHOLARSHIP : beca *f*

grape ['greɪp] *n* : uva *f*

grapefruit ['greɪpˌfruːt] *n* : toronja *f*, pomelo *m*

grapevine ['greɪpˌvaɪn] *n* **1** : vid *f*, parra *f* **2 I heard it through the ~** : me lo dijo un pajarito *fam*

graph ['græf] *n* : gráfica *f*, gráfico *m* — **graphic** ['græfɪk] *adj* : gráfico

grapple ['græpəl] *vi* **-pled; -pling ~ with** : forcejear con (una persona), luchar con (un problema)

grasp ['græsp] *vt* **1** : agarrar **2** UNDERSTAND : comprender, captar — **~** *n* **1** : agarre *m* **2** UNDERSTANDING : comprensión *f* **3** REACH : alcance *m*

grass ['græs] *n* **1** : hierba *f* (planta) **2** LAWN : césped *m*, pasto *m* *Lat* — **grasshopper** ['græsˌhɑpər] *n* : saltamontes *m* — **grassy** ['græsi] *adj* **grassier; -est** : cubierto de hierba

grate¹ ['greɪt] *v* **grated; -ing** *vt* **1** : rallar (en cocina) **2 ~ one's teeth** : hacer rechinar los dientes — *vi* RASP : chirriar

grate² *n* GRATING : reja *f*, rejilla *f*

grateful ['greɪtfəl] *adj* : agradecido — **gratefully** ['greɪtfəli] *adv* : con agradecimiento — **gratefulness** ['greɪtfəlnəs] *n* : gratitud *f*, agradecimiento *m*

grater ['greɪt̬ər] *n* : rallador *m*

gratify ['græt̬əˌfaɪ] *vt* **-fied; -fying** **1** PLEASE : complacer **2** SATISFY : satisfacer

grating ['greɪt̬ɪŋ] *n* : reja *f*, rejilla *f*

gratitude ['græt̬əˌtuːd, -ˌtjuːd] *n* : gratitud *f*

gratuitous [grəˈtuːət̬əs] *adj* : gratuito

grave¹ ['greɪv] *n* : tumba *f*, sepultura *f*

grave² *adj* **graver; -est** : grave

gravel ['grævəl] *n* : grava *f*, gravilla *f*

gravestone ['greɪvˌstoʊn] *n* : lápida *f* — **graveyard** ['greɪvˌjɑrd] *n* : cementerio *m*

gravity ['grævət̬i] *n, pl* **-ties** : gravedad *f*

gravy ['greɪvi] *n, pl* **-vies** : salsa *f* (preparada con jugo de carne)

gray ['greɪ] *adj* **1** : gris **2 ~ hair** : pelo *m* canoso — *n* : gris *m* — *vi* or **turn ~** : encanecer, ponerse gris

graze¹ ['greɪz] *vi* **grazed; grazing** : pastar, pacer

graze² *vt* **1** TOUCH : rozar **2** SCRATCH : rasguñarse

grease ['griːs] *n* : grasa *f* — **~** ['griːs, 'griːz] *vt* **greased; greasing** : engrasar — **greasy** ['griːsi, -zi] *adj* **greasier; -est** **1** : grasiento **2** OILY : graso, grasoso

great ['greɪt] *adj* **1** : grande **2** FANTASTIC : estupendo, fabuloso — **great-grandchild** [ˌgreɪtˈgrændˌtʃaɪld] *n, pl*

-children [-ˌtʃɪldrən] : bisnieto *m*, -ta *f* — **great–grandfather** [ˌɡreɪtˈɡrænd-ˌfɑðər] *n* : bisabuelo *m* — **great-grandmother** [ˌɡreɪtˈɡrænd-ˌmʌðər] *n* : bisabuela *f* — **greatly** [ˈɡreɪtli] *adv* **1** MUCH : mucho **2** VERY : muy — **greatness** [ˈɡreɪtnəs] *n* : grandeza *f*

greed [ˈɡriːd] *n* **1** : codicia *f*, avaricia *f* **2** GLUTTONY : glotonería *f* — **greedily** [ˈɡriːdəli] *adv* : con avaricia — **greedy** [ˈɡriːdi] *adj* **greedier; -est 1** : codicioso, avaro **2** GLUTTONOUS : glotón

Greek [ˈɡriːk] *adj* : griego — ∼ *n* : griego *m* (idioma)

green [ˈɡriːn] *adj* **1** : verde **2** INEXPERIENCED : novato — ∼ *n* **1** : verde *m* (color) **2** ∼s *npl* : verduras *fpl* — **greenery** [ˈɡriːnəri] *n*, *pl* **-eries** : vegetación *f* — **greenhouse** [ˈɡriːnˌhaʊs] *n* : invernadero *m*

greet [ˈɡriːt] *vt* **1** : saludar **2** WELCOME : recibir — **greeting** [ˈɡriːtɪŋ] *n* **1** : saludo *m* **2** ∼s *npl* REGARDS : saludos *mpl*, recuerdos *mpl*

gregarious [ɡrɪˈɡæriəs] *adj* : sociable

grenade [ɡrəˈneɪd] *n* : granada *f*

grew → grow

grey → gray

greyhound [ˈɡreɪˌhaʊnd] *n* : galgo *m*

grid [ˈɡrɪd] *n* **1** GRATING : rejilla *f* **2** NETWORK : red *f* **3** : cuadriculado *m* (de un mapa)

griddle [ˈɡrɪdəl] *n* : plancha *f*

grief [ˈɡriːf] *n* : dolor *m*, pesar *m* — **grievance** [ˈɡriːvəns] *n* : queja *f* — **grieve** [ˈɡriːv] *v* **grieved; grieving** *vt* : entristecer — *vi* ∼ **for** : llorar (a), lamentar — **grievous** [ˈɡriːvəs] *adj* : grave, doloroso

grill [ˈɡrɪl] *vt* **1** : asar a la parrilla **2** INTERROGATE : interrogar — ∼ *n* **1** : parrilla *f* (para cocinar) — **grille** *or* **grill** [ˈɡrɪl] GRATING *n* : reja *f*, rejilla *f*

grim [ˈɡrɪm] *adj* **grimmer; grimmest 1** STERN : severo **2** GLOOMY : sombrío

grimace [ˈɡrɪməs, ɡrɪˈmeɪs] *n* : mueca *f* — ∼ *vi* **-maced; -macing** : hacer muecas

grime [ˈɡraɪm] *n* : mugre *f*, suciedad *f* — **grimy** [ˈɡraɪmi] *adj* **grimier; -est** : mugriento, sucio

grin [ˈɡrɪn] *vi* **grinned; grinning** : sonreír (abiertamente) — ∼ *n* : sonrisa *f* (abierta)

grind [ˈɡraɪnd] *v* **ground; grinding** *vt* **1** : moler (el café, etc.) **2** SHARPEN : afilar **3** ∼ **one's teeth** : rechinar los dientes — *vi* : rechinar — ∼ *n* **the daily** ∼ : la rutina diaria — **grinder** [ˈɡraɪndər] *n* : molinillo *m*

grip [ˈɡrɪp] *vt* **gripped; gripping** : agarrar, asir **2** INTEREST : captar el interés de — ∼ *n* **1** GRASP : agarre *m* **2** CONTROL : control *m*, dominio *m* **3** HANDLE : empuñadura *f* **4 come to** ∼s **with** : llegar a entender de

gripe [ˈɡraɪp] *vi* **griped; griping** : quejarse — ∼ *n* : queja *f*

grisly [ˈɡrɪzli] *adj* **-lier; -est** : espeluznante, horrible

gristle [ˈɡrɪsəl] *n* : cartílago *m*

grit [ˈɡrɪt] *n* **1** : arena *f*, grava *f* **2** GUTS : agallas *fpl fam* **3** ∼s *npl* : sémola *f* de maíz — ∼ *vt* **gritted; gritting** ∼ **one's teeth** : acorazarse

groan [ˈɡroːn] *vi* : gemir — ∼ *n* : gemido *m*

grocery [ˈɡroːsəri, -ʃəri] *n*, *pl* **-ceries 1** *or* ∼ **store** : tienda *f* de comestibles, tienda *f* de abarrotes *Lat* **2 groceries** *npl* : comestibles *mpl*, abarrotes *mpl Lat* — **grocer** [ˈɡroːsər] *n* : tendero *m*, -ra *f*

groggy [ˈɡrɑɡi] *adj* **-gier; -est** : atontado, grogui *fam*

groin [ˈɡrɔɪn] *n* : ingle *f*

groom [ˈɡruːm, ˈɡrʊm] *n* BRIDEGROOM : novio *m* — ∼ *vt* **1** : almohazar (un animal) **2** PREPARE : preparar

groove [ˈɡruːv] *n* : ranura *f*, surco *m*

grope [ˈɡroːp] *vi* **groped; groping 1** : andar a tientas **2** ∼ **for:** buscar a tientas

gross [ˈɡroːs] *adj* **1** SERIOUS : grave **2** OBESE : obeso **3** TOTAL : bruto **4** VULGAR : grosero, basto — ∼ *n* **1** *or* ∼ **income** : ingresos *mpl* brutos **2** *pl* ∼ : gruesa *f* (12 docenas) — **grossly** [ˈɡroːsli] *adv* **1** EXTREMELY : enormemente **2** CRUDELY : groseramente

grotesque [ɡroːˈtɛsk] *adj* : grotesco

grouch [ˈɡraʊtʃ] *n* : gruñón *m*, -ñona *f fam* — **grouchy** [ˈɡraʊtʃi] *adj* **grouchier; -est** : gruñón *fam*

ground¹ [ˈɡraʊnd] → **grind**

ground² *n* **1** : suelo *m*, tierra *f* **2** *or* ∼s LAND : terreno *m* **3** ∼s REASON : razón *f*, motivos *mpl* **4** ∼s DREGS : pozo *m* (de café) — ∼ *vt* **1** BASE : fundar, basar **2** : conectar a tierra (un aparato eléctrico) **3** : restringir (un avión o un piloto) a la tierra — **groundhog** [ˈɡraʊndˌhɔɡ] *n* : marmota *f* (de América) — **groundless** [ˈɡraʊndləs] *adj* : infundado — **groundwork** [ˈɡraʊndˌwərk] *n* : trabajo *m* preparatorio

group [ˈɡruːp] *n* : grupo *m* — ∼ *vt* : agrupar — *vi* or ∼ **together** : agruparse

grove [ˈɡroːv] *n* : arboleda *f*

grovel ['grɑvəl, 'grʌ-] vi -eled or -elled; -eling or -elling : arrastrarse, humillarse

grow ['groː] v grew ['gruː]; grown ['groːn]; growing 1 vi : crecer 2 INCREASE : aumentar 3 BECOME : volverse, ponerse 4 ~ dark : oscurecerse 5 ~ up : hacerse mayor — vt 1 CULTIVATE : cultivar 2 : dejarse crecer (el pelo, etc.) — grower ['groːər] n : cultivador m, -dora f

growl ['grɑʊl] vi : gruñir — ~ n : gruñido m

grown-up ['groːnˌəp] adj : mayor — ~ n : persona f mayor

growth ['groːθ] n 1 : crecimiento m 2 INCREASE : aumento m 3 DEVELOPMENT : desarrollo m 4 TUMOR : tumor m

grub ['grʌb] n 1 LARVA : larva f 2 FOOD : comida f

grubby ['grʌbi] adj grubbier; -est : mugriento, sucio

grudge ['grʌdʒ] vt grudged; grudging : dar de mala gana — ~ n : to hold a ~ : guardar rencor

grueling or gruelling ['gruːlɪŋ, 'gruːə-] adj : extenuante, agotador

gruesome ['gruːsəm] adj : horripilante

gruff ['grʌf] adj 1 BRUSQUE : brusco 2 HOARSE : bronco

grumble ['grʌmbəl] vi -bled; -bling : refunfuñar, rezongar

grumpy ['grʌmpi] adj grumpier; -est : malhumorado, gruñón fam

grunt ['grʌnt] vi : gruñir — ~ n : gruñido m

guarantee [ˌgærənˈtiː] n : garantía f — ~ vt -teed; -teeing : garantizar

guard ['gɑrd] n 1 : guardia f 2 PRECAUTION : protección f — ~ vt : proteger, vigilar — vi ~ against : protegerse contra — guardian ['gɑrdiən] n 1 : tutor m, -tora f (de niños) 2 PROTECTOR : guardián m, -diana f

guava ['gwɑvə] n : guayaba f

guerrilla or guerilla [gəˈrɪlə] n 1 : guerrillero m, -ra f 2 ~ warfare : guerra f de guerrillas

guess ['ges] vt 1 : adivinar 2 SUPPOSE : suponer, creer — vi ~ at : adivinar — ~ n : conjetura f, suposición f

guest ['gest] n 1 : invitado m, -da f 2 : huésped mf (a un hotel)

guide ['gɑɪd] n : guía mf (persona), guía f (libro, etc.) — ~ vt guided; guiding : guiar — guidance ['gɑɪdəns] n : orientación f — guidebook ['gɑɪdˌbʊk] n : guía f — guideline ['gɑɪdlɑɪn] n : pauta f, directriz f

guild ['gɪld] n : gremio m

guile ['gɑɪl] n : astucia f

guilt ['gɪlt] n : culpa f, culpabilidad f — guilty ['gɪlti] adj guiltier; -est : culpable

guinea pig ['gɪni-] n : conejillo m de Indias, cobaya f

guise ['gɑɪz] n : apariencia f

guitar [gəˈtɑr, gɪ-] n : guitarra f

gulf ['gʌlf] n 1 : golfo m 2 ABYSS : abismo m

gull ['gʌl] n : gaviota f

gullet ['gʌlət] n 1 THROAT : garganta f 2 ESOPHAGUS : esófago m

gullible ['gʌləbəl] adj : crédulo

gully ['gʌli] n, pl -lies : barranco m

gulp ['gʌlp] vt or ~ down : tragarse, engullir — vi : tragar saliva — ~ n : trago m

gum[1] ['gʌm] n : encía f (de la boca)

gum[2] n 1 : resina f (de plantas) 2 CHEWING GUM : goma f de mascar, chicle m

gumption ['gʌmpʃən] n : iniciativa f, agallas fpl fam

gun ['gʌn] n 1 FIREARM : arma f de fuego 2 or spray ~ : pistola f 3 → cannon, pistol, revolver, rifle — ~ vt gunned; gunning 1 or ~ down : matar a tiros, asesinar 2 ~ the engine : acelerar (el motor) — gunboat ['gʌnˌboːt] n : cañonero m — gunfire ['gʌnˌfɑɪr] n : disparos mpl — gunman ['gʌnmən] n, pl -men [-mən, -ˌmen] : pistolero m, gatillero m Lat — gunpowder ['gʌnˌpɑʊdər] n : pólvora f — gunshot ['gʌnˌʃɑt] n : disparo m, tiro m

gurgle ['gərgəl] vi -gled; -gling 1 : borbotar, gorgotear 2 : gorjear (dícese de un niño)

gush ['gʌʃ] vi 1 SPOUT : salir a chorros 2 ~ with praise : deshacerse en elogios

gust ['gʌst] n : ráfaga f

gusto ['gʌstoː] n, pl gustoes : entusiasmo m

gusty ['gʌsti] adj gustier; -est : racheado, ventoso

gut ['gʌt] n 1 : intestino m 2 ~s npl INNARDS : tripas fpl 3 ~s npl COURAGE : agallas fpl fam — ~ vt gutted; gutting 1 EVISCERATE : destripar (un pollo, etc.), limpiar (un pescado) 2 : destruir el interior de (un edificio)

gutter ['gʌtər] n : canaleta f (de un techo), cuneta f (de una calle)

guy ['gɑɪ] n : tipo m fam

guzzle ['gʌzəl] vt -zled; -zling : chupar fam, tragar

gym ['dʒɪm] or gymnasium [dʒɪmˈneɪziəm, -zəm] n, pl -siums or -sia [-ziə, -ʒə] : gimnasio m — gymnast

H

h ['eɪtʃ] *n*, *pl* **h's** *or* **hs** ['eɪtʃəz] : h *f*, octava letra del alfabeto inglés

habit ['hæbət] *n* **1** CUSTOM : hábito *m*, costumbre *f* **2** : hábito *m* (religioso)

habitat ['hæbɪˌtæt] *n* : hábitat *m*

habitual [hə'bɪtʃʊəl] *adj* **1** CUSTOMARY : habitual **2** INVETERATE : empedernido

hack¹ ['hæk] *n* **1** : caballo *m* de alquiler **2** *or* ~ **writer** : escritorzuelo *m*, -la *f*

hack² *vt* : cortar — *vi or* ~ **into** : piratear (un sistema informático)

hackneyed ['hæknɪd] *adj* : manido, trillado

hacksaw ['hækˌsɔ] *n* : sierra *f* para metales

had → **have**

haddock ['hædək] *ns & pl* : eglefino *m*

hadn't ['hædənt] (*contraction of* **had not**) → **have**

hag ['hæg] *n* : bruja *f*

haggard ['hægərd] *adj* : demacrado

haggle ['hægəl] *vi* **-gled; -gling** : regatear

hail¹ ['heɪl] *vt* **1** GREET : saludar **2** : llamar (un taxi)

hail² *n* : granizo *m* (en meteorología) — ~ *vi* : granizar — **hailstone** ['heɪlˌstoːn] *n* : piedra *f* de granizo

hair ['hær] *n* **1** : pelo *m*, cabello *m* **2** : vello *m* (en las piernas, etc.) — **hairbrush** ['hærˌbrʌʃ] *n* : cepillo *m* (para el pelo) — **haircut** ['hærˌkʌt] *n* **1** : corte *m* de pelo **2 get a** ~ : cortarse el pelo — **hairdo** ['hærˌduː] *n, pl* **-dos** : peinado *m* — **hairdresser** ['hærˌdrɛsər] *n* : peluquero *m*, -ra *f* — **hairless** ['hærləs] *adj* : sin pelo, calvo — **hairpin** ['hærˌpɪn] *n* : horquilla *f* — **hair-raising** ['hærˌreɪzɪŋ] *adj* : espeluznante — **hairstyle** ['hærˌstaɪl] *n* : peinado *m* — **hair spray** *n* : laca *f* (para el pelo) — **hairy** ['hæri] *adj* **hairier; -est** : peludo, velludo

hale ['heɪl] *adj* : saludable, robusto

half ['hæf, 'haf] *n, pl* **halves** ['hævz, 'havz] **1** : mitad *f* **2** *or* **halftime** : tiempo *m* (en deportes) **3 in** ~ : por la mitad — ~ *adv* **1** : medio **2** ~ **an hour** : una media hora — ~ *adj* : medio — **half brother** *n* : medio hermano *m*, hermanastro *m* — **halfhearted** ['hæfhɑrtəd] *adj* : sin ánimo, poco entusiasta — **half sister** *n* : media her-

mana *f*, hermanastra *f* — **halfway** ['hæfˌweɪ] *adv* : a medio camino — ~ *adj* : medio

halibut ['hæləbət] *ns & pl* : halibut *m*

hall ['hɔl] *n* **1** HALLWAY : corredor *m*, pasillo *m* **2** AUDITORIUM : sala *f* **3** LOBBY : vestíbulo *m* **4** DORMITORY : residencia *f* universitaria

hallmark ['hɔlˌmɑrk] *n* : sello *m* (distintivo)

Halloween [ˌhæləˈwiːn, ˌhɑ-] *n* : víspera *f* de Todos los Santos

hallucination [həˌluːsənˈeɪʃən] *n* : alucinación *f*

hallway ['hɔlˌweɪ] *n* **1** ENTRANCE : entrada *f* **2** CORRIDOR : corredor *m*, pasillo *m*

halo ['heɪˌloː] *n, pl* **-los** *or* **-loes** : aureola *f*, halo *m*

halt ['hɔlt] *n* **1 call a** ~ **to** : poner fin a **2 come to a** ~ : pararse — ~ *vi* : pararse — *vt* : parar

halve ['hæv, 'hav] *vt* **halved; halving 1** DIVIDE : partir por la mitad **2** REDUCE : reducir a la mitad — **halves** → **half**

ham ['hæm] *n* : jamón *m*

hamburger ['hæmˌbərgər] *or* **hamburg** [-ˌbərg] *n* **1** : carne *f* molida **2** *or* **patty** : hamburguesa *f*

hammer ['hæmər] *n* : martillo *m* — ~ *v* : martillar, martillear

hammock ['hæmək] *n* : hamaca *f*

hamper¹ ['hæmpər] *vt* : obstaculizar, dificultar

hamper² *n* : cesto *m*, canasta *f* (para ropa sucia)

hamster ['hæmpstər] *n* : hámster *m*

hand ['hænd] *n* **1** : mano *f* **2** : manecilla *f*, aguja *f* (de un reloj, etc.) **3** HANDWRITING : letra *f*, escritura *f* **4** WORKER : obrero *m*, -ra *f* **5 by** ~ : a mano **6 lend a** ~ : echar una mano **7 on** ~ : a mano, disponible **8 on the other** ~ : por otro lado — ~ *vt* **1** : pasar, dar **2** ~ **out** : distribuir **3** ~ **over** : entregar — **handbag** ['hændˌbæg] *n* : cartera *f Lat*, bolso *m Spain* — **handbook** ['hændˌbʊk] *n* : manual *m* — **handcuffs** ['hændˌkʌfs] *npl* : esposas *fpl* — **handful** ['hændfʊl] *n* : puñado *m* — **handgun** ['hændˌgʌn] *n* : pistola *f*, revólver *m*

handicap ['hændiˌkæp] *n* **1** : minusvalía *f*

(física) **2** : hándicap *m* (en deportes) — ~ *vt* **-capped; -capping 1** : asignar un hándicap a (en deportes) **2** HAMPER : obstaculizar — **handicapped** ['hændi,kæpt] *adj* : minusválido

handicrafts ['hændi,kræfts] *npl* : artesanía(s) *f(pl)*

handiwork ['hændi,wərk] *n* : trabajo *m* (manual)

handkerchief ['hæŋkərtʃəf, -,tʃiːf] *n*, *pl* **-chiefs** : pañuelo *m*

handle ['hændəl] *n* : asa *m* (de una taza, etc.), mango *m* (de un utensilio), pomo *m* (de una puerta), tirador *m* (de un cajón) — ~ *vt* **-dled; -dling 1** TOUCH : tocar **2** MANAGE : tratar, manejar — **handlebars** ['hændəl,bɑrz] *npl* : manillar *m*, manubrio *m* Lat

handmade ['hænd,meid] *adj* : hecho a mano

handout ['hænd,aʊt] *n* **1** ALMS : dádiva *f*, limosna *f* **2** LEAFLET : folleto *m*

handrail ['hænd,reil] *n* : pasamanos *m*

handshake ['hænd,ʃeik] *n* : apretón *m* de manos

handsome ['hæntsəm] *adj* **-somer; -est 1** ATTRACTIVE : apuesto, guapo **2** GENEROUS : generoso **3** SIZABLE : considerable

handwriting ['hænd,raitiŋ] *n* : letra *f*, escritura *f* — **handwritten** ['hænd,ritən] *adj* : escrito a mano

handy ['hændi] *adj* **handier; -est 1** NEARBY : a mano **2** USEFUL : práctico, útil **3** DEFT : habilidoso — **handyman** ['hændi,mən] *n*, *pl* **-men** [-mən, -,men] : hombre *m* habilidoso

hang ['hæŋ] *v* **hung** ['hʌŋ]; **hanging** *vt* **1** : colgar (*past tense often* **hanged**) EXECUTE : ahorcar **3** ~ **one's head** : bajar la cabeza — *vi* **1** : colgar, pender **2** : caer (dícese de la ropa, etc.) **3** ~ **up on s.o.** : colgar a algn — ~ *n* **1** DRAPE : caída *f* **2 get the ~ of** : agarrar la onda de

hangar ['hæŋər, 'hæŋgər] *n* : hangar *m*

hanger ['hæŋər] *n* : percha *f*, gancho *m* (para ropa) Lat

hangover ['hæŋo:vər] *n* : resaca *f*

hanker ['hæŋkər] *vi* ~ **for** : tener ansias de — **hankering** ['hæŋkəriŋ] *n* : ansia *f*, anhelo *m*

haphazard [hæp'hæzərd] *adj* : casual, fortuito

happen ['hæpən] *vi* **1** : pasar, suceder, ocurrir **2** ~ **to do sth** : hacer algo por casualidad **3 it so happens that...** : da la casualidad de que... — **happening** ['hæpəniŋ] *n* : suceso *m*, acontecimiento *m*

happy ['hæpi] *adj* **-pier; -est 1** : feliz **2 be ~** : alegrarse **3 be ~ with** : estar contento con **4 be ~ to do sth** : hacer algo con mucho gusto — **happily** ['hæpili] *adv* : alegremente — **happiness** ['hæpinəs] *n* : felicidad *f* — **happy-go-lucky** ['hæpigo:'lʌki] *adj* : despreocupado

harass [hə'ræs, 'hærəs] *vt* : acosar — **harassment** [hə'ræsmənt, 'hærəsmənt] *n* : acoso *m*

harbor *or Brit* **harbour** ['hɑrbər] *n* : puerto *m* — ~ *vt* **1** SHELTER : albergar **2 ~ a grudge against** : guardar rencor a

hard ['hɑrd] *adj* **1** : duro **2** DIFFICULT : difícil **3 be a ~ worker** : ser muy trabajador **4 ~ liquor** : bebidas *fpl* fuertes **5 ~ water** : agua *f* dura — ~ *adv* **1** FORCEFULLY : fuerte **2 work ~** : trabajar duro **3 take sth ~** : tomarse algo muy mal — **harden** ['hɑrdən] *vt* : endurecer — **hardheaded** ['hɑrd'hedəd] *adj* : testarudo, terco — **hard-hearted** ['hɑrd'hɑrtəd] *adj* : duro de corazón — **hardly** ['hɑrdli] *adv* **1** : apenas **2 ~ ever** : casi nunca — **hardness** ['hɑrdnəs] *n* **1** : dureza *f* **2** DIFFICULTY : dificultad *f* — **hardship** ['hɑrd,ʃip] *n* : dificultad *f* — **hardware** ['hɑrd,wær] *n* **1** : ferretería *f* **2** : hardware *m* (en informática) — **hardworking** ['hɑrd'wərkiŋ] *adj* : trabajador

hardy ['hɑrdi] *adj* **-dier; -est** : fuerte (dícese de personas), resistente (dícese de las plantas)

hare ['hær] *n*, *pl* **hare** *or* **hares** : liebre *f*

harm ['hɑrm] *n* : daño *m* — ~ *vt* : hacer daño a (una persona), dañar (una cosa), perjudicar (la reputación de algn, etc.) — **harmful** ['hɑrmfəl] *adj* : perjudicial — **harmless** ['hɑrmləs] *adj* : inofensivo

harmonica [hɑr'mɑnikə] *n* : armónica *f*

harmony ['hɑrməni] *n*, *pl* **-nies** : armonía *f* — **harmonious** [hɑr'mo:niəs] *adj* : armonioso — **harmonize** ['hɑrmə,naiz] *v* **-nized; -nizing** : armonizar

harness ['hɑrnəs] *n* : arnés *m* — ~ *vt* **1** : enjaezar **2** UTILIZE : utilizar

harp ['hɑrp] *n* : arpa *m* — ~ *vi* ~ **on** : insistir sobre

harpoon [hɑr'puːn] *n* : arpón *m*

harpsichord ['hɑrpsi,kɔrd] *n* : clavicémbalo *m*

harsh ['hɑrʃ] *adj* **1** ROUGH : áspero **2** SEVERE : duro, severo **3** : fuerte (dícese de una luz), discordante (dícese de sonidos) — **harshness** ['hɑrʃnəs] *n* : severidad *f*

harvest ['hɑrvəst] n : cosecha f — v : cosechar

has → have

hash ['hæʃ] vt 1 CHOP : picar 2 ~ over DISCUSS : discutir — ~ n : picadillo m (comida)

hasn't ['hæzənt] (contraction of has not) → has

hassle ['hæsəl] n : problemas mpl, lío m — ~ vt -sled; -sling : fastidiar

haste ['heɪst] n 1 : prisa f, apuro m 2 make ~ : darse prisa, apurarse Lat — **hasten** ['heɪsən] vt : acelerar — vi : apresurarse, apurarse Lat — **hasty** ['heɪsti] adj **hastier; -est** : precipitado

hat ['hæt] n : sombrero m

hatch ['hætʃ] n 1 : escotilla f — ~ vt 1 : empollar (huevos) 2 CONCOCT : tramar — vi : salir del cascarón

hatchet ['hætʃət] n : hacha f

hate ['heɪt] n : odio m — ~ vt **hated; hating** : odiar, aborrecer — **hateful** ['heɪtfəl] adj : odioso, aborrecible — **hatred** ['heɪtrəd] n : odio m

haughty ['hɔti] adj **-tier; -est** : altanero, altivo

haul ['hɔl] vt : arrastrar, jalar Lat — ~ n 1 CATCH : redada f (de peces) 2 LOOT : botín m 3 a long ~ : un trayecto largo

haunch ['hɔntʃ] n : cadera f (de una persona), anca f (de un animal)

haunt ['hɔnt] vt 1 : frecuentar, rondar 2 TROUBLE : inquietar — ~ n : sitio m predilecto — **haunted** ['hɔntəd] adj : embrujado

have ['hæv, in sense 3 as an auxiliary verb usu hæf] v **had** ['hæd]; **having; has** ['hæz, in sense 3 as an auxiliary verb usu hæs] vt 1 : tener 2 CONSUME : comer, tomar 3 ALLOW : permitir 4 : dar (una fiesta, etc.), convocar (una reunión) 5 ~ one's hair cut : cortarse el pelo 6 ~ sth done : mandar hacer algo — v aux 1 : haber 2 ~ just done sth : acabar de hacer algo 4 you've finished, haven't you? : has terminado, ¿no?

haven ['heɪvən] n : refugio m

havoc ['hævək] n : estragos mpl

hawk[1] ['hɔk] n : halcón m

hawk[2] vt : pregonar (mercancías)

hay ['heɪ] n : heno m — **hay fever** n : fiebre f del heno — **haystack** ['heɪˌstæk] n : almiar m — **haywire** ['heɪˌwaɪr] adj **go ~** : estropearse

hazard ['hæzərd] n : peligro m, riesgo m — ~ vt : arriesgar, aventurar — **hazardous** ['hæzərdəs] adj : arriesgado, peligroso

haze ['heɪz] n : bruma f, neblina f

hazel ['heɪzəl] n : color m avellana — **hazelnut** ['heɪzəlˌnʌt] n : avellana f

hazy ['heɪzi] adj **hazier; -est** : nebuloso

he ['hi:] pron : él

head ['hɛd] n 1 : cabeza f 2 END, TOP : cabeza f (de un clavo, etc.), cabecera f (de una mesa) 3 LEADER : jefe m, -fa f 4 be out of one's ~ : estar loco 5 come to a ~ : llegar a un punto crítico 6 ~s or tails : cara o cruz 7 per ~ : por cabeza — ~ adj MAIN : principal — ~ vi : encabezar — vi : dirigirse — **headache** ['hɛdˌeɪk] n : dolor m de cabeza — **headband** ['hɛdˌbænd] n : cinta f del pelo — **headdress** ['hɛdˌdrɛs] n : tocado m — **headfirst** ['hɛdˈfərst] adv : de cabeza — **heading** ['hɛdɪŋ] n : encabezamiento m, título m — **headland** ['hɛdlənd, -ˌlænd] n : cabo m — **headlight** ['hɛdˌlaɪt] n : faro m — **headline** ['hɛdˌlaɪn] n : titular m — **headlong** ['hɛdˌlɔŋ] adv 1 HEADFIRST : de cabeza 2 HASTILY : precipitadamente — **headmaster** ['hɛdˌmæstər] n : director m — **headmistress** ['hɛdˌmɪstrəs, -ˈmɪs-] n : directora f — **head-on** ['hɛdˌɑn, -ˈɔn] adv & adj : de frente — **headphones** ['hɛdˌfoʊnz] npl : auriculares mpl, audífonos mpl Lat — **headquarters** ['hɛdˌkwɔrtərz] ns & pl : oficina f central (de una compañía), cuartel m general (de los militares) — **head start** n : ventaja f — **headstrong** ['hɛdˌstrɔŋ] adj : testarudo, obstinado — **headwaiter** ['hɛdˈweɪtər] n : jefe m, -fa f de comedor — **headway** ['hɛdˌweɪ] n 1 : progreso m 2 make ~ : avanzar — **heady** ['hɛdi] adj **headier; -est** : embriagador

heal ['hi:l] vt : curar — vi : cicatrizar

health ['hɛlθ] n : salud f — **healthy** ['hɛlθi] adj **healthier; -est** : sano, saludable

heap ['hi:p] n : montón m — ~ vt : amontonar

hear ['hɪr] v **heard** ['hərd]; **hearing** vt : oír — vi 1 : oír 2 ~ about : enterarse de 3 ~ from : tener noticias de — **hearing** ['hɪrɪŋ] n 1 : oído m 2 : vista f (en un tribunal) — **hearing aid** n : audífono m — **hearsay** ['hɪrˌseɪ] n : rumores mpl

hearse ['hərs] n : coche m fúnebre

heart ['hɑrt] n 1 : corazón m 2 at ~ : en el fondo 3 by ~ : de memoria 4 lose ~ : descorazonarse 5 take ~ : animarse — **heartache** ['hɑrtˌeɪk] n : pena f, dolor m — **heart attack** n : infarto m, ataque m al corazón — **heartbeat**

['hɑrt,biːt] n : latido m (del corazón) — **heartbreak** ['hɑrt,breɪk] n : congoja f, angustia f — **heartbroken** ['hɑrt,broːkən] adj : desconsolado — **heartburn** ['hɑrt,bərn] n : acidez f estomacal

hearth ['hɑrθ] n : hogar m

heartily ['hɑrt̬əli] adv : de buena gana

heartless ['hɑrtləs] adj : de mal corazón, cruel

hearty ['hɑrt̬i] adj **heartier; -est 1** : cordial, caluroso **2** : abundante (dícese de una comida)

heat ['hiːt] vt : calentar — vi or ~ **up** : calentarse — ~ n **1** : calor m **2** HEATING : calefacción f — **heated** ['hiːt̬əd] adj : acalorado — **heater** ['hiːt̬ər] n : calentador m

heath ['hiːθ] n : brezal m

heathen ['hiːðən] adj : pagano — ~ n, pl **-thens** or **-then** : pagano m, -na f

heather ['hɛðər] n : brezo m

heave ['hiːv] v **heaved** or **hove** ['hoːv]; **heaving** vt **1** LIFT : levantar (con esfuerzo) **2** HURL : lanzar, tirar **3** ~ **a sigh** : suspirar — vi or ~ **up** : levantarse

heaven ['hɛvən] n : cielo m — **heavenly** ['hɛvənli] adj **1** : celestial **2** ~ **body** : cuerpo m celeste

heavy ['hɛvi] adj **heavier; -est 1** : pesado **2** INTENSE : fuerte **3** ~ **sigh** : suspiro m profundo **4** ~ **traffic** : tráfico m denso — **heavily** ['hɛvəli] adv **1** : pesadamente **2** EXCESSIVELY : mucho — **heaviness** ['hɛvinəs] n : peso m, pesadez f — **heavyweight** ['hɛvi,weɪt] n : peso m pesado

Hebrew ['hiːbruː] adj : hebreo — ~ n : hebreo m (idioma)

heckle ['hɛkəl] vt **-led; -ling** : interrumpir (a un orador) con preguntas molestas

hectic ['hɛktɪk] adj : agitado, ajetreado

he'd ['hiːd] (contraction of **he had** or **he would**) → **have, would**

hedge ['hɛdʒ] n : seto m vivo — ~ v **hedged; hedging** vt ~ **one's bets** : cubrirse — vi : contestar con evasivas — **hedgehog** ['hɛdʒ,hɔg, -hɑg] n : erizo m

heed ['hiːd] vt : prestar atención a, hacer caso de — ~ n **take** ~ : tener cuidado — **heedless** ['hiːdləs] adj **be** ~ **of** : hacer caso omiso de

heel ['hiːl] n : talón m (del pie), tacón m (de un zapato)

hefty ['hɛfti] adj **heftier; -est** : robusto y pesado

heifer ['hɛfər] n : novilla f

height ['haɪt] n **1** : estatura f (de una persona), altura f (de un objeto) **2** PEAK : cumbre f **3 the** ~ **of folly** : el colmo de la locura **4 what is your** ~ ? : ¿cuánto mides? — **heighten** ['haɪt̬ən] vt : aumentar, intensificar

heir ['ær] n : heredero m, -ra f — **heiress** ['ærəs] n : heredera f — **heirloom** ['ær,luːm] n : reliquia f de familia

held → **hold**

helicopter ['hɛlə,kɑptər] n : helicóptero m

hell ['hɛl] n : infierno m — **hellish** ['hɛlɪʃ] adj : infernal

he'll ['hiːl, 'hɪl] (contraction of **he shall** or **he will**) → **shall, will**

hello [hə'loː, hɛ-] interj : ¡hola!

helm ['hɛlm] n : timón m

helmet ['hɛlmət] n : casco m

help ['hɛlp] vt **1** : ayudar **2** ~ **oneself** : servirse **3 I can't** ~ **it** : no lo puedo remediar — ~ n **1** : ayuda f **2** STAFF : personal m **3 help!** : ¡socorro!, ¡auxilio! — **helper** ['hɛlpər] n : ayudante mf — **helpful** ['hɛlpfəl] adj **1** OBLIGING : servicial, amable **2** USEFUL : útil — **helping** ['hɛlpɪŋ] n : porción f — **helpless** ['hɛlpləs] adj **1** POWERLESS : incapaz **2** DEFENSELESS : indefenso

hem ['hɛm] n : dobladillo m — ~ vt **hemmed; hemming** ~ **in** : encerrar

hemisphere ['hɛmə,sfɪr] n : hemisferio m

hemorrhage ['hɛmərɪdʒ] n : hemorragia f

hemorrhoids ['hɛmə,rɔɪdz, 'hɛm,rɔɪdz] npl : hemorroides fpl, almorranas fpl

hemp ['hɛmp] n : cáñamo m

hen ['hɛn] n : gallina f

hence ['hɛns] adv **1** : de aquí, de ahí **2** THEREFORE : por lo tanto **3 ten years** ~ : de aquí a 10 años — **henceforth** ['hɛns,forθ, ,hɛns'-] adv : de ahora en adelante

henpeck ['hɛn,pɛk] vt : dominar (al marido)

hepatitis [,hɛpə'taɪt̬əs] n, pl **-titides** [-'tɪt̬ə,diːz] : hepatitis f

her ['hər] adj : su, sus — ~ ['hər, ər] pron **1** (used as direct object) : la **2** (used as indirect object) : le, se **3** (used as object of a preposition) : ella

herald ['hɛrəld] vt : anunciar

herb ['ərb, 'hərb] n : hierba f

herd ['hərd] n : manada f — ~ vt : conducir (en manada) — vi or ~ **together** : reunir

here ['hɪr] adv **1** : aquí, acá **2** ~ **you are!** : ¡toma! — **hereabouts** ['hɪrə,baʊts] or **hereabout** [-,baʊt] adv : por aquí (cerca) — **hereafter** [hɪr'æftər] *adv* : en el futuro — **hereby** [hɪr'baɪ] *adv* : por este medio

hereditary [hə'redə,teri] *adj* : hereditario — **heredity** [hə'redəti] *n* : herencia *f*

heresy ['herəsi] *n*, *pl* **-sies** : herejía *f*

herewith [hɪr'wɪθ] *adv* : adjunto

heritage ['herə,tɪdʒ] *n* **1** : herencia *f* **2** : patrimonio *m* (nacional)

hermit ['hərmət] *n* : ermitaño *m*, -ña *f*

hernia ['hərniə] *n*, *pl* **-nias** *or* **-niae** [-ni:,i:, -ni,aɪ] : hernia *f*

hero ['hi:,ro:, 'hɪr,o:] *n*, *pl* **-roes** : héroe *m* — **heroic** [hɪ'ro:ɪk] *adj* : heroico — **heroine** ['heroən] *n* : heroína *f* — **heroism** ['hero,ɪzəm] *n* : heroísmo *m*

heron ['herən] *n* : garza *f*

herring ['herɪŋ] *n*, *pl* **-ring** *or* **-rings** : arenque *m*

hers ['hərz] *pron* **1** : (el) suyo, (la) suya, (los) suyos, (las) suyas **2 some friends of ~** : unos amigos suyos, unos amigos de ella — **herself** [hər'self] *pron* **1** (*used reflexively*) : se **2** (*used emphatically*) : ella misma

he's ['hiz] (*contraction of* **he** *is or* **he has**) → **be, have**

hesitant ['hezətənt] *adj* : titubeante, vacilante — **hesitate** ['hezə,teɪt] *vi* **-tated; -tating** : vacilar, titubear — **hesitation** [,hezə'teɪʃən] *n* : vacilación *f*, titubeo *m*

heterosexual [,hetəro'sekʃʊəl] *adj* : heterosexual — **~** *n* : heterosexual *mf*

hexagon ['heksə,gɑn] *n* : hexágono *m*

hey ['heɪ] *interj* : ¡eh!, ¡oye!

heyday ['heɪ,deɪ] *n* : auge *m*, apogeo *m*

hi ['haɪ] *interj* : ¡hola!

hibernate ['haɪbər,neɪt] *vi* **-nated; -nating** : hibernar

hiccup ['hɪkəp] *n* **have the ~s** : tener hipo — **~** *vi* **-cuped; -cuping** : tener hipo

hide¹ ['haɪd] *n* : piel *f*, cuero *m*

hide² *v* **hid** ['hɪd]; **hidden** ['hɪdən] *or* **hid; hiding** *vt* **1** : esconder **2** : ocultar (motivos, etc.) — *vi* : esconderse — **hide-and-seek** ['haɪdænd,si:k] *n* : escondite *m*, escondidas *fpl Lat*

hideous ['hɪdiəs] *adj* : horrible, espantoso

hideout ['haɪd,aʊt] *n* : escondite *m*, guarida *f*

hierarchy ['haɪə,rɑrki] *n*, *pl* **-chies** : jerarquía *f* — **hierarchical** [,haɪə'rɑrkɪkəl] *adj* : jerárquico

high ['haɪ] *adj* **1** : alto **2** INTOXICATED : borracho, drogado **3 a ~ voice** : una voz aguda **4 it's two feet ~** : tiene dos pies de alto **5 ~ winds** : fuertes vientos *mpl* — **~** *adv* : alto — **~** *n*

: récord *m*, máximo *m* — **higher** ['haɪər] *adj* **1** : superior **2 ~ education** : enseñanza *f* superior — **highlight** ['haɪ,laɪt] *n* : punto *m* culminante — **highly** ['haɪli] *adv* **1** VERY : muy, sumamente **2 think ~ of** : tener en mucho a — **Highness** ['haɪnəs] *n* **His/Her ~** : Su Alteza *f* — **high school** *n* : escuela *f* superior, escuela *f* secundaria — **high-strung** [,haɪ'strʌŋ] *adj* : nervioso, excitable — **highway** ['haɪ,weɪ] *n* : carretera *f*

hijack ['haɪ,dʒæk] *vt* : secuestrar — **hijacker** ['haɪ,dʒækər] *n* : secuestrador *m*, -dora *f* — **hijacking** *n* : secuestro *m*

hike ['haɪk] *v* **hiked; hiking** *vi* : ir de caminata — *vt* *or* **~ up** RAISE : subir — **~** *n* : caminata *f*, excursión *f* — **hiker** ['haɪkər] *n* : excursionista *mf*

hilarious [hɪ'leriəs, haɪ-] *adj* : muy divertido — **hilarity** [hɪ'lerəti, haɪ-] *n* : hilaridad *f*

hill ['hɪl] *n* **1** : colina *f*, cerro *m* **2** SLOPE : cuesta *f* — **hillside** ['hɪl,saɪd] *n* : ladera *f*, cuesta *f* — **hilly** ['hɪli] *adj* **hillier; -est** : accidentado

hilt ['hɪlt] *n* : puño *m*

him ['hɪm, əm] *pron* **1** (*used as direct object*) : lo **2** (*used as indirect object*) : le, se **3** (*used as object of a preposition*) : él — **himself** [hɪm'self] *pron* **1** (*used reflexively*) : se **2** (*used emphatically*) : él mismo

hind ['haɪnd] *adj* : trasero, posterior

hinder ['hɪndər] *vt* : dificultar, estorbar — **hindrance** ['hɪndrəns] *n* : obstáculo *m*

hindsight ['haɪnd,saɪt] *n* **in ~** : en retrospectiva

Hindu ['hɪn,du:] *adj* : hindú

hinge ['hɪndʒ] *n* : bisagra *f*, gozne *m* — **~** *vi* **hinged; hinging ~ on** : depender de

hint ['hɪnt] *n* **1** : indirecta *f* **2** TIP : consejo *m* **3** TRACE : asomo *m*, toque *m* — **~** *vt* : dar a entender — *vi* **~ at** : insinuar

hip ['hɪp] *n* : cadera *f*

hippopotamus [,hɪpə'pɑtəməs] *n*, *pl* **-muses** *or* **-mi** [-maɪ] : hipopótamo *m*

hire ['haɪr] *n* **1** : alquiler *m* **2 for ~** : se alquila — **~** *vt* **hired; hiring 1** EMPLOY : contratar, emplear **2** RENT : alquilar

his ['hɪz, ɪz] *adj* : su, sus, de él — **~** *pron* **1** : (el) suyo, (la) suya, (los) suyos, (las) suyas **2 some friends of ~** : unos amigos suyos, unos amigos de él

Hispanic [hɪˈspænɪk] *adj* : hispano, hispánico

hiss [ˈhɪs] *vi* : silbar — *n* : silbido *m*

history [ˈhɪstəri] *n, pl* **-ries 1** : historia *f* **2** BACKGROUND : historial *m* — **historian** [hɪˈstɔriən] *n* : historiador *m*, -dora *f* — **historic** [hɪˈstɔrɪk] *or* **historical** [-ɪkəl] *adj* : histórico

hit [ˈhɪt] *v* **hit; hitting** *vt* **1** : golpear, pegar **2** : dar (con un proyectil) **3** AFFECT : afectar **4** REACH : alcanzar **5 the car ~ a tree** : el coche chocó contra un árbol — *vi* : pegar — *n* **1** : golpe *m* **2** SUCCESS : éxito *m*

hitch [ˈhɪtʃ] *vt* ATTACH : enganchar **2** *or* **~ up** RAISE : subirse **3** — *n* PROBLEM : problema *m* — **hitchhike** [ˈhɪtʃˌhaɪk] *vi* **-hiked; -hiking** : hacer autostop — **hitchhiker** [ˈhɪtʃˌhaɪkər] *n* : autostopista *mf*

hitherto [ˈhɪðərˌtuː, ˌhɪðər-] *adv* : hasta ahora

HIV [ˌeɪtʃˌaɪˈviː] *n* : VIH *m*, virus *m* del sida

hive [ˈhaɪv] *n* : colmena *f*

hives [ˈhaɪvz] *ns & pl* : urticaria *f*

hoard [ˈhɔrd] *n* : tesoro *m* (de dinero), reserva *f* (de provisiones) — *vt* : acumular

hoarse [ˈhɔrs] *adj* **hoarser; -est** : ronco

hoax [ˈhoːks] *n* : engaño *m*

hobble [ˈhɑbəl] *vi* **-bled; -bling** : cojear

hobby [ˈhɑbi] *n, pl* **-bies** : pasatiempo *m*

hobo [ˈhoːboː] *n, pl* **-boes** : vagabundo *m*, -da *f*

hockey [ˈhɑki] *n* : hockey *m*

hoe [ˈhoː] *n* : azada *f* — *vt* **hoed; hoeing** : azadonar

hog [ˈhɔg, ˈhɑg] *n* : cerdo *m* — *vt* **hogged; hogging** MONOPOLIZE : acaparar

hoist [ˈhɔɪst] *vt* **1** : izar (una vela, etc.) **2** LIFT : levantar — *n* : grúa *f*

hold[1] [ˈhoːld] *n* : bodega *f* (en un barco o un avión)

hold[2] *v* **held** [ˈhɛld]; **holding** *vt* **1** GRIP : agarrar **2** POSSESS : tener **3** SUPPORT : sostener **4** : celebrar (una reunión, etc.), mantener (una conversación) **5** CONTAIN : contener **6** CONSIDER : considerar **7** *or* **~ back** : detener **8** **~ hands** : agarrarse de la mano **9** **~ up** ROB : atracar **10** **~ up** DELAY : retrasar — *vi* **1** LAST : durar, continuar **2** APPLY : ser válido — *n* **1** GRIP : agarre *m* **2** **get ~ of** : conseguir **3 get ~ of oneself** : controlarse — **holder** [ˈhoːldər] *n* : tenedor *m*, -dora *f* — **holdup** [ˈhoːld-

ˌʌp] *n* **1** ROBBERY : atraco *m* **2** DELAY : retraso *m*, demora *f*

hole [ˈhoːl] *n* : agujero *m*, hoyo *m*

holiday [ˈhɑləˌdeɪ] *n* **1** : día *m* feriado, fiesta *f* **2** *Brit* VACATION : vacaciones *fpl*

holiness [ˈhoːlinəs] *n* : santidad *f*

holler [ˈhɑlər] *vi* : gritar — *n* : grito *m*

hollow [ˈhɑloː] *n* **1** : hueco *m* **2** VALLEY : hondonada *f* — *adj* **hollow-; -est 1** : hueco **2** FALSE : vacío, falso — *vt* *or* **~ out** : ahuecar

holly [ˈhɑli] *n, pl* **-lies** : acebo *m*

holocaust [ˈhɑləˌkɔst, ˈhoː-, ˈhɔ-] *n* : holocausto *m*

holster [ˈhoːlstər] *n* : pistolera *f*

holy [ˈhoːli] *adj* **-lier; -est** : santo, sagrado

homage [ˈɑmɪdʒ, ˈhɑ-] *n* : homenaje *m*

home [ˈhoːm] *n* **1** : casa *f* **2** FAMILY : hogar *m* **3** INSTITUTION : residencia *f*, asilo *m* **4 at ~ and abroad** : dentro y fuera del país — *adv* **go ~** : ir a casa — **homeland** [ˈhoːmˌlænd] *n* : patria *f* — **homeless** [ˈhoːmləs] *adj* : sin hogar — **homely** [ˈhoːmli] *adj* **-lier; -est 1** DOMESTIC : casero **2** UGLY : feo — **homemade** [ˈhoːmˈmeɪd] *adj* : casero, hecho en casa — **homemaker** [ˈhoːmˌmeɪkər] *n* : ama *f* de casa — **home run** *n* : jonrón *m* — **homesick** [ˈhoːmˌsɪk] *adj* **be ~** : echar de menos a la familia — **homeward** [ˈhoːmwərd] *adj* : de vuelta, de regreso — **homework** [ˈhoːmˌwərk] *n* : tarea *f*, deberes *mpl* — **homey** [ˈhoːmi] *adj* **homier; -est** : hogareño, acogedor

homicide [ˈhɑməˌsaɪd, ˈhoː-] *n* : homicidio *m*

homogeneous [ˌhoːməˈdʒiːniəs, -njəs] *adj* : homogéneo

homosexual [ˌhoːməˈsɛkʃuəl] *adj* : homosexual — *n* : homosexual *mf* — **homosexuality** [ˌhoːməˌsɛkʃuˈælət̬i] *n* : homosexualidad *f*

honest [ˈɑnəst] *adj* **1** : honrado **2** FRANK : sincero — **honestly** *adv* : sinceramente — **honesty** [ˈɑnəsti] *n, pl* **-ties** : honradez *f*

honey [ˈhʌni] *n, pl* **-eys** : miel *f* — **honeycomb** [ˈhʌniˌkoːm] *n* : panal *m* — **honeymoon** [ˈhʌniˌmuːn] *n* : luna *f* de miel

honk [ˈhʌŋk, ˈhɔŋk] *vi* : tocar la bocina — *n* : bocinazo *m*

honor *or Brit* **honour** [ˈɑnər] *n* : honor *m* — *vt* **1** : honrar **2** : aceptar (un cheque, etc.), cumplir con (una promesa) — **honorable** *or Brit* **honourable** [ˈɑnərəbəl] *adj* : honorable, honroso — **honorary** [ˈɑnəˌreri] *adj* : honorario

hood ['hʊd] *n* **1** : capucha *f* (de un abrigo, etc.) **2** : capó *m* (de un automóvil)

hoodlum ['hʊdləm, 'huːd-] *n* : matón *m*

hoodwink ['hʊd,wɪŋk] *vt* : engañar

hoof ['hʊf, 'huːf] *n, pl* **hooves** ['hʊvz, 'huːvz] *or* **hoofs** : pezuña *f* (de una vaca, etc.), casco *m* (de un caballo)

hook ['hʊk] *n* **1** : gancho *m* **2** *or* ～ **and eye** : corchete *m* **3** → **fishhook 4 off the** ～ : descolgado — ～ *vt* : enganchar — *vi* : engancharse

hoop ['huːp] *n* : aro *m*

hooray [hʊ'reɪ] → **hurrah**

hoot ['huːt] *vi* **1** : ulular (dícese de un búho) **2** ～ **with laughter** : reírse a carcajadas — ～ *n* **1** : ululato *m* (de un búho) **2 I don't give a** ～ : me importa un comino

hop[1] ['hɑp] *vi* **hopped; hopping** : saltar a la pata coja — ～ *n* : salto *m* a la pata coja

hop[2] *n* ～**s** : lúpulo *m* (planta)

hope ['hoʊp] *v* **hoped; hoping** *vi* : esperar — *vt* : esperar que — ～ *n* : esperanza *f* — **hopeful** ['hoʊpfəl] *adj* : esperanzado — **hopefully** *adv* **1** : con esperanza **2 it will help** : se espera que ayude — **hopeless** ['hoʊpləs] *adj* : desesperado — **hopelessly** ['hoʊpləsli] *adv* : desesperadamente

horde ['hɔrd] *n* : horda *f*

horizon [hə'raɪzən] *n* : horizonte *m* — **horizontal** [,hɔrə'zɑntəl] *adj* : horizontal

hormone ['hɔr,moʊn] *n* : hormona *f*

horn ['hɔrn] *n* **1** : cuerno *m* (de un animal) **2** : trompa *f* (instrumento musical) **3** : bocina *f*, claxon *m* (de un vehículo)

hornet ['hɔrnət] *n* : avispón *m*

horoscope ['hɔrə,skoʊp] *n* : horóscopo *m*

horror ['hɔrər] *n* : horror *m* — **horrendous** [hɔ'rendəs] *adj* : horrendo — **horrible** ['hɔrəbəl] *adj* : horrible — **horrid** ['hɔrɪd] *adj* : horroroso, horrible — **horrify** ['hɔrə,faɪ] *vt* **-fied; -fying** : horrorizar

hors d'oeuvre [ɔr'dərv] *n, pl* **hors d'oeuvres** [-'dərvz] : entremés *m*

horse ['hɔrs] *n* : caballo *m* — **horseback** ['hɔrs,bæk] *n* **on** ～ : a caballo — **horsefly** ['hɔrs,flaɪ] *n, pl* **-flies** : tábano *m* — **horseman** ['hɔrsmən] *n, pl* **-men** [-mən, -,men] : jinete *m* — **horseplay** ['hɔrs,pleɪ] *n* : payasadas *fpl* — **horsepower** ['hɔrs,paʊər] *n* : caballo *m* de fuerza — **horseradish** ['hɔrs,rædɪʃ] *n* : rábano *m* picante — **horseshoe** ['hɔrs,ʃuː] *n* : herradura *f* — **horse-**

woman ['hɔrs,wʊmən] *n, pl* **-women** [-,wɪmən] : jinete *f*

horticulture ['hɔrtə,kʌltʃər] *n* : horticultura *f*

hose ['hoʊz] *n* **1** *pl* **hoses** : manguera *f*, manga *f* **2 hose** *pl* STOCKINGS : medias *fpl* — ～ *vt* **hosed; hosing** : regar (con manguera) — **hosiery** ['hoʊʒəri, 'hoʊzə-] *n* : calcetería *f*

hospice ['hɑspəs] *n* : hospicio *m*

hospital ['hɑs,pɪtəl] *n* : hospital *m* — **hospitable** [hɑ'spɪtəbəl, 'hɑspɪ-] *adj* : hospitalario — **hospitality** [,hɑspə-'tæləʈi] *n, pl* **-ties** : hospitalidad *f* — **hospitalize** ['hɑspɪtə,laɪz] *vt* **-ized; -izing** : hospitalizar

host[1] ['hoʊst] *n* **a** ～ **of** : toda una serie de

host[2] *n* **1** : anfitrión *m*, -triona *f* **2** : presentador *m*, -dora *f* (de televisión, etc.) — ～ *vt* : presentar (un programa de televisión, etc.)

host[3] *n* EUCHARIST : hostia *f*, Eucaristía *f*

hostage ['hɑstɪdʒ] *n* : rehén *m*

hostel ['hɑstəl] *n or* **youth** ～ : albergue *m* juvenil

hostess ['hoʊstɪs] *n* : anfitriona *f*

hostile ['hɑstəl, -,taɪl] *adj* : hostil — **hostility** [hɑ'stɪləʈi] *n, pl* **-ties** : hostilidad *f*

hot ['hɑt] *adj* **hotter; hottest 1** : caliente, caluroso (dícese del tiempo), cálido (dícese del clima) **2** SPICY : picante **3 feel** ～ : tener calor **4 have a** ～ **temper** : tener mal genio **5** ～ **news** : noticias *fpl* de última hora **6 it's** ～ **today** : hace calor

hot dog *n* : perro *m* caliente

hotel [hoʊ'tɛl] *n* : hotel *m*

hotheaded ['hɑt'hedəd] *adj* : exaltado

hound ['haʊnd] *n* : perro *m* (de caza) — ～ *vt* : acosar, perseguir

hour ['aʊər] *n* : hora *f* — **hourglass** ['aʊər,glæs] *n* : reloj *m* de arena — **hourly** ['aʊərli] *adv & adj* : cada hora, por hora

house ['haʊs] *n, pl* **houses** ['haʊzəz, -səz] **1** : casa *f* **2** : cámara *f* (del gobierno) **3** *publishing* ～ : editorial *f* — ～ ['haʊz] *vt* **housed; housing** : albergar — **houseboat** ['haʊs,boʊt] *n* : casa *f* flotante — **housefly** ['haʊs,flaɪ] *n, pl* **-flies** : mosca *f* común — **household** ['haʊs,hoʊld] *adj* **1** : doméstico **2** ～ **name** : nombre *m* muy conocido — ～ *n* : casa *f* — **housekeeper** ['haʊs,kiːpər] *n* : ama *f* de llaves — **housekeeping** ['haʊs,kiːpɪŋ] *n* : gobierno *m* de la casa — **housewarming** ['haʊs,wɔrmɪŋ] *n* : fiesta *f* de estreno de una casa — **housewife** ['haʊs,waɪf] n, pl **-wives** : ama f de casa — **housework** ['haʊs,wərk] n : faenas fpl domésticas — **housing** ['haʊzɪŋ] n 1 : viviendas fpl 2 CASE : caja f protectora

hove → **heave**

hovel ['hʌvəl, 'hɑ-] n : casucha f, tugurio m

hover ['hʌvər, 'hɑ-] vi 1 : cernerse 2 ~ **about** : rondar

how ['haʊ] adv 1 : cómo 2 (used in exclamations) : qué 3 ~ **are you?** : ¿cómo está Ud.? 4 ~ **come** : por qué 5 ~ **much** : cuánto 6 ~ **do you do?** : mucho gusto 7 ~ **old are you?** : ¿cuántos años tienes? — ~ conj : como

however [haʊˈevər] conj 1 : de cualquier manera que 2 ~ **you like** : como quieras — ~ adv 1 NEVERTHELESS : sin embargo, no obstante 2 ~ **difficult it is** : por difícil que sea 3 ~ **hard I try** : por más que me esfuerce

howl ['haʊl] vi : aullar — ~ n : aullido m

hub ['hʌb] n 1 CENTER : centro m 2 : cubo m (de una rueda)

hubbub ['hʌ,bʌb] n : alboroto m, jaleo m

hubcap ['hʌb,kæp] n : tapacubos m

huddle ['hʌdəl] vi **-dled; -dling** or ~ **together** : apiñarse

hue ['hju] n : color m, tono m

huff ['hʌf] n **be in a** ~ : estar enojado

hug ['hʌg] vt **hugged; hugging** : abrazar — ~ n : abrazo m

huge ['hjuːdʒ] adj **huger; hugest** : inmenso, enorme

hull ['hʌl] n : casco m (de un barco, etc.)

hum ['hʌm] v **hummed; humming** vi 1 : tararear 2 BUZZ : zumbar — vt : tararear (una melodía) — ~ n : zumbido m

human ['hjuːmən, 'juː-] adj : humano — ~ n : (ser m) humano m — **humane** [hjuːˈmeɪn, juː-] adj : humano, humanitario — **humanitarian** [hjuːˌmænəˈteriən, juː-] adj : humanitario — **humanity** [hjuːˈmænəti, juː-] n, pl **-ties** : humanidad f

humble ['hʌmbəl] vt **-bled; -bling** 1 : humillar 2 ~ **oneself** : humillarse — ~ adj **-bler; -blest** : humilde

humdrum ['hʌm,drʌm] adj : monótono, rutinario

humid ['hjuːməd, 'juː-] adj : húmedo — **humidity** [hjuːˈmɪdəti, juː-] n, pl **-ties** : humedad f

humiliate [hjuːˈmɪliˌeɪt, juː-] vt **-ated; -ating** : humillar — **humiliating** [hjuːˈmɪliˌeɪtɪŋ, juː-] adj : humillante — **humiliation** [hjuːˌmɪliˈeɪʃən, juː-] n : humillación f — **humility** [hjuːˈmɪləti, juː-] n : humildad f

humor or Brit **humour** ['hjuːmər, 'juː-] n : humor m — ~ vt : seguir la corriente a, complacer — **humorous** ['hjuːmərəs, 'juː-] adj : humorístico, cómico

hump ['hʌmp] n : joroba f

hunch ['hʌntʃ] vi or ~ **over** : encorvarse — ~ n : presentimiento m

hundred ['hʌndrəd] adj : cien, ciento — ~ n, pl **-dreds** or **-dred** : ciento m — **hundredth** ['hʌndrədθ] adj : centésimo — ~ n 1 : centésimo m, -ma f (en una serie) 2 : centésimo m (en matemáticas)

hung → **hang**

Hungarian [hʌŋˈgæriən] adj : húngaro — ~ n : húngaro m (idioma)

hunger ['hʌŋgər] n : hambre m — ~ vi 1 : tener hambre 2 ~ **for** : ansiar, anhelar — **hungry** ['hʌŋgri] adj **-grier; -est** 1 : hambriento 2 **be** ~ : tener hambre

hunk ['hʌŋk] n : pedazo m (grande)

hunt ['hʌnt] vt 1 : cazar 2 ~ **for** : buscar — ~ n 1 : caza f, cacería f 2 SEARCH : búsqueda f, busca f — **hunter** ['hʌntər] n : cazador m, -dora f — **hunting** ['hʌntɪŋ] n 1 : caza f 2 **go** ~ : ir de caza

hurdle ['hərdəl] n 1 : valla f (en deportes) 2 OBSTACLE : obstáculo m

hurl ['hərl] vt : lanzar, arrojar

hurrah [hʊˈrɑ, -ˈrɔ] interj : ¡hurra!

hurricane ['hərəˌkeɪn] n : huracán m

hurry ['həri] n : prisa f, apuro f Lat — v **-ried; -rying** vi : darse prisa, apurarse Lat — vt : apurar, dar prisa a — **hurried** ['hərid] adj : apresurado — **hurriedly** ['həridli] adv : apresuradamente, de prisa

hurt ['hərt] v **hurt; hurting** vt 1 INJURE : hacer daño a, lastimar 2 OFFEND : ofender, herir — vi 1 : doler 2 **my foot** ~**s** : me duele el pie — ~ n 1 INJURY : herida f 2 DISTRESS : dolor m, pena f — **hurtful** ['hərtfəl] adj : hiriente, doloroso

hurtle ['hərtəl] vi **-tled; -tling** : lanzarse, precipitarse

husband ['hʌzbənd] n : esposo m, marido m

hush ['hʌʃ] vt : hacer callar, acallar — ~ n : silencio m

husk ['hʌsk] n : cáscara f

husky[1] ['hʌski] adj **-kier; -est** HOARSE : ronco

husky[2] n, pl **-kies** : perro m, -rra f esquimal

husky³ *adj* BURLY : fornido
hustle ['həsəl] *v* **-tled; -tling** *vt* : dar prisa a, apurar *Lat* — *vi* : darse prisa, apurarse *Lat* — **~** *n* — **and bustle** : ajetreo m, bullicio m
hut ['hʌt] *n* : cabaña f
hutch ['hʌt∫] *n* **or rabbit ~** : conejera f
hyacinth ['haɪəˌsɪnθ] *n* : jacinto m
hybrid ['haɪbrɪd] *n* : híbrido m — **~** *adj* : híbrido
hydrant ['haɪdrənt] *n* **or fire ~** : boca f de incendios
hydraulic [haɪˈdrɔlɪk] *adj* : hidráulico
hydroelectric [ˌhaɪdroˈlektrɪk] *adj* : hidroeléctrico
hydrogen ['haɪdrədʒən] *n* : hidrógeno m
hyena [haɪˈiːnə] *n* : hiena f
hygiene ['haɪdʒiːn] *n* : higiene f — **hygienic** [haɪdʒˈenɪk, -dʒiː-; ˌhaɪdʒiˈenɪk] *adj* : higiénico
hymn ['hɪm] *n* : himno m

hyperactive [ˌhaɪpərˈæktɪv] *adj* : hiperactivo
hyphen ['haɪfən] *n* : guión m
hypnosis [hɪpˈnoːsɪs] *n, pl* **-noses** [-ˌsiːz] : hipnosis f — **hypnotic** [hɪpˈnɑtɪk] *adj* : hipnótico — **hypnotism** ['hɪpnəˌtɪzəm] *n* : hipnotismo m — **hypnotize** ['hɪpnəˌtaɪz] *vt* **-tized; -tizing** : hipnotizar
hypochondriac [ˌhaɪpəˈkɑndriˌæk] *n* : hipocondríaco m, -ca f
hypocrisy [hɪpˈɑkrəsi] *n, pl* **-sies** : hipocresía f — **hypocrite** ['hɪpəˌkrɪt] *n* : hipócrita mf — **hypocritical** [ˌhɪpəˈkrɪtɪkəl] *adj* : hipócrita
hypothesis [haɪˈpɑθəsɪs] *n, pl* **-eses** [-ˌsiːz] : hipótesis f — **hypothetical** [ˌhaɪpəˈθetɪkəl] *adj* : hipotético
hysteria [hɪsˈteriə, -ˈtɪr-] *n* : histeria f, histerismo m — **hysterical** [hɪsˈterɪkəl] *adj* : histérico

I

i ['aɪ] *n, pl* **i's** *or* **is** ['aɪz] : i f, novena letra del alfabeto inglés
I ['aɪ] *pron* : yo
ice ['aɪs] *n* : hielo m — **~** *v* **iced; icing** *vt* **1** FREEZE : congelar **2** CHILL : enfriar **3** : bañar (pasteles, etc.) — *vi* **or ~ up** : helarse, congelarse — **iceberg** ['aɪsˌbərg] *n* : iceberg m — **icebox** ['aɪsˌbɑks] → **refrigerator** — **ice-cold** ['aɪsˈkoːld] *adj* : helado — **ice cream** *n* : helado m — **ice cube** *n* : cubito m de hielo — **ice-skate** ['aɪsˌskeɪt] *vi* **-skated; -skating** : patinar — **ice skate** *n* : patín m de cuchilla — **icicle** ['aɪsɪkəl] *n* : carámbano m — **icing** ['aɪsɪŋ] *n* : baño m
icon ['aɪˌkɑn, -kən] *n* : icono m
icy ['aɪsi] *adj* **icier; -est 1** : cubierto de hielo (dícese de pavimento, etc.) **2** FREEZING : helado
I'd ['aɪd] (*contraction of* **I should** *or* **I would**) → **should, would**
idea [aɪˈdiːə] *n* : idea f
ideal [aɪˈdiːəl] *adj* : ideal — **~** *n* : ideal m — **idealist** [aɪˈdiːəlɪst] *n* : idealista mf — **idealistic** [aɪˌdiːəˈlɪstɪk] *adj* : idealista — **idealize** [aɪˈdiːəˌlaɪz] *vt* **-ized; -izing** : idealizar
identity [aɪˈdentəti] *n, pl* **-ties** : identidad f — **identical** [aɪˈdentɪkəl] *adj* : idéntico — **identify** [aɪˈdentəˌfaɪ] *v* **-fied; -fying** *vt* : identificar — *vi* — **with** : identificarse con — **identifica-**

tion [aɪˌdentəfɪˈkeɪ∫ən] *n* **1** : identificación f **2 ~ card** : carnet m, carné m
ideology [aɪdiˈɑlədʒi, ˌɪ-] *n, pl* **-gies** : ideología f — **ideological** [ˌaɪdiəˈlɑdʒɪkəl, ˌɪ-] *adj* : ideológico
idiocy ['ɪdiəsi] *n, pl* **-cies** : idiotez f
idiom ['ɪdiəm] *n* EXPRESSION : modismo m — **idiomatic** [ˌɪdiəˈmætɪk] *adj* : idiomático
idiosyncrasy [ˌɪdioˈsɪŋkrəsi] *n, pl* **-sies** : idiosincrasia f
idiot ['ɪdiət] *n* : idiota mf — **idiotic** [ˌɪdiˈɑtɪk] *adj* : idiota
idle ['aɪdəl] *adj* **idler; idlest 1** LAZY : haragán, holgazán **2** INACTIVE : parado (dícese de una máquina) **3** UNEMPLOYED : desocupado **4** VAIN : frívolo, vano **5 out of ~ curiosity** : por pura curiosidad — **~** *v* **idled; idling** *vi* : andar al ralentí (dícese de un motor) — *vt* **~ away the hours** : pasar el rato — **idleness** ['aɪdəlnəs] *n* : ociosidad f
idol ['aɪdəl] *n* : ídolo m — **idolize** ['aɪdəˌlaɪz] *vt* **-ized; -izing** : idolatrar
idyllic [aɪˈdɪlɪk] *adj* : idílico
if ['ɪf] *conj* **1** : si **2** THOUGH : aunque, si bien **3 ~ so** : si es así
igloo ['ɪgluː] *n, pl* **-loos** : iglú m
ignite [ɪgˈnaɪt] *v* **-nited; -niting** *vt* : encender — *vi* : encenderse — **ignition** [ɪgˈnɪ∫ən] *n* **1** : ignición f **2 ~ switch** : encendido m

ignore [ɪgˈnor] vt **-nored; -noring** : ignorar, no hacer caso de — **ignorance** [ˈɪgnərənts] n : ignorancia f — **ignorant** [ˈɪgnərənt] adj **1** : ignorante **2 be ~ of** : desconocer, ignorar

ilk [ˈɪlk] n : tipo m, clase f

ill [ˈɪl] adj **worse** [ˈwərs]; **worst** [ˈwərst] **1** SICK : enfermo **2** BAD : malo — adv **worse; worst** : mal — **ill-advised** [ˌɪlædˈvaɪzd, -əd-] adj : imprudente — **ill at ease** : incómodo

I'll [ˈaɪl] (contraction of **I shall** or **I will**) → **shall, will**

illegal [ɪˈliːgəl] adj : ilegal

illegible [ɪˈlɛdʒəbəl] adj : ilegible

illegitimate [ˌɪlɪˈdʒɪtəmət] adj : ilegítimo — **illegitimacy** [ˌɪlɪˈdʒɪtəməsi] n : ilegitimidad f

illicit [ɪˈlɪsət] adj : ilícito

illiterate [ɪˈlɪtərət] adj : analfabeto — **illiteracy** [ɪˈlɪtərəsi] n, pl **-cies** : analfabetismo m

ill-mannered [ˌɪlˈmænərd] adj : descortés, maleducado

ill-natured [ˌɪlˈneɪtʃərd] adj : de mal genio

illness [ˈɪlnəs] n : enfermedad f

illogical [ɪˈlɑdʒɪkəl] adj : ilógico

ill-treat [ˌɪlˈtriːt] vt : maltratar

illuminate [ɪˈluːmənˌeɪt] vt **-nated; -nating** : iluminar — **illumination** [ɪˌluːməˈneɪʃən] n : iluminación f

illusion [ɪˈluːʒən] n : ilusión f — **illusory** [ɪˈluːsəri, -zəri] adj : ilusorio

illustrate [ˈɪləsˌtreɪt] v **-trated; -trating** : ilustrar — **illustration** [ˌɪləˈstreɪʃən] n **1** : ilustración f **2** EXAMPLE : ejemplo m — **illustrative** [ɪˈlʌstrətɪv, ˈɪləˌstreɪtɪv] adj : ilustrativo

illustrious [ɪˈlʌstriəs] adj : ilustre, glorioso

ill will n : animadversión f, mala voluntad f

I'm [ˈaɪm] (contraction of **I am**) → **be**

image [ˈɪmɪdʒ] n : imagen f — **imaginary** [ɪˈmædʒəˌneri] adj : imaginario — **imagination** [ɪˌmædʒəˈneɪʃən] n : imaginación f — **imaginative** [ɪˈmædʒəˌnətɪv, -nəˌtɪv] adj : imaginativo — **imagine** [ɪˈmædʒən] vt **-ined; -ining** : imaginar(se)

imbalance [ɪmˈbæləns] n : desequilibrio m

imbecile [ˈɪmbəsəl, -ˌsɪl] n : imbécil mf

imbue [ɪmˈbjuː] vt **-bued; -buing** : imbuir

imitation [ˌɪməˈteɪʃən] n : imitación f — **~** adj : de imitación, artificial — **imitate** [ˈɪməˌteɪt] vt **-tated; -tating** : imitar, remedar — **imitator** [ˈɪməˌteɪtər] n : imitador m, -dora f

immaculate [ɪˈmækjələt] adj : inmaculado

immaterial [ˌɪməˈtɪriəl] adj : irrelevante, sin importancia

immature [ˌɪməˈtʃur, -ˈtjur, -ˈtur] adj : inmaduro — **immaturity** [ˌɪməˈtʃurəti, -ˈtjur-, -ˈtur-] n, pl **-ties** : inmadurez f

immediate [ɪˈmiːdiət] adj : inmediato — **immediately** [ɪˈmiːdiətli] adv : inmediatamente

immense [ɪˈmɛns] adj : inmenso — **immensity** [ɪˈmɛnsəti] n, pl **-ties** : inmensidad f

immerse [ɪˈmərs] vt **-mersed; -mersing** : sumergir — **immersion** [ɪˈmərʒən] n : inmersión f

immigrate [ˈɪməˌgreɪt] vi **-grated; -grating** : inmigrar — **immigrant** [ˈɪmɪgrənt] n : inmigrante mf — **immigration** [ˌɪməˈgreɪʃən] n : inmigración f

imminent [ˈɪmənənt] adj : inminente — **imminence** [ˈɪmənənts] n : inminencia f

immobile [ɪmˈoːbəl] adj : inmóvil — **immobilize** [ɪˈmoːbəˌlaɪz] vt **-lized; -lizing** : inmovilizar

immoral [ɪˈmɔrəl] adj : inmoral — **immorality** [ˌɪmɔˈræləti, ˌɪmə-] n, pl **-ties** : inmoralidad f

immortal [ɪˈmɔrtəl] adj : inmortal — **~** n : inmortal mf — **immortality** [ˌɪmɔrˈtæləti] n : inmortalidad f

immune [ɪˈmjuːn] adj : inmune — **immunity** [ɪˈmjuːnəti] n, pl **-ties** : inmunidad f — **immunization** [ˌɪmjunəˈzeɪʃən] n : inmunización f — **immunize** [ˈɪmjuˌnaɪz] vt **-nized; -nizing** : inmunizar

imp [ˈɪmp] n RASCAL : diablillo m

impact [ˈɪmpækt] n : impacto m

impair [ɪmˈpær] vt : dañar, perjudicar

impart [ɪmˈpɑrt] vt : impartir (información), conferir (una calidad, etc.)

impartial [ɪmˈpɑrʃəl] adj : imparcial — **impartiality** [ɪmˌpɑrʃiˈæləti] n, pl **-ties** : imparcialidad f

impassable [ɪmˈpæsəbəl] adj : intransitable

impasse [ˈɪmˌpæs] n : impasse m

impassioned [ɪmˈpæʃənd] adj : apasionado

impassive [ɪmˈpæsɪv] adj : impasible

impatience [ɪmˈpeɪʃənts] n : impaciencia f — **impatient** [ɪmˈpeɪʃənt] adj : impaciente — **impatiently** [ɪmˈpeɪʃəntli] adv : con impaciencia

impeccable [ɪmˈpɛkəbəl] adj : impecable

impede [ɪm'piːd] *vt* **-peded; -peding** : dificultar — **impediment** [ɪm-'pɛdəmənt] *n* : impedimento *m*, obstáculo *m*

impel [ɪm'pɛl] *vt* **-pelled; -pelling** : impeler

impending [ɪm'pɛndɪŋ] *adj* : inminente

impenetrable [ɪm'pɛnɪtrəbəl] *adj* : impenetrable

imperative [ɪm'pɛrətɪv] *adj* **1** COMMANDING : imperativo **2** NECESSARY : imprescindible — **~** *n* : imperativo *m*

imperceptible [ˌɪmpər'sɛptəbəl] *adj* : imperceptible

imperfection [ˌɪmpərfɛkʃən] *n* : imperfección *f* — **imperfect** [ɪm'pərfɪkt] *adj* : imperfecto — **~** *n or* **~ tense** : imperfecto *m*

imperial [ɪm'pɪriəl] *adj* : imperial — **imperialism** [ɪm'pɪriəˌlɪzəm] *n* : imperialismo *m* — **imperious** [ɪm'pɪriəs] *adj* : imperioso

impersonal [ɪm'pərsənəl] *adj* : impersonal

impersonate [ɪm'pərsəˌneɪt] *vt* **-ated; -ating** : hacerse pasar por, imitar — **impersonation** [ɪmˌpərsən'eɪʃən] *n* : imitación *f* — **impersonator** [ɪm-'pərsənˌeɪtər] *n* : imitador *m*, -dora *f*

impertinent [ɪm'pərtənənt] *adj* : impertinente — **impertinence** [ɪm'pərtənənts] *n* : impertinencia *f*

impervious [ɪm'pərviəs] *adj* **~ to** : impermeable a

impetuous [ɪm'pɛtʃuəs] *adj* : impetuoso, impulsivo

impetus [ˈɪmpətəs] *n* : ímpetu *m*, impulso *m*

impinge [ɪm'pɪndʒ] *vi* **-pinged; -pinging ~ on** : afectara, incidir en

impish [ˈɪmpɪʃ] *adj* : pícaro, travieso

implant [ɪm'plænt] *vt* : implantar

implausible [ɪm'plɔːzəbəl] *adj* : inverosímil

implement [ˈɪmpləmənt] *n* : instrumento *m*, implemento *m Lat* — **~** [ˈɪmplə-ˌmɛnt] *vt* : poner en práctica

implicate [ˈɪmpləˌkeɪt] *vt* **-cated; -cating** : implicar — **implication** [ˌɪmpləˈkeɪ-ʃən] *n* **1** INVOLVEMENT : implicación *f* **2** CONSEQUENCE : consecuencia *f* **3 by ~** : de forma indirecta

implicit [ɪm'plɪsɪt] *adj* **1** : implícito **2** UNQUESTIONING : absoluto, incondicional

implore [ɪm'plor] *vt* **-plored; -ploring** : implorar, suplicar

imply [ɪm'plaɪ] *vt* **-plied; -plying 1** HINT : insinuar **2** ENTAIL : implicar

impolite [ˌɪmpə'laɪt] *adj* : descortés, maleducado

import [ɪm'port] *vt* : importar (mercancías) — **important** [ɪm'portənt] *adj* : importante — **importance** [ɪm-'portənts] *n* : importancia *f* — **importation** [ˌɪmpor'teɪʃən] *n* : importación *f* — **importer** [ɪm'portər] *n* : importador *m*, -dora *f*

impose [ɪm'poːz] *v* **-posed; -posing** *vt* : imponer — *vi* **~ on** : importunar, molestar — **imposing** [ɪm'poːzɪŋ] *adj* : imponente — **imposition** [ˌɪmpə-'zɪʃən] *n* **1** ENFORCEMENT : imposición *f* **2 be an ~ on** : molestar

impossible [ɪm'pasəbəl] *adj* : imposible — **impossibility** [ɪmˌpasəˈbɪlətɪ] *n, pl* **-ties** : imposibilidad *f*

impostor *or* **imposter** [ɪm'pastər] *n* : impostor *m*, -tora *f*

impotent [ˈɪmpətənt] *adj* : impotente — **impotence** [ˈɪmpətənts] *n* : impotencia *f*

impound [ɪm'paund] *vt* : incautar, embargar

impoverished [ɪm'pavərɪʃt] *adj* : empobrecido

impracticable [ɪm'præktɪkəbəl] *adj* : impracticable

impractical [ɪm'præktɪkəl] *adj* : poco práctico

imprecise [ˌɪmprɪ'saɪs] *adj* : impreciso — **imprecision** [ˌɪmprɪ'sɪʒən] *n* : imprecisión *f*

impregnable [ɪm'prɛgnəbəl] *adj* : impenetrable

impregnate [ɪm'prɛgˌneɪt] *vt* **-nated; -nating 1** : impregnar **2** FERTILIZE : fecundar

impress [ɪm'prɛs] *vt* **1** : causar una buena impresión a **2** AFFECT : impresionar **3 ~ sth on s.o.** : recalcar algo a algn — *vi* : impresionar — **impression** [ɪm'prɛʃən] *n* : impresión *f* — **impressionable** [ɪm'prɛʃənəbəl] *adj* : impresionable — **impressive** [ɪm'prɛsɪv] *adj* : impresionante

imprint [ˈɪmprɪnt, 'ɪm,-] *vt* : imprimir — **~** [ˈɪm,prɪnt] *n* MARK : impresión *f*, huella *f*

imprison [ɪm'prɪzən] *vt* : encarcelar — **imprisonment** [ɪm'prɪzənmənt] *n* : encarcelamiento *m*

improbable [ɪm'prabəbəl] *adj* : improbable — **improbability** [ɪmˌprabə'bɪlətɪ] *n, pl* **-ties** : improbabilidad *f*

impromptu [ɪm'pramptuː, -ˌtjuː] *adj* : improvisado

improper [ɪm'prapər] *adj* **1** UNSEEMLY : indecoroso **2** INCORRECT : impropio

— **impropriety** [ˌɪmprəˈpraɪəti] n, pl -eties : inconveniencia f

improve [ɪmˈpruːv] v -proved; -proving : mejorar — **improvement** [ɪmˈpruːvmənt] n : mejora f

improvise [ˈɪmprəˌvaɪz] v -vised; -vising : improvisar — **improvisation** [ˌɪmprɑvəˈzeɪʃən, ˌɪmprəvə-] n : improvisación f

impudent [ˈɪmpjədənt] adj : insolente — **impudence** [ˈɪmpjədənts] n : insolencia f

impulse [ˈɪmpʌls] n 1 : impulso m 2 on ∼ : sin reflexionar — **impulsive** [ɪmˈpʌlsɪv] adj : impulsivo — **impulsiveness** [ɪmˈpʌlsɪvnəs] n : impulsividad f

impunity [ɪmˈpjuːnəti] n 1 : impunidad f 2 with ∼ : impunemente

impure [ɪmˈpjʊr] adj : impuro — **impurity** [ɪmˈpjʊrəti] n, pl -ties : impureza f

in [ˈɪn] prep 1 : en 2 DURING : por, en Lat 3 WITHIN : dentro de 4 **dressed** ∼ **red** : vestido de rojo 5 ∼ **the rain** : bajo la lluvia 6 ∼ **the sun** : al sol 7 ∼ **this way** : de esta manera 8 **the best** ∼ **the world** : el mejor del mundo 9 **written** ∼ **ink/French** : escrito con tinta/en francés — adv 1 INSIDE : dentro, adentro 2 **be** ∼ : estar (en casa) 3 **be** ∼ **on** : participar en 4 **come in!** : ¡entre!, ¡pase! 5 **he's** ∼ **for a shock** : se va a llevar un shock — adj : de moda

inability [ˌɪnəˈbɪləti] n, pl -ties : incapacidad f

inaccessible [ˌɪnɪkˈsɛsəbəl] adj : inaccesible

inaccurate [ɪnˈækjərət] adj : inexacto

inactive [ɪnˈæktɪv] n : inactivo — **inactivity** [ˌɪnækˈtɪvəti] n, pl -ties : inactividad f

inadequate [ɪnˈædɪkwət] adj : insuficiente

inadvertently [ˌɪnədˈvərtəntli] adv : sin querer

inadvisable [ˌɪnædˈvaɪzəbəl] adj : desaconsejable

inane [ˈɪneɪn] adj **inaner; -est** : estúpido, tonto

inanimate [ɪnˈænəmət] adj : inanimado

inapplicable [ɪnˈæplɪkəbəl, ˌɪnəˈplɪkəbəl] adj : inaplicable

inappropriate [ˌɪnəˈproːpriət] adj : impropio, inoportuno

inarticulate [ˌɪnɑrˈtɪkjələt] adj : incapaz de expresarse

inasmuch as [ˌɪnæzˈmʌtʃˌæz] conj : ya que, puesto que

inattentive [ˌɪnəˈtɛntɪv] adj : poco atento

inaudible [ɪnˈodəbəl] adj : inaudible

inaugural [ɪˈnɔːɡjərəl, -ɡərəl] adj 1 : inaugural 2 ∼ **address** : discurso m de investidura — **inaugurate** [ɪˈnɔːɡjəˌreɪt, -ɡə-] vt **-rated; -rating** 1 : investir (a un presidente, etc.) 2 BEGIN : inaugurar — **inauguration** [ɪˌnɔːɡjəˈreɪʃən, -ɡə-] n : investidura f (de una persona), inauguración f (de un edificio, etc.)

inborn [ˈɪnˌbɔrn] adj : innato

inbred [ˈɪnˌbrɛd] adj INNATE : innato

incalculable [ɪnˈkælkjələbəl] adj : incalculable

incapable [ɪnˈkeɪpəbəl] adj : incapaz — **incapacitate** [ˌɪnkəˈpæsəˌteɪt] vt **-tated; -tating** : incapacitar — **incapacity** [ˌɪnkəˈpæsəti] n, pl -ties : incapacidad f

incarcerate [ɪnˈkɑrsəˌreɪt] vt **-ated; -ating** : encarcelar

incarnate [ɪnˈkɑrnət, -ˌneɪt] adj : encarnado — **incarnation** [ˌɪnkɑrˈneɪʃən] n : encarnación f

incendiary [ɪnˈsɛndiˌɛri] adj : incendiario

incense¹ [ˈɪnˌsɛnts] n : incienso m

incense² [ˈɪnˈsɛns] vt **-censed; -censing** : indignar, enfurecer

incentive [ɪnˈsɛntɪv] n : incentivo m

inception [ɪnˈsɛpʃən] n : comienzo m, principio m

incessant [ɪnˈsɛsənt] adj : incesante

incest [ˈɪnˌsɛst] n : incesto m — **incestuous** [ɪnˈsɛstʃuəs] adj : incestuoso

inch [ˈɪntʃ] n : pulgada f — ∼ v : avanzar poco a poco

incident [ˈɪnsədənt] n : incidente m — **incidence** [ˈɪnsədənts] n : índice m (de crímenes, etc.) — **incidental** [ˌɪnsəˈdɛntəl] adj 1 MINOR : incidental 2 CHANCE : casual — **incidentally** [ˌɪnsəˈdɛntəli, -ˈdɛntli] adv : a propósito

incinerate [ɪnˈsɪnəˌreɪt] vt **-ated; -ating** : incinerar — **incinerator** [ɪnˈsɪnəˌreɪtər] n : incinerador m

incision [ɪnˈsɪʒən] n : incisión f

incite [ɪnˈsaɪt] vt **-cited; -citing** : incitar, instigar

incline [ɪnˈklaɪn] v **-clined; -clining** vt 1 BEND : inclinar 2 **be** ∼**ed to** : inclinarse a, tender a — ∼ vi 1 : inclinarse — ∼ [ˈɪnˌklaɪn] n : pendiente f — **inclination** [ˌɪnkləˈneɪʃən] n 1 : inclinación f 2 DESIRE : deseo m, ganas fpl

include [ɪnˈkluːd] vt **-cluded; -cluding** : incluir — **inclusion** [ɪnˈkluːʒən] n : inclusión f — **inclusive** [ɪnˈkluːsɪv] adj : inclusivo

incognito [ˌɪnkɑɡˈniːto, ɪnˈkɑɡnəˌtoː] adv & adj : de incógnito

incoherent [ˌɪnkoˈhɪrənt, -ˈhɛr-] adj : incoherente — **incoherence** [ˌɪnkoˈhɪrənts, -ˈher-] n : incoherencia f

income [ˈɪnˌkʌm] n : ingresos mpl — **income tax** n : impuesto m sobre la renta

incomparable [ɪnˈkɑmpərəbəl] adj : incomparable

incompatible [ˌɪnkəmˈpætəbəl] adj : incompatible

incompetent [ɪnˈkɑmpətənt] adj : incompetente — **incompetence** [mˈkɑmpətənts] n : incompetencia f

incomplete [ˌɪnkəmˈpliːt] adj : incompleto

incomprehensible [ˌɪnˌkɑmprɪˈhentsəbəl] adj : incomprensible

inconceivable [ˌɪnkənˈsiːvəbəl] adj : inconcebible

inconclusive [ˌɪnkənˈkluːsɪv] adj : no concluyente

incongruous [ɪnˈkɑŋgruəs] adj : incongruente

inconsiderate [ˌɪnkənˈsɪdərət] adj : desconsiderado

inconsistent [ˌɪnkənˈsɪstənt] adj 1 : inconsecuente 2 be ~ with : no concordar con — **inconsistency** [ˌɪnkənˈsɪstəntsi] n, pl -cies : inconsecuencia f

inconspicuous [ˌɪnkənˈspɪkjuəs] adj : que no llama la atención

inconvenient [ˌɪnkənˈvinjənt] adj : incómodo, inconveniente — **inconvenience** [ˌɪnkənˈvinjənts] n 1 BOTHER : incomodidad f, molestia f 2 DRAWBACK : inconveniente m — ~ vt -nienced; -niencing vt : importunar, molestar

incorporate [ɪnˈkɔrpəˌreɪt] vt -rated; -rating : incorporar

incorrect [ˌɪnkəˈrɛkt] adj : incorrecto

increase [ˈɪnˌkriːs, ɪnˈkriːs] n : aumento m — ~ [ɪnˈkriːs, ˈɪnˌkriːs] v -creased; -creasing : aumentar — **increasingly** [ɪnˈkriːsɪŋli] adv : cada vez más

incredible [ɪnˈkrɛdəbəl] adj : increíble

incredulous [ɪnˈkrɛdʒələs] adj : incrédulo

incriminate [ɪnˈkrɪməˌneɪt] vt -nated; -nating : incriminar

incubator [ˈɪŋkjuˌbeɪtər, ˈɪn-] n : incubadora f

incumbent [ɪnˈkʌmbənt] n : titular mf

incur [ɪnˈkər] vt **incurred; incurring** : provocar (al enojo, etc.), incurrir en (gastos)

incurable [ɪnˈkjurəbəl] adj : incurable

indebted [ɪnˈdɛˌtəd] adj 1 : endeudado 2 be ~ to s.o. : estar en deuda con algn

indecent [ɪnˈdiːsənt] adj : indecente — **indecency** [ɪnˈdiːsəntsi] n, pl -cies : indecencia f

indecisive [ˌɪndɪˈsaɪsɪv] adj : indeciso

indeed [ɪnˈdiːd] adv 1 TRULY : verdaderamente, sin duda 2 IN FACT : en efecto 3 ~? : ¿de veras?

indefinite [ɪnˈdɛfənət] adj 1 : indefinido 2 VAGUE : impreciso — **indefinitely** [ɪnˈdɛfənətli] adv : indefinidamente

indelible [ɪnˈdɛləbəl] adj : indeleble

indent [ɪnˈdɛnt] vt : sangrar (un párrafo) — **indentation** [ˌɪnˌdɛnˈteɪʃən] n DENT, NOTCH : mella f

independent [ˌɪndəˈpɛndənt] adj : independiente — **independence** [ˌɪndəˈpɛndənts] n : independencia f

indescribable [ˌɪndɪˈskraɪbəbəl] adj : indescriptible

indestructible [ˌɪndɪˈstrʌktəbəl] adj : indestructible

index [ˈɪndɛks] n, pl **-dexes** or **-dices** [ˈɪndəˌsiːz] : índice m — ~ vt : incluir en un índice — **index finger** n : dedo m índice

Indian [ˈɪndiən] adj : indio m, -dia f

indication [ˌɪndəˈkeɪʃən] n : indicio m, señal f — **indicate** [ˈɪndəˌkeɪt] vt -cated; -cating : indicar — **indicative** [ɪnˈdɪkətɪv] adj : indicativo — **indicator** [ˈɪndəˌkeɪtər] n : indicador m

indict [ɪnˈdaɪt] vt : acusar (de un crimen) — **indictment** [ɪnˈdaɪtmənt] n : acusación f

indifferent [ɪnˈdɪfrənt, -dɪfə-] adj 1 : indiferente 2 MEDIOCRE : mediocre — **indifference** [ɪnˈdɪfrənts, -dɪfə-] n : indiferencia f

indigenous [ɪnˈdɪdʒənəs] adj : indígena

indigestion [ˌɪndaɪrˈdʒɛstʃən, -dɪ-] n : indigestión f — **indigestible** [ˌɪndaɪrˈdʒɛstəbəl, -dɪ-] adj : indigesto

indignation [ˌɪndɪgˈneɪʃən] n : indignación f — **indignant** [ɪnˈdɪgnənt] adj : indignado — **indignity** [ɪnˈdɪgnəˌti] n, pl **-ties** : indignidad f

indigo [ˈɪndɪˌgoː] n, pl **-gos** or **-goes** : añil m

indirect [ˌɪndəˈrɛkt, -daɪ-] adj : indirecto

indiscreet [ˌɪndɪˈskriːt] adj : indiscreto — **indiscretion** [ˌɪndɪˈskrɛʃən] n : indiscreción f

indiscriminate [ˌɪndɪˈskrɪmənət] adj : indiscriminado

indispensable [ˌɪndɪˈspɛntsəbəl] adj : indispensable, imprescindible

indisputable [ˌɪndɪˈspjuːtəbəl, ɪnˈdɪspjuːtə-] adj : indiscutible

indistinct [ˌɪndɪˈstɪŋkt] adj : indistinto

individual [ˌɪndəˈvɪdʒuəl] adj 1 : individual 2 PARTICULAR : particular — ~ n : individuo m — **individuality** [ˌɪndəˌvɪdʒuˈælət̪i] n, pl **-ties** : individualidad f *f* — **individually** [ˌɪndəˈvɪdʒuəli, -dʒəli] *adv* : individualmente

indoctrinate [ɪnˈdɑktrəˌneɪt] *vt* **-nated;** **-nating** : adoctrinar — **indoctrination** [ɪnˌdɑktrəˈneɪʃən] *n* : adoctrinamiento *m*

indoor [ˈɪnˌdor] *adj* **1** : (de) interior **2 ~ plant** : planta *f* de interior **3 ~ pool** : piscina *f* cubierta **4 ~ sports** : deportes *mpl* bajo techo — **indoors** [ˈɪnˈdorz] *adv* : adentro, dentro

induce [ɪnˈdus, -ˈdjus] *vt* **-duced;** **-ducing 1** : inducir **2** CAUSE : provocar — **inducement** [ɪnˈdusmənt, -ˈdjus-] *n* : incentivo *m*

indulge [ɪnˈdʌldʒ] *v* **-dulged;** **-dulging** *vt* **1** GRATIFY : satisfacer **2** PAMPER : consentir — *vi* **~ in** : permitirse — **indulgence** [ɪnˈdʌldʒəns] *n* **1** : indulgencia *f* **2** SATISFYING : satisfacción *f* — **indulgent** [ɪnˈdʌldʒənt] *adj* : indulgente

industry [ˈɪndəstri] *n, pl* **-tries 1** : industria *f* **2** DILIGENCE : diligencia *f* — **industrial** [ɪnˈdʌstriəl] *adj* : industrial — **industrialize** [ɪnˈdʌstriəˌlaɪz] *vt* **-ized;** **-izing** : industrializar — **industrious** [ɪnˈdʌstriəs] *adj* : diligente, trabajador

inebriated [ɪˈniːbriˌeɪtəd] *adj* : ebrio, embriagado

inedible [ɪˈnedəbəl] *adj* : no comestible

ineffective [ˌɪnɪˈfektɪv] *adj* **1** : ineficaz **2** INCOMPETENT : incompetente — **ineffectual** [ˌɪnɪˈfektʃuəl] *adj* : inútil, ineficaz

inefficient [ˌɪnɪˈfɪʃənt] *adj* **1** : ineficiente **2** INCOMPETENT : incompetente — **inefficiency** [ˌɪnɪˈfɪʃənsi] *n, pl* **-cies** : ineficiencia *f*

ineligible [ɪˈneledʒəbəl] *adj* : inelegible

inept [ɪˈnept] *adj* **1** : inepto **2 ~ at** : incapaz para

inequality [ˌɪnɪˈkwɑləti] *n, pl* **-ties** : desigualdad *f*

inert [ɪˈnərt] *adj* : inerte — **inertia** [ɪˈnərʃə] *n* : inercia *f*

inescapable [ˌɪnɪˈskeɪpəbəl] *adj* : ineludible

inevitable [ɪˈnevətəbəl] *adj* : inevitable — **inevitably** [-bli] *adv* : inevitablemente

inexcusable [ˌɪnɪkˈskjuːzəbəl] *adj* : inexcusable

inexpensive [ˌɪnɪkˈspensɪv] *adj* : barato, económico

inexperienced [ˌɪnɪkˈspɪriənɪst] *adj* : inexperto

inexplicable [ˌɪnɪkˈsplɪkəbəl] *adj* : inexplicable

infallible [ɪnˈfæləbəl] *adj* : infalible

infamous [ˈɪnfəməs] *adj* : infame

infancy [ˈɪnfənsi] *n, pl* **-cies** : infancia *f* — **infant** [ˈɪnfənt] *n* : bebé *m*; niño *m*, -ña *f* — **infantile** [ˈɪnfənˌtaɪl, -təl, -ˌtiːl] *adj* : infantil

infantry [ˈɪnfəntri] *n, pl* **-tries** : infantería *f*

infatuated [ɪnˈfætʃuˌeɪtəd] *adj* **be ~ with** : estar encaprichado con — **infatuation** [ɪnˌfætʃuˈeɪʃən] *n* : encaprichamiento *m*

infect [ɪnˈfekt] *vt* : infectar — **infection** [ɪnˈfekʃən] *n* : infección *f* — **infectious** [ɪnˈfekʃəs] *adj* : contagioso

infer [ɪnˈfər] *vt* **inferred; inferring** : deducir, inferir — **inference** [ˈɪnfərəns] *n* : deducción *f*

inferior [ɪnˈfɪriər] *adj* : inferior — **~ n** : inferior *m* — **inferiority** [ɪnˌfɪriˈɔrəti] *n, pl* **-ties** : inferioridad *f*

infernal [ɪnˈfərnəl] *adj* : infernal — **inferno** [ɪnˈfərˌno] *n, pl* **-nos** : infierno *m*

infertile [ɪnˈfərtəl, -ˌtaɪl] *adj* : estéril — **infertility** [ˌɪnfərtɪləti] *n* : esterilidad *f*

infest [ɪnˈfest] *vt* : infestar

infidelity [ˌɪnfəˈdeləti, -faɪ-] *n, pl* **-ties** : infidelidad *f*

infiltrate [ɪnˈfɪlˌtreɪt, ˈɪnfɪl-] *v* **-trated;** **-trating** *vt* : infiltrar — *vi* : infiltrarse

infinite [ˈɪnfənət] *adj* : infinito — **infinitive** [ɪnˈfɪnətɪv] *n* : infinitivo *m* — **infinity** [ɪnˈfɪnəti] *n, pl* **-ties 1** : infinito *m* **2 an ~ of** : una infinidad de

infirm [ɪnˈfərm] *adj* : enfermizo, endeble — **infirmary** [ɪnˈfərməri] *n, pl* **-ries** : enfermería *f* — **infirmity** [ɪnˈfərməti] *n, pl* **-ties 1** FRAILTY : endeblez *f* **2** AILMENT : enfermedad *f*

inflame [ɪnˈfleɪm] *vt* **-flamed;** **-flaming** : inflamar — **inflammable** [ɪnˈflæməbəl] *adj* : inflamable — **inflammation** [ˌɪnfləˈmeɪʃən] *n* : inflamación *f* — **inflammatory** [ɪnˈflæməˌtori] *adj* : inflamatorio

inflate [ɪnˈfleɪt] *vt* **-flated;** **-flating** : inflar — **inflation** [ɪnˈfleɪʃən] *n* : inflación *f* — **inflationary** [ɪnˈfleɪʃəˌneri] *adj* : inflacionario, inflacionista

inflexible [ɪnˈfleksɪbəl] *adj* : inflexible

inflict [ɪnˈflɪkt] *vt* : infligir

influence [ˈɪnˌfluəns, ɪnˈfluəns] *n* **1** : influencia *f* **2 under the ~** : embriagado — *vt* **-enced;** **-encing** : influir en, influenciar — **influential** [ˌɪnfluˈentʃəl] *adj* : influyente

influenza [ˌɪnfluˈenzə] *n* : gripe *f*, influenza *f*

influx [ˈɪnˌflʌks] *n* : afluencia *f*

inform [ɪnˈfɔrm] *vt* **1** : informar **2 keep me ~ed** : manténme al corriente — *vi* **~ on** : delatar, denunciar

informal [ɪɱˈfɔrməl] *adj* **1** : informal **2** : familiar (dícese del lenguaje) — **informality** [ɪɱfɔrˈmæləṭi, -fər-] *n, pl* **-ties** : falta *f* de ceremonia — **informally** [ɪɱˈfɔrməli] *adv* : de manera informal

information [ˌɪɱfərˈmeɪʃən] *n* : información *f* — **informative** [ɪɱˈfɔrməṭɪv] *adj* : informativo — **informer** [ɪɱˈfɔrmər] *n* : informante *mf*

infrared [ˌɪɱfrəˈrɛd] *adj* : infrarrojo

infrastructure [ˈɪɱfrəˌstrʌktʃər] *n* : infraestructura *f*

infrequent [ɪɱˈfriːkwənt] *adj* : infrecuente — **infrequently** [ɪɱˈfriːkwəntli] *adv* : raramente

infringe [ɪɱˈfrɪndʒ] *v* **-fringed; -fringing** *vt* : infringir — *vi* ~ **on** : violar — **infringement** [ɪɱˈfrɪndʒmənt] *n* : violación *f*

infuriate [ɪɱˈfjʊriˌeɪt] *vt* **-ated; -ating** : enfurecer, poner furioso — **infuriating** [ɪɱˈfjʊriˌeɪṭɪŋ] *adj* : exasperante

infuse [ɪɱˈfjuːz] *vt* **-fused; -fusing** : infundir — **infusion** [ɪɱˈfjuːʒən] *n* : infusión *f*

ingenious [ɪnˈdʒiːnjəs] *adj* : ingenioso — **ingenuity** [ˌɪndʒəˈnuːəṭi, -nju-] *n, pl* **-ties** : ingenio

ingenuous [ɪnˈdʒɛnjuəs] *adj* : ingenuo

ingest [ɪnˈdʒɛst] *vt* : ingerir

ingot [ˈɪŋgət] *n* : lingote *m*

ingrained [ɪnˈgreɪnd] *adj* : arraigado

ingratiate [ɪnˈgreɪʃiˌeɪt] *vt* **-ated; -ating** ~ **oneself with** : congraciarse con

ingratitude [ɪnˈgrætəˌtuːd, -ˌtjuːd] *n* : ingratitud *f*

ingredient [ɪnˈgriːdiənt] *n* : ingrediente *m*

ingrown [ˈɪnˌgroːn] *adj* ~ **nail** : uña *f* encarnada

inhabit [ɪnˈhæbət] *vt* : habitar — **inhabitant** [ɪnˈhæbəṭənt] *n* : habitante *mf*

inhale [ɪnˈheɪl] *v* **-haled; -haling** *vt* : inhalar, aspirar — *vi* : inspirar

inherent [ɪnˈhɪrənt, -ˈher-] *adj* : inherente — **inherently** [ɪnˈhɪrəntli, -ˈher-] *adv* : intrínsecamente

inherit [ɪnˈherət] *vt* : heredar — **inheritance** [ɪnˈherəṭəns] *n* : herencia *f*

inhibit [ɪnˈhɪbət] *vt* IMPEDE : inhibir — **inhibition** [ˌɪnhəˈbɪʃən, ˌɪnə-] *n* : inhibición *f*

inhuman [ɪnˈhjuːmən, -ˈjuː-] *adj* : inhumano — **inhumane** [ˌɪnhjuˈmeɪn, -ju-] *adj* : inhumano — **inhumanity** [ˌɪnhjuˈmænəṭi, -ju-] *n, pl* **-ties** : inhumanidad *f*

initial [ɪˈnɪʃəl] *adj* : inicial — *n* : inicial *f* — *vt* **-tialed** *or* **-tialled; -tialing** *or* **-tialling** : poner las iniciales a

initiate [ɪˈnɪʃiˌeɪt] *vt* **-ated; -ating 1** BEGIN : iniciar **2** ~ **s.o. into sth** : iniciar a algn en algo — **initiation** [ɪˌnɪʃiˈeɪʃən] *n* : iniciación *f* — **initiative** [ɪˈnɪʃəṭɪv] *n* : iniciativa *f*

inject [ɪnˈdʒɛkt] *vt* : inyectar — **injection** [ɪnˈdʒɛkʃən] *n* : inyección *f*

injure [ˈɪndʒər] *vt* **-jured; -juring 1** : herir **2** ~ **oneself** : hacerse daño — **injurious** [ɪnˈdʒʊriəs] *adj* : perjudicial — **injury** [ˈɪndʒəri] *n, pl* **-ries 1** : herida *f* **2** HARM : perjuicio *m*

injustice [ɪnˈdʒʌstəs] *n* : injusticia *f*

ink [ˈɪŋk] *n* : tinta *f* — **inkwell** [ˈɪŋkˌwɛl] *n* : tintero *m*

inland [ˈɪnˌlænd, -lənd] *adj* : interior — ~ *adv* : hacia el interior, tierra adentro

in-laws [ˈɪnˌlɔz] *npl* : suegros *mpl*

inlet [ˈɪnˌlɛt, -lət] *n* : ensenada *f*, cala *f*

inmate [ˈɪnˌmeɪt] *n* **1** PATIENT : paciente *mf* **2** PRISONER : preso *m*, -sa *f*

inn [ˈɪn] *n* : posada *f*, hostería *f*

innards [ˈɪnərdz] *npl* : entrañas *fpl*, tripas *fpl fam*

innate [ɪˈneɪt] *adj* : innato

inner [ˈɪnər] *adj* : interior, interno — **innermost** [ˈɪnərˌmoːst] *adj* : más íntimo, más profundo

inning [ˈɪnɪŋ] *n* : entrada *f*

innocent [ˈɪnəsənt] *adj* : inocente — ~ *n* : inocente *mf* — **innocence** [ˈɪnəsənts] *n* : inocencia *f*

innocuous [ɪˈnɑkjəwəs] *adj* : inocuo

innovate [ˈɪnəˌveɪt] *vi* **-vated; -vating** : innovar — **innovation** [ˌɪnəˈveɪʃən] *n* : innovación *f* — **innovative** [ˈɪnəˌveɪṭɪv] *adj* : innovador — **innovator** [ˈɪnəˌveɪṭər] *n* : innovador *m*, -dora *f*

innuendo [ˌɪnjuˈɛndo] *n, pl* **-dos** *or* **-does** : insinuación *f*, indirecta *f*

innumerable [ɪˈnuːmərəbəl, -ˈnjuː-] *adj* : innumerable

inoculate [ɪˈnɑkjəˌleɪt] *vt* **-lated; -lating** : inocular — **inoculation** [ɪˌnɑkjəˈleɪʃən] *n* : inoculación *f*

inoffensive [ˌɪnəˈfɛntsɪv] *adj* : inofensivo

inpatient [ˈɪnˌpeɪʃənt] *n* : paciente *mf* hospitalizado

input [ˈɪnˌpʊt] *n* **1** : contribución *f* **2** : entrada *f* (de datos) — ~ *vt* **-putted** *or* **-put; -putting** : entrar (datos, etc.)

inquire [ɪnˈkwaɪr] *v* **-quired; -quiring** *vi* : preguntar — *vi* **1** ~ **about** : informarse sobre **2** ~ **into** : investigar — **inquiry** [ˈɪnˌkwaɪri, ɪnˈkwaɪri; ˈɪnkwəri, ˈɪŋ-] *n, pl* **-ries 1** QUESTION : pregunta *f* **2** INVESTIGATION : investigación *f* — **inquisition** [ˌɪnkwəˈzɪʃən, ˌɪŋ-] *n* : inquisición *f* — **inquisitive** [ɪnˈkwɪzət̬ɪv] *adj* : curioso

insane [ɪnˈseɪn] *adj* : loco — **insanity** [ɪnˈsænət̬i] *n, pl* **-ties** : locura *f*

insatiable [ɪnˈseɪʃəbəl] *adj* : insaciable

inscribe [ɪnˈskraɪb] *vt* **-scribed; -scribing** : inscribir — **inscription** [ɪnˈskrɪpʃən] *n* : inscripción *f*

inscrutable [ɪnˈskruːt̬əbəl] *adj* : inescrutable

insect [ˈɪnˌsɛkt] *n* : insecto *m* — **insecticide** [ɪnˈsɛktəˌsaɪd] *n* : insecticida *m*

insecure [ˌɪnsɪˈkjʊr] *adj* : inseguro, poco seguro — **insecurity** [ˌɪnsɪˈkjʊrət̬i] *n, pl* **-ties** : inseguridad *f*

insensitive [ɪnˈsɛnsət̬ɪv] *adj* : insensible — **insensitivity** [ɪnˌsɛnsəˈtɪvət̬i] *n, pl* **-ties** : insensibilidad *f*

inseparable [ɪnˈsɛpərəbəl] *adj* : inseparable

insert [ɪnˈsərt] *vt* : insertar (texto), introducir (una moneda, etc.)

inside [ɪnˈsaɪd, ˈɪnˌsaɪd] *n* 1 : interior *m* 2 ~ **out** : al revés — *adv* : dentro, adentro — ~ *adj* : interior — ~ *prep* 1 or ~ **of** : dentro de 2 ~ **an hour** : en menos de una hora

insidious [ɪnˈsɪdiəs] *adj* : insidioso

insight [ˈɪnˌsaɪt] *n* : perspicacia *f*

insignia [ɪnˈsɪɡniə] or **insigne** [-ˌniː] *n, pl* **-nia** or **-nias** : insignia *f*, enseña *f*

insignificant [ˌɪnsɪɡˈnɪfɪkənt] *adj* : insignificante

insincere [ˌɪnsɪnˈsɪr] *adj* : insincero

insinuate [ɪnˈsɪnjuˌeɪt] *vt* **-ated; -ating** : insinuar — **insinuation** [ɪnˌsɪnjuˈeɪʃən] *n* : insinuación *f*

insipid [ɪnˈsɪpəd] *adj* : insípido

insist [ɪnˈsɪst] *v* : insistir — **insistent** [ɪnˈsɪstənt] *adj* : insistente

insofar as [ˌɪnsoˈfɑːræz] *conj* : en la medida en que

insole [ˈɪnˌsoːl] *n* : plantilla *f*

insolent [ˈɪnsələnt] *adj* : insolente — **insolence** [ˈɪnsələns] *n* : insolencia *f*

insolvent [ɪnˈsɑːlvənt] *adj* : insolvente

insomnia [ɪnˈsɑːmniə] *n* : insomnio *m*

inspect [ɪnˈspɛkt] *vt* : inspeccionar, revisar — **inspection** [ɪnˈspɛkʃən] *n* : inspección *f* — **inspector** [ɪnˈspɛktər] *n* : inspector *m*, -tora *f*

inspire [ɪnˈspaɪr] *vt* **-spired; -spiring** : inspirar — **inspiration** [ˌɪnspəˈreɪʃən] *n* : inspiración *f* — **inspirational** [ˌɪnspəˈreɪʃənəl] *adj* : inspirador

instability [ˌɪnstəˈbɪlət̬i] *n, pl* **-ties** : inestabilidad *f*

install [ɪnˈstɔːl] *vt* **-stalled; -stalling** : instalar — **installation** [ˌɪnstəˈleɪʃən] *n* : instalación *f* — **installment** [ɪnˈstɔːlmənt] *n* 1 PAYMENT : plazo *m*, cuota *f* 2 : entrega *f* (de una publicación o telenovela)

instance [ˈɪnstəns] *n* 1 : ejemplo *m* 2 **for** ~ : por ejemplo 3 **in this** ~ : en este caso

instant [ˈɪnstənt] *n* : instante *m* — ~ *adj* 1 IMMEDIATE : inmediato 2 ~ **coffee** : café *m* instantáneo — **instantaneous** [ˌɪnstənˈteɪniəs] *adj* : instantáneo — **instantly** [ˈɪnstəntli] *adv* : al instante, instantáneamente

instead [ɪnˈstɛd] *adv* 1 : en cambio 2 **I went** ~ : fui en su lugar — **instead of** *prep* : en vez de, en lugar de

instep [ˈɪnˌstɛp] *n* : empeine *m*

instigate [ˈɪnstəˌɡeɪt] *vt* **-gated; -gating** : instigar a — **instigation** [ˌɪnstəˈɡeɪʃən] *n* : instigación *f* — **instigator** [ˈɪnstəˌɡeɪt̬ər] *n* : instigador *m*, -dora *f*

instill [ɪnˈstɪl] or *Brit* **instil** *vt* **-stilled; -stilling** : inculcar, infundir

instinct [ˈɪnˌstɪŋkt] *n* : instinto *m* — **instinctive** [ɪnˈstɪŋktɪv] or **instinctual** [ɪnˈstɪŋktʃuəl] *adj* : instintivo

institute [ˈɪnstəˌtuːt, -ˌtjuːt] *vt* **-tuted; -tuting** 1 : instituir 2 INITIATE : iniciar — ~ *n* : instituto *m* — **institution** [ˌɪnstəˈtuːʃən, -ˈtjuː-] *n* : institución *f*

instruct [ɪnˈstrʌkt] *vt* 1 : instruir 2 COMMAND : mandar — **instruction** [ɪnˈstrʌkʃən] *n* : instrucción *f* — **instructor** [ɪnˈstrʌktər] *n* : instructor *m*, -tora *f*

instrument [ˈɪnstrəmənt] *n* : instrumento *m* — **instrumental** [ˌɪnstrəˈmɛntəl] *adj* : instrumental 2 **be** ~ **in** : jugar un papel fundamental en

insubordinate [ˌɪnsəˈbɔrdənət] *adj* : insubordinado — **insubordination** [ˌɪnsəˌbɔrdənˈeɪʃən] *n* : insubordinación *f*

insufferable [ɪnˈsʌfərəbəl] *adj* : insoportable

insufficient [ˌɪnsəˈfɪʃənt] *adj* : insuficiente

insular [ˈɪnsələr, -sjʊ-] *adj* 1 : insular 2 NARROW-MINDED : estrecho de miras

insulate [ˈɪnsəˌleɪt] *vt* **-lated; -lating** : aislar — **insulation** [ˌɪnsəˈleɪʃən] *n* : aislamiento *m*

insulin [ˈɪnsələn] *n* : insulina *f*

insult [ɪnˈsʌlt] *vt* : insultar — ~ [ˈɪnˌsʌlt] *n* : insulto *m* — **insulting** [ɪnˈsʌltɪŋ] *adj* : insultante, ofensivo

insure [ɪnˈʃʊr] *vt* **-sured; -suring** : asegurar — **insurance** [ɪnˈʃʊrəns, ˈɪnˌʃʊr-] *n* : seguro *m*

insurmountable [ˌɪnsərˈmaʊntəbəl] *adj* : insuperable

intact [ɪnˈtækt] *adj* : intacto

intake ['ɪn.teɪk] n : consumo m (de alimentos), entrada f (de aire, etc.)

intangible [ɪn'tændʒəbəl] adj : intangible

integral ['ɪntɪgrəl] adj : integral

integrate ['ɪntəˌgreɪt] v -grated; -grating vt : integrar — vi : integrarse

integrity [ɪn'tegrəti] n : integridad f

intellect ['ɪntəl.ekt] n : intelecto m — **intellectual** [ˌɪntəl'ektʃuəl] adj : intelectual — n : intelectual mf — **intelligence** [ɪn'teləʤəns] n : inteligencia f — **intelligent** [ɪn'teləʤənt] adj : inteligente — **intelligible** [ɪn'teləʤəbəl] adj : inteligible

intend [ɪn'tend] vt 1 be ~ed for : ser para 2 ~ to do : pensar hacer, tener la intención de hacer — **intended** [ɪn'tendəd] adj : intencionado, deliberado

intense [ɪn'tens] adj : intenso — **intensely** [ɪn'tensli] adv : sumamente, profundamente — **intensify** [ɪn'tensəˌfaɪ] v -fied; -fying vt : intensificar — vi : intensificarse — **intensity** [ɪn'tensəti] n, pl -ties : intensidad f — **intensive** [ɪn'tensɪv] adj : intensivo

intent [ɪn'tent] n : intención f — ~ adj 1 : atento, concentrado 2 ~ on doing : resuelto a hacer — **intention** [ɪn'tentʃən] n : intención f — **intentional** [ɪn'tentʃənəl] adj : intencional, deliberado — **intently** [ɪn'tentli] adv : atentamente, fijamente

interact [ˌɪntər'ækt] vi 1 : interactuar 2 ~ with : relacionarse con — **interaction** [ˌɪntər'ækʃən] n : interacción f — **interactive** [ˌɪntər'æktɪv] adj : interactivo

intercede [ˌɪntər'siːd] vi -ceded; -ceding : interceder

intercept [ˌɪntər'sept] vt : interceptar

interchange [ˌɪntər'tʃeɪndʒ] vt -changed; -changing : intercambiar — ~ ['ɪntərtʃeɪndʒ] n 1 : intercambio m 2 JUNCTION : enlace m — **interchangeable** [ˌɪntər'tʃeɪndʒəbəl] adj : intercambiable

intercourse ['ɪntərˌkors] n : relaciones fpl (sexuales)

interest ['ɪntrəst, -təˌrest] n : interés m — ~ vt : interesar — **interested** [-əd] adj : interesado — **interesting** ['ɪntrəstɪŋ, -təˌrestɪŋ] adj : interesante

interface ['ɪntərˌfeɪs] n : interfaz mf (de una computadora)

interfere [ˌɪntər'fɪr] vi -fered; -fering 1 ~ in : entrometerse en, interferir en 2 ~ with DISRUPT : afectar (una actividad, etc.) — **interference** [ˌɪntər-

'fɪrəns] n 1 : interferencia f 2 : intromisión f (en el radio, etc.)

interim ['ɪntərəm] n 1 : interín m 2 in the ~ : mientras tanto — ~ adj : interino, provisional

interior [ɪn'tɪriər] adj : interior — ~ n : interior m

interjection [ˌɪntər'dʒekʃən] n : interjección f

interlock [ˌɪntər'lɑk] vt : engranar

interloper ['ɪntərˌloʊpər] n : intruso m, -sa f

interlude ['ɪntərˌluːd] n 1 : intervalo m 2 : interludio m (en música, etc.)

intermediate [ˌɪntər'miːdiət] adj : intermedio — **intermediary** [ˌɪntər'miːdiˌeri] n, pl -aries : intermediario m, -ria f

interminable [ɪn'tɑrmənəbəl] adj : interminable

intermission [ˌɪntər'mɪʃən] n : intervalo m, intermedio m

intermittent [ˌɪntər'mɪtənt] adj : intermitente

intern¹ ['ɪnˌtərn, ɪn'tərn] vt : confinar

intern² ['ɪnˌtərn] vi : hacer las prácticas — ~ n : interno m, -na f

internal [ɪn'tərnəl] adj : interno

international [ˌɪntər'næʃənəl] adj : internacional

interpret [ɪn'tərprət] vt : interpretar — **interpretation** [ɪnˌtərprə'teɪʃən] n : interpretación f — **interpreter** [ɪn'tərprə-tər] n : intérprete mf

interrogate [ɪn'terəˌgeɪt] vt -gated; -gating : interrogar — **interrogation** [ɪnˌterə'geɪʃən] n QUESTIONING : interrogatorio m — **interrogative** [ˌɪntə-'rɑgətɪv] adj : interrogativo

interrupt [ˌɪntər'ʌpt] v : interrumpir — **interruption** [ˌɪntər'ʌpʃən] n : interrupción f

intersect [ˌɪntər'sekt] vt : cruzar (dícese de calles), cortar (dícese de líneas) — vi : cruzarse, cortarse — **intersection** [ˌɪntər'sekʃən] n : cruce m, intersección f

intersperse [ˌɪntər'spərs] vt -spersed; -spersing : intercalar

interstate [ˌɪntər'steɪt] n or ~ highway : carretera f interestatal

intertwine [ˌɪntər'twaɪn] vi -twined; -twining : entrelazarse

interval ['ɪntərvəl] n : intervalo m

intervene [ˌɪntər'viːn] vi -vened; -vening 1 : intervenir 2 ELAPSE : transcurrir, pasar — **intervention** [ˌɪntər'ven-tʃən] n : intervención f

interview ['ɪntərˌvjuː] n : entrevista f — ~ vt : entrevistar — **interviewer** ['ɪntərˌvjuːər] n : entrevistador m, -dora f

intestine [ɪn'testən] n : intestino m — **intestinal** [ɪn'testənəl] adj : intestinal
intimate¹ ['ɪntəˌmeɪt] vt -**mated; -mating** : insinuar, dar a entender
intimate² ['ɪntəmət] adj : íntimo — **intimacy** ['ɪntəməsi] n, pl -**cies** : intimidad f
intimidate [ɪn'tɪməˌdeɪt] vt -**dated; -dating** : intimidar — **intimidation** [ɪnˌtɪmə'deɪʃən] n : intimidación f
into ['ɪntu:] prep 1 : en, a 2 **bump** ~ : darse contra 3 (used in mathematics) **3** ~ **12** : 12 dividido por 3
intolerable [ɪn'tɑlərəbəl] adj : intolerable — **intolerance** [ɪn'tɑlərənts] n : intolerancia f — **intolerant** [ɪn'tɑlərənt] adj : intolerante
intoxicate [ɪn'tɑksəˌkeɪt] vt -**cated; -cating** : embriagar — **intoxicated** [ɪn'tɑksəˌkeɪtəd] adj 1 : embriagado 2 ~ **with** : ebrio de
intransitive [ɪn'trænsətɪv, -trænzə-] adj : intransitivo
intravenous [ˌɪntrə'vi:nəs] adj : intravenoso
intrepid [ɪn'trepəd] adj : intrépido
intricate ['ɪntrɪkət] adj : complicado, intrincado — **intricacy** ['ɪntrɪkəsi] n, pl -**cies** : complejidad f
intrigue [ɪn'tri:g, 'ɪntri:g] n : intriga f — ~ [ɪn'tri:g] v -**trigued; -triguing** : intrigar — **intriguing** [ɪn'tri:gɪŋ] adj : intrigante
intrinsic [ɪn'trɪnzɪk, -trɪntsɪk] adj : intrínseco
introduce [ˌɪntrə'du:s, -'dju:s] vt -**duced; -ducing** 1 : introducir 2 : presentar (a una persona) — **introduction** [ˌɪntrə'dʌkʃən] n 1 : introducción f 2 : presentación f (de una persona) — **introductory** [ˌɪntrə'dʌktəri] adj : introductorio
introvert ['ɪntrəˌvərt] n : introvertido m, -da f — **introverted** ['ɪntrəˌvərtəd] adj : introvertido
intrude [ɪn'tru:d] vi -**truded; -truding** 1 : entrometerse 2 ~ **on s.o.** : molestar a algn — **intruder** [ɪn'tru:dər] n : intruso m, -sa f — **intrusion** [ɪn'tru:ʒən] n : intrusión f — **intrusive** [ɪn'tru:sɪv] adj : intruso
intuition [ˌɪntu'ɪʃən, -tju-] n : intuición f — **intuitive** [ɪn'tu:ətɪv, -tju:-] adj : intuitivo
inundate ['ɪnənˌdeɪt] vt -**dated; -dating** : inundar
invade [ɪn'veɪd] vt -**vaded; -vading** : invadir
invalid¹ [ɪn'væləd] adj : inválido
invalid² [ɪn'væləd] n : inválido m, -da f

invaluable [ɪn'væljəbəl, -'væljuə-] adj : inestimable, invalorable Lat
invariable [ɪn'væriəbəl] adj : invariable
invasion [ɪn'veɪʒən] n : invasión f
invent [ɪn'vent] vt : inventar — **invention** [ɪn'ventʃən] n : invención f — **inventive** [ɪn'ventɪv] adj : inventivo — **inventor** [ɪn'ventər] n : inventor m, -tora f
inventory ['ɪnvənˌtɔri] n, pl -**ries** : inventario m
invert [ɪn'vərt] vt : invertir
invertebrate [ɪn'vərtəˌbrət, -ˌbreɪt] adj : invertebrado — ~ n : invertebrado m
invest [ɪn'vest] vt : invertir
investigate [ɪn'vestəˌgeɪt] v -**gated; -gating** : investigar — **investigation** [ɪnˌvestə'geɪʃən] n : investigación f — **investigator** [ɪn'vestəˌgeɪtər] n : investigador m, -dora f
investment [ɪn'vestmənt] n : inversión f — **investor** [ɪn'vestər] n : inversor m, -sora f
inveterate [ɪn'vetərət] adj : inveterado
invigorating [ɪn'vɪgəˌreɪtɪŋ] adj : vigorizante
invincible [ɪn'vɪntsəbəl] adj : invencible
invisible [ɪn'vɪzəbəl] adj : invisible
invitation [ˌɪnvə'teɪʃən] n : invitación f — **invite** [ɪn'vaɪt] vt -**vited; -viting** 1 : invitar 2 SEEK : buscar (problemas, etc.) — **inviting** [ɪn'vaɪtɪŋ] adj : atrayente
invoice ['ɪnˌvɔɪs] n : factura f
invoke [ɪn'vo:k] vt -**voked; -voking** : invocar
involuntary [ɪn'vɑlənˌteri] adj : involuntario
involve [ɪn'vɑlv] vt -**volved; -volving** 1 CONCERN : concernir, afectar 2 ENTAIL : suponer — **involved** [ɪn'vɑlvd] adj 1 COMPLEX : complicado 2 CONCERNED : afectado — **involvement** [ɪn'vɑlvmənt] n : participación f
invulnerable [ɪn'vʌlnərəbəl] adj : invulnerable
inward ['ɪnwərd] adj INNER : interior, interno — ~ or **inwards** [-wərdz] adv : hacia adentro, hacia el interior
iodine ['aɪəˌdaɪn, -dən] n : yodo m, tintura f de yodo
ion ['aɪən, 'aɪˌɑn] n : ion m
iota [aɪ'otə] n : pizca f, ápice m
IOU [ˌaɪˌo'ju:] n : pagaré m, vale m
Iranian [ɪ'reɪniən, -'ræ-, -'rɑ-; aɪ'-] adj : iraní
Iraqi [ɪ'rɑki, -'ræk-] adj : iraquí
ire ['aɪr] n : ira f — **irate** [aɪ'reɪt] adj : furioso
iris ['aɪrəs] n, pl **irises** or **irides** ['aɪrə-

diz, 'ir-] **1 :** iris *m* (del ojo) **2 :** lirio *m* (planta)

Irish ['aırıʃ] *adj* : irlandés

irksome ['ərksəm] *adj* : irritante, fastidioso

iron ['aıərn] *n* **1 :** hierro *m*, fierro *m Lat* (metal) **2 :** plancha *f* (para la ropa) — ~ *v* : planchar

ironic [aɪˈrɑnɪk] *or* **ironical** [-nɪkəl] *adj* : irónico

ironing board *n* **1 :** tabla *f* (de planchar)

irony ['aɪrəni] *n, pl* **-nies** : ironía *f*

irrational [ɪˈræʃənəl] *adj* : irracional

irreconcilable [ɪˌrɛkənˈsaɪləbəl] *adj* : irreconciliable

irrefutable [ˌɪrɪˈfjuːt̬əbəl, ɪˈrɛfjə-] *adj* : irrefutable

irregular [ɪˈrɛgjələr] *adj* : irregular — **irregularity** [ɪˌrɛgjəˈlærət̬i] *n, pl* **-ties** : irregularidad *f*

irrelevant [ɪˈrɛləvənt] *adj* : irrelevante

irreparable [ɪˈrɛpərəbəl] *adj* : irreparable

irreplaceable [ˌɪrɪˈpleɪsəbəl] *adj* : irreemplazable

irresistible [ˌɪrɪˈzɪstəbəl] *adj* : irresistible

irresolute [ɪˈrɛzəˌluːt] *adj* : irresoluto

irrespective of [ˌɪrɪˈspɛktɪvə] *prep* : sin tener en cuenta

irresponsible [ˌɪrɪˈspɑntsəbəl] *adj* : irresponsable — **irresponsibility** [ˌɪrɪˌspɑntsəˈbɪlət̬i] *n, pl* **-ties** : irresponsabilidad *f*

irreverent [ɪˈrɛvərənt] *adj* : irreverente

irreversible [ˌɪrɪˈvərsəbəl] *adj* : irreversible, irrevocable

irrigate ['ɪrəˌgeɪt] *vt* **-gated; -gating** : irrigar, regar — **irrigation** [ˌɪrəˈgeɪʃən] *n* : irrigación *f*, riego *m*

irritate ['ɪrəˌteɪt] *vt* **-tated; -tating** : irritar — **irritable** ['ɪrət̬əbəl] *adj* : irritable — **irritably** ['ɪrət̬əbli] *adv* : con irritación — **irritating** ['ɪrəˌteɪt̬ɪŋ] *adj* : irritante — **irritation** [ˌɪrəˈteɪʃən] *n* : irritación *f*

is → be

Islam [ɪsˈlɑm, ɪz-, -ˈlæm; 'ɪsˌlɑm, 'ɪz-, -ˌlæm] *n* : el Islam — **Islamic** [ɪsˈlɑmɪk, ɪz-, -ˈlæ-] *adj* : islámico

island ['aɪlənd] *n* : isla *f* — **isle** ['aɪl] *n* : isla *f*

isolate ['aɪsəˌleɪt] *vt* **-lated; -lating** : aislar — **isolation** [ˌaɪsəˈleɪʃən] *n* : aislamiento *m*

Israeli [ɪzˈreɪli] *adj* : israelí

issue ['ɪˌʃuː] *n* **1** MATTER : asunto *m*, cuestión *f* **2 :** número *m* (de una revista, etc.) **3 make an ~ of :** insistir demasiado sobre **4 take ~ with :** disentir de — ~ *v* **-sued; -suing** *vi* **from :** surgir de — *vt* **1 :** emitir (sellos, etc.), distribuir (provisiones, etc.) **2** PUBLISH : publicar

isthmus ['ɪsməs] *n* : istmo *m*

it ['ɪt] *pron* **1** (*as subject*) : él, ella **2** (*as indirect object*) : le, se **3** (*as direct object*) : lo, la **4** (*as object of a preposition*) : él, ella **5 it's raining :** está lloviendo **6 it's 8 o'clock :** son las ocho **7 it's hot out :** hace calor **8 ~ is necessary :** es necesario **9 who is ~? :** ¿quién es? **10 it's me :** soy yo

Italian [ɪˈtæljən, aɪ-] *adj* : italiano — ~ *n* : italiano *m* (idioma)

italics ['ɪtælɪks, aɪ-] *n* : cursiva *f*

itch ['ɪtʃ] *vi* **1 :** picar **2 be ~ing to :** morirse por — ~ *n* : picazón *f* — **itchy** ['ɪtʃi] *adj* **itchier; -est** : que pica

it'd ['ɪt̬əd] (*contraction of* **it had** *or* **it would**) → **have, would**

item ['aɪt̬əm] *n* **1 :** artículo *m* **2 :** punto *m* (en una agenda) **3 ~ of clothing :** prenda *f* de vestir **4 news ~ :** noticia *f* — **itemize** ['aɪt̬əˌmaɪz] *vt* **-ized; -izing** : detallar, enumerar

itinerant [aɪˈtɪnərənt] *adj* : ambulante

itinerary [aɪˈtɪnəˌrɛri] *n, pl* **-aries** : itinerario *m*

it'll ['ɪt̬əl] (*contraction of* **it shall** *or* **it will**) → **shall, will**

its ['ɪts] *adj* : su, sus

it's ['ɪts] (*contraction of* **it is** *or* **it has**) → **be, have**

itself [ɪt̬ˈsɛlf] *pron* **1** (*used reflexively*) : se **2** (*used for emphasis*) : (él) mismo, (ella) misma, sí (mismo) **3 by ~ :** solo

I've ['aɪv] (*contraction of* **I have**) → **have**

ivory ['aɪvəri] *n, pl* **-ries** : marfil *m*

ivy ['aɪvi] *n, pl* **ivies** : hiedra *f*

J

j ['dʒeɪ] *n, pl* **j's** *or* **js** ['dʒeɪz] : j *f*, décima letra del alfabeto inglés

jab ['dʒæb] *vt* **jabbed; jabbing 1** PIERCE : pinchar **2** POKE : golpear (con la punta de algo) — ~ *n* **1** PRICK : pinchazo *m* **2** POKE : golpe *m* abrupto

jabber ['dʒæbər] *vi* : farfullar

jack ['dʒæk] *n* **1** : gato *m* (mecanismo) **2** : sota *f* (de naipes) — ~ *vt or* ~ **up 1** : levantar (con un gato) **2** INCREASE : subir

jackal ['dʒækəl] *n* : chacal *m*

jackass ['dʒæk,æs] *n* : asno *m*, burro *m*

jacket ['dʒækət] *n* **1** : chaqueta *f* **2** : sobrecubierta *f* (de un libro), carátula *f* (de un disco)

jackhammer ['dʒæk,hæmər] *n* : martillo *m* neumático

jackknife ['dʒæk,naɪf] *n* : navaja *f* — ~ *vi* **-knifed; -knifing** : plegarse (dícese de un camión)

jack-o'-lantern ['dʒækə,læntərn] *n* : linterna *f* hecha de una calabaza

jackpot ['dʒæk,pɑt] *n* : premio *m* gordo

jaded ['dʒeɪdəd] *adj* **1** TIRED : agotado **2** BORED : hastiado

jagged ['dʒægəd] *adj* : dentado

jail ['dʒeɪl] *n* : cárcel *f* — ~ *vt* : encarcelar — **jailer** *or* **jailor** ['dʒeɪlər] *n* : carcelero *m*, -ra *f*

jalapeño [hɑlə'peɪnjo, ,hæ-, -pi:no] *n* : jalapeño *m Lat*

jam¹ ['dʒæm] *v* **jammed; jamming** *vt* **1** CRAM : apiñar, embutir **2** BLOCK : atascar, atorar — *vi* : atascarse, atrancarse — ~ *n* **1** *or* **traffic** ~ : embotellamiento *m* (de tráfico) **2** FIX : lío *m*, aprieto *m*

jam² *n* PRESERVES : mermelada *f*

jangle ['dʒæŋgəl] *v* **-gled; -gling** *vi* : hacer un ruido metálico — *vt* : hacer sonar — ~ *n* : ruido *m* metálico

janitor ['dʒænətər] *n* : portero *m*, -ra *f*; conserje *mf*

January ['dʒænju,eri] *n* : enero *m*

Japanese [,dʒæpə'ni:z, -'ni:s] *adj* : japonés — ~ *n* : japonés *m* (idioma)

jar¹ ['dʒɑr] *v* **jarred; jarring 1** GRATE : chirriar **2** CLASH : desentonar **3** ~ **on** IRRITATE : crispar, enervar (a algn) — *vt* JOLT : sacudir — ~ *n* : sacudida *f*

jar² *n* : tarro *m*

jargon ['dʒɑrgən] *n* : jerga *f*

jaundice ['dʒɔndɪs] *n* : ictericia *f*

jaunt ['dʒɔnt] *n* : excursión *f*

jaunty ['dʒɔnti] *adj* **-tier; -est** : garboso, desenvuelto

jaw ['dʒɔ] *n* : mandíbula *f* (de una persona), quijada *f* (de un animal) — **jawbone** ['dʒɔ,bon] *n* : mandíbula *f*, quijada *f*

jay ['dʒeɪ] *n* : arrendajo *m*

jazz ['dʒæz] *n* : jazz *m* — ~ *vt or* ~ **up** : animar, alegrar — **jazzy** ['dʒæzi] *adj* **jazzier; -est** FLASHY : llamativo

jealous ['dʒɛləs] *adj* : celoso — **jealousy** ['dʒɛləsi] *n* : celos *mpl*, envidia *f*

jeans ['dʒi:nz] *npl* : jeans *mpl*, vaqueros *mpl*

jeer ['dʒɪr] *vt* **1** BOO : abuchear **2** MOCK : mofarse de — *vi* ~ **at** : mofarse de — ~ *n* : mofa *f*

jell ['dʒɛl] *vi* : cuajar

jelly ['dʒɛli] *n, pl* **-lies** : jalea *f* — **jellyfish** ['dʒɛli,fɪʃ] *n* : medusa *f*

jeopardy ['dʒɛpərdi] *n* : peligro *m*, riesgo *m* — **jeopardize** ['dʒɛpər,daɪz] *vt* **-dized; -dizing** : arriesgar, poner en peligro

jerk ['dʒərk] *n* **1** JOLT : sacudida *f* brusca **2** FOOL : idiota *mf* — ~ *vt* : sacudir — *vi* JOLT : dar sacudidas

jersey ['dʒərzi] *n, pl* **-seys** : jersey *m*

jest ['dʒɛst] *n* : broma *f* — ~ *vi* : bromear — **jester** ['dʒɛstər] *n* : bufón *m*

Jesus ['dʒi:zəs, -zəz] *n* : Jesús *m*

jet ['dʒɛt] *n* **1** STREAM : chorro *m* **2** *or* ~ **airplane** : avión *m* a reacción, reactor *m* — **jet-propelled** *adj* : a reacción

jettison ['dʒɛtəsən] *vt* **1** : echar al mar **2** DISCARD : deshacerse de

jetty ['dʒɛti] *n, pl* **-ties** : desembarcadero *m*, muelle *m*

jewel ['dʒu:əl] *n* **1** : joya *f* **2** GEM : piedra *f* preciosa — **jeweler** *or* **jeweller** ['dʒu:ələr] *n* : joyero *m*, -ra *f* — **jewelry** ['dʒu:əlri] *n* : joyas *fpl*, alhajas *fpl*

Jewish ['dʒu:ɪʃ] *adj* : judío

jibe ['dʒaɪb] *vi* **jibed; jibing** AGREE : concordar

jiffy ['dʒɪfi] *n, pl* **-fies** : santiamén *m*, segundo *m*

jig ['dʒɪg] *n* : giga *f*

jiggle ['dʒɪgəl] *vt* **-gled; -gling** : sacudir, zarandear — ~ *n* : sacudida *f*

jigsaw ['dʒɪgˌsɔ] *n* **1** : sierra *f* de vaivén **2** *or* **~ puzzle** : rompecabezas *m*

jilt ['dʒɪlt] *vt* : dejar plantado

jingle ['dʒɪŋgəl] *v* **-gled; -gling** *vi* : tintinear — *vt* : hacer sonar — **~** *n* TINKLE : tintineo *m*

jinx ['dʒɪŋks] *n* CURSE : maldición *f*

jitters ['dʒɪtərz] *npl* **have the ~** : estar nervioso — **jittery** ['dʒɪtəri] *adj* : nervioso

job ['dʒɑb] *n* **1** EMPLOYMENT : empleo *m*, trabajo *m* **2** TASK : trabajo *m*

jockey ['dʒɑki] *n, pl* **-eys** : jockey *mf*

jog ['dʒɑg] *v* **jogged; jogging** *vt* **~ s.o.'s memory** : refrescar la memoria a algn — *vi* : hacer footing — **jogging** *n* : footing *m*

join ['dʒɔɪn] *vt* **1** UNITE : unir, juntar **2** MEET : reunirse con **3** : hacerse socio de (una organización, etc.) — *vi* **1** *or* **~ together** : unirse **2** : hacerse socio (de una organización, etc.)

joint ['dʒɔɪnt] *n* **1** : articulación *f* (en anatomía) **2** JUNCTURE : juntura *f*, unión *f* — **~** *adj* : conjunto : **jointly** ['dʒɔɪntli] *adv* : conjuntamente

joke ['dʒoːk] *n* : chiste *m*, broma *f* — **~** *vi* **joked; joking** : bromear — **joker** ['dʒoːkər] *n* **1** : bromista *mf* **2** : comodín *m* (en los naipes)

jolly ['dʒɑli] *adj* **-lier; -est** : alegre, jovial

jolt ['dʒoːlt] *vt* : sacudir — **~** *n* **1** : sacudida *f* brusca **2** SHOCK : golpe *m* (emocional)

jostle ['dʒɑsəl] *v* **-tled; -tling** *vt* : empujar, dar empujones — *vi* : empujarse

jot ['dʒɑt] *vt* **jotted; jotting** *or* **~ down** : anotar, apuntar

journal ['dʒərnəl] *n* **1** DIARY : diario *m* **2** PERIODICAL : revista *f* — **journalism** ['dʒərnəlˌɪzəm] *n* : periodismo *m* — **journalist** ['dʒərnəlɪst] *n* : periodista *mf*

journey ['dʒərni] *n, pl* **-neys** : viaje *m* — **~** *vi* **-neyed; -neying** : viajar

jovial ['dʒoːviəl] *adj* : jovial

joy ['dʒɔɪ] *n* : alegría *f* — **joyful** ['dʒɔɪfəl] *adj* : alegre, feliz — **joyous** ['dʒɔɪəs] *adj* : jubiloso, alegre

jubilant ['dʒuːbələnt] *adj* : jubiloso — **jubilee** ['dʒuːbəˌliː] *n* : aniversario *m* especial

Judaism ['dʒuːdəˌɪzəm, 'dʒuːdi-, 'dʒuːˌdeɪ-] *n* : judaísmo *m*

judge ['dʒʌdʒ] *vt* **judged; judging** : juzgar — **~** *n* : juez *mf* — **judgment** *or* **judgement** ['dʒʌdʒmənt] *n* **1** RULING : fallo *m*, sentencia *f* **2** VIEW : juicio *m*

judicial ['dʒuˈdɪʃəl] *adj* : judicial — **judicious** ['dʒuˈdɪʃəs] *adj* : juicioso

jug ['dʒʌg] *n* : jarra *f*

juggle ['dʒʌgəl] *vi* **-gled; -gling** : hacer juegos malabares — **juggler** ['dʒʌgələr] *n* : malabarista *mf*

jugular vein ['dʒʌgjələr-] *n* : vena *f* yugular

juice ['dʒuːs] *n* : jugo *m* — **juicy** ['dʒuːsi] *adj* **juicier; -est** : jugoso

jukebox ['dʒuːkˌbɑks] *n* : máquina *f* de discos

July ['dʒuˌlaɪ] *n* : julio *m*

jumble ['dʒʌmbəl] *vt* **-bled; -bling** : mezclar — **~** *n* : revoltijo *m*

jumbo ['dʒʌmˌboː] *adj* : gigante

jump ['dʒʌmp] *vi* **1** LEAP : saltar **2** START : sobresaltarse **3** RISE : subir de un golpe **4** **~ at** : no dejar escapar (una oportunidad, etc.) — *vt* : saltar — **~** *n* **1** LEAP : salto *m* **2** INCREASE : aumento *m* — **jumper** ['dʒʌmpər] *n* **1** : saltador *m*, -dora *f* (en deportes) **2** : jumper *m* (vestido) — **jumpy** ['dʒʌmpi] *adj* **jumpier; -est** : nervioso

junction ['dʒʌŋkʃən] *n* **1** JOINING : unión *f* **2** : cruce *m* (de calles), empalme *m* (de un ferrocarril) — **juncture** ['dʒʌŋktʃər] *n* : coyuntura *f*

June ['dʒuːn] *n* : junio *m*

jungle ['dʒʌŋgəl] *n* : selva *f*

junior ['dʒuːnjər] *adj* **1** YOUNGER : más joven **2** SUBORDINATE : subalterno — **~** *n* **1** : persona *f* de menor edad **2** SUBORDINATE : subalterno *m*, -na *f* **3** : estudiante *mf* de penúltimo año

junk ['dʒʌŋk] *n* : trastos *mpl* (viejos) — **~** *vt* : echar a la basura

junta ['hʊntə, 'dʒʌn-, 'hʌn-] *n* : junta *f* (militar)

jurisdiction [ˌdʒʊrəsˈdɪkʃən] *n* : jurisdicción *f*

jury ['dʒʊri] *n, pl* **-ries** : jurado *m* — **juror** ['dʒʊrər] *n* : jurado *mf*

just ['dʒʌst] *adj* : justo — **~** *adv* **1** BARELY : apenas **2** EXACTLY : exactamente **3** ONLY : sólo, solamente **4** **~ now** : ahora mismo **5 she has ~ left** : acaba de salir **6 we were ~ leaving** : justo íbamos a salir

justice ['dʒʌstɪs] *n* **1** : justicia *f* **2** JUDGE : juez *mf*

justify ['dʒʌstəˌfaɪ] *vt* **-fied; -fying** : justificar — **justification** [ˌdʒʌstəfəˈkeɪʃən] *n* : justificación *f*

jut ['dʒʌt] *vi* **jutted; jutting** *or* **~ out** : sobresalir

juvenile ['dʒuːvənˌaɪl, -vənəl] *adj* **1** YOUNG : juvenil **2** CHILDISH : infantil — **~** *n* : menor *mf*

juxtapose [ˌdʒʌkstəˌpoːz] *vt* **-posed; -posing** : yuxtaponer

K

k ['keɪ] *n, pl* **k's** *or* **ks** ['keɪz] : k *f*, undécima letra del alfabeto inglés

kaleidoscope [kə'laɪdə,skoːp] *n* : caleidoscopio *m*

kangaroo [,kæŋgə'ruː] *n, pl* **-roos** : canguro *m*

karat ['kærət] *n* : quilate *m*

karate [kə'roːṭi] *n* : karate *m*

keel ['kiːl] *n* : quilla *f* — ~ *vi or* ~ **over** : volcarse (dícese de un barco), desplomarse (dícese de una persona)

keen ['kiːn] *adj* **1** SHARP : cortante, penetrante **3** ENTHUSIASTIC : entusiasta **4** ~ **eyesight** : visión aguda

keep ['kiːp] *v* **kept** ['kept]; **keeping** *vt* **1** : guardar **2** : cumplir (una promesa), acudir a (una cita) **3** DETAIN : hacer quedar, detener **4** PREVENT : impedir **5** ~ **up** : mantener — *vi* **1** REMAIN : mantenerse **2** LAST : conservarse **3** *or* ~ **on** CONTINUE : no dejar — ~ *n* **1 earn one's** ~ : ganarse el pan **2 for** ~**s** : para siempre — **keeper** ['kiːpər] *n* : guarda *mf* — **keeping** ['kiːpɪŋ] *n* **1** CARE : cuidado *m* **2 in** ~ **with** : de acuerdo con — **keepsake** ['kiːp,seɪk] *n* : recuerdo *m*

keg ['keg] *n* : barril *m*

kennel ['kenəl] *n* : caseta *f* para perros, perrera *f*

kept → keep

kerchief ['kərtʃəf, -,tʃiːf] *n* : pañuelo *m*

kernel ['kərnəl] *n* **1** : almendra *f* **2** CORE : meollo *m*

kerosene *or* **kerosine** ['kerə,siːn, ,kerə'-] *n* : querosén *m*

ketchup ['ketʃəp, 'kæ-] *n* : salsa *f* de tomate

kettle ['keṭəl] *n* : hervidor *m*, tetera *f* (para hervir)

key ['kiː] *n* **1** : llave *f* **2** : tecla *f* (de un piano o una máquina) — ~ *vt* **be keyed up** : estar nervioso — ~ *adj* : clave — **keyboard** ['kiː,bord] *n* : teclado *m* — **keyhole** ['kiː,hoːl] *n* : ojo *m* (de la cerradura) — **keynote** ['kiː,noːt] *n* : tónica *f* — **key ring** *n* : llavero *m*

khaki ['kæki, 'kɑ-] *adj* : caqui

kick ['kɪk] *vt* **1** : dar una patada a **2** ~ **out** : echar a patadas — *vi* **1** : dar patadas (dícese de una persona), co-

cear (dícese de un animal) **2** RECOIL : dar un culatazo — ~ *n* **1** : patada *f*, coz *f* (de un animal) **2** RECOIL : culatazo **3** PLEASURE, THRILL : placer *m*

kid ['kɪd] *n* **1** GOAT : chivo *m*, -va *f*; cabrito *m* **2** CHILD : niño *m*, -ña *f* — ~ *v* **kidded; kidding** *vi or* ~ **around** : bromear — *vt* TEASE : tomar el pelo a — **kidnap** ['kɪd,næp] *vt* **-napped** *or* **-naped** [-,næpt]; **-napping** *or* **-naping** [-,næpɪŋ] : secuestrar, raptar

kidney ['kɪdni] *n, pl* **-neys** : riñón *m*

kidney bean *n* : frijol *m*

kill ['kɪl] *vt* **1** : matar **2** DESTROY : acabar con **3** ~ **time** : matar el tiempo — ~ *n* **1** KILLING : matanza *f* **2** PREY : presa *f* — **killer** ['kɪlər] *n* : asesino *m*, -na *f* — **killing** ['kɪlɪŋ] *n* **1** : matanza *f* **2** MURDER : asesinato *m*

kiln ['kɪl, 'kɪln] *n* : horno *m*

kilo ['kiːloː] *n, pl* **-los** : kilo *m* — **kilogram** ['kɪlə,græm, 'kiː-] *n* : kilogramo *m* — **kilometer** [kɪ'lɑmətər, 'kɪlə,miː-] *n* : kilómetro *m* — **kilowatt** ['kɪlə,wɑt] *n* : kilovatio *m*

kin ['kɪn] *n* : parientes *mpl*

kind ['kaɪnd] *n* **1** : tipo *m*, clase *f* — ~ *adj* : amable

kindergarten ['kɪndər,gɑrtən, -dən] *n* : jardín *m* infantil, jardín *m* de niños *Lat*

kindhearted [,kaɪnd'hɑrṭəd] *adj* : de buen corazón

kindle ['kɪndəl] *vt* **-dled; -dling 1** : encender (un fuego) **2** AROUSE : despertar

kindly ['kaɪndli] *adj* **-lier; -est** : bondadoso, amable — ~ *adv* **1** : amablemente **2 take** ~ **to** : aceptar de buena gana **3 we** ~ **ask you not smoke** : les rogamos que no fumen — **kindness** ['kaɪndnəs] *n* : bondad *f* — **kind of** *adv* SOMEWHAT : un tanto, algo

kindred ['kɪndrəd] *adj* **1** : emparentado **2** ~ **spirit** : alma *f* gemela

king ['kɪŋ] *n* : rey *m* — **kingdom** ['kɪŋdəm] *n* : reino *m*

kink ['kɪŋk] *n* **1** TWIST : vuelta *f*, curva *f* **2** FLAW : problema *m*

kinship ['kɪn,ʃɪp] *n* : parentesco *m*

kiss ['kɪs] *vt* : besar — *vi* : besarse — ~ *n* : beso *m*

kit ['kɪt] *n* **1** : juego *m*, kit *m* **2 first-aid**

~ : botiquín *m* **3 tool** ~ : caja *f* de herramientas

kitchen ['kɪtʃən] *n* : cocina *f*

kite ['kaɪt] *n* 1 : cometa *f*, papalote *m Lat*

kitten ['kɪtən] *n* : gatito *m*, -ta *f* — **kitty** ['kɪti] *n, pl* **-ties** FUND : fondo *m* común

knack ['næk] *n* : maña *f*, facilidad *f*

knapsack ['næp,sæk] *n* : mochila *f*

knead ['ni:d] *vt* 1 : amasar, sobar **2** MASSAGE : masajear

knee ['ni:] *n* : rodilla *f* — **kneecap** ['ni:-,kæp] *n* : rótula *f*

kneel ['ni:l] *vi* **knelt** ['nɛlt] *or* **kneeled** ['ni:ld]; **kneeling** : arrodillarse

knew → **know**

knickknack ['nɪk,næk] *n* : chuchería *f*

knife ['naɪf] *n, pl* **knives** ['naɪvz] : cuchillo *m* — ~ *vt* **knifed** ['naɪft]; **knifing** : acuchillar

knight ['naɪt] *n* 1 : caballero *m* 2 : caballo *m* (en ajedrez) — **knighthood** ['naɪt,hʊd] *n* : título *m* de Sir

knit ['nɪt] *v* **knit** *or* **knitted** ['nɪtəd]; **knitting** *v* : tejer — ~ *n* : prenda *f* tejida

knob ['nɑb] *n* : tirador *m*, botón *m*, perilla *f Lat*

knock ['nɑk] *vt* 1 : golpear 2 CRITICIZE : criticar 3 ~ **down** : derribar, echar

al suelo — *vi* 1 : dar un golpe, llamar (a la puerta) 2 COLLIDE : darse, chocar — ~ *n* : golpe *m*, llamada *f* (a la puerta)

knot ['nɑt] *n* : nudo *m* — ~ *vt* **knotted**; **knotting** : anudar — **knotty** ['nɑti] *adj* **-tier; -est** 1 : nudoso 2 : enredado (dícese de un problema)

know ['no:] *v* **knew** ['nu:, 'nju:]; **known** ['no:n]; **knowing** *vt* 1 : saber 2 : conocer (a una persona, un lugar) 3 ~ **how to** : saber — *vi* : saber — **knowing** ['no:ɪŋ] *adj* : cómplice — **knowingly** ['no:ɪŋli] *adv* 1 : de manera cómplice 2 DELIBERATELY : a sabiendas — **know-it-all** ['no:ɪt,ɔl] *n* : sabelotodo *mf fam* — **knowledge** ['nɑlɪʤ] *n* 1 : conocimiento *m* 2 LEARNING : conocimientos *mpl*, saber *m* — **knowledgeable** ['nɑlɪʤəbəl] *adj* : informado, entendido

knuckle ['nʌkəl] *n* : nudillo *m*

Koran [kə'rɑn, -'ræn] *n* **the Koran** : el Corán *m*

Korean [kə'ri:ən] *adj* : coreano *m*, -na *f* — ~ *n* : coreano *m* (idioma)

kosher ['ko:ʃər] *adj* : aprobado por la ley judía

L

l ['ɛl] *n, pl* **l's** *or* **ls** ['ɛlz] : l *f*, duodécima letra del alfabeto inglés

lab ['læb] → **laboratory**

label ['leɪbəl] *n* 1 TAG : etiqueta *f* 2 BRAND : marca *f* — ~ *vt* **-beled** *or* **-belled; -beling** *or* **-belling** : etiquetar

labor ['leɪbər] *n* 1 : trabajo *m* 2 WORKERS : mano *f* de obra 3 **in** ~ : de parto — ~ *vi* 1 : trabajar 2 STRUGGLE : avanzar penosamente — ~ *vt* BELABOR : insistir en (un punto)

laboratory ['læbrə,tori, lə'bɔrə-] *n, pl* **-ries** : laboratorio *m*

laborer ['leɪbərər] *n* : trabajador *m*, -dora *f*

laborious [lə'boriəs] *adj* : laborioso

lace ['leɪs] *n* 1 : encaje *m* 2 SHOELACE : cordón *m* (de zapatos), agujeta *f Lat* — ~ *vt* **laced; lacing** 1 TIE : atar 2 **be laced with** : echar licor a (una bebida, etc.)

lacerate ['læsə,reɪt] *vt* **-ated; -ating** : lacerar

lack ['læk] *vt* : carecer de, no tener — *vi* **be lacking** : faltar — ~ *n* : falta *f*, carencia *f*

lackadaisical [,lækə'deɪzɪkəl] *adj* : apático, indolente

lackluster ['læk,lʌstər] *adj* : sin brillo, apagado

laconic [lə'kɑnɪk] *adj* : lacónico

lacquer ['lækər] *n* : laca *f*

lacrosse [lə'krɔs] *n* : lacrosse *f*

lacy ['leɪsi] *adj* **lacier; -est** : como de encaje

lad ['læd] *n* : muchacho *m*, niño *m*

ladder ['lædər] *n* : escalera *f*

laden ['leɪdən] *adj* : cargado

ladle ['leɪdəl] *n* : cucharón *m* — ~ *vt* **-dled; -dling** : servir con cucharón

lady ['leɪdi] *n, pl* **-dies** : señora *f*, dama *f* — **ladybug** ['leɪdi,bʌg] *n* : mariquita *f* — **ladylike** ['leɪdi,laɪk] *adj* : elegante, como señora

lag ['læg] *n* 1 DELAY : retraso *m* 2 INTERVAL : intervalo *m* — ~ *vi* **lagged; lagging** : quedarse atrás, rezagarse

lager ['lɑgər] *n* : cerveza *f* rubia

lagoon [lə'gu:n] *n* : laguna *f*

laid *pp* → **lay¹**

lain *pp* → **lie¹**

lair ['lær] *n* : guarida *f*

lake ['leɪk] n : lago m
lamb ['læm] n : cordero m
lame ['leɪm] adj **lamer; lamest 1** : cojo, renco **2 a ~ excuse** : una excusa poco convincente
lament [lə'mɛnt] vt **1** MOURN : llorar **2** DEPLORE : lamentar — vi : lamentarse m — **lamentable** ['læməntəbəl, lə'mɛntə-] adj : lamentable
laminate ['læmə,neɪt] vt **-nated; -nating** : laminar
lamp ['læmp] n : lámpara f — **lamppost** ['læmp,post] n : farol m — **lampshade** ['læmp,ʃeɪd] n : pantalla f
lance ['læns] n : lanza f — ~ vt **lanced; lancing** : abrir con lanceta (en medicina)
land ['lænd] n **1** : tierra f **2** COUNTRY : país m **3** or **plot of ~** : terreno m — ~ vt **1** : desembarcar (pasajeros de un barco), hacer aterrizar (un avión) **2** CATCH : sacar (un pez) del agua **3** SECURE : conseguir (empleo, etc.) — vi **1** : aterrizar (dícese de un avión) **2** FALL : caer — **landing** ['lændɪŋ] n **1** : aterrizaje m (de aviones) **2** : desembarco m (de barcos) **3** : descanso m (de una escalera) — **landlady** ['lænd,leɪdi] n, pl **-dies** : casera f — **landlord** ['lænd,lord] n : casero m — **landmark** ['lænd,mark] n **1** : punto m de referencia **2** MONUMENT : monumento m histórico — **landowner** ['lænd,onər] n : hacendado m, -da f; terrateniente mf — **landscape** ['lænd,skeɪp] n : paisaje m — ~ vt **-scaped; -scaping** : ajardinar — **landslide** ['lænd,slaɪd] n **1** : desprendimiento m de tierras **2** or **~ victory** : victoria f arrolladora
lane ['leɪn] n **1** : carril m (de una carretera) **2** PATH, ROAD : camino m
language ['læŋgwɪdʒ] n **1** : idioma m, lengua f **2** SPEECH : lenguaje m
languid ['læŋgwɪd] adj : lánguido — **languish** ['læŋgwɪʃ] vi : languidecer
lanky ['læŋki] adj **lankier; -est** : delgado, larguirucho fam
lantern ['læntərn] n : linterna f
lap ['læp] n **1** : regazo m (de una persona) **2** : vuelta f (en deportes) — ~ v **lapped; lapping** vt or ~ **up** : beber a lengüetadas — vi ~ **against** : lamer
lapel [lə'pɛl] n : solapa f
lapse ['læps] n **1** : lapsus m, falla f (de memoria, etc.) **2** INTERVAL : lapso m, intervalo m — ~ vi **lapsed; lapsing 1** EXPIRE : caducar **2** ELAPSE : transcurrir, pasar **3 ~ into** : caer en
laptop ['læp,tɑp] adj : portátil
larceny ['larsəni] n, pl **-nies** : robo m

lard ['lard] n : manteca f de cerdo
large ['lardʒ] adj **larger; largest 1** : grande **2 at ~** : en libertad **3 by and ~** : por lo general — **largely** ['lardʒli] adv : en gran parte
lark ['lark] n **1** : alondra f (pájaro) **2 for a ~** : por divertirse
larva ['larvə] n, pl **-vae** [-,viː, -,vaɪ] : larva f
larynx ['lærɪŋks] n, pl **-rynges** [lə'rɪn,dʒiːz] or **-ynxes** ['lærɪŋksəz] : laringe f — **laryngitis** [,lærən'dʒaɪtəs] n : laringitis f
lasagna [lə'zɑnjə] n : lasaña f
laser ['leɪzər] n : láser m
lash ['læʃ] vt **1** WHIP : azotar **2** BIND : amarrar — vi ~ **out at** : arremeter contra — ~ n **1** BLOW : latigazo m (con un látigo) **2** EYELASH : pestaña f
lass ['læs] or **lassie** ['læsi] n : muchacha f, chica f
lasso ['læ,soː, læ'suː] n, pl **-sos** or **-soes** : lazo m
last ['læst] vi : durar — ~ n **1** : último m, -ma f **2 at ~** : por fin, finalmente — adv **1** : por última vez, en último lugar **2 arrive ~** : llegar el último — adj **1** : último **2 ~ year** : el año pasado — **lastly** ['læstli] adv : por último, finalmente
latch ['lætʃ] n : picaporte m, pestillo m
late ['leɪt] adj **later; latest 1** : tarde **2** : avanzado (dícese de la hora) **3** DECEASED : difunto **4** RECENT : reciente — ~ adv **later; latest** : tarde — **lately** ['leɪtli] adv : recientemente, últimamente — **lateness** ['leɪtnəs] n **1** : retraso m **2** : lo avanzado (de la hora)
latent ['leɪtənt] adj : latente
lateral ['lætərəl] adj : lateral
latest ['leɪtəst] n **at the ~** : a más tardar
lathe ['leɪð] n : torno m
lather ['læðər] n : espuma f — ~ vt : enjabonar — vi : hacer espuma
Latin-American [,lætənə'merɪkən] adj : latinoamericano
latitude ['lætə,tuːd, -,tjuːd] n : latitud f
latter ['lætər] adj **1** : último **2** SECOND : segundo — ~ pron **the ~** : éste, ésta, éstos pl, éstas pl
lattice ['lætəs] n : enrejado m
laugh ['læf] vi : reír(se) — ~ n : risa f — **laughable** ['læfəbəl] adj : risible, ridículo — **laughter** ['læftər] n : risa f, risas fpl
launch ['lɔntʃ] vt : lanzar — ~ n : lanzamiento m
launder ['lɔndər] vt **1** : lavar y planchar (ropa) **2** : blanquear, lavar (dinero) — **laundry** ['lɔndri] n, pl **-dries 1** : ropa f

sucia **2** : lavandería *f* (servicio) **3 do the** ~ : lavar la ropa

lava ['lɑvə, 'læ-] *n* : lava *f*

lavatory ['lævəˌtori] *n, pl* **-ries** BATHROOM : baño *m*, cuarto *m* de baño

lavender ['lævəndər] *n* : lavanda *f*

lavish ['lævɪʃ] *adj* **1** EXTRAVAGANT : pródigo **2** ABUNDANT : abundante **3** LUXURIOUS : lujoso — ~ *vt* : prodigar

law ['lɔ] *n* **1** : ley *f* **2** : derecho *m* (profesión, etc.) **3 practice** ~ : ejercer la abogacía — **lawful** ['lɔfəl] *adj* : legal, legítimo

lawn ['lɔn] *n* : césped *m* — **lawn mower** *n* : cortadora *f* de césped

lawsuit ['lɔˌsuːt] *n* : pleito *m*

lawyer ['lɔjər, 'lɔːjər] *n* : abogado *m*, -da *f*

lax ['læks] *adj* : poco estricto, relajado

laxative ['læksətɪv] *n* : laxante *m*

lay¹ ['leɪ] *vt* **laid** ['leɪd]; **laying 1** PLACE, PUT : poner, colocar **2** ~ **eggs** : poner huevos **3** ~ **off** : dispedir (un empleado) **4** ~ **out** PRESENT : presentar, exponer **5** ~ **out** DESIGN : diseñar (el trazado de)

lay² ['leɪ] → **lie¹**

lay³ *adj* **1** SECULAR : laico **2** NONPROFESSIONAL : lego, profano

layer ['leɪər] *n* : capa *f*

layman ['leɪmən] *n, pl* **-men** : lego *m*, laico *m* (en religión)

layout ['leɪˌaʊt] *n* ARRANGEMENT : disposición *f*

lazy ['leɪzi] *adj* **-zier; -est** : perezoso — **laziness** ['leɪzinəs] *n* : pereza *f*

lead¹ ['liːd] *vt* **led** ['led]; **leading 1** GUIDE : conducir **2** DIRECT : dirigir **3** HEAD : encabezar, ir al frente de — *vi* **1** : llevar, conducir (a algo) — ~ *n* **1** : delantera *f* **2 follow s.o.'s** ~ : seguir el ejemplo de algn

lead² ['led] *n* **1** : plomo *m* (metal) **2** GRAPHITE : mina *f* — **leaden** ['ledən] *adj* **1** : de plomo **2** HEAVY : pesado

leader ['liːdər] *n* : jefe *m*, -fa *f* — **leadership** ['liːdərˌʃɪp] *n* : mando *m*, dirección *f*

leaf ['liːf] *n, pl* **leaves** ['liːvz] **1** : hoja *f* **2 turn over a new** ~ : hacer borrón y cuenta nueva — ~ *vt* ~ **through** : hojear (un libro, etc.) — **leaflet** ['liːflət] *n* : folleto *m*

league ['liːg] *n* **1** : liga *f* **2 be in** ~ **with** : estar confabulado con

leak ['liːk] *vt* **1** : dejar escapar (un líquido o un gas) **2** : filtrar (información) — *vi* **1** : gotear, escaparse (dícese de un líquido o un gas) **2** : filtrarse (dícese de información) — ~ *n* **1** : agujero *m* (en un cubo, etc.), gotera *f*

(de un techo) **2** : fuga *f*, escape *m* (de un líquido o un gas) **3** : filtración *f* (de información) — **leaky** ['liːki] *adj* **leakier; -est** : que hace agua

lean¹ ['liːn] *v* **leaned** *or Brit* **leant** ['lent]; **leaning** *vi* **1** BEND : inclinarse **2** ~ **against** : apoyarse contra — *vt* : apoyar

lean² *adj* **1** THIN : delgado **2** : sin grasa (dícese de la carne)

leaning ['liːnɪŋ] *n* : inclinación *f*

leanness ['liːnnəs] *n* : delgadez *f* (de una persona), lo magro (de la carne)

leap ['liːp] *vi* **leapt** *or* **leaped** ['liːpt, 'lept]; **leaping** : saltar, brincar — ~ *n* : salto *m*, brinco *m* — **leap year** *n* : año *m* bisiesto

learn ['lərn] *v* **learned** ['lərnd, 'lərnt]; **learning** : aprender — **learned** ['lərnəd] *adj* : sabio, erudito — **learner** ['lərnər] *n* : principiante *mf*, estudiante *mf* — **learning** ['lərnɪŋ] *n* : erudición *f*, saber *m*

lease ['liːs] *n* : contrato *m* de arrendamiento — ~ *vt* **leased; leasing** : arrendar

leash ['liːʃ] *n* : correa *f*

least ['liːst] *adj* **1** : menor **2** SLIGHTEST : más mínimo — ~ *n* **1 at** ~ : por lo menos **2** the ~ : lo menos **3 to say the** ~ : por no decir más — ~ *adv* : menos

leather ['leðər] *n* : cuero *m*

leave ['liːv] *v* **left** ['left]; **leaving** *vt* **1** : dejar **2** : salir(se) de (un lugar) **3** ~ **out** : omitir — *vi* DEPART : irse — ~ *n* **1** *or* ~ **of absence** : permiso *m*, licencia *f* **2 take one's** ~ : despedirse

leaves → **leaf**

lecture ['lektʃər] *n* **1** TALK : conferencia *f* **2** REPRIMAND : sermón *m*, reprimenda *f* — ~ *v* **-tured; -turing** *vt* : sermonear — *vi* : dar clase, dar una conferencia

led *pp* → **lead¹**

ledge ['ledʒ] *n* : antepecho *m* (de una ventana), saliente *m* (de una montaña)

leech ['liːtʃ] *n* : sanguijuela *f*

leek ['liːk] *n* : puerro *m*

leer ['lɪr] *vi* : lanzar una mirada lasciva — ~ *n* : mirada *f* lasciva

leery ['lɪri] *adj* : receloso

leeway ['liːˌweɪ] *n* : libertad *f* de acción, margen *m*

left¹ → **leave**

left² ['left] *adj* : izquierdo — ~ *adv* : a la izquierda — ~ *n* : izquierda *f* — **left-handed** ['leftˈhændəd] *adj* : zurdo

leftovers ['leftˌoːvərz] *npl* : restos *mpl*, sobras *fpl*

leg ['lɛg] n 1 : pierna f (de una persona, de ropa), pata f (de un animal, de muebles) 2 : etapa f (de un viaje)

legacy ['lɛgəsi] n, pl **-cies** : legado m

legal ['liːgəl] adj 1 LAWFUL : legítimo, legal 2 JUDICIAL : legal, jurídico — **legality** [li'gælət̬i] n, pl **-ties** : legalidad f — **legalize** ['liːgəˌlaɪz] vt **-ized; -izing** : legalizar

legend ['lɛdʒənd] n : leyenda f — **legendary** ['lɛdʒənˌderi] adj : lengendario

legible ['lɛdʒəbəl] adj : legible

legion ['liːdʒən] n : legión f

legislate ['lɛdʒəsˌleɪt] vi **-lated; -lating** : legislar — **legislation** [ˌlɛdʒəsˈleɪʃən] n : legislación f — **legislative** ['lɛdʒəsˌleɪt̬ɪv] adj : legislativo, legislador — **legislature** ['lɛdʒəsˌleɪtʃər] n : asamblea f legislativa

legitimate [lɪˈdʒɪt̬əmət] adj : legítimo — **legitimacy** [lɪˈdʒɪt̬əməsi] n : legitimidad f

leisure ['liːʒər, 'lɛ-] n 1 : ocio m, tiempo m libre 2 **at your** ~ : cuando te venga bien — **leisurely** ['liːʒərli, 'lɛ-] adj & adv : lento, sin prisas

lemon ['lɛmən] n : limón m — **lemonade** [ˌlɛməˈneɪd] n : limonada f

lend ['lɛnd] vt **lent** ['lɛnt]; **lending** : prestar

length ['lɛŋθ] n 1 : largo m 2 DURATION : duración f 3 **at** ~ FINALLY : por fin 4 **at** ~ EXTENSIVELY : extensamente 5 **go to any** ~s : hacer todo lo posible — **lengthen** ['lɛŋθən] vt 1 : alargar 2 PROLONG : prolongar — vi : alargarse — **lengthways** ['lɛŋθˌweɪz] or **lengthwise** ['lɛŋθˌwaɪz] adv : a lo largo — **lengthy** ['lɛŋθi] adj **lengthier; -est** : largo

lenient ['liːniənt] adj : indulgente — **leniency** ['liːniənsi] n, pl **-cies** : indulgencia f

lens ['lɛnz] n 1 : cristalino m (del ojo) 2 : lente mf (de un instrumento) 3 → **contact lens**

Lent ['lɛnt] n : Cuaresma f

lentil ['lɛntəl] n : lenteja f

leopard ['lɛpərd] n : leopardo m

leotard ['liːəˌtard] n : leotardo m, malla f

lesbian ['lɛzbiən] n : lesbiana f

less ['lɛs] adv (comparative of **little**) : menos — ~ adj (comparative of **little**) : menos — ~ pron : menos — ~ prep MINUS : menos — **lessen** ['lɛsən] v : disminuir — **lesser** ['lɛsər] adj : menor

lesson ['lɛsən] n 1 CLASS : clase f, curso m 2 **learn one's** ~ : aprender la lección

lest ['lɛst] conj ~ **we forget** : para que no olvidemos

let ['lɛt] vt **let; letting** 1 ALLOW : dejar, permitir 2 RENT : alquilar 3 ~**'s go!** : ¡vamos!, ¡vámonos! 4 ~ **down** DISAPPOINT : fallar 5 ~ **in** : dejar entrar 6 ~ **off** FORGIVE : perdonar 7 ~ **up** ABATE : amainar, disminuir

letdown ['lɛtˌdaʊn] n : chasco m, decepción f

lethal ['liːθəl] adj : letal

lethargic [lɪˈθɑrdʒɪk] adj : letárgico

let's ['lɛts] (contraction of **let us**) → **let**

letter ['lɛt̬ər] n 1 : carta f 2 : letra f (del alfabeto)

lettuce ['lɛt̬əs] n : lechuga f

letup ['lɛtˌʌp] n : pausa f, descanso m

leukemia [luˈkiːmiə] n : leucemia f

level ['lɛvəl] n 1 : nivel m 2 **be on the** ~ : ser honrado — ~ vt **-eled** or **-elled; -eling** or **-elling** 1 : nivelar 2 AIM : apuntar 3 RAZE : arrasar — ~ adj 1 FLAT : llano, plano 2 : nivel (de altura) — **levelheaded** ['lɛvəlˈhɛdəd] adj : sensato, equilibrado

lever ['lɛvər, 'liː-] n : palanca f — **leverage** ['lɛvərɪdʒ, 'liː-] n 1 : apalancamiento m (en física) 2 INFLUENCE : influencia f

levity ['lɛvət̬i] n : ligereza f

levy ['lɛvi] n, pl **levies** : impuesto m — ~ vt **levied; levying** : imponer, exigir (un impuesto)

lewd ['luːd] adj : lascivo

lexicon ['lɛksɪˌkɑn] n, pl **-ica** [-kə] or **-icons** : léxico m, lexicón m

liable ['laɪəbəl] adj 1 : responsable 2 LIKELY : probable 3 SUSCEPTIBLE : propenso — **liability** [ˌlaɪəˈbɪlət̬i] n, pl **-ties** 1 RESPONSIBILITY : responsabilidad f 2 DRAWBACK : desventaja f 3 **liabilities** npl DEBTS : deudas fpl, pasivo m

liaison ['liːəˌzɑn, liˈeɪ-] n 1 : enlace m 2 AFFAIR : amorío m

liar ['laɪər] n : mentiroso m, -sa f

libel ['laɪbəl] n : libelo m, difamación f — ~ vt **-beled** or **-belled; -beling** or **-belling** : difamar

liberal ['lɪbrəl, 'lɪbərəl] adj : liberal — ~ n : liberal mf

liberate ['lɪbəˌreɪt] vt **-ated; -ating** : liberar — **liberation** [ˌlɪbəˈreɪʃən] n : liberación f

liberty ['lɪbərt̬i] n, pl **-ties** : libertad f

library ['laɪˌbreri] n, pl **-braries** : biblioteca f — **librarian** [laɪˈbreriən] n : bibliotecario m, -ria f

lice → **louse**

license or **licence** ['laɪsənts] n 1 PERMIT

: licencia *f* **2** FREEDOM : libertad *f* **3** AUTHORIZATION : permiso *m* — ~ *vt* : licensed; licensing : autorizar

lick ['lɪk] *vt* **1** : lamer **2** DEFEAT : dar una paliza a *fam* — ~ *n* : lamida *f*

licorice ['lɪkərɪʃ, -rəs] *n* : regaliz *m*

lid ['lɪd] *n* **1** : tapa *f* **2** EYELID : párpado *m*

lie[1] ['laɪ] *vi* **lay** ['leɪ]; **lain** ['leɪn]; **lying** ['laɪŋ] **1** *or* ~ **down** : acostarse, echarse **2** BE : estar, encontrarse

lie[2] *vi* **lied; lying** ['laɪŋ] : mentir — ~ *n* : mentira *f*

lieutenant [lu:'tɛnənt] *n* : teniente *mf*

life ['laɪf] *n, pl* **lives** ['laɪvz] : vida *f* — **lifeboat** ['laɪf,boːt] *n* : bote *m* salvavidas — **lifeguard** ['laɪf,gɑrd] *n* : socorrista *mf* — **lifeless** ['laɪfləs] *adj* : sin vida — **lifelike** ['laɪf,laɪk] *adj* : natural, realista — **lifelong** ['laɪf,lɔŋ] *adj* : de toda la vida — **life preserver** *n* : salvavidas *m* — **lifestyle** ['laɪf,staɪl] *n* : estilo *m* de vida — **lifetime** ['laɪf,taɪm] *n* : vida *f*

lift ['lɪft] *vt* **1** RAISE : levantar **2** STEAL : robar — *vi* **1** CLEAR UP : despejarse **2** *or* ~ **off** : despegar (dícese de un avión, etc.) — ~ *n* **1** LIFTING : levantamiento *m* **2 give s.o. a** ~ : llevar en coche a algn — **liftoff** ['lɪft,ɔf] *n* : despegue *m*

light[1] ['laɪt] *n* **1** : luz *f* **2** LAMP : lámpara *f* **3** HEADLIGHT : faro *m* **4 do you have a** ~? : ¿tienes fuego? — ~ *adj* **1** BRIGHT : bien iluminado **2** : claro (dícese de los colores), rubio (dícese del pelo) — *v* **lit** ['lɪt] *or* **lighted; lighting** *vt* **1** : encender (un fuego) **2** ILLUMINATE : iluminar — *vi or* ~ **up** : iluminarse — **lightbulb** ['laɪt,bʌlb] *n* : bombilla *f*, bombillo *m Lat* — **lighten** ['laɪtən] *vt* BRIGHTEN : iluminar — **lighter** ['laɪtər] *n* : encendedor *m* — **lighthouse** ['laɪt,haʊs] *n* : faro *m* — **lighting** ['laɪtɪŋ] *n* : alumbrado *m* — **lightning** ['laɪtnɪŋ] *n* : relámpago *m*, rayo *m* — **light-year** ['laɪt,jɪr] *n* : año *m* luz

light[2] *adj* : ligero — **lighten** ['laɪtən] *vt* : aligerar — **lightly** ['laɪtli] *adv* **1** : suavemente **2 let off** ~ : tratar con indulgencia — **lightness** ['laɪtnəs] *n* : ligereza *f* — **lightweight** ['laɪt,weɪt] *adj* : ligero

like[1] ['laɪk] *v* **liked; liking** *vt* **1** : gustarle (a uno) **2** WANT : querer — *vi* **if you** ~ : si quieres — **likes** *npl* : preferencias *fpl*, gustos *mpl* — **likable** *or* **likeable** ['laɪkəbəl] *adj* : simpático

like[2] *adj* SIMILAR : parecido — ~ *prep* : como — ~ *conj* **1** AS : como **2** AS IF

: como si — **likelihood** ['laɪkli,hʊd] *n* : probabilidad *f* — **likely** ['laɪkli] *adj* **-lier; -est** : probable — **liken** ['laɪkən] *vt* : comparar — **likeness** ['laɪknəs] *n* : semejanza *f*, parecido *m* — **likewise** ['laɪk,waɪz] *adv* **1** : lo mismo **2** ALSO : también

liking ['laɪkɪŋ] *n* : afición *f* (por una cosa), simpatía *f* (por una persona)

lilac ['laɪlək, -læk, -lɑk] *n* : lila *f*

lily ['lɪli] *n, pl* **lilies** **1** : lirio *m*, azucena *f* **2 ~ of the valley** : lirio *m* de los valles

lima bean ['laɪmə] *n* : frijol *m* de media luna

limb ['lɪm] *n* **1** : miembro *m* (en anatomía) **2** : rama *f* (de un árbol)

limber ['lɪmbər] *vi or* ~ **up** : calentarse, hacer ejercicios preliminares — ~ *adj* : ágil

limbo ['lɪm,boː] *n, pl* **-bos** : limbo *m*

lime ['laɪm] *n* : lima *f*, limón *m* verde *Lat*

limelight ['laɪm,laɪt] *n* **be in the** ~ : estar en el candelero

limerick ['lɪmərɪk] *n* : poema *m* jocoso de cinco versos

limestone ['laɪm,stoːn] *n* : (piedra *f*) caliza *f*

limit ['lɪmət] *n* : límite *m* — ~ *vt* : limitar, restringir — **limitation** [,lɪmə'teɪʃən] *n* : limitación *f*, restricción *f* — **limited** ['lɪmətəd] *adj* : limitado

limousine ['lɪmə,ziːn, ,lɪmə'-] *n* : limusina *f*

limp[1] ['lɪmp] *vi* : cojear — ~ *n* : cojera *f*

limp[2] *adj* : flojo, fláccido

line ['laɪn] *n* **1** : línea *f* **2** ROPE : cuerda *f* **3** ROW : fila *f* **4** QUEUE : cola *f* **5** WRINKLE : arruga *f* **6 drop a** ~ : mándar unas líneas — *v* **lined; lining** *vt* **1** : forrar (un vestido, etc.), cubrir (las paredes, etc.) **2** MARK : rayar, trazar líneas en **3** BORDER : bordear — *vi* ~ **up** : ponerse en fila, hacer cola

lineage ['lɪniɪdʒ] *n* : linaje *m*

linear ['lɪniər] *adj* : lineal

linen ['lɪnən] *n* : lino *m*

liner ['laɪnər] *n* **1** LINING : forro *m* **2** SHIP : buque *m*, transatlántico *m*

lineup ['laɪn,əp] *n* **1** *or* **police** ~ : fila *f* de sospechosos **2** : alineación *f* (en deportes)

linger ['lɪŋgər] *vi* **1** : quedarse, entretenerse **2** PERSIST : persistir

lingerie [,lɑndʒə'reɪ, ,lænʒə'ri:] *n* : ropa *f* íntima femenina, lencería *f*

lingo ['lɪŋgoː] *n, pl* **-goes** JARGON : jerga *f*

linguistics [lɪŋ'gwɪstɪks] *n* : lingüística *f* — **linguist** ['lɪŋgwɪst] *n* : lingüista *mf*

— **linguistic** [lɪŋˈgwɪstɪk] *adj* : lingüístico

lining [ˈlaɪnɪŋ] *n* : forro *m*

link [ˈlɪŋk] *n* 1 : eslabón *m* (de una cadena) 2 BOND : lazo *m* 3 CONNECTION : conexión *f* — ~ *vt* : enlazar, conectar — *vi* ~ **up** : unirse, conectar

linoleum [ləˈnoːliəm] *n* : linóleo *m*

lint [ˈlɪnt] *n* : pelusa *f*

lion [ˈlaɪən] *n* : león *m* — **lioness** [ˈlaɪənɪs] *n* : leona *f*

lip [ˈlɪp] *n* 1 : labio *m* 2 EDGE : borde *m* — **lipstick** [ˈlɪpˌstɪk] *n* : lápiz *m* de labios

liqueur [lɪˈkʊr, -ˈkər, -ˈkjʊr] *n* : licor *m*

liquid [ˈlɪkwəd] *adj* : líquido — ~ *n* : líquido *m* — **liquidate** [ˈlɪkwəˌdeɪt] *vt* **-dated; -dating** : liquidar — **liquidation** [ˌlɪkwəˈdeɪʃən] *n* : liquidación *f*

liquor [ˈlɪkər] *n* : bebidas *fpl* alcohólicas

lisp [ˈlɪsp] *vi* : cecear — ~ *n* : ceceo *m*

list¹ [ˈlɪst] *n* : lista *f* — ~ *vt* 1 ENUMERATE : hacer una lista de, enumerar 2 INCLUDE : incluir (en una lista)

list² [ˈlɪst] *vi* : escorar (dícese de un barco)

listen [ˈlɪsən] *vi* 1 : escuchar 2 ~ **to** HEED : hacer caso de 3 ~ **to reason** : atender a razones — **listener** [ˈlɪsənər] *n* : oyente *mf*

listless [ˈlɪstləs] *adj* : apático

lit [ˈlɪt] *pp* → **light**

litany [ˈlɪtəni] *n, pl* **-nies** : letanía *f*

liter [ˈliːtər] *n* : litro *m*

literacy [ˈlɪtərəsi] *n* : alfabetismo *m*

literal [ˈlɪtərəl] *adj* : literal — **literally** *adv* : literalmente, al pie de la letra

literate [ˈlɪtərət] *adj* : alfabetizado

literature [ˈlɪtərəˌtʃʊr, -tʃər] *n* : literatura *f* — **literary** [ˈlɪtəˌreri] *adj* : literario

lithe [ˈlaɪð, ˈlaɪθ] *adj* : ágil y grácil

litigation [ˌlɪtəˈgeɪʃən] *n* : litigio *m*

litre → **liter**

litter [ˈlɪtər] *n* 1 RUBBISH : basura *f* 2 : camada *f* (de animales) 3 *or* **kitty** ~ : arena *f* higiénica — ~ *vt* : tirar basura en, ensuciar — *vi* : tirar basura

little [ˈlɪtəl] *adj* **littler** *or* **less** [ˈles] *or* **lesser** [ˈlesər]; **littlest** *or* **least** [ˈliːst] 1 SMALL : pequeño 2 **a** ~ SOME : un poco de 3 **he speaks** ~ **English** : habla poco inglés — ~ *adv* **less** [ˈles], **least** [ˈliːst] : poco — ~ *pron* 1 : poco *m*, -ca *f* 2 ~ **by** ~ : poco a poco

liturgy [ˈlɪtərdʒi] *n, pl* **-gies** : liturgia *f* — **liturgical** [ləˈtərdʒɪkəl] *adj* : litúrgico

live [ˈlɪv] *vi* **lived; living** 1 : vivir 2 RESIDE : residir 3 ~ **on** : vivir de — *vi* : vivir, llevar (una vida) — ~ [ˈlaɪv] *adj* 1 : vivo 2 : con corriente (dícese de cables eléctricos) 3 : en vivo, en di-

recto (dícese de programas de televisión, etc.) — **livelihood** [ˈlaɪvliˌhʊd] *n* : sustento *m*, medio *m* de vida — **lively** [ˈlaɪvli] *adj* **-lier; -est** : animado, alegre — **liven** [ˈlaɪvən] *vt or* ~ **up** : animar — *vi* : animarse

liver [ˈlɪvər] *n* : hígado *m*

livestock [ˈlaɪvˌstɑk] *n* : ganado *m*

livid [ˈlɪvəd] *adj* 1 : lívido 2 ENRAGED : furioso

living [ˈlɪvɪŋ] *adj* : vivo — ~ *n* **make a** ~ : ganarse la vida — **living room** *n* : living *m*, sala *f* (de estar)

lizard [ˈlɪzərd] *n* : lagarto *m*

llama [ˈlɑmə, ˈjɑ-] *n* : llama *f*

load [ˈloːd] *n* 1 CARGO : carga *f* 2 BURDEN : carga *f*, peso *m* 3 ~**s of** : un montón de — ~ *vt* : cargar

loaf¹ [ˈloːf] *n, pl* **loaves** [ˈloːvz] : pan *m*, barra *f* (de pan)

loaf² *vi* : holgazanear — **loafer** [ˈloːfər] *n* 1 : holgazán *m*, -zana *f* 2 : mocasín *m* (zapato)

loan [ˈloːn] *n* : préstamo *m* — ~ *vt* : prestar

loathe [ˈloːð] *vt* **loathed; loathing** : odiar — **loathsome** [ˈloːðsəm, ˈloːð-] *adj* : odioso

lobby [ˈlɑbi] *n, pl* **-bies** 1 : vestíbulo *m* 2 *or* **political** ~ : grupo *m* de presión, lobby *m* — ~ *v* **-bied; -bying** *vi* : ejercer presión política

lobe [ˈloːb] *n* : lóbulo *m*

lobster [ˈlɑbstər] *n* : langosta *f*

local [ˈloːkəl] *adj* : local — ~ *n* **the** ~**s** : los vecinos del lugar — **locale** [loˈkæl] *n* : escenario *m* — **locality** [loˈkæləti] *n, pl* **-ties** : localidad *f* — **locate** [ˈloːkeɪt, loˈkeɪt] *vt* **-cated; -cating** 1 SITUATE : situar, ubicar 2 FIND : localizar — **location** [loˈkeɪʃən] *n* : situación *f*, lugar *m*

lock¹ [ˈlɑk] *n* : mechón *m* (de pelo)

lock² *n* 1 : cerradura *f* (de una puerta, etc.) 2 : esclusa *f* (de un canal) — ~ *vt* 1 : cerrar (con llave) 2 *or* ~ **up** CONFINE : encerrar — *vi* 1 : cerrarse con llave 2 : bloquearse (dícese de una rueda, etc.) — **locker** [ˈlɑkər] *n* : armario *m* — **locket** [ˈlɑkət] *n* : medallón *m* — **locksmith** [ˈlɑkˌsmɪθ] *n* : cerrajero *m*, -ra *f*

locomotive [ˌloːkəˈmoːtɪv] *n* : locomotora *f*

locust [ˈloːkəst] *n* : langosta *f*, chapulín *m Lat*

lodge [ˈlɑdʒ] *v* **lodged; lodging** *vt* 1 HOUSE : hospedar, alojar 2 FILE : presentar — *vi* : hospedarse, alojarse — ~ *n* : pabellón *m* — **lodger** [ˈlɑdʒər] *n*

: huésped *m*, -peda *f* — **lodging** ['lɑdʒɪŋ] *n* 1 : alojamiento *m* 2 **~s** *npl* : habitaciones *fpl*

loft ['lɔft] *n* 1 : desván *m* (en una casa) 2 HAYLOFT : pajar *m* — **lofty** ['lɔfti] *adj* **loftier; -est** 1 : noble, elevado 2 HAUGHTY : altanero

log ['lɔg, 'lɑg] *n* 1 : tronco *m*, leño *m* 2 RECORD : diario *m* — *vi* **logged; logging** 1 : talar (árboles) 2 RECORD : registrar, anotar 3 **~ on** : entrar (en el sistema) 4 **~ off** : salir (del sistema) — **logger** ['lɔgər, 'lɑ-] *n* : leñador *m*, -dora *f*

logic ['lɑdʒɪk] *n* : lógica *f* — **logical** ['lɑdʒɪkəl] *adj* : lógico — **logistics** [lə-'dʒɪstɪks, lo-] *ns & pl* : logística *f*

logo ['loːgoː] *n, pl* **logos** [-goz] : logotipo *m*

loin ['lɔɪn] *n* : lomo *m*

loiter ['lɔɪtər] *vi* : vagar, holgazanear

lollipop *or* **lollypop** ['lɑlipɑp] *n* : pirulí *m*, chupete *m* Lat

lone ['loːn] *adj* : solitario — **loneliness** ['loːnlinəs] *n* : soledad *f* — **lonely** ['loːnli] *adj* **-lier; -est** : solitario, solo — **loner** ['loːnər] *n* : solitario *m*, -ria *f* — **lonesome** ['loːnsəm] *adj* : solo, solitario

long¹ ['lɔŋ] *adj* **longer** ['lɔŋgər]; **longest** ['lɔŋgəst] : largo — **~** *adv* 1 : mucho tiempo **2 all day ~** : todo el día 3 **as ~ as** : mientras 4 **no ~er** : ya no 5 **so ~!** : ¡hasta luego!, ¡adiós! — **~ n 1 before ~** : dentro de poco **2 the ~ and the short** : lo esencial

long² *vi* **~ for** : anhelar, desear

longevity [lɑn'dʒevəti] *n* : longevidad *f*

longing ['lɔŋɪŋ] *n* : ansia *f*, anhelo *m*

longitude ['lɑndʒə,tuːd, -,tjuːd] *n* : longitud *f*

look ['lʊk] *vi* 1 : mirar 2 SEEM : parecer 3 **~ after** : cuidar (de) 4 **~ for** EXPECT : esperar 5 **~ for** SEEK : buscar 6 **~ into** : investigar 7 **~ out** : tener cuidado 8 **~ over** EXAMINE : revisar 9 **~ up to** : respetar — *vt* : mirar — *n* 1 : mirada *f* 2 APPEARANCE : aspecto *m*, aire *m* — **lookout** ['lʊk,aʊt] *n* 1 : puesto de observación 2 WATCHMAN : vigía *mf* 3 **be on the ~ for** : estar al acecho de

loom¹ ['luːm] *n* : telar *m*

loom² *vi* 1 APPEAR : aparecer, surgir 2 APPROACH : ser inminente

loop ['luːp] *n* 1 : lazada *f*, lazo *m* — *vt* : hacer lazadas con — **loophole** ['luːp-ˌhoːl] *n* : escapatoria *f*

loose ['luːs] *adj* **looser; -est** MOVABLE

: flojo, suelto 2 SLACK : flojo 3 ROOMY : holgado 4 APPROXIMATE : libre, aproximado 5 FREE : suelto 6 IMMORAL : relajado — **loosely** ['luːsli] *adv* 1 : sin apretar 2 ROUGHLY : aproximadamente — **loosen** ['luːsən] *vt* : aflojar

loot ['luːt] *n* : botín *m* — *vt* : saquear, robar — **looter** ['luːtər] *n* : saqueador *m*, -dora *f* — **looting** ['luːtɪŋ] *n* : saqueo *m*

lop ['lɑp] *vt* **lopped; lopping** : cortar, podar

lopsided ['lɑp,saɪdəd] *adj* : torcido, chueco Lat

lord ['lɔrd] *n* 1 : señor *m*, noble *m* **2 the Lord** : el Señor

lore ['lor] *n* : saber *m* popular, tradición *f*

lose ['luːz] *v* **lost** ['lɔst]; **losing** ['luːzɪŋ] *vt* 1 : perder 2 **~ one's way** : perderse 3 **~ time** : atrasarse (dícese de un reloj) — *vi* : perder — **loser** ['luːzər] *n* : perdedor *m*, -dora *f* — **loss** ['lɔs] *n* 1 : pérdida *f* 2 DEFEAT : derrota *f* 3 **be at a ~ for words** : no encontrar palabras — **lost** ['lɔst] *adj* 1 : perdido 2 **get ~** : perderse

lot ['lɑt] *n* 1 FATE : suerte *f* 2 PLOT : solar *m* 3 **a ~ of** *or* **~s of** : mucho, un montón de

lotion ['loːʃən] *n* : loción *f*

lottery ['lɑtəri] *n, pl* **-teries** : lotería *f*

loud ['laʊd] *adj* 1 : alto, fuerte 2 NOISY : ruidoso 3 FLASHY : llamativo — **~** *adv* 1 : fuerte 2 **out ~** : en voz alta — **loudly** ['laʊdli] *adv* : en voz alta — **loudspeaker** ['laʊd,spiːkər] *n* : altavoz *m*

lounge ['laʊndʒ] *vi* **lounged; lounging** 1 : repantigarse 2 *or* **~ about** : holgazanear — **~** *n* : salón *m*

louse ['laʊs] *n, pl* **lice** ['laɪs] : piojo *m* — **lousy** ['laʊzi] *adj* **lousier; -est** 1 : piojoso 2 BAD : pésimo, muy malo

love ['lʌv] *n* 1 : amor *m* **2 fall in ~** : enamorarse — *v* **loved; loving** : querer, amar — **lovable** ['lʌvəbəl] *adj* : adorable, amoroso Lat — **lovely** ['lʌvli] *adj* **-lier; -est** : lindo, precioso — **lover** ['lʌvər] *n* : amante *mf* — **loving** ['lʌvɪŋ] *adj* : cariñoso

low ['loː] *adj* **lower** ['loːər]; **-est** 1 : bajo 2 SCARCE : escaso 3 DEPRESSED : deprimido — *adv* 1 : bajo 2 **turn the lights down ~** : bajar las luces — *n* 1 : punto *m* bajo 2 *or* **~ gear** : primera velocidad *f* — **lower** ['loːər] *adj* : inferior, más bajo — *vt* : bajar — **lowly** ['loːli] *adj* **-lier; -est** : humilde

loyal ['lɔɪəl] *adj* : leal, fiel — **loyalty** ['lɔɪəlti] *n, pl* **-ties** : lealtad *f*

lozenge ['lɑzəndʒ] n : pastilla f

lubricate ['lu:brɪ,keɪt] vt **-cated; -cating** : lubricar — **lubricant** ['lu:brɪkənt] n : lubricante m — **lubrication** [,lu:brɪ'keɪʃən] n : lubricación f

lucid ['lu:səd] adj : lúcido — **lucidity** [lu:'sɪdəţi] n : lucidez f

luck ['lʌk] n **1** : suerte f **2 good ~!** : ¡buena suerte! — **luckily** ['lʌkəli] adv : afortunadamente — **lucky** ['lʌki] adj **luckier; -est 1** : afortunado **2 ~ charm** : amuleto m (de la suerte)

lucrative ['lu:krəţɪv] adj : lucrativo

ludicrous ['lu:dəkrəs] adj : ridículo, absurdo

lug ['lʌg] vt **lugged; lugging** : arrastrar

luggage ['lʌgɪdʒ] n : equipaje m

lukewarm ['lu:k'wɔrm] adj : tibio

lull ['lʌl] vt **1** CALM : calmar **2 ~ to sleep** : adormecer — **~** n : período m de calma, pausa f

lullaby ['lʌlə,baɪ] n, pl **-bies** : canción f de cuna, nana f

lumber ['lʌmbər] n : madera f — **lumberjack** ['lʌmbər,dʒæk] n : leñador m, -dora f

luminous ['lu:mənəs] adj : luminoso

lump ['lʌmp] n **1** CHUNK, PIECE : pedazo m, trozo m **2** SWELLING : bulto m **3** : grumo m (en un líquido) — **~** vt or **~ together** : juntar, agrupar — **lumpy** ['lʌmpi] adj **lumpier; -est** : grumoso (dícese de una salsa), lleno de bultos (dícese de un colchón)

lunacy ['lu:nəsi] n, pl **-cies** : locura f

lunar ['lu:nər] adj : lunar

lunatic ['lu:nə,ţɪk] n : loco m, -ca f

lunch ['lʌntʃ] n : almuerzo m, comida f — **~** vi : almorzar, comer — **luncheon** ['lʌntʃən] n : comida f, almuerzo m

lung ['lʌŋ] n : pulmón m

lunge ['lʌndʒ] vi **lunged; lunging 1** : lanzarse **2 ~ at** : arremeter contra

lurch[1] ['lʌrtʃ] vi **1** STAGGER : tambalearse **2** : dar bandazos (dícese de un vehículo)

lurch[2] n **leave in a ~** : dejar en la estacada

lure ['lʊr] n **1** BAIT : señuelo m **2** ATTRACTION : atractivo m — **~** vt **lured; luring** : atraer

lurid ['lʊrəd] adj **1** GRUESOME : espeluznante **2** SENSATIONAL : sensacionalista **3** GAUDY : chillón

lurk ['lɜrk] vi : estar al acecho

luscious ['lʌʃəs] adj : delicioso, exquisito

lush ['lʌʃ] adj : exuberante, suntuoso

lust ['lʌst] n **1** : lujuria f **2** CRAVING : ansia f, anhelo m — **~** vi **after** : desear (a una persona), codiciar (riquezas, etc.)

luster or **lustre** ['lʌstər] n : lustre m

lusty ['lʌsti] adj **lustier; -est** : fuerte, vigoroso

luxurious [,lʌg'ʒʊriəs, ,lʌk'ʃʊr-] adj : lujoso — **luxury** ['lʌkʃəri, 'lʌgʒə-] n, pl **-ries** : lujo m

lye ['laɪ] n : lejía f

lying → lie

lynch ['lɪntʃ] vt : linchar

lynx ['lɪŋks] n : lince m

lyric ['lɪrɪk] or **lyrical** ['lɪrɪkəl] adj : lírico — **lyrics** npl : letra f (de una canción)

M

m ['ɛm] n, pl **m's** or **ms** ['ɛmz] : m f, decimotercera letra del alfabeto inglés

ma'am ['mæm] → **madam**

macabre [mə'kɑb, -'kɑbər, -'kɑbrə] adj : macabro

macaroni [,mækə'ro:ni] n : macarrones mpl

mace ['meɪs] n **1** : maza f (arma o símbolo) **2** : macis f (especia)

machete [mə'ʃeţi] n : machete m

machine [mə'ʃi:n] n : máquina f — **machinery** [mə'ʃi:nəri] n, pl **-eries 1** : maquinaria f **2** WORKS : mecanismo m — **machine gun** n : ametralladora f

mad ['mæd] adj **madder; maddest 1** INSANE : loco **2** FOOLISH : insensato **3** ANGRY : furioso

madam ['mædəm] n, pl **mesdames** [meɪ'dɑm] : señora f

madden ['mædən] vt : enfurecer

made → make

madly ['mædli] adv : como un loco, locamente — **madman** ['mæd,mæn, -mən] n, pl **-men** [-mən, -,men] : loco m — **madness** ['mædnəs] n : locura f

Mafia ['mɑfiə] n : Mafia f

magazine ['mægə,zi:n] n **1** PERIODICAL : revista f **2** : recámara f (de un arma de fuego)

maggot ['mægət] n : gusano m

magic ['mædʒɪk] n : magia f — **~** or **magical** ['mædʒɪkəl] adj : mágico — **magician** [mə'dʒɪʃən] n : mago m, -ga f

magistrate ['mædʒəˌstreɪt] n : magistrado m, -da f

magnanimous [mægˈnænəməs] adj : magnánimo

magnate ['mægˌneɪt, -nət] n : magnate mf

magnet ['mægnət] n : imán m — **magnetic** [mægˈnɛtɪk] adj : magnético — **magnetism** ['mægnəˌtɪzəm] n : magnetismo m — **magnetize** ['mægnəˌtaɪz] vt -tized; -tizing : magnetizar

magnificent [mægˈnɪfəsənt] adj : magnífico — **magnificence** [mægˈnɪfəsənts] n : magnificencia f

magnify ['mægnəˌfaɪ] vt -fied; -fying 1 ENLARGE : ampliar 2 EXAGGERATE : exagerar — **magnifying glass** n : lupa f

magnitude ['mægnəˌtuːd, -ˌtjuːd] n : magnitud f

magnolia [mægˈnoːljə] n : magnolia f

mahogany [məˈhɑgəni] n, pl -nies : caoba f

maid ['meɪd] n : sirvienta f, criada f, muchacha f — **maiden** ['meɪdən] adj FIRST : inaugural — **maiden name** n : nombre m de soltera

mail ['meɪl] n 1 : correo m 2 LETTERS : correspondencia f — ~ vt : enviar por correo — **mailbox** ['meɪlˌbɑks] n : buzón m — **mailman** ['meɪlˌmæn, -mən] n, pl -men [-mən, -ˌmɛn] : cartero m

maim ['meɪm] vt : mutilar

main ['meɪn] n : tubería f principal (de agua o gas), cable m principal (de un circuito) — ~ adj : principal — **mainframe** ['meɪnˌfreɪm] n : computadora f central — **mainland** ['meɪnˌlænd, -lənd] n : continente m — **mainly** ['meɪnli] adv : principalmente — **mainstay** ['meɪnˌsteɪ] n : sostén m (principal) — **mainstream** ['meɪnˌstriːm] n : corriente f principal — ~ adj : dominante, convencional

maintain [meɪnˈteɪn] vt : mantener — **maintenance** ['meɪntənənts] n : mantenimiento m

maize ['meɪz] n : maíz m

majestic [məˈdʒɛstɪk] adj : majestuoso — **majesty** ['mædʒəsti] n, pl -ties : majestad f

major ['meɪdʒər] adj 1 : muy importante, principal 2 : mayor (en música) — ~ n 1 : mayor mf, comandante mf (en las fuerzas armadas) 2 : especialidad f (universitaria) — ~ vi -jored; -joring : especializarse — **majority** [məˈdʒɔrəti] n, pl -ties : mayoría f

make ['meɪk] v made ['meɪd]; making vt 1 : hacer 2 MANUFACTURE : fabricar 3 CONSTITUTE : constituir 4 PREPARE : preparar 5 RENDER : poner 6 COMPEL : obligar 7 ~ **a decision** : tomar una decisión 8 ~ **a living** : ganar la vida — vi 1 ~ **do** : arreglárselas 2 ~ **for** : dirigirse a 3 ~ **good** SUCCEED : tener éxito — ~ n BRAND : marca f — **make-believe** ['meɪkbəˌliːv] n : fantasía f — ~ adj : imaginario — **make out** vt 1 : hacer (un cheque, etc.) 2 DISCERN : distinguir 3 UNDERSTAND : comprender — vi **how did you ~**? : ¿qué tal te fue? — **maker** ['meɪkər] n MANUFACTURER : fabricante mf — **makeshift** ['meɪkˌʃɪft] adj : improvisado — **makeup** ['meɪkˌʌp] n 1 COMPOSITION : composición f 2 COSMETICS : maquillaje m — **make up** vt 1 PREPARE : preparar 2 INVENT : inventar 3 CONSTITUTE : formar — vi RECONCILE : hacer las paces

maladjusted [ˌmæləˈdʒʌstəd] adj : inadaptado

malaria [məˈlɛriə] n : malaria f, paludismo m

male ['meɪl] n : macho m (de animales o plantas), varón m (de personas) — ~ adj 1 : macho 2 MASCULINE : masculino

malevolent [məˈlɛvələnt] adj : malévolo

malfunction [mælˈfʌŋkʃən] vi : funcionar mal — ~ n : mal funcionamiento m

malice ['mælɪs] n : mala intención f, rencor m — **malicious** [məˈlɪʃəs] adj : malicioso

malign [məˈlaɪn] adj : maligno — ~ vt : calumniar

malignant [məˈlɪgnənt] adj : maligno

mall ['mɔl] n or **shopping ~** : centro m comercial

malleable ['mæliəbəl] adj : maleable

mallet ['mælət] n : mazo m

malnutrition [ˌmælnuˈtrɪʃən, -ˌnjuː-] n : desnutrición f

malpractice [ˌmælˈpræktəs] n : mala práctica f, negligencia f

malt ['mɔlt] n : malta f

mama or **mamma** ['mɑmə] n : mamá f

mammal ['mæməl] n : mamífero m

mammogram ['mæməˌgræm] n : mamografía f

mammoth ['mæməθ] adj : gigantesco

man ['mæn] n, pl **men** ['mɛn] : hombre m — ~ vt **manned; manning** : tripular (un barco o avión), encargarse de (un servicio)

manage ['mænɪdʒ] v -aged; -aging vt 1 HANDLE : manejar 2 DIRECT : administrar, dirigir — vi COPE : arreglárselas

— **manageable** ['mænɪdʒəbəl] *adj* : manejable — **management** ['mænɪdʒmənt] *n* : dirección *f* — **manager** ['mænɪdʒər] *n* : director *m*, -tora *f*; gerente *mf* — **managerial** [ˌmænə'dʒɪriəl] *adj* : directivo

mandarin ['mændərən] *n or* ～ **orange** : mandarina *f*

mandate ['mændeɪt] *n* : mandato *m* — **mandatory** ['mændəˌtori] *adj* : obligatorio

mane ['meɪn] *n* : crin *f* (de un caballo), melena *f* (de un león)

maneuver [mə'nuːvər, -'njuː] *n* : maniobra *f* — ～ *v* -vered; -vering : maniobrar

mangle ['mæŋgəl] *vt* -gled; -gling : destrozar

mango ['mæŋgoː] *n*, *pl* **-goes** : mango *m*

mangy ['meɪndʒi] *adj* **mangier; -est** : sarnoso

manhandle ['mænˌhændəl] *vi* -dled; -dling : maltratar

manhole ['mænˌhoːl] *n* : boca *f* de alcantarilla

manhood ['mænˌhʊd] *n* **1** : madurez *f* (de un hombre) **2** VIRILITY : virilidad *f*

mania ['meɪniə, -njə] *n* : manía *f* — **maniac** ['meɪniˌæk] *n* : maníaco *m*, -ca *f*

manicure ['mænəˌkjʊr] *n* : manicura *f* — ～ *vt* -cured; -curing : hacer la manicura a

manifest ['mænəˌfest] *adj* : manifiesto, patente — ～ *vt* : manifestar — **manifesto** [ˌmænə'festoː] *n*, *pl* **-tos** *or* **-toes** : manifiesto *m*

manipulate [mə'nɪpjəˌleɪt] *vt* -lated; -lating : manipular — **manipulation** [məˌnɪpjə'leɪʃən] *n* : manipulación *f*

mankind ['mænˌkaɪnd, ˌkaɪnd] *n* : género *m* humano, humanidad *f*

manly ['mænli] *adj* -lier; -est : viril — **manliness** ['mænlinəs] *n* : virilidad *f*

man-made ['mænˌmeɪd] *adj* : artificial

mannequin ['mænɪkən] *n* : maniquí *m*

manner ['mænər] *n* **1** : manera *f*, clase *f* **3** ～**s** *npl* ETIQUETTE : modales *mpl*, educación *f* — **mannerism** ['mænəˌrɪzəm] *n* : peculiaridad *f* (de una persona)

manoeuvre *Brit* → **maneuver**

manor ['mænər] *n* : casa *f* solariega

manpower ['mænˌpaʊər] *n* : mano *f* de obra

mansion ['mæntʃən] *n* : mansión *f*

manslaughter ['mænˌslɔtər] *n* : homicidio *m* sin premeditación

mantel ['mæntəl] *or* **mantelpiece** ['mæntəlˌpiːs] *n* : repisa *f* de la chimenea

manual ['mænjuəl] *adj* : manual — ～ *n* : manual *m*

manufacture [ˌmænjə'fæktʃər] *n* : fabricación *f* — ～ *vt* -tured; -turing : fabricar — **manufacturer** [ˌmænjə'fæktʃərər] *n* : fabricante *mf*

manure [mə'nʊr, -'njʊr] *n* : estiércol *m*

manuscript ['mænjəˌskrɪpt] *n* : manuscrito *m*

many ['meni] *adj* **more** ['mor]; **most** ['moːst] **1** : muchos **2 as** ～ : tantos **3 how** ～ : cuántos **4 too** ～ : demasiados — ～ *pron* : muchos *pl*, -chas *pl*

map ['mæp] *n* : mapa *m* — ～ *vt* **mapped; mapping 1** : trazar el mapa de **2** *or* ～ **out** : planear, proyectar

maple ['meɪpəl] *n* : arce *m*

mar ['mɑr] *vt* **marred; marring** : estropear

marathon ['mærəˌθɑn] *n* : maratón *f*

marble ['mɑrbəl] *n* **1** : mármol *m* **2** ～**s** *npl* : canicas *fpl* (para jugar)

march ['mɑrtʃ] *n* : marcha *f* — ～ *vi* : marchar, desfilar

March ['mɑrtʃ] *n* : marzo *m*

mare ['mær] *n* : yegua *f*

margarine ['mɑrdʒərən] *n* : margarina *f*

margin ['mɑrdʒən] *n* : margen *m* — **marginal** ['mɑrdʒənəl] *adj* : marginal

marigold ['mærəˌgoːld] *n* : caléndula *f*

marijuana [ˌmærə'hwɑnə] *n* : marihuana *f*

marinate ['mærəˌneɪt] *vt* -nated; -nating : marinar

marine [mə'riːn] *adj* : marino — ～ *n* : soldado *m* de marina

marionette [ˌmæriə'net] *n* : marioneta *f*

marital ['mærətəl] *adj* **1** : matrimonial **2** ～ **status** : estado *m* civil

maritime ['mærəˌtaɪm] *adj* : marítimo

mark ['mɑrk] *n* **1** : marca *f* **2** STAIN : mancha *f* **3** IMPRINT : huella *f* **4** TARGET : blanco *m* **5** GRADE : nota *f* — ～ *vt* **1** : marcar **2** STAIN : manchar **3** POINT OUT : señalar **4** : calificar (un examen, etc.) **5** COMMEMORATE : conmemorar **6** CHARACTERIZE : caracterizar **7** ～ **off** : delimitar — **marked** ['mɑrkt] *adj* : marcado, notable — **markedly** ['mɑrkədli] *adv* : notablemente — **marker** ['mɑrkər] *n* : marcador *m*

market ['mɑrkət] *n* : mercado *m* — ～ *vt* : vender, comercializar — **marketable** ['mɑrkətəbəl] *adj* : vendible — **marketplace** ['mɑrkətˌpleɪs] *n* : mercado *m*

marksman ['mɑrksmən] *n*, *pl* **-men** [-mən, -ˌmen] : tirador *m* — **marksmanship** ['mɑrksmənˌʃɪp] *n* : puntería *f*

marmalade ['mɑrməˌleɪd] *n* : mermelada *f*

maroon[1] [mə'ruːn] vt : abandonar, aislar

maroon[2] n : rojo m oscuro

marquee [mɑr'kiː] n CANOPY : marquesina f

marriage ['mærɪdʒ] n 1 : matrimonio m 2 WEDDING : casamiento m, boda f — **married** ['mærid] adj 1 : casado 2 **get ~** : casarse

marrow ['mæroʊ] n : médula f, tuétano m

marry ['mæri] v **-ried; -rying** vt 1 : casar 2 WED : casarse con — vi : casarse

Mars ['mɑrz] n : Marte m

marsh ['mɑrʃ] n 1 : pantano m 2 or **salt ~** : marisma f

marshal ['mɑrʃəl] n 1 : mariscal m (en el ejército); jefe m, -fa f (de policía, de bomberos, etc.) — ~ vt **-shaled** or **-shalled; -shaling** or **-shalling** : poner en orden (los pensamientos, etc.), reunir (las tropas)

marshmallow ['mɑrʃˌmɛloʊ, -ˌmæloʊ] n : malvavisco m

marshy ['mɑrʃi] adj **marshier; -est** : pantanoso

mart ['mɑrt] n : mercado m

martial ['mɑrʃəl] adj : marcial

martyr ['mɑrtər] n : mártir mf — ~ vt : martirizar

marvel ['mɑrvəl] n : maravilla f — vi **-veled** or **-velled; -veling** or **-velling** : maravillarse — **marvelous** ['mɑrvələs] or **marvellous** adj : maravilloso

mascara [mæs'kærə] n : rímel m

mascot ['mæsˌkɑt, -kət] n : mascota f

masculine ['mæskjələn] adj : masculino — **masculinity** [ˌmæskjə'lɪnəti] n : masculinidad f

mash ['mæʃ] vt 1 CRUSH : aplastar, majar 2 PUREE : hacer puré de — **mashed potatoes** npl : puré m de patatas, puré m de papas Lat

mask ['mæsk] n : máscara f — ~ vt : enmascarar

masochism ['mæsəˌkɪzəm, 'mæzə-] n : masoquismo m — **masochist** ['mæsəkɪst, 'mæzə-] n : masoquista f — **masochistic** [ˌmæsə'kɪstɪk, ˌmæzə-] adj : masoquista

mason ['meɪsən] n : albañil mf — **masonry** ['meɪsənri] n, pl **-ries** : albañilería f

masquerade [ˌmæskə'reɪd] n : mascarada f — ~ vi **-aded; -ading** ~ **as** : disfrazarse de, hacerse pasar por

mass ['mæs] n 1 : masa f 2 MULTITUDE : cantidad f 3 **the ~es** : las masas

Mass ['mæs] n : misa f

massacre ['mæsɪkər] n : masacre f — ~ vt **-cred; -cring** : masacrar

massage [mə'sɑʒ, -'sɑdʒ] n : masaje m — ~ vt **-saged; -saging** : dar masaje a, masajear — **masseur** [mæ'sər] n : masajista m — **masseuse** [mæ'səz, -'sərz, -'suːz] n : masajista f

massive ['mæsɪv] adj 1 BULKY, SOLID : macizo 2 HUGE : enorme, masivo

mast ['mæst] n : mástil m

master ['mæstər] n 1 : amo m, señor m (de la casa) 2 EXPERT : maestro m, -tra f 3 **~'s degree** : maestría f — ~ vt : dominar — **masterful** ['mæstərfəl] adj : magistral — **masterpiece** ['mæstərˌpiːs] n : obra f maestra — **mastery** ['mæstəri] n : maestría f

masturbate ['mæstərˌbeɪt] v **-bated; -bating** vi : masturbarse — **masturbation** [ˌmæstər'beɪʃən] n : masturbación f

mat ['mæt] n 1 DOORMAT : felpudo m 2 RUG : estera f

matador ['mætəˌdɔr] n : matador m

match ['mætʃ] n 1 EQUAL : igual mf 2 : fósforo m, cerilla f (para encender) 3 GAME : partido m, combate m (en boxeo) 4 **be a good ~** : hacer buena pareja — ~ vt 1 or **~ up** : emparejar 2 EQUAL : igualar 3 : combinar con, hacer juego con (ropa, colores, etc.) — vi : concordar, coincidir

mate ['meɪt] n 1 COMPANION : compañero m, -ra f; amigo m, -ga f 2 : macho m, hembra f (de animales) — ~ vi **mated; mating** : aparearse

material [mə'tɪriəl] adj 1 : material 2 IMPORTANT : importante — ~ n 1 : material m 2 CLOTH : tela f, tejido m — **materialistic** [məˌtɪriə'lɪstɪk] adj : materialista — **materialize** [mə'tɪriəˌlaɪz] vi **-ized; -izing** : aparecer

maternal [mə'tərnəl] adj : maternal — **maternity** [mə'tərnəti] n, pl **-ties** : maternidad f — ~ adj 1 : de maternidad 2 **~ clothes** : ropa f de futura mamá

math ['mæθ] → **mathematics**

mathematics [ˌmæθə'mætɪks] ns & pl : matemáticas fpl — **mathematical** [ˌmæθə'mætɪkəl] adj : matemático — **mathematician** [ˌmæθəmə'tɪʃən] n : matemático m, -ca f

matinee or **matinée** [ˌmætə'neɪ] n : matiné(e) f, fonción f de tarde

matrimony ['mætrəˌmoʊni] n : matrimonio m — **matrimonial** [ˌmætrə'moʊniəl] adj : matrimonial

matrix ['meɪtrɪks] n, pl **-trices** ['meɪtrəˌsiz, 'mæ-] or **-trixes** ['meɪtrɪksəz] : matriz f

matte ['mæt] adj : mate

matter ['mætər] n 1 SUBSTANCE : materia

f **2** QUESTION : asunto *m*, cuestión *f* **3** as a ~ of fact : en efecto, en realidad **4** for that ~ : de hecho **5** to make ~s worse : para colmo de males **6** what's the ~? : ¿qué pasa? — ~ *vi* : importar

mattress ['mætrəs] *n* : colchón *m*

mature [mə'tur, -'tjur, -'tʃur] *adj* **-turer; -est** : maduro — ~ *vi* **-tured; -turing** : madurar — **maturity** [mə'turəti, -tjur-, -'tʃur-] *n* : madurez *f*

maul ['mɔl] *vt* : maltratar, aporrear

mauve ['mo:v, 'mov] *n* : malva *m*

maxim ['mæksəm] *n* : máxima *f*

maximum ['mæksəməm] *n, pl* **-ma** ['mæksəmə] *or* **-mums** : máximo *m* — ~ *adj* : máximo — **maximize** ['mæksə,maɪz] *vt* **-mized; -mizing** : llevar al máximo

may ['meɪ] *v aux, past* **might** ['maɪt]; *present s & pl* **may 1** : poder **2 come what** ~ : pase lo que pase **3** it ~ happen : puede pasar **4** ~ the best man win : que gane el mejor

May ['meɪ] *n* : mayo *m*

maybe ['meɪbi] *adv* : quizás, tal vez

mayhem ['meɪˌhem, 'meɪəm] *n* : alboroto *m*

mayonnaise ['meɪəˌneɪz] *n* : mayonesa *f*

mayor ['meɪər, 'mɛr] *n* : alcalde *m*, -desa *f*

maze ['meɪz] *n* : laberinto *m*

me ['mi:] *pron* **1** : me **2 for ~** : para mí **3 give it to ~!** : ¡dámelo! **4 it's ~** : soy yo **5 with ~** : conmigo

meadow ['mɛdo:] *n* : prado *m*, pradera *f*

meager ['mi:gər] *or* **meagre** *adj* : escaso

meal ['mi:l] *n* **1** : comida *f* **2** : harina *f* (de maíz, etc.) — **mealtime** ['mi:l,taɪm] *n* : hora *f* de comer

mean¹ ['mi:n] *vt* **meant** ['mɛnt]; **meaning 1** SIGNIFY : querer decir **2** INTEND : querer, tener la intención de **3** be meant for : estar destinado a **4** he didn't ~ it : no lo dijo en serio

mean² *adj* **1** UNKIND : malo **2** STINGY : mezquino, tacaño **3** HUMBLE : humilde

mean³ *adj* AVERAGE : medio — ~ *n* : promedio *m*

meander [mi'ændər] *vi* **-dered; -dering 1** WIND : serpentear **2** WANDER : vagar

meaning ['mi:nɪŋ] *n* : significado *m*, sentido *m* — **meaningful** ['mi:nɪŋfəl] *adj* : significativo — **meaningless** ['mi:nɪŋləs] *adj* : sin sentido

meanness ['mi:nnəs] *n* **1** UNKINDNESS : maldad *f* **2** STINGINESS : mezquindad *f*

means ['mi:nz] *n* **1** : medio *m* **2 by all ~** : por supuesto **3 by ~ of** : por medio de **4 by no ~** : de ninguna manera

meantime ['mi:nˌtaɪm] *n* **1** : interín *m* **2 in the ~** : mientras tanto — ~ *adv* → **meanwhile**

meanwhile ['mi:n,hwaɪl] *adv* : mientras tanto — ~ *n* → **meantime**

measles ['mi:zəlz] *npl* : sarampión *m*

measly ['mi:zli] *adj* **-slier; -est** : miserable, misero

measure ['mɛʒər, 'meɪ-] *n* : medida *f* — ~ *v* **-sured; -suring** : medir — **measurable** ['mɛʒərəbəl, 'meɪ-] *adj* : mensurable — **measurement** ['mɛʒərmənt, 'meɪ-] *n* : medida *f* — **measure up** *vi* ~ **to** : estar a la altura de

meat ['mi:t] *n* : carne *f* — **meatball** ['mi:t,bɔl] *n* : albóndiga *f* — **meaty** ['mi:ti] *adj* **meatier; -est 1** : carnoso **2** SUBSTANTIAL : sustancioso

mechanic [mɪ'kænɪk] *n* : mecánico *m*, -ca *f* — **mechanical** [mɪ'kænɪkəl] *adj* : mecánico — **mechanics** [mɪ'kænɪks] *ns & pl* **1** : mecánica *f* **2** WORKINGS : mecanismo *m* — **mechanism** ['mɛkəˌnɪzəm] *n* : mecanismo *m* — **mechanize** ['mɛkəˌnaɪz] *vt* **-nized; -nizing** : mecanizar

medal ['mɛdəl] *n* : medalla *f* — **medallion** [mə'dæljən] *n* : medallón *m*

meddle ['mɛdəl] *vi* **-dled; -dling** : entrometerse

media ['mi:diə] *or* **mass ~** *npl* : medios *mpl* de comunicación

median ['mi:diən] *adj* : medio

mediate ['mi:di,eɪt] *vi* **-ated; -ating** : mediar — **mediation** [,mi:di'eɪʃən] *n* : mediación *f* — **mediator** ['mi:di,eɪtər] *n* : mediador *m*, -dora *f*

medical ['mɛdɪkəl] *adj* : médico — **medicated** ['mɛdəˌkeɪtəd] *adj* : medicinal — **medication** [,mɛdə'keɪʃən] *n* : medicamento *m* — **medicinal** [mə-'dɪsənəl] *adj* : medicinal — **medicine** ['mɛdəsən] *n* **1** : medicina *f* **2** MEDICATION : medicina *f*, medicamento *m*

medieval *or* **mediaeval** [,mi:di'val, ,mi:-, ,me-, -'di:vəl] *adj* : medieval

mediocre [,mi:di'o:kər] *adj* : mediocre — **mediocrity** [,mi:di'ɑkrəti] *n, pl* **-ties** : mediocridad *f*

meditate ['mɛdəˌteɪt] *vi* **-tated; -tating** : meditar — **meditation** [,mɛdə'teɪʃən] *n* : meditación *f*

medium ['mi:diəm] *n, pl* **-diums** *or* **-dia** ['mi:diə] **1** MEANS : medio *m* **2** MEAN : punto *m* medio, término *m* medio **3** → **media** — ~ *adj* : mediano

medley ['medli] *n, pl* **-leys 1** : mezcla *f* **2** : popurrí *m* (de canciones)

meek [mi:k] *adj* : dócil

meet [mi:t] *v* **met** ['met]; **meeting** *vt* **1** ENCOUNTER : encontrarse con **2** SATIS-FY : satisfacer **3** pleased to ∼ you : encantado de conocerlo — *vi* **1** : encontrarse **2** ASSEMBLE : reunirse **3** BE INTRODUCED : conocerse — *n* **1** : encuentro *m* — **meeting** ['mi:tɪŋ] *n* : reunión *f*

megabyte ['mega₁baɪt] *n* : megabyte *m*

megaphone ['mega₁fo:n] *n* : megáfono *m*

melancholy ['melən₁kɑli] *n, pl* **-cholies** : melancolía *f* — ∼ *adj* : melancólico, triste

mellow ['melo:] *adj* **1** : suave, dulce **2** CALM : apacible **3** : maduro (dícese de frutas), añejo (dícese de vinos) — ∼ *vt* : suavizar, endulzar — *vi* : suavizarse

melody ['melədi] *n, pl* **-dies** : melodía *f*

melon ['melən] *n* : melón *m*

melt [melt] *vi* : derretirse, fundirse — *vt* : derretir

member ['membər] *n* : miembro *m* — **membership** ['membər₁ʃɪp] *n* **1** : calidad *f* de miembro **2** MEMBERS : miembros *mpl*

membrane ['mem₁breɪn] *n* : membrana *f*

memory ['memri, 'mema-] *n, pl* **-ries 1** : memoria *f* **2** RECOLLECTION : recuerdo *m* — **memento** [mɪ'men₁to:] *n, pl* **-tos** *or* **-toes** : recuerdo *m* — **memo** ['memo:] *n, pl* **memos** *or* **memorandum** [memə'rændəm] *n, pl* **-dums** *or* **-da** [-də] : memorándum *m* — **memoirs** ['mem₁warz] *npl* : memorias *fpl* — **memorable** ['memərəbəl] *adj* : memorable — **memorial** [mə'moriəl] *adj* : conmemorativo — ∼ *n* : monumento *m* (conmemorativo) — **memorize** ['memə₁raɪz] *vt* **-rized; -rizing** : aprender de memoria

men → **man**

menace ['menəs] *n* : amenaza *f* — ∼ *vt* **-aced; -acing** : amenazar — **menacing** ['menəsɪŋ] *adj* : amenazador

mend [mend] *vt* **1** : reparar, arreglar **2** DARN : zurcir — *vi* HEAL : curarse

menial ['mi:niəl] *adj* : servil, bajo

meningitis [menən'dʒaɪtəs] *n, pl* **-gitides** [-'dʒɪtə₁di:z] : meningitis *f*

menopause ['menə₁pɔz] *n* : menopausia *f*

menstruate ['menstru₁eɪt] *vi* **-ated; -ating** : menstruar — **menstruation** [menstru'eɪʃən] *n* : menstruación *f*

mental ['mentəl] *adj* : mental — **men-tality** [men'tæləti] *n, pl* **-ties** : mentalidad *f*

mention ['menʃən] *n* : mención *f* — **mention** *vt* **1** : mencionar **2** don't ∼ it! : ¡de nada!, ¡no hay de qué!

menu ['menju:] *n* : menú *m*

meow [mi'ao] *n* : maullido *m*, miau *m* — ∼ *vi* : maullar

mercenary ['mərsən₁eri] *n, pl* **-naries** : mercenario *m*, -ria *f* — ∼ *adj* : mercenario

merchant ['mərtʃənt] *n* : comerciante *mf* — **merchandise** ['mərtʃən₁daɪz, -₁daɪs] *n* : mercancía *f*, mercadería *f*

merciful ['mərsɪfəl] *adj* : misericordioso, compasivo — **merciless** ['mərsɪləs] *adj* : despiadado

mercury ['mərkjəri] *n, pl* **-ries** : mercurio *m*

Mercury ['mərkjəri] *n* : Mercurio *m*

mercy ['mərsi] *n, pl* **-cies 1** : misericordia *f*, compasión *f* **2** at the ∼ of : a merced de

mere [mɪr] *adj, superlative* **merest** : mero, simple — **merely** ['mɪrli] *adv* : simplemente

merge ['mərdʒ] *v* **merged; merging** *vi* : unirse, fusionarse (dícese de las compañías), confluir (dícese de los ríos, las calles, etc.) — *vt* : unir, fusionar, combinar — **merger** ['mərdʒər] *n* : unión *f*, fusión *f*

merit ['merət] *n* : mérito *m* — ∼ *vt* : merecer

mermaid ['mər₁meɪd] *n* : sirena *f*

merry ['meri] *adj* **-rier; -est** : alegre — **merry-go-round** ['merigo₁raond] *n* : tiovivo *m*

mesa ['meɪsə] *n* : mesa *f*

mesh ['meʃ] *n* : malla *f*

mesmerize ['mezmə₁raɪz] *vt* **-ized; -izing** : hipnotizar

mess [mes] *n* **1** : desorden *m* **2** MUDDLE : lío *m* **3** : rancho *m* (militar) — ∼ *vt* **1** *or* ∼ **up** SOIL : ensuciar **2** *or* ∼ **up** DISARRANGE : desordenar **3** *or* ∼ **up** BUNGLE : echar a perder — *vi* **1** ∼ **around** PUTTER : entretenerse **2** ∼ **with** PROVOKE : meterse con

message ['mesɪdʒ] *n* : mensaje *m* — **messenger** ['mesəndʒər] *n* : mensajero *m*, -ra *f*

messy ['mesi] *adj* **messier; -est** : desordenado, sucio

met → **meet**

metabolism [mə'tæbə₁lɪzəm] *n* : metabolismo *m*

metal ['metəl] *n* : metal *m* — **metallic** [mə'tælɪk] *adj* : metálico

metamorphosis [ˌmɛtəˈmɔrfəsɪs] *n, pl* **-phoses** [-ˌsiːz] : metamorfosis *f*

metaphor [ˈmɛtəˌfor, -fər] *n* : metáfora *f*

meteor [ˈmiːtiər, -tiˌor] *n* : meteoro *m* — **meteorological** [ˌmiːtiərəˈlɑdʒɪkəl] *adj* : meteorológico *m* — **meteorologist** [ˌmiːtiəˈrɑlədʒɪst] *n* : meteorólogo *m*, **-ga** *f* — **meteorology** [ˌmiːtiəˈrɑlədʒi] *n* : meteorología *f*

meter *or Brit* **metre** [ˈmiːtər] *n* **1** : metro *m* **2** : contador *m* (de electricidad, etc.)

method [ˈmɛθəd] *n* : método *m* — **methodical** [məˈθɑdɪkəl] *adj* : metódico *m*

meticulous [məˈtɪkjələs] *adj* : meticuloso

metric [ˈmɛtrɪk] *or* **metrical** [-trɪkəl] *adj* : métrico

metropolis [məˈtrɑpələs] *n* : metrópoli *f* — **metropolitan** [ˌmɛtrəˈpɑlətən] *adj* : metropolitano

Mexican [ˈmɛksɪkən] *adj* : mexicano

mice → **mouse**

microbe [ˈmaɪˌkroːb] *n* : microbio *m*

microfilm [ˈmaɪkrəˌfɪlm] *n* : microfilm *m*

microphone [ˈmaɪkrəˌfoːn] *n* : micrófono *m*

microscope [ˈmaɪkrəˌskoːp] *n* : microscopio *m* — **microscopic** [ˌmaɪkrəˈskɑpɪk] *adj* : microscópico

microwave [ˈmaɪkrəˌweɪv] *n or* **~ oven** : microondas *m*

mid [ˈmɪd] *adj* **1** ~ **morning** : a media mañana **2** in ~-**August** : a mediados de agosto **3 she is in her mid thirties** : tiene alrededor de 35 años — **midair** [ˈmɪdˈær] *n* in ~ : en el aire — **midday** [ˈmɪdˈdeɪ] *n* : mediodía *m*

middle [ˈmɪdəl] *adj* : de en medio, del medio — ~ *n* **1** : medio *m*, centro *m* **2** in the ~ of : en medio de (un espacio), a mitad de (una actividad) **3** in the ~ of the month : a mediados del mes — **middle-aged** [ˈmɪdəlˈeɪdʒd] *adj* : de mediana edad — **Middle Ages** *npl* : Edad *f* Media — **middle class** *n* : clase *f* media — **middleman** [ˈmɪdəlˌmæn] *n, pl* **-men** [-mən, -ˌmɛn] : intermediario *m*, -ria *f*

midget [ˈmɪdʒət] *n* : enano *m*, -na *f*

midnight [ˈmɪdˌnaɪt] *n* : medianoche *f*

midriff [ˈmɪdrɪf] *n* : diafragma *m*

midst [ˈmɪdst] *n* **1** in the ~ of : en medio de **2** in our ~ : entre nosotros

midsummer [ˈmɪdˈsʌmər, -ˌsʌ-] *n* : pleno verano *m*

midway [ˈmɪdˌweɪ] *adv* : a mitad de camino, a medio camino

midwife [ˈmɪdˌwaɪf] *n, pl* **-wives** [-ˌwaɪvz] : comadrona *f*

midwinter [ˈmɪdˈwɪntər, -ˈwɪn-] *n* : pleno invierno *m*

miff [ˈmɪf] *vt* : ofender

might¹ [ˈmaɪt] (*used to express permission or possibility or as a polite alternative to* **may**) → **may**

might² *n* : fuerza *f*, poder *m* — **mighty** [ˈmaɪti] *adj* **mightier; -est 1** : fuerte, poderoso **2** GREAT : enorme — ~ *adv* : muy

migraine [ˈmaɪˌgreɪn] *n* : jaqueca *f*, migraña *f*

migrate [ˈmaɪˌgreɪt] *vi* **-grated; -grating** : emigrar — **migrant** [ˈmaɪgrənt] *n* : trabajador *m*, -dora *f* ambulante

mild [ˈmaɪld] *adj* **1** GENTLE : suave **2** LIGHT : leve **3 a ~ climate** : una clima templada

mildew [ˈmɪlˌduː, -ˌdjuː] *n* : moho *m*

mildly [ˈmaɪldli] *adv* : ligeramente, suavemente — **mildness** [ˈmaɪldnəs] *n* : apacibilidad *f* (de personas), suavedad *f* (de sabores, etc.)

mile [ˈmaɪl] *n* : milla *f* — **mileage** [ˈmaɪlɪdʒ] *n* : distancia *f* recorrida (en millas), kilometraje *m* — **milestone** [ˈmaɪlˌstoːn] *n* : hito *m*

military [ˈmɪləˌteri] *adj* : militar — ~ *n* the ~ : las fuerzas armadas — **militant** [ˈmɪlətənt] *adj* : militante — ~ *n* : militante *mf* — **militia** [məˈlɪʃə] *n* : milicia *f*

milk [ˈmɪlk] *n* : leche *f* — ~ *vt* **1** : ordeñar (una vaca, etc.) **2** EXPLOIT : explotar — **milky** [ˈmɪlki] *adj* **milkier; -est** : lechoso — **Milky Way** *n* the ~ : la Vía Láctea

mill [ˈmɪl] *n* **1** : molino *m* **2** FACTORY : fábrica *f* **3** GRINDER : molinillo *m* — ~ *vt* : moler — *vi or* ~ **about** : arremolinarse

millennium [məˈlɛniəm] *n, pl* **-nia** [-niə] *or* **-niums** : milenio *m*

miller [ˈmɪlər] *n* : molinero *m*, -ra *f*

milligram [ˈmɪləˌgræm] *n* : miligramo *m* — **millimeter** *or Brit* **millimetre** [ˈmɪləˌmiːtər] *n* : milímetro *m*

million [ˈmɪljən] *n, pl* **millions** *or* **million 1** : millón *m* **2 a ~ people** : un millón de personas — ~ *adj* a ~ : un millón de — **millionaire** [ˌmɪljəˈnær, ˈmɪljəˌnær] *n* : millonario *m*, -ria *f* — **millionth** [ˈmɪljənθ] *adj* : millonésimo

mime [ˈmaɪm] *n* **1** : mimo *mf* **2** PANTOMIME : pantomima *f* — ~ *vt* **mimed; miming** *vt* : imitar — *vi* : hacer la mímica — **mimic** [ˈmɪmɪk] *vt* **-icked; -icking** : imitar, remedar — ~ *n* : imitador *m*, -dora *f* — **mimicry** [ˈmɪmɪkri] *n, pl* **-ries** : imitación *f*

mince ['mɪnts] *v* **minced; mincing** *vt* **1** : picar, moler **2 not to ~ one's words** : no tener pelos en la lengua

mind ['maɪnd] *n* **1** : mente *f* **2** INTELLECT : capacidad *f* intelectual **3** OPINION : opinión *f* **4** REASON : razón *f* **5 have a ~ to** : tener intención de — *vt* **1** TEND : cuidar **2** OBEY : obedecer **3** WATCH : tener cuidado con **4 I don't ~ the heat** : no me molesta el calor — *vi* **1** OBEY : obedecer **2 I don't ~** : no me importa, me es igual — **mindful** ['maɪndfəl] *adj* : atento — **mindless** ['maɪndləs] *adj* **1** SENSELESS : estúpido, sin sentido **2** DULL : aburrido

mine¹ ['maɪn] *pron* **1** : (el) mío, (la) mía, (los) míos, (las) mías **2 a friend of ~** : un amigo mío

mine² *n* : mina *f* — *v* **mined; mining 1** : extraer (oro, etc.) **2** : minar (con artefactos explosivos) — **minefield** ['maɪnˌfiːld] *n* : campo *m* de minas — **miner** ['maɪnər] *n* : minero *m*, -ra *f*

mineral ['mɪnərəl] *n* : mineral *m*

mingle ['mɪŋgəl] *v* **-gled; -gling** *vt* : mezclar — *vi* **1** : mezclarse **2** : circular (a una fiesta, etc.)

miniature ['mɪniəˌtʃʊr, 'mɪnɪˌtʃʊr, -tʃər] *n* : miniatura *f* — **~** *adj* : en miniatura

minimal ['mɪnəməl] *adj* : mínimo — **minimize** ['mɪnəˌmaɪz] *vt* **-mized; -mizing** : minimizar — **minimum** ['mɪnəməm] *adj* : mínimo — **~** *n*, *pl* **-ma** ['mɪnəmə] *or* **-mums** : mínimo *m*

mining ['maɪnɪŋ] *n* : minería *f*

minister ['mɪnəstər] *n* **1** : pastor *m*, -tora *f* (de una iglesia) **2** : ministro *m*, -tra *f* (en política) — *vi* **~ to** : cuidar (de), atender a — **ministerial** [ˌmɪnəˈstɪriəl] *adj* : ministerial — **ministry** ['mɪnəstri] *n*, *pl* **-tries** : ministerio *m*

mink ['mɪŋk] *n*, *pl* **mink** *or* **minks** : visón *m*

minnow ['mɪnoʊ] *n*, *pl* **-nows** : pececillo *m* de agua dulce

minor ['maɪnər] *adj* **1** : menor **2** INSIGNIFICANT : sin importancia — **~** *n* **1** : menor *mf* (de edad) **2** : asignatura *f* secundaria (de estudios) — **minority** [məˈnɔrəˌti, maɪ-] *n*, *pl* **-ties** : minoría *f*

mint¹ ['mɪnt] *n* **1** : menta *f* (planta) **2** : pastilla *f* de menta (dulce)

mint² *n* **1 the U.S. Mint** : la casa de la moneda de los EE.UU. **2 be worth a ~** : valer un dineral — *vt* : acuñar — **~** *adj* **in ~ condition** : como nuevo

minus ['maɪnəs] *prep* **1** : menos **2** WITHOUT : sin — **~** *n* *or* **~ sign** : signo *m* de menos

minuscule ['mɪnəsˌkjuːl, mɪˈnʌs-] *adj* : minúsculo

minute¹ ['maɪnuːt, mɪ-, -'njuːt] *n* **1** : minuto *m* **2** MOMENT : momento *m* **3 ~s** *npl* : actas *fpl* (de una reunión)

minute² ['mɪnət] *adj* **-nuter; -est 1** TINY : diminuto, minúsculo **2** DETAILED : minucioso

miracle ['mɪrɪkəl] *n* : milagro *m* — **miraculous** [məˈrækjələs] *adj* : milagroso

mirage ['mɪrɑʒ, mɪˈrɑʒ] *n* : espejismo *m*

mire ['maɪr] *n* : lodo *m*, fango *m*

mirror ['mɪrər] *n* : espejo *m* — *vt* : reflejar

mirth ['mɜrθ] *n* : alegría *f*, risas *fpl*

misapprehension [ˌmɪsˌæprəˈhentʃən] *n* : malentendido *m*

misbehave [ˌmɪsbɪˈheɪv] *vi* **-haved; -having** : portarse mal — **misbehavior** [ˌmɪsbɪˈheɪvjər] *n* : mala conducta *f*

miscalculate [mɪsˈkælkjəˌleɪt] *v* **-lated; -lating** : calcular mal

miscarriage [ˌmɪsˈkærɪdʒ, ˌmɪsˌkærɪdʒ] *n* **1** : aborto *m* **2 ~ of justice** : error *m* judicial

miscellaneous [ˌmɪsəˈleɪniəs] *adj* : diverso, vario

mischief ['mɪstʃəf] *n* : travesuras *fpl* — **mischievous** ['mɪstʃəvəs] *adj* : travieso

misconception [ˌmɪskənˈsɛpʃən] *n* : concepto *m* erróneo

misconduct [mɪsˈkɑndəkt] *n* : mala conducta *f*

misdeed [mɪsˈdiːd] *n* : fechoría *f*

misdemeanor [ˌmɪsdɪˈmiːnər] *n* : delito *m* menor

miser ['maɪzər] *n* : avaro *m*, -ra *f*; tacaño *m*, -ña *f*

miserable ['mɪzərəbəl] *adj* **1** UNHAPPY : triste **2** WRETCHED : miserable **3 ~ weather** : tiempo *m* malo

miserly ['maɪzərli] *adj* : mezquino

misery ['mɪzəri] *n*, *pl* **-eries 1** : sufrimiento *m* **2** WRETCHEDNESS : miseria *f*

misfire [mɪsˈfaɪr] *vi* **-fired; -firing** : fallar

misfit ['mɪsˌfɪt, mɪsˈfɪt] *n* : inadaptado *m*, -da *f*

misfortune [mɪsˈfɔrtʃən] *n* : desgracia *f*

misgiving [mɪsˈgɪvɪŋ] *n* : duda *f*

misguided [mɪsˈgaɪdəd] *adj* : descaminado, equivocado

mishap ['mɪsˌhæp] *n* : contratiempo *m*

misinform [ˌmɪsɪnˈfɔrm] *vt* : informar mal

misinterpret [ˌmɪsɪnˈtərprət] *vt* : interpretar mal

misjudge [mɪsˈdʒʌdʒ] *vt* **-judged; -judging** : juzgar mal

mislay ['mɪsˌleɪ] *vt* **-laid** [-ˌleɪd] ; **-laying** : extraviar, perder

mislead [mɪsˈliːd] *vt* **-led** [-ˈled]; **-leading** : engañar — **misleading** [mɪsˈliːdɪŋ] *adj* : engañoso

misnomer [mɪsˈnoːmər] *n* : nombre *m* inapropiado

misplace [mɪsˈpleɪs] *vt* **-placed**; **-placing** : extraviar, perder

misprint ['mɪsˌprɪnt, mɪs-] *n* : errata *f*, error *m* de imprenta

miss ['mɪs] *vt* **1** : errar, faltar **2** OVER-LOOK : pasar por alto **3** : perder (una oportunidad, un vuelo, etc.) **4** AVOID : evitar **5** OMIT : saltarse **6** I ~ **you** : te echo de menos — ~ *n* **1** : fallo *m* (de un tiro, etc.) **2** FAILURE : fracaso *m*

Miss ['mɪs] *n* : señorita *f*

missile ['mɪsəl] *n* **1** : misil *m* **2** PROJECTILE : proyectil *m*

missing ['mɪsɪŋ] *adj* : perdido, desaparecido

mission ['mɪʃən] *n* : misión *f* — **missionary** ['mɪʃəˌneri] *n, pl* **-aries** : misionero *m*, -ra *f*

misspell [mɪsˈspel] *vt* : escribir mal

mist ['mɪst] *n* : neblina *f*, bruma *f*

mistake [mɪˈsteɪk] *vt* **mistook** [-ˈstʊk]; **mistaken** [-ˈsteɪkən]; **-taking 1** MISINTERPRET : entender mal **2** CONFUSE : confundir — ~ *n* **1** : error *m* **2** **make a** ~ : equivocarse — **mistaken** [mɪˈsteɪkən] *adj* : equivocado

mister ['mɪstər] *n* : señor *m*

mistletoe ['mɪsəlˌtoː] *n* : muérdago *m*

mistreat [mɪsˈtriːt] *vt* : maltratar

mistress ['mɪstrəs] *n* **1** : dueña *f*, señora *f* (de una casa) **2** LOVER : amante *f*

mistrust [mɪsˈtrʌst] *n* : desconfianza *f* — ~ *vt* : desconfiar de

misty ['mɪsti] *adj* **mistier**; **-est** : neblinoso, nebuloso

misunderstand [ˌmɪsʌndərˈstænd] *vt* **-stood**; **-standing** : entender mal — **misunderstanding** [ˌmɪsʌndərˈstændɪŋ] *n* : malentendido *m*

misuse [mɪsˈjuːz] *vt* **-used**; **-using 1** : emplear mal **2** MISTREAT : maltratar — ~ [mɪsˈjuːs] *n* : mal empleo *m*, abuso *m*

mitigate ['mɪtəˌgeɪt] *vt* **-gated**; **-gating** : mitigar

mitt ['mɪt] *n* : manopla *f*, guante *m* (de béisbol) — **mitten** ['mɪtən] *n* : manopla *f*, mitón *m*

mix ['mɪks] *vt* **1** : mezclar **2** ~ **up** : confundir — *vi* : mezclarse — ~ *n* : mezcla *f* — **mixture** ['mɪkstʃər] *n* : mezcla *f* — **mix-up** ['mɪksˌʌp] *n* : confusión *f*, lío *m fam*

moan ['moːn] *n* : gemido *m* — ~ *vi* : gemir

mob ['mɑb] *n* : muchedumbre *f* — ~ *vt* **mobbed**; **mobbing** : acosar

mobile ['moːbəl, -ˌbiːl, -ˌbaɪl] *adj* : móvil — ~ ['moːbiːl] *n* : móvil *m* — **mobile home** *n* : caravana *f* — **mobility** [moːˈbɪləti] *n* : movilidad *f* — **mobilize** ['moːbəˌlaɪz] *vt* **-lized**; **-lizing** : movilizar

moccasin ['mɑkəsən] *n* : mocasín *m*

mock ['mɑk, 'mɔk] *vt* : burlarse de, mofarse de — ~ *adj* : falso — **mockery** ['mɑkəri, 'mɔ-] *n, pl* **-eries** : burla *f* — **mock-up** ['mɑkˌʌp] *n* : maqueta *f*

mode ['moːd] *n* **1** : modo *m* **2** FASHION : moda *f*

model ['mɑdəl] *n* **1** : modelo *m* **2** MOCK-UP : maqueta *f* **3** : modelo *mf* (persona) — ~ *v* **-eled** *or* **-elled**; **-eling** *or* **-elling** *vt* **1** SHAPE : modelar **2** WEAR : lucir — *vi* : trabajar de modelo — ~ *adj* : modelo

modem ['moːdəm, -ˌdem] *n* : módem *m*

moderate ['mɑdərət] *adj* : moderado — ~ *n* : moderado *m*, -da *f* — ~ ['mɑdəˌreɪt] *v* **-ated**; **-ating** *vt* : moderar — *vi* : moderarse — **moderation** [ˌmɑdəˈreɪʃən] *n* : moderación *f* — **moderator** ['mɑdəˌreɪtər] *n* : moderador *m*, -dora *f*

modern ['mɑdərn] *adj* : moderno — **modernize** ['mɑdərˌnaɪz] *vt* **-ized**; **-izing** : modernizar

modest ['mɑdəst] *adj* : modesto — **modesty** ['mɑdəsti] *n* : modestia *f*

modify ['mɑdəˌfaɪ] *vt* **-fied**; **-fying** : modificar

moist ['mɔɪst] *adj* : húmedo — **moisten** ['mɔɪsən] *vt* : humedecer — **moisture** ['mɔɪstʃər] *n* : humedad *f* — **moisturizer** ['mɔɪstʃəˌraɪzər] *n* : crema *f* hidratante

molar ['moːlər] *n* : muela *f*

molasses [məˈlæsəz] *n* : melaza *f*

mold[1] ['moːld] *n* FORM : molde *m* — ~ *vt* : moldear, formar

mold[2] *n* FUNGUS : moho *m* — **moldy** ['moːldi] *adj* **moldier**; **-est** : mohoso

mole[1] ['moːl] *n* : lunar *m* (en la piel)

mole[2] *n* : topo *m* (animal)

molecule ['mɑlɪˌkjuːl] *n* : molécula *f*

molest [məˈlest] *vt* **1** HARASS : importunar **2** : abusar (sexualmente)

molten ['moːltən] *adj* : fundido

mom ['mɑm, 'mʌm] *n* : mamá *f*

moment ['moːmənt] *n* : momento *m* — **momentarily** [ˌmoːmənˈterəli] *adv* **1** : momentáneamente **2** SOON : dentro de poco, pronto — **momentary** ['moːmənˌteri] *adj* : momentáneo

momentous [moˈmentəs] *adj* : muy importante

momentum [moˈmentəm] *n, pl* **-ta** [-t̬ə] *or* **-tums** 1 : momento *m* (en física) 2 IMPETUS : ímpetu *m*

monarch [ˈmɑnərk, -nərk] *n* : monarca *mf* — **monarchy** [ˈmɑnərki, -nər-] *n, pl* **-chies** : monarquía *f*

monastery [ˈmɑnəˌsteri] *n, pl* **-teries** : monasterio *m*

Monday [ˈmʌnˌdeɪ, -di] *n* : lunes *m*

money [ˈmʌni] *n, pl* **-eys** *or* **-ies** [ˈmʌniz] : dinero *m* — **monetary** [ˈmɑnəˌteri, ˈmʌnə-] *adj* : monetario — **money order** *n* : giro *m* postal

mongrel [ˈmɑŋgrəl, ˈmʌŋ-] *n* : perro *m* mestizo

monitor [ˈmɑnət̬ər] *n* : monitor *m* (de una computadora, etc.) — ~ *vt* : controlar

monk [ˈmʌŋk] *n* : monje *m*

monkey [ˈmʌŋki] *n, pl* **-keys** : mono *m*, -na *f* — **monkey wrench** *n* : llave *f* inglesa

monogram [ˈmɑnəˌgræm] *n* : monograma *m*

monologue [ˈmɑnəˌlɔg] *n* : monólogo *m*

monopoly [məˈnɑpəli] *n, pl* **-lies** : monopolio *m* — **monopolize** [məˈnɑpəˌlaɪz] *vt* **-lized; -lizing** : monopolizar

monotonous [məˈnɑt̬ənəs] *adj* : monótono — **monotony** [məˈnɑt̬əni] *n* : monotonía *f*

monster [ˈmɑnstər] *n* : monstruo *m* — **monstrosity** [mɑnˈstrɑsət̬i] *n, pl* **-ties** : monstruosidad *f* — **monstrous** [ˈmɑnstrəs] *adj* 1 : monstruoso 2 HUGE : gigantesco

month [ˈmʌnθ] *n* : mes *m* — **monthly** [ˈmʌnθli] *adv* : mensualmente — ~ *adj* : mensual

monument [ˈmɑnjəmənt] *n* : monumento *m* — **monumental** [ˌmɑnjəˈmentəl] *adj* : monumental

moo [ˈmuː] *vi* : mugir — ~ *n* : mugido *m*

mood [ˈmuːd] *n* : humor *m* — **moody** [ˈmuːdi] *adj* **moodier; -est** 1 GLOOMY : melancólico, deprimido 2 IRRITABLE : malhumorado 3 TEMPERAMENTAL : de humor variable

moon [ˈmuːn] *n* : luna *f* — **moonlight** [ˈmuːnˌlaɪt] *n* : luz *f* de la luna

moor¹ [ˈmʊr, ˈmɔr] *n* : brezal *m*, páramo *m*

moor² *vt* : amarrar — **mooring** [ˈmʊrɪŋ, ˈmɔr-] *n* DOCK : atracadero *m*

moose [ˈmuːs] *ns & pl* : alce *m*

moot [ˈmuːt] *adj* : discutible

mop [ˈmɑp] *n* 1 : trapeador *m* Lat, fre-

gona *f* Spain 2 *or* ~ **of hair** : pelambrera *f* — ~ *vt* **mopped; mopping** : trapear Lat, pasar la fregona a Spain

mope [ˈmoːp] *vi* **moped; moping** : andar deprimido

moped [ˈmoːped] *n* : ciclomotor *m*

moral [ˈmɔrəl] *adj* : moral — ~ *n* 1 : moraleja *f* (de un cuento, etc.) 2 ~**s** *npl* : moral *f*, moralidad *f* — **morale** [məˈræl] *n* : moral *f* — **morality** [məˈrælət̬i] *n, pl* **-ties** : moralidad *f*

morbid [ˈmɔrbɪd] *adj* : morboso

more [ˈmɔr] *adj* : más — ~ *adv* 1 : más 2 ~ **and** ~ : cada vez más 3 ~ **or less** : más o menos 4 **once** ~ : una vez más — ~ *pron* : más — **moreover** [mɔrˈoːvər] *adv* : además

morgue [ˈmɔrg] *n* : depósito *m* de cadáveres

morning [ˈmɔrnɪŋ] *n* 1 : mañana *f* 2 **good** ~! : ¡buenos días! 3 **in the** ~ : por la mañana

moron [ˈmɔrˌɑn] *n* : estúpido *m*, -da *f*; imbécil *mf*

morose [məˈroːs] *adj* : malhumorado

morphine [ˈmɔrˌfiːn] *n* : morfina *f*

morsel [ˈmɔrsəl] *n* 1 BITE : bocado *m* 2 FRAGMENT : pedazo *m*

mortal [ˈmɔrt̬əl] *adj* : mortal — ~ *n* : mortal *mf* — **mortality** [mɔrˈtælət̬i] *n* : mortalidad *f*

mortar [ˈmɔrt̬ər] *n* : mortero *m*

mortgage [ˈmɔrgɪdʒ] *n* : hipoteca *f* — ~ *vt* **-gaged; -gaging** : hipotecar

mortify [ˈmɔrt̬əˌfaɪ] *vt* **-fied; -fying** 1 : mortificar 2 HUMILIATE : avergonzar

mosaic [moˈzeɪɪk] *n* : mosaico *m*

Moslem [ˈmɑzləm] → **Muslim**

mosque [ˈmɑsk] *n* : mezquita *f*

mosquito [məˈskiːt̬o] *n, pl* **-toes** : mosquito *m*, zancudo *m* Lat

moss [ˈmɔs] *n* : musgo *m*

most [ˈmoːst] *adj* 1 : la mayoría de, la mayor parte de 2 **(the)** ~ : más — ~ *adv* : más — ~ *n* : más *m*, máximo *m* — ~ *pron* : la mayoría, la mayor parte — **mostly** [ˈmoːstli] *adv* 1 MAINLY : en su mayor parte, principalmente 2 USUALLY : normalmente

motel [moˈtel] *n* : motel *m*

moth [ˈmɔθ] *n* : palomilla *f*, polilla *f*

mother [ˈmʌðər] *n* : madre *f* — ~ *vt* : cuidar de 2 SPOIL : mimar — **motherhood** [ˈmʌðərˌhʊd] *n* : maternidad *f* — **mother-in-law** [ˈmʌðərɪnˌlɔ] *n, pl* **mothers-in-law** : suegra *f* — **motherly** [ˈmʌðərli] *adj* : maternal — **mother-of-pearl** [ˌmʌðərəvˈpərl] *n* : nácar *m*

motif [moˈtiːf] *n* : motivo *m*

motion ['mo:ʃən] *n* 1 : movimiento *m* 2 PROPOSAL : moción *f* 3 set in ~ : poner en marcha — ~ *vi* ~ to s.o. : hacer una señal a algn — **motionless** ['mo:ʃənləs] *adj* : inmóvil — **motion picture** *n* : película *f*

motive ['mo:ṭɪv] *n* : motivo *m* — **motivate** ['mo:ṭəˌveɪt] *vt* -vated; -vating : motivar — **motivation** [ˌmo:ṭəˈveɪʃən] *n* : motivación *f*

motor ['mo:ṭər] *n* : motor *m* — **motorbike** ['mo:ṭərˌbaɪk] *n* : motocicleta *f* (pequeña), moto *f* — **motorboat** ['mo:ṭərˌbot] *n* : lancha *f* motora — **motorcycle** ['mo:ṭərˌsaɪkəl] *n* : motocicleta *f* — **motorcyclist** ['mo:ṭərˌsaɪkəlɪst] *n* : motociclista *mf* — **motorist** ['mo:ṭərɪst] *n* : automovilista *mf*, motorista *mf Lat*

motto ['mɑṭo:] *n, pl* **-toes** : lema *m*

mould ['mo:ld] → **mold**

mound ['maʊnd] *n* 1 PILE : montón *m* 2 HILL : montículo *m*

mount¹ ['maʊnt] *n* 1 HORSE : montura *f* 2 SUPPORT : soporte *m* — ~ *vt* : montar (un caballo, etc.), subir (una escalera) — *vi* INCREASE : aumentar

mount² *n* HILL : monte *m* — **mountain** ['maʊntən] *n* : montaña *f* — **mountainous** ['maʊntənəs] *adj* : montañoso

mourn ['mo:rn] *vt* : llorar (por) — *vi* : lamentarse — **mourner** ['mo:rnər] *n* : doliente *mf* — **mournful** ['mo:rnfəl] *adj* : triste — **mourning** ['mo:rnɪŋ] *n* : luto *m*

mouse ['maʊs] *n, pl* **mice** ['maɪs] : ratón *m* — **mousetrap** ['maʊsˌtræp] *n* : ratonera *f*

moustache ['mʌˌstæʃ, məˈstæʃ] → **mustache**

mouth ['maʊθ] *n* : boca *f* (de una persona o un animal), desembocadura *f* (de un río) — **mouthful** ['maʊθfʊl] *n* : bocado *m* — **mouthpiece** ['maʊθˌpi:s] *n* : boquilla *f* (de un instrumento musical)

move ['mu:v] *v* **moved; moving** *vi* 1 GO : ir 2 RELOCATE : mudarse 3 STIR : moverse 4 ACT : tomar medidas — *vt* 1 : mover 2 AFFECT : conmover 3 TRANSPORT : transportar, trasladar 4 PROPOSE : proponer — ~ *n* 1 MOVEMENT : movimiento *m* 2 RELOCATION : mudanza *f* 3 STEP : medida *f* — **movable** ['mu:vəbəl] *or* **moveable** *adj* : movible, móvil — **movement** ['mu:vmənt] *n* : movimiento *m*

movie ['mu:vi] *n* 1 : película *f* 2 ~**s** *npl* : cine *m*

mow ['mo:] *vt* **mowed; mowed** *or*

mown ['mo:n]; **mowing** : cortar (la hierba) — **mower** ['mo:ər] → **lawn mower**

Mr. ['mɪstər] *n, pl* **Messrs.** ['mesərz] : señor *m*

Mrs. ['mɪsəz, -səs, *esp South* 'mɪzəz, -zəs] *n, pl* **Mesdames** [meɪˈdeɪm, -ˈdæm] : señora *f*

Ms. ['mɪz] *n* : señora *f*, señorita *f*

much ['mʌtʃ] *adj* **more; most** : mucho — ~ *adv* **more** ['mor]; **most** ['mo:st] 1 : mucho 2 as ~ as : tanto como 3 how ~? : ¿cuánto? 4 too ~ : demasiado — ~ *pron* : mucho, -cha

muck ['mʌk] *n* 1 DIRT : mugre *f*, suciedad *f* 2 MANURE : estiércol *m*

mucus ['mju:kəs] *n* : mucosidad *f*

mud ['mʌd] *n* : barro *m*, lodo *m*

muddle ['mʌdəl] *v* **-dled; -dling** *vt* 1 CONFUSE : confundir 2 JUMBLE : desordenar — *vi* ~ **through** : arreglárselas — ~ *n* : confusión *f*, lío *m fam*

muddy ['mʌdi] *adj* **-dier; -est** : fangoso, lleno de barro

muffin ['mʌfən] *n* : mollete *m*

muffle ['mʌfəl] *vt* **-fled; -fling** : amortiguar (un sonido) — **muffler** ['mʌflər] *n* 1 SCARF : bufanda *f* 2 : silenciador *m*, mofle *m Lat* (de un automóvil)

mug ['mʌɡ] *n, pl* : tazón *m* — ~ *vt* : asaltar, atracar — **mugger** ['mʌɡər] *n* : atracador *m*, -dora *f*

muggy ['mʌɡi] *adj* **-gier; -est** : bochornoso

mule ['mju:l] *n* : mula *f*

mull ['mʌl] *vt or* ~ **over** : reflexionar sobre

multicolored [ˌmʌltiˈkʌlərd, ˌmʌltaɪ-] *adj* : multicolor

multimedia [ˌmʌltiˈmi:diə, ˌmʌltaɪ-] *adj* : multimedia

multinational [ˌmʌltiˈnæʃənəl, ˌmʌltaɪ-] *adj* : multinacional

multiple ['mʌltəpəl] *adj* : múltiple — ~ *n* : múltiplo *m* — **multiplication** [ˌmʌltəpləˈkeɪʃən] *n* : multiplicación *f* — **multiply** ['mʌltəplaɪ] *v* **-plied; -plying** *vt* : multiplicar — *vi* : multiplicarse

multitude ['mʌltəˌtu:d, -ˌtju:d] *n* : multitud *f*

mum ['mʌm] *adj* **keep** ~ : guardar silencio

mumble ['mʌmbəl] *v* **-bled; -bling** *vt* : mascullar — *vi* : hablar entre dientes

mummy ['mʌmi] *n, pl* **-mies** : momia *f*

mumps ['mʌmps] *ns & pl* : paperas *fpl*

munch ['mʌntʃ] *v* : mascar, masticar

mundane [ˌmʌnˈdeɪn, 'mʌn-] *adj* : rutinario, ordinario

municipal [mjʊ'nɪsəpəl] adj : municipal — **municipality** [mjʊ,nɪsə'pæləṱi] n, pl -ties : municipio m

munitions [mjʊ'nɪʃənz] npl : municiónes fpl

mural ['mjʊrəl] n : mural m

murder ['mərdər] n : asesinato m, homicidio m — vt : asesinar, matar — vi : matar — **murderer** ['mərdərər] n : asesino m, -na f; homicida mf — **murderous** ['mərdərəs] adj : asesino, homicida

murky ['mərki] adj -kier; -est : turbio, oscuro

murmur ['mərmər] n : murmullo m — **murmur** v : murmurar

muscle ['mʌsəl] n : músculo m — vi -cled; -cling or ~ in : meterse por la fuerza en — **muscular** ['mʌskjələr] adj 1 : muscular 2 STRONG : musculoso

muse[1] ['mjuz] n : musa f

muse[2] vi **mused; musing** : meditar

museum [mjʊ'ziːəm] n : museo m

mushroom ['mʌʃ,rum, -,rʊm] n 1 : hongo m, seta f 2 : champiñón m (en la cocina) — vi GROW : crecer rápidamente, multiplicarse

mushy ['mʌʃi] adj **mushier; -est 1** SOFT : blando 2 MAWKISH : sensiblero

music ['mjuzɪk] n : música f — **musical** ['mjuzɪkəl] adj : musical — ~ n : comedia f musical — **musician** [mju-'zɪʃən] n : músico m, -ca f

Muslim ['mʌzləm, 'mʊs-, 'muz-] adj : musulmán — ~ n : musulmán m, -mana f

muslin ['mʌzlən] n : muselina f

mussel ['mʌsəl] n : mejillón m

must ['mʌst] v aux 1 : deber, tener que 2 you ~ come : tienes que venir 3 you

~ be tired : debes (de) estar cansado — ~ n : necesidad f

mustache ['mʌ,stæʃ, mʌ'stæʃ] n : bigote m, bigotes mpl

mustang ['mʌ,stæŋ] n : mustang m

mustard ['mʌstərd] n : mostaza f

muster ['mʌstər] vt 1 : reunir 2 or ~ up : armarse de, cobrar (valor, fuerzas, etc.)

musty ['mʌsti] adj **mustier; -est** : que huele a cerrado

mute ['mjut] adj **muter; mutest** : mudo — ~ n : mudo m, -da f

mutilate ['mjuṱə,leɪt] vt **-lated; -lating** : mutilar

mutiny ['mjuṱəni] n, pl **-nies** : motín m — ~ vi **-nied; -nying** : amotinarse

mutter ['mʌtər] vi : murmurar

mutton ['mʌtən] n : carne f de carnero

mutual ['mjutʃuəl] adj 1 : mutuo 2 COMMON : común — **mutually** ['mjutʃuəli, -tʃəli] adv : mutuamente

muzzle ['mʌzəl] n 1 SNOUT : hocico m 2 : bozal m (para un perro, etc.) 3 : boca f (de un arma de fuego) — ~ vt **-zled; -zling** : poner un bozal a (un animal)

my ['maɪ] adj : mi

myopia [maɪ'oːpiə] n : miopía f — **myopic** [maɪ'oːpɪk, -'ɑ-] adj : miope

myself [maɪ'sɛlf] pron 1 (reflexive) : me 2 (emphatic) : yo mismo 3 by ~ : solo

mystery ['mɪstəri] n, pl **-teries** : misterio m — **mysterious** [mɪ'stɪriəs] adj : misterioso

mystic ['mɪstɪk] adj or **mystical** ['mɪstɪkəl] : místico

mystify ['mɪstə,faɪ] vt **-fied; -fying** : dejar perplejo, confundir

mystique [mɪ'stik] n : aura f de misterio

myth ['mɪθ] n : mito m — **mythical** ['mɪθɪkəl] adj : mítico

N

n ['ɛn] n, pl **n's** or **ns** ['ɛnz] : n f, decimocuarta letra del alfabeto inglés

nab ['næb] vt **nabbed; nabbing 1** ARREST : pescar fam 2 GRAB : agarrar

nag ['næg] v **nagged; nagging** vi COMPLAIN : quejarse — vt 1 ANNOY : fastidiar, dar la lata a 2 SCOLD : regañar — **nagging** adj : persistente

nail ['neɪl] n 1 : clavo m 2 : uña f (de un dedo) — ~ vt or ~ **down** : clavar — **nail file** n : lima f de uñas

naive or naïve [nɑ'iv] adj **-iver; -est** : ingenuo — **naïveté** [nɑ,iːvə'teɪ, nɑ-'iːvə-] n : ingenuidad f

naked ['neɪkəd] adj 1 : desnudo 2 the ~ **truth** : la pura verdad 3 to the ~ **eye** : a simple vista

name ['neɪm] n 1 : nombre m 2 REPUTATION : fama f 3 **what is your ~?** : ¿cómo se llama? 4 → first name, surname — ~ vt **named; naming 1** : poner nombre a 2 APPOINT : nombrar 3 ~ **a price** : fijar un precio — **nameless** ['neɪmləs] adj : anónimo — **namely** ['neɪmli] adv : a saber — **namesake** ['neɪm,seɪk] n : tocayo m, -ya f

nap[1] ['næp] vi **napped; napping** : echarse una siesta — ~ n : siesta f

nap² n : pelo m (de una tela)
nape ['neɪp, 'næp] n or ~ **of the neck** : nuca f
napkin ['næpkən] n 1 : servilleta f 2 → **sanitary napkin**
narcotic [nɑr'kɑtɪk] n : narcótico m, estupefaciente m
narrate ['nær,eɪt] vt **-rated; -rating** : narrar — **narration** [næ'reɪʃən] n : narración f — **narrative** ['nærətɪv] n : narración f — **narrator** ['nær,eɪtər] n : narrador m, -dora f
narrow ['nær,oː] adj 1 : estrecho, angosto 2 RESTRICTED : limitado — vi : estrecharse — vt 1 : estrechar 2 or ~ **down** : limitar — **narrowly** ['næroːli] adv : por poco — **narrow-minded** [,næroː'maɪndəd] adj : de miras estrechas
nasal ['neɪzəl] adj : nasal
nasty ['næsti] adj **-tier; -est** 1 MEAN : malo, cruel 2 UNPLEASANT : desagradable 3 REPUGNANT : asqueroso — **nastiness** ['næstinəs] n : maldad f
nation ['neɪʃən] n : nación f — **national** ['næʃənəl] adj : nacional — **nationalism** ['næʃənə,lɪzəm] n : nacionalismo m — **nationality** [,næʃə'næləti] n, pl **-ties** : nacionalidad f — **nationalize** ['næʃənə,laɪz] vt **-ized; -izing** : nacionalizar — **nationwide** ['neɪʃən,waɪd] adj : por todo el país
native ['neɪtɪv] adj 1 : natal (dícese de un país, etc.) 2 INNATE : innato 3 ~ **language** : lengua f materna — ~ n 1 : nativo m, -va f 2 **be a** ~ **of** : ser natural de — **Native American** : indio m americano, india f americana — **nativity** [nə'tɪvəti, neɪ-] n, pl **-ties the Nativity** : la Navidad
nature ['neɪtʃər] n 1 : naturaleza f 2 KIND : índole f, clase f 3 DISPOSITION : carácter m, natural m — **natural** ['nætʃərəl] adj : natural — **naturalize** ['nætʃərə,laɪz] vt **-ized; -izing** : naturalizar — **naturally** ['nætʃərəli] adv : naturalmente
naught ['nɔt] n 1 NOTHING : nada f 2 ZERO : cero m
naughty ['nɔti] adj **-tier; -est** 1 : travieso, pícaro 2 RISQUÉ : picante
nausea ['nɔziə, 'nɔʃə] n : náuseas fpl — **nauseating** ['nɔzi,eɪtɪŋ] adj : nauseabundo — **nauseous** ['nɔʃəs, -ziəs] adj 1 **feel** ~ : sentir náuseas 2 SICKENING : nauseabundo
nautical ['nɔtɪkəl] adj : náutico
naval ['neɪvəl] adj : naval
nave ['neɪv] n : nave f (de una iglesia)
navel ['neɪvəl] n : ombligo m

navigate ['nævə,geɪt] v **-gated; -gating** vi : navegar — vt 1 : gobernar (un barco), pilotar (un avión) 2 : navegar por (un río, etc.) — **navigable** ['nævɪɡəbəl] adj : navegable — **navigation** [,nævə'geɪʃən] n : navegación f — **navigator** ['nævə,geɪtər] n : navegante mf
navy ['neɪvi] n, pl **-vies** 1 : marina f de guerra 2 or ~ **blue** : azul m marino
near ['nɪr] adv : cerca — prep : cerca de — ~ adj : cercano, próximo — ~ vt : acercarse a — **nearby** ['nɪr,baɪ, 'nɪr,baɪ] adv : cerca — ~ adj : cercano — **nearly** ['nɪrli] adv : casi — **nearsighted** ['nɪr,saɪtəd] adj : miope, corto de vista
neat ['niːt] adj 1 TIDY : muy arreglado 2 CLEVER : hábil, ingenioso — **neatly** ['niːtli] adv 1 : ordenadamente 2 CLEVERLY : hábilmente — **neatness** ['niːtnəs] n : pulcritud f, orden m
nebulous ['nɛbjʊləs] adj : nebuloso
necessary ['nɛsə,seri] adj : necesario — **necessarily** [,nɛsə'serəli] adv : necesariamente — **necessitate** [nɪ'sesə,teɪt] vt **-tated; -tating** : exigir, requerir — **necessity** [nɪ'sesəti] n, pl **-ties** 1 : necesidad f 2 **necessities** npl : cosas fpl indispensables
neck ['nɛk] n 1 : cuello m (de una persona o una botella), pescuezo m (de un animal) 2 COLLAR : cuello m — **necklace** ['nɛkləs] n : collar m — **necktie** ['nɛk,taɪ] n : corbata f
nectar ['nɛktər] n : néctar m
nectarine [,nɛktə'riːn] n : nectarina f
need ['niːd] n 1 : necesidad f 2 **if** ~ **be** : si hace falta — ~ vt 1 : necesitar, exigir 2 ~ **to** : tener que — v aux : tener que
needle ['niːdəl] n : aguja f — ~ vt **-dled; -dling** : pinchar
needless ['niːdləs] adj 1 : innecesario 2 ~ **to say** : de más está decir
needlework ['niːdəl,wərk] n : bordado m
needn't ['niːdənt] (contraction of **need not**) → **need**
needy ['niːdi] **needier; -est** adj : necesitado
negative ['nɛɡətɪv] adj : negativo — ~ n 1 : negación f (en gramática) 2 : negativo m (en fotografía)
neglect [nɪ'ɡlɛkt] vt : descuidar — ~ n : descuido m, abandono m
negligee [,nɛɡlə'ʒeɪ] n : negligé m
negligence ['nɛɡlɪdʒəns] n : negligencia f, descuido m — **negligent** ['nɛɡlɪdʒənt] adj : negligente, descuidado
negligible ['nɛɡlɪdʒəbəl] adj : insignificante

negotiate [nɪˈgoːʃieɪt] v **-ated; -ating** : negociar — **negotiable** [nɪˈgoːʃəbəl, -ʃiə-] adj : negociable — **negotiation** [nɪgoːʃiˈeɪʃən, -siˈeɪ-] n : negociación f — **negotiator** [nɪˈgoːʃieɪtər, -siˈeɪt-] n : negociador m, -dora f

Negro [ˈniːgroː] n, pl **-groes** sometimes considered offensive : negro m, -gra f

neigh [neɪ] vi : relinchar — ~ n : relincho m

neighbor or Brit **neighbour** [ˈneɪbər] n : vecino m, -na f — **neighborhood** or Brit **neighbourhood** [ˈneɪbərhʊd] n 1 : barrio m, vecindario m 2 **in the** ~ **of** : alrededor de — **neighborly** or Brit **neighbourly** [ˈneɪbərli] adv : amable

neither [ˈniːðər, ˈnaɪ-] conj 1 ~...**nor** : ni...ni 2 ~ **am/do I** : yo tampoco — ~ pron : ninguno, -na — ~ adj : ninguno (de los dos)

neon [ˈniːɑːn] n : neón m

nephew [ˈnefjuː, chiefly British ˈnevjuː] n : sobrino m

Neptune [ˈneptuːn, -tjuːn] n : Neptuno m

nerve [ˈnərv] n 1 : nervio m 2 COURAGE : coraje m 3 GALL : descaro m 4 ~ **s** npl JITTERS : nervios mpl — **nervous** [ˈnərvəs] adj : nervioso — **nervousness** [ˈnərvəsnəs] n : nerviosismo m — **nervy** [ˈnərvi] adj **nervier; -est** : descarado

nest [ˈnest] n : nido m — ~ vi : anidar

nestle [ˈnesəl] vi **-tled; -tling** : acurrucarse

net¹ [ˈnet] n : red f — ~ vt **netted; netting** : pescar, atrapar (con una red)

net² adj : neto — ~ vt **netted; netting** YIELD : producir neto

nettle [ˈnetəl] n : ortiga f

network [ˈnetwərk] n : red f

neurology [nʊˈrɑːlədʒi, njʊ-] n : neurología f

neurosis [nʊˈroːsɪs, njʊ-] n, pl **-roses** [-siːz] : neurosis f — **neurotic** [nʊˈrɑːtɪk, njʊ-] adj : neurótico

neuter [ˈnuːtər, ˈnjuː-] adj : neutro — ~ vt : castrar

neutral [ˈnuːtrəl, ˈnjuː-] n : punto m muerto (de un automóvil) — ~ adj 1 : neutral 2 : neutro (en electrotecnia o química) — **neutrality** [nuːˈtrælət̬i, njuː-] n : neutralidad f — **neutralize** [ˈnuːtrəˌlaɪz, ˈnjuː-] vt **-ized; -izing** : neutralizar

neutron [ˈnuːtrɑːn, ˈnjuː-] n : neutrón m

never [ˈnevər] adv 1 : nunca, jamás 2 NOT : no 3 ~ **again** : nunca más 4 ~ **mind** : no importa — **nevermore** [ˌnevərˈmor] adv : nunca jamás — **nev-**

ertheless [ˌnevərðəˈles] adv : sin embargo, no obstante

new [ˈnuː, ˈnjuː] adj : nuevo — **newborn** [ˈnuːbɔrn, ˈnjuː-] adj : recién nacido — **newcomer** [ˈnuːˌkʌmər, ˈnjuː-] n : recién llegado m, -da f — **newly** [ˈnuːli, ˈnjuː-] adv : recién, recientemente — **newlywed** [ˈnuːliˌwed, ˈnjuː-] n : recién casado m, -da f — **news** [ˈnuːz, ˈnjuːz] n : noticias fpl — **newscast** [ˈnuːzˌkæst, ˈnjuːz-] n : noticiario m, noticiero m Lat — **newscaster** [ˈnuːzˌkæstər, ˈnjuːz-] n : presentador m, -dora f (de un noticiario) — **newsletter** [ˈnuːzˌletər, ˈnjuːz-] n : boletín m informativo — **newspaper** [ˈnuːzˌpeɪpər, ˈnjuːz-] n : periódico m, diario m — **newsstand** [ˈnuːzˌstænd, ˈnjuːz-] n : puesto m de periódicos

newt [ˈnuːt, ˈnjuːt] n : tritón m

New Year's Day n : día m del Año Nuevo

next [ˈnekst] adj 1 : próximo 2 FOLLOWING : siguiente — ~ adv 1 : la próxima vez 2 AFTERWARD : después, luego 3 NOW : ahora — **next-door** [ˈnekstˈdor] adj : de al lado — **next to** adv ALMOST : casi — ~ prep BESIDE : al lado de

nib [ˈnɪb] n : plumilla f

nibble [ˈnɪbəl] vt **-bled; -bling** : mordisquear

Nicaraguan [ˌnɪkəˈrɑːgwən] adj : nicaragüense

nice [ˈnaɪs] adj **nicer; nicest** 1 PLEASANT : agradable, bueno 2 KIND : amable — **nicely** [ˈnaɪsli] adv 1 WELL : bien 2 KINDLY : amablemente — **niceness** [ˈnaɪsnəs] n : amabilidad f — **niceties** [ˈnaɪsət̬iz] npl : detalles mpl, sutilezas fpl

niche [ˈnɪtʃ] n 1 : nicho m 2 **find one's** ~ : hacerse su hueco

nick [ˈnɪk] n 1 : corte m pequeño, muesca f 2 **in the** ~ **of time** : justo a tiempo — ~ vt : hacer una muesca en

nickel [ˈnɪkəl] n 1 : níquel m (metal) 2 : moneda f de cinco centavos

nickname [ˈnɪkˌneɪm] n : apodo m, sobrenombre m — ~ vt **-named; -naming** : apodar

nicotine [ˈnɪkəˌtiːn] n : nicotina f

niece [ˈniːs] n : sobrina f

niggling [ˈnɪgəlɪŋ] adj 1 PETTY : insignificante 2 PERSISTENT : constante

night [ˈnaɪt] n 1 : noche f 2 **at** ~ : de noche 3 **last** ~ : anoche 4 **tomorrow** ~ : mañana por la noche — **nightclub** [ˈnaɪtˌklʌb] n : club m nocturno — **nightfall** [ˈnaɪtˌfɔl] n : anochecer m — **nightgown** [ˈnaɪtˌgaʊn] n : camisón m (de noche) — **nightly** ['naɪt] *adj* : de todas las noches — ~ *adv* : cada noche — **nightmare** ['naɪtmær] *n* : pesadilla *f* — **nighttime** ['naɪt,taɪm] *n* : noche *f*

nil ['nɪl] *n* NOTHING : nada *f*

nimble ['nɪmbəl] *adj* **-bler; -blest** : ágil

nine ['naɪn] *adj* : nueve — ~ *n* : nueve *m* — **nine hundred** *adj* : novecientos — ~ *n* : novecientos *m* — **nineteen** [naɪn'tiːn] *adj* : diecinueve — ~ *n* : diecinueve *m* — **nineteenth** [naɪn'tiːnθ] *adj* : decimonoveno, -na ~ *n* **1** : decimonoveno *m*, -na *f* **2** : diecinueveavo *m* (en matemáticas) — **ninetieth** ['naɪntiəθ] *adj* : nonagésimo — ~ *n* **1** : nonagésimo *m*, -ma *f* (en una serie) **2** : noventavo *m* (en matemáticas) — **ninety** ['naɪnti] *adj* : noventa — ~ *n, pl* **-ties** : noventa *m* — **ninth** ['naɪnθ] *adj* : noveno — ~ *n* **1** : noveno *m*, -na *f* (en una serie) **2** : noveno *m* (en matemáticas)

nip ['nɪp] *vt* **nipped; nipping 1** PINCH : pellizcar **2** BITE : mordisquear **3** ~ **in the bud** : cortar de raíz — ~ *n* **1** PINCH : pellizco *m* **2** NIBBLE : mordisco *m*

nipple ['nɪpəl] *n* **1** : pezón *m* (de una mujer) **2** : tetilla *f* (de un hombre o un biberón)

nitrogen ['naɪtrədʒən] *n* : nitrógeno *m*

nitwit ['nɪt,wɪt] *n* : idiota *mf*

no ['noː] *adv* : no — ~ *adj* **1** : ninguno **2 I have ~ money** : no tengo dinero **3 it's ~ trouble** : no es ningún problema **4** ~ **smoking** : prohibido fumar — ~ *n, pl* **noes** *or* **nos** ['noːz] : no *m*

noble ['noːbəl] *adj* **-bler; -blest** : noble — ~ *n* : noble *mf* — **nobility** [noˈbɪl-ə̩ti] *n* : nobleza *f*

nobody ['noːbədi, -,bɑdi] *pron* : nadie

nocturnal [nɑk'tərnəl] *adj* : nocturno

nod ['nɑd] *v* **nodded; nodding** *vi* **1** *or* ~ **yes** : asentir con la cabeza **2** ~ **off** : dormirse — *vt* ~ **one's head** : asentir con la cabeza — ~ *n* : señal *m* con la cabeza

noes → **no**

noise ['nɔɪz] *n* : ruido *m* — **noisily** ['nɔɪzəli] *adv* : ruidosamente — **noisy** ['nɔɪzi] *adj* **noisier; -est** : ruidoso

nomad ['noː,mæd] *n* : nómada *mf* — **nomadic** [noˈmædɪk] *adj* : nómada

nominal ['nɑmənəl] *adj* : nominal

nominate ['nɑmə,neɪt] *vt* **-nated; -nating 1** : proponer, postular *Lat* **2** AP-POINT : nombrar — **nomination**

[,nɑmə'neɪʃən] *n* **1** : propuesta *f*, postulación *f Lat* **2** APPOINTMENT : nombramiento *m*

nonalcoholic [,nɑnælkə'hɔlɪk] *adj* : no alcohólico

nonchalant [,nɑnʃə'lɑnt] *adj* : despreocupado

noncommissioned officer [,nɑnkə'mɪʃənd] *n* : suboficial *mf*

noncommittal [,nɑnkə'mɪt̬əl] *adj* : evasivo

nondescript [,nɑndr'skrɪpt] *adj* : anodino, soso

none ['nʌn] *pron* **1** : ninguno, ninguna **2 there are ~ left** : no hay más — ~ *adv* **1 be ~ the worse** : no sufrir daño alguno **2** ~ **too happy** : nada contento **3** ~ **too soon** : a buena hora

nonentity [nɑnˈɛnt̬əti] *n, pl* **-ties** : persona *f* insignificante

nonetheless [,nʌnðə'lɛs] *adv* : sin embargo, no obstante

nonexistent [,nɑnɪg'zɪstənt] *adj* : inexistente

nonfat [nɑn'fæt] *adj* : sin grasa

nonfiction [nɑn'fɪkʃən] *n* : no ficción *f*

nonprofit [nɑn'prɑfət] *adj* : sin fines lucrativos

nonsense ['nɑn,sɛns, 'nɑnsənts] *n* : tonterías *fpl*, disparates *mpl* — **nonsensical** [nɑn'sɛntsɪkəl] *adj* : absurdo

nonsmoker [nɑn'smoːkər] *n* : no fumador *m*, -dora *f*

nonstop [nɑn'stɑp] *adj* : directo — ~ *adv* : sin parar

noodle ['nuːdəl] *n* : fideo *m*

nook ['nʊk] *n* : rincón *m*

noon ['nuːn] *n* : mediodía *m*

no one *pron* : nadie

noose ['nuːs] *n* **1** : dogal *m*, soga *f* **2** LASSO : lazo *m*

nor ['nɔr] *conj* **1 neither...~** : ni...ni **2** ~ **I** : yo tampoco

norm ['nɔrm] *n* **1** : norma *f* **2 the ~** : lo normal — **normal** ['nɔrməl] *adj* : normal — **normality** [nɔr'mæləti] *n* : normalidad *f* — **normally** *adv* : normalmente

north ['nɔrθ] *adv* : al norte — ~ *adj* : norte, del norte — ~ *n* : norte *m* **2 the North** : el Norte — **North American** *adj* : norteamericano — **northeast** [nɔr'θiːst] *adv* : hacia el nordeste — ~ *adj* : nordeste, del nordeste — ~ *n* : nordeste, noreste *m* — **northeastern** [nɔr'θiːstərn] *adj* : nordeste, del nordeste — **northerly** ['nɔrðərli] *adj* : del norte — **northern** ['nɔrðərn] *adj* : del norte, norteño — **northwest** [nɔrθ'wɛst] *adv* : hacia el noroeste —

~ *adj* : noroeste, del noroeste — ~ *n*
: noroeste *m* — **northwestern** [nɔrθ-
'wɛstərn] *adj* : noroeste, del noroeste
Norwegian [nɔr'wiːdʒən] *adj* : noruego —
~ *n* : noruego *m*
nose ['noːz] *n* **1** : nariz *f* (de una persona), hocico *m* (de un animal) **2 blow**
one's ~ : sonarse las narices — ~ *vi*
nosed; nosing *or* ~ **around** : meter
las narices — **nosebleed** ['noːz,bliːd] *n*
: hemorragia *f* nasal — **nosedive**
['noːz,daɪv] *n* : descenso *m* en picada
nostalgia [nɑ'stældʒə, nə-] *n* : nostalgia *f*
— **nostalgic** [nɑ'stældʒɪk, nə-] *adj*
: nostálgico
nostril ['nɑstrəl] *n* : ventana *f* de la nariz
nosy *or* **nosey** ['noːzi] *adj* **nosier; -est**
: entrometido
not ['nɑt] *adv* **1** : no **2 he's** ~ **tired** : no
esta cansado **3 I hope** ~ : espero que
no **4** ~ ... **anything** : no...nada
notable ['noːtəbəl] *adj* : notable — ~ *n*
: personaje *m* — **notably** ['noːtəbli]
adv : notablemente
notary public ['noːtəri-] *n, pl* **notaries**
public *or* **notary publics** : notario *m*,
-ria *f*
notation [noː'teɪʃən] *n* : anotación *f*
notch ['nɑtʃ] *n* : muesca *f*, corte *m* — ~
vt : hacer un corte en
note ['noːt] *vt* **noted; noting 1** NOTICE
: observar, notar **2** RECORD : anotar —
~ *n* **1** : nota *f* **2** *of* ~ : destacado **3**
take ~ *of* : prestar atención a **4 take**
~ **s** : apuntar — **notebook** ['noːt,bʊk]
n : libreta *f*, cuaderno *m* — **noted**
['noːtəd] *adj* : renombrado, célebre —
noteworthy ['noːt,wərði] *adj* : notable
nothing ['nʌθɪŋ] *pron* **1** : nada **2 be** ~
but : no ser más que **3 for** ~ **FREE**
: gratis — ~ *n* **1** ZERO : zero *m* **2** TRI-
FLE : nimiedad *f*
notice ['noːtɪs] *n* **1** SIGN : letrero *m*, aviso
m **2 at a moment's** ~ : sin previo
aviso **3 be given one's** ~ : ser despedido **4 take** ~ *of* : prestar atención
a — ~ *vt* -**ticed; -ticing** : notar — **no-**
ticeable ['noːtɪsəbəl] *adj* : perceptible,
evidente
notify ['noːtə,faɪ] *vt* -**fied; -fying** : notificar, avisar — **notification** [,noːtəfə-
'keɪʃən] *n* : notificación *f*, aviso *m*
notion ['noːʃən] *n* **1** : noción *f*, idea *f* **2**
~ **s** *npl* : artículos *mpl* de mercería
notorious [noː'toːriəs] *adj* : de mala fama
— **notoriety** [,noːtə'raɪəti] *n* : mala
fama *f*, notoriedad *f*
notwithstanding [,nɑtwɪθ'stændɪŋ,
-wɪð-] *prep* : a pesar de, no obstante —
~ *adv* : sin embargo — *conj* : a
pesar de que

nougat ['nuːgət] *n* : turrón *m*
nought ['nɔt, 'nɑt] → **naught**
noun ['naʊn] *n* : nombre *m*, sustantivo *m*
nourish ['nərɪʃ] *vt* : nutrir — **nourish-**
ing ['nərɪʃɪŋ] *adj* : nutritivo — **nour-**
ishment ['nərɪʃmənt] *n* : alimento *m*
novel ['nɑvəl] *adj* : original, novedoso
— ~ *n* : novela *f* — **novelist**
['nɑvəlɪst] *n* : novelista *mf* — **novelty**
['nɑvəlti] *n, pl* **-ties** : novedad *f*
November [noː'vɛmbər] *n* : noviembre *m*
novice ['nɑvɪs] *n* : novato *m*, -ta *f*: principiante *mf*
now ['naʊ] *adv* **1** : ahora **2** THEN : entonces **3 from** ~ **on** : de ahora en
adelante **4** ~ **and then** : de vez en
cuando **5 right** ~ : ahora mismo —
~ *conj* ~ **that** : ahora que, ya que
— ~ *n* **1 a year from** ~ : dentro de
un año **2 by** ~ : ya **3 until** ~ : hasta
ahora — **nowadays** ['naʊə,deɪz] *adv*
: hoy en día
nowhere ['noː,hwɛr] *adv* **1** (*indicating*
location) : por ninguna parte, por
ningún lado **2** (*indicating motion*) : a
ninguna parte, a ningún lado **3 I'm** ~
near finished : aún me falta mucho
para terminar **4 it's** ~ **near here**
: queda bastante lejos de aquí — ~ *n*
: ninguna parte *f*
nozzle ['nɑzəl] *n* : boca *f* (de una
manguera, etc.)
nuance ['nuːˌɑnts, 'njuː-] *n* : matiz *m*
nucleus ['nuːkliəs, 'njuː-] *n, pl* **-clei**
[-kliaɪ] : núcleo *m* — **nuclear** ['nuː-
kliər, 'njuː-] *adj* : nuclear
nude ['nuːd, 'njuːd] *adj* **nuder; nudest**
: desnudo — ~ *n* : desnudo *m*
nudge ['nʌdʒ] *vt* **nudged; nudging**
: dar un codazo a — ~ *n* : toque *m*
(con el codo)
nudity ['nuːdəti, 'njuː-] *n* : desnudez *f*
nugget ['nʌgət] *n* : pepita *f* (de oro, etc.)
nuisance ['nuːsənts, 'njuː-] *n* **1** ANNOY-
ANCE : fastidio *m*, molestia *f* **2** PEST
: pesado *m*, -da *f* fam
null ['nʌl] *adj* ~ **and void** : nulo y sin
efecto
numb ['nʌm] *adj* **1** : entumecido, dormido **2** ~ **with fear** : paralizado de miedo — ~ *vt* : entumecer, adormecer
number ['nʌmbər] *n* **1** : número *m* **2 a**
~ **of** : varios — ~ *vt* **1** : numerar **2**
INCLUDE : contar, incluir **3** TOTAL : ascender a
numeral ['nuːmərəl, 'njuː-] *n* : número *m*
— **numeric** [nʊ'mɛrɪk, njʊ-] *or* **numer-**
ical [nʊ'mɛrɪkəl, njʊ-] *adj* : numérico
— **numerous** ['nuːmərəs, 'njuː-] *adj*
: numeroso

nun ['nʌn] n : monja f
nuptial ['nʌpʃəl] adj : nupcial
nurse ['nərs] n 1 : enfermero m, -ra f 2 →
    nursemaid — **~** vt **nursed; nursing**
    1 : cuidar (de), atender 2 SUCKLE
    : amamantar — **nursemaid** ['nərs-
    ,meɪd] n : niñera f — **nursery** ['nərsəri]
    n, pl -**eries** : cuarto m de los niños 2
    or **day ~** : guardería f 3 : vivero m
    (de plantas) — **nursing home** n
    : asilo m de ancianos
nurture ['nərtʃər] vt -**tured; -turing** 1
    NOURISH : nutrir 2 EDUCATE : criar, ed-
    ucar 3 FOSTER : alimentar
nut ['nʌt] n 1 : nuez f 2 LUNATIC : loco m,
    -ca f 3 ENTHUSIAST : fanático m, -ca f 4
    ~s and bolts : tuercas y tornillos —

nutcracker ['nʌt,krækər] n : cascanue-
    ces m
nutmeg ['nʌt,mɛg] n : nuez f moscada
nutrient ['nu:triənt, 'nju:-] n : nutriente m
nutrition [nu'trɪʃən, nju:-] n : nutrición f
    — **nutritional** [nu'trɪʃənəl, nju:-] adj
    : nutritivo — **nutritious** [nu'trɪʃəs,
    nju:-] adj : nutritivo
nuts ['nʌts] adj : loco
nutshell ['nʌt,ʃel] n 1 : cáscara f de nuez
    2 **in a ~** : en pocas palabras
nutty ['nʌti] adj -**tier; -tiest** : loco
nuzzle ['nʌzəl] v -**zled; -zling** vi : acur-
    rucarse — vt : acariciar con el hocico
nylon ['naɪ,lɑn] n 1 : nilón m 2 **~s** npl
    : medias fpl de nilón
nymph ['nɪmpf] n : ninfa f

O

o ['o:] n, pl **o's** or **os** ['o:z] 1 : o f, deci-
    moquinta letra del alfabeto inglés 2
    ZERO : cero m
O ['o:] → **oh**
oaf ['o:f] n : zoquete m
oak ['o:k] n, pl **oaks** or **oak** : roble m
oar ['o:r] n : remo m
oasis [o'eɪsɪs] n, pl **oases** [-,si:z] : oasis
    m
oath ['o:θ] n, pl **oaths** ['o:ðz, 'o:θs] 1 : ju-
    ramento m 2 SWEARWORD : palabrota f
oats ['o:ts] npl : avena f — **oatmeal** ['o:t-
    ,mi:l] n : harina f de avena
obedient [o'bi:diənt] adj : obediente —
    obedience [o'bi:diəns] n : obediencia
    f
obese [o'bi:s] adj : obeso — **obesity**
    [o'bi:səti] n : obesidad f
obey [o'beɪ] v **obeyed; obeying** : obe-
    decer
obituary [ə'bɪtʃu,eri] n, pl -**aries** : obitu-
    ario m
object ['ɑbdʒɪkt] n 1 : objeto m 2 AIM
    : objetivo m 3 : complemento m (en
    gramática) — **~** [əb'dʒɛkt] vt : objetar
    — vi **~ to** : oponerse a — **objection**
    [əb'dʒɛkʃən] n : objeción f — **objec-
    tionable** [əb'dʒɛkʃənəbəl] adj : de-
    sagradable — **objective** [əb'dʒɛktɪv]
    adj : objetivo — n : objetivo m
oblige [ə'blaɪdʒ] vt **obliged; obliging** 1
    : obligar 2 **be much ~d** : estar muy
    agradecido 3 **~ s.o.** : hacer un favor a
    algn — **obligation** [,ɑblə'geɪʃən] n
    : obligación f — **obligatory** [ə'blɪgə-
    ,tori] adj : obligatorio — **obliging**
    [ə'blaɪdʒɪŋ] adj : atento, servicial

oblique [o'bli:k] adj 1 SLANTING : obli-
    cuo 2 INDIRECT : indirecto
obliterate [ə'blɪtə,reɪt] vt -**ated; -ating** 1
    ERASE : borrar 2 DESTROY : arrasar
oblivion [ə'blɪviən] n : olvido m —
    oblivious [ə'blɪviəs] adj : inconsciente
oblong ['ɑ,blɔŋ] adj : oblongo — **~** n
    : rectángulo m
obnoxious [ɑb'nɑkʃəs, əb-] adj : odioso
oboe ['o:,bo:] n : oboe m
obscene [ɑb'si:n, əb-] adj : obsceno —
    obscenity [ɑb'sɛnəti, əb-] n, pl -**ties**
    : obscenidad f
obscurity [ɑb'skjurəti, əb-] n, pl -**ties**
    : oscuridad f — **obscure** [ɑb'skjur,
    əb-] adj : oscuro — **~** vt -**scured;
    -scuring** 1 DARKEN : oscurecer 2 HIDE
    : ocultar
observe [əb'zərv] v -**served; -serving**
    vt : observar — vi WATCH : mirar —
    observance [əb'zərvəns] n 1 : obser-
    vancia f 2 **religious ~s** : prácticas fpl
    religiosas — **observant** [əb'zərvənt]
    adj : observador — **observation**
    [,ɑbsər'veɪʃən, -zər-] n : observación f
    — **observatory** [əb'zərvə,tori] n, pl
    -**ries** : observatorio m
obsess [əb'sɛs] vt : obsesionar — **ob-
    session** [əb'sɛʃən, ɑb-] n : obsesión f
    — **obsessive** [əb'sɛsɪv, ɑb-] adj : ob-
    sesivo
obsolete [,ɑbsə'li:t, 'ɑbsə-] adj : obsole-
    to, desusado
obstacle ['ɑbstəkəl] n : obstáculo m
obstetrics [əb'stetrɪks] n : obstetricia f
obstinate ['ɑbstənət] adj : obstinado
obstruct [əb'strʌkt] vt 1 BLOCK : obstru-

ir 2 HINDER : obstaculizar — **obstruction** [əbˈstrʌkʃən] n : obstrucción f

obtain [əbˈteɪn] vt : obtener, conseguir — **obtainable** [əbˈteɪnəbəl] adj : asequible

obtrusive [əbˈtruːsɪv] adj : entrometido (dícese de las personas), demasiado prominente (dícese de las cosas)

obtuse [ɑbˈtuːs, əb-, -ˈtjuːs] adj : obtuso

obvious [ˈɑbviəs] adj : obvio, evidente — **obviously** [ˈɑbviəsli] adv 1 CLEARLY : obviamente 2 OF COURSE : claro, por supuesto

occasion [əˈkeɪʒən] n 1 : ocasión f 2 on ~ : de vez en cuando — ~ vt : ocasionar — **occasional** [əˈkeɪʒənəl] adj : poco frecuente, ocasional — **occasionally** [əˈkeɪʒənəli] adv : de vez en cuando

occult [əˈkʌlt, ˈɑˌkʌlt] adj : oculto

occupy [ˈɑkjəˌpaɪ] vt **-pied; -pying** 1 : ocupar 2 ~ **oneself** : entretenerse — **occupancy** [ˈɑkjəpənsi] n, pl **-cies** : ocupación f — **occupant** [ˈɑkjəpənt] n : ocupante mf — **occupation** [ˌɑkjəˈpeɪʃən] n : ocupación f — **occupational** [ˌɑkjəˈpeɪʃənəl] adj : profesional

occur [əˈkər] vi **occurred; -ring** 1 : ocurrir 2 APPEAR : encontrarse 3 ~ **to s.o.** : ocurrirse a algn — **occurrence** [əˈkərənts] n 1 EVENT : acontecimiento m, suceso m 2 INCIDENCE : incidencia f

ocean [ˈoːʃən] n : océano m

ocher or **ochre** [ˈoːkər] n : ocre m

o'clock [əˈklɑk] adv 1 **at 6** ~ : a las seis 2 **it's one** ~ : es la una 3 **it's ten** ~ : son las diez

octagon [ˈɑktəˌgɑn] n : octágono m — **octagonal** [ɑkˈtægənəl] adj : octagonal

octave [ˈɑktɪv] n : octava f

October n : octubre m

octopus [ˈɑktəpəs, -pəs] n, pl **-puses** or **-pi** [-ˌpaɪ] : pulpo m

oculist [ˈɑkjəlɪst] n : oculista mf

odd [ˈɑd] adj 1 STRANGE : extraño, raro 2 : sin pareja (dícese de un calcetín, etc.) 3 **forty** ~ **years** : cuarenta y tantos años 4 ~ **jobs** : algunos trabajos mpl 5 ~ **number** : número m impar — **oddity** [ˈɑdəti] n, pl **-ties** : rareza f — **oddly** [ˈɑdli] adv : de manera extraña — **odds** [ˈɑdz] npl 1 CHANCES : probabilidades fpl 2 **at** ~ : en desacuerdo 3 **five to one** ~ : cinco contra uno (en apuestas) — **odds and ends** npl : cosas fpl sueltas

ode [ˈoːd] n : oda f

odious [ˈoːdiəs] adj : odioso

odor or Brit **odour** [ˈoːdər] n : olor m —

odorless or Brit **odourless** [ˈoːdərləs] adj : inodoro

of [ˈʌv, əv] prep 1 : de 2 **five minutes** ~ **ten** : las diez menos cinco 3 **the eighth** ~ **April** : el ocho de abril

off [ˈɔf] adv 1 ~ LEAVE : irse 2 ~ **cut** : cortar 3 **day** ~ : día m de descanso 4 **fall** ~ : caerse 5 **doze** ~ : dormirse 6 **far** ~ : lejos 7 ~ **and on** : de vez en cuando 8 **shut** ~ : apagar 9 **ten miles** ~ : a diez millas de aquí — ~ prep 1 : de 2 **be** ~ **duty** : estar libre 3 ~ **center** : descentrado — ~ adj 1 CANCELED : cancelado 2 OUT : apagado 3 **an** ~ **chance** : una posibilidad remota

offend [əˈfɛnd] vt : ofender — **offender** [əˈfɛndər] n : delincuente mf — **offense** or **offence** [əˈfɛnts, ˈɔˌfɛnts] n 1 AFFRONT : afrenta f 2 ASSAULT : ataque m 3 : ofensiva f (en deportes) 4 CRIME : delito m 5 **take** ~ : ofenderse — **offensive** [əˈfɛntsɪv, ˈɔˌfɛnt-] adj : ofensivo — ~ n : ofensiva f

offer [ˈɔfər] vt : ofrecer — ~ n : oferta f — **offering** [ˈɔfərɪŋ] n : ofrenda f

offhand [ˈɔfˈhænd] adv : de improviso, en este momento — ~ adj : improvisado

office [ˈɔfəs] n 1 : oficina f 2 POSITION : cargo m 3 **run for** ~ : presentarse como candidato — **officer** [ˈɔfəsər] n 1 : oficial mf 2 or **police** ~ : agente mf (de policía) — **official** [əˈfɪʃəl] n : funcionario m, -ria f — ~ adj : oficial

offing [ˈɔfɪŋ] n **in the** ~ : en perspectiva

offset [ˈɔfˌsɛt] vt **-set; -setting** : compensar

offshore [ˈɔfˈʃɔr] adv : a una distancia de la costa

offspring [ˈɔfˌsprɪŋ] ns & pl : prole f, progenie f

often [ˈɔfən, ˈɔftən] adv 1 : muchas veces, a menudo, con frecuencia 2 **every so** ~ : de vez en cuando

ogle [ˈoːgəl] vt **ogled; ogling** : comerse con los ojos

ogre [ˈoːgər] n : ogro m

oh [ˈoː] interj 1 : ¡oh!, ¡ah! 2 ~ **no!** : ¡ay no! 3 ~ **really?** : ¿de veras?

oil [ˈɔɪl] n 1 : aceite m 2 PETROLEUM : petróleo m 3 or **painting** : óleo m — ~ vt : lubricar — **oilskin** [ˈɔɪlˌskɪn] n : hule m — **oily** [ˈɔɪli] adj **oilier; -est** : aceitoso, grasiento

ointment [ˈɔɪntmənt] n : ungüento m, pomada f

OK or **okay** [ˈoːˈkeɪ] adv 1 : muy bien 2 ~! : ¡de acuerdo!, ¡bueno! — ~ adj :

ALL RIGHT : bien **2** it's ~ with me
: por mí no hay problema — ~ *n*
: visto *m* bueno — **OK'd**
or **okayed** [ˌoʹkeɪd] *vt* **OK'ing** or **okaying**
: dar el visto bueno a

okra [ʹoːkrə, *South also* -krɪ] *n* : quingombó *m*

old [ʹoːld] *adj* **1** : viejo **2** FORMER : antiguo **3** any ~ : cualquier **4** be ten
years ~ : tener diez años (de edad) **5**
~ age : vejez *f* **6** ~ man : anciano *m*
7 ~ woman : anciana *f* — ~ *n* the
~ : los viejos, los ancianos —
old–fashioned [ʹoːldʹfæʃənd] *adj* : anticuado

olive [ʹɑlɪv, -ləv] *n* **1** : aceituna *f* (fruta) **2**
or ~ **green** : verde *m* oliva

Olympic [oʹlɪmpɪk] *adj* : olímpico —
Olympics [oʹlɪmpɪks] *npl* the ~ : las
Olimpíadas, las Olimpíadas

omelet or **omelette** [ʹɑmlət, ʹɑmə-] *n*
: omelette *mf Lat*, tortilla *f* francesa
Spain

omen [ʹoːmən] *n* : agüero *m* — **ominous**
[ʹɑmənəs] *adj* : ominoso, de mal
agüero

omit [oʹmɪt] *vt* **omitted; omitting** : omitir — **omission** [oʹmɪʃən] *n* : omisión *f*

omnipotent [ɑmʹnɪpətənt] *adj* : omnipotente

on [ʹɑn, ʹɔn] *prep* **1** : en **2** ABOUT : sobre
3 ~ foot : a pie **4** ~ Monday : el
lunes **5** ~ the right : a la derecha **6**
~ vacation : de vacaciones **7** talk ~
the phone : hablar por teléfono — ~
adv **1** and so ~ : etcétera **2** from that
moment ~ : a partir de ese momento
3 keep ~ : seguir **4** later ~ : más
tarde **5** ~ and ~ : sin parar **6** put ~
: ponerse (ropa), poner (música, etc.)
7 turn ~ : encender (una luz, etc.),
abrir (una llave) — ~ *adj* **1** : encendido (dícese de luces, etc.), abierto
(dícese de llaves) **2** be ~ to : estar
enterado de

once [ʹwʌns] *adv* **1** : una vez **2** FORMERLY : antes — ~ *n* **1** at ~ : TOGETHER
: al mismo tiempo **2** at ~ : IMMEDIATELY : inmediatamente — ~ *conj* : una
vez que

oncoming [ʹɑnˌkʌmɪŋ, ʹɔn-] *adj* : que
viene

one [ʹwʌn] *adj* **1** : un, uno **2** ONLY : único
3 or ~ **and the same** : el mismo —
~ *n* **1** : uno *m* (número) **2** ~ by ~
: uno a uno — ~ *pron* **1** : uno, una **2**
~ **another** : el uno al otro **3** ~ **never**
knows : nunca se sabe **4** that ~
: aquél, aquélla **5** which ~? : ¿cuál?
— **oneself** [ˌwʌnʹsɛlf] *pron* **1** (*used re-*

flexively) : se **2** (*used after prepositions*) : sí mismo, sí misma **3** (*used emphatically*) : uno mismo, una misma **4**
by ~ : solo — **one–sided** [ʹwʌnʹsaɪdəd] *adj* **1** UNEQUAL : desigual **2** BIASED : parcial — **one–way** [ʹwʌnʹweɪ]
adj **1** : de sentido único (dícese de una
calle) **2** ~ **ticket** : boleto *m* de ida

ongoing [ʹɑnˌgoːɪŋ] *adj* : en curso, corriente

onion [ʹʌnjən] *n* : cebolla *f*

only [ʹoːnli] *adj* : único — ~ *adv* **1**
: sólo, solamente **2** if ~ : ojalá, por lo
menos — ~ *conj* BUT : pero

onset [ʹɑnˌsɛt] *n* : comienzo *m*, llegada *f*

onslaught [ʹɑnˌslɔt, ʹɔn-] *n* : ataque *m*,
arremetida *f*

onto [ʹɑntuː, ʹɔn-] *prep* : sobre

onus [ʹoːnəs] *n* : responsabilidad *f*

onward [ʹɑnwərd, ʹɔn-] *adv & adj* : hacia
adelante

onyx [ʹɑnɪks] *n* : ónix *m*

ooze [ʹuːz] *vi* **oozed; oozing** : rezumar

opal [ʹoːpəl] *n* : ópalo *m*

opaque [oʹpeɪk] *adj* : opaco

open [ʹoːpən] *adj* **1** : abierto **2** AVAILABLE
: vacante, libre **3** an ~ **question**
: una cuestión pendiente — ~ *vt*
: abrir — *vi* **1** : abrirse **2** BEGIN : comenzar — ~ *n* in the ~ **1** OUTDOORS
: al aire libre **2** KNOWN : sacado a la luz
— **open–air** [ʹoːpənʹær] *adj* : al aire
libre — **opener** [ʹoːpənər] *n* **1** : abridor
m **2** or **bottle** ~ : abrebotellas *m* **3** or
can ~ : abrelatas *m* — **opening**
[ʹoːpənɪŋ] *n* **1** : abertura *f* **2** BEGINNING
: comienzo *m*, apertura *f* **3** OPPORTUNITY : oportunidad *f* — **openly** [ʹoːpənli] *adv* : abiertamente

opera [ʹɑprə, ʹɑpərə] *n* : ópera *f*

operate [ʹɑpəˌreɪt] *v* **-ated; -ating** *vi* **1**
FUNCTION : funcionar **2** ~ on s.o.
: operar a algn — *vt* **1** : hacer funcionar (una máquina) **2** MANAGE : dirigir, manejar — **operation** [ˌɑpəʹreɪʃən]
n **1** : operación *f* **2** FUNCTIONING : funcionamiento *m* — **operational** [ˌɑpəʹreɪʃənəl] *adj* : operacional — **operative** [ʹɑpərətɪv, -reɪ-] *adj* : en vigor —
operator [ʹɑpəˌreɪtər] *n* **1** : operador *m*,
-dora *f* **2** or **machine** ~ : operario *m*,
-ria *f*

opinion [əʹpɪnjən] *n* : opinión *f* — **opinionated** [əʹpɪnjəˌneɪtəd] *adj* : dogmático

opium [ʹoːpiəm] *n* : opio *m*

opossum [əʹpɑsəm] *n* : zarigüeya *f*, oposum *m*

opponent [əʹpoːnənt] *n* : adversario *m*,
-ria *f*; contrincante *mf* (en deportes)

opportunity [ˌɑpərˈtunəti, -ˈtju-] n, pl **-ties** : oportunidad f — **opportune** [ˌɑpərˈtun, -ˈtjun] adj : oportuno — **opportunist** [ˌɑpərˈtunɪst, -ˈtju-] n : oportunista mf

oppose [əˈpoːz] vt **-posed; -posing** : oponerse a — **opposed** adj ~ **to** : en contra de

opposite [ˈɑpəzət] adj **1** FACING : enfrente **2** CONTRARY : opuesto — ~ n **the ~** : lo contrario, lo opuesto — ~ adv : enfrente — ~ prep : enfrente de, frente a — **opposition** [ˌɑpəˈzɪʃən] n **1** : oposición f **2 in ~ to** : en contra de

oppress [əˈpres] vt : oprimir — **oppression** [əˈpreʃən] n : opresión f — **oppressive** [əˈpresɪv] adj **1** : opresivo **2** STIFLING : agobiante — **oppressor** [əˈpresər] n : opresor m, -sora f

opt [ˈɑpt] vi ~ **for** : optar por

optic [ˈɑptɪk] or **optical** [-tɪkəl] adj : óptico — **optician** [ɑpˈtɪʃən] n : óptico m, -ca f

optimism [ˈɑptəˌmɪzəm] n : optimismo m — **optimist** [ˈɑptəmɪst] n : optimista mf — **optimistic** [ˌɑptəˈmɪstɪk] adj : optimista

optimum [ˈɑptəməm] n, pl **-ma** [-mə] : lo óptimo, lo ideal

option [ˈɑpʃən] n **1** : opción f **2 have no ~** : no tener más remedio — **optional** [ˈɑpʃənəl] adj : facultativo, opcional

opulence [ˈɑpjələnts] n : opulencia f — **opulent** [ˈɑpjələnt] adj : opulento

or [ˈɔr] conj **1** (indicating an alternative) : o (u before o- or ho-) **2** (following a negative) : ni **3** ~ **else** : si no

oracle [ˈɔrəkəl] n : oráculo m

oral [ˈɔrəl] adj : oral

orange [ˈɔrɪndʒ] n **1** : naranja f (fruta) **2** : naranja m (color)

orator [ˈɔrətər] n : orador m, -dora f

orbit [ˈɔrbət] n : órbita f — ~ vt : girar alrededor de — vi : orbitar

orchard [ˈɔrtʃərd] n : huerto m

orchestra [ˈɔrkəstrə] n : orquesta f

orchid [ˈɔrkɪd] n : orquídea f

ordain [ɔrˈdeɪn] vt **1** : ordenar (un sacerdote, etc.) **2** DECREE : decretar

ordeal [ɔrˈdiːl, ˈɔrˌdiːl] n : prueba f dura

order [ˈɔrdər] vt **1** : ordenar **2** : pedir (mercancías, etc.) — vi : hacer un pedido — ~ n **1** ARRANGEMENT : orden m **2** COMMAND : orden f **3** REQUEST : pedido m **4** : orden f (religiosa) **5 in ~ that** : para que **6 in ~ to** : para **7 out of ~** : averiado, descompuesto — Lat — **orderly** [ˈɔrdərli] adj : ordenado — ~ n, pl **-lies 1** : ordenanza m (en el

ejército) **2** : camillero m (en un hospital)

ordinary [ˈɔrdənˌeri] adj **1** : normal, corriente **2** MEDIOCRE : ordinario — **ordinarily** [ˌɔrdənˈerəli] adv : generalmente

ore [ˈor] n : mena f

oregano [əˈregəˌnoː] n : orégano m

organ [ˈɔrgən] n : órgano m — **organic** [ɔrˈgænɪk] adj : orgánico — **organism** [ˈɔrgəˌnɪzəm] n : organismo m — **organist** [ˈɔrgənɪst] n : organista mf — **organize** [ˈɔrgəˌnaɪz] vt **-nized; -nizing** : organizar — **organization** [ˌɔrgənəˈzeɪʃən] n : organización f — **organizer** [ˈɔrgəˌnaɪzər] n : organizador m, -dora f

orgasm [ˈɔrˌgæzəm] n : orgasmo m

orgy [ˈɔrdʒi] n, pl **-gies** : orgía f

Orient [ˈɔriˌent] n **the ~** : el Oriente — **orient** vt : orientar — **oriental** [ˌɔriˈentəl] adj : del Oriente, oriental — **orientation** [ˌɔriənˈteɪʃən] n : orientación f

orifice [ˈɔrəfəs] n : orificio m

origin [ˈɔrədʒən] n : origen m — **original** [əˈrɪdʒənəl] n : original m — ~ adj **1** : original — **originality** [əˌrɪdʒəˈnæləti] n : originalidad f — **originally** [əˈrɪdʒənəli] adv : originariamente — **originate** [əˈrɪdʒəˌneɪt] v **-nated; -nating** vt : originar — vi **1** : originarse **2** ~ **from** : provenir de — **originator** [əˈrɪdʒəˌneɪtər] n : creador m, -dora f

ornament [ˈɔrnəmənt] n : adorno m — ~ vt : adornar — **ornamental** [ˌɔrnəˈmentəl] adj : ornamental, de adorno — **ornate** [ɔrˈneɪt] adj : elaborado, adornado

ornithology [ˌɔrnəˈθɑlədʒi] n, pl **-gies** : ornitología f

orphan [ˈɔrfən] n : huérfano m, -na f — ~ vt : dejar huérfano — **orphanage** [ˈɔrfənɪdʒ] n : orfelinato m, orfanato m

orthodox [ˈɔrθəˌdɑks] adj : ortodoxo — **orthodoxy** [ˈɔrθəˌdɑksi] n, pl **-doxies** : ortodoxia f

orthopedic [ˌɔrθəˈpiːdɪk] adj : ortopédico

oscillation [ˌɑsəˈleɪʃən] n : oscilación f — **oscillate** [ˈɑsəˌleɪt] vi **-lated; -lating** : oscilar

ostensible [ɑˈstentsəbəl] adj : aparente, ostensible

ostentation [ˌɑstənˈteɪʃən] n : ostentación f — **ostentatious** [ˌɑstənˈteɪʃəs] adj : ostentoso

osteopath [ˈɑstiəˌpæθ] n : osteópata f

ostracism [ˈɑstrəˌsɪzəm] n : ostracismo m — **ostracize** [ˈɑstrəˌsaɪz] vt **-cized; -cizing** : aislar

ostrich [ˈɑstrɪtʃ, ˈɔs-] n : avestruz m

other ['ʌðər] *adj* **1** : otro **2 every ~ day** : cada dos días **3 on the ~ hand** : por otra parte, por otro lado — *pron* **1** : otro, otra **2 the ~s** : los otros, las otras, los demás, las demás — **other than** *prep* : aparte de, fuera de — **otherwise** ['ʌðər,waɪz] *adv* **1** : eso aparte, por lo demás **2** DIFFERENTLY : de otro modo **3** OR ELSE : si no

otter ['ɑtər] *n* : nutria *f*

ought ['ɔt] *v aux* **1** : deber **2 you ~ to have done it** : deberías haberlo hecho

ounce ['aʊns] *n* : onza *f*

our ['ɑr, 'aʊr] *adj* : nuestro — **ours** ['aʊrz, 'ɑrz] *pron* **1** : (el) nuestro, (la) nuestra, (los) nuestros, (las) nuestras **2 a friend of ~** : un amigo nuestro — **ourselves** [ɑr'sɛlvz, aʊr-] *pron* **1** (*used reflexively*) : nos **2** (*used after prepositions*) : nosotros, nosotras **3** (*used for emphasis*) : nosotros mismos, nosotras mismas

oust ['aʊst] *vt* : desbancar

out ['aʊt] *adv* **1** OUTSIDE : fuera, afuera **2 cry ~** : gritar **3 eat ~** : comer afuera **4 go ~** : salir **5 look ~** : mirar para afuera **6 run ~ of** : agotar **7 turn ~** : apagar (una luz) **8 take ~** REMOVE : sacar — *~ prep →* **out of** — *adj* **1** ABSENT : ausente **2** UNFASHIONABLE : fuera de moda **3** EXTINGUISHED : apagado **4 the sun is ~** : hace sol

outboard motor ['aʊt,bɔrd] *n* : motor *m* fuera de borde

outbreak ['aʊt,breɪk] *n* : brote *m* (de una enfermedad), comienzo *m* (de guerra)

outburst ['aʊt,bərst] *n* : arranque *m*, arrebato *m*

outcast ['aʊt,kæst] *n* : paria *mf*

outcome ['aʊt,kʌm] *n* : resultado *m*

outcry ['aʊt,kraɪ] *n, pl* **-cries** : protesta *f*

outdated [aʊt'deɪtəd] *adj* : anticuado

outdo [aʊt'duː] *vt* **-did** [-'dɪd], **-done** [-'dʌn]; **-doing**; **-does** [-'dʌz] : superar

outdoor [aʊt'dɔr] *adj* : al aire libre — **outdoors** ['aʊt'dɔrz] *adv* : al aire libre

outer ['aʊtər] *adj* : exterior — **outer space** *n* : espacio *m* exterior

outfit ['aʊt,fɪt] *n* **1** EQUIPMENT : equipo *m* **2** CLOTHES : conjunto *m* — *~ vt* **-fitted; -fitting** EQUIP : equipar

outgoing ['aʊt,goɪŋ] *adj* **1** SOCIABLE : extrovertido **2 ~ mail** : correo *m* (para enviar) **3 ~ president** : presidente *m*, -ta *f* saliente

outgrow [aʊt'groː] *vt* **-grew** [-'gruː]; **-grown** [-'groːn]; **-growing** : crecer más que

outing ['aʊtɪŋ] *n* : excursión *f*

outlandish [aʊt'lændɪʃ] *adj* : estrafalario

outlast [aʊt'læst] *vt* : durar más que

outlaw ['aʊt,lɔ] *n* : forajido *m*, -da *f* — *~ vt* : declarar ilegal

outlay ['aʊt,leɪ] *n* : desembolso *m*

outlet ['aʊt,lɛt, -lət] *n* **1** EXIT : salida *f* **2** RELEASE : desahogo *m* **3** *or* **electrical ~** : toma *f* de corriente **4** *or* **retail ~** : tienda *f* al por menor

outline ['aʊt,laɪn] *n* **1** CONTOUR : contorno *m* **2** SKETCH : bosquejo *m*, boceto *m* **3** SUMMARY : esquema *m* — *~ vt* **-lined; -lining 1** SKETCH : bosquejar **2** EXPLAIN : delinear, esbozar

outlive [aʊt'lɪv] *vt* **-lived; -living** : sobrevivir a

outlook ['aʊt,lʊk] *n* **1** PROSPECTS : perspectivas *fpl* **2** VIEWPOINT : punto *m* de vista

outlying ['aʊt,laɪɪŋ] *adj* : alejado, distante

outmoded [aʊt'moːdəd] *adj* : pasado de moda, anticuado

outnumber [aʊt'nʌmbər] *vt* : superar en número a

out of *prep* **1** FROM : de **2** THROUGH : por **3** WITHOUT : sin **4 ~ curiosity** : por curiosidad **5 ~ control** : fuera de control **6 one ~ four** : uno de cada cuatro — **out-of-date** [aʊtəv'deɪt] *adj* : anticuado — **out-of-door** [aʊtəv-'dɔr] *or* **out-of-doors** [-'dɔrz] *adj →* **outdoor**

outpatient ['aʊt,peɪʃənt] *n* : paciente *m* externo

outpost ['aʊt,poːst] *n* : puesto *m* avanzado

output ['aʊt,pʊt] *n* **1** : producción *f*, rendimiento *m* **2** : salida *f* (informática) — *~ vt* **-putted** *or* **-put; -putting** : producir

outrage ['aʊt,reɪdʒ] *n* **1** : atrocidad *f*, escándalo *m* **2** ANGER : ira *f*, indignación *f* — *~ vt* **-raged; -raging** : ultrajar — **outrageous** [aʊt'reɪdʒəs] *adj* : escandaloso

outright [,aʊt'raɪt] *adv* **1** COMPLETELY : por completo **2** INSTANTLY : en el acto — *~* ['aʊt,raɪt] *adj* : completo, absoluto

outset ['aʊt,sɛt] *n* : comienzo *m*, principio *m*

outside [aʊt'saɪd, 'aʊt-] *n* **1** : exterior *m* **2 from the ~** : desde fuera, desde afuera — *~ adj* **1** : exterior, externo **2 an ~ chance** : una posibilidad remota — *~ adv* : fuera, afuera — *~ prep or ~* **of** : fuera de — **outsider** [aʊt-'saɪdər] *n* : forastero *m*, -ra *f*

outskirts ['aʊt‚skərts] *npl* : afueras *fpl*, alrededores *mpl*

outspoken [‚aʊt'spo:kən] *adj* : franco, directo

outstanding [‚aʊt'stændɪŋ] *adj* 1 UNPAID : pendiente 2 EXCELLENT : excepcional

outstretched [aʊt'strɛtʃt] *adj* : extendido

outstrip [aʊt'strɪp] *vt* **-stripped** *or* **-strip** ['strɪpt], **-stripping** : aventajar

outward ['aʊtwərd] *adj* 1 : hacia afuera 2 EXTERNAL : externo, external — ~ *or* **outwards** [-wərdz] *adv* : hacia afuera — **outwardly** ['aʊtwərdli] *adv* APPARENTLY : aparentemente

outweigh [aʊt'weɪ] *vt* : pesar más que

outwit [aʊt'wɪt] *vt* **-witted; -witting** : ser más listo que

oval ['o:vəl] *n* : óvalo *m* — ~ *adj* : ovalado

ovary ['o:vəri] *n, pl* **-ries** : ovario *m*

ovation [o:'veɪʃən] *n* : ovación *f*

oven ['ʌvən] *n* : horno *m*

over ['o:vər] *adv* 1 ABOVE : por encima 2 AGAIN : otra vez, de nuevo 3 MORE : más 4 all ~ : por todas partes 5 ask ~ : invitar 6 cross ~ : cruzar 7 fall ~ : caerse 8 ~ and ~ : una y otra vez 9 ~ here : aquí 10 ~ there : allí — ~ *prep* 1 ABOVE, UPON : encima de, sobre 2 ACROSS : por encima de, sobre 3 DURING : en, durante 4 fight ~ : pelearse por 5 ~ $5 : más de $6 6 ~ the phone : por teléfono — ~ *adj* : terminado, acabado

overall [‚o:vər'ɔl] *adv* GENERALLY : en general — *adj* : total, en conjunto — **overalls** ['o:vər‚ɔlz] *npl* : overol *m Lat*

overbearing [‚o:vər'bærɪŋ] *adj* : dominante, imperioso

overboard ['o:vər‚bord] *adv* fall ~ : caer al agua

overburden [‚o:vər'bərdən] *vt* : sobrecargar

overcast [‚o:vər'kæst] *adj* : nublado

overcharge [‚o:vər'tʃɑrdʒ] *vt* **-charged; -charging** : cobrar demasiado

overcoat ['o:vər‚ko:t] *n* : abrigo *m*

overcome [‚o:vər'kʌm] *v* **-came** [-'keɪm], **-come; -coming** *vt* 1 CONQUER : vencer 2 OVERWHELM : agobiar — *vi* : vencer

overcook [‚o:vər'kʊk] *vt* : cocer demasiado

overcrowded [‚o:vər'kraʊdəd] *adj* : abarrotado de gente

overdo [‚o:vər'du:] *vt* **-did** [-'dɪd], **-done** [-'dʌn], **-doing; -does** [-'dʌz] 1 : hacer demasiado 2 EXAGGERATE : exagerar 3 → **overcook**

overdose ['o:vər‚do:s] *n* : sobredosis *f*

overdraw [‚o:vər'drɔ] *vt* **-drew** [-'dru:]; **-drawn** [-'drɔn], **-drawing** : girar en descubierto — **overdraft** ['o:vər‚dræft] *n* : sobregiro *m*, descubierto *m*

overdue [‚o:vər'du:] *adj* : fuera de plazo (dícese de pagos, libros, etc.)

overeat [‚o:vər'i:t] *vi* **-ate** [-'eɪt], **-eaten** [-'i:tən], **-eating** : comer demasiado

overestimate [‚o:vər'ɛstə‚meɪt] *vt* **-mated; -mating** : sobreestimar

overflow [‚o:vər'flo:] *vt* : desbordar — *vi* : desbordarse — ~ ['o:vər‚flo:] *n* : desbordamiento *m* (de un río)

overgrown [‚o:vər'gro:n] *adj* : cubierto (de malas hierbas, etc.)

overhand ['o:vər‚hænd] *adv* : por encima de la cabeza

overhang [‚o:vər'hæn] *v* **-hung** [-'hʌŋ]; **-hanging** : sobresalir

overhaul [‚o:vər'hɔl] *vt* : revisar (un motor, etc.)

overhead [‚o:vər'hɛd] *adv* : por encima — ~ [-'hɛd] *adj* : de arriba — ~ ['o:vər‚hɛd] *n* : gastos *mpl* generales

overhear [‚o:vər'hɪr] *vt* **-heard; -hearing** : oír por casualidad

overheat [‚o:vər'hi:t] *vt* : calentar demasiado — *vi* : recalentarse

overjoyed [‚o:vər'dʒɔɪd] *adj* : encantado

overland [‚o:vər'lænd, -lənd] *adv & adj* : por tierra

overlap [‚o:vər'læp] *v* **-lapped; -lapping** *vt* : traslapar — *vi* : traslaparse

overload [‚o:vər'lo:d] *vt* : sobrecargar

overlook [‚o:vər'lʊk] *vt* 1 : dar a (un jardín, el mar, etc.) 2 MISS : pasar por alto

overly ['o:vərli] *adv* : demasiado

overnight [‚o:vər'naɪt] *adv* 1 : por la noche 2 SUDDENLY : de la noche a la mañana — ~ ['o:vər‚naɪt] *adj* 1 : de noche 2 SUDDEN : repentino

overpass ['o:vər‚pæs] *n* : paso *m* elevado

overpopulated [‚o:vər'pɑpjə‚leɪtəd] *adj* : superpoblado

overpower [‚o:vər'paʊər] *vt* 1 SUBDUE : dominar 2 OVERWHELM : agobiar, abrumar

overrated [‚o:vər'reɪtəd] *adj* : sobreestimado

override [‚o:vər'raɪd] *vt* **-rode** [-'ro:d], **-ridden** [-'rɪdən]; **-riding** 1 : predominar sobre 2 : anular (una decisión, etc.)

overrule [‚o:vər'ru:l] *vt* **-ruled; -ruling** : anular (una decisión), rechazar (una protesta)

overrun [‚o:vər'rʌn] *vt* **-ran** [-'ræn], **-running** 1 INVADE : invadir 2 EXCEED : exceder

overseas [,o:vər'si:z] *adv* : en el extranjero — ~ [o:vər,si:z] *adj* : extranjero, exterior

oversee [,o:vər'si:] *vt* **-saw** [-'sɔ]; **-seen** [-'si:n]; **-seeing** : supervisar

overshadow [,o:vər'ʃædo:] *vt* : eclipsar

oversight ['o:vər,saɪt] *n* : descuido *m*

oversleep [,o:vər'sli:p] *vi* **-slept** [-'slɛpt]; **-sleeping** : quedarse dormido

overstep [,o:vər'stɛp] *vt* **-stepped**; **-stepping** : sobrepasar

overt [o'vərt, 'o:,vərt] *adj* : manifiesto

overtake [,o:vər'teɪk] *vt* **-took** [-'tʊk]; **-taken** [-'teɪkən]; **-taking 1** PASS : adelantar **2** SURPASS : superar

overthrow [,o:vər'θro:] *vt* **-threw** [-'θru:]; **-thrown** [-'θro:n]; **-throwing** : derrocar

overtime ['o:vər,taɪm] *n* **1** : horas *fpl* extras (de trabajo) **2** : prórroga *f* (en deportes)

overtone ['o:vər,to:n] *n* SUGGESTION : tinte *m*, insinuación *f*

overture ['o:vər,tʃʊr, -tʃər] *n* : obertura *f* (en música)

overturn [,o:vər'tərn] *vt* **1** : dar la vuelta a **2** NULLIFY : anular — *vi* : volcar

overweight [,o:vər'weɪt] *adj* : demasiado gordo

overwhelm [,o:vər'hwɛlm] *vt* **1** : abrumar, agobiar **2** : aplastar (a un enemigo) — **overwhelming** [o:vər'hwɛlmɪŋ] *adj* : abrumador, apabullante

overwork [o:vər'wərk] *vt* : hacer trabajar demasiado — *vi* : trabajar demasiado

overwrought [,o:vər'rɔt] *adj* : alterado, sobreexcitado

owe ['o:] *vt* **owed; owing** : deber — **owing to** *prep* : debido a

owl ['aʊl] *n* : búho *m*

own ['o:n] *adj* : propio — ~ *vt* : poseer, tener — *vi* ~ **up** : confesar — ~ *pron* **1 my (your, his/her/their, our)** ~ : el mío, la mía; el tuyo, la tuya; el suyo, la suya; el nuestro, la nuestra **2 be on one's** ~ : estar solo **3 to each his** ~ : cada uno a lo suyo — **owner** ['o:nər] *n* : propietario *m*, -ria *f* — **ownership** ['o:nər,ʃɪp] *n* : propiedad *f*

ox ['ɑks] *n, pl* **oxen** ['ɑksən] : buey *m*

oxygen ['ɑksɪdʒən] *n* : oxígeno *m*

oyster ['ɔɪstər] *n* : ostra *f*

ozone ['o:zo:n] *n* : ozono *m*

P

p ['pi:] *n, pl* **p's** *or* **ps** ['pi:z] : *p f*, decimosexta letra del alfabeto inglés

pace ['peɪs] *n* **1** STEP : paso *m* **2** RATE : ritmo *m* **3 keep** ~ **with** : andar al mismo paso que — ~ *vi* **paced; pacing** *or* ~ **up and down** : caminar de arriba para abajo

pacify ['pæsə,faɪ] *vt* **-fied; -fying** : apaciguar — **pacifier** ['pæsə,faɪər] *n* : chupete *m* — **pacifist** ['pæsəfɪst] *n* : pacifista *mf*

pack ['pæk] *n* **1** BUNDLE : fardo *m* **2** BACKPACK : mochila *f* **3** PACKAGE : paquete *m* **4** : baraja *f* (de naipes) **5** : manada *f* (de lobos, etc.), jauría *f* (de perros) — ~ *vt* **1** PACKAGE : empaquetar **2** FILL : llenar **3** : hacer (una maleta) — *vi* : hacer las maletas — **package** ['pækɪdʒ] *vt* **-aged; -aging** : empaquetar — ~ *n* : paquete *m* — **packet** ['pækət] *n* : paquete *m*

pact ['pækt] *n* : pacto *m*, acuerdo *m*

pad ['pæd] *n* **1** CUSHION : almohadilla *f* **2** TABLET : bloc *m* (de papel) **3** or ink ~ : tampón *m* **4** launching ~ : plataforma *f* (de lanzamiento) — ~ *vt* **padded; padding** : rellenar — pad-

-ding ['pædɪŋ] *n* **1** : relleno *m* **2** : paja *f* (en un discurso, etc.)

paddle ['pædəl] *n* **1** : canalete *m* (de una canoa) **2** : pala *f*, paleta *f* (en deportes) — ~ *vt* **-dled; -dling** : hacer avanzar (una canoa) con canalete

padlock ['pæd,lɑk] *n* : candado *m* — ~ *vt* : cerrar con candado

pagan ['peɪgən] *n* : pagano *m*, -na *f* — ~ *adj* : pagano

page[1] ['peɪdʒ] *vt* **paged; paging** : llamar por altavoz

page[2] *n* : página *f* (de un libro, etc.)

pageant ['pædʒənt] *n* : espectáculo *m* — **pageantry** ['pædʒəntri] *n* : pompa *f*, boato *m*

paid → **pay**

pail ['peɪl] *n* : cubo *m* Spain, cubeta *f* Lat

pain ['peɪn] *n* **1** : dolor *m* **2** : pena *f* (mental) **3** ~**s** *npl* EFFORT : esfuerzos *mpl* — ~ *vt* : doler — **painful** ['peɪnfəl] *adj* : doloroso — **painkiller** ['peɪn,kɪlər] *n* : analgésico *m* — **painless** ['peɪnləs] *adj* : indoloro, sin dolor — **painstaking** ['peɪn,steɪkɪŋ] *adj* : meticuloso, esmerado

paint ['peɪnt] *v* : pintar — ~ *n* : pintura

f — **paintbrush** ['peɪnt,brʌʃ] *n* : pincel *m* (de un artista), brocha *f* (para pintar casas, etc.) — **painter** ['peɪntər] *n* : pintor *m*, -tora *f* — **painting** ['peɪntɪŋ] *n* : pintura *f*

pair ['pær] *n* **1** : par *m* **2** COUPLE : pareja *f* — ~ *vt* : emparejar

pajamas [pə'dʒɑməz, -'dʒæ-] *npl* : pijama *m*, piyama *mf Lat*

Pakistani [pækɪ'stæni, pɑkɪ'stɑni] *adj* : paquistaní

pal ['pæl] *n* : amigo *m*, -ga *f*

palace ['pæləs] *n* : palacio *m*

palate ['pælət] *n* : paladar *m* — **palatable** ['pælətəbəl] *adj* : sabroso

pale ['peɪl] *adj* **paler; palest 1** PALLID : pálido **2** : claro (dícese de los colores, etc.) — ~ *vi* **paled; paling** : palidecer — **paleness** ['peɪlnəs] *n* : palidez *f*

Palestinian [pælə'stɪniən] *adj* : palestino

palette ['pælət] *n* : paleta *f*

pallbearer ['pɔl,berər] *n* : portador *m*, -dora *f* del féretro

pallid ['pæləd] *adj* : pálido — **pallor** ['pælər] *n* : palidez *f*

palm[1] ['pɑm, 'pɔlm] *n* : palma *f* (de la mano)

palm[2] *or* ~ **tree** : palmera *f* — **Palm Sunday** *n* : Domingo *m* de Ramos

palpitate ['pælpə,teɪt] *vi* -**tated; -tating** : palpitar — **palpitation** [pælpə'teɪʃən] *n* : palpitación *f*

paltry ['pɔltri] *adj* -**trier; -est** : mísero, mezquino

pamper ['pæmpər] *vt* : mimar

pamphlet ['pæmpflət] *n* : panfleto *m*, folleto *m*

pan ['pæn] *n* **1** SAUCEPAN : cacerola *f* **2** FRYING PAN : sartén *mf* — ~ *vt* **panned; panning** CRITICIZE : poner por los suelos

pancake ['pæn,keɪk] *n* : crepe *mf*, panqueque *m Lat*

panda ['pændə] *n* : panda *mf*

pandemonium [pændə'moniəm] *n* : pandemonio *m*

pander ['pændər] *vi* ~ **to** : complacer a

pane ['peɪn] *n* : cristal *m*, vidrio *m*

panel ['pænəl] *n* **1** : panel *m* **2** GROUP : jurado *m* **3** *or* **instrument** ~ : tablero *m* (de instrumentos) — ~ *vt* -**eled** *or* -**elled; -eling** *or* -**elling** : adornar con paneles — **paneling** ['pænəlɪŋ] *n* : paneles *mpl*

pang ['pæŋ] *n* : punzada *f*

panic ['pænɪk] *n* : pánico *m* — ~ *v* -**icked; -icking** *vt* : llenar del pánico — *vi* : ser presa del pánico — **panicky** ['pænɪki] *adj* : presa de pánico

panorama [pænə'ræmə, -'rɑ-] *n* : panorama *m* — **panoramic** [pænə'ræmɪk, -'rɑ-] *adj* : panorámico

pansy ['pænzi] *n*, *pl* -**sies** : pensamiento *m*

pant ['pænt] *vi* : jadear, resoplar

panther ['pænθər] *n* : pantera *f*

panties ['pæntiz] *npl* : bragas *fpl Spain*, calzones *mpl Lat*

pantomime ['pæntə,maɪm] *n* : pantomima *f*

pantry ['pæntri] *n*, *pl* -**tries** : despensa *f*

pants ['pænts] *npl* TROUSERS : pantalón *m*, pantalones *mpl*

papa ['pɑpə] *n* : papá *m fam*

papal ['peɪpəl] *adj* : papal

papaya [pə'paɪə] *n* : papaya *f*

paper ['peɪpər] *n* **1** : papel *m* **2** DOCUMENT : documento *m* **3** NEWSPAPER : periódico *m* — ~ *vt* WALLPAPER : empapelar — ~ *adj* : de papel — **paperback** ['peɪpər,bæk] *n* : libro *m* en rústica — **paper clip** *n* : clip *m*, sujetapapeles *m* — **paperweight** ['peɪpər,weɪt] *n* : pisapapeles *m* — **paperwork** ['peɪpər,wɜrk] *n* : papeleo *m*

paprika [pə'priːkə, pæ-] *n* : pimentón *m*

par ['pɑr] *n* **1** : par *m* (en golf) **2 below** ~ : debajo de la par **3 on** ~ **with** ~ : al nivel de

parable ['pærəbəl] *n* : parábola *f*

parachute ['pærə,ʃuːt] *n* : paracaídas *m* — ~ *vi* -**chuted; -chuting** : lanzarse en paracaídas

parade [pə'reɪd] *n* **1** : desfile *m* **2** DISPLAY : alarde *m* — ~ *v* -**raded; -rading** *vi* MARCH : desfilar — *vt* DISPLAY : hacer alarde de

paradise ['pærə,daɪs, -,daɪz] *n* : paraíso *m*

paradox ['pærə,dɑks] *n* : paradoja *f* — **paradoxical** [pærə'dɑksɪkəl] *adj* : paradójico

paraffin ['pærəfən] *n* : parafina *f*

paragraph ['pærə,græf] *n* : párrafo *m*

Paraguayan [pærə'gwaɪən, -'gweɪ-] *adj* : paraguayo

parakeet ['pærə,kiːt] *n* : periquito *m*

parallel ['pærə,lel, -ləl] *adj* : paralelo — ~ *n* **1** : paralelo *m* (en geografía) **2** SIMILARITY : paralelismo *m*, semejanza *f* — ~ *vt* : ser paralelo a

paralysis [pə'ræləsɪs] *n*, *pl* -**yses** [-,siːz] : parálisis *f* — **paralyze** *or Brit* **paralise** ['pærə,laɪz] *vt* -**lyzed** *or Brit* -**lised; -lyzing** *or Brit* -**lising** : paralizar

parameter [pə'ræmətər] *n* : parámetro *m*

paramount ['pærə,maunt] *adj* **of** ~ **importance** : de suma importancia

paranoia [ˌpærəˈnɔɪə] *n* : paranoia *f* — **paranoid** [ˈpærənɔɪd] *adj* : paranoico
paraphernalia [ˌpærəfərˈneɪljə, -fər-] *ns & pl* : parafernalia *f*
paraphrase [ˈpærəˌfreɪz] *n* : paráfrasis *f* — *vt* **-phrased; -phrasing** : parafrasear
paraplegic [ˌpærəˈpliːdʒɪk] *n* : parapléjico *m*, -ca *f*
parasite [ˈpærəˌsaɪt] *n* : parásito *m*
paratrooper [ˈpærəˌtruːpər] *n* : paracaidista *mf* (militar)
parcel [ˈpɑrsəl] *n* : paquete *m*
parch [ˈpɑrtʃ] *vt* : resecar
parchment [ˈpɑrtʃmənt] *n* : pergamino *m*
pardon [ˈpɑrdən] *n* **1** : perdón *m* **2** REPRIEVE : indulto *m* **3 I beg your ~** : perdone Ud., disculpe Ud. *Lat* — *vt* **1** : perdonar **2** REPRIEVE : indultar (a un delincuente)
parent [ˈpærənt] *n* **1** : madre *f*, padre *m* **2 ~s** *npl* : padres *mpl* — **parental** [pəˈrentəl] *adj* : de los padres
parenthesis [pəˈrenθəsɪs] *n, pl* **-theses** [-ˌsiːz] : paréntesis *m*
parish [ˈpærɪʃ] *n* : parroquia *f* — **parishioner** [pəˈrɪʃənər] *n* : feligrés *m*, -gresa *f*
parity [ˈpærəti] *n, pl* **-ties** : igualdad *f*
park [ˈpɑrk] *n* : parque *m* — *v* : estacionar, parquear *Lat*
parka [ˈpɑrkə] *n* : parka *f*
parking [ˈpɑrkɪŋ] *n* : estacionamiento *m*
parliament [ˈpɑrləmənt] *n* : parlamento *m* — **parliamentary** [ˌpɑrləˈmentəri, ˌpɑrljə-] *adj* : parlamentario
parlor *or Brit* **parlour** [ˈpɑrlər] *n* : salón *m*
parochial [pəˈroːkiəl] *adj* **1** : parroquial **2** PROVINCIAL : de miras estrechas
parody [ˈpærədi] *n, pl* **-dies** : parodia *f* — *vt* **-died; -dying** : parodiar
parole [pəˈroːl] *n* : libertad *f* condicional
parrot [ˈpærət] *n* : loro *m*, papagayo *m*
parry [ˈpæri] *vt* **-ried; -rying 1** : parar (un golpe) **2** EVADE : eludir (una pregunta, etc.)
parsley [ˈpɑrsli] *n* : perejil *m*
parsnip [ˈpɑrsnɪp] *n* : chirivía *f*
parson [ˈpɑrsən] *n* : clérigo *m*
part [ˈpɑrt] *n* **1** : parte *f* **2** PIECE : pieza *f* **3** ROLE : papel *m* **4** : raya *f* (del pelo) — *vi* **1** *or* **~ company** : separarse **2 ~ with** : deshacerse de — *vt* SEPARATE : separar
partake [pɑrˈteɪk, pər-] *vi* **-took; -taken; -taking ~ in** : participar en
partial [ˈpɑrʃəl] *adj* **1** : parcial **2 be ~ to** : ser aficionado a

participate [pɑrˈtɪsəˌpeɪt, pər-] *vi* **-pated; -pating** : participar — **participant** [pɑrˈtɪsəpənt, pər-] *n* : participante *mf*
participle [ˈpɑrtəˌsɪpəl] *n* : participio *m*
particle [ˈpɑrtɪkəl] *n* : partícula *f*
particular [pərˈtɪkjələr] *adj* **1** : particular **2** FUSSY : exigente — **~** *n* **1 in ~** : en particular, en especial **2 ~s** *npl* DETAILS : detalles *mpl* — **particularly** [pərˈtɪkjələrli] *adv* : especialmente
partisan [ˈpɑrtəzən, -sən] *n* : partidario *m*, -ria *f*
partition [pɑrˈtɪʃən, pər-] *n* **1** DISTRIBUTION : partición *f* **2** DIVIDER : tabique *m* — *vt* : dividir
partly [ˈpɑrtli] *adv* : en parte
partner [ˈpɑrtnər] *n* **1** : pareja *f* (en un juego, etc.) **2** *or* **business ~** : socio *m*, -cia *f* — **partnership** [ˈpɑrtnərˌʃɪp] *n* : asociación *f*
party [ˈpɑrti] *n, pl* **-ties 1** : partido *m* (político) **2** GATHERING : fiesta *f* **3** GROUP : grupo *m*
pass [ˈpæs] *vi* **1** : pasar **2** CEASE : pasarse **3** *or* **~ away** DIE : morir **5 ~ for** : pasar por **6 ~ out** FAINT : desmayarse — *vt* **1** : pasar **2** *or* **~ in front of** : pasar por **3** OVERTAKE : adelantar **4** : aprobar (un examen, una ley, etc.) **5 ~ down** : transmitir — **~** *n* **1** PERMIT : pase *m*, permiso *m* **2** : pase *m* (en deportes) **3** *or* **mountain ~** : paso *m* de montaña — **passable** [ˈpæsəbəl] *adj* **1** ADEQUATE : adecuado **2** : transitable (dícese de un camino, etc.) — **passage** [ˈpæsɪdʒ] *n* **1** : paso *m* **2** CORRIDOR : pasillo *m* (dentro de un edificio), pasaje *m* (entre edificios) **3** VOYAGE : travesía *f* (por el mar) — **passageway** [ˈpæsɪdʒˌweɪ] *n* : pasillo *m*, corredor *m*
passenger [ˈpæsəndʒər] *n* : pasajero *m*, -ra *f*
passerby [ˌpæsərˈbaɪ, ˈpæsər-] *n, pl* **passersby** [ˌpæsərz-] : transeúnte *mf*
passion [ˈpæʃən] *n* : pasión *f* — **passionate** [ˈpæʃənət] *adj* : apasionado
passive [ˈpæsɪv] *adj* : pasivo
Passover [ˈpæsˌoːvər] *n* : Pascua *f* (en el judaísmo)
passport [ˈpæsˌpɔrt] *n* : pasaporte *m*
password [ˈpæsˌwɜrd] *n* : contraseña *f*
past [ˈpæst] *adj* **1** : pasado **2** FORMER : anterior **3 the ~ few months** : los últimos meses — **~** *prep* **1** IN FRONT OF : por delante de **2** BEYOND : más allá de **3 half ~ two** : las dos y media — **~** *n* : pasado *m* — **~** *adv* : por delante

pasta ['pɑstə, 'pæs-] n : pasta f

paste ['peɪst] n 1 : pasta f 2 GLUE : engrudo m — ~ vt **pasted; pasting** : pegar

pastel [pæ'stɛl] n : pastel m — ~ adj : pastel

pasteurize ['pæstʃəˌraɪz, 'pæstjə-] vt **-ized; -izing** : pasteurizar

pastime ['pæsˌtaɪm] n : pasatiempo m

pastor ['pæstər] n : pastor m, -tora f

pastry ['peɪstri] n, pl **-ries** : pasteles mpl

pasture ['pæstʃər] n : pasto m

pasty ['peɪsti] adj **pastier; -est** 1 DOUGHY : pastoso 2 PALLID : pálido

pat ['pæt] n 1 : palmadita f 2 **a ~ of butter** : una porción de mantequilla — ~ vt **patted; patting** : dar palmaditas — ~ adv **have down ~** : saberse de memoria — ~ adj GLIB : fácil

patch ['pætʃ] n 1 : parche m, remiendo m (para la ropa) 2 SPOT : mancha f, trozo m 3 PLOT : parcela f (de tierra) — ~ vt 1 MEND : remender 2 **~ up** : arreglar — **patchy** ['pætʃi] adj **patchier; -est** 1 : desigual 2 INCOMPLETE : parcial, incompleto

patent adj ['pætənt] 1 or **patented** ['pætənt̬ɪd] : patentado 2 ['pætənt, 'peɪt-] OBVIOUS : patente, evidente — ~ ['pætənt] n : patente f — ~ ['pætənt] vt : patentar

paternal [pə'tərnəl] adj 1 FATHERLY : paternal 2 **~ grandmother** : abuela f paterna — **paternity** [pə'tərnəti] n : paternidad f

path ['pæθ, 'pɑθ] n 1 TRACK, TRAIL : camino m, sendero m 2 COURSE : trayectoria f

pathetic [pə'θɛt̬ɪk] adj : patético

pathology [pə'θɑlədʒi] n, pl **-gies** : patología f

pathway ['pæθˌweɪ] n : camino m, sendero m

patience ['peɪʃənts] n : paciencia f — **patient** ['peɪʃənt] adj : paciente — ~ n : paciente mf — **patiently** adv : con paciencia

patio ['pæt̬iˌoː] n, pl **-tios** : patio m

patriot ['peɪtriət] n : patriota mf — **patriotic** [ˌpeɪtri'ɑt̬ɪk] adj : patriótico

patrol [pə'troːl] n : patrulla f — ~ vt **-trolled; -trolling** : patrullar

patron ['peɪtrən] n 1 SPONSOR : patrocinador m, -dora f 2 CUSTOMER : cliente m, -ta f — **patronage** ['peɪtrənɪdʒ, 'pæ-] n 1 SPONSORSHIP : patrocinio m 2 CLIENTELE : clientela f — **patronize** ['peɪtrəˌnaɪz, 'pæ-] vt **-ized; -izing** 1 : ser cliente de (una tienda, etc.) 2 : tratar (a algn) con condescencia

patter ['pæt̬ər] n : tamborileo m (de la lluvia), correteo m (de los pies)

pattern ['pæt̬ərn] n 1 MODEL : modelo m 2 DESIGN : diseño m 3 STANDARD : pauta f, modo m 4 : patrón m (en costura) — ~ vt : basar (en un modelo)

paunch ['pɔntʃ] n : panza f

pause ['pɔz] n : pausa f — ~ vi **paused; pausing** : hacer una pausa

pave ['peɪv] vt **paved; paving** : pavimentar — **pavement** ['peɪvmənt] n : pavimento m

pavilion [pə'vɪljən] n : pabellón m

paw ['pɔ] n 1 : pata f 2 : garra f (de un gato) — ~ vt : tocar con la pata

pawn¹ ['pɔn] n : peón m (en ajedrez)

pawn² vt : empeñar — **pawnbroker** ['pɔnˌbroːkər] n : prestamista mf — **pawnshop** ['pɔnˌʃɑp] n : casa f de empeños

pay ['peɪ] v **paid** ['peɪd]; **paying** vt 1 : pagar 2 **~ attention** : prestar atención 3 **~ back** : devolver 4 **~ one's respects** : presentar uno sus respetos 5 **~ a visit** : hacer una visita — vi 1 : pagar 2 **crime doesn't ~** : no hay crimen sin castigo — ~ n : paga f — **payable** ['peɪəbəl] adj : pagadero — **paycheck** ['peɪˌtʃɛk] n : cheque m del sueldo — **payment** ['peɪmənt] n 1 : pago m 2 INSTALLMENT : plazo m, cuota f Lat — **payroll** n : nómina f

PC ['piːˌsiː] n, pl **PCs** or **PC's** : PC mf, computadora f personal

pea ['piː] n : guisante m, arveja f Lat

peace ['piːs] n : paz f — **peaceful** ['piːsfəl] adj 1 : pacífico 2 CALM : tranquilo

peach ['piːtʃ] n : melocotón m, durazno m Lat

peacock ['piːˌkɑk] n : pavo m real

peak ['piːk] n 1 SUMMIT : cumbre f, cima f, pico m (de una montaña) 2 APEX : nivel m máximo — ~ adj : máximo — ~ vi : alcanzar su nivel máximo

peal ['piːl] n 1 : repique m 2 **~s of laughter** : carcajadas fpl

peanut ['piːˌnʌt] n : cacahuete m, maní m Lat

pear ['pær] n : pera f

pearl ['pərl] n : perla f

peasant ['pɛzənt] n : campesino m, -na f

peat ['piːt] n : turba f

pebble ['pɛbəl] n : guijarro m

pecan ['piːˌkɑn, -ˌkæn, piˈkæn] n : pacana f, nuez f Lat

peck ['pɛk] vt : picar, picotear — ~ n 1 : picotazo m (de un pájaro) 2 KISS : besito

peculiar [prˈkjuːljər] adj 1 DISTINCTIVE

: peculiar, característico **2** STRANGE : extraño, raro — **peculiarity** [pɪˌkjuːˈljærəti, -kjuˈljær-] *n, pl* **-ties 1** : peculiaridad *f* **2** ODDITY : rareza *f*

pedal ['pɛdəl] *n* : pedal *m* — ~ *vi* **-aled** *or* **-alled; -aling** *or* **-alling** : pedalear

pedantic [pɪˈdæntɪk] *adj* : pedante

peddle ['pɛdəl] *vt* **-dled; -dling** : vender en las calles — **peddler** ['pɛdlər] *n* : vendedor *m*, -dora *f* ambulante

pedestal ['pɛdəstəl] *n* : pedestal *m*

pedestrian [pəˈdɛstriən] *n* : peatón *m*, -tona *f* — ~ *adj* — **crossing** *n* : paso *m* de peatones

pediatrics [ˌpiːdiˈætrɪks] *ns & pl* : pediatría *f* — **pediatrician** [ˌpiːdiəˈtrɪʃən] *n* : pediatra *mf*

pedigree ['pɛdəˌgriː] *n* : pedigrí *m* (de un animal), linaje *m* (de una persona)

peek ['piːk] *vi* : mirar a hurtadillas — ~ *n* : mirada *f* (furtiva)

peel ['piːl] *vt* : pelar (fruta, etc.) — *vi* : pelarse (dícese de la piel), desconcharse (dícese de la pintura) — ~ *n* : piel *f*, cáscara *f*

peep¹ ['piːp] *vi* CHEEP : piar — ~ *n* : pío *m* (de un pajarito)

peep² *vi* **1** PEEK : mirar a hurtadillas **2** *or* **out** : asomar — ~ *n* GLANCE : mirada *f* (furtiva)

peer¹ ['pɪr] *n* : par *mf*

peer² *vi* : mirar (con atención)

peeve ['piːv] *vt* : irritar — **peevish** ['piːvɪʃ] *adj* : malhumorado

peg ['pɛg] *n* **1** : clavija *f* **2** HOOK : gancho *m*

pelican ['pɛlɪkən] *n* : pelícano *m*

pellet ['pɛlət] *n* **1** : bolita *f* **2** SHOT : perdigón *m*

pelt¹ ['pɛlt] *n* : piel *f* (de un animal)

pelt² *vt* : lanzar (algo a algn)

pelvis ['pɛlvɪs] *n, pl* **-vises** *or* **-ves** [-ˌviːz] : pelvis *f* — **pelvic** ['pɛlvɪk] *adj* : pélvico

pen¹ ['pɛn] *vt* **penned; penning** ENCLOSE : encerrar — ~ *n* : corral *m*, redil *m*

pen² *n* **1** *or* **ballpoint** ~ : bolígrafo *m* **2** *or* **fountain** ~ : pluma *f*

penal ['piːnəl] *adj* : penal — **penalize** ['piːnəˌlaɪz, 'pɛn-] *vt* **-ized; -izing** : penalizar — **penalty** ['pɛnəlti] *n, pl* **-ties 1** : pena *f*, castigo *m* **2** : penalty *m* (en deportes)

penance ['pɛnənts] *n* : penitencia *f*

pencil ['pɛntsəl] *n* : lápiz *m* — **pencil sharpener** *n* : sacapuntas *m*

pendant ['pɛndənt] *n* : colgante *m*

pending ['pɛndɪŋ] *adj* : pendiente — ~ *prep* : en espera de

penetrate ['pɛnəˌtreɪt] *v* **-trated; -trating** : penetrar — **penetrating** ['pɛnəˌtreɪtɪŋ] *adj* : penetrante — **penetration** [ˌpɛnəˈtreɪʃən] *n* : penetración *f*

penguin ['pɛŋgwɪn, 'pɛn-] *n* : pingüino *m*

penicillin [ˌpɛnəˈsɪlən] *n* : penicilina *f*

peninsula [pəˈnɪntsələ, -ˈnɪntʃələ] *n* : península *f*

penis ['piːnəs] *n, pl* **-nes** [-ˌniːz] *or* **-nises** : pene *m*

penitentiary [ˌpɛnəˈtɛntʃəri] *n, pl* **-ries** : penitenciaría *f*

pen name *n* : seudónimo *m*

pennant ['pɛnənt] *n* : banderín *m*

penny ['pɛni] *n, pl* **-nies** *or* **pence** ['pɛnts] : centavo *m* (de los Estados Unidos), penique *m* (del Reino Unido) — **penniless** ['pɛnɪləs] *adj* : sin un centavo

pension ['pɛntʃən] *n* : pensión *m*, jubilación *f*

pensive ['pɛntsɪv] *adj* : pensativo

pentagon ['pɛntəˌgɑn] *n* : pentágono *m*

penthouse ['pɛntˌhaʊs] *n* : ático *m*

pent–up ['pɛntˌʌp] *adj* : reprimado

people ['piːpəl] *ns & pl* **1** people *npl* : gente *f*, personas *fpl* **2** *pl* ~**s** : pueblo *m*

pep ['pɛp] *n* **1** : energía *f*, vigor *m* — ~ *vt* *or* ~ **up** : animar

pepper ['pɛpər] *n* **1** : pimienta *f* (condimento) **2** : pimiento *m* (fruta) — **peppermint** ['pɛpərˌmɪnt] *n* : menta *f*

per ['pɜr] *prep* **1** : por **2** ACCORDING TO : según **3** ~ **day** : al día **4 miles** ~ **hour** : millas *fpl* por hora

perceive [pərˈsiːv] *vt* **-ceived; -ceiving** : percibir

percent [pərˈsɛnt] *adv* : por ciento — **percentage** [pərˈsɛntɪdʒ] *n* : porcentaje *m*

perception [pərˈsɛpʃən] *n* : percepción *f* — **perceptive** [pərˈsɛptɪv] *adj* : perspicaz

perch¹ ['pɜrtʃ] *n* : percha *f* (para los pájaros) — ~ *vi* : posarse

perch² *n* : perca *f* (pez)

percolate ['pɜrkəˌleɪt] *v* **-lated; -lating** : filtrarse — **percolator** ['pɜrkəˌleɪtər] *n* : cafetera *f* de filtro

percussion [pərˈkʌʃən] *n* : percusión *f*

perennial [pəˈrɛniəl] *adj* : perenne — ~ *n* : planta *f* perenne

perfect ['pɜrfɪkt] *adj* : perfecto — ~ [pərˈfɛkt] *vt* : perfeccionar — **perfection** [pərˈfɛkʃən] *n* : perfección *f* — **perfectionist** [pərˈfɛkʃənɪst] *n* : perfeccionista *mf*

perforate ['pǝrfǝ,reɪt] vt -rated; -rating : perforar

perform [pǝr'fɔrm] vt 1 CARRY OUT : realizar, hacer 2 : representar (una obra teatral), interpretar (una obra musical) — vi 1 FUNCTION : funcionar 2 ACT : actuar — **performance** [pǝr'fɔrmǝnts] n 1 : realización f 2 INTERPRETATION : interpretación f 3 PRESENTATION : representación f — **performer** [pǝr'fɔrmǝr] n : actor m, -triz f; intérprete mf (de música)

perfume ['pǝr,fju:m, pǝr'-] n : perfume m

perhaps [pǝr'hæps] adv : tal vez, quizá, quizás

peril ['perǝl] n : peligro m — **perilous** ['perǝlǝs] adj : peligroso

perimeter [pǝ'rɪmǝtǝr] n : perímetro m

period ['pɪriǝd] n 1 : período m (de tiempo) 2 : punto m (en puntuación) 3 ERA : época f — **periodic** [,pɪri'ɑdɪk] adj : periódico — **periodical** [,pɪri'ɑdɪkǝl] n : revista f

peripheral [pǝ'rɪfǝrǝl] adj : periférico

perish ['perɪʃ] vi : perecer — **perishable** ['perɪʃǝbǝl] adj : perecedero — **perishables** ['perɪʃǝbǝlz] npl : productos mpl perecederos

perjury ['pǝrdʒǝri] n : perjurio m

perk ['pǝrk] vi ~ up : animarse, reanimarse — ~ n : extra m — **perky** ['pǝrki] adj perkier; -est : alegre

permanence ['pǝrmǝnǝnts] n : permanencia f — **permanent** ['pǝrmǝnǝnt] adj : permanente — ~ n : permanente f

permeate ['pǝrmi,eɪt] v -ated; -ating : penetrar

permission [pǝr'mɪʃǝn] n : permiso m — **permissible** [pǝr'mɪsǝbǝl] adj : permisible — **permissive** [pǝr'mɪsɪv] adj : permisivo — **permit** [pǝr'mɪt] vt -mitted; -mitting : permitir — ~ ['pǝr,mɪt, pǝr'-] n : permiso m

peroxide [pǝ'rɑk,saɪd] n : peróxido m

perpendicular [,pǝrpǝn'dɪkjǝlǝr] adj : perpendicular

perpetrate ['pǝrpǝ,treɪt] vt -trated; -trating : cometer — **perpetrator** ['pǝrpǝ,treɪtǝr] n : autor m, -tora f (de un delito)

perpetual [pǝr'petʃuǝl] adj : perpetuo

perplex [pǝr'pleks] vt : dejar perplejo — **perplexing** [pǝr'pleksɪŋ] adj : desconcertante — **perplexity** [pǝr'pleksǝti] n, pl -ties : perplejidad f

persecute ['pǝrsɪ,kju:t] vt -cuted; -cuting : perseguir — **persecution** [,pǝrsɪ'kju:ʃǝn] n : persecución f

persevere [,pǝrsǝ'vɪr] vi -vered; -vering

: perseverar — **perseverance** [,pǝrsǝ-'vɪrǝnts] n : perseverancia f

persist [pǝr'sɪst] vi : persistir — **persistence** [pǝr'sɪstǝnts] n : persistencia f — **persistent** [pǝr'sɪstǝnt] adj : persistente

person ['pǝrsǝn] n : persona f — **personal** ['pǝrsǝnǝl] adj : personal — **personality** [,pǝrsǝn'ælǝti] n, pl -ties : personalidad f — **personally** ['pǝrsǝnǝli] adv : personalmente, en persona — **personnel** [,pǝrsǝn'el] n : personal m

perspective [pǝr'spektɪv] n : perspectiva f

perspiration [,pǝrspǝ'reɪʃǝn] n : transpiración f — **perspire** [pǝr'spaɪr] vi -spired; -spiring : transpirar

persuade [pǝr'sweɪd] vt -suaded; -suading : persuadir — **persuasion** [pǝr'sweɪʒǝn] n : persuasión f

pertain [pǝr'teɪn] vi ~ to : estar relacionado con — **pertinent** ['pǝrtǝnǝnt] adj : pertinente

perturb [pǝr'tǝrb] vt : perturbar

Peruvian [pǝ'ru:viǝn] adj : peruano

pervade [pǝr'veɪd] vt -vaded; -vading : penetrar — **pervasive** [pǝr'veɪsɪv, -zɪv] adj : penetrante

perverse [pǝr'vǝrs] adj 1 CORRUPT : perverso 2 STUBBORN : obstinado — **pervert** ['pǝr,vǝrt] n : pervertido m, -da f

peso ['peɪ,so:] n, pl -sos : peso m

pessimism ['pesǝ,mɪzǝm] n : pesimismo m — **pessimist** ['pesǝmɪst] n : pesimista mf — **pessimistic** [,pesǝ'mɪstɪk] adj : pesimista

pest ['pest] n 1 : insecto m nocivo, animal m nocivo 2 : peste f fam (persona) — **pester** ['pestǝr] vt -tered; -tering : molestar

pesticide ['pestǝ,saɪd] n : pesticida m

pet ['pet] n 1 : animal m doméstico 2 FAVORITE : favorito m, -ta f — ~ vt petted; petting : acariciar

petal ['petǝl] n : pétalo m

petite [pǝ'ti:t] adj : chiquita

petition [pǝ'tɪʃǝn] n : petición f — ~ vt : dirigir una petición a

petrify ['petrǝ,faɪ] vt -fied; -fying : petrificar

petroleum [pǝ'tro:liǝm] n : petróleo m

petticoat ['peti,ko:t] n : enagua f, fondo m Lat

petty ['peti] adj -tier; -est 1 UNIMPORTANT : insignificante, nimio 2 MEAN : mezquino — **pettiness** ['petinǝs] n : mezquindad f

petulant ['petʃǝlǝnt] adj : irritable, de mal genio

pew ['pju:] n : banco m (de iglesia)

pewter ['pjutər] n : peltre m

phallic ['fælɪk] adj : fálico

phantom ['fæntəm] n : fantasma m

pharmacy ['fɑrməsi] n, pl **-cies** : farmacia f — **pharmacist** ['fɑrməsɪst] n : farmacéutico m, -ca f

phase ['feɪz] n : fase f — ~ vt **phased; phasing** ~ **in** : introducir progresivamente 2 ~ **out** : retirar progresivamente

phenomenon [fɪ'nɑmə nɑn, -nən] n, pl **-na** [-nə] or **-nons** : fenómeno m — **phenomenal** [fɪ'nɑmənəl] adj : fenomenal

philanthropy [fə'lænθrəpi] n, pl **-pies** : filantropía f — **philanthropist** [fə'lænθrəpɪst] n : filántropo m, -pa f

philosophy [fə'lɑsəfi] n, pl **-phies** : filosofía f — **philosopher** [fə'lɑsəfər] n : filósofo m, -fa f

phlegm ['flɛm] n : flema f

phobia ['foʊbiə] n : fobia f

phone ['foʊn] → **telephone**

phonetic ['fo neɪɪk] adj : fonético

phony or **phoney** ['foʊni] adj **-nier; -est** : falso — ~ n, pl **-nies** : farsante mf

phosphorus ['fɑsfərəs] n : fósforo m

photo ['foʊtoː] n, pl **-tos** : foto f — **photocopier** ['foʊtoˌkɑpiər] n : fotocopiadora f — **photocopy** ['foʊtoˌkɑpi] n, pl **-copies** : fotocopia f — ~ vt **-copied; -copying** : fotocopiar — **photograph** ['foʊtəˌgræf] n : fotografía f, foto f — ~ vt : fotografiar — **photographer** [fə'tɑgrəfər] n : fotógrafo m, -fa f — **photographic** [ˌfoʊtə'græfɪk] adj : fotográfico — **photography** [fə'tɑgrəfi] n : fotografía f

phrase ['freɪz] n : frase f — ~ vt **phrased; phrasing** : expresar

physical ['fɪzɪkəl] adj : físico — ~ n : reconocimiento m médico

physician [fə'zɪʃən] n : médico m, -ca f

physics ['fɪzɪks] ns & pl : física f — **physicist** ['fɪzəsɪst] n : físico m, -ca f

physiology [ˌfɪzi'ɑlədʒi] n : fisiología f

physique [fə'ziːk] n : físico m

piano ['pjænoː] n, pl **-anos** : piano m — **pianist** ['pjænɪst, pi'ænɪst] n : pianista mf

pick ['pɪk] vt **1** CHOOSE : escoger **2** GATHER : recoger **3** REMOVE : quitar (poco a poco) **4** ~ **a fight** : buscar camorra — vi **1** ~ **and choose** : ser exigente **2** ~ **on** : meterse con — ~ n **1** CHOICE : selección f **2** or **pickax** ['pɪkˌæks] : pico m **3** **the** ~ **of** : lo mejor de

picket ['pɪkət] n **1** STAKE : estaca f **2** or ~ **line** : piquete m — ~ v : piquetear

pickle ['pɪkəl] n **1** : pepinillo m (encurtido) **2** JAM : lío m fam, apuro m — ~ vt **-led; -ling** : encurtir

pickpocket ['pɪkˌpɑkət] n : carterista mf

pickup ['pɪkˌʌp] n **1** IMPROVEMENT : mejora f **2** or ~ **truck** : camioneta f — **pick up** vt **1** LIFT : levantar **2** TIDY : arreglar, ordenar — vi IMPROVE : mejorar

picnic ['pɪkˌnɪk] n : picnic m — ~ vi **-nicked; -nicking** : ir de picnic

picture ['pɪktʃər] n **1** PAINTING : cuadro m **2** DRAWING : dibujo m **3** PHOTO : fotografía f **4** IMAGE : imagen f **5** MOVIE : película f — ~ vt **-tured; -turing 1** DEPICT : representar **2** IMAGINE : imaginarse — **picturesque** [ˌpɪktʃə'rɛsk] adj : pintoresco

pie ['paɪ] n : pastel m (con fruta o carne), empanada f (con carne)

piece ['piːs] n **1** : pieza f **2** FRAGMENT : trozo m, pedazo m **3 a** ~ **of advice** : un consejo — ~ vt **pieced; piecing** or ~ **together** : juntar, componer — **piecemeal** ['piːsˌmiːl] adv : poco a poco — ~ adj : poco sistemático

pier ['pɪr] n : muelle m

pierce ['pɪrs] vt **pierced; piercing** : perforar — **piercing** adj : penetrante

piety ['paɪəti] n, pl **-eties** : piedad f

pig ['pɪg] n : cerdo m, -da f; puerco m, -ca f

pigeon ['pɪdʒən] n : paloma f — **pigeonhole** ['pɪdʒənˌhoʊl] n : casilla f

piggyback ['pɪgiˌbæk] adv & adj : a cuestas

pigment ['pɪgmənt] n : pigmento m

pigpen ['pɪgˌpɛn] n : pocilga f

pigtail ['pɪgˌteɪl] n : coleta f, trenza f

pile[1] ['paɪl] n HEAP : montón m, pila f — ~ vt **piled; piling** vt : amontonar, apilar — vi ~ **up** : amontonarse, acumularse

pile[2] n NAP : pelo m (de telas)

pilfer ['pɪlfər] vt : robar, hurtar

pilgrim ['pɪlgrəm] n : peregrino m, -na f — **pilgrimage** ['pɪlgrəmɪdʒ] n : peregrinación f

pill ['pɪl] n : pastilla f, píldora f

pillage ['pɪlɪdʒ] v : saquear — ~ n — ~ **-laged; -laging** : saquear

pillar ['pɪlər] n : pilar m, columna f

pillow ['pɪloː] n : almohada f — **pillowcase** ['pɪloːˌkeɪs] n : funda f (de almohada)

pilot ['paɪlət] n : piloto m — ~ vt : pilotar, pilotear — **pilot light** n : piloto m

pimp ['pɪmp] n : proxeneta m

pimple ['pɪmpəl] n : grano m

pin ['pɪn] n **1** : alfiler m **2** BROOCH

: broche *m* **3** *or* **bowling ~** : bolo *m* — **~** *vt* **pinned; pinning 1** FASTEN : prender, sujetar (con alfileres) **2** *or* **~ down** : inmovilizar

pincers ['pɪntsərz] *npl* : tenazas *fpl*

pinch ['pɪntʃ] *vt* **1** : pellizcar **2** STEAL : robar — *vi* : apretar — **~** *n* **1** : pellizco *m* **2** BIT : pizca *f* **3 in a ~** : en caso necesario

pine[1] ['paɪn] *n* : pino *m* (árbol)

pine[2] *vi* **pined; pining 1** LANGUISH : languidecer **2 ~ for** : suspirar por

pineapple ['paɪnˌæpəl] *n* : piña *f*, ananás *m*

pink ['pɪŋk] *n* : rosa *m*, rosado *m* — **~** *adj* : rosa, rosado

pinnacle ['pɪnɪkəl] *n* : pináculo *m*

pinpoint ['pɪnˌpɔɪnt] *vt* : localizar, precisar

pint ['paɪnt] *n* : pinta *f*

pioneer [ˌpaɪəˈnɪr] *n* : pionero *m*, -ra *f*

pious ['paɪəs] *adj* : piadoso

pipe ['paɪp] *n* **1** : tubo *m*, caño *m* **2** : pipa *f* (para fumar) — **pipeline** ['paɪpˌlaɪn] *n* **1** : conducto *m*, oleoducto *m* (para petróleo)

piquant ['piːkənt, 'pɪkwənt] *adj* : picante

pique ['piːk] *n* : resentimiento *m*

pirate ['paɪrət] *n* : pirata *mf*

pistachio [pəˈstæʃiˌoː, -staˈ-] *n, pl* **-chios** : pistacho *m*

pistol ['pɪstəl] *n* : pistola *f*

piston ['pɪstən] *n* : pistón *m*

pit ['pɪt] *n* **1** HOLE : hoyo *m*, fosa *f* **2** MINE : mina *f* **3** : hueso *m* (de una fruta) **4 ~ of the stomach** : boca *f* del estómago — **~** *vt* **pitted; pitting 1** : marcar de hoyos **2** : deshuesar (una fruta) **3 ~ against** : enfrentar a

pitch ['pɪtʃ] *vt* **1** : armar (una tienda) **2** THROW : lanzar — *vi* **1** *or* **~ forward** : caerse **2** LURCH : cabecear (dícese de un barco o un avión) — **~** *n* **1** DEGREE, LEVEL : grado *m*, punto *m* **2** TONE : tono *m* **3** THROW : lanzamiento *m* **4** *or* **sales ~** : presentación *f* (de un vendedor)

pitcher ['pɪtʃər] *n* **1** JUG : jarro *m* **2** : lanzador *m*, -dora *f* (en béisbol, etc.)

pitchfork ['pɪtʃˌfɔrk] *n* : horquilla *f*, horca *f*

pitfall ['pɪtˌfɔl] *n* : riesgo *m*, dificultad *f*

pith ['pɪθ] *n* **1** : médula *f* (de un hueso, etc.) **2** CORE : meollo *m* — **pithy** ['pɪθi] *adj* **pithier; -est** : conciso y sustancioso

pity ['pɪti] *n, pl* **pities 1** COMPASSION : compasión *f* **2 what a ~!** : ¡qué lástima! — **~** *vt* **pitied; pitying** : compadecerse de — **pitiful** ['pɪtɪfəl] *adj*

: lastimoso — **pitiless** ['pɪtɪləs] *adj* : despiadado

pivot ['pɪvət] *n* : pivote *m* — **~** *vi* **1** : girar sobre un eje **2 ~ on** : depender de

pizza ['piːtsə] *n* : pizza *f*

placard ['plækərd, -ˌkard] *n* POSTER : cartel *m*, póster *m*

placate ['pleɪˌkeɪt, 'plæ-] *vt* **-cated; -cating** : apaciguar

place ['pleɪs] *n* **1** : sitio *m*, lugar *m* **2** SEAT : asiento *m* **3** POSITION : puesto *m* **4** ROLE : papel *m* **5 take ~** : tener lugar **6 take the ~ of** : sustituir a — **~** *vt* **placed; placing 1** PUT, SET : poner, colocar **2** IDENTIFY : identificar, recordar **3 ~ an order** : hacer un pedido — **placement** ['pleɪsmənt] *n* : colocación *f*

placid ['plæsəd] *adj* : plácido, tranquilo

plagiarism ['pleɪdʒəˌrɪzəm] *n* : plagio *m* — **plagiarize** ['pleɪdʒəˌraɪz] *vt* **-rized; -rizing** : plagiar

plague ['pleɪg] *n* **1** : plaga *f* (de insectos, etc.) **2** : peste *f* (en medicina)

plaid ['plæd] *n* : tela *f* escocesa — **~** *adj* : escocés

plain ['pleɪn] *adj* **1** SIMPLE : sencillo **2** CLEAR : claro, evidente **3** CANDID : franco **4** HOMELY : poco atractivo **5 in ~ sight** : a la vista (de todos) — *n* : llanura *f*, planicie *f* — **plainly** ['pleɪnli] *adv* **1** CLEARLY : claramente **2** FRANKLY : francamente **3** SIMPLY : sencillamente

plaintiff ['pleɪntɪf] *n* : demandante *mf*

plan ['plæn] *n* **1** : plan *m*, proyecto *m* **2** DIAGRAM : plano *m* — **~** *v* **planned; planning** *vt* **1** : planear, proyectar **2** INTEND : tener planeado — *vi* : hacer planes

plane[1] ['pleɪn] *n* **1** LEVEL : plano *m*, nivel *m* **2** AIRPLANE : avión *m*

plane[2] *n or* **carpenter's ~** : cepillo *m*

planet ['plænət] *n* : planeta *m*

plank ['plæŋk] *n* : tabla *f*

planning ['plænɪŋ] *n* : planificación *f*

plant ['plænt] *vt* : plantar (flores, árboles), sembrar (semillas) — **~** *n* **1** : planta *f* **2** FACTORY : fábrica *f*

plantain ['plæntən] *n* : plátano *m* (grande)

plantation [plænˈteɪʃən] *n* : plantación *f*

plaque ['plæk] *n* : placa *f*

plaster ['plæstər] *n* : yeso *m* — **~** *vt* **1** : enyesar **2** COVER : cubrir — **plaster cast** *n* : escayola *f*

plastic ['plæstɪk] *adj* **1** : de plástico **2** FLEXIBLE : plástico, flexible **3 ~ surgery** : cirugía *f* plástica — **~** *n* : plástico *m*

plate 334 pneumatic

plate ['pleɪt] *n* **1** SHEET : placa *f* **2** DISH : plato *m* **3** ILLUSTRATION : lámina *f* — ~ *vt* **plated**; **plating** : chapar (en metal)

plateau [plæ'to:] *n, pl* **-teaus** *or* **-teaux** ['-'toz] : meseta *f*

platform ['plæt,fɔrm] *n* **1** : plataforma *f* **2** : andén *m* (de una estación de ferrocarril) **3** *or* **political** ~ : programa *m* electoral

platinum ['plætənəm] *n* : platino *m*

platitude ['plætə,tu:d, -,tju:d] *n* : lugar *m* común

platoon [plə'tu:n] *n* : sección *f* (en el ejército)

platter ['plætər] *n* : fuente *f*

plausible ['plɔzəbəl] *adj* : creíble, verosímil

play ['pleɪ] *n* **1** : juego *m* **2** DRAMA : obra *f* de teatro — ~ *vi* **1** : jugar **2** ~ **in a band** : tocar en un grupo — ~ *vt* **1** : jugar (deportes, etc.), jugar a (juegos) **2** : tocar (música o un instrumento) **3** ~ **the role of** : representar el papel de — **player** ['pleɪər] *n* **1** : jugador *m*, -dora *f* **2** ACTOR : actor *m*, actriz *f* **3** MUSICIAN : músico *m*, -ca *f* — **playful** ['pleɪfəl] *adj* : juguetón — **playground** ['pleɪ,graʊnd] *n* : patio *m* de recreo — **playing card** *n* : naipe *m*, carta *f* — **playmate** ['pleɪ,meɪt] *n* : compañero *m*, -ra *f* de juego — **play-off** ['pleɪ,ɔf] *n* : desempate *m* — **playpen** ['pleɪ,pɛn] *n* : corral *m* (para niños) — **plaything** ['pleɪ,θɪŋ] *n* : juguete *m* — **playwright** ['pleɪ,raɪt] *n* : dramaturgo *m*, -ga *f*

plea ['pli:] *n* **1** : acto *m* de declararse (en derecho) **2** APPEAL : ruego *m*, súplica *f* — **plead** ['pli:d] *v* **pleaded** *or* **pled** ['plɛd]; **pleading** — *vi* **1** ~ **for** : suplicar **2** ~ **guilty** : declararse culpable **3** ~ **not guilty** : negar la acusación — *vt* **1** : alegar, pretextar **2** ~ **a case** : defender un caso

pleasant ['plɛzənt] *adj* : agradable, grato — **please** ['pli:z] *v* **pleased**; **pleasing** *vt* **1** GRATIFY : complacer **2** SATISFY : satisfacer — *vi* **1** : agradar **2 do as you** ~ : haz lo que quieras — ~ *adv* : por favor — **pleased** ['pli:zd] *adj* : contento — **pleasing** ['pli:zɪŋ] *adj* : agradable — **pleasure** ['plɛʒər] *n* : placer *m*, gusto *m*

pleat ['pli:t] *vt* : plisar — ~ *n* : pliegue *m*

pledge ['plɛdʒ] *n* **1** SECURITY : prenda *f* **2** PROMISE : promesa *f* — ~ *vt* **pledged**; **pledging 1** PAWN : empeñar **2** PROMISE : prometer

plenty ['plɛnti] *n* **1** : abundancia *f* **2** ~ **of time** : tiempo *m* de sobra — **plentiful** ['plɛntɪfəl] *adj* : abundante

pliable ['plaɪəbəl] *adj* : flexible

pliers ['plaɪərz] *npl* : alicates *mpl*

plight ['plaɪt] *n* : situación *f* difícil

plod ['plɑd] *vi* **plodded**; **plodding 1** : caminar con paso pesado **2** DRUDGE : trabajar laboriosamente

plot ['plɑt] *n* **1** LOT : parcela *f* **2** : argumento *m* (de una novela, etc.) **3** CONSPIRACY : complot *m*, intriga *f* — ~ *v* **plotted**; **plotting 1** : tramar (un plan), trazar (una gráfica, etc.) — *vi* CONSPIRE : conspirar

plow *or* **plough** ['plaʊ] *n* **1** : arado *m* **2** ~ **snowplow** — ~ *v* : arar

ploy ['plɔɪ] *n* : estratagema *f*

pluck ['plʌk] *vt* **1** : arrancar **2** : desplumar (un pollo, etc.) **3** : recoger (flores) **4** ~ **one's eyebrows** : depilarse las cejas

plug ['plʌg] *n* **1** STOPPER : tapón *m* **2** : enchufe *m* (eléctrico) — ~ *vt* **plugged**; **plugging 1** BLOCK : tapar **2** ADVERTISE : dar publicidad a **3** ~ **in** : enchufar

plum ['plʌm] *n* : ciruela *f*

plumb ['plʌm] *adj* : a plomo, vertical — **plumber** ['plʌmər] *n* : fontanero *m*, -ra *f*; plomero *m*, -ra *f Lat* — **plumbing** ['plʌmɪŋ] *n* **1** : fontanería *f*, plomería *f Lat* **2** PIPES : cañerías *fpl*

plume ['plu:m] *n* : pluma *f*

plummet ['plʌmət] *vi* : caer en picado

plump ['plʌmp] *adj* : rechoncho *fam*

plunder ['plʌndər] *vi* : saquear, robar — ~ *n* : botín *m*

plunge ['plʌndʒ] *v* **plunged**; **plunging** *vt* **1** IMMERSE : sumergir **2** THRUST : hundir — *vi* **1** : zambullirse (en el agua) **2** DESCEND : descender en picada — ~ *n* **1** DIVE : zambullida *f* **2** DROP : descenso *m* abrupto

plural ['plʊrəl] *adj* : plural — ~ *n* : plural *m*

plus ['plʌs] *adj* : positivo — ~ *n* **1** *or* ~ **sign** : signo *m* (de) más **2** ADVANTAGE : ventaja *f* — ~ *prep* : más — ~ *conj* : y, además

plush ['plʌʃ] *n* : felpa *f* — ~ *adj* **1** : de felpa **2** LUXURIOUS : lujoso

plutonium [plu:'to:niəm] *n* : plutonio *m*

ply ['plaɪ] *vt* **plied**; **plying 1** : ejercer (un oficio) **2** ~ **with questions** : acosar con preguntas

plywood ['plaɪ,wʊd] *n* : contrachapado *m*

pneumatic [nʊ'mætɪk, nju-] *adj* : neumático

pneumonia [nʊˈmoːnjə, njuː-] n : pulmonía f

poach[1] ['poːtʃ] vt : cocer a fuego lento

poach[2] vt or ~ **game** : cazar ilegalmente — **poacher** ['poːtʃər] n : cazador m furtivo, cazadora f furtiva

pocket ['pɑkət] n : bolsillo m — ~ vt : meterse en el bolsillo — **pocketbook** ['pɑkətˌbʊk] n : cartera f, bolsa f Lat — **pocketknife** ['pɑkətˌnaɪf] n, pl **-knives** : navaja f

pod ['pɑd] n : vaina f

poem ['poːəm] n : poema m — **poet** ['poːət] n : poeta mf — **poetic** [poˈɛtɪk] or **poetical** [-tɪkəl] adj : poético — **poetry** ['poːətri] n : poesía f

poignant ['pɔɪnjənt] adj : conmovedor

point ['pɔɪnt] n 1 : punto m 2 PURPOSE : sentido m 3 TIP : punta f 4 FEATURE : cualidad f 5 **be beside the** ~ : no venir al caso 6 **there's no** ~ ... : no sirve de nada...— ~ vt 1 AIM : apuntar 2 or ~ **out** : señalar, indicar — vi ~ **at** : señalar (con el dedo) — **point-blank** ['pɔɪntˈblæŋk] adv : a quemarropa — **pointer** ['pɔɪntər] n 1 NEEDLE : aguja f 2 : perro m de muestra 3 TIP : consejo m — **pointless** ['pɔɪntləs] adj : inútil — **point of view** n : perspectiva f, punto m de vista

poise ['pɔɪz] n 1 : elegancia f 2 COMPOSURE : aplomo m

poison ['pɔɪzən] n : veneno m — ~ vt : envenenar — **poisonous** ['pɔɪzənəs] adj : venenoso (dícese de una culebra, etc.), tóxico (dícese de una sustancia)

poke ['poːk] vt **poked; poking** 1 JAB : golpear (con la punta de algo), dar 2 THRUST : introducir, asomar — ~ n : golpe m abrupto (con la punta de algo)

poker[1] ['poːkər] n : atizador m (para el fuego)

poker[2] n : póquer m (juego de naipes)

polar ['poːlər] adj : polar — **polar bear** n : oso m blanco — **polarize** ['poːləˌraɪz] vt **-ized; -izing** : polarizar

pole[1] ['poːl] n : palo m, poste m

pole[2] n : polo m (en geografía)

police [pəˈliːs] vt **-liced; -licing** : mantener el orden en — ~ ns & pl **the** ~ : la policía — **policeman** [pəˈliːsmən] n, pl **-men** [-mən, -ˌmɛn] : policía m — **police officer** n : policía mf, agente mf de policía — **policewoman** [pəˈliːsˌwʊmən] n, pl **-women** [-ˌwɪmən] : (mujer f) policía f

policy ['pɑləsi] n, pl **-cies** 1 : política f 2 or **insurance** ~ : póliza f de seguros

polio ['poːliˌoː] or **poliomyelitis** [ˌpoːliˌoːˌmaɪəˈlaɪtəs] n : polio f, poliomielitis f

polish ['pɑlɪʃ] vt 1 : pulir 2 : limpiar (zapatos), encerar (un suelo) — ~ n 1 LUSTER : brillo m, lustre m 2 : betún m (para zapatos), cera f (para suelos y muebles), esmalte m (para las uñas)

Polish ['poːlɪʃ] adj : polaco — ~ n : polaco m (idioma)

polite [pəˈlaɪt] adj **-liter; -est** : cortés — **politeness** [pəˈlaɪtnəs] n : cortesía f

political [pəˈlɪtɪkəl] adj : político — **politician** [ˌpɑləˈtɪʃən] n : político m, -ca f — **politics** ['pɑləˌtɪks] ns & pl : política f

polka ['poːlkə, 'poːkə] n : polka f — **polka dot** ['poːkəˌdɑt] n : lunar m

poll ['poːl] n 1 : encuesta f, sondeo m 2 **the** ~**s** : las urnas — ~ vt 1 : obtener (votos) 2 CANVASS : encuestar, sondear

pollen ['pɑlən] n : polen m

pollute [pəˈluːt] vt **-luted; -luting** : contaminar — **pollution** [pəˈluːʃən] n : contaminación f

polyester ['pɑliˌɛstər, ˌpɑliˈ-] n : poliéster m

polygon ['pɑliˌgɑn] n : polígono m

pomegranate ['pɑməˌgrænət, 'pɑmˌgrænət] n : granada f

pomp ['pɑmp] n : pompa f — **pompous** ['pɑmpəs] adj : pomposo

pond ['pɑnd] n : charca f (natural), estanque m (artificial)

ponder ['pɑndər] vt : considerar — vi ~ **over** : reflexionar sobre

pony ['poːni] n, pl **-nies** : poni m — **ponytail** ['poːniˌteɪl] n : cola f de caballo

poodle ['puːdəl] n : caniche m

pool ['puːl] n 1 PUDDLE : charco m 2 : fondo m común (de recursos) 3 BILLIARDS : billar m 4 or **swimming** ~ : piscina f — ~ vt : hacer un fondo común de

poor ['pʊr, 'pɔr] adj 1 : pobre 2 INFERIOR : malo 3 **the** ~ : los pobres — **poorly** ['pʊrli, 'pɔr-] adv : mal

pop[1] ['pɑp] v **popped; popping** vt 1 : hacer reventar 2 ~ **sth into** : meter algo en — vi 1 BURST : reventar, estallar 2 ~ **in** : entrar (un momento) 3 ~ **out** : saltar (dícese de los ojos) 4 ~ **up** APPEAR : aparecer — ~ n 1 : ruido m seco 2 → **soda pop**

pop[2] n or ~ **music** : música f popular

popcorn ['pɑpˌkɔrn] n : palomitas fpl

pope ['poːp] n : papa m

poplar ['pɑplər] n : álamo m

poppy ['pɑpi] n, pl **-pies** : amapola f

popular ['pɑpjələr] adj : popular — **pop-**

ularity [ˌpɑpjəˈlærət̬i] n : popularidad f — **popularize** [ˈpɑpjələˌraɪz] vt **-ized; -izing** : popularizar

populate [ˈpɑpjəˌleɪt] vt **-lated; -lating** : poblar — **population** [ˌpɑpjəˈleɪʃən] n : población f

porcelain [ˈpɔrsələn] n : porcelana f

porch [ˈpɔrtʃ] n : porche m

porcupine [ˈpɔrkjəˌpaɪn] n : puerco m espín

pore¹ [ˈpɔr] vi **pored; poring** ~ **over** : estudiar esmeradamente

pore² n : poro m

pork [ˈpɔrk] n : carne f de cerdo

pornography [pɔrˈnɑɡrəfi] n : pornografía f — **pornographic** [ˌpɔrnəˈɡræfɪk] adj : pornográfico

porous [ˈpɔrəs] adj : poroso

porpoise [ˈpɔrpəs] n : marsopa f

porridge [ˈpɔrɪdʒ] n : avena f (cocida), gachas fpl (de avena)

port¹ [ˈpɔrt] n HARBOR : puerto m

port² n or ~ **side** : babor m

port³ n : oporto m (vino)

portable [ˈpɔrt̬əbəl] adj : portátil

portent [ˈpɔrˌtent] n : presagio m

porter [ˈpɔrt̬ər] n : maletero m, mozo m (de estación)

portfolio [pɔrtˈfoːliˌo] n, pl **-lios** : cartera f

porthole [ˈpɔrtˌhoːl] n : portilla f

portion [ˈpɔrʃən] n : porción f

portrait [ˈpɔrtrət, -ˌtreɪt] n : retrato m

portray [pɔrˈtreɪ] vt **1** : representar, retratar **2** : interpretar (un personaje)

Portuguese [ˌpɔrt̬əˈɡiːz, -ˈɡiːs] adj : portugués — ~ n : portugués m (idioma)

pose [ˈpoːz] v **posed; posing** vt : plantear (una pregunta, etc.), representar (una amenaza) — vi **1** : posar **2** ~ **as** : hacerse pasar por — ~ n : pose f

posh [ˈpɑʃ] adj : elegante, de lujo

position [pəˈzɪʃən] n **1** : posición f **2** JOB : puesto m — ~ vt : colocar, situar

positive [ˈpɑzət̬ɪv] adj **1** : positivo **2** CERTAIN : seguro

possess [pəˈzes] vt : poseer — **possession** [pəˈzeʃən] n **1** : posesión f **2** ~ s npl BELONGINGS : bienes mpl — **possessive** [pəˈzesɪv] adj : posesivo

possible [ˈpɑsəbəl] adj : posible — **possibility** [ˌpɑsəˈbɪlət̬i] n, pl **-ties** : posibilidad f — **possibly** [ˈpɑsəbli] adv : posiblemente

post¹ [ˈpoːst] n POLE : poste m, palo m

post² n POSITION : puesto m

post³ n MAIL : cartas fpl — ~ vt **1** : echar al correo **2 keep** ~**ed** : tener al corriente — **postage** [ˈpoːstɪdʒ] n

: franqueo m — **postal** [ˈpoːstəl] adj : postal — **postcard** [ˈpoːstˌkɑrd] n : tarjeta f postal

poster [ˈpoːstər] n : cartel m

posterity [pɑˈsterət̬i] n : posteridad f

posthumous [ˈpɑstʃəməs] adj : póstumo

postman [ˈpoːstmən, -ˌmæn] → **mailman** — **post office** : oficina f de correos

postpone [ˌpoːstˈpoːn] vt **-poned; -poning** : aplazar — **postponement** [ˌpoːstˈpoːnmənt] n : aplazamiento m

postscript [ˈpoːstˌskrɪpt] n : posdata f

posture [ˈpɑstʃər] n : postura f

postwar [ˈpoːstˈwɔr] adj : de (la) posguerra

pot [ˈpɑt] n **1** : olla f (de cocina) **2** FLOWERPOT : maceta f **3** ~ **s and pans** : cacharros mpl

potassium [pəˈtæsiəm] n : potasio m

potato [pəˈteɪt̬o] n, pl **-toes** : patata f, papa f Lat

potent [ˈpoːt̬ənt] adj **1** POWERFUL : poderoso **2** EFFECTIVE : eficaz

potential [pəˈtentʃəl] adj : potencial — ~ n : potencial m

pothole [ˈpɑtˌhoːl] n : bache m

potion [ˈpoːʃən] n : poción f

pottery [ˈpɑt̬əri] n, pl **-teries** : cerámica f

pouch [ˈpaʊtʃ] n **1** BAG : bolsa f pequeña **2** : bolsa f (de un animal)

poultry [ˈpoːltri] n : aves fpl de corral

pounce [ˈpaʊns] vi **pounced; pouncing** : abalanzarse

pound¹ [ˈpaʊnd] n : libra f (unidad de dinero o de peso)

pound² n or **dog** ~ : perrera f

pound³ vt **1** CRUSH : machacar **2** HIT : golpear — vi : palpitar (dícese del corazón)

pour [ˈpɔr] vt : verter — vi **1** FLOW : fluir, salir **2 it's** ~**ing** : está lloviendo a cántaros

pout [ˈpaʊt] vi : hacer pucheros — ~ n : puchero m

poverty [ˈpɑvərt̬i] n : pobreza f

powder [ˈpaʊdər] vt **1** : empolvar **2** CRUSH : pulverizar — ~ n **1** : polvo m **2** or **face** ~ : polvos mpl — **powdery** [ˈpaʊdəri] adj : polvoriento

power [ˈpaʊər] n **1** CONTROL : poder m **2** ABILITY : capacidad f **3** STRENGTH : fuerza f **4** : potencia f (política) **5** ENERGY : energía f **6** ELECTRICITY : electricidad f — ~ vt : impulsar — **powerful** [ˈpaʊərfəl] adj : poderoso — **powerless** [ˈpaʊərləs] adj : impotente

practical [ˈpræktɪkəl] adj : práctico — **practically** [ˈpræktɪkli] adv : casi, prácticamente

practice or **practise** [ˈpræktəs] v **-ticed**

or **-tised; -ticing** *or* **-tising** *vt* **1** : practicar **2** : ejercer (una profesión) — *vi* : practicar — **practice** *n* **1** : práctica *f* **2** CUSTOM : costumbre *f* **3** : ejercicio *m* (de una profesión) **4 be out of ~** : no estar en forma — **practitioner** [præk-'tɪʃənər] *n* **1** : profesional *mf* **2 general ~** : médico *m*, -ca *f* de medicina general

pragmatic [præg'mæt̬ɪk] *adj* : pragmático

prairie ['preri] *n* : pradera *f*

praise ['preɪz] *vt* **praised; praising** : elogiar, alabar — **~** *n* : elogio *m*, alabanza *f* — **praiseworthy** ['preɪz,wərði] *adj* : loable

prance ['prænts] *vi* **pranced; prancing** : hacer cabriolas

prank ['præŋk] *n* : travesura *f*

prawn ['prɔn] *n* : gamba *f*

pray ['preɪ] *vi* **1** : rezar **2 ~ for** : rogar — **prayer** ['prer] *n* : oración *f*

preach ['priːtʃ] *v* : predicar — **preacher** ['priːtʃər] *n* MINISTER : pastor *m*, -tora *f*

precarious [prɪ'kæriəs] *adj* : precario

precaution [prɪ'kɔʃən] *n* : precaución *f*

precede [prɪ'siːd] *vt* **-ceded; -ceding** : preceder a — **precedence** ['presədənts, prɪ'siːdənts] *n* : precedencia *f* — **precedent** ['presədənt] *n* : precedente *m*

precinct ['priː,sɪŋkt] *n* **1** DISTRICT : distrito *m* **2 ~s** *npl* : recinto *m*

precious ['prefəs] *adj* : precioso

precipice ['presəpəs] *n* : precipicio *m*

precipitate [prɪ'sɪpə,teɪt] *vt* **-tated; -tating** : precipitar — **precipitation** [prɪsɪpə'teɪʃən] *n* **1** HASTE : precipitación *f* **2** : precipitaciones *fpl* (en meteorología)

precise [prɪ'saɪs] *adj* : preciso — **precisely** *adv* : precisamente — **precision** [prɪ'sɪʒən] *n* : precisión *f*

preclude [prɪ'kluːd] *vt* **-cluded; -cluding** **1** PREVENT : impedir **2** EXCLUDE : excluir

precocious [prɪ'koːʃəs] *adj* : precoz

preconceived [priːkən'siːv] *adj* : preconcebido

predator ['predət̬ər] *n* : depredador *m*

predecessor ['predə,sesər, 'priː-] *n* : antecesor *m*, -sora *f*; predecesor *m*, -sora *f*

predicament [prɪ'dɪkəmənt] *n* : apuro *m*

predict [prɪ'dɪkt] *vt* : pronosticar, predecir — **predictable** [prɪ'dɪktəbəl] *adj* : previsible — **prediction** [prɪ'dɪkʃən] *n* : pronóstico *m*, predicción *f*

predispose [priːdɪ'spoːz] *vt* **-posed; -posing** : predisponer

predominant [prɪ'dɑmənənt] *adj* : predominante

preeminent [prɪ'emənənt] *adj* : preeminente

preempt [prɪ'empt] *vt* : adelantarse a (un ataque, etc.)

preen ['priːn] *vt* **1** : arreglarse (las plumas) **2 ~ oneself** : acicalarse

prefabricated [priː'fæbrə,keɪt̬əd] *adj* : prefabricado

preface ['prefəs] *n* : prefacio *m*, prólogo *m*

prefer [prɪ'fər] *vt* **-ferred; -ferring** : preferir — **preferable** ['prefərəbəl] *adj* : preferible — **preference** ['prefrənts, 'prefər-] *n* : preferencia *f* — **preferential** [prefə'rentʃəl] *adj* : preferente

prefix ['priː,fɪks] *n* : prefijo *m*

pregnancy ['pregnəntsi] *n*, *pl* **-cies** : embarazo *m* — **pregnant** ['pregnənt] *adj* : embarazada

prehistoric [priːhɪ'stɔrɪk] *or* **prehistorical** [-ɪkəl] *adj* : prehistórico

prejudice ['predʒədəs] *n* **1** BIAS : prejuicio *m* **2** HARM : perjuicio *m* — **~** *vt* **-diced; -dicing** **1** BIAS : predisponer **2** HARM : perjudicar — **prejudiced** ['predʒədəst] *adj* : parcial

preliminary [prɪ'lɪmə,neri] *adj* : preliminar

prelude ['preˌluːd, 'prelˌjuːd; 'preiˌluːd, 'priː-] *n* : preludio *m*

premarital [prɪ'mærət̬əl] *adj* : prematrimonial

premature [priːmə'tʊr, -'tjʊr, -'tʃʊr] *adj* : prematuro

premeditated [prɪ'medə,teɪt̬əd] *adj* : premeditado

premier [prɪ'mɪr, -'mjɪr; 'priː,mɪər] *adj* : principal — **~** *n* PRIME MINISTER : primer ministro *m*, primera ministra *f*

premiere [prɪ'mjer, -'mɪr] *n* : estreno *m*

premise ['premɪs] *n* **1** : premisa *f* (de un argumento) **2 ~s** *npl* : recinto *m*, local *m*

premium ['priːmiəm] *n* **1** : premio *m* **2 ~ insurance ~** : prima *f* (de seguro)

preoccupied [prɪ'ɑkjə,paɪd] *adj* : preocupado

prepare [prɪ'pær] *v* **-pared; -paring** *vt* : preparar — *vi* : prepararse — **preparation** [prepə'reɪʃən] *n* **1** : preparación *f* **2 ~s** *npl* ARRANGEMENTS : preparativos *mpl* — **preparatory** [prɪ'pærə,tori] *adj* : preparatorio

prepay [priː'peɪ] *vt* **-paid; -paying** : pagar por adelantado

preposition [prepə'zɪʃən] *n* : preposición *f*

preposterous [prɪˈpɑstərəs] adj : absurdo, ridículo

prerequisite [priˈrekwəzət] n : requisito m previo

prerogative [priˈrɑgətɪv] n : prerrogativa f

prescribe [priˈskraɪb] vt **-scribed; -scribing 1** : prescribir **2** : recetar (en medicina) — **prescription** [priˈskrɪpʃən] n : receta f

presence [ˈprezənts] n : presencia f

present[1] [ˈprezənt] adj **1** CURRENT : actual **2 be ~ at** : estar presente en — **~ n 1** : presente m **2 at ~** : actualmente

present[2] [ˈprezənt] n GIFT : regalo m — **~** [priˈzent] vt **1** INTRODUCE : presentar **2** GIVE : entregar — **presentation** [priːˌzenˈteɪʃən, ˌprezən-] n **1** : presentación f **2 or ~ ceremony** : ceremonia f de entrega

presently [ˈprezəntli] adv **1** SOON : dentro de poco **2** NOW : actualmente

preserve [priˈzərv] vt **-served; -serving 1** : conservar **2** MAINTAIN : mantener — **~ n 1** JAM : confitura f **2 or game ~** : coto m de caza — **preservation** [ˌprezərˈveɪʃən] n : preservación f, conservación f — **preservative** [priˈzərvətɪv] n : conservante m

president [ˈprezədənt] n : presidente m, -ta f — **presidency** [ˈprezədəntsi] n, pl **-cies** : presidencia f — **presidential** [ˌprezəˈdentʃəl] adj : presidencial

press [ˈpres] n : prensa f — **~** vt **1** : apretar **2** IRON : planchar — **~** vi **1** : apretar **2** URGE : presionar — **pressing** [ˈpresɪŋ] adj : urgente — **pressure** [ˈpreʃər] n : presión f — **~** vt **-sured; -suring** : presionar, apremiar

prestige [preˈstiːʒ, -ˈstiːdʒ] n : prestigio m — **prestigious** [preˈstɪdʒəs] adj : prestigioso

presume [priˈzuːm] vt **-sumed; -suming** : presumir — **presumably** [priˈzuːməbli] adv : es de suponer, supuestamente — **presumption** [priˈzʌmpʃən] n : presunción f — **presumptuous** [priˈzʌmptʃʊəs] adj : presuntuoso

pretend [priˈtend] vt **1** CLAIM : pretender **2** FEIGN : fingir — vi : fingir — **pretense** or **pretence** [priˈtents, ˈpriːˌtents] n **1** CLAIM : pretensión f **2 under false ~s** : con pretextos falsos — **pretentious** [priˈtentʃəs] adj : pretencioso

pretext [ˈpriːˌtekst] n : pretexto m

pretty [ˈprɪti] adj **-tier; -est** : lindo, bonito — **~** adv FAIRLY : bastante

pretzel [ˈpretsəl] n : galleta f salada

prevail [priˈveɪl] vi **1** TRIUMPH : prevalecer **2** PREDOMINATE : predominar **3 ~ upon** : persuadir — **prevalent** [ˈprevələnt] adj : extendido

prevent [priˈvent] vt : impedir — **prevention** [priˈventʃən] n : prevención f — **preventive** [priˈventɪv] adj : preventivo

preview [ˈpriːˌvjuː] n : preestreno m

previous [ˈpriːviəs] adj : previo, anterior — **previously** [ˈpriːviəsli] adv : anteriormente

prey [ˈpreɪ] n, pl **preys** : presa f — **prey on** vt **1** : alimentarse de **2 ~ on one's mind** : atormentar a algn

price [ˈpraɪs] n : precio m — **~** vt **priced; pricing** : poner un precio a — **priceless** [ˈpraɪsləs] adj : inestimable

prick [ˈprɪk] n : pinchazo m — **~** vt **1** : pinchar **2 ~ up one's ears** : levantar las orejas — **prickly** [ˈprɪkəli] adj : espinoso

pride [ˈpraɪd] n : orgullo m — **~** vt **prided; priding ~ oneself on** : enorgullecerse de

priest [ˈpriːst] n : sacerdote m — **priesthood** [ˈpriːstˌhʊd] n : sacerdocio m

prim [ˈprɪm] adj **primmer; primmest** : remilgado

primary [ˈpraɪˌmeri, ˈpraɪməri] adj **1** FIRST : primario **2** PRINCIPAL : principal — **primarily** [praɪˈmerəli] adv : principalmente

prime[1] [ˈpraɪm] adj **1** MAIN : principal, primero **2** EXCELLENT : excelente — **prime minister** n : primero ministro m, primera ministra f

prime[2] n **the ~ of one's life** : la flor de la vida — **~** vt **primed; priming 1** : cebar (un arma de fuego, etc.) **2** PREPARE : preparar

primer[1] [ˈpraɪmər] n : base f (de pintura)

primer[2] [ˈprɪmər] n READER : cartilla f

primitive [ˈprɪmətɪv] adj : primitivo

primrose [ˈprɪmˌroz] n : primavera f

prince [ˈprɪnts] n : príncipe m — **princess** [ˈprɪntsəs, -ˌses] n : princesa f

principal [ˈprɪntsəpəl] adj : principal — **~** n : director m, -tora f (de un colegio)

principle [ˈprɪntsəpəl] n : principio m

print [ˈprɪnt] n **1** MARK : huella f **2** LETTERING : letra f **3** ENGRAVING : grabado m **4** : estampado m (de tela) **5** : copia f (en fotografía) **6 out of ~** : agotado — **~** vt : imprimir (libros, etc.) — vi : escribir con letra de molde — **printer** [ˈprɪntər] n **1** : impresor m, -sora f (persona) **2** : impresora f (máquina) — **printing** [ˈprɪntɪŋ] n **1** : impresión f **2**

: imprenta *f* (profesión) **3** LETTERING : letras *fpl* de molde

prior ['praɪər] *adj* **1** : previo **2 ~ to** : antes de — **priority** [praɪ'ɔrəṭi] *n*, *pl* **-ties** : prioridad *f*

prison ['prɪzən] *n* : prisión *f*, cárcel *f* — **prisoner** ['prɪzənər] *n* **1** : preso *m*, -sa *f* **2 ~ of war** : prisionero *m*, -ra *f* de guerra

privacy ['praɪvəsi] *n*, *pl* **-cies** : intimidad *f* — **private** ['praɪvət] *adj* **1** : privado **2** SECRET : secreto — *~ n* : soldado *m* raso — **privately** ['praɪvətli] *adv* : en privado

privilege ['prɪvlɪdʒ, 'prɪvə-] *n* : privilegio *m* — **privileged** ['prɪvlɪdʒd, 'prɪvə-] *adj* : privilegiado

prize ['praɪz] *n* : premio *m* — *~ adj* : premiado — *~ vt* **prized; prizing** : valorar, apreciar — **prizefighter** ['praɪz,faɪṭər] *n* : boxeador *m*, -dora *f* profesional — **prizewinning** ['praɪz,wɪnɪŋ] *adj* : premiado

pro ['proː] *n* **1** → **professional 2 the ~s and cons** : los pros y los contras

probability [,prɑbə'bɪləṭi] *n*, *pl* **-ties** : probabilidad *f* — **probable** ['prɑbəbəl] *adj* : probable — **probably** [-bli] *adv* : probablemente

probation [proˈbeɪʃən] *n* **1** : período *m* de prueba (de un empleado, etc.) **2** : libertad *f* condicional (de un preso)

probe ['proːb] *n* **1** : sonda *f* (en medicina, etc.) **2** INVESTIGATION : investigación *f* — *~ vt* **probed; probing 1** : sondar **2** INVESTIGATE : investigar

problem ['prɑbləm] *n* : problema *m*

procedure [prəˈsiːdʒər] *n* : procedimiento *m*

proceed [proˈsiːd] *vi* **1** ACT : proceder **2** CONTINUE : continuar **3** ADVANCE : avanzar — **proceedings** [proˈsiːdɪŋz] *npl* **1** EVENTS : actos *mpl* **2** : proceso *m* (en derecho) — **proceeds** ['proː,siːdz] *npl* : ganancias *fpl*

process ['prɑ,ses, 'proː-] *n*, *pl* **-cesses** ['prɑ,sesəz, 'proː-, -səsəz, -sə,siːz] **1** : proceso *m* **2 in the ~ of** : en vías de — *~ vt* : procesar — **procession** [prəˈseʃən] *n* : desfile *m*

proclaim [proˈkleɪm] *vt* : proclamar — **proclamation** [,prɑklə'meɪʃən] *n* : proclamación *f*

procrastinate [prəˈkræstə,neɪt] *vi* **-nated; -nating** : demorar, aplazar

procure [prəˈkjʊr] *vt* **-cured; -curing** : obtener

prod ['prɑd] *vt* **prodded; prodding** : pinchar, aguijonear

prodigal ['prɑdɪgəl] *adj* : pródigo

prodigy ['prɑdədʒi] *n*, *pl* **-gies** : prodigio *m*

produce [prəˈduːs, -ˈdjuːs] *vt* **-duced; -ducing 1** : producir **2** CAUSE : causar **3** SHOW : presentar, mostrar **4** : poner en escena (una obra de teatro) — *~* ['prɑ,duːs, 'proː-, -,djuːs] *n* : productos *mpl* agrícolas — **producer** [prəˈduːsər, -ˈdjuː-] *n* : productor *m*, -tora *f* — **product** ['prɑdʌkt] *n* : producto *m* — **productive** [prəˈdʌktɪv] *adj* : productivo

profane [proˈfeɪn] *adj* **1** : profano **2** IRREVERENT : blasfemo — **profanity** [proˈfænəṭi] *n*, *pl* **-ties** : blasfemia *f*

profess [prəˈfes] *vt* : profesar — **profession** [prəˈfeʃən] *n* : profesión *f* — **professional** [prəˈfeʃənəl] *adj* : profesional — *~ n* : profesional *mf* — **professor** [prəˈfesər] *n* : profesor *m*, -sora *f*

proficiency [prəˈfɪʃəntsi] *n* : competencia *f* — **proficient** [prəˈfɪʃənt] *adj* : competente

profile ['proː,faɪl] *n* **1** : perfil *m* **2 keep a low ~** : no llamar la atención

profit ['prɑfət] *n* **1** : beneficio *m*, ganancia *f* — *~ vi* : sacar provecho (de), beneficiarse (de) — **profitable** ['prɑfəṭəbəl] *adj* : provechoso

profound [prəˈfaʊnd] *adj* : profundo

profuse [prəˈfjuːs] *adj* : profuso — **profusion** [prəˈfjuːʒən] *n* : profusión *f*

prognosis [prɑgˈnoːsɪs] *n*, *pl* **-noses** [-,siːz] : pronóstico *m*

program ['proː,græm, -grəm] *n* : programa *m* — *~ vt* **-grammed** *or* **-gramed; -gramming** *or* **-graming** : programar

progress ['prɑgrəs, -gres] *n* **1** : progreso *m* **2** ADVANCE : avance *m* — *~* [prəˈgres] *vi* : progresar, avanzar — **progressive** [prəˈgresɪv] *adj* **1** : progresista (dícese de la política, etc.) **2** INCREASING : progresiva

prohibit [proˈhɪbət] *vt* : prohibir — **prohibition** [,proːə'bɪʃən, ,proːhə-] *n* : prohibición *f*

project ['prɑdʒekt, -dʒɪkt] *n* : proyecto *m* — *~* [prəˈdʒekt] *vt* : proyectar — *vi* PROTRUDE : sobresalir — **projectile** [prəˈdʒektəl, -taɪl] *n* : proyectil *m* — **projection** [prəˈdʒekʃən] *n* **1** : proyección *f* **2** PROTRUSION : saliente *m* — **projector** [prəˈdʒektər] *n* : proyector *m*

proliferate [proˈlɪfə,reɪt] *vi* **-ated; -ating** : proliferar — **proliferation** [prə,lɪfə'reɪʃən] *n* : proliferación *f* — **prolific** [prəˈlɪfɪk] *adj* : prolífico

prologue ['proː,lɔg] *n* : prólogo *m*

prolong [prəˈlɔŋ] *vt* : prolongar

prom ['prɑm] *n* : baile *m* formal (en un colegio)

prominent ['prɑmənənt] *adj* : prominente — **prominence** ['prɑmənənts] *n* 1 : prominencia *f* 2 IMPORTANCE : eminencia *f*

promiscuous [prə'mɪskjuəs] *adj* : promiscuo

promise ['prɑməs] *n* : promesa *f* — ~ *v* **-ised; -ising** *vt* : prometer — **promising** ['prɑməsɪŋ] *adj* : prometedor

promote [prə'moːt] *vt* **-moted; -moting** 1 : ascender (a un alumno o un empleado) 2 FURTHER : promover, fomentar 3 ADVERTISE : promocionar — **promoter** [prə'moːtər] *n* : promotor *m*, -tora *f*; empresario *m*, -ria *f* (en deportes) — **promotion** [prə'moːʃən] *n* 1 : ascenso *m* (de un alumno o un empleado) 2 ADVERTISING : publicidad *f*, propaganda *f*

prompt ['prɑmpt] *vt* 1 INCITE : provocar (una cosa), inducir (a una persona) 2 : apuntar (a un actor, etc.) — ~ *adj* 1 : rápido 2 PUNCTUAL : puntual

prone ['proːn] *adj* 1 : boca abajo, decúbito prono 2 **be** ~ **to** : ser propenso a

prong ['prɔŋ] *n* : punta *f*, diente *m*

pronoun ['proːnaʊn] *n* : pronombre *m*

pronounce [prə'naʊnts] *vt* **-nounced; -nouncing** : pronunciar — **pronouncement** [prə'naʊntsmənt] *n* : declaración *f* — **pronunciation** [prə-ˌnʌntsi'eɪʃən] *n* : pronunciación *f*

proof ['pruːf] *n* : prueba *f* — ~ *adj* ~ **against** : a prueba de — **proofread** ['pruːfˌriːd] *vt* **-read; -reading** : corregir

prop ['prɑp] *n* 1 SUPPORT : puntal *m*, apoyo *m* 2 : accesorio *m* (en teatro) — ~ *vt* **propped; propping 1** ~ **against** : apoyar contra 2 ~ **up** SUPPORT : apoyar

propaganda [ˌprɑpə'gændə, ˌproː-] *n* : propaganda *f*

propagate ['prɑpəˌgeɪt] *v* **-gated; -gating** *vt* : propagar — *vi* : propagarse

propel [prə'pel] *vt* **-pelled; -pelling** : propulsar — **propeller** [prə'pelər] *n* : hélice *f*

propensity [prə'pentsəti] *n*, *pl* **-ties** : propensión *f*

proper ['prɑpər] *adj* 1 SUITABLE : apropiado 2 REAL : verdadero 3 CORRECT : correcto 4 GENTEEL : cortés 5 ~ **name** : nombre *m* propio — **properly** ['prɑpərli] *adv* : correctamente

property ['prɑpərti] *n*, *pl* **-ties 1** : propiedad *f* 2 BUILDING : inmueble *m* 3 LAND, LOT : parcela *f*

prophet ['prɑfət] *n* : profeta *m*, profetisa *f* — **prophecy** ['prɑfəsi] *n*, *pl* **-cies** : profecía *f* — **prophesy** ['prɑfəˌsaɪ] *v* **-sied; -sying** *vt* : profetizar — *vi* : hacer profecías — **prophetic** [prə-'fetɪk] *adj* : profético

proportion [prə'porʃən] *n* 1 : proporción *f* 2 SHARE : parte *f* — **proportional** [prə'porʃənəl] *adj* : proporcional — **proportionate** [prə'porʃənət] *adj* : proporcional

proposal [prə'poːzəl] *n* : propuesta *f*

propose [prə'poːz] *v* **-posed; -posing** *vt* 1 SUGGEST : proponer 2 ~ **to do sth** : pensar hacer algo — *vi* : proponer matrimonio — **proposition** [ˌprɑpə-'zɪʃən] *n* : proposición *f*

proprietor [prə'praɪətər] *n* : propietario *m*, -ria *f*

propriety [prə'praɪəti] *n*, *pl* **-eties** : decencia *f*, decoro *m*

propulsion [prə'pʌlʃən] *n* : propulsión *f*

prose ['proːz] *n* : prosa *f*

prosecute ['prɑsɪˌkjuːt] *vt* **-cuted; -cuting** : procesar — **prosecution** [ˌprɑsɪ'kjuːʃən] *n* 1 : procesamiento *m* 2 **the** ~ : la acusación — **prosecutor** ['prɑsɪˌkjuːtər] *n* : acusador *m*, -dora *f*

prospect ['prɑspekt] *n* 1 : perspectiva *f* 2 POSSIBILITY : posibilidad *f* — **prospective** [prə'spektɪv, 'prɑspek-] *adj* : futuro, posible

prosper ['prɑspər] *vi* : prosperar — **prosperity** [prɑ'sperəti] *n* : prosperidad *f* — **prosperous** ['prɑspərəs] *adj* : próspero

prostitute ['prɑstəˌtuːt, -ˌtjuːt] *n* : prostituta *f* — **prostitution** [ˌprɑstə'tuːʃən, -ˌtjuː-] *n* : prostitución *f*

prostrate ['prɑˌstreɪt] *adj* : postrado

protagonist [proː'tægənɪst] *n* : protagonista *mf*

protect [prə'tekt] *vt* : proteger — **protection** [prə'tekʃən] *n* : protección *f* — **protective** [prə'tektɪv] *adj* : protector — **protector** [prə'tektər] *n* : protector *m*, -tora *f*

protégé ['proːtəˌʒeɪ] *n* : protegido *m*, -da *f*

protein ['proːˌtiːn] *n* : proteína *f*

protest ['proːˌtest] *n* : protesta *f* — ~ [proː'test] *vt* : protestar — *vi* ~ **against** : protestar contra — **Protestant** ['prɑtəstənt] *n* : protestante *mf* — **protester** *or* **protestor** ['proːˌtestər, proː'-] *n* : manifestante *mf*

protocol ['proːtəˌkɔl] *n* : protocolo *m*

prototype ['proːtəˌtaɪp] *n* : prototipo *m*

protract [proː'trækt] *vt* : prolongar

protrude [proː'truːd] *vi* **-truded; -truding** : sobresalir

proud ['praʊd] adj : orgulloso

prove ['pruːv] v **proved; proved** or **proven** ['pruːvən]; **proving** vt : probar — vi : resultar

proverb ['prɑˌvərb] n : proverbio m, refrán m — **proverbial** [prə'vərbiəl] adj : proverbial

provide [prə'vaɪd] v **-vided; -viding** vt : proveer — vi **~ for** SUPPORT : mantener — **provided** [prə'vaɪdəd] or **~ that** conj : con tal (de) que, siempre que — **providence** ['prɑvədənts] n : providencia f

province ['prɑvɪnts] n 1 : provincia f 2 SPHERE : campo m, competencia f — **provincial** [prə'vɪntʃəl] adj : provinciano

provision [prə'vɪʒən] n 1 : provisión f, suministro m 2 STIPULATION : condición f 3 **~s** npl : víveres mpl — **provisional** [prə'vɪʒənəl] adj : provisional — **proviso** [prə'vaɪzoː] n, pl **-sos** or **-soes** : condición f

provoke [prə'voːk] vt **-voked; -voking** : provocar — **provocation** [prɑvə'keɪʃən] n : provocación f — **provocative** [prə'vɑkətɪv] adj : provocador, provocativo

prow ['praʊ] n : proa f

prowess ['praʊəs] n 1 BRAVERY : valor m 2 SKILL : habilidad f

prowl ['praʊl] vi : merodear, rondar — vt : merodear por — **prowler** ['praʊlər] n : merodeador m, -dora f

proximity [prɑk'sɪmət̬i] n : proximidad f — **proxy** ['prɑksi] n, pl **proxies by ~** : por poder

prude ['pruːd] n : mojigato m, -ta f

prudence ['pruːdənts] n : prudencia f — **prudent** ['pruːdənt] adj : prudente

prune¹ ['pruːn] n : ciruela f pasa

prune² vt **pruned; pruning** : podar (arbustos, etc.)

pry ['praɪ] v **pried; prying** vi **~ into** : entrometerse en — vt or **~ open** : abrir (a la fuerza)

psalm ['sɑm, 'sɑlm] n : salmo m

pseudonym ['suːdəˌnɪm] n : seudónimo m

psychiatry [sə'kaɪətri, saɪ-] n : psiquiatría f — **psychiatric** [ˌsaɪki'ætrɪk] adj : psiquiátrico — **psychiatrist** [sə'kaɪətrɪst, saɪ-] n : psiquiatra mf

psychic ['saɪkɪk] adj : psíquico

psychoanalysis [ˌsaɪkoːə'næləsɪs] n, pl **-yses** : psicoanálisis m — **psychoanalyst** [ˌsaɪkoː'ænəlɪst] n : psicoanalista mf — **psychoanalyze** [ˌsaɪkoː'ænəˌlaɪz] vt **-lyzed; -lyzing** : psicoanalizar

psychology [saɪ'kɑlədʒi] n, pl **-gies** : psicología f — **psychological** [ˌsaɪkə'lɑdʒɪkəl] adj : psicológico — **psychologist** [saɪ'kɑlədʒɪst] n : psicólogo m, -ga f

psychopath ['saɪkəˌpæθ] n : psicópata mf

psychotherapy [ˌsaɪkoː'θerəpi] n, pl **-pies** : psicoterapia f

psychotic [saɪ'kɑt̬ɪk] adj : psicótico

puberty ['pjuːbərt̬i] n : pubertad f

pubic ['pjuːbɪk] adj : púbico

public ['pʌblɪk] adj : público — **~** n : público m — **publication** [ˌpʌblə'keɪʃən] n : publicación f — **publicity** [pə'blɪsət̬i] n : publicidad f — **publicize** ['pʌbləˌsaɪz] vt **-cized; -cizing** : publicitar, divulgar

publish ['pʌblɪʃ] vt : publicar — **publisher** ['pʌblɪʃər] n 1 : editor m, -tora f (persona) 2 : casa f editorial (negocio)

pucker ['pʌkər] vt : fruncir, arrugar — vi : arrugarse

pudding ['pʊdɪŋ] n : budín m, pudín m

puddle ['pʌdəl] n : charco m

pudgy ['pʌdʒi] adj **pudgier; -est** : rechoncho fam

Puerto Rican [pwert̬o'riːkən, ˌportə-] adj : puertorriqueño

puff ['pʌf] vi 1 BLOW : soplar 2 PANT : resoplar 3 **~ up** SWELL : hincharse — vt : hinchar — **~** n 1 : bocanada f (de humo) 2 : chupada f (a un cigarrillo) 3 or **cream ~** : pastelito m de crema 4 or **powder ~** : borla f — **puffy** ['pʌfi] adj **puffier; -est** : hinchado

pull ['pʊl, 'pʌl] vt 1 : tirar de 2 EXTRACT : sacar 3 TEAR : desgarrarse (un músculo, etc.) 4 **~ off** REMOVE : quitar 5 **~ oneself together** : calmarse 6 **~ up** : levantar, subir — vi 1 : tirar 2 **~ through** RECOVER : reponerse 3 **~ together** COOPERATE : reunir 4 **~ up** STOP : parar — **~** n 1 : tirón m 2 INFLUENCE : influencia f — **pulley** ['pʊli] n, pl **-leys** : polea f — **pullover** ['pʊlˌoːvər] n : suéter m

pulp ['pʌlp] n 1 : pulpa f (de frutas, etc.) 2 or **wood ~** : pasta f de papel

pulpit ['pʊlˌpɪt] n : púlpito m

pulsate ['pʌlˌseɪt] vi **-sated; -sating** : palpitar — **pulse** ['pʌls] n : pulso m

pulverize ['pʌlvəˌraɪz] vt **-ized; -izing** : pulverizar

pummel ['pʌməl] vt **-meled; -meling** : aporrear

pump¹ ['pʌmp] n : bomba f — **~** vt 1 : bombear 2 **~ up** : inflar

pump² n SHOE : zapato m de tacón

pumpernickel ['pʌmpərˌnɪkəl] n : pan m negro de centeno

pumpkin ['pʌmpkɪn, 'pʌŋkən] n : calabaza f, zapallo m Lat

pun ['pʌn] n : juego m de palabras — ~ vi punned; punning : hacer juegos de palabras

punch¹ ['pʌntʃ] vt 1 : dar un puñetazo a 2 PERFORATE : perforar (papeles, etc.), picar (un boleto) — ~ n 1 : golpe m, puñetazo m 2 or paper ~ : perforadora f

punch² n : ponche m (bebida)

punctual ['pʌŋktʃʊəl] adj : puntual — **punctuality** [,pʌŋktʃʊ'æləʈi] n : puntualidad f

punctuate ['pʌŋktʃʊeɪt] vt -ated; -ating : puntuar — **punctuation** [,pʌŋktʃʊ-'eɪʃən] n : puntuación f

puncture ['pʌŋktʃər] n : pinchazo m, ponchadura f Lat — ~ vt -tured; -turing : pinchar, ponchar Lat

pungent ['pʌndʒənt] adj : acre

punish ['pʌnɪʃ] vt : castigar — **punishment** ['pʌnɪʃmənt] n : castigo m — **punitive** ['pjuːnəʈɪv] adj : punitivo

puny ['pjuːni] adj -nier; -est : enclenque

pup ['pʌp] n : cachorro m, -rra f (de un perro); cría f (de otros animales)

pupil¹ ['pjuːpəl] n : alumno m, -na f (de colegio)

pupil² n : pupila f (del ojo)

puppet ['pʌpət] n : títere m

puppy ['pʌpi] n, pl -pies : cachorro m, -rra f

purchase ['pərtʃəs] vt -chased; -chasing : comprar — ~ n : compra f

pure ['pjʊr] adj purer; purest : puro

puree [pjʊ'reɪ, -'riː] n : puré m

purely ['pjʊrli] adv : puramente

purgatory ['pərgə,tɔri] n, pl -ries : purgatorio m — **purge** ['pərdʒ] vt purged; purging : purgar — ~ n : purga f

purify ['pjʊrə,faɪ] vt -fied; -fying : purificar — **purification** [,pjʊrəfə'keɪʃən] n : purificación f

puritanical [,pjʊrə'tænɪkəl] adj : puritano

purity ['pjʊrəʈi] n : pureza f

purple ['pərpəl] n : morado m

purport [pər'pɔrt] vt ~ to be : pretender ser

purpose ['pərpəs] n 1 : propósito m 2 RESOLUTION : determinación f 3 on ~

: a propósito — **purposeful** ['pərpəs-fəl] adj : resuelto — **purposely** ['pər-pəsli] adv : a propósito

purr ['pər] n : ronroneo m — ~ vi : ronronear

purse ['pərs] n 1 or change ~ : monedero m 2 HANDBAG : cartera f, bolso m Spain, bolsa f Lat — ~ vt pursed; pursing : fruncir

pursue [pər'suː] vt -sued; -suing 1 CHASE : perseguir 2 SEEK : buscar — **pursuer** [pər'suːər] n : perseguidor m, -dora f — **pursuit** [pər'suːt] n 1 CHASE : persecución f 2 SEARCH : búsqueda f 3 OCCUPATION : actividad f

pus ['pʌs] n : pus m

push ['pʊʃ] vt 1 SHOVE : empujar 2 PRESS : apretar 3 URGE : presionar 4 ~ around BULLY : mangonear — vi 1 : empujar 2 ~ for : presionar para — ~ n 1 SHOVE : empujón m 2 DRIVE : dinamismo m 3 EFFORT : esfuerzo m — **pushy** ['pʊʃi] adj pushier; -est : mandón, prepotente

pussy ['pʊsi] n, pl pussies : gatito m, -ta f; minino m, -na f

put ['pʊt] v put; putting vt 1 : poner 2 INSERT : meter 3 EXPRESS : decir 4 ~ one's mind to sth : proponerse hacer algo — vi ~ up with : aguantar — **put away** vt 1 STORE : guardar 2 or ~ aside : dejar a un lado — **put down** vt 1 SUPPRESS : aplastar, sofocar 2 ATTRIBUTE : atribuir — **put off** vt DEFER : aplazar, posponer — **put on** vt 1 ASSUME : adoptar 2 PRESENT : presentar (una obra de teatro, etc.) 3 WEAR : ponerse — **put out** vt INCONVENIENCE : incomodar — **put up** vt 1 BUILD : construir 2 LODGE : alojar 3 PROVIDE : poner (dinero)

putrefy ['pjuːtrə,faɪ] vi -fied; -fying : pudrirse

putty ['pʌʈi] n, pl -ties : masilla f

puzzle ['pʌzəl] v -zled; -zling : confundir, dejar perplejo — vi ~ over : tratar de descifrar — ~ n 1 : rompecabezas m 2 MYSTERY : enigma m

pylon ['paɪˌlɑn, -lən] n : pilón m

pyramid ['pɪrə,mɪd] n : pirámide f

python ['paɪθɑn, -θən] n : pitón f

Q

q ['kjuː] *n*, *pl* **q's** *or* **qs** ['kjuːz] : q *f*, decimoséptima letra del alfabeto inglés

quack¹ ['kwæk] *vi* : graznar (dícese del pato) — ~ *n* : graznido *m*

quack² *n* CHARLATAN : charlatán *m*, -tana *f*

quadruple [kwɑ'druːpəl, -'drʌ-; 'kwɑdrə-] *v* **-pled; -pling** *vt* : cuadruplicar — *vi* : cuadruplicarse

quagmire ['kwæg.maɪr, 'kwɑg-] *n* : atolladero *m*

quail ['kweɪl] *n*, *pl* **quail** *or* **quails** : codorniz *f*

quaint ['kweɪnt] *adj* **1** ODD : curioso **2** PICTURESQUE : pintoresco

quake ['kweɪk] *vi* **quaked; quaking** : temblar — ~ *n* → **earthquake**

qualify ['kwɑlə.faɪ] *v* **-fied; -fying** *vt* **1** LIMIT : matizar **2** : calificar (en gramática) **3** EQUIP : habilitar — *vi* **1** : titularse (de abogado, etc.) **2** : clasificarse (en deportes) — **qualification** [.kwɑləfə'keɪʃən] *n* **1** REQUIREMENT : requisito *m* **2** ~**s** *npl* ABILITY : capacidad *f* **3** **without** ~ : sin reservas — **qualified** ['kwɑlə.faɪd] *adj* : capacitado

quality ['kwɑləti] *n*, *pl* **-ties 1** : calidad *f* **2** PROPERTY : cualidad *f*

qualm ['kwɑm, 'kwɑlm, 'kwɔm] *n* **1** DOUBT : duda *f* **2 have no** ~**s about** : no tener ningún escrúpulo en

quandary ['kwɑndri] *n*, *pl* **-ries** : dilema *m*

quantity ['kwɑntəti] *n*, *pl* **-ties** : cantidad *f*

quarantine ['kwɔrən.tiːn] *n* : cuarentena *f* — ~ *vt* **-tined; -tining** : poner en cuarentena

quarrel ['kwɔrəl] *n* : pelea *f*, riña *f* — ~ *vi* **-reled** *or* **-relled; -reling** *or* **-relling** : pelearse, reñir — **quarrelsome** ['kwɔrəlsəm] *adj* : pendenciero

quarry¹ ['kwɔri] *n*, *pl* **quarries** PREY : presa *f*

quarry² *n*, *pl* **quarries** EXCAVATION : cantera *f*

quart ['kwɔrt] *n* : cuarto *m* de galón

quarter ['kwɔrtər] *n* **1** : cuarto *m* (en matemáticas) **2** : moneda *f* de 25 centavos **3** DISTRICT : barrio *m* **4** ~ **after three** : las tres y cuarto **5** ~**s** *npl* LODGING : alojamiento *m* — ~ *vt* **1**

: dividir en cuatro partes **2** : acuartelar (tropas) — **quarterly** ['kwɔrtərli] *adv* : cada tres meses — ~ *adj* : trimestral — ~ *n*, *pl* **-lies** : publicación *f* trimestral

quartet ['kwɔr'tɛt] *n* : cuarteto *m*

quartz ['kwɔrts] *n* : cuarzo *m*

quash ['kwɑʃ, 'kwɔʃ] *vt* **1** ANNUL : anular **2** SUPPRESS : aplastar, sofocar

quaver ['kweɪvər] *vi* : temblar

quay ['kiː, 'keɪ, 'kweɪ] *n* : muelle *m*

queasy ['kwiːzi] *adj* **-sier; -est** : mareado

queen ['kwiːn] *n* : reina *f*

queer ['kwɪr] *adj* ODD : extraño

quell ['kwɛl] *vt* SUPPRESS : sofocar, aplastar

quench ['kwɛntʃ] *vt* **1** EXTINGUISH : apagar **2** ~ **one's thirst** : quitar la sed

query ['kwɪri, 'kwɛr-] *n*, *pl* **-ries** : pregunta *f* — ~ *vt* **-ried; -rying 1** ASK : preguntar **2** QUESTION : cuestionar

quest ['kwɛst] *n* : búsqueda *f*

question ['kwɛstʃən] *n* **1** QUERY : pregunta *f* **2** ISSUE : cuestión *f* **3 be out of the** ~ : ser indiscutible **4 call into** ~ : poner en duda **5 without** ~ : sin duda — ~ *vt* **1** ASK : preguntar **2** DOUBT : cuestionar **3** INTERROGATE : interrogar — *vi* : preguntar — **questionable** ['kwɛstʃənəbəl] *adj* : discutible — **question mark** *n* : signo *m* de interrogación — **questionnaire** [.kwɛstʃə'nær] *n* : cuestionario *m*

queue ['kjuː] *n* : cola *f* — ~ *vi* **queued; queuing** *or* **queueing** : hacer cola

quibble ['kwɪbəl] *vi* **-bled; -bling** : discutir, quejarse por nimiedades

quick ['kwɪk] *adj* **1** : rápido **2** CLEVER : agudo — ~ *n* **to the** ~ : en lo vivo — ~ *adv* : rápidamente — **quicken** ['kwɪkən] *vt* : acelerar — **quickly** ['kwɪkli] *adv* : rápidamente — **quicksand** ['kwɪk.sænd] *n* : arena *f* movediza — **quick-tempered** ['kwɪk'tɛmpərd] *adj* : irascible — **quick-witted** ['kwɪk-'wɪtəd] *adj* : agudo

quiet ['kwaɪət] *n* **1** : silencio *m* **2** CALM : tranquilidad *f* — ~ *adj* **1** : silencioso **2** CALM : tranquilo **3** RESERVED : callado **4** : discreto (dícese de colores, etc.) — ~ *vt* **1** SILENCE : hacer callar **2** CALM : calmar — *vi* *or* ~ **down** : calmarse — **quietly** adv 1 : silenciosamente 2 CALMLY : tranquilamente

quilt ['kwɪlt] n : edredón m

quintet [kwɪn'tet] n : quinteto m

quip ['kwɪp] n : ocurrencia f, salida f — ~ vt **quipped; quipping** : decir bromeando

quirk ['kwərk] n : peculiaridad f

quit ['kwɪt] v **quit; quitting** vt 1 LEAVE : dejar, abandonar 2 ~ **doing** : dejar de hacer — vi 1 STOP : parar 2 RESIGN : dimitir, renunciar

quite ['kwaɪt] adv 1 COMPLETELY : completamente 2 RATHER : bastante

quits ['kwɪts] adj **call it** ~ : quedar en paz

quiver ['kwɪvər] vi : temblar

quiz ['kwɪz] n, pl **quizzes** TEST : prueba f — ~ vt **quizzed; quizzing** : interrogar

quota ['kwoʊtə] n : cuota f, cupo m

quotation [kwoʊ'teɪʃən] n 1 : cita f 2 ESTIMATE : presupuesto m — **quotation marks** npl : comillas fpl — **quote** ['kwoʊt] vt **quoted; quoting** 1 CITE : citar 2 : cotizar (en finanzas) — ~ n 1 → quotation 2 ~**s** npl → **quotation marks**

quotient ['kwoʊʃənt] n : cociente m

R

r ['ɑr] n, pl **r's** or **rs** ['ɑrz] : r f, decimoctava letra del alfabeto inglés

rabbi ['ræˌbaɪ] n : rabino m, -na f

rabbit ['ræbət] n, pl **-bit** or **-bits** : conejo m, -ja f

rabble ['ræbəl] n : chusma f, populacho m

rabies ['reɪbiːz] ns & pl : rabia f — **rabid** ['ræbəd] adj 1 : rabioso 2 FANATIC : fanático

raccoon [ræ'kuːn] n, pl **-coon** or **-coons** : mapache m

race¹ ['reɪs] n 1 : raza f 2 **human** ~ : género m humano

race² n : carrera f (competitiva) — ~ vi **raced; racing** 1 : correr (en una carrera) 2 RUSH : ir corriendo — **racehorse** ['reɪsˌhɔrs] n : caballo m de carreras — **racetrack** ['reɪsˌtræk] n : pista f (de carreras)

racial ['reɪʃəl] adj : racial — **racism** ['reɪˌsɪzəm] n : racismo m — **racist** ['reɪsɪst] n : racista mf

rack ['ræk] n 1 SHELF : estante m 2 **luggage** ~ : portaequipajes m — ~ vt 1 ~**ed with** : atormentado por 2 ~ **one's brains** : devanarse los sesos

racket¹ ['rækət] n : raqueta f (en deportes)

racket² n 1 DIN : alboroto m, bulla f 2 SWINDLE : estafa f

racy ['reɪsi] adj **racier, -est** : subido de tono, picante

radar ['reɪˌdɑr] n : radar m

radiant ['reɪdiənt] adj : radiante — **radiance** ['reɪdiəns] n : resplandor m — **radiate** ['reɪdiˌeɪt] v **-ated; -ating** vi : irradiar — vi 1 : irradiar 2 or ~ **out** : extenderse (desde un centro) — **radi-ation** [ˌreɪdi'eɪʃən] n : radiación f — **radiator** ['reɪdiˌeɪtər] n : radiador m

radical ['rædɪkəl] adj : radical — ~ n : radical mf

radii → **radius**

radio ['reɪdiˌoʊ] n, pl **-dios** : radio mf (aparato), radio f (medio) — ~ vt : transmitir por radio — **radioactive** [ˌreɪdioʊˈæktɪv] adj : radioactivo, radiactivo

radish ['rædɪʃ] n : rábano m

radius ['reɪdiəs] n, pl **radii** [-diˌaɪ] : radio m

raffle ['ræfəl] vt **-fled; -fling** : rifar — ~ n : rifa f

raft ['ræft] n : balsa f

rafter ['ræftər] n : cabrio m

rag ['ræg] n 1 : trapo m 2 ~**s** npl TATTERS : harapos mpl, andrajos mpl

rage ['reɪdʒ] n 1 : cólera f, rabia f 2 **be all the** ~ : hacer furor — ~ vi **raged; raging** 1 : estar furioso 2 : bramar (dícese del viento, etc.)

ragged ['rægəd] adj UNEVEN : irregular 2 TATTERED : andrajoso, harapiento

raid ['reɪd] n 1 : invasión f (militar) 2 : asalto m (por delincuentes), redada f (por la policía) — ~ vt 1 INVADE : invadir 2 ROB : asaltar 3 : hacer una redada en (dícese de la policía) — **raider** ['reɪdər] n ATTACKER : asaltante mf

rail¹ ['reɪl] vi ~ **at s.o.** : recriminar a algn

rail² n 1 BAR : barra f 2 HANDRAIL : pasamanos m 3 TRACK : riel m 4 **by** ~ : por ferrocarril — **railing** ['reɪlɪŋ] n 1 : baranda f (de un balcón), pasamanos m (de una escalera) 2

RAILS : reja f — **railroad** ['reɪlˌroːd] n : ferrocarril m — **railway** ['reɪlˌweɪ] → **railroad**

rain ['reɪn] n : lluvia f — ~ vi : llover —
rainbow ['reɪnˌboː] n : arco m iris —
raincoat ['reɪnˌkoːt] n : impermeable m
— **rainfall** ['reɪnˌfɔl] n : precipitación f
— **rainy** ['reɪni] adj **rainier; -est** : lluvioso

raise ['reɪz] vt **raised; raising 1** : levantar **2** COLLECT : recaudar **3** REAR : criar **4** GROW : cultivar **5** INCREASE : aumentar **6** : sacar (objeciones, etc.) — ~ n : aumento m

raisin ['reɪzən] n : pasa f

rake ['reɪk] n : rastrillo m — ~ vt
raked; raking : rastrillar

rally ['ræli] v **-lied; -lying** vi **1** : unirse, reunirse **2** RECOVER : recuperarse — vt : conseguir (apoyo), unir a (la gente) — ~ n, pl **-lies** : reunión f, mitin m

ram ['ræm] n : carnero m (animal) — ~ vt **rammed; ramming 1** CRAM : meter con fuerza **2** or ~ **into** : chocar contra

RAM ['ræm] n : RAM f

ramble ['ræmbəl] vi **-bled; -bling 1** WANDER : pasear **2** or ~ **on** : divagar — ~ n : paseo m, excursión f

ramp ['ræmp] n : rampa f

rampage ['ræmˌpeɪdʒ, ˌræm'peɪdʒ] vi **-paged; -paging** : andar arrasando todo — ~ ['ræmˌpeɪdʒ] n : frenesí m (de violencia)

rampant ['ræmpənt] adj : desenfrenado

rampart ['ræmˌpɑrt] n : muralla f

ramshackle ['ræmˌʃækəl] adj : destartalado

ran → **run**

ranch ['ræntʃ] n GRASSLAND : hacienda f — **rancher** ['ræntʃər] n : hacendado m, -da f

rancid ['rænsɪd] adj : rancio

rancor ['ræŋkər] n : rencor m

random ['rændəm] adj **1** : aleatorio **2 at** ~ : al azar

rang → **ring**

range ['reɪndʒ] n GRASSLAND : pradera f **2** STOVE : cocina f **3** VARIETY : gama f **4** SCOPE : amplitud f **5** or **mountain** ~ : cordillera f — ~ v **ranged; ranging 1** EXTEND : extenderse **2 from...to...** : variar entre...y... — **ranger** ['reɪndʒər] n or **forest** ~ : guardabosque mf

rank¹ ['ræŋk] adj **1** SMELLY : fétido **2** OUTRIGHT : completo

rank² n **1** ROW : fila f **2** : rango m (militar) **3** ~ s npl : soldados mpl rasos **4 the** ~ **and file** : las bases — ~ vt RATE : clasificar — vi : clasificarse

rankle ['ræŋkəl] vi **-kled; -kling** : causar rencor, doler

ransack ['rænˌsæk] vt **1** SEARCH : registrar **2** LOOT : saquear

ransom ['rænsəm] n : rescate m — ~ vt : rescatar

rant ['rænt] vi or ~ **and rave** : despotricar

rap¹ ['ræp] n KNOCK : golpecito m — ~ v **rapped; rapping** : golpear

rap² n or ~ **music** : rap m

rapacious [rə'peɪʃəs] adj : rapaz

rape ['reɪp] vt **raped; raping** : violar — ~ n : violación f

rapid ['ræpɪd] adj : rápido — **rapids** ['ræpɪdz] npl : rápidos mpl

rapist ['reɪpɪst] n : violador m, -dora f

rapport [ræ'por] n **have a good** ~ : entenderse bien

rapt ['ræpt] adj : absorto, embelesado

rapture ['ræptʃər] n : éxtasis m

rare ['ræer] adj **rarer; rarest 1** FINE : excepcional **2** UNCOMMON : raro **3** : poco cocido (dícese de la carne) — **rarely** ['ræerli] adv : raramente — **rarity** ['ræerəˌti] n, pl **-ties** : rareza f

rascal ['ræskəl] n : pillo m, -lla f; pícaro m, -ra f

rash¹ ['ræʃ] adj : imprudente, precipitado

rash² n : sarpullido m, erupción f

rasp ['ræsp] vt SCRAPE : raspar — ~ n : escofina f

raspberry ['ræzˌberi] n, pl **-ries** : frambuesa f

rat ['ræt] n : rata f

rate ['reɪt] n **1** PACE : velocidad f, ritmo m **2** : tipo m, tasa m (de interés, etc.) **3** PRICE : tarifa f **4 at any** ~ : de todos modos **5 birth** ~ : índice m de natalidad — ~ vt **rated; rating 1** REGARD : considerar **2** DESERVE : merecer

rather ['ræðər, 'rɑ-, 'rʌ-] adv **1** FAIRLY : bastante **2 I'd** ~... : prefiero... **3** or ~ : o mejor dicho

ratify ['ræṯəˌfaɪ] vt **-fied; -fying** : ratificar — **ratification** [ˌræṯəfə'keɪʃən] n : ratificación f

rating ['reɪṯɪŋ] n **1** : clasificación f **2** ~ s npl : índice m de audiencia

ratio ['reɪʃioː] n, pl **-tios** : proporción f

ration ['ræʃən, 'reɪʃən] n **1** : ración f **2** ~ s npl PROVISIONS : víveres mpl — ~ vt **rationed; rationing** : racionar

rational ['ræʃənəl] adj : racional — **rationale** [ˌræʃə'næl] n : lógica f, razones fpl — **rationalize** ['ræʃənəˌlaɪz] vt **-ized; -izing** : racionalizar

rattle ['ræṯəl] v **-tled; -tling** vi : traquetear — ~ vt **1** SHAKE : agitar **2** UPSET : desconcertar 3 ~ **off** : decir de corrido — ~ n 1 : traqueteo m 2 or baby's ~ : sonajero m — **rattlesnake** ['ræt_əl-,sneɪk] n : serpiente f de cascabel

raucous ['rɔkəs] adj 1 HOARSE : ronco 2 BOISTEROUS : bullicioso

ravage ['rævɪdʒ] vt -aged; -aging : estragar, asolar — **ravages** ['rævɪdʒəz] npl : estragos mpl

rave ['reɪv] vi **raved; raving** 1 : delirar 2 ~ **about** : hablar con entusiasmo sobre

raven ['reɪvən] n : cuervo m

ravenous ['rævənəs] adj 1 HUNGRY : hambriento 2 VORACIOUS : voraz

ravine [rə'viːn] n : barranco m

ravishing ['rævɪʃɪŋ] adj : encantador

raw ['rɔ] adj **rawer; rawest** 1 UNCOOKED : crudo 2 INEXPERIENCED : inexperto 3 CHAFED : en carne viva 4 : frío y húmedo (dícese del tiempo) 5 ~ **deal** : trato m injusto 6 ~ **materials** : materias fpl primas

ray ['reɪ] n : rayo m

rayon ['reɪˌɑn] n : rayón m

raze ['reɪz] vt **razed; razing** : arrasar

razor ['reɪzər] n : maquinilla f de afeitar — **razor blade** n : hoja f de afeitar

reach ['riːtʃ] vt 1 : alcanzar 2 or ~ **out** : extender 3 : llegar a (un acuerdo, un límite, etc.) 4 CONTACT : contactar — vi 1 : extenderse 2 ~ **for** : tratar de agarrar — ~ n 1 : alcance m 2 **within** ~ : al alcance

react [ri'ækt] vi : reaccionar — **reaction** [ri'ækʃən] n : reacción f — **reactionary** [ri'ækʃəˌneri] adj : reaccionario — ~ n, pl **-ries** : reaccionario m, -ria f — **reactor** [ri'æktər] n : reactor m

read ['riːd] v **read** ['rɛd]; **reading** vt 1 : leer 2 INTERPRET : interpretar 3 SAY : decir 4 INDICATE : marcar — vi 1 : leer 2 **it ~s as follows** : dice lo siguiente — **readable** ['riːdəbəl] adj : legible — **reader** ['riːdər] n : lector m, -tora f

readily ['redəli] adv 1 WILLINGLY : de buena gana 2 EASILY : fácilmente

reading ['riːdɪŋ] n : lectura f

readjust [ˌriːə'dʒʌst] vt : reajustar — vi : volverse a adaptar

ready ['redi] adj **readier; -est** 1 : listo, preparado 2 WILLING : dispuesto 3 AVAILABLE : disponible 4 **get** ~ : prepararse — ~ vt **readied; readying** : preparar

real ['riːl] adj 1 : verdadero, real 2 GENUINE : auténtico — ~ adv VERY : muy — **real estate** n : propiedad f inmobiliaria, bienes mpl raices — **realism**

['riːəˌlɪzəm] n : realismo m — **realist** ['riːəlɪst] n : realista mf — **realistic** [ˌriːə'lɪstɪk] adj : realista — **reality** [ri'æləti] n, pl **-ties** : realidad f

realize ['riːəˌlaɪz] vt **-ized; -izing** 1 : darse cuenta de 2 ACHIEVE : realizar — **realization** [ˌriːələ'zeɪʃən] n 1 : comprensión f 2 FULFILLMENT : realización f

really ['rili, 'riː-] adv : verdaderamente

realm ['relm] n 1 KINGDOM : reino m 2 SPHERE : esfera f

ream ['riːm] n : resma f (de papel)

reap ['riːp] v : cosechar

reappear [ˌriːə'pɪr] vi : reaparecer

rear[1] ['rɪr] vt 1 RAISE : levantar 2 : criar (niños, etc.) — vi or ~ **up** : encabritarse

rear[2] n 1 BACK : parte f de atrás 2 BUTTOCKS : trasero m fam — ~ adj : trasero, posterior

rearrange [ˌriːə'reɪndʒ] vt **-ranged; -ranging** : reorganizar, cambiar

reason ['riːzən] n : razón f — ~ vt THINK : pensar — vi : razonar — **reasonable** ['riːzənəbəl] adj : razonable — **reasoning** ['riːzənɪŋ] n : razonamiento m

reassure [ˌriːə'ʃʊr] vt **-sured; -suring** : tranquilizar — **reassurance** [ˌriːə-'ʃʊrənts] n : (palabras fpl de) consuelo m

rebate ['riːbeɪt] n : reembolso m

rebel ['rebəl] n : rebelde mf — ~ [rɪ'bɛl] vi **-belled; -belling** : rebelarse — **rebellion** [rɪ'beljən] n : rebelión f — **rebellious** [rɪ'beljəs] adj : rebelde

rebirth [ˌriː'bərθ] n : renacimiento m

rebound [ˌriː'baʊnd, 'riːˌbaʊnd] vi : rebotar — ~ ['riːˌbaʊnd] n : rebote m

rebuff [rɪ'bʌf] vt : rechazar — ~ n : desaire m

rebuild [ˌriː'bɪld] vt **-built; -building** : reconstruir

rebuke [rɪ'bjuːk] vt **-buked; -buking** : reprender — ~ n : reprimenda f

rebut [rɪ'bʌt] vt **-butted; -butting** : rebatir — **rebuttal** [rɪ'bʌtəl] n : refutación f

recall [rɪ'kɔl] vt 1 : llamar (al servicio, etc.) 2 REMEMBER : recordar 3 REVOKE : revocar — ~ [rɪ'kɔl, 'riːˌkɔl] n 1 : retirada f 2 MEMORY : memoria f

recant [rɪ'kænt] vi : retractarse

recapitulate [ˌriːkə'pɪtʃəˌleɪt] v **-lated; -lating** : recapitular

recapture [ˌriː'kæptʃər] vt **-tured; -turing** 1 : recobrar 2 RELIVE : revivir

recede [ri'siːd] vi **-ceded; -ceding** : retirarse

receipt [rɪˈsiːt] n 1 : recibo m 2 ~s npl : ingresos mpl

receive [rɪˈsiːv] vt -ceived; -ceiving : recibir — **receiver** [rɪˈsiːvər] n 1 : receptor m (de radio, etc.) 2 or **telephone** ~ : auricular m

recent [ˈriːsənt] adj : reciente — **recently** [-li] adv : recientemente

receptacle [rɪˈsɛptɪkəl] n : receptáculo m, recipiente m

reception [rɪˈsɛpʃən] n : recepción f — **receptionist** [rɪˈsɛpʃənɪst] n : recepcionista mf — **receptive** [rɪˈsɛptɪv] adj : receptivo

recess [ˈriːˌsɛs, rɪˈsɛs] n 1 ALCOVE : hueco m 2 : recreo m (escolar) 3 ADJOURNMENT : suspensión f de actividades Spain, receso m Lat — **recession** [rɪˈsɛʃən] n : recesión f

recharge [ˌriːˈtʃɑrdʒ] vt -charged; -charging : recargar — **rechargeable** [ˌriːˈtʃɑrdʒəbəl] adj : recargable

recipe [ˈrɛsəpi] n : receta f

recipient [rɪˈsɪpiənt] n : recipiente mf

reciprocal [rɪˈsɪprəkəl] adj : recíproco

recite [rɪˈsaɪt] vt -cited; -citing 1 : recitar (un poema, etc.) 2 LIST : enumerar — **recital** [rɪˈsaɪtəl] n : recital m

reckless [ˈrɛkləs] adj : imprudente — **recklessness** [ˈrɛkləsnəs] n : imprudencia f

reckon [ˈrɛkən] vt 1 COMPUTE : calcular 2 CONSIDER : considerar — **reckoning** [ˈrɛkənɪŋ] n : cálculos mpl

reclaim [rɪˈkleɪm] vt 1 : reclamar 2 RECOVER : recuperar

recline [rɪˈklaɪn] vi -clined; -clining : reclinarse — **reclining** adj : reclinable (dícese de un asiento, etc.)

recluse [ˈrɛˌkluːs, rɪˈkluːs] n : solitario m, -ria f

recognition [ˌrɛkɪɡˈnɪʃən] n : reconocimiento m — **recognizable** [ˈrɛkɪɡˌnaɪzəbəl] adj : reconocible — **recognize** [ˈrɛkɪɡˌnaɪz] vt -nized; -nizing : reconocer

recoil [rɪˈkɔɪl] vi : retroceder — ~ [ˈriːˌkɔɪl, rɪˈ-] n : culatazo m (de un arma de fuego)

recollect [ˌrɛkəˈlɛkt] v : recordar — **recollection** [ˌrɛkəˈlɛkʃən] n : recuerdo m

recommend [ˌrɛkəˈmɛnd] vt : recomendar — **recommendation** [ˌrɛkəmənˈdeɪʃən] n : recomendación f

reconcile [ˈrɛkənˌsaɪl] v -ciled; -ciling 1 : reconciliar (personas), conciliar (datos, etc.) 2 ~ oneself to : resignarse a — vi MAKE UP : reconciliarse — **reconciliation** [ˌrɛkənˌsɪliˈeɪʃən] n : reconciliación f

reconnaissance [rɪˈkɑnəzənts, -sənts] n : reconocimiento m (militar)

reconsider [ˌriːkənˈsɪdər] vt : reconsiderar

reconstruct [ˌriːkənˈstrʌkt] vt : reconstruir

record [rɪˈkɔrd] vt 1 WRITE DOWN : anotar, apuntar 2 REGISTER : registrar 3 : grabar (música, etc.) — ~ [ˈrɛkərd] n 1 DOCUMENT : documento m 2 REGISTER : registro m 3 HISTORY : historial m 4 : disco m (de música, etc.) 5 criminal ~ : antecedentes mpl penales 6 world ~ : récord m mundial — **recorder** [rɪˈkɔrdər] n 1 : flauta f dulce 2 or tape ~ : grabadora f — **recording** [-ɪŋ] n : disco m — **record player** n : tocadiscos m

recount¹ [rɪˈkaʊnt] vt NARRATE : narrar, relatar

recount² [ˈriːˌkaʊnt, riˈ-] vt : volver a contar (votos, etc.) — ~ n : recuento m

recourse [ˈriːˌkors, rɪˈ-] n 1 : recurso m 2 have ~ to : recurrir a

recover [rɪˈkʌvər] vt : recobrar — vi RECUPERATE : recuperarse — **recovery** [rɪˈkʌvəri] n, pl -eries : recuperación f

recreation [ˌrɛkriˈeɪʃən] n : recreo m — **recreational** [ˌrɛkriˈeɪʃənəl] adj : de recreo

recruit [rɪˈkruːt] vt : reclutar — ~ n : recluta mf — **recruitment** [rɪˈkruːtmənt] n : reclutamiento m

rectangle [ˈrɛkˌtæŋɡəl] n : rectángulo m — **rectangular** [rɛkˈtæŋɡjələr] adj : rectangular

rectify [ˈrɛktəˌfaɪ] vt -fied; -fying : rectificar

rector [ˈrɛktər] n 1 : párroco m (clérigo) 2 : rector m, -tora f (de una universidad) — **rectory** [ˈrɛktəri] n, pl -ries : rectoría f

rectum [ˈrɛktəm] n, pl -tums or -ta [-tə] : recto m

recuperate [rɪˈkuːpəˌreɪt, -ˈkjuː-] v -ated; -ating vt : recuperar — vi : recuperarse — **recuperation** [rɪˌkuːpəˈreɪʃən, -ˌkjuː-] n : recuperación f

recur [rɪˈkər] vi -curred; -curring : repetirse — **recurrence** [rɪˈkərənts] n : repetición f — **recurrent** [rɪˈkərənt] adj : que se repite

recycle [riˈsaɪkəl] vt -cled; -cling : reciclar

red [ˈrɛd] adj : rojo — ~ n : rojo m — **redden** [ˈrɛdən] vt : enrojecer — vi : enrojecerse — **reddish** [ˈrɛdɪʃ] adj : rojizo

redecorate [riˈdɛkəˌreɪt] vt -rated; -rating : pintar de nuevo

redeem [rɪˈdiːm] vt 1 SAVE : salvar,

rescatar **2** : desempeñar (de un monte de piedad) **3** : canjear (cupones, etc.) — **redemption** [rɪ'dempʃən] *n* : redención *f*

red–handed ['rɛd'hændəd] *adv or adj* : con las manos en la masa

redhead ['rɛd,hɛd] *n* : pelirrojo *m*, -ja *f*

red–hot ['rɛd'hɑt] *adj* : al rojo vivo

redness ['rɛdnəs] *n* : rojez *f*

redo [ri'du:] *vt* **-did** [-dɪd]; **-done** ['-dʌn]; **-doing** : hacer de nuevo

redouble [ri'dʌbəl] *vt* **-bled; -bling** : redoblar

red tape *n* : papeleo *m*

reduce [rɪ'du:s, -'dju:s] *v* **-duced; -ducing** *vt* : reducir — *vi* SLIM : adelgazar — **reduction** [rɪ'dʌkʃən] *n* : reducción *f*

redundant [rɪ'dʌndənt] *adj* : redundante

reed ['ri:d] *n* **1** : caña *f* **2** : lengüeta *f* (de un instrumento)

reef ['ri:f] *n* : arrecife *m*

reek ['ri:k] *vi* : apestar

reel ['ri:l] *n* : carrete *m* (de hilo, etc.) — ~ *vt* **1** ~ **in** : enrollar (un sedal), sacar (un pez) del agua **2** ~ **off** : enumerar — *vi* SPIN : dar vueltas **2** STAGGER : tambalearse

reestablish [,ri:ə'stæblɪʃ] *vt* : restablecer

refer [rɪ'fər] *v* **-ferred; -ferring** *vt* **1** DIRECT : enviar, mandar **2** SUBMIT : remitir — *vi* ~ **to 1** MENTION : referirse a **2** CONSULT : consultar

referee [,rɛfə'ri:] *n* : árbitro *m*, -tra *f* — ~ *v* **-eed; -eeing** : arbitrar

reference ['rɛfrənts, 'rɛfə-] *n* **1** : referencia *f* **2** CONSULTATION : consulta *f* **3 or** ~ **book** : libro *m* de consulta **4 in** ~ **to** : con referencia a

refill [ri'fɪl] *vt* : rellenar — ~ ['ri:,fɪl] *n* : recambio *m*

refine [rɪ'faɪn] *vt* **-fined; -fining** : refinar — **refined** [rɪ'faɪnd] *adj* : refinado — **refinement** [rɪ'faɪnmənt] *n* : refinamiento *m* — **refinery** [rɪ'faɪnəri] *n*, *pl* **-eries** : refinería *f*

reflect [rɪ'flɛkt] *vt* : reflejar — *vi* **1** : reflejarse **2** ~ **badly on** : desacreditar **3** ~ **upon** : reflexionar sobre — **reflection** [rɪ'flɛkʃən] *n* **1** : reflexión *f* **2** IMAGE : reflejo *m* — **reflector** [rɪ'flɛktər] *n* : reflector *m*

reflex ['ri:,flɛks] *n* : reflejo *m*

reflexive [rɪ'flɛksɪv] *adj* : reflexivo

reform [rɪ'fɔrm] *vt* : reformar — *vi* : reformarse — ~ *n* : reforma *f* — **reformer** [rɪ'fɔrmər] *n* : reformador *m*, -dora *f*

refrain¹ [rɪ'freɪn] *vi* ~ **from** : abstenerse de

refrain² *n* : estribillo *m* (en música)

refresh [rɪ'frɛʃ] *vt* : refrescar — **refreshments** [rɪ'frɛʃmənts] *npl* : refrigerio *m*

refrigerate [rɪ'frɪdʒə,reɪt] *vt* **-ated; -ating** : refrigerar — **refrigeration** [rɪ,frɪdʒə'reɪʃən] *n* : refrigeración *f* — **refrigerator** [rɪ'frɪdʒə,reɪtər] *n* : nevera *f*, refrigerador *m* *Lat*, frigorífico *m* *Spain*

refuel [ri'fju:əl] *v* **-eled** *or* **-elled; -eling** *or* **-elling** *vt* : llenar de carburante — *vi* : repostar

refuge ['rɛ,fju:dʒ] *n* : refugio *m* — **refugee** [,rɛfju'dʒi:] *n* : refugiado *m*, -da *f*

refund [rɪ'fʌnd, 'ri:,fʌnd] *vt* : reembolsar — ~ ['ri:,fʌnd] *n* : reembolso *m*

refurbish [rɪ'fərbɪʃ] *vt* : renovar, restaurar

refuse¹ [rɪ'fju:z] *v* **-fused; -fusing** *vt* **1** : rehusar, rechazar **2** ~ **to do sth** : negarse a hacer algo — *vi* : negarse — **refusal** [rɪ'fju:zəl] *n* : negativa *f*

refuse² ['rɛ,fju:s, -,fju:z] *n* : residuos *mpl*, desperdicios *mpl*

refute [rɪ'fju:t] *vt* **-futed; -futing** : refutar

regain [ri'geɪn] *vt* : recuperar, recobrar

regal ['ri:gəl] *adj* : regio, majestuoso — **regalia** [rɪ'geɪljə] *n* : ropaje *m*, insignias *fpl*

regard [rɪ'gɑrd] *n* **1** : consideración *f* **2** ESTEEM : estima *f* **3 in this** ~ : en este sentido **4** ~**s** *npl* : saludos *mpl* **5 with** ~ **to** : respecto a — ~ *vt* **1** : mirar (con recelo, etc.) **2** HEED : tener en cuenta **3** ESTEEM : estimar **4 as** ~**s** : en lo que se refiere a **5** ~ **as** : considerar — **regarding** [rɪ'gɑrdɪŋ] *prep* : respecto a — **regardless** [rɪ'gɑrdləs] *adv* : a pesar de todo — **regardless of** *prep* **1** : sin tener en cuenta **2** IN SPITE OF : a pesar de

regent ['ri:dʒənt] *n* : regente *mf*

regime [reɪ'ʒi:m, rɪ-] *n* : régimen *m* — **regimen** ['rɛdʒəmən] *n* : régimen *m*

regiment ['rɛdʒəmənt] *n* : regimiento *m*

region ['ri:dʒən] *n* : región *f* — **regional** ['ri:dʒənəl] *adj* : regional

register ['rɛdʒəstər] *n* : registro *m* — ~ *vt* **1** : registrar (a personas), matricular (vehículos) **2** SHOW : marcar, manifestar **3** : certificar (correo) — *vi* ENROLL : inscribirse, matricularse — **registrar** ['rɛdʒə,strɑr] *n* : registrador *m*, -dora *f* oficial — **registration** [,rɛdʒə'streɪʃən] *n* **1** : inscripción *f*, matriculación *f* **2 or** ~ **number** : número *m* de matrícula — **registry** ['rɛdʒəstri] *n*, *pl* **-tries** : registro *m*

regret [rɪ'grɛt] *vt* **-gretted; -gretting** : lamentar — ~ *n* **1** REMORSE : arrepentimiento *m* **2** SORROW : pesar *m*

— **regrettable** [rɪ'grɛt̬əbəl] *adj* : lamentable

regular ['rɛgjələr] *adj* **1** : regular **2** CUSTOMARY : habitual — ~ *n* : cliente *mf* habitual — **regularity** [rɛgjə'lærət̬i] *n*, *pl* **-ties** : regularidad *f* — **regularly** ['rɛgjələrli] *adv* : regularmente — **regulate** ['rɛgjəleɪt] *vt* **-lated; -lating** : regular — **regulation** [rɛgjə'leɪʃən] *n* **1** CONTROL : regulación *f* **2** RULE : regla *f*

rehabilitate [riːhə'bɪlə̩teɪt, rɪə-] *vt* **-tated; -tating** : rehabilitar — **rehabilitation** [riːhə̩bɪlə'teɪʃən, rɪə-] *n* : rehabilitación *f*

rehearse [rɪ'hərs] *v* **-hearsed; -hearsing** : ensayar — **rehearsal** [rɪ'hərsəl] *n* : ensayo *m*

reign ['reɪn] *n* : reinado *m* — ~ *vi* : reinar

reimburse [riːəm'bərs] *vt* **-bursed; -bursing** : reembolsar — **reimbursement** [riːəm'bərsmənt] *n* : reembolso *m*

rein ['reɪn] *n* : rienda *f*

reincarnation [riːɪn̩kɑr'neɪʃən] *n* : reencarnación *f*

reindeer ['reɪn̩dɪr] *n* : reno *m*

reinforce [riːən'fɔrs] *vt* **-forced; -forcing** : reforzar — **reinforcement** [riːən'fɔrsmənt] *n* : refuerzo *m*

reinstate [riːən'steɪt] *vt* **-stated; -stating 1** : restablecer **2** : restituir (a algn en su cargo)

reiterate [riː'ɪt̬ə̩reɪt] *vt* **-ated; -ating** : reiterar

reject [rɪ'dʒɛkt] *vt* : rechazar — **rejection** [rɪ'dʒɛkʃən] *n* : rechazo *m*

rejoice [rɪ'dʒɔɪs] *vi* **-joiced; -joicing** : regocijarse

rejuvenate [rɪ'dʒuːvə̩neɪt] *vt* **-nated; -nating** : rejuvenecer

rekindle [riː'kɪndəl] *vt* **-dled; -dling** : reavivar

relapse [rɪ'læps, 'riːˌlæps] *n* : recaída *f* — ~ [rɪ'læps] *vi* **-lapsed; -lapsing** : recaer

relate [rɪ'leɪt] *v* **-lated; -lating** *vt* **1** TELL : relatar **2** ASSOCIATE : relacionar — *vi* ~ **to 1** CONCERN : estar relacionado con **2** UNDERSTAND : identificarse con **3** : relacionarse con (socialmente) — **related** [rɪ'leɪt̬əd] *adj* ~ **to** : emparentado con — **relation** [rɪ'leɪʃən] *n* **1** CONNECTION : relación *f* **2** RELATIVE : pariente *mf* **3** in ~ to : en relación con **4** ~s *npl* : relaciones *fpl* — **relationship** [rɪ'leɪʃən̩ʃɪp] *n* **1** : relación *f* **2** KINSHIP : parentesco *m* — **relative** ['rɛlət̬ɪv] *n* : pariente *mf* — ~ *adj* : relativo — **relatively** *adv* : relativamente

relax [rɪ'læks] *vt* : relajar — *vi* : relajarse — **relaxation** [riːˌlæk'seɪʃən] *n* **1** : relajación *f* **2** RECREATION : esparcimiento *m*

relay ['riːˌleɪ] *n* **1** : relevo *m* **2** *or* ~ **race** : carrera *f* de relevos — ~ ['riːˌleɪ, rɪ'leɪ] *vt* **-layed; -laying** : transmitir

release [rɪ'liːs] *vt* **-leased; -leasing 1** FREE : liberar, poner en libertad **2** : soltar (un freno, etc.) **3** EMIT : despedir **4** : sacar (un libro, etc.), estrenar (una película) — ~ *n* **1** : liberación *f* **2** : estreno *m* (de una película), publicación *f* (de un libro) **3** : fuga *f* (de gases)

relegate ['rɛlə̩geɪt] *vt* **-gated; -gating** : relegar

relent [rɪ'lɛnt] *vi* : ceder — **relentless** [rɪ'lɛntləs] *adj* : implacable

relevant ['rɛləvənt] *adj* : pertinente — **relevance** ['rɛləvənts] *n* : pertinencia *f*

reliable [rɪ'laɪəbəl] *adj* : fiable (dícese de personas), fidedigno (dícese de información, etc.) — **reliability** [rɪˌlaɪə'bɪlət̬i] *n*, *pl* **-ties** : fiabilidad *f* (de una cosa), responsabilidad *f* (de una persona) — **reliance** [rɪ'laɪənts] *n* **1** : dependencia *f* **2** TRUST : confianza *f* — **reliant** [rɪ'laɪənt] *adj* : dependiente

relic ['rɛlɪk] *n* : reliquia *f*

relief [rɪ'liːf] *n* **1** : alivio *m* **2** AID : ayuda *f* **3** : relieve *m* (en la escultura) **4** REPLACEMENT : relevo *m* — **relieve** [rɪ'liːv] *vt* **-lieved; -lieving 1** : aliviar **2** REPLACE : relevar (a algn) **3** ~ **s.o. of** : liberar a algn de

religion [rɪ'lɪdʒən] *n* : religión *f* — **religious** [rɪ'lɪdʒəs] *adj* : religioso

relinquish [rɪ'lɪŋkwɪʃ, -lɪn-] *vt* : renunciar a, abandonar

relish [rɛlɪʃ] *n* **1** : salsa *f* (condimento) **2** **with** ~ : con gusto — ~ *vt* : saborear

relocate [riːˌloʊˌkeɪt, riːloʊˈkeɪt] *vt* **-cated; -cating** : trasladar — *vi* : trasladarse — **relocation** [riːloʊ'keɪʃən] *n* : traslado *m*

reluctance [rɪ'lʌktənts] *n* : reticencia *f*, desgana *f* — **reluctant** [rɪ'lʌktənt] *adj* : reacio, reticente — **reluctantly** [rɪ'lʌktəntli] *adv* : a regañadientes

rely [rɪ'laɪ] *vi* **-lied; -lying** ~ **on 1** DEPEND ON : depender de **2** TRUST : confiar en

remain [rɪ'meɪn] *vi* **1** : quedar **2** STAY : quedarse **3** CONTINUE : seguir, continuar — **remainder** [rɪ'meɪndər] *n* : resto *m* — **remains** [rɪ'meɪnz] *npl* : restos *mpl*

remark [rɪ'mɑrk] *n* : comentario *m*, observación *f* — ~ *vt* : observar — *vi* ~

on : observar — **remarkable** [ri-'markəbəl] adj : extraordinario, notable
remedy ['remədi] n, pl **-dies** : remedio m — ~ vt **-died; -dying** : remediar — **remedial** [ri'mi:diəl] adj : correctivo
remember [ri'membər] vt 1 : acordarse de, recordar 2 ~ **to** : acordarse de — vi : acordarse, recordar — **remembrance** [ri'membrəns] n : recuerdo m
remind [ri'maind] vt : recordar — **reminder** [ri'maindər] n : recordatorio m
reminiscence [remə'nisənts] n : recuerdo m, reminiscencia f — **reminisce** [remə'nis] vi **-nisced; -niscing** : rememorar los viejos tiempos — **reminiscent** [remə'nisənt] adj **be ~ of** : recordar
remiss [ri'mis] adj : negligente, remiso
remit [ri'mit] vt **-mitted; -mitting 1** PARDON : perdonar 2 : enviar (dinero) — **remission** [ri'miʃən] n : remisión f
remnant ['remnənt] n 1 : resto m 2 TRACE : vestigio m
remorse [ri'mɔrs] n : remordimiento m — **remorseful** [ri'mɔrsfəl] adj : arrepentido
remote [ri'mo:t] adj **-moter; -est 1** : remoto 2 ALOOF : distante 3 ~ **from** : apartado de, alejado de — **remote control** n : control m remoto — **remotely** [ri'mo:tli] adv SLIGHTLY : remotamente
remove [ri'mu:v] vt **-moved; -moving 1** : quitar (una tapa, etc.), quitarse (ropa) **2** EXTRACT : sacar 3 DISMISS : destituir **4** ELIMINATE : eliminar — **removable** [ri'mu:vəbəl] adj : separable, de quita y pon — **removal** [ri'mu:vəl] n 1 : eliminación f 2 EXTRACTION : extracción f
remunerate [ri'mju:nə,reit] vt **-ated; -ating** : remunerar
render ['rendər] vt 1 : rendir (homenaje), prestar (ayuda) 2 MAKE : hacer 3 TRANSLATE : traducir
rendezvous ['rɑndɪ,vu:, -deɪ-] n & pl : cita f
rendition [ren'diʃən] n : interpretación f
renegade ['reni,geid] n : renegado m, -da f
renew [ri'nu:, -'nju:] vt 1 : renovar 2 RESUME : reanudar — **renewal** [ri'nu:əl, -'nju:-] n : renovación f
renounce [ri'naunts] vt **-nounced; -nouncing** : renunciar a
renovate ['renə,veit] vt **-vated; -vating** : renovar — **renovation** [renə'veiʃən] n : renovación f
renown [ri'naun] n : renombre m — **renowned** [ri'naund] adj : célebre, renombrado

rent ['rent] n 1 : alquiler m, arrendamiento m, renta f 2 **for ~** : se alquila — ~ v : alquilar — **rental** ['rentəl] n : alquiler m — ~ adj : de alquiler — **renter** ['rentər] n : arrendatario m, -ria f
renunciation [ri,nʌntsi'eiʃən] n : renuncia f
reopen [ri:'o:pən] vt : volver a abrir
reorganize [ri:'ɔrgə,naiz] vt **-nized; -nizing** : reorganizar — **reorganization** [ri:,ɔrgənə'zeiʃən] n : reorganización f
repair [ri'pær] vt : reparar, arreglar — n 1 : reparación f, arreglo m 2 **in bad ~** : en mal estado
repay [ri'pei] vt **-paid; -paying 1** : devolver (dinero), pagar (una deuda) 2 : corresponder a (un favor, etc.)
repeal [ri'pi:l] vt : abrogar, revocar — n : abrogación f, revocación f
repeat [ri'pi:t] vt : repetir — n : repetición f — **repeatedly** [ri'pi:tədli] adv : repetidas veces
repel [ri'pel] vt **-pelled; -pelling** : repeler — **repellent** [ri'pelənt] n : repelente m
repent [ri'pent] vi : arrepentirse — **repentance** [ri'pentəns] n : arrepentimiento m
repercussion [ri:pər'kʌʃən, repər-] n : repercusión f
repertoire ['repər,twar] n : repertorio m
repetition [repə'tiʃən] n : repetición f — **repetitious** [repə'tiʃəs] adj : repetitivo — **repetitive** [ri'petətiv] adj : repetitivo
replace [ri'pleis] vt **-placed; -placing 1** : reponer 2 SUBSTITUTE : reemplazar, sustituir 3 EXCHANGE : cambiar — **replacement** [ri'pleismənt] n 1 : sustitución f 2 : sustituto m, -ta f (persona) 3 **or ~ part** : repuesto m
replenish [ri'pleniʃ] vt 1 : reponer 2 REFILL : rellenar
replete [ri'pli:t] adj ~ **with** : repleto de
replica ['replikə] n : réplica f
reply [ri'plai] vi **-plied; -plying** : contestar, responder — ~ n, pl **-plies** : respuesta f
report [ri'port] n 1 : informe m 2 RUMOR : rumor m 3 **or ~ news** : reportaje m 4 **weather ~** : boletín m meteorológico — ~ vt 1 RELATE : anunciar 2 ~ **a crime** : denunciar un delito 2 **or ~ on** : informar sobre — vi 1 : informar 2 ~ **for duty** : presentarse — **report card** n : boletín m de calificaciones — **reportedly** [ri'portədli] adv

: según se dice — **reporter** [rɪ'portər] *n* : periodista *mf*; reportero *m*, -ra *f*

repose [rɪ'po:z] *vi* **-posed; -posing** : reposar — ~ *n* : reposo *m*

reprehensible [ˌreprɪ'hensəbəl] *adj* : reprensible

represent [ˌreprɪ'zent] *vt* **1** : representar **2** PORTRAY : presentar — **representation** [ˌreprɪzen'teɪʃən] *n* : representación *f* — **representative** [ˌreprɪ'zentətɪv] *adj* : representativo — ~ *n* : representante *mf*

repress [rɪ'pres] *vt* : reprimir — **repression** [rɪ'preʃən] *n* : represión *f*

reprieve [rɪ'pri:v] *n* : indulto *m*

reprimand ['reprə,mænd] *n* : reprimenda *f* — ~ *vt* : reprender

reprint [rɪ'prɪnt] *vt* : reimprimir — ~ ['ri:,prɪnt, rɪ'prɪnt] *n* : reedición *f*

reprisal [rɪ'praɪzəl] *n* : represalia *f*

reproach [rɪ'proːtʃ] *n* **1** : reproche *m* **2 beyond** ~ : irreprochable — ~ *vt* : reprochar — **reproachful** [rɪ'proːtʃfəl] *adj* : de reproche

reproduce [ˌri:prə'du:s, -'dju:s] *v* **-duced; -ducing** *vt* : reproducir — *vi* : reproducirse — **reproduction** [ˌri:prə'dʌkʃən] *n* : reproducción *f* — **reproductive** [ˌri:prə'dʌktɪv] *adj* : reproductor

reproof [rɪ'pru:f] *n* : reprobación *f*

reptile ['reptaɪl] *n* : reptil *m*

republic [rɪ'pʌblɪk] *n* : república *f* — **republican** [rɪ'pʌblɪkən] *n* : republicano *m*, -na *f* — ~ *adj* : republicano

repudiate [rɪ'pju:di,eɪt] *vt* **-ated; -ating** : repudiar

repugnant [rɪ'pʌgnənt] *adj* : repugnante, asqueroso — **repugnance** [rɪ'pʌgnəns] *n* : repugnancia *f*

repulse [rɪ'pʌls] *vt* **-pulsed; -pulsing** : repeler, rechazar — **repulsive** [rɪ'pʌlsɪv] *adj* : repulsivo

reputation [ˌrepjə'teɪʃən] *n* : reputación *f* — **reputable** ['repjətəbəl] *adj* : de confianza, acreditado — **reputed** [rɪ'pju:təd] *adj* : supuesto

request [rɪ'kwest] *n* : petición *f* — ~ *vt* : pedir

requiem ['rekwiəm, 'rei-] *n* : réquiem *m*

require [rɪ'kwaɪr] *vt* **-quired; -quiring 1** CALL FOR : requerir **2** NEED : necesitar — **requirement** [rɪ'kwaɪrmənt] *n* **1** NEED : necesidad *f* **2** DEMAND : requisito *m* — **requisite** ['rekwəzɪt] *adj* : necesario

resale ['ri:,seɪl, ri:'seɪl] *n* : reventa *f*

rescind [rɪ'sɪnd] *vt* : rescindir (un contrato), revocar (una ley, etc.)

rescue ['reskju:] *vt* **-cued; -cuing** : rescatar, salvar — ~ *n* : rescate *m* —

rescuer ['reskjuər] *n* : salvador *m*, -dora *f*

research [rɪ'sɑrtʃ, 'ri:,sɑrtʃ] *n* : investigación *f* — ~ *vt* : investigar — **researcher** [rɪ'sɑrtʃər, 'ri:,-] *n* : investigador *m*, -dora *f*

resemble [rɪ'zembəl] *vt* **-sembled; -sembling** : parecerse a — **resemblance** [rɪ'zembləns] *n* : parecido *m*

resent [rɪ'zent] *vt* : resentirse de, ofenderse por — **resentful** [rɪ'zentfəl] *adj* : resentido — **resentment** [rɪ'zentmənt] *n* : resentimiento *m*

reserve [rɪ'zɑrv] *vt* **-served; -serving** : reservar — ~ *n* **1** : reserva *f* **2** ~**s** *npl* : reservas *fpl* (militares) — **reservation** [ˌrezər'veɪʃən] *n* : reserva *f* — **reserved** [rɪ'zɑrvd] *adj* : reservado — **reservoir** ['rezər,vwɑr, -,vwɔr, -,vɔr] *n* : embalse *m*

reset [ˌri:'set] *vt* **-set; -setting** : volver a poner (un reloj, etc.)

residence ['rezədəns] *n* : residencia *f* — **reside** [rɪ'zaɪd] *vi* **-sided; -siding** : residir — **resident** ['rezədənt] *adj* : residente — ~ *n* : residente *mf* — **residential** [ˌrezə'dentʃəl] *adj* : residencial

residue ['rezə,du:, -,dju:] *n* : residuo *m*

resign [rɪ'zaɪn] *vt* **1** QUIT : dimitir **2** ~ **oneself to** : resignarse a — **resignation** [ˌrezɪg'neɪʃən] *n* **1** : dimisión *f* **2** ACCEPTANCE : resignación *f*

resilient [rɪ'zɪljənt] *adj* **1** : resistente (dícese de personas) **2** ELASTIC : elástico — **resilience** [rɪ'zɪljəns] *n* **1** : resistencia *f* **2** ELASTICITY : elasticidad *f*

resin ['rezən] *n* : resina *f*

resist [rɪ'zɪst] *vt* : resistir — *vi* : resistirse — **resistance** [rɪ'zɪstəns] *n* : resistencia *f* — **resistant** [rɪ'zɪstənt] *adj* : resistente

resolve [rɪ'zɑlv] *vt* **-solved; -solving** : resolver — ~ *n* : resolución *f* — **resolution** [ˌrezə'lu:ʃən] *n* **1** : resolución *f* **2** DECISION, INTENTION : propósito *m* — **resolute** ['rezə,lu:t] *adj* : resuelto

resonance ['rezənəns] *n* : resonancia *f* — **resonant** ['rezənənt] *adj* : resonante

resort [rɪ'zort] *n* **1** RECOURSE : recurso *m* **2** *or* **tourist** ~ : centro *m* turístico — *vi* ~ **to** : recurrir a

resounding [rɪ'zaʊndɪŋ] *adj* **1** RESONANT : resonante **2** ABSOLUTE : rotundo

resource ['ri:,sors, rɪ'sors] *n* : recurso *m* — **resourceful** [rɪ'sorsfəl, -'zors-] *adj* : ingenioso

respect [rɪ'spekt] *n* **1** ESTEEM : respeto *m* **2 in some** ~**s** : en algún sentido **3 pay one's** ~**s** : presentar uno sus respetos 4 with ~ to : (con) respecto a — ~ vt : respetar — **respectable** [rɪ'spɛktəbəl] adj : respetable — **respectful** [rɪ'spɛktfəl] adj : respetuoso — **respective** [rɪ'spɛktɪv] adj : respectivo — **respectively** adv : respectivamente

respiration [ˌrɛspə'reɪʃən] n : respiración f — **respiratory** ['rɛspərə,tori, rɪ'spaɪrə-] adj : respiratorio

respite ['rɛspɪt, rɪ'spaɪt] n : respiro m

response [rɪ'spɑns] n : respuesta f — **respond** [rɪ'spɑnd] vi : responder — **responsibility** [rɪˌspɑnsə'bɪləti] n, pl -ties : responsabilidad f — **responsible** [rɪ'spɑnsəbəl] adj : responsable — **responsive** [rɪ'spɑnsɪv] adj : sensible, receptivo

rest¹ ['rɛst] n 1 : descanso m 2 SUPPORT : apoyo m 3 : silencio m (en música) — ~ vi 1 : descansar 2 LEAN : apoyarse 3 — **on** DEPEND ON : depender de — vt 1 RELAX : descansar 2 LEAN : apoyar

rest² n REMAINDER : resto m

restaurant ['rɛstərənt, -rɑnt] n : restaurante m

restful ['rɛstfəl] adj : tranquilo, apacible

restitution [ˌrɛstə'tuːʃən, -'tjuː-] n : restitución f

restless ['rɛstləs] adj : inquieto, agitado

restore [rɪ'stor] vt -stored; -storing 1 RETURN : devolver 2 REESTABLISH : restablecer 3 REPAIR : restaurar — **restoration** [ˌrɛstə'reɪʃən] n 1 : restablecimiento m 2 REPAIR : restauración f

restrain [rɪ'streɪn] vt 1 : contener 2 ~ **oneself** : contenerse — **restrained** [rɪ'streɪnd] adj : comedido, moderado — **restraint** [rɪ'streɪnt] n 1 : restricción f 2 SELF-CONTROL : moderación f, control m de sí mismo

restriction [rɪ'strɪkʃən] n : restricción f — **restrict** [rɪ'strɪkt] vt : restringir — **restricted** [rɪ'strɪktəd] adj : restringido — **restrictive** [rɪ'strɪktɪv] adj : restrictivo

result [rɪ'zʌlt] vi : resultar — ~ n 1 : resultado m 2 **as a** ~ **of** : como consecuencia de

resume [rɪ'zuːm] v -sumed; -suming vt : reanudar — vi : reanudarse

résumé or **resume** or **resumé** ['rɛzəˌmeɪ, ˌrɛzə'-] n : currículum m (vitae)

resumption [rɪ'zʌmpʃən] n : reanudación f

resurgence [rɪ'sərdʒəns] n : resurgimiento m

resurrection [ˌrɛzə'rɛkʃən] n : resurrección f — **resurrect** [ˌrɛzə'rɛkt] vt : resucitar

resuscitate [rɪ'sʌsəˌteɪt] vt -tated; -tating : resucitar

retail ['riːˌteɪl] vt : vender al por menor — ~ n : venta f al por menor — ~ adj : detallista, minorista — adv : al detalle, al por menor — **retailer** ['riːˌteɪlər] n : detallista mf, minorista mf

retain [rɪ'teɪn] vt : retener

retaliate [rɪ'tæliˌeɪt] vi -ated; -ating : tomar represalias — **retaliation** [rɪˌtæli-'eɪʃən] n : represalias fpl

retard [rɪ'tɑrd] vt : retardar, retrasar — **retarded** [rɪ'tɑrdəd] adj : retrasado

retention [rɪ'tɛnʃən] n : retención f

reticence ['rɛt̬əsəns] n : reticencia f — **reticent** ['rɛt̬əsənt] adj : reticente

retina ['rɛt̬ənə] n, pl -nas or -nae [-əni, -ənaɪ] : retina f

retinue ['rɛt̬ənˌuː, -ˌjuː] n : séquito m

retire [rɪ'taɪr] vi -tired; -tiring 1 WITHDRAW : retirarse 2 : jubilarse, retirarse (de un trabajo) 3 : acostarse (en la cama) — **retirement** [rɪ'taɪrmənt] n : jubilación f — **retiring** [rɪ'taɪrɪŋ] adj SHY : retraído

retort [rɪ'tɔrt] vt : replicar — ~ n : réplica f

retrace [ˌriː'treɪs] vt -traced; -tracing ~ **one's steps** : volver sobre sus pasos

retract [rɪ'trækt] vt 1 WITHDRAW : retirar 2 : retraer (garras, etc.) — vi : retractarse

retrain [ˌriː'treɪn] vt : reciclar

retreat [rɪ'triːt] n 1 : retirada f 2 REFUGE : refugio m — vi : retirarse

retribution [ˌrɛtrə'bjuːʃən] n : castigo m

retrieve [rɪ'triːv] vt -trieved; -trieving 1 : cobrar, recuperar 2 RESCUE : salvar — **retrieval** [rɪ'triːvəl] n : recuperación f — **retriever** [rɪ'triːvər] n : perro m cobrador

retroactive [ˌrɛtro'æktɪv] adj : retroactivo

retrospect ['rɛtrəˌspɛkt] n in ~ : mirando hacia atrás — **retrospective** [ˌrɛtrə-'spɛktɪv] adj : retrospectivo

return [rɪ'tərn] vi 1 : volver, regresar 2 REAPPEAR : reaparecer — vt 1 : devolver 2 YIELD : producir — ~ n 1 : regreso m, vuelta f 2 : devolución f 3 YIELD : rendimiento m 4 **in** ~ **for** : a cambio de 5 **or tax** ~ : declaración f de impuestos — ~ adj : de vuelta

reunite [ˌriːjʊ'naɪt] vt -nited; -niting : reunir — **reunion** [riː'juːnjən] n : reunión f

revamp [riː'væmp] vt : renovar

reveal [rɪ'viːl] vt 1 : revelar 2 SHOW : dejar ver

revel ['revəl] *vi* **-eled** *or* **-elled; -eling** *or* **-elling** ~ **in** : deleitarse en

revelation [ˌrevəˈleɪʃən] *n* : revelación *f*

revelry ['revəlri] *n, pl* **-ries** : jolgorio *m*, regocijos *mpl*

revenge [rɪˈvɛndʒ] *vt* **-venged; -venging** : vengar — ~ *n* 1 : venganza *f* 2 **take** ~ **on** : vengarse de

revenue ['revəˌnuː, -ˌnjuː] *n* : ingresos *mpl*

reverberate [rɪˈvərbəˌreɪt] *vi* **-ated; -ating** : retumbar, resonar

reverence ['revərənts] *n* : reverencia *f*, veneración *f* — **revere** [rɪˈvɪr] *vt* **-vered; -vering** : venerar — **reverend** ['revərənd] *adj* : reverendo — **reverent** ['revərənt] *adj* : reverente

reverie ['revəri] *n, pl* **-eries** : ensueño *m*

reverse [rɪˈvərs] *adj* : inverso, contrario — ~ *v* **-versed; -versing** *vt* 1 : invertir 2 : cambiar (una política), revocar (una decisión) 3 : dar marcha atrás a (un automóvil) — *vi* : invertirse — ~ *n* 1 BACK : dorso *m*, revés *m* 2 *or* ~ **gear** : marcha *f* atrás 3 **the** ~ : lo contrario — **reversible** [rɪˈvərsəbəl] *adj* : reversible — **reversal** [rɪˈvərsəl] *n* 1 : inversión *f* 2 CHANGE : cambio *m* total 3 SETBACK : revés *m* — **revert** [rɪˈvərt] *vi* : revertir

review [rɪˈvjuː] *n* 1 : revisión *f* 2 OVERVIEW : resumen *m* 3 CRITIQUE : reseña *f*, crítica *f* 4 : repaso *m* (para un examen) — ~ *vt* 1 EXAMINE : examinar 2 : repasar (una lección) 3 CRITIQUE : reseñar — **reviewer** [rɪˈvjuːər] *n* : crítico *m*, -ca *f*

revile [rɪˈvaɪl] *vt* **-viled; -viling** : injuriar

revise [rɪˈvaɪz] *vt* **-vised; -vising** 1 : modificar (una política, etc.) 2 : revisar, corregir (una publicación) — **revision** [rɪˈvɪʒən] *n* : corrección *f*, modificación *f*

revive [rɪˈvaɪv] *v* **-vived; -viving** *vt* 1 : reanimar, reactivar 2 : resucitar (a una persona) 3 RESTORE : restablecer — *vi* 1 : reanimarse, reactivarse 2 COME TO : volver en sí — **revival** [rɪˈvaɪvəl] *n* : reanimación *f*, reactivación *f*

revoke [rɪˈvoːk] *vt* **-voked; -voking** : revocar

revolt [rɪˈvoːlt] *vi* : rebelarse, sublevarse — *vt* : dar asco a — ~ *n* : revuelta *f*, sublevación *f* — **revolting** [rɪˈvoːltɪŋ] *adj* : asqueroso

revolution [ˌrevəˈluːʃən] *n* : revolución *f* — **revolutionary** [ˌrevəˈluːʃəˌneri] *adj* : revolucionario — ~ *n, pl* **-aries** : revolucionario *m*, -ria *f* — **revolutionize** [ˌrevəˈluːʃəˌnaɪz] *vt* **-ized; -izing** : revolucionar

revolve [rɪˈvɑlv] *v* **-volved; -volving** *vt* : hacer girar — *vi* : girar

revolver [rɪˈvɑlvər] *n* : revólver *m*

revue [rɪˈvjuː] *n* : revista *f* (teatral)

revulsion [rɪˈvʌlʃən] *n* : repugnancia *f*

reward [rɪˈword] *vt* : recompensar — ~ *n* : recompensa *f*

rewrite [riːˈraɪt] *vt* **-wrote; -written; -writing** : volver a escribir

rhetoric ['retərɪk] *n* : retórica *f* — **rhetorical** [rɪˈtorɪkəl] *adj* : retórico

rheumatism ['ruːməˌtɪzəm, 'ru-] *n* : reumatismo *m* — **rheumatic** [rʊˈmætɪk] *adj* : reumático

rhino ['raɪnoː] *n, pl* **-no** *or* **-nos** → **rhinoceros** — **rhinoceros** [raɪˈnɑsərəs] *n, pl* **-noceroses** *or* **-noceros** *or* **-noceri** [-ˌraɪ] : rinoceronte *m*

rhubarb ['ruːˌbɑrb] *n* : ruibarbo *m*

rhyme [raɪm] *n* 1 : rima *f* 2 VERSE : verso *m* (en rima) — ~ *vi* **rhymed; rhyming** : rimar

rhythm ['rɪðəm] *n* : ritmo *m* — **rhythmic** ['rɪðmɪk] *or* **rhythmical** [-mɪkəl] *adj* : rítmico

rib [rɪb] *n* : costilla *f* — ~ *vt* TEASE : tomar el pelo a

ribbon ['rɪbən] *n* : cinta *f*

rice [raɪs] *n* : arroz *m*

rich ['rɪtʃ] *adj* 1 : rico 2 ~ **foods** : comidas *fpl* pesadas — **riches** ['rɪtʃəz] *npl* : riquezas *fpl* — **richness** ['rɪtʃnəs] *n* : riqueza *f*

rickety ['rɪkəti] *adj* : desvencijado, destartalado

ricochet ['rɪkəˌʃeɪ, -ˌʃet] *n* : rebote *m* — ~ *vi* **-cheted** [-ˌʃeɪd] *or* **-chetted** [-ˌʃetəd]; **-cheting** [-ˌʃeɪŋ] *or* **-chetting** [-ˌʃetɪŋ] : rebotar

rid [rɪd] *vt* **rid; ridding** 1 : librar 2 **get** ~ **of** : deshacerse de — **riddance** ['rɪdənts] *n* **good** ~! : ¡adiós y buen viaje!

riddle[1] ['rɪdəl] *n* : acertijo *m*, adivinanza *f*

riddle[2] *vt* **-dled; -dling** 1 : acribillar 2 **riddled with** : lleno de

ride [raɪd] *v* **rode** ['roːd]; **ridden** ['rɪdən]; **riding** *vt* 1 : montar (a caballo, en bicicleta), ir (en autobús, etc.) 2 TRAVERSE : recorrer — *vi* 1 *or* ~ **horseback** : montar a caballo 2 : ir (en auto, etc.) — ~ *n* 1 : paseo *m*, vuelta *f* 2 : aparato *m* (en un parque de diversiones) — **rider** ['raɪdər] *n* 1 : jinete *mf* (a caballo) 2 CYCLIST : ciclista *mf*, motociclista *mf*

ridge [rɪdʒ] *n* : cadena *f* (de montañas)

ridiculous [rəˈdɪkjələs] *adj* : ridículo — **ridicule** ['rɪdəˌkjuːl] *n* : burlas *fpl* — ~ *vt* **-culed; -culing** : ridiculizar

rife ['raɪf] *adj* **1** : extendido **2 be** ~ **with** : estar plagado de

rifle[1] ['raɪfəl] *vi* **-fled; -fling** ~ **through** : revolver

rifle[2] *n* : rifle *m*, fusil *m*

rift ['rɪft] *n* **1** : grieta *f* **2** : ruptura *f* (entre personas)

rig[1] ['rɪg] *vt* : amañar (una elección)

rig[2] *vt* **rigged; rigging 1** : aparejar (un barco) **2** EQUIP : equipar **3** *or* ~ **out** DRESS : vestir **4** *or* ~ **up** CONSTRUCT : construir — ~ *n* **1** : aparejo *m* (de un barco) **2** *or* **oil** ~ : plataforma *f* petrolífera — **rigging** ['rɪgɪŋ, -gən] *n* : aparejo *m*

right ['raɪt] *adj* **1** JUST : bueno, justo **2** CORRECT : correcto **3** APPROPRIATE : apropiado, adecuado **4** STRAIGHT : recto **5 be** ~ : tener razón **6** → **right-hand** — ~ *n* **1** GOOD : bien *m* **2** ENTITLEMENT : derecho *m* **3 on the** ~ : a la derecha **4** *or* ~ **side** : derecha *f* — ~ *adv* **1** WELL : bien **2** PRECISELY : justo **3** DIRECTLY : directamente **4** IMMEDIATELY : inmediatamente **5** COMPLETELY : completamente **6** *or* **to the** ~ : a la derecha — ~ *vt* STRAIGHTEN : enderezar **2** ~ **a wrong** : reparar un daño — **right angle** *n* : ángulo *m* recto — **righteous** ['raɪtʃəs] *adj* : recto, honrado — **rightful** ['raɪtfəl] *adj* : legítimo — **right-hand** ['raɪthænd] *adj* : derecho — **right-handed** ['raɪthændəd] *adj* : diestro — **rightly** ['raɪtli] *adv* **1** : justamente **2** CORRECTLY : correctamente — **right-wing** ['raɪtwɪŋ] *adj* : derechista

rigid ['rɪdʒɪd] *adj* : rígido

rigor *or Brit* **rigour** ['rɪgər] *n* : rigor *m* — **rigorous** ['rɪgərəs] *adj* : riguroso

rim ['rɪm] *n* **1** EDGE : borde *m* **2** : llanta *f* (de una rueda) **3** : montura *f* (de anteojos)

rind ['raɪnd] *n* : corteza *f*

ring[1] ['rɪŋ] *v* **rang** ['ræŋ]; **rung** ['rʌŋ]; **ringing** *vi* **1** : sonar (dícese de un timbre, etc.) **2** RESOUND : resonar — *vt* **1** : tocar (un timbre, etc.) — ~ *n* **1** : toque *m* (de un timbre, etc.) **2** CALL : llamada *f* (por teléfono)

ring[2] *n* **1** : anillo *m*, sortija *f* **2** BAND, HOOP : aro *m* **3** CIRCLE : círculo *m* **4** *or* **boxing** ~ : cuadrilátero *m* **5** NETWORK : red *f* — ~ *vt* : cercar, rodear — **ringleader** ['rɪŋˌliːdər] *n* : cabecilla *mf*

ringlet ['rɪŋlət] *n* : rizo *m*, bucle *m*

rink ['rɪŋk] *n* : pista *f* (de patinaje)

rinse ['rɪns] *vt* **rinsed; rinsing** : enjuagar — ~ *n* : enjuague *m*

riot ['raɪət] *n* : disturbio *m* — ~ *vi* : causar disturbios — **rioter** ['raɪətər] *n* : alborotador *m*, -dora *f*

rip ['rɪp] *v* **ripped; ripping** *vt* **1** : rasgar, desgarrar **2** ~ **off** : arrancar — *vi* : rasgarse — ~ *n* **1** : rasgón *m*, desgarrón *m*

ripe ['raɪp] *adj* **riper; ripest 1** : maduro **2** ~ **for** : listo para — **ripen** ['raɪpən] *v* : madurar — **ripeness** ['raɪpnəs] *n* : madurez *f*

rip-off ['rɪpˌɔf] *n* : timo *m fam*

ripple ['rɪpəl] *v* **-pled; -pling** *vi* : rizarse (dícese de agua) — *vt* : rizar — ~ *n* : onda *f*, rizo *m*

rise ['raɪz] *vi* **rose** ['roʊz]; **risen** ['rɪzən]; **rising 1** GET UP : levantarse **2** : salir (dícese del sol, etc.) **3** ASCEND : subir **4** INCREASE : aumentar **5** ~ **up** REBEL : sublevarse — ~ *n* **1** ASCENT : subida *f* **2** INCREASE : aumento *m* **3** SLOPE : cuesta *f* — **riser** ['raɪzər] *n* **1 early** ~ : madrugador *m*, -dora *f* **2 late** ~ : dormilón *m*, -lona *f*

risk ['rɪsk] *n* : riesgo *m* — ~ *vt* : arriesgar — **risky** ['rɪski] *adj* **riskier; -est** : arriesgado, riesgoso *Lat*

rite ['raɪt] *n* : rito *m* — **ritual** ['rɪtʃʊəl] *adj* : ritual — ~ *n* : ritual *m*

rival ['raɪvəl] *n* : rival *mf* — ~ *adj* : rival — ~ *vt* **-valed** *or* **-valled; -valing** *or* **-valling** : rivalizar con — **rivalry** ['raɪvəlri] *n, pl* **-ries** : rivalidad *f*

river ['rɪvər] *n* : río *m*

rivet ['rɪvət] *n* : remache *m* — ~ *vt* **1** : remachar **2** FIX : fijar (los ojos, etc.) **3 be** ~**ed by** : estar fascinando con

roach ['roʊtʃ] → **cockroach**

road ['roʊd] *n* **1** : carretera *f* **2** STREET : calle *f* **3** PATH : camino *m* — **roadblock** ['roʊdˌblɑk] *n* : control *m* — **roadside** ['roʊdˌsaɪd] *n* : borde *m* de la carretera — **roadway** ['roʊdˌweɪ] *n* : carretera *f*

roam ['roʊm] *vi* : vagar — *vt* : vagar por

roar ['ror] *vi* **1** : rugir **2** ~ **with laughter** : reírse a carcajadas — *vt* : decir a gritos — ~ *n* **1** : rugido *m* (de un animal), estruendo *m* (de un avión, etc.)

roast ['roʊst] *vt* : asar (carne, etc.), tostar (café, etc.) — *vi* : asarse — ~ *n* : asado *m* — ~ *adj* : asado — **roast beef** *n* : rosbif *m*

rob ['rɑb] *v* **robbed; robbing** *vt* **1** : robar **2** ~ **of** : privar de — *vi* : robar — **robber** ['rɑbər] *n* : ladrón *m*, -drona *f* — **robbery** ['rɑbəri] *n, pl* **-beries** : robo *m*

robe ['roʊb] *n* **1** : toga *f* (de un magistrado, etc.) **2** → **bathrobe**

robin ['rɑbən] *n* : petirrojo *m*

robot ['roːbʌt, -bət] n : robot m
robust [roˈbʌst, ˈroːbʌst] adj : robusto
rock[1] ['rɑk] vt 1 : acunar (a un niño), mecer (una cuna) 2 SHAKE : sacudir — vi : mecerse — ~ n or ~ **music** : música f rock
rock[2] n 1 : roca f (sustancia) 2 BOULDER : peña f, peñasco m 3 STONE : piedra f
rocket ['rɑkət] n : cohete m
rocking chair n : mecedora f
rocky ['rɑki] adj **rockier; -est** 1 : rocoso 2 SHAKY : tambaleante
rod ['rɑd] n : varilla f 2 **fishing ~** : caña f de pescar
rode → **ride**
rodent ['roːdənt] n : roedor m
rodeo ['roːdiˌoː, roˈdeɪoː] n, pl **-deos** : rodeo m
roe ['roː] n : hueva f
rogue ['roːg] n : pícaro m, -ra f
role ['roːl] n : papel m
roll ['roːl] n 1 : rollo m (de película, etc.) 2 LIST : lista f 3 : redoble m (de un tambor) 4 SWAYING : balanceo m 5 BUN : pancito m Lat, panecillo m Spain — ~ vt 1 : hacer rodar 2 or ~ **out** : estirar (masa) 3 ~ **up** : enrollar (papel, etc.), arremangar (una manga) — vi 1 : rodar 2 SWAY : balancearse 3 ~ **around** : revolcarse 4 ~ **over** : dar la vuelta — **roller** ['roːlər] n 1 : rodillo m 2 CURLER : rulo m — **roller coaster** ['roːlərˌkoːstər] n : montaña f rusa — **roller-skate** ['roːlərˌskeɪt] vi **-skated; -skating** : patinar (sobre ruedas) — **roller skate** n : patín m de (ruedas)
Roman ['roːmən] adj : romano — **Roman Catholic** adj : católico
romance [roˈmæns, ˈroːˌmæns] n 1 : novela f romántica 2 AFFAIR : romance m
Romanian [ruˈmeɪniən, ro-] adj : rumano — ~ n : rumano m (idioma)
romantic [roˈmæntɪk] adj : romántico
romp ['rɑmp] n : retozo m — vi : retozar
roof ['ruːf, 'rʊf] n, pl **roofs** ['ruːfs, 'rʊfs; 'ruːvz, 'rʊvz] 1 : tejado m, techo m 2 ~ **of the mouth** : paladar m — **roofing** ['ruːfɪŋ, 'rʊfɪŋ] n : techumbre f — **rooftop** ['ruːfˌtɑp, 'rʊf-] n : tejado m, techo m
rook[1] ['rʊk] n : grajo m (ave)
rook[2] n : torre f (en ajedrez)
rookie ['rʊki] n : novato m, -ta f
room ['ruːm, 'rʊm] n 1 : cuarto m, habitación f 2 BEDROOM : dormitorio m 3 SPACE : espacio m 4 OPPORTUNITY : posibilidad f — **roommate** ['ruːmˌmeɪt, 'rʊm-] n : compañero m, -ra f de

cuarto — **roomy** ['ruːmi, 'rʊmi] adj **roomier; -est** : espacioso
roost ['ruːst] n : percha f — ~ vi : posarse — **rooster** ['ruːstər, 'rʊs-] n : gallo m
root[1] ['ruːt, 'rʊt] n : raíz f — ~ vt ~ **out** : extirpar
root[2] vi ~ **around in** : hurgar en
root[3] vi ~ **for** SUPPORT : alentar
rope ['roːp] n : cuerda f — ~ vt **roped; roping** 1 : atar (con cuerda) 2 ~ **off** : acordonar
rosary ['roːzəri] n, pl **-ries** : rosario m
rose[1] → **rise**
rose[2] ['roːz] n 1 : rosa f (flor), rosa m (color) — ~ adj : rosa — **rosebush** ['roːzˌbʊʃ] n : rosal m
rosemary ['roːzˌmeri] n, pl **-maries** : romero m
Rosh Hashanah [ˌrɑʃhəˈʃɑnə, ˌroːʃ-] n : el Año Nuevo judío
roster ['rɑstər] n : lista f
rostrum ['rɑstrəm] n, pl **-tra** or **-trums** [-trə] : tribuna f
rosy ['roːzi] adj **rosier; -est** 1 : sonrosado 2 PROMISING : halagüeno
rot ['rɑt] v **rotted; rotting** vi : pudrirse — vt : pudrir — ~ n : putrefacción f
rotary ['roːtəri] adj : rotativo — ~ n : rotonda f, glorieta f Spain
rotate ['roːˌteɪt] v **-tated; -tating** vi : girar — vt 1 : girar 2 ALTERNATE : alternar — **rotation** [roˈteɪʃən] n : rotación f
rote ['roːt] n **by** ~ : de memoria
rotor ['roːtər] n : rotor m
rotten ['rɑtən] adj 1 : podrido 2 BAD : malo
rouge ['ruːʒ, 'ruːdʒ] n : colorete m
rough ['rʌf] adj 1 COARSE : áspero 2 RUGGED : accidentado 3 CHOPPY : agitado 4 DIFFICULT : duro 5 FORCEFUL : brusco 6 APPROXIMATE : aproximado 7 UNREFINED : tosco 8 ~ **draft** : borrador m — ~ vt 1 ~ **up** BEAT : dar una paliza a — **roughage** ['rʌfɪdʒ] n : fibra f — **roughen** ['rʌfən] vt : poner áspero — vi : ponerse áspero — **roughly** ['rʌfli] adv 1 : bruscamente 2 ABOUT : aproximadamente — **roughness** ['rʌfnəs] n COARSENESS : aspereza f
roulette [ruˈlet] n : ruleta f
round ['raʊnd] adj : redondo — ~ adv → **around** — ~ n 1 : círculo m 2 : ronda f (de bebidas, negociaciones, etc.) 3 : asalto m (en boxeo), vuelta f (en juegos) 4 ~ **of applause** : aplauso m 5 ~ s npl : visitas fpl (de un médico), rondas fpl (de un policía, etc.) — ~ vt 1 TURN : doblar 2 ~ **off**

: redondear **3** ~ **off** *or* ~ **out** COMPLETE : rematar **4** ~ **up** GATHER : reunir (personas), rodear (ganado) — ~ *prep* → **around** — **roundabout** ['raʊndə,baʊt] *adj* : indirecto — **round–trip** ['raʊnd,trɪp] *n* : viaje *m* de ida y vuelta — **roundup** ['raʊnd,ʌp] *n* : rodeo *m* (de animales), redada *f* (de delincuentes, etc.)

rouse ['raʊz] *vt* **roused; rousing 1** AWAKEN : despertar **2** EXCITE : excitar

rout ['raʊt] *n* : derrota *f* aplastante — ~ *vt* : derrotar

route ['ru:t, 'raʊt] *n* **1** : ruta *f* **2** *or* **delivery ~** : recorrido *m*

routine [ru:'ti:n] *n* : rutina *f* — ~ *adj* : rutinario

rove ['ro:v] *v* **roved; roving** *vi* : errar, vagar — *vt* : errar por

row¹ ['ro:] *vt* **1** : llevar a remo **2** ~ **a boat** : remar — *vi* : remar

row² *n* **1** : fila *f* (de gente o asientos), hilera *f* (de casas, etc.) **2 in a ~** SUCCESSIVELY : seguido

row³ ['raʊ] *n* **1** RACKET : bulla *f* **2** QUARREL : pelea *f*

rowboat ['ro:,bo:t] *n* : bote *m* de remos

rowdy ['raʊdi] *adj* **-dier; -est** : escandaloso, alborotador — ~ *n*, *pl* **-dies** : alborotador *m*, -dora *f*

royal ['rɔɪəl] *adj* : real — **royalty** ['rɔɪəlti] *n*, *pl* **-ties 1** : realeza *f* **2 royalties** *npl* : derechos *mpl* de autor

rub ['rʌb] *v* **rubbed; rubbing** *vt* **1** : frotar **2** CHAFE : rozar **3** ~ **in** : aplicar frotando — *vi* **1** ~ **against** : rozar **2** ~ **off** : salir (al frotar) — *n* : frotamiento *m*

rubber ['rʌbər] *n* **1** : goma *f*, caucho *m* **2** ~**s** *npl* : chanclos *mpl* — **rubber band** *n* : goma *f* (elástica) — **rubber stamp** *n* : sello *m* (de goma) — **rubbery** ['rʌbəri] *adj* : gomoso

rubbish ['rʌbɪʃ] *n* **1** : basura *f* **2** NONSENSE : tonterías *fpl*

rubble ['rʌbəl] *n* : escombros *mpl*

ruby ['ru:bi] *n*, *pl* **-bies** : rubí *m*

rudder ['rʌdər] *n* : timón *m*

ruddy ['rʌdi] *adj* **-dier; -est** : rubicundo

rude ['ru:d] *adj* **ruder; rudest 1** IMPOLITE : grosero, mal educado **2** ABRUPT : brusco — **rudely** ['ru:dli] *adv* : groseramente — **rudeness** ['ru:dnəs] *n* : mala educación *f*

rudiment ['ru:dəmənt] *n* : rudimento *m* — **rudimentary** [,ru:də'mentəri] *adj* : rudimentario

rue ['ru:] *vt* **rued; ruing** : lamentar — **rueful** ['ru:fəl] *adj* : triste, arrepentido

ruffle ['rʌfəl] *vt* **-fled; -fling 1** : despeinar (pelo), erizar (plumas) **2** VEX : alterar, contrariar — ~ *n* : volante *m* (de un vestido, etc.)

rug ['rʌg] *n* : alfombra *f*, tapete *m*

rugged ['rʌgəd] *adj* **1** : escabroso (dícese del terreno), escarpado (dícese de montañas) **2** HARSH : duro **3** STURDY : fuerte

ruin ['ru:ən] *n* : ruina *f* — ~ *vt* : arruinar

rule ['ru:l] *n* **1** : regla *f* **2** CONTROL : dominio *m* **3 as a ~** : por lo general — ~ *v* **ruled; ruling** *vt* **1** GOVERN : gobernar **2** : fallar (dícese de un juez) **3** ~ **out** : descartar — *vi* : gobernar, reinar — **ruler** ['ru:lər] *n* **1** : gobernante *mf*; soberano *m*, -na *f* **2** : regla *f* (para medir) — **ruling** ['ru:lɪŋ] *n* VERDICT : fallo *m*

rum ['rʌm] *n* : ron *m*

Rumanian [ru'meɪniən] → **Romanian**

rumble ['rʌmbəl] *vi* **-bled; -bling 1** : retumbar **2** : hacer ruidos (dícese del estómago) — ~ *n* : retumbo *m*, estruendo *m*

rummage ['rʌmɪdʒ] *vi* **-maged; -maging** : hurgar

rumor ['ru:mər] *n* : rumor *m* — ~ *vt* **be ~ed** : rumorearse

rump ['rʌmp] *n* **1** : grupa *f* (de un animal) **2** ~ **steak** : filete *m* de cadera

rumpus ['rʌmpəs] *n* : lío *m*, jaleo *m fam*

run ['rʌn] *v* **ran** ['ræn]; **run; running** *vi* **1** : correr **2** FUNCTION : funcionar **3** LAST : durar **4** : desteñir (dícese de colores) **5** EXTEND : correr, extenderse **6** : presentarse (como candidato) **7** ~ **away** : huir **8** ~ **into** ENCOUNTER : tropezar con **9** ~ **into** HIT : chocar contra **10** ~ **late** : ir retrasado **11** ~ **out of** : quedarse sin **12** ~ **over** : atropellar — *vt* **1** : correr **2** OPERATE : hacer funcionar **3** : hacer correr (agua) **4** MANAGE : dirigir **5** ~ **a fever** : tener fiebre — ~ *n* **1** : carrera *f* **2** TRIP : viaje *m*, paseo *m* (en coche) **3** SERIES : serie *f* **4 in the long ~** : a la larga **5 in the short ~** : a corto plazo — **runaway** ['rʌnə,weɪ] *n* : fugitivo *m*, -va *f* — ~ *adj* : fugitivo — **rundown** ['rʌn,daʊn] *n* : resumen *m* — **run-down** ['rʌn'daʊn] *adj* **1** : destartalado **2** EXHAUSTED : agotado

rung¹ → **ring**¹

rung² ['rʌŋ] *n* : peldaño *m* (de una escalera, etc.)

runner ['rʌnər] *n* **1** : corredor *m*, -dora *f* **2** : patín *m* (de un trineo), riel *m* (de un cajón, etc.) — **runner-up** [,rʌnə'rʌp] *n*, *pl* **runners–up** : subcampeón *m*, -peona *f* — **running** ['rʌnɪŋ] *adj* **1**

FLOWING : corriente **2** CONTINUOUS : continuo **3** CONSECUTIVE : seguido

runt ['rʌnt] *n* : animal *m* más pequeño (de una camada)

runway ['rʌn,weɪ] *n* : pista *f* de aterrizaje

rupture ['rʌptʃər] *n* : ruptura *f* — ~ *v* **-tured; -turing** *vt* : romper — *vi* : reventar

rural ['rʊrəl] *adj* : rural

ruse ['ruːs, 'ruːz] *n* : ardid *m*

rush[1] ['rʌʃ] *n* : junco *m* (planta)

rush[2] *vi* : ir de prisa — *vt* **1** : apresurar, apurar **2** ATTACK : asaltar **3** : llevar rápidamente (al hospital, etc.) — ~ *n* **1** : prisa *f*, apuro *m* **2** : ráfaga *f* (de aire), torrente *m* (de agua) — ~ *adj* : ur-

gente — **rush hour** *n* : hora *f* punta

russet ['rʌsət] *n* : color *m* rojizo

Russian ['rʌʃən] *adj* : ruso — ~ *n* : ruso *m* (idioma)

rust ['rʌst] *n* : herrumbre *f*, óxido *m* — ~ *vi* : oxidarse — *vt* : oxidar

rustic ['rʌstɪk] *adj* : rústico

rustle ['rʌsəl] *v* **-tled; -tling** *vt* **1** : hacer susurrar **2** : robar (ganado) — *vi* : susurrar — ~ *n* : susurro *m*

rusty ['rʌsti] *adj* **rustier; -est** : oxidado

rut ['rʌt] *n* **1** : surco *m* **2 be in a ~** : ser esclavo de la rutina

ruthless ['ruːθləs] *adj* : despiadado, cruel

rye ['raɪ] *n* : centeno *m*

S

s ['ɛs] *n*, *pl* **s's** *or* **ss** ['ɛsəz] : s *f*, decimonovena letra del alfabeto inglés

Sabbath ['sæbəθ] *n* **1** : sábado *m* (día santo judío) **2** : domingo *m* (día santo cristiano)

sabotage ['sæbə,tɑːʒ] *n* : sabotaje *m* — ~ *vt* **-taged; -taging** : sabotear

saccharin ['sækərən] *n* : sacarina *f*

sack ['sæk] *n* : saco *m* — ~ *vt* **1** FIRE : despedir **2** PLUNDER : saquear

sacrament ['sækrəmənt] *n* : sacramento *m*

sacred ['seɪkrəd] *adj* : sagrado

sacrifice ['sækrə,faɪs] *n* : sacrificio *m* — ~ *vt* **-ficed; -ficing** : sacrificar

sacrilege ['sækrəlɪdʒ] *n* : sacrilegio — **sacrilegious** [,sækrə'lɪdʒəs, -'liː-] *adj* : sacrílego

sad ['sæd] *adj* **sadder; saddest** : triste — **sadden** ['sædən] *vt* : entristecer

saddle ['sædəl] *n* : silla *f* (de montar) — ~ *vt* **-dled; -dling 1** : ensillar (un caballo, etc.) **2** ~ **s.o. with sth** : cargar a algn con algo

sadistic [sə'dɪstɪk] *adj* : sádico

sadness ['sædnəs] *n* : tristeza *f*

safari [sə'fɑri, -'fær-] *n* : safari *m*

safe ['seɪf] *adj* **safer; safest 1** : seguro **2** UNHARMED : ileso **3** CAREFUL : prudente **4** ~ **and sound** : sano y salvo — ~ *n* : caja *f* fuerte — **safeguard** ['seɪf,ɡɑrd] *n* : salvaguarda *f* : salvaguardar — **safely** ['seɪfli] *adv* **1** : sin peligro **2** arrive ~ : llegar sin novedad — **safety** ['seɪfti] *n*, *pl* **-ties** : seguridad *f* — **safety belt** *n* : cinturón *m* de seguridad — **safety pin** *n* : imperdible *m*

saffron ['sæfrən] *n* : azafrán *m*

sag ['sæɡ] *vi* **sagged; sagging 1** : combarse **2** GIVE : aflojarse **3** FLAG : flaquear

saga ['sɑɡə, 'sæ-] *n* : saga *f*

sage[1] ['seɪdʒ] *n* : salvia *f* (planta)

sage[2] *adj* **sager; -est** : sabio — ~ *n* : sabio *m*, -bia *f*

said → **say**

sail ['seɪl] *n* **1** : vela *f* (de un barco) **2 go for a ~** : salir a navegar **3 set ~** : zarpar — *vi* : navegar — *vt* : gobernar (un barco), navegar (el mar) — **sailboat** ['seɪl,boʊt] *n* : velero *m* — **sailor** ['seɪlər] *n* : marinero *m*

saint ['seɪnt, *before a name* seɪnt *or* sənt] *n* : santo *m*, -ta *f* — **saintly** ['seɪntli] *adj* **saintlier; -est** : santo

sake ['seɪk] *n* **1 for goodness' ~!** : ¡por Dios! **2 for the ~ of** : por (el bien de)

salad ['sæləd] *n* : ensalada *f*

salamander ['sælə,mændər] *n* : salamandra *f*

salami [sə'lɑmi] *n* : salami *m*

salary ['sæləri] *n*, *pl* **-ries** : sueldo *m*

sale ['seɪl] *n* **1** : venta *f* **2 for ~** : se vende **3 on ~** : de rebaja — **salesman** ['seɪlzmən] *n*, *pl* **-men** [-mən, -,mɛn] : vendedor *m*, dependiente *m* — **saleswoman** ['seɪlz,wʊmən] *n*, *pl* **-women** [-,wɪmən] : vendedora *f*, dependienta *f*

salient ['seɪljənt] *adj* : saliente

saliva [sə'laɪvə] *n* : saliva *f*

sallow ['sæloʊ] *adj* : amarillento, cetrino

salmon ['sæmən] *ns & pl* : salmón *m*

salon [sə'lɑn, 'sæ,lɑn] *n* → **beauty salon**

saloon [sə'lu:n] n : bar m

salsa ['sɔlsə, 'sɑl-] n : salsa f mexicana, salsa f picante

salt ['sɔlt] n : sal f — ~ vt : salar — saltwater ['sɔlt,wɔtər, -,wɑ-] adj : de agua salada — salty ['sɔlti] adj saltier; -est : salado

salute [sə'lu:t] v -luted; -luting vt : saludar — vi : hacer un saludo — ~ n : saludo m

salvage ['sælvɪdʒ] n : salvamento m — ~ vt -vaged; -vaging : salvar

salvation [sæl'veɪʃən] n : salvación f

salve ['sæv, 'sɑv] n : ungüento m

same ['seɪm] adj 1 : mismo 2 be the ~ (as) : ser igual (que) 3 the ~ thing (as) : la misma cosa (que) — ~ pron 1 all the ~ : igual 2 the ~ : lo mismo — ~ adv the ~ : igual

sample ['sæmpəl] n : muestra f — ~ vt -pled; -pling : probar

sanatorium [,sænə'toriəm] n, pl -riums or -ria [-iə] : sanatorio m

sanctify ['sæŋktə,faɪ] vt -fied; -fying : santificar

sanction n ['sæŋkʃən] : sanción f — ~ vt : sancionar

sanctity ['sæŋktəti] n, pl -ties : santidad f

sanctuary ['sæŋktʃu,eri] n, pl -aries : santuario m

sand ['sænd] n : arena f — ~ vt : lijar (madera)

sandal ['sændəl] n : sandalia f

sandpaper ['sænd,peɪpər] n : papel m de lija — ~ vt : lijar

sandwich ['sænd,wɪtʃ] n : sandwich m, bocadillo m Spain — ~ vt ~ between : meter entre

sandy ['sændi] adj sandier; -est : arenoso

sane ['seɪn] adj saner; sanest 1 : cuerdo 2 SENSIBLE : sensato

sang → sing

sanitarium [,sænə'teriəm] n, pl -iums or -ia [-iə] → sanatorium

sanitary ['sænə,teri] adj 1 : sanitario 2 HYGIENIC : higiénico — sanitary napkin n : compresa f (higiénica) — sanitation [,sænə'teɪʃən] n : sanidad f

sanity ['sænəti] n : cordura f

sank → sink

Santa Claus ['sæntə,klɔz] : Papá m Noel

sap[1] ['sæp] n 1 : savia f (de una planta) 2 SUCKER : inocentón m, -tona f

sap[2] vt sapped; sapping : minar (la fuerza, etc.)

sapphire ['sæ,faɪr] n : zafiro m

sarcasm ['sɑr,kæzəm] n : sarcasmo m — sarcastic [sɑr'kæstɪk] adj : sarcástico

sardine [sɑr'di:n] n : sardina f

sash ['sæʃ] n : faja f (de un vestido), fajín m (de un uniforme)

sat → sit

satanic [sə'tænɪk, seɪ-] adj : satánico

satchel ['sætʃəl] n : cartera f

satellite ['sætə,laɪt] n : satélite m

satin ['sætən] n : raso m

satire ['sæ,taɪr] n : sátira f — satiric [sə-'tɪrɪk] or satirical [-ɪkəl] adj : satírico

satisfaction [,sætəs'fækʃən] n : satisfacción f — satisfactory [,sætəs'fæktəri] adj : satisfactorio — satisfy ['sætəs-,faɪ] v -fied; -fying vt 1 : satisfacer 2 CONVINCE : convencer — satisfying adj : satisfactorio

saturate ['sætʃə,reɪt] vt -rated; -rating 1 : saturar 2 DRENCH : empapar — saturation [,sætʃə'reɪʃən] n : saturación f

Saturday ['sætər,deɪ, -di] n : sábado m

Saturn ['sætərn] n : Saturno m

sauce ['sɔs] n : salsa f — saucepan ['sɔs,pæn] n : cacerola f — saucer ['sɔsər] n : platillo m — saucy ['sɔsi] adj saucier; -est IMPUDENT : descarado

sauna ['sɔnə, 'saʊnə] n : sauna mf

saunter ['sɔntər, 'sɑn-] vi : pasear

sausage ['sɔsɪdʒ] n : salchicha f

sauté [sɔ'teɪ, soʊ-] vt -téed or -téd; -téing : saltear, sofreír

savage ['sævɪdʒ] adj : salvaje, feroz — ~ n : salvaje mf — savagery ['sævɪdʒri, -dʒəri] n, pl -ries : ferocidad f

save ['seɪv] vt saved; saving 1 RESCUE : salvar 2 RESERVE : guardar 3 : ahorrar (dinero, tiempo, etc.) — ~ prep EXCEPT : salvo

savior ['seɪvjər] n : salvador m, -dora f

savor ['seɪvər] v : saborear — savory ['seɪvəri] adj : sabroso

saw[1] → see

saw[2] ['sɔ] n : sierra f — ~ vt sawed; sawed or sawn; sawing : serrar — sawdust ['sɔ,dʌst] n : serrín m, aserrín m

saxophone ['sæksə,foʊn] n : saxofón m

say ['seɪ] v said ['sed]; saying; says ['sez] vt 1 : decir 2 INDICATE : marcar (dícese de relojes, etc.) — vi 1 : decir 2 that is to ~ : es decir — ~ n, pl says ['seɪz] I have no ~ : no tener ni voz ni voto 2 have one's ~ : dar su opinión — saying ['seɪŋ] n : refrán m

scab ['skæb] n 1 : costra f (en una herida) 2 STRIKEBREAKER : esquirol mf

scaffold ['skæfəld, -,foʊld] n : andamio m (en construcción)

scald ['skɔld] vt : escaldar

scale¹ ['skeɪl] *n* : balanza *f* (para pesar)

scale² *n* : escama *f* (de un pez, etc.) — ~ *vt* **scaled; scaling** : escamar

scale³ *vt* **scaled; scaling 1** CLIMB : escalar **2** ~ **down** : reducir — ~ *n* : escala *f* (musical, salarial, etc.)

scallion ['skæljən] *n* : cebolleta *f*

scallop ['skɑləp, 'skæ-] *n* : vieira *f*

scalp ['skælp] *n* : cuero *m* cabelludo

scam ['skæm] *n* : estafa *f*, timo *m fam*

scamper ['skæmpər] *vi* ~ **away** : irse corriendo

scan ['skæn] *vt* **scanned; scanning 1** : escandir (versos) **2** EXAMINE : escudriñar **3** SKIM : echar un vistazo a **4** : escanear (en informática)

scandal ['skændəl] *n* **1** : escándalo *m* **2** GOSSIP : habladurías *fpl* — **scandalous** ['skændələs] *adj* : escandaloso

Scandinavian [ˌskændəˈneɪviən] *adj* : escandinavo

scant ['skænt] *adj* : escaso

scapegoat ['skeɪpˌgoʊt] *n* : chivo *m* expiatorio

scar ['skɑr] *n* : cicatriz *f* — ~ *v* **scarred; scarring 1** : dejar una cicatriz en — *vi* : cicatrizar

scarce ['skers] *adj* **scarcer; -est** : escaso — **scarcely** ['skersli] *adv* : apenas — **scarcity** ['skersəti] *n, pl* **-ties** : escasez *f*

scare ['sker] *vt* **scared; scaring 1** : asustar **2 be ~d of** : tener miedo a — ~ *n* **1** FRIGHT : susto *m* **2** ALARM : pánico *m* — **scarecrow** ['sker,kroː] *n* : espantapájaros *m*, espantajo *m*

scarf ['skɑrf] *n, pl* **scarves** ['skɑrvz] *or* **scarfs 1** : bufanda *f* **2** KERCHIEF : pañuelo *m*

scarlet ['skɑrlət] *adj* : escarlata — **scarlet fever** *n* : escarlatina *f*

scary ['skeri] *adj* **scarier; -est** : que da miedo

scathing ['skeɪðɪŋ] *adj* : mordaz

scatter ['skætər] *vt* **1** STREW : esparcir **2** DISPERSE : dispersar — *vi* : dispersarse

scavenger ['skævəndʒər] *n* : carroñero *m*, -ra *f* (animal)

scenario [səˈnæriˌoː, -ˈnɑr-] *n, pl* **-ios 1** : guión *m* (cinemático) **2 the worst-case** ~ : el peor de los casos

scene ['siːn] *n* **1** : escena *f* **2 behind the** ~**s** : entre bastidores **3 make a** ~ : armar un escándalo — **scenery** ['siːnəri] *n, pl* **-eries 1** : decorado *m* **2** LANDSCAPE : paisaje *m* — **scenic** ['siːnɪk] *adj* : pintoresco

scent ['sent] *n* **1** : aroma *m* **2** PERFUME : perfume *m* **3** TRAIL : rastro *m* — **scented** ['sentəd] *adj* : perfumado

sceptic ['skeptɪk] → **skeptic**

schedule ['ske,dʒuːl, -dʒəl, *esp Brit* 'ʃed-juːl] *n* **1** : programa *m* **2** TIMETABLE : horario *m* **3 behind** ~ : atrasado, con retraso **4 on** ~ : según lo previsto — ~ *vt* **-uled; -uling** : planear, programar

scheme ['skiːm] *n* **1** PLAN : plan *m* **2** PLOT : intriga *f* **3** DESIGN : esquema *m* — ~ *vi* **schemed; scheming** : intrigar

schism ['sɪzəm, 'skɪ-] *n* : cisma *m*

schizophrenia [ˌskɪtsəˈfriːniə, ˌskɪzə-, -friː-] *n* : esquizofrenia *f* — **schizophrenic** [ˌskɪtsəˈfrenɪk, ˌskɪzə-] *adj* : esquizofrénico

scholar ['skɑlər] *n* : erudito *m*, -ta *f* — **scholarly** ['skɑlərli] *adj* : erudito — **scholarship** ['skɑlərˌʃɪp] *n* **1** : erudición *f* **2** GRANT : beca *f*

school¹ ['skuːl] *n* : banco *m* (de peces)

school² *n* **1** : escuela *f* **2** COLLEGE : universidad *f* **3** DEPARTMENT : facultad *f* — ~ *vt* : instruir — **schoolboy** ['skuːlˌbɔɪ] *n* : colegial *m* — **schoolgirl** ['skuːlˌgərl] *n* : colegiala *f* — **schoolteacher** ['skuːlˌtiːtʃər] *n* → **teacher**

science ['saɪənts] *n* : ciencia *f* — **scientific** [ˌsaɪənˈtɪfɪk] *adj* : científico — **scientist** ['saɪəntɪst] *n* : científico *m*, -ca *f*

scissors ['sɪzərz] *npl* : tijeras *fpl*

scoff ['skɑf] *vi* ~ **at** : burlarse de, mofarse de

scold ['skoːld] *vt* : regañar

scoop ['skuːp] *n* **1** : pala *f* **2** : noticia *f* exclusiva (en periodismo) — ~ *vt* **1** : sacar (con pala) **2** ~ **out** : ahuecar **3** ~ **up** : recoger

scoot ['skuːt] *vi* : ir rápidamente — **scooter** ['skuːtər] *n* **1** : patinete *m* **2** *or* **motor** ~ : escúter *m*

scope ['skoːp] *n* **1** RANGE : alcance *m* **2** OPPORTUNITY : posibilidades *fpl*

scorch ['skɔrtʃ] *vt* : chamuscar

score ['skɔr] *n, pl* **scores 1** : tanteo *m* (en deportes) **2** RATING : puntuación *f* **3** : partitura *f* (musical) **4** *or pl* **score** TWENTY : veintena *f* **5 keep** ~ : llevar la cuenta **6 on that** ~ : en ese sentido — ~ *v* **scored; scoring** *vt* **1** : marcar, anotarse *Lat* (un tanto) **2** : sacar (una nota) — *vi* : marcar (en deportes)

scorn ['skɔrn] *n* : desdén *m* — ~ *vt* : desdeñar — **scornful** ['skɔrnfəl] *adj* : desdeñoso

scorpion ['skɔrpiən] *n* : alacrán *m*, escorpión *m*

Scot ['skɑt] *n* : escocés *m*, -cesa *f* — **Scotch** ['skɑtʃ] *adj* → **Scottish** — ~ *n or* ~ **whiskey** : whisky *m* escocés — **Scottish** ['skɑtɪʃ] *adj* : escocés

scoundrel ['skaʊndrəl] n : sinvergüenza mf

scour ['skaʊər] vt 1 SCRUB : fregar 2 SEARCH : registrar

scourge ['skərdʒ] n : azote m

scout ['skaʊt] n : explorador m, -dora f

scowl ['skaʊl] vi : fruncir el ceño — ~ n : ceño m fruncido

scram ['skræm] vi scrammed; scramming : largarse

scramble ['skræmbəl] v -bled; -bling vi 1 CLAMBER : trepar 2 ~ for : pelearse por — vt : mezclar — ~ n : rebatiña f, pelea f — **scrambled eggs** npl : huevos mpl revueltos

scrap¹ ['skræp] n 1 PIECE : pedazo m 2 or ~ metal : chatarra f 3 ~s npl : sobras — ~ vt scrapped; scrapping : desechar

scrap² n FIGHT : pelea f

scrapbook ['skræp,bʊk] n : álbum m de recortes

scrape ['skreɪp] v scraped; scraping vt 1 : rascar 2 : rasparse (la rodilla, etc.) 3 or ~ off : raspar 4 ~ together : reunir — vi 1 RUB : rozar 2 ~ by : arreglárselas — ~ n 1 : rasguño m 2 PREDICAMENT : apuro m

scratch ['skrætʃ] vt 1 CLAW : arañar 2 MARK : rayar 3 : rascarse (la cabeza, etc.) 4 ~ out : tachar — ~ n 1 : arañazo m 2 MARK : rayón m 3 start from ~ : empezar desde cero

scrawl ['skrɔl] v : garabatear — ~ n : garabato m

scrawny ['skrɔni] adj scrawnier; -est : escuálido

scream ['skriːm] vi : gritar, chillar — ~ n : grito m, chillido m

screech ['skriːtʃ] n 1 : chillido m (de personas) 2 : chirrido m (de frenos, etc.) — ~ vi 1 : chillar 2 : chirriar (dícese de los frenos, etc.)

screen ['skriːn] n 1 : pantalla f 2 PARTITION : mampara f 3 or window ~ : mosquitero m — ~ vt 1 SHIELD : proteger 2 HIDE : ocultar 3 : seleccionar (candidatos, etc.)

screw ['skruː] n : tornillo m — ~ vt 1 : atornillar 2 ~ up RUIN : fastidiar — **screwdriver** ['skruː,draɪvər] n : destornillador m

scribble ['skrɪbəl] v -bled; -bling : garabatear — ~ n : garabato m

script ['skrɪpt] n 1 HANDWRITING : escritura f 2 : guión m (de cine, etc.) — **scripture** ['skrɪptʃər] n : escritos mpl sagrados 2 the Scriptures npl : las Escrituras fpl

scroll ['skroːl] n : rollo m (de pergamino, etc.)

scrounge ['skraʊndʒ] v **scrounged; scrounging** vt : gorrear fam — vi ~ around for sth : andar buscando algo

scrub¹ ['skrʌb] n UNDERBRUSH : maleza f

scrub² vt **scrubbed; scrubbing** SCOUR : fregar — n : fregado m

scruff ['skrʌf] n by the ~ of the neck : por el pescuezo

scruple ['skruːpəl] n : escrúpulo m — **scrupulous** ['skruːpjələs] adj : escrupuloso

scrutiny ['skruːtəni] n, pl -nies : análisis m cuidadoso — **scrutinize** ['skruːtən,aɪz] vt : escudriñar

scuff ['skʌf] vt : raspar, rayar

scuffle ['skʌfəl] n : refriega f

sculpture ['skʌlptʃər] n : escultura f — **sculpt** ['skʌlpt] v : esculpir — **sculptor** ['skʌlptər] n : escultor m, -tora f

scum ['skʌm] n 1 FROTH : espuma f 2 : escoria f (dícese de personas)

scurry ['skəri] vi -ried; -rying : corretear

scuttle¹ ['skʌtəl] n : cubo m (para carbón)

scuttle² vt -tled; -tling : hundir (un barco)

scuttle³ vi SCAMPER : corretear

sea ['siː] n 1 : mar mf 2 at ~ : en el mar — ~ adj : del mar — **seafarer** ['siː,færər] n : marinero m — **seafood** ['siː,fuːd] n : mariscos mpl — **seagull** ['siː,gʌl] n : gaviota f

seal¹ ['siːl] n : foca f (animal)

seal² n 1 STAMP : sello m 2 CLOSURE : cierre m (hermético) — ~ vt : sellar

seam ['siːm] n 1 : costura f 2 VEIN : veta f

seaman ['siːmən] n, pl -men [-mən, -,men] : marinero m

seamy ['siːmi] adj seamier; -est : sórdido

seaplane ['siː,pleɪn] n : hidroavión m

seaport ['siː,pɔrt] n : puerto marítimo

search ['sərtʃ] vt : registrar — vi ~ for : buscar — ~ n 1 : registro m 2 : búsqueda f — **searchlight** ['sərtʃ,laɪt] n : reflector m

seashell ['siː,ʃɛl] n : concha f (marina) — **seashore** ['siː,ʃɔr] n : orilla f del mar — **seasick** ['siː,sɪk] adj 1 : mareado 2 be ~ : marearse — **seasickness** ['siː,sɪknəs] n : mareo m

season ['siːzən] n 1 : estación f (del año) 2 : temporada f (en deportes, etc.) — ~ vt 1 FLAVOR : sazonar 2 : secar (madera) — **seasonal** ['siːzənəl] adj

: estacional — **seasoned** adj EXPERI-
ENCED : veterano — **seasoning**
['si:zənɪŋ] n : condimento m
seat ['si:t] n 1 : asiento m 2 : fondillos
mpl (de un pantalón) 3 BUTTOCKS
: trasero m 4 CENTER : sede f — ~ vt 1
be ~ed : sentarse 2 the bus ~s 30
: el autobús tiene cabida para 30 —
seat belt n : cinturón m de seguridad
seaweed ['si:,wi:d] n : alga f marina
secede [sɪ'si:d] vi -ceded; -ceding
: separarse (de una nación, etc.)
secluded [sɪ'klu:dəd] adj : aislado —
seclusion [sɪ'klu:ʒən] n : aislamiento
m
second ['sekənd] adj : segundo — ~ or
secondly ['sekəndli] adv : en segundo
lugar — ~ n 1 : segundo m, -da f 2
MOMENT : segundo m 3 have ~s
: repetir (en una comida) — ~ vt : secundar — **secondary** ['sekən,deri] adj
: secundario — **secondhand** ['sekənd-
'hænd] adj : de segunda mano — **second-rate** ['sekənd'reɪt] adj : mediocre
secret ['si:krət] adj : secreto — ~ n
: secreto m — **secrecy** ['si:krəsi] n, pl
-**cies** : secreto m
secretary ['sekrə,teri] n, pl -**taries** 1
: secretario m, -ria f 2 : ministro m, -tra
f (del gobierno)
secretion [sɪ'kri:ʃən] n : secreción f —
secrete [sɪ'kri:t] vt -**creted; -creting**
: secretar
secretive ['si:krətɪv, sɪ'kri:tɪv] adj
: reservado — **secretly** ['si:krətli] adv
: en secreto
sect ['sekt] n : secta f
section ['sekʃən] n : sección f, parte f
sector ['sektər] n : sector m
secular ['sekjələr] adj : secular
security [sɪ'kjurəti] n, pl -**ties** 1 : seguridad f 2 GUARANTEE : garantía f 3 **securities** npl : valores mpl — **secure** [sɪ-
'kjur] adj -**curer; -est** : seguro — ~ vt
-**cured; -curing** 1 FASTEN : asegurar 2
GET : conseguir
sedan [sɪ'dæn] n : sedán m
sedate [sɪ'deɪt] adj : sosegado
sedative ['sedətɪv] adj : sedante — ~ n
: sedante m
sedentary ['sedən,teri] adj : sedentario
sediment ['sedəmənt] n : sedimento m
seduce [sɪ'du:s, -'dju:s] vt -**duced; -duc-
ing** : seducir — **seduction** [sɪ'dʌkʃən]
n : seducción f — **seductive** [sɪ'dʌktɪv]
adj : seductor
see ['si:] v **saw** ['sɔ]; **seen** ['si:n]; **seeing**
vt 1 : ver 2 UNDERSTAND : entender 3
ESCORT : acompañar 4 ~ **s.o. off** : despedirse de algn 5 ~ **sth through** : ll-

evar algo a cabo 6 ~ **you later!**
: ¡hasta luego! — vi 1 : ver 2 UNDER-
STAND : entender 3 **let's** ~ : vamos a
ver 4 ~ **to** : ocuparse de
seed ['si:d] n, pl **seed** or **seeds** 1
: semilla f 2 SOURCE : germen m —
seedy ['si:di] adj **seedier; -est**
SQUALID : sórdido
seek ['si:k] v **sought** ['sɔt]; **seeking** vt 1
or ~ **out** : buscar 2 REQUEST : pedir 3
~ **to** : tratar de — vi SEARCH : buscar
seem ['si:m] vi : parecer
seep ['si:p] vi : filtrarse
seesaw ['si:,sɔ] n : balancín m
seethe ['si:ð] vi **seethed; seething** : rabiar, estar furioso
segment ['segmənt] n : segmento m
segregate ['segrɪ,geɪt] vt -**gated;
-gating** : segregar — **segregation**
[,segrɪ'geɪʃən] n : segregación f
seize ['si:z] v **seized; seizing** vt 1
GRASP : agarrar 2 CAPTURE : tomar 3
: aprovechar (una oportunidad) — vi
or ~ **up** : agarrotarse — **seizure**
['si:ʒər] n 1 CAPTURE : toma f 2 : ataque
m (en medicina)
seldom ['seldəm] adv : pocas veces,
raramente
select [sə'lekt] adj : selecto — ~ vt
: seleccionar — **selection** [sə'lekʃən] n
: selección f — **selective** [sə'lektɪv]
adj : selectivo
self ['self] n, pl **selves** ['selvz] 1 : ser m
2 **her better** ~ : su lado bueno —
self-addressed [,selfə'drest] adj : con
la dirección del remitente — **self-assured** [,selfə'ʃurd] adj : seguro de sí
mismo — **self-centered** [,self'sentərd]
adj : egocéntrico — **self-confidence**
[,self'kɑnfədənts] n : confianza f en sí
mismo — **self-confident** [,self'kɑn-
fədənt] adj : seguro de sí mismo —
self-conscious [,self'kɑntʃəs] adj
: cohibido — **self-control** [,self'kən-
'troːl] n : dominio m de sí mismo —
self-defense [,selfdɪ'fents] n : defensa
f propia — **self-employed** [,selfɪm-
'ploɪd] adj : que trabaja por cuenta
propia — **self-esteem** [,selfɪ'sti:m] n
: amor m propio — **self-evident** [,self-
'evədənt] adj : evidente — **self-help**
[,self'help] n : autoayuda f — **self-
important** [,selfɪm'pɔrtənt] adj : presumido — **self-interest** [,self'ɪntrəst,
-tə,rest] n : interés m personal — **selfish** ['selfɪʃ] adj : egoísta — **selfish-
ness** ['selfɪʃnəs] n : egoísmo m — **self-
less** ['selfləs] adj : desinteresado —
self-pity [,self'pɪti] n, pl -**ties** : autocompasión f — **self-portrait** [,self-

'portrət] n : autorretrato m — **self-
respect** [ˌselfri'spekt] n : amor m propio — **self-righteous** [ˌself'raɪtʃəs] adj
: santurrón — **self-service** [ˌself-
'sərvɪs] adj : de autoservicio — **self-
sufficient** [ˌselfsə'fɪʃənt] adj : autosuficiente — **self-taught** [ˌself'tɔt] adj
: autodidacta

sell ['sel] v **sold** ['soːld]; **selling** vt
: vender — vi : venderse — **seller**
['selər] n : vendedor m, -dora f

selves → **self**

semantics [sɪ'mæntɪks] ns & pl : semántica f

semblance ['semblənts] n : apariencia f

semester [sə'mestər] n : semestre m

semicolon ['semiˌkoːlən, ˌse.maɪ-] n
: punto y coma m

semifinal ['semiˌfaɪnəl, ˌse.maɪ-] n : semifinal f

seminary ['semɪˌneri] n, pl **-naries**
: seminario m — **seminar** ['semɪˌnɑr] n
: seminario m

senate ['senət] n : senado m — **senator**
['senətər] n : senador m, -dora f

send ['send] vt **sent** ['sent]; **sending** 1
: mandar, enviar 2 ~ **away for** : pedir
3 ~ **back** : devolver (mercancías,
etc.) 4 ~ **for** : mandar a buscar —
sender ['sendər] n : remitente mf

senile ['siːˌnaɪl] adj : senil — **senility**
[sɪ'nɪlə ̩ti] n : senilidad f

senior ['siːnjər] n 1 SUPERIOR : superior
m 2 : estudiante mf de último año (en
educación) 3 or ~ **citizen** : persona f
mayor 4 **be s.o.'s** ~ : ser mayor que
algn — ~ adj 1 : superior (en rango)
2 ELDER : mayor — **seniority** [ˌsiː-
'njorə ̩ti] n : antigüedad f

sensation [sen'seɪʃən] n : sensación f —
sensational [sen'seɪʃənəl] adj : sensacional

sense ['sents] n 1 : sentido m 2 FEELING
: sensación f 3 COMMON SENSE : sentido
m común 4 **make** ~ vt : tener sentido — ~ vt **sensed; sensing** : sentir
— **senseless** ['sentsləs] adj 1 : sin
sentido 2 UNCONSCIOUS : inconsciente
— **sensible** ['sentsəbəl] adj : sensato,
práctico — **sensibility** [ˌsentsə'bɪlə ̩ti]
n, pl **-ties** : sensibilidad f — **sensitive**
['sentsə ̩tɪv] adj 1 : sensible 2 TOUCHY
: susceptible — **sensitivity** [ˌsentsə-
'tɪvə ̩ti] n, pl **-ties** : sensibilidad f —
sensual ['sentʃuəl] adj : sensual —
sensuous ['sentʃuəs] adj : sensual

sent → **send**

sentence ['sentən ̩ts, -ənz] n 1 : frase f 2
JUDGMENT : sentencia f — ~ vt
-tenced; -tencing : sentenciar

sentiment ['sentəmənt] n 1 : sentimiento m 2 BELIEF : opinión f — **sentimental** [ˌsentə'mentəl] adj : sentimental —
sentimentality [ˌsentəmen'tælə ̩ti] n, pl
-ties : sentimentalismo m

sentry ['sentri] n, pl **-tries** : centinela m

separation [ˌsepə'reɪʃən] n : separación
f — **separate** ['sepə ̩reɪt] v **-rated;
-rating** vt 1 : separar 2 DISTINGUISH
: distinguir — vi : separarse — ~
['seprət, 'sepə-] adj 1 : separado 2 DE-
TACHED : aparte 3 DISTINCT : distinto
— **separately** ['seprətli, 'sepə-] adv
: por separado

September [sep'tembər] n : septiembre
m, setiembre m

sequel ['siːkwəl] n 1 : continuación f 2
CONSEQUENCE : secuela f

sequence ['siːkwənts] n 1 ORDER : orden
m 2 : secuencia f (de números o esce-
nas)

Serb ['sərb] or **Serbian** ['sərbiən] adj
: serbio

serene [sə'riːn] adj : sereno — **serenity**
[sə'renə ̩ti] n : serenidad f

sergeant ['sɑrdʒənt] n : sargento mf

serial ['siriəl] adj : seriado — ~ n : serial m — **series** ['siriːz] n, pl **series**
: serie f

serious ['siriəs] adj : serio — **seriously**
['siriəsli] adv 1 : seriamente 2 GRAVELY
: gravemente 3 **take** ~ : tomar en
serio

sermon ['sərmən] n : sermón m

serpent ['sərpənt] n : serpiente f

servant ['sərvənt] n : criado m, -da f

serve ['sərv] v **served; serving** vi 1
: servir 2 : sacar (en deportes) 3 ~ **as**
: servir de — vt 1 : servir 2 ~ **time**
: cumplir una condena — **server**
['sərvər] n 1 WAITER : camarero m, -ra f
2 : servidor m (en informática)

service ['sərvəs] n 1 : servicio m 2 CER-
EMONY : oficio m 3 MAINTENANCE : revisión f 4 **armed** ~**s** : fuerzas fpl armadas — ~ vt **-viced; -vicing**
: revisar (un vehículo, etc.) — **serv-
iceman** ['sərvəsˌmæn, -mən] n, pl **-men**
[-mən, -ˌmen] : militar m — **service
station** n : estación f de servicio —
serving ['sərvɪŋ] n : porción f, ración f

session ['seʃən] n : sesión f

set ['set] n 1 : juego m (de platos, etc.) 2
: set m (en tenis, etc.) 3 or **stage** ~
: decorado m 4 **television** ~ : aparato m de televisión — ~ v **set; setting**
vt 1 or ~ **down** : poner 2 : poner en
hora (un reloj) 3 FIX : fijar (una fecha,
etc.) 4 ~ **fire to** : prender fuego a 5
~ **free** : poner en libertad 6 ~ **off**

: hacer sonar (una alarma), hacer estallar (una bomba) **7 — out to (do sth)** : proponerse (hacer algo) **8 — up** ASSEMBLE : montar, armar **9 — up** ESTABLISH : establecer — *vi* **1** : cuajarse (dícese de la gelatina, etc.), fraguar (dícese del cemento) **2** : ponerse (dícese del sol, etc.) **3 — in** BEGIN : empezar **4 — off** *or* **— out** : salir (de viaje) — ~ *adj* **1** FIXED : fijo **2** READY : listo, preparado — **setback** ['set₁bæk] *n* : revés *m* — **setting** ['setɪŋ] *n* **1** : posición *f* (de un control) **2** MOUNTING : engaste *m* (de joyas) **3** SCENE : escenario *m*

settle ['setəl] *v* **settled; settling** *vi* **1** : asentarse (dícese de polvo, colonos, etc.) **2 — down** RELAX : calmarse **3 ~ for** : conformarse con **4 ~ in** : instalarse — *vt* **1** DECIDE : fijar, decidir **2** RESOLVE : resolver **3** PAY : pagar **4** CALM : calmar **5** COLONIZE : colonizar — **settlement** ['setəlmənt] *n* **1** PAYMENT : pago *m* **2** COLONY : colonia *f*, poblado *m* **3** AGREEMENT : acuerdo *m* — **settler** ['setələr] *n* : colono *m*, -na *f*

seven ['sevən] *adj* : siete — ~ *n* : siete *m* — **seven hundred** *n* : setecientos *m* — ~ *n* : setecientos *m* — **seventeen** [₁sevən'tiːn] *adj* : diecisiete — ~ *n* : diecisiete *m* — **seventeenth** [₁sevən'tiːnθ] *adj* **1** : decimoséptimo — ~ *n* **1** : decimoséptimo *m*, -ma *f* (en una serie) **2** : diecisieteavo *m* (en matemáticas) — **seventh** ['sevənθ] *adj* : séptimo — ~ *n* **1** : séptimo *m*, -ma *f* (en una serie) **2** : séptimo *m* (en matemáticas) — **seventieth** ['sevəntiəθ] *adj* **1** : septuagésimo — ~ *n* **1** : septuagésimo *m*, -ma *f* (en una serie) **2** : setentavo *m* (en matemáticas) — **seventy** ['sevənti] *adj* : setenta — ~ *n*, *pl* **-ties** : setenta *m*

sever ['sevər] *vt* **-ered; -ering** : cortar, romper

several ['sevrəl, 'sevə-] *adj* : varios — ~ *pron* : varios, varias

severance ['sevrəns, sevə-] *n* : ruptura *f*

severe [sə'vɪr] *adj* **severer; -est 1** : severo **2** SERIOUS : grave — **severely** *adv* **1** : severamente **2** SERIOUSLY : gravemente — **severity** [sə'verəti] *n* **1** : severidad *f* **2** SERIOUSNESS : gravedad *f*

sew ['soː] *v* **sewed; sewn** ['soːn] *or* **sewed; sewing** : coser

sewer ['suːər] *n* : cloaca *f* — **sewage** ['suːɪdʒ] *n* : aguas *fpl* negras

sewing ['soːɪŋ] *n* : costura *f*

sex ['seks] *n* **1** : sexo *m* **2** INTERCOURSE

: relaciones *fpl* sexuales — **sexism** ['sek₁sɪzəm] *n* : sexismo *m* — **sexist** ['seksɪst] *adj* : sexista — **sexual** ['sekʃʊəl] *adj* : sexual — **sexuality** [₁sekʃʊ'æləti] *n* : sexualidad *f* — **sexy** ['seksi] *adj* **sexier; -est** : sexy

shabby ['ʃæbi] *adj* **shabbier; -est 1** WORN : gastado **2** UNFAIR : malo, injusto

shack ['ʃæk] *n* : choza *f*

shackle ['ʃækəl] *n* : grillete *m*

shade ['ʃeɪd] *n* **1** : sombra *f* **2** : tono *m* (de un color) **3** NUANCE : matiz *m* **4** *or* **lampshade** : pantalla *f* **5** *or* **window** ~ : persiana *f* — ~ *vt* **shaded; shading** : proteger de la luz — **shadow** ['ʃædoʊ] *n* : sombra *f* — **shadowy** ['ʃædoʊi] *adj* INDISTINCT : vago — **shady** ['ʃeɪdi] *adj* **shadier; -est 1** : sombreado **2** DISREPUTABLE : sospechoso

shaft ['ʃæft] *n* **1** : asta *f* (de una flecha, etc.) **2** HANDLE : mango *m* **3** AXLE : eje *m* **4** : rayo *m* (de luz) **5** *or* **mine** ~ : pozo *m*

shaggy ['ʃægi] *adj* **shaggier; -est** : peludo

shake ['ʃeɪk] *v* **shook** ['ʃʊk], **shaken** ['ʃeɪkən]; **shaking** *vt* **1** : sacudir **2** MIX : agitar **3 ~ hands with s.o.** : dar la mano a algn **4 ~ one's head** : negar con la cabeza **5 ~ up** UPSET : afectar — *vi* : temblar — **shake** *n* **1** : sacudida *f* **2 → handshake** — **shaker** ['ʃeɪkər] *n* **1 salt** ~ : salero *m* **2 pepper** ~ : pimentero *m* — **shaky** ['ʃeɪki] *adj* **shakier; -est 1** : tembloroso **2** UNSTABLE : poco firme

shall ['ʃæl] *v aux*, *past* **should** ['ʃʊd]; *pres sing & pl* **shall 1** (*expressing volition or futurity*) → **will 2** (*expressing possibility or obligation*) → **should 3 ~ we go?** : ¿nos vamos?

shallow ['ʃæloː] *adj* **1** : poco profundo **2** SUPERFICIAL : superficial

sham ['ʃæm] *n* : farsa *f* — ~ *v* **shammed; shamming** : fingir

shambles ['ʃæmbəlz] *ns* & *pl* : caos *m*, desorden *m*

shame ['ʃeɪm] *n* **1** : vergüenza *f* **2 what a** ~**!** : ¡qué lástima! — ~ *vt* **shamed; shaming** : avergonzar — **shameful** ['ʃeɪmfəl] *adj* : vergonzoso — **shameless** ['ʃeɪmləs] *adj* : desvergonzado

shampoo [ʃæm'puː] *vt* : lavar (el pelo) — ~ *n*, *pl* **-poos** : champú *m*

shamrock ['ʃæm₁rɑk] *n* : trébol *m*

shan't ['ʃænt] (*contraction of* **shall not**) → **shall**

shape ['ʃeɪp] v **shaped; shaping** vt **1** : formar **2** DETERMINE : determinar **3 be —d like** : tener forma de — vi or **~ up** : tomar forma — **~** n **1** : forma f **2 get in ~** : ponerse en forma — **shapeless** ['ʃeɪpləs] adj : informe

share ['ʃer] n **1** : porción f **2** : acción f (en una compañía) — **~** v **shared; sharing** vt **1** : compartir **2** DIVIDE : dividir — vi : compartir — **shareholder** ['ʃer,hoːldər] n : accionista mf

shark ['ʃɑrk] n : tiburón m

sharp ['ʃɑrp] adj **1** : afilado **2** POINTY : puntiagudo **3** ACUTE : agudo **4** HARSH : duro, severo **5** CLEAR : nítido **6** : sostenido (en música) **7 a — curve** : una curva cerrada — **~** adv **at two o'clock ~** : a las dos en punto — **~** n : sostenido (en música) — **sharpen** ['ʃɑrpən] vt : afilar (un cuchillo, etc.), sacar punta a (un lápiz) — **sharpener** ['ʃɑrpənər] n **1** or **knife ~** : afilador m **2** or **pencil ~** : sacapuntas m — **sharply** ['ʃɑrpli] adv : bruscamente

shatter ['ʃæṭər] vt **1** : hacer añicos **2** DEVASTATE : destrozar — vi : hacerse añicos

shave ['ʃeɪv] v **shaved; shaved** or **shaven** ['ʃeɪvən]; **shaving** vt **1** : afeitar **2** SLICE : cortar — vi : afeitarse — **~** n : afeitada f — **shaver** ['ʃeɪvər] n : máquina f de afeitar

shawl ['ʃɔl] n : chal m

she ['ʃiː] pron : ella

sheaf ['ʃiːf] n, pl **sheaves** ['ʃiːvz] **1** : gavilla f **2** : fajo m (de papeles)

shear ['ʃɪr] vt **sheared; sheared** or **shorn** ['ʃɔrn]; **shearing** : esquilar — **shears** ['ʃɪrz] npl : tijeras fpl (grandes)

sheath ['ʃiːθ] n, pl **sheaths** ['ʃiːðz, 'ʃiːðs] : funda f, vaina f

shed¹ ['ʃed] v **shed; shedding** vt **1** : derramar (lágrimas, etc.) **2** : mudar (de piel, etc.), quitarse (ropa) **3 — light on** : aclarar

shed² n : cobertizo m

she'd ['ʃiːd] (contraction of **she had** or **she would**) → **have, would**

sheen ['ʃiːn] n : brillo m, lustre m

sheep ['ʃiːp] n, pl **sheep** : oveja f — **sheepish** ['ʃiːpɪʃ] adj : avergonzado

sheer ['ʃɪr] adj **1** THIN : transparente **2** PURE : puro **3** STEEP : escarpado

sheet ['ʃiːt] n **1** : sábana f (de la cama) **2** : hoja f (de papel) **3** : capa f (de hielo, etc.) **4** PLATE : placa f, lámina f

shelf ['ʃelf] n, pl **shelves** ['ʃelvz] : estante m

shell ['ʃel] n **1** : concha f **2** : caparazón m (de un crustáceo, etc.) **3** : cáscara f

(de un huevo, etc.) **4** : armazón mf (de un edificio, etc.) **5** POD : vaína f **6** MISSILE : proyectil m — **~** vt **1** : pelar (nueces, etc.) **2** BOMBARD : bombardear

she'll ['ʃiːl, 'ʃɪl] (contraction of **she shall** or **she will**) → **shall, will**

shellfish ['ʃel,fɪʃ] n : marisco m

shelter ['ʃeltər] n **1** : refugio m **2 take ~** : refugiarse — **~** vt **1** PROTECT : proteger **2** HARBOR : albergar

shelve ['ʃelv] vt **shelved; shelving** DEFER : dar carpetazo a

shepherd ['ʃepərd] n : pastor m — **~** vt GUIDE : conducir, guiar

sherbet ['ʃɑrbət] n : sorbete m

sheriff ['ʃerɪf] n : sheriff mf

sherry ['ʃeri] n, pl **-ries** : jerez m

she's ['ʃiːz] (contraction of **she is** or **she has**) → **be, have**

shield ['ʃiːld] n : escudo m — **~** vt : proteger

shier, shiest → **shy**

shift ['ʃɪft] vt **1** MOVE : mover **2** SWITCH : transferir — vi **1** CHANGE : cambiar **2** MOVE : moverse **3** or **~ gears** : cambiar de velocidad — **~** n **1** CHANGE : cambio m **2** : turno m (de trabajo) — **shiftless** ['ʃɪftləs] adj : holgazán — **shifty** ['ʃɪfti] adj **shiftier, -est** : sospechoso

shimmer ['ʃɪmər] vi : brillar, relucir

shin ['ʃɪn] n : espinilla f

shine ['ʃaɪn] v **shone** ['ʃoːn] or **shined; shining** vi : brillar — vt **1** : alumbrar (una luz) **2** POLISH : sacar brillo a — **~** n : brillo m

shingle ['ʃɪŋgəl] n : teja f plana y delgada (en construcción) — **~** vt **-gled; -gling** : techar — **shingles** ['ʃɪŋgəlz] npl : herpes m

shiny ['ʃaɪni] adj **shinier, -est** : brillante

ship ['ʃɪp] n **1** : barco m, buque m **2 — spaceship** — **~** vt **shipped; shipping** : transportar, enviar (por barco) — **shipbuilding** ['ʃɪp,bɪldɪŋ] n : construcción f naval — **shipment** ['ʃɪpmənt] n : envío m — **shipping** ['ʃɪpɪŋ] n **1** : transporte m **2** SHIPS : barcos mpl — **shipshape** ['ʃɪp,ʃeɪp] adj : ordenado — **shipwreck** ['ʃɪp,rek] n : naufragio m — **~** vt **be —ed** : naufragar — **shipyard** ['ʃɪp,jɑrd] n : astillero m

shirk ['ʃɑrk] vt : esquivar

shirt ['ʃɑrt] n : camisa f

shiver ['ʃɪvər] vi : temblar (del frío, etc.) — **~** n : escalofrío m

shoal ['ʃoːl] n : banco m

shock ['ʃɑk] n 1 IMPACT : choque m 2 SURPRISE, UPSET : golpe m emocional 3 : shock m (en medicina) 4 or **electric ~** : descarga f (eléctrica) — **~** vt : escandalizar — **shock absorber** n : amortiguador m — **shocking** ['ʃɑkɪŋ] adj : escandaloso

shoddy ['ʃɑdi] adj **shoddier; -est** : de mala calidad

shoe ['ʃu:] n : zapato m — **~** vt **shod** ['ʃɑd]; **shoeing** : herrar (un caballo) — **shoelace** ['ʃu:ˌleɪs] n : cordón m (de zapato) — **shoemaker** ['ʃu:ˌmeɪkər] n : zapatero m, -ra f

shone → **shine**

shook → **shake**

shoot ['ʃu:t] v **shot** ['ʃɑt]; **shooting** vt 1 : disparar 2 : echar (una mirada) 3 PHOTOGRAPH : fotografiar 4 FILM : rodar — vi 1 : disparar 2 — **by** : pasar como una bala — **~** n : brote m, retoño m (de una planta) — **shooting star** n : estrella f fugaz

shop ['ʃɑp] n 1 : tienda f 2 WORKSHOP : taller m — **~** vi **shopped; shopping** 1 : hacer compras 2 **go shopping** : ir de compras — **shopkeeper** ['ʃɑpˌki:pər] n : tendero m, -ra f — **shoplift** ['ʃɑpˌlɪft] vi : hurtar mercancía (en tiendas) — **shoplifter** ['ʃɑpˌlɪftər] n : ladrón m, -drona f (que roba en tiendas) — **shopper** ['ʃɑpər] n : comprador m, -dora f

shore ['ʃor] n : orilla f

shorn → **shear**

short ['ʃɔrt] adj 1 : corto 2 : bajo (estatura) 3 CURT : brusco 4 a **~ time ago** : hace poco 5 **be ~ of** : estar corto de — **~** adv 1 **stop ~** : parar en seco 2 **fall ~** : quedarse corto — **shortage** ['ʃɔrtɪdʒ] n : escasez f, carencia f — **shortcake** ['ʃɔrtˌkeɪk] n : tarta f de fruta — **shortcoming** ['ʃɔrtˌkʌmɪŋ] n : defecto m — **shortcut** ['ʃɔrtˌkʌt] n : atajo m — **shorten** ['ʃɔrtən] vt : acortar — **shorthand** ['ʃɔrtˌhænd] n : taquigrafía f — **short-lived** ['ʃɔrtˈlɪvd, -ˈlaɪvd] adj : efímero — **shortly** ['ʃɔrtli] adv : dentro de poco — **shortness** ['ʃɔrtnəs] n 1 : lo corto (de una cosa), baja estatura f (de una persona) 2 **~ of breath** : falta f de aliento — **shorts** npl 1 : shorts mpl, pantalones mpl cortos — **shortsighted** ['ʃɔrtˌsaɪtəd] → **nearsighted**

shot ['ʃɑt] n 1 : disparo m, tiro m 2 : tiro m (en deportes) 3 ATTEMPT : intento m 4 PHOTOGRAPH : foto f 5 INJECTION : inyección f 6 : trago m (de licor) — **shotgun** ['ʃɑtˌgʌn] n : escopeta f

should ['ʃʊd] past of **shall** 1 **if she ~ call** : si llama 2 **I ~ have gone** : debería haber ido 3 **they ~ arrive soon** : deben llegar pronto 4 **what ~ we do?** : ¿qué hacemos?

shoulder ['ʃoldər] n 1 : hombro m 2 : arcén m (de una carretera) — **~** vt : cargar con (la responsabilidad, etc.) — **shoulder blade** n : omóplato m

shouldn't ['ʃʊdənt] (contraction of **should not**) → **should**

shout ['ʃaʊt] v : gritar — **~** n : grito m

shove ['ʃʌv] v **shoved; shoving** : empujar — **~** n : empujón m

shovel ['ʃʌvəl] n : pala f — **~** vt **-veled** or **-velled; -veling** or **-velling** 1 : mover (tierra, etc.) con una pala 2 DIG : cavar (con una pala)

show ['ʃo] v **showed; shown** ['ʃon] or **showed; showing** vt 1 : mostrar 2 TEACH : enseñar 3 PROVE : demostrar 4 ESCORT : acompañar 5 : proyectar (una película), dar (un programa de televisión) 6 — **off** : hacer alarde de — vi 1 : notarse, verse 2 — **off** : lucirse 3 — **up** ARRIVE : aparecer — **~** n 1 : demostración f 2 EXHIBITION : exposición f 3 : espectáculo m (teatral), programa m (de televisión, etc.) — **showdown** ['ʃoˌdaʊn] n : confrontación f

shower ['ʃaʊər] n 1 : ducha f 2 : chaparrón m (en meteorología) 3 PARTY : fiesta f — **~** vt 1 SPRAY : regar 2 **~ s.o. with** : colmar a algn de — vi 1 : ducharse 2 RAIN : llover

showy ['ʃoi] adj **showier; -est** : llamativo, ostentoso

shrank → **shrink**

shrapnel ['ʃræpnəl] ns & pl : metralla f

shred ['ʃred] n 1 : tira f (de tela, etc.) 2 IOTA : pizca f — **~** vt **shredded; shredding** 1 : hacer tiras 2 GRATE : rallar

shrewd ['ʃru:d] adj : astuto

shriek ['ʃri:k] vi : chillar — **~** n : chillido m, alarido m

shrill ['ʃrɪl] adj : agudo, estridente

shrimp ['ʃrɪmp] n : camarón m

shrine ['ʃraɪn] n 1 TOMB : sepulcro m 2 SANCTUARY : santuario m

shrink ['ʃrɪŋk] v **shrank** ['ʃræŋk]; **shrunk** ['ʃrʌŋk] or **shrunken** ['ʃrʌŋkən]; **shrinking** vi : encoger — vi 1 : encogerse (dícese de ropa), reducirse (dícese de números, etc.) 2 — **back** : retroceder

shrivel ['ʃrɪvəl] vi **-veled** or **-velled; -veling** or **-velling** or **~ up** : arrugarse, marchitarse

shroud ['ʃraʊd] n 1 : sudario m, mortaja f 2 VEIL : velo m — ~ vt : envolver

shrub ['ʃrʌb] n : arbusto m, mata f

shrug ['ʃrʌg] vi **shrugged; shrugging** : encogerse de hombros

shrunk → shrink

shudder ['ʃʌdər] vi : estremecerse — ~ n : estremecimiento m

shuffle ['ʃʌfəl] v **-fled; -fling** : barajar (naipes), revolver (papeles, etc.) — vi : caminar arrastrando los pies

shun ['ʃʌn] vi **shunned; shunning** : evitar, esquivar

shut ['ʃʌt] v **shut; shutting** vt 1 CLOSE : cerrar 2 ~ **off → turn off** 3 ~ **down** CONFINE : encerrar — vi 1 or ~ **down** : cerrarse 2 ~ **up!** : ¡cállate! — **shutter** ['ʃʌtər] n 1 or **window** ~ : contraventana f 2 : obturador m (de una cámara)

shuttle ['ʃʌtəl] n 1 : lanzadera f (para tejer) 2 or ~ **bus** : autobús m (de corto recorrido) 3 → **space shuttle** — ~ **-tled; -tling** vt : transportar — vi : ir y venir

shy ['ʃaɪ] adj **shier** or **shyer** ['ʃaɪər]; **shiest** or **shyest** ['ʃaɪəst] : tímido — ~ vi **shied; shying** or ~ **away** : retroceder — **shyness** ['ʃaɪnəs] n : timidez f

sibling ['sɪblɪŋ] n : hermano m, hermana f

sick ['sɪk] adj 1 : enfermo 2 **be** ~ VOMIT : vomitar 3 **be** ~ **of** : estar harto de 4 **feel** ~ : tener náuseas — **sicken** ['sɪkən] vt DISGUST : dar asco a — **sickening** ['sɪkənɪŋ] adj : nauseabundo

sickle ['sɪkəl] n : hoz f

sickly ['sɪkli] adj **sicklier; -est** UNHEALTHY : enfermizo 2 → **sickening** — **sickness** ['sɪknəs] n : enfermedad f

side ['saɪd] n 1 : lado m 2 : costado m (de una persona), ijada f (de un animal) 3 : parte f (en una disputa, etc.) 4 ~ **by** ~ : uno al lado de otro 5 **take** ~**s** : tomar partido — vi ~ **with** : ponerse de parte de — **sideboard** ['saɪd,bord] n : aparador m — **sideburns** ['saɪd,bərnz] npl : patillas fpl — **side effect** n : efecto m secundario — **sideline** ['saɪd,laɪn] n : línea f de banda (en deportes) — **sidestep** ['saɪd,step] vt **-stepped; -stepping** : eludir, esquivar — **sidetrack** ['saɪd,træk] vt **get** ~**ed** : distraerse — **sidewalk** ['saɪd-,wɔk] n : acera f — **sideways** ['saɪd-,weɪz] adj & adv : de lado — **siding** ['saɪdɪŋ] n : revestimiento m exterior

siege ['siːdʒ, 'siːʒ] n : sitio m

sieve ['sɪv] n : tamiz m, cedazo m

sift ['sɪft] vt 1 : cerner, tamizar 2 or ~ **through** : pasar por el tamiz

sigh ['saɪ] vi : suspirar — ~ n : suspiro m

sight ['saɪt] n 1 : vista f 2 SPECTACLE : espectáculo m 3 : lugar m de interés (turístico) 4 **catch** ~ **of** : avistar — ~ vt : avistar — **sightseer** ['saɪt,siːər] n : turista mf

sign ['saɪn] n 1 : signo m 2 NOTICE : letrero m 3 GESTURE : seña f, señal f — ~ vt : firmar (un cheque, etc.) — vi 1 : firmar 2 ~ **up** ENROLL : inscribirse

signal ['sɪgnəl] n : señal f — v **-naled** or **-nalled; -naling** or **-nalling** vt 1 : hacer señas a 2 INDICATE : señalar — vi 1 : hacer señas 2 : señalizar (en un vehículo)

signature ['sɪgnətʃər] n : firma f

significance [sɪg'nɪfɪkənts] n 1 : significado m 2 IMPORTANCE : importancia f — **significant** [sɪg'nɪfɪkənt] adj : importante — **signify** ['sɪgnə,faɪ] vt **-fied; -fying** : significar

sign language n : lenguaje m gestual — **signpost** ['saɪn,post] n : poste m indicador

silence ['saɪlənts] n : silencio m — ~ vt **-lenced; -lencing** : silenciar — **silent** ['saɪlənt] adj 1 : silencioso 2 MUM : callado 3 : mudo (dícese de películas y letras)

silhouette [,sɪlə'wet] n : silueta f — ~ vt **-etted; -etting be** ~**d against** : perfilarse contra

silicon ['sɪlɪkən, -,kɑn] n : silicio m

silk ['sɪlk] n : seda f — **silky** ['sɪlki] adj **silkier; -est** : sedoso

sill ['sɪl] n : alféizar m (de una ventana), umbral m (de una puerta)

silly ['sɪli] adj **sillier; -est** : tonto, estúpido

silt ['sɪlt] n : cieno m

silver ['sɪlvər] n 1 : plata f 2 → **silverware** — ~ adj : de plata — **silverware** ['sɪlvər,wær] n : plata f — **silvery** ['sɪlvəri] adj : plateado

similar ['sɪmələr] adj : similar, parecido — **similarity** [,sɪmə'lærəţi] n, pl **-ties** : semejanza f, parecido m

simmer ['sɪmər] v : hervir a fuego lento

simple ['sɪmpəl] adj **simpler; -plest** 1 : simple 2 EASY : sencillo — **simplicity** [sɪm'plɪsəţi] n : simplicidad f, sencillez f — **simplify** ['sɪmplə,faɪ] vt **-fied; -fying** : simplificar — **simply** ['sɪmpli] adv 1 : sencillamente 2 ABSOLUTELY : realmente

simulate ['sɪmjə,leɪt] *vt* -lated; -lating : simular

simultaneous [,saɪməl'teɪniəs] *adj* : simultáneo

sin ['sɪn] *n* : pecado *m* — ~ *vi* sinned; sinning : pecar

since ['sɪns] *adv* 1 *or* ~ then : desde entonces 2 long ~ : hace mucho — ~ *conj* 1 : desde que 2 BECAUSE : ya que, como 3 it's been years ~.. : hace años que... — ~ *prep* : desde

sincere [sɪn'sɪr] *adj* -cerer; -est : sincero — **sincerely** *adv* : sinceramente — **sincerity** [sɪn'serəti] *n* : sinceridad *f*

sinful ['sɪnfəl] *adj* : pecador (dícese de las personas), pecaminoso (dícese de las acciones)

sing ['sɪŋ] *v* sang ['sæŋ] *or* sung ['sʌŋ]; sung; singing : cantar

singe ['sɪndʒ] *vt* singed; singeing : chamuscar

singer ['sɪŋər] *n* : cantante *mf*

single ['sɪŋgəl] *adj* 1 : solo, único 2 UNMARRIED : soltero 3 every ~ day : cada día, todos los días — ~ *n* 1 : soltero *m*, -ra *f* 2 *or* ~ room : habitación *f* individual — ~ *vt* -gled; -gling ~ out 1 SELECT : escoger 2 DISTINGUISH : señalar — **single-handed** ['sɪŋgəl'hændəd] *adj* : sin ayuda, solo

singular ['sɪŋgjələr] *adj* : singular — ~ *n* : singular *m*

sinister ['sɪnəstər] *adj* : siniestro

sink ['sɪŋk] *v* sank ['sæŋk] *or* sunk ['sʌŋk]; sunk; sinking *vi* 1 : hundirse (en un líquido) 2 DROP : bajar, caer — *vt* 1 : hundir 2 ~ sth into : clavar algo en — ~ *n* 1 *or* kitchen ~ : fregadero *m* 2 *or* bathroom ~ : lavabo *m*, lavamanos *m*

sinner ['sɪnər] *n* : pecador *m*, -dora *f*

sip ['sɪp] *v* sipped; sipping *vt* : sorber — *vi* : beber a sorbos — ~ *n* : sorbo *m*

siphon ['saɪfən] *n* : sifón *m* — ~ *vt* : sacar con sifón

sir ['sər] *n* 1 (*in titles*) : sir *m* 2 (*as a form of address*) : señor *m* 3 Dear Sir : Estimado señor

siren ['saɪrən] *n* : sirena *f*

sirloin ['sər,lɔɪn] *n* : solomillo *m*

sissy ['sɪsi] *n*, *pl* -sies : mariquita *mf fam*

sister ['sɪstər] *n* : hermana *f* — **sister-in-law** ['sɪstərɪn,lɔ] *n*, *pl* **sisters-in-law** : cuñada *f*

sit ['sɪt] *v* sat ['sæt]; sitting *vi* 1 *or* ~ down : sentarse 2 LIE : estar (ubicado) 3 MEET : estar en sesión 4 *or* ~ up : incorporarse — *vt* : sentar

site ['saɪt] *n* 1 : sitio *m*, lugar *m* 2 LOT : solar *m*

sitter ['sɪtər] → **baby-sitter**

sitting room → **living room**

situated ['sɪtʃu,eɪtəd] *adj* : ubicado, situado — **situation** [,sɪtʃu'eɪʃən] *n* : situación *f*

six ['sɪks] *adj* : seis — ~ *n* : seis *m* — **six hundred** *adj* : seiscientos — ~ *n* : seiscientos *m* — **sixteen** [sɪks'tiːn] *adj* : dieciséis — ~ *n* : dieciséis *m* — **sixteenth** [sɪks'tiːnθ] *adj* : decimosexto — ~ *n* 1 : decimosexto *m*, -ta *f* (en una serie) 2 : dieciseisavo *m*, dieciseisava parte *f* — **sixth** ['sɪksθ, 'sɪks] *adj* : sexto — ~ *n* 1 : sexto *m*, -ta *f* (en una serie) 2 : sexto *m* (en matemáticas) — **sixtieth** ['sɪkstiəθ] *adj* : sexagésimo — ~ *n* 1 : sexagésimo *m*, -ma *f* (en una serie) 2 : sesentavo *m* (en matemáticas) — **sixty** ['sɪksti] *adj* : sesenta — ~ *n*, *pl* -ties : sesenta *m*

size ['saɪz] *n* 1 : tamaño *m*, talla *f* (de ropa), número *m* (de zapatos) 2 EXTENT : magnitud *f* — ~ *vt* sized; sizing ~ up : evaluar — **sizable** *or* **sizeable** ['saɪzəbəl] *adj* : considerable

sizzle ['sɪzəl] *vi* -zled; -zling : chisporrotear

skate¹ ['skeɪt] *n* : raya *f* (pez)

skate² *n* : patín *m* — ~ *vi* skated; skating : patinar — **skateboard** ['skeɪt,bord] *n* : monopatín *m* — **skater** ['skeɪtər] *n* : patinador *m*, -dora *f*

skeleton ['skelətən] *n* : esqueleto *m*

skeptic ['skeptɪk] *n* : escéptico *m*, -ca *f* — **skeptical** ['skeptɪkəl] *adj* : escéptico — **skepticism** ['skeptə,sɪzəm] *n* : escepticismo *m*

sketch ['sketʃ] *n* 1 : esbozo *m*, bosquejo *m* 2 SKIT : sketch *m* — ~ *vt* : bosquejar — *vi* : hacer bosquejos — **sketchy** ['sketʃi] *adj* sketchier; -est : incompleto

skewer ['skjuːər] *n* : brocheta *f*, broqueta *f*

ski ['skiː] *n*, *pl* skis : esquí *m* — ~ *vi* skied; skiing : esquiar

skid ['skɪd] *n* : derrape *m*, patinazo *m* — ~ *vi* skidded; skidding : derrapar, patinar

skier ['skiːər] *n* : esquiador *m*, -dora *f*

skill ['skɪl] *n* 1 : habilidad *f*, destreza *f* 2 TECHNIQUE : técnica *f* — **skilled** *adj* : hábil

skillet ['skɪlət] *n* : sartén *mf*

skillful ['skɪlfəl] *adj* : hábil, diestro

skim ['skɪm] *v* skimmed; skimming 1 : espumar (sopa, etc.), descremar (leche) 2 : pasar rozando (una superfi-

cie) **3** *or* **~ through** : echar un vistazo a — **~** *adj* : descremado
skimp ['skɪmp] *vi* **~ on** : escatimar — **skimpy** ['skɪmpi] *adj* **skimpier; -est 1** : exiguo, escaso **2** : brevísimo (dícese de ropa)
skin ['skɪn] *n* : piel *f* — *vt* **skinned; skinning** : despellejar — **skin diving** *n* : buceo *m*, submarinismo *m* — **skinny** ['skɪni] *adj* **skinnier; -est** : flaco
skip ['skɪp] *v* **skipped; skipping** *vi* : ir brincando — *vt* OMIT : saltarse — *n* : brinco *m*, salto *m*
skipper ['skɪpər] *n* : capitán *m*, -tana *f*
skirmish ['skərmɪʃ] *n* : escaramuza *f*
skirt ['skərt] *n* : falda *f* — *~ vt* **1** BORDER : bordear **2** EVADE : eludir
skull ['skʌl] *n* : cráneo *m* (de una persona viva), calavera *f* (de un esqueleto)
skunk ['skʌŋk] *n* : mofeta *f*, zorrillo *m* *Lat*
sky ['skaɪ] *n, pl* **skies** : cielo *m* — **skylight** ['skaɪ,laɪt] *n* : claraboya *f*, tragaluz *m* — **skyline** ['skaɪ,laɪn] *n* : horizonte *m* — **skyscraper** ['skaɪ,skreɪpər] *n* : rascacielos *m*
slab ['slæb] *n* : bloque *m* (de piedra, etc.)
slack ['slæk] *adj* **1** LOOSE : flojo **2** CARELESS : descuidado — *n* **1 take up the ~** : tensar (una cuerda, etc.) **2** **~s** *npl* : pantalones *mpl* — **slacken** ['slækən] *vt* : aflojar — *vi* : aflojarse
slain → slay
slam ['slæm] *n* : golpe *m*, portazo *m* (de una puerta) — *~ v* **slammed; slamming** *vt* **1** *or* **~ down** : tirar, plantar **2** *or* **~ shut** : cerrar de golpe **3 ~ the door** : dar un portazo — *vi* **1** : cerrarse de golpe **2 ~ into** : chocar contra
slander ['slændər] *vt* : calumniar, difamar — *~ n* : calumnia *f*, difamación *f*
slang ['slæŋ] *n* : argot *m*
slant ['slænt] *n* : inclinación *f* — *~ vi* : inclinarse
slap ['slæp] *vt* **slapped; slapping 1** : dar una bofetada a **2 ~ s.o. on the back** : dar una palmada en la espalda a algn — *~ n* **1** : bofetada *f*, cachetada *f* *Lat*
slash ['slæʃ] *vt* **1** : hacer un tajo en **2** : rebajar (precios) drásticamente — *~ n* : tajo *m*
slat ['slæt] *n* : tablilla *f*
slate ['sleɪt] *n* : pizarra *f*
slaughter ['slɔtər] *n* : matanza *f* — *~ vt* **1** : matar (animales) **2** MASSACRE : masacrar — **slaughterhouse** ['slɔtər,haʊs] *n* : matadero *m*
slave ['sleɪv] *n* : esclavo *m*, -va *f* — *~*

slaved; slaving : trabajar como un burro — **slavery** ['sleɪvəri] *n* : esclavitud *f*
Slavic ['slɑvɪk, 'slæ-] *adj* : eslavo
slay ['sleɪ] *vt* **slew** ['slu:]; **slain** ['sleɪn]; **slaying** : asesinar
sleazy ['sli:zi] *adj* **sleazier; -est** : sórdido
sled ['sled] *n* : trineo *m*
sledgehammer ['sledʒ,hæmər] *n* : almádena *f*
sleek ['sli:k] *adj* : liso y brillante
sleep ['sli:p] *n* **1** : sueño *m* **2 go to ~** : dormirse — *~ vi* **slept** ['slept]; **sleeping** : dormir — **sleeper** ['sli:pər] *n* **be a light ~** : tener el sueño ligero — **sleepless** ['sli:pləs] *adj* **have a ~ night** : pasar la noche en blanco — **sleepwalker** ['sli:p,wɔkər] *n* : sonámbulo *m*, -la *f* — **sleepy** ['sli:pi] *adj* **sleepier; -est 1** : somnoliento, soñoliento **2 be ~** : tener sueño
sleet ['sli:t] *n* : aguanieve *f* — *~ vi* : caer aguanieve
sleeve ['sli:v] *n* : manga *f* — **sleeveless** ['sli:vləs] *adj* : sin mangas
sleigh ['sleɪ] *n* : trineo *m*
slender ['slendər] *adj* : delgado
slew ['slu:] → **slay**
slice ['slaɪs] *vt* **sliced; slicing** : cortar — *~ n* : trozo *m*, rebanada *f* (de pan, etc.), tajada *f* (de carne)
slick ['slɪk] *adj* SLIPPERY : resbaladizo, resbaloso *Lat*
slide ['slaɪd] *v* **slid** ['slɪd]; **sliding** ['slaɪdɪŋ] *vi* : deslizarse — *vt* : deslizar — *~ n* **1** : deslizamiento *m* **2** : tobogán *m* (para niños) **3** : diapositiva *f* (fotográfica) **4** DECLINE : descenso *m*
slier, sliest → sly
slight ['slaɪt] *adj* **1** : ligero, leve **2** SLENDER : delgado — *~ vt* : desairar — **slightly** ['slaɪtli] *adv* : ligeramente, un poco
slim ['slɪm] *adj* **slimmer; slimmest 1** : delgado **2 a ~ chance** : escasas posibilidades *fpl* — *~ v* **slimmed; slimming** : adelgazar
slime ['slaɪm] *n* **1** : baba *f* (de un caracol, etc.) **2** MUD : limo *m* — **slimy** ['slaɪmi] *adj* **slimier; -est** : viscoso
sling ['slɪŋ] *vt* **slung** ['slʌŋ]; **slinging 1** THROW : lanzar **2** HANG : colgar — *~ n* **1** : honda *f* **2** : cabestrillo *m* (en medicina) — **slingshot** ['slɪŋ,ʃɑt] *n* : tirachinas *m*
slink ['slɪŋk] *vi* **slunk** ['slʌŋk]; **slinking** : andar furtivamente
slip¹ ['slɪp] *v* **slipped; slipping** *vi* **1** SLIDE : resbalarse **2 let sth ~** : dejar

escapar algo **3 ~ away** : escabullirse **4 ~ up** : equivocarse — *vt* **1** : deslizar **2 ~ into** : ponerse (una prenda) **3 it slipped my mind** : se me olvidó — **~** *n* **1** MISTAKE : error *m*, desliz *m* **2 ~ of the tongue** : lapsus *m* **3** PETTICOAT : enagua *f*

slip[2] *n* **~ of paper** : papelito *m*

slipper ['slɪpər] *n* : zapatilla *f*, pantufla *f*

slippery ['slɪpəri] *adj* **slipperier; -est** : resbaladizo, resbaloso *Lat*

slit ['slɪt] *n* **1** OPENING : rendija *f* **2** CUT : corte *m*, raja *f* — **~** *vt* **slit; slitting** : cortar

slither ['slɪðər] *vi* : deslizarse

sliver ['slɪvər] *n* : astilla *f*

slogan ['sloːgən] *n* : eslogan *m*

slop ['slɑp] *v* **slopped; slopping** *vt* : derramar — *vi* : derramarse

slope ['sloːp] *vi* **sloped; sloping** : inclinarse — **~** *n* : pendiente *f*, declive *m*

sloppy ['slɑpi] *adj* **sloppier; -est 1** CARELESS : descuidado **2** UNKEMPT : desaliñado

slot ['slɑt] *n* : ranura *f*

sloth ['slɔːθ, 'sloːθ] *n* : pereza *f*

slouch ['slaʊtʃ] *vi* : andar con los hombros caídos (en una silla)

slovenly ['slʌvənli, 'slɑv-] *adj* : desaliñado

slow ['sloː] *adj* **1** : lento **2 be ~** : estar atrasado (dícese de un reloj) — *adv* → **slowly** — **~** *vt* : retrasar, retardar — *vi or* **~ down** : ir más despacio — **slowly** ['sloːli] *adv* : lentamente, despacio — **slowness** ['sloːnəs] *n* : lentitud *f*

sludge ['slʌdʒ] *n* SEWAGE : aguas *fpl* negras

slug[1] *n* **1** : babosa *f* (molusco) **2** BULLET : bala *f* **3** TOKEN : ficha *f*

slug[2] *vt* **slugged; slugging** : pegar un porrazo a

sluggish ['slʌgɪʃ] *adj* : lento

slum ['slʌm] *n* : barrio *m* bajo

slumber ['slʌmbər] *vi* : dormir — **~** *n* : sueño *m*

slump ['slʌmp] *vi* **1** DROP : bajar **2** COLLAPSE : dejarse caer **3** → **slouch** — **~** *n* : bajón *m*

slung → sling

slunk → slink

slur[1] ['slər] *n* ASPERSION : calumnia *f*, difamación *f*

slur[2] *vt* **slurred; slurring** : arrastrar (las palabras)

slurp ['slərp] *v* : beber haciendo ruido — **~** *n* : sorbo *m* (ruidoso)

slush ['slʌʃ] *n* : nieve *f* medio derretida

sly ['slaɪ] *adj* **slier; sliest** : astuto, taimado **2 on the ~** : a escondidas

smack[1] ['smæk] *vi* **~ of** : oler a

smack[2] *vt* **1** : pegar una bofetada a **2** KISS : besar **3 ~ one's lips** : relamerse — **~** *n* **1** SLAP : bofetada *f* **2** KISS : beso *m* — **~** *adv* : justo, exactamente

small ['smɔl] *adj* : pequeño, chico — **smallpox** ['smɔl,pɑks] *n* : viruela *f*

smart ['smɑrt] *adj* **1** : listo, inteligente **2** STYLISH : elegante — *vi* STING : escocer — **smartly** ['smɑrtli] *adv* : elegantemente

smash ['smæʃ] *n* **1** BLOW : golpe *m* **2** COLLISION : choque *m* **3** BANG, CRASH : estrépito *m* — **~** *vt* **1** BREAK : romper **2** DESTROY : aplastar — *vi* **1** SHATTER : hacerse pedazos **2 ~ into** : estrellarse contra

smattering ['smætərɪŋ] *n* : nociones *fpl*

smear ['smɪr] *n* : mancha *f* — **~** *vt* **1** : embadurnar (de pinta, etc.), untar (de aceite, etc.) **2** SMUDGE : manchar

smell ['smel] *v* **smelled** *or* **smelt** ['smelt]; **smelling** : oler — *n* **1** : (sentido *m* del) olfato *m* **2** ODOR : olor *m* — **smelly** ['smeli] *adj* **smellier; -est** : maloliente

smelt[1] ['smelt] *vt* : fundir

smile ['smaɪl] *vi* **smiled; smiling** : sonreír — **~** *n* : sonrisa *f*

smirk ['smərk] *vi* : sonreír con suficiencia — **~** *n* : sonrisa *f* satisfecha

smitten ['smɪtən] *adj* **be ~ with** : estar enamorado de

smith ['smɪθ] → **blacksmith**

smock ['smɑk] *n* : blusón *m*, bata *f*

smog ['smɑg, 'smɔg] *n* : smog *m*

smoke ['smoːk] *n* : humo *m* — *v* **smoked; smoking** *vi* **1** : humear (dícese de fuegos, etc.) **2** : fumar (dícese de personas) — *vt* **1** : ahumar (carne, etc.) **2** : fumar (cigarrillos) — **smoker** ['smoːkər] *n* : fumador *m*, -dora *f* — **smokestack** ['smoːkˌstæk] *n* : chimenea *f* — **smoky** ['smoːki] *adj* **smokier; -est 1** : lleno de humo **2** : a humo (dícese de sabores, etc.)

smolder ['smoːldər] *vi* : arder (sin llama)

smooth ['smuːð] *adj* **1** : liso (dícese de superficies), suave (dícese de movimientos), tranquilo (dícese del mar) **2** : sin grumos (dícese de salsas, etc.) — *vt* : alisar — **smoothly** ['smuːðli] *adv* : suavemente — **smoothness** ['smuːðnəs] *n* : suavidad *f*

smother ['smʌðər] *vt* : asfixiar (a algn), sofocar (llamas, etc.)

smudge ['smʌdʒ] *v* **smudged; smudg-**

ing *vt* : emborronar — *vi* : correrse — **~** *n* : mancha *f*, borrón *m*

smug ['smʌg] *adj* **smugger; smuggest** : suficiente

smuggle ['smʌgəl] *vt* **-gled; -gling** : pasar de contrabando — **smuggler** ['smʌgələr] *n* : contrabandista *mf*

snack ['snæk] *n* : refrigerio *m*, tentempié *m fam*

snag ['snæg] *n* : problema *m* — **~** *v* **snagged; snagging** *vt* : enganchar — *vi* : engancharse

snail ['sneɪl] *n* : caracol *m*

snake ['sneɪk] *n* : culebra *f*, serpiente *f*

snap ['snæp] *v* **snapped; snapping** *vi* **1** BREAK : romperse **2** : intentar morder (dícese de un perro, etc.) **3 ~ at** : contestar bruscamente a — *vt* **1** BREAK : romper **2 ~ one's fingers** : chasquear los dedos **3 ~ open/shut** : abrir/cerrar de golpe — **~** *n* **1** : chasquido *m* **2** FASTENER : broche *m* (de presión) **3 be a ~** : ser facilísimo — **snappy** ['snæpi] *adj* **snappier; -est 1** FAST : rápido **2** STYLISH : elegante —

snapshot ['snæp,ʃɑt] *n* : instantánea *f*

snare ['snær] *n* : trampa *f* — **~** *vt* **snared; snaring** : atrapar

snarl¹ ['snɑrl] *vi* TANGLE : enmarañar, enredar — **~** *n* : enredo *m*, maraña *f*

snarl² *vi* GROWL : gruñir — **~** *n* : gruñido *m*

snatch ['snætʃ] *vt* : arrebatar

sneak ['snik] *vi* : ir a hurtadillas — *vt* : hacer furtivamente — **~** *n* : soplón *m*, -plona *f fam* — **sneakers** ['snikərz] *npl* : tenis *mpl*, zapatillas *fpl* — **sneaky** ['sniki] *adj* **sneakier; -est** : solapado

sneer ['snɪr] *vi* : sonreír con desprecio — **~** *n* : sonrisa *f* de desprecio

sneeze ['sniz] *vi* **sneezed; sneezing** : estornudar — **~** *n* : estornudo *m*

snide ['snaɪd] *adj* : sarcástico

sniff ['snɪf] *vi* : oler — *vt* : oler **2** → **sniffle** — **~** *n* : aspiración *f* por la nariz — **sniffle** ['snɪfəl] *vi* **-fled; -fling** : sorberse la nariz — **sniffles** ['snɪfəlz] *npl* **have the ~** : estar resfriado

snip ['snɪp] *n* : tijeretada *f* — **~** *vt* **snipped; snipping** : cortar (con tijeras)

snivel ['snɪvəl] *vi* **-veled** *or* **-velled; -veling** *or* **-velling** : lloriquear

snob ['snɑb] *n* : esnob *mf* — **snobbish** ['snɑbɪʃ] *adj* : esnob

snoop ['snuːp] *vi* : husmear — **~** *n* : fisgón *m*, -gona *f*

snooze ['snuːz] *vi* **snoozed; snoozing** : dormitar — **~** *n* : siestecita *f*, siesta *f*

snore ['snor] *vi* **snored; snoring** : roncar — **~** *n* : ronquido *m*

snort ['snort] *vi* : bufar — **~** *n* : bufido *m*

snout ['snaʊt] *n* : hocico *m*, morro *m*

snow ['snoː] *n* : nieve *f* — **~** *vi* : nevar — **snowfall** ['snoːfɔl] *n* : nevada *f* — **snowflake** ['snoːfleɪk] *n* : copo *m* de nieve — **snowman** ['snoːmæn] *n* : muñeco *m* de nieve — **snowplow** ['snoːplaʊ] *n* : quitanieves *m* — **snowshoe** ['snoːʃuː] *n* : raqueta *f* (para nieve) — **snowstorm** ['snoːstɔrm] *n* : tormenta *f* de nieve — **snowy** ['snoːi] *adj* **snowier; -est 1 a ~ day** : un día nevoso **2 ~ mountains** : montañas *fpl* nevadas

snub ['snʌb] *vt* **snubbed; snubbing** : desairar — **~** *n* : desaire *m*

snuff ['snʌf] *vt or* **~ out** : apagar

snug ['snʌg] *adj* **snugger; snuggest 1** : cómodo **2** TIGHT : ajustado — **snuggle** ['snʌgəl] *vi* **-gled; -gling** : acurrucarse

so ['soː] *adv* **1** LIKEWISE : también **2** THUS : así **3** THEREFORE : por lo tanto **4** *or* **~ much** : tanto **5** *or* **~ very** : tan **6 and ~ on** : etcétera **7 I think ~** : creo que sí **8 I told you ~** : te lo dije — **~** *conj* **1** THEREFORE : así que **2** *or* **~ that** : para que **3 ~ what?** : ¿y qué? — **~** *adj* TRUE : cierto — **~** *pron or* **~** : más o menos

soak ['soːk] *vi* : estar en remojo — *vt* **1** : poner en remojo **2 ~ up** : absorber — **~** *n* : remojo *m*

soap ['soːp] *n* : jabón *m* — **~** *vt or* **~ up** : enjabonar — **soapy** ['soːpi] *soapier; -est* *adj* : jabonoso

soar ['sor] *vi* **1** : planear **2** SKYROCKET : dispararse

sob ['sɑb] *vi* **sobbed; sobbing** : sollozar — **~** *n* : sollozo *m*

sober ['soːbər] *adj* **1** : sobrio **2** SERIOUS : serio — **sobriety** [sə'braɪəṭi, so-] *n* **1** : sobriedad *f* **2** SERIOUSNESS : seriedad *f*

so-called ['soːkɔld] *adj* : supuesto, presunto

soccer ['sɑkər] *n* : futbol *m*, fútbol *m*

social ['soːʃəl] *adj* : social — *n* : reunión *f* social — **sociable** ['soːʃəbəl] *adj* : sociable — **socialism** ['soːʃə,lɪzəm] *n* : socialismo *m* — **socialist** ['soːʃəlɪst] *n* : socialista *mf* — *adj* : socialista — **socialize** ['soːʃə,laɪz] *v* **-ized; -izing** *vt* : socializar — *vi* **~ with** : alternar con — **society** [sə'saɪəṭi] *n, pl* **-eties** : sociedad *f* — **sociology** [,soːsi'ɑlədʒi] *n* : sociología *f*

sock[1] ['sak] n, pl **socks** or **sox** ['saks] : calcetín m

sock[2] vt : pegar, golpear — **~** n PUNCH : puñetazo m

socket ['sakət] n 1 or **electric ~** : enchufe m, toma f de corriente 2 or **eye ~** : órbita f, cuenca f 3 : glena f (de una articulación)

soda ['so:də] n 1 or **~ pop** : refresco m, gaseosa f 2 or **~ water** : soda f

sodium ['so:diəm] n : sodio m

sofa ['so:fə] n : sofá m

soft ['sɔft] adj 1 : blando 2 SMOOTH : suave — **softball** ['sɔft,bɔl] n : softbol m — **soft drink** n : refresco m — **soften** ['sɔfən] vt 1 : ablandar 2 EASE, SMOOTH : suavizar — vi 1 : ablandarse 2 EASE : suavizarse — **softly** ['sɔftli] adv : suavemente — **software** ['sɔft,wær] n : software m

soggy ['sɔgi] adj **soggier; -est** : empapado

soil ['sɔɪl] vt : ensuciar — **~** n DIRT : tierra f

solace ['saləs] n : consuelo m

solar ['so:lər] adj : solar

sold → **sell**

solder ['sadər, 'sɔ-] n : soldadura f — **~** vt : soldar

soldier ['so:ldʒər] n : soldado mf

sole[1] ['so:l] n : lenguado m (pez)

sole[2] n : planta f (del pie), suela f (de un zapato)

sole[3] adj : único — **solely** ['so:li] adv : únicamente, sólo

solemn ['saləm] adj : solemne — **solemnity** [sə'lemnəti] n, pl **-ties** : solemnidad f

solicit [sə'lisət] vt : solicitar

solid ['saləd] adj 1 : sólido 2 UNBROKEN : continuo 3 **~ gold** : oro m macizo 4 **two ~ hours** : dos horas seguidas — **~** n : sólido m — **solidarity** [salə'dærəti] n : solidaridad f — **solidify** [sə'lɪdə,faɪ] v **-fied; -fying** vt : solidificar — vi : solidificarse — **solidity** [sə'lɪdəti] n, pl **-ties** : solidez f

solitary ['salə,teri] adj : solitario — **solitude** ['salə,tu:d, -,tju:d] n : soledad f

solo ['so:,lo:] n, pl **-los** : solo m — **soloist** ['so:loɪst] n : solista mf

solution [sə'lu:ʃən] n : solución f — **soluble** ['saljəbəl] adj : soluble — **solve** ['salv] vt **solved; solving** : resolver — **solvent** ['salvənt] n : solvente m

somber ['sambər] adj : sombrío

some ['sʌm] adj 1 (of unspecified identity) : un 2 (of an unspecified amount) : algo de, un poco de 3 (of an unspecified number) : unos 4 CERTAIN : al-

gunos 5 **that was ~ game!** : ¡fue un partidazo! — **~** pron 1 SEVERAL : algunos, unos 2 PART : un poco, algo — **~** adv — **twenty people** : unas veinte personas — **somebody** ['sʌmbədi, -,badi] pron : alguien — **someday** ['sʌm,deɪ] adv : algún día — **somehow** ['sʌm,hau] adv 1 : de algún modo 2 **~ or other** : de alguna manera u otra — **someone** ['sʌm,wʌn] pron : alguien

somersault ['sʌmər,sɔlt] n : voltereta f, salto m mortal

something ['sʌmθɪŋ] pron 1 : algo 2 **~ else** : otra cosa — **sometime** ['sʌm,taɪm] adv 1 : algún día, en algún momento 2 **~ next month** : (durante) el mes que viene — **sometimes** ['sʌm,taɪmz] adv : a veces — **somewhat** ['sʌm,hwat, -,hwɑt] adv : algo — **somewhere** ['sʌm,hwer] adv 1 : en alguna parte, en algún lado 2 **~ around** : alrededor de 3 **~ else** → **elsewhere**

son ['sʌn] n : hijo m

song ['sɔŋ] n : canción f

son-in-law ['sʌnɪn,lɔ] n, pl **sons-in-law** : yerno m

sonnet ['sanət] n : soneto m

soon ['su:n] adv 1 : pronto 2 SHORTLY : dentro de poco 3 **as ~ as** : en cuanto 4 **as ~ as possible** : lo más pronto posible 5 **~ after** : poco después 6 **~er or later** : tarde o temprano 7 **the ~er the better** : cuanto antes mejor

soot ['sut, 'su:t, 'sʌt] n : hollín m

soothe ['su:ð] vt **soothed; soothing** 1 CALM : calmar 2 RELIEVE : aliviar

sop ['sap] vt **sopped; sopping ~ up** : absorber

sophistication [sə,fɪstə'keɪʃən] n : sofisticación f — **sophisticated** [sə'fɪstə,keɪtəd] adj : sofisticado

sophomore ['saf,mor, 'safə,mor] n : estudiante mf de segundo año

soprano [sə'præ,no:] n, pl **-nos** : soprano mf

sorcerer ['sɔrsərər] n : hechicero m, brujo m — **sorcery** ['sɔrsəri] n : hechicería f, brujería f

sordid ['sɔrdəd] adj : sórdido

sore ['sor] adj **sorer; sorest** 1 : dolorido 2 ANGRY : enfadado 3 **~ throat** : dolor m de garganta 4 **I have a ~ throat** : me duele la garganta — **~** n : llaga f — **sorely** ['sorli] adv : muchísimo — **soreness** ['sornəs] n : dolor m

sorrow ['saro] n : pesar m, pena f — **sorry** ['sari] adj **sorrier; -est** 1 PITIFUL : lamentable 2 **feel ~ for** : compadecer 3 **I'm ~** : lo siento

sort ['sɔrt] n 1 : tipo m, clase f 2 a — of : una especie de — ~ vt : clasificar — **sort of** adv 1 SOMEWHAT : algo 2 MORE OR LESS : más o menos

SOS [ˌɛsˌoːˈɛs] n : SOS m

so-so ['soːˈsoː] adj & adv : así así fam

soufflé [suːˈfleɪ] n : suflé m

sought → **seek**

soul ['soːl] n : alma f

sound[1] ['saʊnd] adj 1 HEALTHY : sano 2 FIRM : sólido 3 SENSIBLE : lógico 4 a ~ **sleep** : un sueño profundo 5 **safe and** ~ : sano y salvo

sound[2] n : sonido m — vt : hacer sonar, tocar (una trompeta, etc.) — vi 1 : sonar 2 SEEM : parecer

sound[3] n CHANNEL : brazo m de mar — vt 1 : sondar (en navegación) 2 or ~ **out** : sondear

soundly ['saʊndli] adv 1 SOLIDLY : sólidamente 2 DEEPLY : profundamente

soundproof ['saʊndˌpruːf] adj : insonorizado

soup ['suːp] n : sopa f

sour ['saʊər] adj 1 : agrio 2 ~ **milk** : leche f cortada — ~ vt : agriar

source ['sɔrs] n : fuente f, origen m

south ['saʊθ] adv : al sur — ~ adj : (del) sur — ~ n : sur m — **South African** adj : sudafricano — **South American** adj : sudamericano — **southeast** [saʊˈθiːst] adv : hacia el sureste — ~ adj : (del) sureste — ~ n : sureste m, sudeste m — **southeastern** [saʊˈθiːstərn] adj → **southeast** — **southerly** ['sʌðərli] adv & adj : del sur — **southern** ['sʌðərn] adj : del sur, meridional — **southwest** [saʊˈθwɛst] adv : hacia el suroeste — ~ adj : (del) suroeste — ~ n : suroeste m, sudoeste m — **southwestern** [saʊˈθwɛstərn] adj → **southwest**

souvenir [ˌsuːvəˈnɪr, 'suːvə-] n : recuerdo m

sovereign ['sɑvərən] n : soberano m, -na f — ~ adj : soberano — **sovereignty** ['sɑvərənti] n, pl -ties : soberanía f

Soviet ['soːviˌɛt, 'sɑ-, -viət] adj : soviético

sow[1] ['saʊ] n : cerda f

sow[2] ['soː] vt sowed; sown ['soːn] or sowed; sowing : sembrar

sox → **sock**

soybean ['sɔɪˌbiːn] n : soya f, soja f

spa ['spɑ] n : balneario m

space ['speɪs] n 1 : espacio m 2 ROOM, SPOT : sitio m, lugar m — ~ vt **spaced; spacing** : espaciar — **spaceship** ['speɪsˌʃɪp] n : nave f espacial — **space shuttle** n : transbordador m espacial — **spacious** ['speɪʃəs] adj : espacioso, amplio

spade[1] ['speɪd] n SHOVEL : pala f

spade[2] n : pica f (naipe)

spaghetti [spəˈɡɛti] n : espaguetis mpl

span ['spæn] n 1 PERIOD : espacio m 2 : luz f (entre dos soportes) — ~ vt **spanned; spanning** 1 : abarcar (un período) 2 CROSS : extenderse sobre

Spaniard ['spænjərd] n : español m, -ñola f

spaniel ['spænjəl] n : spaniel m

Spanish ['spænɪʃ] adj : español — ~ n : español m (idioma)

spank ['spæŋk] vt : dar palmadas a (en las nalgas)

spar ['spɑr] vi sparred; sparring : entrenarse (en boxeo)

spare ['spær] vt spared; sparing 1 PARDON : perdonar 2 SAVE : ahorrar 3 **can you** ~ **a dollar?** : ¿me das un dólar? 4 **I can't** ~ **the time** : no tengo tiempo 5 ~ **no expense** : no reparar en gastos 6 **to** ~ : de sobra — ~ adj 1 : de repuesto 2 EXCESS : de más 3 LEAN : delgado — ~ n or ~ **part** : repuesto m — **spare time** n : tiempo m libre — **sparing** ['spærɪŋ] adj : parco, económico

spark ['spɑrk] n : chispa f — ~ vi : chispear, echar chispas — vt : despertar (interés), provocar (crítica) — **sparkle** ['spɑrkəl] vi -**kled; -kling** : destellar, centellear — ~ n : destello m, centelleo m — **spark plug** n : bujía f

sparrow ['spæroː] n : gorrión m

sparse ['spɑrs] adj sparser; -est : escaso

spasm ['spæzəm] n : espasmo m

spat[1] → **spit**

spat[2] n QUARREL : disputa f, pelea f

spatter ['spætər] vt : salpicar

spawn ['spɔn] vi : desovar — vt : engendrar, producir — ~ n : hueva f

speak ['spiːk] v spoke ['spoːk]; spoken ['spoːkən]; **speaking** vi 1 : hablar 2 ~ **out against** : denunciar 3 ~ **up** : hablar más alto 4 ~ **up for** : defender — vt 1 : decir 2 : hablar (un idioma) — **speaker** ['spiːkər] n 1 ORATOR : orador m, -dora f 2 : hablante mf (de un idioma) 3 LOUDSPEAKER : altavoz m

spear ['spɪr] n : lanza f — **spearhead** ['spɪrˌhɛd] n : punta f de lanza — ~ vt : encabezar — **spearmint** ['spɪrmɪnt] n : menta f verde

special ['spɛʃəl] adj : especial — **specialist** ['spɛʃəlɪst] n : especialista mf — **specialization** [ˌspɛʃələˈzeɪʃən] n : especialización f — **specialize** ['spɛʃə-

.larz] *vi* **-ized; -izing** : especializarse — **specially** *adv* : especialmente — **specialty** ['speʃəlṭi], *n, pl* **-ties** : especialidad *f*

species ['spiːʃiːz, -sɪz] *ns & pl* : especie *f*

specify ['spesəˌfaɪ] *vt* **-fied; -fying** : especificar — **specific** [sprɪsɪfɪk] *adj* : específico — **specifically** [sprɪsɪfɪkli] *adv* **1** : específicamente **2** EXPLICITLY : expresamente — **specification** [spesəfəˈkeɪʃən] *n* : especificación *f*

specimen ['spesəmən] *n* : espécimen *m*

speck ['spek] *n* **1** SPOT : mancha *f* **2** BIT : mota *f* — **speckled** ['spekəld] *adj* : moteado

spectacle ['spektɪkəl] *n* **1** : espectáculo *m* **2** ~**s** *npl* GLASSES : gafas *fpl*, lentes *fpl*, anteojos *mpl* — **spectacular** [spekˈtækjələr] *adj* : espectacular — **spectator** ['spekˌteɪtər] *n* : espectador *m*, -dora *f*

specter *or* **spectre** ['spektər] *n* : espectro *m*

spectrum ['spektrəm] *n, pl* **-tra** [-trə] *or* **-trums** : espectro *m* **2** RANGE : gama *f*

speculation [spekjəˈleɪʃən] *n* : especulación *f*

speech ['spiːtʃ] *n* **1** : habla *f* **2** ADDRESS : discurso *m* — **speechless** ['spiːtʃləs] *adj* : mudo

speed ['spiːd] *n* **1** : rapidez *f* **2** VELOCITY : velocidad *f* — ~ *v* **sped** ['sped] *or* **speeded; speeding** *vi* **1** : conducir a exceso de velocidad **2** ~ **off** : irse a toda velocidad **3** ~ **up** : acelerarse — *vt or* ~ **up** : acelerar — **speed limit** *n* : velocidad *f* máxima — **speedometer** [sprˈdɑmətər] *n* : velocímetro *m* — **speedy** ['spiːdi] *adj* **speedier, -est** : rápido

spell¹ ['spel] *vt* **1** : escribir (las letras de) **2** *or* ~ **out** : deletrear **3** MEAN : significar

spell² *n* ENCHANTMENT : hechizo *m*

spell³ *n* : período *m* (de tiempo)

spellbound ['spelˌbaʊnd] *adj* : embelesado

spelling ['spelɪŋ] *n* : ortografía *f*

spend ['spend] *vt* **spent** ['spent]; **spending 1** : gastar (dinero) **2** : pasar (las vacaciones, etc.) **3** ~ **time on** : dedicar tiempo a

sperm ['spərm] *n, pl* **sperm** *or* **sperms** : esperma *mf*

spew ['spjuː] *vt* : vomitar, arrojar (lava, etc.)

sphere ['sfɪr] *n* : esfera *f* — **spherical** ['sfɪrɪkəl, 'sfer-] *adj* : esférico

spice ['spaɪs] *n* : especia *f* — ~ *vt* **spiced; spicing** : condimentar, sazonar — **spicy** ['spaɪsi] *adj* **spicier; -est** : picante

spider ['spaɪdər] *n* : araña *f*

spigot ['spɪɡət, -kət] *n* : grifo *m* Spain, llave *f* Lat

spike ['spaɪk] *n* **1** : clavo *m* (grande) **2** POINT : punta *f* — **spiky** ['spaɪki] *adj* : puntiagudo

spill ['spɪl] *vt* : derramar — *vi* : derramarse

spin ['spɪn] *v* **spun** ['spʌn]; **spinning** *vi* **1** : girar — *vt* **1** : hilar (lana, etc.) **2** TWIRL : hacer girar — *n* **1** : vuelta *f*, giro *m* **2 go for a** ~ : dar una vuelta (en auto)

spinach ['spɪnɪtʃ] *n* : espinacas *fpl*

spinal cord ['spaɪnəl] *n* : médula *f* espinal

spindle ['spɪndəl] *n* : huso *m* (para hilar) — **spindly** ['spɪndli] *adj* : larguirucho *fam*

spine ['spaɪn] *n* **1** : columna *f* vertebral **2** QUILL : púa *f* **3** THORN : espina *f* **4** : lomo *m* (de un libro)

spinster ['spɪnstər] *n* : soltera *f*

spiral ['spaɪrəl] *adj* : de espiral, en espiral — ~ *n* : espiral *f* — *vi* **-raled** *or* **-ralled; -raling** *or* **-ralling** : ir en espiral

spire ['spaɪr] *n* : aguja *f*

spirit ['spɪrət] *n* **1** : espíritu *m* **2 in good** ~**s** : animado **3** ~**s** *npl* : licores *mpl* — **spirited** ['spɪrətəd] *adj* : animado — **spiritual** ['spɪrɪtʃuəl, -tʃəl] *adj* : espiritual — **spirituality** [spɪrɪtʃuˈæləṭi] *n, pl* **-ties** : espiritualidad *f*

spit¹ ['spɪt] *n* ROTISSERIE : asador *m*

spit² *v* **spit** *or* **spat** ['spæt]; **spitting** : escupir — *n* SALIVA : saliva *f*

spite ['spaɪt] *n* **1** : rencor *m* **2 in** ~ **of** : a pesar de — ~ *vt* **spited; spiting** : fastidiar — **spiteful** ['spaɪtfəl] *adj* : rencoroso

spittle ['spɪtəl] *n* : saliva *f*

splash ['splæʃ] *vt* : salpicar — *vi* **1** : salpicar **2** *or* ~ **about** : chapotear — ~ *n* **1** : salpicadura *f* **2** : mancha *f* (de color, etc.)

splatter ['splætər] → **spatter**

spleen ['spliːn] *n* : bazo *m* (órgano)

splendor ['splendər] *n* : esplendor *m* — **splendid** ['splendəd] *adj* : espléndido

splint ['splɪnt] *n* : tablilla *f*

splinter ['splɪntər] *n* : astilla *f* — *vi* : astillarse

split ['splɪt] *v* **split; splitting** *vt* **1** : partir **2** BURST : reventar **3** *or* ~ **up** : dividir — *vi* **1** : partirse, rajarse **2** *or* ~ **up**

: dividirse — ~ *n* **1** CRACK : rajadura *f* **2** *or* ~ **seam** : descosido *m* **3** DIVISION : división *f*

splurge ['splərdʒ] *vi* **splurged; splurging** : derrochar dinero

spoil ['spɔɪl] *vt* **spoiled** *or* **spoilt** ['spɔɪlt]; **spoiling 1** RUIN : estropear **2** PAMPER : consentir, mimar — **spoils** *npl* : botín *m*

spoke¹ ['spoːk] → **speak**

spoke² *n* : rayo *m* (de una rueda)

spoken → **speak**

spokesman ['spoːksmən] *n, pl* **-men** [-mən, -ˌmɛn] : portavoz *mf* — **spokeswoman** ['spoːksˌwʊmən] *n, pl* **-women** [-ˌwɪmən] : portavoz *f*

sponge ['spʌndʒ] *n* : esponja *f* — **sponged; sponging** : limpiar con una esponja — **spongy** ['spʌndʒi] *adj* **spongier; -est** : esponjoso

sponsor ['spɑntsər] *n* : patrocinador *m*, -dora *f* — ~ *vt* : patrocinar — **sponsorship** ['spɑntsərˌʃɪp] *n* : patrocinio *m*

spontaneity [ˌspɑntəˈniːəti, -ˈneɪ-] *n* : espontaneidad *f* — **spontaneous** [spɑnˈteɪniəs] *adj* : espontáneo

spooky ['spuːki] *adj* **spookier; -est** : espeluzante

spool ['spuːl] *n* : carrete *m*

spoon ['spuːn] *n* : cuchara *f* — **spoonful** ['spuːnˌfʊl] *n* : cucharada *f*

sporadic [spəˈrædɪk] *adj* : esporádico

spore ['spor] *n* : espora *f*

sport ['sport] *n* **1** : deporte *m* **2 be a good ~** : tener espíritu deportivo — **sportsman** ['sportsmən] *n, pl* **-men** [-mən, -ˌmɛn] : deportista *m* — **sportswoman** ['sportsˌwʊmən] *n, pl* **-women** [-ˌwɪmən] : deportista *f* — **sporty** ['sporti] *adj* **sportier; -est** : deportivo

spot ['spɑt] *n* **1** : mancha *f* **2** DOT : punto *m* **3** PLACE : lugar *m*, sitio *m* **4 in a tight ~** : en apuros **5 on the ~** : INSTANTLY : en ese mismo momento — ~ *vt* **spotted; spotting 1** STAIN : manchar **2** DETECT, NOTICE : ver, descubrir — **spotless** ['spɑtləs] *adj* : impecable — **spotlight** ['spɑtˌlaɪt] *n* **1** : foco *m*, reflector *m* **2 be in the ~** : ser el centro de atención — **spotty** ['spɑti] *adj* **spottier; -est** : irregular

spouse ['spaʊs] *n* : cónyuge *mf*

spout ['spaʊt] *vi* : salir a chorros — ~ *n* **1** : pico *m* (de una jarra, etc.) **2** STREAM : chorro *m*

sprain ['spreɪn] *n* : esguince *m* — ~ *vt* : sufrir un esguince en

sprawl ['sprɔl] *vi* **1** : repantigarse (en un sillón, etc.) **2** EXTEND : extenderse — ~ *n* : extensión *f*

spray¹ ['spreɪ] *n* BOUQUET : ramillete *m*

spray² *n* **1** MIST : rocío *m* **2** *or* **aerosol** : spray *m* **3** *or* ~ **bottle** : atomizador *m* — ~ *vt* : rociar (una superficie), pulverizar (un líquido)

spread ['spred] *v* **spread; spreading** *vt* **1** : propagar (enfermedades), difundir (noticias, etc.) **2** *or* ~ **out** : extender **3** : untar (con mantequilla, etc.) — *vi* **1** : propagarse, difundirse **2** *or* ~ **out** : extenderse — ~ *n* **1** : propagación *f*, difusión *f* **2** PASTE : pasta *f* (para untar) — **spreadsheet** ['spredˌʃiːt] *n* : hoja *f* de cálculo

spree ['spri] *n* **go on a ~** : ir de juerga *fam*

sprig ['sprɪg] *n* : ramito *m*

sprightly ['spraɪtli] *adj* **sprightlier; -est** : vivo

spring ['sprɪŋ] *v* **sprang** ['spræŋ] *or* **sprung** ['sprʌŋ]; **sprung; springing** *vi* **1** : saltar **2** ~ **from** : surgir de **3** ~ **up** : surgir — *vt* **1** ACTIVATE : accionar **2** ~ **a leak** : hacer agua **3** ~ **sth on s.o.** : sorprender a algn con algo — ~ *n* **1** : manantial *m* (de aguas) **2** : primavera *f* (estación) **3** LEAP : salto *m* **4** RESILIENCE : elasticidad *f* **5** : resorte *m* (mecanismo) **6** *or* **bedspring** : muelle *m* — **springboard** ['sprɪŋˌbord] *n* : trampolín *m* — **springtime** ['sprɪŋˌtaɪm] *n* : primavera *f* — **springy** ['sprɪŋi] *adj* **springier; -est** : mullido

sprinkle ['sprɪŋkəl] *vt* **-kled; -kling 1** : salpicar, rociar **2** DUST : espolvorear — ~ *n* : llovizna *f* — **sprinkler** ['sprɪŋkələr] *n* : aspersor *m*

sprint ['sprɪnt] *vi* **1** : correr **2** : esprintar (en deportes) — ~ *n* : esprint *m* (en deportes)

sprout ['spraʊt] *vi* : brotar — ~ *n* : brote *m*

spruce¹ ['spruːs] *vt* **spruced; sprucing** ~ **up** : arreglar

spruce² *n* : picea *f* (árbol)

spry ['spraɪ] *adj* **sprier** *or* **spryer** ['spraɪər]; **spriest** *or* **spryest** ['spraɪəst] : ágil, activo

spun → **spin**

spur ['spər] *n* **1** : espuela *f* **2** STIMULUS : acicate *m* **3 on the ~ of the moment** : sin pensarlo — ~ *vt* **spurred; spurring** *or* ~ **on 1** : espolear (un caballo) **2** MOTIVATE : motivar

spurn ['spərn] *vt* : desdeñar, rechazar

spurt¹ ['spərt] *vi* : salir a chorros — ~ *n* : chorro *m*

spurt² *n* **1** : arranque *m* (de energía, etc.) **2 work in ~s** : trabajar por rachas

spy ['spaɪ] *v* **spied; spying** *vt* : ver, divisar — *vi* — **on s.o.** : espiar a algn — ~ *n* : espía *mf*

squabble ['skwɑbəl] *n* : riña *f*, pelea *f* — ~ *vi* **-bled; -bling** : reñir, pelearse

squad ['skwɑd] *n* : pelotón *m* (militar), brigada *f* (de policías)

squadron ['skwɑdrən] *n* : escuadrón *m* (de soldados), escuadra *f* (de aviones o naves)

squalid ['skwɑlɪd] *adj* : miserable

squall ['skwɔl] *n* : turbión *m*

squalor ['skwɑlər] *n* : miseria *f*

squander ['skwɑndər] *vt* : derrochar (dinero, etc.), desperdiciar (oportunidades, etc.)

square ['skwær] *n* **1** : cuadrado *m* **2** : plaza *f* (de una ciudad) — ~ *adj* **squarer; -est 1** : cuadrado **2** HONEST : justo **3** EVEN : en paz **4 a ~ meal** : una comida decente — ~ *vt* **squared; squaring 1** : elevar al cuadrado (un número) **2** : saldar (una cuenta) — **square root** *n* : raíz *f* cuadrada

squash[1] ['skwɑʃ, 'skwɔʃ] *vt* **1** : aplastar **2** : acallar (protestas, etc.) — ~ *n* **1** : squash *m* (deporte)

squash[2] *n, pl* **squashes** *or* **squash** : calabaza *f* (vegetal)

squat ['skwɑt] *vi* **squatted; squatting 1** *or* **~ down** : ponerse en cuclillas **2** : ocupar un lugar sin derecho — ~ *adj* : achaparrado — **squatter; squattest** : achaparrado

squawk ['skwɔk] *n* : graznido *m* — ~ *vi* : graznar

squeak ['skwiːk] *vi* **1** : chillar **2** CREAK : chirriar — ~ *n* **1** : chillido *m* **2** CREAK : chirrido *m* — **squeaky** ['skwiːki] *adj* **squeakier; -est** : chirriante

squeal ['skwiːl] *vi* **1** : chillar (dícese de personas, etc.), chirriar (dícese de frenos, etc.) **2** PROTEST : quejarse — ~ *n* **1** : chillido *m* (de una persona), chirrido *m* (de frenos, etc.)

squeamish ['skwiːmɪʃ] *adj* : impresionable, delicado

squeeze ['skwiːz] *vt* **squeezed; squeezing 1** : apretar **2** : exprimir (frutas, etc.) **3** : extraer (jugo, etc.) — ~ *n* : apretón *m*

squid ['skwɪd] *n, pl* **squid** *or* **squids** : calamar *m*

squint ['skwɪnt] *vi* : entrecerrar los ojos — ~ *n* : estrabismo *m*

squirm ['skwərm] *vi* : retorcerse

squirrel ['skwərəl] *n* : ardilla *f*

squirt ['skwərt] *vt* : lanzar un chorro de — *vi* : salir a chorros — ~ *n* : chorrito *m*

stab ['stæb] *n* **1** : puñalada *f* **2** ~ **of pain** : pinchazo *m* **3 take a ~ at** : intentar — ~ *vt* **stabbed; stabbing 1** KNIFE : apuñalar **2** STICK : clavar

stable[1] ['steɪbəl] *n* **1** : establo *m* (para ganado) **2** *or* **horse ~** : caballeriza *f* — ~ *adj* **-bler; -blest** : estable — **stability** [stə'bɪləti] *n, pl* **-ties** : estabilidad *f* — **stabilize** ['steɪbəˌlaɪz] *vt* **-lized; -lizing** : estabilizar

stack ['stæk] *n* : montón *m*, pila *f* — ~ *vt* : amontonar, apilar

stadium ['steɪdiəm] *n, pl* **-dia** *or* **-diums** : estadio *m*

staff ['stæf, stævz] *n, pl* **staffs** *or* **staves** ['steɪvz, 'steɪvz] **1** : bastón *m* **2** *pl* **staffs** PERSONNEL : personal *m* **3** *pl* **staffs** : pentagrama *m* (en música) — ~ ['stæf] *vt* : proveer de personal

stag ['stæg] *n, pl* **stags** *or* **stag** : ciervo *m*, venado *m* — ~ *adj* : sólo para hombres — ~ *adv* **go** ~ : ir solo

stage ['steɪdʒ] *n* **1** : escenario *m* (de un teatro) **2** PHASE : etapa *f* **3 the ~** : el teatro — ~ *vt* **staged; staging 1** : poner en escena **2** ARRANGE : montar — **stagecoach** ['steɪdʒˌkoːtʃ] *n* : diligencia *f*

stagger ['stægər] *vi* : tambalearse — *vt* **1** : escalonar (turnos, etc.) **2 be ~ed by** : quedarse estupefacto por — ~ *n* : tambaleo *m* — **staggering** ['stægərɪŋ] *adj* : asombroso

stagnant ['stægnənt] *adj* : estancado — **stagnate** ['stægneɪt] *vi* **-nated; -nating** : estancarse

stain ['steɪn] *vt* **1** : manchar **2** : teñir (madera) — ~ *n* **1** : mancha *f* **2** DYE : tinte *m*, tintura *f* — **stainless steel** ['steɪnləs-] *n* : acero inoxidable

stair ['stær] *n* **1** STEP : escalón *m*, peldaño *m* **2** ~**s** *npl* : escalera(s) *f(pl)* — **staircase** ['stærˌkeɪs] *n* : escalera(s) *f(pl)* — **stairway** ['stærˌweɪ] *n* : escalera(s) *f(pl)*

stake ['steɪk] *n* **1** POST : estaca *f* **2** BET : apuesta *f* **3** INTEREST : intereses *mpl* **4 be at ~** : estar en juego — ~ *vt* **staked; staking 1** : estacar **2** BET : jugarse **3** ~ **a claim to** : reclamar

stale ['steɪl] *adj* **staler; stalest 1** : duro (dícese del pan) **2** OLD : viejo **3** STUFFY : viciado

stalk[1] ['stɔk] *n* : tallo *m* (de una planta)

stalk[2] ['stɔk] *vt* : acechar — *vi or* ~ **off** : irse con altivez

stall[1] ['stɔl] *n* **1** : compartimiento *m* (de un establo) **2** STAND : puesto *m* — ~ *vt* : parar (un motor) — *vi* : pararse

stall² vt DELAY : entretener — vi : andar con rodeos

stallion ['stæljən] n : caballo m semental

stalwart ['stɔlwərt] adj 1 STRONG : fornido 2 ~ **supporter** : partidario m leal

stamina ['stæmənə] n : resistencia f

stammer ['stæmər] vi : tartamudear — ~ n : tartamudeo m

stamp ['stæmp] n 1 SEAL : sello m 2 DIE : cuño m 3 or **postage** ~ : sello m, estampilla f Lat, timbre m Lat — vt 1 : franquear (una carta) 2 IMPRINT : sellar 3 MINT : acuñar 4 ~ **one's foot** : dar una patada (en el suelo)

stampede [stæm'pi:d] n : estampida f — ~ vi **-peded; -peding** : salir en estampida

stance ['stænts] n : postura f

stand ['stænd] v **stood** ['stʊd], **standing** vi 1 : estar de pie, estar parado Lat 2 BE : estar 3 CONTINUE : seguir vigente 4 LIE, REST : reposar 5 ~ **aside** or ~ **back** : apartarse 6 ~ **out** : sobresalir 7 or ~ **up** : ponerse de pie, pararse Lat — vt 1 PLACE : poner, colocar 2 ENDURE : soportar 3 ~ **a chance** : tener una posibilidad — **stand by** vt 1 : mantener (una promesa, etc.) 2 SUPPORT : apoyar — **stand for** vt 1 MEAN : significar 2 PERMIT : permitir — **stand up** vi 1 ~ **for** : defender 2 ~ **up to** : resistir a — ~ n 1 RESISTANCE : resistencia f 2 STALL : puesto m 3 BASE : base f 4 POSITION : posición f 5 ~**s** npl : tribuna f

standard ['stændərd] n 1 : norma f 2 BANNER : estandarte m 3 CRITERION : criterio m 4 ~ **of living** : nivel m de vida — ~ adj : estándar — **standardize** ['stændər,daɪz] vt **-ized; -izing** : estandarizar

standing ['stændɪŋ] n 1 RANK : posición f 2 DURATION : duración f

standpoint ['stænd,pɔɪnt] n : punto m de vista

standstill ['stænd,stɪl] n 1 **be at a** ~ : estar paralizado 2 **come to a** ~ : pararse

stank → **stink**

stanza ['stænzə] n : estrofa f

staple¹ ['steɪpəl] n : producto m principal — ~ adj : principal, básico

staple² ['steɪpəl] n : grapa f (para papeles) — vt **-pled; -pling** : grapar, engrapar Lat — **stapler** ['steɪplər] n : grapadora f, engrapadora f Lat

star ['stɑr] n : estrella f — v **starred; starring** vt FEATURE : estar protagonizado por — vi ~ **in** : protagonizar

starboard ['stɑrbərd] n : estribor m

starch ['stɑrtʃ] vt : almidonar — ~ n 1 : almidón m 2 : fécula f (comida)

stardom ['stɑrdəm] n : estrellato m

stare ['stær] vi **stared; staring** : mirar fijamente — ~ n : mirada f fija

starfish ['stɑr,fɪʃ] n : estrella f de mar

stark ['stɑrk] adj 1 PLAIN : austero 2 HARSH : severo, duro 3 SHARP : marcado — ~ adv 1 : completamente 2 ~ **naked** : en cueros (vivos)

starlight ['stɑr,laɪt] n : luz f de las estrellas

starling ['stɑrlɪŋ] n : estornino m

starry ['stɑri] adj **starrier; -est** : estrellado

start ['stɑrt] vi 1 : empezar, comenzar 2 SET OUT : salir 3 JUMP : sobresaltarse 4 or ~ **up** : arrancar — vt 1 : empezar, comenzar 2 CAUSE : provocar 3 or ~ **up** ESTABLISH : montar 4 or ~ **up** : arrancar (un motor, etc.) — ~ n 1 : principio m 2 **get an early** ~ : salir temprano 3 **give s.o. a** ~ : asustar a algn — **starter** ['stɑrtər] n : motor m de arranque (de un vehículo)

startle ['stɑrtəl] vt **-tled; -tling** : asustar

starve ['stɑrv] v **starved; starving** vi : morirse de hambre — vt : privar de comida — **starvation** [stɑr'veɪʃən] n : inanición f, hambre f

stash ['stæʃ] vt : esconder

state ['steɪt] n 1 : estado m 2 **the States** : los Estados Unidos — ~ vt **stated; stating** 1 SAY : decir 2 REPORT : exponer — **stately** ['steɪtli] adj **statelier; -est** : majestuoso — **statement** ['steɪtmənt] n 1 : declaración f 2 or **bank** ~ : estado m de cuenta — **statesman** ['steɪtsmən] n, pl **-men** [-mən, -mɛn] : estadista mf

static ['stætɪk] adj : estático — ~ n : estática f

station ['steɪʃən] n 1 : estación f (de trenes, etc.) 2 RANK : condición f (social) 3 : canal m (de televisión), emisora f (de radio) 4 ~ **fire station, police station** — vt : apostar, estacionar — **stationary** ['steɪʃəneri] adj : estacionario

stationery ['steɪʃəneri] n : papel m y sobres mpl (para cartas)

station wagon n : camioneta f (familiar)

statistic [stə'tɪstɪk] n : estadística f — **statistical** [stə'tɪstɪkəl] adj : estadístico

statue ['stætʃu] n : estatua f

stature ['stætʃər] n : estatura f, talla f

status ['steɪtəs, 'stæ-] n 1 : situación f 2 or **social** ~ : estatus m 3 **marital** ~ : estado m civil

statute ['stætʃuːt] *n* : estatuto *m*

staunch ['stɔntʃ] *adj* : leal

stave ['steɪv] *vt* **staved** *or* **stove** ['stoːv]; **staving 1 ~ in** : romper **2 ~ off** : evitar

staves → staff

stay[1] ['steɪ] *vi* **1** REMAIN : quedarse, permanecer **2** LODGE : alojarse **3 ~ awake** : mantenerse despierto **4 ~ in** : quedarse en casa — *vt* : suspender (una ejecución, etc.) — **~** *n* **1** : estancia *f*, estadía *f Lat* **2** SUSPENSION : suspensión *f*

stay[2] *n* SUPPORT : soporte *m*

stead ['sted] *n* **1 in s.o.'s ~** : en lugar de algn **2 stand s.o. in good ~** : ser muy útil a algn — **steadfast** ['sted,fæst] *adj* **1** FIRM : firme **2** LOYAL : leal, fiel — **steadily** ['stedəli] *adv* **1** : progresivamente **2** INCESSANTLY : sin parar **3** FIXEDLY : fijamente — **steady** ['stedi] *adj* **steadier; -est** FIRM, SURE : firme, seguro **2** FIXED : fijo **3** DEPENDABLE : responsable **4** CONSTANT : constante — **~** *vt* **steadied; steadying 1** : mantener firme **2** : calmar (los nervios)

steak ['steɪk] *n* : bistec *m*, filete *m*

steal ['stiːl] *v* **stole** ['stoːl]; **stolen** ['stoːlən]; **stealing** *vt* : robar — *vi* **1** : robar **2 ~ away** : escabullirse

stealth ['stelθ] *n* : sigilo *m* — **stealthy** ['stelθi] *adj* **stealthier; -est** : furtivo, sigiloso

steam ['stiːm] *n* **1** : vapor *m* **2 let off ~** : desahogarse — *vi* : echar vapor — *vt* **1** : cocer al vapor **2 ~ up** : empañar — **steam engine** *n* : motor *m* de vapor — **steamship** ['stiːm,ʃɪp] *n* : (barco *m* de) vapor *m* — **steamy** ['stiːmi] *adj* **steamier; -est 1** : lleno de vapor **2** PASSIONATE : tórrido

steel ['stiːl] *n* : acero *m* — **~** *vt* **~ oneself** : armarse de valor — **~** *adj* : de acero

steep[1] ['stiːp] *adj* **1** : empinado **2** CONSIDERABLE : considerable **3** : muy alto (dícese de precios)

steep[2] *vt* : dejar (té, etc.) en infusión

steeple ['stiːpəl] *n* : aguja *f*, campanario *m*

steer[1] ['stɪr] *n* : buey *m*

steer[2] *vt* : dirigir (un auto, etc.), pilotear (un barco) — **steering wheel** *n* : volante *m*

stem[1] ['stem] *n* : tallo *m* (de una planta), pie *m* (de una copa) — **~** *vi* **~ from** : provenir de

stem[2] *vt* **stemmed; stemming** : contener, detener

stench ['stentʃ] *n* : hedor *m*, mal olor *m*

stencil ['stensəl] *n* : plantilla *f* (para marcar)

step ['step] *n* **1** : paso *m* **2** RUNG, STAIR : escalón *m* **3 ~ by ~** : paso por paso **4 take ~s** : tomar medidas **5 watch your ~** : mira por dónde caminas — **~** *vi* **stepped; stepping 1** : dar un paso **2 ~ back** : retroceder **3 ~ down** RESIGN : retirarse **4 ~ in** : intervenir **5 ~ out** : salir (por un momento) **6 this way** : pase por aquí — **step up** *vt* INCREASE : aumentar

stepbrother ['step,brʌðər] *n* : hermanastro *m* — **stepdaughter** ['step,dɔtər] *n* : hijastra *f* — **stepfather** ['step,fɑðər, -fɑ-] *n* : padrastro *m*

stepladder ['step,lædər] *n* : escalera *f* de tijera

stepmother ['step,mʌðər] *n* : madrastra *f* — **stepsister** ['step,sɪstər] *n* : hermanastra *f* — **stepson** ['step,sʌn] *n* : hijastro *m*

stereo ['sterioː, -stɪr-] *n, pl* **stereos** : estéreo *m* — **~** *adj* : estéreo

stereotype ['sterio,taɪp, 'stɪr-] *n* **-typed; -typing** : estereotipar — **~** *n* : estereotipo *m*

sterile ['sterəl] *adj* : estéril — **sterility** [stə'rɪləti] *n* : esterilidad *f* — **sterilization** [,sterələ'zeɪʃən] *n* : esterilización *f* — **sterilize** ['sterə,laɪz] *vt* **-ized; -izing** : esterilizar

sterling ['stɜrlɪŋ] *adj* : excelente — **sterling silver** *n* : plata *f* de ley

stern[1] ['stɜrn] *adj* : severo, adusto

stern[2] *n* : popa *f*

stethoscope ['steθə,skoːp] *n* : estetoscopio *m*

stew ['stuː, 'stjuː] *n* : estofado *m*, guiso *m* — **~** *vt* : estofar, guisar — *vi* **1** : cocer **2** FRET : preocuparse

steward ['stuːərd, 'stjuː-] *n* **1** : administrador *m*, -dora *f* **2** : auxiliar *m* de vuelo (en un avión) **3** : camarero *m* (en un barco) — **stewardess** ['stuːərdəs, 'stjuː-] *n* **1** : auxiliar *f* de vuelo, azafata *f* (en un avión) **2** : camarera *f* (en un barco)

stick[1] ['stɪk] *n* **1** : palo *m* **2** TWIG : ramita *f* (suelta) **3** WALKING STICK : bastón *m*

stick[2] *v* **stuck** ['stʌk]; **sticking** *vt* **1** : pegar **2** STAB : clavar **3** PUT : poner **4 ~ out** : sacar (la lengua, etc.) — *vi* **1** : pegarse **2** JAM : atascarse **3 ~ around** : quedarse **4 ~ out** PROTRUDE : sobresalir **5 ~ out** SHOW : asomar **6 ~ up** : sobresalir **7 ~ up for** : defender — **sticker** ['stɪkər] *n* : etiqueta *f*

adhesiva — **stickler** ['stɪklər] *n* be a ~
for : insistir mucho en — **sticky** ['stɪki]
adj **stickier; -est** : pegajoso

stiff ['stɪf] *adj* **1** RIGID : rígido, tieso **2**
STILTED : forzado **3** STRONG : fuerte **4**
DIFFICULT : difícil **5** : entumecido
(dícese de músculos) — **stiffen**
['stɪfən] *vt* : fortalecer, hacer más duro
— *vi* **1** HARDEN : endurecerse **2** : entumecerse (dícese de músculos) — **stiffness** ['stɪfnəs] *n* : rigidez *f*

stifle ['staɪfəl] *vt* **-fled; -fling** : sofocar

stigmatize ['stɪɡmətaɪz] *vt* **-tized; -tizing** : estigmatizar

still ['stɪl] *adj* **1** : inmóvil **2** SILENT : callado — ~ *adv* **1** : todavía, aún **2** NEVERTHELESS : de todos modos, aún así **3** sit ~! : ¡quédate quieto! — ~ *n* : quietud *f*, calma *f* — **stillborn** ['stɪl,bɔrn] *adj* : nacido muerto — **stillness** ['stɪlnəs] *n* : calma *f*, silencio *m*

stilt ['stɪlt] *n* : zanco *m* — **stilted** ['stɪltəd] *adj* : forzado

stimulate ['stɪmjə,leɪt] *vt* **-lated; -lating** : estimular — **stimulant** ['stɪmjələnt] *n* : estimulante *m* — **stimulation** [,stɪmjə'leɪʃən] *n* : estimulación *f* — **stimulus** ['stɪmjələs] *n, pl* **-li** [-,laɪ] : estímulo *m*

sting ['stɪŋ] *v* **stung** ['stʌŋ]; **stinging** : picar — ~ *n* : picadura *f* — **stinger** ['stɪŋər] *n* : aguijón *m*

stingy ['stɪndʒi] *adj* **stingier; -est** : tacaño — **stinginess** ['stɪndʒinəs] *n* : cañería *f*

stink ['stɪŋk] *vi* **stank** ['stæŋk] *or* **stunk** ['stʌŋk]; **stunk; stinking** : apestar, oler mal — ~ *n* : hedor *m*, peste *f* *fam*

stint ['stɪnt] *vi* ~ **on** : escatimar — ~ *n* : período *m*

stipulate ['stɪpjə,leɪt] *vt* **-lated; -lating** : estipular

stir ['stər] *v* **stirred; stirring** *vt* **1** : remover, revolver **2** MOVE : mover **3** INCITE : incitar **4** *or* ~ **up** : despertar (memorias, etc.), provocar (ira, etc.) — *vi* : moverse, agitarse — ~ *n* COMMOTION : revuelo *m*

stirrup ['stərəp, 'stɪr-] *n* : estribo *m*

stitch ['stɪtʃ] *n* **1** : puntada *f* **2** PAIN : punzada *f* (en el costado) — ~ *v* : coser

stock ['stɑk] *n* **1** INVENTORY : existencias *fpl* **2** SECURITIES : acciones *fpl* **3** ANCESTRY : linaje *m*, estirpe *f* **4** BROTH : caldo *m* **5 out of** ~ : agotado **6 take** ~ **of** : evaluar — ~ *vt* : surtir, abastecer — *vi* ~ **up on** : abastecerse de — **stockbroker** ['stɑk,broʊkər] *n* : corredor *m*, -dora *f* de bolsa

stocking ['stɑkɪŋ] *n* : media *f*

---

stock market *n* : bolsa *f* — **stockpile** ['stɑk,paɪl] *n* : reservas *fpl* — ~ *vt* **-piled; -piling** : almacenar — **stocky** ['stɑki] *adj* **stockier; -est** : robusto, fornido

stodgy ['stɑdʒi] *adj* **stodgier; -est 1** DULL : pesado **2** OLD-FASHIONED : anticuado

stoic ['stoʊɪk] *n* : estoico *m*, -ca *f* — ~ *or* **stoical** [-ɪkəl] *adj* : estoico — **stoicism** ['stoʊə,sɪzəm] *n* : estoicismo *m*

stoke ['stoʊk] *vt* **stoked; stoking** : echar carbón o leña a

stole[1] ['stoʊl] → **steal**

stole[2] *n* : estola *f*

stolen → **steal**

stomach ['stʌmɪk] *n* : estómago *m* — ~ *vt* : aguantar, soportar — **stomachache** ['stʌmɪk,eɪk] *n* : dolor *m* de estómago

stone ['stoʊn] *n* **1** : piedra *f* **2** : hueso *m* (de una fruta) — ~ *vt* **stoned; stoning** : apedrear — **stony** ['stoʊni] *adj* **stonier; -est 1** : pedregoso **2 a** ~ **silence** : un silencio sepulcral

stood → **stand**

stool ['stuːl] *n* : taburete *m*

stoop ['stuːp] *vi* **1** : agacharse **2** ~ **to** : rebajarse a — ~ *n* **have a** ~ : ser encorvado

stop ['stɑp] *v* **stopped; stopping** *vt* **1** PLUM : tapar **2** PREVENT : impedir **3** HALT : parar, detener **4** CEASE : dejar de — *vi* **1** : detenerse, parar **2** CEASE : cesar, dejar **3** ~ **by** : visitar — ~ *n* **1** : parada *f*, alto *m* **2 come to a** ~ : pararse, detenerse **3 put a** ~ **to** : poner fin a — **stopgap** ['stɑp,ɡæp] *n* : arreglo *m* provisorio — **stoplight** ['stɑp,laɪt] *n* : semáforo *m* — **stoppage** ['stɑpɪdʒ] *n or* **work** ~ : paro *m* — **stopper** ['stɑpər] *n* : tapón *m*

store ['stɔr] *vt* **stored; storing** : guardar (comida, etc.), almacenar (datos, mercancías, etc.) — ~ *n* **1** SUPPLY : reserva *f* **2** SHOP : tienda *f* — **storage** ['stɔrɪdʒ] *n* : almacenamiento *m* — **storehouse** ['stɔr,haʊs] *n* : almacén *m* — **storekeeper** ['stɔr,kiːpər] *n* : tendero *m*, -ra *f* — **storeroom** ['stɔr,ruːm, -,rʊm] *n* : almacén *m*

stork ['stɔrk] *n* : cigüeña *f*

storm ['stɔrm] *n* : tormenta *f*, tempestad *f* — ~ *vi* **1** RAGE : ponerse furioso **2** ~ **in/out** : entrar/salir furioso — *vt* ATTACK : asaltar — **stormy** ['stɔrmi] *adj* **stormier; -est** : tormentoso

story[1] ['stɔri] *n, pl* **stories 1** TALE : cuento *m* **2** ACCOUNT : historia *f* **3** RUMOR : rumor *m*

story *n* FLOOR : piso *m*, planta *f*

stout ['staʊt] *adj* **1** BRAVE : valiente **2** RESOLUTE : tenaz **3** STURDY : fuerte **4** FAT : corpulento

stove[1] ['stoːv] *n* **1** : estufa *f* (para calentar) **2** RANGE : cocina *f*

stove[2] → **stave**

stow ['stoː] *vt* **1** : guardar **2** LOAD : cargar — *vi* ~ **away** : viajar de polizón

stowaway ['stoːəˌweɪ] *n* : polizón *m*

straddle ['strædəl] *vt* **-dled; -dling** : sentarse a horcajadas sobre

straggle ['strægəl] *vi* **-gled; -gling** : rezagarse, quedarse atrás — **straggler** ['strægələr] *n* : rezagado *m*, -da *f*

straight ['streɪt] *adj* **1** : recto, derecho **2** : lacio (dícese del pelo) **3** HONEST : franco **4** TIDY : arreglado — ~ *adv* **1** DIRECTLY : derecho **2** EXACTLY : justo **3** CLEARLY : con claridad **4** FRANKLY : con franqueza — **straightaway** ['streɪtˌweɪ, -ˌweɪ] *adv* : inmediatamente — **straighten** ['streɪtən] *vt* **1** : enderezar **2** ~ **up** : arreglar — **straightforward** [streɪtˈfɔrwərd] *adj* **1** FRANK : franco **2** CLEAR : claro, sencillo

strain[1] ['streɪn] *n* **1** LINEAGE : linaje *m* **2** STREAK : veta *f* **3** VARIETY : variedad *f* **4** ~**s** *npl* : acordes *mpl* (de música)

strain[2] *vt* **1** : forzar (la vista o la voz) **2** FILTER : colar **3** : tensar (relaciones, etc.) **4** ~ **a muscle** : sufrir un esguince **5** ~ **oneself** : hacerse daño — *vi* : esforzarse (por) — ~ *n* **1** STRESS : tensión *f* **2** SPRAIN : esguince *m* — **strainer** ['streɪnər] *n* : colador *m*

strait ['streɪt] *n* **1** : estrecho *m* **2 in dire** ~**s** : en grandes apuros

strand[1] ['strænd] *vt* **be** ~**ed** : quedar(se) varado

strand[2] *n* **1** : hebra *f* **2 a** ~ **of hair** : un pelo

strange ['streɪndʒ] *adj* **stranger; -est 1** : extraño, raro **2** UNFAMILIAR : desconocido — **strangely** ['streɪndʒli] *adv* : de manera extraña — **strangeness** ['streɪndʒnəs] *n* **1** : rareza *f* **2** UN-FAMILIARITY : lo desconocido — **stranger** ['streɪndʒər] *n* : desconocido *m*, -da *f*

strangle ['stræŋgəl] *vt* **-gled; -gling** : estrangular

strap ['stræp] *n* **1** : correa *f* **2** *or* **shoulder** ~ : tirante *m* — ~ *vt* **strapped; strapping** : sujetar con una correa — **strapless** ['stræpləs] *n* : sin tirantes — **strapping** ['stræpɪŋ] *adj* : robusto, fornido

strategy ['strætədʒi] *n, pl* **-gies** : estrate-

gia *f* — **strategic** [strəˈtiːdʒɪk] *adj* : estratégico

straw ['strɔ] *n* **1** : paja *f* **2** *or* **drinking** ~ : pajita *f* **3 the last** ~ : el colmo

strawberry ['strɔˌberi] *n, pl* **-ries** : fresa *f*

stray ['streɪ] *n* : animal *m* perdido — ~ *vi* **1** : perderse, extraviarse **2** : apartarse (de un grupo, etc.) **3** DEVIATE : desviarse — ~ *adj* : perdido

streak ['striːk] *n* **1** : raya *f* **2** VEIN : veta *f* **3** ~ **of luck** : racha *f* de suerte — *vi* ~ **by** : pasar como una flecha

stream ['striːm] *n* **1** : arroyo *m*, riachuelo *m* **2** FLOW : chorro *m*, corriente *f* — *vi* : correr — **streamer** ['striːmər] *n* **1** PENNANT : banderín *m* **2** : serpentina *f* (de papel) — **streamlined** ['striːmˌlaɪnd] *adj* **1** : aerodinámico **2** EFFICIENT : eficiente

street ['striːt] *n* : calle *f* — **streetcar** ['striːtˌkɑr] *n* : tranvía *m* — **streetlight** ['striːtˌlaɪt] *n* : farol *m*

strength ['streŋkθ] *n* **1** : fuerza *f* **2** FORTITUDE : fortaleza *f* **3** TOUGHNESS : resistencia *f*, solidez *f* **4** INTENSITY : intensidad *f* **5** ~**s and weaknesses** : virtudes y defectos — **strengthen** ['streŋkθən] *vt* **1** : fortalecer **2** REINFORCE : reforzar **3** INTENSIFY : intensificar

strenuous ['strenjuəs] *adj* **1** : enérgico **2** ARDUOUS : duro, riguroso

stress ['stres] *n* **1** : tensión *f* **2** EMPHASIS : énfasis *m* **3** : acento *m* (en lingüística) — ~ *vt* **1** EMPHASIZE : enfatizar **2** *or* ~ **out** : estresar — **stressful** ['stresfəl] *adj* : estresante

stretch ['stretʃ] *vt* **1** : estirar (músculos, elástico, etc.) **2** EXTEND : extender **3** ~ **the truth** : forzar la verdad — *vi* **1** : estirarse **2** EXTEND : extenderse — ~ *n* **1** : extensión *f* **2** ELASTICITY : elasticidad *f* **3** EXPANSE : tramo *m* **4** : período *m* (de tiempo) — **stretcher** ['stretʃər] *n* : camilla *f*

strew ['struː] *vt* **strewed; strewed** *or* **strewn** ['struːn] **strewing** : esparcir (semillas, etc.), desparramar (papeles, etc.)

stricken ['strɪkən] *adj* ~ **with** : aquejado de (una enfermedad), afligido por (tristeza, etc.)

strict ['strɪkt] *adj* : estricto — **strictly** *adv* ~ **speaking** : en rigor

stride ['straɪd] *vi* **strode** ['stroːd]; **stridden** ['strɪdən] **striding** : ir dando zancadas — ~ *n* **1** : zancada *f* **2 make great** ~**s** : hacer grandes progresos

strident ['straɪdənt] *adj* : estridente

strife ['straɪf] *n* : conflictos *mpl*

strike ['straɪk] v struck ['strʌk]; struck; striking vt 1 HIT : golpear 2 or ~ against : chocar contra 3 or ~ out DELETE : tachar 4 : dar (la hora) 5 IMPRESS : impresionar 6 : descubrir (con oro o petróleo) 7 it ~s me as... : me parece... 8 ~ up START : entablar — vi 1 : golpear 2 ATTACK : atacar 3 : declararse en huelga 4 : sobrevenir (dícese de una enfermedad, etc.) — ~ n 1 BLOW : golpe m 2 : huelga f, paro m Lat (de trabajadores) 3 ATTACK : ataque m — strikebreaker ['straɪk,breɪkər] n : esquirol mf — striker ['straɪkər] n : huelgista mf — striking ['straɪkɪŋ] adj : notable, llamativo

string ['strɪŋ] n 1 : cordel m 2 : sarta f (de perlas, insultos, etc.), serie f (de eventos, etc.) 3 ~s npl : cuerdas fpl (en música) — ~ vt strung ['strʌŋ]; stringing 1 : ensartar 2 or ~ up : colgar — string bean n : habichuela f verde

stringent ['strɪndʒənt] adj : estricto, severo

strip¹ ['strɪp] v stripped; stripping vt 1 REMOVE : quitar 2 UNDRESS : desnudar 3 ~ s.o. of sth : despojar a algn de algo — vi UNDRESS : desnudarse

strip² n : tira f

stripe ['straɪp] n : raya f, lista f — striped ['straɪpt, 'straɪpəd] adj : a rayas, rayado

strive ['straɪv] vi strove ['stroːv]; striven ['strɪvən] or strived; striving 1 ~ for : luchar por 2 ~ to : esforzarse por

strode → stride

stroke ['stroːk] vt stroked; stroking : acariciar — ~ n 1 : golpe m 2 : derrame m cerebral (en medicina)

stroll ['stroːl] vi : pasearse — ~ n : paseo m — stroller ['stroːlər] n : cochecito m (para niños)

strong ['strɔŋ] adj : fuerte — stronghold ['strɔŋ,hoːld] n : bastión m — strongly ['strɔŋli] adv 1 DEEPLY : profundamente 2 WHOLEHEARTEDLY : totalmente 3 VIGOROUSLY : enérgicamente

strove → strive

struck → strike

structure ['strʌktʃər] n : estructura f — structural ['strʌktʃərəl] adj : estructural

struggle ['strʌgəl] vi -gled; -gling 1 : forcejear 2 STRIVE : luchar — ~ n : lucha f

strum ['strʌm] vt strummed; strumming : rasguear

strung → string

strut ['strʌt] vi strutted; strutting : pavonearse — ~ n : puntal m (en construcción)

stub ['stʌb] n : colilla f (de un cigarrillo), cabo m (de un lápiz, etc.), talón m (de un cheque) — ~ vt stubbed; stubbing ~ one's toe : darse en el dedo

stubble ['stʌbəl] n : barba f de varios días

stubborn ['stʌbərn] adj : terco, obstinado 2 PERSISTENT : tenaz

stucco ['stʌkoː] n, pl stuccos or stuccoes : estuco m

stuck → stick — stuck-up ['stʌk,ʌp] adj : engreído, creído fam

stud¹ ['stʌd] n 1 NAIL, TACK : tachuela f, tachón m 2 or ~ earring : arete m Lat, pendiente m Spain 3 : montante m (en construcción)

stud² n 1 : semental m (animal)

student ['stuːdənt, 'stjuː-] n : estudiante mf; alumno m, -na f (de un colegio) — studio ['stuːdioː, 'stjuː-] n, pl studios : estudio m — study ['stʌdi] n, pl studies : estudio m — ~ v studied; studying : estudiar — studious ['stuːdiəs, 'stjuː-] adj : estudioso

stuff ['stʌf] n 1 : cosas fpl 2 MATTER, SUBSTANCE : cosa f 3 know one's ~ : ser experto — ~ vt 1 FILL : rellenar 2 CRAM : meter — stuffing ['stʌfɪŋ] n : relleno m — stuffy ['stʌfi] adj stuffier; -est 1 STODGY : pesado, aburrido 2 : tapado (dícese de la nariz) 3 ~ rooms : salas fpl mal ventiladas

stumble ['stʌmbəl] vi -bled; -bling 1 : tropezar 2 ~ across or upon : tropezar con

stump ['stʌmp] n 1 : muñón m (de una pierna, etc.) 2 or tree ~ : tocón m — ~ vt : dejar perplejo

stun ['stʌn] vt stunned; stunning 1 : aturdir (con un golpe) 2 ASTONISH : dejar atónito

stung → sting

stunk → stink

stunning ['stʌnɪŋ] adj 1 : increíble, sensacional 2 STRIKING : imponente

stunt¹ ['stʌnt] vt : atrofiar

stunt² n : proeza f (acrobática)

stupendous ['stupendəs, stju-] adj : estupendo

stupid ['stupəd, 'stjuː-] adj 1 : estúpido 2 SILLY : tonto, bobo — stupidity [stu'pɪdəti, stju-] n : tontería f, estupidez f

sturdy ['stərdi] adj sturdier; -est 1 : fuerte, resistente 2 ROBUST : robusto

stutter ['stʌtər] vi : tartamudear — ~ n : tartamudeo m

sty ['staɪ] n 1 pl sties PIGPEN : pocilga f

2 pl **sties** or **styes** : orzuelo m (en el ojo)

style ['staɪl] n **1** : estilo m **2** FASHION : moda f **3 be in ~** : estar de moda — **~** vt **styled; styling** : peinar (pelo), diseñar (vestidos, etc.) — **stylish** ['staɪlɪʃ] adj : elegante, chic — **stylist** ['staɪlɪst] n : estilista f

suave ['swɑv] adj : refinado y afable

sub¹ ['sʌb] vi **subbed; subbing → substitute — ~** n → substitute

sub² n → submarine

subconscious [ˌsʌb'kɑntʃəs] adj : subconsciente — **~** n : subconsciente m

subdivide [ˌsʌbdə'vaɪd, 'sʌbdəˌvaɪd] vt **-vided; -viding** : subdividir — **subdivision** [ˈsʌbdəˌvɪʒən] n : subdivisión f

subdue [səb'du:, -'dju:] vt **-dued; -duing 1** CONQUER : sojuzgar **2** CONTROL : dominar **3** SOFTEN : atenuar — **subdued** adj : apagado

subject ['sʌbdʒɪkt] n **1** : sujeto m **2** : súbdito m, -ta f (de un gobierno) **3** TOPIC : tema m — **~** adj **1** : sometido **2 ~ to** : sujeto a — **~** [səb'dʒɛkt] vt **~ to** : someter a — **subjective** [səb'dʒɛktɪv] adj : subjetivo

subjunctive [səb'dʒʌŋktɪv] n : subjuntivo m — **subjunctive** adj : subjuntivo

sublime [sə'blaɪm] adj : sublime

submarine ['sʌbməˌriːn, ˌsʌbmə-] adj : submarino — **~** n : submarino m

submerge [səb'mərdʒ] v **-merged; -merging** vt : sumergir — vi : sumergirse

submit [səb'mɪt] v **-mitted; -mitting** vt **1** YIELD : rendirse **2 ~ to** : someterse a — vi : presentar — **submission** [səb'mɪʃən] n **1** : sumisión f **2** PRESENTATION : presentación f — **submissive** [səb'mɪsɪv] adj : sumiso

subordinate [sə'bɔrdənət] adj : subordinado — **~** n : subordinado m, -da f — **~** [sə'bɔrdənˌeɪt] vt **-nated; -nating** : subordinar

subpoena [sə'piːnə] n : citación f

subscribe [səb'skraɪb] vi **-scribed; -scribing ~ to** : suscribirse a (una revista, etc.), suscribir (una opinión, etc.) — **subscriber** [səb'skraɪbər] n : suscriptor m, -tora f (de una revista, etc.); abonado m, -da f (de un servicio) — **subscription** [səb'skrɪpʃən] n : suscripción f

subsequent ['sʌbsɪkwənt, -səˌkwent] adj **1** : subsiguiente **2 ~ to** : posterior a — **subsequently** ['sʌbsɪkwentli, -kwənt-] adv : posteriormente

subservient [səb'sərviənt] adj : servil

subside [səb'saɪd] vi **-sided; -siding 1**

SINK : hundirse **2** : amainar (dícese de tormentas, pasiones, etc.), remitir (dícese de fiebres, etc.)

subsidiary [səb'sɪdiˌeri] adj : secundario — **~** n, pl **-ries** : filial f

subsidy ['sʌbsədi] n, pl **-dies** : subvención f — **subsidize** ['sʌbsəˌdaɪz] vt **-dized; -dizing** : subvencionar

subsistence [səb'sɪstəns] n : subsistencia f — **subsist** [səb'sɪst] vi : subsistir

substance ['sʌbstəns] n : sustancia f

substandard [ˌsʌb'stændərd] adj : inferior

substantial [səb'stæntʃəl] adj **1** CONSIDERABLE : considerable **2** STURDY : sólido **3** : sustancioso (dícese de una comida, etc.) — **substantially** [səb'stæntʃəli] adv : considerablemente

substitute ['sʌbstəˌtuːt, -ˌtjuːt] n : sustituto m, -ta f (de una persona); sucedáneo m (de una cosa) — **~** vt **-tuted; -tuting** : sustituir — **substitution** [ˌsʌbstə'tuːʃən, -'tjuː-] n : sustitución f

subterranean [ˌsʌbtə'reɪniən] adj : subterráneo

subtitle ['sʌbˌtaɪtəl] n : subtítulo m

subtle ['sʌtəl] adj **-tler; -tlest** : sutil — **subtlety** ['sʌtəlti] n, pl **-ties** : sutileza f

subtraction [səb'trækʃən] n : resta f — **subtract** [səb'trækt] vt : restar

suburb ['sʌˌbərb] n **1** : barrio m residencial, suburbio m **2 the ~s** : las afueras — **suburban** [sə'bərbən] adj : de las afueras (de una ciudad)

subversion [səb'vərʒən] n : subversión f — **subversive** [səb'vərsɪv] adj : subversivo

subway ['sʌbˌweɪ] n : metro m

succeed [sək'siːd] vt : suceder a — vi : tener éxito (dícese de personas), dar resultado (dícese de planes, etc.) — **success** [sək'ses] n : éxito m — **successful** [sək'sesfəl] adj : de éxito, exitoso Lat — **successfully** adv : con éxito

succession [sək'sɛʃən] n **1** : sucesión f **2 in ~** : sucesivamente, seguidos — **successive** [sək'sɛsɪv] adj : sucesivo — **successor** [sək'sɛsər] n : sucesor m, -sora f

succinct [sək'sɪŋkt, sə'sɪŋkt] adj : sucinto

succulent ['sʌkjələnt] adj : suculento

succumb [sə'kʌm] vi : sucumbir

such ['sʌtʃ] adj **1** : tal **2 ~ as** : como **3 ~ a pity!** : ¡qué lástima! — **~** pron **1** : tal **2 and ~** : y cosas por el estilo **3 as ~** : como tal — **~** adv **1** VERY : muy **2 ~ a nice man!** : ¡qué hombre tan simpático! **3 ~ that** : de tal manera que

suck ['sʌk] *vt* 1 *or* ~ **on** : chupar 2 *or* ~ **up** : sorber (bebidas), aspirar (con una máquina) — **sucker** ['sʌkər] *n* 1 SHOOT : chupón *m* 2 FOOL : imbécil *mf* — **suckle** ['sʌkəl] *vt* **-led; -ling** : amamantar — **suction** ['sʌkʃən] *n* : succión *f*

sudden ['sʌdən] *adj* 1 : repentino 2 **all of a** ~ : de repente — **suddenly** ['sʌdənli] *adv* : de repente

suds ['sʌdz] *npl* : espuma *f* (de jabón)

sue ['suː] *vt* **sued; suing** : demandar (por)

suede ['sweɪd] *n* : ante *m*, gamuza *f*

suet ['suːət] *n* : sebo *m*

suffer ['sʌfər] *vi* : sufrir — *vt* 1 : sufrir 2 BEAR : tolerar — **suffering** ['sʌfərɪŋ] *n* : sufrimiento *m*

suffice [sə'faɪs] *vi* **-ficed; -ficing** : bastar — **sufficient** [sə'fɪʃənt] *adj* : suficiente — **sufficiently** [sə'fɪʃəntli] *adv* : (lo) suficientemente

suffix ['sʌˌfɪks] *n* : sufijo *m*

suffocate ['sʌfəˌkeɪt] *v* **-cated; -cating** *vt* : asfixiar — *vi* : asfixiarse — **suffocation** [ˌsʌfə'keɪʃən] *n* : asfixia *f*

suffrage ['sʌfrɪdʒ] *n* : sufragio *m*

sugar ['ʃʊgər] *n* : azúcar *mf* — **sugarcane** ['ʃʊgərˌkeɪn] *n* : caña *f* de azúcar — **sugary** ['ʃʊgəri] *adj* : azucarado

suggestion [səg'dʒɛstʃən, sə-] *n* 1 : sugerencia *f* 2 TRACE : indicio *m* — **suggest** [səg'dʒɛst, sə-] *vt* 1 : sugerir 2 INDICATE : indicar

suicide ['suːəˌsaɪd] *n* 1 : suicidio *m* (acto) 2 : suicida *mf* (persona) — **suicidal** [ˌsuːə'saɪdəl] *adj* : suicida

suit ['suːt] *n* 1 LAWSUIT : pleito *m* 2 : traje *m* (ropa) 3 : palo *m* (de naipes) — ~ *vt* 1 ADAPT : adaptar 2 BEFIT : ser apropiado para 3 ~ **s.o.** : convenir a algn (dícese de fechas, etc.), quedar bien a algn (dícese de ropa) — **suitable** ['suːtəbəl] *adj* : apropiado — **suitcase** ['suːtˌkeɪs] *n* : maleta *f*, valija *f* Lat

suite ['swiːt, *for 2 also* 'suːt] *n* 1 : suite *f* (de habitaciones) 2 : juego *m* (de muebles)

suitor ['suːtər] *n* : pretendiente *m*

sulfur ['sʌlfər] *n* : azufre *m*

sulk ['sʌlk] *vi* : enfurruñarse *fam* — **sulky** ['sʌlki] *adj* **sulkier; -est** : malhumorado

sullen ['sʌlən] *adj* : hosco

sultry ['sʌltri] *adj* **sultrier; -est** 1 : bochornoso 2 SENSUAL : sensual

sum ['sʌm] *n* : suma *f* — ~ *vt* **summed; summing** — **up** : resumir — **summarize** ['sʌməˌraɪz] *v* **-rized; -rizing** : resumir — **summary** ['sʌməri] *n, pl* **-ries** : resumen *m*

summer ['sʌmər] *n* : verano *m*

summit ['sʌmət] *n* : cumbre *f*

summon ['sʌmən] *vt* 1 : llamar (a algn), convocar (una reunión) 2 : citar (en derecho) — **summons** ['sʌmənz] *n, pl* **summonses** SUBPOENA : citación *f*

sumptuous ['sʌmptʃuəs] *adj* : suntuoso

sun ['sʌn] *n* : sol *m* — **sunbathe** ['sʌnˌbeɪθ] *vi* **-bathed; -bathing** : tomar el sol — **sunbeam** ['sʌnˌbiːm] *n* : rayo *m* de sol — **sunburn** ['sʌnˌbərn] *n* : quemadura *f* de sol

Sunday ['sʌnˌdeɪ, -di] *n* : domingo *m*

sundry ['sʌndri] *adj* : varios, diversos

sunflower ['sʌnˌflaʊər] *n* : girasol *m*

sung → **sing**

sunglasses ['sʌnˌglæsəz] *npl* : gafas *fpl* de sol, lentes *mpl* de sol

sunk → **sink** — **sunken** ['sʌŋkən] *adj* : hundido

sunlight ['sʌnˌlaɪt] *n* : (luz *f* del) sol *m* — **sunny** ['sʌni] *adj* **-nier; -est** : soleado — **sunrise** ['sʌnˌraɪz] *n* : salida *f* del sol — **sunset** ['sʌnˌsɛt] *n* : puesta *f* del sol — **sunshine** ['sʌnˌʃaɪn] *n* : sol *m*, luz *f* del sol — **suntan** ['sʌnˌtæn] *n* : bronceado *m*

super ['suːpər] *adj* : súper *fam*

superb [sʊ'pərb] *adj* : magnífico, espléndido

superficial [ˌsuːpər'fɪʃəl] *adj* : superficial

superfluous [sʊ'pərfluəs] *adj* : superfluo

superimpose [ˌsuːpərɪm'poːz] *vt* **-posed; -posing** : sobreponer

superintendent [ˌsuːpərɪn'tɛndənt] *n* 1 : superintendente *mf* (de policía) 2 *or* **building** ~ : portero *m*, -ra *f* 3 *or* **school** ~ : director *m*, -tora *f* (de un colegio)

superior [sʊ'pɪriər] *adj* : superior — ~ *n* : superior *m* — **superiority** [sʊˌpɪriˈɔrəti] *n, pl* **-ties** : superioridad *f*

superlative [sʊ'pərlətɪv] *adj* 1 : superlativo (en gramática) 2 EXCELLENT : excepcional — ~ *n* : superlativo *m*

supermarket ['suːpərˌmɑrkət] *n* : supermercado *m*

supernatural [ˌsuːpər'nætʃərəl] *adj* : sobrenatural

superpower ['suːpərˌpaʊər] *n* : superpotencia *f*

supersede [ˌsuːpər'siːd] *vt* **-seded; -seding** : reemplazar, suplantar

supersonic [ˌsuːpər'sɑnɪk] *adj* : supersónico

superstition [ˌsuːpər'stɪʃən] *n* : superstición *f* — **superstitious** [ˌsuːpər'stɪʃəs] *adj* : supersticioso

supervisor ['suːpərˌvaɪzər] *n* : supervisor

m, **-sora** *f* — **supervise** ['su:pər‚vaɪz] *vt*
-**vised; -vising** : supervisar — **super-**
vision [‚su:pər'vɪʒən] *n* : supervisión *f*
— **supervisory** [‚su:pər'vaɪzəri] *adj*
: de supervisor

supper ['sʌpər] *n* : cena *f*, comida *f*

supplant [sə'plænt] *vt* : suplantar

supple ['sʌpəl] *adj* **-pler; -plest** : flexible

supplement ['sʌpləmənt] *n* : suplemento *m* — ~ ['sʌplə‚ment] *vt* : complementar — **supplementary** [‚sʌplə-
'mentəri] *adj* : suplementario

supply [sə'plaɪ] *vt* **-plied; -plying 1**
: suministrar **2** ~ **with** : proveer de —
~ *n*, *pl* -**plies 1** : suministro *m*, provisión *f* **2** ~ **and demand** : oferta y
demanda **3 supplies** *npl* PROVISIONS
: provisiones *fpl*, víveres *mpl* — **sup-**
plier [sə'plaɪər] *n* : proveedor *m*, -dora *f*

support [sə'pɔrt] *vt* **1** BACK : apoyar **2**
: mantener (una familia, etc.) **3** PROP
UP : sostener — ~ *n* **1** : apoyo *m*
(moral), ayuda *f* (económica) **2** PROP
: soporte *m* — **supporter** [sə'pɔrtər] *n*
: partidario *m*, -ria *f*

suppose [sə'poz] *vt* **-posed; -posing 1**
: suponer **2 be** ~**d to (do sth)** : tener
que (hacer algo) — **supposedly** *adv*
: supuestamente

suppress [sə'prɛs] *vt* **1** : reprimir **2**
: suprimir (noticias, etc.) — **suppres-**
sion [sə'prɛʃən] *n* **1** : represión *f* **2**
: supresión *f* (de información)

supreme [su'prim] *adj* : supremo — **su-**
premacy [su'prɛməsi] *n*, *pl* -**cies** : supremacía *f*

sure ['ʃʊr] *adj* **surer; -est** : seguro **1**
make ~ **that** : asegurarse de que —
~ *adv* **1** OF COURSE : por supuesto,
claro **2 it** ~ **is hot!** : ¡qué calor! —
surely ['ʃʊrli] *adv* : seguramente

surfing ['sərfɪŋ] *n* : surf *m*, surfing *m*

surface ['sərfəs] *n* : superficie *f* — *v*
-faced; -facing *vi* : salir a la superficie
— *vt* : revestir

surfeit ['sərfət] *n* : exceso *m*

surfing ['sərfɪŋ] *n* : surf *m*, surfing *m*

surge ['sərdʒ] *vi* **surged; surging 1**
SWELL : hincharse (dícese del mar) **2**
SWARM : moverse en tropel — ~ *n* **1**
: oleaje *m* (del mar), oleada *f* (de gente)
2 INCREASE : aumento *m* (súbito)

surgeon ['sərdʒən] *n* : cirujano *m*, -na *f*
— **surgery** ['sərdʒəri] *n*, *pl* -**geries**
: cirugía *f* — **surgical** ['sərdʒɪkəl] *adj*
: quirúrgico

surly ['sərli] *adj* **surlier; -est** : hosco,
arisco

surmount [sər'maʊnt] *vt* : superar

surname ['sər‚neɪm] *n* : apellido *m*

surpass [sər'pæs] *vt* : superar

surplus ['sər‚plʌs] *n* : excedente *m*

surprise [sə'praɪz, sər-] *n* **1** : sorpresa *f* **2**
take by ~ : sorprender — ~ *vt*
-prised; -prising : sorprender — **sur-**
prising [sə'praɪzɪŋ, sər-] *adj* : sorprendente

surrender [sə'rendər] *vt* : entregar,
rendir — *vi* : rendirse — ~ *n* : rendición *f* (de una ciudad, etc.), entrega *f*
(de posesiones)

surrogate ['sərəgət, -‚geɪt] *n* : sustituto *m*

surround [sə'raʊnd] *vt* : rodear — **sur-**
roundings [sə'raʊndɪŋz] *npl* : ambiente *m*

surveillance [sər'veɪlənts, -veɪljənts,
-veɪənts] *n* : vigilancia *f*

survey [sər'veɪ] *vt* **-veyed; -veying 1**
: medir (un solar) **2** INSPECT : inspeccionar **3** POLL : sondear — ~ ['sər‚veɪ]
n, *pl* -**veys 1** INSPECTION : inspección *f*
2 : medición *f* (de un solar) **3** POLL
: encuesta *f*, sondeo *m* — **surveyor**
[sər'veɪər] *n* : agrimensor *m*, -sora *f*

survive [sər'vaɪv] *v* **-vived; -viving** *vi*
: sobrevivir — *vt* : sobrevivir a — **sur-**
vival [sər'vaɪvəl] *n* : supervivencia *f* —
survivor [sər'vaɪvər] *n* : superviviente
mf

susceptible [sə'septəbəl] *adj* ~ **to**
: propenso a — **susceptibility** [sə-
‚septə'bɪləti] *n*, *pl* -**ties** : propensión *f* (a
enfermedades, etc.)

suspect ['sʌs‚pekt, sə'spekt] *adj* : sospechoso — ~ ['sʌs‚pekt] *n* : sospechoso
m, -sa *f* — ~ [sə'spekt] *vt* **1** : sospechar
(algo), sospechar de (algn)

suspend [sə'spend] *vt* : suspender —
suspense [sə'spents] *n* **1** : incertidumbre *f* **2** : suspenso *m Lat*, suspense *m*
Spain (en el cine, etc.) — **suspension**
[sə'spentʃən] *n* : suspensión *f*

suspicion [sə'spɪʃən] *n* : sospecha *f* —
suspicious [sə'spɪʃəs] *adj* **1** QUESTION-
ABLE : sospechoso **2** DISTRUSTFUL
: suspicaz

sustain [sə'steɪn] *vt* **1** : sostener **2** SUF-
FER : sufrir

swagger ['swægər] *vi* : pavonearse

swallow[1] ['swɑlo] *v* : tragar — ~ *n*
: trago *m*

swallow[2] *n* : golondrina *f* (pájaro)

swam → **swim**

swamp ['swɑmp] *n* : pantano *m*, ciénaga
f — *vt* : inundar — **swampy**
['swɑmpi] *adj* **swampier; -est** : pantanoso, cenagoso

swan ['swɑn] *n* : cisne *m*

swap ['swɑp] *vt* **swapped; swapping 1**

: intercambiar **2** ~ **sth for sth** : cambiar algo por algo **3** ~ **sth with s.o.** : cambiar algo a algn — ~ *n* : cambio *m*

swarm ['swɔrm] *n* : enjambre *m* — ~ *vi* : enjambrar

swat ['swɑt] *vt* **swatted; swatting** : aplastar (un insecto)

sway ['sweɪ] *n* **1** : balanceo *m* **2** INFLUENCE : influjo *m* — ~ *vi* : balancearse — *vt* : influir en

swear ['swæer] *v* **swore** ['swor]; **sworn** ['sworn]; **swearing** *vi* **1** : jurar **2** CURSE : decir palabrotas — *vt* : jurar — **swearword** ['swæer,wɔrd] *n* : palabrota *f*

sweat ['swɛt] *vi* **sweat** or **sweated; sweating** : sudar — ~ *n* : sudor *m* — **sweater** ['swɛt̬ər] *n* : suéter *m* — **sweatshirt** ['swɛt,ʃərt] *n* : sudadera *f* — **sweaty** ['swɛt̬i] *adj* **sweatier; -est** : sudado

Swedish ['swiːdɪʃ] *adj* : sueco — *n* : sueco *m* (idioma)

sweep ['swiːp] *v* **swept** ['swɛpt]; **sweeping** *vt* **1** : barrer **2** ~ **aside** : apartar **3** ~ **through** : extenderse por — *vi* : barrer — ~ *n* **1** : barrido *m* **2** : movimiento *m* circular (de la mano, etc.) **3** SCOPE : alcance *m* — **sweeping** ['swiːpɪŋ] *adj* **1** WIDE : amplio **2** EXTENSIVE : extenso — **sweepstakes** ['swiːp,steɪks] *ns* & *pl* : lotería *f*

sweet ['swiːt] *adj* **1** : dulce **2** PLEASANT : agradable — ~ *n* : dulce *m* — **sweeten** ['swiːt̬ən] *vt* : endulzar — **sweetener** ['swiːt̬ənər] *n* : endulzante *m* — **sweetheart** ['swiːt,hɑrt] *n* **1** : novio *m*, -via *f* **2** (*used as a form of address*) : cariño *m* — **sweetness** ['swiːtnəs] *n* : dulzura *f* — **sweet potato** *n* : batata *f*, boniato *m*

swell ['swɛl] *vi* **swelled; swelled** or **swollen** ['swoːlən, 'swɑl-]; **swelling 1** or ~ **up** : hincharse **2** INCREASE : aumentar, crecer — ~ *n* : oleaje *m* (del mar) — **swelling** ['swɛlɪŋ] *n* : hinchazón *f*

sweltering ['swɛltərɪŋ] *adj* : sofocante

swept → **sweep**

swerve ['swərv] *vi* **swerved; swerving** : virar bruscamente

swift ['swɪft] *adj* : rápido — **swiftly** *adv* : rápidamente

swig ['swɪg] *n* : trago *m* — ~ *vi* **swigged; swigging** : beber a tragos

swim ['swɪm] *vi* **swam** ['swæm]; **swum** ['swʌm]; **swimming 1** : nadar **2** REEL : dar vueltas — ~ *n* **1** : baño *m* **2 go for a** ~ : ir a nadar — **swimmer** ['swɪmər] *n* : nadador *m*, -dora *f*

swindle ['swɪndəl] *vt* **-dled; -dling** : estafar, timar — ~ *n* : estafa *f*, timo *m fam*

swine ['swaɪn] *ns* & *pl* : cerdo *m*, -da *f*

swing ['swɪŋ] *v* **swung** ['swʌŋ]; **swinging** *vt* **1** : balancear, hacer oscilar **2** MANAGE : arreglar — *vi* **1** : balancearse, oscilar **2** SWIVEL : girar — ~ *n* **1** : vaivén *m*, balanceo *m* **2** SHIFT : cambio *m* **3** : columpio *m* (para niños) **4 in full** ~ : en pleno proceso

swipe ['swaɪp] *v* **swiped; swiping** *vt* STEAL : birlar *fam*, robar — *vi* ~ **at** : intentar pegar

swirl ['swərl] *vi* : arremolinarse — ~ *n* **1** EDDY : remolino *m* **2** SPIRAL : espiral *f*

swish ['swɪʃ] *vt* : agitar (haciendo un sonido) — *vi* **1** RUSTLE : hacer frufrú **2** ~ **by** : pasar silbando

Swiss ['swɪs] *adj* : suizo

switch ['swɪtʃ] *n* **1** WHIP : vara *f* **2** CHANGE : cambio *m* **3** : interruptor *m*, llave *f* (de la luz, etc.) — ~ *vt* **1** CHANGE : cambiar de **2** EXCHANGE : intercambiar **3** ~ **on** : encender, prender *Lat* **4** ~ **off** : apagar — *vi* **1** : cambiar **2** CHANGE : cambiar **2** SWAP : intercambiarse — **switchboard** ['swɪtʃ,bɔrd] *n* : centralita *f*, conmutador *m Lat*

swivel ['swɪvəl] *vi* **-veled** or **-velled; -veling** or **-velling** : girar (sobre un pivote)

swollen → **swell**

swoon ['swuːn] *vi* : desvanecerse

swoop ['swuːp] *vi* ~ **down on** : abatirse sobre — ~ *n* : descenso *m* en picada

sword ['sɔrd] *n* : espada *f* — **swordfish** ['sɔrd,fɪʃ] *n* : pez *m* espada

swore, sworn → **swear**

swum → **swim**

swung → **swing**

syllable ['sɪləbəl] *n* : sílaba *f*

syllabus ['sɪləbəs] *n*, *pl* **-bi** [-,baɪ] or **-buses** : programa *m* (de estudios)

symbol ['sɪmbəl] *n* : símbolo *m* — **symbolic** ['sɪm'bɑlɪk] *adj* : simbólico — **symbolism** ['sɪmbə,lɪzəm] *n* : simbolismo *m* — **symbolize** ['sɪmbə,laɪz] *vt* **-ized; -izing** : simbolizar

symmetry ['sɪmətri] *n*, *pl* **-tries** : simetría *f* — **symmetrical** [sə'mɛtrɪkəl] *adj* : simétrico

sympathy ['sɪmpəθi] *n*, *pl* **-thies 1** COMPASSION : compasión *f* **2** UNDERSTANDING : comprensión *f* **3** CONDOLENCES : pésame *m* **4 sympathies** *npl* LOYALTY : simpatías *fpl* — **sympathize** ['sɪmpə,θaɪz] *vi* **-thized; -thizing 1** ~ **with** PITY : compadecerse de **2** ~

with UNDERSTAND : comprender — **sympathetic** [ˌsɪmpəˈθetɪk] *adj* **1** COMPASSIONATE : compasivo **2** UNDERSTANDING : comprensivo

symphony [ˈsɪmfəni] *n, pl* **-nies** : sinfonía *f*

symposium [sɪmˈpoːziəm] *n, pl* **-sia** [-ziə] *or* **-siums** : simposio *m*

symptom [ˈsɪmptəm] *n* : síntoma *m* — **symptomatic** [ˌsɪmptəˈmætɪk] *adj* : sintomático

synagogue [ˈsɪnəˌgɑg, -ˌgɔg] *n* : sinagoga *f*

synchronize [ˈsɪŋkrəˌnaɪz, ˈsɪn-] *vt* **-nized; -nizing** : sincronizar

syndrome [ˈsɪnˌdroːm] *n* : síndrome *m*

synonym [ˈsɪnəˌnɪm] *n* : sinónimo *m* —

synonymous [səˈnɑnəməs] *adj* : sinónimo

synopsis [səˈnɑpsɪs] *n, pl* **-opses** [-ˌsiːz] : sinopsis *f*

syntax [ˈsɪnˌtæks] *n* : sintaxis *f*

synthesis [ˈsɪnθəsɪs] *n, pl* **-theses** [-ˌsiːz] : síntesis *f* — **synthesize** [ˈsɪnθəˌsaɪz] *vt* **-sized; -sizing** : sintetizar — **synthetic** [sɪnˈθetɪk] *adj* : sintético

syphilis [ˈsɪfələs] *n* : sífilis *f*

Syrian [ˈsɪriən] *adj* : sirio

syringe [səˈrɪndʒ, ˈsɪrɪndʒ] *n* : jeringa *f*, jeringuilla *f*

syrup [ˈsərəp, ˈsɪrəp] *n* : jarabe *m*

system [ˈsɪstəm] *n* **1** : sistema *m* **2** BODY : organismo *m* **3** digestive ~ : aparato *m* digestivo — **systematic** [ˌsɪstəˈmætɪk] *adj* : sistemático

T

t [ˈtiː] *n, pl* **t's** *or* **ts** [ˈtiːz] : t *f*, vigésima letra del alfabeto inglés

tab [ˈtæb] *n* **1** TAG : etiqueta *f* **2** FLAP : lengüeta *f* **3** ACCOUNT : cuenta *f* **4 keep ~s on** : vigilar

table [ˈteɪbəl] *n* **1** : mesa *f* **2** LIST : tabla *f* **3** ~ **of contents** : índice *m* de materias — **tablecloth** [ˈteɪbəlˌklɔθ] *n* : mantel *m* — **tablespoon** [ˈteɪbəlˌspuːn] *n* **1** : cuchara *f* grande **2** : cucharada *f* (cantidad)

tablet [ˈtæblət] *n* **1** PAD : bloc *m* **2** PILL : pastilla *f* **3** *or* **stone ~** : lápida *f*

tabloid [ˈtæˌblɔɪd] *n* : tabloide *m*

taboo [təˈbuː, tæ-] *adj* : tabú — ~ *n* : tabú *m*

tacit [ˈtæsɪt] *adj* : tácito

taciturn [ˈtæsɪˌtərn] *adj* : taciturno

tack [ˈtæk] *vt* **1** : fijar con tachuelas **2** ~ **on** ADD : añadir — ~ *n* **1** : tachuela *f* **2 change ~** : cambiar de rumbo

tackle [ˈtækəl] *n* **1** GEAR : aparejo *m* **2** : placaje *m*, tacle *m* Lat (acción) — ~ *vt* **-led; -ling 1** : placar, taclear Lat **2** CONFRONT : abordar

tacky [ˈtæki] *adj* **tackier; -est 1** : pegajoso **2** GAUDY : de mal gusto

tact [ˈtækt] *n* : tacto *m* — **tactful** [ˈtæktfəl] *adj* : diplomático, discreto

tactical [ˈtæktɪkəl] *adj* : táctico — **tactic** [ˈtæktɪk] *n* : táctica *f* — **tactics** [ˈtæktɪks] *ns & pl* : táctica *f*

tactless [ˈtæktləs] *adj* : indiscreto

tadpole [ˈtædˌpoːl] *n* : renacuajo *m*

tag[1] [ˈtæg] *n* LABEL : etiqueta *f* — ~ *vi* **tagged; tagging** *vt* : etiquetar — *vi*

~ **along with s.o.** : acompañar a algn

tag[2] *vt* : tocar (en varios juegos)

tail [ˈteɪl] *n* **1** : cola *f* **2** ~**s** *npl* : cruz *f* (de una moneda) — ~ *vt* FOLLOW : seguir

tailor [ˈteɪlər] *n* : sastre *m*, -tra *f* — ~ *vt* **1** : confeccionar (ropa) **2** ADAPT : adaptar

taint [ˈteɪnt] *vt* : contaminar

take [ˈteɪk] *v* **took** [ˈtʊk], **taken** [ˈteɪkən]; **taking** *vt* **1** : tomar **2** BRING : llevar **3** REMOVE : sacar **4** BEAR : soportar, aguantar **5** ACCEPT : aceptar **6 I ~ it that...** : supongo que... **7** ~ **a bath** : bañarse **8** ~ **a walk** : dar un paseo **9** ~ **back** : retirar (palabras, etc.) **10** ~ **in** ALTER : achicar **11** ~ **in** GRASP : entender **12** ~ **in** TRICK : engañar **13** ~ **off** REMOVE : quitar, quitarse (ropa) **14** ~ **on** : asumir (una responsabilidad, etc.) **15** ~ **out** : sacar **16** ~ **over** : tomar el poder de **17** ~ **place** : tener lugar **18** ~ **up** SHORTEN : acortar **19** ~ **up** OCCUPY : ocupar — *vi* **1** : prender (dícese de una vacuna, etc.) **2** ~ **off** : despegar (dícese de aviones, etc.) **3** ~ **over** : asumir el mando — ~ *n* **1** PROCEEDS : ingresos *mpl* **2** : toma *f* (en el cine) — **takeoff** [ˈteɪkˌɔf] *n* : despegue *m* (de un avión, etc.) — **takeover** [ˈteɪkˌoːvər] *n* : toma *f* (de poder, etc.), adquisición *f* (de una empresa)

talcum powder [ˈtælkəm] *n* : polvos *mpl* de talco

tale [ˈteɪl] *n* : cuento *m*

talent ['tælənt] *n* : talento *m* — **talented** ['tæləntəd] *adj* : talentoso

talk ['tɔk] *vi* **1** : hablar **2** ~ **about** : hablar de **3** ~ **to/with** : hablar con — *vt* **1** SPEAK : hablar **2** ~ **over** : hablar de, discutir — ~ *n* **1** CHAT : conversación *f* **2** SPEECH : charla *f* — **talkative** ['tɔkətɪv] *adj* : hablador

tall ['tɔl] *adj* **1** : alto **2 how ~ are you?** : ¿cuánto mides?

tally ['tæli] *n, pl* **-lies** : cuenta *f* — ~ **-lied; -lying** *vt* RECKON : calcular — *vi* MATCH : concordar, cuadrar

talon ['tælən] *n* : garra *f*

tambourine [,tæmbə'rin] *n* : pandereta *f*

tame ['teɪm] *adj* **tamer; -est 1** : domesticado **2** DOCILE : manso **3** DULL : insípido, soso — ~ *vt* **tamed; taming** : domar

tamper ['tæmpər] *vi* ~ **with** : forzar (una cerradura), amañar (documentos, etc.)

tampon ['tæm,pɑn] *n* : tampón *m*

tan ['tæn] *v* **tanned; tanning** *vt* : curtir (cuero) — *vi* : broncearse — ~ *n* **1** SUNTAN : bronceado *m* **2** : (color *m*) café *m* con leche

tang ['tæŋ] *n* : sabor *m* fuerte

tangent ['tændʒənt] *n* : tangente *f*

tangerine [,tændʒə'rin, 'tændʒə-] *n* : mandarina *f*

tangible ['tændʒəbəl] *adj* : tangible

tangle ['tæŋgəl] *v* **-gled; -gling** *vt* : enredar — *vi* : enredarse — ~ *n* : enredo *m*

tango ['tæŋgo] *n, pl* **-gos** : tango *m*

tank ['tæŋk] *n* **1** : tanque *m*, depósito *m* **2** : tanque *m* (militar) — **tanker** ['tæŋkər] *n* **1** : buque *m* tanque **2** or ~ **truck** : camión *m* cisterna

tantalizing ['tæntə,laɪzɪŋ] *adj* : tentador

tantrum ['tæntrəm] *n* **throw a ~** : hacer un berrinche

tap[1] ['tæp] *n* FAUCET : llave *f*, grifo *m* *Spain* — ~ *vt* **tapped; tapping 1** : sacar (un líquido, etc.), sangrar (un árbol) **2** : intervenir (un teléfono)

tap[2] *vt* **tapped; tapping** STRIKE : tocar, dar un golpecito en — ~ *n* **1** : golpecito *m*, toque *m* **1**

tape ['teɪp] *n* : cinta *f* — ~ *vt* **taped; taping 1** : pegar con cinta **2** RECORD : grabar — **tape measure** *n* : cinta *f* métrica

taper ['teɪpər] *n* : vela *f* (larga) — ~ *vi* **1** NARROW : estrecharse **2** or ~ **off** : disminuir

tapestry ['tæpəstri] *n, pl* **-tries** : tapiz *m*

tar ['tɑr] *n* : alquitrán *m* — ~ *vt* **tarred; tarring** : alquitranar

tarantula [tə'ræntʃələ, -'ræntələ] *n* : tarántula *f*

target ['tɑrgət] *n* **1** : blanco *m* **2** GOAL : objetivo *m*

tariff ['tærɪf] *n* : tarifa *f*, arancel *m*

tarnish ['tɑrnɪʃ] *vt* **1** : deslustrar **2** : empañar (una reputación, etc.) — *vi* : deslustrarse

tart[1] ['tɑrt] *adj* SOUR : ácido, agrio

tart[2] *n* : pastel *m*

tartan ['tɑrtən] *n* : tartán *m*

task ['tæsk] *n* : tarea *f*

tassel ['tæsəl] *n* : borla *f*

taste ['teɪst] *v* **tasted; tasting** *vt* TRY : probar — *vi* **1** : saber **2** ~ **like** : saber a — ~ *n* **1** FLAVOR : gusto *m*, sabor *m* **2 have a ~ of** : probar **3 in good/bad** ~ : de buen/mal gusto — **tasteless** ['teɪstləs] *adj* **1** : sin sabor **2** COARSE : de mal gusto — **tasty** ['teɪsti] *adj* **tastier; -est** : sabroso

tasteful ['teɪstfəl] *adj* : de buen gusto

tatters ['tætərz] *npl* : harapos *mpl* — **tattered** ['tætərd] *adj* : harapiento

tattle ['tætəl] *vi* **-tled; -tling** ~ **on s.o.** : acusar a algn

tattoo [tæ'tu] *vt* : tatuar — ~ *n* : tatuaje *m*

taught → **teach**

taunt ['tɔnt] *n* : pulla *f*, burla *f* — ~ *vt* : mofarse de, burlarse de

taut ['tɔt] *adj* : tirante, tenso

tavern ['tævərn] *n* : taberna *f*

tax ['tæks] *vt* **1** : gravar **2** STRAIN : poner a prueba — ~ *n* **1** : impuesto *m* **2** BURDEN : carga *f* — **taxable** ['tæksəbəl] *adj* : imponible — **taxation** [tæk-'seɪʃən] *n* : impuestos *mpl* — **tax-exempt** ['tæksɪg'zempt, -eg-] *adj* : libre de impuestos

taxi ['tæksi] *n, pl* **taxis** : taxi *m* — ~ *vi* **taxied; taxiing** *or* **taxying; taxis** *or* **taxies** : rodar por la pista (dícese de un avión)

taxpayer ['tæks,peɪər] *n* : contribuyente *mf*

tea ['ti:] *n* : té *m*

teach ['ti:tʃ] *v* **taught** ['tɔt]; **teaching** *vt* : enseñar, dar clases de (una asignatura) — *vi* : dar clases — **teacher** ['ti:tʃər] *n* : profesor *m*, -sora *f*; maestro *m*, -tra *f* (de niños pequeños) — **teaching** ['ti:tʃɪŋ] *n* : enseñanza *f*

teacup ['ti:,kʌp] *n* : taza *f* de té

team ['ti:m] *n* : equipo *m* — ~ *vi or* ~ **up** : asociarse — **teammate** ['ti:m-,meɪt] *n* : compañero *m*, -ra *f* de equipo — **teamwork** ['ti:m,wərk] *n* : trabajo *m* de equipo

teapot ['ti:,pɑt] *n* : tetera *f*

tear¹ ['tær] v **tore** ['tor]; **torn** ['torn]; **tearing** vt 1 : romper, rasgar 2 **~ apart** : destrozar 3 **~ down** : derribar 4 **~ off** or **~ out** : arrancar 5 **~ up** : romper (papel, etc.) — vi 1 : romperse, rasgarse 2 RUSH : ir a toda velocidad — **~ n** : desgarro m, rasgón m

tear² ['tɪr] n : lágrima f — **tearful** ['tɪrfəl] adj : lloroso

tease ['tiz] vt **teased; teasing** 1 : tomar el pelo a, burlarse de 2 ANNOY : fastidiar

teaspoon ['ti.spun] n 1 : cucharita f 2 : cucharadita f (cantidad)

technical ['tɛknɪkəl] adj : técnico — **technicality** [tɛknəˈkæləti] n, pl **-ties** : detalle m técnico — **technically** [-kli] adv : técnicamente — **technician** [tɛkˈnɪʃən] n : técnico m, -ca f

technique [tɛkˈnik] n : técnica f

technological [tɛknəˈlɑdʒɪkəl] adj : tecnológico — **technology** [tɛkˈnɑlədʒi] n, pl **-gies** : tecnología f

teddy bear ['tɛdi] n : oso m de peluche

tedious ['tidiəs] adj : tedioso, aburrido — **tedium** ['tidiəm] n : tedio m

tee ['ti] n : tee m (en deportes)

teem ['tim] vi 1 POUR : llover a cántaros 2 **be ~ing with** : estar repleto de

teenage ['tin.eɪdʒ] or **teenaged** [-.eɪdʒd] adj : adolescente — **teenager** ['tin.eɪdʒər] n : adolescente mf — **teens** ['tinz] npl : adolescencia f

teepee → tepee

teeter ['titər] vi : tambalearse

teeth → tooth — teethe ['tið] vi **teethed; teething** : echar los dientes

telecommunication [tɛləkəˌmjunəˈkeɪʃən] n : telecomunicación f

telegram ['tɛləgræm] n : telegrama m — **telegraph** ['tɛləgræf] n : telégrafo m — **~ v** : telegrafiar

telephone ['tɛləfon] n : teléfono m — **~ v -phoned; -phoning** : llamar por teléfono

telescope ['tɛləskop] n : telescopio m

televise ['tɛləvaɪz] vt **-vised; -vising** : televisar — **television** ['tɛləˌvɪʒən] n : televisión f

tell ['tɛl] v **told** ['told]; **telling** vt 1 : decir 2 RELATE : contar 3 DISTINGUISH : distinguir 4 **~ s.o. off** : regañar a algn — vi 1 : decir 2 KNOW : saber 3 SHOW : tener efecto 4 **~ on s.o.** : acusar a algn — **teller** ['tɛlər] n or **bank ~** : cajero m, -ra f

temp ['tɛmp] n : empleado m, -da f temporal

temper ['tɛmpər] vt MODERATE : temper-

ar — **~ n** 1 MOOD : humor m 2 **have a bad ~** : tener mal genio 3 **lose one's ~** : perder los estribos — **temperament** ['tɛmpərmənt, -prə-, -pərə-] n : temperamento m — **temperamental** [ˌtɛmpərˈmɛntəl, -prə-, -pərə-] adj : temperamental — **temperate** ['tɛmpərət] adj 1 : moderado 2 **~ zone** : zona f templada

temperature ['tɛmpərˌtʃur, -prə-, -pərə-, -tʃər] n 1 : temperatura f 2 **have a ~** : tener fiebre

tempest ['tɛmpəst] n : tempestad f

temple ['tɛmpəl] n 1 : templo m 2 : sien f (en anatomía)

tempo ['tɛmpoː] n, pl **-pi** [-ˌpiː] or **-pos** 1 : tiempo m 2 PACE : ritmo m

temporarily [tɛmpəˈrɛrəli] adv : temporalmente — **temporary** ['tɛmpəˌrɛri] adj : temporal

tempt ['tɛmpt] vt : tentar — **temptation** [tɛmpˈteɪʃən] n : tentación f

ten ['tɛn] adj : diez — **~ n** : diez m

tenacity [təˈnæsəti] n : tenacidad f — **tenacious** [təˈneɪʃəs] adj : tenaz

tenant ['tɛnənt] n : inquilino m, -na f; arrendatario m, -ria f

tend¹ ['tɛnd] vt MIND : cuidar

tend² vi **~ to** : tender a — **tendency** ['tɛndənsi] n, pl **-cies** : tendencia f

tender¹ ['tɛndər] adj 1 : tierno 2 PAINFUL : dolorido

tender² vt : presentar — **~ n** 1 : oferta f 2 **legal ~** : moneda f de curso legal

tenderloin ['tɛndərˌlɔɪn] n : lomo m (de cerdo o vaca)

tenderness ['tɛndərnəs] n : ternura f

tendon ['tɛndən] n : tendón m

tenet ['tɛnət] n : principio m

tennis ['tɛnəs] n : tenis m

tenor ['tɛnər] n : tenor m

tense¹ ['tɛns] n : tiempo m (de un verbo)

tense² vt **tensed; tensing** vt : tensar — vi : tensarse — **~ adj** : tenser; **tensest** : tenso — **tension** ['tɛntʃən] n : tensión f

tent ['tɛnt] n : tienda f de campaña

tentacle ['tɛntɪkəl] n : tentáculo m

tentative ['tɛntətɪv] adj 1 HESITANT : vacilante 2 PROVISIONAL : provisional

tenth ['tɛnθ] adj : décimo — **~ n** 1 : décimo m, -ma f (en una serie) 2 : décimo m (en matemáticas)

tenuous ['tɛnjuəs] adj : tenue, endeble

tepid ['tɛpɪd] adj : tibio

term ['tərm] n 1 WORD : término m 2 PERIOD : período m 3 **be on good ~s** : tener buenas relaciones 4 **in ~s of** : con respecto a — **~ vt** : calificar de

terminal ['tərmənəl] *adj* : terminal — ~ *n* **1** : terminal *m* **2** *or* **bus** ~ : terminal *f*

terminate ['tərmə‚neɪt] *v* **-nated; -nating** *vi* : terminar(se) — *vt* : poner fin a — **termination** [‚tərmə'neɪʃən] *n* : terminación *f*

termite ['tər‚maɪt] *n* : termita *f*

terrace ['terəs] *n* : terraza *f*

terrain [tə'reɪn] *n* : terreno *m*

terrestrial [tə'restriəl] *adj* : terrestre

terrible ['terəbəl] *adj* : espantoso, terrible — **terribly** ['terəbli] *adv* : terriblemente

terrier ['teriər] *n* : terrier *mf*

terrific [tə'rɪfɪk] *adj* **1** HUGE : tremendo **2** EXCELLENT : estupendo

terrify ['terə‚faɪ] *vt* **-fied; -fying** : aterrar, aterrorizar — **terrifying** ['terə‚faɪɪŋ] *adj* : aterrador

territory ['terə‚tori] *n, pl* **-ries** : territorio *m* — **territorial** [‚terə'toriəl] *adj* : territorial

terror ['terər] *n* : terror *m* — **terrorism** ['terər‚ɪzəm] *n* : terrorismo *m* — **terrorist** ['terərɪst] *n* : terrorista *mf* — **terrorize** ['terər‚aɪz] *vt* **-ized; -izing** : aterrorizar

terse ['tərs] *adj* **terser; tersest** : seco, lacónico

test ['test] *n* **1** TRIAL : prueba *f* **2** EXAM : examen *m*, prueba *f* **3** : análisis *m* (en medicina) — ~ *vt* **1** TRY : probar **2** QUIZ : analizar **3** : analizar (la sangre, etc.), examinar (los ojos, etc.)

testament ['testəmənt] *n* **1** WILL : testamento *m* **2** **the Old/New Testament** : el Antiguo/Nuevo Testamento

testicle ['testɪkəl] *n* : testículo *m*

testify ['testə‚faɪ] *v* **-fied; -fying** : testificar

testimony ['testə‚moni] *n, pl* **-nies** : testimonio *m*

test tube *n* : probeta *f*, tubo *m* de ensayo

tetanus ['tetənəs] *n* : tétano *m*

tether ['teðər] *vt* : atar

text ['tekst] *n* : texto *m* — **textbook** ['tekst‚bʊk] *n* : libro *m* de texto

textile ['tek‚staɪl, 'tekstəl] *n* : textil *m*

texture ['tekstʃər] *n* : textura *f*

than ['ðæn] *conj & prep* : que, de (con cantidades)

thank ['θæŋk] *vt* **1** : agradecer, dar (las) gracias a **2** ~ **you!** : ¡gracias! — **thankful** ['θæŋkfəl] *adj* : agradecido — **thankfully** ['θæŋkfəli] *adv* **1** : con agradecimiento **2** FORTUNATELY : gracias a Dios — **thanks** ['θæŋks] *npl* **1** : agradecimiento *m* **2** ~! : ¡gracias!

Thanksgiving [θæŋks'gɪvɪŋ, 'θæŋks‚-] *n* : día *m* de Acción de Gracias

that ['ðæt] *pron, pl* **those** ['ðoz] **1** : ése, ésa, eso **2** (*more distant*) : aquél, aquélla, aquello **3 is** ~ **you?** : ¿eres tú? **4 like** ~ : así **5** ~ **is...** : es decir... **6 those who...** : los que... — ~ *conj* : que — ~ *adj, pl* **those 1** : ese, esa **2** (*more distant*) : aquel, aquella **3** ~ **one** : ése, ésa — ~ *adv* : tan

thatched ['θætʃt] *adj* : con techo de paja

thaw ['θɔ] *vt* : descongelar (alimentos), derretir (hielo) — *vi* **1** : descongelarse **2** MELT : derretirse — ~ *n* : deshielo *m*

the [ðə, *before vowel sounds usu* ði:] *art* **1** : el, la, los, las **2** PER : por — ~ *adv* **1** ~ **sooner** ~ **better** : cuanto más pronto, mejor **2 I like this one** ~ **best** : éste es el que más me gusta

theater *or* **theatre** ['θiətər] *n* : teatro *m* — **theatrical** [θi'ætrɪkəl] *adj* : teatral

theft ['θeft] *n* : robo *m*, hurto *m*

their ['ðer] *adj* : su, sus, de ellos, de ellas — **theirs** ['ðerz] *pron* **1** : (el) suyo, (la) suya, (los) suyos, (las) suyas **2 some friends of** ~ : unos amigos suyos, unos amigos de ellos

them ['ðem] *pron* **1** (*used as direct object*) : los, las **2** (*used as indirect object*) : les, se **3** (*used as object of a preposition*) : ellos, ellas

theme ['θim] *n* **1** : tema *m* **2** ESSAY : trabajo *m* (escrito)

themselves [ðəm'selvz, ðem-] *pron* **1** (*used reflexively*) : se **2** (*used emphatically*) : ellos mismos, ellas mismas **3** (*used after a preposition*) : sí (mismos), sí (mismas)

then ['ðen] *adv* **1** : entonces **2** NEXT : luego, después **3** BESIDES : además — ~ *adj* : entonces

thence ['ðens, 'θens] *adv* : de ahí (en adelante)

theology [θi'ɑlədʒi] *n, pl* **-gies** : teología *f* — **theological** [‚θiə'lɑdʒɪkəl] *adj* : teológico

theorem ['θiərəm, 'θirəm] *n* : teorema *m* — **theoretical** [‚θiə'retɪkəl] *adj* : teórico — **theory** ['θiəri, 'θiri] *n, pl* **-ries** : teoría *f*

therapeutic [‚θerə'pjutɪk] *adj* : terapéutico — **therapist** ['θerəpɪst] *n* : terapeuta *mf* — **therapy** ['θerəpi] *n, pl* **-pies** : terapia *f*

there ['ðer] *adv* **1** *or* **over** ~ : allí, allá **2** *or* **right** ~ : ahí **3 in** ~ : ahí (dentro) **4** ~**, it's done!** : ¡listo! **5 up/down** ~ : ahí arriba/abajo **6**

who's ~? : ¿quién es? — **~** *pron* **1** : is/are — hay **2** — **are three of us** : somos tres — **thereabouts** *or* **thereabout** [ðærə'baʊts, -'baʊt; 'ðærə-] *adv or* ~ : por ahí — **thereafter** [ðær-'æftər] *adv* : después — **thereby** [ðær-'baɪ, 'ðær,baɪ] *adv* : así — **therefore** [ðær,for] *adv* : por lo tanto

thermal ['θərməl] *adj* : térmico

thermometer [θər'mɑmətər] *n* : termómetro *m*

thermos ['θərməs] *n* : termo *m*

thermostat ['θərmə,stæt] *n* : termostato *m*

thesaurus [θɪ'sɔrəs] *n, pl* **-sauri** [-'sɔr,aɪ] *or* **-sauruses** [-'sɔrəsəz] : diccionario *m* de sinónimos

these → this

thesis ['θisɪs] *n, pl* **theses** ['θi:si:z] : tesis *f*

they ['ðeɪ] *pron* **1** : ellos, ellas **2 where are ~?** : ¿dónde están? **3 as ~ say** : como dicen — **they'd** ['ðeɪd] (*contraction of* **they had** *or* **they would**) → **have, would** — **they'll** ['ðeɪl, 'ðel] (*contraction of* **they shall** *or* **they will**) → **shall, will** — **they're** ['ðer] (*contraction of* **they are**) → **be** — **they've** ['ðeɪv] (*contraction of* **they have**) → **have**

thick ['θɪk] *adj* **1** : grueso **2** DENSE : espeso **3 a ~ accent** : un acento marcado **4 it's two inches ~** : tiene dos pulgadas de grosor — **~** *n* **in the ~ of** : en medio de — **thicken** ['θɪkən] *vt* : espesar — *vi* : espesarse — **thicket** ['θɪkət] *n* : matorral *m* — **thickness** ['θɪknəs] *n* : grosor *m*, espesor *m*

thief ['θi:f] *n, pl* **thieves** ['θi:vz] : ladrón *m*, -drona *f*

thigh ['θaɪ] *n* : muslo *m*

thimble ['θɪmbəl] *n* : dedal *m*

thin ['θɪn] *adj* **thinner; -est 1** : delgado **2** : ralo (dícese del pelo) **3** WATERY : claro, aguado **4** FINE : fino — *v* **thinned; thinning** *vt* DILUTE : diluir — *vi* : ralear (dícese del pelo)

thing ['θɪŋ] *n* **1** : cosa *f* **2 for one ~** : en primer lugar **3 how are ~s?** : ¿qué tal? **4 it's a good ~ that...** : menos mal que... **5 the important ~ is...** : lo importante es...

think ['θɪŋk] *v* **thought** ['θɔt]; **thinking** *vt* **1** : pensar **2** BELIEVE : creer **3 ~ up** : idear — *vi* **1** : pensar **2 ~ about** *or* **~ of** CONSIDER : pensar en **3 ~ of** REMEMBER : acordarse de **4 what do you ~ of it?** : ¿qué te parece? — **thinker** ['θɪŋkər] *n* : pensador *m*, -dora *f*

third ['θərd] *adj* : tercero — *or* **third-**

ly [-li] *adv* : en tercer lugar — **~** *n* **1** : tercero *m*, -ra *f* (en una serie) **2** : tercero *m* (en matemáticas) — **Third World** *n* : Tercer Mundo *m*

thirst ['θərst] *n* : sed *f* — **thirsty** ['θərsti] *adj* **thirstier; -est 1** : sediento **2 be ~** : tener sed

thirteen [θər'ti:n] *adj* : trece — **~** *n* : trece *m* — **thirteenth** [,θər'ti:nθ] *adj* : décimo tercero — **~** *n* **1** : decimotercero *m*, -ra *f* (en una serie) **2** : treceavo *m* (en matemáticas)

thirty ['θərti] *adj* : treinta — **~** *n, pl* **thirties** : treinta *m* — **thirtieth** ['θərtiəθ] *adj* : trigésimo — **~** *n* **1** : trigésimo *m*, -ma *f* (en una serie) **2** : treintavo *m* (en matemáticas)

this ['ðɪs] *pron, pl* **these** ['ði:z] **1** : éste, ésta, esto **2 like ~** : así — **~** *adj, pl* **these 1** : este, esta **2 ~ one** : éste, ésta **3 ~ way** : por aquí — **~** *adv* **~ big** : así de grande

thistle ['θɪsəl] *n* : cardo *m*

thong ['θɔŋ] *n* **1** : correa *f* **2** SANDAL : chancla *f*

thorn ['θɔrn] *n* : espina *f* — **thorny** ['θɔrni] *adj* : espinoso

thorough ['θəro] *adj* **1** : meticuloso **2** COMPLETE : completo — **thoroughly** *adv* **1** : a fondo **2** COMPLETELY : completamente — **thoroughbred** ['θərobred] *adj* : de pura sangre — **thoroughfare** ['θəro,fær] *n* : vía *f* pública

those → that

though ['ðo:] *conj* : aunque — **~** *adv* **1** : sin embargo **2 as ~** : como si

thought ['θɔt] → **think** — **~** *n* **1** : pensamiento *m* **2** IDEA : idea *f* — **thoughtful** ['θɔtfəl] *adj* **1** : pensativo **2** KIND : amable — **thoughtless** ['θɔtləs] *adj* **1** CARELESS : descuidado **2** RUDE : desconsiderado

thousand ['θaʊzənd] *adj* : mil — **~** *n, pl* **-sands** *or* **-sand** : mil *m* — **thousandth** ['θaʊzən(t)θ] *adj* : milésimo — **~** *n* **1** : milésimo *m*, -ma *f* (en una serie) **2** : milésimo *m* (en matemáticas)

thrash ['θræʃ] *vt* : dar una paliza a — *vi* **or ~ around** : agitarse, revolcarse

thread ['θrɛd] *n* **1** : hilo *m* **2** : rosca *f* (de un tornillo) — **~** *vt* : enhilar (una aguja), ensartar (cuentas) — **threadbare** ['θrɛdbær] *adj* : raído

threat ['θrɛt] *n* : amenaza *f* — **threaten** ['θrɛtən] *v* : amenazar — **threatening** ['θrɛtənɪŋ] *adj* : amenazador

three ['θri:] *adj* : tres — *n* : tres *m* — **three hundred** *adj* : trescientos — **~** *n* : trescientos *m*

threshold ['θrɛʃˌhoːld, -ˌoːld] *n* : umbral *m*

threw → throw

thrift ['θrɪft] *n* : frugalidad *f* — **thrifty** ['θrɪfti] *adj* **thriftier; -est** : económico, frugal

thrill ['θrɪl] *vt* : emocionar — *n* : emoción *f* — **thriller** ['θrɪlər] *n* : película *f* de suspense *Spain*, película *f* de suspenso *Lat* — **thrilling** ['θrɪlɪŋ] *adj* : emocionante

thrive ['θraɪv] *vi* **throve** ['θroːv] *or* **thrived; thriven** ['θrɪvən] **1** FLOURISH : florecer **2** PROSPER : prosperar

throat ['θroːt] *n* : garganta *f*

throb ['θrɑb] *vi* **throbbed; throbbing** **1** PULSATE : palpitar **2** VIBRATE : vibrar **3** ~ **with pain** : tener un dolor punzante

throes ['θroːz] *npl* **1** PANGS : agonía *f* **2** **in the** ~ **of** : en medio de

throne ['θroːn] *n* : trono *m*

throng ['θrɔŋ] *n* : muchedumbre *f*, multitud *f*

throttle ['θrɑtəl] *vt* **-tled; -tling** : estrangular — ~ *n* : válvula *f* reguladora

through ['θruː] *prep* **1** : por, a través de **2** BETWEEN : entre **3** BECAUSE OF : a causa de **4** DURING : durante **5** ~ **throughout 6 Monday** ~ **Friday** : de lunes a viernes — ~ *adv* **1** : de un lado a otro (en el espacio), de principio a fin (en el tiempo) **2** COMPLETELY : completamente — ~ *adj* **1 be** ~ : haber terminado **2** ~ **traffic** : tráfico *m* de paso — **throughout** [θruːˈaʊt] *prep* : por todo (un lugar), a lo largo de (un período de tiempo)

throw ['θroː] *v* **threw** ['θruː]; **thrown** ['θroːn]; **throwing** *vt* **1** : tirar, lanzar **2** : proyectar (una sombra) **3** CONFUSE : desconcertar **4** ~ **a party** : dar una fiesta **5** ~ **away** *or* ~ **out** : tirar, botar *Lat* — ~ **up** VOMIT : vomitar — ~ *n* : tiro *m*, lanzamiento *m*

thrush ['θrʌʃ] *n* : tordo *m*, zorzal *m*

thrust ['θrʌst] *vt* **thrust; thrusting** **1** : empujar (bruscamente) **2** PLUNGE : clavar **3** ~ **upon** : imponer a — ~ *n* **1** : empujón *m* **2** : estocada *f* (en esgrima)

thud ['θʌd] *n* : ruido *m* sordo

thug ['θʌg] *n* : matón *m*

thumb ['θʌm] *n* : (dedo *m*) pulgar *m* — ~ *vt* ~ **through** : hojear — **thumbnail** ['θʌmˌneɪl] *n* : uña *f* del pulgar — **thumbtack** ['θʌmˌtæk] *n* : tachuela *f*, chinche *f Lat*

thump ['θʌmp] *vt* : golpear — *vi* : latir

con fuerza (dícese del corazón) — ~ *n* : ruido *m* sordo

thunder ['θʌndər] *n* : truenos *mpl* — *vi* : tronar — *vt* SHOUT : bramar — **thunderbolt** ['θʌndərˌboːlt] *n* : rayo *m* — **thunderous** ['θʌndərəs] *adj* : atronador — **thunderstorm** ['θʌndərˌstorm] *n* : tormenta *f* eléctrica

Thursday ['θərzˌdeɪ, -di] *n* : jueves *m*

thus ['ðʌs] *adv* **1** : así **2** THEREFORE : por lo tanto

thwart ['θwɔrt] *vt* : frustrar

thyme ['taɪm, 'θaɪm] *n* : tomillo *m*

thyroid ['θaɪˌrɔɪd] *n* : tiroides *mf*

tiara [tiˈærə, -ˈɑr-] *n* : diadema *f*

tic ['tɪk] *n* : tic *m* (nervioso)

tick¹ ['tɪk] *n* : garrapata *f* (insecto)

tick² ['tɪk] *n* **1** : tictac *m* (sonido) **2** CHECK : marca *f* — ~ *vi* : hacer tictac — *vt* **1** *or* ~ **off** CHECK : marcar **2** ~ **off** ANNOY : fastidiar

ticket ['tɪkət] *n* **1** : pasaje *m* (de avión), billete *m Spain* (de tren, avión, etc.), boleto *m Lat* (de tren o autobús) **2** : entrada *f* (al teatro, etc.) **3** FINE : multa *f*

tickle ['tɪkəl] *v* **-led; -ling** *vt* **1** : hacer cosquillas a **2** AMUSE : divertir — *vi* : picar — ~ *n* : cosquilleo *m* — **ticklish** ['tɪkəlɪʃ] *adj* **1** : cosquilloso **2** TRICKY : delicado

tidal wave ['taɪdəl] *n* : maremoto *m*

tidbit ['tɪdˌbɪt] *n* MORSEL : golosina *f*

tide ['taɪd] *n* : marea *f* — ~ *vt* **tided; tiding** ~ **over** : ayudar a superar un apuro

tidy ['taɪdi] *adj* **-dier; -est** : ordenado, arreglado — ~ *vt* **-died; -dying** *or* ~ **up** : ordenar, arreglar

tie ['taɪ] *n* **1** : atadura *f*, cordón *m* **2** BOND : lazo *m* **3** : empate *m* (en deportes) **4** NECKTIE : corbata *f* — ~ *vt* **tied; tying** *or* **tieing** *vt* **1** : atar, amarrar *Lat* **2** ~ **a knot** : hacer un nudo — *vi* : empatar (en deportes)

tier ['tɪr] *n* : nivel *m*, piso *m* (de un pastel), grada *f* (de un estadio)

tiger ['taɪgər] *n* : tigre *m*

tight ['taɪt] *adj* **1** : apretado **2** SNUG : ajustado, ceñido **3** TAUT : tirante **4** STINGY : agarrado **5** SCARCE : escaso **6 a** ~ **seal** : un cierre hermético **7 a** ~ **spot** : un aprieto — ~ *adv* **closed** ~ : bien cerrado — **tighten** ['taɪtən] *vt* **1** : apretar **2** TENSE : tensar **3** : hacer más estricto (reglas, etc.) — **tightly** ['taɪtli] *adv* : bien, fuerte — **tightrope** ['taɪtˌroːp] *n* : cuerda *f* floja — **tights** ['taɪts] *npl* : leotardo *m*, mallas *fpl*

tile ['taɪl] *n* **1** : azulejo *m*, baldosa *f* (de

piso) **2** *or* roofing ~ : teja *f* — ~ *vt*
tiled; tiling **1** : revestir de azulejos,
embaldosar (un piso) **2** : tejar (un
techo)
till¹ ['til] *prep & conj* → until
till² *vt* : cultivar
till³ *n* : caja *f* (registradora)
tilt ['tilt] *n* **1** : inclinación *f* **2 at full ~** : a
toda velocidad — ~ *vt* : inclinar — *vi*
: inclinarse
timber ['timbər] *n* **1** : madera *f* (para
construcción) **2** BEAM : viga *f*
timbre ['tæmbər, 'tim-] *n* : timbre *m*
time ['taim] *n* **1** : tiempo *m* **2** AGE : época
f **3** : compás *m* (en música) **4 at ~s**
: a veces **5 at this ~** : en este momento **6 for the ~ being** : por el momento **7 from ~ to ~** : de vez en
cuando **8 have a good ~** : pasarlo
bien **9 many ~s** : muchas veces **10
on ~** : a tiempo **11 ~ after ~** : una
y otra vez **12 what ~ is it?** : ¿qué
hora es? — ~ *vt* : timed; timing
: tomar el tiempo a (algn), cronometrar (una carrera, etc.) — **timeless**
['taimləs] *adj* : eterno — **timely** ['taim-
li] *adj* **-lier; -est** : oportuno — **timer**
['taimər] *n* : temporizador *m*, avisador
m (de cocina) — **times** ['taimz] *prep* **3
~ 4 is 12** : 3 por 4 son 12 — **timetable** ['taim,teibəl] *n* : horario *m*
timid ['timid] *adj* : tímido
tin ['tin] *n* **1** : estaño *m* **2** CAN : lata *f*,
bote *m* *Spain* — **tinfoil** ['tin,foil] *n*
: papel *m* (de) aluminio
tinge ['tindʒ] *vt* tinged; tingeing *or*
tinging ['tindʒiŋ] : matizar — ~ *n* **1**
TINT : matiz *m* **2** TOUCH : dejo *m*
tingle ['tiŋgəl] *vi* **-gled; -gling** : sentir
(un) hormigueo — ~ *n* : hormigueo
m
tinker ['tiŋkər] *vi* ~ **with** : intentar
arreglar (con pequeños ajustes)
tinkle ['tiŋkəl] *vi* **-kled; -kling** : tintinear
— ~ *n* : tintineo *m*
tint ['tint] *n* : tinte *m* — ~ *vt* : teñir
tiny ['taini] *adj* **-nier; -est** : diminuto,
minúsculo
tip¹ ['tip] *v* **tipped; tipping** *vt* TILT : inclinar **2** *or* ~ **over** : volcar — *vi* : inclinarse
tip² *n* END : punta *f*
tip³ *n* ADVICE : consejo *m* — ~ *vt* ~
off : avisar
tip⁴ *vt* : dar una propina a — ~ *n* GRA-
TUITY : propina *f*
tipsy ['tipsi] *adj* **-sier; -est** : achispado
tiptoe ['tip,to:] *n* **on** ~ : de puntillas —
~ *vi* **-toed; -toeing** : caminar de puntillas

tip–top ['tip,tap, -,tap] *adj* : excelente
tire¹ ['tair] *n* : neumático *m*, llanta *f* *Lat*
tire² *v* **tired; tiring** *vt* : cansar — *vi*
: cansarse — **tired** ['taird] *adj* **1** ~ **of**
: cansado de, harto de **2** ~ **out** : agotado — **tireless** ['tairləs] *adj* : incansable — **tiresome** ['tairsəm] *adj* : pesado
tissue ['tiʃu:] *n* **1** : pañuelo *m* de papel **2**
: tejido *m* (en biología)
title ['taitəl] *n* **1** : título *m* — ~ *vt* **-tled;
-tling** : titular
to ['tu:] *prep* **1** : a **2** TOWARD : hacia **3** IN
ORDER TO : para **4** UP TO : hasta **5 a
quarter ~ seven** : las siete menos
cuarto **6 be nice ~ them** : trátalos
bien **7 from ~ the box** : diez por caja **8
the mate ~ this shoe** : el compañero de este zapato **9 two ~ four
years old** : entre dos y cuatro años de
edad **10 want ~ do** : querer hacer —
~ *adv* **1 come** ~ : volver en sí **2** ~
and fro : de un lado a otro
toad ['to:d] *n* : sapo *m*
toast ['to:st] *vt* **1** : tostar (pan, etc.) **2**
: brindar por (una persona) — ~ *n* **1**
: pan *m* tostado, tostadas *fpl* **2** DRINK
: brindis *m* — **toaster** ['to:stər] *n*
: tostador *m*
tobacco [tə'bæko:] *n, pl* **-cos** : tabaco *m*
toboggan [tə'bagən] *n* : tobogán *m*
today [tə'dei] *adv* : hoy — ~ *n* : hoy *m*
toddler ['tadlər] *n* : niño *m* pequeño,
niña *f* pequeña (que comienza a caminar)
toe ['to:] *n* : dedo *m* (del pie) — **toenail**
['to:,neil] *n* : uña *f* (del pie)
together [tə'geðər] *adv* **1** : juntos **2** ~
with : junto con
toil ['toil] *n* : trabajo *m* duro — ~ *vi*
: trabajar duro
toilet ['toilət] *n* **1** BATHROOM : baño *m*,
servicio *m* **2** : inodoro *m* (instalación)
— **toilet paper** *n* : papel *m* higiénico
— **toiletries** ['toilətriz] *npl* : artículos
mpl de tocador
token ['to:kən] *n* **1** SIGN : muestra *f* **2** ME-
MENTO : recuerdo *m* **3** : ficha *f* (para un
tren, etc.)
told → tell
tolerable ['talərəbəl] *adj* : tolerable
tolerance ['talərəns] *n* : tolerancia *f* —
tolerant ['talərənt] *adj* : tolerante —
tolerate ['talə,reit] *vt* **-ated; -ating**
: tolerar
toll¹ ['to:l] *n* **1** : peaje *m* **2 death ~**
: número *m* de muertos **3 take a ~ on**
: afectar
toll² *vi* RING : tocar, doblar — ~ *n*
: tañido *m*

tomato [təˈmeɪt̬o, -ˈmɑ-] *n, pl* **-toes** : tomate *m*

tomb [ˈtuːm] *n* : tumba *f*, sepulcro *m* — **tombstone** [ˈtuːmˌstoʊn] *n* : lápida *f*

tome [ˈtoʊm] *n* : tomo *m*

tomorrow [təˈmɑro] *adv* : mañana — ~ *n* : mañana *m*

ton [ˈtʌn] *n* : tonelada *f*

tone [ˈtoʊn] *n* : tono *m* — ~ *vt* **toned; toning** *or* ~ **down** : atenuar

tongs [ˈtɑŋz, ˈtɔŋz] *npl* : tenazas *fpl*

tongue [ˈtʌŋ] *n* : lengua *f*

tonic [ˈtɑnɪk] *n* **1** : tónico *m* **2** *or* ~ **water** : tónica *f*

tonight [təˈnaɪt] *adv* : esta noche — ~ *n* : esta noche *f*

tonsil [ˈtɑnsəl] *n* : amígdala *f*

too [ˈtuː] *adv* **1** ALSO : también **2** EXCESSIVELY : demasiado

took → **take**

tool [ˈtuːl] *n* : herramienta *f* — **toolbox** [ˈtuːlˌbɑks] *n* : caja *f* de herramientas

toot [ˈtuːt] *vt* : sonar (un claxon, etc.) — ~ *n* **1** WHISTLE : pitido *m* **2** HONK : bocinazo *m*

tooth [ˈtuːθ] *n, pl* **teeth** [ˈtiːθ] : diente *m* — **toothache** [ˈtuːθˌeɪk] *n* : dolor *m* de muelas — **toothbrush** [ˈtuːθˌbrʌʃ] *n* : cepillo *m* de dientes — **toothpaste** [ˈtuːθˌpeɪst] *n* : pasta *f* de dientes, pasta *f* dentífrica

top¹ [ˈtɑp] *n* **1** : parte *f* superior **2** SUMMIT : cima *f*, cumbre *f* **3** COVER : tapa *f*, cubierta *f* **4 on** ~ **of** : encima de — ~ *vt* **topped; topping** COVER : rematar (un edificio, etc.), bañar (un pastel, etc.) **2** SURPASS : superar **3** ~ **off** : llenar — *adj* **1** : de arriba, superior **2** BEST : mejor **3 a** ~ **executive** : un alto ejecutivo

top² *n* : trompo *m* (juguete)

topic [ˈtɑpɪk] *n* : tema *m* — **topical** [ˈtɑpɪkəl] *adj* : de interés actual

topmost [ˈtɑpˌmoʊst] *adj* : más alto

topple [ˈtɑpəl] *v* **-pled; -pling** *vi* : caerse — *vt* **1** OVERTURN : volcar **2** OVERTHROW : derrocar

torch [ˈtɔrtʃ] *n* : antorcha *f*

tore → **tear¹**

torment [ˈtɔrˌmɛnt] *n* : tormento *m* — ~ [ˈtɔrˌmɛnt, ˈtɔr-] *vt* : atormentar

torn → **tear¹**

tornado [tɔrˈneɪdo] *n, pl* **-does** *or* **-dos** : tornado *m*

torpedo [tɔrˈpiːdo] *n, pl* **-does** : torpedo *m* — ~ *vt* : torpedear

torrent [ˈtɔrənt] *n* : torrente *m*

torrid [ˈtɔrɪd] *adj* : tórrido

torso [ˈtɔrˌso] *n, pl* **-sos** *or* **-si** [-ˌsiː] : torso *m*

tortilla [tɔrˈtiːjə] *n* : tortilla *f*

tortoise [ˈtɔrt̬əs] *n* : tortuga *f* (terrestre) — **tortoiseshell** [ˈtɔrt̬əsˌʃɛl] *n* : carey *m*, concha *f*

tortuous [ˈtɔrtʃuəs] *adj* : tortuoso

torture [ˈtɔrtʃər] *n* : tortura *f* — ~ *vt* **-tured; -turing** : torturar

toss [ˈtɔs, ˈtɑs] *vt* **1** : tirar, lanzar **2** : mezclar (una ensalada) — ~ *vi* **and turn** : dar vueltas — ~ *n* : lanzamiento *m*

tot [ˈtɑt] *n* : pequeño *m*, -ña *f*

total [ˈtoʊt̬əl] *adj* : total — ~ *n* : total *m* — ~ *vt* **-taled** *or* **-talled; -taling** *or* **-talling** **1** : ascender a **2** *or* ~ **up** : totalizar, sumar

totalitarian [toˌtæləˈteriən] *adj* : totalitario

tote [ˈtoʊt] *vt* **toted; toting** : llevar

totter [ˈtɑt̬ər] *vi* : tambalearse

touch [ˈtʌtʃ] *vt* **1** : tocar **2** MOVE : conmover **3** AFFECT : afectar **4** ~ **up** : retocar — *vi* : tocarse — ~ *n* **1** : tacto *m* (sentido) **2** HINT : toque *m* **3** BIT : pizca *f* **4 keep in** ~ : mantenerse en contacto **5 lose one's** ~ : perder la habilidad — **touchdown** [ˈtʌtʃˌdaʊn] *n* : touchdown *m* — **touchy** [ˈtʌtʃi] *adj* **touchier; -est 1** : delicado **2 be** ~ **about** : picarse a la mención de

tough [ˈtʌf] *adj* **1** : duro **2** STRONG : fuerte **3** STRICT : severo **4** DIFFICULT : difícil — **toughen** [ˈtʌfən] *vt* *or* ~ **up** : endurecer — *vi* : endurecerse — **toughness** [ˈtʌfnəs] *n* : dureza *f*

tour [ˈtʊr] *n* **1** : viaje *m* (por un país, etc.), visita *f* (a un museo, etc.) **2** : gira *f* (de un equipo, etc.) — ~ *vi* **1** TRAVEL : viajar **2** : hacer una gira (dícese de equipos, etc.) — *vt* **1** : viajar por, recorrer — **tourist** [ˈtʊrɪst, ˈtɔr-] *n* : turista *mf*

tournament [ˈtɔrnəmənt, ˈtʊr-] *n* : torneo *m*

tousle [ˈtaʊzəl] *vt* **-sled; -sling** : despeinar

tout [ˈtaʊt] *vt* : promocionar

tow [ˈtoː] *vt* : remolcar — ~ *n* : remolque *m*

toward [ˈtord, təˈword] *or* **towards** [ˈtordz, təˈwordz] *prep* : hacia

towel [ˈtaʊəl] *n* : toalla *f*

tower [ˈtaʊər] *n* : torre *f* — ~ *vi* **over** : descollar sobre — **towering** [ˈtaʊərɪŋ] *adj* : altísimo

town [ˈtaʊn] *n* **1** VILLAGE : pueblo *m* **2** CITY : ciudad *f* — **township** [ˈtaʊnˌʃɪp] *n* : municipio *m*

tow truck [ˈtoːˌtrʌk] *n* : grúa *f*

toxic [ˈtɑksɪk] *adj* : tóxico

toy ['tɔɪ] *n* : juguete *m* — *vi* ~ **with** : juguetear con

trace ['treɪs] *n* **1** SIGN : rastro *m*, señal *f* **2** HINT : dejo *m* — *vt* **traced; tracing 1** : calcar (un dibujo, etc.) **2** DRAW : trazar **3** FIND : localizar

track ['træk] *n* **1** : pista *f* **2** PATH : sendero *m* **3** *or* **railroad** ~ : vía *f* (férrea) **4 keep** ~ **of** : llevar la cuenta de — ~ *vt* TRAIL : seguir la pista de

tract[1] ['trækt] *n* **1** EXPANSE : extensión *f* **2** : tracto *m* (en anatomía)

tract[2] *n* PAMPHLET : folleto *m*

traction ['trækʃən] *n* : tracción *f*

tractor ['træktər] *n* **1** : tractor *m* **2** *or* ~ **-trailer** : camión *m* (con remolque)

trade ['treɪd] *n* **1** PROFESSION : oficio *m* **2** COMMERCE : comercio *m* **3** INDUSTRY : industria *f* **4** EXCHANGE : cambio *m* — *v* **traded; trading** : comerciar — *vt* ~ **sth with s.o.** : cambiar algo a algn — **trademark** ['treɪd,mɑrk] *n* : marca *f* registrada

tradition [trə'dɪʃən] *n* : tradición *f* — **traditional** [trə'dɪʃənəl] *adj* : tradicional

traffic ['træfɪk] *n* : tráfico *m* — *vi* **trafficked; trafficking** ~ **in** : traficar con — **traffic light** *n* : semáforo *m*

tragedy ['trædʒədi] *n, pl* **-dies** : tragedia *f* — **tragic** ['trædʒɪk] *adj* : trágico

trail ['treɪl] *vi* **1** DRAG : arrastrar **2** LAG : rezagarse **3** ~ **off** : apagarse — *vt* **1** DRAG : arrastrar **2** PURSUE : seguir la pista de — ~ *n* **1** : rastro *m*, huellas *fpl* **2** PATH : sendero *m* — **trailer** ['treɪlər] *n* **1** : remolque *m* **2** : caravana *f* (vivienda)

train ['treɪn] *n* **1** : tren *m* **2** : cola *f* (de un vestido) **3** SERIES : serie *f* **4** ~ **of thought** : hilo *m* (de las ideas) — *vt* **1** : adiestrar, entrenar (atletas, etc.) **2** AIM : apuntar — *vi* : prepararse, entrenarse (en deportes, etc.) — **trainer** ['treɪnər] *n* : entrenador *m*, -dora *f*

trait ['treɪt] *n* : rasgo *m*

traitor ['treɪtər] *n* : traidor *m*, -dora *f*

tramp ['træmp] *vi* : caminar (pesadamente) — ~ *n* VAGRANT : vagabundo *m*, -da *f*

trample ['træmpəl] *vt* **-pled; -pling** : pisotear

trampoline [,træmpə'lin, 'træmpə,-] *n* : trampolín *m*

trance ['trænts] *n* : trance *m*

tranquillity *or* **tranquility** [træŋ'kwɪləti] *n* : tranquilidad *f* — **tranquil** ['træŋkwəl] *adj* : tranquilo — **tranquilize** ['træŋkwə,laɪz] *vt* **-ized; -izing** : tranquilizar — **tranquilizer** ['træŋkwə,laɪzər] *n* : tranquilizante *m*

transaction [træn'zækʃən] *n* : transacción *f*

transatlantic [,træntsət'læntɪk, ,trænz-] *adj* : transatlántico

transcend [træn'send] *vt* **1** : ir más allá de **2** OVERCOME : superar

transcribe [træn'skraɪb] *vt* **-scribed; -scribing** : transcribir — **transcript** ['træn,skrɪpt] *n* : transcripción *f*

transfer [træn'sfər, 'træns,fər] *v* **-ferred; -ferring** *vt* **1** : transferir (fondos, etc.) **2** : trasladar (a un empleado, etc.) — *vi* **1** : cambiarse (de escuelas, etc.) **2** : hacer transbordo (entre trenes, etc.) — ~ ['trænts,fər] *n* **1** : transferencia *f* (de fondos, etc.), traslado *m* (de una persona) **2** : boleto *m* (para hacer transbordo) **3** DECAL : calcomanía *f*

transform [træn'sfɔrm] *vt* : transformar — **transformation** [,træntsfər'meɪʃən] *n* : transformación *f*

transfusion [trænts'fjuʒən] *n* : transfusión *f*

transgression [trænts'greʃən, trænz-] *n* : transgresión *f* — **transgress** [trænts'gres, trænz-] *vt* : transgredir

transient ['trænʃənt, 'trænsiənt] *adj* : pasajero

transit ['trænsɪt, 'trænzɪt] *n* **1** : tránsito *m* **2** TRANSPORTATION : transporte *m* — **transition** [træn'sɪʃən, -'zɪʃ-] *n* : transición *f* — **transitive** ['træntsətɪv, 'trænzə-] *adj* : transitivo — **transitory** ['træntsə,tori, 'trænzə,-] *adj* : transitorio

translate [trænts'leɪt, trænz-; 'trænts,-, 'trænz,-] *vt* **-lated; -lating** : traducir — **translation** [trænts'leɪʃən, trænz-] *n* : traducción *f* — **translator** [trænts'leɪtər, trænz-; 'trænts,-, 'trænz,-] *n* : traductor *m*, -tora *f*

translucent [trænts'lusənt, trænz-] *adj* : translúcido

transmit [trænts'mɪt, trænz-] *vt* **-mitted; -mitting** : transmitir — **transmission** [trænts'mɪʃən, trænz-] *n* : transmisión *f* — **transmitter** [trænts'mɪtər, trænz-; 'trænts,-, 'trænz,-] *n* : transmisor *m*

transparent [trænts'pærənt] *adj* : transparente — **transparency** [trænts'pærəntsi] *n, pl* **-cies** : transparencia *f*

transpire [trænts'paɪr] *vi* **-spired; -spiring** **1** TURN OUT : resultar **2** HAPPEN : suceder

transplant [trænts'plænt] *vt* : trasplantar — ~ ['trænts,plænt] *n* : trasplante *m*

transport [trænts'port, 'trænts,-] *vt* : transportar — ~ ['trænts,port] *n* : transporte *m* — **transportation** [,træntspor'teɪʃən] *n* : transporte *m*

transpose [trænts'poz] *vt* **-posed;**

-posing 1 : trasponer **2** : transportar (en música)

trap ['træp] *n* : trampa *f* — **~** *vi* **trapped; trapping** : atrapar — **trapdoor** ['træp,dor] *n* : trampilla *f*

trapeze [træ'pi:z] *n* : trapecio *m*

trappings ['træpɪŋz] *npl* : adornos *mpl*, atavíos *mpl*

trash ['træʃ] *n* : basura *f*

trauma ['trɔmə, 'trɑu-] *n* : trauma *m* — **traumatic** [trə'mætɪk, trɔ-, trɑu-] *adj* : traumático

travel ['trævəl] *vi* **-eled** *or* **-elled; -eling** *or* **-elling 1** : viajar **2** MOVE : desplazarse — **~** *n* : viajes *mpl* — **traveler** *or* **traveller** ['trævələr] *n* : viajero *m*, -ra *f*

traverse [trə'vərs, træ'vərs, 'trævərs] *vt* **-versed; -versing** : atravesar

travesty ['trævəsti] *n, pl* **-ties** : parodia *f*

trawl ['trɔl] *vi* : pescar (con red de arrastre) — **trawler** ['trɔlər] *n* : barco *m* de pesca

tray ['treɪ] *n* : bandeja *f*

treachery ['trɛtʃəri] *n, pl* **-eries** : traición *f* — **treacherous** ['trɛtʃərəs] *adj* **1** : traidor **2** DANGEROUS : peligroso

tread ['trɛd] *v* **trod** ['trɑd], **trodden** ['trɑdən] *or* **trod; treading** *vt* **1** *or* **~ on** : pisar **2 ~ water** : flotar — *vi* **1** STEP : pisar **2** WALK : caminar — *n* **1** STEP : paso *m* **2** : banda *f* de rodadura (de un neumático) — **treadmill** ['trɛd,mɪl] *n* : rueda *f* de andar

treason ['tri:zən] *n* : traición *f* (a la patria)

treasure ['trɛʒər, 'treɪ-] *n* : tesoro *m* — *vt* **-sured; -suring** : apreciar — **treasurer** ['trɛʒərər, 'treɪ-] *n* : tesorero *m*, -ra *f* — **treasury** ['trɛʒəri, 'treɪ-] *n, pl* **-suries** : erario *m*, tesoro *m*

treat ['tri:t] *vt* **1** : tratar **2** CONSIDER : considerar **3 ~ s.o. to (dinner, etc.)** : invitar a algn (a cenar, etc.) — *n* **1** : gusto *m*, placer *m* **2 it's my ~** : invito yo

treatise ['tri:tɪs] *n* : tratado *m*

treatment ['tri:tmənt] *n* : tratamiento *m*

treaty ['tri:ti] *n, pl* **-ties** : tratado *m*

treble ['trɛbəl] *adj* **1** TRIPLE : triple **2** : de tiple (en música) — *n* **1** : tiple *m* — **-bling** : triplicar — **treble clef** : clave *f* de sol

tree ['tri:] *n* : árbol *m*

trek ['trɛk] *vi* **trekked; trekking** : viajar (con dificultad) — **~** *n* : viaje *m* difícil

trellis ['trɛlɪs] *n* : enrejado *m*

tremble ['trɛmbəl] *vi* **-bled; -bling** : temblar

tremendous [trɪ'mɛndəs] *adj* : tremendo

tremor ['trɛmər] *n* : temblor *m*

trench ['trɛntʃ] *n* **1** : zanja *f* **2** : trinchera *f* (militar)

trend ['trɛnd] *n* **1** : tendencia *f* **2** FASHION : moda *f* — **trendy** ['trɛndi] *adj* **trendier; -est** : de moda

trepidation [,trɛpə'deɪʃən] *n* : inquietud *f*

trespass ['trɛspəs, -pæs] *vi* : entrar ilegalmente (en propiedad ajena)

trial ['traɪəl] *n* **1** : juicio *m*, proceso *m* **2** TEST : prueba *f* **3** ORDEAL : dura prueba *f* — **~** *adj* : de prueba

triangle ['traɪˌæŋgəl] *n* : triángulo *m* — **triangular** [traɪˈæŋgjələr] *adj* : triangular

tribe ['traɪb] *n* : tribu *f* — **tribal** ['traɪbəl] *adj* : tribal

tribulation [,trɪbjə'leɪʃən] *n* : tribulación *f*

tribunal [traɪ'bju:nəl, trɪ-] *n* : tribunal *m*

tribute ['trɪbju:t] *n* : tributo *m* — **tributary** ['trɪbjəˌteri] *n, pl* **-taries** : afluente *m*

trick ['trɪk] *n* **1** : trampa *f* **2** PRANK : broma *f* **3** KNACK, FEAT : truco *m* **4** : baza *f* (en naipes) — **~** *vt* : engañar — **trickery** ['trɪkəri] *n* : engaño *m*

trickle ['trɪkəl] *vi* **-led; -ling** : gotear — **~** *n* : goteo *m*

tricky ['trɪki] *adj* **trickier; -est 1** SLY : astuto, taimado **2** DIFFICULT : difícil

tricycle ['traɪsəkəl, -sɪkəl] *n* : triciclo *m*

trifle ['traɪfəl] *n* **1** TRIVIALITY : nimiedad *f* **2 a ~** : un poco — *vi* **-fled; -fling** **~ with** : jugar con — **trifling** ['traɪflɪŋ] *adj* : insignificante

trigger ['trɪgər] *n* : gatillo *m* — **~** *vt* : causar, provocar

trill ['trɪl] *n* : trino *m* — **~** *vi* : trinar

trillion ['trɪljən] *n* : billón *m*

trilogy ['trɪlədʒi] *n, pl* **-gies** : trilogía *f*

trim ['trɪm] *vt* **trimmed; trimming 1** : recortar **2** ADORN : adornar — **~** *adj* **trimmer; trimmest 1** SLIM : esbelto **2** NEAT : arreglado — *n* **1** : recorte *m* **2** DECORATION : adornos *mpl* **3 in ~** : en buena forma — **trimmings** ['trɪmɪŋz] *npl* **1** : adornos *mpl* **2** GARNISH : guarnición *f*

Trinity ['trɪnəti] *n* : Trinidad *f*

trinket ['trɪŋkət] *n* : chuchería *f*

trio ['tri:o] *n, pl* **trios** : trío *m*

trip ['trɪp] *v* **tripped; tripping** *vi* **1** : caminar (a paso ligero) **2** STUMBLE : tropezar **3 ~ up** : equivocarse — *vt* **1** ACTIVATE : activar **2 ~ s.o.** : hacer una zancadilla a algn **3 ~ s.o. up** : hacer equivocar a algn — **~** *n* **1** : viaje *m* **2** STUMBLE : traspié *m*

tripe ['traɪp] n 1 : mondongo m, callos mpl 2 NONSENSE : tonterías fpl

triple ['trɪpəl] vt **-pled; -pling** : triplicar — ~ n : triple m — ~ adj : triple —

triplet ['trɪplət] n 1 : trillizo m, -za f

triplicate ['trɪplɪkət] n : triplicado m

tripod ['traɪpɑd] n : trípode m

trite ['traɪt] adj **triter; tritest** : trillado

triumph ['traɪəmpf] n : triunfo m — vi : triunfar — **triumphal** [traɪˈʌmpfəl] adj : triunfal — **triumphant** [traɪˈʌmpfənt] adj : triunfante

trivial ['trɪviəl] adj : trivial — **trivia** ['trɪviə] ns & pl : trivialidades fpl — **triviality** [ˌtrɪviˈæləʤi] n, pl **-ties** : trivialidad f

trod, trodden → **tread**

trolley ['trɑli] n, pl **-leys** : tranvía m

trombone [trɑmˈboːn] n : trombón m

troop ['truːp] n 1 : escuadrón m (de caballería), compañía f (de soldados) 2 ~s npl : tropas fpl — vi : in/out : entrar/salir en tropel — **trooper** ['truːpər] n 1 : soldado m 2 or **state** ~ : policía mf estatal

trophy ['troːfi] n, pl **-phies** : trofeo m

tropic ['trɑpɪk] n 1 : trópico m 2 **the** ~s : el trópico — ~ or **tropical** [-pɪkəl] adj : tropical

trot ['trɑt] n : trote m — vi **trotted; trotting** : trotar

trouble ['trʌbəl] v **-bled; -bling** vt 1 WORRY : preocupar 2 BOTHER : molestar — vi : molestarse — ~ n 1 PROBLEMS : problemas mpl 2 EFFORT : molestia f 3 **be in** ~ : estar en apuros 4 **get in** ~ : meterse en problemas 5 **I had** ~ **doing it** : me costó hacerlo — **troublemaker** ['trʌbəlˌmeɪkər] n : alborotador m, -dora f — **troublesome** ['trʌbəlsəm] adj : problemático

trough ['trɔf] n, pl **troughs** ['trɔfs, 'trɔvz] 1 : depresión f 2 or **feeding** ~ : comedero m 3 or **drinking** ~ : bebedero m

troupe ['truːp] n : compañía f (de teatro)

trousers ['traʊzərz] npl : pantalón m, pantalones mpl

trout ['traʊt] n, pl **trout** : trucha f

trowel ['traʊəl] n : paleta f (de albañil), desplantador m (de jardinero)

truant ['truːənt] n : alumno m, -na f que falta a clase

truce ['truːs] n : tregua f

truck ['trʌk] vt : transportar en camión — ~ n 1 : camión m 2 CART : carro m — **trucker** ['trʌkər] n : camionero m, -ra f

trudge ['trʌʤ] vi **trudged; trudging** : caminar a paso pesado

true ['truː] adj **truer; truest** 1 : verdadero 2 LOYAL : fiel 3 GENUINE : auténtico 4 **be** ~ : ser cierto, ser verdad

truffle ['trʌfəl] n : trufa f

truly ['truːli] adv : verdaderamente

trump ['trʌmp] n : triunfo m (en naipes)

trumpet ['trʌmpət] n : trompeta f

trunk ['trʌŋk] n 1 STEM, TORSO : tronco m 2 : trompa f (de un elefante) 3 : baúl m (equipaje) 4 : maletero m (de un auto) 5 ~s npl : traje m de baño (de hombre)

truss ['trʌs] n 1 FRAMEWORK : armazón m 2 : braguero m (en medicina)

trust ['trʌst] n 1 CONFIDENCE : confianza f 2 HOPE : esperanza f 3 CREDIT : crédito m 4 : trust m (en finanzas) 5 **in** ~ : en fideicomiso — ~ vt 1 : confiar 2 HOPE : esperar — vt 1 : confiar en, fiarse de (en frases negativas) 2 ~ **s.o. with sth** : confiar algo a algn — **trustee** [trʌˈstiː] n : fideicomisario m, -ria f — **trustworthy** ['trʌstˌwərði] adj : digno de confianza

truth ['truːθ] n, pl **truths** ['truːðz, 'truːθs] : verdad f — **truthful** ['truːθfəl] adj : sincero, veraz

try ['traɪ] v **tried; trying** vt 1 ATTEMPT : tratar (de), intentar 2 : juzgar (un caso, etc.) 3 TEST : poner a prueba 4 or ~ **out** : probar 5 ~ **on** : probarse (ropa) — vi : hacer un esfuerzo — ~ n, pl **tries** : intento m — **trying** adj 1 ANNOYING : irritante, pesado 2 DIFFICULT : duro — **tryout** ['traɪˌaʊt] n : prueba f

tsar ['zɑr, 'sɑr, 'tsɑr] → **czar**

T-shirt ['tiːˌʃərt] n : camiseta f

tub ['tʌb] n 1 : cuba f, tina f 2 CONTAINER : envase m 3 BATHTUB : bañera f

tuba ['tuːbə, 'tjuː-] n : tuba f

tube ['tuːb, 'tjuːb] n 1 : tubo m 2 or **inner** ~ : cámara f 3 **the** ~ : la tele

tuberculosis [tuˌbərkjəˈloːsɪs, tjuː-] n, pl **-loses** [-ˌsiːz] : tuberculosis f

tubing ['tuːbɪŋ, 'tjuː-] n : tubería f — **tubular** ['tuːbjələr, 'tjuː-] adj : tubular

tuck ['tʌk] vt 1 : meter 2 ~ **away** : guardar 3 ~ **in** : meter por dentro (una blusa, etc.) 4 ~ **s.o. in** : arropar a algn — ~ n : jareta f

Tuesday ['tuːzˌdeɪ, 'tjuːz-, -di] n : martes m

tuft ['tʌft] n : mechón m (de pelo), penacho m (de plumas)

tug ['tʌg] v **tugged; tugging** or ~ **at** : tirar de, jalar de — ~ n 1 : tirón m, jalón m — **tugboat** ['tʌgˌboːt] n : remolcador m — **tug-of-war** [ˌtʌgəvˈwɔr] n, pl **tugs-of-war** : tira y afloja m

tuition [tuːˈɪʃən, tjuː-] n 1 : enseñanza f 2 or ~ **fees** : matrícula f
tulip [ˈtuːlɪp, ˈtjuː-] n : tulipán m
tumble [ˈtʌmbəl] vi -**bled**; -**bling** : caerse — ~ n : caída f — **tumbler** [ˈtʌmblər] n : vaso m (sin pie)
tummy [ˈtʌmi] n, pl -**mies** : barriga f, panza f
tumor [ˈtuːmər ˈtjuː-] n : tumor m
tumult [ˈtuːmʌlt ˈtjuː-] n : tumulto m — **tumultuous** [tʊˈmʌltʃʊəs, tjuː-] adj : tumultuoso
tuna [ˈtuːnə ˈtjuː-] n, pl -**na** or -**nas** : atún m
tune [ˈtuːn, ˈtjuːn] n 1 MELODY : melodía f 2 SONG : tonada f 3 in ~ : afinado 4 out of ~ : desafinado — v ~ **tuned**; **tuning** vt : afinar — vi ~ **in** : sintonizar — **tuner** [ˈtuːnər, ˈtjuː-] n 1 : afinador m, -dora f (de pianos, etc.) 2 : sintonizador m (de un receptor)
tunic [ˈtuːnɪk, ˈtjuː-] n : túnica f
tunnel [ˈtʌnəl] n : túnel m — vi -**neled** or -**nelled**; -**neling** or -**nelling** : hacer un túnel
turban [ˈtərbən] n : turbante m
turbine [ˈtərbən, -ˌbaɪn] n : turbina f
turbulent [ˈtərbjələnt] adj : turbulento — **turbulence** [ˈtərbjələns] n : turbulencia f
turf [ˈtərf] n 1 GRASS : césped m 2 SOD : tepe m
turgid [ˈtərdʒɪd] adj : ampuloso (dícese de prosa, etc.)
turkey [ˈtərki] n, pl -**keys** : pavo m
turmoil [ˈtərˌmɔɪl] n : confusión f
turn [ˈtərn] vt 1 : hacer girar (una rueda, etc.), volver (la cabeza, una página, etc.) 2 : dar la vuelta a (una esquina) 3 SPRAIN : torcer 4 ~ **down** REFUSE : rechazar 5 ~ **down** LOWER : bajar 6 ~ **in** : entregar 7 ~ **off** : cerrar (una llave), apagar (la luz, etc.) 8 ~ **on** : abrir (una llave), encender, prender Lat (la luz, etc.) 9 ~ **out** EXPEL : echar 10 ~ **out** PRODUCE : producir 11 ~ **out** → **turn off** 12 or ~ **over** FLIP : dar la vuelta a, voltear Lat 13 ~ **over** TRANSFER : entregar 14 ~ **s.o.'s stomach** : revolver el estómago a algn 15 ~ **sth into** sth : convertir algo en algo 16 ~ **up** RAISE : subir — vi 1 ROTATE : girar, dar vueltas 2 BECOME : ponerse 3 SOUR : agriarse 4 RESORT : recurrir 5 or ~ **around** : dar la vuelta, volverse 6 ~ **into** : convertirse en 7 ~ **left** : doblar a la izquierda 8 ~ **out** COME : acudir 9 ~ **out** RESULT : resultar 10 ~ **up** APPEAR : aparecer — ~ n 1 : vuelta f 2

CHANGE : cambio m 3 CURVE : curva f 4 **do a good** ~ : hacer un favor 5 **whose** ~ **is it?** : ¿a quién le toca?
turnip [ˈtərnəp] n : nabo m
turnout [ˈtərnaʊt] n : concurrencia f — **turnover** [ˈtərnˌovər] n 1 : tartaleta f (postre) 2 : volumen m (de ventas) 3 : movimiento f (de personal) — **turnpike** [ˈtərnˌpaɪk] n : carretera f de peaje — **turntable** [ˈtərnˌteɪbəl] n : plato m giratorio
turpentine [ˈtərpənˌtaɪn] n : trementina f
turquoise [ˈtərˌkɔɪz, -ˌkwɔɪz] n : turquesa f
turret [ˈtərət] n 1 : torrecilla f 2 : torreta f (de un tanque, etc.)
turtle [ˈtərtəl] n : tortuga f (marina) — **turtleneck** [ˈtərtəlˌnek] n : cuello m de tortuga
tusk [ˈtʌsk] n : colmillo m
tussle [ˈtʌsəl] n : pelea f — vi -**sled**; -**sling** : pelearse
tutor [ˈtuːtər, ˈtjuː-] n : profesor m, -sora f particular — vt : dar clases particulares a
tuxedo [təkˈsiːdo] n, pl -**dos** or -**does** : esmoquin m, smoking m
TV [ˌtiːˈviː, ˈtiːˌviː] → **television**
twang [ˈtwæŋ] n 1 : tañido m 2 : acento m nasal (de la voz)
tweak [ˈtwiːk] vt : pellizcar — ~ n : pellizco m
tweed [ˈtwiːd] n : tweed m
tweet [ˈtwiːt] n : gorjeo m, pío m — vi : piar
tweezers [ˈtwiːzərz] npl : pinzas fpl
twelve [ˈtwelv] adj : doce — ~ n 1 : doce m — **twelfth** [ˈtwelfθ] adj : duodécimo — ~ n 1 : duodécimo m, -ma f (en una serie) 2 : doceavo m (en matemáticas)
twenty [ˈtwʌnti, ˈtwen-] adj : veinte — ~ n, pl -**ties** : veinte m — **twentieth** [ˈtwʌntiəθ, ˈtwen-] adj : vigésimo — ~ n 1 : vigésimo m, -ma f (en una serie) 2 : veinteavo m (en matemáticas)
twice [ˈtwaɪs] adv 1 : dos veces 2 ~ **as much/many as** : el doble de (algo), el doble que (algo)
twig [ˈtwɪg] n : ramita f
twilight [ˈtwaɪˌlaɪt] n : crepúsculo m
twin [ˈtwɪn] n : gemelo m, -la f; mellizo m, -za f — ~ adj : gemelo, mellizo
twine [ˈtwaɪn] n : cordel m, bramante m Spain
twinge [ˈtwɪndʒ] n : punzada f
twinkle [ˈtwɪŋkəl] vi -**kled**; -**kling** 1 : centellear 2 : brillar (dícese de los ojos) — ~ n : centelleo m, brillo m (de los ojos)

twirl ['twərl] *vt* : girar, dar vueltas a — *vi* : girar, dar vueltas — ~ *n* : giro *m*, vuelta *f*

twist ['twɪst] *vt* **1** : retorcer **2** TURN : girar **3** SPRAIN : torcerse **4** : tergiversar (palabras) — *vi* **1** : retorcerse **2** COIL : enrollarse **3** : serpentear (entre montañas, etc.) — ~ *n* **1** BEND : vuelta *f* **2** TURN : giro *m* **3** ~ **of lemon** : rodajita *f* de limón — **twister** ['twɪstər] *n* → **tornado**

twitch ['twɪtʃ] *vi* : moverse (espasmódicamente) — ~ *n* **nervous** ~ : tic *m* nervioso

two ['tu:] *adj* : dos — ~ *n, pl* **twos** : dos *m* — **twofold** ['tu:fo:ld] *adj* : doble — ~ ['tu:fo:ld] *adv* : al doble — **two**

hundred *adj* : doscientos — ~ *n* : doscientos *m*

tycoon [taɪ'ku:n] *n* : magnate *mf*

tying → **tie**

type ['taɪp] *n* : tipo *m* — ~ *v* **typed; typing** : escribir a máquina — **typewritten** ['taɪp,rɪtən] *adj* : escrito a máquina — **typewriter** ['taɪp,raɪtər] *n* : máquina *f* de escribir

typhoon [taɪ'fu:n] *n* : tifón *m*

typical ['tɪpɪkəl] *adj* : típico, característico — **typify** ['tɪpə,faɪ] *vt* **-fied; -fying** : tipificar

typist ['taɪpɪst] *n* : mecanógrafo *m*, -fa *f*

typography [taɪ'pɑgrəfi] *n* : tipografía *f*

tyranny ['tɪrəni] *n, pl* **-nies** : tiranía *f* — **tyrant** ['taɪrənt] *n* : tirano *m*, -na *f*

tzar ['zɑr, 'tsɑr, 'sɑr] → **czar**

U

u ['ju:] *n, pl* **u's** *or* **us** ['ju:z] : u *f*, vigésima primera letra del alfabeto inglés

udder ['ʌdər] *n* : ubre *f*

UFO [ju:,ef'o:, 'ju:,fo:] (*unidentified flying object*) *n, pl* **UFO's** *or* **UFOs** : ovni *m*, OVNI *m*

ugly ['ʌgli] *adj* **uglier; -est** : feo — **ugliness** ['ʌglinəs] *n* : fealdad *f*

ulcer ['ʌlsər] *n* : úlcera *f*

ulterior [ʌl'tɪriər] *adj* ~ **motive** : segunda intención *f*

ultimate ['ʌltəmət] *adj* **1** FINAL : final, último **2** UTMOST : máximo **3** FUNDAMENTAL : fundamental — **ultimately** ['ʌltəmətli] *adv* **1** FINALLY : por último, finalmente **2** EVENTUALLY : a la larga

ultimatum [ʌltə'meɪtəm, -mɑ-] *n, pl* **-tums** *or* **-ta** [-tə] : ultimátum *m*

ultraviolet [ʌltrə'vaɪələt] *adj* : ultravioleta

umbilical cord [ʌm'bɪlɪkəl] *n* : cordón *m* umbilical

umbrella [ʌm'brɛlə] *n* : paraguas *m*

umpire ['ʌm,paɪr] *n* : árbitro *m*, -tra *f* — *vt* **-pired; -piring** : arbitrar

umpteenth [ʌmp'ti:nθ] *adj* : enésimo

unable [ʌn'eɪbəl] *adj* **1** : incapaz **2 be ~ to** : no poder

unabridged [ʌnə'brɪdʒd] *adj* : íntegro

unacceptable [ʌnɪk'sɛptəbəl] *adj* : inaceptable

unaccountable [ʌnə'kaʊntəd] *adj* : inexplicable

unaccustomed [ʌnə'kʌstəmd] *adj* **be ~ to** : no estar acostumbrado a

unadulterated [ʌnə'dʌltə,reɪtəd] *adj* : puro

unaffected [ʌnə'fɛktəd] *adj* **1** : no afectado **2** NATURAL : sin afectación, natural

unafraid [ʌnə'freɪd] *adj* : sin miedo

unaided [ʌn'eɪdəd] *adj* : sin ayuda

unanimous [ju'nænəməs] *adj* : unánime

unannounced [ʌnə'naʊnst] *adj* : sin dar aviso

unarmed [ʌn'ɑrmd] *adj* : desarmado

unassuming [ʌnə'su:mɪŋ] *adj* : modesto, sin pretensiones

unattached [ʌnə'tætʃt] *adj* **1** : suelto **2** UNMARRIED : soltero

unattractive [ʌnə'træktɪv] *adj* : poco atractivo

unauthorized [ʌn'ɔθə,raɪzd] *adj* : no autorizado

unavailable [ʌnə'veɪləbəl] *adj* : no disponible

unavoidable [ʌnə'vɔɪdəbəl] *adj* : inevitable

unaware [ʌnə'wær] *adj* **1** : inconsciente **2 be ~ of** : ignorar — **unawares** [ʌnə'wærz] *adv* **catch s.o.** ~ : agarrar a algn desprevenido

unbalanced [ʌn'bælənst] *adj* : desequilibrado

unbearable [ʌn'bærəbəl] *adj* : inaguantable, insoportable

unbelievable [ʌnbə'li:vəbəl] *adj* : increíble

unbending [ʌn'bɛndɪŋ] *adj* : inflexible

unbiased [ʌn'baɪəst] *adj* : imparcial

unborn [ʌn'bɔrn] *adj* : aún no nacido

unbreakable [ʌn'breɪkəbəl] *adj* : irrompible

unbridled [ʌn'braɪdəld] *adj* : desenfrenado

unbroken [ʌn'broːkən] *adj* **1** INTACT : intacto **2** CONTINUOUS : continuo

unbutton [ʌn'bʌtən] *vt* : desabrochar, desabotonar

uncalled–for [ʌn'kɔːldˌfor] *adj* : inapropiado, innecesario

uncanny [ən'kæni] *adj* -nier; -est : extraño, misterioso

unceasing [ʌn'siːsɪŋ] *adj* : incesante

unceremonious [ʌnˌserəˈmoːniəs] *adj* **1** INFORMAL : poco ceremonioso **2** ABRUPT : brusco

uncertain [ʌn'sərtən] *adj* **1** : incierto **2** **in no ～ terms** : de forma vehemente — **uncertainty** [ʌn'sərtənti] *n, pl* -ties : incertidumbre *f*

unchanged [ʌn'tʃeɪndʒd] *adj* : igual, sin alterar — **unchanging** [ʌn'tʃeɪdʒɪŋ] *adj* : inmutable

uncivilized [ʌn'sɪvəˌlaɪzd] *adj* : incivilizado

uncle [ʌŋkəl] *n* : tío *m*

unclear [ʌn'klɪr] *adj* : poco claro

uncomfortable [ʌn'kʌmpfərˌtəbəl] *adj* **1** : incómodo **2** DISCONCERTING : inquietante, desagradable

uncommon [ʌn'kɑmən] *adj* : raro

uncompromising [ʌn'kɑmprəˌmaɪzɪŋ] *adj* : intransigente

unconcerned [ʌnkən'sərnd] *adj* : indiferente

unconditional [ʌnkən'dɪʃənəl] *adj* : incondicional

unconscious [ʌn'kɑntʃəs] *adj* : inconsciente

unconstitutional [ʌnˌkɑntstəˈtuːʃənəl, -'tjuː-] *adj* : inconstitucional

uncontrollable [ʌnkən'troːləbəl] *adj* : incontrolable

unconventional [ʌnkən'ventʃənəl] *adj* : poco convencional

uncouth [ʌn'kuːθ] *adj* : grosero

uncover [ʌn'kʌvər] *vt* **1** : destapar **2** REVEAL : descubrir

undecided [ʌndɪ'saɪdəd] *adj* : indeciso

undeniable [ʌndɪ'naɪəbəl] *adj* : innegable

under ['ʌndər] *adv* **1** : debajo **2** LESS : menos **3** *or* **～ anesthetic** : bajo los efectos de la anestesia — *prep* **1** BELOW, BENEATH : debajo de, abajo de **2** **～ 20 minutes** : menos de 20 minutos **3** **～ the circumstances** : dadas las circunstancias

underage [ʌndər'eɪdʒ] *adj* : menor de edad

underclothes ['ʌndərˌkloːz, -ˌkloːðz] → **underwear**

undercover [ʌndər'kʌvər] *adj* : secreto

undercurrent ['ʌndərˌkərənt] *n* : tendencia *f* oculta

underdeveloped [ʌndərdɪ'veləpt] *adj* : subdesarrollado

underestimate [ʌndər'estəˌmeɪt] *vt* -mated; -mating : subestimar

underfoot [ʌndər'fʊt] *adv* : bajo los pies

undergo [ʌndər'goː] *vt* -went [-'went]; -gone [-'gɔn]; -going : sufrir, experimentar

undergraduate [ʌndər'grædʒuət] *n* : estudiante *m* universitario, estudiante *f* universitaria

underground [ʌndər'graʊnd] *adv* **1** : bajo tierra **2** **go ～** : pasar a la clandestinidad — ～ ['ʌndərˌgraʊnd] *adj* **1** : subterráneo **2** SECRET : secreto, clandestino — ～ ['ʌndərˌgraʊnd] *n* : movimiento *m* clandestino

undergrowth [ʌndər'groːθ] *n* : maleza *f*

underhanded [ʌndər'hændəd] *adj* SLY : solapado

underline ['ʌndərˌlaɪn] *vt* -lined; -lining : subrayar

underlying [ʌndər'laɪɪŋ] *adj* : subyacente

undermine [ʌndər'maɪn] *vt* -mined; -mining : socavar, minar

underneath [ʌndər'niːθ] *adv* : debajo, abajo — ～ *prep* : debajo de, abajo de Lat

underpants ['ʌndərˌpænts] *npl* : calzoncillos *mpl*, calzones *mpl* Lat

underpass ['ʌndərˌpæs] *n* : paso *m* inferior

underprivileged [ʌndər'prɪvɪlɪdʒd] *adj* : desfavorecido

underrate [ʌndər'reɪt] *vt* -rated; -rating : subestimar

undershirt ['ʌndərˌʃərt] *n* : camiseta *f*

understand [ʌndər'stænd] *v* -stood [-'stʊd]; -standing : comprender, entender — **understandable** [ʌndər'stændəbəl] *adj* : comprensible — **understanding** [ʌndər'stændɪŋ] *adj* : comprensivo, compasivo — ～ *n* **1** : comprensión *f* **2** AGREEMENT : acuerdo *m*

understatement [ʌndər'steɪtmənt] *n* **that's an ～** : decir sólo eso es quedarse corto

understudy ['ʌndərˌstʌdi] *n, pl* -dies : sobresaliente *mf* (en el teatro)

undertake [ʌndər'teɪk] *vt* -took [-'tʊk]; -taken [-'teɪkən]; -taking : emprender (una tarea), encargarse de (una responsabilidad) — **undertaker** ['ʌndərˌteɪkər] *n* : director *m*, -tora *f* de una funeraria — **undertaking** ['ʌndərˌteɪkɪŋ, ʌndər'-] *n* : empresa *f*, tarea *f*

undertone ['ʌndər,toːn] n 1 : voz f baja 2 SUGGESTION : matiz m

undertow ['ʌndər,toː] n : resaca f

underwater [,ʌndər'woṭər, -'woː-] adj : submarino — adv : debajo (del agua)

under way [,ʌndər'weɪ] adv get ~ : ponerse en marcha

underwear ['ʌndər,wær] n : ropa f interior

underwent → **undergo**

underworld ['ʌndər,wərld] n the ~ CRIMINALS : la hampa, los bajos fondos

underwriter ['ʌndər,raɪṭər, ,ʌndər'-] n : asegurador m, -dora f

undesirable [,ʌndɪ'zaɪrəbəl] adj : indeseable

undeveloped [,ʌndɪ'veləpt] adj : sin desarrollar

undignified [ʌn'dɪgnəfaɪd] adj : indecoroso

undisputed [,ʌndɪ'spjuːṭəd] adj : indiscutible

undo [ʌn'duː] vt **-did** [-'dɪd]; **-done** [-'dʌn]; **-doing** 1 UNFASTEN : deshacer, desatar 2 : reparar (daños, etc.)

undoubtedly [ʌn'daʊṭədli] adv : indudablemente

undress [ʌn'dres] vt : desnudar — vi : desnudarse

undue [ʌn'duː, -'djuː] adj : indebido, excesivo

undulate ['ʌndʒə,leɪt] vi **-lated; -lating** : ondular

unduly [ʌn'duːli, -'djuː-] adv : excesivamente

undying [ʌn'daɪɪŋ] adj : eterno

unearth [ʌn'ərθ] vt : desenterrar

unearthly [ʌn'ərθli] adj **-lier; -est** : sobrenatural, de otro mundo

uneasy [ʌn'iːzi] adj **-easier; -est** 1 AWKWARD : incómodo 2 WORRIED : inquieto 3 RESTLESS : agitado — **uneasily** [ʌn'iːzəli] adv : inquietamente — **uneasiness** [ʌn'iːzinəs] n : inquietud f

uneducated [ʌn'edʒə,keɪṭəd] adj : inculto

unemployed [,ʌnɪm'plɔɪd] adj : desempleado — **unemployment** [,ʌnɪm'plɔɪmənt] n : desempleo m

unerring [ʌn'erɪŋ, -'ər-] adj : infalible

unethical [ʌn'eθɪkəl] adj : poco ético

uneven [ʌn'iːvən] adj 1 : desigual 2 : impar (dícese de un número)

unexpected [,ʌnɪk'spektəd] adj : inesperado

unfailing [ʌn'feɪlɪŋ] adj 1 CONSTANT : constante 2 INEXHAUSTIBLE : inagotable

unfair [ʌn'fær] adj : injusto — **unfairly** [ʌn'færli] adv : injustamente — **unfairness** [ʌn'færnəs] n : injusticia f

unfaithful [ʌn'feɪθfəl] adj : infiel — **unfaithfulness** [ʌn'feɪθfəlnəs] n : infidelidad f

unfamiliar [,ʌnfə'mɪljər] adj 1 : desconocido 2 be ~ with : desconocer

unfasten [ʌn'fæsən] vt 1 : desabrochar (ropa, etc.) 2 UNDO : desatar (una cuerda, etc.)

unfavorable [ʌn'feɪvərəbəl] adj : desfavorable

unfeeling [ʌn'fiːlɪŋ] adj : insensible

unfinished [ʌn'fɪnɪʃt] adj : sin terminar

unfit [ʌn'fɪt] adj 1 UNSUITABLE : impropio 2 UNSUITED : no apto, incapaz

unfold [ʌn'foːld] vt 1 : desplegar, desdoblar 2 REVEAL : revelar (un plan, etc.) — vi 1 : extenderse, desplegarse 2 DEVELOP : desarrollarse

unforeseen [,ʌnfor'siːn] adj : imprevisto

unforgettable [,ʌnfər'geṭəbəl] adj : inolvidable

unforgivable [,ʌnfər'gɪvəbəl] adj : imperdonable

unfortunate [ʌn'fortʃənət] adj 1 UNLUCKY : desgraciado, desafortunado 2 INAPPROPRIATE : inoportuno — **unfortunately** [ʌn'fortʃənətli] adv : desgraciadamente

unfounded [ʌn'faʊndəd] adj : infundado

unfriendly [ʌn'frendli] adj **-lier; -est** : poco amistoso

unfurl [ʌn'fərl] vt : desplegar

unfurnished [ʌn'fərnɪʃt] adj : desamueblado

ungainly [ʌn'geɪnli] adj : desgarbado

ungodly [ʌn'godli, -'gɑd-] adj 1 : impío 2 an ~ hour : una hora intempestiva

ungrateful [ʌn'greɪtfəl] adj : desagradecido

unhappy [ʌn'hæpi] adj **-pier; -est** 1 SAD : infeliz, triste 2 UNFORTUNATE : desafortunado — **unhappily** [ʌn'hæpəli] adv 1 SADLY : tristemente 2 UNFORTUNATELY : desgraciadamente — **unhappiness** [ʌn'hæpinəs] n : tristeza f

unharmed [ʌn'hɑrmd] adj : salvo, ileso

unhealthy [ʌn'helθi] adj **-thier; -est** 1 : malsano 2 SICKLY : enfermizo

unheard-of [ʌn'hərdəv] adj : sin precedente, insólito

unhook [ʌn'huk] vt : desenganchar

unhurt [ʌn'hərt] adj : ileso

unicorn ['juːnə,kɔrn] n : unicornio m

unification [,juːnəfə'keɪʃən] n : unificación f

uniform ['juːnə,fɔrm] adj : uniforme —

~ *n* : uniforme *m* — **uniformity** [ˌjuːnəˈfɔrməti] *n, pl* **-ties** : uniformidad *f*

unify [ˈjuːnəˌfaɪ] *vt* **-fied; -fying** : unificar

unilateral [ˌjuːnəˈlætərəl] *adj* : unilateral

unimaginable [ˌʌnɪˈmædʒənəbəl] *adj* : inconcebible

unimportant [ˌʌnɪmˈpɔrtənt] *adj* : insignificante

uninhabited [ˌʌnɪnˈhæbətəd] *adj* : deshabitado, despoblado

uninjured [ˌʌnˈɪndʒərd] *adj* : ileso

unintentional [ˌʌnɪnˈtentʃənəl] *adj* : involuntario

union [ˈjuːnjən] *n* **1** : unión *f* **2** *or* **labor ~** : sindicato *m*, gremio *m Lat*

unique [juˈniːk] *adj* : único — **uniquely** [juˈniːkli] *adv* EXCEPTIONALLY : excepcionalmente

unison [ˈjuːnəsən, -zən] *n* **in ~** : al unísono

unit [ˈjuːnɪt] *n* **1** : unidad *f* **2** : módulo *m* (de un mobiliario)

unite [juˈnaɪt] *v* **united; uniting** *vt* : unir — *vi* : unirse — **unity** [ˈjuːnəti] *n, pl* **-ties 1** : unidad *f* **2** HARMONY : acuerdo *m*

universe [ˈjuːnəˌvərs] *n* : universo *m* — **universal** [ˌjuːnəˈvərsəl] *adj* : universal

university [ˌjuːnəˈvərsəti] *n, pl* **-ties** : universidad *f*

unjust [ˌʌnˈdʒʌst] *adj* : injusto — **unjustified** [ˌʌnˈdʒʌstəˌfaɪd] *adj* : injustificado

unkempt [ˌʌnˈkempt] *adj* **1** : descuidado, desaseado **2** : despeinado (dícese del pelo)

unkind [ˌʌnˈkaɪnd] *adj* : poco amable, cruel — **unkindness** [ˌʌnˈkaɪndnəs] *n* : falta *f* de amabilidad, crueldad *f*

unknown [ˌʌnˈnoːn] *adj* : desconocido

unlawful [ˌʌnˈlɔfəl] *adj* : ilegal

unless [ənˈles] *conj* : a menos que, a no ser que

unlike [ˌʌnˈlaɪk] *adj* : diferente — **~** *prep* : a diferencia de — **unlikelihood** [ˌʌnˈlaɪkliˌhʊd] *n* : improbabilidad *f* — **unlikely** [ˌʌnˈlaɪkli] *adj* **-lier; -est** : improbable

unlimited [ˌʌnˈlɪmətəd] *adj* : ilimitado

unload [ˌʌnˈloːd] *v* : descargar

unlock [ˌʌnˈlɑk] *vt* : abrir (con llave)

unlucky [ˌʌnˈlʌki] *adj* **-luckier; -est** UNFORTUNATE : desgraciado **2** : de mala suerte (dícese de un número, etc.)

unmarried [ˌʌnˈmærid] *adj* : soltero

unmask [ˌʌnˈmæsk] *vt* : desenmascarar

unmistakable [ˌʌnmɪˈsteɪkəbəl] *adj* : inconfundible

unnatural [ˌʌnˈnætʃərəl] *adj* **1** : anormal **2** AFFECTED : afectado, forzado

unnecessary [ˌʌnˈnesəˌseri] *adj* : innecesario — **unnecessarily** [-ˌnesəˈserəli] *adv* : innecesariamente

unnerving [ˌʌnˈnərvɪŋ] *adj* : desconcertante

unnoticed [ˌʌnˈnoːtəst] *adj* : inadvertido

unobtainable [ˌʌnəbˈteɪnəbəl] *adj* : inasequible

unobtrusive [ˌʌnəbˈstruːsɪv] *adj* : discreto

unofficial [ˌʌnəˈfɪʃəl] *adj* : no oficial

unorthodox [ˌʌnˈɔrθəˌdɑks] *adj* : poco ortodoxo

unpack [ˌʌnˈpæk] *vt* **1** : desempaquetar, desempacar *Lat* (un paquete, etc.) **2** : deshacer (una maleta) — *vi* : deshacer las maletas

unparalleled [ˌʌnˈpærəˌleld] *adj* : sin igual

unpleasant [ˌʌnˈplezənt] *adj* : desagradable

unplug [ˌʌnˈplʌg] *vt* **-plugged; -plugging** : desconectar, desenchufar

unpopular [ˌʌnˈpɑpjələr] *adj* : poco popular

unprecedented [ˌʌnˈpresəˌdentəd] *adj* : sin precedente

unpredictable [ˌʌnprɪˈdɪktəbəl] *adj* : imprevisible

unprepared [ˌʌnprɪˈpærd] *adj* **1** : no preparado **2** UNREADY : desprevenido

unqualified [ˌʌnˈkwɑləˌfaɪd] *adj* **1** : no calificado, sin título **2** COMPLETE : absoluto

unquestionable [ˌʌnˈkwestʃənəbəl] *adj* : indiscutible — **unquestioning** [ˌʌnˈkwestʃənɪŋ] *adj* : incondicional

unravel [ˌʌnˈrævəl] *v* **-eled** *or* **-elled; -eling** *or* **-elling** *vt* : desenmarañar — *vi* : deshacerse

unreal [ˌʌnˈriːl] *adj* : irreal — **unrealistic** [ˌʌnriːəˈlɪstɪk] *adj* : poco realista

unreasonable [ˌʌnˈriːzənəbəl] *adj* **1** : irrazonable **2** EXCESSIVE : excesivo

unrecognizable [ˌʌnrekəgˈnaɪzəbəl] *adj* : irreconocible

unrelated [ˌʌnrɪˈleɪtəd] *adj* : no relacionado

unrelenting [ˌʌnrɪˈlentɪŋ] *adj* : implacable

unreliable [ˌʌnrɪˈlaɪəbəl] *adj* : que no es de fiar

unrepentant [ˌʌnrɪˈpentənt] *adj* : impenitente

unrest [ˌʌnˈrest] *n* **1** : inquietud *f*, malestar *m* **2** *or* **political ~** : disturbios *mpl*

unripe [ˌʌnˈraɪp] *adj* : verde, no maduro

unrivaled or **unrivalled** [ʌnˈraɪvəld] adj : incomparable, sin par

unroll [ʌnˈroːl] vt : desenrollar — vi : desenrollarse

unruly [ʌnˈruːli] adj : indisciplinado

unsafe [ʌnˈseɪf] adj : inseguro

unsaid [ʌnˈsed] adj : sin decir

unsanitary [ʌnˈsænəˌteri] adj : antihigiénico

unsatisfactory [ʌnˌsætəsˈfæktəri] adj : insatisfactorio

unscathed [ʌnˈskeɪðd] adj : ileso

unscrew [ʌnˈskruː] vt : destornillar

unscrupulous [ʌnˈskruːpjələs] adj : sin escrúpulos

unseemly [ʌnˈsiːmli] adj -lier; -est : indecoroso

unseen [ʌnˈsiːn] adj 1 : no visto 2 UNNOTICED : inadvertido

unselfish [ʌnˈselfɪʃ] adj : desinteresado

unsettle [ʌnˈsetəl] vt -tled; -tling DISTURB : perturbar — **unsettled** [ʌnˈsetəld] adj 1 CHANGEABLE : inestable 2 DISTURBED : agitado, inquieto 3 : variable (dícese del tiempo)

unsightly [ʌnˈsaɪtli] adj : feo

unskilled [ʌnˈskɪld] adj : no calificado — **unskillful** [ʌnˈskɪlfəl] adj : torpe, poco hábil

unsociable [ʌnˈsoːʃəbəl] adj : poco sociable

unsound [ʌnˈsaʊnd] adj 1 : defectuoso, erróneo 2 **of ~ mind** : demente

unspeakable [ʌnˈspiːkəbəl] adj 1 : indecible 2 TERRIBLE : atroz

unstable [ʌnˈsteɪbəl] adj : inestable

unsteady [ʌnˈstedi] adj 1 : inestable 2 SHAKY : tembloroso

unsuccessful [ʌnsəkˈsesfəl] adj 1 : fracasado 2 **be ~** : no tener éxito

unsuitable [ʌnˈsuːtəbəl] adj 1 : inadecuado 2 INCONVENIENT : inconveniente

unsure [ʌnˈʃʊr] adj : inseguro

unsuspecting [ʌnsəˈspektɪŋ] adj : confiado

unsympathetic [ʌnˌsɪmpəˈθetɪk] adj : indiferente

unthinkable [ʌnˈθɪŋkəbəl] adj : inconcebible

untidy [ʌnˈtaɪdi] adj : desordenado (dícese de una sala, etc.), desaliñado (dícese de una persona)

untie [ʌnˈtaɪ] vt -tied; -tying or -tieing : desatar

until [ʌnˈtɪl] prep : hasta — conj : hasta que

untimely [ʌnˈtaɪmli] adj 1 PREMATURE : prematuro 2 INOPPORTUNE : inoportuno

untold [ʌnˈtoːld] adj : incalculable

untoward [ʌnˈtord, -ˌtoːrd, -təˈwɔrd] adj 1 ADVERSE : adverso 2 IMPROPER : indecoroso

untroubled [ʌnˈtrʌbəld] adj 1 : tranquilo 2 **be ~ by** : no estar afectado por

untrue [ʌnˈtruː] adj : falso

unused [ʌnˈjuːzd, in sense 2 usually -ˈjuːst] adj 1 NEW : nuevo 2 **be ~ to** : no estar acostumbrado a

unusual [ʌnˈjuːʒuəl] adj : poco común, insólito — **unusually** [ʌnˈjuːʒuəl, -ˈjuːʒəli] adv : excepcionalmente

unveil [ʌnˈveɪl] vt : descubrir, revelar

unwanted [ʌnˈwɒntəd] adj : superfluo (dícese de un objeto), no deseado (dícese de un niño, etc.)

unwarranted [ʌnˈwɔrəntəd] adj : injustificado

unwelcome [ʌnˈwelkəm] adj : inoportuno, molesto

unwell [ʌnˈwel] adj **be ~** : sentirse mal

unwieldy [ʌnˈwiːldi] adj : difícil de manejar

unwilling [ʌnˈwɪlɪŋ] adj : poco dispuesto — **unwillingly** [ʌnˈwɪlɪŋli] adv : de mala gana

unwind [ʌnˈwaɪnd] v -wound [-ˈwaʊnd], -winding vt : desenrollar — vi 1 : desenrollarse 2 RELAX : relajarse

unwise [ʌnˈwaɪz] adj : imprudente

unworthy [ʌnˈwərði] adj **be ~ of** : no ser digno de

unwrap [ʌnˈræp] vt -wrapped; -wrapping : desenvolver

up [ʌp] adv 1 ABOVE : arriba 2 UPWARDS : hacia arriba 3 **ten miles farther ~** : diez millas más adelante 4 **~ here/there** : aquí/allí arriba 5 **~ north** : en el norte 6 **~ until** : hasta — adj 1 AWAKE : levantado 2 FINISHED : terminado 3 **be ~ against** : enfrentarse con 4 **be ~ on** : estar al corriente de 5 **it's ~ to you** : depende de ti 6 **prices are ~** : los precios han aumentado 7 **the sun is ~** : ha salido el sol 8 **what's ~?** : ¿qué pasa? — prep 1 **go ~ the river** : ir río arriba 2 **go ~ the stairs** : subir la escalera 3 **~ the coast** : a lo largo de la costa — v **upped** [ʌpt]; **upping**; **ups** vt : aumentar — vi **she ~ and left** : agarró y se fue

upbringing [ˈʌpˌbrɪŋɪŋ] n : educación f

upcoming [ˈʌpˌkʌmɪŋ] adj : próximo

update [ˈʌpˌdeɪt] vt -dated; -dating : poner al día, actualizar — [ˈʌpˌdeɪt] n : puesta f al día

upgrade [ˈʌpˌɡreɪd, ˌʌpˈ-] vt -graded; -grading : elevar la categoría de (un puesto, etc.), mejorar (una facilidad, etc.)

upheaval [ˌʌpˈhiːvəl] n : trastorno m
uphill [ˌʌpˈhɪl] adv : cuesta arriba — ~ [ˈʌpˌhɪl] adj 1 : en subida 2 **be an battle** : ser muy difícil
uphold [ʌpˈhoːld] vt **-held; -holding** : sostener, apoyar
upholstery [ʌpˈhoːlstəri] n, pl **-steries** : tapicería f
upkeep [ˈʌpˌkiːp] n : mantenimiento m
upon [əˈpɔn, əˈpɑn] prep 1 : en, sobre 2 ~ **leaving** : al salir
upper [ˈʌpər] adj : superior — ~ n : parte f superior (del calzado, etc.)
uppercase [ˌʌpərˈkeɪs] adj : mayúsculo
upper class n : clase f alta
upper hand n : ventaja f, dominio m
uppermost [ˈʌpərˌmoːst] adj : más alto
upright [ˈʌpˌraɪt] adj 1 VERTICAL : vertical 2 ERECT : derecho 3 JUST : recto, honesto — ~ n : montante m, poste m
uprising [ˈʌpˌraɪzɪŋ] n : insurrección f, revuelta f
uproar [ˈʌpˌror] n COMMOTION : alboroto m
uproot [ʌpˈruːt, -ˈrʊt] vt : desarraigar
upset [ʌpˈset] vt **-set; -setting 1** OVERTURN : volcar 2 DISTRESS : alterar, inquietar 3 DISRUPT : trastornar — ~ adj 1 DISTRESSED : alterado 2 **have an** ~ **stomach** : estar mal del estómago — ~ [ˈʌpˌset] n : trastorno m
upshot [ˈʌpˌʃɑt] n : resultado m final
upside down [ˌʌpˌsaɪdˈdaʊn] adv 1 : al revés 2 **turn** ~ : volver — **upside-down** [ˌʌpˌsaɪdˈdaʊn] adj : al revés
upstairs [ˈʌpˈstærz] adv : arriba — ~ [ˈʌpˌstærz, ˌʌpˈ-] adj : de arriba — ~ [ˈʌpˌstærz, ˌʌpˈ-] ns & pl : piso m de arriba
upstart [ˈʌpˌstɑrt] n : advenedizo m, -za f
upstream [ˈʌpˈstrim] adv : río arriba
upswing [ˈʌpˌswɪŋ] n **be on the** ~ : estar mejorándose
up-to-date [ˌʌptəˈdeɪt] adj 1 : corriente, al día 2 MODERN : moderno
uptown [ˈʌpˈtaʊn] adv : hacia la parte alta de la ciudad, hacia el distrito residencial
upturn [ˈʌpˌtərn] n : mejora f, auge m (económico)
upward [ˈʌpwərd] or **upwards** [-wərdz] adv : hacia arriba — **upward** adj : ascendente, hacia arriba
uranium [jʊˈreɪniəm] n : uranio m
urban [ˈərbən] adj : urbano
urbane [ˌərˈbeɪn] adj : urbano, cortés
urge [ˈərdʒ] vt **urged; urging 1** PRESS : instar, exhortar 2 ~ **on** : animar — ~ n : impulso m, ganas fpl — **ur-**

gency [ˈərdʒəntsi] n, pl **-cies** : urgencia f — **urgent** [ˈərdʒənt] adj 1 : urgente 2 **be** ~ : urgir
urine [ˈjʊrən] n : orina f — **urinate** [ˈjʊrəˌneɪt] vi **-nated; -nating** : orinar
urn [ˈərn] n : urna f
Uruguayan [ˌʊrəˈgwaɪən, ˌjʊr-, -ˈgweɪ-] adj : uruguayo
us [ˈʌs] pron 1 (as direct or indirect object) : nos 2 (as object of a preposition) : nosotros, nosotras 3 **both of** ~ : nosotros dos 4 **it's** ~! : ¡somos nosotros!
usage [ˈjuːsɪdʒ, -zɪdʒ] n : uso m
use [ˈjuːz] v **used** [ˈjuːzd, the phrase "used to" is usually ˈjuːstu]; **using** vt 1 : usar 2 CONSUME : consumir, tomar (drogas, etc.) 3 ~ **up** : agotar, consumir — vi 1 **she** ~**d to dance** : acostumbraba bailar 2 **winters** ~**d to be colder** : los inviernos solían ser más fríos — ~ [ˈjuːs] n 1 : uso m 2 **have no** ~ **for** : no necesitar 3 **have the** ~ **of** : poder usar, tener acceso a 4 **it's no** ~! : ¡es inútil! — **used** [ˈjuːzd, in sense 2 usually ˈjuːst] adj 1 SECONDHAND : usado 2 **be** ~ **to** : estar acostumbrado a — **useful** [ˈjuːsfəl] adj : útil, práctico — **usefulness** [ˈjuːsfəlnəs] n : utilidad f — **useless** [ˈjuːsləs] adj : inútil — **user** [ˈjuːzər] n : usuario m, -ria f
usher [ˈʌʃər] vt 1 : acompañar, conducir 2 ~ **in** : hacer entrar — ~ n : acomodador m, -dora f
usual [ˈjuːʒuəl] adj 1 : habitual, usual 2 **as** ~ : como de costumbre — **usually** [ˈjuːʒuəli, ˈjuːʒəli] adv : usualmente
usurp [jʊˈsərp, -ˈzərp] vt : usurpar
utensil [juːˈtentsəl] n : utensilio m
uterus [ˈjuːtərəs] n, pl **uteri** [-ˌraɪ] : útero m, matriz f
utility [juːˈtɪləti] n, pl **-ties 1** : utilidad f 2 or **public** ~ : empresa f de servicio público
utilize [ˈjuːtəˌlaɪz] vt **-lized; -lizing** : utilizar
utmost [ˈʌtˌmoːst] adj 1 FARTHEST : extremo 2 **of the** ~ **importance** : de suma importancia — ~ n **do one's** ~ : hacer todo lo posible
utopia [juːˈtoːpiə] n : utopía f — **utopian** [juːˈtoːpiən] adj : utópico
utter¹ [ˈʌtər] adj : absoluto, completo
utter² vt : decir, pronunciar (palabras) — **utterance** [ˈʌtərənts] n : declaración f, expresión f
utterly [ˈʌtərli] adv : completamente, totalmente

V

v ['viː] *n*, *pl* **v's** *or* **vs** ['viːz] : v *f*, vigésima segunda letra del alfabeto inglés

vacant ['veɪkənt] *adj* **1** AVAILABLE : libre **2** UNOCCUPIED : desocupado **3** : vacante (dícese de un puesto) **4** : ausente (dícese de una mirada) — **vacancy** ['veɪkənsi] *n*, *pl* **-cies 1** : (puesto *m*) vacante *f* **2** : habitación *f* libre (en un hotel, etc.)

vacate ['veɪkeɪt] *vt* **-cated; -cating** : desalojar, desocupar

vacation [veɪ'keɪʃən, və-] *n* : vacaciones *fpl*

vaccination [ˌvæksə'neɪʃən] *n* : vacunación *f* — **vaccinate** ['væksəneɪt] *vt* **-nated; -nating** : vacunar — **vaccine** ['væksiːn, 'væk,-] *n* : vacuna *f*

vacuum ['væk,juːm, -kjəm] *n*, *pl* **vacuums** *or* **vacua** : vacío *m* — ~ *vt* : pasar la aspiradora por — **vacuum cleaner** *n* : aspiradora *f*

vagina [və'dʒaɪnə] *n*, *pl* **-nae** [-ˌniː, -ˌnaɪ] *or* **-nas** : vagina *f*

vagrant ['veɪgrənt] *n* : vagabundo *m*, -da *f*

vague ['veɪg] *adj* **vaguer; -est** : vago, indistinto

vain ['veɪn] *adj* **1** CONCEITED : vanidoso **2 in ~** : en vano

valentine ['vælənˌtaɪn] *n* : tarjeta *f* del día de San Valentín

valiant ['væljənt] *adj* : valiente, valeroso

valid ['væləd] *adj* : válido — **validate** ['væləˌdeɪt] *vt* **-dated; -dating** : validar — **validity** [və'lɪdət̬i, væ-] *n* : validez *f*

valley ['væli] *n*, *pl* **-leys** : valle *m*

valor ['vælər] *n* : valor *m*, valentía *f*

value ['væljuː] *n* : valor *m* — ~ *vt* **-ued; -uing** : valorar — **valuable** ['væljuəbəl, 'væljəbəl] *adj* : valioso — **valuables** *npl* : objetos *mpl* de valor

valve ['vælv] *n* : válvula *f*

vampire ['væmˌpaɪr] *n* : vampiro *m*

van ['væn] *n* : furgoneta *f*, camioneta *f*

vandal ['vændəl] *n* : vándalo *m* — **vandalism** ['vændəlˌɪzəm] *n* : vandalismo *m* — **vandalize** ['vændəlˌaɪz] *vt* : destrozar, destruir

vane ['veɪn] *n* *or* **weather ~** : veleta *f*

vanguard ['vænˌgɑrd] *n* : vanguardia *f*

vanilla [və'nɪlə, -'nɛ-] *n* : vainilla *f*

vanish ['vænɪʃ] *vi* : desaparecer

vanity ['vænət̬i] *n*, *pl* **-ties 1** : vanidad *f* **2** *or* ~ **table** : tocador *m*

vantage point ['væntɪdʒ] *n* : posición *f* ventajosa

vapor ['veɪpər] *n* : vapor *m*

variable ['vɛriəbəl] *adj* : variable — ~ *n* : variable *f* — **variance** ['vɛriəns] *n* **at ~ with** : en desacuerdo con — **variant** ['vɛriənt] *n* : variante *f* — **variation** [ˌvɛri'eɪʃən] *n* : variación *f*

varied ['vɛrid] *adj* : variado — **variegated** ['vɛriəˌgeɪt̬əd] *adj* : abigarrado, multicolor — **variety** [və'raɪət̬i] *n*, *pl* **-ties 1** : variedad *f* **2** ASSORTMENT : surtido *m* **3** SORT : clase *f* — **various** ['vɛriəs] *adj* : varios, diversos

varnish ['vɑrnɪʃ] *n* : barniz *m* — ~ *vt* : barnizar

vary ['vɛri] *v* **varied; varying** : variar

vase ['veɪs, 'veɪz, 'vɑz] *n* **1** : jarrón *m* **2** *or* **flower ~** : florero *m*

vast ['væst] *adj* : vasto, enorme — **vastness** ['væstnəs] *n* : inmensidad *f*

vat ['væt] *n* : cuba *f*

vault¹ ['vɔlt] *vi* LEAP : saltar — ~ *n* : salto *m*

vault² *n* **1** DOME : bóveda *f* **2** *or* **bank ~** : cámara *f* acorazada, bóveda *f* de seguridad *Lat* **3** CRYPT : cripta *f*

VCR [ˌviːsiːˈɑr] *n* (*videocassette recorder*) : video *m*

veal ['viːl] *n* : (carne *f* de) ternera *f*

veer ['vɪr] *vi* : virar

vegetable ['vɛdʒtəbəl, 'vɛdʒət̬ə-] *adj* : vegetal — ~ *n* **1** : vegetal *m* (planta) **2** ~**s** *npl* : verduras *fpl* — **vegetarian** [ˌvɛdʒə'tɛriən] *n* : vegetariano *mf* — **vegetation** [ˌvɛdʒə'teɪʃən] *n* : vegetación *f*

vehemence ['viːəmənts] *n* : vehemencia *f* — **vehement** ['viːəmənt] *adj* : vehemente

vehicle ['viːəkəl, 'viːˌhɪkəl] *n* : vehículo *m*

veil ['veɪl] *n* : velo *m* — ~ *vt* **1** : cubrir con un velo **2** CONCEAL : velar

vein ['veɪn] *n* **1** : vena *f* **2** : veta *f* (de un mineral, etc.)

velocity [və'lɑsət̬i] *n*, *pl* **-ties** : velocidad *f*

velvet ['vɛlvət] *n* : terciopelo *m* — **velvety** ['vɛlvət̬i] *adj* : aterciopelado

vending machine ['vɛndɪŋ-] *vt* : máquina *f* expendedora

vendor ['vɛndər] *n* : vendedor *m*, -dora *f*

veneer [və'nɪr] *n* **1** : chapa *f* **2** FACADE : apariencia *f*

venerable ['vɛnərəbəl] *adj* : venerable — **venerate** ['vɛnəˌreɪt] *vt* **-ated; -ating** : venerar — **veneration** [ˌvɛnə'reɪʃən] *n* : veneración *f*

venereal [və'nɪriəl] *adj* : venéreo

venetian blind [və'niːʃən-] *n* : persiana *f* veneciana

Venezuelan [ˌvɛnə'zweɪlən, -'zʊɛ-] *adj* : venezolano

vengeance ['vɛndʒəns] *n* **1** : venganza *f* **2 take ~ on** : vengarse de — **vengeful** ['vɛndʒfəl] *adj* : vengativo

venison ['vɛnəsən, -zən] *n* : (carne *f* de) venado *m*

venom ['vɛnəm] *n* : veneno *m* — **venomous** ['vɛnəməs] *adj* : venenoso

vent ['vɛnt] *vt* : desahogar — **~** *n* **1** or **air ~** : rejilla *f* de ventilación **2** OUTLET : desahogo *m* — **ventilate** ['vɛntəˌleɪt] *vt* **-lated; -lating** : ventilar — **ventilation** [ˌvɛntə'leɪʃən] *n* : ventilación *f* — **ventilator** ['vɛntəˌleɪtər] *n* : ventilador *m*

ventriloquist [vɛn'trɪləkwɪst] *n* : ventrílocuo *m*, -cua *f*

venture ['vɛntʃər] *v* **-tured; -turing** *vt* **1** RISK : arriesgar **2** : aventurar (una opinión, etc.) — *vi* : atreverse — **~** *n* or **business ~** : empresa *f*

venue ['vɛnjuː] *n* : lugar *m*

Venus ['viːnəs] *n* : Venus *m*

veranda or **verandah** [və'rændə] *n* : veranda *f*

verb ['vərb] *n* : verbo *m* — **verbal** ['vərbəl] *adj* : verbal — **verbatim** [vər'beɪtəm] *adv* : palabra por palabra — **~** *adj* : literal — **verbose** [vər'boːs] *adj* : verboso

verdict ['vərdɪkt] *n* **1** : veredicto *m* **2** OPINION : opinión *f*

verge ['vərdʒ] *n* **1** : borde *m* **2 on the ~ of** : a punto de (hacer algo), al borde de (algo) — **~** *vi* **verged; verging ~ on** : rayar en

verify ['vɛrəˌfaɪ] *vt* **-fied; -fying** : verificar — **verification** [ˌvɛrəfə'keɪʃən] *n* : verificación *f*

vermin ['vərmən] *ns & pl* : alimañas *fpl*

vermouth [vər'muːθ] *n* : vermut *m*

versatile ['vərsətəl] *adj* : versátil — **versatility** [ˌvərsə'tɪləti] *n* : versatilidad *f*

verse ['vərs] *n* **1** LINE : verso *m* **2** POETRY : poesía *f* **3** : versículo *m* (en la Biblia) — **versed** ['vərst] *adj* **be well ~ in** : ser muy versado en

version ['vərʒən] *n* : versión *f*

versus ['vərsəs] *prep* : versus

vertebra ['vərtəbrə] *n*, *pl* **-brae** [-ˌbreɪ, -ˌbriː] or **-bras** : vértebra *f*

vertical ['vərtɪkəl] *adj* : vertical — **~** *n* : vertical *f*

vertigo ['vərtɪˌgoː] *n*, *pl* **-goes** or **-gos** : vértigo *m*

verve ['vərv] *n* : brío *m*

very ['vɛri] *adv* **1** : muy **2 at the ~ least** : por lo menos **3 the ~ same thing** : la misma cosa **4 ~ much** : mucho **5 ~ well** : muy bien — **~** *adj* **verier; -est 1** PRECISE, SAME : mismo **2** MERE : solo, mero **3 the ~ thing** : justo lo que hacía falta

vessel ['vɛsəl] *n* **1** CONTAINER : recipiente *m* **2** SHIP : nave *f*, buque *m* **3** or **blood ~** : vaso *m* sanguíneo

vest ['vɛst] *n* **1** : chaleco *m* **2** *Brit* UNDERSHIRT : camiseta *f*

vestibule ['vɛstəˌbjuːl] *n* : vestíbulo *m*

vestige ['vɛstɪdʒ] *n* : vestigio *m*

vet ['vɛt] *n* **1** → **veterinarian 2** → **veteran**

veteran ['vɛtərən, 'vɛtrən] *n* : veterano *m*, -na *f*

veterinarian [ˌvɛtərə'nɛriən, ˌvɛtrə'nɛr-] *n* : veterinario *m*, -ria *f* — **veterinary** ['vɛtrəˌnɛri] *adj* : veterinario

veto ['viːtoː] *n*, *pl* **-toes** : veto *m* — **~** *vt* : vetar

vex ['vɛks] *vt* ANNOY : irritar

via ['vaɪə, 'viːə] *prep* : por, vía

viable ['vaɪəbəl] *adj* : viable

viaduct ['vaɪəˌdʌkt] *n* : viaducto *m*

vial ['vaɪəl] *n* : frasco *m*

vibrant ['vaɪbrənt] *adj* : vibrante — **vibrate** ['vaɪˌbreɪt] *vi* **-brated; -brating** : vibrar — **vibration** [vaɪ'breɪʃən] *n* : vibración *f*

vicar ['vɪkər] *n* : vicario *m*, -ria *f*

vicarious [vaɪ'kæriəs, vɪ-] *adj* : indirecto

vice ['vaɪs] *n* : vicio *m*

vice president *n* : vicepresidente *m*, -ta *f*

vice versa [ˌvaɪsɪ'vərsə, ˌvaɪs'vər-] *adv* : viceversa

vicinity [və'sɪnəti] *n*, *pl* **-ties 1** : inmediaciones *fpl* **2 in the ~ of** ABOUT : alrededor de

vicious ['vɪʃəs] *adj* **1** SAVAGE : feroz **2** MALICIOUS : malicioso

victim ['vɪktəm] *n* : víctima *f*

victor ['vɪktər] *n* : vencedor *m*, -dora *f*

victory ['vɪktəri] *n*, *pl* **-ries** : victoria *f* — **victorious** [vɪk'toːriəs] *adj* : victorioso

video ['vɪdioː] *n* : video *m*, vídeo *m* *Spain* — **~** *adj* : de video — **videocassette** [ˌvɪdiokə'sɛt] *n* : videocasete *m* — **videotape** ['vɪdioˌteɪp] *n* : videocinta *f* — ~ *vt* **-taped; -taping** : videograbar

vie ['vaɪ] *vi* **vied; vying** ['vaɪɪŋ] : competir

Vietnamese [ˌvi̯ˌetnəˈmiːz, -ˈmiːs] *adj* : vietnamita

view ['vjuː] *n* **1** : vista **2** OPINION : opinión **3 come into** ~ : aparecer **4 in** ~ **of** : en vista de (que) — ~ *vt* **1** : ver **2** CONSIDER : considerar — **viewer** ['vjuːər] *n or* **television** ~ : televidente *mf* — **viewpoint** ['vjuːˌpɔɪnt] *n* : punto *m* de vista

vigil ['vɪdʒəl] *n* : vela *f* — **vigilance** ['vɪdʒələns] *n* : vigilancia *f* — **vigilant** ['vɪdʒələnt] *adj* : vigilante

vigor *or Brit* **vigour** ['vɪgər] *n* : vigor *m* — **vigorous** ['vɪgərəs] *adj* **1** : enérgico **2** ROBUST : vigoroso

Viking ['vaɪkɪŋ] *n* : vikingo *m*, -ga *f*

vile ['vaɪl] *adj* **viler; vilest 1** : vil **2** REVOLTING : asqueroso **3** TERRIBLE : horrible

villa ['vɪlə] *n* : casa *f* de campo

village ['vɪlɪdʒ] *n* : pueblo *m* (grande), aldea *f* (pequeña) — **villager** ['vɪlɪdʒər] *n* : vecino *m*, -na *f* (de un pueblo); aldeano *m*, -na *f* (de una aldea)

villain ['vɪlən] *n* : villano *m*, -na *f*

vindicate ['vɪndəˌkeɪt] *vt* **-cated; -cating 1** : vindicar **2** JUSTIFY : justificar

vindictive [vɪnˈdɪktɪv] *adj* : vengativo

vine ['vaɪn] *n* **1** : enredadera *f* **2** GRAPEVINE : vid *f*

vinegar ['vɪnɪgər] *n* : vinagre *m*

vineyard ['vɪnjərd] *n* : viña *f*, viñedo *m*

vintage ['vɪntɪdʒ] *n* **1** : cosecha *f* (de vino) **2** ERA : época *f* — ~ *adj* **1** : añejo (dícese de un vino) **2** CLASSIC : de época

vinyl ['vaɪnəl] *n* : vinilo

viola [viˈoːlə] *n* : viola *f*

violate ['vaɪəˌleɪt] *vt* **-lated; -lating** : violar — **violation** [ˌvaɪəˈleɪʃən] *n* : violación *f*

violence ['vaɪləns, 'vaɪə-] *n* : violencia *f* — **violent** ['vaɪlənt, 'vaɪə-] *adj* : violento

violet ['vaɪlət, 'vaɪə-] *n* : violeta *f* (flor), violeta *m* (color)

violin [ˌvaɪəˈlɪn] *n* : violín *m* — **violinist** [ˌvaɪəˈlɪnɪst] *n* : violinista *mf* — **violoncello** [ˌvaɪələnˈtʃɛloː, ˌviː-] → **cello**

VIP [ˌviːˌaɪˈpiː] *n, pl* **VIPs** [-ˈpiːz] : VIP *mf*

viper ['vaɪpər] *n* : víbora *f*

virgin ['vərdʒən] *n* : virgen *mf* — ~ *adj* **1** : virgen (dícese de la lana, etc.) **2** CHASTE : virginal — **virginity** [vərˈdʒɪnəti] *n* : virginidad *f*

virile ['vɪrəl, -ˌaɪl] *adj* : viril — **virility** [vəˈrɪləti] *n* : virilidad *f*

virtual ['vərtʃuəl] *adj* : virtual — **virtually** ['vərtʃuəli, 'vərtʃəli] *adv* : prácticamente

virtue ['vərtʃuː] *n* **1** : virtud *f* **2 by** ~ **of** : en virtud de

virtuoso [ˌvərtʃuˈoːsoː, -zoː] *n, pl* **-sos** *or* **-si** [-ˌsiː, -ziː] : virtuoso *m*, -sa *f*

virtuous ['vərtʃuəs] *adj* : virtuoso

virulent ['vɪrələnt, 'vɪrjə-] *adj* : virulento

virus ['vaɪrəs] *n* : virus *m*

visa ['viːzə, -sə] *n* : visado *m*, visa *f* Lat

vis-à-vis [ˌviːzəˈviː, -sə-] *prep* : con respecto a

viscous ['vɪskəs] *adj* : viscoso

visible ['vɪzəbəl] *adj* **1** : visible **2** NOTICEABLE : evidente — **visibility** [ˌvɪzəˈbɪləti] *n, pl* **-ties** : visibilidad *f*

vision ['vɪʒən] *n* **1** : visión *f* **2 have** ~ **s of** : imaginarse — **visionary** ['vɪʒəˌneri] *adj* : visionario — ~ *n, pl* **-ries** : visionario *m*, -ria *f*

visit ['vɪzət] *vt* : visitar — *vi* **1** : hacer una visita **2 be** ~**ing** : estar de visita — ~ *n* : visita *f* — **visitor** ['vɪzətər] *n* **1** : visitante *mf* **2** GUEST : visita *f*

visor ['vaɪzər] *n* : visera *f*

vista ['vɪstə] *n* : vista *f*

visual ['vɪʒuəl] *adj* : visual — **visualize** ['vɪʒuˌlaɪz] *vt* **-ized; -izing** : visualizar

vital ['vaɪtəl] *adj* **1** CRUCIAL : esencial **2** : vital — **vitality** [vaɪˈtæləti] *n, pl* **-ties** : vitalidad *f*, energía *f*

vitamin ['vaɪtəmən] *n* : vitamina *f*

vivacious [vəˈveɪʃəs, var-] *adj* : vivaz, animado

vivid ['vɪvəd] *adj* : vivo (dícese de colores), vívido (dícese de sueños, etc.)

vocabulary [voˈkæbjəˌleri] *n, pl* **-laries** : vocabulario *m*

vocal ['voːkəl] *adj* **1** : vocal **2** OUTSPOKEN : vociferante — **vocal cords** *npl* : cuerdas *fpl* vocales — **vocalist** ['voːkəlɪst] *n* : cantante *mf*, vocalista *mf*

vocation [voˈkeɪʃən] *n* : vocación *f* — **vocational** [voˈkeɪʃənəl] *adj* : profesional

vociferous [voˈsɪfərəs] *adj* : vociferante, ruidoso

vodka ['vɑdkə] *n* : vodka *m*

vogue ['voːg] *n* **1** : moda *f*, boga *f* **2 be in** ~ : estar de moda, estar en boga

voice ['vɔɪs] *n* : voz *f* — ~ *vt* **voiced; voicing** : expresar

void ['vɔɪd] *adj* **1** INVALID : nulo **2** ~ **of** : falto de — ~ *n* : vacío *m* — ~ *vt* : anular

volatile ['vɑlət̬əl] *adj* : volátil — **volatility** [,vɑlə'tɪlət̬i] *n* : volatilidad *f*

volcano [vɑl'keɪnoː] *n, pl* **-noes** *or* **-nos** : volcán *m* — **volcanic** [vɑl'kænɪk] *adj* : volcánico

volition [voʊ'lɪʃən] *n* **of one's own ~** : por voluntad propia

volley ['vɑli] *n, pl* **-leys 1** : descarga *f* (de tiros) **2** : torrente *m* (de insultos, etc.) **3** : volea *f* (en deportes) — **volleyball** ['vɑli,bɔl] *n* : voleibol *m*

volt ['voːlt] *n* : voltio *m* — **voltage** ['voːltɪdʒ] *n* : voltaje *m*

voluble ['vɑljəbəl] *adj* : locuaz

volume ['vɑljəm, -,juːm] *n* : volumen *m* — **voluminous** [və'luːmənəs] *adj* : voluminoso

voluntary ['vɑlən,teri] *adj* : voluntario — **volunteer** [,vɑlən'tɪr] *n* : voluntario *m*, -ria *f* — **~** *vt* : ofrecer — *vi* **~ to** : ofrecerse a

voluptuous [və'lʌptʃʊəs] *adj* : voluptuoso

vomit ['vɑmət] *n* : vómito *m* — **~** *v* : vomitar

voracious [vɔ'reɪʃəs, və-] *adj* : voraz

vote ['voːt] *n* **1** : voto *m* **2** SUFFRAGE : derecho *m* al voto — **~** *vi* **voted; voting** : votar — **voter** ['voːt̬ər] *n* : votante *mf* — **voting** ['voːt̬ɪŋ] *n* : votación *f*

vouch ['vaʊtʃ] *vi* **~ for** : responder de (algo), responder por (algn) — **voucher** ['vaʊtʃər] *n* : vale *m*

vow ['vaʊ] *n* : voto *m* — **~** *vt* : jurar

vowel ['vaʊəl] *n* : vocal *m*

voyage ['vɔɪɪdʒ] *n* : viaje *m*

vulgar ['vʌlɡər] *adj* **1** COMMON : ordinario **2** CRUDE : grosero, vulgar — **vulgarity** [,vʌl'ɡærət̬i] *n, pl* **-ties** : vulgaridad *f*

vulnerable ['vʌlnərəbəl] *adj* : vulnerable — **vulnerability** [,vʌlnərə'bɪlət̬i] *n, pl* **-ties** : vulnerabilidad *f*

vulture ['vʌltʃər] *n* : buitre *m*

vying → vie

W

w ['dʌbəl,juː] *n, pl* **w's** *or* **ws** [-,juːz] : w *f*, vigésima tercera letra del alfabeto inglés

wad ['wɑd] *n* : taco *m* (de papel, etc.), fajo *m* (de billetes)

waddle ['wɑdəl] *vi* **-dled; -dling** : andar como un pato

wade ['weɪd] *v* **waded; wading** *vi* : caminar por el agua — *vt or* **~ across** : vadear

wafer ['weɪfər] *n* : barquillo *m*

waffle ['wɑfəl] *n* : gofre *m* *Spain*, wafle *m* *Lat*

waft ['wɑft, 'wæft] *vt* : llevar por el aire — *vi* : flotar

wag ['wæɡ] *v* **wagged; wagging** *vt* : menear — *vi* : menearse

wage ['weɪdʒ] *n or* **wages** *npl* : salario *m* — **~** *vt* **waged; waging ~ war** : hacer la guerra

wager ['weɪdʒər] *n* : apuesta *f* — **~** *v* : apostar

wagon ['wæɡən] *n* **1** CART : carrito *m* **2 → station wagon**

waif ['weɪf] *n* : niño *m* abandonado

wail ['weɪl] *vi* : lamentarse — **~** *n* : lamento *m*

waist ['weɪst] *n* : cintura *f* — **waistline** ['weɪst,laɪn] *n* : cintura *f*

wait ['weɪt] *vi* : esperar — *vt* **1** AWAIT : esperar **2 ~ tables** : servir a la mesa

~ *n* **1** : espera *f* **2 lie in ~** : estar al acecho — **waiter** ['weɪt̬ər] *n* : camarero *m*, mozo *m* *Lat* — **waiting room** *n* : sala *f* de espera — **waitress** ['weɪtrəs] *n* : camarera *f*, moza *f* *Lat*

waive ['weɪv] *vt* **waived; waiving** : renunciar a — **waiver** ['weɪvər] *n* : renuncia *f*

wake[1] ['weɪk] *v* **woke** ['woːk], **woken** ['woːkən] *or* **waked; waking** *vi or* **~ up** : despertarse — *vt* : despertar — **~** *n* : velatorio *m* (de un difunto)

wake[2] *n* **1** : estela *f* (de un barco) **2 in the ~ of** : tras, como consecuencia de

waken ['weɪkən] *vt* : despertar — *vi* : despertarse

walk ['wɔk] *vi* **1** : caminar, andar **2** STROLL : pasear **3 too far to ~** : demasiado lejos para ir a pie — *vt* **1** : caminar por **2** : sacar a pasear (a un perro) — **~** *n* **1** : paseo *m* **2** PATH : camino *m* **3** GAIT : andar *m* — **walker** ['wɔkər] *n* **1** : paseante *mf* **2** HIKER : excursionista *mf* — **walking stick** *n* : bastón *m* — **walkout** ['wɔk,aʊt] *n* STRIKE : huelga *f* — **walk out** *vi* **1** STRIKE : declararse en huelga **2** LEAVE : salir, irse **3 ~ on** : abandonar

wall ['wɔl] *n* : muro *m* (exterior), pared *f* (interior), muralla *f* (de una ciudad)

wallet ['wɑlət] n : billetera f, cartera f
wallflower ['wɔl,flaʊər] n be a ~
: comer pavo
wallop ['wɑləp] vt : pegar fuerte — ~ n
: golpe m fuerte
wallow ['wɑ,loː] vi : revolcarse
wallpaper ['wɔl,peɪpər] n : papel m pintado — ~ vt : empapelar
walnut ['wɔl,nʌt] n : nuez f
walrus ['wɔlrəs, 'wɑl-] n, pl -rus or
-ruses : morsa f
waltz ['wɔlts] n : vals m — ~ vi : valsar
wan ['wɑn] adj wanner; -est : pálido
wand ['wɑnd] n : varita f (mágica)
wander ['wɑndər] vi 1 : vagar, pasear 2
STRAY : divagar — vt : pasear por —
wanderer ['wɑndərər] n : vagabundo
m, -da f — wanderlust ['wɑndər,lʌst] n
: pasión f por viajar
wane ['weɪn] vi waned; waning : menguar — ~ n be on the ~ : estar dis-
minuyendo
want ['wɑnt, 'wɔnt] vt 1 DESIRE : querer 2
NEED : necesitar 3 LACK : carecer de —
~ n 1 NEED : necesidad f 2 LACK
: falta f 3 DESIRE : deseo m — wanting
['wɑntɪŋ, 'wɔn-] adj be ~ : carecer
wanton ['wɑntən, 'wɔn-] adj 1 LEWD
: lascivo 2 ~ cruelty : crueldad f des-
piadada
war ['wɔr] n : guerra f
ward ['wɔrd] n 1 : sala f (de un hospital,
etc.) 2 : distrito m electoral 3 : pupilo
m, -la f (de un tutor, etc.) — ~ vt ~
off : protegerse contra — warden
['wɔrdən] n 1 : guardián m, -diana f 2
or game ~ : guardabosque mf 3 or
prison ~ : alcaide m
wardrobe ['wɔrd,roːb] n 1 CLOSET : armario m 2 CLOTHES : vestuario m
warehouse ['wær,haʊs] n : almacén m,
bodega f Lat — wares ['wærz] npl
: mercancías fpl
warfare ['wɔr,fær] n : guerra f
warily ['wærəli] adv : cautelosamente
warlike ['wær,laɪk] adj : belicoso
warm ['wɔrm] adj 1 : caliente 2 LUKE-
WARM : tibio 3 CARING : cariñoso 4 I
feel ~ : tengo calor 5 ~ clothes
: ropa f de abrigo — ~ vt or ~ up
: calentar — vi 1 or ~ up : calentarse
2 ~ to : tomar simpatía a (algn),
entusiasmarse con (algo) — warm-
blooded ['wɔrm'blʌdəd] adj : de sangre caliente — warmhearted ['wɔrm-
'hɑrtəd] adj : cariñoso — warmly
['wɔrmli] adv 1 : calurosamente 2
dress ~ : abrigarse — warmth
['wɔrmθ] n 1 : calor m 2 AFFECTION
: cariño m, afecto m

warn ['wɔrn] vt : advertir, avisar—
warning ['wɔrnɪŋ] n : advertencia f,
aviso m
warp ['wɔrp] vt 1 : alabear (madera,
etc.) 2 DISTORT : deformar — vi
: alabearse
warrant ['wɔrənt] n 1 : autorización f 2
arrest ~ : orden f judicial — ~ vt
: justificar — warranty ['wɔrənti,
,wɔrən'ti:] n, pl -ties : garantía f
warrior ['wɔriər] n : guerrero m, -ra f
warship ['wɔr,ʃɪp] n : buque m de guerra
wart ['wɔrt] n : verruga f
wartime ['wɔr,taɪm] n : tiempo m de
guerra
wary ['wæri] adj warier; -est : cauteloso
was → be
wash ['wɑʃ, 'wɔʃ] vt 1 : lavar(se) 2
CARRY : arrastrar 3 ~ away : llevarse
4 ~ over : bañar — vi : lavarse —
~ n 1 : lavado m 2 LAUNDRY : ropa f sucia
— washable ['wɑʃəbəl, 'wɔ-] adj
: lavable — washcloth ['wɑʃ,klɔθ,
'wɔʃ-] n : toallita f (para lavarse) —
washed-out ['wɑʃt'aʊt, 'wɔʃt-] adj 1
: desvaído (dícese de colores) 2 EX-
HAUSTED : agotado — washer ['wɑʃər,
'wɔ-] n 1 → washing machine 2
: arandela f (de una llave, etc.) —
washing machine n : máquina f de
lavar, lavadora f — washroom ['wɑʃ-
,ruːm, 'wɔʃ-, -,rʊm] n : servicios mpl
(públicos), baño m
wasn't ['wɑzənt] (contraction of was
not) → be
wasp ['wɑsp, 'wɔsp] n : avispa f
waste ['weɪst] v wasted; wasting vt 1
: desperdiciar, derrochar, malgastar 2
~ time : perder tiempo — vi or ~
away : consumirse — ~ adj : de
desecho — ~ n 1 : derroche m, desperdicio m 2 RUBBISH : desechos mpl 3
a ~ of time : una pérdida de tiempo
— wastebasket ['weɪst,bæskət] n : papelera f — wasteful ['weɪstfəl] adj
: derrochador — wasteland ['weɪst-
,lænd, -lənd] n : yermo m
watch ['wɑtʃ] vi 1 : mirar 2 or keep ~
: velar 3 ~ out! : ¡ten cuidado!, ¡ojo!
— vt 1 : mirar 2 or ~ over : vigilar,
cuidar 3 ~ what you do : ten cuidado con lo que haces — ~ n 1 reloj m
2 SURVEILLANCE : vigilancia f 3 LOOK-
OUT : guardia mf — watchdog ['wɑtʃ-
,dɔg] n : perro m guardián — watchful
['wɑtʃfəl] adj : vigilante — watchman
['wɑtʃmən] n, pl -men [-mən, -,men]
: vigilante m, guarda m — watchword
['wɑtʃ,wərd] n : santo m y seña
water ['wɔtər, 'wɑ-] n : agua f — ~ vt 1

: regar (el jardín, etc.) **2 ~ down** DI-LUTE : diluir, aguar — *vi* **1** : lagrimar (dícese de los ojos) **2 my mouth is ~ing** : se me hace agua la boca — **watercolor** ['wɔt̬ər,kʌlər, 'wɑ-] *n* : acuarela *f* — **watercress** ['wɔt̬ər,krɛs, 'wɑ-] *n* : berro *m* — **waterfall** ['wɔt̬ər,fɔl, 'wɑ-] *n* : cascada *f*, salto *m* de agua — **water lily** *n* : nenúfar *m* — **water-logged** ['wɔt̬ər,lɔgd, 'wɑt̬ər,lɑgd] *adj* : lleno de agua, empapado — **water-melon** ['wɔt̬ər,mɛlən, 'wɑ-] *n* : sandía *f* — **waterpower** ['wɔt̬ər,pauər, 'wɑ-] *n* : energía *f* hidráulica — **waterproof** ['wɔt̬ər,pruf, 'wɑ-] *adj* : impermeable — **watershed** ['wɔt̬ər,ʃɛd, 'wɑ-] *n* **1** : cuenca *f* (de un río) **2** : momento *m* crítico — **waterskiing** ['wɔt̬ər,skiːɪŋ, 'wɑ-] *n* : esquí *m* acuático — **water-tight** ['wɔt̬ər,taɪt, 'wɑ-] *adj* : hermético — **waterway** ['wɔt̬ər,weɪ, 'wɑ-] *n* : vía *f* navegable — **waterworks** ['wɔt̬ər,wərks, 'wɑ-] *npl* : central *f* de abastecimiento de agua — **watery** ['wɔt̬əri, 'wɑ-] *adj* **1** : acuoso **2** DILUTED : aguado, diluido **3** WASHED-OUT : desvaído (dícese de colores)

watt ['wɑt] *n* : vatio *m* — **wattage** ['wɑt̬ɪdʒ] *n* : vataje *m*

wave ['weɪv] *v* **waved; waving** *vi* **1** : saludar con la mano **2** : flotar (dícese de una bandera) — *vt* **1** SHAKE : agitar **2** CURL : ondular SIGNAL : hacer señas a (con la mano) — *n* **1** : ola *f* (de agua) **2** CURL : onda *f* **3** : onda *f* (en física) **4** : señal *f* (con la mano) **5** SURGE : oleada *f* — **wavelength** ['weɪv,lɛŋkθ] *n* : longitud *f* de onda

waver ['weɪvər] *vi* : vacilar

wax[1] ['wæks] *vi* : crecer (dícese de la luna)

wax[2] *n* : cera *f* (para pisos, etc.) — *vt* : encerar — **waxy** ['wæksi] *adj* **waxier, -est** : ceroso

way ['weɪ] *n* **1** : camino *m* **2** MEANS : manera *f*, modo *m* **3 by the ~** : a propósito, por cierto **4 by ~ of** : vía, pasando por **5 come a long ~** : hacer grandes progresos **6 get in the ~** : meterse en el camino **7 get one's own ~** : salirse uno con la suya **8 mend one's ~s** : dejar las malas costumbres **9 out of the ~** REMOTE : remoto, recóndito **10 which ~ did he go?** : ¿por dónde fue?

we ['wiː] *pron* : nosotros, nosotras

weak ['wiːk] *adj* **1** : débil **2** DILUTED : aguado **3 a ~ excuse** : una excusa poco convincente — **weaken** ['wiːkən] *vt* : debilitar — *vi* : debilitarse —

weakling ['wiːklɪŋ] *n* : debilucho *m*, -cha *f* — **weakly** ['wiːkli] *adv* : débilmente — *~ adj* **weaklier; -est** : enfermizo — **weakness** ['wiːknəs] *n* **1** : debilidad *f* **2** FLAW : flaqueza *f*, punto *m* débil

wealth ['wɛlθ] *n* : riqueza *f* — **wealthy** ['wɛlθi] *adj* **wealthier; -est** : rico

weapon ['wɛpən] *n* : arma *f*

wear ['wær] *v* **wore** ['wor]; **worn** ['worn]; **wearing** *vt* **1** : llevar (ropa, etc.), calzar (zapatos) **2** *or* **~ away** : desgastar **3 ~ oneself out** : agotarse **4 ~ out** : gastar — *vi* **1** LAST : durar **2 ~ off** : desaparecer **3 ~ out** : gastarse — *n* **1** USE : uso *m* **2** CLOTHING : ropa *f* **3 be the worse for ~** : estar deteriorado — **wear and tear** *n* : desgaste *m*

weary ['wɪri] *adj* **-rier; -est** : cansado — *~ v* **-ried; -rying** *vt* : cansar — *vi* : cansarse — **weariness** ['wɪrinəs] *n* : cansancio *m* — **wearisome** ['wɪrisəm] *adj* : cansado

weasel ['wiːzəl] *n* : comadreja *f*

weather ['wɛðər] *n* : tiempo *m* — *~ vt* **1** WEAR : erosionar, desgastar **2** EN-DURE, OVERCOME : superar — **weath-er-beaten** ['wɛðər,biːt̬ən] *adj* : curtido — **weatherman** ['wɛðər,mæn] *n, pl* **-men** [-mən, -mɛn] : meteorólogo *m*, -ga *f* — **weather vane** *n* : valeta *f*

weave ['wiːv] *v* **wove** ['woːv] *or* **weaved; woven** ['woːvən] *or* **weaved; weaving** *vt* **1** : tejer (tela) **2** INTERLACE : entretejer **3 ~ one's way** : abrirse camino — *vi* : tejer — *n* **1** : tejido *m* — **weaver** ['wiːvər] *n* : tejedor *m*, -dora *f*

web ['wɛb] *n* **1** : telaraña *f* (de araña) **2** : membrana *f* interdigital (de aves) **3** NETWORK : red *f*

wed ['wɛd] *v* **wedded; wedding** *vt* : casarse con — *vi* : casarse

we'd ['wiːd] *(contraction of we had, we should, or we would)* → **have, should, would**

wedding ['wɛdɪŋ] *n* : boda *f*, casamiento *m*

wedge ['wɛdʒ] *n* **1** : cuña *f* **2** PIECE : porción *f*, trozo *m* — *~ vt* **wedged; wedging 1** : apretar (con una cuña) **2** CRAM : meter

Wednesday ['wɛnzdeɪ, -di] *n* : miércoles *m*

wee ['wiː] *adj* **1** : pequeñito **2 in the ~ hours** : a las altas horas

weed ['wiːd] *n* : mala hierba *f* — *~ vt* **1** : desherbar **2 ~ out** : eliminar

week ['wiːk] n : semana f — **weekday** ['wiːkˌdeɪ] n : día m laborable — **weekend** ['wiːkˌɛnd] n : fin m de semana — **weekly** ['wiːkli] adv : semanalmente — ~ adj : semanal — ~ n, pl **-lies** : semanario m

weep ['wiːp] v **wept** ['wɛpt]; **weeping** : llorar — **weeping willow** n : sauce m llorón — **weepy** ['wiːpi] adj **weepier; -est** : lloroso

weigh ['weɪ] vt **1** : pesar **2** CONSIDER : sopesar **3** ~ **down** : sobrecargar (con una carga), abrumar (con preocupaciones, etc.) — vi : pesar

weight ['weɪt] n : peso m **2 gain** ~ : engordar **3 lose** ~ : adelgazar — **weighty** ['weɪti] adj **weightier; -est 1** HEAVY : pesado **2** IMPORTANT : importante, de peso

weird ['wɪrd] adj **1** : misterioso **2** STRANGE : extraño

welcome ['wɛlkəm] vt **-comed; -coming** : dar la bienvenida a, recibir — ~ adj **1** : bienvenido **2 you're** ~ : de nada — ~ n : bienvenida f, acogida f

weld ['wɛld] v : soldar

welfare ['wɛlˌfær] n **1** WELL-BEING : bienestar m **2** AID : asistencia f social

well[1] ['wɛl] adv **better** ['bɛtər]; **best** ['bɛst] **1** : bien **2** CONSIDERABLY : bastante **3 as** ~ : también **4 as** ~ **as** : además de — ~ adj : bien — ~ interj **1** (used to introduce a remark) : bueno **2** (used to express surprise) : ¡vaya!

well[2] n : pozo m — ~ vi or ~ **up** : brotar, manar

we'll ['wiːl, wɪl] (contraction of **we shall** or **we will**) → **shall, will**

well-being ['wɛlˈbiːɪŋ] n : bienestar m — **well-bred** ['wɛlˈbrɛd] adj : fino, bien educado — **well-done** ['wɛlˈdʌn] adj **1** : bien hecho **2** : bien cocido (dícese de la carne, etc.) — **well-known** ['wɛlˈnoːn] adj : famoso, bien conocido — **well-meaning** ['wɛlˈmiːnɪŋ] adj : bienintencionado — **well-off** ['wɛlˈɔf] adj : acomodado — **well-rounded** ['wɛlˈraʊndəd] adj : completo — **well-to-do** [ˌwɛltəˈduː] adj : próspero, adinerado

Welsh ['wɛlʃ] adj : galés — ~ n **1** : galés m (idioma) **2 the** ~ : los galeses

went → **go**
wept → **weep**
were → **be**
we're ['wɪr, 'wər, 'wiːər] (contraction of **we are**) → **be**

weren't ['wɛrənt, 'wɔrnt] (contraction of **were not**) → **be**

west ['wɛst] adv : al oeste — ~ adj : oeste, del oeste — ~ n **1** : oeste m **2 the West** : el Oeste, el Occidente — **westerly** ['wɛstərli] adv & adj : del oeste — **western** ['wɛstərn] adj **1** : del oeste **2 Western** : occidental — **Westerner** ['wɛstərnər] n : habitante mf del oeste — **westward** ['wɛstwərd] adv & adj : hacia el oeste

wet ['wɛt] adj **wetter; wettest 1** : mojado **2** RAINY : lluvioso **3** ~ **paint** : pintura f fresca — ~ vt **wet** or **wetted; wetting** : mojar, humedecer

we've ['wiːv] (contraction of **we have**) → **have**

whack ['hwæk] vt : golpear fuertemente — ~ n : golpe m fuerte

whale ['hweɪl] n, pl **whales** or **whale** : ballena f

wharf ['hwɔrf] n, pl **wharves** ['hwɔrvz] : muelle m, embarcadero m

what ['hwʌt, 'hwɑt] adj **1** (used in questions and exclamations) : qué **2** WHATEVER : cualquier — ~ pron **1** (used in questions) : qué **2** (used in indirect statements) : lo que, qué **3** ~ **does it cost?** : ¿cuánto cuesta? **4** ~ **for?** : ¿por qué? **5** ~ **if** : y si — **whatever** [hwʌtˈɛvər, ˌhwʌt-] adj **1** : cualquier **2 there's no chance** ~ : no hay ninguna posibilidad **3 nothing** ~ : nada en absoluto — ~ pron **1** ANYTHING : lo que **2** (used in questions) : qué **3** ~ **it may be** : sea lo que sea — **whatsoever** [ˌhwʌtsoˈɛvər, ˌhwʌt-] adj & pron → **whatever**

wheat ['hwiːt] n : trigo m

wheedle ['hwiːdəl] vt **-dled; -dling** : engatusar

wheel ['hwiːl] n **1** : rueda f **2** or **steering** ~ : volante m (de automóviles, etc.), timón m (de barcos) — ~ vt : empujar (algo sobre ruedas) — vi or ~ **around** : darse la vuelta — **wheelbarrow** ['hwiːlˌbæroː] n : carretilla f — **wheelchair** ['hwiːlˌtʃær] n : silla f de ruedas

wheeze ['hwiːz] vi **wheezed; wheezing** : resollar — ~ n : resuello m

when ['hwɛn] adv : cuándo — ~ conj **1** : cuando **2 the days** ~ **I clean the house** : los días (en) que limpio la casa — ~ pron : cuándo — **whenever** [hwɛnˈɛvər] adv : cuando sea — ~ conj **1** : cada vez que **2** ~ **you like** : cuando quieras

where ['hwɛr] adv **1** : dónde **2** ~ **are you going?** : ¿adónde vas? — ~ conj

& pron : donde — **whereabouts** ['hwerə,bauts] adv : (por) dónde — ~ ns & pl : paradero m — **wherever** [hwer'evər] adv 1 : en cualquier parte 2 WHERE : dónde, adónde — ~ conj : dondequiera que

whet ['hwɛt] vt **whetted; whetting** 1 : afilar 2 ~ **the appetite** : estimular el apetito

whether ['hweðər] conj 1 : si 2 **we doubt** ~ **he'll show up** : dudamos que aparezca 3 ~ **you like it or not** : tanto si quieras como si no

which ['hwɪtʃ] adj 1 : qué, cuál 2 **in** ~ **case** : en cuyo caso — ~ pron 1 (used in questions) : cuál 2 (used in relative clauses) : que, el (la) cual — **whichever** [hwɪtʃ'evər] adj : cualquier ~ — pron : el (la) que, cualquiera que

whiff ['hwɪf] n 1 PUFF : soplo m 2 SMELL : olorcillo m

while ['hwaɪl] n 1 : rato m 2 **be worth one's** ~ : valer la pena 3 **in a** ~ : dentro de poco — ~ conj 1 : mientras 2 WHEREAS : mientras que 3 ALTHOUGH : aunque — ~ vt **whiled; whiling** ~ **away the time** : matar el tiempo

whim ['hwɪm] n : capricho m, antojo m

whimper ['hwɪmpər] vi : lloriquear— ~ n : quejido m

whimsical ['hwɪmzɪkəl] adj : caprichoso, fantasioso

whine ['hwaɪn] vi **whined; whining** 1 : gimotear 2 COMPLAIN : quejarse — ~ n : quejido m, gemido m

whip ['hwɪp] v **whipped; whipping** vt 1 : azotar 2 BEAT : batir (huevos, crema, etc.) 3 ~ **up** AROUSE : avivar, despertar — vi FLAP : agitarse — ~ n : látigo m

whir ['hwər] vi **whirred; whirring** : zumbar — ~ n : zumbido m

whirl ['hwərl] vi 1 : dar vueltas, girar 2 or ~ **about** : arremolinarse — ~ n 1 : giro m 2 SWIRL : torbellino m — **whirlpool** ['hwərl,pu:l] n : remolino m — **whirlwind** ['hwərl,wɪnd] n : torbellino m

whisk ['hwɪsk] vt 1 : batir 2 ~ **away** : llevarse — ~ n or **egg** ~ : batidor m — **whisk broom** n : escobilla f

whisker ['hwɪskər] n 1 : pelo m (de la barba) 2 ~ **s** npl : bigotes mpl (de animales)

whiskey or **whisky** ['hwɪski] n, pl -**keys** or -**kies** : whisky m

whisper ['hwɪspər] vi : cuchichear, susurrar — vt : susurrar — ~ n : susurro m

whistle ['hwɪsəl] v -**tled; -tling** vi 1 : silbar, chiflar Lat 2 : pitar (dícese de un tren, etc.) — vt : silbar — ~ n 1 : silbido m, chiflido m (sonido) 2 : silbato m, pito m (instrumento)

white ['hwaɪt] adj **whiter; -est** : blanco — ~ n 1 : blanco m (color) 2 : clara f (de huevos) 3 or ~ **person** : blanco m, -ca f — **white-collar** ['hwaɪt'kalər] adj 1 : de oficina 2 ~ **worker** : oficinista m — **whiten** ['hwaɪtən] vt : blanquear — **whiteness** ['hwaɪtnəs] n : blancura f — **whitewash** ['hwaɪt,waʃ] vt 1 : enjalbegar 2 CONCEAL : encubrir (un escándalo, etc.) — ~ n 1 : jalbegue m, lechada f 2 COVER-UP : encubrimiento m

whittle ['hwɪtəl] vt -**tled; -tling** 1 : tallar (madera) 2 or ~ **down** : reducir

whiz or **whizz** ['hwɪz] vi **whizzed; whizzing** 1 BUZZ : zumbar 2 ~ **by** : pasar muy rápido — ~ or **whizz** n, pl **whizzes** : zumbido m — **whiz kid** n : joven m prometedor

who ['hu:] pron 1 (used in direct and indirect questions) : quién 2 (used in relative clauses) : que, quien — **whodunit** [hu:'dʌnɪt] n : novela f policíaca — **whoever** [hu:'evər] pron 1 : quienquiera que, quien 2 (used in questions) : quién

whole ['ho:l] adj 1 : entero 2 INTACT : intacto 3 **a** ~ **lot** : muchísimo — ~ n 1 : todo m 2 **as a** ~ : en conjunto 3 **on the** ~ : en general — **wholehearted** ['ho:l'hartəd] adj : sincero — **wholesale** ['ho:l,seɪl] n : venta f al por mayor — ~ adj 1 : al por mayor 2 ~ **slaughter** : matanza f sistemática — ~ adv : al por mayor — **wholesaler** ['ho:l,seɪlər] n : mayorista m — **wholesome** ['ho:lsəm] adj : sano — **whole wheat** : de trigo integral — **wholly** ['ho:li] adv : completamente

whom ['hu:m] pron 1 (used in direct questions) : a quién 2 (used in indirect questions) : de quién, con quién, en quién 3 (used in relative clauses) : que, a quien

whooping cough n : tos f ferina

whore ['hor] n : puta f

whose ['hu:z] adj 1 (used in questions) : de quién 2 (used in relative clauses) : cuyo — ~ pron : de quién

why ['hwaɪ] adv : por qué — ~ n, pl **whys** : porqué m — ~ conj : por qué — ~ interj (used to express surprise) : ¡vaya!, ¡mira!

wick ['wɪk] n : mecha f

wicked ['wɪkəd] adj 1 : malo, malvado 2

MISCHIEVOUS : travieso **3** TERRIBLE : terrible, horrible — **wickedness** ['wɪkədnəs] n : maldad f

wicker ['wɪkər] n : mimbre m — ~ adj : de mimbre

wide ['waɪd] adj **wider; widest 1** : ancho **2** VAST : amplio, extenso **3** or ~ **of the mark** : desviado — ~ adv **1** ~ **apart** : muy separados **2 far and** ~ : por todas partes **3** ~ **open** : abierto de par en par — **wide-awake** ['waɪdə'weɪk] adj : (completamente) despierto — **widely** ['waɪdli] adv : extensivamente — **widespread** ['waɪd'spred] adj : extendido

widow ['wɪdo:] n : viuda f — ~ vt : dejar viuda — **widower** ['wɪdowər] n : viudo m

width ['wɪdθ] n : ancho m, anchura f

wield ['wi:ld] vt **1** : usar, manejar **2** EXERT : ejercer

wiener ['wi:nər] → **frankfurter**

wife ['waɪf] n, pl **wives** ['waɪvz] : esposa f, mujer f

wig ['wɪg] n : peluca f

wiggle ['wɪgəl] v **-gled; -gling** vt : menear, contonear — vi : menearse — ~ n : meneo m

wigwam ['wɪg,wɑm] n : wigwam m

wild ['waɪld] adj **1** : salvaje **2** DESOLATE : agreste **3** UNRULY : desenfrenado **4** RANDOM : al azar **5** FRANTIC : frenético **6** OUTRAGEOUS : extravagante — ~ adv **1** ~ **wildly 2 run** ~ : volver al estado silvestre (dícese de las plantas), desmandarse (dícese de los niños) — **wildcat** ['waɪld,kæt] n : gato m montés — **wilderness** ['wɪldərnəs] n : yermo m, desierto m — **wildfire** ['waɪld,faɪr] n **1** : fuego m descontrolado **2 spread like** ~ : propagarse como un reguero de pólvora — **wildflower** ['waɪld,flaʊər] n : flor f silvestre — **wildlife** ['waɪld,laɪf] n : fauna f — **wildly** ['waɪldli] adv **1** FRANTICALLY : frenéticamente **2** EXTREMELY : locamente

will¹ ['wɪl] v past **would** ['wʊd]; pres sing & pl **will** vi WISH : querer — v aux **1 tomorrow we** ~ **go shopping** : mañana iremos de compras **2 he** ~ **get angry over nothing** : se pone furioso por cualquier cosa **3 I** ~ **go despite them** : iré a pesar de ellos **4 I won't do it** : no lo haré **5 that** ~ **be the mailman** : eso ha de ser el cartero **6 the couch** ~ **hold three people** : en el sofá cabrán tres personas **7 accidents** ~ **happen** : los accidentes ocurrirán **8 you** ~ **do as I say** : harás lo que digo

will² n **1** : voluntad f **2** TESTAMENT : testamento m **3 free** ~ : libre albedrío m — **willful** or **wilful** ['wɪlfəl] adj **1** OBSTINATE : terco **2** INTENTIONAL : intencionado — **willing** ['wɪlɪŋ] adj **1** : complaciente **2 be** ~ **to** : estar dispuesto a — **willingly** ['wɪlɪŋli] adv : con gusto — **willingness** ['wɪlɪŋnəs] n : buena voluntad f

willow ['wɪlo:] n : sauce m

willpower ['wɪl,paʊər] n : fuerza f de voluntad

wilt ['wɪlt] vi : marchitarse

wily ['waɪli] adj **wilier; -est** : artero, astuto

win ['wɪn] v **won** ['wʌn]; **winning** vi : ganar — vt **1** : ganar, conseguir **2** ~ **over** : ganarse a — ~ n : triunfo m, victoria f

wince ['wɪns] vi **winced; wincing** : hacer una mueca de dolor — ~ n : mueca f de dolor

winch ['wɪntʃ] n : torno m

wind¹ ['wɪnd] n **1** : viento m **2** BREATH : aliento m **3** FLATULENCE : flatulencia f **4 get** ~ **of** : enterarse de

wind² ['waɪnd] v **wound** ['waʊnd]; **winding** vi : serpentear — vt **1** COIL : enrollar **2** ~ **a clock** : dar cuerda a un reloj

windfall ['wɪnd,fɔl] n : beneficio m imprevisto

winding ['waɪndɪŋ] adj : tortuoso

wind instrument n : instrumento m de viento

windmill ['wɪnd,mɪl] n : molino m de viento

window ['wɪndo:] n : ventana f (de un edificio o una computadora), ventanilla f (de un vehículo), vitrina f (de una tienda) — **windowpane** ['wɪndo:,peɪn] n : vidrio m — **windowsill** ['wɪndo:,sɪl] n : repisa f de la ventana

windpipe ['wɪnd,paɪp] n : tráquea f

windshield ['wɪndʃi:ld] n **1** : parabrisas m **2** ~ **wiper** : limpiaparabrisas m

window-shop ['wɪndo:,ʃɑp] vi **-shopped; -shopping** : mirar las vitrinas

wind up ['waɪnd,ʌp] vt : terminar, concluir — vi : terminar, acabar — **windup** n : conclusión f

windy ['wɪndi] adj **windier; -est 1** : ventoso **2 it's** ~ : hace viento

wine ['waɪn] n : vino m — **wine cellar** n : bodega f

wing ['wɪŋ] n **1** : ala f **2 under s.o.'s** ~ : bajo el cargo de algn — **winged** ['wɪŋd, 'wɪŋəd] adj : alado

wink ['wɪŋk] vi : guiñar — ~ n **1** : guiño m **2 not sleep a** ~ : no pegar el ojo

winner ['wɪnər] n : ganador m, -dora f —

winning ['wɪnɪŋ] adj 1 : ganador 2 CHARMING : encantador — winnings ['wɪnɪŋz] npl : ganancias fpl

winter ['wɪntər] n : invierno m — adj : invernal, de invierno — wintergreen ['wɪntərˌgrin] n : gaulteria f — wintertime ['wɪntərˌtaɪm] n : invierno m — wintry ['wɪntri] adj wintrier; -est : invernal, de invierno

wipe ['waɪp] vt wiped; wiping 1 : limpiar 2 ~ away : enjugar (lágrimas), borrar (una memoria) 3 ~ out : aniquilar, destruir — ~ n : pasada f (con un trapo, etc.)

wire ['waɪr] n 1 : alambre m 2 : cable m (eléctrico o telefónico) 3 TELEGRAM : telegrama m — ~ vt -wired; wiring 1 : instalar el cableado en (una casa, etc.) 2 BIND : atar con alambre 3 TELEGRAPH : enviar un telegrama a — wireless ['waɪrləs] adj : inalámbrico — wiring ['waɪrɪŋ] n : cableado m — wiry ['waɪri] adj wirier; -est 1 : hirsuto, tieso (dícese del pelo) 2 : esbelto y musculoso (dícese del cuerpo)

wisdom ['wɪzdəm] n : sabiduría f — wisdom tooth n : muela f de juicio

wise ['waɪz] adj wiser; wisest 1 : sabio 2 SENSIBLE : prudente — wisecrack ['waɪzˌkræk] n : broma f, chiste m — wisely ['waɪzli] adv : sabiamente

wish ['wɪʃ] vt 1 : desear 2 ~ s.o. well : desear lo mejor a algn — vi 1 : pedir (como deseo) 2 as you ~ : como quieras — ~ n 1 : deseo m 2 best ~es : muchos recuerdos — wishbone ['wɪʃˌbon] n : espoleta f — wishful ['wɪʃfəl] adj : deseoso 2 ~ thinking : ilusiones fpl

wishy-washy ['wɪʃiˌwɔʃi, -ˌwɑʃi] adj : insípido, soso

wisp ['wɪsp] n 1 : mechón m (de pelo) 2 : voluta f (de humo)

wistful ['wɪstfəl] adj : melancólico

wit ['wɪt] n 1 CLEVERNESS : ingenio m 2 HUMOR : agudeza f 3 at one's ~'s end : desesperado 4 scared out of one's ~s : muerto de miedo

witch ['wɪʧ] n : bruja f — witchcraft ['wɪʧˌkræft] n : brujería f, hechicería f

with ['wɪð, 'wɪθ] prep 1 : con 2 I'm going ~ you : voy contigo 3 it varies ~ the season : varía según la estación 4 the girl ~ red hair : la muchacha de pelo rojo 5 ~ all his work, the business failed : a pesar de su trabajo, el negocio fracasó

withdraw [wɪð'drɔ, wɪθ-] v -drew [-'dru:]; -drawn [-'drɔn]; -drawing vt : retirar — vi : apartarse — withdraw-

al [wɪð'drɔːl, wɪθ-] n 1 : retirada f 2 : abandono (de drogas, etc.) — withdrawn [wɪð'drɔn, wɪθ-] adj : introvertido

wither ['wɪðər] vi : marchitarse

withhold [wɪð'hold, wɪθ-] vt -held [-'held]; -holding : retener (fondos), negar (permiso, etc.)

within [wɪð'ɪn, wɪθ-] adv : dentro — ~ prep 1 : dentro de 2 (in expressions of distance) : a menos de 3 (in expressions of time) : dentro de, en menos de 4 ~ reach : al alcance de la mano

without [wɪð'aʊt, wɪθ-] adv do ~ : pasar sin algo — ~ prep : sin

withstand [wɪð'stænd, wɪθ-] vt -stood [-'stʊd]; -standing 1 BEAR : aguantar 2 RESIST : resistir

witness ['wɪtnəs] n 1 : testigo mf 2 EVIDENCE : testimonio m 3 bear ~ : atestiguar — ~ vt 1 SEE : ser testigo de 2 : atestiguar (una firma, etc.)

witticism ['wɪtəˌsɪzəm] n : agudeza f, ocurrencia f

witty ['wɪti] adj -tier; -est : ingenioso, ocurrente

wives → wife

wizard ['wɪzərd] n 1 : mago m, brujo m 2 a math ~ : un genio de matemáticas

wizened ['wɪzənd, 'wi:-] adj : arrugado

wobble ['wɑbəl] vi -bled; -bling 1 : tambalearse 2 : temblar (dícese de la voz, etc.) — wobbly ['wɑbəli] adj : cojo

woe ['wo:] n 1 : aflicción f 2 ~s npl TROUBLES : penas fpl — woeful ['wo:fəl] adj : triste

woke, woken → wake

wolf ['wʊlf] n, pl wolves ['wʊlvz] : lobo m, -ba f — ~ vt or ~ down : engullir

woman ['wʊmən] n, pl women ['wɪmən] : mujer f — womanly ['wʊmənli] adj : femenino

womb ['wuːm] n : útero m, matriz f

won → win

wonder ['wʌndər] n 1 MARVEL : maravilla f 2 AMAZEMENT : asombro m — ~ vi : preguntarse — wonderful ['wʌndərfəl] adj : maravilloso, estupendo

won't ['wont] (contraction of will not) → will

woo ['wu:] vt 1 COURT : cortejar 2 : buscar el apoyo de (clientes, votantes, etc.)

wood ['wʊd] n 1 : madera f (materia) 2 FIREWOOD : leña f 3 or ~s npl FOREST : bosque m — ~ adj : de madera — woodchuck ['wʊdˌʧʌk] n : marmota f de América — wooded ['wʊdəd] adj : arbolado, boscoso — wooden ['wʊdən] adj : de madera — **woodpecker** ['wʊd,pɛkər] n : pájaro m carpintero — **woodshed** ['wʊd,ʃɛd] n : leñera f — **woodwind** ['wʊd,wɪnd] n : instrumento m de viento de madera — **woodwork** ['wʊd,wərk] n : carpintería f

wool ['wʊl] n : lana f — **woolen** or **woollen** ['wʊlən] adj : de lana — n 1 : lana f (tela) 2 ~s npl : prendas fpl de lana — **woolly** ['wʊli] adj **-lier; -est** : lanudo

word ['wərd] n 1 : palabra f 2 NEWS : noticias fpl 3 ~s npl : letra f (de una canción, etc.) 4 **have ~s with** : reñir con 5 **just say the ~** : no tienes que decirlo 6 **keep one's ~** : cumplir su palabra — ~ vt : expresar — **word processing** n : procesamiento m de textos — **word processor** n : procesador m de textos — **wordy** ['wərdi] adj **wordier; -est** : prolijo

wore → **wear**

work ['wərk] n 1 LABOR : trabajo m 2 EMPLOYMENT : trabajo m, empleo m 3 : obra f (de arte, etc.) 4 ~s npl FACTORY : fábrica f 5 ~s npl MECHANISM : mecanismo m — v **worked** ['wərkt] or **wrought** ['rɔt]; **working** vt 1 : hacer trabajar (a una persona) 2 : manejar, operar (una máquina, etc.) — vi 1 : trabajar 2 FUNCTION : funcionar 3 : surtir efecto (dícese de una droga), resultar (dícese de una idea, etc.) — **worked up** adj : nervioso — **worker** ['wərkər] n : trabajador m, -dora f; obrero m, -ra f — **working** ['wərkɪŋ] adj 1 : que trabaja (dícese de personas), de trabajo (dícese de la ropa, etc.) 2 **be in ~ order** : funcionar bien — **working class** n : clase f obrera — **workingman** ['wərkɪŋmæn] n, pl **-men** [-mən, -,mɛn] : obrero m — **workman** ['wərkmən] n, pl **-men** [-mən, -,mɛn] 1 : obrero m 2 ARTISAN : artesano m — **workmanship** ['wərkmən,ʃɪp] n : artesanía f, destreza f — **workout** ['wərk,aʊt] n : ejercicios mpl (físicos) — **work out** vt 1 DEVELOP : elaborar 2 SOLVE : resolver — vi 1 TURN OUT : resultar 2 SUCCEED : lograr, salir bien 3 EXERCISE : hacer ejercicio — **workshop** ['wərk,ʃɑp] n : taller m — **work up** vt 1 EXCITE : ponerse como loco 2 GENERATE : desarrollar

world ['wərld] n : mundo m 2 **think the ~ of s.o.** : tener a algn en alta estima — ~ adj : mundial, del mundo — **worldly** ['wərldli] adj : mundano —

worldwide ['wərld,waɪd] adv : en todo el mundo — ~ adj : global, mundial

worm ['wərm] n 1 : gusano m, lombriz f 2 ~s npl : lombrices fpl (parásitos)

worn → **wear** — **worn-out** ['wɔrn'aʊt] adj 1 USED : gastado 2 TIRED : agotado

worry ['wəri] v **-ried; -rying** vt : preocupar, inquietar — vi : preocuparse, inquietarse — ~ n, pl **-ries** : preocupación f — **worried** ['wərid] adj : preocupado — **worrisome** ['wərisəm] adj : inquietante

worse ['wərs] adv (comparative of **bad** or of **ill**) : peor — adj (comparative of **bad** or of **ill**) 1 : peor 2 **from bad to ~** : de mal en peor 3 **get ~** : empeorar — ~ n 1 **the ~** : el (la) peor, lo peor 2 **take a turn for the ~** : ponerse peor — **worsen** ['wərsən] v : empeorar

worship ['wərʃəp] v **-shiped** or **-shipped; -shiping** or **-shipping** vt : adorar — vi : practicar una religión — ~ n : adoración f, culto m — **worshiper** or **worshipper** ['wərʃəpər] n : adorador m, -dora f

worst ['wərst] adv (superlative of **ill** or of **bad** or **badly**) : peor — adj (superlative of **bad** or of **ill**) : peor — n **the ~** : lo peor, el (la) peor

worth ['wərθ] n 1 : valor m (monetario) 2 MERIT : mérito m, valía f 3 **ten dollars' ~ of gas** : diez dólares de gasolina — ~ prep 1 **it's ~ $ 10** : vale $ 10 2 **it's ~ doing** : vale la pena hacerlo — **worthless** ['wərθləs] adj 1 : sin valor 2 USELESS : inútil — **worthwhile** [wərθ'hwaɪl] adj : que vale la pena — **worthy** ['wərði] adj **-thier; -est** : digno

would ['wʊd] past of **will** 1 **he ~ often take his children to the park** : solía llevar a sus hijos al parque 2 **I ~ go if I had the money** : iría yo si tuviera el dinero 3 **I ~ rather go alone** : preferiría ir sola 4 **she ~ have won if she hadn't tripped** : habría ganado si no hubiera tropezado 5 **~ you kindly help me with this?** : ¿tendría la bondad de ayudarme con esto? — **would-be** ['wʊd'bi] adj **a ~ poet** : un aspirante a poeta — **wouldn't** ['wʊdənt] (contraction of **would not**) → **would**

wound¹ ['wuːnd] n : herida f — ~ vt : herir

wound² ['waʊnd] → **wind**

wove, woven → **weave**

wrangle ['ræŋgəl] vi **-gled; -gling** : reñir — ~ n : riña f, disputa f

wrap ['ræp] *vt* **wrapped; wrapping 1** : envolver 2 — **up** FINISH : dar fin a — **~** *n* **1** : prenda *f* que envuelve (como un chal) **2** WRAPPER : envoltura *f* — **wrapper** ['ræpər] *n* **1** : envoltura *f*, envoltorio *m* — **wrapping** ['ræpɪŋ] *n* : envoltura *f*, envoltorio *m*

wrath ['ræθ] *n* : ira *f*, cólera *f* — **wrathful** ['ræθfəl] *adj* : iracundo

wreath ['riːθ] *n*, *pl* **wreaths** ['riːðz, 'riːθs] : corona *f* (de flores, etc.)

wreck ['rɛk] *n* **1** WRECKAGE : restos *mpl* **2** RUIN : ruina *f*, desastre *m* **3 be a nervous ~** : tener los nervios destrozados — **~** *vt* : destrozar (un automóvil), naufragar (un barco) — **wreckage** ['rɛkɪdʒ] *n* : restos *mpl* (de un buque naufragado, etc.), ruinas *fpl* (de un edificio)

wren ['rɛn] *n* : chochín *m*

wrench ['rɛntʃ] *vt* **1** PULL : arrancar (de un tirón) **2** SPRAIN, TWIST : torcerse — **~** *n* **1** TUG : tirón *m*, jalón *m* **2** SPRAIN : torcedura *f* **3** *or* **monkey ~** : llave *f* inglesa

wrestle ['rɛsəl] *vi* **-tled; -tling** : luchar — **wrestler** ['rɛslər] *n* : luchador *m*, -dora *f* — **wrestling** ['rɛslɪŋ] *n* : lucha *f*

wretch ['rɛtʃ] *n* : desgraciado *m*, -da *f* — **wretched** ['rɛtʃəd] *adj* **1** : miserable **2 ~ weather** : tiempo *m* espantoso

wriggle ['rɪgəl] *vi* **-gled; -gling** : retorcerse, menearse

wring ['rɪŋ] *vt* **wrung** ['rʌŋ]; **wringing 1** *or* **~ out** : escurrir (el lavado, etc.) **2**

TWIST : retorcer **3** EXTRACT : arrancar (información, etc.)

wrinkle ['rɪŋkəl] *n* : arruga *f* — **~** *v* **-kled; -kling** *vt* : arrugar — *vi* : arrugarse

wrist ['rɪst] *n* : muñeca *f* — **wristwatch** ['rɪst,wɑtʃ] *n* : reloj *m* de pulsera

writ ['rɪt] *n* : orden *f* (judicial)

write ['raɪt] *v* **wrote** ['roːt]; **written** ['rɪtən]; **writing** : escribir — **write down** *vt* : apuntar, anotar — **write off** *vt* CANCEL : cancelar — **writer** ['raɪtər] *n* : escritor *m*, -tora *f*

writhe ['raɪð] *vi* **writhed; writhing** : retorcerse

writing ['raɪtɪŋ] *n* : escritura *f*

wrong ['rɔŋ] *n* **1** INJUSTICE : injusticia *f*, mal *m* **2** : agravio *m* (en derecho) **3 be in the ~** : haber hecho mal — **~** *adj* **1** UNSUITABLE : inadecuado, inapropiado **2** INCORRECT : incorrecto, equivocado **4 be ~** : no tener razón — **~** *adv* : mal, incorrectamente — **~** *vt* **wronged; wronging** : ofender, ser injusto con — **wrongful** ['rɔŋfəl] *adj* **1** UNJUST : injusto **2** UNLAWFUL : ilegal — **wrongly** ['rɔŋli] *adv* **1** UNJUSTLY : injustamente **2** INCORRECTLY : mal

wrote → write

wrought iron ['rɔt] *n* : hierro *m* forjado

wrung → wring

wry ['raɪ] *adj* **wrier** ['raɪər]; **wriest** ['raɪəst] : irónico, sardónico (dícese del humor)

XYZ

x *n*, *pl* **x's** *or* **xs** ['ɛksəz] : x *f*, vigésima cuarta letra del alfabeto inglés

xenophobia [,zɛnəˈfoːbiə, ,ziː-] *n* : xenofobia *f*

Xmas ['krɪsməs] *n* : Navidad *f*

X ray ['ɛks,reɪ] *n* **1** : rayo *m* X **2** *or* **~ photograph** : radiografía *f* — **x-ray** *vt* : radiografiar

xylophone ['zaɪlə,foːn] *n* : xilófono *m*

y ['waɪ] *n*, *pl* **y's** *or* **ys** ['waɪz] : y *f*, vigésima quinta letra del alfabeto inglés

yacht ['jɑt] *n* : yate *m*

yam ['jæm] *n* **1** : ñame *m* **2** SWEET POTATO : batata *f*, boniato *m*

yank ['jæŋk] *vt* : tirar de, jalar *Lat* — **~** *n* : tirón *m*, jalón *m* *Lat*

Yankee ['jæŋki] *n* : yanqui *mf*

yap ['jæp] *vi* **yapped; yapping** : ladrar — **~** *n* : ladrido *m*

yard ['jɑrd] *n* **1** : yarda *f* (medida) **2** COURTYARD : patio *m* **3** : jardín *m* (de una casa) — **yardstick** ['jɑrd,stɪk] *n* **1** : vara *f* (de medir) **2** CRITERION : criterio *m*

yarn ['jɑrn] *n* **1** : hilado *m* **2** TALE : historia *f*, cuento *m*

yawn ['jɔn] *vi* : bostezar — **~** *n* : bostezo *m*

year ['jɪr] *n* **1** : año *m* **2 she's ten ~s old** : tiene diez años **3 I haven't seen them in ~s** : hace siglos que no los veo — **yearbook** ['jɪr,bʊk] *n* : anuario *m* — **yearling** ['jɪrlɪŋ, 'jərlən] *n* : animal *m* menor de dos años — **yearly** ['jɪrli] *adv* **1** : anualmente **2 three**

times ~ : tres veces al año — ~ *adj* : anual

yearn ['jərn] *vi* : anhelar — **yearning** ['jərnɪŋ] *n* : anhelo *m*, ansia *f*

yeast ['ji:st] *n* : levadura *f*

yell ['jɛl] *vi* : gritar, chillar — *vt* : gritar — ~ *n* : grito *m*, chillido *m*

yellow ['jɛlo] *adj* : amarillo — ~ *n* : amarillo *m* — **yellowish** ['jɛloɪʃ] *adj* : amarillento

yelp ['jɛlp] *n* : gañido *m* — ~ *vi* : dar un gañido

yes ['jɛs] *adv* 1 : sí 2 **say** ~ : decir que sí — ~ *n* : sí *m*

yesterday ['jɛstərˌdeɪ, -di] *adv* : ayer — ~ *n* 1 : ayer *m* 2 **the day before** ~ : anteayer

yet ['jɛt] *adv* 1 : aún, todavía 2 **has he come** ~? : ¿ya ha venido? 3 **not** ~ : todavía no 4 — **more problems** : más problemas aún 5 NEVERTHELESS : sin embargo — ~ *conj* : pero

yield ['ji:ld] *vt* 1 PRODUCE : producir 2 — **the right of way** : ceder el paso — *vi* : ceder — ~ *n* : rendimiento *m*, rédito *m* (en finanzas)

yoga ['jo:gə] *n* : yoga *m*

yogurt ['jo:gərt] *n* : yogur *m*, yogurt *m*

yoke ['jo:k] *n* : yugo *m*

yolk ['jo:k] *n* : yema *f* (de un huevo)

you ['ju:] *pron* 1 (*used as subject—familiar*) : tú; vos (*in some Latin American countries*); ustedes *pl*; vosotros, vosotras *pl Spain* 2 (*used as subject—formal*) : usted, ustedes *pl* 3 (*used as indirect object—familiar*) : te, les *pl* (se *before lo, la, los, las*), os *pl Spain* 4 (*used as indirect object—formal*) : lo (*Spain sometimes* le), la; los (*Spain sometimes* les), las *pl Spain* 5 (*used after a preposition—familiar*) : ti; vos (*in some Latin American countries*); ustedes *pl*; vosotros, vosotras *pl Spain* 6 (*used after a preposition—formal*) : usted, ustedes *pl* 7 **with** — *pl* (*familiar*) : contigo; con ustedes *pl*; con vosotros, con vosotras *pl Spain* 8 **with** — ~ (*formal*) : con usted, con ustedes *pl* 9 — **never know** : nunca se sabe — **you'd** ['ju:d, 'jʊd] (*contraction of* you had *or* you would) → **have**, **would** — **you'll** ['ju:l, 'jʊl] (*contraction of* you shall *or* you will) → **shall**, **will**

young ['jʌŋ] *adj* **younger** ['jʌŋgər]; **youngest** [-gəst] 1 : joven 2 **my** ~**er brother** : mi hermano menor 3 **she is the** ~**est** : es la más pequeña 4 **the** ~ : los jóvenes — ~ *npl* : jóvenes *mfpl* (de los humanos), crías *fpl* (de los animales) — **youngster** ['jʌŋkstər] *n* : chico *m*, -ca *f*; joven *mf*

your ['jʊr, 'jɔr, jər] *adj* 1 (*familiar singular*) : tu 2 (*familiar plural*) su, vuestro *Spain* 3 (*formal*) : su 4 **on** ~ **left** : a la izquierda

you're ['jʊr, 'jɔr, 'jʊər] (*contraction of* you are) → **be**

yours ['jʊrz, 'jɔrz] *pron* 1 (*belonging to one person—familiar*) : (el) tuyo, (la) tuya, (los) tuyos, (las) tuyas 2 (*belonging to more than one person—familiar*) : (el) suyo, (la) suya, (los) suyos, (las) suyas; (el) vuestro, (la) vuestra, (los) vuestros, (las) vuestras *Spain* 3 (*formal*) : (el) suyo, (la) suya, (los) suyos, (las) suyas

yourself [jər'sɛlf] *pron*, *pl* **yourselves** [-'sɛlvz] 1 (*used reflexively—familiar*) : te, se *pl*, os *pl Spain* 2 (*used reflexively—formal*) : se 3 (*used for emphasis*) : tú mismo, tú misma; usted mismo, usted misma; ustedes mismos, ustedes mismas *pl*; vosotros mismos, vosotras mismas *pl Spain*

youth ['ju:θ], *n*, *pl* **youths** ['ju:ðz, 'ju:θs] 1 : juventud *f* 2 BOY : joven *m* 3 **today's** ~ : los jóvenes de hoy — **youthful** ['ju:θfəl] *adj* 1 : juvenil, de juventud 2 YOUNG : joven

you've ['ju:v] (*contraction of* you have) → **have**

yowl ['jaʊl] *vi* : aullar — ~ *n* : aullido *m*

yucca ['jʌkə] *n* : yuca *f*

Yugoslavian ['ju:goˌslaviən] *adj* : yugoslavo

yule ['ju:l] *n* CHRISTMAS : Navidad *f* — **yuletide** ['ju:lˌtaɪd] *n* : Navidades *fpl*

z ['zi:], *n*, *pl* **z's** *or* **zs** : z *f*, vigésima sexta letra del alfabeto inglés

zany ['zeɪni] *adj* **-nier**; **-est** : alocado, disparatado

zeal ['zi:l] *n* : fervor *m*, celo *m* — **zealous** ['zɛləs] *adj* : entusiasta

zebra ['zi:brə] *n* : cebra *f*

zenith ['zi:nəθ] *n* 1 : cenit *m* (en astronomía) 2 PEAK : apogeo *m*

zero ['zi:ro, 'zɪro] *n*, *pl* **-ros** : cero *m*

zest ['zɛst] *n* 1 : gusto *m* 2 FLAVOR : sazón *f*

zigzag ['zɪgˌzæg] *n* : zigzag *m* — ~ *vi* **-zagged**; **-zagging** : zigzaguear

zinc ['zɪŋk] *n* : cinc *m*, zinc *m*

zip ['zɪp] *v* **zipped**; **zipping** *vt* or ~ **up** : cerrar la cremallera de, cerrar el cierre de *Lat* — *vi* SPEED : pasarse volando — **zip code** *n* : código *m* postal — **zipper** ['zɪpər] *n* : cremallera *f*, cierre *m* *Lat*

zodiac ['zo:di̩æk] *n* : zodíaco *m*
zone ['zo:n] *n* : zona *f*
zoo ['zu:] *n, pl* **zoos** : zoológico *m*, zoo *m* — **zoology** [zo'alədʒi, zu:-] *n* : zoología *f*

zoom ['zu:m] *vi* : zumbar, ir volando — ~ *n* **1** : zumbido *m* **2** *or* ~ **lens** : zoom *m*
zucchini [zʊ'ki:ni] *n, pl* **-ni** *or* **-nis** : calabacín *m*, calabacita *f Lat*

Common Spanish Abbreviations

SPANISH ABBREVIATION AND EXPANSION		ENGLISH EQUIVALENT	
abr.	abril	**Apr.**	April
A.C., a.C.	antes de Cristo	**BC**	before Christ
a. de J.C.	antes de Jesucristo	**BC**	before Christ
admon., admón.	administración	—	administration
a/f	a favor	—	in favor
ago.	agosto	**Aug.**	August
Apdo.	apartado (de correos)	—	P.O. box
aprox.	aproximadamente	**approx.**	approximately
Aptdo.	apartado (de correos)	—	P.O. box
Arq.	arquitecto	**arch.**	architect
A.T.	Antiguo Testamento	**O.T.**	Old Testament
atte.	atentamente	—	sincerely
atto., atta.	atento, atenta	—	kind, courteous
av., avda.	avenida	**ave.**	avenue
a/v	a vista	—	on receipt
BID	Banco Interamericano de Desarrollo	**IDB**	Interamerican Development Bank
Bo	banco	—	bank
BM	Banco Mundial	—	World Bank
c/, C/	calle	**st.**	street
C	centígrado, Celsius	**C**	centigrade, Celsius
C.	compañía	**Co.**	company
CA	corriente alterna	**AC**	alternating current
cap.	capítulo	**ch., chap.**	chapter
c/c	cuenta corriente	—	current account, checking account
c.c.	centímetros cúbicos	**cu. cm**	cubic centimeters
CC	corriente continua	**DC**	direct current
c/d	con descuento	—	with discount
Cd.	ciudad	—	city
CE	Comunidad Europea	**EC**	European Community
CEE	Comunidad Económica Europea	**EEC**	European Economic Community
cf.	confróntese	**cf.**	compare
cg.	centígramo	**cg**	centigram
CGT	Confederación General de Trabajadores *o* del Trabajo	—	confederation of workers, workers' union
CI	coeficiente intelectual *o* de inteligencia	**IQ**	intelligence quotient
Cía.	compañía	**Co.**	company
cm.	centímetro	**cm**	centimeter
Cnel.	coronel	**Col.**	colonel
col.	columna	**col.**	column
Col. *Mex*	colonia	—	residential area
Com.	comandante	**Cmdr.**	commander
comp.	compárese	**comp.**	compare
Cor.	coronel	**Col.**	colonel
C.P.	código postal	—	zip code

SPANISH ABBREVIATION AND EXPANSION		ENGLISH EQUIVALENT	
CSF, c.s.f.	coste, seguro y flete	c.i.f.	cost, insurance, and freight
cta.	cuenta	ac., acct.	account
cte.	corriente	cur.	current
c/u	cada uno, cada una	ea.	each
CV	caballo de vapor	hp	horsepower
D.	Don	—	—
Da., D.ª	Doña	—	—
d.C.	después de Cristo	AD	anno Domini (in the year of our Lord)
dcha.	derecha	—	right
d. de J.C.	después de Jesucristo	AD	anno Domini (in the year of our lord)
dep.	departamento	dept.	department
DF, D.F.	Distrito Federal	—	Federal District
dic.	diciembre	Dec.	December
dir.	director, directora	dir.	director
dir.	dirección	—	address
Dña.	Doña	—	—
do.	domingo	Sun.	Sunday
dpto.	departamento	dept.	department
Dr.	doctor	Dr.	doctor
Dra.	doctora	Dr.	doctor
dto.	descuento	—	discount
E, E.	Este, este	E	East, east
Ed.	editorial	—	publishing house
Ed., ed.	edición	ed.	edition
edif.	edificio	bldg.	building
edo.	estado	st.	state
EEUU, EE.UU.	Estados Unidos	US, U.S.	United States
ej.	por ejemplo	e.g.	for example
E.M.	esclerosis multiple	MS	multiple sclerosis
ene.	enero	Jan.	January
etc.	etcétera	etc.	et cetera
ext.	extensión	ext.	extension
F	Fahrenheit	F	Fahrenheit
f.a.b.	franco a bordo	f.o.b.	free on board
FC	ferrocarril	RR	railroad
feb.	febrero	Feb.	February
FF AA, FF.AA.	Fuerzas Armadas	—	armed forces
FMI	Fondo Monetario Internacional	IMF	International Monetary Fund
g.	gramo	g., gm, gr.	gram
G.P.	giro postal	M.O.	money order
gr.	gramo	g., gm, gr.	gram
Gral.	general	Gen.	general
h.	hora	hr.	hour
Hnos.	hermanos	Bros.	brothers
I+D, I & D, I y D	investigación y desarrollo	R & D	research and development
i.e.	esto es, es decir	i.e.	that is
incl.	inclusive	incl.	inclusive, inclusively

SPANISH ABBREVIATION AND EXPANSION		ENGLISH EQUIVALENT	
Ing.	ingeniero, ingeniera	eng.	engineer
IPC	índice de precios al consumo	CPI	consumer price index
IVA	impuesto al valor agregado	VAT	value-added tax
izq.	izquierda	l.	left
juev.	jueves	Thurs.	Thursday
jul.	julio	Jul.	July
jun.	junio	Jun.	June
kg.	kilogramo	kg	kilogram
km.	kilómetro	km	kilometer
km/h	kilómetros por hora	kph	kilometers per hour
kv, kV	kilovatio	kw, kW	kilowatt
l.	litro	l, lit.	liter
Lic.	licenciado, licenciada	—	—
Ltda.	limitada	Ltd.	limited
lun.	lunes	Mon.	Monday
m	masculino	m	masculine
m	metro	m	meter
m	minuto	m	minute
mar.	marzo	Mar.	March
mart.	martes	Tues.	Tuesday
mg.	miligramo	mg	milligram
miérc.	miércoles	Wed.	Wednesday
min	minuto	min.	minute
mm.	milímetro	mm	millimeter
M-N, m/n	moneda nacional	—	national currency
Mons.	monseñor	Msgr.	monsignor
Mtra.	maestra	—	teacher
Mtro.	maestro	—	teacher
N, N.	Norte, norte	N, no.	North, north
n/o	nuestro	—	our
n.º	número	no.	number
N. de (la) R.	nota de (la) redacción	—	editor's note
NE	nordeste	NE	northeast
NN.UU.	Naciones Unidas	UN	United Nations
NO	noroeste	NW	northwest
nov.	noviembre	Nov.	November
N.T.	Nuevo Testamento	N.T.	New Testament
ntra., ntro.	nuestra, nuestro	—	our
NU	Naciones Unidas	UN	United Nations
núm.	número	num.	number
O, O.	Oeste, oeste	W	West, west
oct.	octubre	Oct.	October
OEA, O.E.A.	Organización de Estados Americanos	OAS	Organization of American States
OMS	Organización Mundial de la Salud	WHO	World Health Organization
ONG	organización no gubernamental	NGO	non-governmental organization
ONU	Organización de las Naciones Unidas	UN	United Nations
OTAN	Organización del Tratado del Atlántico Norte	NATO	North Atlantic Treaty Organization

SPANISH ABBREVIATION AND EXPANSION		ENGLISH EQUIVALENT	
p.	página	p.	page
P, P.	padre	Fr.	father
pág.	página	pg.	page
pat.	patente	pat.	patent
PCL	pantalla de cristal líquido	LCD	liquid crystal display
P.D.	post data	P.S.	postscript
p. ej.	por ejemplo	e.g.	for example
PNB	Producto Nacional Bruto	GNP	gross national product
pº	paseo	Ave.	avenue
p.p.	porte pagado	ppd.	postpaid
PP, p.p.	por poder, por poderes	p.p.	by proxy
prom.	promedio	av., avg.	average
ptas., pts.	pesetas	—	—
q.e.p.d.	que en paz descanse	R.I.P.	may he/she rest in peace
R, R/	remite	—	sender
RAE	Real Academia Española	—	—
ref., ref.ª	referencia	ref.	reference
rep.	república	rep.	republic
r.p.m.	revoluciones por minuto	rpm.	revolutions per minute
rte.	remite, remitente	—	sender
s.	siglo	c., cent.	century
s/	su, sus	—	his, her, your, their
S, S.	Sur, sur	S, so.	South, south
S.	san, santo	St.	saint
S.A.	sociedad anónima	Inc.	incorporated (company)
sáb.	sábado	Sat.	Saturday
s/c	su cuenta	—	your account
SE	sudeste, sureste	SE	southeast
seg.	segundo, segundos	sec.	second, seconds
sep., sept.	septiembre	Sept.	September
s.e.u.o.	salvo error u omisión	—	errors and omissions excepted
Sgto.	sargento	Sgt.	sergeant
S.L.	sociedad limitada	Ltd.	limited (corporation)
S.M.	Su Majestad	HM	His Majesty, Her Majesty
s/n	sin número	—	no (street) number
s.n.m.	sobre el nivel de mar	a.s.l.	above sea level
SO	sudoeste/suroeste	SW	southwest
S.R.C.	se ruega contestación	R.S.V.P.	please reply
ss.	siguientes	—	the following ones
SS, S.S.	Su Santidad	H.H.	His Holiness
Sta.	santa	St.	Saint
Sto.	santo	St.	saint
t, t.	tonelada	t., tn	ton
TAE	tasa anual efectiva	APR	annual percentage rate
tb.	también	—	also
tel., Tel.	teléfono	tel.	telephone
Tm.	tonelada métrica	MT	metric ton
Tn.	tonelada	t., tn	ton
trad.	traducido	tr., trans., transl.	translated
UE	Unión Europea	EU	European Union
Univ.	universidad	Univ., U.	university

SPANISH ABBREVIATION AND EXPANSION		ENGLISH EQUIVALENT	
UPC	unidad procesadora central	**CPU**	central processing unit
Urb.	urbanización	—	residential area
v	versus	**v., vs.**	versus
v	verso	**v., ver., vs.**	verse
v.	véase	**vid.**	see
Vda.	viuda	—	widow
v.g., v.gr.	verbigracia	**e.g.**	for example
vier., viern.	viernes	**Fri.**	Friday
V.M.	Vuestra Majestad	—	Your Majesty
V^{O}B^O, V.^{O}B.^{O}	visto bueno	—	OK, approved
vol, vol.	volumen	**vol.**	volume
vra., vro.	vuestra, vuestro	—	your

Spanish Numbers

Cardinal Numbers

1	uno	28	veintiocho
2	dos	29	veintinueve
3	tres	30	treinta
4	cuatro	31	treinta y uno
5	cinco	40	cuarenta
6	seis	50	cincuenta
7	siete	60	sesenta
8	ocho	70	setenta
9	nueve	80	ochenta
10	diez	90	noventa
11	once	100	cien
12	doce	101	ciento uno
13	trece	200	doscientos
14	catorce	300	trescientos
15	quince	400	cuatrocientos
16	dieciséis	500	quinientos
17	diecisiete	600	seiscientos
18	dieciocho	700	setecientos
19	diecinueve	800	ochocientos
20	veinte	900	novecientos
21	veintiuno	1,000	mil
22	veintidós	1,001	mil uno
23	veintitrés	2,000	dos mil
24	veinticuatro	100,000	cien mil
25	veinticinco	1,000,000	un millón
26	veintiséis	1,000,000,000	mil millones
27	veintisiete	1,000,000,000,000	un billón

Ordinal Numbers

1st	primero, -ra	17th	decimoséptimo, -ma
2nd	segundo, -da	18th	decimoctavo, -va
3rd	tercero, -ra	19th	decimonoveno, -na; *or*
4th	cuarto, -ta		decimonono, -na
5th	quinto, -ta	20th	vigésimo, -ma
6th	sexto, -ta	21st	vigésimoprimero,
7th	séptimo, -ta		vigésimaprimera
8th	octavo, -ta	30th	trigésimo, -ma
9th	noveno, -na	40th	cuadragésimo, -ma
10th	décimo, -ma	50th	quincuagésimo, -ma
11th	undécimo, -ma	60th	sexagésimo, -ma
12th	duodécimo, -ma	70th	septuagésimo, -ma
13th	decimotercero, -ra	80th	octogésimo, -ma
14th	decimocuarto, -ta	90th	nonagésimo, -ma
15th	decimoquinto, -ta	100th	centésimo, -ma
16th	decimosexto, -ta	1,000th	milésimo, -ma

English Numbers

Cardinal Numbers

1	one	20	twenty
2	two	21	twenty-one
3	three	30	thirty
4	four	40	forty
5	five	50	fifty
6	six	60	sixty
7	seven	70	seventy
8	eight	80	eighty
9	nine	90	ninety
10	ten	100	one hundred
11	eleven	101	one hundred and one
12	twelve	200	two hundred
13	thirteen	1,000	one thousand
14	fourteen	1,001	one thousand and one
15	fifteen	2,000	two thousand
16	sixteen	100,000	one hundred thousand
17	seventeen	1,000,000	one million
18	eighteen	1,000,000,000	one billion
19	nineteen	1,000,000,000,000	one trillion

Ordinal Numbers

1st	first	16th	sixteenth
2nd	second	17th	seventeenth
3rd	third	18th	eighteenth
4th	fourth	19th	nineteenth
5th	fifth	20th	twentieth
6th	sixth	21st	twenty-first
7th	seventh	30th	thirtieth
8th	eighth	40th	fortieth
9th	ninth	50th	fiftieth
10th	tenth	60th	sixtieth
11th	eleventh	70th	seventieth
12th	twelfth	80th	eightieth
13th	thirteenth	90th	ninetieth
14th	fourteenth	100th	hundredth
15th	fifteenth	1,000th	thousandth